ENCYCLOPEDIA OF AMERICAN HISTORY

Comprehensive Index

VOLUME XI

ENCYCLOPEDIA OF AMERICAN HISTORY

Volume I
THREE WORLDS MEET
Beginnings to 1607

Volume II
COLONIZATION AND SETTLEMENT
1608 to 1760

Volume III
REVOLUTION AND NEW NATION
1761 to 1812

Volume IV
EXPANSION AND REFORM
1813 to 1855

Volume V
CIVIL WAR AND RECONSTRUCTION
1856 to 1869

Volume VI
THE DEVELOPMENT OF THE INDUSTRIAL UNITED STATES
1870 to 1899

Volume VII
THE EMERGENCE OF MODERN AMERICA
1900 to 1928

Volume VIII
THE GREAT DEPRESSION AND WORLD WAR II
1929 to 1945

Volume IX
POSTWAR UNITED STATES
1946 to 1968

Volume X
CONTEMPORARY UNITED STATES
1969 to the Present

Volume XI
COMPREHENSIVE INDEX

ENCYCLOPEDIA OF AMERICAN HISTORY

Comprehensive Index

VOLUME XI

Facts On File, Inc.

Encyclopedia of American History:
Comprehensive Index

Editorial Director: Laurie E. Likoff
Editor in Chief: Owen Lancer
Chief Copy Editor: Michael G. Laraque
Associate Editor: Dorothy Cummings
Production Director: Olivia McKean
Production Manager: Rachel L. Berlin
Production Associate: Theresa Montoya
Art Director: Cathy Rincon
Interior Designer: Joan M. Toro
Desktop Designers: Erika K. Arroyo and David C. Strelecky
Maps and Illustrations: Dale E. Williams and Jeremy Eagle

Facts On File, Inc.
132 West 31st Street
New York NY 10001

Library of Congress Cataloging-in-Publication Data

Encyclopedia of American history / Gary B. Nash, general editor.
p.   cm.
Includes bibliographical references and indexes.
Contents: v. 1. Three worlds meet — v. 2. Colonization and settlement —
v. 3. Revolution and new nation — v. 4. Expansion and reform — v. 5. Civil War
and Reconstruction — v. 6. The development of the industrial United States —
v. 7. The emergence of modern America — v. 8. The Great Depression and
World War II — v. 9. Postwar United States — v. 10. Contemporary
United States. — v. 11 Comprehensive index
ISBN 0-8160-4371-X (set)   ISBN 0-8160-5079-1 (v. 11)
1. United States—History—Encyclopedias. I. Nash, Gary B.
E174 .E53 2002
973′.03—dc21   2001051278

About the Editors

General Editor: Gary B. Nash received a Ph.D from Princeton University. He is currently director of the National Center for History in the Schools at the University of California, Los Angeles, where he teaches American history of the colonial and Revolutionary era. He is a published author of college and precollegiate history texts. Among his best-selling works is *The American People: Creating a Nation and Society* (Addison Wesley, Longman), now in its fifth edition.

Nash is an elected member of the Society of American Historians, American Academy of Arts and Sciences, and the American Philosophical Society. He has served as past president of the Organization of American Historians, 1994–95, and was a founding member of the National Council for History Education, 1990.

Volume I Editor: Peter Mancall, University of Kansas, received a Ph.D. at Harvard University. He is a published author of several books, including *Envisioning America: English Plans for Colonization of North America, 1580–1640* (St. Martin's Press, 1995) and *American Encounters: Natives and Newcomers from European Contact to Indian Removal* (Routledge, 2000).

Volume II Editor: Billy G. Smith, Montana State University, received a Ph.D. from the University of California, Los Angeles. He is a published author of several books, including *The "Lower Sort": Philadelphia's Laboring People, 1750–1800* (Cornell University Press) and the forthcoming *Down and Out in Early America* (Penn State University Press).

Volume III Editor: Paul A. Gilje, University of Oklahoma, holds a Ph.D from Brown University. He is the author of several books, including *Rioting in America*

(Indiana University Press, 1996) and *The Road to Mobocracy: Popular Disorder in New York City, 1763–1834* (University of North Carolina Press, 1987).

Volume IV Editor: Malcolm J. Rohrbough, University of Iowa, holds a Ph.D. from the University of Wisconsin. He is the author of several books, including *Days of Gold: The California Gold Rush and the American Nation* (University of California Press, 1996), and is coeditor of a 10-volume history of the trans-Appalachian frontier to be published by the University of Illinois Press.

Volume V Editor: Joan Waugh is a professor of history at the University of California, Los Angeles, where she specializes in the Civil War and Reconstruction periods. She is the author of *Unsentimental Reformer: The Life of Josephine Shaw Lowell* (Harvard University Press, 1998) and the forthcoming *Ulysses S. Grant and the Union Cause* (University of North Carolina Press, 2004).

Volume VI Editor: Ari Hoogenboom, professor emeritus, Brooklyn College, City University of New York, received a Ph.D. from Columbia University. He is the author of *The Gilded Age* (Prentice Hall, 1967) and *Rutherford B. Hayes: Warrior and President* (University Press of Kansas, 1995), among other books and articles.

Volume VII Editor: Elizabeth Faue, Wayne State University, received a Ph.D. from the University of Minnesota. She is the author of *Community of Suffering and Struggle: Women, Men, and the Labor Movement in Minneapolis, 1915–1945* (University of North Carolina Press, 1991) and *Writing the Wrongs: Eva McDonald and the Political Culture of American Labor Reform* (Cornell University Press, 2002).

Volume VIII Editor: John W. Jeffries, University of Maryland, Baltimore County, received a Ph.D. from Yale University. He is the author of several books, including *Wartime America: The World War II Homefront* (Ivan Dee, 1996).

Volume IX Editor: Allan M. Winkler, Miami University of Ohio, received a Ph.D from Yale University. He is the author of several books, including *Life Under a Cloud: American Anxiety about the Atom* (Oxford University Press, 1993) and a best-selling textbook, *The American People: Creating a Nation and Society* (with Gary Nash), now in its fifth edition.

Volume X Editor: Donald T. Critchlow, St. Louis University, received a Ph.D from the University of California, Berkeley. He is the author of several books, including *Intended Consequences: Birth Control, Abortion and the Federal Government in Modern America* (Oxford University Press, 1999) and coauthor of the textbook *America: A Concise History* (Wadsworth, 1993).

Foreword

The Encyclopedia of American History series is designed as a handy reference to the most important individuals, events, and topics in U.S. history. In 10 volumes, the encyclopedia covers the period from the 15th century, when European explorers first made their way across the Atlantic Ocean to the Americas, to the present day. The encyclopedia is written for precollegiate as well as college students, for parents of young learners in the schools, and for the general public. The volume editors are distinguished historians of American history. In writing individual entries, each editor has drawn upon the expertise of scores of specialists. This ensures the scholarly quality of the entire series. Articles contributed by the various volume editors are uncredited.

This 10-volume encyclopedia of "American history" is broadly conceived to include the historical experience of the various peoples of North America. Thus, in the first volume, many essays treat the history of a great range of indigenous people before contact with Europeans. In the same vein, readers will find essays in the first several volumes that sketch Spanish, Dutch, and French explorers and colonizers who opened up territories for European settlement that later would become part of the United States. The venues and cast of characters in the American historical drama are thus widened beyond traditional encyclopedias.

In creating the eras of American history that define the chronological limits of each volume, and in addressing major topics in each era, the encyclopedia follows the architecture of *The National Standards for United States History, Revised Edition* (Los Angeles: National Center for History in the Schools, 1996). Mandated by the U.S. Congress, the national standards for U.S. history have been widely used by states and school districts in organizing curricular frameworks and have been followed by many other curriculum-building efforts.

Entries are cross-referenced, when appropriate, with *See also* citations at the end of articles. At the end of most entries, a listing of articles and books allows readers to turn to specialized sources and historical accounts. In each volume, an array of maps provide geographical context, while numerous illustrations help vivify the material covered in the text. A time line is included to provide students with a chronological reference to major events occurring in the given era. The selection of historical documents in the back of each volume gives students experience with the raw documents that historians use when researching history. A comprehensive index to each volume also facilitates the reader's access to particular information.

In each volume, long entries are provided for major categories of American historical experience. These categories may include: African Americans, agriculture, art and architecture, business, economy, education, family life, foreign policy, immigration, labor, Native Americans, politics, population, religion, urbanization, and women. By following these essays from volume to volume, the reader can access what might be called a mini-history of each broad topic, for example, family life, immigration, or religion.

—Gary B. Nash
University of California, Los Angeles

Index

Boldface page numbers denote extensive treatment of a topic. *Italic* page numbers refer to illustrations; *c* refers to the Chronology; and *m* indicates a map.

A

AA (American Association)
baseball league **VI:** 22
AAA. *See* Agricultural
Adjustment Administration
AAAS (American Association for
the Advancement of Science)
IV: 308
AABA. *See* American Anti-
Boycott Association
AALL. *See* American
Association for Labor
Legislation
AAPA (Association Against the
Prohibition Amendment)
VII: 241
Aaron, Henry L.(Hank) **IX:** 5;
X: 1, 325c
AARP (American Association of
Retired Persons) **X:** 189
AASS. *See* American Anti-
Slavery Society
Aataentsic **I:** 1, 171; **II:** 160
ABA (American Basketball
Association) **X:** 285
Abakuas **I:** 48
Abamacho **I:** 225
Abbe, Cleveland **VI:** 310
Abbey, Edwin Austin **VI:** 137
Abbott, Grace **VII:** 1, 3; **VIII:**
383
Abbott and Costello **VIII:** 217
ABC network
popular culture **X:** 239,
241
television **X:** 295, 296
"Abdul Scam." *See* Abscam
Abenaki **I:** 1–2
Duston, Hannah Emerson
II: 97
Maliseet **I:** 219

Native Americans **II:** 243
New Hampshire **II:** 250,
251
Passamaquoddy **I:** 278
Vermont **II:** 381
Abercromby, James **II:** 158
Aberdeen, Lord **IV:** 270
Abernathy, Ralph **IX:** 38, 161,
274
Abington Township v. Schempp
IX: 257, 333c
AbioCor **X:** 275
*Ableman v. Booth; United States
v. Booth* **V:** 405c
ABM Treaty. *See* Anti-Ballistic
Missile Treaty
abolition/abolition movement
II: *1*, 1–2; **III:** 15–17, *16*,
393c, 394c; **IV:** xiii, 1–4, *2,
5*, 376c–379c; **V:** 1–4, *3*,
405c
AASS **IV:** 13–15, *14*
ACS **IV:** 15–16
African Americans **III:** 5;
IV: 8–9
AME Church **V:** 5
American Missionary
Association **V:** 8
Banneker, Benjamin **III:**
33–34
Barnum, Phineas T. **VI:**
20
Beecher, Henry Ward **VI:**
24
Benezet, Anthony **II:**
31–32
Birth of a Nation **VII:** 31
Blackwell, Antoinette
Brown **VI:** 30
Blair, Francis P., Jr. **V:** 30
Bleeding Kansas **V:** 31–32
Booth, John Wilkes **V:** 32

Brown, John **V:** 37–38
Brown, William Wells **V:**
39–40
Burns, Anthony **IV:** 59
Calhoun, John C. **IV:** 63
Carney, William H. **V:** 49
Chase, Salmon P. **V:** 56
Christiana, Pennsylvania,
riot **V:** 59
Civil Rights Act of 1866 **V:**
62
Civil War **V:** 63–67
Compromise of 1850 **IV:**
93, 95
Confiscation Acts **V:** 78
cotton culture **IV:** 98
Cuffe, Paul **III:** 98
Dana, Charles A. **V:** 88
Dana, Richard Henry **IV:**
103
Davis, Jefferson **V:** 89, 90
Delany, Martin Robinson
V: 93
Democratic Party **IV:** 108
Douglass, Frederick **V:**
99–100
Dred Scott decision **V:** 102
Dunmore, Lord **III:** 109
emancipation **V:** 111
Emerson, Ralph Waldo **IV:**
126–127
entertainment, popular **VI:**
95
Equiano, Olaudah **III:**
118–119
female antislavery societies
IV: 135–136
54th Massachusetts
Regiment **V:** 124
Finney, Charles Grandison
IV: 139
Fitzhugh, George **V:** 128

Forten, James **III:**
131–132
Foster, Abigail Kelley **IV:**
147–148
Fourteenth Amendment
V: 138
Franklin, Benjamin **III:**
135
Free-Soil Party **IV:** 150
Frémont, John C. **IV:** 154
fugitive slave laws **IV:** 154,
155
Fuller, Margaret **IV:** 156
Gabriel's Rebellion **III:**
145
Garfield, James A. **VI:** 108
Garrison, William Lloyd **V:**
145–147
*Genius of Universal
Emancipation* **IV:**
160–161
Greeley, Horace **V:** 158
Greenhow, Rose O'Neal **V:**
159
Grimké, Angelina and
Sarah **IV:** 164–165
Grimké, Charlotte Forten
V: 160
Haiti **III:** 159
Hall, Prince **III:** 160
Hammon, Jupiter **II:**
153–154
Harper, Frances Ellen
Watkins **V:** 164
Herndon, William H. **V:**
166
Hicks, Elias **IV:** 173
Higginson, Thomas
Wentworth **V:** 166–167
Howe, Julia Ward **V:** 174
humanitarianism **III:** 170
Jay, John **III:** 182

abolition/abolition movement
(*continued*)
  jayhawkers **V:** 186–187
  Johnson, Andrew **V:** 187
  Joint Committee on the
    Conduct of War **V:** 191
  Jones, Absalom **III:** 189
  journalism **II:** 178; **IV:** 194
  Julian, George W. **V:** 194
  Juneteenth **V:** 194–195
  Kansas-Nebraska Act of
    1854 **V:** 197–198
  Kelley, William D. **V:** 198
  King, Rufus **III:** 195, 196
  labor and labor movements
    III: 199
  Langston, John Mercer **VI:**
    171
  Laurens, Henry **III:**
    202–203
  Liberia **IV:** 209
  Liberty Party **IV:** 210–211
  Lincoln, Abraham **V:** 208
  literature **IV:** 212; **V:** 212
  Livingston, William **III:**
    217
  Lovejoy, Elijah **IV:**
    214–215
  Madison, James **III:** 230
  Mason-Dixon Line **V:** 224
  Massachusetts Emigrant
    Aid Society **IV:** 223–224
  Methodism **III:** 242
  monuments **V:** 239
  Mott, Lucretia **IV:**
    246–247
  Negro Convention
    movement **IV:** 261
  Niles, Hezekiah **III:**
    258–259
  NWSA **V:** 248
  Oglethorpe, James Edward
    II: 267
  Ostend Manifesto **V:** 260
  Paine, Thomas **III:** 271
  Peale, Charles Willson **3:**
    273
  Pennington, James William
    Charles **V:** 270
  personal liberty laws **IV:**
    280
  Phillips, Wendell **IV:**
    280–281
  Pierce, Franklin **V:** 275
  Port Royal, South
    Carolina, Experiment **V:**
    279
  Quakers **II:** 309; **III:** 291
  race and racial conflict **IV:**
    291; **V:** 287
  religion **IV:** 296; **V:** 299,
    300

  Republican Party **IV:** 300,
    301; **V:** 301
  Revels, Hiram R. **V:** 303
  Rush, Benjamin **III:** 313
  Schurz, Carl **VI:** 256
  Seneca Falls **IV:** 313–314
  Sewall, Samuel **II:** 334
  Seward, William H. **V:** 314
  slavery **III:** 326, 327; **IV:**
    316; **V:** 328
  Society of Friends **V:** 331
  spiritualism **IV:** 325, 326
  Stanton, Edwin M. **V:** 333
  Stanton, Elizabeth Cady **V:**
    334
  Stevens, Thaddeus **V:** 337,
    338
  Stewart, Maria **IV:** 327
  Still, William **IV:** 327–328
  Stone, Lucy **VI:** 278
  Stowe, Harriet Beecher **V:**
    338–339
  Sumner, Charles **V:** 342,
    343
  Tappan, Arthur and Lewis
    IV: 333–334
  Taylor, Susie King **V:** 350
  Thoreau, Henry David **IV:**
    342
  Truth, Sojourner **V:** 357
  Tubman, Harriet **V:** 358
  Underground Railroad **V:**
    361
  Van Lew, Elizabeth **V:** 378
  Wade, Benjamin **V:** 385
  Weld, Theodore Dwight
    IV: 362
  Welles, Gideon **V:** 391
  Wheatley, Phillis **III:**
    373–374
  Whig Party **IV:** 364
  Williams, Peter, Jr. **IV:** 366
  Wilmot Proviso **V:** 395
  Women's National Loyal
    League **V:** 396
  women's status and rights
    IV: 368; **V:** 397
  Woolman, John **II:** 410
  Wright, Fanny **IV:** 369
  Yancey, William Lowndes
    V: 401
abortion **X:** 1–4, *2*, 324*c*, 327*c*,
  330*c*, 331*c*
  *Akron v. Akron Center for
    Reproductive Health* **X:**
    16–17
  birth control **X:** 36, 37
  birthrates **X:** 38
  Brennan, William J. **X:** 41
  Burger, Warren E. **X:** 44
  Christian Coalition **X:** 61
  Clinton, William **X:** 66

  conservative movement **X:**
    79, 80
  ERA **X:** 106
  feminism **X:** 114–116
  fertility **II:** 118
  Ford, Gerald R. **X:** 121
  Ginsburg, Ruth Bader **X:**
    130–131
  Gore, Albert, Jr. **X:** 133
  Helms, Jesse A., Jr. **X:** 141
  Kennedy, Edward M. **X:**
    164
  Libertarian Party **X:** 176
  marriage and family life
    VIII: 204; **X:** 182, 183
  NOW **X:** 211
  O'Connor, Sandra Day **X:**
    226
  Powell, Lewis **X:** 247
  pro-life and pro-choice
    movements **X:** 248–249
  public health **VII:** 243
  Reagan, Ronald W. **X:** 259,
    260
  Roe v. Wade **X:** 268,
    335–338
  Scalia, Antonin **X:** 271
  sexual revolution **X:** 277,
    278
  Souter, David **X:** 279
  Steinem, Gloria **X:** 288
  Supreme Court **X:** 290,
    291
  televangelism **X:** 293
  United Nations **X:** 307
  WEAL **IX:** 323–325
  *Webster v. Reproductive
    Health Services* **X:**
    318–319
  White, Byron R. **X:** 319
  women's rights and status
    X: 320
"Abortion and the Conscience
  of the Nation" (Reagan) **X:** 3
Abraham Levitt and Sons **VIII:**
  343
Abraham Lincoln Brigade **VIII:**
  276, 335
Abrams v. United States **VII:**
  123, 275, 280; **VIII:** 54
*Abridgement of the Debates of
  Congress from 1789 to 1856*
  (Benton) **IV:** 50
Absalom! Absalom! (Faulkner)
  VIII: 192
Absarokee. *See* Crow
Abscam **X:** 4–5
abstract art **VII:** 19, 20; **VIII:**
  24, 25
abstract expressionism **VIII:** 25;
  IX: 19–20
Abyssinia. *See* Ethiopia

Abzug, Bella **IX:** 115; **X:** 116,
  211
AC. *See* alternating current
Academy Award **VIII:** 406*c*
Acadia **I:** 2–3. *See also* Nova
  Scotia
Acadians **I:** 2; **II:** **2,** 419*c*
  Creole **II:** 74
  French colonies **II:** 129
  Monckton, Robert **II:** 232
  New Orleans **II:** 258
  Queen Anne's War **II:** 309
  Seven Years' War **II:** 332
Acamapichtli **I:** 17
Acapulco **I:** 318
accidents, workplace **X:** 225
Accomac nation **II:** 295
Account of Denmark
  (Molesworth) **III:** 79
Acheson, Dean **IX:** *1,* **1–2,** 330*c*
  Asia (foreign policy) **IX:** 21
  Hiss, Alger **IX:** 134
  Korean War **IX:** 163
  military-industrial complex
    IX: 203
  NATO **IX:** 233
  NSC-68 **IX:** 233
  White Paper **IX:** 321
Achille Lauro **X:** 222, 298
acid rain **X:** 195
ACLU. *See* American Civil
  Liberties Union
Acoma pueblo **I:** 13, 257, 271,
  295; **II:** 254, 303
Acosta, Jorge **I:** 354
Acosta, José de **I:** **3,** 207
acquired immune deficiency
  syndrome (AIDS) **X:** 5–6,
  326*c*
  African Americans **X:** 10
  gay rights movement **X:**
    127
  sexual revolution **X:** 278
Acropolis (Copán) **I:** 86
ACS. *See* American
  Colonization Society
Act Against Papists (1593) **I:**
  121
Act Concerning Religion **II:**
  144, 323
Act in Restraint of Appeals
  (1533) **I:** 73
ACTION agency **IX:** 311
activism. *See also* judicial
  activism
  "Chicago Eight" **X:** 61
  Christian Coalition **X:**
    61–62
  conservation,
    environmentalism, and
    environmental policy **X:**
    77

conservative movement **X:** 79
ERA **X:** 105–107
feminism **X:** 113–116
gay rights movement **X:** 127–128
gun control **X:** 137
liberalism **X:** 175
Moral Majority **X:** 197
NAACP **X:** 208–209
Native Americans **X:** 214
NOW **X:** 210–211
nuclear freeze movement **X:** 224
pro-life and pro-choice movements **X:** 248–249
race and racial conflict **X:** 256
Schlafly, Phyllis **X:** 271–272
South Africa **X:** 279
Steinem, Gloria **X:** 287, 288
Weather Underground **X:** 317–318
Act of 1873 **VII:** 60
Act of Chapultepec **VIII:** 410c
act of faith. See auto-da-fé
Act of Supremacy (1534) **I:** 309; **II:** 19
Act of Supremacy (1559) **I:** 120, 309
Act of Supremacy and Uniformity (1559) **I:** 74
Act of the Six Articles (1536) **I:** 73
Act of Toleration **II:** 144
Act of Union **II:** 87, 232
Acts of Trade **III:** 360
Acts of Trade and Navigation **II:** 2–3, 418c, **III:** 322
   animals **II:** 20–21
   Boston **II:** 35
   British Empire **II:** 41
   Lloyd, David **II:** 197
   Maryland **II:** 210
   Massachusetts **II:** 214
   mercantilism **II:** 221
   monarchy, British **II:** 232
   piracy **II:** 285
   rum trade **II:** 326
   smuggling **II:** 349
Act to Combat International Terrorism of 1984 **X:** 298
Act Up **X:** 127
Acuff, Roy **VIII:** 222
ACW. See Amalgamated Clothing Workers of America
ADA. See Americans for Democratic Action; Americans with Disabilities Act

Adal **I:** 109, 124
Adams, Abigail **III:** 1, 3, 365; **IV:** 4
Adams, Ansel **VII:** 19; **VIII:** 24, 268
Adams, Brock **X:** 276
Adams, Charles F. **IV:** 151; **V:** 314; **VI:** 174
Adams, Henry **VI:** 1–2
   Gilded Age, The **VI:** 114
   King, Clarence **VI:** 160
   literature **VI:** 177
   Saint-Gaudens, Augustus **VI:** 253
   Victorianism **VI:** 304
Adams, John **II:** 405; **III:** 1–4, 2, 392c–397c; **IV:** 4, 106, 168; **V:** 372
   Adams, Abigail **III:** 1
   Alien and Sedition Acts **III:** 9
   art **III:** 23
   Attucks, Crispus **III:** 28
   Bache, Benjamin Franklin **III:** 29
   Boston Massacre **III:** 43
   Chase, Samuel **III:** 65
   Common Sense (Paine) **III:** 79
   Constitutional Convention **III:** 81
   constitutions, state **III:** 82
   Continental Congress, First **III:** 87
   Continental Congress, Second **III:** 88
   Conway Cabal **III:** 90
   Copley, John Singleton **III:** 91
   Coxe, Tench **III:** 96
   Declaration of Independence **III:** 102
   Duane, William **III:** 108
   education **III:** 114
   election of 1800 **III:** 116
   Federalist Party **III:** 126
   foreign affairs **III:** 130
   Franklin, Benjamin **III:** 135
   Fries's Rebellion **III:** 140
   Gerry, Elbridge **III:** 152, 153
   Hamilton, Alexander **III:** 162
   Jay, John **III:** 181
   Jefferson, Thomas **III:** 183, 185, 186
   Judiciary Act of 1801 **III:** 193
   Loyalists **III:** 219
   Loyal Nine **III:** 222
   Madison, Dolley **III:** 227

Madison, James **III:** 229
Marbury v. Madison **III:** 230
Marshall, John **III:** 235
Mayhew, Jonathan **III:** 238
Paris, Treaty of **III:** 273
Pickering, John **III:** 276
Quasi War **III:** 292
Quincy, Josiah **III:** 293
Rush, Benjamin **III:** 313
suffrage **III:** 336
Supreme Court **III:** 338
Taylor, John, of Caroline **III:** 344
Virginia dynasty **III:** 361
Warren, Joseph **III:** 363
Warren, Mercy Otis **III:** 364
Washington, George **III:** 366
Weems, "Parson" **III:** 371
writs of assistance **III:** 384
XYZ affair **III:** 385
Adams, John Quincy **II:** 220; **IV:** 4–5, 375c, 376c; **X:** 102
   AASS **IV:** 14
   Adams, Abigail **III:** 1
   Adams-Onís Treaty **IV:** 5
   American System **IV:** 19
   Amistad incident **IV:** 20
   Calhoun, John C. **IV:** 62
   Clay, Henry **IV:** 87
   Copley, John Singleton **III:** 91
   Cuba **IV:** 100
   Democratic Party **IV:** 106–107
   election of 1828 **IV:** 122–124
   election of 1840 **IV:** 125
   Era of Good Feelings **IV:** 127
   Florida **III:** 129
   foreign affairs **III:** 131
   foreign policy **IV:** 141–142
   Harrison, William Henry **IV:** 169
   Jackson, Andrew **IV:** 192, 193
   King, Rufus **III:** 195
   Monroe Doctrine **IV:** 241
   political parties **III:** 279
   Polk, James K. **IV:** 282
   Tappan, Arthur and Lewis **IV:** 333
   Van Buren, Martin **IV:** 351
   Virginia dynasty **III:** 361
   Whig Party **IV:** 363
Adams, Samuel **II:** 72, 182, 215, 216; **III:** 4, 4–5, 392c
   anti-Federalists **III:** 14
   Boston Massacre **III:** 44

Boston Tea Party **III:** 45
Cincinnati, Order of **III:** 69
committees of correspondence **III:** 77
Continental Congress, First **III:** 87
Continental Congress, Second **III:** 88
Conway Cabal **III:** 90
Gerry, Elbridge **III:** 152
Hancock, John **III:** 163
Lee, Arthur **III:** 205
Lee, Charles **III:** 205
Lexington and Concord, Battles of **III:** 212
Loyal Nine **III:** 222
Old South Church **III:** 265, 266
Revere, Paul **III:** 304
Suffolk Resolves **III:** 335
Adams, Samuel Hopkins **VII:** 178
Adams Memorial (Saint-Gaudens) **VI:** 253
Adamson Act **VII:** 1–2, 358c
   AFL **VII:** 11
   Democratic Party **VII:** 66
   lobbying groups **VII:** 162
   Railroad Administration **VII:** 255
   Wilson, Woodrow **VII:** 334
Adams-Onís Treaty **III:** 129, 131, 258; **IV:** 5–6, 6m, 375c, 386–387
   Adams, John Quincy **IV:** 5
   Austin, Moses **IV:** 36
   Florida **IV:** 139
   foreign policy **IV:** 142
   Manifest Destiny **IV:** 218m
   Native Americans **IV:** 256
   Oregon Treaty of 1846 **IV:** 269
   Seminole wars **IV:** 312
   Texas **IV:** 337
Adarand Constructors Inc. v. Pena (1995) **X:** 264
'Adawiyya, Rabi'a al- **I:** 337
ADD. See Attention Deficit Disorder
Addams, Jane **VI:** 326c; **VII:** 2, 2–3, 358c
   criminal justice **VII:** 59
   immigration **VI:** 140
   Kelley, Florence **VII:** 146
   NAACP **VII:** 198
   National Women's Trade Union League **VII:** 205
   New Woman **VII:** 214
   progressivism in the 1890s **VI:** 233

Addams, Jane *(continued)*
   religion **VII:** 260
   settlement houses **VI:** 259
   social work **VII:** 289
   Wells-Barnett, Ida Bell **VI:**
      312
   "Why Women Should
      Vote" **VII:** 372–376
   Women's International
      League for Peace and
      Freedom **VII:** 337
   women's status and rights
      VII: 340
Address to the Inhabitants of the
   British Settlements in
   America, upon Slave-Keeping
   (Rush) **III:** 329
Address to the People of Great
   Britain **III:** 181
adelantado **I:** 3–4, 38, 78, 288
Adena **I:** 244
ADHD (Attention Deficit and
   Hyperactivity Disorder) **X:**
   190
Adirondack Forest Preserve **VI:**
   65
Adirondack Park **VI:** 65
Adja kingdom **I:** 101, 131
Adjusted Compensation Act
   VII: 291
Adkins v. Children's Hospital
   VII: 3, 87, 360c
Adler, Dankmar **VI:** 279–280
Adler, Felix **VI:** 158
Administration of Justice Act
   III: 76, 392c
Adobe Walls, Battle of **IV:** 76
adolescents. *See* children
Adolf of Nassau, archbishop of
   Mainz **I:** 147
Adopting Act **II:** 296
adoption (by Indians)
      captivity **II:** 51–52
      ethnocentrism **II:** 113
      Hendrick **II:** 155
      Jemison, Mary **II:** 173
      Native Americans **II:** 244
      Powhatan Confederacy **II:**
         295
      Smith, John **II:** 346
      South Carolina **II:** 353
      Zeisberger, David **II:** 415
adoption (in general) **X:** 128, 183
Adrian, Robert **III:** 321
Adrian of Utrecht **I:** 198
adult education **IV:** 215
adultery **II:** 409; **IV:** 222, 367
Advanced Research Projects
   Agency (ARPA) **X:** 152
Advance-Newhouse **X:** 244
adventism **IV:** 299; **VI:** 75,
   242–243

Adventures of Dollie (film) **VII:**
   115
Adventures of Huckleberry
   Finn, The (Twain) **IV:** 98; **V:**
   213; **VI:** 177, 298, 325c
Adventures of Tom Sawyer
   (Twain) **V:** 213
advertising **II:** 7, 292, 299; **IV:**
   196; **VI:** 2, **2–3,** 274; **VII:** 4,
   4–5; VIII: 1–2; **IX:** 2, 2–3,
   332c, 334c; **X: 6–8,** 7
   abortion **X:** 3
   agriculture **X:** 16
   business **VII:** 38; **IX:** 46
   campaign finance **X:** 53
   censorship **VIII:** 55
   consumer movement **IX:**
      69
   cosmetics industry **VII:**
      58
   Dukakis, Michael **X:** 91
   elections **IX:** 95
   FCC **VIII:** 116
   Food, Drug, and Cosmetic
      Act **VIII:** 123
   General Motors **IX:** 121
   Horton, Willie (campaign
      ad) **X:** 143–144
   illustration, photography,
      and the graphic arts **VI:**
      137
   journalism **VII:** 141; **IX:**
      153
   magazines **VI:** 185
   McDonald's **IX:** 191
   media **X:** 184, 186, 187
   miracle drugs **IX:** 206
   newspapers **VI:** 211, 212
   Packard, Vance **IX:** 239
   PACs **X:** 236
   political parties **X:** 239
   popular culture **VIII:** 273
   postwar planning **VIII:**
      279
   public opinion polls **VIII:**
      283
   radio **VII:** 254, 255
   SANE **IX:** 267, 268
   sexuality **VII:** 283
   sexual revolution **X:** 277
   suburbs **VIII:** 342
   television **IX:** 296–297; **X:**
      295
   tobacco suits **X:** 303, 305
   trade **VI:** 290
   trade, foreign **VII:** 309
   war bonds **VIII:** 374
   work, household **VII:** 342
   World War II home front
      VIII: 396
   yellow journalism **VI:** 321
Advertising Council **VIII:** 1–2

AEA (American Enterprise
   Association) **X:** 301
AEC. *See* Atomic Energy
   Commission
AEF. *See* American
   Expeditionary Force
AEI (American Enterprise
   Institute) **X:** 301
AERA. *See* American Equal
   Rights Association
aerial warfare **V:** 21–22
aerospace aviation **IX:** 28
aestheticism **VI:** 312
Aesthetic movement **VI:** 3, 15,
   248
Afar people **I:** 109
AFDC (Aid to Families with
   Dependent Children) **X:** 110
affirmative action **X: 8–9,** 329c
   African Americans **X:** 11
   Bakke **X:** 34–35
   Brennan, William J. **X:** 41
   Burger, Warren E. **X:** 44
   Civil Rights Act of 1991 **X:**
      63
   federalism **X:** 112
   liberalism **X:** 175
   militia movement **X:** 193
   NAACP **X:** 208
   Powell, Lewis **X:** 247
   race and racial conflict **X:**
      256
   Rehnquist, William H. **X:**
      264
   Supreme Court **X:** 291
Affluent Society, The (John
   Kenneth Galbraith) **IX:** 69,
   117, 332c
Afghanistan **X:** 330c, 331c
   Carter, James Earl, Jr. **X:**
      58
   Clinton, William **X:** 69
   cold war (end of) **X:** 71,
      72
   defense policy **X:** 86, 89
   economy **X:** 96
   foreign policy **X:** 123–125
   Powell, Colin L. **X:** 247
   Reagan, Ronald W. **X:** 260,
      261
   Strategic Arms Limitation
      Treaties **X:** 289
   terrorism **X:** 299, 301
AFL. *See* American Federation
   of Labor; American Football
   League
AFL-CIO **VIII:** 165, 291; **IX:**
   332c; **X:** 106, 169, 171, 329c
   American Federation of
      Labor **IX:** 11, 12
   labor **IX:** 170
   Reuther, Walter **IX:** 259

Teamsters Union **IX:** 292,
   293
union movement **IX:** 303
United Farm Workers **IX:**
   304
Afognak Forest and Fish-
   Culture Reserve **VI:** 65
Africa **I:** 138m, 386c; **II: 3–5;**
   IV: 209–210; **V:** 1, 328; **VI:** 5,
   103, 296–297; **VII:** 32, 33,
   105; **IX:** 332c. *See also*
   specific countries
   African Americans **II:** 5
   AIDS **X:** 5
   art and architecture **I:** 12
   Blaeu, Willem **I:** 31
   Brazil **I:** 33
   bubonic plague **I:** 285
   Cameroon **I:** 52–53
   Cathay (China) **I:** 65
   cold war (end of) **X:** 70, 71
   Columbian Exchange **I:**
      77, 78
   corn (maize) **I:** 88
   Creole **II:** 74
   Dias, Bartholomeu **I:** 105
   Djenne-Djeno **I:** 108–109
   Djibouti **I:** 109
   Dutch West India
      Company **II:** 98
   Ethiopia **I:** 123–125
   foreign policy **IX:** 3–4; **X:**
      12–14, 123
   Gama, Vasco da **I:** 137
   Georgia **II:** 138
   Ghana **I:** 140–141
   gold **I:** 142
   Gold Coast **I:** 143–144
   Gomes, Diogo **I:** 144
   Guinea-Bisseau **I:** 146–147
   Gullah **II:** 151
   horses **I:** 168–169
   Ibn Battuta **I:** 173
   Ibn Khaldûn **I:** 174
   invention and technology
      I: 180
   Islam **I:** 184
   Jamestown **II:** 172
   Johnson, Mary **II:** 175
   Kongo **I:** 195–196
   labor **II:** 189
   Leo Africanus **I:** 203–204
   Louisiana **II:** 199, 200
   Luba **I:** 209–210
   Mali **I:** 217–218
   manufacturing and
      industry **II:** 204
   marabout **I:** 222
   mariners **II:** 204
   Massachusetts **II:** 215
   mulattoes **II:** 237
   music **II:** 239

Newport **II:** 258
New York **II:** 259
Niger River **I:** 263
Point Four Program **IX:** 242–243
population trends **I:** 290
Prester, John **I:** 293
Sahara **I:** 315–317
Senegambia **I:** 321–322
Seven Years' War **II:** 332
slavery **I:** 326–327; **II:** 338–340
slave trade **I:** 330; **II:** 343–344
smallpox **I:** 330
Songhai **I:** 331–332
South Africa **X:** 279–280
Soviet Union **IX:** 277
Sudan **I:** 336–337
Sufism **I:** 337
Suleiman I **I:** 339
terrorism **X:** 298m
United Nations **X:** 307
Virginia **II:** 384
wars of national liberation **IX:** 317
witches **I:** 374
yellow fever **II:** 414
African-American churches, growth of **VI: 3–5**
African Americans **VI:** 6
AME Church **VI:** 4
AME Zion Church **VI:** 4–5
Baptists **VI:** 3–4
religion **VI:** 241
African-American education **II:** 6–7; **IV:** 7, 379c; **VI:** 5, 6; **X:** 10–11
Bruce, Blanche K. **V:** 40
Eastman, George **VI:** 87
education **V:** 108; **VI:** 89–91
education, federal aid to **VI:** 92
education, philanthropy and **VI:** 94
Morrill Land-Grant Act **V:** 241
Tubman, Harriet **V:** 358
African-American enlisted men, Union navy **V:** 368
African-American history **V:** 270
African-American labor **V:** 116
African-American movement **IX: 4–7**
Baker, Ella **IX:** 30–31
Black Panthers **IX:** 38–40
Black Power **IX:** 40–41
Carmichael, Stokely **IX:** 47–48
King, Martin Luther, Jr. **IX:** 160–162

Malcolm X **IX:** 186–187
Muhammad, Elijah **IX:** 214–215
NAACP **IX:** 220
Powell, Adam Clayton **IX:** 245–246
race and racial conflict **IX:** 253–255
Robeson, Paul **IX:** 261
Southern Christian Leadership Conference **IX:** 274–276
African-American music **VI:** 202
African-American newspapers **VII:** 113
African-American prisoners of war **V:** 282
African-American regiments **V: 4–5,** 5, 407c. See also African-American soldiers (Union army)
Carney, William H. **V:** 49
Corps d'Afrique **V:** 83–84
54th Massachusetts Regiment **V:** 124–126
Milliken's Bend, Battle of **V:** 232–233
Pinchback, Pinckney B. S. **V:** 275
Revels, Hiram R. **V:** 303
Taylor, Susie King **V:** 350
Truth, Sojourner **V:** 357
volunteer army **V:** 383
African Americans **II: 5–7,** 6t, 229, 237, 419c; **III: 5–7,** 394c, 396c; **IV:** xiii, **6–9,** 7, 8m, 376c–379c; **V:** 408c; **VI: 5–7,** 323c, 325c, 327c, 328c; **VII:** 77, 358c; **VIII: 2, 2–5,** 4, 406c–410c; **IX:** 332c; **X: 9–12,** 10m, 329c
AASS **IV:** 13
abolition/abolition movement **II:** 1–2; **III:** 15–17; **IV:** 1–4, 2
abortion **X:** 3
ACS **IV:** 15–16
African-American regiments **V:** 4–5
agriculture **II:** 7, 12; **VII:** 7
AIDS **X:** 5
aircraft industry **VIII:** 11
Allen, Richard **III:** 10–11
AME Church **V:** 5–6
American Federation of Labor **VI:** 11
American Missionary Association **V:** 8
Amistad incident **IV:** 20
Anglican Church **II:** 20
Annapolis Naval Academy **V:** 373

architecture **III:** 18
Army, U.S. **VIII:** 20
Army Air Forces, U.S. **VIII:** 21
art **IV:** 27; **VII:** 19–20
art and architecture **VIII:** 23–24; **X:** 26
Attucks, Crispus **III:** 27–28
automobile industry **VIII:** 30
banks **III:** 32
Banneker, Benjamin **III:** 33–34
Baptists **II:** 29
baseball **VI:** 22; **VII:** 27
Beckwourth, Jim **IV:** 46–47
Benezet, Anthony **II:** 31
Bethune, Mary McLeod **VIII:** 36
bicycling, 1870–1900 **VI:** 28
birth control **X:** 37
birthrates **X:** 38
Black Cabinet **VIII:** 37–38
Black Codes **V:** 29–30
black nationalism. See black nationalism
blues **VII:** 32
Boas, Franz **VII:** 33
Bridges, Harry **VIII:** 43
Brown, John **V:** 37
Brown, William Wells **V:** 39–40
Brownsville Riot **VII:** 35
Bruce, Blanche K. **V:** 40–41
Buffalo Soldiers **VI:** 39
Burns, Anthony **IV:** 59
Byrnes, James F. **VIII:** 48
camp followers **III:** 59
Canada **III:** 60
Caribbean **II:** 53
Carney, William H. **V:** 49
carpetbaggers **V:** 50
Cary, Ann Shadd **V:** 52
Catholics **VIII:** 54
Catto, Octavius **V:** 52–53
CCC **VIII:** 63
Charleston **II:** 56, 57
childhood **II:** 60
children **VIII:** 56
CIO **VIII:** 69
cities and urban life **III:** 70–71; **VII:** 48, 49–50; **VIII:** 59, 60
civil rights. See civil rights
Civil Rights Act of 1866 **V:** 62
Civil Rights Act of 1875 **V:** 62–63

civil rights cases **VI:** 55
Colored National Labor Union **V:** 68–69
Communists **VIII:** 65
Connecticut **II:** 69
conservative coalition **VIII:** 73
corruption, political **VI:** 66
cosmetics industry **VII:** 58
crime **X:** 82
crowd action **II:** 78
Crummell, Alexander **VI:** 70–71
Cuffe, Paul **III:** 98–99
dance **II:** 82
Dartmoor Prison **IV:** 103–104
Davis Bend, Mississippi, freedmen's colony **V:** 91–92
Delany, Martin Robinson **V:** 92–93
Democratic Party **V:** 95; **VII:** 67; **VIII:** 80, 81
disease **II:** 90, 91, 93
Douglass, Frederick **V:** 99–100
Dred Scott decision **V:** 100–102
Du Bois, W. E. B. **VII:** 71–72
Dunbar, Paul Laurence **VI:** 82–83
Dunmore, Lord **III:** 108, 109
Eaton, John, Jr. **V:** 104
education **II:** 104; **IV:** 120, 121; **V:** 108
education, higher **X:** 97
election of 1932 **VIII:** 96
election of 1936 **VIII:** 97
elections **V:** 111
Ellington, Duke **VIII:** 99–100
Elliot, Robert B. **V:** 111
emancipation **V:** 111–114
Emancipation Proclamation **V:** 114–115, 424
enemy aliens **VIII:** 102
Enlightenment **II:** 110
entertainment **VII:** 85
entertainment, popular **VI:** 95–97
ethnocentrism **II:** 112–113
Executive Order 8802 **VIII:** 106
exploration **IV:** 131
Fair Labor Standards Act **VIII:** 110
Farrakhan, Louis A. **X:** 111
FEPC **VIII:** 109

African Americans (continued)
  fertility **II:** 117–118
  Florida **III:** 129
  FMP **VIII:** 119
  food **II:** 121, 122
  Forten, James **III:**
    131–132
  Fort Mose **II:** 123
  Foster, Stephen C. **V:** 138
  Freedman's Saving Bank
    V: 141–142
  FSA **VIII:** 112
  fugitive slave laws **IV:**
    154–155
  Gabriel's Rebellion **III:**
    145
  Garvey, Marcus **VII:**
    105–106
  gender **II:** 137
  Gershwin, George **VII:**
    109
  Great Awakening **II:** 148
  Great Depression **VIII:**
    140
  Great Migration. *See* Great
    Migration
  Griffith, D. W. **VII:**
    115–116
  *Griggs et al. v. Duke Power
    Company* **X:** 136
  Grimké, Charlotte Forten
    V: 160
  Gullah **II:** 151–152
  Haiti **III:** 159
  Hall, Prince **III:** 160
  Hammon, Jupiter **II:** 154
  Harlan, John Marshall **VI:**
    122
  Harlem Renaissance. *See*
    Harlem Renaissance
  Harper, Frances Ellen
    Watkins **V:** 164
  Harpers Ferry, West
    Virginia **V:** 166
  Harrison, Benjamin **VI:**
    123
  Hayes, Rutherford B. **VI:**
    126, 127
  Helms, Jesse A., Jr. **X:** 141
  Hemmings, Sally **III:**
    164–165
  Hicks, Elias **IV:** 173
  Holiday, Billie **VIII:**
    148–149
  homefront **V:** 169
  housing **II:** 157
  Howard, O. O. **V:** 173
  immigration **V:** 176
  Islam **I:** 185
  Jackson, Jesse L. **X:** 159,
    160
  Jamestown **II:** 172
  jazz **VII:** 137

Jefferson, Thomas **III:** 184
Jim Crow. *See* Jim Crow
Johnson, Anthony **II:**
  175–176
Johnson, Jack **VII:**
  138–139
Johnson, Mary **II:** 175
Jones, Absalom **III:** 189
Joplin, Scott **VII:** 140–141
Juneteenth **V:** 194–195
Knights of Labor **VI:** 162
Kościuszko, Tadeusz **III:**
  198
Kuhn, Justus Engelhardt
  II: 186
Ku Klux Klan **V:** 199–201;
  VI: 162–163; **VII:** 147
Ku Klux Klan Act **V:** 201
labor and labor movements
  II: 188; **III:** 199; **VI:**
  171; **VII:** 154; **VIII:**
  179, 181
land **II:** 192
Langston, John Mercer **VI:**
  171–172
liberalism **VIII:** 188
Liberia **IV:** 209–210
Liberia, immigration to **VI:**
  174–175
literature **II:** 195; **IV:** 211,
  212; **V:** 213; **VII:** 161,
  162; **VIII:** 190, 192; **X:**
  177
lobbying groups **VII:** 163
Locke, Alain **VII:** 164
Locke, John **II:** 198
Louis, Joe **VIII:** 195–196
Louisiana **II:** 200
Lovejoy, Elijah **IV:** 214
Loyalists **III:** 219
lumbering **II:** 201
lynching. *See* lynching
mariners **II:** 204
Marines, U.S. **VIII:** 203
marriage and family life **II:**
  208; **III:** 232–235; **IV:**
  221; **VIII:** 204, 205; **X:**
  109
Maryland **II:** 211
medicine **II:** 220; **III:** 241;
  VII: 180; **VIII:** 208
Memphis riot **V:** 232
Methodism **III:** 242
midwives **II:** 225
migration **VIII:** 212, 213;
  IX: 201
miscegenation **II:** 228; **V:**
  233–234
modernism **VII:** 188
mortality **II:** 235
movies **X:** 198
MOWM **VIII:** 201–202
mulattoes **II:** 237–238

multiculturalism **X:** 200,
  201
music **II:** 239; **III:** 251; **V:**
  244–245; **VII:** 194,
  195; **VIII:** 221, 224; **X:**
  201
Myrdal, Gunnar **VIII:**
  224–225
NAACP. *See* National
  Association for the
  Advancement of
  Colored People
National Association of
  Colored Women **VII:**
  199–200
Nation of Islam **X:** 213
Native Americans **X:** 215
Navy, U.S. **VIII:** 237
Negro Convention
  movement **IV:** 261
Negro Plot of 1741 **II:**
  247–248
New Deal **VIII:** 242
New Jersey **II:** 253
New Netherland **II:** 257
Newport **II:** 258
news media **VIII:** 243
newspapers **VI:** 212
New York City **II:** 263
New York City draft riots
  V: 254–255
Niagara Movement **VII:**
  214–215
NYA **VIII:** 234
Owens, Jesse **VIII:**
  260–261
OWI **VIII:** 257–258
Paul, Alice **VII:** 226
Pennington, James William
  Charles **V:** 270
Petersburg campaign **V:**
  271
Phillips, Wendell **IV:** 281
photography **VIII:** 268
Pinchback, Pinckney B. S.
  V: 275–276
plantations **V:** 277
Plessy v. Ferguson **VI:**
  224–225
political parties **X:** 238
politics in the Roosevelt
  era **VIII:** 271
popular culture **VII:** 233;
  VIII: 275; **IX:** 243; **X:**
  241
population trends **II:**
  290–292; **III:** 284; **V:**
  279; **VI:** 226; **VII:** 233;
  VIII: 277; **X:** 243
Port Royal, South
  Carolina, Experiment **V:**
  279–280
postal service **II:** 292

postwar planning **VIII:**
  279
poverty **X:** 245, 246
POWs **VIII:** 282
Prince, Lucy Terry **II:** 298
race and racial conflict **II:**
  311–312; **III:** 295; **IV:**
  289–292; **V:** 287–288;
  VII: 247–249; **VIII:**
  287–289; **X:** 255–257
Radical Republicans **V:**
  289
radio **VII:** 254–255
railroads **V:** 290
Rainey, Joseph H. **V:**
  290–291
Randolph, A. Philip **VIII:**
  291
Ray, Charlotte **V:** 291
Reconstruction **V:** 291,
  293–295
Reconstruction Acts **V:**
  295, *295*, 296
redemption **V:** 296, 297
Red Scare **VII:** 259
refugees **V:** 298
relief **VIII:** 301
religion **II:** 313–314; **III:**
  299; **IV:** 296–297; **V:**
  300; **VII:** 261; **VIII:** 304
Republican Party **IV:** 301;
  VIII: 305
Revels, Hiram R. **V:** 303
Rhode Island **II:** 321
Robeson, Paul **VIII:**
  309–310
Roosevelt, Eleanor **VIII:**
  310–311, 411*c*
Roosevelt, Franklin D.
  VIII: 313
rural life **III:** 312
St. Mary's City **II:** 328
scalawags **V:** 307
Scottsboro Boys **VIII:**
  319–320
Second Great Awakening
  IV: 311
segregation **VII:** 280–281
Selective Service **VIII:**
  323–324
Seward, William H. **V:** 315
sharecropping **V:** 315–316
Sherman, William T. **V:**
  321
Sherman's March through
  Georgia **V:** 322–323
shipbuilding **VIII:** 325
Singleton, Benjamin **V:**
  327
slavery. *See* slaves/slavery
Social Security Act **VIII:**
  329
social work **VII:** 291

society, British American **II:** 351
Society for the Propagation of the Gospel in Foreign Parts **II:** 352
Society of Friends **V:** 332
Solid South **VI:** 270
South **VIII:** 331, 332
South Carolina **II:** 354
Special Field Order No. 15 **V:** 332–333
sports **VII:** 293–295; **VIII:** 336–338; **X:** 285, 286
Stevens, Thaddeus **V:** 338
Stewart, Maria **IV:** 327
STFU **VIII:** 333
Still, William **IV:** 327–328
Stowe, Harriet Beecher **V:** 339
strikes **V:** 340
suffrage **II:** 364; **III:** 336
Sumner, Charles **V:** 343
Supreme Court **VIII:** 344, 347
Tanner, Benjamin Tucker **VI:** 283
Tappan, Arthur and Lewis **IV:** 333
Taylor, Susie King **V:** 350
Terrell, Mary Church **VII:** 308
theater **V:** 352
Thirteenth Amendment **V:** 352–353
Tin Pan Alley **VII:** 309
tobacco **II:** 375
Tourgée, Albion W. **V:** 354
transportation **V:** 355
Truth, Sojourner **V:** 356–358
Tubman, Harriet **V:** 358–359
Turner, Henry McNeal **VI:** 296, 297
Turner, Nat **IV:** 346–348
Underground Railroad **V:** 361–362
unemployment **VIII:** 363, 364
Union League **V:** 367–368
United States v. Cruikshank **V:** 375–376
Universal Negro Improvement Association (UNIA) **VII:** 315–316
Urban League **IX:** 305–306
veterans, Civil War **V:** 379
Virginia **II:** 384, 385
Voting Rights Act of 1965 **IX:** 311–312
WAC **VIII:** 381

Wagner, Robert F. **VIII:** 372
Washington, Booker T. **VI:** 307–309
WASP **VIII:** 380
Watts uprising **IX:** 317–318
WAVES **VIII:** 380
Welles, Gideon **V:** 392
Welles, Orson **VIII:** 376
Wells-Barnett, Ida Bell **VI:** 311–312
Wheatley, Phillis **III:** 373–374
White, Walter **VIII:** 378
Williams, Peter, Jr. **IV:** 366
woman suffrage **VII:** 335
Women's National Loyal League **V:** 396, 397
women's rights and status **II:** 407, 410; **III:** 383; **V:** 399; **VII:** 340; **VIII:** 384–386; **IX:** 326; **X:** 320
World's Columbian Exposition **VI:** 320
World War II **VIII:** 389, 390
World War II home front **VIII:** 394
WPA **VIII:** 387
Wright, Richard **VIII:** 399–400
yellow fever **II:** 414
zambos **I:** 381–382
zoot-suiters **VIII:** 403–404
African-American soldiers (Confederate army) **V:** 169
African-American soldiers (Union army). *See also* African-American regiments
Butler, Benjamin **V:** 46
Carney, William H. **V:** 49
Catto, Octavius **V:** 52–53
Civil War **V:** 67
contrabands **V:** 80–81
Delany, Martin Robinson **V:** 93
Douglass, Frederick **V:** 100
emancipation **V:** 113
Emancipation Proclamation **V:** 115
Fort Pillow, Tennessee **V:** 135
Grant, Ulysses S. **V:** 156
Higginson, Thomas Wentworth **V:** 167
Kelley, William D. **V:** 198
Milliken's Bend, Battle of **V:** 232, 233
Petersburg campaign **V:** 272

Pinchback, Pinckney B. S. **V:** 275
prisons **V:** 282
race and racial conflict **V:** 287
Reconstruction **V:** 292
Revels, Hiram R. **V:** 303
slavery **V:** 330
Stanton, Edwin M. **V:** 334
African-American suffrage **V:** 408*c*; **VI:** 323*c*, 327*c*
AME Church **V:** 5
amnesty, acts of **V:** 8
Blackwell, Antoinette Brown **VI:** 30
Brown, Olympia **VI:** 36
Catto, Octavius **V:** 52
Chase, Salmon P. **V:** 57
elections **V:** 109
elections, conduct of **VI:** 95
emancipation **V:** 112
Enforcement Acts **V:** 117
Fifteenth Amendment **V:** 123–124, 428
Fourteenth Amendment **V:** 138–139, 427–428
Freedmen's Bureau **V:** 144
grandfather clause **VI:** 118–119
Grant, Ulysses S. **V:** 156
Great Migration **VII:** 112
Harrison, Benjamin **VI:** 123
Higginson, Thomas Wentworth **V:** 167
Hoar, George Frisbie **VI:** 130
impeachment of Andrew Johnson **V:** 178
Johnson, Andrew **V:** 188
Julian, George W. **V:** 194
Kelley, William D. **V:** 198
Langston, John Mercer **VI:** 171
Mallory, Stephen R. **V:** 222
NAACP **VII:** 199
Oates, William C. **V:** 257
Paul, Alice **VII:** 226
race and racial conflict **VII:** 248
Radical Republicans **V:** 288, 289
Reconstruction **V:** 293, 294
Reconstruction Acts **V:** 296
Republican Party **V:** 302
scalawags **V:** 307
Schurz, Carl **VI:** 256
segregation **VII:** 281
slavery **V:** 330
southern demagogues **VII:** 292

Stanton, Elizabeth Cady **V:** 334–335
Stone, Lucy **VI:** 278
Thirteenth Amendment **V:** 353
Union League **V:** 368
United States v. Cruikshank **V:** 375–376
Wells-Barnett, Ida Bell **VI:** 312
woman suffrage **VII:** 335
women's status and rights **V:** 398, 399
African-American theater **VI:** 203–204
African ethnic groups
Asante **I:** 13
Bantu **I:** 24–25
Benin **I:** 28
Dagomba **I:** 101
Ewe **I:** 125
Fang **I:** 127
Fon **I:** 131–132
Fulani **I:** 135
Gonja **I:** 144
Hausa **I:** 155
Igbo **I:** 175
Kotoko **I:** 196
Luba **I:** 209–210
Luhya **I:** 210
Maravi **I:** 223
Mbundu **I:** 229–230
Mossi **I:** 243–244
Mpongwe **I:** 246–247
in New Spain **I:** 260, 261
Oyo **I:** 273
Taureg **I:** 360–361
Téké **I:** 343
Yoruba **I:** 377
African Intelligencer, The **IV:** 209
African Masonic Lodge **III:** 160
African Methodist Episcopal (AME) Church **III:** 396*c*; **V:** 5–6; **X:** 11
ACS **IV:** 15
African-American churches, growth of **VI:** 4, 5
African Americans **III:** 6; **VI:** 6
Allen, Richard **III:** 11
Great Awakening **II:** 148
Liberia, immigration to **VI:** 175
Methodism **III:** 242
Negro Convention movement **IV:** 261
religion **III:** 299; **IV:** 297
Revels, Hiram R. **V:** 303
Tanner, Benjamin Tucker **VI:** 283–284

African Methodist Episcopal
(AME) Church *(continued)*
Tubman, Harriet **V:** 358
Turner, Henry McNeal **VI:**
296
Vesey, Denmark **IV:** 353
African Methodist Episcopal
Zion (AMEZ) Church **IV:**
297; **VI:** 4–6
African National Congress
(ANC) **X:** 280
African nations (foreign policy)
X: 12–14
African Repository, The **IV:** 15
Africans **II:** 417*c;* **IV:** 100, 333
English immigrants **II:**
109
mortality **II:** 235
New York City **II:** 263
slavery **II:** 339–340
slave trade **II:** 343–344
Spanish colonies **II:** 358
Virginia **II:** 382, 384
Africans' School **II:** 31
Afro-American Steamship and
Mercantile Company **VI:**
175
Afrocentrism **X:** 200
Afro-Christianity **II:** 384
afterlife. *See* death and afterlife,
beliefs about
"After the Ball" (Harris) **VII:**
309
Agadja. *See* Fon
Agassiz, Louis **IV:** 290; **VI:** 195
Agasu **I:** 101, 131–132
age (average) **V:** 278
age (median) **VIII:** 278
age (population trends) **X:**
243–244
Age Discrimination Act of 1975
X: 14, 113
Age Discrimination and
Employment Act of 1967 **X:**
113
Age Discrimination in
Employment Act of 1967 **IX:**
103
Agee, James **VIII:** 268
Agency for International
Development **IX:** 242
Age of Discovery **I:** 106
Age of Reason (Paine) **III:** 104,
249, 272
AGF (Army Ground Forces)
VIII: 381
aggravated assault **X:** 81
Agnew, Spiro T. **X:** 14, 120,
220, 221, 324*c*
Agona **I:** 59
agrarian reform **VII:** 331–332
agribusiness **VII:** 268; **VIII:**
390, 395

Agricultural Adjustment Act
VIII: 5–6, 406*c,* 407*c;* **IX:** 8
agriculture **VIII:** 7
Communists **VIII:** 65
Congress **VIII:** 67
conservatism **VIII:** 71
court-packing plan **VIII:**
76
economy **VIII:** 92
First New Deal **VIII:** 122
liberalism **VIII:** 188
New Deal **VIII:** 240
RA **VIII:** 307
socialists **VIII:** 327
STFU **VIII:** 333
Supreme Court **VIII:** 345
taxation **VIII:** 351, 352
Tugwell, Rexford G. **VIII:**
361
wage and price controls
VIII: 371
Wallace, Henry A. **VIII:**
373
Agricultural Adjustment
Administration (AAA)
African Americans **VIII:** 3
Agricultural Adjustment
Act **VIII:** 6
agriculture **VIII:** 8
Brain Trust **VIII:** 41
Communists **VIII:** 66
South **VIII:** 332
STFU **VIII:** 332–333
unemployment **VIII:** 363
agricultural and mechanical
(A&M) colleges **VI:** 8
Agricultural and Mechanical
Colleges Acts. *See* Morrill
Land-Grant Act
Agricultural and Technical
College (A&T) **IX:** 272–273
agricultural consolidation **V:**
175
agricultural cooperatives **VII:**
360*c;* **VIII:** 7, 405*c*
Agricultural Marketing Act
VII: 6
agriculture **VII:** 7
Capper-Volstead Act **VII:**
42–43
cities and urban life **VII:**
48
agricultural corporations
(agribusiness) **VII:** 268
agricultural depression
(1870–90) **VI:** 8–9, 69–70,
206
agricultural depression (1920s)
VII: xiv
Agricultural Adjustment
Act **VIII:** 5
Agricultural Marketing Act
VII: 5–6

agriculture **VII:** 7; **VIII:** 7
Capper-Volstead Act **VII:**
42
economy **VII:** 75; **VIII:** 90
Great Depression **VIII:**
138
Harding, Warren G. **VII:**
118
marriage and family life
VIII: 204
McNary-Haugen Farm
Bill **VII:** 175
rural life **VII:** 269
suburbs **VII:** 300
tariffs **VII:** 306
agricultural equipment **IV:**
105–106, 224–225
agricultural experiment stations
VI: 8, 45
agricultural exports **V:** 264;
VIII: 5, 9
agricultural implements **VI:**
221, 292
agricultural labor **VIII:** 409*c*
immigration **VIII:** 162
Mexican Americans **VIII:**
210
Mexican Repatriation
Program **VIII:** 211
Steinbeck, John **VIII:** 339
Agricultural Labor Relations Act
of 1975 (ALRA) **IX:** 305
Agricultural Marketing Act **VII:**
5–6, 7; **VIII:** 6–7, 405*c*
Agricultural Adjustment
Act **VIII:** 5, 6–7
agriculture **VIII:** 7
Congress **VIII:** 66
FCA **VIII:** 112
Hoover presidency **VIII:**
153, 154
agricultural prices **VIII:** 254
agricultural price supports **VII:**
175
agricultural processors **VIII:** 6
Agricultural Society, U.S. **IV:** 11
agricultural surplus. *See* crop
surplus
agricultural workers **VIII:** 65
Agricultural Workers
Organization **VII:** 130
agriculture **I:** 385*c;* **II:** 7–13, *9;*
III: 7–8, 398*c;* **IV:** 9–12; **V:**
6–7; **VI:** 7*m,* 7–9, 131–132,
327*c;* **VII:** 6–8; **VIII:** 7–9,
407*c;* **IX:** 7–9, 331*c,* 334*c;* **X:**
14–16, *15,* 149, 225. *See also*
specific crops
Abenaki **I:** 2
abolition movement **IV:** 1
Acadia **I:** 2
Acadians **II:** 2
Africa **II:** 4

African Americans **II:** 6;
IV: 7; **VI:** 5
Agricultural Adjustment
Act **VIII:** 5–7
Agricultural Marketing Act
VII: 5–6
Akan **I:** 5
Algonquin **II:** 17
Amazon River **I:** 8
Apalachee **I:** 11
Asian Americans **VIII:** 26
Azores **I:** 16–17
Bantu **I:** 25
barbed wire **VI:** 20
Barton, Clara **V:** 25
BIA **IV:** 180
Bidwell, John **IV:** 51
Black Codes **V:** 29
borderlands **II:** 35
braceros **IX:** 41–42
Brain Trust **VIII:** 41
Brazil **I:** 31
Brook Farm **IV:** 58
Cahokia **I:** 47
California **IV:** 64–66
California gold rush **IV:** 69
California missions **IV:** 70
Capper-Volstead Act **VII:**
42–43
Carib **I:** 56
Carver, George
Washington **VI:** 45
Cayuga **I:** 67
Champlain, Samuel de **II:**
56
children **VIII:** 56
chinampas **I:** 72
Church of Jesus Christ of
Latter-day Saints **IV:** 81
class **II:** 62–63
Columbian Exchange **I:** 77
Connecticut **II:** 69
corn (maize) **I:** 87–88
cotton culture **IV:** 97–99
Cuba **I:** 98
Deere, John **IV:** 105–106
Democratic Party **VIII:**
80
depression **VI:** 8–9
Dust Bowl **VIII:** 85–87
Economic Opportunity Act
of 1964 **IX:** 87
economy **II:** 101; **IV:**
117–118; **V:** 104, 107;
VII: 73; **VIII:** 90
employment **V:** 116
employment in (1950) **IX:**
45*m*
environment **II:** 110, 111
environmental issues **VIII:**
104
Erie Canal **IV:** 129
ethnocentrism **II:** 113

expansion **VI:** 7–8
Fair Labor Standards Act **VIII:** 110
fairs, agricultural **III:** 123
Farmer-Labor Party **VII:** 91
farmers' alliances **VI:** 99
FCA **VIII:** 111–112
Federal Farm Loan Act **VII:** 91–92
First New Deal **VIII:** 122
fishing **II:** 118
Florida **I:** 130; **II:** 120
food **II:** 121
food riots **V:** 129
foreign policy **VI:** 103; **VII:** 101
Fourier, Charles **IV:** 149
Free-Silver movement **VI:** 104–105
French colonies **II:** 127
frontier **III:** 141
FSA **VIII:** 112–113
fur trade **II:** 131
Gates, Sir Thomas **II:** 135
George III, king of Great Britain **III:** 151
Great Migration **VII:** 111–112
Great Plains **III:** 154
Great Plains Indians **II:** 149, 150
Greenland **I:** 145
Guadalajara **II:** 151
haciendas **I:** 149–150
Handsome Lake **III:** 164
Havasupai **I:** 156
Hawaiian Islands **IV:** 172
Hidatsa **I:** 161
Hohokam **I:** 163
homefront **V:** 168
Hoover presidency **VIII:** 153
Hopi **I:** 166–167
Huron **I:** 171; **II:** 160
immigration **IV:** 177; **V:** 175
indentured servitude **II:** 164
Indian Removal Act (1830) **IV:** 182–183
Indians of the Desert Southwest **II:** 165, 166
indigo **II:** 166
industrialization **IV:** 187
Iroquois **I:** 181; **II:** 168
Jamaica **I:** 187
Jamestown **II:** 171
Johnson, Mary **II:** 175
Kalm, Peter **II:** 181
labor **II:** 187–190
labor and labor movements **II:** 187; **III:** 199, 200

La Follette, Robert **VII:** 154
Lincoln, Abraham **V:** 209
lobbying groups **VII:** 163
Louisiana **II:** 199
machines **VI:** 8
Madeira **I:** 214
Maine **II:** 203
markets **VI:** 8
marriage and family life **II:** 206; **III:** 232, 235; **IV:** 222; **V:** 222; **VIII:** 204
Maryland **II:** 210
Massachusett **I:** 225
Massachusetts **II:** 215
Maya **I:** 226, 227
McGillivray, Alexander **III:** 240
McNary-Haugen Farm Bill **VII:** 175
Mexican Americans **VIII:** 210
Mexican immigration **VII:** 182, 183
Mexican Revolution **VII:** 184
migration **IV:** 235; **VIII:** 212–213
missions **II:** 229
Mississippian culture **I:** 236
Mississippi River **V:** 236
Morrill Land-Grant Act **V:** 241
mortality **II:** 235
Mossi **I:** 244
Natchez **I:** 251
National Reclamation Act **VII:** 203–204
Native American religion **I:** 252
Native Americans **II:** 243, 244, 246
New Hampshire **II:** 250
New Jersey **II:** 253
New Mexico **I:** 255, 257; **II:** 254
New Netherland **II:** 257
Newport **II:** 258
New Spain **I:** 261
New York **II:** 259
Non-Partisan League **VII:** 215–216
North Carolina **II:** 264
Northwest Coast Indians **II:** 265
Nullification Controversy **IV:** 264
Owen, Robert **IV:** 273
Panic of 1819 **IV:** 275, 276
Panic of 1837 **IV:** 276
Panic of 1857 **V:** 264

Patrons of Husbandry **VI:** 221
Pennsylvania **II:** 276
People's Party **VI:** 222
Peru **I:** 279
plantation system **II:** 286–287
Point Four Program **IX:** 243
population trends **III:** 284
Powhatan **I:** 292
Powhatan Confederacy **II:** 294–295
primogeniture and entail **II:** 297
pueblo **I:** 295
Pueblo Indians **II:** 303
Puerto Ricans **IX:** 250
RA **VIII:** 307
race and racial conflict **III:** 295
REA **VIII:** 315–316
Republican Party **VIII:** 305
Rhode Island **II:** 320, 321
rural life **III:** 312; **VII:** 268–269
Sandys, George **II:** 329
science **II:** 331
Secotan **I:** 320–321
service sector **IX:** 272
sharecropping. *See* sharecropping
Shenandoah Valley: Jackson's campaign **V:** 316
Sherman's March through Georgia **V:** 322
slavery **II:** 339, 342; **IV:** 316–319
society, British American **II:** 351
South **VIII:** 331, 332
South Carolina **II:** 353
South Carolina Regulation **III:** 330–331
Spanish colonies **II:** 355, 357
Special Field Order No. 15 **V:** 332–333
specialization **VI:** 8
STFU **VIII:** 332–333
suburbs **VII:** 300
Sudan **I:** 336–337
sugar **I:** 338–339
Sutter, John **IV:** 332
Swedish colonies **II:** 365
Taino **I:** 342
Taylor, John, of Caroline **III:** 344
techniques **VI:** 8
technology **II:** 369; **VIII:** 353
tenants **II:** 370

Teotihuacán **I:** 346
Texas **IV:** 337
Timucua **I:** 351
tobacco **I:** 353–354; **II:** 374
trade **III:** 351
Trail of Tears **IV:** 343
Tugwell, Rexford G. **VIII:** 361
Tuscarora **II:** 378–379
unemployment **VIII:** 363
United Farm Workers **IX:** 304–305
wage and price controls **VIII:** 371
Wallace, Henry A. **VIII:** 373
WMC **VIII:** 374
women's status and rights **II:** 406, 407
World War II **VIII:** 390
World War II home front **VIII:** 395
Yoruba **I:** 377
Agriculture Department **IV:** 11; **V:** 7; **VII:** 244; **VIII:** 63, 373; **IX:** 8, 9
agriculture **VI:** 8
conservation **VI:** 65
education, federal aid to **VI:** 92, 93
medicine **VI:** 191
Weather Bureau, U.S. **VI:** 310
Agriculture Labor Relations Act (California) **X:** 16
Aguado, Juan **I:** 78, 82
Aguilar, Francisco de **I:** 4
Aguilar, Gerónimo (Jerónimo) de **I:** 5, 92, 97, 146
Aguilar, Martin de **IV:** 93
Aguilera, Christina **X:** 241
Aguinaldo, Emilio **VI:** 100; **VII:** 8, 98, 355c
Aguirre, Lope de **I:** 8, 9, 119
Agustín I, emperor of Mexico **IV:** 303
ahaw (ahau) **I:** 227–228
Ahmar, Ibn al-, Muhammad V **I:** 174
Ahuitzotl **I:** 18, 97
Ai **I:** 130
Aideed, Muhammad Farah **X:** 66, 88, 328c
AIDS. *See* acquired immune deficiency syndrome
aid societies. *See* United States Christian Commission; United States Sanitary Commission; Women's National Loyal League
Aid to Dependent Children **VII:** 189; **VIII:** 328, 329, 383, 416–417. *See also* Title IV

Aid to Families with Dependent Children (AFDC) **X:** 110
Aid to the Blind **VIII:** 329, 418–419. *See also* Title X
AIM. *See* American Indian Movement
Ainsworth, Henry **II:** 238–239
"Ain't I a Woman?" speech **IV:** 379*c*
AIP. *See* American Independent Party
AIPO (American Institute for Public Opinion) **VIII:** 284
air brake **V:** 409*c*
Air Commerce Act of 1926 **VII:** 23, 147
air conditioning **VIII:** 353
aircraft **VI:** 150; **X:** 275
aircraft carriers **V:** 21; **VIII:** 74, 211
aircraft industry **VIII: 9–11,** *10*
air power **VIII:** 12
CIO **VIII:** 70
economy **VIII:** 92
labor **VIII:** 181
migration **VIII:** 213
mobilization **VIII:** 214
South **VIII:** 332
Sunbelt **VIII:** 344
technology **VIII:** 353
transportation **VIII:** 361
Air Force, U.S. **VII:** 160, 186–187; **IX:** 77, 329*c. See also* Army Air Forces
Air Force Department **IX:** 224
airlifts **IX:** 37, 299
airline industry **VII:** 147
Air Mail Act of 1934 **VII:** 24
airplane hijackings **X:** 297–298, 300, 327*c,* 331*c*
air power **VIII: 11–12**
aircraft industry **VIII:** 9–11
Army Air Forces, U.S. **VIII:** 20–21
Arnold, "Hap" **VIII:** 21–22
blitzkrieg **VIII:** 39
Britain, Battle of **VIII:** 43
Coral Sea, Battle of the **VIII:** 74
demobilization **VIII:** 79
Forrestal, James V. **VIII:** 126
Guadalcanal **VIII:** 141
Midway, Battle of **VIII:** 211
Navy, U.S. **VIII:** 236
North African campaign **VIII:** 249–250
Pearl Harbor **VIII:** 264
Philippine Sea, Battle of the **VIII:** 267
Solomon Islands **VIII:** 331

World War II European theater **VIII:** 392
World War II Pacific theater **VIII:** 398
Air Quality Act of 1967 **IX:** 334*c*
air raid drills **VIII:** 254
air traffic controllers' strike **X:** 170, 326*c*
air travel. *See* aviation
Aix-la-Chapelle, Peace (Treaty) of **II:** 182
Akan **I:** 5–6, 13, 144
Akerman, Amos **V:** 200
Akimel Au Authm **II:** 165, 166
Akimel O'odham (Pima) **I:** 164
Akron, Ohio, Women's Rights Convention of 1851 **V:** 357, 398
Akron v. Akron Center for Reproductive Health (1981) **X: 16–17,** 226
Akwamu **I:** 5
Alabama **I:** 85, 130, 213; **II:** 57, 60–61, 353; **VI:** 4, 210; **IX:** 333*c,* 334*c;* **X:** 107, 242, 313–314
Civil Rights Act of 1957 **IX:** 54
cotton culture **IV:** 99
freedom rides **IX:** 114
Horseshoe Bend, Battle of **IV:** 173
Indian Removal Act (1830) **IV:** 181
King, Martin Luther, Jr. **IX:** 161
migration **IV:** 235
Mobile campaign **V:** 236
NAACP **IX:** 220
Native Americans **IV:** 256
plantations **V:** 276
public land policy **IV:** 286
Reconstruction **V:** 294
Reynolds v. Simms **IX:** 259–260
secession **V:** 313
Trail of Tears **IV:** 344
Travis, William Barret **IV:** 345
Voting Rights Act of 1965 **IX:** 311
Wheeler, Joseph **V:** 392
White Citizens' Councils **IX:** 320
Yancey, William Lowndes **V:** 401
Alabama (music group) **X:** 202
Alabama (ship) **VI:** 43, 309, 310
Alabama, CSS
Confederate navy **V:** 74
foreign policy **V:** 132
Semmes, Raphael **V:** 313

Seward, William H. **V:** 315
Union navy **V:** 370
Alabama claims
foreign policy **V:** 132, 133
Seward, William H. **V:** 315
Sumner, Charles **V:** 343
Alabama Midland decision **VI:** 40, 239
Alamance, Battle of **III: 8,** 170, 261, 392*c*
Alamo, The **IV: 12–13,** 377*c*
Bowie, Jim **IV:** 56, 57
Crockett, Davy **IV:** 100
Gadsden Purchase **IV:** 159
Houston, Sam **IV:** 174
Mexican-American War **IV:** 232
Santa Anna, Antonio López de **IV:** 303
Texas **IV:** 338
Texas, Republic of **IV:** 341
Travis, William Barret **IV:** 346
Alarcón, Hernando de **I:** 90
Alaska **III: 8–9; IV:** 241, 269; **V:** 408*c;* **VI:** 65, 160–162; **VII:** 356*c*
abortion **X:** 2
Alaska Native Claim Settlement Act **X:** 17
Aleut **II:** 16
amendments to the Constitution **X:** 19
Bering, Vitus Jonassen **II:** 32
foreign policy **V:** 133
Green Party **X:** 135
Inuit **II:** 167
Jackson, Jesse L. **X:** 160
literature **II:** 195
marriage **X:** 183
Native Americans **X:** 215
population trends **X:** 242
Russia in **II: 13–14**
Russian settlements **II:** 326
Seward, William H. **V:** 315
Alaska Commercial Company **VI:** 26
Alaskan Aleuts **X:** 63, 327*c*
Alaska Native Claim Settlement Act (ANSCA) of 1971 **X: 17,** 214
Alaskan Natives **X:** 243. *See also* Native Americans
Albany, New York **IV:** 128
Beaver Wars **II:** 31
fur trade **II:** 130–131
Hudson, Henry **II:** 158
New Netherland **II:** 255
New York **II:** 259, 262
Protestantism **II:** 301
Albany Congress **II: 14,** *14,* 85, 155; **III:** 134, 170–171

Albany Plan of Union **II:** 14
Albany Regency **IV:** 351
Albee, Edward **VI:** 96; **IX:** 181
Albemarle Point, South Carolina **II:** 354
Albert, Carl B. **X: 17–18,** 120, 144
Albert of Mainz **I:** 211
Albright, Horace **VII:** 203
Albright, Madeleine K. **X: 18,** 329*c*
defense policy **X:** 88
feminism **X:** 116
Remarks to the Fourth World Conference on Women **X:** 353–355
United Nations **X:** 308
Albuquerque **I:** 90
alcaldes **I:** 39
alcaldías **II:** 355
Alcatraz **IX:** 13, 228; **X:** 214, 323*c*
alcohol/alcoholism **II: 14–15; III:** 346; **V:** 176, 230–231, 270; **VI:** 226, 233–235; **VII:** 327, 358*c*
American Fur Company **IV:** 17
Conestoga **II:** 67
French colonies **II:** 127
Indian Removal Act (1830) **IV:** 183
Jemison, Mary **II:** 173
marriage and family life **II:** 207
medicine **IV:** 230
merchants **II:** 222
Montour, Andrew **II:** 233
Neolin **II:** 248
New Netherland **II:** 257
Prohibition. *See* Prohibition; Prohibition Party
Rensselaerswyck **II:** 319
revitalization movements **II:** 320
taverns and inns **II:** 367, 368
temperance movement. *See* temperance movement; Woman's Christian Temperance Union
Virginia **II:** 384
Alcorn, James L. **V:** 307
Alcorn University **V:** 303
Alcott, Bronson **IV:** 155, 212, 345; **VI:** 9
Alcott, Louisa May **V:** 408*c;* **VI: 9**
Alcott, William **IV:** 111
Alden, John **II: 15,** 16, 361
Alden, Priscilla **II: 15–16,** 361

Alder and Sullivan **VI:** 279–280
Aldine Press **I:** 365
Aldrich, Nelson W. **VII:** 227,
    305
    Congress **VI:** 63, 64
    corruption, political **VI:** 67
    lobbies and pressure
        groups **VI:** 180
    tariff issue **VI:** 284
Aldrich, Thomas Bailey **VI:**
    176–177
Aldrin, Edwin "Buzz" **X:** 281
Aleman, Arnoldo **X:** 218
Aleut **II:** 13, 14, **16**, 166, 326
Aleutian Islands **VIII:** 398
Alexander, Charles **IV:** 196
Alexander, Edward P. **V: 7–8,**
    22, **150**
Alexander, Harold R. L. G.
    VIII: 249, 325
Alexander, James **II:** 16, 153,
    415
Alexander, Lamar **X:** 35
Alexander, Mary Spratt Provoost
    II: 16–17
Alexander, William **IV:** 239
Alexander, Sir William **I:** 3
Alexander, Will W. **VIII:** 112
Alexander I, czar of Russia **IV:**
    241
Alexander II, czar of Russia **VII:**
    109
Alexander III, Pope **I:** 292
"Alexander's Ragtime Band"
    (Berlin) **VII:** 194
Alexander VI **I: 6,** 203, 311,
    358, 369, 386*c*
Alexander VI, Pope **I:** 6
Alexander the Great **I:** 338
Alexandria Confederate
    Memorial **V:** 239
Alexie, Sherman **X:** 177
Alfonso V, king of Portugal **I:**
    127
Alfred, USS **III:** 36, 190
Alger, Horatio **VI: 9–10,** 81
Algeria **I:** 317, 360; **V:** 403;
    VIII: 249, 392; **IX:** 316; **X:**
    156, 228–229
Algiers **IV:** 104
Algonquian **I: 6,** 388*c*
    Hakluyt, Richard, the
        Younger **I:** 151
    Harriot, Thomas **I:** 154
    Iroquois **I:** 181, 183
    Maliseet **I:** 219
    Manteo **I:** 220
    Mantoac **I:** 221
    Massachusett **I:** 224
    Montagnais-Naskapi **I:**
        241
    Secotan **I:** 320–321
    werowance **I:** 372

Algonquin **I:** 6; **II: 17,** *318*
    agriculture **II:** 22
    Brulé, Étienne **II:** 44
    calumet **II:** 50
    Chesapeake Bay **II:** 58
    Connecticut **II:** 68
    Delaware **II:** 86
    disease **II:** 90
    Dutch-Indian Wars **II:**
        98–99
    Eliot, John **II:** 107
    ethnocentrism **II:** 113
    exploration **II:** 114
    French colonies **II:** 126,
        127
    Great Plains Indians **II:**
        149
    housing **II:** 157
    Huron **II:** 160
    Kieft, Willem **II:** 182
    Logan, James **II:** 198
    Maryland **II:** 209
    Massachusetts **II:** 212
    Massasoit **II:** 217
    Native Americans **II:**
        242–243
    New Hampshire **II:** 250
    New Netherland **II:** 256
    New York **II:** 259, 260
    Nicolet, Jean **II:** 263
    North Carolina **II:** 264
    Pennsylvania **II:** 274
    Powhatan (chief) **II:** 293
    Powhatan Confederacy **II:**
        294–295
    religion, Native American
        II: 317–318
    sachems **II:** 327
    Squanto **II:** 360–361
    Virginia **II:** 382
    wampum **II:** 390
    Wingina **II:** 401
    women's status and rights
        II: 406, 410
Algonquin (Kieft) War **II:** 99
Algonquin park wolf **II:** 405
Alhama **I:** 306
'Ali **I:** 184
Ali, Muhammad **IX:** 5–6, 9,
    9–10, 297, 334*c*
Alianza Federal de Mercedes
    IX: 298, 334*c*
Alianza para el Progreso. *See*
    Alliance for Progress
Alice Paul Amendment. *See*
    Equal Rights Amendment
    (ERA)
Alien Act of 1798 **III:** 9, 396*c*
Alien and Sedition Acts **III:**
    9–10, 396*c*; **IV:** 106
    Adams, John **III:** 3
    Bache, Benjamin Franklin
        III: 29

    Catholics **III:** 63
    Democratic-Republican
        Party **III:** 104
    Duane, William **III:** 108
    election of 1800 **III:** 116
    Federalist Party **III:** 126
    Fries's Rebellion **III:** 140
    Gallatin, Albert **III:** 147
    Jefferson, Thomas **III:** 185
    journalism **III:** 192
    liberty tree/pole **III:** 214
    literature **III:** 214
    Macon, Nathaniel **III:** 226
    Madison, James **III:** 229
    Quasi War **III:** 291–292
    states' rights **III:** 333
    Virginia and Kentucky
        Resolutions **III:** 360
Alien Exclusion Act. *See*
    Immigration Act of 1917
Alien Registration Act. *See*
    Smith Act
aliens, enemy. *See* enemy aliens
Allah Temple of Islam (ATI) **IX:**
    214
All-America Football
    Conference **IX:** 280
All-American Girls' Baseball
    League **IX:** 281
Allegheny County Buildings
    (Pittsburgh) **VI:** 248
Allegheny Mountains **V:** 305
Allen, Ethan **II:** 381; **III: 10,**
    392*c*, 393*c*
    Arnold, Benedict **III:** 21
    deism **III:** 104
    Fort Ticonderoga **III:** 133
    Green Mountain Boys **III:**
        156
    land riots **III:** 202
Allen, Florence **VIII:** 384
Allen, James **V:** 21
Allen, Leroy **IX:** 38
Allen, Richard **II:** 31, 148; **III:**
    6, **10–11,** 17, 189, 396*c*; **IV:**
    15, 261, 297; **V:** 1, 5; **VI:** 4; **X:**
    139
Allen, Steve **IX:** 267
Allen, William "Foghorn Bill"
    IV: 270
Allen, William Francis **VI:** 202
Allende, Salvador **X:** 173, 325*c*
Allen University **VI:** 4
All God's Chillun Got Wings
    (O'Neill) **VIII:** 309
Alliance, USS **III:** 36, 90
Alliance for Progress **IX: 10–11,**
    241, **317,** 333*c*; **X:** 172
Alliance movement. *See*
    farmers' alliances
Allied Control Council **IX:** 37
Allies **VII:** 343, 359*c. See also*
    Grand Alliance

All in the Family (TV program)
    X: 295
Allison, William B. **VI:** 32
All My Sons (Arthur Miller) **IX:**
    181
allotments **VIII:** 163
All-Star Game **VIII:** 336
Allston, Washington **IV:** 245
Almagro, Diego de **I:** 276, 277,
    283, 363
Almanack and Ephemeris
    (Banneker) **III:** 395*c*
almanacs **II:** 220; **III:** 33, 34,
    395*c*
Almohads **I:** 184, 222
"almonds" **I:** 46
Almoravids **I:** 141, 184, 217,
    222, 317
almshouses **II: 18,** 24, **34, 70,**
    282
Almy, Brown, & Slater **IV:** 184
Almy, William **III:** 325, 326
Alpert, Richard **IX:** 175, 184
alphabet, Mormon **IV:** 110
"alphabet" educational method
    IV: 228
Alpha Suffrage Club **VI:** 312
al-Qaeda **X:** 125, 300, 301, 331*c*
ALRA (Agricultural Labor
    Relations Act of 1975) **IX:**
    305
Alsace **VII:** *344*
Alsop, Joseph **IX:** 13, 14
Alsop, Stewart **IX:** 13, 14
Alta California **I:** 48; **II:** 331–332
Altamont, California **IX:** 244
altar screens **II:** 25
altepetl **I:** 18, 249, 352
alternating current (AC) **VI:**
    146, 149, 285, 326*c*
alternative service **V:** 331
Altgeld, John Peter **VI: 10–11,**
    127, **236; VII:** 62, 64
Altiplano **I:** 10
Altman, Robert **X:** 198, 240
Alton Observer **IV:** 214
aluminum **VI:** 145
Alvarado, Hernando de **I:** 90
Alvarado, Juan Bautista **IV:** 207,
    332
Alvarado, Pedro de **I: 6–8,** 7
    Aguilar, Francisco de **I:** 4
    Aztecs **I:** 21
    Cuauhtémoc **I:** 97
    Cuitláhuac **I:** 99
    Las Casas, Bartolomé de **I:**
        198, 199
    Maya **I:** 227
    New Spain **I:** 258
    Tezcatlipoca **I:** 348
    Tlaxcala **I:** 353
Alvares, Francisco **I:** 125
Alvord, John W. **V:** 141

A&M (agricultural and mechanical) colleges **VI:** 8
AMA. *See* American Medical Association
Amadas, Philip **I:** 26, 220, 313, 372; **II:** 264, 401
Amalecite. *See* Maliseet
Amalgamated Association of Iron and Steel Workers **VI:** 44, 132, 327*c*; **VII:** 297
Amalgamated Association of Miners **VI:** 57
Amalgamated Clothing Workers **VII:** 152
Amalgamated Clothing Workers of America (ACW) **VII:** 152; **VIII:** 145, 172, 186
Amalgamated Trades and Labor Assembly **VI:** 167
amalgamation **V:** 233
Amana **X:** 273
Amana Church Society **IV:** 299
Amana Community **VI:** 301
Amantacha **II:** 44
Amateur Athletic Union **VI:** 290
"Amazing Grace" (Newton) **II:** 239
Amazon **II:** 374
Amazon.com **X:** 178
Amazon River **I:** 8, 9*m*, 386*c*
    Andes Mountains **I:** 10
    Brazil **I:** 31, 33
    Vespucci, Amerigo **I:** 368
Amazons (female warriors) **I:** 102, 132
ambassadors. *See* diplomacy; United Nations
ambergris **I:** 9, 29
Amboise, Charles d' **I:** 204
Ambon, Indonesia **I:** 117
Ambrister, John **III:** 129
ambulance corps **V:** 230
AMCA (American Medical College Association) **VI:** 192
AME Church. *See* African Methodist Episcopal Church
amendments to the Constitution **X:** 18–20. *See also specific amendments*
America and the World War (Roosevelt) **VII:** 235
America First Committee **VIII:** 12–13, 409*c*
    Communists **VIII:** 65
    conservatism **VIII:** 72
    destroyers-for-bases deal **VIII:** 82
    isolationists **VIII:** 166
    Johnson, Hugh S. **VIII:** 174
    Neutrality Acts **VIII:** 239
    socialists **VIII:** 327

Wheeler, Burton K. **VIII:** 378
American, The (James) **VI:** 154
American Academy of Arts and Sciences **III:** 321, 394*c*; **V:** 174; **VI:** 195
American Academy of Sciences **VI:** 65
American Airlines **VII:** 147; **IX:** 27
American Almanac **IV:** 121
American and Foreign Anti-Slavery Society **IV:** 15, 334; **V:** 3
American Anti-Boycott Association (AABA)
    Buck's Stove **VII:** 36
    Danbury Hatters **VII:** 61
    National Civic Federation **VII:** 201
    open shop movement **VII:** 219
American Anti-Imperialist League **VI:** 13, 357–358
American Anti-Slavery Society (AASS) **IV:** 13–15, 14, 377*c*; **V:** 3, 146, 147, 331; **VI:** 12
    abolition movement **IV:** 3, 4
    female antislavery societies **IV:** 135–136
    Foster, Abigail Kelley **IV:** 148
    Liberty Party **IV:** 210
    Lovejoy, Elijah **IV:** 215
    Mott, Lucretia **IV:** 247
    Phillips, Wendell **IV:** 281
    religion **IV:** 296
    Seneca Falls **IV:** 313
    Tappan, Arthur and Lewis **IV:** 333
    Weld, Theodore Dwight **IV:** 362
    Williams, Peter, Jr. **IV:** 366
American-Arab relations **VIII:** 403
American Association (AA) (baseball league) **VI:** 22
American Association for Labor Legislation (AALL) **VII:** 342, 343
American Association for the Advancement of Science (AAAS) **IV:** 308; **VI:** 25, 195
American Association of Advertising Agents **VII:** 5
American Association of Education of Colored Youth **V:** 164
American Association of Retired Persons (AARP) **X:** 189
American Association of Social Workers **VII:** 290

American Association of the Red Cross **V:** 24, 25
American Association of University Women **VI:** 247
American Atheists **X:** 266
American Bandstand **X:** 202
American Baptist Anti-Slavery Convention **V:** 299
American Baptist churches **II:** 321
American Baptist Home Mission Society **V:** 299
American Basketball Association (ABA) **X:** 285
American Bible Society **III:** 169; **IV:** 296
American Biograph Company **VII:** 115
American Board of Commissioners for Foreign Missions **IV:** 183
American Bridge Company **VI:** 35
American Bund **VIII:** 19, 60, 131
American Capitalism (John Kenneth Galbraith) **IX:** 117
American Catholic Church **VI:** 243, 249
"American Century, The" (Luce) **VIII:** 196
American Citizens Equal Rights Association **V:** 276
"American Civilization" (Emerson) **IV:** 126
American Civil Liberties Union (ACLU) **VII:** 11, 62, 278; **VIII:** 13, 405*c*; **IX:** 104; **X:** 5, 118, 162, 245, 266
    Asian Americans **VIII:** 26
    civil liberties **VIII:** 60
    Korematsu v. United States **VIII:** 178
    Thomas, Norman **VIII:** 358
American Claimant, The (Howells) **VI:** 115
American Collegiate Association **VI:** 247
American Colonization Society (ACS) **IV:** 15, 15–16, 375*c*; **V:** 1, 270, 328; **VI:** 174, 296
    AASS **IV:** 14–15
    abolition/abolition movement **III:** 17; **IV:** 1, 2
    Cuffe, Paul **III:** 99
    Forten, James **III:** 132
    Genius of Universal Emancipation **IV:** 160
    Jones, Absalom **III:** 189
    Liberia **IV:** 209, 210

Madison, James **III:** 230
    race and race relations **IV:** 291
    religion **IV:** 296
American Commonwealth, The (Bryce) **VI:** 38, 326*c*
American Communist Party **VII:** 52
American Conflict, The (Greeley) **V:** 158
American Convention of Abolition Societies **IV:** 16
American Cotton Oil Company **VI:** 294
American Council of Learned Societies **IX:** 221
American Council on Race Relations **VIII:** 289
American Daily Advertiser **III:** 396*c*
American Democrat, The (Cooper) **IV:** 197
American Dilemma (Myrdal) **VIII:** 410*c*
    African Americans **VIII:** 5
    civil rights **VIII:** 62
    liberalism **VIII:** 189
    Myrdal, Gunnar **VIII:** 224, 225
    race and racial conflict **VIII:** 287, 289
American dream **VI:** 57, 233
American Emigrant Company **VI:** 66
American Enterprise Association (AEA) **X:** 301
American Enterprise Institute (AEI) **X:** 301
American Equal Rights Association (AERA) **V:** 397, 398; **VI:** 12, 36, 278
American Exodus: A Record of Human Erosion (Lange and Taylor) **VIII:** 87, 268
American Expeditionary Force (AEF) **VII:** 8–10, 9
    American Legion **VII:** 11
    Dawes, Charles **VII:** 63
    Pershing, John **VII:** 227
    veterans **VII:** 324
    Wilson, Woodrow **VII:** 334
    World War I **VII:** 344
American Express **IX:** 330*c*
American Farm Bureau **VII:** 359*c*
    agriculture **VII:** 7
    Capper-Volstead Act **VII:** 42
    lobbying groups **VII:** 163
    McNary-Haugen Farm Bill **VII:** 175
    rural life **VII:** 268

American Farm Bureau Federation **VIII:** 113; **IX:** 8, 330c

American Federationist **VII:** 252

American Federation of Labor (AFL) **VI: 11,** 325c; **VII: 10–11; VIII: 14,** 407c, 408c; **IX: 11–12,** 65, 66, 89, 292, 331c; **X:** 169. *See also* National Labor Union
   Adamson Act **VII:** 2
   Bridges, Harry **VIII:** 43
   Buck's Stove **VII:** 36
   CIO **VIII:** 69
   Clayton Antitrust Act **VII:** 51
   Communists **VIII:** 65
   Coolidge, Calvin **VII:** 56
   Democratic Party **VII:** 66
   Fair Labor Standards Act **VIII:** 110
   Gompers, Samuel **VI:** 117
   Hillman, Sidney **VIII:** 145, 146
   Homestead Strike **VI:** 132
   immigration restrictions **VI:** 141
   Industrial Relations Commission **VII:** 128
   IWW **VII:** 129
   Knights of Labor **VI:** 162
   labor, radical **VI:** 167
   labor and labor movements **VII:** 152–154; **VIII:** 179–181
   labor organizations **VI:** 170
   Lawrence Strike **VII:** 155
   Lewis, John L. **VIII:** 186
   lobbying groups **VII:** 162
   Mitchell, John **VII:** 186
   Murray, Philip **VIII:** 221
   National Civic Federation **VII:** 201
   National War Labor Board **VII:** 204
   New Unionism **VII:** 212, 213
   NLRB **VIII:** 231
   NWLB **VIII:** 233
   Paterson Strike **VII:** 225
   Perkins, Frances **VIII:** 265
   Pullman Strike **VI:** 236
   radicalism **VII:** 250
   radical press **VII:** 252
   Railroad Administration **VII:** 255
   Seattle General Strike **VII:** 279
   Shirtwaist Makers Strike **VII:** 285
   Socialist Labor Party **VI:** 268

steel industry **VII:** 297
Steel Strike of 1919 **VII:** 298, 299
Workmen's Compensation Act **VII:** 342
American Federation of State, County, and Municipal Employees **IX:** 304
American Federation of Teachers **X:** 100
American Folksongs **VIII:** 410c
American Football League (AFL) **IX:** 280; **X:** 284
American Football League Players Association **X:** 163
American Fur Company **IV: 16–17**
   Ashley, William Henry **IV:** 30
   Astor, John Jacob **IV:** 30–32
   Astoria **IV:** 32
   Beckwourth, Jim **IV:** 46
   Bodmer, Karl **IV:** 55
   Bridger, James **IV:** 57
   Catlin, George **IV:** 77
   Chouteau family **IV:** 79
   Fort Laramie **IV:** 143
   Fort Vancouver **IV:** 145
   fur trade **IV:** 156, 157
   Missouri Fur Company **IV:** 239
   mountain men **IV:** 247, 248
   rendezvous **IV:** 299
   Rocky Mountain Fur Company **IV:** 302
   Sublette, William **IV:** 330
American Gothic (Wood) **VIII:** 25
American Guide series **VIII:** 121
American Hebrew magazine **VI:** 172
American Heritage Rivers Initiative **X:** 250
American Home Economics Association **VI:** 247
American Independent Party (AIP) **X: 20,** 314
American Indian Movement (AIM) **IX:** *12,* **12–13,** 228, 334c; **X:** 214, 324c
American Indian Religious Freedom Act of 1978 **X:** 215
American Indians. *See* Native Americans
American in Paris (Gershwin) **VII:** 195
American Institute for Public Opinion (AIPO) **VIII:** 284
American Institute of Architects **VI:** 15

American Institute of Mining **VI:** 194
American Institutionalist School of economic thought **IX:** 117
American Institution of Public Opinion **IX:** 118
American Iron and Steel Association **VI:** 180
Americanism **VII:** 260–261
"Americanization" **X:** 132
American Jewish Congress **VIII:** 173
American Jockey Club **VI:** 134
American Journal of Education **IV:** 121
American Journal of Science and Arts **IV:** 308
American League **VI:** 22; **VII:** 294; **VIII:** 336; **X:** 284
American Legion **VII: 11–12,** 162, 291, 324–326; **VIII:** 131, 381
"American Liberty" (Freneau) **III:** 139
American Liberty League **VIII: 14–15,** 71, 72, 81, 305
American Magazine **III:** 61; **VII:** 192, 299, 305
American Medical Association (AMA) **IV:** 113, 231, 308; **VI:** 192; **VII:** 178–180, 242, 244, 355c; **VIII:** 113, 208, 209; **IX:** 196, 250
American Medical College Association (AMCA) **VI:** 192
American Medical Society **III:** 11
American Mercury **VII:** 181
American Mining Congress **IX:** 226
American Missionary Association **V:** 8, 52; **VI:** 94
American Missionary Society **IV:** 334
American Motors **IX:** 24
American Museum **IV:** 77
American Museum of Natural History **IV:** 78; **VII:** 177
American Mutoscope and Biograph Company **VII:** 190
American National Baptist convention **VI:** 4
American National Cattlemen's Association **IX:** 226
"American Negro, The" (Moynihan) **X:** 109
American Negro Academy **VI:** 71, 328c
American News Company **VI:** 81
American Newspaper Publishers Association **VI:** 212

American Party **V:** 251, 300–301, 405c; **X:** 20. *See also* Know-Nothings
   Fillmore, Millard **IV:** 138
   Frémont, John C. **IV:** 154
   immigration **IV:** 180
   Know-Nothing Party **IV:** 202
   Republican Party **IV:** 300, 301
American Peace Society **V:** 266
American Philosophical Society **II: 18–19; III: 11–12,** 392c; **IV:** 120
   Bartram, John **II:** 30
   Bond, Thomas **II:** 33
   Crèvecoeur, J. Hector St. John de **III:** 98
   Enlightenment **II:** 109
   Franklin, Benjamin **III:** 133
   Franklin, Deborah Read **II:** 125
   Jefferson, Thomas **III:** 185
   Pennsylvania **II:** 278
   Philadelphia **II:** 282
   Priestley, Joseph **III:** 285
   Rittenhouse, David **II:** 322; **III:** 310
   science **II:** 330; **III:** 321
   Shippen, William, Jr. **II:** 336
   Smith, Robert **II:** 348
American Plan **VII: 12,** 220, 359c
American Protective Association (APA) **VI: 11–12,** 326c
   immigration restrictions **VI:** 140, 141
   nativism **VI:** 209
   religion **VI:** 243
   Roman Catholicism **VI:** 249
American Protective League **VII:** 54
American Psychiatric Association **IV:** 308; **X:** 127, 324c
American Public Health Association **VI:** 192, 323c
American Pulpwood Association **IX:** 226
American race **IV:** 290
American Railroad Journal **IV:** 40
American Railway Union (ARU) **VII:** 62, 64, 65
   Cleveland, Grover **VI:** 59
   Lloyd, Henry Demarest **VI:** 179
   Pullman Strike **VI:** 235–236
   Socialist Party **VI:** 268

American Red Cross **V:** 25, 97; **VI:** 325*c;* **VIII:** 207, 297
American Red Cross Liberty Fund **X:** 195
American Reform Party **X:** 264
American Register **IV:** 196
American Renaissance
    art and architecture **VI:** 15
    painting **VI:** 219
    Saint-Gaudens, Augustus **VI:** 253
    sculpture **VI:** 258–259
    White, Stanford **VI:** 313–314
American Republican Party **IV:** 180
American Revolution **III:** 12–13; **V:** 5, 69, 76. *See also* Revolutionary War
    Adams, Abigail **III:** 1
    Adams, John **III:** 3
    African Americans **III:** 5
    Algonquin **II:** 17
    American Philosophical Society **III:** 11
    Anglican Church **II:** 20
    antislavery and abolition **III:** 16
    Arnold, Benedict **III:** 21
    art **III:** 22–23
    Bernard, Francis **III:** 37–38
    Billings, William **III:** 38
    Brackenridge, Hugh Henry **III:** 46–47
    Burgesses, House of **II:** 45
    Chauncy, Charles **II:** 57
    Cherokee **II:** 58
    Church, Benjamin **III:** 68–69
    cities and urban life **II:** 62
    Colden, Cadwallader **II:** 66
    Connecticut **II:** 70
    Connecticut Wits **III:** 80
    De Lancey, James **II:** 86
    De Lancey family **II:** 86
    Delaware **II:** 88
    Democratic Party **IV:** 106
    Democratic-Republican societies **III:** 105
    Dunmore, Lord **III:** 109
    education **III:** 114
    Flashman, Edward **II:** 119
    Florida **II:** 121; **IV:** 139
    Franklin, Deborah Read **II:** 125
    French Revolution **III:** 138
    frontier **III:** 141
    fur trade **II:** 132
    Hancock, John **III:** 162–164

iron manufacturing **II:** 168
Iroquois **II:** 170
Jews **III:** 187
journalism **III:** 190
labor and labor movements **III:** 199
Lafayette, marquis de **III:** 200–201
land riots **III:** 202
lawyers **III:** 204
Livingston, Robert R. **III:** 216
marriage and family life **III:** 232
Massachusetts **II:** 216
Methodism **III:** 242
Morris, Gouverneur **III:** 246
North Carolina **II:** 264
North Carolina Regulation **III:** 261
Olive Branch Petition **III:** 266
Paine, Thomas **III:** 271
popular culture **III:** 282–283
privateering **II:** 300
Quebec, Battle of **III:** 293
race and racial conflict **III:** 295
religion **III:** 297–299
religious liberty **III:** 300
Rensselaerswyck **II:** 319
riots **III:** 309
Rittenhouse, David **II:** 322; **III:** 310
Scotch-Irish **III:** 322
Seneca Falls **IV:** 313
Seven Years' War **II:** 332, 334
Shippen, William, Jr. **II:** 336
slavery **IV:** 316
slave trade **II:** 329
Smith, Robert **II:** 348
South Carolina **II:** 353
Stono Rebellion **II:** 361
suffrage **III:** 336
Tyler, Royall **III:** 352–353
Virginia and Kentucky Resolutions **III:** 360
Warren, Mercy Otis **III:** 363
Whig Party **IV:** 362
Whigs **III:** 375
writs of assistance **III:** 384
American Samoa **VII:** 177
American Scholar, The (Emerson) **IV:** 126, 212
American School of Ethnology **IV:** 290

Americans for Democratic Action (ADA) **VIII:** 145, 311; **IX:** 13–14
American Slavery as It Is (Weld) **IV:** 14, 362
American Social Science Association **VI:** 305
American Society for the Promotion of Temperance **IV:** 336
American Society of Composers, Authors, and Publishers (ASCAP) **VI:** 129, 272
American Sociological Association **VI:** 280
American Spelling Book (Webster) **III:** *114*, 370, 394*c;* **IV:** 120
American Steel and Wire Company **VI:** 20
American Sugar Refining Company
    business and government **VI:** 40
    Congress **VI:** 63
    corruption, political **VI:** 67
    trusts **VI:** 294
American Sunday School movement **VI:** 241
American Sunday School Union **IV:** 296
Americans United for Separation of Church and State **X:** 266
Americans with Disabilities Act (ADA) of 1990 **X:** 20–21, *21,* 46, 327*c,* 351–353
American System **IV:** 17–19; **V:** 348
    Clay, Henry **IV:** 86
    internal improvements **IV:** 188
    National Road **IV:** 253
    Polk, James K. **IV:** 283
    Whig Party **IV:** 363
American System of Manufactures **VII:** 133
American Telegraph Company **V:** 351
American Telephone and Telegraph (AT&T) **VI:** 147, 198; **VII:** 253, 254, 358*c;* **VIII:** 116; **X:** 50*m,* 244
American Temperance Society (ATS) **IV:** 336
American Temperance Union **IV:** 296
American Tobacco **X:** 305
American Transcendentalists **IV:** 26
American Way of Death, The (Jessica Mitford) **IX:** 69

American Woman Suffrage Association (AWSA) **V:** 248, 335, 397, 398; **VI:** 326*c;* **VII:** 198
    Anthony, Susan B. **VI:** 12, 13
    Blackwell, Antoinette Brown **VI:** 30
    Bradwell, Myra Colby **VI:** 34
    Brown, Olympia **VI:** 36
    Shaw, Anna Howard **VI:** 260
    Stone, Lucy **VI:** 278
    women's rights **VI:** 317
American Women report **IX:** 246; **X:** 210
American Woolen Company. *See* Lawrence Strike
American Zionist Emergency Council **VIII:** 403
America Online (AOL) **X:** 51
America's Funniest Home Videos (TV program) **X:** 295
America's Most Wanted (TV program) **X:** 295
Americorps ° VISTA **IX:** 311
Ameritech **X:** 50*m*
Ames, Adelbert **V:** 40, 49, 303
Ames, Fisher **III:** 13, 215
Ames, Mary Clemmer **VI:** 212
Ames, Oakes **V:** 84–85
AMEZ Church. *See* African Methodist Episcopal Zion Church
Amherst, Jeffrey **II:** 332, 333, 404; **III:** 146, 280–281
Amherst College **III:** 370; **VI:** 290
amino acids **IX:** 270
Amish **II:** 139
Amistad incident **III:** 334; **IV:** 19–21, *20,* 377*c;* **V:** 8
    Adams, John Quincy **IV:** 5
    Supreme Court decision **IV:** 331
    Tappan, Arthur and Lewis **IV:** 333–334
    United States v. Libellants and Claimants of the Schooner Amistad **IV:** 398–402
Amlak, Yekuno **I:** 124
Ammons, Elias **VII:** 167
ammunition **V:** 356
amnesty **V:** 8–9, 96, 142, 408*c,* 425–426
Amnesty Act of 1872 **VI:** 323*c*
Amnesty Proclamation of 1863 **V:** 219
Amnesty Proclamation of 1865 **V:** 142

Amonute. *See* Pocahontas

Amos 'n Andy **VII:** 232, 253–255, 361*c;* **VIII:** 274, 275, 289

amphetamines **X:** 206

amphibious warfare **VIII:** **15–16,** *16*
    King, Ernest J. **VIII:** 177
    Marines, U.S. **VIII:** 203
    Navy, U.S. **VIII:** 236
    Nimitz, Chester W. **VIII:** 246
    Normandy, invasion of **VIII:** 247–248
    Philippine Sea, Battle of the **VIII:** 267
    shipbuilding **VIII:** 324
    Sicily **VIII:** 325
    Tarawa **VIII:** 350
    World War II European theater **VIII:** 393
    World War II Pacific theater **VIII:** 398

amusement parks **VII:** 231–232, 256–257

Anabaptists **I:** 309; **II:** 29

Anaconda Plan **IV:** 310
    Civil War **V:** 66
    Porter, David Dixon **V:** 280
    tactics and strategy **V:** 347
    Union army **V:** 367

Ana de Sousa. *See* Nzinga, queen of Angola

Anahuac **IV:** 341, 345, 346

Analco pueblo **I:** 319

"Anarchiad, The" **III:** 80

anarchist press **VI:** 167

anarchists/anarchism **IV:** 358–359; **VI:** 127, 136, 167, 227, 325*c;* **VII:** 361*c*
    Goldman, Emma **VII:** 109–110
    radicalism **VII:** 250–251
    Sacco and Vanzetti **VII:** 273
    socialism **VII:** 289

Anasazi **I:** 255, 385*c;* **II:** 317

ANC (African National Congress) **X:** 280

Anchisaurus **IV:** 308

Ancient Order of Hibernians (AOH) **VI:** 195–196

Ancon, Treaty of (1883) **VI:** 50

Anderson, "Bloody Bill" **V:** 46, 285

Anderson, Howard **V:** 406*c*

Anderson, James **VI:** 44

Anderson, John B. **X:** **21,** 59, 238, 259, 326*c*

Anderson, Joseph Reid **V:** 356

Anderson, Kenneth A. N. **VIII:** 249

Anderson, Laurie **X:** 26

Anderson, Margaret **VII:** 188

Anderson, Marian **VIII:** 3, 227, 408*c*

Anderson, Mary **VIII:** 383

Anderson, Richard **V:** 13, 333, 395

Anderson, Robert **V:** **9–10,** 136, 137, 320

Anderson, Terry **X:** 297

Anderson, Thomas **X:** 20

Andersonville Prison, Georgia **V:** **10–11,** 25, 239, 282

Andes Mountains **I:** **9–10,** 175, 213, 279, 291, 325

Andre, John **III:** **13–14**
    Arnold, Benedict **III:** 21
    theater **III:** 347
    Trumbull, John **III:** 352
    West Point **III:** 372

Andreessen, Marc **X:** 153, 274

Andrew, John A. **V:** 49, 124–136

Andrews, Eliza **V:** 113

Andrews, George **IX:** 100

Andrews, James J. **V:** 11

Andrews, Samuel **VII:** 296

Andrews, Stephen Pearl **VI:** 318

Andrews, T. Coleman **IX:** 282

Andrews Sisters **VIII:** 224, *367*

Andrews's Raid **V:** 11, 228

Andros, Sir Edmund **II:** **19,** 418*c*
    Boston **II:** 35
    Boston Philosophical Society **II:** 37
    Carteret, Philip **II:** 54
    Connecticut **II:** 69
    Dominion of New England **II:** 94–95
    Dudley, Joseph **II:** 95
    Glorious Revolution **II:** 141
    government, British American **II:** 144, 145
    Massachusetts **II:** 214
    Mather, Cotton **II:** 217

anesthesia **IV:** 230, 307; **V:** 230, 231, 310

anesthesiology **VI:** 192

Angel Island (San Francisco) **V:** 176

Angles **I:** 10–11

Anglican Church **II:** **19–20.** *See also* Church of England
    Baptists **III:** 34
    Bradford, William (1663–1752) **II:** 39
    Chauncy, Charles **II:** 57
    Connecticut **II:** 70
    Cotton, John **II:** 73
    education **II:** 103, 104
    Great Awakening **II:** 147

Harrison, Peter **II:** 154

Heathcote, Caleb **II:** 155

Henry, Patrick **III:** 166

Hooker, Thomas **II:** 156

Hyde, Edward, Viscount Cornbury **II:** 162

Iroquois **II:** 170

Johnson, Samuel **II:** 176–177

King's College **II:** 184–185

Leverett, John **II:** 194

Loyalists **III:** 219

Lutherans **II:** 201

Maryland **II:** 209, 210

Massachusetts **II:** 212, 214

Massachusetts Bay Company **II:** 216

Mayflower Compact **II:** 219

midwives **II:** 225

monarchy, British **II:** 231

Morton, Thomas **II:** 236

music **II:** 239

New Hampshire **II:** 251

New Jersey **II:** 253

Penn, William **II:** 273

Pennsylvania **II:** 275, 276

Pilgrims **II:** 283

Presbyterians **II:** 296

Protestantism **II:** 301

religion **III:** 298

religion, Euro-American **II:** 316

religious liberty **III:** 300

Roman Catholics **II:** 323, 324

science **II:** 330

Seabury, Samuel **III:** 323

Society for the Propagation of the Gospel in Foreign Parts **II:** 352–353

Tennent, William, Sr. **II:** 372

Virginia **II:** 385

Wesley, John **II:** 393

Whitefield, George **II:** 397

women's status and rights **II:** 408

Anglo-American Arbitration treaty of 1892 **VI:** 27

Anglo-American Food Committee **VIII:** 9, 52

Anglo-American law **IV:** 221, 222

Anglo-American Protestants **V:** 340

Anglo-American relations **VIII:** **16–17,** 409*c*
    Arnold, "Hap" **VIII:** 22
    Atlantic Charter **VIII:** 28
    Cairo Conference **VIII:** 51

destroyers-for-bases deal **VIII:** 82–83

foreign policy **VIII:** 125

Grand Alliance **VIII:** 136

Lend-Lease Act **VIII:** 184–185

Roosevelt, Franklin D. **VIII:** 314

World War II European theater **VIII:** 391

Anglo-Dutch wars **II:** 257, 260, 261

Anglo-French War, 1793–1815 **III:** 395*c*–396*c;* **IV:** 355, 358
    Adams, John **III:** 3
    Democratic-Republican Party **III:** 104
    economy **III:** 113
    Howe, Richard, Lord **III:** 168
    impressment **III:** 176
    Neutrality Proclamation **III:** 256
    San Lorenzo, Treaty of **III:** 317
    trade **III:** 350
    West Indies **III:** 372
    XYZ affair **III:** 385

Anglo-Normans **I:** **10–11,** 12–13, **120,** 385*c*

Anglo-Powhatan War **II:** 268, 294, 295

Anglo-Protestantism **VIII:** 302

Anglo-Saxons **IV:** 289, 291, 292
    immigration restrictions **VI:** 141
    imperialism **VI:** 142
    literature **VI:** 176
    Social Gospel **VI:** 267
    Strong, Josiah **VI:** 279

Angola **I:** 267, 329, 330; **II:** 343; **IX:** 4, 316
    African nations **X:** 13
    antiwar movement— Vietnam **X:** 24
    cold war (end of) **X:** 70, 71
    foreign policy **X:** 124
    Reagan, Ronald W. **X:** 260
    South Africa **X:** 279
    United Nations **X:** 307

Angra Pequena **I:** 105

animal rights **X:** 16

animals **II:** **20–22; IV:** 9–10, 35
    Acadians **II:** 2
    agriculture **II:** 11, 12
    Canary Islands **I:** 53
    Columbian Exchange **I:** 76–78
    Connecticut **II:** 69
    Crow **II:** 77
    economy **II:** 101, 102

animals *(continued)*
environment **II:** 110, 111
food **II:** 121–122
forests **II:** 122
fur trade **II:** 130
Gesner, Conrad von **I:** 140
Great Plains Indians **II:** 150
Guadalajara **II:** 151
haciendas **I:** 150
Hanno the elephant **I:** 153
horses **I:** 167–169
indentured servitude **II:** 163
Indians of the Desert Southwest **II:** 166
Inuit **II:** 167
Iroquois **II:** 168
literature **II:** 195
Native American religion **I:** 252
Native Americans **II:** 243
New Jersey **II:** 253
New Netherland **II:** 257
New Spain **I:** 261
North Carolina **II:** 265
Northwest Coast Indians **II:** 265
Olmecs **I:** 270
population trends **I:** 289
religion, Native American **II:** 317
Spanish colonies **II:** 355
trade and shipping **II:** 375, 376
Virginia **II:** 382, 385
wolves **II:** 405
animation **VIII:** 408c
Anishinaabe **I:** 252
"Annabelle Lee" (Poe) **IV:** 213
Annales The True and Royall History of the Famous Empresse Elizabeth (William Camden) **I:** 52, 121
Annan, Kofi **X:** *308*
Annapolis, Maryland **II:** 178, 210, 377
Annapolis Convention **III: 14,** 394c
Articles of Confederation **III:** 25
Constitutional Convention **III:** 81
Coxe, Tench **III:** 96
Dickinson, John **III:** 106
Hamilton, Alexander **III:** 161
Madison, James **III:** 228
Mason, George **III:** 237
Anne, queen of Great Britain **II:** 232, 352

annexation **IV:** 175; **VI:** 43, 123–124, 130, 255, 327c, 328c
Annual Register **III:** 52
Another Country (James Baldwin) **IX:** 33
ANSCA. *See* Alaska Native Claim Settlement Act
Anshutz **VII:** 18
Antarctica **IV:** 133, 375c
Antequera (Oaxaca) **I:** 258
Anthony, Dan **V:** 186, 187
Anthony, Susan B. **IV:** 53, 54, 336; **V:** 409c; **VI:** *12,* **12–13,** 324c; **VII:** 198, 335, 355c
abolition **V:** 3
Blackwell, Antoinette Brown **VI:** 30
Brown, Olympia **VI:** 36
Fourteenth Amendment **V:** 139
Gage, Matilda Joslyn **VI:** 107
Hooker, Isabella Beecher **VI:** 132–133
Lockwood, Belva Ann Bennett McNall **VI:** 180
NWSA **V:** 248
Philadelphia Centennial Exposition **VI:** 224
prostitution **V:** 283
Shaw, Anna Howard **VI:** 260
Speech on Woman Suffrage **VI:** 329
Stanton, Elizabeth Cady **V:** 334
Stone, Lucy **VI:** 278
Women's National Loyal League **V:** 396
women's rights and status **V:** 397, 398; **VI:** 317
Woodhull, Victoria **VI:** 318
Anthracite Coal Strike **VII: 12–13,** 356c
Darrow, Clarence **VII:** 62
Mitchell, John **VII:** 186
muckrakers **VII:** 192
National Civic Federation **VII:** 201
New Unionism **VII:** 212
Roosevelt, Theodore **VII:** 266
United Mine Workers of America (UMWA) **VII:** 314
anthracite mining **VII:** 313–314
anthrax **X:** 331c
anthropology **IV:** 290; **VII:** 357c, 361c
Boas, Franz **VII:** 32–33
literature **VII:** 162

Mead, Margaret **VII:** 176–177
race and racial conflict **VII:** 248
anthropophagy. *See* cannibalism
Anti-Ballistic Missile (ABM) Treaty **X:** *22,* **22–23,** 331c
arms race **X:** 25
détente **X:** 89
Kissinger, Henry A. **X:** 166
SDI **X:** 289
Strategic Arms Limitation Treaties **X:** 289
antiballistic missile systems **IX:** 16
antibiotics **VIII:** 8–9; **IX:** 205–206, 295; **X:** 188
anti-Catholicism/anti-Catholic movement **IV:** 201, 298; **VI:** 11–12, 209
anti-Catholic riots **IV: 21–23,** *22,* 180
anti-Chinese agitation, rise of **IV: 23,** 65
anti-Comintern treaty **VIII:** 31, 124, 199
anticommunism **VIII:** 73, 184, 276; **IX: 14–15**
American Federation of Labor **IX:** 11
Americans for Democratic Action **IX:** 13–14
antiwar movement—Vietnam **X:** 24
Army-McCarthy hearings **IX:** 17–19
Buckley, William F.. Jr. **X:** 43
Bunche, Ralph **IX:** 43
Carter, James Earl, Jr. **X:** 58
Chambers, Whittaker **IX:** 50–51
cold war **IX:** 60
communism **IX:** 61
Congress of Industrial Organizations **IX:** 66
conservatism **IX:** 68–69
conservative movement **X:** 78, 79
elections **IX:** 94
Federal Employee Loyalty Program **IX:** 109–110
folk music revival **IX:** 111
foreign policy **X:** 122–124
gays and lesbians **IX:** 119
Hoover, J. Edgar **IX:** 136
House Un-American Activities Committee **IX:** 137–138
Internal Security Act of 1950 **IX:** 143–144

Iran-contra affair **X:** 154–155
militia movement **X:** 193
movies **IX:** 212
Nixon, Richard M. **X:** 219
Reagan, Ronald W. **X:** 260
Southeast Asia Treaty Organization **IX:** 274
Truman Doctrine **IX:** 300, 301
Anti-Defamation League **VIII:** 19
Anti-Drug Abuse Act of 1986 **X:** 82, 207
Antietam/Sharpsburg, Battle of **V: 11–13,** *12m,* 406c
Armistead, Lewis A. **V:** 15
Balloon Corps **V:** 21
Burnside, Ambrose E. **V:** 45
Civil War **V:** 66
desertion **V:** 96
Early, Jubal A. **V:** 103
Emancipation Proclamation **V:** 115
Fredericksburg, Battle of **V:** 139
Hancock, Winfield Scott **V:** 163
Hill, Ambrose P. **V:** 168
Hood, John Bell **V:** 170
Hooker, Joseph **V:** 171
Howard, O. O. **V:** 173
Irish-American regiments **V:** 181–182
Jackson, "Stonewall" **V:** 186
Lee, Robert E. **V:** 206
Longstreet, James **V:** 215
McClellan, George B. **V:** 226
Meade, George Gordon **V:** 226
medicine and hospitals **V:** 230
Native Americans **V:** 249
nurses **V:** 256
photography **V:** 273
science and technology **V:** 308
Zouaves **V:** 403
anti-Federalists **III: 14–15**
Adams, Samuel **III:** 5
Bank of the United States (First) **III:** 31
Bill of Rights **III:** 38
Clinton, George **III:** 75
Constitutional Convention **III:** 82
Federalist Papers **III:** 125
Federalists **III:** 127

Henry, Patrick **III:** 165, 166
Macon, Nathaniel **III:** 226
Madison, James **III:** 228
Mason, George **III:** 238
political parties **III:** 278
religious liberty **III:** 300
states' rights **III:** 333
Taylor, John, of Caroline **III:** 344
Yates, Abraham, Jr. **III:** 387
Antigua **II:** 374
anti-immigration legislation. *See* nativism
Anti-Imperialist League **VI: 13; VII:** 292
Antilla islands **I:** 27
antilynching legislation **VII:** 360*c*
Bethune, Mary McLeod **VIII:** 36
Byrnes, James F. **VIII:** 48
civil rights **VIII:** 61
conservative coalition **VIII:** 73–74
race and racial conflict **VIII:** 287
Roosevelt, Eleanor **VIII:** 311
White, Walter **VIII:** 378
Anti-Masonic Party **IV:** 137, 363
anti-Masonry **IV: 24**
antimonopoly **VIII: 17–18,** *18.* *See also* antitrust issues
Brain Trust **VIII:** 41
Frankfurter, Felix **VIII:** 127
Henderson, Leon **VIII:** 145
liberalism **VIII:** 188
New Deal **VIII:** 242
Public Utility Holding Company Act **VIII:** 284
recession of 1937–38 **VIII:** 293
Second New Deal **VIII:** 321
TNEC **VIII:** 355
anti-Nebraska movement **IV:** 300
Antinomian Controversy of 1636–1638
Cotton, John **II:** 73
Hooker, Thomas **II:** 157
Hutchinson, Anne Marbury **II:** 161
Massachusetts **II:** 212
Rhode Island **II:** 320
Willard, Samuel **II:** 399
Winthrop, John **II:** 402

anti-nuke movement **X:** 325*c*
Antioch College **IV:** 220
Antipodes **I:** 80, 82
antipoverty programs. *See* War on Poverty
Antiquities Act **VII: 13,** 203, **266,** 356*c*–357*c*
Antiquities Act of 1906 **X:** 250
Anti-Saloon League (ASL) **VI:** 234, 235; **VII:** 239, 240, 327
anti-Semitism **I:** 191–192; **V:** 28, 407*c;* **VI:** 172; **VII: 13–15; VIII: 18–19; X:** 111, 160
America First Committee **VIII:** 12
Catholics **VIII:** 53
conservatism **VIII:** 72
Coughlin, Father Charles E. **VIII:** 75
Ford, Henry **VII:** 97
Goldman, Emma **VII:** 109
Hearst, William Randolph **VII:** 121
Hillman, Sidney **VIII:** 146
Holocaust **VIII:** 150
immigration **VIII:** 162
Jews **VIII:** 172, 173
Leo Frank case **VII:** 157
Mencken, H. L. **VII:** 181
postwar planning **VIII:** 279
race and racial conflict **VIII:** 288
refugees **VIII:** 298
Union Party **VIII:** 365
World War II **VIII:** 389
World War II home front **VIII:** 395
Zionism **VIII:** 403
antisepsis **V:** 229, 231
antislavery. *See* abolition/abolition movement
Anti-Slavery Almanac, The **IV:** *14*
Anti-Slavery Convention of American Women **IV:** 165, 246
Anti-Slavery Record **IV:** 14
Anti-Slavery Society **VI:** 278
antismoking **IX:** 158, 249, 333*c*
anti-suffragists **VII: 15,** 335
Anti-Terrorism Act of 1987 **X:** 298
Anti-Terrorism Act of 1990 **X:** 298
Anti-Terrorism and Effective Death Penalty Act of 1996 **X:** 299
antitrust issues **VI:** 191, 261–262; **VII:** 356*c,* 357*c;* **IX:** 210, 334*c;* **X:** 330*c. See also* antimonopoly; trust-busting

AFL **VII:** 10
agriculture **VII:** 7
Breyer, Stephen **X:** 42
business **VII:** 39; **X:** 49
Capper-Volstead Act **VII:** 42–43
Clayton Antitrust Act. *See* Clayton Antitrust Act
computers **X:** 73
Elkins Act **VII:** 83–84
Federal Trade Commission Act **VII:** 94
muckrakers **VII:** 192
New Freedom **VII:** 211
New Nationalism **VII:** 211
Northern Securities Co. v. U.S. **VII:** 216
oil industry **VII:** 217–218
Payne-Aldrich Tariff Act **VII:** 226
politics **VII:** 230
progressivism **VII:** 237
Rockefeller, John D. **VII:** 264
Sherman Antitrust Act. *See* Sherman Antitrust Act
sports **X:** 284
Standard Oil **VII:** 296
tobacco suits **X:** 304
Wilson, Woodrow **VII:** 334
Antitrust Paradox, The (Bork) **X:** 39
antiwar movement
civil disobedience **IX:** 54
Clinton, William **X:** 65
conscription **X:** 76
folk music revival **IX:** 111
Hayden, Tom **IX:** 131
Jackson State University **X:** 160
Johnson, Lyndon **IX:** 152
Kent State University **X:** 164
McCarthy, Eugene **IX:** 189
New Left **IX:** 231
popular culture **IX:** 244
sexual revolution **X:** 277
Steinem, Gloria **X:** 288
Students for a Democratic Society **IX:** 286
television **IX:** 297
Twenty-sixth Amendment **X:** 306
Vietnam antiwar movement **X: 24**
Vietnam War **IX:** 309–310
Weather Underground **X:** 318
Antonioni, Michelangelo **X:** 239
Anuszkiewicz, Richard **X:** 26
Anzinka. *See* Téké

AOH (Ancient Order of Hibernians) **VI:** 195–196
AOL (America Online) **X:** 51
AOL Time Warner **X:** 132
A&P. *See* Great Atlantic and Pacific Tea Company (A&P)
APA. *See* American Protective Association
Apache nation **I:** 166, 255, 257, 320; **III:** 155; **V:** 173; **VI:** 14, 112–113, 207, 323*c,* 325*c*
Carson, Kit **IV:** 76
Colt revolver **IV:** 92
De Vargas, Diego **II:** 89
Great Plains Indians **II:** 150
Indians of the Desert Southwest **II:** 165, 166
missions **II:** 229
Native Americans **IV:** 258
Navajo **II:** 247
New Mexico **II:** 255
Pueblo Indians **II:** 303
Pueblo Revolt **II:** 304
Texas **IV:** 337
Apache War **VI: 14,** 113, 145, 207, 325*c,* 326*c*
Apalachee **I: 11–12,** 130, 131; **II:** 120, 309
apartheid **IX:** 4; **X:** 13, 71, 279–280
Apess, William **IV:** 211
aphrodisiac, ambergris as **I:** 9
apocalypse **I:** 81; **X:** 293
Apollo space program **IX:** 219, 269, 279, 294; **X:** 281
Apologetica Historia (Bartolomé de Las Casas) **I:** 200
Apology for African Methodism, An (Tanner) **VI:** 283
Apomatack **II:** 30
Appalachia **IX:** 130
Appalachian Mountains **I:** 202–203; **II:** 115, 264, 265, 385; **IV:** 162, 253
Appalachian Regional Commission **IX:** 15–16
Appalachian Regional Development Act **IX: 15–16,** 334*c*
Appalachian Trail **IX:** 225, 226
Appeal in Favor of that Class of Americans Called Africans (Child) **V:** 2
Appeal to Reason (journal) **VII:** 286, 288
Appeal to the Christian Women of the South (A. Grimké) **IV:** 135, 164, 368, 395–398
Appeal to the Colored Citizens of the World (Walker) **IV:** 16, 376*c*

Appendix Theatri Ortelii et Atlantis Mercatoris (Willem and Joan Blaeu) **I:** 31
Apple Computers **X:** 72, 273
Appomattox Court House, Virginia **V:** 13–15, *14*, 408*c*
    Chamberlain, Joshua L. **V:** 54
    Civil War **V:** 66
    Confederate States of America **V:** 77
    emancipation **V:** 114
    fire-eaters **V:** 127
    Five Forks, Battle of **V:** 128–129
    Grant, Ulysses S. **V:** 156
    Lee, Robert E. **V:** 207
    Longstreet, James **V:** 215
    Louisiana Tigers **V:** 218
    marine corps **V:** 222
    Parker, Ely Samuel **V:** 265
    Petersburg campaign **V:** 272–273
    Pickett, George Edward **V:** 274
    Richmond, Virginia **V:** 304
    Sheridan, Philip H. **V:** 319
    Union army **V:** 367
Appomatuc **II:** 294
apprenticeship **VI:** 170–171; **VII:** 76
    artisans **II:** 25; **III:** 25
    childhood **II:** 60
    class **II:** 63
    education **II:** 104; **III:** 113
    labor and labor movements **II:** 187; **III:** 200
    lawyers **III:** 203
    marriage and family life **II:** 208
    midwives **II:** 224
    Moraley, William **II:** 234
    spinsters **II:** 360
Apsaruke. *See* Crow
Aquidneck **II:** 65, 66, 258, 320, 321
Aquinas, Thomas **I:** 109, 189
Arabella (fictional character) **II:** 193
Arab-Israeli conflict **IX:** 43, 146–147, 201, 277, 299, 330*c;* **X:** 54–55, 122, 166
Aragón
    Castile **I:** 62, 63
    Charles V **I:** 67
    Ferdinand and Isabella **I:** 127
    Philip II **I:** 281
    Reconquista **I:** 306
    Seville **I:** 323
Arapaho nation **IV:** 75, 79, 144; **V:** 213, 405*c*, 407*c*

Araucanians **I:** 85, 363; **II:** 229
Arawak **I:** 12, 26, 82; **II:** 51, 52
Arbenz Guzmán, Jacobo **IX:** 172, 331*c*
Arbuckle, Fatty **VII:** 143
Arbués, Pedro de **I:** 178
Arbuthnot, Alexander **III:** 129
Arcadia **II:** 174
archaeological classicism **X:** 27
archaeology **I:** 13; **IV:** 308
Architectural Barriers Act of 1968 **X:** 20
architecture. *See* art and architecture
Architecture for Country Houses (Downing) **IV:** 28
arc lighting **VI:** 148
Arctic region **II:** 166–167, 242
Ardennes Forest **VIII:** 44
Arecibo Observatory **IX:** 278
Arendaronon **I:** 170–172
Argall, Samuel **II:** 81, 274, 288
Argentina **I:** 10, 38, 167–168, 175, 306; **II:** 229; **IV:** 242; **X:** 122, 173, 174, 218
argonauts
    California gold rush **IV:** 66
    California Trail **IV:** 71
    Colorado gold rush **IV:** 89
    gold, discovery and mining **IV:** 162, 163
Argonne Offensive **VII:** 359*c*
Arikara nation **II:** 150; **IV:** 28, 113, 329, 377*c*
Aristide, Jean-Bertrand **X:** 67, 88, 140
Aristotle **I:** 369; **II:** 330, 338; **IV:** 215
Arizona **II:** 419*c;* **IV:** xiii; **VI:** 14, 207, 323*c;* **VIII:** 343
    agriculture **II:** 8
    Alvarado, Pedro de **I:** 8
    Bent's Fort **IV:** 51
    Bilingual Education Act of 1968 **X:** 36
    cotton culture **IV:** 99
    ERA **X:** 107
    exploration **II:** 115
    Frémont, John C. **IV:** 154
    Hispanic Americans **X:** 143
    Hohokam **I:** 163–164
    Hopi **I:** 166–167
    Indians of the Desert Southwest **II:** 165, 166
    missions **II:** 229
    Native Americans **X:** 215
    New Mexico **I:** 255; **II:** 255
    O'Connor, Sandra Day **X:** 226
    Pima revolt **II:** 283–284
    population trends **X:** 242

Protestantism **II:** 300
pueblo **I:** 295–296
Pueblo Indians **II:** 303
Sunbelt **X:** 290
Texas **IV:** 339
Arizona, USS **VIII:** 264
Arizona Territory **V:** 406*c;* **VI:** 51*m*
Arkansas **II:** 178; **IV:** 48, 99, 235; **VI:** 156; **IX:** 108–109; **X:** 329*c*
    Cleburne, Patrick Ronayne **V:** 67
    Clinton, Hillary Rodham **X:** 64
    Clinton, William **X:** 65
    ERA **X:** 107
    governors **V:** 152
    Ku Klux Klan **V:** 199
    Pea Ridge/Elkhorn Tavern, Battle of **V:** 265
    population trends **X:** 242
    Reconstruction **V:** 292, 294
    Wade-Davis Bill of 1864 **V:** 385
Arkansas nation **II:** 206
Arkes, Hadley **X:** 43
Arkhangelsk, Russia **I:** 43
Arlington, Virginia **V:** 389
Armada Portrait of 1588 **I:** 121
Armageddon, Battle of **VI:** 242, 283
Armco **IX:** 282
armed forces **VII:** 186–187; **VIII:** 205, 291, 366–367, 408*c*. *See also specific headings, e.g.:* Navy, U.S.
    African-American movement **IX:** 4, 6
    American Expeditionary Force **VII:** 8–9
    Bay of Pigs **IX:** 34
    Brownsville Riot **VII:** 35
    Clinton, William **X:** 66
    cold war (end of) **X:** 71
    conscription **VII:** 54–55; **X:** 75–76
    defense budget **IX:** 77–78
    defense policy **X:** 86–88
    demobilization **IX:** 78
    foreign policy **VII:** 99; **X:** 124
    gay rights movement **X:** 127, 128
    gays and lesbians **IX:** 119
    intelligence tests **VII:** 131
    Korean War **IX:** 163–165
    military-industrial complex **IX:** 203–204
    NASA **IX:** 219
    National Defense Act **VII:** 201

National Security Act of 1947 **IX:** 224–225
Naval Disarmament Conference **VII:** 209–210
Progressive Party **IX:** 248
Truman Doctrine **IX:** 300
veterans **VII:** 324–326; **IX:** 307–308
Vietnam War **IX:** 308–310
War Powers Act **X:** 315
Armenia **X:** 281
Armijo, Manuel **IV:** 47, 306
Arminius, Jacob **II:** 301
Armistead, Lewis A. **V:** 15, 163
Armistice Day **VII:** 9
armor **II:** 150
Armored Forces **VIII:** 349
armories **V:** 164
Armory Show **VII:** 17, 358*c*
    art **VII:** 18
    Ashcan school **VII:** 20
    Greenwich Village **VII:** 115
    modernism **VII:** 188
Armour, George **VI:** 196
Armour, Philip D. **VI:** 191
arms control **X:** 326*c*
    cold war (end of) **X:** 71
    foreign policy **X:** 124
    Gore, Albert, Jr. **X:** 134
    INF Treaty **X:** 151–152
    Kemp, Jack F. **X:** 163
    Kissinger, Henry A. **X:** 165–165
    nuclear freeze movement **X:** 224
    Reagan, Ronald W. **X:** 260–261
arms embargo **VIII:** 105
arms race **IX:** 16–17; **X:** 25
    ABM Treaty **X:** 22–23
    Catholic Bishops' Letter **X:** 59
    cold war **IX:** 60; **X:** 70
    defense policy **X:** 85–86
    hydrogen bomb **IX:** 140
    Limited Test Ban Treaty of 1963 **IX:** 180
    Mills, C. Wright **IX:** 205
    SANE **IX:** 267
    Strategic Arms Limitation Treaties **X:** 288–289
    U.S. nuclear weapons facilities **IX:** 17*m*
Armstrong, Edwin Howard **VII:** 134
Armstrong, Louis **VII:** 137, 194, 195, 361*c;* **VIII:** 149, 223
Armstrong, Neil **IX:** 219; **X:** 281, 323*c*
Armstrong, Samuel **VI:** 308

Armstrong, Scott **X**: 44
army, Confederate. *See*
  Confederate army
army, U.S. **V**: 408*c*; **VI**: 324*c*;
  VII: 227; **VIII**: **19–20**; **IX**:
  17–19, 77, 185–186, 329*c*,
  331*c*; **X**: 13. *See also* Union
  army
    African Americans **VIII**: 3
    amphibious warfare **VIII**:
      15
    Army Air Forces, U.S.
      VIII: 20
    Asian Americans **VIII**: 26
    Axis **VIII**: 32
    Beckwourth, Jim **IV**: 47
    Bent's Fort **IV**: 50
    BIA **IV**: 181
    Black Hawk War **IV**: 52, 53
    Black Hills gold rush **VI**:
      29
    Bradley, Omar N. **VIII**: 40
    buffalo, extermination of
      VI: 38
    Buffalo Soldiers **VI**: 39
    Capra, Frank **VIII**: 52
    censorship **VIII**: 55
    code breaking **VIII**: 64
    Confederate army **V**: 71
    demobilization **VIII**: 79
    DiMaggio, Joe **VIII**: 84
    exploration **IV**: 133
    foreign policy **VI**: 103
    Fort Leavenworth **IV**: 145
    Fort Vancouver **IV**: 146
    Frémont, John C. **IV**: 153
    gays and lesbians **VIII**: 130
    Gorgas, Josiah **V**: 151
    Great Strike of 1877 **VI**:
      119
    Guadalcanal **VIII**: 141
    Johnston, Joseph E. **V**: 190
    King, Ernest J. **VIII**: 178
    Lee, Robert E. **V**: 205
    Louis, Joe **VIII**: 196
    Marines, U.S. **VIII**: 203
    Marshall, George C. **VIII**:
      205–207
    Mauldin, Bill **VIII**: 207
    mobilization **VIII**: 214
    Mormon War **IV**: 244–245
    MOWM **VIII**: 201
    Native Americans **V**: 251
    Nimitz, Chester W. **VIII**:
      246
    Normandy, invasion of
      VIII: 247
    North African campaign
      VIII: 249
    Okinawa **VIII**: 259
    Pearl Harbor **VIII**: 264
    Philippines **VIII**: 266

    Philippine Sea, Battle of
      the **VIII**: 267
    Pike, Zebulon
      Montgomery **IV**: 281,
      282
    propaganda **VIII**: 283
    redemption **V**: 297
    Santa Fe Trail **IV**: 306
    Scott, Winfield **IV**:
      309–310
    Sheridan, Philip H. **V**: 319
    Sherman, William T. **V**:
      321
    Sicily **VIII**: 325
    Sioux wars **VI**: 263
    Solomon Islands **VIII**: 331
    steel industry **VIII**: 339
    Stimson, Henry L. **VIII**:
      340
    strikes **V**: 340
    tanks **VIII**: 349
    Tarawa **VIII**: 350
    Taylor, Zachary **IV**: 334
    volunteer army **V**: 384
    WAC **VIII**: 381–382
    Wheeler, Joseph **V**: 392
    World War II **VIII**: 388
    World War II Pacific
      theater **VIII**: 398
    WPB **VIII**: 375
Army Air Forces, U.S. **VIII**:
  20–21. *See also* Air Force,
  U.S.
    air power **VIII**: 11–12
    Army, U.S. **VIII**: 19
    Arnold, "Hap" **VIII**: 21–22
    Atlantic, Battle of the
      VIII: 28
    demobilization **VIII**: 79
    Mariana Islands **VIII**: 202
    Marshall, George C. **VIII**:
      206
    Okinawa **VIII**: 259
    OSS **VIII**: 257
    photography **VIII**: 269
    WAC **VIII**: 381
    WASP **VIII**: 380–381
Army Appropriation Act of 1901
  VI: 72
Army Corps of Engineers **IV**:
  188; **V**: **370–371**; **IX**: 16
    cartography **V**: 51
    Petersburg campaign **V**:
      271
    Red River campaign **V**:
      297, 298
    West Point **V**: 372
Army Department **IX**: 224
Army Ground Forces (AGF)
  VIII: 381
Army Life in a Black Regiment
  (Higginson) **V**: 167

Army-McCarthy hearings **IX**:
  17–19, *18*, 190, 297, 331*c*
Army Medical Department **V**:
  230
Army of the Cumberland
    Chattanooga, Battle of **V**:
      57
    Chickamauga, Battle of **V**:
      58
    Hooker, Joseph **V**:
      171–172
    Lookout Mountain, Battle
      of **V**: 216
    Murfreesboro/Stones
      River, Battle of **V**: 242
    Rosecrans, William S. **V**:
      305
    Sheridan, Philip H. **V**: 318
    Thomas, George H. **V**: 354
Army of the Mississippi **V**: 36,
  83, 305
Army of New Mexico **V**: 73
Army of Northern Virginia
    Antietam, Battle of **V**: 11
    Balloon Corps **V**: 22
    Chancellorsville, Battle of
      V: 54
    Cold Harbor, Battle of **V**:
      68
    Confederate army **V**:
      72–73
    Confederate States of
      America **V**: 77
    Fredericksburg, Battle of
      V: 139
    Gettysburg, Battle of **V**:
      147–150
    Halleck, Henry W. **V**: 162
    Hancock, Winfield Scott **V**:
      163
    Hill, Ambrose P. **V**:
      167–168
    Jackson, "Stonewall" **V**:
      186
    Lee, Robert E. **V**: 206,
      207
    Longstreet, James **V**: 215
    Louisiana Tigers **V**: 218
    McClellan, George B. **V**:
      225, 226
    Meade, George Gordon **V**:
      227
    Oates, William C. **V**: 257
    Overland campaign **V**: 261
    Pickett, George Edward **V**:
      274
    Shenandoah Valley:
      Sheridan's campaign **V**:
      317, 318
    Stuart, J. E. B. **V**: 341
    tactics and strategy **V**: 346,
      347

    Union army **V**: 367
    Zouaves **V**: 403
Army of the Ohio **V**: 19, 324,
  353, 354
Army of the Potomac **V**: 406*c*,
  407*c*
    Antietam, Battle of **V**: 11
    Balloon Corps **V**: 21
    Burnside, Ambrose E. **V**:
      44, 45
    Chancellorsville, Battle of
      V: 54–56
    Cold Harbor, Battle of **V**:
      68
    Confederate States of
      America **V**: 77
    Fredericksburg, Battle of
      V: 139, 141
    Gettysburg, Battle of **V**:
      147–150
    Hancock, Winfield Scott **V**:
      163
    homefront **V**: 169
    Hooker, Joseph **V**: 171
    Jackson, "Stonewall" **V**:
      186
    Longstreet, James **V**: 215
    Lookout Mountain, Battle
      of **V**: 216
    McClellan, George B. **V**:
      224–225
    Meade, George Gordon **V**:
      226, 227
    medicine and hospitals **V**:
      230
    Overland campaign **V**:
      260–261
    Peninsular campaign **V**:
      267, 269
    Petersburg campaign **V**:
      271, 272
    Richmond, Virginia **V**: 304
    science and technology **V**:
      309
    Shenandoah Valley:
      Jackson's campaign **V**:
      316
    Sheridan, Philip H. **V**: 318
    Stuart, J. E. B. **V**: 341
    tactics and strategy **V**: 347
    Union army **V**: 366, 367
    Wilderness, Battle of the
      V: 395
Army of the Shenandoah Valley
  V: 318
Army of the Southwest **V**: 265
Army of Tennessee
    Atlanta campaign **V**: 19, 20
    Bragg, Braxton **V**: 36
    Chickamauga, Battle of **V**:
      58
    Confederate army **V**: 73

Army of Tennessee (*continued*)
Cumming, Kate **V:** 85
Hood, John Bell **V:** 170, 171
Howard, O. O. **V:** 173
Johnston, Joseph E. **V:** 190
Longstreet, James **V:** 215
Murfreesboro/Stones River, Battle of **V:** 242, 243
Orphan Brigade **V:** 258
Rosecrans, William S. **V:** 305
Sherman, William T. **V:** 321
Vicksburg campaign **V:** 380
Wheeler, Joseph **V:** 392
Army of the Trans-Mississippi **V:** 73
Army of Vicksburg **V:** 73
Army of Virginia **V:** 186
Army Service Forces (ASF) **VIII:** 382
Army Signal Corps **V:** 351
Army War College **VII:** 201–202, 235
Arnarson, Ingólfur **I:** 174, 263
Arnim, Jürgen von **VIII:** 249
Arnold, Benedict **III: 21–22,** *22,* 393c; **V:** 372
Allen, Ethan **III:** 10
Andre, John **III:** 13, 14
Brant, Joseph **III:** 49
Burr, Aaron **III:** 53
Canada **III:** 60
Carleton, Guy **III:** 62
Conway Cabal **III:** 91
Fort Ticonderoga **III:** 133
Jefferson, Thomas **III:** 184
McDougall, Alexander **III:** 239
Morgan, Daniel **III:** 246
Quebec, Battle of **III:** 293
Saratoga, surrender at **III:** 320
Valcour Island, Battle of **III:** 357
West Point **III:** 372
Yorktown, surrender at **III:** 388
Arnold, Henry H. "Hap" **VIII: 21–22**
Army, U.S. **VIII:** 20
Army Air Forces, U.S. **VIII:** 20, 21
Marshall, George C. **VIII:** 206
photography **VIII:** 269
Arnold, Matthew **VI:** 15, 205
Arnold, Samuel **V:** 17
Arnold, Thurman **VIII:** 18; **X:** 125

Aroostook War **IV: 25,** 360
Arouet, François-Marie. *See* Voltaire
ARPA (Advanced Research Projects Agency) **X:** 152
ARPANET **X:** 152–153
Arrangement in Gray and Black (Whistler) **VI:** 312, *313*
"arsenal of democracy" **VIII:** 374–375, 394
arsenals, Confederate **V:** 152
arson **II:** 78, 247, 262, 337
art and architecture **I: 12–13; II: 22, 22–25,** *23, 24;* **III: 17–20,** *19,* **22–24,** *23,* 50, 184–185, 323; **IV:** 25–{4: }28, *26,* 34–35, 54–55, 77–78, 82; **V: 15–16,** 247–248, 253, 405c; **VI: 14–16,** 325c; **VII: 15–20,** *19,* 346, 357c, 358c; **VIII: 22–25,** *23, 24,* 114, 140, 268–269, 407c; **IX: 19–21; X: 26–27,** *27*
Aesthetic movement **VI:** 3
Africa **II:** 4
African-American movement **IX:** 5, 7
Andes Mountains **I:** 10
Anglican Church **II:** 20
Anglo-Normans **I:** 11
Armory Show **VII:** 17
Ashcan school **VII:** 20
Beat Generation **IX:** 35
Benin **I:** 28
Boston **II:** 35
Burgis, William **II:** 45–46
Caribbean **II:** 53
Carver, George Washington **VI:** 45
Catesby, Mark **II:** 55
Cholula **I:** 72
Comstock, Anthony **VI:** 62
Copán **I:** 86
Copley, John Singleton **III:** 91
Cozumel **I:** 96
Cuzco **I:** 99
Dummer, Jeremiah **II:** 96
Dürer, Albrecht **I:** 113–114
Eakins, Thomas **VI:** 85–87
Feke, Robert **II:** 117
forests **II:** 122
forts **II:** 124
Franklin, Deborah Read **II:** 125
Fulton, Robert **III:** 141
Gedi **I:** 139
gold **I:** 142
Great Plains Indians **II:** 149

Greenwich Village **VII:** 114–115
Haida **I:** 150
Harlem Renaissance **VII:** 120
Harrison, Peter **II:** 154–155
Herrman, Augustine **II:** 156
Hesselius, John **II:** 156
Hohokam **I:** 163–164
Hopewell culture **I:** 166
Hopi **I:** 167
housing **II:** 158
Igbo **I:** 175
invention and technology **I:** 180
Iroquois **I:** 181
Jemison, Mary **II:** 173
Johnston, Henrietta Deering **II:** 177–178
Kuhn, Justus Engelhardt **II:** 186
Le Moyne, Jacques **I:** 202–203
Leonardo da Vinci **I:** 204–205
Lima **I:** 206
limners **II:** 194
London **I:** 208
Machu Picchu **I:** 213–214
Mansa Musa I **I:** 220
Maryland **II:** 211
Massachusetts **II:** 215–216
Maya **I:** 227, 228
métis **II:** 223
Mexico **I:** 235
Michelangelo **I:** 235–236
modernism **VII:** 187–188
music **VI:** 201
National Endowment for the Arts **IX:** 221
Native American religion **I:** 252
Navajo **II:** 247
New Mexico **I:** 255
Olmecs **I:** 269, 270
painting **VI:** 219–220
Palenque **I:** 275
Peale, Charles Willson **III:** 273, 275
Philadelphia Centennial Exposition **VI:** 224
pueblo **I:** 295
Pueblo Indians **II:** 303
Remington, Frederic **VI:** 245–246
Richardson, Henry Hobson **VI:** 247–248
Saint-Gaudens, Augustus **VI:** 253
Santa Fe **I:** 319

Sargent, John Singer **VI:** 255–256
Savannah **II:** 329
sculpture **VI:** 258–259
skyscrapers **VI:** 264–265
Smibert, John **II:** 345–346
Smith, Robert **II:** 347–348
society, British American **II:** 352
Stuart, Gilbert **III:** 335
Sullivan, Louis H. **VI:** 279–280
taverns and inns **II:** 367
Tenochtitlán **I:** 344
Theus, Jeremiah **II:** 373
Tiffany, Louis Comfort **VI:** 288
Tikal **I:** 349, 350
Timbuktu **I:** 350
Toltecs **I:** 356, 357
Trumbull, John **III:** 352
Venice **I:** 365
Victorianism **VI:** 304
Virginia **II:** 384, 385
West, Benjamin **III:** 371–372
Whistler, James Abbott McNeill **VI:** 312
White, John **I:** 372, 373
White, Stanford **VI:** 313–314
World's Columbian Exposition **VI:** 319–320
Yucatán Peninsula **I:** 378
art deco **VII:** 19; **VIII:** 22
Arteaga, Ignacio de **I:** 266
Arte de Navigae (Martin Cortes) **I:** 118
Arthur, Chester Alan **V:** 25; **VI:** *16,* **16–17,** *325c*
Chinese Exclusion Act **VI:** 50, 52
civil service reform **VI:** 56
Congress **VI:** 63
Conkling, Roscoe **VI:** 64
Geological Survey, U.S. **VI:** 110
Hayes, Rutherford B. **VI:** 126
the presidency **VI:** 230
star route frauds **VI:** 275
tariff issue **VI:** 284
Arthur Mervyn (Brown) **III:** 49
Articles of Association **III:** 325
Articles of Confederation **III:** *24,* **24–25,** 393c–395c, 401–405; **IV:** 263
Adams, John **III:** 3
American Revolution **III:** 12
Annapolis Convention **III:** 14

antislavery and abolition
   III: 16
Constitutional Convention
   III: 81
constitutions, state III: 82
Continental Congress,
   Second III: 89
Federalist Papers III: 125
Federalists III: 127
Jay, John III: 181
Jay-Gardoqui treaty
   negotiations III: 182
King, Rufus III: 195
Lee, Richard Henry III:
   207
Madison, James III: 227,
   228
Morris, Gouverneur III:
   246
Morris, Robert III: 247
national debt III: 253
Newburgh conspiracy III:
   256
Northwest Ordinances III:
   261
Randolph, Edmund III:
   296
Shays's Rebellion III: 325
Sherman, Roger III: 325
states' rights III: 333
Witherspoon, John III:
   380
Articles of Impeachment for
   President William Jefferson
   Clinton X: 357–359
artificial organs X: 190, 275
artillery V: 72, 345, 356
artillery corps V: 364–364
artisans II: 25–26; III: 25–26
   childhood II: 60
   cities and urban life III: 70
   class II: 63
   crafts II: 73–74
   deism III: 104
   Dummer, Jeremiah II: 96
   economy II: 102
   education III: 113
   freemasonry III: 137
   Gabriel's Rebellion III:
      145
   Hutchinson, Anne
      Marbury II: 161
   indentured servitude II:
      165
   industrial revolution III:
      177
   Jamestown II: 171, 172
   Jews III: 187
   Keith, William II: 181
   labor and labor movements
      II: 187–188; III: 200
   limners II: 194

Loyalists III: 219
lumbering II: 201
MacIntosh, Ebenezer III:
   225
Maryland II: 210
Massachusetts II: 215
mills II: 225
Morris, Robert III: 248
Navajo II: 247
New Jersey II: 253
Newport II: 258
pewter II: 280–281
Philadelphia II: 282
Phyfe, Duncan III: 275
printing and publishing II:
   299
religion, Euro-American
   II: 316
Rittenhouse, David III:
   309–310
shipbuilding II: 335
Sons of Liberty III: 330
Spanish colonies II: 359
Tammany Society III: 341
technology II: 369
trade III: 350
trade and shipping II:
   377
Virginia II: 384
voluntary associations III:
   362
women's status and rights
   II: 407
*Artist's Wife and His Setter Dog,
   The* (Eakins) VI: 87
art music VI: 201–202
Art Nouveau VI: 15–16
*Art of Moneymaking; or Hints
   and Helps on How to Make a
   Fortune* (Barnum) VI: 21
Arts and Crafts style VII: 16
art songs VI: 23
Art Students League VI: 48
ARU. *See* American Railway
   Union
ARVN IX: 308
Aryan Nations X: 257
Asante I: 13, 125, 144
Asante state (Africa) II: 344
Asbury, Francis III: 26–27, 27,
   242; IV: 296
ASCAP. *See* American Society of
   Composers, Authors, and
   Publishers
aseptic surgery V: 231
ASF (Army Service Forces)
   VIII: 382
ASGP (Association of State
   Green Parties) X: 135
Ashbrook, John X: 79
Ashburton, Lord. *See* Baring,
   Alexander, Lord Ashburton

Ashcan school VII: 18, 20, 115,
   357c
Ashcroft, John X: 305, 318
Ashkenazic Jews I: 191–192; II:
   175; VI: 243
Ashley, William Henry IV:
   28–30, 29m, 375c
   American Fur Company
      IV: 17
   Astor, John Jacob IV: 32
   Atkinson, Henry IV: 33
   Beckwourth, Jim IV: 46
   Bridger, James IV: 57
   exploration IV: 131
   fur trade IV: 157
   McLoughlin, John IV: 229
   Missouri Fur Company IV:
      239
   mountain men IV: 247
   rendezvous IV: 300
   Rocky Mountain Fur
      Company IV: 302
   Smith, Jedediah Strong IV:
      320, 321
   South Pass IV: 324
   Sublette, William IV: 329,
      330
Ashmolean Museum (Oxford,
   England) I: 40
Ashmun, Jehudi IV: 209
Ashwander case VIII: 356
Asia I: 65m; II: 332; IV: 143,
   219; VI: 103; X: 5, 307
   Blaeu, Willem I: 31
   bubonic plague I: 285
   cities and urban life IX: 52
   cold war IX: 58
   Columbus, Christopher I:
      79, 81, 82
   corn (maize) I: 88
   dollar diplomacy VII: 70
   Dutch East India
      Company I: 114–115
   foreign policy VII: 99
   and foreign policy IX:
      21–22
   Great White Fleet VII:
      114
   immigration VII: 127
   Islam I: 184
   Open Door Policy VII:
      218–219
   Point Four Program IX:
      242–243
   Polo, Marco I: 286, 287
   Prester John I: 293
   Root-Takahira Agreement
      VII: 267–268
   Southeast Asia Treaty
      Organization IX:
      273–274
   trade, foreign VII: 310

Asian American movement IX:
   22
Asian Americans VIII: 25–26,
   26, 61, 162, 171–172; X:
   27–30, 29m
   Civil Liberties Act of 1988
      X: 63
   Dillingham Commission
      VII: 69
   education, higher X: 97
   Gentlemen's Agreement
      VII: 107–108
   Great White Fleet VII:
      114
   literature X: 177
   multiculturalism X: 200,
      201
   National Origins Act VII:
      202
   nativism VII: 208, 209
   population trends X: 243
   Quota Act VII: 245
   race and racial conflict
      VII: 247, 248; X: 255,
      256
   Russo-Japanese War VII:
      271
   segregation VII: 281
Asian economic crisis X: 69, 96
Asian Exclusion League VIII:
   26
asiento I: 261
Askia al-Hajj Muhammad Ibn
   Alik Bakr Turé (Touré). *See*
   Askia Muhammad I
Askia Dawud I: 244
Askia dynasty I: 14
Askia Muhammad I
   (Muhammad Turé [Askia al-
   Hajj Muhammad Ibn Alik
   Bakr Turé (Touré)]) I: 14,
   139, 243–244, 332, 350
ASL. *See* Anti-Saloon League
Aspin, Les X: 13, 66, 87, 88
assassination of Abraham
   Lincoln V: 17–19, 18, 208,
   211, 408c
   amnesty, acts of V: 9
   Booth, John Wilkes V:
      32–33
   impeachment of Andrew
      Johnson V: 177
   Johnson, Andrew V: 187
   Lincoln, Mary Todd
      V: 212
   photography V: 273
   Republican Party V: 302
   Seward, William H.
      V: 315
   Stanton, Edwin M. V: 334
   Stevens, Thaddeus V: 338
   theater V: 351

assassination of Abraham
   Lincoln (continued)
   Welles, Gideon **V:** 392
   Whitman, Walt **V:** 394
assassinations/assassination
   attempts **VI:** 106, 325c; **IX:**
   333c, 334c; **X:** 30, **30–31,**
   326c
   American Independent
      Party **X:** 20
   Arthur, Chester Alan **VI:**
      17
   Bush, George H. W. **X:** 45
   civil service reform **VI:** 56
   Farrakhan, Louis A. **X:**
      111
   Garfield, James A. **VI:** 109
   gun control **X:** 136
   Iranian hostage crisis **X:**
      155
   Kennedy, John F. **IX:** 158
   Kennedy, Robert F. **IX:**
      159
   King, Martin Luther, Jr.
      IX: 162
   Koreagate **X:** 166
   labor, radical **VI:** 167
   Mafia incident **VI:** 185
   Malcolm X **IX:** 187
   Operation Mongoose **IX:**
      236
   Oswald, Lee Harvey **IX:**
      237–238
   Pizarro, Francisco **I:** 283
   race and racial conflict **IX:**
      253; **X:** 255
   Reagan, Ronald W. **X:**
      259
   television **IX:** 297
   terrorism **X:** 297
   Wallace, George C. **X:** 314
   Weathermen **IX:** 319
Assemblies of God **VIII:** 304
assembly line **IV:** 91; **VII:** 357c.
   See also mass production
   business **VII:** 38
   economy **VII:** 74
   invention and technology
      VII: 133
   socialism **VII:** 288
Assertive Multilateralism **X:** 66
assimilation **IV:** 221; **VI:** 98,
   144; **VII:** 37; **VIII:** 25, 131,
   235, 236
Assiniboine nation **II:** 159; **IV:**
   55
Associated Artists **VI:** 288
associate degrees **X:** 97–98
Associated Press **IV:** 196; **V:**
   192; **VII:** 143; **IX:** 153
Association, the **III:** **27,** 87,
   101, 335

Association against the
   Prohibition Amendment
   (AAPA) **VII:** 241
Association for the
   Advancement of Women **VI:**
   30, 195
Association of Advertising Clubs
   of America **VII:** 4
Association of American
   Medical Colleges **VI:** 192,
   326c
Association of American
   Painters and Sculptors **VII:**
   18
Association of State Green
   Parties (ASGP) **X:** 135
Association of the Army of
   Northern Virginia **V:** 217,
   379
Astaire, Fred **VII:** 108; **VIII:**
   218
Astor, John Jacob **II:** 133; **III:**
   65, 142, 153, 397c; **IV:**
   30–32, 31
   American Fur Company
      IV: 16–17
   Ashley, William Henry **IV:**
      30
   Astoria **IV:** 32–33
   Chouteau family **IV:** 79
   Columbia River **IV:** 93
   economy **IV:** 118
   Fort Vancouver **IV:** 145
   fur trade **IV:** 157
   Missouri Fur Company **IV:**
      239
   mountain men **IV:** 247
   Oregon Trail **IV:** 267
   Oregon Treaty of 1846 **IV:**
      269
   Rocky Mountain Fur
      Company **IV:** 302
   South Pass **IV:** 324
Astoria **IV:** **32–33**
   American Fur Company
      IV: 16
   Astor, John Jacob **IV:** 31
   exploration **IV:** 131
   Fort Vancouver **IV:** 145
   Oregon Trail **IV:** 267
   South Pass **IV:** 324
astrology **II:** 220, 331
astronauts **IX:** 219, 334c
astronomy **I:** 242, 270; **II:** 141,
   277, 322, 330, 331; **III:** 395c;
   IV: 308; **VI:** 194–195,
   257–258; **VII:** 275–276; **VIII:**
   318
   American Philosophical
      Society **III:** 11
   Banneker, Benjamin **III:**
      33

Rittenhouse, David **III:**
   310
   science **III:** 321
Aswan Dam **IX:** 288
A&T. See Agricultural and
   Technical College
Atabrine **VIII:** 208
Atahualpa **I:** **14–15,** 15, 143,
   177, 283, 387c
Atchison, David Rice **V:** 31,
   197
ATF. See Bureau of Alcohol,
   Tobacco, and Firearms
Athabascan **II:** 149, 165
athletes **X:** 285, 286
ATI (Allah Temple of Islam) **IX:**
   214
Atkinson, Henry **IV:** **33–34,** 52
Atkinson, Samuel C. **IV:** 196
Atkinson, Ti-Grace **X:** 211
Atlanta, Battle of
   Atlanta campaign **V:** 20
   Civil War **V:** 66
   Copperheads **V:** 82
   elections **V:** 110
   emancipation **V:** 113
   homefront **V:** 169
Atlanta, CSS **V:** 132
Atlanta, Georgia **X:** 299
   homefront **V:** 169
   Hood, John Bell **V:** 171
   Petersburg campaign **V:**
      272
   refugees **V:** 298
   Sherman, William T. **V:**
      321
   Sherman's March through
      Georgia **V:** 321
   tactics and strategy **V:** 347
Atlanta, siege of **V:** 168, 407c
Atlanta Baptist Female
   Seminary **VI:** 4
Atlanta Braves **X:** 1
Atlanta campaign **V:** **19–20,** 20
   Blair, Francis P., Jr. **V:** 30
   Cleburne, Patrick Ronayne
      V: 68
   Confederate army **V:** 73
   Hooker, Joseph **V:** 173
   Johnston, Joseph E. **V:** 190
   Orphan Brigade **V:** 258
   Sherman, William T. **V:**
      321
   Sherman's March through
      Georgia **V:** 321–322
   Thomas, George H. **V:** 354
   Union army **V:** 367
Atlanta Compromise speech
   (Washington) **VI:** 6, 327c,
   348–349
Atlanta Constitution **VII:** 332
Atlanta University **VI:** 94

Atlantic, Battle of the **VIII:**
   26–28, 27m
   Casablanca Conference
      VIII: 52
   cash-and-carry **VIII:** 53
   destroyers-for-bases deal
      VIII: 82
   Navy, U.S. **VIII:** 236
   shipbuilding **VIII:** 324
   submarines **VIII:** 342
Atlantic Charter **VIII:** **28,** 409c,
   423
   Anglo-American relations
      VIII: 17
   Arnold, "Hap" **VIII:** 22
   foreign policy **VIII:** 125
   Grand Alliance **VIII:** 136
   OWI **VIII:** 257
   propaganda **VIII:** 283
   Soviet-American relations
      VIII: 333, 334
   UN **VIII:** 365
   Welles, Sumner **VIII:** 377
Atlantic Charter of 1941 **IX:** 3
Atlantic Conference (1941)
   VIII: 377
Atlantic Monthly **V:** 160; **VI:** 80,
   176, 177, 179
Atlantic Ocean
   Cabot, John **I:** 41m
   Columbus, Christopher **I:**
      79–80
Atlantic Provinces **II:** 167
atlases **I:** 31, 232
atomic bomb **VIII:** **28–30,**
   408c, 409c, 411c; **IX:** 330c.
   See also Manhattan Project
   air power **VIII:** 12
   Anglo-American relations
      VIII: 17
   arms race **IX:** 16
   Axis **VIII:** 32
   Bush, Vannevar **VIII:** 45
   business **VIII:** 47
   Communists **VIII:** 66
   computers **IX:** 64
   demobilization **VIII:** 79
   ENIAC **IX:** 98
   espionage **VIII:** 104
   foreign policy **VIII:** 125
   Forrestal, James V. **VIII:**
      126
   Grand Alliance **VIII:** 137
   Hiroshima and Nagasaki
      VIII: 146–148
   intelligence **VIII:** 164
   Iwo Jima **VIII:** 169
   Jews **VIII:** 173
   Lilienthal, David E. **VIII:**
      190
   Manhattan Project **VIII:**
      200–201

Mariana Islands **VIII:** 202

mobilization **VIII:** 215

Okinawa **VIII:** 259

Oppenheimer, J. Robert **IX:** 236–237

OSRD **VIII:** 255, 256

Potsdam Conference **VIII:** 280

Roosevelt, Franklin D. **VIII:** 314

science **VIII:** 318; **IX:** 268–269

Soviet-American relations **VIII:** 333

Stimson, Henry L. **VIII:** 340

technology **VIII:** 353; **IX:** 293–294

Truman, Harry **IX:** 299

Truman's Announcement of the Atomic Bombing of Hiroshima **VIII:** 431–433

TVA **VIII:** 356

V-J Day **VIII:** 369

Wallace, Henry A. **VIII:** 373

World War II **VIII:** 389, 390

World War II Pacific theater **VIII:** 399

atomic energy. *See* nuclear energy

Atomic Energy Act of 1946 **IX:** 23, 329*c*

Atomic Energy Act of 1954 **IX:** 24, 331*c*

Atomic Energy Commission (AEC) **VIII:** 190, 201; **IX:** **23–24,** 329*c*

hydrogen bomb **IX:** 139, 140

medicine **IX:** 197

Oppenheimer, J. Robert **IX:** 237

technology **IX:** 293

atomic weight **VII:** 276

Atotarho **I:** 161

atrocities **V:** 191

ATS (American Temperance Society) **IV:** 336

AT&T. *See* American Telephone and Telegraph

Attakullakulla **II:** 269

Attention Deficit and Hyperactivity Disorder (ADHD) **X:** 190

Attention Deficit Disorder (ADD) **X:** 185, 190

Attignawantan **I:** 170–172

Attigneenongnahac **I:** 170–172

Attlee, Clement **VIII:** 29, 137, 279, 280, 410*c*

attorneys general, Confederate **V:** 27

attorneys. *See* lawyers

attorneys general **V:** 334

Attucks, Crispus **III:** 6, **27–28,** 43

Atzerodt, George **V:** 17, 18

audiencia(s) **I:** 15–16; **II:** 355

Brazil **I:** 33

Council of the Indies **I:** 95

Ferdinand and Isabella **I:** 128

New Spain **I:** 259

Philip II **I:** 281

Zumárraga, Juan de **I:** 382

Audubon, John James **IV:** **34–35,** 35, 308, 376*c*

Audubon, John Woodhouse **IV:** 35

Audubon Society **VI:** 65

Augsburg confession **I:** 212

Augusta **II:** 138, 267

Augusta, USS **VIII:** 246

Augusta Institute **VI:** 4

"August ham" **II:** 122

Aum Shinrikyo **X:** 299

Aunt Jemima and the Pillsbury Doughboy (Jeff Donaldson) **IX:** 21

Aurora (newspaper) **III:** 29, 107, 108, 192

Auschwitz-Birkenau **VIII:** 150

Austin, Hudson **X:** 135

Austin, Moses **IV:** **35–36**

Austin, Stephen F. **IV:** 36

lead mines **IV:** 208

Texas **IV:** 338

Texas Revolution **IV:** 339

Austin, Stephen F. **IV:** 36, **36–38**

Alamo, The **IV:** 12

Austin, Moses **IV:** 36

Houston, Sam **IV:** 174, 175

lead mines **IV:** 208

Santa Anna, Antonio López de **IV:** 303

Santa Fe Trail **IV:** 305

Texas **IV:** 338

Texas, Republic of **IV:** 339–341

Texas Revolution **IV:** 339

Austin, Texas **IV:** 175

Australia **I:** 114; **II:** 119; **VIII:** 398; **IX:** 273–274; **X:** 131

Austria **II:** 332, 378; **IV:** 241; **IX:** 194

Austria-Hungary **VII:** 127*t*, 343

autobiographies **II:** 179, 234

Autobiography of an Idea (Sullivan) **VI:** 280

Autobiography of Benjamin Franklin **III:** 135, 215

Autobiography of Malcolm X, The (Alex Haley) **IX:** 7, 334*c*

auto-da-fé **I:** 16, 178, 190

automation (agriculture) **IX:** 7

automobiles/automobile industry **VI:** 150, 327*c;* **VII:** 21, **21–23,** 82, *174;* **VIII:** **30–31,** 38, 46, 297, 407*c;* **IX:** **24–26,** 25, 26; **X:** **31–32,** 32, 275

advertising **X:** 6

African Americans **VIII:** 3

Chrysler Corporation Loan Guarantee Act **X:** 62–63

CIO **VIII:** 69

consumer movement **IX:** 69

economy **VII:** 74; **VIII:** 90, 92; **IX:** 89; **X:** 94

Ford, Henry **VII:** 95–97

Ford Motor Corporation **IX:** 112

Fuel Administration **VII:** 102

General Motors **IX:** 120–121

Great Depression **VIII:** 138

invention and technology **VII:** 133

Kaiser, Henry J. **VIII:** 175

labor **VIII:** 179; **X:** 170

mass production **VII:** 174–175

mobilization **VIII:** 214

Murray, Philip **VIII:** 221

Nader, Ralph **X:** 205

National Traffic and Motor Vehicle Safety Act of 1966 **IX:** 225

oil industry **VII:** 217, 218

OPM **VIII:** 255

rationing **VIII:** 292

Reuther, Walter **IX:** 258–259

rust belt **X:** 269

steel industry **VII:** 297, 298; **VIII:** 339

suburbanization **IX:** 288

suburbs **VII:** 300

technology **VIII:** 353; **IX:** 294

transportation **VIII:** 360

unemployment **VIII:** 363

urban transportation **VII:** 318–319

WPB **VIII:** 375

auto theft **X:** 81

Autry, Gene **VIII:** 218, 222

Avalon. *See* Newfoundland

Avery, Henry **II:** 285

Avery, Oswald **X:** 191

Avery, Sewell L. **VIII:** 15

Avery, Waightstill **II:** 367

aviation **VII:** **23–24,** 356*c,* 361*c;* **VIII:** 4, 9–12; **IX:** **26–28,** 27, 269, 294, 330*c,* 331*c. See also* space exploration

invention and technology **VII:** 133

Kelly Air Mail Act **VII:** 147

Lindbergh, Charles **VII:** 158–159

Mitchell, Billy **VII:** 186–187

Wright Brothers **VII:** 347–348

aviation disasters **X:** 275

Ávila, Pedro Arias de. *See* Dávilar, Pedrarias

Avis car-rental company **IX:** 3

awards **V:** 227–228

Awatixa **I:** 161

Awatovi **I:** 167

Awaxawi **I:** 161

AWSA. *See* American Woman Suffrage Association

Axayácatl **I:** 237, 343

Axim **I:** 144

Axis **VIII:** *31,* **31–32,** 409*c,* 410*c*

America First Committee **VIII:** 13

Army, U.S. **VIII:** 19

atomic bomb **VIII:** 29

Britain, Battle of **VIII:** 43

Casablanca Conference **VIII:** 52

cash-and-carry **VIII:** 53

code breaking **VIII:** 64

conservatism **VIII:** 72

destroyers-for-bases deal **VIII:** 82

election of 1940 **VIII:** 98

enemy aliens **VIII:** 102

espionage **VIII:** 104

Ethiopia **VIII:** 105

FBI **VIII:** 115

foreign policy **VIII:** 124, 125

Four Freedoms **VIII:** 126

German Americans **VIII:** 131

Good Neighbor Policy **VIII:** 133

Grand Alliance **VIII:** 136

Axis *(continued)*
  Hiroshima and Nagasaki
    VIII: 147
  Italian Americans **VIII:**
    167
  Italian campaign **VIII:** 168
  Munich Conference **VIII:**
    220
  North African campaign
    VIII: 249, 250
  OSS **VIII:** 256–257
  Polish Americans **VIII:**
    269
  Popular Front **VIII:** 276
  POWs **VIII:** 281–282
  submarines **VIII:** 342
  Teheran Conference **VIII:**
    354
  World War II **VIII:** 389
  World War II European
    theater **VIII:** 391
Axis radio stations **VIII:**
  116–117
Ayer, F. Wayland **VI:** 2; **VII:** 4
Ayers, Bill **X:** 317, 318
Ayllón, Lucas Vázquez de **I:** 76,
  130
ayllus **I:** 280
Ayrer, Jacob **I:** 344
ayuntamiento. See cabildo(s)
Azambuja, Diogo d' **I:** 104
Azcapotzalco **I:** 17, 185, 342, 346
Azerbaijan **X:** 281
Azikiwe Nnamdi **IX:** 261
'Azîz, 'Abd-al' **I:** 174
Azores **I:** **16–17,** 53, 386*c*
Aztecs **I:** 7, **17–22,** *18,* 19*m,*
  107; **II:** 244
  Aguilar, Francisco de **I:** 4
  Aguilar, Gerónimo
    (Jerónimo) de **I:** 5
  Alvarado, Pedro de **I:** 6–8
  art and architecture **I:** 12,
    13
  Aztlán **I:** 22
  cacao **I:** 45, 46
  chinampas **I:** 72
  Cholula **I:** 72
  conquistadores **I:** 85
  Cortés, Hernán **I:** 93
  Cuauhtémoc **I:** 97
  Cuitláhuac **I:** 98–99
  Díaz de Castillo, Bernal **I:**
    106
  Durán, Diego **I:** 113
  Escalante, Juan de **I:** 123
  flowery wars **I:** 131
  Grijalva, Juan de **I:** 146
  Huitzilopochtli **I:** 170
  invention and technology
    I: 180
  Itzcóatl **I:** 185
  Malinche **I:** 218

Maya **I:** 227
Mendoza, Antonio de **I:**
  231
Mexico **I:** 234, 235
Moctezuma II **I:** 237–238
Nahua **I:** 249
Nahuatl **I:** 250
Native American religion
  I: 252
New Spain **I:** 258
Olmecs **I:** 269
Quetzalcoatl **I:** 301
Sahagún, Bernardino de **I:**
  315
Sandoval, Gonzalo de **I:**
  317–318
smallpox **I:** 331
Tabasco **I:** 341
Tacuba **I:** 342
Tarascan **I:** 343
Tenochtitlán **I:** 344–346
Teotihuacán **I:** 346
Tezcatlipoca **I:** 347, 348
Tlacacla **I:** 351
Tláloc **I:** 352
Tlaxcala **I:** 352, 353
Toltecs **I:** 356, 357
Velázquez, Diego de **I:** 364
Veracruz **I:** 366
Aztlán **I:** 22
Azusa Street Revival **VII:** 261

B

B-17 Flying Fortress **VIII:** *10*
  aircraft industry **VIII:** *10*
  air power **VIII:** 12
  Mariana Islands **VIII:** 202
  WASP **VIII:** 380
B-24 Liberator bomber
  aircraft industry **VIII:** 11
  Atlantic, Battle of the
    VIII: 28
  automobile industry **VIII:**
    30
  Mariana Islands **VIII:** 202
B-25 **VIII:** 380
B-26 **VIII:** 380
B-29 Superfortress
  air power **VIII:** 12
  Army Air Forces, U.S.
    VIII: 21
  atomic bomb **VIII:** 29
  Hiroshima and Nagasaki
    VIII: 146
  Mariana Islands **VIII:** 202
  World War II Pacific
    theater **VIII:** 399
Baba, Ahmad **I:** **23,** 351
Babbitt (Lewis) **VIII:** 191
Babcock, Orville **V:** 133, 157,
  393; **VI:** 255
Babson, Roger Q. **VIII:** 272*t*

baby boom **IX:** **29–30,** 46, 192,
  244–245, 329*c*
  marriage and family life
    VIII: 205
  population trends **VIII:**
    277
  World War II **VIII:** 390
  World War II home front
    VIII: 394
baby boomers **X:** **33–34,** 38
Bacall, Lauren **IX:** 212
Bacchante and Infant Faun
  (MacMonnie) **VI:** 259
Bache, Benjamin Franklin **III:**
  29, 108, 135, 192
Bache, Margaret **III:** 108
Bache, Sarah Franklin **II:** 125
bachelor's degrees **X:** 97, 98
Bacher, Robert F. **IX:** 23
Backstreet Boys **X:** 202
"back-to-Africa" movement. *See*
  colonization
Backus, Isaac **II:** 29; **III:**
  29–30, 34, 329
Bacon, Francis **II:** 109
Bacon, Henry **VI:** 259, 313
Bacon, Nathaniel **II:** 27–28, 32,
  77, 383, 423–424
Bacon's Rebellion **II:** **27–28,**
  28, 418*c*
  Berkeley, Lady Frances **II:**
    32
  Berkeley, Sir William **II:**
    33
  Burgesses, House of **II:** 45
  class **II:** 63
  Conestoga **II:** 67
  crowd action **II:** 77
  Culpeper, Thomas, Lord
    II: 79
  indentured servitude **II:**
    165
  Jamestown **II:** 172–173
  Maryland **II:** 209
  North Carolina **II:** 265
  Susquehannock War **II:**
    364
  Virginia **II:** 383
bacteria **V:** 97
bacterial resistance **X:** 188
bacteriology **VI:** 191; **VII:** 276
Bad Axe, Battle of **IV:** 52, 334
Badlay, Ahmad **I:** 124
Badoglio, Pietro **VIII:** 105
Baehr v. Miike (1993) **X:** 183
Baermann, Karl **VI:** 23
Baez, Buenaventura **VI:** 255
Baez, Joan **IX:** 84–85, 111, 191,
  217, 244, 268; **X:** 240
Baffin Island **I:** 83, 133
Baga **I:** 321
Bahamas **I:** 81, 288, 386*c;* **II:**
  52, 285, 368

Bahía **I:** **23–24,** 33
Bahía de Santa María. *See*
  Chesapeake Bay
Bailey, Francis **III:** 139
Bailey, James Anthony **VI:** 21,
  97, 98
Bailey, Joseph **V:** 280
*Bailey v. Drexel Furniture
  Company* **VII:** 360*c*
Bainuk **I:** 321
Baja California **I:** 48, 132
Bajío **II:** 357
Baker, Charles **IX:** 31
Baker, Ella Josephine **VIII:** 228;
  IX: 30–31, 160, 284
Baker, Howard **X:** 276
Baker, James **X:** 139
Baker, Ray Stannard **VII:** 192,
  299
Baker, Theodore **VI:** 202
Baker's Progressive Union **VII:**
  163
Baker v. Carr (1962) **IX:**
  31–32, 316, 333*c;* **X:** 41
Baker v. Vermont (1999) **X:**
  183
Bakeshop Act **VII:** 163, 164
Baki **I:** 339
Bakke, Allan **X:** 34–35
*Bakke (Regents of the University
  of California v. Allan Bakke)*
  (1978) **X:** 34–35, 325*c*
  affirmative action **X:** 8
  Brennan, William J. **X:** 41
  Burger, Warren E. **X:** 44
  NAACP **X:** 208
  Powell, Lewis **X:** 247
  Supreme Court **X:** 291
Bakker, Jim **X:** 197, 293, 294
Bakker, Tammy Faye **X:** 294
Bakr, Abu **I:** 141, 184
Bakri, al- **I:** 140–141
Bakweri **I:** 52
Balaguer, Joaquin **IX:** 172
balanced budget
  Bonus Army **VIII:** 39
  Eccles, Marriner S. **VIII:**
    89
  Great Depression **VIII:**
    139–140
  Hoover presidency **VIII:**
    154
  Keynesianism **VIII:** 176
  Morgenthau, Henry **VIII:**
    216
  recession of 1937–38 **VIII:**
    293
  taxation **VIII:** 351
  TNEC **VIII:** 355
Balanced Budget and
  Emergency Deficit Control
  Act of 1985. *See* Gramm-
  Rudman-Hollings Act of 1985

Balanced Budget and Emergency Deficit Control Reaffirmation Act of 1987 **X:** 134–135

Balboa, Vasco Núñez de **I: 24,** 25*m*, 386*c*
  adelantado **I:** 3–4
  conquistadores **I:** 84
  Panama **I:** 275, 276
  Soto, Hernando de **I:** 332

Baldanzi, George **IX:** 235

Baldwin, James **IX:** 5, *32,* **32–33,** 182, 191, 331*c*

Baldwin, Matthias **IV:** 307

Baldwin, Roger **IV:** 20, 333

Baldwin Locomotive Works **IV:** 307

Balinese Character (Mead and Bateson) **VII:** 177

Balkans **VIII:** 393; **X:** 307

Ball, Elias **II:** 373

Ball, George W. **X:** 307

Ballinger, Richard **VII:** 228, 236, 304

ballistic missiles **IX:** 16, 28

Balloon Corps **V: 21–22,** 309

balloons, hot-air **V:** 309, 346

Ball's Bluff, Battle of **V:** 191

Baltimore, Battle of **III:** 230; **IV: 39,** 201, 358

Baltimore, Lord. *See* Calvert, Cecilius

Baltimore, Maryland **II:** 204, 210
  Baltimore & Ohio Railroad (B&O) **IV:** 39–40
  Bank of the United States, Second **IV:** 44
  cities and urban life **IV:** 81
  diseases and epidemics **IV:** 112
  industrialization **IV:** 185
  railroads **IV:** 293, 295
  religion **IV:** 298
  riots **V: 22,** 46, 389
  Seton, Elizabeth Ann **IV:** 316

Baltimore, USS **VI:** 50

Baltimore & Ohio Railroad (B&O) **IV: 39–40,** 376*c;* **V:** 164–165, 242, 355; **VI:** 119, 126
  economy **IV:** 118
  industrialization **IV:** 185
  internal improvements **IV:** 188
  National Road **IV:** 255
  railroads **IV:** 295
  science and technology **IV:** 307

Baltimore Evening Post **III:** 258

Baltimore *Herald* **VII:** 181

Baltimore Orioles **VI:** 22

Baltimore Sun **IV:** 82, 197

Balzac v. Puerto Rico **VII:** 360*c*

Banai, Eddie Benton **IX:** 12, 334*c*

Bancroft, Anne **IX:** 214

Bancroft, George **VI:** 266

bandeirantes **I:** 33

banding birds **IV:** 34

bandits **IV:** 249

B&O. *See* Baltimore & Ohio Railroad

bands, military **III:** 251; **V:** 243–244

Banister, Marion Glass **VIII:** 384

banjo **II:** 239

BankAmericard **IX:** 330*c*

bankers, international **VIII:** 75

bank failures **VIII:** 33

Bankhead-Jones Act of 1935 **VIII:** 94

Bankhead-Jones Farm Tenant Act of 1937 **VIII:** 112, 307, 407*c*

"bank holidays" **VIII:** 33, 100, *101*

banking, finance and credit **II: 28–29,** 221, 222, 368, 375; **III: 32–33; IV: 40–44,** *41,* 44; **V: 22–24,** *23,* 409*c;* **VI:** 327*c;* **VII:** 75, 91–92, 268–269, 358*c;* **VIII:** 405*c*–407*c;* **X:** 144–145. *See also* state banks
  agriculture **VIII:** 8, 9
  architecture **III:** 20
  Austin, Moses **IV:** 36
  Banking Act of 1933 **VIII:** 33
  Banking Act of 1935 **VIII:** 33–34
  Bank of North America **III:** 30
  Bank of Pennsylvania **III:** 247
  Bank of the United States, Second **IV:** 44
  Bank of the United States (First) **III:** 30–31
  Benton, Thomas Hart **IV:** 49
  Big Stick diplomacy **VII:** 28
  business **X:** 49
  business and government **VI:** 40
  business cycles **VI:** 41
  canal era **IV:** 73–74
  Church of Jesus Christ of Latter-day Saints **IV:** 79
  Clay, Henry **IV:** 87
  Comstock Lode **IV:** 96

Cooke, Jay **V:** 81

Crédit Mobilier **V:** 84–85

Crime of '73 **VI:** 70

Democratic Party **IV:** 108; **V:** 94; **VII:** 66

Eccles, Marriner S. **VIII:** 89

economy **IV:** 118–119; **V:** 105–106; **VII:** 74–75; **VIII:** 91

election of 1840 **IV:** 124

Emergency Banking Act of 1933 **VIII:** 100–101

Era of Good Feelings **IV:** 127

FCA **VIII:** 111

Federal Reserve Act **VII:** 93–94

Federal Trade Commission Act **VII:** 94

foreign policy **VII:** 101

Gallatin, Albert **III:** 147

Girard Bank **III:** 153

globalization **X:** 131–132

Gould, Jay **VI:** 117–118

Great Depression **VIII:** 138

greenbacks **V:** 159

HOLC **VIII:** 150–151

Hoover presidency **VIII:** 154

housing **VI:** 135

industrialization **IV:** 184–185

industrial revolution **III:** 177

Laffer curve **X:** 172

McCormick, Cyrus Hall **IV:** 225

McCulloch v. Maryland **IV:** 227

Mellon, Andrew **VII:** 180–181

Morgan, John Pierpont **VI:** 197–198

Morris, Robert **III:** 247

national banking system **VI:** 205–206

New Freedom **VII:** 211

New Orleans, Battle of **V:** 252

New York City **V:** 253

New York City bailout **X:** 217

OMB **X:** 226–227

Panic of 1819 **IV:** 275

Panic of 1837 **IV:** 276, 277

Panic of 1857 **V:** 264

Patrons of Husbandry **VI:** 221

public land policy **IV:** 286

railroads **V:** 290; **VI:** 238

rural life **VII:** 268

Second Bank of the United States **III:** 33, 153

Sherman, William T. **V:** 320

stock market crash (1929) **VIII:** 341

televangelism **X:** 294

trade **III:** 350

transportation **V:** 354

Tredegar Iron Works **V:** 356

War of 1812 **IV:** 356

Wilson, Woodrow **VII:** 334

banking, investment **V:** 81; **VI: 19–20; VIII:** 33, 321

Banking Act of 1933 **VIII: 33,** 406*c*
  Banking Act of 1935 **VIII:** 34
  FDIC **VIII:** 117
  Hoover presidency **VIII:** 154
  New Deal **VIII:** 241

Banking Act of 1935 **VIII: 33–34**
  Banking Act of 1933 **VIII:** 33
  Eccles, Marriner S. **VIII:** 89
  FDIC **VIII:** 117
  New Deal **VIII:** 241

banking crisis **VIII:** 95, 117

banking reform **VIII:** 35

banking regulation **IV:** 43; **VIII:** 134

banking system **VI:** 223; **VIII:** 138–139

banknotes **IV:** 44, 119; **VI:** 205–206

Bank of California **IV:** 96

Bank of England **IV:** 42, 276

Bank of North America **III: 30,** 394*c*
  banks **III:** 32
  Morris, Gouverneur **III:** 247
  Morris, Robert **III:** 247–248
  trade **III:** 351

Bank of Pennsylvania **III:** 247, 394*c*

Bank of the United States, First **III: 30–31,** *31,* 395*c,* 398*c;* **IV:** 41, 356
  banks **III:** 32
  Carey, Mathew **III:** 62
  Federalist Party **III:** 126
  Gallatin, Albert **III:** 147
  Girard, Stephen **III:** 153
  Hamilton, Alexander **III:** 162
  King, Rufus **III:** 195

Bank of the United States, First
(*continued*)
  Macon, Nathaniel **III**: 226
  national debt **III**: 253
  Panic of 1792 **III**: 272
  Rittenhouse, David **III**:
    310
  states' rights **III**: 333
  trade **III**: 351
Bank of the United States,
  Second **III**: 33, 153; **IV**:
  44–45, 375*c*, 377*c*; **VI**: 205.
  See also Bank War
    American System **IV**: 18,
      19
    architecture **IV**: 27
    banking and currency **IV**:
      41, *41*, 42
    Benton, Thomas Hart **IV**:
      49
    Bonus Bill **IV**: 56
    Calhoun, John C. **IV**: 62
    Clay, Henry **IV**: 87
    Democratic Party **IV**: 107
    economy **IV**: 119
    election of 1828 **IV**:
      122–123
    election of 1840 **IV**: 124
    Era of Good Feelings **IV**:
      127
    Jackson, Andrew **IV**: 193
    McCulloch v. Maryland
      IV: 227
    Monroe, James **IV**: 240
    Panic of 1819 **IV**: 275, 276
    Panic of 1837 **IV**: 276, 277
    Polk, James K. **IV**: 282
    Supreme Court decision
      IV: 330
    Tyler, John **IV**: 348
    Van Buren, Martin **IV**: 351
    Webster, Daniel **IV**: 360
    Whig Party **IV**: 363
bankruptcy **IV**: 34, 36
banks (commercial) **VIII**: 33
Banks, Dennis **IX**: 12, 334*c*
Banks, Nathaniel P.
    Cedar Mountain, Battle of
      V: 53
    Jackson, "Stonewall" **V**:
      185
    Mississippi River **V**: 235
    Peninsular campaign **V**:
      267
    Porter, David Dixon **V**: 280
    Red River campaign **V**:
      297, 298
    Shenandoah Valley:
      Jackson's campaign **V**:
      316, 317
    Union army **V**: 365
    Vicksburg campaign **V**: 382

Wakeman, Sarah Rosetta
  V: 386
  Zouaves **V**: 404
banks, national **V**: 106
banks, southern **V**: 23, 106
Bank War
    banking and currency **IV**:
      42
    Benton, Thomas Hart **IV**:
      49
    Democratic Party **IV**: 107
    economy **IV**: 119
    Jackson, Andrew **IV**: 193
    Panic of 1837 **IV**: 276
Bannan, Benjamin **VI**: 195, 196
Banneker, Benjamin **III**: *33,*
  33–34, 395*c*
Banner of Light (newspaper)
  IV: 326
Bantu **I**: **24–26,** 52, 210
Bao Dai **IX**: 308–310
Baptism in Kansas (Curry) **VIII**:
  25
Baptist Church **IV**: 59, 296–298,
  311*t*; **V**: 209, 299
Baptists **II**: **29–30**; **III**: **34–35**;
  VI: 3–4, 6; **VII**: 261; **VIII**:
  303; **X**: 11, 107
    antislavery and abolition
      III: 15
    Backus, Isaac **III**: 30
    Connecticut **II**: 70
    education **II**: 103; **III**: 115
    Great Awakening **II**:
      148–149
    Loyalists **III**: 221
    Madison, James **III**: 227
    New Jersey **II**: 254
    Protestantism **II**: 301
    religion **III**: 298–299
    religion, African American
      II: 314
    religion, Euro-American
      II: 316
    Virginia **II**: 385
    Willard, Samuel **II**: 399
    Williams, Roger **II**: 399
Baptists, Northern **V**: 299
Baptists, Southern **V**: 299
baracoons **II**: 343
Baraka, Amiri **IX**: 7. *See also*
  Jones, Leroi
Baramendana, king of Mali **I**:
  217
Baranov, Alexander **II**: 326
Barbadoes, James G. **IV**: 13
Barbados **I**: 26, 338; **II**: 56, 229,
  349, 354, 374
Barbary pirates **III**: 35, 394*c*,
  397*c*; **IV**: 104, 105, 328
    Chauncey, Isaac **III**: 65
    Constitution, USS **III**: 80

Continental navy **III**: 90
  foreign affairs **III**: 130,
    131
  Rowson, Susanna **III**: 311
Barbastro, Lois Cancer de **I**:
  130
barbed wire **VI**: 20, 46, 324*c*;
    VII: *344*
Barbee, George **VI**: 134
Barber, Samuel **IX**: 217
barbiturates **X**: 206
Barbizon art community **IV**: 55
Barbotiere **I**: 29
"Barcelona Letter" of 1493
  (Christopher Columbus) **I**:
  294, 392–394
Barclay, Robert **II**: 307; **IV**: 206
Bard, John **III**: 240
Bardeen, John **X**: 72
Bardot, Bridgitte **IX**: 213
Barents, William **I**: 114, 265
Baring, Alexander, Lord
  Ashburton **IV**: 360–361, 387*c*
Baring Brothers **VI**: 42
Barkley, Alben **VIII**: 67
Barletta, Nicolas Ardito **X**: 231
Barlow, Francis Channing **V**:
  384
Barlow, Joel **III**: **35–36**, 80
Barlow, Roger **I**: 35
Barlowe, Arthur **I**: **26–27,** 220,
  313, 372; **II**: 264, 401
barn, round **IV**: 308
Barnard, George Gray **VI**: 259
Barnard, George N. **V**: 273
Barnard, Henry **IV**: 120; **V**: 104
Barnard College **VI**: 316
"Barnburners" **IV**: 150
Barnes and Noble **X**: 178
Barnett, Ferdinand **VI**: 311–312
Barnett, Ross **IX**: 200
Barnett, Samuel **VI**: 259
Barnum, Phineas T. **IV**: 82, 250;
    VI: **20–21**, 97, 323*c*
Barnum & Bailey Circus **VI**: 97
Barnwell, John **II**: 379
Baronov, Aleksandr
  Andreyevich **III**: 8–9
Baroody, William, Sr. **X**: 301
barrel making **II**: 101, 111, 250
Barret, James **III**: 212
Barrin, Roland-Michel **II**: 129
Barron, Frank **IX**: 175
Barron, James **III**: 67; **IV**: 105
Barron v. Baltimore **IV**: 377*c*
Barros, João de **I**: 105
Barry, John **III**: **36**
Barry, Leonora Marie **VI**: 169
"Bars Fight" (Prince) **II**: 195,
  298
barter **II**: 222; **IV**: 260; **V**: 106
Barth, Karl **VIII**: 304

Barthelme, Frederick **X**: 177
Bartholdi, Auguste **VI**: 276
"Bartleby the Scrivener"
  (Melville) **IV**: 213
Bartlett, Charlie **IX**: 156
Bartók, Béla **VIII**: 223
Barton, Bruce **VII**: 5
Barton, Clara **V**: 11, **24–26,** 25,
  97, 256; **VI**: 157, 325*c*
Bartram, John **II**: 30; **III**: 321
    American Philosophical
      Society **II**: 18
    animals **II**: 21
    Colden, Jane **II**: 66
    Kalm, Peter **II**: 181
    Logan, James **II**: 198
    Pennsylvania **II**: 277
    Philadelphia **II**: 282
    science **II**: 330
Bartram, William **II**: 66; **III**:
    37, *37,* 321, 395*c*
Baruch, Bernard M. **VII**: 25,
  235, 330; **VIII**: 34; **IX**: 57
    Byrnes, James F. **VIII**: 48
    dollar-a-year men **VIII**: 84
    Johnson, Hugh S. **VIII**:
      173
    reconversion **VIII**: 295
Baruch-Hancock Report **VIII**:
  295
baseball **VI**: **21–22**, 22; **VII**:
  25–27, 26, 360*c*, 361*c*; **VIII**:
  83–84, 297, 335–336,
  407*c*–409*c*; **IX**: 329*c*, 332*c*; **X**:
  1, 262, 284, 325*c*
    African-American
      movement **IX**: 5
    popular culture **VII**: 232
    recreation **VII**: 256, 258;
      IX: 255
    Rickey, Branch **IX**: 260
    Robinson, Jackie **IX**:
      262–263
    sports **VII**: 293, 294; **IX**:
      280, 281
    Sunday, Billy **VII**: 301,
      302
Basie, William "Count" **VIII**: 3,
  223
Basilica of San Marco **I**: 142
basketball **VI**: 275; **VII**: 295;
    VIII: 336; **IX**: 280, 281; **X**:
    285, 296
basket-naming **II**: 152
Basque **II**: 243
Basques **I**: 74–75, 241
Bass, Rick **X**: 178
Bataan Death March **VIII**:
  34–35, 35, 147, 267, 282,
  409*c*
Bates, Edward **V**: 301
Bateson, Gregory **VII**: 177

Bat God **I:** 242
Batista, Fulgencio **IX:** 33, 60
Baton Rouge, Louisiana **II:** 74;
  IV: 5
Battel, Andrew **I: 27,** 297
battlefield photography **V:** 273
battle flags **V: 26,** *26*
"Battle Hymn of the Republic"
  (Howe) **V:** 174, 244
battleships **VII:** 187; **VIII:** 264,
  264
Batts, Thomas **II: 30–31,** 115
Battuta, Ibn **I:** 204
Bauer, Gary **X:** 79
Baugh, Sammy **VIII:** 336
Baum, L. Frank **VI:** 73
Bavin, Thomas **I:** 373
Baxter, Irving **VI:** 290
Bayard, James **III:** 117
Bayard, Thomas F. **VI:** 26
Bayard-Chamberlain Treaty of
  1888 **VI:** 26
Bayh, Birch **X:** 105, 253
Bay Indians **II:** 88
Bay Islands, Colony of the **IV:**
  89
Bay of Pigs **IX: 33–35,** *34m,* 50,
  158, 204, *333c*
BBN (Bolt Beranek and
  Newman, Inc.) **X:** 152
B. Dalton **X:** 178
BE (Bureau of Ethnology) **VI:**
  228
Beach, Alfred **VI:** 292
Beach, Amy Marcy Cheney **VI:**
  22–23, 201, 202
Beadle, Erastus **VI:** 80–81
Beafada **I:** 321
Beale, Fred **VII:** 106
Beall, Lloyd J. **V:** 222
Beal v. Doe **X:** 3
Beame, Abraham **X:** 217
Bean, James Baxter **V:** 231
Beanes, William **IV:** 201
Beard, Charles and Mary **V:**
  180; **VII:** 161
Bear Flag Revolt **IV: 45**
  Bidwell, John **IV:** 51
  California **IV:** 65
  Carson, Kit **IV:** 75
  exploration **IV:** 132
  Frémont, John C. **IV:** 153
  Larkin, Thomas Oliver **IV:**
    208
Bear Lake **IV:** 302
Beat Generation **IX: 35–36,**
  331c, 332c
  counterculture **IX:** 71
  Ginsberg, Allen **IX:**
    122–123
  Kerouac, Jack **IX:** 159–160
  literature **IX:** 182

music **IX:** 217
religion **IX:** 256
Beatles **IX:** *36,* **36–37; X:** 202,
  240
  counterculture **IX:** 72
  Ginsberg, Allen **IX:** 123
  movies **IX:** 214
  music **IX:** 218
  popular culture **IX:** 244
  rock and roll **IX:** 264
Beatriz, Doña **I:** 8
Beattie, Ann **X:** 177
Beatty, Warren **VII:** 260; **IX:**
  214
Beaufort, Battle of **III:** 187
Beaujeu, Anne de **I:** 78
Beaumont, Texas **VII:** *355c*
Beaumont, William **IV:** 230
Beauregard, Pierre Gustave
  Toutant **V: 26–27,** *406c*
  Alexander, Edward P. **V:** 7
  Anderson, Robert **V:** 9
  Boyd, Belle **V:** 34
  Bull Run, First Battle of **V:**
    42
  Confederate army **V:** 73
  Fort Sumter, South
    Carolina **V:** 136
  Greenhow, Rose O'Neal **V:**
    159
  Johnston, Albert Sidney **V:**
    189
  Johnston, Joseph E. **V:** 190
  Mississippi River **V:** 234
  Shiloh, Battle of **V:** 324,
    326
Beaux, Cecilia **VI:** 219
Beaux Hommes **II:** 77
Beaver Island **IV:** 329
beavers/beaver trade **I:** 182; **IV:**
  131, 248
  environment **II:** 111
  fur trade **II:** 130–131, 133
  Great Plains Indians **II:**
    150
  Hudson's Bay Company **II:**
    159
  Iroquois **II:** 168
  Native Americans **II:** 243
  Stuyvesant, Peter **II:** 363
Beaver Wars **II: 31,** 160, 169
bebop **VIII:** 223, *410c*
Beccaria, Cesare **III:** 286; **IV:**
  277
Bechet, Sidney **VII:** 137
Beck, David **IX:** 292–293, 303
Beck, Martin **VI:** 96
Becknell, William **IV: 45–46,**
  131, 305, 306
Beckwourth, Jim **IV:** *46,* **46–47,**
  131, 247, 302, *375c*
Beckwourth Pass **IV:** 47

Bedford, New York **II:** 372
Bedini, Gaetano **IV:** 23
Beecher, Catharine
  cities and urban life **IV:** 83
  education **IV:** 120–121
  female antislavery societies
    IV: 135
  women's status and rights
    IV: 368
Beecher, Henry Ward **IV:** *378c;*
  VI: 23–24, *24*
  Beecher-Tilton scandal **VI:**
    24
  Darwinism and religion
    VI: 75
  Hooker, Isabella Beecher
    VI: 133
  music **VI:** 202
  religion **VI:** 241, 242
  Social Darwinism **VI:** 266
Beecher, Lyman **III:** 346; **IV:**
  21, 296; **V:** 251
Beecher-Tilton scandal **VI:**
  24–25, 319
"Beef Trust" **VI:** 191
Bee Gees **X:** 240
beepers **IX:** 270
beer **III:** 281; **IV:** 336
Begin, Menachem **X: 54–55,** 58
Behaim, Martin **I: 27**
Beijing **I:** 312
Belafonte, Harry **IX:** 191, 267
Belarus **X:** 124, 152, 281
Belasco, David **VI:** 287
Bel Geddes, Norman **VIII:** 22
Belgian Congo **IX:** 316, 317
Belgian settlers **II:** 260
Belgium **VII:** 343, *360c;* **VIII:**
  39, 44, 151, *410c;* **IX:** 194,
  231–233; **X:** 223
Belize **I:** 225–229
Belknap, William Worth **V:** 157
Bell, Alexander Graham **V:** 351;
  VI: 25, 62, 147, 149, *324c*
Bell, Cool Papa **VII:** 295
Bell, Derrick **X:** 12
Bell, John **IV:** 301; **V:** *406c;* **VI:**
  121
Bellamy, Black Sam **II:** 286
Bellamy, Edward **VI: 26; VII:**
  229
  business cycles **VI:** 41
  literature **VI:** 178
  Social Gospel **VI:** 267
  socialism **VI:** 267
  Socialist Party **VI:** 269
  utopianism **VI:** 301
Bell Atlantic **X:** *50m*
Belle Boyd in Camp and Prison
  (Boyd) **V:** 35, 213
Bellecourt, Clyde **IX:** 12, *334c*
Bell family **V:** 37

Bell Laboratories **IX:** 64, 293;
  X: *325c*
Bellomont, earl of **II:** 285
Bellotti v. Baird **X:** 17
Bellow, Saul **VIII:** 193; **X:** 177
Bellows, Henry **V:** 203, 204, 373
Bell South **X:** *50m*
Bell Telephone Company **VI:** 25
Bell Telephone Laboratories **X:**
  72, 274
Belmont, August **V:** *295;* **VI:**
  134; **VII:** 201
Belmont Stakes **VI:** 134
Belmont v. Belmont (1979) **X:**
  211
Belon, Pierre **I:** 40
Belzec **VIII:** 150
Bembo, Pietro **I:** 304
Bemis Heights, Battle of **III:**
  21, 320
Benatar, Pat **X:** 203
Benedict College **VI:** 4
Benezet, Anthony **II: 31–32**
  abolitionism **II:** 2
  African Americans **II:** 7
  education **II:** 104
  Enlightenment **II:** 110
  Quakers **II:** 309
  Woolman, John **II:** 410
Ben Gurion, David **IX:** 146
Benin **I: 28; II:** 344; **X:** 13
  Dahomey **I:** 101–102
  Ewe **I:** 125
  Fon **I:** 131–132
  Mossi **I:** 243
  slavery **I:** 327
  slave trade **I:** 330
  Yoruba **I:** 377
"Benito Cereno" (Melville) **IV:**
  213
Benjamin, Judah P. **V: 27–28,**
  75, 180
Benjamin, Patricia **X:** 263
Bennett, Henry **II:** 79
Bennett, James Gordon **IV:** 194;
  V: 192
Bennett, James Gordon, Jr. **VI:**
  211, 289
Bennett, Ned **IV:** 354
Bennett, Richard **II:** 174, 175,
  209
Bennett, Rolla **IV:** 354
Bennett, S. Fillmore **VI:** 203
Bennett, William J. **X: 35**
  conservative movement **X:**
    80
  crime **X:** 82
  Kemp, Jack F. **X:** 163
  NEA, NEH **X:** 209
  neoconservative **X:** 216
Benny, Jack **VIII:** *274, 405c*
Benson, Martin **II:** 397

Bent, Charles **IV: 47–48,** 50, 51, **200**
Bent, George **IV:** 47
Bent, Robert **IV:** 47, 48
Bent, St. Vrain and Company **IV:** 47, 50
Bent, William **IV:** 47, **48,** 50
Benteen, Frederick **V:** 214
Benton, Thomas Hart **IV:** *49,* **49–50; VIII:** 25
    American Fur Company **IV:** 16
    Astor, John Jacob **IV:** 32
    exploration **IV:** 132
    Frémont, Jessie Benton **IV:** 152
    Frémont, John C. **IV:** 153
    Manifest Destiny **IV:** 217
    Panic of 1837 **IV:** 276
    Santa Fe Trail **IV:** 306
    Sublette, William **IV:** 330
Bentonville, Battle of **V:** 28
Bentsen, Lloyd **X:** 45, 91
Bent's Fort **IV: 50–51**
    Beckwourth, Jim **IV:** 47
    Bent, Charles **IV:** 47
    Bent, William **IV:** 48
    Fort Laramie **IV:** 143
    Santa Fe Trail **IV:** 306
Benzedrine **X:** 206
Benzoni, Girolamo **I:** 30
Berbers **I:** 184, 321, 360
Berg, Paul **X:** 191
Berger, Samuel R. "Sandy" **X:** 88
Berger, Victor **VI:** 268
Bergman, Ingrid **VIII:** 409c; **IX:** 212
Bergmann, Carl **IV:** 179
Bering, Vitus **II:** 13, **32,** 115, 167, 195, 326; **III:** 8
Bering Sea dispute **VI: 26–27**
    Blaine, James Gillespie **VI:** 32
    Canada and the United States **VI:** 43
    Harlan, John Marshall **VI:** 122
    Harrison, Benjamin **VI:** 123
Bering Strait **I:** 289, 385c; **II:** 167
Berkeley, Lady Frances **II: 32**
Berkeley, George **II:** 105, 346, 413
Berkeley, Sir William **II: 32–33**
    Bacon's Rebellion **II:** 27–28
    Batts, Thomas **II:** 30
    Berkeley, Lady Frances **II:** 32

Burgesses, House of **II:** 44–45
Byrd family **II:** 47
Jamestown **II:** 172
printing and publishing **II:** 298
Virginia **II:** 383
Berkley, John, Lord **II:** 144, 252
Berkman, Alexander **VI:** 106, 132, 167; **VII:** 110, 252
Berle, Adolf A., Jr. **VIII: 35–36,** 41
Berlin, Germany **IX:** 77–78; **X:** 89
Berlin, Irving **VII:** 108, 194, 308, 309; **VIII:** 223
Berlin blockade **IX: 37,** 58, 232, 299, **330c**
Berlin Conference **VI:** 32
Berlin Decree **III:** 267
Berlin Olympics (1936) **VIII:** 260–261, 275, 338
Berlin Wall **IX:** 277, 333c; **X:** 327c
    Bush, George H. W. **X:** 46
    cold war (end of) **X:** 70, 72
    INF Treaty **X:** 151
    Iron Curtain **X:** 157
Bermuda **I: 28–29,** 29–30; **II:** 135, 374, 387; **VI:** 4
Bermuda Company **I: 29–30,** 318
Bermudez, Juan **I:** 29
Bernadotte, Folke **IX:** 43
Bernard, Francis **III: 37–38,** 43, 171, 349
Berners-Lee, Tim **X:** 153, 274
Bernhardt, Sarah **VI:** 286
Bernstein, Carl **X:** 185, 196
Bernstein, Leonard **VIII:** 410c; **IX:** 216, *216*
Berrio, Don Antonio de **I:** 119
Berry, Carrie **V:** 168
Berwanger, Jay **VIII:** 336
Besant, Annie Wood **VI:** 245
Bessemer, Henry **VI:** 27, 276
Bessemer-Kelly process **IV:** 105
Bessemer process **VI: 27**
    bridges **VI:** 35
    Carnegie, Andrew **VI:** 44
    industrial revolution, second **VI:** 145
    steel **VI:** 276, 277
Bessie, Alvah **IX:** 134–135, *211*
Best, Pete **IX:** 36
Bethlehem Steel **VII:** 297, 306; **IX:** 282
Bethune, Mary McLeod **VIII: 36,** *36*
    African Americans **VIII:** 3
    Black Cabinet **VIII:** 37
    Democratic Party **VIII:** 81

NYA **VIII:** 234
    Roosevelt, Eleanor **VIII:** 311
    WPA **VIII:** 387
Beveridge, Albert J. **IV:** 219
Beverley, Robert **II: 33,** 172, 179, 289
Bèze, Théodore de **I:** 170
BIA. *See* Indian Affairs, Bureau of
Biafra **I:** 330
Biberman, Herbert **IX:** 135, *211*
Bible **I:** 147; **II:** 208, 215; **V:** 5, 108; **VI:** 75, 88, 242, 243; **VII:** 260, 278; **X:** 293–294. *See also* Scopes Trial
    Common Sense (Paine) **III:** 78
    deism **III:** 103
    education **III:** 113, 115; **IV:** 120
    Hicks, Elias **IV:** 172
    immigration **IV:** 180
    Indian Removal Act (1830) **IV:** 183
    literature **III:** 214
    Mayhew, Jonathan **III:** 238
    Native Americans **IV:** 257
    Paine, Thomas **III:** 272
    race and race relations **IV:** 290, 291
    religion **IV:** 296
    spiritualism **IV:** 325
    Unitarianism **III:** 355
"Bible Commonwealth" **II:** 19
Bible reading (in schools) **X:** 104–105
Bible schools **IV:** 311
biblical criticism **VIII:** 303
Bibliotheca universalis (Conrad von Gesner) **I:** 140
bicameral legislatures **II:** 325
bicentennial celebration **X:** 325c
Bickel, Alexander **X:** 39
Bickerdyke, Mary Ann **V: 28–29**
bicycling, 1870–1900 **VI: 27–28,** *28*
Bicycling World **VI:** 27
Biddle, Nicholas
    banking and currency **IV:** 42
    Bank of the United States, Second **IV:** 44
    election of 1840 **IV:** 124
Bidlack Treaty (1846) **IV:** 88, 378c
Bidwell, John **IV: 51,** 71; **VI:** 234
Bienville, Sieur de **IV:** 208
Bierstadt, Albert **V:** 16, 405c; **VI:** 219
big bands **VIII:** 132, 223

Big Black River **V:** 382
Big Bopper **IX:** 263
Big Brother (TV program) **X:** 295
Bigelow v. Virginia **X:** 3
Big Foot, Chief **VI:** 263
Big Four **VII:** 323
Big Money, The (Dos Passos) **VIII:** 191
Bigotes **I:** 88.**I:** 90
"big science" **VIII:** 317
Big Six meatpacking companies **VI:** 191
Big Sleep, The (Chandler) **VIII:** 193
"Big Steel." *See* United States Steel Corporation
Big Stick diplomacy **VII: 27–29,** *28,* 266, 267, 310, 357c
Big Three automakers **VII:** 22, 74; **VIII:** 30; **IX:** 24–25
"Big Three" leaders
    Cairo Conference **VIII:** 51
    Potsdam Conference **VIII:** 279, 280
    Roosevelt, Franklin D. **VIII:** 314
    Soviet-American relations **VIII:** 334
    Teheran Conference **VIII:** 354
    World War II European theater **VIII:** 391
    Yalta Conference **VIII:** 401
Big Tree, Treaty of **II:** 173
Biko, Stephen **X:** 279
Bilbo, Theodore **VII:** 292
bilingual education **IX:** 251; **X:** 142
Bilingual Education Act of 1968 **X: 35–36**
billboard advertising **X:** 8
Bill Haley and the Comets **IX:** 217, 263, 331c
Billing, George **II:** 252, 253
Billings, John **V:** 213
Billings, Warren **VII:** 188
Billings, William **II:** 239; **III: 38,** 250, 251; **VI:** 183, 201
Billings and Holden Collection of Ancient Psalmody, The **IV:** 250
"Billion Dollar Congress"
    Harrison, Benjamin **VI:** 123
    the presidency **VI:** 230
    Reed, Thomas Brackett **VI:** 240
    tariff issue **VI:** 284

Bill of Rights **III: 38–39**, 393*c*,
395*c*, 410–412; **IV:** 377*c*;
VIII: 60, 61, 126; **X:** 19–20.
See also specific amendments
   anti-Federalists **III:** 14
   Catholics **III:** 63
   Federalist Papers **III:** 125
   Gallatin, Albert **III:** 147
   Henry, Patrick **III:** 166
   Madison, James **III:** 229
   Mason, George **III:** 237,
      238
   states' rights **III:** 333
Bill of Rights (English) **II:** 140
bill of rights (state) **III:** 84
bill of rights for women **X:** 211
bills of exchange **II:** 222
Billy Budd (Melville) **IV:** 213;
   VI: 178
Billy the Kid (Copland) **VIII:**
   223
"Billy Yank" **V:** 69, 362
Biloxi Indians **II:** 246
Bimbia **I:** 52
bimetallism **IV:** 43, 118–119;
   VI: 28–29
   Bland-Allison Act **VI:** 32
   Bryan, William Jennings
      VI: 37
   Crime of '73 **VI:** 69–70
   currency issue **VI:** 72
   McKinley, William **VI:**
      189
Bimini **I:** 288
binders **VI:** 8
Binet, Alfred **VII:** 131
Bingham, Arthur **III:** 216
Bingham, Eula **X:** 225
Bingham, George Caleb **III:** 43;
   IV: 26, 378*c*; **V:** 16
bingo **VIII:** 296
bin Laden, Osama **X:** 331*c*
   Clinton, William **X:** 69
   defense policy **X:** 88–89
   foreign policy **X:** 125
   Powell, Colin L. **X:** 247
   terrorism **X:** 301
biographers **V:** 166
Bioko **I:** 129
biological hazards **X:** 225
biological weapons **X:** 152, 236,
   298, 299
Biological Weapons Anti-
   Terrorism Act of 1989 **X:** 298
Biologics Control Act of 1902
   IX: 222
biology **II:** 330; **VII:** 278; **VIII:**
   318
Bipartisan Campaign Reform
   Act of 2002 **X:** 53–54
bird paintings **IV:** 34–35
Birdsall, Mary **IV:** 54

Birds of America, The
   (Audubon) **IV:** 34, 308, 376*c*
Birmingham (Alabama)
   confrontation **IX: 37–38,**
   333*c*
   African-American
      movement **IX:** 6
   civil disobedience **IX:** 54
   Civil Rights Act of 1964
      IX: 56
   King, Martin Luther, Jr.
      IX: 160–161
   race and racial conflict **IX:**
      253
   Southern Christian
      Leadership Conference
      IX: 275
Birney, James **IV:** 210, 211, 283
birth control **II:** 118; **IV:** 369; **V:**
   223; **VI:** 173; **VII: 29–30,**
   358*c*, 359*c*; **VIII:** 54, 204; **X:**
   36–38
   abortion **X:** 3
   birthrates **X:** 38
   Ellis, Havelock **VII:** 84
   Flynn, Elizabeth Gurley
      VII: 95
   Goldman, Emma **VII:** 110
   Greenwich Village **VII:**
      115
   marriage and family life
      VII: 171; **X:** 109, 183
   population trends **VII:**
      233
   public health **VII:** 243
   radical press **VII:** 252
   Sanger, Margaret **VII:**
      273–274
   sexuality **VII:** 282, 283
   sexual revolution **X:** 277
   White, Byron R. **X:** 319
   women's status and rights
      VII: 338, 339
birth control pills. *See* "pill, the"
Birth Control Review
   (magazine) **VII:** 29
Birth of a Nation (Griffith) **VII:**
   30–31, 358*c*
   entertainment **VII:** 85
   Griffith, D. W. **VII:**
      115–116
   Ku Klux Klan **VII:** 147
   movie industry **VII:**
      190–191
   NAACP **VII:** 199
   popular culture **VII:** 232
   race and racial conflict
      VII: 249
birthrates **II:** 215, 291; **V:** 277;
   X: 38, 109, 290
   baby boom **IX:** 29–30
   children **VIII:** 56–57

marriage and family life
   VIII: 204, 205; **IX:** 192,
   193
population trends **VIII:**
   277; **IX:** 245
public health **IX:** 249
suburbanization **IX:** 287
women's status and rights
   VIII: 385
World War II home front
   VIII: 394
births, out-of-wedlock **X:** 181,
   182
Birú **I:** 24
Bishop, Maurice **X:** 135
bison. *See also* buffalo,
   extermination of
BITNET **X:** 153
Bittner, Van **IX:** 235–236
bituminous mining **VII:** 313
Bizaillon, Pierre **II:** 130
Black, Hugo L. **VIII: 36–37,**
   110, 178, 346, 346*t*, 407*c*; **IX:**
   315; **X:** 125
   Baker v. Carr **IX:** 31
   Dennis v. United States **IX:**
      80
   Engel v. Vitale **IX:** 100
   Gideon v. Wainwright **IX:**
      121
   *Heart of Atlanta Motel
      Inc., v. United States* **IX:**
      132–133
   Warren Court **IX:** 315
Black, Jeremiah Sullivan **V:** 128
black aesthetic **IX:** 7, 40
Black Arts movement **IX:** 5, 21
Black Arts Repertory Theatre
   IX: 7, 334*c*
"Blackbeard." *See* Teach,
   Edward
black bile (melancholy) **II:** 220
Black Boy (Wright) **VIII:** 191,
   399
Black, Brown, and Beige
   (Ellington) **VIII:** 99, 223
Blackburn, Harry **X:** 268
Blackburn's Ford **V:** 214
Black Cabinet **VIII: 37–38**
   African Americans **VIII:** 3
   Bethune, Mary McLeod
      VIII: 36
   civil rights **VIII:** 61
   Democratic Party **VIII:**
      81
   NYA **VIII:** 234
Black Carib **I:** 56
black churches **V:** 299
Black Codes **V: 29–30,** 408*c*
   Civil Rights Act of 1866 **V:**
      62
   Democratic Party **V:** 95

Fifteenth Amendment **V:**
   124
Fourteenth Amendment
   V: 138
Freedmen's Bureau **V:** 143
Johnson, Andrew **V:** 188
New Orleans riot **V:** 252
Reconstruction Acts **V:** 295
Thirteenth Amendment **V:**
   353
Black Crook, The (musical) **VI:**
   203, 286
Black Death. *See* plague
   (bubonic)
blackface **VI:** 95–97
Blackfeet nation **II:** 50
   American Fur Company
      IV: 17
   Astor, John Jacob **IV:** 32
   Bent, Charles **IV:** 47
   Bodmer, Karl **IV:** 55
   Missouri Fur Company **IV:**
      239
black free labor. *See* labor, free
Blackfriars Theatre **I:** 324
"Black Friday" **VI:** 118
Black Hawk **IV:** 51–53, 375*c*,
   377*c*
Black Hawk War **III:** 73, 398*c*;
   IV: 33–34, **51–53,** 52, 256,
   334, 377*c*
   Anderson, Robert **V:** 9
   Davis, Jefferson **V:** 88
   Johnston, Albert Sidney **V:**
      189
   Johnston, Joseph E. **V:**
      190
   Lincoln, Abraham **V:** 209
Black Hills **IV:** 131; **V:** 213–214
Black Hills, War for the **VI:**
   207–209, 240, 324*c*
Black Hills gold rush **VI: 29,**
   324*c*
   Crazy Horse **VI:** 69
   Red Cloud **VI:** 240
   Sioux wars **VI:** 263
   Sitting Bull **VI:** 264
"Black Hole of Calcutta" **II:**
   119
Black Jacks **II:** 337
Black Justice **VIII:** 405*c*
black legend **I: 30–31,** 198,
   294, 322
blacklisting **VII:** 251; **VIII:** 310
black market **VIII: 38**
   OPA **VIII:** 254
   rationing **VIII:** 292
   wage and price controls
      VIII: 372
   World War II **VIII:** 389
   World War II home front
      VIII: 394

black-marketing **X:** 258
"Black Monday" **VIII:** 317, 345; **IX:** 276
Black Monday (Thomas P. Brady) **IX:** 320
Blackmun, Harry A. **X:** 290, 291
Black Muslims. *See* Nation of Islam
Black National Convention **IV:** 13
black nationalism **VI:** 283; **VII:** 105–106, 315–316; **IX:** 5–7, 47, 68, 257; **X:** 12, 37, 111, 257
blackouts **VIII:** 253, 254
Black Panthers **IX:** 38–40, 39, 334c; **X:** 37, 297
   African-American movement **IX:** 7
   Black Power **IX:** 40
   Carmichael, Stokely **IX:** 48
   race and racial conflict **IX:** 255
   Weathermen **IX:** 319
"black pews" **IV:** 333
Black Power **IX:** *40*, **40–41,** 334c
   African-American movement **IX:** 6
   Carmichael, Stokely **IX:** 47
   race and racial conflict **IX:** 255
   Student Nonviolent Coordinating Committee **IX:** 285
Black Power Movement **X:** 208
Black Republicans **IV:** 301
   Grant, Ulysses S. **V:** 156
   Reconstruction **V:** 294
   redemption **V:** 297
   scalawags **V:** 307
Black Riders, The (Crane) **VI:** 68, 178
"Black Robes" **II:** 174
blacks. *See* African Americans
black separatism **X:** 12, 213
Black Shriners **IX:** 214
Black Sox **X:** 198
"Black Sox" scandal **VII:** 26, 294, 360c
Black Star Line **VII:** 105, 106, 315
Blackstone, William **II:** 35; **III:** **39–40,** 203, 391c; **IV:** 221–222
"Black Thursday" **VIII:** 341
"Black Tuesday" **VIII:** 341, 405c
Blackwell, Alice Stone **VII:** 335
Blackwell, Antoinette Brown **V:** 396; **VI:** **29–30,** 35, 317, 318

Blackwell, Elizabeth **IV:** 230–231, 378c; **VI:** **30–31,** 318
   disease and epidemics **V:** 97
   ladies aid societies **V:** 203, 204
   nurses **V:** 255
   prostitution **V:** 283
Blackwell, Emily **VI:** 31
Blackwell, Henry **VI:** 36, 278; **VII:** 198
Bladensburgh, Battle of **IV:** 358
Blaeu, Joan **I:** 31
Blaeu, Willem **I:** **31**
Blaine, James Gillespie **VI:** **31–32,** 325c
   Chilean-American relations **VI:** 50
   Civil Rights Act of 1875 **V:** 63
   Cleveland, Grover **VI:** 58
   Congress **VI:** 63
   Conkling, Roscoe **VI:** 64
   corruption, political **VI:** 67
   Crédit Mobilier **V:** 84
   Garfield, James A. **VI:** 108, 109
   Harrison, Benjamin **VI:** 122, 123
   Mafia incident **VI:** 185–186
   mugwumps **VI:** 199
   Nast, Thomas **V:** 247
   newspapers **VI:** 211
   Pan-American Union **VI:** 220
   presidential campaigns **VI:** 231, 232
   Radical Republicans **V:** 288
   Republican Party **V:** 302; **VI:** 246
   Schurz, Carl **VI:** 257
Blair, Francis Preston, Jr. **V:** **30–31,** 152
Blair, Henry **IV:** 308, 377c
Blair, Henry W. **VI:** 92
Blair, James **II:** 19, 20, 67
Blair, John **III:** 338
Blair, Montgomery **VI:** 61
Blair, Samuel **II:** 84, 372
Blaize, Herbert A. **X:** 135
Blake, Eubie **VII:** 85
Blake, James W. **VI:** 204
Blake, John Lauris **IV:** 167
Blakey, G. Robert **X:** 258
Blalock, Alfred **VIII:** 207
Blamaceda, José Manuel **VI:** 50
Blanchard, Joshua P. **V:** 266
Blanck, Max **VII:** 312

Blanco y Erenas, Ramón **VI:** 272
Bland, Edward **II:** 115
Bland, James **VI:** 203
Bland, Richard **III:** **40**
Bland, Richard P. **VI:** 32
Bland-Allison Act of 1878 **VI:** **32,** 324c
   bimetallism **VI:** 29
   Congress **VI:** 63
   Crime of '73 **VI:** 70
   currency issue **VI:** 73
   Free-Silver movement **VI:** 105
   Hayes, Rutherford B. **VI:** 126
Blashfield, Edwin Howland **VI:** 219
Blast, The **VII:** 252
blast furnaces **VI:** 27
Blatch, Harriot Eaton Stanton **VII:** **31–32,** 335, 336
Blatchford, Herbert **IX:** 229
Blavatsky, Helena Petrovna **VI:** *244,* 244–245
Blease, Cole **VII:** 292
Bledsoe family **V:** 36
Bleeding Kansas **IV:** 151, *151,* 155, 285–286; **V:** **31–32,** 32m, 405c
   abolition **V:** 4
   Brown, John **V:** 38
   Buchanan, James **V:** 41–42
   bushwhackers **V:** 46
   Douglas, Stephen A. **V:** 98
   Higginson, Thomas Wentworth **V:** 166
   jayhawkers **V:** 186–187
   Kansas-Nebraska Act of 1854 **V:** 198
   Quantrill, William Clarke **V:** 285
   Republican Party **V:** 301
   slavery **V:** 328–329
   Stuart, J. E. B. **V:** 341
   Sumner, Charles **V:** 342
Blennerhassett, Harman **III:** 54
Bletchley Park **VIII:** 64, 164
Blind, Aid to. *See* Title X
Blind Fiddler, The (Krimmel) **IV:** 26
Bliss, Philip P. **VI:** 203
Blithedale Romance, The (Hawthorne) **IV:** 345
blitzkrieg **VIII:** **39,** 408c
   aircraft industry **VIII:** 11
   air power **VIII:** 11
   Anglo-American relations **VIII:** 17
   Britain, Battle of **VIII:** 43
   election of 1940 **VIII:** 98
   mobilization **VIII:** 214

   refugees **VIII:** 298
   Selective Service **VIII:** 322
   tanks **VIII:** 349
   World War II European theater **VIII:** 391
Bliven, Bruce **VII:** 382–384
Block, Adriaen **II:** 68, 249
blockade, British **IV:** 104, 141, 358
blockade, Union
   Confederate States of America **V:** 76, 77
   Dahlgren, John A. B. **V:** 87
   food riots **V:** 129
   foreign policy **V:** 131, 132
   Galveston, Battle of **V:** 145
   ladies aid societies **V:** 203
   Mallory, Stephen R. **V:** 221
   medicine and hospitals **V:** 231
   Mobile campaign **V:** 236
   plantations **V:** 276
   Porter, David Dixon **V:** 280
   Port Royal, South Carolina, Experiment **V:** 279
   Seward, William H. **V:** 314
   tactics and strategy **V:** 347
   Union navy **V:** 368–369
   war contracting **V:** 387
blockade runners
   Confederate navy **V:** 74
   foreign policy **V:** 131
   impressment **V:** 180
   medicine and hospitals **V:** 231
   Semmes, Raphael **V:** 313
   Tredegar Iron Works **V:** 356
blockbusters
   movies **X:** 198, 199
   popular culture **X:** 239, 240, 242
Block Island **II:** 107
blood banks **VIII:** 207
Bloodless Revolution. *See* Glorious Revolution
bloodletting **IV:** 229
blood transfusions **X:** 5
"Bloody Arm" **IV:** 46
Bloody Marsh, Battle of **II:** 267
"Bloody Monday" **IV:** 23
Bloody Sunday **IX:** 275
Bloom, Allan **X:** 80
Bloomer, Amelia **IV:** **53–54,** *54,* 314, 336, 378c
"bloomers" **IV:** 54; **V:** 123
Blount, James H. **VI:** 124
Blount, William **III:** **40–41,** 175
Blow, Kurtis **X:** 202
Blow, Peter **V:** 101

"Blowin' in the Wind" **IX:** 111, 191

Blow Up (movie) **X:** 239

"blue-backed speller" **III:** *114*

bluebacks **V:** 23, 106

Blue Cross **VIII:** 209

"Blue Eagle" campaign **VIII:** 1, 173, *231*, 232

Blue Jacket **III: 41,** 123; **IV:** 168

Bluemner, Oscar **VII:** 20

blues **VI:** 202–203; **VII: 32; VIII:** 222–224

  entertainment **VII:** 86

  Gershwin, George **VII:** 108, 109

  Great Migration **VII:** 113

  Harlem Renaissance **VII:** 120

  jazz **VII:** 137

  music **VII:** 194, 195

"blue" v. "gray" **V:** 362

Blum, Leon **VIII:** 276

Bly, Nellie **VI:** 212

Blyden, Edward W. **VI:** 174, 175

Board of Economic Warfare **VIII:** 373

Board of Education of Westside Community Schools v. Mergens (1990) **X:** 104

Board of Mediation **VII:** 361c

Board of Trade **II:** 419c

Board of Trade and Plantations **II:** 43

board system **III:** 89

Boas, Franz Uri **VII: 32–33,** 357c

  literature **VII:** 162

  Locke, Alain **VII:** 164

  Mead, Margaret **VII:** 177

  race and racial conflict **VII:** 248, 249

Boating Party, The (Cassatt) **VI:** 45

boats **IV:** 74

Bobadilla, Francisco de **I:** 79, 82

bobbysoxers **VIII:** 326

Bockscar bomber **VIII:** 146

Bodmer, Karl **IV: 54–56,** 377c

Boehm, Johann Phillip **II:** 139, 140

Boeing **VIII:** *10;* **IX:** 28, 294; **X:** 275

Boeing B-47 Stratojet **IX:** 27

Boeing 747 **VII:** 160

Boesky, Ivan **X:** 49, 50

Bogardus, James **IV:** 82, 308

Bogart, Humphrey **VIII:** 218, 409c; **IX:** 135, 212

bogernaciones **II:** 355

Boggs, Hale **IX:** 145; **X:** 228

Boggs, Lillburn W. **IV:** 79, 323

Bogotá **I:** 118

Bok, Edward W. **VI:** 185

Boker, George **VI:** 176

Boland, Edward **X:** 38, 154

Boland Amendment **X: 38,** 326c

  cold war (end of) **X:** 71

  contras **X:** 81

  Iran-contra affair **X:** 154

  North, Oliver L. **X:** 222

  War Powers Act **X:** 315

Boleyn, Anne **I:** 73, 119, 160, 224, 309

Bolingbroke, Viscount **III:** 54, 278

Bolívar, Simón **IV:** 170; **VI:** 220

Bolivia **I:** 10, 175, 277, 291; **II:** 355; **VI:** 49, 50; **X:** 46, 174

Bolling, Richard **X:** 75

"Boll Weevils" **X:** 144

Bolsec, Jérome **I:** 50

Bolshevik Revolution **VII:** 359c; **VIII:** 333

  Hearst, William Randolph **VII:** 121

  radical press **VII:** 252

  Red Scare **VII:** 258

  Reed, John **VII:** 259, 260

Bolsheviks **VII:** 360c

  foreign policy **VII:** 100

  Goldman, Emma **VII:** 110

  Red Scare **VII:** 259

  Russian Revolution **VII:** 270

  Seattle General Strike **VII:** 278, 279

  Siberian Expedition **VII:** 285

Bolt Beranek and Newman, Inc. (BBN) **X:** 152

bolting cloth **II:** 225

Bolton, Herbert Eugene **II:** 34

Bomber, Daniel (Aldo Manuzio) **I:** 191

bombing campaigns **VIII:** 20, 21

bomb shelters **VIII:** 29

Bonanza Creek **VI:** 160–161

Bonaparte, Napoleon **III: 41–42,** 397c; **V:** 192, 345

  Barlow, Joel **III:** 36

  California missions **IV:** 70

  Dartmoor Prison **IV:** 104

  embargo of 1807 **III:** 117

  Florida **IV:** 139

  foreign affairs **III:** 130, 131

  foreign policy **IV:** 141

  French Revolution **III:** 138, 139

  Fulton, Robert **III:** 141, 142

George III, king of Great Britain **III:** 151

Ghent, Treaty of (1814) **IV:** 161

Lafayette, marquis de **III:** 201

Lewis and Clark Expedition **III:** 210

Louisiana Purchase **III:** 218

Monroe-Pinkney Treaty **III:** 246

New Orleans, Battle of (1815) **IV:** 262

New Spain (Mexico), northern frontier of **III:** 258

Orders in Council **III:** 267

Quasi War **III:** 292

Rochambeau, comte de **III:** 310

Talleyrand, Prince **III:** 341

War of 1812 **IV:** 355, 358

XYZ affair **III:** 385

Bond, Julian **X:** 209

Bond, Thomas **II:** 18, **33–34**

Bond, W. C. **III:** 321

bonds **VI:** 19, 146

  banking and currency **V:** 23, 24

  Confederate States of America **V:** 77

  Cooke, Jay **V:** 81

  economy **V:** 105, 106

  taxation **V:** 349

bonds, Confederate **V:** 106

Bonhomme Richard, USS **III:** 190, 394c

Bonner, Robert **VI:** 80

Bonner, Thomas D. **IV:** 47

Bonnet, Stede **II: 34,** 285–286, 369

Bonneville, Benjamin **IV:** 325

Bonney, Anne **II:** 286

"Bonny Blue Flag, The" **V:** 244

Bontemps, Arna **III:** 145

Bonus Army **VIII: 39–40,** 406c

  election of 1932 **VIII:** 96

  Hoover presidency **VIII:** 155

  Patton, George **VIII:** 263

  relief **VIII:** 300

Bonus Bill **IV: 56,** 253; **VII:** 11

bonuses **V:** 80, 364

Bonus March of 1932 **VII:** 292, 326

boogie-woogie **VIII:** 223

Book of Common Prayer (Church of England) **I:** 73–74, 298, 309

"Book of General Laws and Libertyes" **II:** 144

Book of Mormon

  Church of Jesus Christ of Latter-day Saints **IV:** 79

  Deseret, State of **IV:** 109

  religion **IV:** 298

  Smith, Joseph, Jr. **IV:** 322

  Young, Brigham **IV:** 371

Book-of-the-Month Club **VIII:** 297

books **X:** 185. *See also* literature

  cabinet of curiosities **I:** 40

  Cozumel **I:** 97

  Gutenberg, Johann Gensfleisch zum **I:** 147

  Maya **I:** 229

  printing press **I:** 293–295

bookstores **X:** 178, 185

"boondoggles" **VIII:** 63, 118, 387

Boone, Daniel **II:** 115; **III: 42–43,** 107, 141, 378, 391c, 393c

Boone, Pat **IX:** 263

boosterism **VIII:** 1

Booth, Edwin **VI:** 286

Booth, John Wilkes **V: 32–33,** 33, 408c

  assassination of Abraham Lincoln **V:** 17, 18

  espionage **V:** 118

  Seward, William H. **V:** 315

  theater **V:** 351, 352

Booth, Junius Brutus **V:** 352

Booth, Lionel F. **V:** 135

Borah, William E. **VII:** 62, 331; **VIII:** 17, **40,** 305

Borden, Gail **IV:** 308

borderlands **II:** 25, **34–35,** 47, 113, 267

Border Patrol **VII:** 127, 182, 361c; **X:** 192

"border ruffians"

  Bleeding Kansas **V:** 31, 32

  Brown, John **V:** 38

  jayhawkers **V:** 186

  Quantrill, William Clarke **V:** 285

border states

  brothers' war **V:** 37

  Confiscation Acts **V:** 78

  desertion **V:** 95

  race and racial conflict **V:** 287, 288

  refugees **V:** 298–299

  Washington, D.C. **V:** 389

Borgia, Cesare **I:** 204

Borgia family **I:** 6

Bork, Robert **X: 38–39,** 327c

  abortion **X:** 4

  conservative movement **X:** 80

  Cox, Archibald, Jr. **X:** 81

Bork, Robert *(continued)*
  Nixon, Richard M. **X:** 221
  Reagan, Ronald W. **X:** 260
  Richardson, Elliot L. **X:** 268
  Ruckelshaus, William D. **X:** 269
  Senate **X:** 276
  Supreme Court **X:** 291
  think tanks **X:** 301
  Watergate scandal **X:** 317
born-again status **X:** 107, 108
Borneo **I:** 114; **VIII:** 399
Born on the Fourth of July (movie) **X:** 198
Bornu **I:** 317
Borresen, Kari **IX:** 257
Bosch, Juan **IX:** 172, 317
Bosch Loopers **II:** 130–131
Bosnia **X:** 329*c*
  Clinton, William **X:** 67
  Dayton accords **X:** 85
  defense policy **X:** 88
  Kosovo **X:** 166
  NATO **X:** 224
Boss, Charlotte **IX:** 249
Boston, Massachusetts **II:** 35–37, 36*m*; **III:** 391*c*–394*c*; **IV:** 379*c*; **IX:** 52; **X:** 325*c*
  Adams, Samuel **III:** 4
  African-American churches, growth of **VI:** 4
  African Americans **IV:** 8
  agriculture **II:** 12
  almshouses **II:** 18
  Andros, Sir Edmund **II:** 19
  Anglican Church **II:** 20
  architecture **II:** 24; **IV:** 28
  Boylston, Zabdiel **II:** 37
  Brown, William Wells **V:** 40
  Bulfinch, Charles **III:** 50
  Bunker Hill, Battle of **III:** 50–51
  Burgis, William **II:** 46
  Burns, Anthony **IV:** 59
  cities and urban life **II:** 61; **IV:** 81; **VI:** 55
  class **II:** 63
  Coddington, William **II:** 65
  committees of correspondence **III:** 77
  Connecticut **II:** 69
  Cotton, John **II:** 73
  crafts **II:** 73–74
  crowd action **II:** 78
  Davenport, James **II:** 83–84
  disease and epidemics **II:** 91, 92; **IV:** 112

Dominion of New England **II:** 95
Dorchester Heights, Battle of **III:** 107
Dummer, Jeremiah **II:** 96
Dyer, Mary **II:** 99
education **IV:** 121
Edwards, Jonathan **II:** 106
entertainment, popular **VI:** 96
Estaing, comte d' **III:** 120
French colonies **II:** 129
French immigrants **II:** 130
fugitive slave laws **IV:** 155
Fuller, Margaret **IV:** 155
Garland, Hamlin **VI:** 109
Glorious Revolution **II:** 141
Harris, Benjamin **II:** 154
Harrison, Peter **II:** 154
homefront **V:** 168
Hooker, Thomas **II:** 156–157
Hutchinson, Anne Marbury **II:** 161
immigration **IV:** 180
industrialization **IV:** 185
journalism **II:** 178
King George's War **II:** 182
King Philip's War **II:** 183
Knight, Sarah Kemble **II:** 185
Know-Nothing Party **IV:** 201
labor **II:** 187
ladies aid societies **V:** 204
Lee, Charles **III:** 205
limners **II:** 194
lotteries **II:** 199
MacIntosh, Ebenezer **III:** 225
Mason, John **II:** 211
Massachusetts **II:** 212, 214
Massachusetts Bay Company **II:** 216
Mather, Cotton **II:** 217
Mather, Increase **II:** 218
Miantonomo **II:** 224
midwives **II:** 225
mills **II:** 225
monuments **V:** 239
Morton, Thomas **II:** 236
mulattoes **II:** 238
music **VI:** 201
New Hampshire **II:** 250, 251
Old South Church **III:** 265
Pelham, Peter **II:** 272–273
Phillips, Wendell **IV:** 280
piracy **II:** 285
population trends **II:** 292
postal service **II:** 292

printing and publishing **II:** 299
railroads **IV:** 292, 293, 295
Randolph, Edward **II:** 312
religion **IV:** 296
Revere, Paul **III:** 304
settlement houses **VI:** 259
Sewall, Samuel **II:** 334
shipbuilding **II:** 335
smallpox **II:** 345
Smibert, John **II:** 346
society, British American **II:** 350
Stamp Act **III:** 332
Stewart, Maria **IV:** 327
Sumner, Charles **V:** 342
taverns and inns **II:** 368
Taylor, Susie King **V:** 350
temperance movement **IV:** 335–336
Townshend Duties **III:** 349
trade and shipping **II:** 377
transportation **V:** 356
travel **II:** 377, 378
Turell, Jane Colman **II:** 378
Van Rensselaer, Maria Van Cortlandt **II:** 381
Webster, Daniel **IV:** 359–360
Willard, Samuel **II:** 399
Winthrop, John **II:** 401
witchcraft **II:** 402
wolves **II:** 405
yellow fever **II:** 414
Boston, USS **IV:** 172
Boston & Maine Railroad **IV:** 295
Boston Athletic Association **VI:** 290
Boston Bicycling Club **VI:** 27
Boston Caucus **II:** 72
Boston Celtics **VII:** 295; **X:** 285
"Boston classicists"
Boston Common **IV:** 28
Boston Female Anti-Slavery society **IV:** 8, 14, 135
Boston Gazette **III:** 293, 304
Boston Handel and Haydn Society Collection of Church Music (Mason) **IV:** 250
"Boston Hymn" (Emerson) **IV:** 127
Boston Journeymen Bootmakers' Society **IV:** 204
Boston Manufacturing Company **IV:** 184
Boston Massacre **III:** 43–45, 44, 392*c*
  Adams, John **III:** 2
  Adams, Samuel **III:** 4

African Americans **III:** 6
Attucks, Crispus **III:** 27–28
Gage, Thomas **III:** 146
Gerry, Elbridge **III:** 152
Hancock, John **III:** 163
Hutchinson, Thomas **III:** 171
Knox, Henry **III:** 197
Quincy, Josiah **III:** 293
Revere, Paul **III:** 304
Townshend Duties **III:** 349
Warren, Joseph **III:** 363
Boston Philosophical Society **II:** 37, 330
Boston Police Strike of 1919 **VII:** 56
Boston Port Bill **III:** 76, 237, 293–294, 392*c*
Boston Public Library **VI:** 176, 256
Boston Red Sox **VII:** 294
Boston Red Stockings **VI:** 21
Boston Spectator **IV:** 167
Boston Symphony Orchestra **VI:** 23, 201
Boston Tea Party **II:** 179; **III:** 45, 392*c*
  Adams, John **III:** 2
  Adams, Samuel **III:** 4
  artisans **III:** 26
  Coercive Acts **III:** 76
  committees of correspondence **III:** 77
  Dickinson, John **III:** 105
  economy **III:** 111
  Hancock, John **III:** 163
  Hutchinson, Thomas **III:** 171
  MacIntosh, Ebenezer **III:** 225
  North, Lord **III:** 260
  Old South Church **III:** 265–266
  Pitt, William **III:** 277
  Quartering Act **III:** 291
  Quincy, Josiah **III:** 293
  Revere, Paul **III:** 304
  riots **III:** 308, 309
  Tea Act **III:** 344
  Warren, Joseph **III:** 363
  Young, Thomas **III:** 390
Boswell, James **II:** 267
botany **II:** 30, 55, 66, 277, 330; **III:** 37, 321, 395*c*
Botany Woolen Mill **VII:** 224
Boucher, Jonathan **III:** 46
Boucicault, Dion **V:** 352; **VI:** 156, 286–287
Boudin, Kathy **IX:** 319; **X:** 318
Boughton, George **VI:** 219
Boulder Dam **VIII:** 103

boundaries of America, post–Revolutionary War **III:** 273, 274*m*
Boundary 2 **X:** 178
boundary disputes **VI:** 309
bound labor **III:** 199
bounties **II:** 329, 405
"bounty jumpers" **V:** 95
bounty system **V: 34,** 364, 383
Bouquet, Henry **II:** 52, 333–334
Bourbons **VI:** 77–78
"Bourbon Triumvirate" **V:** 39
Bourke-White, Margaret **VIII:** 268, 275
Boutwell, George S. **VI:** 13
Bow, Clara **VII:** *86,* 87
Bowdoin, James **III:** 353
Bowdoin College **IV:** 376*c*
Bower Award and Prize **IV:** 149
Bowers, Henry F. **VI:** 11, 326*c*
Bowers v. Hardwick (1986) **X:** 41, 319, 327*c*
Bowery Theater, New York City **V:** 352
Bowie, Duncan **VI:** 289
Bowie, Jim **IV:** 13, **56–57,** 341, 346
Bowie, Rezin **IV:** 56
Bowie knife **IV:** 56
Bowlegs, Billy **IV:** 312
Bowles, Chester **VIII:** 255
bowling **VIII:** 297
Boxer Rebellion **VI:** 217; **VII: 33–34,** 355*c;* **VIII:** 183
    foreign policy **VII:** 98
    Open Door Policy **VII:** 219
    Russo-Japanese War **VII:** 271
    World War I **VII:** 343
boxing **V:** 192; **VI: 32–34,** 33, 325*c;* **VII:** 67, *139,* 258, 293–294, 357*c,* 359*c;* **VIII:** 195–196, 336–337, 408*c;* **IX:** 9, 10, 280, 334*c*
boy bands **X:** 202
boycotts **III:** 87, 392*c*–393*c;* **IV:** 141, 173; **VI:** 170; **VII:** 357*c;* **VIII:** 14, 173; **IX:** 331*c;* **X:** 16
    AFL **VII:** 10
    African-American movement **IX:** 5
    Buck's Stove **VII:** 36
    Clayton Antitrust Act **VII:** 51
    Congress of Racial Equality **IX:** 67
    Danbury Hatters **VII:** 61
    King, Martin Luther, Jr. **IX:** 160
    labor movement **VII:** 152
    Parks, Rosa **IX:** 240

segregation **IX:** 271
    Taft-Hartley Act **IX:** 291
    United Farm Workers **IX:** 304
    White Citizens' Councils **IX:** 320
Boyd, Belle **V: 34–35,** 118, 213
Boyer, Elizabeth **IX:** 323
Boyer, Herbert **X:** 191
Boyers, Peggy **X:** 177
Boyers, Robert **X:** 177
Boyle, Robert **II:** 40, 67
Boyle, T. Coraghessan **X:** 178
Boylston, Thomas **III:** 350
Boylston, Zabdiel **II: 37–38,** 92, 217, 345
Boy Scouts **VIII:** 298
Boy Scouts of America v. Dale **X:** 330*c*
Bozell, Brent **X:** 42, 43
Bozell, Priscilla **X:** 42, 43
Bozeman Trail **IV:** 58
Bozeman Trail, War for the **VI:** 69, 208, 240
Bozeman Wagon Road **VI:** 263
Bosnia-Herzegovina **X:** 85
Bozo people **I:** 109
BP (Brotherhood of Professional Base Ball Players) **VI:** 22
braceros **IX: 41–42,** 173, 330*c*
braceros program **VIII:** 162, 210, 211, 409*c*
Brackenridge, Hugh Henry **III: 46–47,** 139, 215
Bradbury, John **IV:** 345–346
Bradbury, Ray **IX:** 183
Braddock, Edward **II:** 38, 419*c*
    Boone, Daniel **III:** 42
    Cornplanter **III:** 91
    Flashman, Edward **II:** 119
    Fort Necessity **II:** 123
    Franklin, Benjamin **III:** 134
    French colonies **II:** 129
    Gage, Thomas **III:** 146
    Gates, Horatio **III:** 149
    Lee, Charles **III:** 205
    Pennsylvania **II:** 276
    Seven Years' War **II:** 332
    Washington, George **III:** 366
Braddock, James **VIII:** 195
Bradford, Andrew **II:** 38
Bradford, Cornelia Smith **II:** 38
Bradford, David **III:** 375, 376
Bradford, Sarah **V:** 358
Bradford, William **II: 38–39;** **III:** 11
    alcohol **II:** 15
    Bradford, Cornelia Smith **II:** 38

journalism **II:** 179
    literature **II:** 195
    Mayflower Compact **II:** 219
    Morton, Thomas **II:** 236
    Pilgrims **II:** 283
    Plymouth **II:** 287
    Zenger, John Peter **II:** 415
Bradford, William E. **V:** 135
Bradford Patent **II:** 287
Bradley, Bill **X:** 134
Bradley, Joseph P. **VI:** 55, 318
Bradley, Omar N. **VIII: 40–41,** 410*c;* **IX:** 203
Bradley, Will **VI:** 138
Bradstreet, Anne Dudley **II: 39,** 96, 195
Bradstreet, Simon **II:** 39
Bradwell, Myra Colby **VI: 34,** 318
Bradwell v. Illinois **VI:** 34, 318, 324*c*
Brady, James S. **X:** 31, 136–137
Brady, Mathew B. **V:** 35, **35–36,** 273
Brady, Sarah **X:** 136–137
Brady, Thomas J. **VI:** 275
Brady, Thomas P. **IX:** 320
Brady Handgun Violence Prevention Act of 1993 **X:** 82, 113, 137, 328*c*
Bragg, Braxton **V: 36**
    Atlanta campaign **V:** 19
    Beauregard, Pierre **V:** 27
    Chattanooga, Battle of **V:** 57
    Chickamauga, Battle of **V:** 58
    Confederate army **V:** 73
    Corinth, Battle of **V:** 83
    Davis, Jefferson **V:** 90
    Forrest, Nathan Bedford **V:** 134
    Johnston, Joseph E. **V:** 190
    Longstreet, James **V:** 215
    Lookout Mountain, Battle of **V:** 216
    Murfreesboro/Stones River, Battle of **V:** 242, 243
    Rosecrans, William S. **V:** 305
    Shiloh, Battle of **V:** 323, 324
Braham, Dave **VI:** 203
Brainerd, David **II: 39–40**
Brainerd, John **II:** 40
brain tan **II:** 21
Brain Trust **VII:** 25; **VIII: 41–42**
    Baruch, Bernard M. **VIII:** 34

Berle, Adolf A., Jr. **VIII:** 35
First New Deal **VIII:** 122
Johnson, Hugh S. **VIII:** 173
London Economic Conference **VIII:** 193
Moley, Raymond C. **VIII:** 215
NIRA **VIII:** 228
NRA **VIII:** 231
Tugwell, Rexford G. **VIII:** 361
brake, air **V:** 409*c*
Branch Davidians **X: 39–40,** 328*c*
    militia movement **X:** 194
    Oklahoma City bombing **X:** 228
    Reno, Janet **X:** 267
    terrorism **X:** 299
Brandeis, Louis Dembitz **VII: 34, 34–35,** 358*c,* **IX:** 1
    antimonopoly **VIII:** 17
    court-packing plan **VIII:** 76
    Frankfurter, Felix **VIII:** 127
    Goldmark, Josephine **VII:** 111
    Holmes, Oliver Wendell **VII:** 122
    Muller v. Oregon **VII:** 193
    New Nationalism **VII:** 212
    Supreme Court **VIII:** 345, 346*t*
Brandenburg v. Ohio (1969) **X:** 60
branding **II:** 188
Brando, Marlon **IX:** 213
Brandt, Willy **X:** 70
Brandy Station, Battle of **V:** 148
Brandywine, Battle of **III:** 47*m,* **47–48,** 393*c;* **IV:** 239
    Cornwallis, Lord **III:** 92
    Germantown, Battle of **III:** 151
    Greene, Nathanael **III:** 155
    Howe, Sir William **III:** 168
    Knox, Henry **III:** 197
    Lafayette, marquis de **III:** 201
    Pinckney, Charles Cotesworth **III:** 277
    Pulaski, Casimir **III:** 289
    Revolutionary War **III:** 305
    St. Clair, Arthur **III:** 316
    Sullivan, John **III:** 337

Brant, John **IV:** 259
Brant, Joseph **II:** 76, 395; **III:** 48–49, *49*, 179, 255, 393*c*
Brant, Sebastian **I:** 241
Brantley, Etheldred T. **IV:** 347
Branzburg v. Hayes (1972) **X:** 324*c*
brass **IV:** 186*m*
Brattain, Walter H. **X:** 72
Brattle, Thomas **II: 40,** 194
Brattle, William **II:** 40, 193, 194
Braudel, Fernand **I:** 75
Bray, Thomas **II:** 20
Brazil **I: 31–34,** *32m,* 386*c;* **V:** 114; **IX:** 172; **X:** 69, 122, 172–174
   Amazon River **I:** 8
   Bahía **I:** 23–24
   Battel, Andrew **I:** 27
   Cabral, Pedro Álvares **I:** 44
   cannibalism **I:** 54
   castas **I:** 62
   coffee **I:** 76
   Dutch West India Company **II:** 98
   Jesuits **I:** 189
   Jews (Judaism) **I:** 192; **II:** 175
   John III **I:** 193
   Léry, Jean de **I:** 205–206
   missions **II:** 229
   plantation system **II:** 286
   slavery **II:** 338
   slave trade **I:** 330; **II:** 343
   smallpox **I:** 331
   Spanish colonies **II:** 358, 359
   Stade, Hans **I:** 335–336
   sugar **I:** 338
   Tordesillas, Treaty of **I:** 358, 359
   Tupinambá **I:** 361
   Vespucci, Amerigo **I:** 368
brazilwood trees. *See* dyewood trees
bread **II:** 389
"bread colonies" **II:** 225
breadline **VIII:** *139,* 299
bread riots **V:** 116
Breckenridge, Henry **VII:** 202, 236
Breckinridge, John C. **IV:** 108, 301, **V:** 405*c,* 406*c*
   Chattanooga, Battle of **V:** 57
   Democratic Party **V:** 94
   Douglas, Stephen A. **V:** 99
   Murfreesboro/Stones River, Battle of **V:** 243
   Orphan Brigade **V:** 258
Breed's Hill. *See* Bunker Hill, Battle of

Breezing Up (Homer) **VI:** 130–131
Breintnall, Joseph **II:** 30, 277
Bremer, Arthur H. **X:** 314
Brendan the Navigator, Saint **I:** 34
Brennan, William J., Jr. **IX:** 31, 315; **X: 40–42,** *41*
   Burger, Warren E. **X:** 44
   flag burning **X:** 117
   Meese, Edwin C. **X:** 191
   Supreme Court **X:** 291
Brent, Margaret Reed **II:** 40
Brentwood, Long Island **IV:** 359
Brer Rabbit **II:** 152
Brest-Litovsk, Treaty of **VII:** 270
Brethren, The (Woodward and Armstrong) **X:** 44
Bretton Woods Conference (1944) **VIII: 42,** 410*c*
   Congress **VIII:** 68
   Eccles, Marriner S. **VIII:** 89
   economy **VIII:** 93
   foreign policy **VIII:** 125
   Morgenthau, Henry **VIII:** 216
   postwar planning **VIII:** 279
   Roosevelt, Franklin D. **VIII:** 314
Brewer, David **VII:** 193
Brewster, Mary **VI:** 259
Brewster, William **II:** 38, 68, 283
Breyer, Stephen **X: 42,** 130, **134,** 291
Brezhnev, Leonid I. **IX:** 106, 278; **X:** 324*c,* 325*c*
   ABM Treaty **X:** 22
   cold war (end of) **X:** 70, 71
   defense policy **X:** 86
   détente **X:** 89
   Ford, Gerald R. **X:** 121
   foreign policy **X:** 123
   Kennedy, Edward M. **X:** 164
   Nixon, Richard M. **X:** 220
Brezhnev Doctrine of 1968 **X:** 124
Briand, Aristide **VII:** 43, 146
bribery **X:** 121–122
Brice's Crossroads, Battle of **V:** 134
Bricker, John **VIII:** 99
brides, purchase of **II:** 414
bridge, contract (card game) **VIII:** 296
Bridger, James **IV: 57–58**
   Astor, John Jacob **IV:** 32
   exploration **IV:** 131

   mountain men **IV:** 247
   Rocky Mountain Fur Company **IV:** 302
   Sublette, William **IV:** 330
bridges **VI: 34–35,** 44, 85, 324*c*
Bridges, Harry **II: 42–43**
Bridgman, Frederick **VI:** 219
Brief Account of the Destruction of the Indies (Bartolomé de Las Casas) **I:** 30
Briefe and True Report of the New Found Land of Virginia (Thomas Harriot) **I:** 102, 154, *154,* 388*c*
   Hakluyt, Richard, the Younger **I:** 152
   Native American religion **I:** 253
   Picts **I:** 282
   Roanoke **I:** 313
   White, John **I:** 373
Brief Summe of Geographie **I:** 35
brig **I:** 35
brigades **IV:** 131, 248
brigantine(s) **I: 34–35,** 179, 317
Briggs, Charles A. **VI:** 242
Briggs, Emily **VI:** 212
Brigham, Judge **IX:** 80
Bright Eyes **VI:** 153
Brimm, Benjamin **V:** 375
Brims **II: 41**
Bringing It All Back Home (Bob Dylan) **IX:** 85
Brinkley, David **IX:** 153
Bristol **I: 35,** 41, 42, 75, 151
Bristow, Benjamin H. **V:** 393; **VI:** 122
Britain. *See* England
Britain (William Camden) **I:** 51–52
Britain, Battle of **VIII: 43–44**
   air power **VIII:** 11
   Anglo-American relations **VIII:** 17
   destroyers-for-bases deal **VIII:** 82
   Kennedy, Joseph P. **VIII:** 176
   news media **VIII:** 243
   radio **VIII:** 290
   refugees **VIII:** 298
British . . . *See also under* English . . .
British Aggression in Venezuela (Scruggs) **VI:** 303
British Broadcasting Corporation **VIII:** 283
British colonies
   art **II:** 24–25
   Chickasaw **II:** 59
   class **II:** 63–64

   indentured servitude **II:** 163
   medicine **II:** 220
   mercantilism **II:** 221
   miscegenation **II:** 228
   monarchy, British **II:** 232
   Monckton, Robert **II:** 233
   mulattoes **II:** 238
   music **II:** 238–239
   Native Americans **II:** 246, 247
   New Amsterdam **II:** 250
   New Hampshire **II:** 250–252
   New Jersey **II:** 252–254
   North Carolina **II:** 263–265
   printing and publishing **II:** 299
   Queen Anne's War **II:** 309
   race and racial conflict **II:** 311–312
   Red Shoes **II:** 313
   Roman Catholics **II:** 323
   society, British American **II:** 349–352
   theater **II:** 373
   trade and shipping **II:** 375–377
   Tuscarora **II:** 378, 379
   war and warfare **II:** 391
   Weiser, Johann Conrad **II:** 393
   women's status and rights **II:** 409
British Columbia **I:** 150; **IV:** 113
British East India Company. *See* East India Company (British)
British Empire **II: 41–44,** *42;* **III:** 203; **VIII:** 17, 125
   Beverley, Robert **II:** 33
   Boston **II:** 35
   cities and urban life **II:** 61
   consumption **II:** 71
   Florida **II:** 120, 121
   Fort Mose **II:** 123
   forts **II:** 124
   Fort William Henry Massacre **II:** 124–125
   French colonies **II:** 128*m*
   fur trade **II:** 132
   Georgia **II:** 137–138
   government, British American **II:** 144
   Hendrick **II:** 155
   Howe, George Augustus, Viscount **II:** 158
   indentured servitude **II:** 163
   Iron Acts **II:** 167
   iron manufacturing **II:** 168
   Iroquois **II:** 170

Jesuits **II:** 174
Johnson, Sir William **II:** 177
Keith, William **II:** 181
King George's War **II:** 182
Louisiana **II:** 199
manufacturing and industry **II:** 203
Massachusetts **II:** 214
mercantilism **II:** 221
monarchy, British **II:** 231–232
New Jersey **II:** 252
New York City **II:** 263
piracy **II:** 285
Seven Years' War **II:** 334
technology **II:** 369
Virginia **II:** 385
British exploration **IV:** 93
British Guiana **VI:** 4, 59, 303
British immigrants **IV:** 301
British Isles **I:** 290
British Museum **II:** 30
British North American Act **VI:** 43
British North West Company **IV:** 269
British Political Warfare Executive **VIII:** 283
Briton, The **III:** 378
broadcasting **VII:** 254, 360*c*
broadcasting industry **X:** 49, 294–297, 329*c*
Broaddrick, Juanita **X:** 162
broad-spectrum antibiotics **IX:** 205, 295
Broadway **V:** 352; **VII:** 108; **VIII:** 273, 289, 410*c*
Broadway productions **X:** 241–242, 277
Brock, Sir Isaac **IV:** 175
Brody, Fawn **III:** 164
bronchitis **V:** 230
Bronson, Eli **II:** 298
Bronzeville (Chicago) **IX:** 4
Brook, Phillips **VI:** 241
Brooke, John Mercer **V:** 74, 237
Brook Farm **IV: 58; V:** 88
   Emerson, Ralph Waldo **IV:** 126
   Fourier, Charles **IV:** 149
   Fuller, Margaret **IV:** 155
   religion **IV:** 299
   transcendental movement **IV:** 345
Brookhiser, Richard **X:** 43
Brookings Institution **VIII:** 235; **X:** 301
Brooklyn Bridge **VI:** 14, 35, 325*c*
Brooklyn *Daily Eagle* **V:** 393

Brooklyn Dodgers **IX:** 5, 260, 262–263, 280, 329*c*, 332*c*
Brooklyn Philharmonic **VI:** 201
Brooks, Garth **X:** 202, 203, 240
Brooks, James **V:** 85
Brooks, Ned **IX:** *296*
Brooks, Preston
   abolition **V:** 4
   Bleeding Kansas **V:** 31
   slavery **V:** 329
   Sumner, Charles **V:** 342, 343
Brooks Brothers **VI:** 78
Broteer. *See* Smith, Venture
Brotherhood of Locomotive Firemen **VII:** 64
Brotherhood of Professional Base Ball Players (BP) **VI:** 22
Brotherhood of Sleeping Car Porters **VIII:** 4, 291
brothers' war **V: 36–37,** 165. *See also* Civil War
Broughton, William **IV:** 93
Browder, Earl
   Communists **VIII:** 65
   FBI **VIII:** 115
   politics in the Roosevelt era **VIII:** 272*t*
   Popular Front **VIII:** 276
   Thomas, Norman **VIII:** 358
Brower, David **IX:** 101
Brown, Charles Brockden **III: 49–50,** 215; **IV:** 196
Brown, Dee **X:** 324*c*
Brown, Earle **IX:** 216
Brown, Edmund G. (Pat) **VII:** 189; **X:** 220
Brown, H. Rap **IX:** 285
Brown, Henry B. **VI:** 224
Brown, Jacob **IV:** 309
Brown, James **IX:** 263–264; **X:** 201
Brown, Jerry **X:** 16
Brown, John **III:** 148; **IV:** 40, 301, 342; **V: 37–39,** 38, 405*c*; **VI:** 171
   abolition **V:** 4
   Bleeding Kansas **V:** 31
   Booth, John Wilkes **V:** 32–33
   Civil War **V:** 64
   Douglass, Frederick **V:** 100
   Harpers Ferry, West Virginia **V:** 164–166, *165*
   Higginson, Thomas Wentworth **V:** 167
   Lee, Robert E. **V:** 205
   slavery **V:** 329
   Stuart, J. E. B. **V:** 341

Brown, John, Jr. **V:** 186
Brown, Bishop John M. **VI:** 283
Brown, Joseph Emerson **V: 39**
   Confederate States of America **V:** 77
   conscription **V:** 79
   elections **V:** 110
   governors **V:** 152, 153
   homespun **V:** 170
   states' rights **V:** 336
Brown, Lewis **X:** 301
Brown, Linda **IX:** 42, 316
Brown, Moses **III:** 325, 326; **IV:** 184
Brown, Oliver **IX:** 42
Brown, Olympia **VI: 35–36,** 133, **317,** 318
Brown, Prentiss **VIII:** 255
Brown, Ron **X:** 162
Brown, Walter **VII:** 24
Brown, Wells **V:** 39–40
Brown, William Wells **IV:** 14, 379*c*; **V: 39–40,** 125, 328
Brown & Williams **X:** 305
Brown Berets **IX:** 328
Browne, Edmund **II:** 405
Browne, Richard **I:** 177
Browne, Robert **II:** 68
Brownell, Herbert **X:** 43–44
Brownie camera **VI:** 87
Browning, Robert **VI:** 172
Brownlow, William G. **V:** 199
Brownson, Orestes **IV:** 212; **VI:** 243, 249, 250
Brownsville Raid, The (Weaver) **VII:** 35
Brownsville Riot **VII: 35,** 356*c*
Brown University **II:** 149. *See also* College of Rhode Island
Brown v. Board of Education (1954) **V:** 354; **IX: 42–43,** 331*c*; **X:** 256, 279
   African-American movement **IX:** 4–5
   African Americans **VIII:** 5
   civil rights **VIII:** 61
   Civil Rights Act of 1957 **IX:** 55
   Eisenhower, Dwight D. **IX:** 93
   Marshall, Thurgood **IX:** 193
   Murray, Pauli **IX:** 215
   Myrdal, Gunnar **VIII:** 224
   NAACP **VIII:** 228; **IX:** 220
   segregation **IX:** 271
   sit-ins **IX:** 272
   Southern Manifesto **IX:** 276
   Supreme Court **VIII:** 347
   Warren Court **IX:** 316

White Citizens' Councils **IX:** 319
Wilkins, Roy **IX:** 322
browsers, Internet **X:** 153
Bruce, Blanche Kelso **V: 40–41,** **VI:** 5
Brulé, Étienne **II: 44,** 115, 263
Brunner, Emil **VIII:** 304
Brush, Charles F. **VI:** 148
Bryan, Jonathan **II:** 138
Bryan, William Jennings **VI: 36,** **36–37,** 327*c;* **VII:** *278,* 355*c,* 357*c,* 361*c*
   Anti-Imperialist League **VI:** 13
   bimetallism **VI:** 29
   class consciousness **VI:** 57
   Cleveland, Grover **VI:** 59
   Congress **VI:** 63
   "Cross of Gold" speech **VI:** 354–357
   Currency Act **VII:** 60
   currency issue **VI:** 73
   Darrow, Clarence **VII:** 62
   Democratic Party **VI:** 78; **VII:** 65–66
   elections **VII:** 80
   Free-Silver movement **VI:** 105
   Hanna, Marcus Alonzo **VI:** 121
   Lease, Mary Elizabeth **VI:** 173
   McKinley, William **VI:** 189
   Mencken, H. L. **VII:** 181
   New Nationalism **VII:** 212
   People's Party **VI:** 223
   presidential campaigns **VI:** 231–233
   Republican Party **VII:** 262
   Scopes Trial **VII:** 278
   Simpson, Jerry **VI:** 262
   Sunday, Billy **VII:** 302
   Taft, William Howard **VII:** 303
   Watson, Tom **VII:** 332
Bryant, Carolyn **IX:** 253
Bryant, Louise **VII:** 259
Bryant, William Cullen **IV:** 26, 212, 224
Bryce, James, first viscount Bryce **VI: 37–38,** 205, 326*c*
Bryne, Ethel **VII:** 29
Bryn Mawr College **VI:** 287–288, 316
Brzezinski, Zbigniew **X:** 18
Buber, Martin **VIII:** 303
bubonic plague. *See* plague (bubonic)
buccaneers **II:** 284–285
Bucer, Martin **I:** 298

Buchanan, Franklin
  Annapolis Naval Academy
    V: 373
  brothers' war **V:** 37
  Confederate navy **V:** 74
  Monitor-Merrimack **V:**
    237, 238
Buchanan, George **I:** 187
Buchanan, James **V:** *41*, **41–42**,
  405*c*; **VI:** 78, 92, 198
  Benton, Thomas Hart **IV:**
    50
  Bleeding Kansas **V:** 32
  Cass, Lewis **IV:** 77
  Church of Jesus Christ of
    Latter-day Saints **IV:** 81
  Democratic Party **IV:** 108;
    V: 94
  Deseret, State of **IV:** 110
  Douglas, Stephen A. **V:**
    98
  filibustering **V:** 127
  foreign policy **V:** 131
  Fort Sumter, South
    Carolina **V:** 136
  Frémont, John C. **IV:** 154
  Homestead Act of 1862 **V:**
    170
  Larkin, Thomas Oliver **IV:**
    207, 208
  Manifest Destiny **IV:** 218
  Mormon War **IV:** 244
  Morrill Land-Grant Act **V:**
    241
  nativism **V:** 251
  Oregon Treaty of 1846 **IV:**
    270
  Ostend Manifesto **V:** *259*,
    260
  popular sovereignty **IV:**
    286
  public land policy **IV:**
    287–288
  Republican Party **IV:** 301;
    V: 301
  Sickles, Daniel E. **V:** 326
  Stanton, Edwin M. **V:** 333
  Young, Brigham **IV:** 372
Buchanan, McKean **V:** 37
Buchanan, Patrick J. **X:** **42**
  conservative movement **X:**
    80
  Dole, Robert **X:** 90
  Nader, Ralph **X:** 206
  Perot, H. Ross **X:** 234
  Reform Party **X:** 264
  World Trade Organization
    X: 321
Buchenwald **VIII:** *149*
Buck, Dudley **VI:** 201
Buck, Pearl S. **VIII:** 408*c*

Buckley, James **X:** 141, 216,
  217
Buckley, William F., Jr. **IX:** 68;
  X: **42–43**, 78, 297
Buckley v. Valeo (1976) **X:** 53,
  236
Buck's Stove **VII:** 10, **35–36**,
  201
Buddhism **IV:** 298; **IX:** 256; **X:**
  265
Budge, Don **VIII:** 337
budget, national. *See* national
  budget
Budget and Accounting Act
  VII: **36–37**, 118, 360*c*
Budget and Accounting Act of
  1921 **X:** 226
budget cuts **VIII:** 93
Budget Enforcement Acts of
  1990 and 1993 **X:** 135
budget reform **VII:** 63
Buell, Don Carlos **V:** 324, 326,
  354
Buena Vista, Battle of **V:** 36,
  88–89
Buena Vista, Mexico **IV:** 334
Buenos Aires Inter-American
  Conference of 1936 **VIII:**
  377
buffalo **II:** 133, 159; **IV:** 248; **V:**
  251
  extermination of **VI:** **38**,
    46, 206, 208
Buffalo, New York **III:** 167; **IV:**
  128; **V:** 40
Buffalo Bill. *See* Cody, William
  Frederick
*Buffalo Bill: King of the Border
  Men* (Buntline) **VI:** 59
Buffalo Bills **X:** 163
Buffalo Bill's Wild West Show
  VI: 59–60, *97*, 209, 325*c*
Buffalo Creek Reservation **II:**
  173
buffalo robes **V:** 251
Buffalo Soldiers **VI:** **39**
Buffon **IV:** 34
Buford, John **V:** 148
Bugs Bunny **VIII:** 275
Buick Motor Car Company **IX:**
  120
building materials **IV:** 27
building standards **II:** 23
Buler, Pierce **VIII:** 76
Bulfinch, Charles **III:** 20, **50**
Bulgaria **IX:** 58, 105; **X:** 72
Bulge, Battle of the **VIII:** 41,
  44, 263, 393, 410*c*
Bull, Dixey **II:** 285
Bull, William **II:** 361
bullion **II:** 221–222
Bullivant, Benjamin **II:** 367

Bull Moose Party **VIII:** 161,
  248, 305. *See also* election of
  1912
Bulloch, James D. **V:** 132
Bull Run/Manassas, First and
  Second Battles of **V:** **42–44**,
  169
Bull Run/Manassas, First Battle
  of **V:** 42, 43*m*, 406*c*
  Alexander, Edward P. **V:** 7
  Barton, Clara **V:** 24
  Beauregard, Pierre **V:** 27
  Brady, Mathew **V:** 36
  Burnside, Ambrose E. **V:**
    45
  Early, Jubal A. **V:** 103
  espionage **V:** 118
  Greenhow, Rose O'Neal **V:**
    159
  Hooker, Joseph **V:** 171
  Howard, O. O. **V:** 173
  Irish-American regiments
    V: 181
  Jackson, "Stonewall" **V:**
    185
  Johnston, Joseph E. **V:** 190
  Joint Committee on the
    Conduct of War **V:** 190,
    191
  McClellan, George B. **V:**
    224
  medicine and hospitals **V:**
    229–230
  Sherman, William T. **V:**
    320
  Stuart, J. E. B. **V:** 341
  tactics and strategy **V:** 347
  uniforms **V:** 362
  Union army **V:** 365
  Washington, D.C. **V:** 389
  Zouaves **V:** 404
Bull Run/Manassas, Second
  Battle of **V:** 42–44, 44*m*, 406*c*
  Early, Jubal A. **V:** 103
  Ewell, Richard Stoddert **V:**
    118–119
  German-American
    regiments **V:** 147
  Hill, Ambrose P. **V:** 168
  Hood, John Bell **V:** 170
  Hooker, Joseph **V:** 171
  Jackson, "Stonewall" **V:**
    186
  Lee, Robert E. **V:** 206
  Longstreet, James **V:** 215
  Louisiana Tigers **V:** 218
  McClellan, George B. **V:**
    225
  Meade, George Gordon **V:**
    226
  Native Americans **V:** 249
  Stuart, J. E. B. **V:** 341

Bulwer, Sir Henry Lytton **IV:** 88
Bunau-Varilla, Philippe **VII:**
  224, 356*c*
Bunche, Ralph **VIII:** 225, 288;
  IX: *43*, **43–44**, 191, 330*c*
Bundy, McGeorge **X:** 43
Bunker Hill, Battle of **III:**
  50–51, 393*c*
  Burgoyne, John **III:** 51
  Clinton, Sir Henry **III:** 75
  Dorchester Heights, Battle
    of **III:** 107
  Gage, Thomas **III:** 147
  Howe, Sir William **III:** 169
  Putnam, Israel **III:** 290
  Revolutionary War **III:**
    305
  Warren, Joseph **III:** 363
Bunker Hill Monument **IV:** 293
Buntline, Ned **IV:** 58; **VI:** 59, 98
Bureau of African Affairs **IX:** 3,
  332*c*
Bureau of Alcohol, Tobacco, and
  Firearms (ATF) **X:** 39, 194,
  267
Bureau of Drug Abuse Control
  X: 206
Bureau of Ethnology (BE) **VI:**
  228
Bureau of Fisheries **IX:** 48–49
Bureau of Indian Affairs. *See*
  Indian Affairs, Bureau of
Bureau of Investigation **VII:**
  361*c*
Bureau of Narcotics and
  Dangerous Drugs **X:** 206
Bureau of Reclamation **VIII:**
  103
Burford, Anne Gorsuch **X:** 260
Burger, Warren E. **X:** **43–44**,
  323*c*
  Brennan, William J. **X:** 40,
    41
  Ford, Gerald R. **X:** 120
  Ginsburg, Ruth Bader **X:**
    130
  Rehnquist, William H. **X:**
    264
  Supreme Court **X:** 290,
    291
  United States v. Nixon **X:**
    309
  Watergate scandal **X:** 317
Burgesses, House of **II:** *28*,
  44–45, *45*, 417*c*
  Beverley, Robert **II:** 33
  Byrd, William II **II:** 47
  Carter, Landon **II:** 53–54
  Carter, Robert "King" **II:**
    54
  government, British
    American **II:** 142

Parsons' Cause **II:** 271–272
Virginia **II:** 382, 384
Burgis, William **II:** 25, **45–46**, 194
Burgoyne, John **III:** *51*, **51–52**, 393*c*
Arnold, Benedict **III:** 21
Brant, Joseph **III:** 49
Carleton, Guy **III:** 62
Clinton, George **III:** 74
Clinton, Sir Henry **III:** 75
Fort Ticonderoga **III:** 133
Gage, Thomas **III:** 147
Gates, Horatio **III:** 149
Howe, Richard, Lord **III:** 168
Howe, Sir William **III:** 168
Lee, Charles **III:** 205
Lyon, Matthew **III:** 222
McRea, Jane **III:** 239
North, Lord **III:** 260
Revolutionary War **III:** 305
Saratoga, surrender at **III:** 317–320
Valcour Island, Battle of **III:** 357
Washington, George **III:** 367
Burgundy **I:** 67
burial **II:** 314
Cahokia **I:** 47
Hopewell culture **I:** 166
Huron **I:** 171
Monte Albán **I:** 242
mound builders **I:** 244–245
Burke, Edmund **III: 52–53**, 260, 271, 278
Burke, Fielding **VII:** 106
Burke, Tom **VI:** 290
Burke Act **VII: 37**, 206, 356*c*
Burke Act of 1906 **VI:** 76
Burkina Faso **I:** 243, 360
Burleigh, A. Peter **X:** 308
Burleson, Albert S. **VII:** 252
burlesque **VI:** 95, 96, 286
Burlingame Treaty of 1868 **V:** 177
Burlington Railroad **VIII:** 360
Burma **VIII:** 51, 398, 399
"burned-over district"
Erie Canal **IV:** 129
Second Great Awakening **IV:** 311
Smith, Joseph, Jr. **IV:** 322
spiritualism **IV:** 325
Burnet, William **II:** 234
Burnham, Daniel **VI:** 15, 319
Burnham, James **X:** 43
Burns, Anthony **IV: 59**, *59*, 103, 155, 379*c;* **V:** 59, 166

Burns, Arnold **X:** 191
Burns, Lucy **VI:** 36
Burns, Tommy **VII:** 138, 293, 357*c*
Burnside, Ambrose E. **V: 44–45**, *45*, 406*c*
Antietam, Battle of **V:** 13
Fredericksburg, Battle of **V:** 139, 141
Joint Committee on the Conduct of War **V:** 191
Lee, Robert E. **V:** 206
McClellan, George B. **V:** 226
Vallandigham, Clement L. **V:** 377
Burnt Corn, Battle of **IV:** 173
Burr, Aaron **II:** 106, 298; **III:** *53*, **53–54**, 397*c;* **IV:** 76, 84, 85, 106
Adams, John **III:** 3
Clinton, George **III:** 75
Democratic-Republican Party **III:** 104
election of 1800 **III:** 116–117
Hamilton, Alexander **III:** 162
Jefferson, Thomas **III:** 185
Madison, Dolley **III:** 227
Madison, James **III:** 229
Marshall, John **III:** 236
Randolph, Edmund **III:** 296
Tammany Society **III:** 341
Wilkinson, James **III:** 379
Burr, Esther Edwards **II: 46**
Burriel, Juan **VI:** 71, 305, 306
Burrites **III:** 104
Burritt, Elihu **V:** 266
Burros, Daniel **IX:** 166
Burroughs, John **V:** 394; **VI:** 172
Burroughs, William **VI:** 150
Burroughs, William S.
Beat Generation **IX:** 35, 36
counterculture **IX:** 71
Ginsberg, Allen **IX:** 122
Kerouac, Jack **IX:** 159, 160
literature **IX:** 182
Burr's Conspiracy **IV:** 85
Burton, Harold **IX:** 315
Burton, Harold H. **VIII:** 346*t*
Burton, Mary **II:** 247–248
Burton, Phillip **X:** 144
Burwell family **II:** 172
Bury My Heart at Wounded Knee (Brown) **X:** 324*c*
Bush, George H. W. **IX:** 17; **X: 44–47**, *45*, 327*c*, 328*c*
ABM Treaty **X:** 23
abortion **X:** 4

ADA **X:** 21
African nations **X:** 13
arms race **X:** 25
Bennett, William J. **X:** 35
Buchanan, Patrick J. **X:** 42
Bush, George W. **X:** 47
Civil Rights Act of 1991 **X:** 63
Clinton, William **X:** 66
cold war (end of) **X:** *71*
conservative movement **X:** 80
crime **X:** 82
defense policy **X:** 87, 88
Dole, Robert **X:** 90
Dukakis, Michael **X:** 91
economy **X:** 95
foreign policy **X:** 124
GRH Act of 1985 **X:** 135
Haig, Alexander M., Jr. **X:** 139–140
Helms, Jesse A., Jr. **X:** 141
Horton, Willie (campaign ad) **X:** 143–144
immigration **X:** 148
INF Treaty **X:** 152
Kemp, Jack F. **X:** 163
Latin America **X:** 173
Mexico **X:** 192
Mitchell, George **X:** 195
Mondale, Walter F. **X:** 196
NAACP **X:** 208
narcotics **X:** 207
Nixon, Richard M. **X:** 221
North Vietnam **X:** 224
Panama invasion **X:** 231
Persian Gulf War **X:** 234–235
Powell, Colin L. **X:** 247
pro-life and pro-choice movements **X:** 249
Quayle, J. Danforth **X:** 253–254
Reagan, Ronald W. **X:** 259
SDI **X:** 289
Souter, David **X:** 279
South Africa **X:** 280
Starr, Kenneth **X:** 286
Supreme Court **X:** 291
Thomas, Clarence **X:** 302
"Thousand Points of Light" speech **X:** 347–351
United Nations **X:** 308
veto, presidential **X:** 311
Walsh, Lawrence E. **X:** 315
Bush, George W. **X:** *47*, **47–48**, 331*c*
ABM Treaty **X:** 23
Bilingual Education Act of 1968 **X:** 36

Bush, George H. W. **X:** 46
campaign finance **X:** 54
conservation, environmentalism, and environmental policy **X:** 78
conservative movement **X:** 80
defense policy **X:** 88–89
economy **X:** 96
elections **X:** 101–103
federalism **X:** 113
flag burning **X:** *118*
foreign policy **X:** 125
Gore, Albert, Jr. **X:** 134
immigration **X:** 148
Judicial Watch **X:** 162
Kennedy, Edward M. **X:** 164
Latin America **X:** 174
Mexico **X:** 193
Nader, Ralph **X:** 206
NEPA **X:** 210
O'Connor, Sandra Day **X:** 226
Oklahoma City bombing **X:** 228
PACs **X:** 236
political parties **X:** 237
Powell, Colin L. **X:** 247
Presidential Address to a Joint Session of Congress and the American People **X:** 359–362
Reform Party **X:** 264
SDI **X:** 290
Supreme Court **X:** 291
terrorism **X:** 300
United Nations **X:** 308
veto, presidential **X:** 311
Bush, John (Jeb) **X:** 46, 47
Bush, Vannevar **VIII: 44–45**, *45*, 200, 201, 255; **X:** 153
Bush-Brown, H. K. **II:** 173
Bushnell, Horace **IV:** 298
Bush v. Gore (2000) **X:** 331*c*
Breyer, Stephen **X:** 42
Ginsburg, Ruth Bader **X:** 131
Gore, Albert, Jr. **X:** 134
O'Connor, Sandra Day **X:** 226
Rehnquist, William H. **X:** 265
Scalia, Antonin **X:** 271
Souter, David **X:** 279
Supreme Court **X:** 291
Thomas, Clarence **X:** 302
Bush v. Vera (1996) **X:** 329*c*
bushwhackers **V:** 31, 32, **46**, 285, 328

business **IV:** 375*c;* **VI:** 327*c,*
328*c;* **VII:** 37; **VIII:** 45–48;
IX: 44–46; **X:** 49–51, 50*m.*
See also banking, finance and
credit; corporations;
manufacturing and industry
advertising **VII:** 4–5; **VIII:**
1–2
Africa **II:** 4
African Americans **X:** 11
Alexander, Mary Spratt
Provoost **II:** 16–17
almshouses **II:** 18
American Federation of
Labor **VIII:** 14
animals **II:** 21
antimonopoly **VIII:** 17–18
automobile industry **VIII:**
30
Aztecs **I:** 19–20
Baruch, Bernard M. **VII:**
25; **VIII:** 34
Brain Trust **VIII:** 41
Bridges, Harry **VIII:** 43
chain stores **VI:** 46–47
Charleston **II:** 56
Chrysler Corporation Loan
Guarantee Act **X:** 62–63
Columbian Exchange **I:** 78
Congress **VIII:** 68
Connecticut **II:** 69
conservatism **VIII:** 71
Dartmouth College case
IV: 104
dollar-a-year men **VIII:** 84
domesticity **II:** 93
East India Company **I:** 117
economy **II:** 102; **IX:** 89
environment **II:** 111
Ewe **I:** 125
Fair Labor Standards Act
VIII: 110
First New Deal **VIII:** 122
Foreign Corrupt Practices
Act **X:** 121–122
foreign policy **VI:** 103, 104
fur trade **IV:** 156–158
globalization **X:** 131
Good Neighbor Policy
VIII: 133
government **VIII:** 134
and government **VI:**
39–41
Harriman, Averell **VIII:**
143
Hayes, Rutherford B. **VI:**
126, 127
Hepburn Act **VII:** 122
Hoover presidency **VIII:**
154
Hopkins, Harry **VIII:** 157
isolationists **VIII:** 166

Johnson, Hugh S. **VIII:**
173
Jones, Jesse H. **VIII:** 174
Kennedy, Joseph P. **VIII:**
176
Keynesianism **VIII:** 177
labor **VIII:** 179
liberalism **VIII:** 187
mail-order houses **VI:** 186
merchants **II:** 221–222
mobilization **VIII:** 214
Moley, Raymond C. **VIII:**
216
NAFTA **X:** 222–223
Native Americans **X:** 215
NEPA **X:** 210
New Deal **VIII:** 242
news media **VIII:** 243
newspapers **VI:** 211–212
NIRA **VIII:** 228
NLRA **VIII:** 229
NOW **X:** 211
NRA **VIII:** 231–232
NWLB **VIII:** 233
Nye Committee **VIII:** 250
Occupational Safety and
Health Act of 1970 **X:**
225
OPM **VIII:** 255
OWMR **VIII:** 259
Packard, Vance **IX:** 239
PACs **X:** 236
Philadelphia **II:** 281
Pinckney, Elizabeth Lucas
II: 284
pornography **X:** 244
postwar planning **VIII:**
278
Progressive Party **IX:**
248–249
public opinion polls **VIII:**
283
Public Utility Holding
Company Act **VIII:** 284
Quakers **II:** 308
railroads **VI:** 237
recession of 1937-38 **VIII:**
293
Reciprocal Trade
Agreements Act **VIII:**
294
Republican Party **VII:** 263;
VIII: 305
Revenue Act of 1935 **VIII:**
308
Rockefeller, John D. **VII:**
264–265
St. Mary's City **II:** 328
science and technology **IV:**
307; **X:** 273
scientific management
VII: 277

Second New Deal **VIII:**
321
society, British American
II: 350
South **VIII:** 332
Spanish colonies **II:** 357
spinsters **II:** 360
sports **X:** 286
Stearns, Abel **IV:** 326–327
steel industry **VIII:**
338–339
suburbanization **IX:** 288
Sunbelt **X:** 290
taxation **VIII:** 351
Taylor, Frederick W. **VII:**
306–307
technology **VIII:** 353; **IX:**
293
Tenochtitlán **I:** 344, 345
theater **VI:** 287
Third New Deal
VIII: 358
TNEC **VIII:** 355
trusts **VI:** 292–295
Vanderbilt, Cornelius **IV:**
352–353
wage and price controls
VIII: 371
Wells-Barnett, Ida Bell **VI:**
311
Wistar, Caspar **II:**
402–403
women's status and rights
II: 406, 407
WPB **VIII:** 375
Young, Brigham **IV:** 372,
373
Business: A Profession
(Brandeis) **VII:** 34
"business class" **VII:** 185
business cycles **VI:** **41–42**, 142,
206
business pages **IV:** 196
Bustamante, Anastasio
IV: 303
Busta Rhymes **X:** 240
bustles **V:** 122
Bute, John Stuart, earl of **III:**
54–55, 151, 213
Butler, Andrew P. **V:** 31, 197,
342
Butler, Benjamin Franklin **IV:**
103; **V:** **46–47**, 407*c;* **VI:** 120
Baltimore, Maryland, riots
V: 22
Confiscation Acts **V:** 78
contrabands **V:** 80
emancipation **V:** 112
Grant, Ulysses S. **V:** 156
Joint Committee on the
Conduct of War **V:** 191
loyalty oaths **V:** 218

New Orleans, Battle of **V:**
252
prisons **V:** 281
Union army **V:** 365
Butler, Matthew **VI:** 175
Butler, Nicholas Murray **VI:**
102, 183; **VII:** 43
Butler, Pierce **VIII:** 165, 345,
346*t*
Butler, W. O. **V:** 189
Butterfield, Daniel **V:** 227
Butterfield, John **IV:** 272
Butterworth, Mary Peck **II:**
46–47
Butz, Earl **X:** 120
bypass surgery **VIII:** 207–208
Byrd, Richard **VII:** 361*c*
Byrd, Robert **X:** 51, 164, 276
Byrd, Ursala **II:** 33
Byrd, William, I **II:** 30, 47
Byrd, William, II **II:** 11, **47,**
179, 377
Byrd, William, III **II:** 55
Byrd family **II:** **47,** 172
Byrne, William **X:** 233
Byrnes, James F. **VIII:** **48–49**
Democratic Party **VIII:** 81
Hillman, Sidney
VIII: 146
mobilization **VIII:** 214
OPA **VIII:** 254
OWM **VIII:** 258
OWMR **VIII:** 259
reconversion **VIII:** 295
sports **VIII:** 338
Supreme Court **VIII:** 346*t*
wage and price controls
VIII: 371
WMC **VIII:** 375
WPB **VIII:** 376
Byron, Lord **III:** 43

C

CAAA. *See* Comprehensive
Anti-Apartheid Act of 1986
Cabet, Étienne **IV:** **61**
Cabeza de Vaca, Álvar Núñez **I:**
37–38, 88, 251, 256, 295,
383; **IV:** 337
cabildo(s) **I:** **38–40; II:** 355
cacique **I:** 46–47
corregidores **I:** 91
Cuba **I:** 98
encomienda **I:** 122
New Mexico **I:** 257
New Spain **I:** 259
Cabin Creek, Battles of **V:** 391
cabinetmaking **II:** 215; **III:** 275
cabinet of curiosities **I:** **40,** 348
Cable, George Washington **VI:**
177

Cable, John **VII:** 41
Cable Act **VII: 41–42,** 87, 340, 360*c*
cable cars **VI:** 292; **VII:** 317
Cable Communications Policy Act of 1984 **X:** 294
Cable News Network (CNN) **X:** 241, 296
cable television
    movies **X:** 199
    music **X:** 202–203
    popular culture **X:** 239, 241
    pornography **X:** 244
    recreation **X:** 262, 263
    science and technology **X:** 273
    sports **X:** 284
    television **X:** 294–296
Cabot, George **IV:** 170
Cabot, John **I:** 41*m*, **41–42,** 386*c*; **II:** 41, 191, 231
    Acadia **I:** 3
    Bristol **I:** 35
    Cabot, Sebastian **I:** 42
    Cathay (China) **I:** 65
    Hakluyt, Richard, the Younger **I:** 151
    Patent Granted by King Henry VII to John Cabot and His Sons, March 1496 **I:** 394–395
Cabot, Sebastian **I: 42–43,** *43,* 386*c*; **II:** 41
    Bermuda **I:** 29
    Bristol **I:** 35
    Cabot, John **I:** 41
    cod **I:** 75
    Hakluyt, Richard, the Younger **I:** 151
    Northeast Passage **I:** 265
    Northwest Passage **I:** 266
Cabo Tormentoso **I:** 105. *See also* Cape of Good Hope
Cabral, Gonçalo **I:** 386*c*
Cabral, Pedro Álvares **I: 43–44,** 105*m*, 386*c*
    Brazil **I:** 32*m*, 33
    Dias, Bartholomeu **I:** 106
    Ramusio, Giovanni Battista **I:** 305
    Tordesillas, Treaty of **I:** 358
    Vespucci, Amerigo **I:** 368
Cabrillo, Joan Rodriguez **I:** 48
Cacamatzin (Cacama) **I: 44–45**
cacao **I:** 45–46, 150, 261, 353
cacique(s) **I: 46–47,** 79, 88, 90, 342; **II:** 357
Caddoan **II:** 149
Caddo nation **IV:** 57; **V:** 250

Cadillac, Lamonthe. *See* Lamothe, Antoine de, sieur de Cadillac
Cadillac Automobile Company **IX:** 120; **X:** 275
Cadillac Motor Car Company **VII:** 95
Cádiz **II:** 258
Cadman, Charles **VII:** 194
Caesar (slave) **II:** 247
Caesar's Column (Donnelly) **VI:** 178, 301
Cage, John **VIII:** 223; **IX:** 216
Cagney, James **VIII:** 218
Cahan, Abraham **VI:** 177; **VII:** 252
Cahill, Holger **VIII:** 114
Cahokia **I:** 47; **II:** 133
Caine Mutiny (Wouk) **VIII:** 192
Cairo **I:** 75, 220, 230
Cairo Conference, Second **VIII:** 51
Cairo Conference (1943) **VIII: 50,** 144, 157, 200
Cairo Conference Statement **VIII:** 410*c*
Caitlin, George **V:** 16
Cajamarca **I:** 15
Cajun music **VIII:** 222
Cajuns **II:** 74, 129, 332
Calabar **I: 47–48,** 52
calculators, mechanical **VIII:** 353
Calcutta, India **II:** 119
Calder, Alexander **VIII:** 22–23
Calder, Alexander Milne **VI:** 259
Calderon, Ricardo Arias **X:** 231
Caldwell, Erskine **VIII:** 191
calendars **I:** 21, 228–230, 270
calendar stone **I:** *18*
Calhoun, John C. **III:** 360; **IV: 62–64,** *63,* 376*c*, 379*c*; **VI:** 143
    American System **IV:** 19
    Atkinson, Henry **IV:** 33
    Benton, Thomas Hart **IV:** 49
    BIA **IV:** 180
    Bonus Bill **IV:** 56
    Clay, Henry **IV:** 87
    Compromise of 1850 **IV:** 94
    Davis, Jefferson **V:** 89
    Democratic Party **V:** 94
    election of 1840 **IV:** 124
    Greenhow, Rose O'Neal **V:** 159
    internal improvements **IV:** 188
    National Road **IV:** 253

    Nullification Controversy **IV:** 264
    railroads **IV:** 293
    secession **V:** 311, 312
    Tyler, John **IV:** 348–349
    Van Buren, Martin **IV:** 351
    War Hawks **IV:** 355
    Webster, Daniel **IV:** 360
    Whig Party **IV:** 363
    Yancey, William Lowndes **V:** 401
Calhoun, Thomas **V:** 20
Calicut **I:** 44, 137
California **I:** 24, **48–49,** 388*c*; **II:** 49, 165, 230, 420*c*; **III: 57,** 258; **IV:** xiii, **64–66; V:** 405*c*; **VII:** 137–138, 248, 249; **X:** 329*c*, 331*c*
    affirmative action **X:** 9
    African-American churches, growth of **VI:** 4
    agriculture **V:** 7
    American Independent Party **X:** 20
    Asian Americans **VIII:** 25; **X:** 28, 29
    automobile industry **IX:** 26
    Bear Flag Revolt **IV:** 45
    Beckwourth, Jim **IV:** 47
    Bent's Fort **IV:** 51
    Bidwell, John **IV:** 51
    Bilingual Education Act of 1968 **X:** 36
    Calhoun, John C. **IV:** 63
    California Trail **IV:** 70–71
    Carson, Kit **IV:** 75
    Chinese Exclusion Act **VI:** 50, 52
    Chinese workers in **VI:** 51*m*
    Clay, Henry **IV:** 87, 88
    Clayton-Bulwer Treaty **IV:** 88
    Compromise of 1850 **IV:** 94, 94*m*, 95
    conservation **VI:** 65
    cotton culture **IV:** 99
    Dana, Richard Henry **IV:** 103
    Davis, Jefferson **V:** 89
    diseases and epidemics **IV:** 111, 113
    Donner party **IV:** 114–115
    economy **IV:** 117
    energy crisis **X:** 104
    exploration **IV:** 132
    Fifteenth Amendment **V:** 124
    Figueroa, José **IV:** 136
    foreign policy **IV:** 142

    Fort Laramie **IV:** 143
    Fort Leavenworth **IV:** 145
    Frémont, John C. **IV:** 153, 154
    Gadsden Purchase **IV:** 159
    gold, discovery and mining **IV:** 162–164
    Guadalupe Hidalgo, Treaty of (1848) **IV:** 165, 166
    Hispanic Americans **X:** 141–143
    immigration **X:** 148
    immigration restrictions **VI:** 141
    IRCA **X:** 149
    Kearny, Stephen Watts **IV:** 200
    La Raza Unida **IX:** 171
    Larkin, Thomas Oliver **IV:** 207–208
    Latino movement **IX:** 174
    Manifest Destiny **IV:** 217
    marriage **X:** 181
    Mexican-American War **IV:** 232, 234
    Mexico **X:** 192
    migration **IV:** 236; **VIII:** 212, 213; **IX:** 202
    Monroe Doctrine **IV:** 241
    multiculturalism **X:** 200
    Murrieta, Joaquín **IV:** 248–249
    narcotics **X:** 208
    Native Americans **X:** 215
    nativism **VI:** 209
    oil **VI:** 215
    Oregon Treaty of 1846 **IV:** 269
    overland mail **IV:** 271
    Patrons of Husbandry **VI:** 221
    Permanent Indian Frontier **IV:** 279
    Polk, James K. **IV:** 284
    population trends **V:** 279; **X:** 242
    pro-life and pro-choice movements **X:** 248
    race and racial conflict **X:** 256
    Reagan, Ronald W. **X:** 258–259
    religion **IV:** 298
    rust belt **X:** 269
    Smith, Jedediah Strong **IV:** 322
    South Pass **IV:** 325
    Stearns, Abel **IV:** 326–327
    Stockton, Robert Field **IV:** 328
    Submerged Lands Act **IX:** 286–287

California (continued)
  Sunbelt **X:** 290
  Sunbelt **VIII:** 344
  Sutter, John **IV:** 332
  Taylor, Zachary **IV:** 335
  Texas **IV:** 339
  World War II **VIII:** 390
California gold rush
  IV: 66–69, 67, 68m, 378c;
  V: 177, 319
    anti-Chinese agitation, rise
      of **IV:** 23
    Beckwourth, Jim **IV:** 47
    Bidwell, John **IV:** 51
    California **IV:** 65
    California Trail **IV:** 71
    Clayton-Bulwer Treaty **IV:**
      88
    Colt revolver **IV:** 92
    Comstock Lode **IV:** 95
    Deseret, State of **IV:** 110
    diseases and epidemics **IV:**
      111
    exploration **IV:** 132
    Fort Laramie **IV:** 143, 144
    Forty-niners **IV:** 146–147
    gold, discovery and mining
      IV: 162
    immigration **IV:** 177, 180
    Larkin, Thomas Oliver **IV:**
      208
    lead mines **IV:** 208
    migration **IV:** 236
    Murrieta, Joaquín **IV:**
      248–249
    music **IV:** 249
    Native Americans **IV:** 258
    race and race relations **IV:**
      292
    religion **IV:** 298
    Santa Fe Trail **IV:** 306
    Strauss, Levi **IV:** 329
    Sutter, John **IV:** 332
    Vanderbilt, Cornelius **IV:**
      352
California Indians **II: 49,** 49,
  115, 324, 331, 332; **IV:** 163
California Institute of
  Technology **IX:** 293
California Medical School **X:**
  34–35
California missions **IV: 69–70,**
  207
California Rangers **IV:** 249
California Trail **IV: 70–71,**
  268m
  Bidwell, John **IV:** 51
  California **IV:** 65
  California gold rush **IV:** 66
  Donner party **IV:** 114, 115
  exploration **IV:** 132
  Fort Laramie **IV:** 143

mountain men **IV:** 248
Oregon Trail **IV:** 267
Smith, Jedediah Strong **IV:**
  321
Sublette, William **IV:** 330
Sutter, John **IV:** 332
"call and response" **II:** 239
Callender, James **III:** 165, 185
Call Home the Heart (Burke)
  VII: 106
Calliope, HMS **VI:** 255
Call of the Wild (London) **VII:**
  356c
Calloway, Cab **VIII:** 3
calméac **I:** 97
calmecac **I:** 20
calpolli **I:** 249
calpulli **I:** 18, 20
calumet **II: 50**
Calusa **I:** 130, 288; **II:** 120
Calvert, Benedict Leonard **II:**
  210
Calvert, Cecilius **II:** 50, 174,
  209, 323, 328, 396
Calvert, Charles **II:** 274
Calvert, George **II: 50,** 144,
  209–210, 328
Calvert, Leonard **II:** 40, **50–51,**
  144, 209, 328
Calvert family **II:** 156, 209–210,
  300; **V:** 224
Calverton, V. F. **VII:** 253
Calvin, John **I: 49–51; II:** 140,
  212, 296, 300, 316; **III:** 169;
  IV: 138, 298
    Huguenots **I:** 169
    Léry, Jean de **I:** 205
    printing press **I:** 294
    Puritans **I:** 298
    Reformation **I:** 307, 309
Calvinism **I:** 64, 170, 282; **III:**
  113, 298, 299, 355; **IX:** 256
    Finney, Charles Grandison
      IV: 138
    Hammon, Jupiter **II:** 154
    Leverett, John **II:** 193
    Osborn, Sarah Haggar
      Wheaten **II:** 268
    Protestantism **II:** 300, 301
    religion **IV:** 298
    religion, Euro-American
      II: 316
    science **II:** 330
    Second Great Awakening
      IV: 310
    spiritualism **IV:** 325
    Tennent, William, Jr. **II:**
      372
    Tennent, William, Sr. **II:**
      372
    Whitefield, George **II:**
      397

Cambodia **IX:** 310; **X:** 260, 311,
  323c, 325c
Cambodian Americans
    Asian Americans **X:** 28
    cold war (end of) **X:** 70
    foreign policy **X:** 122
    Kent State University **X:**
      164
    North Vietnam **X:** 224
Cambridge, Massachusetts **IV:**
  114
Cambridge Platform
  (Congregationalists) **II:** 68,
  73
Camden, Battle of **III: 57–59,**
  58m
    Cornwallis, Lord **III:** 93
    Gates, Horatio **III:** 149
    Greene, Nathanael **III:**
      155, 156
    Jefferson, Thomas **III:** 184
    Kalb, baron de **III:** 195
    Tarleton, Banastre **III:** 343
Camden, William **I: 51–52,**
  112–113, 121, 208
Camden & Amboy (C&A)
  Railroad **IV:** 295
cameras **VI:** 87, 137, 150, 326c;
  VII: 134
cameras (movies) **IX:** 210–211
Cameron, Donald **VI:** 184
Cameron, James **X:** 240
Cameron, Lucille **VII:** 139
Cameron, Simon **V:** 334, 387;
  VI: 184
Cameroon **I: 52–53**
    Bantu **I:** 24, 25
    Calabar **I:** 48
    Fang **I:** 127
    Fulani **I:** 135
    Islam **I:** 185
    Kotoko **I:** 196
Caminha, Álvaro da **I:** 320
Camm, John **II:** 272
Camp, Walter **VI:** 101
campaign finance **X: 53–54,**
  324c, 325c
    Clinton, William **X:** 68
    Gore, Albert, Jr. **X:** 134
    Judicial Watch **X:** 162
    Nader, Ralph **X:** 206
    Nixon, Richard M. **X:** 220,
      221
    NRA **X:** 213
    PACs **X:** 236
    political parties **X:** 238
    Senate **X:** 276
    Supreme Court **X:** 291
campaigns. *See* political
  campaigns
Campanella, Roy **IX:** 260
Campann, Klass **X:** 239

Campbell, Albert H. **V:** 51
Campbell, Jabez **VI:** 296
Campbell, John **II:** 299
Campbell, Robert **IV:** 143
Campbell, Thomas **IV:** 17,
  71–72, 298
Campbell, W. Glenn **X:** 301
Campbellites **IV:** 299
Camp David accords **X: 54–55,**
  55, 139, 196, 325c
Campeche **I:** 87
Campfire Girls **VIII:** 298
Camp Floyd **IV:** 244
camp followers **III: 59,**
  243–244, 307, 382
Camp Grant **VI:** 14
camp meetings **IV:** 310–311
"Camptown Races" (Foster) **V:**
  137
Campus, Pedro a **I:** 26
Canada **III: 59–61,** 391c, 392c,
  398c; **V:** 132, 133; **VII:** 127,
  127t, 135, 356c; **VIII:** 162,
  408c; **IX:** 231–233; **X:** 328c
    abolition movement **IV:** 3
    African-American
      churches, growth of **VI:**
      4, 5
    African Americans **III:** 5
    agriculture **II:** 8
    Algonquin **II:** 17
    Allen, Ethan **II:** 10
    Andre, John **III:** 13
    Arnold, Benedict **III:** 21
    Aroostook War **IV:** 25
    art **II:** 25
    Beaver Wars **II:** 31
    Bering Sea dispute **VI:**
      26–27
    British Empire **II:** 43
    Burgoyne, John **III:** 51
    Canada and the United
      States **VI:** 43
    Carleton, Guy **III:** 62
    Caroline affair **IV: 74–75**
    Cartier, Jacques **I:** 57m,
      57–59
    Champlain, Samuel de **II:**
      56
    Cornplanter **III:** 91
    Delaware **II:** 87
    economy **III:** 111; **X:** 95
    exploration **II:** 114; **IV:**
      132
    foreign affairs **III:** 130
    foreign policy **IV:** 141, 142;
      VI: 103; **X:** 124
    Fort Ticonderoga **III:** 133
    French alliance **III:** 137
    French colonies **II:**
      126–127, 129
    French immigrants **II:** 130

frontier **III:** 141
fur trade **II:** 132; **III:** 142;
  IV: 156
Gage, Thomas **III:** 146
Gates, Horatio **III:** 149
GATT **X:** 129
Genet, Edmond **III:** 150
Ghent, Treaty of (1814) **IV:**
  161, 162
Green Mountain Boys **III:**
  156
Greenville, Treaty of **III:**
  157
Hessians **III:** 167
Howe, Sir William **III:** 168
Hudson, Henry **II:**
  158–159
Hudson's Bay Company **II:**
  159
Hull, William **IV:** 175
immigration **IV:** 178
Inuit **II:** 167
Iroquois **II:** 168, 170
Iroquois Confederacy **III:**
  178, 179
Jesuits **II:** 174
Johnson, Sir John **III:** 188,
  189
Jolliet, Louis **II:** 178
Kalb, baron de **III:** 195
Kalm, Peter **II:** 181
King George's War **II:** 182
King William's War **II:** 185
Klondike gold rush **VI:**
  160–162
Lafayette, marquis de **III:**
  201
Lake Erie, Battle of **IV:**
  206, 207
La Salle, René-Robert
  Cavelier, sieur de **II:**
  192
Louisiana **II:** 199
Loyalists **III:** 219, 221
Manifest Destiny **IV:** 217
Marquette, Jacques **II:** 205
medicine **VI:** 192
Mexico **X:** 192
monarchy, British **II:** 232
Montagnais-Naskapi **I:** 241
NAFTA **X:** 222
Native Americans **II:** 243;
  IV: 256
Native Americans in the
  War of 1812 **IV:** 258,
  259
NATO **X:** 223
New Orleans, Battle of
  (1815) **IV:** 262
New York **II:** 262
Oregon Treaty of 1846 **IV:**
  269, 270

Pontiac's Rebellion **III:**
  280–281
Proclamation of 1763 **III:**
  287
Prophet, the Shawnee **III:**
  289
Protestantism **II:** 300
Quebec, Battle of **III:**
  293
Queen Anne's War **II:**
  309
Ramusio, Giovanni Battista
  I: 305
Red Jacket **III:** 297
Revolutionary War **III:**
  305, 307
St. Clair, Arthur **III:** 315
Saratoga, surrender at **III:**
  318
Schuyler, Philip John **III:**
  320
Scott, Winfield **IV:** 310
Seven Years' War **II:**
  332–334
space policy **X:** 283
Still, William **IV:** 328
Tecumseh **III:** 345
Thames, Battle of the **IV:**
  342
Tippecanoe, Battle of **III:**
  347
trade and shipping **II:** 375
Treaty of Paris **II:** 378
and the United States **VI:**
  43
Valcour Island, Battle of
  III: 357
Van Buren, Martin **IV:**
  352
Verrazano, Giovanni da **I:**
  367
Vinland **I:** 369
War Hawks **IV:** 355
War of 1812 **IV:** 356, 358
Washington, Treaty of **VI:**
  309–310
Wayne, Anthony **III:** 369
Webster, Daniel **IV:** 360
Webster-Ashburton Treaty
  (1842) **IV:** 360–361
West Indies **III:** 372
Canada West **V:** 52
canal, isthmian **V:** 131–133
canal era **IV: 72–74,** 73m
  agriculture **IV:** 11
  American System **IV:** 18
  Clayton-Bulwer Treaty **IV:**
  88–89
  economy **IV:** 118
  Erie Canal **IV:** 127–130
  internal improvements **IV:**
  188

"canal ring" **VI:** 289
canals **I:** 163, 344, 365; **III:**
  11–12, 141; **IV:** 379c; **V:** 59,
  355
  Bonus Bill **IV:** 56
  industrialization **IV:** 185
  internal improvements **IV:**
  189m, 190
  science and technology **IV:**
  307
Canarsie **II:** 249
Canary Islands **I: 53,** 79–81; **II:**
  250
Canby, Edward **V:** 236
Canby, William **III:** 310, 311
cancer **VIII:** 207, 208; **X:** 303
candles **IV:** 184
Cane Ridge camp meeting **IV:**
  311
Canisius, Peter **I:** 189
canned goods **VIII:** 47, 292
"canned music" **VI:** 271
Cannery Row (Steinbeck) **VIII:**
  339
cannibalism **I: 53–55**
  Aztecs **I:** 18
  Carib **I:** 56
  El Dorado **I:** 119
  Fang **I:** 127
  Laudonnière, René de **I:**
  201
  Léry, Jean de **I:** 205
  Stade, Hans **I:** 336
  Tupinambá **I:** 361
Cannibal Queen. *See* Nzinga,
  queen of Angola
*Cannibals All!, or Slaves
  without Masters* (Fitzhugh)
  V: 128, 212, 328
Canning, George **III:** 246; **IV:**
  241
canning industry **VI:** 165; **VII:**
  45
Cannon, James P. **VII:** 53
Cannon, Joseph Gurney **VII:**
  42, 356c
  Congress **VII:** 53
  Democratic Party **VII:** 66
  elections **VII:** 80
  Meat Inspection Act **VII:**
  178
  National Reclamation Act
  VII: 203
  Progressive Party **VII:** 236
  Republican Party **VII:** 263
  Taft, William Howard **VII:**
  303
Canonicus **II: 51,** 224, 400
Canoy **II:** 396
Canterbury, Robert **X:** 164
Cantor, Eddie **VI:** 96
Cantril, Hadley **VIII:** 284

Cantwell v. Connecticut **VIII:**
  408c
Cão, Diogo **I:** 195–196
CAP. *See* Community Action
  Program
Cape architecture **II:** 215
Cape Breton (Île Royal) **II:** 2,
  43, 332. *See also* Louisbourg
Cape Cod **II:** 130–131, 212, 219
Cape Cod (Thoreau) **IV:** 342
Cape Horn **I:** 56; **IV:** 146
Cape of Good Hope **I:** 44,
  104–106
Capes, Battle of the **III:** 93,
  390
Cape Verde Islands **I:** 44, 146;
  II: 286
Capira **II:** 246
capital **IV:** 118; **V:** 181
Capital Airlines **IX:** 27
capitalism
  Fourier, Charles **IV:** 149
  fur trade **IV:** 157
  gold, discovery and mining
  IV: 163
  Republican Party **IV:** 301
capital punishment **II:** 75–76,
  300, 337, 409; **VII:** 158; **IX:**
  264–265; **X: 55–56,** 324c. *See
  also* executions
  Brennan, William J. **X:** 41
  Horton, Willie (campaign
  ad) **X:** 143
  Kennedy, Edward M. **X:**
  164
  Rehnquist, William H. **X:**
  264
  Reno, Janet **X:** 266, 267
  Supreme Court **X:** 290,
  291
  terrorism **X:** 299
Capitol building **IV:** 27, 161,
  375c; **V:** 389
capitulaciós **I:** 84
Caplovitz, David **IX:** 69
Capone, Al **VII:** 60, 241
Capote, Truman **IX:** 182, 334c
Capper, Arthur **VII:** 42–43
Capper-Volstead Act **VII: 7,
  42–43,** 118, 163, 360c
Capra, Frank **VIII: 50–52,** 218
captaincy system **I:** 33, 193
"Captain Thomas." *See* Bonnet,
  Stede
captivity **II: 51–52**
  African Americans **II:** 5–6
  Chesapeake Bay **II:** 58
  Chickasaw **II:** 59
  Connecticut **II:** 68
  Deerfield Massacre **II:** 85
  Jemison, Mary **II:** 173
  literature **II:** 195

captivity (*continued*)
 "Mary Jemison's Account of Her Capture by the Iroquois" **II:** 426
 Montour, Madame **II:** 233
 Native Americans **II:** 244
 "Olaudah Equiano's Account of his Capture and Enslavement" **II:** 427–429
 Opechancanough **II:** 268
 Pequot War **II:** 280
 Pocahontas **II:** 288
 Powhatan Confederacy **II:** 295
 Rowlandson, Mary White **II:** 324–325
 slavery **II:** 340
 slave trade **II:** 343–344
Caracol **I:** 349
caravela latina **I:** 55
caravela redonda **I:** 55
caravel(s) **I:** 55, **55–56,** 78, 82, 105, 179
Carawan, Guy **IX:** 111, 217
carbines **V:** 318
Cárdenas, Garcia López de **I:** 90, 167
Cárdenas, Juan de **I:** 46
card games **VIII:** 296
Cardinal Mindszenty Foundation **X:** 79
cardiovascular diseases **IX:** 198
Cardozo, Benjamin N. **VIII:** 76, 127, 344, 345, 346*t*
cards **VIII:** 296
Carey, Hugh **X:** 217
Carey, Mathew **III:** **61–62,** 371
Carey plow **IV:** 10
Carib **I:** **56–57; II:** 52
 Arawak **I:** 12
 Barbados **I:** 26
 cannibalism **I:** 54
 El Dorado **I:** 119
 Jamaica **I:** 187
 Martinique **I:** 223
 Montserrat **I:** 243
 Taino **I:** 342
Cariban language **I:** 56
Caribbean **II:** **52–53; IV:** 137, 142, 218–219; **VII:** 70, 310
 Acadians **II:** 2
 African-American churches, growth of **VI:** 5
 Barbados **I:** 26
 British Empire **II:** 43
 Carib **I:** 56
 class **II:** 63
 coffee **I:** 76
 Columbian Exchange **I:** 77
 Columbus, Christopher **I:** 79

convict labor **II:** 72
Cozumel **I:** 96–97
Creole **II:** 74
disease **II:** 92
Dutch West India Company **II:** 98
El Dorado **I:** 119
emancipation **V:** 114
filibustering **V:** 126, 127
foreign policy **V:** 131, 133; **VI:** 103
French colonies **II:** 129
French immigrants **II:** 130
Gullah **II:** 151
Hay, John Milton **VI:** 125
imperialism **VI:** 141
indigenous peoples **II:** 52
indigo **II:** 166
labor **II:** 189
mariners **II:** 204
Metacom **II:** 223
Minuit, Peter **II:** 227
miscegenation **II:** 228
Monckton, Robert **II:** 233
Natchez Revolt **II:** 242
Native Americans **II:** 244, 246
New Hampshire **II:** 250
New Spain **I:** 258
New York **II:** 260
Ostend Manifesto **V:** 259
piracy **II:** 284–285
plantation system **II:** 286
Quakers **II:** 308
Santo Domingo **VI:** 255
slave trade **II:** 343
smallpox **II:** 345
society and daily life **II:** 53
Spanish colonies **II:** 355, 357–359
sugar **I:** 338
sugar cultivation **II:** 53
Teach, Edward **II:** 368
tobacco **II:** 374
trade and shipping **II:** 375
Verrazano, Giovanni da **I:** 367
Virginia **II:** 382
Caristauga **II:** 67
Carleill, Christopher **I:** 111
Carleton, Guy, first baron of Dorchester **III:** 60, **62**
Carleton, James **V:** 406*c*
Carlin, George **X:** 295
Carlisle, John G. **VI:** 73
Carlos, John **IX:** 40, 41
Carlton, James H. **IV:** 76
Carlyle, Thomas **IV:** 126, 345
Carmichael, Stokely **IX:** **47–48,** 48, 334*c*
 African-American movement **IX:** 6
 Black Power **IX:** 40–41

freedom rides **IX:** 114
 Lewis, John **IX:** 178
 Meredith, James **IX:** 200
 Student Nonviolent Coordinating Committee **IX:** 285
 women's status and rights **IX:** 325
Carnation, Lily, Lily Rose (Sargent) **VI:** 256
Carnegie, Andrew **VI:** **43–45,** 44, 326*c;* **VII:** 37–38, 296–297, 319–320, 355*c*
 Anti-Imperialist League **VI:** 13
 Bessemer process **VI:** 27
 bridges **VI:** 35
 class consciousness **VI:** 57
 Frick, Henry Clay **VI:** 105, 106
 Homestead Strike **VI:** 132
 industrial revolution, second **VI:** 145, 147
 Morgan, John Pierpont **VI:** 198
 Pan-American Union **VI:** 220
 Scott, Thomas Alexander **VI:** 258
 Social Darwinism **VI:** 266
 steel **VI:** 277
 trusts **VI:** 295
 Washington, Booker T. **VI:** 308, 309
 "Wealth" Essay **VI:** 339–342
Carnegie Brothers and Company **VI:** 105
Carnegie Endowment for International Peace **VI:** 44; **VII:** 43; **X:** 301
Carnegie Foundation **X:** 99–100
Carnegie Hall **VII:** 194; **VIII:** 100, 132, 223, 408*c*
Carnegie Institute **VI:** 45
Carnegie Steel Company **VI:** 327*c;* **VII:** 37, 319
 Carnegie, Andrew **VI:** 44
 Frick, Henry Clay **VI:** 106
 Homestead Strike **VI:** 132
 industrial revolution, second **VI:** 146
 steel **VI:** 277
Carney, William Harvey **V:** **49,** 125, 228
Carnia Americana (Morton) **IV:** 290
Carolina Algonquian **I:** 253, 290, 313–314, 372, 373
Carolina charter **II:** 418*c*
Carolina colony government, British American **II:** 144

Graffenried, Christopher, baron de **II:** 146
 Native Americans **II:** 244
 travel **II:** 377
 Westo **II:** 394–395
Carolina language **I:** 6
Carolinas. *See also* North Carolina; South Carolina
 agriculture **II:** 8, 10
 class **II:** 63
 economy **II:** 101
 Iroquois **II:** 168
 Native Americans **II:** 246
 piracy **II:** 285
 Teach, Edward **II:** 368
 trade and shipping **II:** 375
 Tuscarora War **II:** 379
 women's status and rights **II:** 407
Caroline, Fort **I:** 57
Caroline affair **IV:** **74–75**
Caroline Islands **VII:** 360*c*
Carolingian Empire **I:** 165
carpentry **II:** 190
carpetbaggers **V:** **49–51,** 50
 Reconstruction **V:** 291, 294
 redemption **V:** 297
 Republican Party **V:** 302
 scalawags **V:** 307
 Warmoth, Henry C. **V:** 388
carpet bombing **VIII:** 12
Carr, Lucien **IX:** 35
Carr, Sir Robert **II:** 87
Carranza, Venustiano **VII:** 358*c*
 Big Stick diplomacy **VII:** 28
 foreign policy **VII:** 99
 Mexican invasion **VII:** 183
 Mexican Revolution **VII:** 183, 185
 Zimmermann telegram **VII:** 353
Carrere, John M. **VI:** 313
Carroll, Charles **III:** 63
Carroll, John **III:** 63
Carroll family **II:** 186
cars. *See* automobiles/automobile industry
Carson, Fiddlin' John **VII:** 86
Carson, Kit **IV:** 75, **75–76,** 378*c;* **V:** 406*c*
 exploration **IV:** 131
 Frémont, Jessie Benton **IV:** 152
 Frémont, John C. **IV:** 153, 154
 Rocky Mountain Fur Company **IV:** 302
Carson, Rachel **IX:** **48–49,** 49, 333*c;* **X:** 76, 210
 business **IX:** 46

consumer movement **IX:** 69

environmental movement **IX:** 101

literature **IX:** 182

science **IX:** 270

Cartagena, Juan de **I:** 215, 272, 277; **II:** 135

Carter, Billy **X:** 59

Carter, James Earl (Jimmy), Jr. **V:** 228; **X: 56–59,** 57, 325*c*, 326*c*, 328*c*

African nations **X:** 13

Anderson, John B. **X:** 21

antiwar movement— Vietnam **X:** 24

arms race **IX:** 16

Bilingual Education Act of 1968 **X:** 36

Bush, George H. W. **X:** 45

Camp David accords **X:** 54–55, 55

Chrysler Corporation Loan Guarantee Act **X:** 62

Clinton, William **X:** 65, 67

cold war (end of) **X:** 71

conservative movement **X:** 79

defense policy **X:** 86

détente **X:** 89

Dole, Robert **X:** 90

economy **X:** 94

education, primary and secondary **X:** 100

Energy, U.S. Department of **X:** 103

energy crisis **X:** 104

ERA **X:** 107

evangelical Christians **X:** 108

Ford, Gerald R. **X:** 119, 121

foreign policy **X:** 123

Ginsburg, Ruth Bader **X:** 130

Haiti, U.S. intervention in **X:** 140

Helms, Jesse A., Jr. **X:** 141

independent counsel **X:** 150

Iranian hostage crisis **X:** 156

Kennedy, Edward M. **X:** 164

Koreagate **X:** 166

Latin America **X:** 172, 173

"Malaise " speech **X:** 341–344

Mitchell, George **X:** 194

Mondale, Walter F. **X:** 196

neoconservatism **X:** 216

NEPA **X:** 210

Nicaragua **X:** 218

Nobel Peace Prize **X:** 59

nuclear freeze movement **X:** 224

OMB **X:** 227

O'Neill, Thomas P., Jr. **X:** 228

Panama Canal turnover **X:** 232, 233

Peace Corps **IX:** 241

political parties **X:** 238

Reagan, Ronald W. **X:** 259

Richardson, Elliot L. **X:** 268

South Africa **X:** 279

Soviet Union **X:** 280

Strategic Arms Limitation Treaties **X:** 289

Supreme Court **X:** 291

terrorism **X:** 297

United Nations **X:** 308

veto, presidential **X:** 311

wage and price controls **X:** 313

Weather Underground **X:** 318

Carter, Landon **II: 53–54**

Carter, Robert **III:** 250, 251

Carter, Robert "King" **II:** 11, 53–54, **54,** 104

Carteret, Sir George **II:** 54, 144–145, 252, 253

Carteret, Philip **II: 54**

Carter family **II:** 172; **VIII:** 222

Cartier, Jacques **I: 57–59,** 58*m*, 387*c*; **II:** 126

Acadia **I:** 2

Hochelaga **I:** 163

Iroquois **I:** 182

Maliseet **I:** 219

Montagnais-Naskapi **I:** 241

Northwest Passage **I:** 266

Ramusio, Giovanni Battista **I:** 305

cartography **V: 51–52,** 309; **VI:** 160, 227, 228. *See also mappae mundi*

art **II:** 25

Behaim, Martin **I:** 27

Blaeu, Willem **I:** 31

Brendan the Navigator, Saint **I:** 34

Cabot, Sebastian **I:** 42

Cathay (China) **I:** 66

Champlain, Samuel de **II:** 56

Columbia River **IV:** 93

Columbus, Bartholomew **I:** 78–79

Columbus, Christopher **I:** 79, 80, 82

Eden, Richard **I:** 118

exploration **II:** 114, 115; **IV:** 132, 133

fur trade **IV:** 157

Harriot, Thomas **I:** 154

Henry the Navigator **I:** 158

Jolliet, Louis **II:** 178

Le Moyne, Jacques **I:** 202–203

Leonardo da Vinci **I:** 204

mappae mundi **I:** 221

Marquette, Jacques **II:** 205, 206

Mercator, Gerhardus **I:** 231–232

Norumbega **I:** 266

Pennsylvania **II:** 277

Pike, Zebulon Montgomery **IV:** 281–282

Ricci, Matteo **I:** 312

T-O maps **I:** 358

Vespucci, Amerigo **I:** 368

Waldseemüller, Martin **I:** 371

Wood, William **II:** 410

cartoons **II:** 179; **VIII:** 207, 275

cartoons, political **V:** 247–248

Caruso, Enrico **VII:** 194, *195*

Carver, George Washington **VI: 45, 308,** 327*c*

Carver, John **II:** 217, 283

Carver, Jonathan **IV:** 93

Carver, Raymond **X:** 177, 178

Cary, Mary Ann Shadd **V:** 52

Casablanca **VIII:** 392

Casablanca (film) **VIII:** 218, 409*c*

Casablanca Conference (1943) **VIII: 52,** 409*c*

Arnold, "Hap" **VIII:** 22

Hopkins, Harry **VIII:** 157

Italian campaign **VIII:** 168

Marshall, George C. **VIII:** 206

second front **VIII:** 320

Sicily **VIII:** 325

World War II European theater **VIII:** 393

Yalta Conference **VIII:** 401

Casa de Contratación **I: 59–61,** 60*m*, 95, **142,** 323

Case, Clifford **X:** 24

casemates **V:** 183

Casey, William **X:** 43

Casey v. Planned Parenthood (1992) **X:** 17

cash-and-carry **VIII: 52–53,** 408*c*

Anglo-American relations **VIII:** 16

foreign policy **VIII:** 124

Lend-Lease Act **VIII:** 184

Neutrality Acts **VIII:** 239

casinos **X:** 7, 263

Casola, Pietro **I:** 365

Casor, John **II:** 176

Cass, Lewis **X: 76–77,** 378*c*

American Fur Company **IV:** 16

Benton, Thomas Hart **IV:** 50

Fillmore, Millard **IV:** 137

Free-Soil Party **IV:** 150

Polk, James K. **IV:** 283

popular sovereignty **IV:** 285

Taylor, Zachary **IV:** 335

Cassady, Neal **IX:** 35, 71, 159–160

Cassatt, Mary **V:** 16; **VI: 45–46,** 138, 325*c*

cassava **I:** 77

Cassell, John **VI:** 116

castas **I: 61–62,** 261; **II:** 356

Castelar, Emilio **VI:** 305

Castellion, Sébastien **I:** 50

castes **II:** 53, 356

Castile **I: 62–64**

Acosta, José de **I:** 3

Charles V **I:** 67, 69

Columbus, Christopher **I:** 80, 81

conquistadores **I:** 84

corregidores **I:** 90

Ferdinand and Isabella **I:** 127, 128

Ibn Khaldûn **I:** 174

Jews (Judaism) **I:** 190

Philip II **I:** 281

Reconquista **I:** 306

Seville **I:** 323

smallpox **I:** 330

Tordesillas, Treaty of **I:** 358

Castillo, Alonso del **I:** 37–38

Castillo, Diego del **II: 54–55**

Castillo Armas, Carlos **IX:** 172

Castillo de San Marcos **II:** 121, 327

castizos **I:** 233, 234

Castle Garden, New York **IV:** 178; **V:** 176

castles **I:** 11

Casto, Don M. **IX:** 288

Castro, Fidel **IX:** 332*c*; **X:** 31, 135, 142, 172, 326*c*

anticommunism **IX:** 14

Bay of Pigs **IX:** 33–35

cold war **IX:** 60

Cuban missile crisis **IX:** 73

Latin America **IX:** 172

Operation Mongoose **IX:** 236

Castro, Dona Izabel de **I:** 44
casualties, Civil War **V:** 67, 77
Catalina Island **IX:** 328
Catawba **II: 55,** 353; **V:** 249
    disease **II:** 90
    fur trade **II:** 130–131
    Montour, Madame **II:** 233
    Native Americans **II:** 244
    North Carolina **II:** 263,
        264
    society, British American
        II: 352
    Tuscarora **II:** 378
Catcher in the Rye, The (J. D.
    Salinger) **IX:** 182
Catchings, Waddill **VIII:** 89
Catch-22 (Joseph Heller) **IX:**
    181
Catesby, Mark **II: 55–56,** 405
Cathay (China) **I: 64–66,** 65*m*
    Cabot, John **I:** 41–42
    Columbus, Christopher **I:**
        79
    Company of Cathay **I:** 83
    Dutch East India
        Company **I:** 115
    Ibn Battuta **I:** 173
    Jesuits **I:** 189
    Polo, Marco **I:** 286, 287
    printing press **I:** 293
    Ricci, Matteo **I:** 311–312
    silver **I:** 325
    slave trade **I:** 328
    sugar **I:** 338
Cathay Company **I:** 133
cathedrals (London) **I:** 208
Cather, Willa **VII:** 160
Catherine of Aragón **I:** 387*c*
    Church of England **I:** 73,
        74
    Henry VII **I:** 159
    Henry VIII **I:** 159, 160
    Mary I **I:** 223–224
    Reformation **I:** 309
Catherine the Great **III:** 190
Catherwood, Frederick **I:** 86;
    IV: 133
Catholic Bishops' Letter **X:**
    59–60
Catholic Church. *See* Roman
    Catholic Church/Roman
    Catholicism
Catholic Conference of Bishops
    X: 248
Catholic immigrants **VII:** 59
Catholic Interracial Council
    VIII: 54
Catholicism. *See* Roman
    Catholic Church/Roman
    Catholicism
Catholic League **I:** 158
Catholic Reformation. *See*
    Counterreformation

Catholic University of America
    VI: 249–250
Catholic Worker (newspaper)
    VIII: 406*c*
Catholic Worker movement
    VIII: 54, 303
Catlin, George **IV:** 55, **77–78**
*Catlin's North American Indian
    Portfolio* **IV:** 78
*Catlin's Notes of Eight Years'
    Travels and Residence in
    Europe* **IV:** 78
Cato Institute **X:** 177, 302
Cato's Letters (Trenchard and
    Gordon) **III:** 79
Cats (musical) **X:** 201
CAT scan machine **X:** 189
Catt, Carrie Lane Chapman **VI:**
    260, 261; **VII: 43–44,** 198,
    335–337, 339–340, 355*c*
cattle **I:** 77, 150, 214; **IV:** 9, 10,
    339; **VI:** 20
    agriculture **II:** 11–13
    animals **II:** 21
    Caribbean **II:** 52
    Johnson, Anthony **II:** 175
    Johnson, Mary **II:** 175
    Navajo **II:** 247
    tenants **II:** 370
    Ward, Nancy **II:** 392
    wolves **II:** 405
cattle kingdom **VI: 46–47,** 47*m*
Catto, Octavius **V: 52–53**
"caudle" **II:** 15
Causton, Thomas **II:** 394
cavalry **V:** 72, 133–134, 364
Caverly, John R. **VII:** 62
Cayor **I: 66,** 185
Cayuga **I: 66–67,** 160, 181–183,
    271; **II:** 67, 85, 168, 243, 256;
    III: 178
CB&Q. *See* Chicago, Burlington
    & Quincy Railway Company
CBN (Christian Broadcasting
    Network) **X:** 294
CBS. *See* Columbia
    Broadcasting System
CBS Evening News **X:** 296
CC. *See* Christian Coalition
CCA. *See* Citizens' Council of
    America
CCC. *See* Civilian Conservation
    Corps
CDA. *See* Communications
    Decency Act of 1996
CDC. *See* Centers for Disease
    Control
CD-ROMs **X:** 187. *See also*
    compact discs
CEA. *See* Council of Economic
    Advisors
Ce Actl Topiltzin Quetzalcoatl **I:**
    301

Ceaușescu, Nicolae **X:** 157
Cecil, Sir Robert **II:** 50, 81
Cedar Creek, Battle of
    De Forest, John William
        V: 92
    Early, Jubal A. **V:** 103
    Shenandoah Valley:
        Sheridan's campaign **V:**
        318
    Sheridan, Philip H. **V:** 318
Cedar Mountain, Battle of **V:**
    43, **53,** 168, 186
Cedars Tavern **III:** 160
cedar trees **I:** 30
Cedras, Raoul **X:** 67, 328*c*
"Celebrated Jumping Frog of
    Calaveras County" (Twain) **V:**
    213, 408*c*; **VI:** 297
Celera Genomics **X:** 146
Celler, Emanuel **X:** 105
Cempoala **I:** 93
cenotes **I:** 69, 378
Censor, The **III:** 267
censorship **V:** 351, 370, 394;
    VIII: 54–55; X: 60–61
    American Civil Liberties
        Union **VIII:** 13
    Birth of a Nation **VII:** 31
    Catholics **VIII:** 54
    civil liberties **VIII:** 60
    conservatism **VIII:** 72
    Coughlin, Father Charles
        E. **VII:** 76
    Greenwich Village **VII:** 115
    Libertarian Party **X:** 176
    movies **VIII:** 218; **X:** 198
    news media **VIII:** 243
    OWI **VIII:** 257
    popular culture **VIII:** 274,
        275
    pornography **X:** 244, 245
    Schenk v. United States
        VII: 275
    television **X:** 295, 297
    Trading with the Enemy
        Act **VII:** 311
    World War I **VII:** 344
    World War II **VIII:** 389,
        394
census **IV:** 6, 187
Center for Strategic and
    International Studies **X:** 302
Center for the Study of
    Responsive Law **IX:** 69; **X:**
    205
Centers for Disease Control
    (CDC) **IX:** 198, 199,
    249–250, 329*c*; **X:** 5
Central America **II:** 285, 337,
    355, 358, 359; **IV:** 379*c*; **V:**
    126, 127, 276; **X:** 71, 123,
    124, 149. *See also specific
    countries*

Clayton-Bulwer Treaty **IV:**
    88
Columbus, Christopher **I:**
    82
    corn (maize) **I:** 87–88
    foreign policy **IV:** 142
    Manifest Destiny **IV:**
        218–219
    Monroe Doctrine **IV:**
        241–242
Central American Court of
    Justice **VI:** 44–45
Central American descent,
    Americans of **X:** 143
Central Andes **I:** 10
Central and Southern States
    Pension fund **IX:** 11–12
central Europe **X:** 86, 223
central European immigrants
    VI: 139, 140
Central Intelligence Agency
    (CIA) **VIII:** 164, 257, 409*c*;
    IX: 49–50, 329*c*, 331*c*
    Bay of Pigs **IX:** 33–35
    Boland Amendment **X:** 38
    Bush, George H. W. **X:** 45
    cold war **IX:** 60; **X:** 71
    foreign policy **X:** 124
    impeachment **X:** 149–150
    Iran-contra affair **X:** 154
    Latin America **IX:** 172; **X:**
        173
    LSD **IX:** 183
    military-industrial complex
        IX: 204
    National Security Act of
        1947 **IX:** 224
    Nicaragua **X:** 218
    North, Oliver L. **X:** 222
    Operation Mongoose **IX:**
        236
    Reagan, Ronald W. **X:** 260
    terrorism **X:** 297, 298, 300
    wars of national liberation
        IX: 317
Central Labor Union **VI:** 167
Central Pacific Railroad **V:** 409*c*;
    VI: 40, 179–180, 237
    Crédit Mobilier **V:** 85
    Pacific Railroad Act of
        1862 **V:** 263
    railroads **V:** 290
    transportation **V:** 355
Central Park, New York City **V:**
    61, 253, 257
Central Powers **VII:** 343
Central Trust Company of
    Illinois **VII:** 62–63
centrifugal cream separator **VI:**
    8
Century magazine **V:** 212, 216
Century of Dishonor, A
    (Jackson) **VI:** 325*c*, 330–332

CEQ. *See* Council on
 Environmental Quality
cerebral meningitis **IV:** 82
ceremonies and rituals. *See also*
 sacrifices
  cacao **I:** 45
  feudalism **I:** 129
  Haida **I:** 150
  Huron **I:** 171
  Igbo **I:** 175
  Inca **I:** 176
  Iroquois **I:** 181, 182
  Maya **I:** 228
  Native American religion
   I: 252–253
  Olmecs **I:** 269
  Puerto Rico **I:** 296
  tobacco **I:** 353
  Zuni **I:** 383
CERN. *See* European
 Laboratory for Particle
 Physics
Cerro Gordo, Battle of **IV:** 304
Cerro Rico **I:** 291
CERT (Computer Emergency
 Response Team) **X:** 153
certification (for aid) **X:**
 192–193
Cervera, Pascual **VI:** 272
CES. *See* Committee on
 Economic Security
Ceylon **I:** 76
chac-mool **I:** 70
Chaco Canyon **I:** 255; **II:** 303
Chad **I:** 155, 196
CHADD (Children and Adults
 with ADD) **X:** 190
Chadwick, George W. **VI:** 201,
 202
Chadwick, Henry **VI:** 21
Chaffee, Roger **IX:** 219, 279
"chain migration" **V:** 176
chain stores **VI: 47–48,** 290;
 VII: 75
Chak the Thunderer **I:** 228
Chak Toh Ich'ak **I:** 349
Chalco **I:** 71
Challenge of Peace, The. *See*
 Catholic Bishops' Letter
Challenger space shuttle **X:** 283,
 327*c*
Chamberlain, George Earl **VII:**
 255
Chamberlain, John **X:** 43
Chamberlain, Joshua L. **V:**
 53–54, 148, **365,** 384
Chamberlain, Neville **VIII:** 16,
 176, 220
Chamberlin, Thomas C. **VI:**
 257
Chambers, Whittaker **IX:**
 50–51, 134, 137; **X:** 43, 219
Chamorro, Antonio **I:** 216

Chamorro, Violeta Barrios de **X:**
 218
Champlain, Samuel de **II: 56,**
 64, 417*c*
  Brulé, Étienne **II:** 44
  exploration **II:** 114
  French colonies **II:**
   126–127
  Hochelaga **I:** 163
  Huron **I:** 172
  Iroquois **I:** 183
  literature **II:** 195
  Maliseet **I:** 219
  Native Americans **II:** 243
  New Hampshire **II:** 250
  Norumbega **I:** 266
  Passamaquoddy **I:** 278
  Squanto **II:** 360–361
  Vermont **II:** 381
Champlain Canal **IV:** 128
Champoton **I:** 92, 93
Chamuscado, Francisco **I:** 256
Chanca, Diego Álvarez **I:** 54
Chanca people **I:** 175
Chancellor, Richard **I:** 265
Chancellorsville, Battle of **V:**
 54–56, 55*m*, **56,** 407*c*
  Alexander, Edward P. **V:** 7
  Early, Jubal A. **V:** 103
  Ewell, Richard Stoddert **V:**
   119
  German-American
   regiments **V:** 147
  Hancock, Winfield Scott **V:**
   163
  Hill, Ambrose P. **V:** 168
  Howard, O. O. **V:** 173
  Irish-American regiments
   V: 182
  Jackson, "Stonewall" **V:**
   186
  Lee, Robert E. **V:** 206
  Longstreet, James **V:** 215
  Meade, George Gordon **V:**
   226
  Sickles, Daniel E. **V:** 326
  Stuart, J. E. B. **V:** 341
  Wilderness, Battle of the
   V: 395
  Zouaves **V:** *404*
Chandler, Raymond **VIII:** 193
Chandler, Zechariah **V:** 178,
 191
Chaney, James **IX:** 66, 67, 207,
 254, 334*c*
Chango (Shango) **I:** 263, 273
channeling **X:** 216, 217
Channing, William Ellery **III:**
 355
  Brook Farm **IV:** 58
  Fuller, Margaret **IV:** 155
  literature **IV:** 212
  religion **IV:** 298

Chaplin, Charlie **VII:** 85, 190,
 190, 191, 359*c*; **VIII:** 217,
 274
Chapman, J. Wilburn **VII:** 302
Chapman, Mark David **X:** 31
character, American **III:** 97
Charbonneau, Toussaint **III:**
 210, 315
Charge, A (Hall) **III:** 160
"Charges Against the Virginia
 Governor" (Bacon) **II:**
 423–424
Charismatic movement **IX:** 256
charitable societies **VIII:** 304
charity schools **II:** 20
Charlemagne (Charles I) **I:** 165,
 306
Charles (Carlos) V, king of Spain
 and Holy Roman Emperor **I:**
 67–69, 68*m*
  Barbados **I:** 26
  Cabeza de Vaca, Álvar
   Núñez **I:** 38
  cabildo **I:** 39
  Cabot, Sebastian **I:** 43
  Castile **I:** 63
  Church of England **I:** 73
  Council of the Indies **I:** 95
  Holy Roman Empire **I:**
   165–166
  Las Casas, Bartolomé de **I:**
   198–200
  Luther, Martin **I:** 211, 212
  Magellan, Ferdinand **I:**
   215
  Mary I **I:** 224
  Mendoza, Antonio de **I:**
   231
  Mercator, Gerhardus **I:**
   232
  Oviedo y Valdés, Gonzalo
   Fernández de **I:** 272
  Philip II **I:** 281
  Reformation **I:** 307, 309
  Sepúlveda, Juan Ginés de
   I: 322
  Trent, Council of **I:** 360
  Vitoria, Francisco de **I:** 370
  Zumárraga, Juan de **I:** 382
Charles I, king of England
  English Civil War **II:** 108
  Gorton, Samuel **II:** 142
  government, British
   American **II:** 142
  Maryland **II:** 209
  Massachusetts **II:** 212
  monarchy, British **II:** 232
  North Carolina **II:** 265
  St. Mary's City **II:** 328
  South Carolina **II:** 353
  Virginia Company of
   London **II:** 387
  Wyatt, Sir Francis **II:** 411

Charles II, king of England **II:**
 418*c*
  Charleston **II:** 56
  Culpeper, Thomas, Lord
   II: 79
  English Civil War **II:** 108
  Glorious Revolution **II:**
   140–141
  government, British
   American **II:** 144, 145
  Maryland **II:** 209
  monarchy, British **II:** 232
  New Jersey **II:** 252
  New York **II:** 260
  North Carolina **II:** 265
  Penn, William **II:** 273
  Pennsylvania **II:** 275
  piracy **II:** 285
  postal service **II:** 292
  Quakers **II:** 308
  Royal African Company **II:**
   325
  South Carolina **II:** 353
Charles III, king of Spain **II:**
 199; **III:** 205
Charles IV, king of Spain **II:** 199
Charles Manson "family" **X:** 31
Charles River Bridge case **IV:**
 331
Charleston, siege of **III: 63–64,**
 394*c*
  Clinton, Sir Henry **III:** 75
  Continental navy **III:** 90
  Cornwallis, Lord **III:** 93
  Estaing, comte d' **III:** 120
  Greene, Nathanael **III:**
   156
  Jefferson, Thomas **III:** 184
  Jews **III:** 187
  Kościuszko, Tadeusz **III:**
   198
  L'Enfant, Pierre-Charles
   III: 207
  Marion, Francis **III:** 231,
   232
  Revolutionary War **III:**
   305
Charleston, South Carolina **II:**
 56–57, 418*c*; **IV:** 376*c*
  Balloon Corps **V:** 22
  Beauregard, Pierre **V:** 27
  Bonnet, Stede **II:** 34
  Carney, William H. **V:** 49
  cities and urban life **II:** 61,
   62
  crafts **II:** 73–74
  Dahlgren, John A. B. **V:** 87
  disease and epidemics **II:**
   90–92; **IV:** 112
  economy **II:** 102
  54th Massachusetts
   Regiment **V:** 126
  Great Awakening **II:** 148

Charleston, South Carolina
(*continued*)
    Grimké, Angelina and
      Sarah **IV:** 164
    Hume, Sophia Wigington
      II: 159–160
    Jews **II:** 175
    Johnston, Henrietta
      Deering **II:** 177
    journalism **II:** 178
    Lining, John **II:** 194
    Mallory, Stephen R. **V:** 221
    marine corps **V:** 222
    Middleton, Arthur **II:** 224
    mills **II:** 225
    miscegenation **II:** 229
    Morton, Thomas **II:** 236
    mulattoes **II:** 238
    music **II:** 239
    Ostenaco **II:** 269
    Pinckney, Elizabeth Lucas
      II: 284
    piracy **II:** 285
    Priber, Christian Gottlieb
      II: 297
    Queen Anne's War **II:** 309
    railroads **IV:** 293, 295
    Reconstruction **V:** 295
    refugees **V:** 298
    secession **V:** 313
    slave resistance **II:** 337
    smallpox **II:** 345
    South Carolina **II:** 354
    Teach, Edward **II:** 369
    theater **II:** 373
    Theus, Jeremiah **II:** 373
    travel **II:** 377
    Union navy **V:** 370
    Vesey, Denmark **IV:**
      353–354
    Whitefield, George **II:** 397
    yellow fever **II:** 414
Charleston Daily Courier **V:** 102
Charleston Mercury **V:** 135–136
Charles Town. *See* Charleston,
  South Carolina
Charlestown, Massachusetts **IV:**
  21
Charles Towne **I:** 76
Charlotte, a Tale of Truth
  (Rowson) **III:** 282, 311
Charlottesville, Virginia **III:**
  184, 185
charnel houses **I:** 244, 245
Charred Body **I:** 161
Charter of Liberties **II:** 261
Charter of Privileges **II:** 276
Chartier, Martin **II:** 130
Chase, Salmon P. **V: 56–57; VI:**
  205
    assassination of Abraham
      Lincoln **V:** 19

banking and currency **V:**
  24
economy **V:** 105
greenbacks **V:** 159
impeachment of Andrew
  Johnson **V:** 178
Kansas-Nebraska Act of
  1854 **V:** 198
Port Royal, South
  Carolina, Experiment **V:**
  279
Republican Party **V:** 301
Wade, Benjamin **V:** 385
Chase, Samuel **III: 64–65,** 65,
  397*c*
    Brackenridge, Hugh
      Henry **III:** 46
    impeachment **III:** 175
    Marbury v. Madison **III:**
      231
    Marshall, John **III:** 236
    Randolph, John **III:** 296
    Supreme Court **III:** 338
Chase, William Merritt **VI:**
  48–49, 138, 219
Chatham Chest **I:** 112
Chattanooga, Battle of **V:** 57,
  407*c*
    Blair, Francis P., Jr. **V:** 30
    Bragg, Braxton **V:** 36
    Civil War **V:** 66
    Grant, Ulysses S. **V:** 156
    Hooker, Joseph **V:** 173
    Howard, O. O. **V:** 173
    Johnston, Joseph E. **V:** 190
    Longstreet, James **V:** 215
    Morgan, John Hunt **V:**
      240
    Rosecrans, William S. **V:**
      305
    Sherman, William T. **V:**
      321
    Thomas, George H. **V:** 354
Chattanooga, Tennessee **V:** 58,
  59. *See also* Lookout
  Mountain, Battle of
Chauncey, Isaac **III: 65**
Chauncy, Charles **II: 57,** 68,
  155; **III:** 355
Chautauqua Institute **VI: 49**
Chautauqua movement **VI:** 92,
  241
Chauvin, Pierre **II:** 126
Chávez, César Estrada **IX:** 41,
  174, 304, 334*c*; **X:** 16, 141,
  288
Chavis, Benjamin **X:** 209
Cheatham, Benjamin **V:** 324
"Checkers" speech (Nixon) **IX:**
  297; **X:** 220
Checkley, John **II:** 390
cheese **IV:** 9, 10

Chemawa Indian School
  (Oregon) **VII:** 207
chemical industry **VII:** 311,
  360*c*
chemical weapons **IX:** 82; **X:**
  152, 236
chemistry **II:** 330; **III:** 312, 321;
  VI: 257; **VIII:** 318
La Chenette. *See* Montour,
  Madame
Cheney, Lynne **X:** 209
Cheney, Richard B. **X:** 46, 48,
  129, 276
Chepian **I:** 225
Cher (singer) **X:** 203
Cheraw **II:** 379
Chernomyrdin, Viktor **X:** 134
Cherokee, Confederate **V:** 250,
  391
Cherokee, Union **V:** 250
Cherokee/Cherokee nation **I:**
  85; **II: 57–58; III: 65–66,**
  392*c*; **IV:** 310, 376*c*–378*c*; **V:**
  250, 390–391; **VI:** 209; **VIII:**
  236; **X:** 215. *See also* Five
  Civilized Tribes
    agriculture **II:** 8
    BIA **IV:** 181
    Brims **II:** 41
    Charleston **II:** 56
    cotton culture **IV:** 98
    Creek nation **III:** 97
    disease **II:** 90
    Dragging Canoe **III:** 107
    Franklin, state of **III:** 135
    fur trade **II:** 130–131
    Georgia **II:** 138
    Handsome Lake **III:** 164
    Horseshoe Bend, Battle of
      IV: 173
    Houston, Sam **IV:** 174
    Indian Removal Act (1830)
      IV: 181, 182*m*, 183
    Iroquois **II:** 168
    Lyon, Matthew **III:** 223
    Marion, Francis **III:** 231
    Native Americans **IV:** 256,
      257
    Native Americans and the
      Revolution **III:** 254, 255
    Native Americans in the
      War of 1812 **IV:** 259
    North Carolina **II:** 263,
      264
    Nullification Controversy
      IV: 263–264
    Ostenaco **II:** 269
    Pontiac's Rebellion **III:**
      281
    Priber, Christian Gottlieb
      II: 297
    South Carolina **II:** 353

    South Carolina Regulation
      III: 330
    Supreme Court decision
      IV: 331
    trade and shipping **II:** 375
    Trail of Tears **IV:** 343, 344
    Ward, Nancy **II:** 391–392
Cherokee Nation v. Georgia **IV:**
  376*c*
    Jackson, Andrew **IV:** 193
    Nullification Controversy
      IV: 264
    Supreme Court decision
      IV: 331
    Trail of Tears **IV:** 344
Cherokee Phoenix, The **IV:** 183
Cherokee Reconstruction Treaty
  of 1866 **V:** 391
Cherokee War **II:** 420*c*
Cherry, Francis **IX:** 108
Cherry Creek, Colorado **IV:** 282
Chesapeake, USS **IV:** 152, 161,
  358
Chesapeake & Ohio Canal **IV:**
  73, 73*m*, 83
Chesapeake Bay **I:** 292, 367; **II:**
  58–59, 59*m*; **IV:** 39, 358; **V:**
  303
    fertility **II:** 117
    Gates, Sir Thomas **II:** 135
    Glorious Revolution **II:**
      141
    housing **II:** 157
    indentured servitude **II:**
      163–165
    iron manufacturing **II:** 167
    Jamestown **II:** 171
    labor **II:** 187–188
    manufacturing and
      industry **II:** 204
    marriage and family life **II:**
      206
    Maryland **II:** 209, 211
    miscegenation **II:** 228
    mortality **II:** 234–235
    Mount Vernon **II:** 237
    Newport, Christopher **II:**
      259
    Smith, John **II:** 346
    Virginia **II:** 382
Chesapeake-Leopard affair **III:**
  66–67, 397*c*; **IV:** 105
    embargo of 1807 **III:** 117
    foreign affairs **III:** 130
    Jefferson, Thomas **III:** 186
    Little Belt incident **III:**
      216
    Orders in Council **III:** 267
Chesapeake region
    African Americans **II:** 6
    agriculture **II:** 10
    Anglican Church **II:** 19

architecture **II:** 23
Calvert, George **II:** 50
class **II:** 63
convict labor **II:** 71–72
disease **II:** 90
domesticity **II:** 93
economy **II:** 101
education **II:** 104
English immigrants **II:** 108
New Jersey **II:** 253
population trends **II:** 291
primogeniture and entail
  II: 297
shipbuilding **II:** 335
slavery **II:** 338, 340
society, British American
  II: 349, 350
tobacco **II:** 374
travel **II:** 377
Virginia **II:** 382, 385
Westo **II:** 394–395
women's status and rights
  II: 407
Chesepioc. *See* Chesapeake Bay
Chesnut, James, Jr. **V:** 58
Chesnut, Mary B. **V: 58**
Chesnutt, Charles W. **VI:** 6, 177
Chest at Chatham **I:** 157
Chester, Thomas Morris **IV:** 15
Chestnut Street Theater,
  Philadelphia **III:** *347*
cheveaux-de-frise **II:** 348
Cheves, Langdon **IV:** 42
Chevrolet Motor Company **IX:**
  120
Cheyenne/Cheyenne nation **II:**
  50; **V:** 213, 341, 405*c*, 407*c;*
  VI: 324*c*
  Bent, William **IV:** 48
  Carson, Kit **IV:** 75
  Colorado gold rush **IV:** 90
  Fort Laramie **IV:** 144
Chiang Kai-shek. *See* Jiang
  Jieshi
Chicago and Northwestern
  Railroad **IV:** 188
Chicago and Rock Island
  Railroad **IV:** 188
Chicago blues **VIII:** 223, 224
Chicago, Burlington & Quincy
  Railway Company (CB&Q)
  IV: 188
  Hill, James J. **VI:** 129
  Morgan, John Pierpont **VI:**
    197, 198
  railroads **VI:** 239
  transportation, urban **VI:**
    292
  Wells-Barnett, Ida Bell **VI:**
    312
Chicago Defender **VII:** 113;
  VIII: 243

"Chicago Eight" **X: 61,** 323*c*
Chicago Fire of 1871 **V:** 107
  Bradwell, Myra Colby **VI:**
    34
  inventions and technology
    VI: 149
  Moody, Dwight Lyman **VI:**
    196
  Sullivan, Louis H. **VI:** 279
Chicago, Illinois **II:** 61; **V:** 168,
  204; **VI:** 323*c;* **VIII:** 120, 210,
  211; **IX:** 319. *See also*
  Democratic National
  Convention of 1968
  Altgeld, John Peter **VI:** 10
  cities and urban life **IV:** 82,
    84; **VI:** 53, 55
  gun control **X:** 137
  Haymarket riot **VI:**
    127–128
  industrialization **IV:** 187
  internal improvements **IV:**
    188
  Jackson, Jesse L. **X:** 159
  McCormick, Cyrus Hall
    IV: 225
  population trends **VI:** 226
  Pullman Strike **VI:**
    235–236
  race and racial conflict **X:**
    255
  settlement houses **VI:**
    259
  skyscrapers **VI:** 264
  temperance movement **IV:**
    337
  Weather Underground **X:**
    318
  World's Columbian
    Exposition **VI:** 319–320
Chicago, Milwaukee, and St.
  Paul Railroad **IV:** 188
Chicago Public Library **VI:** 176
"Chicago School" of
  architecture **VI:** 280
Chicago Seven **IX:** 131
Chicago Stock Exchange **VI:**
  280
Chicago Symphony Orchestra
  VI: 201
Chicago Tribune **V:** 101; **VI:**
  179, 181, 304, 325*c*
Chicago White Sox **VII:** 26, 301,
  360*c*
Chicago Women's Liberation
  Union **X:** 114
Chicago World's Fair (1893). *See*
  World Columbian Exposition
Chicano civil rights **IX:** 171,
  327–328. *See also* Latino
  movement
Chicano movement **X:** 142

Chicano Youth Liberation
  conferences **IX:** 125
Chicaza **I:** 333
Chichén Itzá **I: 69–71,** *70*
  art and architecture **I:** 12
  Maya **I:** 227
  Native American religion
    I: 252
  Toltecs **I:** 356
  Yucatán Peninsula **I:** 378
Chichimeca **I:** 356
chichimecos **II:** 394
Chickahominy **II:** 294, 295
Chickamauga, Battle of **V:**
  58–59
  Chattanooga, Battle of **V:**
    57
  Cleburne, Patrick Ronayne
    V: 68
  homefront **V:** 169
  Hood, John Bell **V:** 171
  Longstreet, James **V:** 215
  Lookout Mountain, Battle
    of **V:** 216
  Orphan Brigade **V:** 258
  Rosecrans, William S. **V:**
    305
  Sheridan, Philip H. **V:** 318
  Thomas, George H. **V:** 354
Chickamaugan nation
  Cherokee nation **III:** 66
  Dragging Canoe **III:** 107
  Franklin, state of **III:** 135
  Wilderness Road **III:** 378
Chickasaw Bayou, Mississippi **V:**
  320, 380
Chickasaw/Chickasaw nation **II:**
  59; III: 72; **IV:** 98, 181,
  182*m*, 343, 344; **V:** 250; **VI:**
  209. *See also* Five Civilized
  Tribes
  agriculture **II:** 8
  Choctaw **II:** 61
  French colonies **II:** 129
  fur trade **II:** 130–131
  Le Moyne, Jean-Baptiste,
    sieur de Bienville **II:**
    193
  Louisiana **II:** 199
  Natchez Revolt **II:** 242
  Native Americans **II:** 246
  Red Shoes **II:** 313
  society, British American
    II: 352
Chickasaw War **II:** 129, 246
chickens **II:** 21, 122, 370
chief justices **VIII:** 409*c*. *See
  also* Supreme Court
Chihuahua **II:** 231
Chilapa **I:** 4
Child, Lydia Maria **IV:** 167, 213;
  V: 2

child abuse **X:** 266, 267
childbirth **I:** 20
  alcohol **II:** 15
  fertility **II:** 117–118
  marriage and family life **II:**
    207
  midwives **II:** 224–225
  mortality **II:** 234, 235
  women's status and rights
    II: 409
child care **VIII:** 205; **X:**
  114–116, 183
childhood. *See*
  children/childhood
child labor **III:** 177, 178; **IV:**
  273; **VII: 44–47,** *45,* 358*c,*
  359*c;* **VIII:** 56, 110
  Abbott, Grace **VII:** 1
  Adamson Act **VII:** 2
  AFL **VII:** 10
  Democratic Party **VII:** 66
  Goldmark, Josephine **VII:**
    111
  Keating-Owen Act **VII:**
    145
  Kelley, Florence **VII:** 146
  marriage and family life
    VII: 172
  Muller v. Oregon **VII:**
    192
  Smith, Alfred E. **VII:** 287
  Wald, Lillian **VII:** 329
  youth **VII:** 351
Child Labor Act of 1919 **VII:**
  359*c,* 360*c*
*Child Labor Legislation
  Handbook* (Goldmark) **VII:**
  111
Child Online Protection Act of
  1998 **X:** 245
child pornography **X:** 74, 245,
  258
childrearing **VII:** 172, 213. *See
  also* youth
Children and Adults with ADD
  (CHADD) **X:** 190
children/childhood **I:** 320; **II:**
  59–60; V: 108, 222–223; **VI:**
  159; **VII: 350–352; VIII:**
  55–57
  AASS **IV:** 14
  African Americans **X:** 10
  baby boomers **X:** 33
  *Brown v. Board of
    Education* **IX:** 42
  child labor **VII:** 44–46
  Children's Bureau **VII:** 47
  Clinton, Hillary Rodham
    X: 64
  computers **X:** 74
  cosmetics industry **VII:**
    57–58

children/childhood (continued)
　crime and punishment **II:** 75
　criminal justice **VII:** 59
　disease **II:** 92
　economy **II:** 101
　education **II:** 103, 104; **IV:** 120; **VII:** 76–79; **VIII:** 93
　FSA **X:** 110
　gay rights movement **X:** 128
　German immigrants **II:** 139
　Heathcote, Caleb **II:** 155
　Huron **II:** 160
　industrialization **IV:** 185
　labor **II:** 188, 189
　marriage and family life **II:** 206–208; **IV:** 221; **VII:** 172; **VIII:** 204; **X:** 109, 110, 181, 183
　Massachusetts School Act **II:** 216–217
　media **X:** 185
　medicine **VIII:** 208; **X:** 190
　mortality **II:** 234, 235
　mothers' pensions **VII:** 189
　NYA **VIII:** 234–235
　popular culture **X:** 239
　population trends **X:** 244
　pornography **X:** 244, 245
　poverty **X:** 245, 246
　recreation **VIII:** 296, 298
　refugees **VIII:** 298
　Reno, Janet **X:** 267
　sexuality **VII:** 283
　slave trade **II:** 344
　smallpox **II:** 345
　social work **VII:** 290
　society, British American **II:** 350
　Spock, Benjamin **IX:** 279
　tobacco suits **X:** 305
　Turell, Jane Colman **II:** 378
　Virginia **II:** 384
　War on Poverty **IX:** 313
　women's network **VIII:** 383
　women's status and rights **II:** 407, 408
　yellow fever **II:** 414
　Yep, Laurence **IX:** 327
　YMCA/YWCA **VII:** 349–350
Children's Bureau **VII: 47; VIII:** 383
　Abbott, Grace **VII:** 1
　Kelley, Florence **VII:** 146

　mothers' pensions **VII:** 189
　public health **VII:** 243
　Sheppard-Towner Act **VII:** 284
　Wald, Lillian **VII:** 329
children's crusade **IX:** 38, 253
"Children's Era" speech (Sanger) **VII:** 384–386
Children's Gun Violence Prevention Act of 1998 **X:** 137
Children's Health Act of 1997 **X:** 164
children's television programming **X:** 296
Chile **II:** 229; **IV:** 130, 241; **VI:** 49–50, 103, 123; **X:** 122, 173, 174, 325c
　Andes Mountains **I:** 10
　Balboa, Vasco Núñez de **I:** 24
　conquistadores **I:** 85
　Inca **I:** 175
　Monte Verde **I:** 242
　Panama **I:** 277
　Valdivia, Pedro de **I:** 363
Chilean-American relations **VI: 49–50**
Chilean immigrants **IV:** 163
Chimalpahin, Domingo Francisco de San Antón Muñón **I: 71**
China **III:** 67; **V:** 405c; **VII:** 355c, 357c, 359c, 360c; **VIII:** 408c, 410c; **IX:** 21, 58; **X:** 324c, 330c, 331c. See also Cathay; Taiwan
　Asia (foreign policy) **IX:** 21
　Asian Americans **VIII:** 26
　Astor, John Jacob **IV:** 30, 31
　Astoria **IV:** 32
　Boxer Rebellion **VII:** 33–34
　Cairo Conference **VIII:** 51
　Carter, James Earl, Jr. **X:** 58
　cash-and-carry **VIII:** 53
　Chinese Exclusion Act **VI:** 50
　Clinton, William **X:** 68
　cold war **IX:** 58; **X:** 70
　détente **X:** 89
　diseases and epidemics **IV:** 111
　dollar diplomacy **VII:** 70
　Ford, Gerald R. **X:** 121
　foreign policy **VI:** 103; **VII:** 98; **VIII:** 124, 125; **X:** 122, 123

Gentlemen's Agreement **VII:** 107
Great White Fleet **VII:** 114
Hay, John Milton **VI:** 125
Hull, Cordell **VIII:** 160
imperialism **VI:** 143
Kissinger, Henry A. **X:** 165
Korean War **IX:** 163–165
labor **X:** 171
Leahy, William D. **VIII:** 183
Lend-Lease Act **VIII:** 184
Luce, Henry R. **VIII:** 196
Mahan, Alfred Thayer **VI:** 186
Manchuria **VIII:** 199–200
Manifest Destiny **IV:** 219
Marshall, George C. **VIII:** 206
McKinley, William **VI:** 190
Nelson, Donald M. **VIII:** 238
Nixon, Richard M. **X:** 220
Open Door notes **VI:** 216–217
Open Door Policy **VII:** 218–219
Root-Takahira Agreement **VII:** 267, 268
Russo-Japanese War **VII:** 271
Southeast Asia Treaty Organization **IX:** 274
Soviet Union **IX:** 277
space policy **X:** 281
sports **X:** 285
Taft, Robert A. **VIII:** 349
technology **IX:** 294
trade, foreign **IX:** 310
Truman Doctrine **IX:** 301
Tyler, John **IV:** 348
UN **VIII:** 366
Washington Conference on Naval Disarmament **VII:** 331
White Paper **IX:** 320–321
Women's International League for Peace and Freedom **VII:** 338
World Trade Organization **X:** 321, 322
World War I **VII:** 343
World War II Pacific theater **VIII:** 396–399
China-Burma-India theater **VIII:** 398
chinampas **I:** 17, **72,** 344
China Sea **IV:** 279
China trade **III: 67–68,** 350; **IV:** 280, 378c
Chinese **II:** 133, 174

Chinese Americans **VI:** 130, 141; **VII:** 69, 208, 245, 355c; **VIII:** 25, 26; **IX:** 22; **X:** 28, 29, 243
　anti-Chinese agitation, rise of **IV:** 23
　California **IV:** 65
　cities and urban life **V:** 60
　Fifteenth Amendment **V:** 124
　gold, discovery and mining **IV:** 163
　immigration **IV:** 177, 180; **V:** 177
　Pacific Railroad Act of 1862 **V:** 263
　population trends **V:** 278
　race and race relations **IV:** 292
　religion **IV:** 298
　transportation **V:** 355
Chinese Exclusion Act of 1882 **VI:** 17, **50–52,** 51m, 52, 141, 325c, 332–334; **VII:** 355c; **IX:** 22
　AFL **VII:** 10
　Gentlemen's Agreement **VII:** 107
　immigration **VII:** 127
　race and racial conflict **VII:** 247
　Root-Takahira Agreement **VII:** 267
Chinese exclusion laws **VIII:** 162
chino **I:** 234
Chinook **II:** 266
Chippawa Creek, Canada **IV:** 309
Chippewa, Battle of **IV:** 358
Chippewa/Chippewa nation **II:** 191, 246; **IV:** 76; **X:** 215
Chiricahua Apache **V:** 406c; **VI:** 14, 112
Chirikov, Aleksei **II:** 13, 32, 326
Chisholm, Shirley **X:** 111
Chisholm v. Georgia (1793) **III:** 182, 338, 396c; **IV:** 330; **X:** 236
Chitomachon **II:** 396
Chivington, John M. **IV:** 48, 90; **V:** 407c
chloramphenicol **IX:** 205
chloroform **IV:** 230
chlorpromazine **X:** 190
Choanoke **II:** 401
Choate, Pat **X:** 263
chocolate **II:** 43, 71. See also cacao
Choctaw, USS **V:** 233
Choctaw/Choctaw nation **I:** 333; **II: 60–61; III: 68,** 97; **V:**

250; **VI:** 209. *See also* Five
  Civilized Tribes
    agriculture **II:** 8
    Chickasaw **II:** 59
    cotton culture **IV:** 98
    French colonies **II:** 129
    fur trade **II:** 130–131
    Indian Removal Act (1830)
      IV: 181, 182*m*
    Louisiana **II:** 199
    Natchez Revolt **II:** 242
    Native Americans **II:** 246;
      IV: 256
    Native Americans in the
      War of 1812 **IV:** 259
    New Orleans, Battle of
      (1815) **IV:** 262
    Red Shoes **II:** 312–313
    religion, Native American
      II: 317
    Trail of Tears **IV:** 343, 344
Chodorov, Frank **X:** 78
Choice, Not an Echo, A
  (Schlafly) **X:** 272
cholera **V:** 15, 175, 338
    Bowie, Jim **IV:** 57
    cities and urban life **IV:**
      82
    diseases and epidemics **IV:**
      111
    Forty-niners **IV:** 147
    immigration **IV:** 178
    Oregon Trail **IV:** 269
    Trail of Tears **IV:** 344
Cholula (Cholollan) **I: 72–73**
    Aztecs **I:** 18, 21
    Cortés, Hernán **I:** 93
    Malinche **I:** 218
    Quetzalcoatl **I:** 301
    Tabasco **I:** 341
    Tlaxcala **I:** 352, 353
    Toltecs **I:** 356
Chopin, Kate **VI:** 177
Chorus Line (musical) **X:** 201,
  241
Chouart, Médard, sieur des
  Groseilliers **II:** 115, 159
Chouteau, Auguste Pierre **IV:**
  79
Chouteau, Jean Pierre **IV:**
  78–79
Chouteau, Pierre, Jr. **IV:** 17, 79
Chouteau, René Auguste **IV:**
  78
Chouteau family **IV: 78–79,**
  156, 247
Christadelphians **IV:** 299
Christiana, Pennsylvania, riot **V:**
  59
Christian American **X:** 62
Christian Anticommunist
  Crusade **X:** 79

Christian Association of
  Washington, Pennsylvania **IV:**
  72, 298
Christian Broadcasting Network
  (CBN) **X:** 294
Christian Church (Disciples of
  Christ) **IV:** 71–72, 323
Christian Coalition (CC) **X:**
  61–62, 108, 197, 268
Christian Crusade **X:** 79
Christian Front **VIII:** 19
Christianity **VI:** 324*c;* **VIII:** 130,
  302–304; **IX:** 255–257. *See
  also* Protestantism; Roman
  Catholic Church/Roman
  Catholicism; *specific headings*
    Africa **II:** 4
    African Americans **II:** 7
    Anglo-Normans **I:** 10
    anti-Masonry **IV:** 24
    art **II:** 25
    auto-da-fé **I:** 16
    Brendan the Navigator,
      Saint **I:** 34
    Bush, George W. **X:** 47
    Canary Islands **I:** 53
    Castile **I:** 62
    Chauncy, Charles **II:** 57
    Church of England **I:**
      73–74
    Columbus, Christopher **I:**
      81
    Cortés, Hernán **I:** 92
    Cozumel **I:** 97
    Darfur **I:** 102
    Darwinism and religion
      VI: 75
    Deseret, State of **IV:** 109
    education **VI:** 91
    Ethiopia **I:** 123–125
    ethnocentrism **II:** 112–113
    evangelical Christians **X:**
      107–108
    Gage, Matilda Joslyn **VI:**
      107
    Garrison, William Lloyd **V:**
      146
    Greenland **I:** 145
    Handsome Lake **III:** 164
    Hawaii **III:** 164
    humanitarianism **III:** 170
    Iceland **I:** 175
    Indian Rights Association
      VI: 144
    Jews (Judaism) **I:** 190
    Liberia **IV:** 209
    Liberty Party **IV:** 210
    London **I:** 208
    mappae mundi **I:** 221
    marriage and family life **V:**
      222
    Methodism **III:** 242–243

music **III:** 251
Native Americans **II:** 244,
  246; **IV:** 256
New Mexico **II:** 254
New Spain (Mexico),
  northern frontier of **III:**
  258
Norse **I:** 264
Nzinga **I:** 267
Paine, Thomas **III:** 272
Powhatan (chief) **II:**
  293–294
Powhatan Confederacy **II:**
  295
praying towns **II:** 295–296
Prester John **I:** 292
prostitution **V:** 283
Protestantism **II:** 300–302
Pueblo Revolt **II:** 304
race and race relations **IV:**
  290
Rauschenbusch, Walter
  VII: 255–256
Reconquista **I:** 306
Reformation **I:** 307–310
religion **III:** 297–299; **IV:**
  296; **V:** 299–300; **VI:**
  241–242; **VII:** 260; **X:**
  265
religion, African-American
  II: 314
religion, Euro-American
  II: 314
religion, Native American
  II: 317–318
revitalization movements
  II: 320
RFRA **X:** 266
Roman Catholicism **VI:**
  249–250
Roman Catholics **II:**
  323–324
slave codes **II:** 336
slavery **II:** 340
Social Darwinism **VI:**
  265–266
Sunday, Billy **VII:** 301–302
Tanner, Benjamin Tucker
  VI: 283
televangelism **X:** 293–294
Trent, Council of **I:**
  359–360
USCC **V:** 371–372
Virginia **II:** 384, 385
Vitoria, Francisco de **I:**
  369
Witherspoon, John **III:**
  380
women's status and rights
  II: 408
YMCA/YWCA **VII:**
  349–350

*Christianity and the Social
  Crisis* (Rauschenbusch) **VI:**
  267; **VII:** 256, 260
Christian Liberty (Martin
  Luther) **I:** 210
Christian Nurture (Bushnell)
  IV: 298
Christian Realism **VIII:** 304
Christian Recorder (newspaper)
  V: 5
Christian Science **VI: 52–53,**
  87–88, 324*c*
Christian Science Monitor **VI:**
  88
Christian Union **VI:** 24
Christo **X:** 26
Christy, Arthur **X:** 150
Chrysler **IX:** 24, 294; **X:** 31, 32,
  51, 62–63
Chrysler, Walter P. **VII:** 74
Chrysler Building **VIII:** 22
Chrysler Corporation **VII:** 22,
  74; **VIII:** 30
Chrysler Corporation Loan
  Guarantee Act of 1979 **X:**
  62–63, 326*c*
Chumash **I:** 48
Church, Benjamin **II:** 309; **III:**
  68–69, 241
Church, Frank **X:** 24, 31
Church, Frederic Edwin **V:** 16
Church, William C. **X:** 212
Church and Modern Life, The
  (Gladden) **VI:** 115
church and state, separation of
  I: 51, 262; **II:** 149, 156–157,
  161, 301, 314, 316–317; **III:**
  103, 184; **VI:** 243, 250; **IX:**
  98; **X:** 326*c*
    conservative movement **X:**
      79–80
    pornography **X:** 245
    religion **X:** 265
    RFRA **X:** 266
    Supreme Court **X:** 291
churches **I:** 12, 13, 175, 364,
  365; **V:** 295; **VIII:** 304
Churchill, Winston **VIII:** *125,*
  409*c,* 410*c;* **IX:** 299; **X:** 156
    Anglo-American relations
      VIII: 16–17
    Arnold, "Hap" **VIII:** 22
    Atlantic Charter **VIII:** 28
    Britain, Battle of **VIII:** 44
    Bulge, Battle of the **VIII:**
      44
    Cairo Conference **VIII:**
      51
    Casablanca Conference
      VIII: 52
    destroyers-for-bases deal
      VIII: 82

Churchill, Winston (*continued*)
  foreign policy **VIII:** 125, *125*
  Grand Alliance **VIII:** 136, 137
  Harriman, Averell **VIII:** 144
  Hopkins, Harry **VIII:** 157
  Munich Conference **VIII:** 220
  North African campaign **VIII:** 249
  Potsdam Conference **VIII:** 279, 280
  Roosevelt, Franklin D. **VIII:** 314
  second front **VIII:** 320
  Soviet-American relations **VIII:** 334
  Teheran Conference **VIII:** 354
  UN **VIII:** 365, 366
  V-E Day **VIII:** 369
  World War II European theater **VIII:** 391
  Yalta Conference **VIII:** 401, *402*
Church of Christ **IV:** 311
Church of England **I: 73–74**.
  See also Anglican Church
  Elizabeth I **I:** 120
  Henry VIII **I:** 160
  James I **I:** 188
  Puritans **I:** 298–299
  Reformation **I:** 309
Church of God in Christ **X:** 11
Church of Jesus Christ of Latter-day Saints (Mormons) **IV: 79–81,** 376*c*; **VI: 198–199; X:** 79, 106, 265
  Bridger, James **IV:** 57
  Deseret, State of **IV:** 109–111
  exploration **IV:** 132
  marriage and family life **IV:** 223
  migration **IV:** 236
  Mormon Trail **IV:** 242–243, 243*m*
  Mormon War **IV:** 244–245
  Native Americans **IV:** 258
  Nauvoo, Illinois **IV:** 260–261
  polygamy **IV:** 285
  religion **IV:** 296, 298; **VI:** 243, 244
  Second Great Awakening **IV:** 311
  Smith, Joseph, Jr. **IV:** 322–324
  South Pass **IV:** 325
  Strang, James Jesse **IV:** 329

Young, Brigham **IV:** 371–373
Church of Scotland **II:** 296
Church of the Four-Square Gospel **VII:** 175–176
Churchyard, Thomas **I:** 141
Churubusco, Battle of **V:** 15
CIA. *See* Central Intelligence Agency
Cíbola
  Coronado, Francisco **I:** 88
  Hopi **I:** 167
  Zuni **I:** 383
Cicippio, Joseph **X:** 297
Ciconicin **II:** 88
cider **IV:** 336
Cigarmakers International **VI:** 11, 116–117
cihuacoatl **I:** 185, 237, 351
cimarrones **I:** 277
Cincinnati **IV:** 187
Cincinnati, Order of **III: 69,** 197, 207
Cincinnati Gazette **V:** 82
Cincinnati Reds **VI:** 21; **VII:** 26, 294
Cincinnati Symphony Orchestra **VI:** 201
cinematography **VII:** 134
Cinerama **IX:** 211
Cinqué, Joseph **IV:** 20, *20*, 21, 377*c*. *See also* Pieh, Sengbe
CIO. *See* Congress of Industrial Organizations
Cipangu. *See also* Japan
  Behaim, Martin **I:** 27
  Cabot, John **I:** 41, 42
  Cathay (China) **I:** 65
  Columbus, Christopher **I:** 79
  Dutch East India Company **I:** 115
  printing press **I:** 294
Cipollone, Rose **X:** 303
circuit courts
  Judiciary Act of 1789 **III:** 192
  Judiciary Act of 1801 **III:** 193
  Supreme Court **III:** 338
circuit riders **IV:** 115, 296, 298
Circular Letter **III:** 349
circumnavigation of the globe
  Drake, Sir Francis **I:** 110–111, 111*m*
  Magellan, Ferdinand **I:** 215–217
  Pigafetta, Antonio **I:** 283
circuses **VI:** 20–21, 97
Cisneros, Francisco Jiménez **I:** 198
Cisneros, Sandra **X:** 177

cities and urban life **II: 61–62; III:** 19, *69,* **69–71,** 178, 284–285; **IV:** 11, **81–84,** *83,* 119; **V:** 6, 7, **59–61,** *60,* 61, 278; **VI:** xv, **53–55,** 54*m,* 90, 233, 241, 242; **VII: 47–50,** *48,* 49*m;* **VIII:** 2, **57–60,** *58,* 217; **IX: 51–52; X:** 9, 11, 243. *See also* suburbs/ suburbanization; urban reform; urban transportation
  African-American movement **IX:** 4, 6
  African Americans **IV:** 7; **VIII:** 5; **X:** 9
  Amazon River **I:** 8
  American Indian Movement **IX:** 12
  American System **IV:** 19
  Appalachian Regional Development Act **IX:** 15–16
  architecture **VII:** 16
  art and architecture **I:** 12, 13; **VIII:** 25
  artisans **II:** 25, 26
  automobile industry **VII:** 22
  Boston **II:** 35–37
  cabildo **I:** 38–39
  Cahokia **I:** 47
  Calabar **I:** 47–48
  Catholics **VIII:** 53
  Charleston **II:** 56–57
  Chichén Itzá **I:** 69–71
  child labor **VII:** 44–46
  Cholula **I:** 72
  class **II:** 63
  communications **VI:** 61
  Copán **I:** 86
  Coronado, Francisco **I:** 88, 90
  crime **X:** 82, 83
  Cuzco **I:** 99
  Democratic Party **V:** 95; **VIII:** 80
  Dillingham Commission **VII:** 68–69
  disease and epidemics **II:** 91, 92; **IV:** 111, 112; **V:** 97
  economy **IV:** 119; **VII:** 74
  education **V:** 108; **X:** 99
  election of 1936 **VIII:** 97
  election of 1940 **VIII:** 98
  elections **X:** 101, 103
  Federal Housing Administration **VIII:** 119; **IX:** 110
  forts **II:** 124
  Gao **I:** 137, 139
  gays and lesbians **VIII:** 129, 130

Gedi **I:** 139
German-American regiments **V:** 147
Ghana **I:** 141
GI Bill of Rights **VIII:** 132
government (state and local) **IX:** 125
Great Depression **VIII:** 140
Great Migration **VII:** 111–113
Guadalajara **II:** 151
HOLC **VIII:** 151
homefront **V:** 169
housing **VI:** 134–135; **VIII:** 158
immigration **IV:** 177, 178; **VII:** 127; **IX:** 142
Indian Claims Commission **IX:** 143
industrialization **IV:** 185
invention and technology **I:** 180
IRCA **X:** 149
Irish Americans **VIII:** 165
Jamestown **II:** 172
Johnson, Tom **VII:** 139–140
journalism **IV:** 194
kindergarten **VI:** 159
labor **II:** 190
Lima **I:** 206
Lisbon **I:** 207–208
literature **IV:** 213; **VIII:** 191
London **I:** 208
Mann Act **VII:** 169
marriage and family life **IV:** 222; **V:** 222; **VII:** 171
Massachusetts School Act **II:** 216–217
Masses, The **VII:** 173
Maya **I:** 226, 227
Mecca **I:** 230
media **X:** 185
medicine **VI:** 191, 192
Mexican Americans **VIII:** 210
migration **IX:** 201–203
Model Cities program **IX:** 207–208
Monte Albán **I:** 241–242
mortality **II:** 235
mulattoes **II:** 238
music **II:** 239
New Orleans **II:** 258
New Spain **I:** 258
newspapers **VI:** 211
New York City **II:** 262–263; **V:** 253–254
Olmecs **I:** 269

Olmstead, Frederick Law
V: 257–258
Panic of 1819 **IV:** 275
Panic of 1837 **IV:** 277
penitentiary movement **IV:**
277–278
Philadelphia **II:** 281–282
popular culture **VII:** 230
population trends **VI:** 226;
VII: 235; **VIII:**
277–278; **X:** 243
poverty **X:** 245–246
progressivism in the 1890s
VI: 233
Prohibition Party **VI:** 234
prostitution **V:** 283–284
RA **VIII:** 307
race and racial conflict
VIII: 287; **X:** 256
recreation **VII:** 258
religion **VI:** 241, 242; **VIII:**
302
rust belt **X:** 269
St. Augustine **II:** 327–328
St. Mary's City **II:** 328
Santa Fe **I:** 319–320
Savannah **II:** 329
settlement houses **VI:**
259–260
Seville **I:** 322–323
sexuality **VII:** 283
slave resistance **II:** 337
slavery **IV:** 319
socialism **VII:** 288
society, British American
II: 350
South **VIII:** 331, 332
Spanish colonies **II:** 356
suburbs **VII:** 299–301;
VIII: 342
Sunbelt **X:** 290
Tacuba **I:** 342
taverns and inns **II:**
367–368
Tenochtitlán **I:** 344–346
Teotihuacán **I:** 346
Termination policy **IX:** 298
Tesla, Nikola **VI:** 285
theater **II:** 373; **V:** 352
Tikal **I:** 349–350
Timbuktu **I:** 350–351
Toltecs **I:** 356
transportation **V:** 356
transportation, urban **VI:**
291–292
Urban League **IX:**
305–306
urban reform **VII:**
316–317
urban transportation **VII:**
317–319
USHA **VIII:** 367–368
Venice **I:** 364–366

Veracruz **I:** 366
women's status and rights
II: 407
World War II home front
VIII: 394
yellow fever **II:** 414
YMCA/YWCA **VII:**
349–350
Yoruba **I:** 377
youth **VII:** 350–351
Yucatán Peninsula **I:** 378
Zacatecas **I:** 381
Citizen Kane **VIII:** 376, 377,
409*c*
Citizens' Council of America
(CCA) **IX:** 320, 332*c*
citizenship **III:** 173, 176; **IV:**
289; **VI:** 6; **VII:** 41, 360*c*
Asian Americans **VIII:** 26
civil rights **VIII:** 61
immigration **VIII:** 162
Native American
movement **IX:** 228
Native Americans **VIII:**
235
Oswald, Lee Harvey **IX:**
237
Puerto Ricans **IX:** 250
Termination policy **IX:** 297
citizen-soldier **IV:** 170; **V:**
61–62
common soldier **V:** 69
Confederate army **V:** 71
governors **V:** 152
Grant, Ulysses S. **V:** 156
Union army **V:** 364
Citizens United **X:** 143
citrus fruit **VII:** 6
citterns **II:** 239
City Beautiful movement **VI:**
14, 320
City College of New York **VI:** 93
city government **VI:** 108
City of Brotherly Love. *See*
Philadelphia
city of gold. *See* El Dorado
city planning **VII:** 16
cityscapes **II:** 194
city-states
Benin **I:** 28
Palenque **I:** 275
Yoruba **I:** 377
Yucatán Peninsula **I:** 378
Ciudad de los Reyes. *See* Lima
Ciudad Hidalgo **I:** 348
Civil Aeronautics Act **VIII:** 408*c*
Civil Aeronautics Authority
VIII: 10
Civil Air Patrol **VIII:** 253
civil aviation **IX:** 27, 28
Civil Crusade (Panama) **X:** 231
civil defense **VIII:** 253–254,
395; **IX:** **52–53**

civil disobedience **IX:** **53–54,**
240, 273
"Civil Disobedience" (Thoreau)
IV: 212, 342, 345, 378*c*,
407–410; **IX:** 53
Civiletti, Benjamin **X:** 5
civil government **II:** 197
Civilian Conservation Corps
(CCC) **VIII:** **63–64**
African Americans **VIII:** 3
Black Cabinet **VIII:** 37
children **VIII:** 56
Congress **VIII:** 68
conscientious objectors
VIII: 70
conservatism **VIII:** 71
environmental issues **VIII:**
103
Native Americans **VIII:**
235
New Deal **VIII:** 241
recreation **VIII:** 296
relief **VIII:** 301
Civilian Public Service (CPS)
VIII: 70
Civility (Conestoga leader) **II:** 67
civil liberties **V:** 66, 161–162;
VII: 355*c*; **VIII:** **60–61,** 409*c*
American Civil Liberties
Union **VIII:** 13
Asian Americans **VIII:** 26
Black, Hugo L. **VIII:** 37
Brandeis, Louis **VII:** 35
censorship **VIII:** 54–55
civil rights **VIII:** 61
conscientious objectors
VIII: 70
Douglas, William O. **VIII:**
85
Espionage Act **VII:** 88
Frankfurter, Felix **VIII:**
127
Greenwich Village **VII:**
115
Holmes, Oliver Wendell
VII: 122, 123
Korematsu v. United States
VIII: 178
liberalism **VIII:** 189
Mauldin, Bill **VIII:** 207
Roosevelt, Eleanor **VIII:**
311
Roosevelt, Franklin D.
VIII: 314
Smith Act **VIII:** 326–327
Supreme Court **VIII:** 347
Thomas, Norman **VIII:**
358
World War II **VIII:** 389
World War II home front
VIII: 394, 395
Civil Liberties Act of 1988 **X:**
63, 327*c*

civil protests **II:** 204
civil rights **V:** 408*c*; **VI:** 6,
81–82; **VII:** 356*c*; **VIII:** 5,
61–62, *62,* 409*c*; **IX:** 332*c*; **X:**
329*c*. *See also* Civil Rights
movement
abortion **X:** 1
ADA **X:** 21
American Missionary
Association **V:** 8
Black Codes **V:** 29
Blair, Francis P., Jr. **V:** 30,
31
Bruce, Blanche K. **V:** 40
Byrnes, James F. **VIII:** 48
Catholics **VIII:** 54
Chase, Salmon P. **V:** 57
Civil Rights Act of 1866 **V:**
62
Civil Rights Act of 1875 **V:**
62–63
Civil Rights Act of 1991 **X:**
63
Communist Party **VII:** 53
conservatism **VIII:** 72
Democratic Party **VIII:** 82
Douglas, William O. **VIII:**
85
Dred Scott decision **V:**
100–102
Du Bois, W. E. B. **VII:**
71–72
election of 1944 **VIII:** 99
elections **IX:** 95
emancipation **V:** 112
Enforcement Acts **V:** 117
Executive Order 8802
VIII: 106
Fair Deal **IX:** 107
Farmer, James L. **X:**
110–111
feminism **X:** 114
FEPC **VIII:** 109
Fifteenth Amendment **V:**
123–124
Fourteenth Amendment
V: 138–139
Freedmen's Bureau **V:** 143
Free Speech Movement
IX: 112–113
Garrison, William Lloyd **V:**
147
gay rights movement **X:**
127
Grant, Ulysses S. **V:** 157
Grimké, Charlotte Forten
V: 160
Harlem Renaissance **VII:**
119
Hayes, Rutherford B. **VI:**
126
Hispanic Americans **X:**
141–142

civil rights (*continued*)
  Hoar, George Frisbie **VI:** 130
  impeachment of Andrew Johnson **V:** 178
  Johnson, Andrew **V:** 188
  Johnson, Lyndon **IX:** 151
  Kennedy, John F. **IX:** 158
  Langston, John Mercer **VI:** 172
  League of Women Voters **IX:** 175
  liberalism **VIII:** 187, 189; **IX:** 179; **X:** 175
  Liberty Party **IV:** 210
  Lincoln, Abraham **V:** 211
  Lovejoy, Elijah **IV:** 214
  MOWM **VIII:** 201–202
  Myrdal, Gunnar **VIII:** 224–225
  NAACP. *See* National Association for the Advancement of Colored People
  National Association of Colored Women **VII:** 199–200
  National Organization for Women **IX:** 223
  Native Americans **VIII:** 235, 236
  New Deal **VIII:** 242
  New Frontier **IX:** 230
  newspapers **VI:** 211
  Niagara Movement **VII:** 214–215
  NOW **X:** 210–211
  O'Connor, Sandra Day **X:** 226
  Phillips, Wendell **IV:** 281
  Pinchback, Pinckney B. S. **V:** 276
  political parties **X:** 237
  race and racial conflict **IV:** 291; **V:** 287–288; **VIII:** 287
  Radical Republicans **V:** 288
  Randolph, A. Philip **VIII:** 291
  Reconstruction **V:** 292
  Republican Party **V:** 300, 302
  Roosevelt, Eleanor **VIII:** 310–311, 411c
  Roosevelt, Franklin D. **VIII:** 314
  scalawags **V:** 307
  Scottsboro Boys **VIII:** 319–320
  Selective Service **VIII:** 323–324
  Singleton, Benjamin **V:** 327

  slavery **IV:** 316
  Society of Friends **V:** 332
  South **VIII:** 332
  States' Rights Party **IX:** 281
  Stevens, Thaddeus **V:** 338
  Stewart, Maria **IV:** 327
  Still, William **IV:** 328
  Sumner, Charles **V:** 342, 343
  Supreme Court **VIII:** 347
  Thirteenth Amendment **V:** 353
  Thomas, Norman **VIII:** 358
  Tourgée, Albion W. **V:** 354
  Truman, Harry **IX:** 300
  United States v. Cruikshank **V:** 375–376
  Urban League **IX:** 305–306
  Vesey, Denmark **IV:** 353
  Voting Rights Act of 1965 **IX:** 311–312
  Wagner, Robert F. **VIII:** 372
  Wallace, Henry A. **VIII:** 373
  Warren Court **IX:** 316
  Welles, Gideon **V:** 392
  Wells-Barnett, Ida Bell **VI:** 312
  White, Byron R. **X:** 319
  White, Walter **VIII:** 378
  Williams, Peter, Jr. **IV:** 366
  Willkie, Wendell L. **VIII:** 379
  Women's National Loyal League **V:** 397
  women's status and rights **V:** 399
  World War II **VIII:** 389, 390
  World War II home front **VIII:** 395
  Wright, Richard **VIII:** 399
Civil Rights Act of 1866 **V: 62,** 408c
  carpetbaggers **V:** 50
  impeachment of Andrew Johnson **V:** 178
  Johnson, Andrew **V:** 188
  Radical Republicans **V:** 289
  Reconstruction **V:** 293
  Reconstruction Acts **V:** 296
  Thirteenth Amendment **V:** 353
Civil Rights Act of 1875 **V: 62–63; VI:** 324c, 325c
  African Americans **VI:** 5, 6
  Butler, Benjamin **V:** 47

  civil rights cases **VI:** 55–56
  Elliot, Robert B. **V:** 111
  Grant, Ulysses S. **V:** 157
  Jim Crow laws **VI:** 156
  Langston, John Mercer **VI:** 172
  Plessy v. Ferguson **VI:** 224
  Republican Party **V:** 302
  Sumner, Charles **V:** 343
  Thirteenth Amendment **V:** 353
Civil Rights Act of 1957 **IX: 54–55,** 332c; **X:** 220
Civil Rights Act of 1960 **IX: 55–56,** 332c
Civil Rights Act of 1964 **V:** 63; **VIII:** 110; **IX:** 5, **56–57,** 333c, 334c
  affirmative action **X:** 8
  African Americans **X:** 10
  Bakke **X:** 34
  Civil Rights Act of 1991 **X:** 63
  Equal Employment Opportunity Commission **IX:** 103
  feminism **X:** 114
  Great Society **IX:** 127
  Griggs et al. v. Duke Power Company **X:** 135–136
  Heart of Atlanta Motel Inc., v. United States **IX:** 132–133
  Humphrey, Hubert H. **IX:** 138
  Johnson, Lady Bird **IX:** 150
  labor **IX:** 170
  liberalism **X:** 175
  National Organization for Women (NOW) **IX:** 223; **X:** 210, 211
  race and racial conflict **X:** 255
  segregation **IX:** 271
  Southern Manifesto **IX:** 276
  Student Nonviolent Coordinating Committee **IX:** 284
  Title IX—Prohibition of Sex Discrimination **X:** 334–335
  White Citizens' Councils **IX:** 320
  women's rights and status **IX:** 324–325; **X:** 320
Civil Rights Act of 1991 **X: 63,** 328c
  affirmative action **X:** 9
  Bush, George H. W. **X:** 46

  race and racial conflict **X:** 256
civil rights cases **VI: 55–56**
  due process clause **VI:** 81
  Harlan, John Marshall **VI:** 122
  Jim Crow laws **VI:** 156
  Supreme Court **VI:** 281
Civil Rights movement **V:** 201, 295; **IX:** 275, 332c, 334c
  African-American movement **IX:** 4–7
  American Indian Movement **IX:** 12–13
  Americans for Democratic Action **IX:** 14
  Asian-American movement **IX:** 22–23
  Baker, Ella **IX:** 30
  Baker v. Carr **IX:** 31–32
  Baldwin, James **IX:** 32–33
  Birmingham confrontation **IX:** 38
  Carmichael, Stokely **IX:** 47
  Congress of Racial Equality **IX:** 66–68
  Equal Employment Opportunity Commission **IX:** 103
  folk music revival **IX:** 111
  Gonzáles, Rodolfo "Corky" **IX:** 124–125
  Graham, Billy **IX:** 126
  Hamer, Fannie Lou **IX:** 129–130
  Hoover, J. Edgar **IX:** 136
  Jackson, Jesse L. **X:** 159
  journalism **IX:** 153–154
  King, Martin Luther, Jr. **IX:** 160–162
  Ku Klux Klan **IX:** 166
  Latino movement **IX:** 173–174
  Lewis, John **IX:** 178–179
  March on Washington **IX:** 191–192
  Meredith, James **IX:** 200
  modern Republicanism **IX:** 209
  multiculturalism **X:** 200
  Murray, Pauli **IX:** 215–216
  music **IX:** 217–218
  NAACP **IX:** 220; **X:** 208
  Nation of Islam **X:** 213
  Native American movement **IX:** 227–229
  Native Americans **X:** 214
  Parks, Rosa **IX:** 240
  race and racial conflict **IX:** 253–255; **X:** 255
  religion **IX:** 256

Robinson, Jackie **IX:** 262–263

Savio, Mario **IX:** 268

segregation **IX:** 271

sexual revolution **X:** 277

sit-ins **IX:** 272–273

Southern Christian Leadership Conference **IX:** 274–276

Student Nonviolent Coordinating Committee **IX:** 284–285

United Farm Workers **IX:** 304

Wallace, George C. **X:** 314

Watts uprising **IX:** 317–318

Civil Rights Restoration Act of 1988 **X:** 136

Civil Service **VI:** 95, 110, 230, 325c; **VII:** 266; **VIII:** 375, 384; **IX:** 247; **X:** 114

civil service reform **V:** 302; **VI:** **56–57,** 325c

Arthur, Chester Alan **VI:** 16

Beecher, Henry Ward **VI:** 24

Blaine, James Gillespie **VI:** 31

Cleveland, Grover **VI:** 58

Congress **VI:** 63

Conkling, Roscoe **VI:** 64

corruption, political **VI:** 67

elections, conduct of **VI:** 95

foreign policy **VI:** 103, 104

Garfield, James A. **VI:** 108, 109

Godkin, Edwin Lawrence **VI:** 116

Harrison, Benjamin **VI:** 123

Hayes, Rutherford B. **VI:** 126

Liberal Republican Party **VI:** 174

mugwumps **VI:** 199

The Nation **VI:** 205

the presidency **VI:** 230

presidential campaigns **VI:** 232

Schurz, Carl **VI:** 256, 257

Villard, Henry **VI:** 305

Civil War **II:** 61; **III:** 326, 327, 333, 360; **IV:** 238; **V:** 63–67, 64m, 65m; **VIII:** 61, 64, 80, 322. *See also* Reconstruction

abolition/abolition movement **IV:** 3–4; **V:** 3, 4

African-American regiments **V:** 4–5

agriculture **V:** 6–7

AME Church **V:** 5

American Missionary Association **V:** 8

amnesty, acts of **V:** 8

Anderson, Robert **V:** 9–10

Andersonville Prison **V:** 10–11

Andrews's Raid **V:** 11

Annapolis Naval Academy **V:** 373

Antietam, Battle of **V:** 11–13

Appomattox Court House, Virginia **V:** 13–15

Armistead, Lewis A. **V:** 15

Army Corps of Engineers **V:** 370–371

art **V:** 16

Arthur, Chester Alan **VI:** 16

assassination of Abraham Lincoln **V:** 17

Atlanta campaign **V:** 19–20

Balloon Corps **V:** 21–22

Baltimore, Maryland, riots **V:** 22

Baltimore & Ohio Railroad (B&O) **IV:** 40

banking, investment **VI:** 19

banking and currency **IV:** 43; **V:** 22–24

Barton, Clara **V:** 24–25

battle flags **V:** 26

Beauregard, Pierre **V:** 26–27

Bent, William **IV:** 48

Bentonville, Battle of **V:** 28

Bickerdyke, "Mother" **V:** 28–29

Birth of a Nation **VII:** 30

Blackwell, Elizabeth **VI:** 31

Blair, Francis P., Jr. **V:** 30

Bleeding Kansas **V:** 31–32

Bloomer, Amelia **IV:** 54

Booth, John Wilkes **V:** 33

bounty system **V:** 34

Boyd, Belle **V:** 34–35

Brady, Mathew **V:** 36

Bragg, Braxton **V:** 36

bridges **VI:** 34–35

brothers' war **V:** 36–37

Brown, John **V:** 38

Brown, William Wells **V:** 40

Bruce, Blanche K. **V:** 40

Buffalo Soldiers **VI:** 39

Bull Run/Manassas, First and Second Battles of **V:** 42–44

Burnside, Ambrose E. **V:** 45

bushwhackers **V:** 46

business and government **VI:** 39

Butler, Benjamin **V:** 46

Carney, William H. **V:** 49

Carson, Kit **IV:** 76

cartography **V:** 51–52

Cedar Mountain, Battle of **V:** 53

Chancellorsville, Battle of **V:** 54–56

Chattanooga, Battle of **V:** 57

Chesnut, Mary B. **V:** 58

Chickamauga, Battle of **V:** 58–59

citizen-soldier **V:** 61–62

civil service reform **VI:** 56

Cleburne, Patrick Ronayne **V:** 67–68

Cody, William Frederick **VI:** 59

Cold Harbor, Battle of **V:** 68

Colored National Labor Union **V:** 68

common soldier **V:** 69–71

Confederate army **V:** 71–73

Confederate navy **V:** 73–74

Confederate States of America **V:** 75–77

Confiscation Acts **V:** 78

conscription **V:** 78–80; **VII:** 54

contrabands **V:** 80–81

Cooke, Jay **V:** 81

Corinth, Battle of **V:** 83

Corps d'Afrique **V:** 83–84

Cumming, Kate **V:** 85

Dahlgren, John A. B. **V:** 87

Dana, Charles A. **V:** 88

Davis, Jefferson **V:** 88–90

Davis, Varina Howell **V:** 91

Davis Bend, Mississippi, freedmen's colony **V:** 91–92

Deere, John **IV:** 105

De Forest, John William **V:** 92

Delany, Martin Robinson **V:** 93

Democratic Party **IV:** 108; **V:** 94; **VI:** 77

desertion **V:** 95–96

Dewey, George **VI:** 79

disease and epidemics **V:** 96–97

Dix, Dorothea **IV:** 114

Douglas, Stephen A. **V:** 99

Douglass, Frederick **V:** 100

Eads, James Buchanan **VI:** 85

Early, Jubal A. **V:** 103

Eaton, John, Jr. **V:** 104

economy **IV:** 119; **V:** 105

education **V:** 108

elections **V:** 109

emancipation **V:** 111–114

Emancipation Proclamation **V:** 114–115

Emerson, Ralph Waldo **IV:** 126–127

employment **V:** 115–117

espionage **V:** 117–118

Ewell, Richard Stoddert **V:** 118–119

Farragut, David G. **V:** 121–122

federal income tax **VII:** 92

54th Massachusetts Regiment **V:** 124–126

Fillmore, Millard **IV:** 136, 138

fire-eaters **V:** 127

Fitzhugh, George **V:** 128

Five Forks, Battle of **V:** 128–129

food riots **V:** 129–130

foraging **V:** 130–131

foreign policy **IV:** 143; **V:** 131–132

Forrest, Nathan Bedford **V:** 133–134

Fort Laramie **IV:** 145

Fort Pillow, Tennessee **V:** 135

Fort Sumter, South Carolina **V:** 135–137

Foster, Stephen C. **V:** 138

Fredericksburg, Battle of **V:** 139–141

Frémont, Jessie Benton **IV:** 152

Frémont, John C. **IV:** 154

fugitive slave laws **IV:** 155

Galveston, Battle of **V:** 145

Garfield, James A. **VI:** 108

Garrison, William Lloyd **V:** 146

German-American regiments **V:** 147

Gettysburg, Battle of **V:** 147–150

Gettysburg Address **V:** 151

Godkin, Edwin Lawrence **VI:** 116

Civil War (*continued*)
   governors **V:** 152–153
   Grand Army of the
     Republic **VI:** 118
   Grant, Julia Dent **V:** 154
   Grant, Ulysses S. **V:** 154,
     156
   Great Migration **VII:** 111
   Greeley, Horace **V:** 158
   Greenback-Labor Party
     VI: 120
   greenbacks **V:** 159
   Greenhow, Rose O'Neal **V:**
     159
   Griffith, D. W. **VII:**
     115–116
   habeas corpus, writ of **V:**
     161–162
   Halleck, Henry W. **V:**
     162–163
   Harpers Ferry, West
     Virginia **V:** 164–166
   Harrison, Benjamin **VI:**
     122
   Hayes, Rutherford B. **VI:**
     125
   Higginson, Thomas
     Wentworth **V:** 167
   Hill, Ambrose P. **V:**
     167–168
   Holmes, Oliver Wendell
     VII: 123
   homefront **V:** 168–170
   Homer, Winslow **VI:** 130
   homespun **V:** 170
   Homestead Act of 1862 **V:**
     170
   Hood, John Bell **V:**
     170–171
   Hooker, Joseph **V:**
     171–172
   Houston, Sam **IV:** 175
   Howard, O. O. **V:** 173
   immigration **IV:** 180; **V:**
     175, 176–177
   impressment **V:** 179–180
   industrial development **V:**
     180–181
   Internal Revenue taxes **VI:**
     147
   Irish-American regiments
     V: 181–182
   ironclad oath **V:** 182–183
   ironclads **V:** 183–184
   Jackson, "Stonewall" **V:**
     185–186
   jayhawkers **V:** 186–187
   Johnson, Andrew **V:** 187
   Johnston, Albert Sidney **V:**
     189
   Johnston, Joseph E. **V:**
     189–190

Joint Committee on the
   Conduct of War **V:**
   190–191
Jomini, Antoine-Henri,
   baron de **V:** 192
journalism **V:** 192–194
Kansas-Nebraska Act of
   1854 **V:** 197–198
Kelley, William D. **V:** 198
ladies aid societies **V:**
   203–204
Langston, John Mercer **VI:**
   172
Lee, Robert E. **V:** 205–207
letters **V:** 207–208
Liberia, immigration to **VI:**
   174
Lincoln, Abraham **V:** 208,
   210–211
Lincoln, Mary Todd **V:** 212
literature **V:** 212–213
Longstreet, James **V:**
   214–216
Lookout Mountain, Battle
   of **V:** 216–217
lost cause, the **V:** 217–218
Louisiana Tigers **V:** 218
loyalty oaths **V:** 218–219
lyceum movement **IV:** 215
Manifest Destiny **IV:** 219
marine corps **V:** 222
Marx, Karl **V:** 223–224
Mason-Dixon Line **V:** 224
McClellan, George B. **V:**
   224–226
McCormick, Cyrus Hall
   IV: 225
McKinley, William **VI:**
   189
Medal of Honor **V:**
   227–228
medicine and hospitals **V:**
   228–232
merchant marine **VI:** 192
Milliken's Bend, Battle of
   V: 232–233
Mississippi River **V:**
   234–236
Mobile campaign **V:** 236
Monitor-Merrimack **V:**
   237–239
monuments **V:** 239–240
Moody, Dwight Lyman **VI:**
   196
Morgan, John Hunt **V:**
   240
Morgan, John Pierpont **VI:**
   197
Mormon War **IV:** 244
Morse, Samuel F. B. **IV:**
   246
Mott, Lucretia **IV:** 247

Murfreesboro/Stones
   River, Battle of **V:**
   242–243
music **V:** 243–245
Nast, Thomas **V:** 247
Native Americans **V:**
   249–251
New Orleans, Battle of **V:**
   251–252
New York City **V:** 253
New York City draft riots
   V: 254–255
Nullification Controversy
   IV: 265
nurses **V:** 255–256
Oates, William C. **V:** 257
Olmstead, Frederick Law
   V: 258
Orphan Brigade **V:** 258
Overland campaign **V:**
   260–261
overland mail **IV:** 272
Pacific Railroad Act of
   1862 **V:** 263
Parker, Ely Samuel **V:** 265
peace movements **V:**
   265–266
Pea Ridge/Elkhorn Tavern,
   Battle of **V:** 265
Pember, Phoebe Yates
   Levy **V:** 266–267
Peninsular campaign **V:**
   267–270
Petersburg campaign **V:**
   270–273
Phillips, Wendell **IV:** 281
photography **V:** 273–274
Pickett, George Edward **V:**
   274–275
Pierce, Franklin **V:** 275
plantations **V:** 276–277
Porter, David Dixon **V:**
   280
Port Royal, South
   Carolina, Experiment **V:**
   279–280
Powell, John Wesley **VI:**
   227
prisons **V:** 281–283
prostitution **V:** 283–284
public land policy **IV:** 288
Quantrill, William Clarke
   V: 285–286
race and racial conflict **IV:**
   291, 292; **V:** 287–288
railroads **V:** 289–290
Rainey, Joseph H. **V:** 290
Red River campaign **V:**
   297–298
refugees **V:** 298–299
religion **V:** 300; **VI:** 241
Republican Party **IV:** 302

Revels, Hiram R. **V:** 303
Richmond, Virginia **V:**
   303–304
Rosecrans, William S. **V:**
   305
rules of war **V:** 305–306
Santa Fe Trail **IV:** 306
Schurz, Carl **VI:** 256
science and technology **V:**
   308–310
Scott, Thomas Alexander
   VI: 258
Scott, Winfield **IV:** 310
secession **V:** 310–313
Selective Service Act **VII:**
   282
Seminole wars **IV:** 312
Semmes, Raphael **V:** 313
Seton, Elizabeth Ann **IV:**
   316
Seward, William H. **V:**
   313–315
Shenandoah Valley
   Jackson's campaign **V:**
     316–317
   Sheridan's campaign **V:**
     317–318
Sheridan, Philip H. **V:**
   318–319
Sherman, William T. **V:**
   319–321
Sherman's March through
   Georgia **V:** 321–323
Shiloh, Battle of **V:**
   323–326
Sickles, Daniel E. **V:**
   326–327
Singleton, Benjamin **V:**
   327
slavery **IV:** 318; **V:** 330
Society of Friends **V:**
   331–332
Spotsylvania, Battles of **V:**
   333
Stanton, Edwin M. **V:**
   333–334
states' rights **V:** 335–336
steel **VI:** 277
Stewart, Maria **IV:** 327
Still, William **IV:** 328
strikes **V:** 339–340
Stuart, J. E. B. **V:** 340–341
Sumner, Charles **V:** 343
Supreme Court decision
   IV: 331
tactics and strategy **V:**
   345–348
tariffs **V:** 348
taxation **V:** 349–350
Taylor, Susie King **V:** 350
telegraph **V:** 350–351
Texas **IV:** 339

Thirteenth Amendment **V:** 352–353

Thomas, George H. **V:** 353–354

Tilden, Samuel Jones **VI:** 289

Tourgée, Albion W. **V:** 354

trade, foreign **VII:** 309

transportation **V:** 355

Tredegar Iron Works **V:** 356

Truth, Sojourner **V:** 357

Tubman, Harriet **V:** 358

UDC **V:** 370

uniforms **V:** 362–364

Union army **V:** 364–367

Union League **V:** 367–368

Union navy **V:** 368–370

USCC **V:** 371–372

USSC **V:** 373–375

Van Lew, Elizabeth **V:** 378

Vesey, Denmark **IV:** 354

veterans **V:** 378–379; **VII:** 324

Vicksburg campaign **V:** 380–383

volunteer army **V:** 383–384

Wade, Benjamin **V:** 385

Wakeman, Sarah Rosetta **V:** 386

Walker, Mary Edwards **V:** 386

war contracting **V:** 387–388

Washington, D.C. **V:** 388–390

Watie, Stand **V:** 390–391

Weather Bureau, U.S. **VI:** 310

Welles, Gideon **V:** 391–392

West Point **V:** 372–373

Whig Party **IV:** 364

Whitman, Walt **V:** 394

Wilderness, Battle of the **V:** 395

Wilmot Proviso **V:** 396

Women's National Loyal League **V:** 396–397

women's status and rights **V:** 398

Yancey, William Lowndes **V:** 401

Zouaves **V:** 403–404

"Civil War Bench" **V:** 239

Civil War bonds **V:** 81

Civil War memorials **VI:** 259

Civil Works Administration (CWA) **VIII: 62–63,** 406*c*

cities and urban life **VIII:** 59

FERA **VIII:** 118

Hopkins, Harry **VIII:** 156

New Deal **VIII:** 241

PWA **VIII:** 285

relief **VIII:** 301

Social Security Act **VIII:** 328

WPA **VIII:** 387

Claflin, Tennessee **VI:** 267

Claiborne, William **II:** 50, 51, 209, 328

Claiborne, William C. C. **IV: 84–85**

claim clubs **IV: 85–86,** 287

Clansman, The (Dixon) **VII:** 30, 147

Clap, Thomas **II:** 184

Clare, Strigul de. *See* Strongbow, Richard

Clarel (Melville) **VI:** 178

Clarenbach, Kathryn **X:** 211

Clarenbach, Kay **IX:** 223

Clark, Daniel **III:** 379

Clark, Dick **X:** 202

Clark, Edward E. **X:** 176

Clark, Ellery **VI:** 290

Clark, George Rogers **III: 71,** 72, 255, 394*c*

Clark, J. Reuben **VII:** 50

Clark, Kenneth **IX:** 42

Clark, Mamie **IX:** 42

Clark, Mark **VIII:** *26,* 168; **IX:** 39

Clark, Thomas **IX:** 31, 80, 132–133, 315, 316

Clark, William **III: 72–73,** 208, *209,* 210, 315; **X:** 260. *See also* Lewis and Clark Expedition

Astor, John Jacob **IV:** 30

Astoria **IV:** 32

Catlin, George **IV:** 77

Chouteau family **IV:** 79

Columbia River **IV:** 93

exploration **IV:** 130, 131

Missouri Fur Company **IV:** 239

Clarke, Herbert L. **VI:** 271

Clarke, John **II:** 29, 321, 399

Clarke, Samuel **II:** 109

Clark Memorandum **VII: 50–51,** 361*c*

Clarkson, Thomas **III:** 98

class **II: 62–64**

Aleut **II:** 16

art **II:** 25

Bacon's Rebellion **II:** 28

Caribbean **II:** 53

Carter, Robert "King" **II:** 54

cities and urban life **II:** 62

clothing **II:** 64, 65

consumption **II:** 71

crime and punishment **II:** 75, 76

Dale, Sir Thomas **II:** 81

dance **II:** 82

domesticity **II:** 93

economy **II:** 102

English Civil War **II:** 107

environment **II:** 112

ethnocentrism **II:** 113

fertility **II:** 117

government, British American **II:** 145

Great Awakening **II:** 148

Harvard College **II:** 155

Hesselius, John **II:** 156

housing **II:** 157, 158

Hume, Sophia Wigington **II:** 159

Jamestown **II:** 171–172

Jesuits **II:** 174

Johnston, Henrietta Deering **II:** 177–178

journalism **II:** 179

Kuhn, Justus Engelhardt **II:** 186

labor **II:** 187–188, 190

La Salle, René-Robert Cavelier, sieur de **II:** 192

Leisler's Rebellion **II:** 192

marriage and family life **II:** 206, 208

Massachusetts **II:** 215

medicine **II:** 220

midwives **II:** 225

miscegenation **II:** 228, 229

mortality **II:** 235

mulattoes **II:** 238

music **II:** 239

Newport **II:** 258

North Carolina **II:** 265

Pennsylvania **II:** 275

postal service **II:** 292

Powhatan Confederacy **II:** 294

Quakers **II:** 307

race and racial conflict **II:** 311

religion, Native American **II:** 317

Rolfe, John **II:** 323

slave resistance **II:** 337

slavery **II:** 338, 339, 341

society, British American **II:** 349, 350

Spanish colonies **II:** 356

Spanish immigration **II:** 359

taverns and inns **II:** 367

Theus, Jeremiah **II:** 373

tobacco **II:** 374

travel **II:** 377

Virginia **II:** 384, 385

Winthrop, John **II:** 402

women's status and rights **II:** 406

class consciousness **VI:** 14, **57–58,** 223, 286

classical architecture **VII:** 16

classical art **X:** 26–27

classical education **IV:** 121

classical liberalism **X:** 174, 175

classical music **VII:** 194–195, 254; **VIII:** 119, 410*c;* **X:** 201

classicism **VI:** 15

Classic Taino **I:** 342

classified documents, publication of **X:** 233

class structure. *See* social classes

class warfare **VIII:** 15

Clatyon, Powell **V:** 199

Clausewitz, Karl von **V:** 345

Clay, Cassius Marcellus, Jr. **IX:** 5, 9, 334*c*. *See also* Ali, Muhammad

Clay, Henry **III:** 214; **IV: 86–88,** *87,* 376*c*–378*c;* **V:** 1, 209, 348; **VI:** 220

ACS **IV:** 15

Adams, John Quincy **IV:** 5

American System **IV:** 18–19

anti-Masonry **IV:** 24

banking and currency **IV:** 42

Benton, Thomas Hart **IV:** 49

Bonus Bill **IV:** 56

Compromise of 1850 **IV:** 94, 410–413

Democratic Party **IV:** 108

election of 1828 **IV:** 122

election of 1840 **IV:** 124, 125

Fillmore, Millard **IV:** 137

Free Trade and Sailor's Rights **IV:** 152

Harrison, William Henry **IV:** 169

internal improvements **IV:** 188

Jackson, Andrew **IV:** 192, 193

Liberia **IV:** 209

Liberty Party **IV:** 210

Mexican-American War **IV:** 232

Missouri Compromise of 1820 **IV:** 237

music **IV:** 250

National Road **IV:** 253

Nullification Controversy **IV:** 264

Oregon Treaty of 1846 **IV:** 270

Polk, James K. **IV:** 283

Taylor, Zachary **IV:** 335

Clay, Henry *(continued)*
    Tyler, John **IV:** 348, 349
    War Hawks **IV:** 355
    Webster, Daniel **IV:** 360
    Whig Party **IV:** 362–364
Clay, Lucius **IX:** 145
Clay, Margaret Meuse **II:** 29
Clayton, John **IV:** 88
Clayton, William **IV:** 109
Clayton Antitrust Act **VII: 51,**
    358*c*
    Adamson Act **VII:** 2
    AFL **VII:** 10
    business **VII:** 39
    Capper-Volstead Act **VII:**
        43
    Danbury Hatters **VII:** 61
    Democratic Party **VII:** 66
    Federal Trade Commission
        Act **VII:** 94
    labor movement **VII:** 152,
        154
    lobbying groups **VII:** 162
    New Unionism **VII:** 212
    progressivism **VII:** 237
Clayton-Bulwer Treaty of 1850
    IV: 88–89, 379*c;* **V:** 131; **VI:**
    190; **VII:** 222
Clean Air Act amendments **X:**
    249
Clean Air Act of 1970 **X:** 31, 77,
    210, 323*c,* 334
Clean Air Act of 1989 **X:** 46
Clean Air Act of 1990 **X:** 195,
    327*c*
Clean Water Act of 1972 **X:** 249,
    324*c*
Clean Water Act of 1981 **X:** 195
Cleaver, Eldridge **IX:** 33, 39
Cleburne, Patrick Ronayne **V:**
    57, **67–68,** 384
Clem, Ohio **V:** 243
Clemenceau, Georges **VII:** 156,
    323, 334
Clemens, Samuel Langhorne.
    See Twain, Mark
Clements, Arch **V:** 46
Clement VIII, Pope **I:** 75, 235
Clement XIV, Pope **I:** 189
clergy **VI:** 318
    gay rights movement **X:** 128
    religion **X:** 265
clerical work **VI:** 169; **VIII:** 385,
    386, 395
Clermont (steamboat) **III:** 142,
    216, 322, 397*c;* **IV:** 118, 185,
    307
Cleveland, Grover **V:** 7, 378,
    379; **VI:** 58, **58–59,** 232,
    325*c*–327*c;* **VII:** 64
    Altgeld, John Peter **VI:** 10
    Beecher, Henry Ward **VI:**
        24

Bering Sea dispute **VI:** 26
bimetallism **VI:** 29
Blaine, James Gillespie **VI:**
    31–32
Bryan, William Jennings
    VI: 37
Congress **VI:** 63–64
Cuba **VI:** 71
currency issue **VI:** 73
Dawes Severalty Act **VI:**
    76
Democratic Party **VI:** 78
Forest Reserve Act of 1891
    VI: 104
Free-Silver movement **VI:**
    105
Geological Survey, U.S.
    VI: 110, 111
Grand Army of the
    Republic **VI:** 118
Great Strike of 1877 **VI:**
    119
Harrison, Benjamin **VI:**
    122
Hawaii **VI:** 124
immigration restrictions
    VI: 141
Morgan, John Pierpont **VI:**
    198
mugwumps **VI:** 199
Muir, John **VI:** 200
Pan-American Union **VI:**
    220
political parties, third **VI:**
    226
the presidency **VI:** 230
presidential campaigns **VI:**
    231, 232
Pullman Strike **VI:** 236
Republican Party **VI:**
    246–247
Samoa **VI:** 255
Schurz, Carl **VI:** 257
Statue of Liberty **VI:** 276
tariff issue **VI:** 284
Venezuela boundary
    dispute **VI:** 303
Cleveland, Ohio **IV:** 82; **V:** 204;
    VII: 140; **X:** 256, 269
Cleveland Spiders **VI:** 22
Clinton, Bill. *See* Clinton,
    William Jefferson
Clinton, DeWitt **III: 73–74,**
    104; **IV:** 77, 128, 365, 375*c;*
    V: 355
Clinton, George **II:** 155; **III:** 74,
    74–75
    Bank of the United States
        (First) **III:** 31
    Burr, Aaron **III:** 54
    Clinton, DeWitt **III:** 73
    Democratic-Republican
        Party **III:** 104

Gallatin, Albert **III:** 147
Shays's Rebellion **III:** 324
Sullivan, John **III:** 337
Yates, Abraham, Jr. **III:**
    387
Clinton, Sir Henry **III: 75–76,**
    393*c,* 394*c*
    Andre, John **III:** 14
    Arnold, Benedict **III:** 21,
        22
    Burgoyne, John **III:** 52
    Charleston, siege of **III:**
        63–64
    Cornwallis, Lord **III:** 92,
        93
    Estaing, comte d' **III:** 120
    Howe, Richard, Lord **III:**
        168
    Monmouth, Battle of **III:**
        244, 245
    Revolutionary War **III:**
        305
    Saratoga, surrender at **III:**
        320
    Yorktown, surrender at
        III: 388
Clinton, Hillary Rodham **X:**
    63–65, *64,* 331*c*
    African nations **X:** 13
    Clinton, William **X:** 65, 68
    Mondale, Walter F. **X:** 196
    Starr, Kenneth **X:** 286, 287
Clinton, Joseph J. **VI:** 4
Clinton, William **II:** 85
Clinton, William Jefferson (Bill)
    VIII: 178; **IX:** 240; **X:**
    65–70, *67,* 328*c*–330*c*
    ABM Treaty **X:** 23
    abortion **X:** 4
    African nations **X:** 13
    Albright, Madeleine K. **X:**
        18
    amendments to the
        Constitution **X:** 19
    Articles of Impeachment
        for **X:** 357–359
    baby boomers **X:** 33
    Breyer, Stephen **X:** 42
    Bush, George H. W. **X:** 44,
        46
    campaign finance **X:** 53
    capital punishment **X:** 56
    Clinton, Hillary Rodham
        X: 64, 65
    Dayton accords **X:** 85
    defense policy **X:** 87–88
    Dole, Robert **X:** 90
    Dukakis, Michael **X:** 91
    economy **X:** 95–96
    elections **X:** 101
    Farmer, James L. **X:** 111
    federalism **X:** 113
    feminism **X:** 116

Ferraro, Geraldine A. **X:**
    117
Ford, Gerald R. **X:** 121
foreign policy **X:** 124
gay rights movement **X:**
    128
Gingrich, Newton L. **X:**
    129, 130
Ginsburg, Ruth Bader **X:**
    130
Gore, Albert, Jr. **X:**
    133–134
GRH Act of 1985 **X:** 135
gun control **X:** 137
Haiti, U.S. intervention in
    X: 140
Helms, Jesse A., Jr. **X:** 141
House of Representatives
    X: 145
immigration **X:** 148–149
impeachment **X:** 150
independent counsel **X:**
    150–151
Judicial Watch **X:** 162
Kemp, Jack F. **X:** 163
Kosovo **X:** 166
Latin America **X:** 173, 174
marriage **X:** 183
Mitchell, George **X:** 195
Nader, Ralph **X:** 206
neoconservatism **X:** 216
NEPA **X:** 210
Nixon, Richard M. **X:** 221
North Vietnam **X:** 224
OMB **X:** 227
Perot, H. Ross **X:** 234
Persian Gulf War **X:** 236
political parties **X:** 237
pornography **X:** 245
Powell, Colin L. **X:** 247
pro-life and pro-choice
    movements **X:** 249
property rights **X:** 250
Reno, Janet **X:** 267
RFRA **X:** 266
SDI **X:** 289
Second Inaugural Address
    X: 355–357
Senate **X:** 276
Shriver, Sargent **X:** 278
South Africa **X:** 280
Starr, Kenneth **X:** 286–287
Supreme Court **X:** 291
terrorism **X:** 299
tobacco suits **X:** 305
United Nations **X:** 308
veto, presidential **X:** 311
War Powers Act **X:** 315
Weather Underground **X:**
    318
Clintonians **III:** 104
clipper ships **VI:** 193
Clive, Robert **II:** 119

Cloak Makers' Strike **VII:** 132
clock making **IV:** 184, 186*m*
cloning **X:** 146, 329*c*
Close, Chuck **X:** 26
Closing of the American Mind, The (Bloom) **X:** 80
Clotel, or The President's Daughter (Brown) **IV:** 379*c*
clothing **I:** 56, 320, 361; **II:** *64,* **64–65,** *65;* **V:** 122–123
   agriculture **II:** 8; **IV:** 10
   Bloomer, Amelia **IV:** 53–54
   childhood **II:** 60
   consumption **II:** 70, 71
   crafts **II:** 74
   Crow **II:** 77
   fashion **V:** 122–123
   fur trade **II:** 133
   homespun **V:** 170
   Hyde, Edward, Viscount Cornbury **II:** 162
   indentured servitude **II:** 163
   indigo **II:** 166
   industrialization **IV:** 186*m*
   labor **II:** 187, 188, 190
   marriage and family life **II:** 206
   Maryland **II:** 211
   Massachusetts **II:** 215
   mountain men **IV:** 248
   Northwest Coast Indians **II:** 266
   science and technology **V:** 310
   Shiloh, Battle of **V:** 324
   society, British American **II:** 351–352
   Strauss, Levi **IV:** 329
   strikes **V:** 340
   uniforms **V:** 362–364
   Union army **V:** 365
   Washington, D.C. **V:** 390
   Woolman, John **II:** 410
clothing industry **V:** 181
Clovis Man **I:** 254–255
Clovis people **I:** 242
Club of Rome **X:** 76
Clyman, James **IV:** 114
CNN. *See* Cable News Network
Coahuila **II:** 231
Coahuila-Texas **IV:** 174, 340
coal/coal industry **III:** 178; **IV:** 40, 292, 295; **V:** 180; **VI:** 193, 292, 293; **VII:** 12–13, 44–45, 82, 102–103, 313–314
Coalition for the Free Exercise of Religion **X:** 266
Coalition of American Public Employees **X:** 111
coastal defense **V:** 74
Coast Guard **VIII:** 237, 386; **X:** 207

Coast Tsimshian **I:** 150
Coatlicue **I:** 170
Co. Aytch (Watkins) **V:** 213
Cobain, Kurt **X:** 202, 240
Cobb, Robert **V:** 258
Cobb, Ty **VIII:** 407*c*
Cobbett, William **III:** 62
Cobden, Richard **V:** 40
Coca, Antonio de **I:** 215
Coca-Cola **IX:** 44
Coca Cola Export Corporation **VIII:** 111
cocaine **VI:** 192; **X:** 206–208
Cochimi **I:** 48
cochineal **I:** 261; **II:** 355
Cochise **V:** 406*c*
Cochran, Jacqueline **VIII:** 380, 381
Cochrane, Sir Alexander **IV:** 39
Cociyo **I:** 242
Cocke, Abraham **I:** 27
cock fighting **II:** 21
Cocoanuts, The **VIII:** 405*c*
cod **I:** **74–75,** 263, 264
Coddington, William **II:** **65–66,** 258, 321
Code and Cypher School **VIII:** 64, 164
code breaking **V:** 216; **VIII:** **64–65**
   Atlantic, Battle of the **VIII:** 28
   Coral Sea, Battle of the **VIII:** 74
   espionage **VIII:** 104
   intelligence **VIII:** 164
   Midway, Battle of **VIII:** 211
   Native Americans **VIII:** 236
   Stimson, Henry L. **VIII:** 340
   technology **VIII:** 353
   WAVES **VIII:** 380
coded messages **V:** 351
code duello **II:** 96
codeine **X:** 206
Code Noir **II:** 53, 193
Code of 1650 (Connecticut) **II:** 70
"Code of Good Practices" (TV) **X:** 295
"code talkers" **VIII:** 236, *236*
Codex Aubin **I:** 400
Codex Mendoza **I:** 231, 250, 349
Cody, William Frederick (Buffalo Bill) **VI:** **59–60,** *60*
   Buffalo Bill's Wild West Show **VI:** *97,* 209
   entertainment, popular **VI:** 98
   literature **VI:** 176

Native Americans **VI:** 209
   Sioux wars **VI:** 263
   Sitting Bull **VI:** 264
Coelho, Anthony **X:** 21, 322
Coelho, Goncalo **I:** 32*m,* 215
Coen brothers **X:** 240
Coercive Acts **III:** **76–77,** 392*c*
   Adams, John **III:** 2
   Adams, Samuel **III:** 4
   Association, the **III:** 27
   Boston Tea Party **III:** 45
   Burke, Edmund **III:** 52
   committees of correspondence **III:** 77
   Continental Congress, First **III:** 87
   Declaration of Independence **III:** 101
   Dickinson, John **III:** 105
   Franklin, Benjamin **III:** 134
   Gage, Thomas **III:** 146
   Hutchinson, Thomas **III:** 171
   Lexington and Concord, Battles of **III:** 211
   Mason, George **III:** 237
   North, Lord **III:** 260
   Proclamation of 1763 **III:** 287
   Quartering Act **III:** 291
   resistance movement **III:** 303
   Revere, Paul **III:** 304
   Suffolk Resolves **III:** 335
   Tea Act **III:** 345
   Wayne, Anthony **III:** 369
"coercive assimilation" **VIII:** 235
"Coetus of the German Reformed Congregations in Pennsylvania" **II:** 140
Coeur d'Alene miners' strike **VI:** **60–61,** 167
coffee **I:** 75–76; **II:** 43, 71, 376; **VI:** 291; **VIII:** 38
coffeehouses **I:** 75
Cofitachequi **I:** 76
cofradias **II:** 357
Cogswell, William **V:** 28
cohabitation **X:** 181, 182
Cohan, George M. **VII:** 85, 309
Cohen, Benjamin **X:** 125
Cohen, Stanley **X:** 191
Cohen, William **X:** 88, 195
Cohens v. Virginia **IV:** 330–331
Cohen v. California (1971) **X:** 319
Cohn, Roy **IX:** 18
Coinage Act of 1792 **IV:** 43
Coinage Act of 1834 **IV:** 43
Coinage Act of 1837 **IV:** 43
Coinage Act of 1873 **VI:** 324*c*

bimetallism **VI:** 28
   Bland-Allison Act **VI:** 32
   Crime of '73 **VI:** 69, 70
   currency issue **VI:** 72
coins **I:** 142, 325, 353; **V:** 23
Coin's Financial School (Harvey) **VI:** 29
Coke, Thomas **III:** 27
Coker v. Georgia (1977) **X:** 56
COLA. *See* cost-of-living adjustment
Colambu, Rajah **I:** 216
Colbert, Claudette **VIII:** 218
Colbert, Jean-Baptiste **I:** 223; **II:** 129
Colden, Cadwallader **II:** **66**
   American Philosophical Society **II:** 18
   Colden, Jane **II:** 66
   De Lancey family **II:** 86
   King's College **II:** 184
   Logan, James **II:** 198
   Pennsylvania **II:** 277
   science **II:** 330
Colden, Jane **II:** **66,** 277, 330
"cold funnel" **I:** 77
Cold Harbor, Battle of **V:** **68**
   Grant, Ulysses S. **V:** 156
   Hancock, Winfield Scott **V:** 163
   Hill, Ambrose P. **V:** 168
   homefront **V:** 169
   Irish-American regiments **V:** 182
   Lee, Robert E. **V:** 207
   Meade, George Gordon **V:** 227
   Overland campaign **V:** 261
   Petersburg campaign **V:** 270–271
Cold Mountain (Frazier) **V:** 213
Cold Springs, New York, strike (1864) **V:** 340
cold war **IX:** **57–60,** *59,* 330*c*
   ABM Treaty **X:** 22
   Acheson, Dean **IX:** 2
   African nations **X:** 12–13
   anticommunism **IX:** 14–15
   arms race **X:** 16–17; **X:** 25
   Asia (foreign policy) **IX:** 21
   atomic bomb **VIII:** 29
   Atomic Energy Commission **IX:** 23
   aviation **IX:** 28
   Berlin blockade **IX:** 37
   Bush, George H. W. **X:** 44, 46
   Catholic Bishops' Letter **X:** 59
   CIA **IX:** 50
   Clinton, William **X:** 66
   Communists **VIII:** 66
   conservatism **VIII:** 73

cold war *(continued)*
  conservative movement **X:** 79
  defense policy **X:** 87
  demobilization **VIII:** 80
  détente **X:** 89
  end of **X: 70–72,** *71*
  Federal Employee Loyalty Program **IX:** 109–110
  foreign policy **VIII:** 126; **X:** 122, 124
  Forrestal, James V. **VIII:** 126
  Good Neighbor Policy **VIII:** 133
  Graham, Billy **IX:** 126
  Grand Alliance **VIII:** 138
  Hiroshima and Nagasaki **VIII:** 148
  Hispanic Americans **X:** 142
  hydrogen bomb **IX:** 139
  immigration **IX:** 141
  INF Treaty **X:** 152
  Interstate Highway Act of 1956 **IX:** 144
  Keynesianism **VIII:** 177
  Latin America **X:** 172, 173
  marriage and family life **IX:** 192
  Marshall Plan **IX:** 194
  Middle East **IX:** 201
  military-industrial complex **IX:** 203
  National Endowment for the Arts **IX:** 221
  NATO **X:** 223
  neoconservatism **X:** 215
  New Frontier **IX:** 230
  NSC-68 **IX:** 233–234
  Peace Corps **IX:** 241
  Point Four Program **IX:** 242–243
  Popular Front **VIII:** 276
  Reagan, Ronald W. **X:** 261
  religion **IX:** 255
  space policy **X:** 281
  Suez crisis **IX:** 289
  technology **VIII:** 354
  Teheran Conference **VIII:** 355
  Truman Doctrine **IX:** 300–301
  United Nations **VIII:** 366; **X:** 307
  wars of national liberation **IX:** 316
Cole, Lester **IX:** 134–135, *211*
Cole, Thomas **IV:** 26; **V:** 16
Cole, USS **X:** 299–300, 331*c*
Colegrove v. Green **IX:** 31
Coleman, William **II:** 18

Coleridge, Samuel Taylor **IV:** 345
Colgate, William **IV:** 118, 184, 187
Colgate Company **VII:** 255
Colhuacan **I:** 17
Coligny, Gaspard de **I:** 201
Colima **I:** 258, 318
collective bargaining **VIII:** 30, 179, 407*c*; **IX:** 11, 291. *See also* unions/union movement
College and Academy of Philadelphia **II:** 104
college football **VIII:** 336; **IX:** 255
College of New Jersey **II:** 104–106, 296, 298. *See also* Princeton College/University
College of New York **II:** 184
College of Philadelphia **II: 66–67,** 104, 220
College of Physicians **II:** 282, 335–336
College of Physicians and Surgeons **VI:** 191
College of Rhode Island **II:** 104–105, 321
College of San Fernando (Mexico City) **II:** 331
College of William and Mary **II:** 20, **67,** 104, 109, 385; **III:** 203, 235
colleges **III:** 114, 115; **IV:** 121; **V:** 240–241, 406*c*; **VIII:** 94–95, 131, 384; **IX:** 91–92. *See also* education, higher
  African-American churches, growth of **VI:** 4
  African Americans **V:** 108, 241; **VI:** 5, 6
  agriculture **VI:** 8
  education **VII:** 77, 78–79
  education, higher **VI:** 93
  education, philanthropy and **VI:** 94
  football **VI:** 101–102
  New Woman **VII:** 213
  social work **VII:** 290
  sports **VII:** 295
  sports and recreation **VI:** 275
  women **V:** 108
College Settlement Association **VI:** 259
Collegiate School **II:** 70, 413. *See also* Yale College/University
collegiate sports **VII:** 293, 295
Collier, John **VII:** 208; **VIII:** 163, 235, 236
Collinson, Peter **II:** 30, 66, 277

Colloquy of Regensburg (1541) **I:** 96
Colluchio **I:** 177
Colman, Samuel **VI:** 288
Colmer, William **VIII:** 295
Colombia **I:** 10, 24, 277, **II:** 356; **IV:** 88, 169, 241, 378*c*; **V:** 131, 133; **VII:** 99, 223–224, 356*c*, 358*c*; **X:** 46
Colón, Bartolomé. *See* Columbus, Bartholomew
Colón, Cristobal. *See* Columbus, Christopher
Colón, Diego. *See* Columbus, Diego
Colonel Dismounted, The (Bland) **III:** 40
Colonel Sellers **VI:** 115
colonialism **IX:** 3
colonial unity **II:** *14*
colonization **VII:** 106. *See also* slaves, colonization/repatriation of; *specific headings, e.g.:*
  English colonies/colonization
  art and architecture **I:** 13
  black legend **I:** 30
  bubonic plague **I:** 286
  gold **I:** 142
  horses **I:** 169
  Las Casas, Bartolomé de **I:** 199
  New World **I:** 263
  Parmenius, Stephen **I:** 278
  smallpox **I:** 330
Colorado **I:** 255; **VI:** 51*m*, 317; **IX:** 171; **X:** 329*c*
  affirmative action **X:** 9
  amendments to the Constitution **X:** 20
  Bent, William **IV:** 48
  Bent's Fort **IV:** 50–51
  Frémont, John C. **IV:** 154
  gay rights movement **X:** 128
  Ginsburg, Ruth Bader **X:** 131
  medicine **X:** 190
  population trends **X:** 242
  pro-life and pro-choice movements **X:** 248
  Supreme Court **X:** 291
  Texas **IV:** 339
Colorado Fuel and Iron Company **VII:** 167
Colorado gold rush **IV: 89–90; V:** 405*c*
  Beckwourth, Jim **IV:** 47
  Bent, William **IV:** 48
  Fort Laramie **IV:** 145
  gold, discovery and mining **IV:** 164

"Pike's Peak or Bust" **IV:** 282
Colorado Republican Federal Campaign Committee v. Federal Election Committee (1998) **X:** 53
Colorado volunteers **V:** 407*c*
Colored Farmers' Alliance **VI:** 99
Colored National Labor Union **V: 68–69**
Colquitt, Alfred **V:** 39
Colson, Charles **X:** 308, 317
Colt, Samuel **IV: 90–92,** *91*
  Colt revolver **IV:** 92
  economy **IV:** 118
  industrialization **IV:** 184, 187
  science and technology **IV:** 307
Colter, John **IV:** 130
Colt revolver **IV:** 91, **92,** 184, 307
Columbia (space shuttle) **X:** 326*c*
Columbia Broadcasting System (CBS) **VIII:** 290; **IX:** 153, 244; **X:** 239, 241, 296
  entertainment **VII:** 86
  journalism **VII:** 143
  music **VII:** 195
  popular culture **VII:** 232
Columbia College **II:** 199. *See also* King's College
Columbiad, The (Barlow) **III:** 36
Columbia Fur Company **IV:** 16–17
Columbian Exchange **I: 76–78**
  bubonic plague **I:** 286
  cacao **I:** 46
  conquistadores **I:** 85
  Coosa **I:** 85
  diseases **I:** 107
  population trends **I:** 289, 290
  slavery **I:** 327
  smallpox **I:** 330–331
  Soto, Hernando de **I:** 333
Columbian Magazine **III:** 61
Columbia River **IV: 92–93**
  American Fur Company **IV:** 16
  Astor, John Jacob **IV:** 31
  Astoria **IV:** 33
  Fort Vancouver **IV:** 145
  McLoughlin, John **IV:** 228–229
  migration **IV:** 236
  Oregon Trail **IV:** 267
  Oregon Treaty of 1846 **IV:** 269

Rocky Mountain Fur
Company **IV:** 302
Columbia studios **X:** 197
Columbia University **VI:** 324c;
VII: 68; **IX:** 319; **X:** 273
football **VI:** 101
MacDowell, Edward
Alexander **VI:** 183
mining: metal and coal **VI:**
194
Pulitzer, Joseph **VI:** 235
track and field **VI:** 289
Columbine High School
shooting **X:** 137, 330c
Columbus, Bartholomew
(Bartolomé Colón) **I:** 3–4,
78–79, 80, 82
Columbus, Christopher
(Cristobal Colón) **I: 79–83,**
80m, 81, 128, 386c, 387c; **II:**
22, 51, 93, 174, 204
adelantado **I:** 3–4
Azores **I:** 17
"Barcelona Letter" of 1493
I: 392–394
Behaim, Martin **I:** 27
cabildo **I:** 39
cabinet of curiosities **I:** 40
Cabot, John **I:** 41
cacao **I:** 45
Canary Islands **I:** 53
cannibalism **I:** 54
caravel **I:** 55, 55
Cathay (China) **I:** 64–65
Columbian Exchange **I:** 76
Columbus, Bartholomew
I: 78–79
conquistadores **I:** 84
corn (maize) **I:** 87–88
Cortés, Hernán **I:** 91
Cuba **I:** 98
Ferdinand and Isabella **I:**
128, 128
Gama, Vasco da **I:** 137
gold **I:** 142
Hispaniola **I:** 161
horses **I:** 167, 169
invention and technology
I: 179
Jamaica **I:** 187
Jews (Judaism) **I:** 190–191
Las Casas, Bartolomé de **I:**
198
Mandeville, Sir John **I:** 219
mappae mundi **I:** 221
Montserrat **I:** 243
New World **I:** 262
Oviedo y Valdés, Gonzalo
Fernández de **I:** 272
Peter Martyr **I:** 280
Ponce de León, Juan **I:**
288

printing press **I:** 294
Puerto Rico **I:** 297
sugar **I:** 338
Taino **I:** 342
Velázquez, Diego de **I:**
363–364
Columbus, Diego (Diego
Colón) **I:** 79, 82, 98, 297
columns **IV:** 27; **V:** 346
Colwell, James **V:** 208
Comanche/Comanche nation **II:**
150, 229, 247, 255; **III:** 154,
155, 258; **IV:** 377c
Bent, Charles **IV:** 47
Chouteau family **IV:** 79
Colt revolver **IV:** 92
exploration **IV:** 131
Rocky Mountain Fur
Company **IV:** 302
Santa Fe Trail **IV:** 306
Smith, Jedediah Strong **IV:**
322
Texas **IV:** 337
Combating Terrorism Act of
2001 **X:** 300
combine, grain **IV:** 10
Combined Bomber Offensive
VIII: 52
Combined Food Board **VIII:** 9
Combined Joint Task Forces
(NATO) **X:** 223
combines **VI:** 8
Comcast **X:** 244
COMECON **IX:** 277
comedies **VIII:** 218
comedy television programs **X:**
295
Comenius, John Amos **VI:** 159
Comet (airplane) **IX:** 28
comets **IV:** 308; **VI:** 194–195
comic operas **VI:** 286
comic strips **VI:** 321
Coming of Age in Samoa
(Mead) **VII:** 162, 177, 361c
Comintern **VII:** 360c, 361c;
VIII: 275–276
Commentaries on the Laws of
England (Blackstone) **III:** 39,
40, 203, 391c
commerce **IV:** 39, 45–46; **VII:**
94, 122, 170. See also trade,
domestic and foreign
Commerce, Illinois **IV:** 323
Commerce Department **VII:**
200; **IX:** 57
commerce raiding **V:** 74, 221,
369–370
commercial agriculture **V:** 7
commercial aviation **IX:** 27
commercial sponsorship **VII:**
254, 255
commissary system **II:** 20

commission government **VI:**
108; **VII:** 316
Commission on Civil Rights **IX:**
54, 55, 57
Commission on Immigration
Reform **X:** 147
Commission on the Status of
Women **X:** 114, 210
Committee for Industrial
Organization **VIII:** 407c,
408c
American Federation of
Labor **VIII:** 14
CIO **VIII:** 69–70
Hillman, Sidney **VIII:** 146
labor **VIII:** 180
Lewis, John L. **VIII:** 186
Committee for Public
Information (CPI) **VII:**
51–52, 359c
advertising **VII:** 5
conscription **VII:** 54
Espionage Act **VII:** 88
Fuel Administration **VII:**
102
Palmer, A. Mitchell **VII:**
221
Selective Service Act **VII:**
282
World War I **VII:** 344
Committee for the First
Amendment **IX:** 135
Committee for the Suppression
of Legalized Vice **V:** 283
Committee of One Hundred
III: 393c
Committee of Secret
Correspondence **III:** 205
Committee of Style **III:** 161
Committee on Economic
Security (CES) **VIII:** 265,
328
Committee on Foreign
Relations **V:** 343
Committee on Maternal Health
VII: 30
Committee on the Present
Danger **X:** 86
committees of correspondence
III: 77, 392c
Adams, Samuel **III:** 4
Association, the **III:** 27
Bland, Richard **III:** 40
Boston Tea Party **III:** 45
Church, Benjamin **III:** 68
Clinton, George **III:** 74
Coercive Acts **III:** 76–77
Democratic-Republican
societies **III:** 105
Dunmore, Lord **III:** 109
Gaspée affair **III:** 149
Henry, Patrick **III:** 166

Lexington and Concord,
Battles of **III:** 211
Livingston, William **III:**
217
Quakers **III:** 291
Quincy, Josiah **III:** 293
Revere, Paul **III:** 304
voluntary associations **III:**
362
Wilson, James **III:** 379
Yates, Abraham, Jr. **III:**
387
Young, Thomas **III:** 390
"committees of vigilance" **IV:** 66
Committee to Reelect the
President (CREEP) **X:** 196,
220, 315–316
Commodity Credit Corporation
VIII: 8
commodity prices **IV:** 275, 276;
VIII: 406c
Commodore **X:** 273
Common Cause **X:** 81
Commoner, Barry **X:** 76
common law **IV:** 221
common law marriage **X:** 181
Commons, John **IX:** 117
Common School Journal (Mann)
IV: 120, 220
common schools **IV:** 120; **VI:** 92
Common Sense (Paine) **III:**
77–79, 78, 393c
corporatism **III:** 94, 95
Declaration of
Independence **III:** 102
deism **III:** 104
literature **III:** 214
Paine, Thomas **III:** 271
republicanism **III:** 302
resistance movement **III:**
303
Common Sense Book of Baby
and Child Care, The (Spock)
IX: 279, 329c; **X:** 33
common soldier **V: 69–71**
bounty system **V:** 34
citizen-soldier **V:** 61–62
letters **V:** 207–208
literature **V:** 213
lost cause, the **V:** 217
uniforms **V:** 363
veterans, Civil War **V:** 379
volunteer army **V:** 383–384
Commonwealth and Southern
VIII: 356, 378–379
commonwealthmen **III: 79–80**
anti-Federalists **III:** 15
Declaration of
Independence **III:** 102
Livingston, William **III:**
217
Whigs **III:** 375

Commonwealth of Independent
States **X:** 280–281
Commonwealth v. Hunt **IV:** 204
communal farms **VIII:** 307
communal riots **X:** 255, 256
communes **IV:** 345; **V:** 357, 358;
VI: 301
   Brook Farm **IV:** 58
   Owen, Robert **IV:** 273
   religion **IV:** 299
   Warren, Josiah **IV:** 358
   Wright, Fanny **IV:** 369
communication(s) **IV:** 234,
245–246; **VI: 61–62; VII:**
311; **VIII:** 353. *See also*
languages
   Aguilar, Gerónimo
    (Jerónimo) de **I:** 5
   business cycles **VI:** 41
   Cabeza de Vaca, Álvar
    Núñez **I:** 37, 38
   Cartier, Jacques **I:** 58
   Cortés, Hernán **I:** 93
   foreign policy **VI:** 103
   Harriot, Thomas **I:** 154
   illustration, photography,
    and the graphic arts **VI:**
    137–138
   Inca **I:** 175
   industrial revolution,
    second **VI:** 146, 147
   invention and technology
    I: 179
   labor, woman **VI:** 169
   magazines **VI:** 185
   Malinche **I:** 218
   Manteo **I:** 220
   Nahuatl **I:** 250
   newspapers **VI:** 211–212
   New York City **V:** 253
   printing press **I:** 293–295
   Puerto Rico **I:** 296
   Roanoke **I:** 313
   science and technology **V:**
    310
   Sheridan, Philip H. **V:** 318
   Tabasco **I:** 341
   telegraph **V:** 350–351
Communications Act of 1934
VIII: 406*c*
Communications Decency Act
(CDA) of 1996 **X:** 60,
153–154, 245, 329*c*
communications industry **VII:**
132–133
communications technology
   advertising **X:** 8
   business **X:** 49
   computers **X:** 72–75
   economy **X:** 95
   globalization **X:** 131
   Internet **X:** 152–154

   science and technology **X:**
    273–275
communication technology **IX:**
270
*Communication Workers of
America v. Beck* (1988) **X:** 53
communion **IV:** 336
communism **VIII: 65–66; IX:
60–62,** 329*c*–331*c;* **X:** 328*c.*
   See also anticommunism; Red
   Scare
   Africa **IX:** 3, 4
   America First Committee
    VIII: 13
   American Legion **VII:** 11
   anti-Semitism **VIII:** 19
   Asia (foreign policy) **IX:**
    21–22
   Asian-American movement
    IX: 22
   Baker v. Carr **IX:** 32
   Bay of Pigs **IX:** 33–34
   censorship **VIII:** 55
   CIO **VIII:** 70
   civil liberties **VIII:** 60
   cold war **IX:** 57–60; **X:**
    70–72
   Congress of Industrial
    Organizations **IX:** 66
   conservatism **IX:** 68
   contras **X:** 80
   Dennis v. United States **IX:**
    80
   election of 1944 **VIII:** 99
   FBI **VIII:** 115
   FTP **VIII:** 120
   FWP **VIII:** 121
   Goldwater, Barry **IX:** 123
   Graham, Billy **IX:** 126
   Hillman, Sidney **VIII:**
    146
   International Ladies'
    Garment Workers
    Union **VII:** 132
   Iron Curtain **X:** 156–157
   labor **VIII:** 181
   Latin America **IX:** 172
   Lewis, John L. **VIII:** 186
   Luce, Henry R. **VIII:** 196
   marriage and family life
    IX: 192
   McCarthy, Joseph **IX:**
    189–190
   Murray, Philip **VIII:** 221
   NATO **IX:** 231–233
   Nixon, Richard M. **X:** 220
   NLRB **VIII:** 230
   Oppenheimer, J. Robert
    IX: 237
   political correctness **X:** 236
   Popular Front **VIII:**
    275–276

   race and racial conflict
    VIII: 287, 288
   Reagan, Ronald W. **X:** 258
   Robeson, Paul **IX:** 261
   Russian Revolution **VII:**
    270–271
   Scottsboro Boys **VIII:**
    319–320
   socialism **VII:** 289; **VIII:**
    327
   Soviet Union **IX:** 277–279
   Spanish Civil War **VIII:**
    335
   Truman Doctrine **IX:**
    300–301
   U.S. European foreign
    policy **IX:** 105
   Vietnam War **IX:** 308–310;
    X: 312
   wars of national liberation
    IX: 317
   White Paper **IX:** 320–321
   Wright, Richard **VIII:**
    399–400
Communist Labor Party
   Communist Party **VII:** 52
   radicalism **VII:** 251
   Reed, John **VII:** 259
   Russian Revolution **VII:**
    270
Communist Manifesto (Marx
and Engels) **V:** 223; **IX:** 61
Communist Party (CP) **VII:
52–53,** 360*c;* **IX:** 61; **X:** 280
   anticommunism **IX:** 14
   Army-McCarthy hearings
    IX: 17–19
   Chambers, Whittaker **IX:**
    50
   Flynn, Elizabeth Gurley
    VII: 95
   Gastonia Strike **VII:** 106
   Hiss, Alger **IX:** 134
   Internal Security Act of
    1950 **IX:** 144
   labor movement **VII:** 154
   Passaic Strike **VII:** 224
   radicalism **VII:** 251
   radical press **VII:** 253
   Red Scare **VII:** 259
   Reed, John **VII:** 259
   Rosenberg, Julius and
    Ethel **IX:** 264–265
   Russian Revolution **VII:**
    270
   socialism **VII:** 289
   Soviet Union **IX:** 277
Communist Party of the United
   States of America (CPUSA)
   VII: 52–53, 251, 361*c;* **IX:**
   12, 80
   Bridges, Harry **VIII:** 43

   Communists **VIII:** 65–66
   election of 1932 **VIII:** 96
   FBI **VIII:** 115
   politics in the Roosevelt
    era **VIII:** 270, 272*t*
   Popular Front **VIII:** 276
   race and racial conflict
    VIII: 287
   Robeson, Paul **VIII:** 310
   Scottsboro Boys **VIII:** 319
   Wright, Richard **VIII:**
    399
Community Action Program
(CAP) **IX:** 52, **62–63,** 127,
208, 313, 334*c*
community life **VI:** 241
   Abenaki **I:** 2
   Acadia **I:** 2
   Apalachee **I:** 11
   Aztecs **I:** 18, 20–21
   Bantu **I:** 25
   Benin **I:** 28
   California **I:** 48
   Cuba **I:** 98
   Florida **I:** 130
   Huron **I:** 170–171
   Iroquois **I:** 181–183
   Luhya **I:** 210
   Maliseet **I:** 219
   Massachusett **I:** 225
   Natchez **I:** 251
   population trends **I:** 289,
    290
   slave trade **I:** 328
   Zuni **I:** 383
commutation
   Confederate army **V:** 72
   conscription **V:** 79
   New York City draft riots
    V: 254
   Society of Friends **V:** 331
   Union army **V:** 364
compact cars **IX:** 25
compact discs (CDs) **X:** 203,
239, 240, 273
Compagnie du Saint Sacrament
II: 127
company boats **IV:** 74
Company of Cathay **I: 83**
Company of Far East Regions **I:**
114
Company of New Netherland **I:**
115
Company of One Hundred
Associates **II:** 127
Company of the Indies **II:** 199
company towns **IV:** 185, 186
competition **VI:** 292, 293
composers **VI:** 22–23; **VIII:** 119
Comprehensive Anti-Apartheid
Act of 1986 (CAAA) **X:** 280,
327*c*

Comprehensive Crime Control Act of 1984 **X:** 82, 207, 326c

Comprehensive Drug Abuse Prevention and Control Act of 1970 **X:** 206–207

Comprehensive Environmental Response Compensation and Liability Act of 1980 **X:** 78, 210

Compromise of 1850 **IV:** **93–95,** 94m, 379c, 410–413; **V:** 406c. *See also* Fugitive Slave Act of 1850

  Benton, Thomas Hart **IV:** 50

  Calhoun, John C. **IV:** 63

  California **IV:** 65

  Cass, Lewis **IV:** 77

  Chase, Salmon P. **V:** 56

  Civil War **V:** 64

  Clay, Henry **IV:** 88

  Democratic Party **IV:** 108; **V:** 94

  Douglas, Stephen A. **V:** 98

  Fillmore, Millard **IV:** 137

  fire-eaters **V:** 128

  Free-Soil Party **IV:** 150, 151

  fugitive slave laws **IV:** 154–155

  Guadalupe Hidalgo, Treaty of (1848) **IV:** 166

  Julian, George W. **V:** 194

  Kansas-Nebraska Act of 1854 **V:** 197

  Know-Nothing Party **IV:** 201

  Missouri Compromise of 1820 **IV:** 237

  Mormon War **IV:** 244

  personal liberty laws **IV:** 280

  Pierce, Franklin **V:** 275

  popular sovereignty **IV:** 285

  Taylor, Zachary **IV:** 335

  Texas **IV:** 339

  Underground Railroad **V:** 362

  Vallandigham, Clement L. **V:** 377

  Webster, Daniel **IV:** 360

  Welles, Gideon **V:** 391

  Whig Party **IV:** 364

Compromise of 1876 **V:** 297

Compromise Tariff of 1833 **IV:** 87, 265

Compton, Arthur H. **IX:** 236

Compton, Henry **II:** 19–20

Comptroller of the Currency **VI:** 205, 206

compulsory education laws **VII:** 76

Computer Emergency Response Team (CERT) **X:** 153

Computer Matching and Privacy Protection Act of 1988 **X:** 112

computer punch cards **VI:** 150

computers **VIII:** 353, 390; **IX:** 63–65, 329c, 331c; **X:** 72–75, 73, 326c

  agriculture **X:** 15–16

  business **X:** 49

  economy **X:** 95

  ENIAC **IX:** 97–98

  Federal Information Act **X:** 112

  globalization **X:** 131

  Internet **X:** 152–154

  literature **X:** 178

  media **X:** 185, 187

  medicine **X:** 190

  movies **X:** 198

  Reagan, Ronald W. **X:** 260

  science **IX:** 269

  science and technology **X:** 273, 275

  technology **IX:** 293, 295

computer tomography (CT) scan **X:** 190

Comstock, Anthony **VI:** **62–63,** 198

Comstock Law of 1873 **VI:** 324c

Comstock Laws **VII:** 29, 115, 252

Comstock Lode **IV:** 90, 95, **95–96,** 163, 164

Conant, Roger **II:** 212

concentration camp bill. *See* Internal Security Act of 1950

concentration camps **VIII:** 149–150, 281–282

Concepción (ship) **I:** 215, 216

Concepción (town) **I:** 363

Concerned Women for America **X:** 108

Concerning Women (La Follette) **VII:** 340

Concha, Hernando de la **II:** 54

Concord, Battle of. *See* Lexington and Concord, Battles of

Concordat of Worms (1122) **I:** 165

Concorde (jet) **IX:** 27

Concord Sonata (Ives) **VII:** 195

concrete **VII:** 16

concubinage **I:** 61, 233, 234; **II:** 53; **V:** 233

concurrent majorities **IV:** 62, 63

Condition, Elevation, Emigration and Destiny of the Colored People of the United States (Delany) **V:** 93

Condorcet, marquis de **III:** 34

Conestoga **II:** **67,** 272, 274

Conestoga wagon **II:** 276; **IV:** 255, 268

Coney Island, New York **VII:** *231,* 256

Confederate army **V:** **71–73**

  African-American regiments **V:** 4

  Alexander, Edward P. **V:** 7–8

  Antietam, Battle of **V:** 11, 13

  Armistead, Lewis A. **V:** 15

  Balloon Corps **V:** 21–22

  battle flags **V:** 26

  Beauregard, Pierre **V:** 26–27

  Bentonville, Battle of **V:** 28

  bounty system **V:** 34

  Boyd, Belle **V:** 34–35

  Bragg, Braxton **V:** 36

  brothers' war **V:** 36–37

  Bull Run, First Battle of **V:** 42

  cartography **V:** 51

  Chattanooga, Battle of **V:** 57

  Chickamauga, Battle of **V:** 58

  Cleburne, Patrick Ronayne **V:** 67–68

  common soldier **V:** 69

  Confederate States of America **V:** 76

  conscription **V:** 78–79

  Corps d'Afrique **V:** 83

  Cumming, Kate **V:** 85

  Davis, Jefferson **V:** 90

  desertion **V:** 96

  Early, Jubal A. **V:** 103

  economy **V:** 107

  emancipation **V:** 112

  Emancipation Proclamation **V:** 114

  espionage **V:** 118

  Ewell, Richard Stoddert **V:** 118–119

  food riots **V:** 129

  foraging **V:** 130

  Forrest, Nathan Bedford **V:** 133–134

  German-American regiments **V:** 147

  Gettysburg, Battle of **V:** 147–150

  Gettysburg Address **V:** 151

  Gorgas, Josiah **V:** 151–152

  Greenhow, Rose O'Neal **V:** 159

  Harpers Ferry, West Virginia **V:** 165–166

  Hill, Ambrose P. **V:** 167–168

  homefront **V:** 169

  Hood, John Bell **V:** 170–171

  ironclad oath **V:** 183

  Jackson, "Stonewall" **V:** 185–186

  Johnston, Albert Sidney **V:** 189

  Johnston, Joseph E. **V:** 189–190

  Ku Klux Klan **V:** 199

  Lee, Robert E. **V:** 205–207

  letters **V:** 207, 208

  Longstreet, James **V:** 214–216

  Lookout Mountain, Battle of **V:** 216

  Louisiana Tigers **V:** 218

  McClellan, George B. **V:** 225

  Medal of Honor **V:** 228

  medicine and hospitals **V:** 231

  monuments **V:** 239

  Morgan, John Hunt **V:** 240

  Mosby, John Singleton **V:** 241–242

  Murfreesboro/Stones River, Battle of **V:** 242–243

  Native Americans **V:** 249

  Oates, William C. **V:** 257

  Orphan Brigade **V:** 258

  peace movements **V:** 266

  Pickett, George Edward **V:** 274–275

  plantations **V:** 276

  Quantrill, William Clarke **V:** 285–286

  railroads **V:** 289

  Red River campaign **V:** 297

  refugees **V:** 298

  Richmond, Virginia **V:** 304

  Rosecrans, William S. **V:** 305

  rules of war **V:** 306

  science and technology **V:** 310

  Shenandoah Valley

    Jackson's campaign **V:** 316–317

    Sheridan's campaign **V:** 317

  slavery **V:** 330

  Stuart, J. E. B. **V:** 340–341

Confederate army (continued)
tactics and strategy **V:** 345, 346
telegraph **V:** 351
UDC **V:** 370
uniforms **V:** 362–364
Union army **V:** 364, 365
veterans, Civil War **V:** 379
volunteer army **V:** 383
war contracting **V:** 387, 388
Washington, D.C. **V:** 388
West Point **V:** 373
Wheeler, Joseph **V:** 392
Wilderness, Battle of the **V:** 395
Zouaves **V:** 403
Confederate Congress
Confederate army **V:** 71
Confederate States of America **V:** 75
conscription **V:** 79
economy **V:** 106
elections **V:** 110
habeas corpus, writ of **V:** 161
homefront **V:** 169
impressment **V:** 180
Mallory, Stephen R. **V:** 221
taxation **V:** 349
Yancey, William Lowndes **V:** 401
Confederate Constitutional Convention **V:** 336–337
Confederate flag **V:** 217–218
"Confederate Flag Pole" **V:** 239
Confederate marine corps **V:** 222
Confederate Medical Department **V:** 229, 230
Confederate navy **V: 73–74**
Annapolis Naval Academy **V:** 373
espionage **V:** 118
foreign policy **V:** 132
Galveston, Battle of **V:** 145
ironclads **V:** 183, 184
Mallory, Stephen R. **V:** 221–222
Monitor-Merrimack **V:** 237
science and technology **V:** 309, 310
Semmes, Raphael **V:** 313
Union navy **V:** 369
war contracting **V:** 387, 388
Confederate Ordnance Department **V:** 387–388
Confederate Partisan Rangers **V:** 285

Confederate States of America **IV:** 265; **V: 75–78,** 76, 406c
amnesty, acts of **V:** 8
Appomattox Court House, Virginia **V:** 13
assassination of Abraham Lincoln **V:** 17
Baltimore, Maryland, riots **V:** 22
banking and currency **V:** 23
Benjamin, Judah P. **V:** 27–28
Booth, John Wilkes **V:** 33
Brown, Joseph **V:** 39
bushwhackers **V:** 46
Chesnut, Mary B. **V:** 58
Civil War **V:** 63, 66
Davis, Jefferson **V:** 88–90
Davis, Varina Howell **V:** 91
Democratic Party **V:** 94
economy **V:** 105–107
fire-eaters **V:** 127–128
food riots **V:** 129–130
foreign policy **V:** 131–132
Forrest, Nathan Bedford **V:** 133–135
Gorgas, Josiah **V:** 151–152
governors **V:** 152
habeas corpus, writ of **V:** 161, 162
homespun **V:** 170
Houston, Sam **IV:** 175
impressment **V:** 179–180
ironclad oath **V:** 182–183
journalism **V:** 193
ladies aid societies **V:** 203
Lincoln, Abraham **V:** 210
literature **V:** 212
lost cause, the **V:** 217–218
McCormick, Cyrus Hall **IV:** 225
music **V:** 244
Native Americans **V:** 249–251
nurses **V:** 256
Republican Party **V:** 301
Richmond, Virginia **V:** 303–304
secession **V:** 310–313
slavery **V:** 330
states' rights **V:** 336
Stephens, Alexander H. **V:** 336–337
taxation **V:** 349
Texas **IV:** 339
transportation **V:** 355
Tredegar Iron Works **V:** 356
Tyler, John **IV:** 349
Union League **V:** 367
Union navy **V:** 368–369

Vicksburg campaign **V:** 380
war contracting **V:** 387–388
Confederate Veteran magazine **V:** 217
Confederate veterans **V:** 379
Confederation Congress **IV:** 240. *See also* Continental Congress, Second
Conference for Progressive Political Action (CPPA) **VII:** 91
Confidence Man, The (Melville) **IV:** 213
Confiscation Acts **V: 78,** 406c
contrabands **V:** 80
emancipation **V:** 112
Emancipation Proclamation **V:** 114
race and racial conflict **V:** 287
slavery **V:** 330
Confucianism **IV:** 298
Congo **IX:** 4
Congolese National Liberation Council **IX:** 4
congregaciones **II:** 357
Congregational Church **II:** 20, **67–68,** 70, 212, 214; **III:** 298, 300; **IV:** 297, 298; **VI:** 115
Cotton, John **II:** 73
Great Awakening **II:** 147, 148
Harvard College **II:** 155
Hooker, Thomas **II:** 156–157
Johnson, Samuel **II:** 176
New Jersey **II:** 253, 254
New Netherland **II:** 257
Osborn, Sarah Haggar Wheaten **II:** 268
Pilgrims **II:** 283
Protestantism **II:** 301
religion, Euro-American **II:** 316
Turell, Jane Colman **II:** 378
Williams, Roger **II:** 399
Congress **IV:** 375c, 378c, 379c; **V:** 406c–408c; **VI: 63–64,** 323c; **VII: 53–54,** 357c, 361c; **VIII: 66–69,** 68t, 406c, 407c, 409c, 410c; **IX:** 2, 310, 329c. *See also* Continental Congress, First; Continental Congress, Second; House of Representatives, U.S.; Senate, U.S.
AASS **IV:** 14
abolition/abolition movement **IV:** 1; **V:** 1

African Americans **IV:** 6; **VIII:** 2
African nations **X:** 13
Agricultural Adjustment Act **VIII:** 5
agriculture **VIII:** 7
amnesty, acts of **V:** 8
antiwar movement— Vietnam **X:** 24
Arnold, "Hap" **VIII:** 22
Aroostook War **IV:** 25
assassinations **X:** 31
Astor, John Jacob **IV:** 31, 32
Banking Act of 1935 **VIII:** 33
banking and currency **IV:** 41–42
Bank of the United States, Second **IV:** 44
Bering Sea dispute **VI:** 26, 27
BIA **IV:** 180–181
bimetallism **VI:** 28–29
Black Codes **V:** 29–30
Blaine, James Gillespie **VI:** 31
Blair, Francis P., Jr. **V:** 30
Bland-Allison Act **VI:** 32
Bonus Army **VIII:** 39
Bonus Bill **IV:** 56
bounty system **V:** 34
Bush, George W. **X:** 48
Byrnes, James F. **VIII:** 48
Calhoun, John C. **IV:** 62
California **IV:** 65
Canada and the United States **VI:** 43
Carson, Kit **IV:** 75
Carter, James Earl, Jr. **X:** 58
cash-and-carry **VIII:** 52
Cass, Lewis **IV:** 77
Catlin, George **IV:** 78
Chinese Exclusion Act **VI:** 50, 52
civil service reform **VI:** 56
Clinton, William **X:** 68
Compromise of 1850 **IV:** 93–95
computers **X:** 74
Congressional Budget and Impoundment Act **X:** 75
Conkling, Roscoe **VI:** 64
conscientious objectors **VIII:** 70
conservatism **VIII:** 71
conservative coalition **VIII:** 73
court-packing plan **VIII:** 76–77

defense policy **X:** 86, 87
Democratic Party **V:** 93; **VI:** 77; **VIII:** 80, 81
destroyers-for-bases deal **VIII:** 82
Dix, Dorothea **IV:** 114
Economic Bill of Rights **VIII:** 90
economy **IV:** 119; **V:** 105, 106
education, federal aid to **VI:** 92
election of 1932 **VIII:** 96
election of 1936 **VIII:** 97
election of 1940 **VIII:** 98
election of 1944 **VIII:** 99
elections **VII:** 80
Enforcement Acts **V:** 117
ERA **X:** 105, 106
federalism **X:** 113
Fillmore, Millard **IV:** 137
foreign policy **X:** 122
Fourteenth Amendment **V:** 138
Free-Silver movement **VI:** 105
fugitive slave laws **IV:** 154, 155
Gadsden Purchase **IV:** 159
Garfield, James A. **VI:** 108
Geological Survey, U.S. **VI:** 111
Gingrich, Newton L. **X:** 130
government **VIII:** 134, 136
Grand Army of the Republic **VI:** 118
Greenback-Labor Party **VI:** 120
Hartford Convention **IV:** 171
Hayes, Rutherford B. **VI:** 126
homefront **V:** 169
Homestead Act of 1862 **V:** 170
House of Representatives **X:** 144–145
immigration **VI:** 138; **X:** 147
immigration restrictions **VI:** 141
impeachment of Andrew Johnson **V:** 178
Indian Affairs, Office of **VI:** 144
Indian Removal Act (1830) **IV:** 183
Interior, Department of **IV:** 187
internal improvements **IV:** 188, 190

Internal Revenue taxes **VI:** 147
Iran-contra affair **X:** 154
IRCA **X:** 149
Jackson, Andrew **IV:** 191
Johnston, Joseph E. **V:** 190
Joint Committee on the Conduct of War **V:** 190–191
Julian, George W. **V:** 194
Kansas-Nebraska Act of 1854 **V:** 197
Kelley, William D. **V:** 198–199
Ku Klux Klan **V:** 200
Langston, John Mercer **VI:** 172
lobbies and pressure groups **VI:** 179–180
loyalty oaths **V:** 218
Massachusetts Emigrant Aid Society **IV:** 223
McCulloch v. Maryland **IV:** 227
McNary-Haugen Farm Bill **VII:** 175
Medal of Honor **V:** 228
medicine and hospitals **V:** 230
Mellon, Andrew **VII:** 180
Mexican-American War **IV:** 232–233
Missouri Compromise of 1820 **IV:** 236–238
Monroe Doctrine **IV:** 241–242
Mormon War **IV:** 244
Morrill Land-Grant Act **V:** 241
Morse, Samuel F. B. **IV:** 245
national banking system **VI:** 205
National Road **IV:** 253
newspapers **VI:** 211
NRPB **VIII:** 232, 233
Oates, William C. **V:** 257
OWMR **VIII:** 259
Pacific Railroad Act of 1862 **V:** 263
PACs **X:** 236
Panic of 1819 **IV:** 276
Panic of 1857 **V:** 264
People's Party **VI:** 222, 223
Persian Gulf War **X:** 235
political parties **X:** 238
political parties, third **VI:** 225
politics in the Roosevelt era **VIII:** 270, 271
Polk, James K. **IV:** 282

polygamy **IV:** 285
population trends **V:** 279
pornography **X:** 245
postwar planning **VIII:** 279
presidency **VI:** 229, 230; **VIII:** 280
presidential campaigns **VI:** 231
public land policy **IV:** 286–288
public opinion polls **VIII:** 284
railroads **IV:** 293
Rainey, Joseph H. **V:** 291
Reconstruction **V:** 294
Reconstruction Acts **V:** 296
reconversion **VIII:** 295
Rehnquist, William H. **X:** 264
relief **VIII:** 301
Relief and Reconstruction Act **VIII:** 302
Republican Party **IV:** 300; **V:** 301; **VIII:** 304, 305
Revenue Act of 1935 **VIII:** 308
Rosecrans, William S. **V:** 305
Samoa **VI:** 255
Senate **X:** 275–276
Seventeenth Amendment **VII:** 69–70
Sherman, John **VI:** 261
Sherman Antitrust Act **VI:** 261
Sooners **VI:** 270
South **VIII:** 331
South Africa **X:** 280
states' rights **V:** 335
Stephens, Alexander H. **V:** 336, 337
Supreme Court **X:** 291
tariff issue **VI:** 284
taxation **VIII:** 351
television **X:** 294
terrorism **X:** 299, 300
Texas **IV:** 338–339
TNEC **VIII:** 355
tobacco suits **X:** 305
Tower Commission **X:** 306
Townsend, Francis E. **VIII:** 359
Twenty-sixth Amendment **X:** 306
Tyler, John **IV:** 349
United States v. Cruikshank **V:** 375
USHA **VIII:** 367
Vallandigham, Clement L. **V:** 377–378

Venezuela boundary dispute **VI:** 303
Versailles, Treaty of **VII:** 324
Wagner, Robert F. **VIII:** 372
Walsh, Lawrence E. **X:** 314
War Powers Act **X:** 315
West Point **V:** 372
Whig Party **IV:** 363, 364
Wilmot Proviso **V:** 395
WMC **VIII:** 375
women's rights and status **VIII:** 384; **X:** 321
World War II home front **VIII:** 396
Wright, Fanny **IV:** 369
Zouaves **V:** 403
Congress (frigate) **III:** 90
Congress, Confederate. *See* Confederate Congress
Congress, First Federal **III:** 89, 327
Congress, USS **V:** 37, 238
Congressional Black Caucus **X:** 256
Congressional Budget and Impoundment Act of 1974 **X: 75,** 134, 325*c*
Congressional Budget Office **X:** 75
Congressional Medal of Honor **VII:** 159, 187
Congressional Military Reform Caucus **X:** 129
congressional pay raises **X:** 19–20
Congressional Reconstruction **V:** 294
Congressional Scorecard **X:** 62
Congressional Space Caucus **X:** 129
Congressional Union for Woman Suffrage **VII:** 204–205, 336
Congress of Industrial Organizations (CIO) **VII:** 154; **VIII:** *69,* **69–70,** 408*c;* **IX: 65–66,** 329*c,* 331*c;* **X:** 169. *See also* AFL-CIO
  African Americans **VIII:** 3
  American Federation of Labor **VIII:** 14; **IX:** 11
  automobile industry **VIII:** 30
  Bridges, Harry **VIII:** 43
  Byrnes, James F. **VIII:** 48
  Communists **VIII:** 65
  conservative coalition **VIII:** 74
  economy **IX:** 90

Congress of Industrial
  Organizations (continued)
    Hillman, Sidney **VIII:** 145,
      146
    Irish Americans **VIII:** 165
    Jews **VIII:** 172
    labor **VIII:** 179–181
    Lewis, John L. **VIII:** 185,
      186
    Murray, Philip **VIII:** 221
    NLRB **VIII:** 231
    NWLB **VIII:** 233
    Operation Dixie **IX:**
      235–236
    Polish Americans **VIII:**
      269
    Popular Front **VIII:** 276
    Reuther, Walter **IX:** 259
    South **VIII:** 332
Congress on Racial Equality
  (CORE) **VIII:** 409c; **IX:**
  66–68, 67, 333c, 334c; **X:**
  111
    African-American
      movement **IX:** 5
    Carmichael, Stokely **IX:** 47
    freedom rides **IX:** 113–114
    Mississippi Freedom
      Democratic Party **IX:**
      207
    NAACP **IX:** 220
    race and racial conflict **IX:**
      253–254
    sit-ins **IX:** 273
    Voting Rights Act of 1965
      IX: 311
conjuring **II:** 314
Conkling, Roscoe **V:** 156, 302;
  VI: 64–65
    Arthur, Chester Alan **VI:**
      16, 17
    civil service reform **VI:** 56
    Congress **VI:** 63
    Garfield, James A. **VI:** 108,
      109
    Hayes, Rutherford B. **VI:**
      126
    Liberal Republican Party
      VI: 174
    newspapers **VI:** 211
    presidential campaigns **VI:**
      232
    Republican Party **VI:** 246
Connally, John B. **IX:** 238
Connecticut **II: 68–70; IV:** 20,
  161, 280; **V:** 92, 391; **VI:** 8; **X:**
  190, 242
    agriculture **II:** 12, 13
    Albany Congress **II:** 14
    Anglican Church **II:** 20
    Arnold, Benedict **III:** 22
    Connecticut **II:** 68

Dartmouth College **II:** 83
Davenport, James **II:** 83
Dominion of New England
  II: 94
Dwight, Timothy **III:** 109
Hooker, Thomas **II:**
  156–157
indentured servitude **II:**
  164
Ingersoll, Jared **III:** 178
Iroquois **II:** 169
Johnson, Samuel **II:** 176
Knight, Sarah Kemble **II:**
  186
land **II:** 191
lumbering **II:** 201
Mason, John **II:** 211
Massachusetts **II:** 212
Massachusetts School Act
  II: 216
mills **II:** 225
monarchy, British **II:** 232
New Netherland **II:** 256
Pequot **II:** 278
Pequot War **II:** 279–280
religion, Euro-American
  II: 316
religious liberty **III:** 300
Rhode Island **II:** 321
Sherman, Roger **III:** 325
shipbuilding **II:** 335
Winthrop, John **II:** 402
witchcraft **II:** 402
Wyoming Valley War **III:**
  384
Youngs, John **II:** 414
"Connecticut Compromise" **III:**
  228, 395c
Connecticut Observer **IV:** 148
Connecticut Wits **III:** 35, **80,**
  109, 214–215
Connecticut Woman Suffrage
  Association **VI:** 133
*Connecticut Yankee in King
  Arthur's Court* (Twain) **V:**
  213
Connolly, John **VI:** 290
Connolly, Richard B. **VI:** 298,
  299
Connor, Eugene "Bull" **IX:** 38,
  114, 154, 253, 275
Connors, Jimmy **X:** 262
Conoco Inc. **IX:** 84
Conoy **II:** 274
conquistadores **I:** 84, **84–85,**
  168, 387c; **II:** 136, 355, 359
    adelantado **I:** 3–4
    Aguilar, Francisco de **I:** 4
    Aguilar, Gerónimo
      (Jerónimo) de **I:** 5
    Alvarado, Pedro de **I:** 6–8
    Aztecs **I:** 21–22

Balboa, Vasco Núñez de **I:**
  24
Barbados **I:** 26
black legend **I:** 30
Cabeza de Vaca, Álvar
  Núñez **I:** 38
castas **I:** 61
Charles V **I:** 69
Córdoba, Francisco
  Hernández de **I:** 86–87
Coronado, Francisco **I:** 88,
  89m, 90
Cortés, Hernán **I:** 91–95
Council of the Indies **I:** 95
Cuauhtémoc **I:** 97
encomienda **I:** 122
gold **I:** 142, 143
Guerrero, Gonzalo **I:** 146
haciendas **I:** 149
Hopi **I:** 167
Las Casas, Bartolomé de **I:**
  198–200
Maya **I:** 227, 229
Mendoza, Antonio de **I:**
  231
Narváez, Pánfilo de **I:**
  250–251
New Spain **I:** 258, 259
Panama **I:** 277
Peru **I:** 280
Pizarro, Francisco **I:** 283,
  284m, 285
Sandoval, Gonzalo de **I:**
  317–318
Soto, Hernando de **I:**
  332–333
Tenochtitlán **I:** 344, 346
Valdivia, Pedro de **I:** 363
Velázquez, Diego de **I:**
  363–364
Yucatán Peninsula **I:** 378
Zumárraga, Juan de **I:** 382
Conrad, Joseph **VI:** 68
*Conscience of a Conservative,
  The* (Barry Goldwater) **IX:**
  123, 332c
Conscience Whigs **IV:** 150, 364;
  V: 158, 342
conscientious objectors **V:** 266,
  331; **VII:** 55; **VIII: 70–71;**
  IX: 9–10; **X:** 323c
    American Civil Liberties
      Union **VIII:** 13
    civil liberties **VIII:** 60–61
    Selective Service **VIII:**
      323
    Supreme Court **VIII:** 347
    Thomas, Norman **VIII:**
      358
consciousness raising **X:** 114
conscription **V: 78–80; VII:**
  54–55; X: 324c. *See also* draft

bounty system **V:** 34
Civil War **V:** 66
cold war (end of) **X:** 71
Confederate army **V:** 71
Eagleton, Thomas F. **X:** 93
elections **V:** 110
end of **X: 75–76**
ERA **X:** 105
governors **V:** 153
habeas corpus, writ of **V:**
  161
homefront **V:** 169
Kennedy, Edward M. **X:**
  163
peace movements **V:** 266
Schenk v. United States
  VII: 275
Selective Service Act **VII:**
  282
socialism **VII:** 289
Soldiers' Bonus **VII:** 291
states' rights **V:** 336
Stephens, Alexander H. **V:**
  337
Union army **V:** 364
volunteer army **V:** 383
Conscription Act of 1862 **V:** 76,
  79, 153
Conscription Act of 1863 **V:** 34,
  90, 254
Conscription Act of 1864 **V:** 79
conservation/conservationism
  IV: 11; **VI: 65–66,** 199–200,
  257; **VII: 55–56; VIII:** 63,
  103; **IX:** 150–151, 321–322.
  See also environmentalism/
  environmental policy
    Antiquities Act **VII:** 13
    Lindbergh, Charles **VII:**
      160
    National Park Service **VII:**
      203
    Pinchot, Gifford **VII:**
      227–228
    Roosevelt, Theodore **VII:**
      265, 266
    science **VII:** 276
    Teapot Dome **VII:** 307
conservatism/conservative
  movement **VIII: 71–73; IX:**
  68–69, 123, 124, 127; **X:**
  78–80. *See also*
  neoconservatism
    American Liberty League
      VIII: 14
    antimonopoly **VIII:** 18
    Bennett, William J. **X:** 35
    Buchanan, Patrick J. **X:**
      42
    Buckley, William F., Jr. **X:**
      42–43
    Byrnes, James F. **VIII:** 49

Congress **VIII:** 67
conservative coalition
  VIII: 73
Democratic Party **VIII:** 81
education **VIII:** 93–94
election of 1936 **VIII:** 97
ERA **X:** 107
FBI **VIII:** 115
Garner, John Nance **VIII:**
  129
Gingrich, Newton L. **X:**
  129
Helms, Jesse A., Jr. **X:** 140,
  141
House of Representatives
  X: 145
Kemp, Jack F. **X:** 163
Laffer curve **X:** 172
liberalism **X:** 174, 176
Libertarian Party **X:** 176
marriage **X:** 182
NEPA **X:** 210
New Deal **VIII:** 242
political correctness **X:** 237
political parties **X:** 237
politics in the Roosevelt
  era **VIII:** 271
pornography **X:** 245
property rights **X:** 250
Quayle, J. Danforth **X:** 253
Reagan, Ronald W. **X:** 259,
  260
Reaganomics **X:** 261
relief **VIII:** 301–302
Schlafly, Phyllis **X:**
  271–272
Selective Service **VIII:** 322
Supreme Court **VIII:** 344,
  345; **X:** 291
unemployment **VIII:** 364
USHA **VIII:** 367
World War II **VIII:** 390
WPA **VIII:** 387
conservative coalition **VIII:**
  73–74, 408c
  CCC **VIII:** 64
  Congress **VIII:** 67, 69
  conservatism **VIII:** 72
  court-packing plan **VIII:**
    77
  Democratic Party **VIII:**
    81–82
  Executive Reorganization
    Act **VIII:** 107
  Fair Labor Standards Act
    VIII: 110
  Full Employment Bill
    VIII: 128
  Garner, John Nance **VIII:**
    129
  government **VIII:** 134
  liberalism **VIII:** 188

New Deal **VIII:** 242
NRPB **VIII:** 233
politics in the Roosevelt
  era **VIII:** 271
postwar planning **VIII:**
  278
presidency **VIII:** 281
recession of 1937–38 **VIII:**
  293
Republican Party **VIII:**
  306
Roosevelt, Franklin D.
  VIII: 313
South **VIII:** 332
Supreme Court **VIII:** 346
Taft, Robert A. **VIII:** 349
taxation **VIII:** 352
Third New Deal **VIII:** 357
Wagner, Robert F. **VIII:**
  373
World War II home front
  VIII: 396
Conservative Judaism **VI:** 158,
  243; **X:** 161, 265
"Conservative Manifesto" **VIII:**
  408c
  conservatism **VIII:** 72
  conservative coalition
    VIII: 73, 74
Conservative Mind, The (Kirk)
  X: 78
conservative theology **IV:** 298;
  VII: 261–262, 302
*Considerations on the Propriety
  of Imposing Taxes in the
  British Colonies* (Dulany)
  III: 108, 391c
"consolidated democracy" **IV:**
  63
consolidation **VI:** 146, 147; **VII:**
  74–75, 143
conspiracies **II:** 248, 262, 419c
  assassinations **X:** 31
  Clinton, Hillary Rodham
    X: 64, 65
Constantinople **I:** 191
Constitution, Cherokee nation
  IV: 376c
Constitution, Confederate **V:**
  420–421
  Confederate States of
    America **V:** 75
  Dred Scott decision **V:** 101
  elections **V:** 109
  habeas corpus, writ of **V:**
    161
  race and racial conflict **V:**
    287
Constitution, Massachusetts **III:**
  3, 4, 84, 394c
constitution, NAACP **VIII:**
  411c

Constitution, New York **III:**
  181, 216
Constitution, Pennsylvania
  Morris, Robert **III:** 247
  Peale, Charles Willson **III:**
    275
  Rittenhouse, David **III:**
    310
  taverns **III:** 343
  Young, Thomas **III:** 390
Constitution, U.S. **II:** 88, 110,
  149, 197, 278, 317; **III:** 394c,
  395c, 398c, 406–412; **V:** 408c;
  VIII: 60, 61; **IX:** 281. *See
  also specific amendments*
  abolition **V:** 1, 2–3
  Adams, John **III:** 3
  African Americans **III:** 6
  amendments to **X:** 18–20
  American Revolution **III:**
    12, 13
  American System **IV:** 18,
    19
  Ames, Fisher **III:** 13
  amnesty, acts of **V:** 9
  anti-Federalists **III:** 15
  banking and currency **IV:**
    41
  BIA **IV:** 180
  Bill of Rights **III:** 38–39
  Bonus Bill **IV:** 56
  Brackenridge, Hugh
    Henry **III:** 47
  Calhoun, John C. **IV:** 63
  Chase, Samuel **III:** 64–65
  citizen-soldier **V:** 62
  Civil War **V:** 63–64
  Clinton, George **III:** 75
  Compromise of 1850 **IV:**
    94
  constitutions, state **III:** 84
  Democratic Party **IV:** 106;
    V: 93
  ERA **X:** 105–107
  federalism **X:** 112
  Federalist Papers **III:**
    124–125
  Federalist Party **III:** 126
  Federalists **III:** 127
  Fifteenth Amendment **V:**
    123–124
  Fourteenth Amendment
    V: 138
  fugitive slave laws **IV:** 154
  Garrison, William Lloyd **V:**
    146
  gay rights movement **X:**
    127, 128
  habeas corpus, writ of **V:**
    161, 162
  Hamilton, Alexander **III:**
    161–162

Hancock, John **III:** 163
Henry, Patrick **III:** 165,
  166
impeachment **III:** 175
impeachment of Andrew
  Johnson **V:** 179
Jews **III:** 188
journalism **III:** 191
Judiciary Act of 1789 **III:**
  192
Lee, Henry **III:** 206
Macon, Nathaniel **III:** 226
Madison, James **III:** 227
Marbury v. Madison **III:**
  231
McCulloch v. Maryland
  IV: 227
Meese, Edwin C. **X:** 191
Morris, Gouverneur **III:**
  247
Nullification Controversy
  IV: 263
personal liberty laws **IV:**
  280
Phillips, Wendell **IV:** 281
Polk, James K. **IV:** 284
public land policy **IV:** 286
race and race relations **IV:**
  289, 290; **V:** 287
Randolph, Edmund **III:**
  296
republicanism **III:** 302
Republican Party **IV:** 301
secession **V:** 311
Seward, William H. **V:** 314
Sherman, Roger **III:** 325
slavery **IV:** 317
slave trade **III:** 329
states' rights **III:** 333; **V:**
  335
Sumner, Charles **V:** 342
Supreme Court **III:**
  337–338
Supreme Court decision
  IV: 330
Constitution, USS **III:** **80–81,**
  291, 304, 397c; **IV:** 356
Constitution, Virginia **III:** 296
Constitution Act (1791) **III:**
  60–61
Constitutional Convention **III:**
  81–82, 394c–395c; **IV:** 56,
  237
  Annapolis Convention **III:**
    14
  Bill of Rights **III:** 38
  Blount, William **III:** 40
  Brackenridge, Hugh
    Henry **III:** 47
  Continental Congress,
    Second **III:** 89
  Dickinson, John **III:** 106

Constitutional Convention
(*continued*)
   Federalist Papers **III:**
     124–125
   Federalists **III:** 127
   Franklin, Benjamin **III:** 135
   Gerry, Elbridge **III:** 152
   Hamilton, Alexander **III:**
     161
   Henry, Patrick **III:** 166
   impeachment **III:** 175
   Independence Hall **III:**
     176
   Jay, John **III:** 182
   King, Rufus **III:** 195
   Laurens, Henry **III:** 203
   Livingston, William **III:**
     216–217
   Madison, James **III:** 228
   Mason, George **III:**
     237–238
   Morris, Gouverneur **III:**
     247
   national debt **III:** 253
   Pinckney, Charles
     Cotesworth **III:** 277
   Randolph, Edmund **III:**
     295, 296
   Shays's Rebellion **III:** 324
   Sherman, Roger **III:** 325
   slave trade **III:** 329
   states' rights **III:** 333
   trade **III:** 350
   Virginia dynasty **III:** 361
   Washington, George **III:**
     367
   Wilson, James **III:** 379
Constitutional League **VII:** 199
Constitutional Post **II:** 292
Constitutional Union Party **IV:**
   301, 364; **V:** 405*c;* **VI:**
   121–122
Constitutional View of the Late
*   War Between the States*
   (Stephens) **V:** 337
Constitution of 1824 (Mexico)
   IV: 341
Constitution Party **X:** 20
constitutions, state **III:** 12,
   82–84, 83*m,* 175, 188; **VI:** 5
construction/construction
   industry **VIII:** 57, 90, 407*c;*
   X: 225. *See also* housing
   Bell, Alexander Graham
     VI: 25
   bridges **VI:** 34–35
   cities and urban life **VI:** 53
   inventions and technology
     VI: 149
   railroads **VI:** 237, 238
consulado **I:** 15
Consular Service **VII:** 135

Consumer Bill of Rights of 1962
   IX: 69
consumer goods **V:** 60–61; **VII:**
   268, 351–352; **VIII:** 46, 339,
   394
consumerism **VI:** 2–3; **X:** 8, 33,
   263
   advertising **IX:** 2
   credit cards **IX:** 72–73
   Galbraith, John Kenneth
     IX: 117
   General Motors **IX:** 121
   television **IX:** 296–297
consumer movement **IX:** 46,
   69–70, 88–89, 91
Consumer Price Index (CPI)
   VIII: 254, 371; **IX:** 70
Consumer Product Safety
   Administration **X:** 205
Consumer Product Safety
   Commission **IX:** 69
consumer rights movement **X:**
   205–206
consumers' leagues **VII:** 146
consumer spending **VIII:** 292
Consumers Research, Inc. **VIII:**
   1
Consumers Union **VIII:** 1
consumption **II: 70–71**
   alcohol **II:** 15
   Caribbean **II:** 52
   Carter, Robert "King" **II:**
     54
   Cherokee **II:** 58
   cities and urban life **II:** 61
   economy **II:** 102
   indentured servitude **II:**
     165
   manufacturing and
     industry **II:** 204
   marriage and family life **II:**
     206
   Massachusetts **II:** 215
   mills **II:** 225
   missions **II:** 229
   rum trade **II:** 326
   society, British American
     II: 351, 352
   South Carolina **II:** 353
   tobacco **II:** 373–374
   trade and shipping **II:**
     377
contador **I:** 60
contagion **IV:** 308
containment policy **X:** 89, 124
   cold war **IX:** 58
   Europe **IX:** 105
   Kennan, George **IX:** 155
   Korean War **IX:** 163
   modern Republicanism
     IX: 209
   NSC-68 **IX:** 234

   "Sources of Soviet
     Conduct" **IX:** 341–344
   Truman Doctrine **IX:**
     300–301
   wars of national liberation
     IX: 316
   White Paper **IX:** 321
Continental army **III: 84–86,**
   85, 393*c,* 394*c*
   Andre, John **III:** 13
   Arnold, Benedict **III:** 21
   Articles of Confederation
     III: 25
   banks **III:** 32
   Barlow, Joel **III:** 35
   Brandywine, Battle of **III:**
     47
   Brant, Joseph **III:** 49
   Burgoyne, John **III:** 52
   Burr, Aaron **III:** 53
   Camden, Battle of **III:** 57
   camp followers **III:** 59
   Charleston, siege of **III:** 64
   Cincinnati, Order of **III:**
     69
   Clinton, George **III:** 74
   Constitutional Convention
     III: 81
   Continental army, mutinies
     of **III:** 86
   Continental Congress,
     Second **III:** 88
   Conway Cabal **III:** 90
   Cowpens, Battle of **III:** 95
   disease and epidemics **III:**
     106
   Dorchester Heights, Battle
     of **III:** 107
   Dragging Canoe **III:** 107
   Dwight, Timothy **III:** 109
   Fort Washington, capture
     of **III:** 133
   freemasonry **III:** 137
   French alliance **III:** 137
   Gates, Horatio **III:** 149
   Germantown, Battle of
     III: 151
   Greene, Nathanael **III:**
     155, 156
   Green Mountain Boys **III:**
     156
   Guilford Courthouse,
     Battle of **III:** 158
   Hale, Nathan **III:** 160
   Hancock, John **III:** 163
   Howe, Richard, Lord **III:**
     167–168
   Howe, Sir William **III:** 168
   Independence Hall **III:**
     176
   Jews **III:** 187
   Kalb, baron de **III:** 195

   Knox, Henry **III:** 197
   Kościuszko, Tadeusz **III:**
     198
   Lafayette, marquis de **III:**
     201
   Lee, Charles **III:** 205, 206
   Lee, Henry **III:** 206
   L'Enfant, Pierre-Charles
     III: 207
   Long Island, Battle of **III:**
     217
   Lyon, Matthew **III:** 222
   Marion, Francis **III:** 231
   Marshall, John **III:** 235
   McDougall, Alexander **III:**
     239
   medicine **III:** 241
   minutemen **III:** 243
   Monmouth, Battle of **III:**
     244–245
   Morgan, Daniel **III:** 246
   Morris, Robert **III:** 247
   Morristown, New Jersey,
     encampment of **III:** 248
   music **III:** 251
   mutinies of **III: 86**
   Native Americans and the
     Revolution **III:** 255
   Newburgh conspiracy **III:**
     256
   Ohio Company of
     Associates **III:** 265
   Pickering, John **III:** 276
   Pulsaki, Casimir **III:** 289
   Putnam, Israel **III:** 290
   Red Jacket **III:** 297
   Revolutionary War **III:**
     305, 307
   Rhode Island, Battle of
     III: 308
   Rush, Benjamin **III:** 312
   Sampson, Deborah **III:**
     316
   Steuben, Frederick von
     III: 334
   Sullivan, John **III:** 337
   Taylor, John, of Caroline
     III: 344
   temperance **III:** 346
   Trenton and Princeton,
     Battles of **III:** 351
   Trumbull, John **III:** 352
   Valley Forge, encampment
     of **III:** 357–359
   Washington, George **III:**
     366
   Wayne, Anthony **III:** 369
   White Plains, Battle of **III:**
     376
   Wilkinson, James **III:** 379
   women's rights and status
     III: 382

"Yankee Doodle" **III:** 387
Yorktown, surrender at
    III: 388
Continental Association **III:**
    393*c*
Continental Congress **II:** 196,
    222, 348, 389
Continental Congress, First **III:**
    86–88, 87, 392*c–393c*
    Adams, John **III:** 2
    Adams, Samuel **III:** 4
    Association, the **III:** 27
    Bland, Richard **III:** 40
    Chase, Samuel **III:** 64
    Coercive Acts **III:** 77
    Continental Congress,
        Second **III:** 88
    Deane, Silas **III:** 101
    Declaration of
        Independence **III:** 101
    Dickinson, John **III:** 105
    Galloway, Joseph **III:** 148
    Hamilton, Alexander **III:**
        161
    Henry, Patrick **III:** 166
    Jay, John **III:** 181
    lawyers **III:** 203
    Lee, Arthur **III:** 205
    Lee, Richard Henry **III:**
        207
    Livingston, William **III:**
        217
    Mason, George **III:** 237
    Peale, Charles Willson **III:**
        273
    resistance movement **III:**
        303
    Revere, Paul **III:** 304
    Seabury, Samuel **III:** 323
    Suffolk Resolves **III:** 335
    Sullivan, John **III:** 337
    voluntary associations **III:**
        362
    Washington, George **III:**
        366
    Wilson, James **III:** 380
Continental Congress, Second
    II: 292–293; **III: 88–89,**
    393*c–395c*
    Adams, John **III:** 2
    Adams, Samuel **III:** 4
    African Americans **III:** 6
    Annapolis Convention **III:**
        14
    antislavery and abolition
        III: 16
    Articles of Confederation
        III: 24
    Backus, Isaac **III:** 30
    Bank of North America
        III: 30
    Barry, John **III:** 36

Bland, Richard **III:** 40
Burgoyne, John **III:** 52
Burke, Edmund **III:** 53
Burr, Aaron **III:** 53
Canada **III:** 60
Chase, Samuel **III:** 64
Clinton, George **III:** 74
Constitutional Convention
    III: 81
constitutions, state **III:** 82
Continental army **III:**
    84–86
Continental navy **III:** 90
Deane, Silas **III:** 101
Declaration of
    Independence **III:**
    101–102, *103*
Dickinson, John **III:**
    105–106
foreign affairs **III:** 130
Franklin, Benjamin **III:**
    134
French alliance **III:** 137
Gates, Horatio **III:** 149
George III, king of Great
    Britain **III:** 150
Gerry, Elbridge **III:** 152
Greene, Nathanael **III:**
    155
Green Mountain Boys **III:**
    156
Hancock, John **III:** 163
Henry, Patrick **III:** 166
Independence Hall **III:**
    176
Jay, John **III:** 181
Jefferson, Thomas **III:**
    183, 184
Jersey, HMS **III:** 187
Knox, Henry **III:** 197
Lafayette, marquis de **III:**
    201
Laurens, Henry **III:** 203
Lee, Arthur **III:** 205
Lee, Charles **III:** 205
Lee, Henry **III:** 206
Lee, Richard Henry **III:**
    207
Livingston, Robert R. **III:**
    216
Livingston, William **III:**
    217
Loyalists **III:** 221
Madison, James **III:**
    227–229
Marion, Francis **III:** 232
McDougall, Alexander **III:**
    240
medicine **III:** 241
Morris, Gouverneur **III:**
    246–247
Morris, Robert **III:** 247

national debt **III:** 253
Newburgh conspiracy **III:**
    256
Olive Branch Petition **III:**
    266
Paris, Treaty of **III:** 273
Peale, Charles Willson **III:**
    273
Pitt, William **III:** 277
privateering **III:** 287
Randolph, Edmund **III:**
    296
resistance movement **III:**
    303
Rush, Benjamin **III:** 313
St. Clair, Arthur **III:** 316
Schuyler, Philip John **III:**
    320
Sherman, Roger **III:** 325
Steuben, Frederick von
    III: 334
Sullivan, John **III:** 337
tariffs **III:** 342
Valley Forge encampment
    of **III:** 358
Washington, George **III:**
    366
Witherspoon, John **III:**
    380
Yates, Abraham, Jr. **III:** 387
Continental Divide **IV:** 324
Continental navy **III: 90,** 393*c*
    African Americans **III:** 6
    Barry, John **III:** 36
    Jones, John Paul **III:** 190
    privateering **III:** 287
contour plowing **IX:** 7
contrabands **V: 80–81**
    Butler, Benjamin **V:** 46
    Confiscation Acts **V:** 78
    Eaton, John, Jr. **V:** 104
    emancipation **V:** 112
    Freedmen's Bureau **V:** 142
    Memphis riot **V:** 232
    nurses **V:** 256
    Port Royal, South
        Carolina, Experiment **V:**
        279
    slavery **V:** 330
    Thirteenth Amendment **V:**
        352
contraception. *See* birth control
Contract Air Mail Act. *See* Kelly
    Air Mail Act
contract bridge **VIII:** 296
Contraction Act of 1866 **VI:** 72
contract labor **VI: 66,** 138, **141,**
    162, 325*c*
Contract Labor Act of 1864 **VI:**
    66
contract law **IV:** 104, 330, 331,
    375*c*

"Contract with America" **X:**
    328*c*
    Gingrich, Newton L. **X:**
        129
    House of Representatives
        X: 145
    NEPA **X:** 210
    Senate **X:** 276
contras **X:** 80, 327*c*
    Boland Amendment **X:** 38
    cold war (end of) **X:** 71
    foreign policy **X:** 124
    Gore, Albert, Jr. **X:** 133
    Iran-contra affair **X:** 154
    Nicaragua **X:** 218
    North, Oliver L. **X:** 222
    War Powers Act **X:** 315
Contrast, The (Tyler) **III:** 347,
    352, 353, 395*c*
Controlled Substance Act of
    1970 **X:** 206–207, 323*c*
Conventional Armed Forces in
    Europe Treaty **X:** 327*c*
Convention of 1800 **III:** 292
Convention of London, 1818 **IV:**
    269, 375*c*
Conventuals **I:** 132
conversos **I:** 178, 190, 191; **II:**
    174
convicencia **I:** 128
convict labor **II: 71–72,** 108,
    286; **VI:** 66
Conway, Martin F. **IV:** 224
Conway, Thomas **III:** 90, 91
Conway Cabal **III: 90–91,** 358
Conyers, John, Jr. **IX:** 240
Conyngham, Gustavus **III:** 90
Coode, John **II:** 141, 209, 210,
    323, 328
Cook, Clarence **VI:** 3
Cook, James **I:** 266; **II:** 32, 266;
    III: 164; **IV:** 171, 199; **VI:**
    123–124
Cook, Mrs. Enoch Hooper **V:** 37
Cook, Will Marion **VI:** 204; **VII:**
    194
Cook and Brother Armory **V:**
    387
Cooke, Alistair **VII:** 5
Cooke, Elisha, Jr. **II: 72,** 217
Cooke, Elisha, Sr. **II:** 217
Cooke, Jay **V:** 56, **81,** 105, 107;
    VI: 19, 41, 324*c*
Cooke, W. F. **IV:** 307
cooking class **VII:** *77, 207*
Cook v. Gralike (2001) **X:** 113
Coolidge, Calvin John **VII:** xiv,
    56, **56–57,** 360*c*
    advertising **VII:** 5
    AFL **VII:** 11
    agriculture **VII:** 8; **VIII:** 7
    aviation **VII:** 23

Coolidge, Calvin John
(*continued*)
  conservatism **VIII:** 71
  Dawes, Charles **VII:** 63
  elections **VII:** 81
  Garvey, Marcus **VII:** 106
  Harding, Warren G. **VII:**
    118
  Hoover, Herbert **VIII:** 152
  Hoover presidency **VIII:**
    153
  Hughes, Charles Evans
    VII: 124
  Kelly Air Mail Act **VII:** 147
  Lindbergh, Charles **VII:**
    159
  McNary-Haugen Farm
    Bill **VII:** 175
  Naval Disarmament
    Conference **VII:** 209
  progressivism **VII:** 238
  Republican Party **VII:** 263
  socialism **VII:** 289
  TVA **VIII:** 356
  Universal Negro
    Improvement
    Association (UNIA)
    VII: 316
  veterans **VII:** 326
  Veterans Bureau **VII:** 327
  Women's International
    League for Peace and
    Freedom **VII:** 338
Cooper, Anthony Ashley, Lord
  II: 144, 265, 353
Cooper, Douglas **V:** 249
Cooper, Gary **IX:** 135
Cooper, George **V:** 138
Cooper, James Fenimore **IV:**
  197, 211, 212, 376c; **VI:** 80;
  X: 179
Cooper, Myles **II:** 83
Cooper, Peter **IV:** 40, 118, 184,
  185, 187; **VI:** 72, 120
"cooperationists" **V:** 311, 336,
  337
cooperative farming **IV:** 345
cooperative organizations **IV:**
  149
cooperatives. *See* agricultural
  cooperatives
Cooper Union **IV:** 121
Cooper v. Aaron (1958) **X:** 41
Cooper v. Boren (1976) **X:** 41
Coors, Joseph **X:** 79
Coosa **I:** **85–86**
Coosaponakeesa **II:** 238
Copán **I:** 69, **86**, 346, 349; **IV:**
  133
Cope, Edward **VI:** 188, 257
Copland, Aaron **VII:** 195; **VIII:**
  119, 223; **IX:** 216, 217

Copley, John Singleton **II:** 25,
  215–216, 273, 346; **III:** 22,
  23, *23*, **91**, 273
Copley, Leonard **II:** 328
Coppage v. Kansas **VII:** 358c
copper **I:** 10; **VI:** 145, 193,
  194m
Copperheads **V:** **81–83**. *See also*
  Peace Democrats
  Burnside, Ambrose E. **V:**
    45
  Democratic Party **V:** 94
  homefront **V:** 169
  Lincoln, Abraham **V:** 211
  Murfreesboro/Stones
    River, Battle of **V:** 243
  Nast, Thomas **V:** 247
  peace movements **V:** 266
  Union League **V:** 367
  Vallandigham, Clement L.
    V: 377–378
  Women's National Loyal
    League **V:** 396
Coppola, Francis Ford **X:** 198,
  239
copyrights **V:** 137; **VI:** 129, 220,
  327c; **X:** 74, 273, 330c
Coral Sea, Battle of the **VIII:**
  74
  air power **VIII:** 11
  Midway, Battle of **VIII:**
    211
  Nimitz, Chester W. **VIII:**
    246
  World War II Pacific
    theater **VIII:** 399
Corbett, Boston **V:** 33
Corbett, James J. **VI:** 33, 34
Corby, William **V:** 181–182
Corcoran, Michael **V:** 181
Corcoran, Thomas **X:** 125
Córdoba (city) **I:** 62
Córdoba, Francisco Hernández
  de **I:** **86–87**, 145, 146
"cordon strategy" **V:** 346
CORE. *See* Congress on Racial
  Equality
Corey, Giles **II:** 402
Corinth, Battle of **V:** **83**, 305,
  354
Corinthian columns **IV:** 27
Corliss engine **VI:** 223–224
Cornelius, Don **X:** 202
Cornell, Ezra **VI:** 94
Cornell University **VI:** 94, 289,
  290; **X:** 211
Cornell University Medical
  College **VI:** 318
Corn God **I:** 242
corn harvester **IV:** 308, 377c
Cornish, Samuel E. **IV:** 194,
  376c

Corn Laws **IV:** 270
corn (maize) **I:** 87, **87–88**, 385c;
  IV: 10, 11; **VI:** 8
  agriculture **II:** 8, 10–13
  Cahokia **I:** 47
  Columbian Exchange **I:**
    77, 78
  Connecticut **II:** 69
  Crow **II:** 77
  Delaware **II:** 89
  diseases **I:** 107
  food **II:** 121
  Gates, Sir Thomas **II:** 135
  Hopewell culture **I:** 166
  Huron **I:** 171
  Indians of the Desert
    Southwest **II:** 165
  Jamestown **II:** 171
  Maine **II:** 203
  Mississippian culture **I:**
    236
  Native American religion
    I: 252
  Navajo **II:** 247
  New Hampshire **II:** 250
  North Carolina **II:**
    263–265
  Pennsylvania **II:** 276
  tenants **II:** 370
  Virginia **II:** 382
  Zuni **I:** 383
Cornplanter **III:** **91–92**, 92,
  164, 297; **IV:** 259
corn planters **IV:** 10
Cornstalk **II:** **72–73**
Cornu, Sebastian **IV:** 55
Cornwallis, Charles, Lord **III:**
  92–93, 394c
  Brandywine, Battle of **III:**
    48
  Camden, Battle of **III:** 57,
    58
  Charleston, siege of **III:** 64
  Clinton, Sir Henry **III:**
    75–76
  Cowpens, Battle of **III:** 95
  Eutaw Springs, Battle of
    III: 120
  Fort Washington, capture
    of **III:** 133
  Gage, Thomas **III:** 147
  Grasse, comte de **III:** 154
  Greene, Nathanael **III:**
    156
  Guilford Courthouse,
    Battle of **III:** 158
  Howe, Sir William **III:**
    168
  Jefferson, Thomas **III:** 184
  Kalb, baron de **III:** 195
  King's Mountain, Battle of
    III: 196, 197

  Lafayette, marquis de **III:**
    201
  Laurens, Henry **III:** 203
  Monmouth, Battle of **III:**
    245
  Revolutionary War **III:**
    305, 307
  Rochambeau, comte de
    III: 310
  Tarleton, Banastre **III:**
    342
  Trenton and Princeton,
    Battles of **III:** 352
  Washington, George **III:**
    367
  Yorktown, surrender at
    III: 388, 390
Cornwallis, Edward **II:** 2
Coronado, Francisco **I:** 88,
  88–90, 89m, 387c, 400–402;
  II: 303; **IV:** 337
  Franciscans **I:** 132
  gold **I:** 143
  Hopi **I:** 167
  New Mexico **I:** 256
  Panama **I:** 276
  Ponce de León, Juan **I:**
    288
  pueblo **I:** 296
  Zuni **I:** 383
corporate income tax **VIII:** 308,
  351, 352
corporate land distribution **II:**
  11
"corporate welfare" **X:** 206
Corporation for National
  Service **IX:** 311
Corporation for Public
  Broadcasting **X:** 296
corporations **III:** 31, **93–94**; **IV:**
  104, 375c; **V:** 290; **VI:** 146,
  277–278, 281; **VII:** xiii. *See
  also* transnational
  corporations
  business **VII:** 37; **X:** 49
  cities and urban life **VII:**
    48
  computers **X:** 74
  economy **X:** 94, 96
  Foreign Corrupt Practices
    Act **X:** 121–122
  IWW **VII:** 129
  labor **X:** 171
  liberalism **X:** 175
  Nader, Ralph **X:** 206
  New Nationalism **VII:** 211
  *Northern Securities Co. v.
    U.S.* **VII:** 216
  oil industry **VII:** 217
  progressivism **VII:** 237
corporatism **III:** **94–95**, 308
Corps d'Afrique **V:** **83–84**

Corps of Discovery **III:** 185–186, 315, 397*c*

Corps of Engineers. *See* Army Corps of Engineers **V:** 371

Corps of Topographical Engineers **IV:** 131

corrective advertising **X:** 7

corregidor **I: 90–91**
  audiencia **I:** 15
  Brazil **I:** 33
  cabildo **I:** 39
  Mendoza, Antonio de **I:** 231
  New Spain **I:** 259
  Tlaxcala **I:** 353

corregidores de españoles **I:** 91

corregidores de indios **I:** 91, 259; **II:** 357

Corregidor Island **VIII:** 35, 266, 267

corregimientos **I:** 90; **II:** 355

Correll, Charles **VII:** 254

"corrupt bargain" **IV:** 87, 122, 192

corruption and scandal **II:** 95, 119, 162, 199; **IV:** 260; **V:** 154, 294, 388; **VI:** 24–25, **66–67,** 67, 211, 323*c*, 325*c*; **VII:** 118, 154–155, 326–327, 360*c*; **X:** 324*c*. *See also* ethical issues
  Abscam **X:** 4–5
  Agnew, Spiro T. **X:** 14
  baseball **VI:** 21; **VII:** 26
  Butler, Benjamin **V:** 46
  Carter, James Earl, Jr. **X:** 57
  civil service reform **VI:** 56
  Clinton, Hillary Rodham **X:** 64, 65
  Clinton, William **X:** 68–69
  Coolidge, Calvin **VII:** 57
  Crédit Mobilier **V:** 84–85
  Foreign Corrupt Practices Act **X:** 121–122
  Garfield, James A. **VI:** 108
  Godkin, Edwin Lawrence **VI:** 116
  Grant, Ulysses S. **V:** 157
  Harding, Warren G. **VII:** 117
  House of Representatives **X:** 144–145
  impeachment **X:** 149–150
  Iran-contra affair **X:** 154–155
  Jaworski, Leon **X:** 161
  Judicial Watch **X:** 162
  Koreagate **X:** 166
  Meese, Edwin C. **X:** 191
  Mitchell, John N. **X:** 196
  mugwumps **VI:** 199

newspapers **VI:** 211

New York City **V:** 253

Nixon, Richard M. **X:** 219–221

North, Oliver L. **X:** 222

presidential campaigns **VI:** 231

progressivism in the 1890s **VI:** 233

railroads **VI:** 238

Reagan, Ronald W. **X:** 260

Reconstruction **V:** 294

religion **X:** 265

Republican Party **V:** 302; **VI:** 246

Ruckelshaus, William D. **X:** 269

Senate **X:** 276

Sickles, Daniel E. **V:** 326

sports **VII:** 294

star route frauds **VI:** 275

Teapot Dome **VII:** 307–308

televangelism **X:** 294

Tweed Ring **VI:** 298–299

war contracting **V:** 387

Watergate **X:** 315–317

Whiskey Ring **V:** 392–393

Corrupt Practices Act of 1925 **X:** 53

Corso, Gregory **IX:** 35

Cortés, Hernán (Fernando, Fernan) **I: 91–95,** *92,* 94*m,* 386*c,* 387*c;* **II:** 359
  Aguilar, Francisco de **I:** 4
  Aguilar, Gerónimo (Jerónimo) de **I:** 5
  Alvarado, Pedro de **I:** 6–8
  Aztecs **I:** 21–22
  black legend **I:** 30
  cabildo **I:** 39
  Cacamatzin **I:** 45
  castas **I:** 61
  Charles V **I:** 69
  chinampas **I:** 72
  Cholula **I:** 72
  Columbian Exchange **I:** 77
  conquistadores **I:** 84, 85
  Cozumel **I:** 97
  Cuauhtémoc **I:** 97
  Díaz de Castillo, Bernal **I:** 106
  Escalante, Juan de **I:** 123
  Franciscans **I:** 132
  Grijalva, Juan de **I:** 146
  Guerrero, Gonzalo **I:** 146
  horses **I:** 167
  Las Casas, Bartolomé de **I:** 198
  Malinche **I:** 218
  Mendoza, Antonio de **I:** 231

Moctezuma II **I:** 237, 238

Narváez, Pánfilo de **I:** 250–251

New Spain **I:** 258

Quetzalcoatl **I:** 301

Ramusio, Giovanni Battista **I:** 305

Sahagún, Bernardino de **I:** 315

Sandoval, Gonzalo de **I:** 317–318

Tabasco **I:** 341

Tacuba **I:** 342

Tlaxcala **I:** 353

Velázquez, Diego de **I:** 364

Veracruz **I:** 366

Cortes, Martin **I:** 118

Cosby, William **II:** 85, 153, 234, 261, 415

Cosby Show (TV program) **X:** 241, 295

Cosell, Howard **X:** 241

cosmetics **VIII:** 408*c*

cosmetics and beauty industry **VII: 57–58,** 355*c*

Cosmographie Universelle, La (André Thevet) **I:** 348, 403–408

cosmopolitanism **VI:** 15

cost accounting **VII:** 307

Costanoan **I:** 48

Costa Rica **V:** 7, 127

Costigan-Wagner antilynching bill **VIII:** 61

cost-of-living adjustment (COLA) **IX:** 46, **70,** 330*c*

Cost of Living Council **X:** 94

Côte d'Ivoire **I:** 13, 144, 243

Cotesworth, Charles **II:** 284

Cotesworth, Harriot **II:** 284

Cotesworth, Thomas **II:** 284

Cotopaxi Iron Works **IV:** 224

Cottage Residences (Downing) **IV:** 28

Cottier, Daniel **VI:** 3

cotton **II:** 3, 8, 43, 193, 247, 374; **III:** 7, 326–327, 376, 396*c;* **VI:** 8, 291; **VII:** 7
  abolition **V:** 1
  African Americans **IV:** 7
  agriculture **IV:** 9–11; **V:** 6
  Confederate States of America **V:** 76
  Davis Bend, Mississippi, freedmen's colony **V:** 92
  economy **IV:** 117–119; **V:** 104–105, 107
  emancipation **V:** 113–114
  Era of Good Feelings **IV:** 127
  foreign policy **V:** 131–132
  Grant, Ulysses S. **V:** 156

Indian Removal Act (1830) **IV:** 181, 183

industrial development **V:** 180

industrialization **IV:** 184

Mississippi River **V:** 236

Mobile campaign **V:** 236

New York City **V:** 253

Panic of 1819 **IV:** 275

Panic of 1837 **IV:** 276

plantations **V:** 276

Port Royal, South Carolina, Experiment **V:** 279–280

public land policy **IV:** 286

Reconstruction **V:** 294

Red River campaign **V:** 297, 298

sharecropping **V:** 315

slavery **IV:** 318; **V:** 329

slave trade, internal **IV:** 319–320

Trail of Tears **IV:** 343

Union navy **V:** 369

war contracting **V:** 387

Cotton, John **II: 73,** 73
  Boston **II:** 35
  Dudley, Thomas **II:** 96
  Hooker, Thomas **II:** 156, 157
  Hutchinson, Anne Marbury **II:** 161
  Massachusetts **II:** 212
  Mather, Cotton **II:** 217
  Wheelwright, John **II:** 396
  Williams, Roger **II:** 399
  Winthrop, John **II:** 402

"Cotton Belt" **V:** 276

cotton culture **IV: 96–99,** 97*m*
  migration **IV:** 235
  Missouri Compromise of 1820 **IV:** 237
  slave trade, internal **IV:** 320
  Texas **IV:** 337, 339

cotton gin **III:** 396*c;* **V:** 1, 276
  agriculture **III:** 7; **IV:** 10, 11
  cotton culture **IV:** 98
  industrialization **IV:** 184
  Missouri Compromise of 1820 **IV:** 237
  science **III:** 322
  slavery **III:** 327
  Whitney, Eli **III:** 376, 377

Cotton Is King (King) **IV:** 97

cotton mills **VI:** 209

Cottonseed Oil Trust **VI:** 294

Cotton Whigs **IV:** 364

Couc, Elizabeth. *See* Montour, Madame

Coughlin, Father Charles E.
VIII: 74–76, 75
America First Committee
VIII: 13
anti-Semitism **VIII:** 19
Catholics **VIII:** 53
censorship **VIII:** 55
conservatism **VIII:** 72
election of 1936 **VIII:** 97
Irish Americans **VIII:** 165
Long, Huey P. **VIII:** 195
religion **VIII:** 303
Townsend, Francis E.
VIII: 359
Union Party **VIII:** 365
Council for New England **II:**
250
Council of Basel **I:** 190
Council of Castile **I:** 128
Council of Economic Advisors
(CEA) **VIII:** 128; **IX: 70–71,**
88, **100,** 329c
Council of Prairie du Chien **IV:**
376c
Council of the Indies **I:** 15, 69,
95, 259, 281; **II:** 355
Council of Trent **II:** 174. *See*
Trent, Council of
Council of Twelve **IV:** 371
Council of Virginia **I:** 103
Council on Environmental
Quality (CEQ) **X:** 77, 210
Council on National Defense
VII: 25, 255
counterculture **IX: 71–72,**
333c
antiwar movement—
Vietnam **X:** 24
Beatles **IX:** 36–37
Dylan, Bob **IX:** 85
environmental movement
IX: 102
folk music revival **IX:** 111
Leary, Timothy **IX:**
175–176
LSD **IX:** 183–184
movies **IX:** 214
music **IX:** 218
narcotics **X:** 206, 207
Native American
movement **IX:** 229
New Age movement **X:**
216–217
New Left **IX:** 231
religion **IX:** 256
rock and roll **IX:** 264
sexual revolution **X:** 277
Weathermen **IX:** 319
Woodstock **X:** 321
counterfeiting **II:** 46, 76, 391
Counterreformation **I: 95–96,**
209, 307, 309

country music **VII:** 86, 254;
VIII: 222, 224; **X:** 201–203,
240
couriers de bois **I:** 149; **II:**
129–131, 178
Courses of Popular Lectures
(Wright) **IV:** 369
Court of Oyer and Terminer **II:**
402
court-packing **III:** 397c; **VII:**
124; **VIII: 76–77,** 407c
Adams, John **III:** 3
Black, Hugo L. **VIII:** 37
Borah, William E. **VIII:** 40
Byrnes, James F. **VIII:** 48
Congress **VIII:** 67
conservatism **VIII:** 72
conservative coalition
VIII: 74
Democratic Party **VIII:** 82
Executive Reorganization
Act **VIII:** 107
Garner, John Nance **VIII:**
129
government **VIII:** 134
Hoover, Herbert **VIII:** 152
Ickes, Harold L. **VIII:** 161
isolationists **VIII:** 166
Jefferson, Thomas **III:** 185
Johnson, Hugh S. **VIII:**
174
Judiciary Act of 1801 **III:**
193
La Follette, Robert M., Jr.
VIII: 182
Marbury v. Madison **III:**
230
Marshall, John **III:**
235–236
New Deal **VIII:** 242
Norris, George W. **VIII:**
249
politics in the Roosevelt
era **VIII:** 271
Republican Party **VIII:**
306
Roosevelt, Franklin D.
VIII: 313
*Schechter Poultry
Corporation v. United
States* **VIII:** 317
Supreme Court **VIII:** 345,
346
Third New Deal **VIII:** 357
Wheeler, Burton K. **VIII:**
378
courts and judiciary
audiencia **I:** 15–16
cabildo **I:** 39
Casa de Contratación **I:**
60, 61
Council of the Indies **I:** 95

crime and punishment **II:**
76
Livingston, Robert R. **II:**
196
Lloyd, David **II:** 197
royal colonies **II:** 325
Sewall, Samuel **II:** 334
society, British American
II: 349
wage and price controls **II:**
389
witchcraft **II:** 402
women's status and rights
II: 409
courtship **VII:** 283
courts martial **IV:** 176, 309; **VII:**
187
court system **IV:** 340
Cousins, Norman **IX:** 267
Coutourier, Henri **II:** 25
Covenant Chain **II:** 19, 184
cover crops **IX:** 7
covered wagons **IV:** 268, 376c
covert activities **IX:** 49, 50, 60,
204, 236
Boland Amendment **X:** 38
cold war (end of) **X:** 71
contras **X:** 81
foreign policy **X:** 124
Iranian hostage crisis **X:**
155
Covilhão, Pero da **I:** 125
Covode, John **V:** 191
Cowley, Malcolm **IX:** 160
Cowpens, Battle of **III:** 95m,
95–96, 394c
Cornwallis, Lord **III:** 93
Greene, Nathanael **III:**
156
Guilford Courthouse,
Battle of **III:** 158
Morgan, Daniel **III:** 246
Revolutionary War **III:** 305
Tarleton, Banastre **III:** 343
Cowskin Prairie **V:** 391
Cox, Archibald, Jr. **X: 81,** 324c
Bork, Robert **X:** 39
independent counsel **X:**
150
Jaworski, Leon **X:** 161
Nixon, Richard M. **X:** 221
Richardson, Elliot L. **X:**
267, 268
Ruckelshaus, William D.
X: 269
United States v. Nixon **X:**
308
Watergate scandal **X:** 316,
317
Cox, James **VII:** 360c
Coolidge, Calvin **VII:** 57
elections **VII:** 81

Harding, Warren G. **VII:**
118
Republican Party **VII:** 263
Cox, James M. **VIII:** 312
Cox, Kenyon **VI:** 219; **VII:** 17
Cox, Samuel **V:** 33
Cox Communications **X:** 244
Coxe, Daniel **II:** 253
Coxe, Tench **III: 96**
Coxey, Jacob S. **VI:** 68, 327c
Coxey's Army **VI: 67–68,** 327c
Cozumel **I:** 91, 92, **96–97**
Cozzens, James Gould **VIII:**
192
CP. *See* Communist Party
CPI. *See* Committee for Public
Information; Consumer Price
Index
CPPA (Conference for
Progressive Political Action)
VII: 91
CPS (Civilian Public Service)
VIII: 70
CPUSA. *See* Communist Party
of the United States of
America
"cradle," gold **IV:** 163
cradleboards **II:** 60
Cradock, Mathew **II:** 216
crafts **II:** 25–26, **73–74,** 104,
369, 407; **VI:** 3. *See also*
artisans
"craft unionism" **VI:** 170; **VIII:**
14, 43. *See also* "industrial
unionism"
Craftus, Richard **IV:** 103
Crane, Stephen **VI: 68–69,** 81,
136, **177–178**
Cranfield, Edward **II:** 252
craniology **IV:** 290
Cranmer, Thomas **I:** 73–74; **II:**
301
Cranston, Alan **X:** 276
Cranston, Samuel **II:** 321
crash of 1929 **VIII: 340–342,**
405c
African Americans **VIII:** 3
Banking Act of 1933 **VIII:**
33
economy **VIII:** 91
FCA **VIII:** 111
Federal Reserve Act **VII:**
93–94
Great Depression **VIII:**
138, 140
Hoover, Herbert **VIII:** 152
literature **VIII:** 191
Mellon, Andrew **VII:** 180
politics in the Roosevelt
era **VIII:** 270
popular culture **VIII:**
273–274

SEC **VIII:** 321, 322
tariffs **VII:** 306
trade, foreign **VII:** 310
Crater, Battle of the **V:** 45, 272
Craven, Charles **II:** 178
Crawford, William H. **IV:** 122, 192, 286, 376*c*
Cray T3E-1200™ computer **X:** 73
"Crazy Blues" (Smith) **VII:** 194
Crazy Horse **V:** 214; **VI:** **69,** 324*c*
 Black Hills gold rush **VI:** 29
 Native Americans **VI:** 207
 Red Cloud **VI:** 239, 240
 Sioux wars **VI:** 263
 Sitting Bull **VI:** 264
cream tester machine **VI:** 8
creation, beliefs about **I:** 228, 275
credit. *See* banking, finance and credit
credit cards **IX:** **72–73,** 90, 330*c*
Credit Island **IV:** 334
Crédit Mobilier **V:** **84–85,** 294, 393
 corruption, political **VI:** 67
 Garfield, James A. **VI:** 108
 Hoar, George Frisbie **VI:** 130
 railroads **VI:** 238
credit-rating services **IV:** 333
Creek Confederacy **I:** 85, 252; **IV:** 258. *See also* Muscogee alliance system
Creek/Creek nation **III:** **96–97;** **IV:** 375*c;* **VI:** 209. *See also* Five Civilized Tribes; Red Sticks
 agriculture **II:** 8
 Brims **II:** 41
 Cherokee **II:** 58
 Cherokee nation **III:** 66
 Choctaw **II:** 61
 cotton culture **IV:** 98
 Dragging Canoe **III:** 107
 frontier **III:** 141
 fur trade **II:** 130–131
 Georgia **II:** 138
 Horseshoe Bend, Battle of **IV:** 173
 Indian Removal Act (1830) **IV:** 181, 182*m*, 183
 Jackson, Andrew **IV:** 191
 McGillivray, Alexander **III:** 240
 Middleton, Arthur **II:** 224
 Musgrove, Mary Bosomworth **II:** 238
 Natchez Revolt **II:** 242

Native Americans **II:** 246; **IV:** 256
Native Americans and the Revolution **III:** 254
Native Americans in the War of 1812 **IV:** 259–260
 New Orleans, Battle of (1815) **IV:** 262
 Pontiac's Rebellion **III:** 281
 race and race relations **IV:** 291
 Seminole wars **IV:** 311
 Tomochichi **II:** 375
 trade and shipping **II:** 375
 Trail of Tears **IV:** 343, 344
 War of 1812 **IV:** 356
Creek War **III:** 66, 68; **IV:** 259
Creel, George **VII:** 5, 51, 52, 282
Creel Committee. *See* Committee for Public Information
Cree nation **IV:** 55
CREEP. *See* Committee to Reelect the President
Creole **II:** **74**
 African Americans **II:** 5, 6
 class **II:** 62
 fertility **II:** 117
 Gullah **II:** 151–152
 Maryland **II:** 210
 slavery **II:** 340
 Virginia **II:** 384
creolization **II:** 151, 211
Crescent City Live Stock Landing and Slaughterhouse Company **VI:** 82
Creswell, John A. J. **VI:** 62
Crèvecoeur, J. Hector St. John de **II:** 349, 352; **III:** **97–98,** 214, 394*c*
Crick, Francis H. C. **IX:** 269, 295
crillos **I:** 233, 259–260; **II:** 356
Crime Act of 1994 **X:** 328*c*
"Crime against Kansas" speech **V:** 405*c*
crime and punishment **II:** **74–76,** 75; **III:** 169; **IV:** 83, 129, 277–278; **IX:** 53–56, 208; **X:** **81–83,** 83, 329*c*, 330*c. See also* espionage; organized crime; terrorism
 abortion **X:** 1
 African Americans **II:** 7; **VI:** 6
 capital punishment **X:** 55–56
 cities and urban life **V:** 61
 computers **X:** 74

consumption **II:** 71
convict labor **II:** 71–72
crowd action **II:** 78
gay rights movement **X:** 127
gun control **X:** 136, 137
Horton, Willie (campaign ad) **X:** 143–144
House of Representatives **X:** 145
Ku Klux Klan **V:** 199–201
Libertarian Party **X:** 176
marriage and family life **II:** 208
missions **II:** 229
Mitchell, John N. **X:** 196
Molly Maguires **VI:** 195–196
NAACP **X:** 208
narcotics **X:** 206–{10: }208
newspapers **VI:** 211
NRA **X:** 213
piracy **II:** 284–286
postal service **II:** 292
prostitution **V:** 283–284
Quakers **II:** 307
Reno, Janet **X:** 266–267
Richmond, Virginia **V:** 304
RICO **X:** 257–258
slave codes **II:** 336
slave resistance **II:** 337
Swedish colonies **II:** 365
terrorism **X:** 297–301
Tweed Ring **VI:** 298–299
women's status and rights **II:** 409
Crimean War
 economy **V:** 104
 ironclads **V:** 183
 medicine and hospitals **V:** 230
 Monitor-Merrimack **V:** 237
 Panic of 1857 **V:** 264
 USSC **V:** 373
 Zouaves **V:** 403
Crime of '73 **VI:** **69–70,** 324*c*
 bimetallism **VI:** 28
 Bland-Allison Act **VI:** 32
 Free-Silver movement **VI:** 105
 Sherman, John **VI:** 261
criminal court cases **I:** 15
criminal evidence **X:** 264
criminal justice **VII:** **58–60.** *See also* juvenile justice
"crimping" **II:** 204
criollo bourgeoisie **IV:** 100
criollos **II:** 355
Cripple Creek strike **VII:** 120, 129
Crisis, The (magazine) **VII:** 71, 72, 119, 199, 357*c;* **VIII:** 227

Crittenden, John J. **V:** 37
Crittenden Compromise of 1860 **V:** 406*c*
Croatia **X:** 85, 88, 166, 329*c*
Croatoan **I:** 220, 313–314
Crocker, Betty **VII:** 5
Crockett, Davy **IV:** 13, 99, **99–100,** 341, 346, 375*c*
Crockett, George **IX:** 80
Croghan, Catherine **II:** 76
Croghan, George **II:** **76**
Croly, David **V:** 233
Croly, Herbert **VII:** 211
Cromwell, Oliver **II:** 19, 108, 209, 211, 232
Cronkite, Walter **X:** 296
Crook, George
 Apache War **VI:** 14
 Black Hills gold rush **VI:** 29
 Crazy Horse **VI:** 69
 Red Cloud **VI:** 240
 Sioux wars **VI:** 263
 Sitting Bull **VI:** 264
Crooks, Ramsay **IV:** 17
crop failures **IV:** 276
crop rotation **IV:** 11
Cropsey, Jasper **VI:** 219
crop stabilization corporations **VIII:** 7
crop surplus **VIII:** 5, 7–9
Crosby, Bing **VIII:** 217, 224
Cross Keys, Battle of **V:** 316
Crossley, Archibald **VIII:** 284
"Cross of Gold" speech (Bryan) **VI:** 327*c,* 354–357
Crosweeksung **II:** 40
Crouching Tiger, Hidden Dragon (movie) **X:** 240
crowd actions **II:** **77–78**
Crowder, Enoch **VII:** 54, 282
Crow nation **I:** 161; **II:** **76–77**
 Beckwourth, Jim **IV:** 46
 exploration **IV:** 131
 Fort Laramie **IV:** 144
 South Pass **IV:** 324
Crown Victoria automobile **IX:** 25
Crummell, Alexander **VI:** **70–71,** 328*c*
Crusade for Justice **IX:** 124
crusade journalism **II:** 299
Crusades **I:** 190, 306
Cruz, Juana Inés de la **II:** 357
Cruzan v. Missouri (1990) **X:** 264–265
crypto-Jews **I:** 191
CSNET **X:** 153
CT (computer tomography) scan **X:** 190
cuauhpipiltin **I:** 19
Cuauhtémoc **I:** 95, **97**

Cuba **I: 97–98**, 387c; **IV: 100–101**; **VI: 71–72**; **VII:** 355c, 356c; **VIII:** 133; **IX:** 332c, 333c; **X:** 326c, 330c
   African nations **X:** 12, 13
   Amistad incident **IV:** 19
   Anti-Imperialist League **VI:** 13
   Barbados **I:** 26
   Barton, Clara **V:** 25
   Bay of Pigs **IX:** 33–35
   Big Stick diplomacy **VII:** 27
   Buchanan, James **V:** 41
   Caribbean **II:** 52, 53
   CIA **IX:** 50
   Cleveland, Grover **VI:** 59
   cold war **IX:** 60; **X:** 70
   Columbus, Christopher **I:** 82
   conquistadores **I:** 85
   Córdoba, Francisco Hernández de **I:** 86, 87
   Cortés, Hernán **I:** 91
   Crane, Stephen **VI:** 68
   de Lôme letter **VI:** 76–77
   Democratic Party **V:** 94
   emancipation **V:** 114
   Fillmore, Millard **IV:** 137
   foreign policy **IV:** 142; **V:** 131, 133; **VI:** 103, 104; **VII:** 98, 99
   Fort Mose **II:** 123
   Grant, Ulysses S. **V:** 156
   Hearst, William Randolph **VII:** 121
   Hispanic Americans **X:** 141, 142
   Hoar, George Frisbie **VI:** 130
   immigration **IX:** 142
   imperialism **VI:** 142–143
   investments, American, abroad **VI:** 150
   Las Casas, Bartolomé de **I:** 198
   Latin America **X:** 172, 173
   Latin America (foreign policy) **IX:** 172
   Manifest Destiny **IV:** 218, 219
   McKinley, William **VI:** 189
   Mexico **X:** 192
   Mills, C. Wright **IX:** 205
   missile crisis **IX:** 73–75
   Monroe Doctrine **IV:** 241
   Narváez, Pánfilo de **I:** 250–251
   Nicaragua **X:** 218
   Operation Mongoose **IX:** 236
   Ostend Manifesto **V:** 259–260
   Pershing, John **VII:** 227
   Reagan, Ronald W. **X:** 261
   "Remember the *Maine*" **VI:** 187–188
   Remington, Frederic **VI:** 245
   Republican Party **IV:** 301
   Roosevelt, Theodore **VII:** 266
   Roosevelt Corollary **VII:** 267
   Rough Riders **VI:** 250
   slavery **II:** 338
   Soto, Hernando de **I:** 332
   Spanish-American War **VI:** 272–273
   Spanish colonies **II:** 355, 358
   Strategic Arms Limitation Treaties **X:** 289
   Taino **I:** 342
   Treaty of Paris **II:** 378
   Velázquez, Diego de **I:** 364
   Virginius affair **VI:** 305–306
   Weather Underground **X:** 318
Cuba **VI:** 328c
Cuban Americans **X:** 142, 143, 200
Cuban Communist Party **IX:** 33
Cuban missile crisis **IX: 73–75,** 74, 333c
   Acheson, Dean **IX:** 2
   arms race **IX:** 16
   cold war **IX:** 60
   Kennedy, John F. **IX:** 158
   Limited Test Ban Treaty of 1963 **IX:** 180
   Soviet Union **IX:** 277
Cuban Student Directorate **IX:** 238
Cudahy **VI:** 191
Cuffe, Paul **III: 98–99,** 394c
Cuguano, Ottobah **II:** 344
Cuicuilco **I:** 346
Cuicuitzca **I:** 45
Cuitláhuac **I:** 21, 22, 45, 93, 97, **98–99**
Culberson, Charles **VII:** 88, 280
Culhuacán **I:** 72
Culiacan **I:** 38
Culp, Wesley **V:** 37
Culpeper, Thomas, Lord **II: 79**
Culpeper family **II:** 172
cultivation. *See* agriculture
"cult of otherness" **X:** 176, 201
cultural history **II:** 35, 74, 390
cultural identity **II:** 52
cultural prejudice **IV:** 182
culture **VI:** 6, 201, 207, 208; **VII:** 361c. *See also* popular culture
   African Americans **II:** 5, 6
   art and architecture **IX:** 19–21
   childhood **II:** 60
   Crow **II:** 77
   dance **II:** 82
   Delaware **II:** 88
   dueling **II:** 96
   globalization **X:** 131–132
   Hispanic Americans **X:** 143
   immigration **X:** 148
   Jews and Judaism **X:** 162
   Kennedy, Jacqueline **IX:** 156
   La Raza Unida **IX:** 171
   literature **IX:** 180–183
   media **X:** 187
   militia movement **X:** 194
   multiculturalism **X:** 200–201
   music **IX:** 216–218; **X:** 201, 202
   National Endowment for the Arts **IX:** 221
   National Endowment for the Humanities **IX:** 221–222
   Native Americans **II:** 242–243; **X:** 215
   Neolin **II:** 248
   New York **II:** 261
   New York City **II:** 263
   North Carolina **II:** 264
   Northwest Coast Indians **II:** 265–266
   political correctness **X:** 236–237
   praying towns **II:** 296
   religion **IX:** 256
   religion, African-American **II:** 314
   Rhode Island **II:** 321
   slavery **II:** 338, 340–342
   society, British American **II:** 351
   South Carolina **II:** 354
   Spanish colonies **II:** 357, 359
   technology **II:** 369
   television **X:** 296–297
   tobacco **II:** 375
   urban **IX:** 52
   Virginia **II:** 384
Culture and Democracy in the United States (Kallen) **VII:** 162
Culture Club (music group) **X:** 240
Cumberland, Rhode Island **II:** 321
Cumberland, USS **V:** 238
Cumberland Hospital **V:** 371
Cumberland River **V:** 234
Cumberland Road **IV:** 18, 56, 188. *See also* National Road
Cumming, Alfred **IV:** 110
Cumming, Kate **V: 85**
cummings, e. e. **VII:** 166
Cummings, Homer **VIII:** 115
Cunha, Tristão da **I:** 153
Cunningham, Andrew B. **VIII:** 325
Curaçao **II:** 98, 257, 362
Curley, James Michael **VIII:** 165
Curran, Charles Courtney **VI:** 219
currency **I:** 45, 345, 353; **IV: 40–44,** 41, 377c; **V: 22–24,** 23; **VI: 72–73,** 73, 324c, 326c; **VII:** 73, 334; **VIII:** 5–6, 42, 406c; **IX:** 256. *See also* banking, finance and credit
   banking **III:** 32; **IV:** 42–43; **V:** 23
   Bank of the United States, Second **IV:** 44
   bimetallism **VI:** 28–29
   Blaine, James Gillespie **VI:** 31
   Bland-Allison Act **VI:** 32
   Bryan, William Jennings **VI:** 37
   business cycles **VI:** 42
   Butterworth, Mary Peck **II:** 46
   Chase, Salmon P. **V:** 56
   Cleveland, Grover **VI:** 58–59
   Confederate States of America **V:** 77
   Conkling, Roscoe **VI:** 64
   Connecticut **II:** 69
   Crime of '73 **VI:** 69–70
   Currency Act **III:** 99
   currency issue **VI:** 72–73
   Democratic Party **VI:** 77
   Dummer, Jeremiah **II:** 96
   economy **IV:** 118–119; **V:** 105, 106
   farmers' alliances **VI:** 99
   foreign policy **VIII:** 124
   Free-Silver movement **VI:** 104–105
   Geological Survey, U.S. **VI:** 111
   government, British American **II:** 145
   Greenback-Labor Party **VI:** 120
   greenbacks **V:** 159

Hayes, Rutherford B. **VI:** 126
Hutchinson, Thomas **III:** 170
Jefferson, Thomas **III:** 184
labor **II:** 190
London Economic Conference **VIII:** 193
Maryland **II:** 210
Massachusetts **II:** 212
mercantilism **II:** 221
merchants **II:** 221–222
Miantonomo **II:** 224
Middleton, Arthur **II:** 224
national banking system **VI:** 205–206
New Jersey **II:** 253
newspapers **VI:** 211
Panic of 1819 **IV:** 275
People's Party **VI:** 223
political parties, third **VI:** 225, 226
Reciprocal Trade Agreements Act **VIII:** 294
slavery **II:** 341
Stephens, Alexander H. **V:** 337
Stevens, Thaddeus **V:** 338
taxation **V:** 349
trade **III:** 349–350
Villard, Henry **VI:** 305
wampum **II:** 390–391
World Disarmament Conference **VIII:** 388
Currency Act **III:** 32, **99,** 111, 157, 391*c;* **VII: 60,** 262, 355*c*
Currency Act of 1834 **IV:** 377*c*
curriculum, college **IV:** 121
Curry, John Steuart **VIII:** 25
Curtin, Andrew **V:** 53
Curtis, Benjamin **V:** 101, 178
Curtis, Charles **VIII:** 96; **X:** 105
Curtis, Cyrus H. K. **VI:** 2, 138, 185
Curtis, George William **V:** 247; **VI:** 56, 64, 199
Curtis, Samuel R. **V:** 265
Curtis, Tom **VI:** 290
Curtis, William **V:** 113
Curtis Act **VII:** 206
Cusabo nation **I:** 130, 131; **II:** 353
Cushing, William **III:** 338
Cushman, Robert **II:** 283
Custer, George **II:** 50
Custer, George Armstrong **V:** 129, 213, 214, 318, 319; **VI:** 324*c*
   Black Hills gold rush **VI:** 29
   Crazy Horse **VI:** 69

entertainment, popular **VI:** 98
   Native Americans **VI:** 207
   Red Cloud **VI:** 240
   Sioux wars **VI:** 263
   Sitting Bull **VI:** 264
Custer, Tom **V:** 228
Custer's Last Stand **V:** 213–214; **VI:** 29
Custis, John Parke **III:** 46
custody rights **VI:** 317
customs (trade)
   Acts of Trade and Navigation **II:** 3
   British Empire **II:** 41
   Heathcote, Caleb **II:** 155
   Massachusetts **II:** 214
   piracy **II:** 285
   Randolph, Edward **II:** 312
customshouses
   Arthur, Chester Alan **VI:** 16
   civil service reform **VI:** 56
   Conkling, Roscoe **VI:** 64
   corruption, political **VI:** 67
Cutler, Timothy **II:** 70, 184
Cuzco **I:** 14, 15, **99,** 177, 283
CWA. *See* Civil Works Administration
Cyane, HMS **III:** 81
cybernetic organs **X:** 275
cyclopes **I:** 239
Cyclops Iron Company **VI:** 44
cyclotron **VIII:** 318
cylinder press **IV:** 196
Czechoslovakia **VII:** 285, 323; **IX:** 58, 105, 106, 277; **X:** 72, 151, 156–157
   foreign policy **VIII:** 124
   isolationists **VIII:** 166
   Munich Conference **VIII:** 220
   Neutrality Acts **VIII:** 239
Czech Republic **X:** 223

D

Dabney, Charles **VI:** 197
Dabney, Morgan & Company **VI:** 197
Da Costa, Uriel **I:** 192
Dacre, Harry **VI:** 204
Dade, Francis L. **IV:** 312
Dagomba **I: 101,** 243
Daguerre, Louis **V:** 35
daguerreotype **V:** 35
Dahlgren, John A. B. **V: 87,** 87, 368
Dahomey **I: 101–102,** 125, 131–132, 377
Dahomey (Cook) **VII:** 194
Dai, Bao **IX:** 308–310

Daily Graphic **VII:** 143
Daily Southern Argus **IV:** 112
Daily Worker **VII:** 53, 253
Daimler-Benz **X:** 32, 51
Daimler Chrysler **X:** 49
dairy farming **V:** 6
dairy industry **VI:** 8
dairy products **II:** 102; **IV:** 10
"Daisy Bell" **VI:** 28
"Daisy" commercial **IX:** 3
Daisy Miller (James) **VI:** 154
Dakota, North **VII:** 215–216
Daladier, Edouard **VIII:** 220
Dale, David **IV:** 273
Dale, Samuel **II:** 55
Dale, Sir Thomas **II: 81–82**
   agriculture **II:** 10
   Gates, Sir Thomas **II:** 135
   Pocahontas **II:** 288, 289
   Powhatan (chief) **II:** 294
   Rolfe, John **II:** 322
Daley, Richard **IX:** 131; **X:** 61
Dallas **X:** 290
Dallas, Battle of **V:** 19
Dallas, George M. **IV:** 283
Daly, Mary **IX:** 257
Damadian, Raymond **X:** 190
Damascus **I:** 230
"dame schools" **II:** 216, 407
Damrosche, Walter **VI:** 23
dams **VII:** 55, 204; **VIII:** 103, 104, 175, 356, 410*c*
Dana, Charles A. **IV:** 58; **V: 88;** **VI:** 211
Dana, Francis **IV:** 4
Dana, Richard Henry **IV: 103**
   Burns, Anthony **IV:** 59
   California **IV:** 65
   California Trail **IV:** 70
   journalism **IV:** 196
Danakil people **I:** 109
Danbury Hatters **VII:** 10, 36, **61,** 152
dance **II: 82; III:** 251; **IX:** 221
   Africa **II:** 4
   art **II:** 24
   Creole **II:** 74
   education **II:** 104
   Massachusetts **II:** 215
   religion, Native American **II:** 317
   society, British American **II:** 351
   Virginia **II:** 384
dance crazes **VII:** 233
dance halls **VII:** 257
dance music **VI:** 194
dancing, exotic **VI:** 96
Dancing Rabbit Creek, Treaty of **IV:** 344
Danforth, John C. **X:** 40, 267, 302

Daniel Boone Escorting Settlers through the Cumberland Gap (Bingham) **III:** 43
Daniels, Josephus **VIII:** 183, 379
Danish merchants **I:** 5
Danites **IV:** 79, 323
Danks, Hart Pease **VI:** 203
D'Anville, duc **II:** 182
DAR. *See* Daughters of the American Revolution
Dare, Virginia **I:** 388*c;* **II: 82–83**
Darfur **I: 102**
Darién **I:** 24, 276, 368
Darien, Georgia **II:** 267
Dario, Giovanni **I:** 365
Dark Victory (film) **VIII:** 218
Darlan, Jean **VIII:** 249
Darnall family **II:** 186
Darnley, Lord (Henry Stuart) **I:** 187
DARPA. *See* Defense Advanced Research Projects Agency
Darrow, Clarence Seward **VI:** 10; **VII: 61–62,** 278, 361*c;* **VIII:** 319
   Haywood, "Big Bill" **VII:** 120
   Leopold and Loeb **VII:** 158
   Mencken, H. L. **VII:** 181
   Scopes Trial **VII:** 278
Dartmoor Prison **IV: 103–104,** 152
Dartmouth, William, Lord **III:** 211, 266
Dartmouth College **II: 83,** 83; **X:** 215
   education **II:** 104–105
   Great Awakening **II:** 149
   lotteries **II:** 199
   Wheelock, Eleazar **II:** 395, 396
Dartmouth College v. Woodward **IV: 104,** 330, 359, 375*c*
   corporations **III:** 94
   education **III:** 115
   Marshall, John **III:** 237
   Supreme Court **III:** 338
Darwin, Charles **II:** 330; **IV:** 291, 307; **VII:** 62, 278, 361*c*
   Blackwell, Antoinette Brown **VI:** 30
   Darwinism and religion **VI:** 75
   literature **VI:** 178
   Marsh, Othniel Charles **VI:** 188
   religion **VI:** 242
   science **VI:** 257

Darwin, Charles (*continued*)
    Social Darwinism **VI:** 265
    Sumner, William Graham
        VI: 280
    Victorianism **VI:** 304
Darwinism **V:** 16; **VI: 75–76,**
    241, 242, 324*c*; **VII:** 275. *See*
    also Social Darwinism
Dasamonquepeuc **II:** 264, 401
Das Capital (Marx) **V:** 223
Daschle, Tom **X:** *137,* 276, 331*c*
Dash for the Timber, A
    (Remington) **VI:** 245–246
Dass, Baba Ram. *See* Alpert,
    Richard
data storage (computers) **IX:** 63,
    64, 98
Daugherty, Harry **VII:** 57, 117,
    118, 307, 308
Daughter of the Middle Border
    (Garland) **VI:** 110
Daughters of Bilitis (DOB) **IX:**
    119; **X:** 277
Daughters of Edwin D. Boit
    (Sargent) **VI:** 256
Daughters of Saint Crispin **VI:**
    169
Daughters of the American
    Revolution (DAR) **VIII:** 3,
    94, 227, 408*c*
Dauti (David) **II:** *See* Dengel,
    Lebna
DAV (Disabled American
    Veterans) **VII:** 326
Davenport, Charles **VII:** 276
Davenport, James **II: 83–84**
Davenport, John **II:** 68
Daves, Delmar **IX:** 229
David, Jacques-Louis **IV:** 34
Davies, Arthur B. **VII:** 18
Davies, Ronald **IX:** 109
Davies, Samuel **II: 84,** 371
Dávilar, Pedrarias **I:** 24, 146,
    272, 276, 332
da Vinci, Leonardo. *See*
    Leonardo da Vinci
Davis, Alexander Jackson **IV:** 28
Davis, Andrew Jackson **IV:** 299
Davis, Benjamin O. **VIII:** 340,
    408*c*
Davis, Bette **VIII:** 219; **IX:** 13
Davis, Chester **VIII:** 6
Davis, David **V:** 248; **VI:** 231
Davis, Dwight **VI:** 274
Davis, Dwight F. **VII:** 187
Davis, Edmund J. **V:** 199, 242
Davis, Edwin H. **IV:** 308
Davis, Harry **VII:** 86, 191, 356*c*
Davis, Henry Winter **V:** 385,
    386
Davis, Isaac **IV:** 171–172, 199
Davis, Jacob **IV:** 329

Davis, Jeff **VII:** 292, 293
Davis, Jeff C. (Union general) **V:**
    323
Davis, Jefferson **IV:** 159, 234; **V:**
    88–90, 89, 406*c*
    assassination of Abraham
        Lincoln **V:** 18
    Atlanta campaign **V:** 19
    Beauregard, Pierre **V:** 27
    Benjamin, Judah P. **V:** 27,
        28
    Bragg, Braxton **V:** 36
    Brown, Joseph **V:** 39
    Chattanooga, Battle of **V:**
        57
    Chesnut, Mary B. **V:** 58
    Civil War **V:** 66
    Confederate States of
        America **V:** 75, 77
    conscription **V:** 79
    Davis, Varina Howell **V:** 91
    Davis Bend, Mississippi,
        freedmen's colony **V:**
        91–92
    Democratic Party **V:** 94
    economy **V:** 107
    elections **V:** 110–111
    employment **V:** 116
    filibustering **V:** 127
    food riots **V:** 130
    foreign policy **V:** 132
    Forrest, Nathan Bedford
        V: 134
    Fort Sumter, South
        Carolina **V:** 136, 137
    Freedmen's Bureau **V:**
        142
    governors **V:** 153
    Greeley, Horace **V:** 158
    Greenhow, Rose O'Neal **V:**
        159
    habeas corpus, writ of **V:**
        161
    homefront **V:** 169
    Hood, John Bell **V:** 170,
        171
    Inaugural Address (1861)
        V: 418–420
    Jackson, "Stonewall" **V:**
        186
    Johnston, Albert Sidney **V:**
        189
    Johnston, Joseph E. **V:**
        189, 190
    journalism **V:** 193
    Lee, Robert E. **V:** 205
    literature **V:** 212
    Mallory, Stephen R. **V:** 221
    Medal of Honor **V:** 228
    Milliken's Bend, Battle of
        V: 232
    monuments **V:** 239

    Morrill Land-Grant Act **V:**
        241
    Murfreesboro/Stones
        River, Battle of **V:** 243
    New York City draft riots
        V: 254
    Pacific Railroad Act of
        1862 **V:** 263
    Peninsular campaign **V:**
        269
    prisons **V:** 282
    Revels, Hiram R. **V:** 303
    Richmond, Virginia **V:** 304
    secession **V:** 313
    Semmes, Raphael **V:** 313
    Shenandoah Valley:
        Jackson's campaign **V:**
        316
    Shiloh, Battle of **V:** 323
    states' rights **V:** 336
    Stephens, Alexander H. **V:**
        337
    tactics and strategy **V:** 346
    Vicksburg campaign **V:**
        380
    Yancey, William Lowndes
        V: 401
Davis, John **I:** 145, 266
Davis, John P. **VIII:** 227
Davis, John W. **VII:** 57, 81,
    360*c*; **VIII:** 15, 71; **IX:** 42
Davis, Joseph **V:** 91, 92
Davis, Rennie **X:** 61
Davis, Sammy, Jr. **IX:** 191
Davis, Stuart **VII:** 19; **VIII:** 25
Davis, Varina Howell **V:** 91
Davis Bend, Mississippi,
    freedmen's colony **V: 91–92,**
    113, 142
Davis Cup **VI:** 274
"Davis Guard" medals **V:** 228
Dawes, Charles Gates **VII:**
    62–63
    Budget and Accounting
        Act **VII:** 36–37
    Coolidge, Calvin **VII:** 57
    Dawes Plan **VII:** 64
    foreign policy **VII:** 101
    Harding, Warren G. **VII:**
        118
Dawes, Henry L. **VI:** 76
Dawes, William **III:** 212, 304,
    363, 393*c*
"Dawes Bank" **VII:** 62–63
Dawes Plan **VII:** 57, **63–64,** 75,
    101
Dawes Severalty Act of 1887 **IV:**
    221; **VI: 76,** 326*c,* 334–336;
    VII: 37, 165, 206; **VIII:** 163,
    235; **IX:** 227
    Indian Affairs, Office of
        VI: 144

    Indian Rights Association
        VI: 144
    Native Americans **VI:** 206,
        207, 209
    the presidency **VI:** 230
    Red Cloud **VI:** 240
    Sooners **VI:** 271
Dawit I **I:** 124
Day, Benjamin **IV:** 194
Day, Doris **IX:** 244
Day, Dorothy **VII:** 205; **VIII:**
    54, 303, 406*c*
Day, Stephen **II: 84**
day care **VIII:** 56; **X:** 110
"Day of Infamy" speech **VIII:**
    428
Days of Rage **IX:** 319; **X:** 318,
    323*c*
Dayton accords **X: 85,** 88, 329*c*
D.C. *See* Washington, District
    of Columbia
DC-3 airliner **VIII:** 10
DC current **VI:** 149
D day **VIII:** 247–248, 410*c*
DDT **VIII:** 9; **IX:** 48, 49, 101,
    270
Dead Indian Land Act **VII:**
    206
Dean, Dizzy **VIII:** 275
Dean, James **IX:** 213, 244
Dean, John **X:** 315, 316
Deane, Francis B. **V:** 356
Deane, Silas **III: 101,** 195, 205
Dearborn, Henry **IV:** 309
Dearborn Independent **VII:** 14,
    97
death, causes of **X:** 10
death and afterlife, beliefs
    about. *See also* burial
    Aztecs **I:** 20–21
    flowery wars **I:** 131
    Huron **I:** 171
    Maya **I:** 228
Death of a Salesman (Arthur
    Miller) **IX:** 181, 330*c*
Death of General Wolfe (West)
    III: 22
death penalty. *See* capital
    punishment
death rates **VIII:** 278. *See also*
    disease and epidemics
    Bay of Pigs **IX:** 34
    birthrates **X:** 38
    bubonic plague **I:** 285
    California **I:** 49
    disease **I:** 106–107
    Korean War **IX:** 164, 165
    medicine **X:** 187
    miracle drugs **IX:** 205
    Occupational Safety and
        Health Act of 1970 **X:**
        225

population trends **IX:** 245; **X:** 243
public health **IX:** 249
Vietnam War **IX:** 310
Deaver, Michael **X:** 260
DeBow's Review **IV:** 197; **V:** 128, 260
Debra Damo monastery **I:** 123, 124
DeBry, Theodor **I:** *102–103, 103, 143, 179*
    black legend **I:** 31
    cannibalism **I:** 55
    Harriot, Thomas **I:** 154, 155
    Native American religion **I:** 253
    Picts **I:** 282
    Stade, Hans **I:** 336
    White, John **I:** 373
Debs, Eugene Victor **VII:** *64, 64–65, 355c, 359c;* **VIII:** 327
    Bellamy, Edward **VI:** 26
    Cleveland, Grover **VI:** 59
    Communist Party **VII:** 53
    Darrow, Clarence **VII:** 62
    elections **VII:** 80
    Espionage Act **VII:** 88
    Federal Trade Commission Act **VII:** 94
    IWW **VII:** 130
    Lloyd, Henry Demarest **VI:** 179
    National Civic Federation **VII:** 201
    politics **VII:** 229, 230
    Pullman Strike **VI:** 235–236
    radicalism **VII:** 250, 251
    Red Scare **VII:** 259
    socialism **VII:** 288, 289
    Socialist Party **VI:** 268, 269
debt (agricultural) **V:** 315–316
debt (Confederate) **V:** 138
debt (in general) **VII:** 118; **VIII:** 138–139. *See also* federal debt; national debt
    Audubon, John James **IV:** 34
    banking and currency **IV:** 42
    economy **IV:** 118*t*, 119
    national **III:** 126, 162, **253**
    Panic of 1819 **IV:** 275
    state **III:** 162
    Texas **IV:** 339
debt peonage **IV:** 64
debt relief **V:** 307; **X:** 173
debt (war)
    Fordney-McCumber Tariff **VII:** 97
    Revolutionary War **III:** 89

tariffs **VII:** 306
trade, foreign **VII:** 310
War Revenue Act **VII:** 330
Decades of the New Worlde, or West India, The (Richard Eden) **I:** 117
Decatur, Stephen **III:** 35, 131, 142; **IV:** **104–105**
DEC (Digital Equipment Corporation) **IX:** 65
"Decennium Luctuosum" **II:** 214
De Chepart, Sieur **II:** 241, 242
Declaration and an Address, A (Campbell) **IV:** 72
Declaration by United Nations **VIII:** 365
Declaration of Independence **II:** 110, 149, 196, 278; **III:** **101–103,** *102, 103,* 393*c,* 399–401; **IV:** 289; **V:** 151
    Adams, John **III:** 2
    American Revolution **III:** 12
    art **III:** 22
    Catholics **III:** 63
    Chase, Samuel **III:** 64
    Common Sense (Paine) **III:** 78
    Continental Congress, Second **III:** 88
    corporatism **III:** 94, 95
    Dickinson, John **III:** 106
    Forten, James **III:** 131
    Franklin, Benjamin **III:** 134
    Galloway, Joseph **III:** 148
    George III, king of Great Britain **III:** 150
    Hancock, John **III:** 163
    immigration **III:** 173
    Independence Hall **III:** 176
    Jefferson, Thomas **III:** 183
    Livingston, William **III:** 217
    Mason, George **III:** 237
    Olive Branch Petition **III:** 266
    resistance movement **III:** 303
    Rush, Benjamin **III:** 313
    Sherman, Roger **III:** 325
    slave trade **III:** 329
    Trumbull, John **III:** 352
    Wilson, James **III:** 379, 380
    Witherspoon, John **III:** 380
Declaration of Independence, The (Trumbull painting) **III:** 352, 396*c*

Declaration of Independence for Women **VI:** 224
Declaration of Independence (Texas) **IV:** 174, 303, 393–394
Declaration of Lima **VIII:** 133, 408*c*
Declaration of Negro Rights **VII:** 315
Declaration of Panama of 1939 **VIII:** 408*c*
Declaration of Rights (Virginia) **III:** 237
Declaration of Rights and Grievances **III:** 101
Declaration of Rights and Sentiments **V:** 397
Declaration of Rights of Women **V:** 399
Declaration of Sentiments **IV:** 314, 315, 368, 405–407
"Declaration of the Causes and Necessity of Taking up Arms" **III:** 266
Declaration of the Indies **I:** 35
Declaration of the Rights of Man **III:** 138
"Declaration of War against Amerikkka" **X:** 317
Declaration on Liberated Europe **VIII:** 401
Declaratory Act **III:** 52, **103,** 268, 332
Decline and Fall of the Roman Empire (Gibbon) **III:** 302
decolonization **IX:** 3
DeConcini, Dennis **X:** 276
deconstructionism **X:** 27
decorative arts **VI:** 288
Decter, Midge **X:** 216
Deep South. *See* Lower South states
Deere, John **IV:** 10, **105–106,** 185
Deerfield Massacre **II:** **84–85,** 214, 309, 352
deerskins
    animals **II:** 21
    Catawba **II:** 55
    Charleston **II:** 56
    Chickasaw **II:** 59
    economy **II:** 101
    forests **II:** 122
    fur trade **II:** 130–131, 133
    Hudson's Bay Company **II:** 159
    Louisiana **II:** 199
    Native Americans **II:** 243
    North Carolina **II:** 264
    South Carolina **II:** 353
    trade and shipping **II:** 375
de facto segregation. **IX:** 4, 271
    See also segregation

defense, civil. *See* civil defense
Defense Advanced Research Projects Agency (DARPA) **X:** 152, 153
defense budget **IX:** **77–78**
    economy **IX:** 89
    Korean War **IX:** 165
    military-industrial complex **IX:** 203
    NSC-68 **IX:** 234
    Truman Doctrine **IX:** 301
Defense Department (DOD) **IX:** 88–89, 225, 233–234, 330*c*
    Boland Amendment **X:** 38
    computers **X:** 73
    defense policy **X:** 88
    Internet **X:** 153
    terrorism **X:** 297, 300
defense industries **IX:** 4, 65
Defense of Brig. Gen. Wm. Hull **IV:** 176
Defense of Marriage Acts (DOMA) **X:** 128, 183
Defense of the Constitutions of the Government of the United States (Adams) **III:** 3
Defense Plant Corporation **VIII:** 295
defense policy **X:** **85–89**
    ABM Treaty **X:** 22–23
    arms race **X:** 25
    Carter, James Earl, Jr. **X:** 58
    cold war (end of) **X:** 71
    conservative movement **X:** 79
    Federal Information Act **X:** 112
    NATO **X:** 223–224
    nuclear freeze movement **X:** 224
    Powell, Colin L. **X:** 247
    Reagan, Ronald W. **X:** 260
    SDI **X:** 289–290
    terrorism **X:** 297
    Vietnam War **X:** 311–312
defense production **V:** 77; **VIII:** 409*c,* 410*c*
    automobile industry **VIII:** 30
    FEPC **VIII:** 109–110
    migration **VIII:** 213
    MOWM **VIII:** 201, 202
    NAACP **VIII:** 228
    NYA **VIII:** 235
    OPM **VIII:** 255
    race and racial conflict **VIII:** 289
    Randolph, A. Philip **VIII:** 291
    RFC **VIII:** 295

defense production *(continued)*
  South **VIII:** 332
  steel industry **VIII:** 339
  transportation **VIII:** 361
  WMC **VIII:** 374–375
  women's status and rights
    VIII: 385
  World War II home front
    VIII: 394
  zoot-suiters **VIII:** 404
defensive warfare **V:** 189, 190,
  215, 346
deficit, federal **VIII:** 351, 355
deficit spending **VIII:** 177, 216,
  286
deflation **VI:** 120
Defoe, Daniel **II:** 285
De Forest, John William **V: 92,**
  213; **VI:** 177
De Forest, Lee **VII:** 134
de Forest, Lockwood **VI:** 288
Deganwidah **I:** 161,182, 238,
  387c. *See also* Dekanawideh
Degas, Edgar **VI:** 45
de Gaulle, Charles **IX:** 106, 233
DeGolyer McClelland
  Company **VI:** 108
Dehgewanus **II:** 173
Deidesheimer, Philip **IV:** 96
deism **II:** 109, 149, 316; **III:** 10,
  103–104, 249, 272
deities. *See* gods and goddesses
de jure segregation **IX:** 271
Dekanawideh (Deganawideh,
  Dekanahwidah) **II: 85,** 168
De Klerk, F. W. **X:** 280
de Kooning, Willem **VIII:** 23,
  25, 114; **IX:** 20
Delagrange, Leon **VII:** 23
De Lancey, Anne **II:** 86
De Lancey, Étienne (Stephen)
  II: 86
De Lancey, James **II: 85–86,**
  185, **415**
De Lancey, John **II:** 86
De Lancey, Oliver **II:** 86
De Lancey, Peter **II:** 86
De Lancey, Susannah **II:** 86
De Lancey family **II: 86,** 130,
  196
Delancy, James **II:** 18
Delany, Martin Robinson **IV:**
  15, 261; **V: 92–93,** 93, 100,
  125; **VI:** 175
Delaware **I:** 104; **II: 86–88; III:**
  106; **IV:** 184; **X:** 160, 242
  agriculture **II:** 11
  economy **II:** 88, 101
  English immigrants **II:**
    108
  European control of **II:**
    87–88

Great Awakening **II:** 147,
  148
Lutherans **II:** 201
Minuit, Peter **II:** 227
New Jersey **II:** 252
original inhabitants **II:**
  86–87
Penn, William **II:** 273
Pennsylvania **II:** 276
slavery **II:** 88
Delaware, USS **III:** 291
Delaware & Hudson (D&H)
  Canal Company **IV:** 292
Delaware Indians **II: 88–89; V:**
  249
  Brainerd, David **II:**
    39–40
  captivity **II:** 52
  Croghan, George **II:** 76
  Delaware **II:** 86–87
  fur trade **II:** 133
  land **II:** 191
  Montour, Andrew **II:** 233
  Neolin **II:** 248
  New Jersey **II:** 252
  New York **II:** 259, 260
  Paxton Boys **II:** 272
  Penn, William **II:** 273
  Pennsylvania **II:** 274
  revitalization movements
    II: 320
  Swedish colonies **II:** 364
  Teedyuscung **II:** 370
  Walking Purchase of 1737
    II: 389–390
  Weiser, Johann Conrad **II:**
    393
  Zeisberger, David **II:** 415
Delaware Prophet. *See* Neolin
De La Warr, Lord **I: 103–104;**
  II: 135, 274, 413
De Leon, Daniel **VI:** 167, 267,
  268; **VII:** 130, 250, 288
de Lesseps, Ferdinand. *See*
  Lesseps, Ferdinand de
Delett, James **IV:** 345
DeLisi, Charles **X:** 145, 191
Deliverance **I:** 29
Dell, Floyd **VII:** 253
Dell 'historia naturale (Ferrante
  Imperato) **I:** 40
Dellinger, Dave **X:** 61
Delmarva Peninsula **II:** 86, 87
de Lôme letter **VI:** 71, **76–77,**
  188, 272, 327–328c
Deloria, Vine, Jr. **IX:** 229
del Valle, Eric Arturo **X:** 231
demagogues, southern **VII:**
  292–293
demerits **V:** 372
Demerol **X:** 206
De Mille, Cecil B. **VII:** 191

demobilization **V:** 334, 367, 384;
  VIII: 79–80
  children **VIII:** 57
  elderly **VIII:** 95
  mobilization **VIII:** 215
  OWMR **VIII:** 258–259
  postwar planning **VIII:**
    279
  V-J Day **VIII:** 370
  WAC **VIII:** 382
  Wagner, Robert F. **VIII:**
    372
  WAVES **VIII:** 380
  World War II **IX:** 78
  World War II home front
    VIII: 396
democracy **VII:** 237
Democracy and Education
  (Dewey) **VII:** 68
Democracy in America
  (Tocqueville) **IV:** 308, 377c
Democratic Alliance for
  Cooperative Hemisphere
  Security **X:** 174
Democratic Conservatives **IV:**
  363
Democratic donkey **V:** 247
"democratic enlargement" **X:**
  124–125
Democratic-Farmer-Labor
  (DFL) Party **X:** 196
democratic government **II:** 252,
  418c
Democratic Leadership Council
  X: 66
Democratic National
  Committee (DNC)
    Farley, James A. **VIII:** 110,
      111
    Flynn, Edward J. **VIII:**
      122
    Henderson, Leon **VIII:**
      145
    Irish Americans **VIII:** 165
Democratic National
  Convention of 1896 **VI:** 37,
  327c
Democratic National
  Convention of 1948 **IX:** 14,
  138, 281, 330c
Democratic National
  Convention of 1964 **IX:** 207;
  X: 196
Democratic National
  Convention of 1968
  (Chicago) **IX:** 334c; **X:** 18, 24,
  61, 323c
    counterculture **IX:** 72
    Democratic Party **IX:** 79
    Ginsberg, Allen **IX:** 123
    Hayden, Tom **IX:** 131
    McCarthy, Eugene **IX:** 189

Mississippi Freedom
  Democratic Party **IX:**
  207
New Left **IX:** 231
Students for a Democratic
  Society **IX:** 286
Weathermen **IX:** 319
Democratic National
  Convention of 1972 **X:** 288
Democratic National
  Convention of 1976 **X:** 325c
Democratic Party **III:** 279, 341;
  IV: 106–109, *107,* 378c; **V:**
  93–95, 405c; **VI: 77–78,**
  323c; **VII: 65–67,** 357c;
  VIII: xiii, **80–82,** 410c; **IX:**
  79, 334c
  abortion **X:** 3, 4
  Adamson Act **VII:** 2
  African Americans **VIII:** 2
  Altgeld, John Peter **VI:**
    10
  America First Committee
    VIII: 13
  American Federation of
    Labor **VIII:** 14
  American Liberty League
    VIII: 14, 15
  Americans for Democratic
    Action **IX:** 13, 14
  American System **IV:** 19
  antiwar movement—
    Vietnam **X:** 24
  banking and currency **IV:**
    42
  Baruch, Bernard M. **VII:**
    25; **VIII:** 34
  Benjamin, Judah P. **V:** 27
  Benton, Thomas Hart **IV:**
    49–50
  Black Cabinet **VIII:** 38
  Blair, Francis P., Jr. **V:** 30,
    31
  Brain Trust **VIII:** 41
  Brown, Joseph **V:** 39
  Bryan, William Jennings
    VI: 36–37
  Buchanan, James **V:** 41, 42
  Byrd, Robert **X:** 51
  Byrnes, James F. **VIII:** 48,
    49
  Cannon, Joseph **VII:** 42
  carpetbaggers **V:** 50
  Carter, James Earl, Jr. **X:**
    56, 59
  Cass, Lewis **IV:** 76–77
  Catholics **VIII:** 53
  Chase, Salmon P. **V:** 56, 57
  CIO **VIII:** 70
  cities and urban life **VIII:**
    59
  civil rights **VIII:** 61, 62

Civil Rights Act of 1866 **V:** 62

Civil Rights Act of 1957 **IX:** 54, 55

Civil War **V:** 64, 67

class consciousness **VI:** 57

Clayton Antitrust Act **VII:** 51

Cleveland, Grover **VI:** 58, 59

Clinton, William **X:** 66

common soldier **V:** 70

Congress **VI:** 63; **VIII:** 66–68, 68*t*

conservatism **VIII:** 72; **IX:** 68, 69

conservative coalition **VIII:** 73, 74

conservative movement **X:** 80

Coolidge, Calvin **VII:** 57

Copperheads **V:** 81–82

corruption, political **VI:** 66

Crockett, Davy **IV:** 100

Currency Act **VII:** 60

currency issue **VI:** 73

Davis, Jefferson **V:** 88

Debs, Eugene V. **VII:** 64

Dewson, "Molly" **VIII:** 83

Douglas, Stephen A. **V:** 97–99

Dred Scott decision **V:** 101

Dukakis, Michael **X:** 91

Eagleton, Thomas F. **X:** 93

education, federal aid to **VI:** 92

Elliot, Robert B. **V:** 111

employment **V:** 117

enemy aliens **VIII:** 102–103

ERA **X:** 105, 107

Era of Good Feelings **IV:** 127

evangelical Christians **X:** 108

Fair Deal **IX:** 107

Farley, James A. **VIII:** 111

farmers' alliances **VI:** 100

federal income tax **VII:** 92, 93

feminism **X:** 116

Ferraro, Geraldine A. **X:** 117

Fifteenth Amendment **V:** 124

Fillmore, Millard **IV:** 137

Flynn, Edward J. **VIII:** 122, 123

Foley, Thomas S. **X:** 118–119

Free-Silver movement **VI:** 105

Free-Soil Party **IV:** 150

Frémont, John C. **IV:** 154

fugitive slave laws **IV:** 155

Garner, John Nance **VIII:** 129

gender gap **X:** 128

German Americans **VIII:** 131

Gore, Albert, Jr. **X:** 133–134

governors **V:** 152, 153

Great Depression **VIII:** 138, 140

Guadalupe Hidalgo, Treaty of (1848) **IV:** 166

habeas corpus, writ of **V:** 162

Hamer, Fannie Lou **IX:** 129

Hancock, Winfield Scott **V:** 163, 164

Harding, Warren G. **VII:** 118

Harriman, Averell **VIII:** 143

Harrison, William Henry **IV:** 170

Hayes, Rutherford B. **VI:** 125–127

Henderson, Leon **VIII:** 145

Hillman, Sidney **VIII:** 146

Hispanic Americans **X:** 143

homefront **V:** 169

House of Representatives **X:** 144, 145

Hull, Cordell **VIII:** 159

immigration **V:** 176; **VI:** 138, 140; **X:** 148

internal improvements **IV:** 188

Internal Revenue taxes **VI:** 147

Internal Security Act of 1950 **IX:** 143

isolationists **VIII:** 166

Italian Americans **VIII:** 167

Jackson, Andrew **IV:** 192

Jackson, Jesse L. **X:** 160

Jackson, "Stonewall" **V:** 185

Jews **VIII:** 173

Johnson, Hugh S. **VIII:** 173

Jones, Jesse H. **VIII:** 174

Judicial Watch **X:** 162

Kansas-Nebraska Act of 1854 **V:** 197, 198

Kelley, William D. **V:** 198

Kennedy, Edward M. **X:** 164

Know-Nothing Party **IV:** 201, 202

Ku Klux Klan **V:** 199

Ku Klux Klan Act **V:** 201

labor and labor movements **IV:** 204; **VII:** 152; **VIII:** 179, 181

Lease, Mary Elizabeth **VI:** 173

liberalism **VIII:** 188, 189; **IX:** 179–180; **X:** 175

Liberal Republican Party **VI:** 174

Liberty Party **IV:** 210, 211

Lincoln, Abraham **V:** 210

Lloyd, Henry Demarest **VI:** 179

machine politics **VI:** 184

Mallory, Stephen R. **V:** 221

Manifest Destiny **IV:** 217

marriage **X:** 182–183

McClellan, George B. **V:** 225, 226

McCormick, Cyrus Hall **IV:** 225

McGovern, George Stanley **X:** 184

McKinley, William **VI:** 189

Mexican-American War **IV:** 232

miscegenation **V:** 233

Mississippi Freedom Democratic Party **IX:** 206–207

Mitchell, George **X:** 194, 195

Mondale, Walter F. **X:** 196

Morgenthau, Henry **VIII:** 216

Mormon War **IV:** 244

Morrill Land-Grant Act **V:** 241

Murray, Philip **VIII:** 221

Nader, Ralph **X:** 205

nativism **V:** 251; **VI:** 209

Nauvoo, Illinois **IV:** 260

neoconservatism **X:** 215, 216

New Deal **VIII:** 240

New Freedom **VII:** 211

New York City draft riots **V:** 254

NRA **X:** 213

Oates, William C. **V:** 257

O'Neill, Thomas P., Jr. **X:** 228

Oregon Treaty of 1846 **IV:** 270

Ostend Manifesto **V:** 260

Overland campaign **V:** 261

Palmer, A. Mitchell **VII:** 221

Panic of 1837 **IV:** 277

Panic of 1857 **V:** 264

Paul, Alice **VII:** 226

peace movements **V:** 266

People's Party **VI:** 222, 223

Perkins, Frances **VIII:** 265

Perot, H. Ross **X:** 234

Petersburg campaign **V:** 272

Pierce, Franklin **V:** 275

Plunkitt, George Washington **VI:** 225

Polish Americans **VIII:** 269

political parties **X:** 237–239 third parties **VI:** 226

politics **VII:** 228

politics in the Roosevelt era **VIII:** 270–273, 272*t*

Polk, James K. **IV:** 283, 284

Popular Front **VIII:** 276

popular sovereignty **IV:** 285

presidential campaigns **VI:** 230–232

Progressive Party **VII:** 236–237; **IX:** 248

progressivism **VII:** 238

Prohibition Party **VI:** 234

pro-life and pro-choice movements **X:** 249

public opinion polls **VIII:** 284

race and racial conflict **V:** 288

Reconstruction **V:** 291, 292, 294, 295

Reconstruction Acts **V:** *295*

redemption **V:** 296, 297

Reed, Thomas Brackett **VI:** 240

Republican Party **IV:** 300, 301; **V:** 301–303; **VI:** 246–247; **VIII:** 305, 306

Revels, Hiram R. **V:** 303

Revenue Act of 1935 **VIII:** 308

Roosevelt, Eleanor **VIII:** 311

Roosevelt, Franklin D. **VIII:** 312, 313

scalawags **V:** 308

secession **V:** 311

Senate **X:** 275, 276

Shriver, Sargent **X:** 278

Sickles, Daniel E. **V:** 326

Smith, Alfred E. **VII:** 287

socialists **VIII:** 327

Solid South **VI:** 270

South **VIII:** 332

Democratic Party (*continued*)
  southern demagogues **VII:** 292–293
  Stanton, Edwin M. **V:** 333
  Stanton, Elizabeth Cady **V:** 335
  states' rights **V:** 335
  States' Rights Party **IX:** 281–282
  Stephens, Alexander H. **V:** 336
  Sublette, William **IV:** 330
  tariff issue **VI:** 284
  tariffs **VII:** 305
  Thirteenth Amendment **V:** 353
  Thomas, Norman **VIII:** 358
  Thurmond, J. Strom **X:** 303
  Tilden, Samuel Jones **VI:** 289
  TVA **VIII:** 356
  Tyler, John **IV:** 348
  Underwood-Simmons Tariff **VII:** 313
  Union army **V:** 365
  United States v. Cruikshank **V:** 375, 376
  Vallandigham, Clement L. **V:** 377–378
  Versailles, Treaty of **VII:** 324
  Vietnam War **X:** 312
  volunteer army **V:** 384
  Wallace, George C. **X:** 314
  Wallace, Henry A. **VIII:** 373
  Watson, Tom **VII:** 332
  Welles, Gideon **V:** 391, 392
  West Point **V:** 373
  Whig Party **IV:** 362–364
  Willkie, Wendell L. **VIII:** 378, 379
  Wilmot Proviso **V:** 396
  Wilson, Woodrow **VII:** 333
  women's network **VIII:** 383
  women's status and rights **VIII:** 384
  World War II home front **VIII:** 396
  Wright, Fanny **IV:** 369
  Yancey, William Lowndes **V:** 401
  Zionism **VIII:** 403
Democratic People's Republic of Korea (North Korea) **IX:** 21, 60; **X:** 328c. *See also* Korean War
  Clinton, William **X:** 67
  cold war (end of) **X:** 70
  Koreagate **X:** 166

Democratic-Republican Party **III:** 104, 395c–398c; **IV:** 375c
  Adams, John **III:** 3
  Alien and Sedition Acts **III:** 9
  Ames, Fisher **III:** 13
  artisans **III:** 26
  Bache, Benjamin Franklin **III:** 29
  Bank of the United States (First) **III:** 30–31
  banks **III:** 32
  Baptists **III:** 34
  Blount, William **III:** 41
  Brackenridge, Hugh Henry **III:** 47
  Burr, Aaron **III:** 54
  Carey, Mathew **III:** 62
  Catholics **III:** 63
  Chase, Samuel **III:** 65
  cities and urban life **III:** 70
  Clinton, DeWitt **III:** 73
  Clinton, George **III:** 75
  Coxe, Tench **III:** 96
  Democratic Party **IV:** 106
  Democratic-Republican societies **III:** 105
  Duane, William **III:** 108
  Dwight, Timothy **III:** 109
  election of 1800 **III:** 116, 117
  embargo of 1807 **III:** 118
  Federalist Party **III:** 126
  foreign affairs **III:** 131
  French Revolution **III:** 138
  Freneau, Philip **III:** 139
  Fries's Rebellion **III:** 140
  Gallatin, Albert **III:** 147
  Gates, Horatio **III:** 149
  Gerry, Elbridge **III:** 153
  Hamilton, Alexander **III:** 162
  Hartford Convention **IV:** 170
  Hull, William **IV:** 175
  immigration **III:** 173
  impeachment **III:** 175
  Jackson, Andrew **IV:** 192
  Jay, John **III:** 182
  Jay's Treaty **III:** 183
  Jefferson, Thomas **III:** 185
  journalism **III:** 191, 192
  Judiciary Act of 1801 **III:** 193
  liberty tree/pole **III:** 214
  literature **III:** 215
  Livingston, Robert R. **III:** 216
  Lyon, Matthew **III:** 222
  Macon, Nathaniel **III:** 226

  Madison, James **III:** 229
  Marbury v. Madison **III:** 230
  Marshall, John **III:** 235, 236
  music **III:** 251
  national debt **III:** 253
  Niles, Hezekiah **III:** 258
  Non-Importation Act **III:** 259
  Pickering, John **III:** 275, 276
  political parties **III:** 279
  popular culture **III:** 282, 283
  Priestley, Joseph **III:** 285
  Quasi War **III:** 291
  Randolph, John **III:** 296
  religious liberty **III:** 300
  riots **III:** 309
  states' rights **III:** 333
  Story, Joseph **III:** 334
  Tammany Society **III:** 341
  tariffs **III:** 342
  Taylor, John, of Caroline **III:** 344
  Van Buren, Martin **IV:** 351
  Virginia and Kentucky Resolutions **III:** 360
  Virginia dynasty **III:** 361
  War Hawks **IV:** 355
  War of 1812 **IV:** 355
  West Point **III:** 373
  Whiskey Rebellion **III:** 375
Democratic-Republican societies **III:** 26, 104, 104–105, 343, 396c
Democratic Republic of the Congo **I:** 209–210
Democratic Review **IV:** 197
Democratic Vistas (Whitman) **VI:** 178
Democratic Washington Union, The **IV:** 150
demonstrations, protests, and rallies **VII:** 188–189; **VIII:** 65; **X:** 323c, 324c. *See also* Civil Rights movement; land riots; resistance movement; riots
  abortion **X:** 2, 4
  ADA **X:** 21
  agriculture **X:** 15, 16
  antiwar movement—Vietnam **X:** 24
  birth control **X:** 37
  Brennan, William J. **X:** 41
  feminism **X:** 114
  flag burning **X:** 118
  foreign policy **X:** 123
  globalization **X:** 132, 132

  Jackson State University **X:** 160
  Kent State University **X:** 164
  labor **X:** 170
  marriage **X:** 182
  Native Americans **X:** 214
  NOW **X:** 211
  pro-life and pro-choice movements **X:** 249
  sexual revolution **X:** 277
  tobacco suits **X:** 304
  Watergate scandal **X:** 316
  Weather Underground **X:** 318
  World Trade Organization **X:** 322
Dempsey, William Harrison "Jack" **VII:** 67, 258, 294, 359c; **VIII:** 336
Demuth, Charles **VII:** 19
DeMuth, Christopher **X:** 301
Dengel, Lebna (Dauti [David] II) **I:** 104, 124, 293
Dengel, Sarsa **I:** 125
dengue fever **IV:** 112
Denison House **VI:** 259
Denkyira **I:** 5
Denmark **I:** 175; **VIII:** 39; **IX:** 194, 231–233; **X:** 223
Dennett, Mary Ware **VII:** 29, 339
Dennie, Joseph **IV:** 196
Dennis, Eugene **IX:** 80
Dennis Miller Live (TV program) **X:** 295
Dennison, William **V:** 152, 383
Dennis v. United States (1951) **VIII:** 326; **IX:** 80, 331c
denominationalism **II:** 300–301
Densmore, Frances **VI:** 202
Densmore, George **VI:** 115
dental drills **IX:** 270
dentistry **IV:** 308
Denver, Colorado **IV:** 89, 90, 164
Denyankan kingdom **I:** 322
De omni rerum fossilium (Conrad von Gesner) **I:** 140
De Orbe Novo (Peter Martyr) **I:** 387c
Department of. . . *See under specific name, e.g.: Agriculture Department*
Department of Energy Organization Act of 1977 **X:** 104
department stores **V:** 60–61; **VI:** 78–79, 326c
  advertising **VI:** 2
  mail-order houses **VI:** 186

trade **VI:** 290

transportation, urban **VI:** 291

dependencies, U.S. **VI:** 142*m*

Dependent and Disability Pension Act of 1890 **VI:** 123

Dependents Pension Act of 1890 **VI:** 326*c*

depreciation of currency **III:** 113

depression **II:** 145, 420*c. See also* Great Depression

depression, Mexican **VII:** 184

depression of 1819 **IV:** 204, 275–276

depression of 1839–43 **IV:** 204–205, 260, 276–277

depression of 1870 **IV:** 225

depression of 1873–79 **V:** 81; **VI:** 324*c*

Bland-Allison Act **VI:** 32

Crime of '73 **VI:** 69

Hayes, Rutherford B. **VI:** 126

labor organizations **VI:** 169, 170

national banking system **VI:** 206

Patrons of Husbandry **VI:** 222

Solid South **VI:** 270

trusts **VI:** 293

depression of 1893–97 **VI:** 327*c*

Bellamy, Edward **VI:** 26

bimetallism **VI:** 29

Cleveland, Grover **VI:** 58

Coxey's Army **VI:** 67–68

currency issue **VI:** 73

imperialism **VI:** 141

national banking system **VI:** 206

New South **VI:** 210

presidential campaigns **VI:** 232

tariff issue **VI:** 285

DePriest, Oscar **VIII:** 2

DePugh, Robert **X:** 193

deregulation **X:** 331*c*

business **X:** 49, 50

labor **X:** 171

NEPA **X:** 210

Reagan, Ronald W. **X:** 260

science and technology **X:** 274

television **X:** 294–295

desegregation **V:** 373; **VIII:** 13, 340; **X:** 323*c. See also* school desegregation

federalism **X:** 112

militia movement **X:** 193

race and racial conflict **X:** 256

Supreme Court **X:** 290, 291

Thurmond, J. Strom **X:** 303

Deseret, State of **IV:** **109–111**

Church of Jesus Christ of Latter-day Saints **IV:** 80–81

migration **IV:** 236

Mormon Trail **IV:** 243*m*

religion **IV:** 298

Young, Brigham **IV:** 372

Deseret News **IV:** 111

deserters/desertion **IV:** 234; **V:** **95–96**

bounty system **V:** 34

Confederate States of America **V:** 77

filibustering **V:** 127

homefront **V:** 169

Lee, Robert E. **V:** 206

Louisiana Tigers **V:** 218

Petersburg campaign **V:** 272

Union army **V:** 364

volunteer army **V:** 384

Désirade **II:** 378

De Smet, Pierre Jean **IV:** 132

Des Moines River **IV:** 131

d'Estaing, comte. *See* Estaing, Charles-Henri Theodat, comte d'

destroyers-for-bases deal **VIII:** **82–83,** 409*c*

America First Committee **VIII:** 12

Britain, Battle of **VIII:** 43

foreign policy **VIII:** 124

Willkie, Wendell L. **VIII:** 379

Desverney, Peter Prioleau **IV:** 354

détente **X:** **89–90**

cold war (end of) **X:** 70, 71

defense policy **X:** 85, 87

Ford, Gerald R. **X:** 121

foreign policy **X:** 122–124

Helms, Jesse A., Jr. **X:** 141

INF Treaty **X:** 151

Nixon, Richard M. **X:** 220

Reagan, Ronald W. **X:** 259

Detroit **II:** 133; **IV:** 169, 175, 176, 259; **VIII:** 288; **X:** 269

Detroit Lions **X:** 319

devaluation **V:** 23

De Vargas, Diego **II:** **89,** 244

Devin, Thomas A. **V:** 129

Devine, Annie **IX:** 207

devolution **X:** 113

Dewey, George **VI:** **79,** 100, 124, 272, 328*c;* **VII:** 8

Dewey, John **VI:** 155, 229; **VII:** **67–68,** 172, 198, 229; **VIII:** 93, 161, 410*c*

Dewey, Thomas E. **VIII:** 410*c;* **IX:** **80–82,** *81,* 330*c;* **X:** 314

Americans for Democratic Action **IX:** 14

Democratic Party **IX:** 79

election of 1940 **VIII:** 98

election of 1944 **VIII:** 99

elections **IX:** 94

politics in the Roosevelt era **VIII:** 272*t,* 273

Republican Party **VIII:** 306; **IX:** 258

Roosevelt, Franklin D. **VIII:** 314

Taft, Robert A. **VIII:** 349

Wallace, Henry A. **VIII:** 374

Dewing, Thomas Wilmer **VI:** 314

DeWitt's Corner, Treaty of **III:** 66

Dewson, Mary **VIII:** **83**

Democratic Party **VIII:** 81

Perkins, Frances **VIII:** 265

women's network **VIII:** 383

women's status and rights **VIII:** 384

DFL (Democratic-Farmer-Labor) Party **X:** 196

diagnostics **IV:** 230

Dial, The

Emerson, Ralph Waldo **IV:** 126

Fuller, Margaret **IV:** 155

journalism **IV:** 196

Thoreau, Henry David **IV:** 342

transcendental movement **IV:** 345

dialect poetry **VI:** 82

dialect songs **V:** 245

Diallo, Amadou **X:** 330*c*

"Dialogue Between a European and an American Englishman" (Hutchinson) **III:** 171

"Dialogue Entitled the Kind Master and the Dutiful Servant, A" (Hammon) **II:** 154

diamond hoax **VI:** 160

Diana Ross and the Supremes **IX:** 217; **X:** 240

diaries **II:** 268–269

Diario (Chimalpahin) **I:** 71

diarrhea **V:** 230

Diary from Dixie, as Written by Mary Boykin Chesnut **V:** 58

Dias, Bartholomeu **I:** 44, 56, **104–106,** 105*m,* 180

Díaz, Porfirio **VI:** 150; **VII:** 28, 182, 183–185, 357*c*

Díaz del Castillo, Bernal **I:** **106**

Charles V **I:** 69

chinampas **I:** 72

Córdoba, Francisco Hernández de **I:** 86

Grijalva, Juan de **I:** 145

Tenochtitlán **I:** 344

Dickinson, Daniel S. **IV:** 285

Dickinson, Emily Elizabeth **V:** 166; **VI:** **79–80,** 325*c*

Crane, Stephen **VI:** 68

Howells, William Dean **VI:** 136

Jackson, Helen Hunt **VI:** 153

literature **VI:** 178

Dickinson, John **III:** **105–106,** 392*c*

Articles of Confederation **III:** 24

Continental Congress, First **III:** 87

literature **III:** 214

Olive Branch Petition **III:** 266

Townshend Duties **III:** 349

Wilson, James **III:** 379

Dickinson, Jonathan **II:** 298

Dickinson, Preston **VII:** 19

Dickinson, Robert Litou **VII:** 30

Dickinson-Ayon Treaty **V:** 133

Dickson, W. K. Laurie **VII:** 190

dictionaries **III:** 370

Didion, Joan **X:** 177

Didrikson, Babe **VIII:** 275, 337, *337,* 338

Dieffmatten, Alsace **VII:** *344*

Diem, Ngo Dinh **IX:** 308, 317

Dieppe **VIII:** 15

Dies, Martin **VIII:** 120, 121

Dies Committee **VIII:** 120–121

diet. *See* food

Diet of Augsburg **I:** 212

Diet of Worms **I:** 211

Dietrich, Marlene **VIII:** 217

differential pay **VII:** 306

DiGerland, Benedict **IX:** 103–104

Digges family **II:** 172, 186

Diggio, John **III:** 215

digital appliances **X:** 273

Digital Equipment Corporation (DEC) **IX:** 65

digital mapping **X:** 281

digital video discs (DVD) **X:** 263, 273

dike systems **I:** 2

Dillinger, John **IX:** 136
Dillingham, William P. **VII:** 69, 127
Dillingham Commission **VII:** 68–69, 357*c*
   Cable Act **VII:** 41
   immigration **VII:** 127
   Immigration Act of 1917 **VII:** 128
   National Origins Act **VII:** 202
   race and racial conflict **VII:** 248
   science **VII:** 276
DiMaggio, Joe **VIII: 83–84,** 336, 409*c;* **IX:** 210
dime novels **V:** 168; **VI: 80–81,** *81,* 98, 176
Diners Club **IX:** 73, 330*c*
Dingley Tariff **VI:** 328*c;* **VII:** 73, 357*c*
   Bryan, William Jennings **VI:** 37
   Congress **VI:** 64
   McKinley, William **VI:** 189
   the presidency **VI:** 230
   Reed, Thomas Brackett **VI:** 241
   tariff issue **VI:** 285
Dinner Pail Brigade. *See* Democratic Party
dinosaurs **IV:** 308
Dinwiddie, Robert **II:** 269; **III:** 366
Diogo I, king of Kongo **I:** 196
Diola **I:** 321
diphtheria **II:** 91, 92, 235; **X:** 188
diplomacy **III:** 2–3; **V:** 405*c;* **VI:** 103, 184–185; **VII:** 70, 180. *See also* foreign policy
   Adams, John Quincy **IV:** 4
   Berle, Adolf A., Jr. **VIII:** 36
   Buchanan, James **V:** 41
   Cass, Lewis **IV:** 76
   Catholics **VIII:** 53
   Chouteau family **IV:** 78–79
   Cuba **IV:** 101
   Gadsden Purchase **IV:** 159–160
   Ghent, Treaty of (1814) **IV:** 161–162
   Guadalupe Hidalgo, Treaty of (1848) **IV:** 165–166
   Habib, Philip C. **X:** 139
   Harriman, Averell **VIII:** 144
   Harrison, William Henry **IV:** 169
   Herrman, Augustine **II:** 233

Iran-contra affair **X:** 155
Jackson, Jesse L. **X:** 160
Johnson, Sir William **II:** 177
Kennedy, Joseph P. **VIII:** 175, 176
Kissinger, Henry A. **X:** 165–166
Leahy, William D. **VIII:** 184
Mondale, Walter F. **X:** 197
Monroe, James **IV:** 240
Montour, Madame **II:** 233
Nixon, Richard M. **X:** 220
Ostenaco **II:** 269
Pocahontas **II:** 288
Richardson, Elliot L. **X:** 268
Rosecrans, William S. **V:** 305
scalawags **V:** 308
Seward, William H. **V:** 314–315
Sickles, Daniel E. **V:** 327
Teedyuscung **II:** 370
Tourgée, Albion W. **V:** 354
Ward, Nancy **II:** 392
Weiser, Johann Conrad **II:** 393
Yancey, William Lowndes **V:** 401
"Direct Cinema" movement **IX:** 211
direct current (DC) **VI:** 149
direct election of presidents **IV:** 49
direct election of senators **VII: 69–70,** 358*c*
   journalism **VII:** 142
   La Follette, Robert **VII:** 155
   New Freedom **VII:** 211
   politics **VII:** 228, 229
   progressivism **VII:** 237
   Wilson, Woodrow **VII:** 335
direct mail **VIII:** 1; **X:** 6, 7
Directorate of Intelligence (CIA) **IX:** 50
Directorate of Operations (CIA) **IX:** 50
directors, movie **IX:** 214
DirecTV **X:** 244
Dirksen, Everett McKinley **IX:** 56, 127
disabilities, people with **X:** 327*c*
   ADA **X:** 20–21
   education, primary and secondary **X:** 100
   liberalism **X:** 175
Disabled American Veterans (DAV) **VII:** 326

disarmament **VII:** 338. *See also* Naval Disarmament Conference; Washington Conference on Naval Disarmament; World Disarmament Conference
Disciples of Christ (Christian Church) **IV:** 71–72, 297–299
disco music **X:** 202, 240
Discourse Concerning Unlimited Submission and Non-Resistance to the Higher Powers (Mayhew) **III:** 238
"Discourse Concerning Western Planting, A" (1584) (Richard Hakluyt, the Younger) **I:** 152, 388*c,* 413–415
"Discourse on the Constitution" (Calhoun) **IV:** 63
Discourses on Davila (Adams) **III:** 3
Discourses on Women (Mott) **IV:** 247
Discovery, HMS **IV:** 171
Discovery, Settlement, and Present State of Kentucke, The (Filson) **III:** 43
Discovery Charter School (Tracy, Colorado) **X:** 99
discrimination **VI:** 324*c;* **VII:** 113, 281; **VIII:** 408*c,* 409*c;* **IX:** 333*c,* 334*c;* **X:** 325*c,* 327*c,* 328*c. See also* gender discrimination; Jim Crow laws; segregation
   ADA **X:** 21
   affirmative action **X:** 8–9
   African-American movement **IX:** 4
   African Americans **IV:** 8; **VI:** 5, 6; **VIII:** 3–5
   Age Discrimination Act of 1975 **X:** 14
   AME Church **V:** 5
   American Indian Movement **IX:** 12–13
   Asian-American movement **IX:** 22
   Baker v. Carr **IX:** 31–32
   Black Cabinet **VIII:** 37
   Brennan, William J. **X:** 41
   Bridges, Harry **VIII:** 43
   Burger, Warren E. **X:** 44
   civil rights **VIII:** 62
   Civil Rights Act of 1875 **V:** 63
   Civil Rights Act of 1964 **IX:** 56, 57
   Civil Rights Act of 1991 **X:** 63
   civil rights cases **VI:** 55

Crummell, Alexander **VI:** 70
employment **V:** 116
Equal Access Act **X:** 104
Equal Employment Opportunity Commission **IX:** 103
Executive Order 8802 **VIII:** 106
feminism **X:** 114, 115
FERA **VIII:** 118
gay rights movement **X:** 127–128
Ginsburg, Ruth Bader **X:** 131
Griggs et al. v. Duke Power Company **X:** 135–136
Heart of Atlanta Motel Inc., v. United States **IX:** 132–133
Hispanic Americans **X:** 142
immigration **IV:** 179, 180
labor trends **VI:** 171
Levitt, William **IX:** 178
liberalism **X:** 175
McCarran-Walter Act **IX:** 188
Morrill Land-Grant Act **V:** 241
Myrdal, Gunnar **VIII:** 225
NAACP **X:** 208
political correctness **X:** 237
President's Commission on the Status of Women **IX:** 246–247
race and racial conflict **IV:** 289, 291; **VIII:** 289
railroads **VI:** 239
Ray, Charlotte **V:** 291
relief **VIII:** 301
Robeson, Paul **VIII:** 309
Selective Service **VIII:** 323–324
Shiloh, Battle of **V:** 324
Singleton, Benjamin **V:** 327
Stewart, Maria **IV:** 327
suburbanization **IX:** 287
Supreme Court **X:** 291
Thomas, Clarence **X:** 302
Title IX—Prohibition of Sex Discrimination **X:** 334–335
Urban League **IX:** 305
Washington, Booker T. **VI:** 309
Williams, Peter, Jr. **IV:** 366
World War II **VIII:** 389
disease and epidemics **I: 106–108,** *107;* **II: 90–93,** *91,* 417*c;* **III: 106–107,** 396*c;* **IV: 111–113,** *112,*

377c; **V:** 96–97; **VI:** 46, 55, 191, 192; **VII:** 242; **VIII:** 8, 35. *See also* medicine and public health
Abenaki **I:** 1
Acadia **I:** 2
agriculture **X:** 16
AIDS **X:** 5–6
Andersonville Prison **V:** 10
animals **II:** 21
Apalachee **I:** 11
Aztecs **I:** 22
Bahía **I:** 24
Bickerdyke, "Mother" **V:** 28–29
Bowie, Jim **IV:** 57
Boylston, Zabdiel **II:** 37
Brazil **I:** 33
Brown, Charles Brockden **III:** 49
bubonic plague **I:** 285–286
California **I:** 49
Calusa **I:** 49
Carib **I:** 56
Cartier, Jacques **I:** 59
Catawba **II:** 55
Cathay (China) **I:** 64
cities and urban life **III:** 70; **V:** 82
Cofitachequi **I:** 76
Columbian Exchange **I:** 76–78
Columbus, Christopher **I:** 82
Coosa **I:** 85
Cozumel **I:** 97
De La Warr, Lord **I:** 104
diseases **I:** 106–108
economy **V:** 107
fishing **II:** 118
Forty-niners **IV:** 147
French colonies **II:** 127
fur trade **II:** 130–131; **IV:** 158
Great Plains **III:** 155
Great Plains Indians **II:** 150
Gullah **II:** 151
Hawaiian Islands **III:** 164; **IV:** 171
Hopi **I:** 167
horses **I:** 169
Huron **II:** 160
Iceland **I:** 175
immigration **IV:** 178; **V:** 175
Inuit **II:** 167
Iroquois **I:** 183
Jamestown **II:** 171
Johnston, Henrietta Deering **II:** 178
King George's War **II:** 182

King Philip's War **II:** 184
King William's War **II:** 185
labor **II:** 189
La Salle, René-Robert Cavelier, sieur de **II:** 192
Las Casas, Bartolomé de **I:** 199, 201
Lining, John **II:** 194
marriage and family life **II:** 207
Maryland **II:** 209, 210
Massachusett **I:** 225
Massachusetts **II:** 212
medicine **II:** 220; **III:** 240; **IV:** 229; **V:** 230; **IX:** 197–200; **X:** 188
Mexican-American War **IV:** 234
Miantonomo **II:** 224
miracle drugs **IX:** 205–206
Mississippi River **V:** 234–235
Mormon Trail **IV:** 242
mortality **II:** 235–236
Narragansett **II:** 241
Natchez **I:** 251
Native Americans **II:** 242–244, 246; **IV:** 258
New Mexico **II:** 254
New Orleans **II:** 258
New Spain **I:** 260
North Carolina **II:** 264
Occupational Safety and Health Act **X:** 225
Oregon Trail **IV:** 268–269
Peninsular campaign **V:** 269
Pizarro, Francisco **I:** 283
population trends **I:** 289; **II:** 290, 291
Powhatan Confederacy **II:** 295
prisons **V:** 282
prostitution **V:** 283
public health **IX:** 249, 250
reducción **I:** 307
revitalization movements **II:** 320
Rush, Benjamin **III:** 312
sexual revolution **X:** 278
shamans **II:** 335
slavery **II:** 340, 344
smallpox **I:** 330–331; **II:** 345
South Carolina **II:** 353
Stowe, Harriet Beecher **V:** 338
Thoreau, Henry David **IV:** 342
tobacco suits **X:** 303–304
Trail of Tears **IV:** 344

travel **II:** 377
Union army **V:** 364, 365
Virginia **II:** 382, 384
Virginia Company of London **II:** 387
Wakeman, Sarah Rosetta **V:** 386
Washington, D.C. **V:** 389
Webster, Noah **III:** 370
Wingina **II:** 401
yellow fever **II:** 414
Disney, Walt **VIII:** 218, 274, 408c; **IX:** 135
Disney animation **X:** 240
Disney Channel **X:** 296
Disney studios **VIII:** 219
Disney World **X:** *262*
dispensationalism **VI:** 242–243
dispensational premillenialism **X:** 107
"Disquisition on Government, The" (Calhoun) **IV:** 63
Disraeli, Benjamin **VI:** 157
dissent **VII:** 274–275
Dissertation on Canon and Feudal Law (Adams) **III:** 2
Dissertation upon Parties, A (Bolingbroke) **III:** 278
Disston Company **IV:** 184
distilling **II:** 203, 204, 215, 258, 368; **IV:** 336
Distribution-Preemption Act (1841) **IV:** 190
district courts **III:** 192
District of Columbia. *See* Washington, District of Columbia
district schools **IV:** 120
Di Varthema, Ludovico **I:** 230
Divers Voyages Touching on America (Richard Hakluyt, the Younger) **I:** 117, 118, 152, 266, 388c
divorce **IV:** 222, 326, 367; **V:** 222; **VI:** 30, 317; **VII:** 170, 171, 233, 234, 283; **VIII:** 204, 205, 395
Burgis, William **II:** 46
Connecticut **II:** 70
feminism **X:** 116
gender **II:** 137
Iroquois **II:** 168
marriage and family life **II:** 206; **X:** 109, 110, 181–183
Protestantism **II:** 301
religion, Euro-American **II:** 316
women's rights and status **II:** 406; **X:** 320
divorce rates **VIII:** 277; **IX:** 29, 192, 193

Dix, Dorothea **IV:** *113*, **113–114**, 219, 278, 378c; **V:** 256
Dix, John A. **V:** 281; **VI:** 289
Dix-Hill cartel **V:** 281–282
"Dixie" **V:** 244
Dixiecrat Party **VIII:** 82, 189; **IX:** 14, 330c. *See also* States' Rights Party
Dixon, Jeremiah **V:** 224
Dixon, Thomas **VII:** 30, 31, 115, 147
Djenne-Djeno (Jenne-Jeno) **I:** 14, **108–109**
Djibouti **I:** 109
Djolof Empire **I:** 66
Dmytryk, Edward **IX:** 135, *211*
DNA **IX:** 269, 295; **X:** 145–146, 191
DNC. *See* Democratic National Committee
DOB. *See* Daughters of Bilitis
Dobbs, Arthur **I:** 266
Dobrynin, Anatoly **X:** 289
Doctorow, E. L. **X:** 177
doctor's degrees **X:** 97, 98
Doctor's Riot **III:** 309
Doctrina Christiana y Catecismo para Instruccion de los Indios (José de Acosta) **I:** 3
documentary programs (television) **X:** 296
DOD. *See* Department of Defense
Dodd, S. C. T. **VI:** 146, 293
Dodge, Grenville M. **IV:** 58; **V:** 118, 263
Dodge, Henry **IV:** 145
Dodge, Josephine **VII:** 15
DOE. *See* Energy Department
Doeg **II:** 27
Doenitz, Karl **VIII:** 28
Doe v. Bolton (1973) **X:** 1, 2, 248, 249
Dogbari **I:** 101, 132
dogs **II:** 21–22, 149
Dog's Life, A (film) **VII:** *190*
Doheny, Edward **VII:** 307
Dohrn, Bernadine **IX:** 319; **X:** 317, 318
DOJ. *See* Justice Department
Dolby systems **X:** 198, 273
Dole, Elizabeth **X:** 90
Dole, Robert **X:** **90–91**, 329c
Buchanan, Patrick J. **X:** 42
Bush, George H. W. **X:** 45
Clinton, William **X:** 68
Ford, Gerald R. **X:** 121
immigration **X:** 148
Kemp, Jack F. **X:** 163
Senate **X:** 276

Dole, Sanford B. **IV:** 172; **VI:** 124

dollar **VIII:** 42

dollar-a-year men **VIII: 84**
  mobilization **VIII:** 214
  Nelson, Donald M. **VIII:** 238
  technology **VIII:** 354
  World War II home front **VIII:** 395

dollar diplomacy **VII: 70,** 99

DOMA. *See* Defense of Marriage Acts

Domagaya **I:** 58, 59

domestic allotment plan **VIII:** 5, 6

Domestic Council **X:** 226–227

Domestic Counter-Terrorism Center **X:** 299

domestic craft labor **IV:** 186–187

domestic help **VII:** 172

domesticity **II: 93**

domestic life **IV:** 67–69

domestic policy
  Americans for Democratic Action **IX:** 14
  anticommunism **IX:** 14
  Council of Economic Advisors **IX:** 71
  Eisenhower, Dwight D. **IX:** 92–93
  Employment Act of 1946 **IX:** 99
  Fair Deal **IX:** 107–108
  Galbraith, John Kenneth **IX:** 117, 118
  Great Society **IX:** 126–127
  Indian Claims Commission **IX:** 142–143
  Model Cities program **IX:** 207–208
  modern Republicanism **IX:** 209
  Native American movement **IX:** 227
  New Frontier **IX:** 230
  Progressive Party **IX:** 248–249
  Termination policy **IX:** 297–298
  Truman, Harry **IX:** 299–300
  Volunteers in Service to America **IX:** 310–311
  War on Poverty **IX:** 313–314

domestic violence **X:** 266

Dominican Americans **X:** 200

Dominican Republic **VII:** 28, 99, 267, 356c, 359c; **IX:** 172, 316, 317, 334c

Dominicans **I: 109–110,** 113, 189, 197–199, 291; **II:** 43, **93–94,** 324

Dominion of New England **II:** 94m, **94–95**
  Andros, Sir Edmund **II:** 19
  Boston Philosophical Society **II:** 37
  Connecticut **II:** 69
  Dudley, Joseph **II:** 95
  Glorious Revolution **II:** 141
  King Philip's War **II:** 184
  Massachusetts **II:** 214
  monarchy, British **II:** 232
  New Hampshire **II:** 251
  New York **II:** 261
  Plymouth **II:** 288
  Randolph, Edward **II:** 312
  Rhode Island **II:** 321

domino theory **IX:** 21, 33

Dona Ana de Sousa. *See* Nzinga, queen of Angola

Donahue, Phil **X:** 295

Donaldson, Jeff **IX:** 21

donatário (captaincy) system **I:** 33, 193

Dongan, Thomas **II:** 144, 324

donkey (Democratic symbol) **V:** 247

Donnacona **I:** 58, 59

Donnelly, Ignatius
  bimetallism **VI:** 29
  currency issue **VI:** 73
  literature **VI:** 178
  Omaha Platform **VI:** 216
  Patrons of Husbandry **VI:** 221
  People's Party **VI:** 222
  utopianism **VI:** 301

Donner, George **IV:** 114, 115

Donner, Jacob **IV:** 114, 115

Donner party **IV:** 71, **114–115**

Donovan, Mike **VI:** 33

Donovan, William J. **VIII:** 256, 257, 409c

Doolittle, Amos **III:** 111

Doors, The **IX:** 244

Doppler radar **X:** 281

Dorantes, Andres **I:** 38

Dorchester Heights, Battle of **III: 107,** 133, 352, 393c

Doric columns **IV:** 27

Dorr Rebellion **IV:** 378c

Dorsey, Stephen W. **VI:** 275

Dorsey, Tommy **VIII:** 223, 326

Dos Passos, John **VII:** 162, 166; **VIII:** 191; **X:** 43

DOT (Department of Transportation) **IX:** 225

double agents **VIII:** 105

Doubleday, Abner **V:** 148, 227; **VII:** 26

double standard **VII:** 283

"Double-V" campaign
  African Americans **VIII:** 4
  civil rights **VIII:** 62
  race and racial conflict **VIII:** 289
  World War II home front **VIII:** 395

Douglas, Ann **VII:** 161

Douglas, Helen Gahagan **X:** 105, 219

Douglas, Stephen A. **IV:** 379c; **V: 97–99,** 98, 405c, 406c
  Bleeding Kansas **V:** 31
  Buchanan, James **V:** 42
  Compromise of 1850 **IV:** 95
  Davis, Jefferson **V:** 89
  Democratic Party **IV:** 108; **V:** 94
  Fillmore, Millard **IV:** 137
  Kansas-Nebraska Act of 1854 **V:** 197
  Lincoln, Abraham **V:** 210
  Pacific Railroad Act of 1862 **V:** 263
  Pierce, Franklin **V:** 275
  popular sovereignty **IV:** 285, 286
  Republican Party **IV:** 300–302; **V:** 300, 301
  Sumner, Charles **V:** 342, 343

Douglas, William O. **VIII: 84–85,** 322, 346t; **IX:** 31, 80, 315, 315; **X:** 125, 319

Douglas Aircraft **VIII:** 10; **IX:** 28, 294

Douglas DC-3 **VIII:** 353, 360

Douglass, Frederick **III:** 131; **IV:** 377c; **V:** 99, **99–100**
  AASS **IV:** 14
  abolition **V:** 3, 4
  African Americans **IV:** 9; **VI:** 6
  Brown, John **V:** 37, 38
  Brown, William Wells **V:** 40
  Catto, Octavius **V:** 52
  Delany, Martin Robinson **V:** 93
  emancipation **V:** 114
  Emancipation Proclamation **V:** 114
  entertainment, popular **VI:** 96
  female antislavery societies **IV:** 135
  54th Massachusetts Regiment **V:** 125

Free-Soil Party **IV:** 150

Garrison, William Lloyd **V:** 146

Harpers Ferry, West Virginia **V:** 166

Langston, John Mercer **VI:** 171

literature **IV:** 212; **V:** 212

lyceum movement **IV:** 215

NEA, NEH **X:** 209

Negro Convention movement **IV:** 261

newspapers **VI:** 212

Pennington, James William Charles **V:** 270

Pinchback, Pinckney B. S. **V:** 276

race and race relations **IV:** 291

Seneca Falls **IV:** 314

slavery **V:** 328

Thirteenth Amendment **V:** 353

Truth, Sojourner **V:** 357

Wells-Barnett, Ida Bell **VI:** 311

World's Columbian Exposition **VI:** 320

Douglass, Lewis **V:** 125

Douglass, Mrs. **IV:** 379c

Dove, Arthur **VII:** 20

Dow, Herbert **IX:** 82

Dow, Lorenzo **III:** 115; **IV: 115–116**

Dow Chemical Corporation **IX: 82**

Dowding, Nancy **IX:** 323

dower **II:** 406, 407

Dow Jones Industrial Average **VIII:** 293; **X:** 51, 95

Downing, Andrew Jackson **IV:** 28

"downtown" **VI:** 291

Doyle, Arthur Conan **VII:** 124

Doz, André **II:** 130

Dr. Dre **X:** 240

draft **V:** 78–80; **VII:** 54–55; **VIII:** 409c; **X:** 324c. *See also* conscientious objectors; conscription
  Army, U.S. **VIII:** 20
  bounty system **V:** 34
  children **VIII:** 57
  Civil War **V:** 66
  cold war (end of) **X:** 71
  Confederate army **V:** 71
  Eagleton, Thomas F. **X:** 93
  elections **V:** 110
  end of **X:** 75–76
  ERA **X:** 105

governors **V:** 153
habeas corpus, writ of **V:** 161
homefront **V:** 169
Japanese Americans, relocation of **VIII:** 171
Kennedy, Edward M. **X:** 163
peace movements **V:** 266
Schenk v. United States **VII:** 275
Selective Service **VIII:** 322–324
Selective Service Act **VII:** 282
socialism **VI:** 289
Soldiers' Bonus **VII:** 291
sports **VIII:** 336
states' rights **V:** 336
Stephens, Alexander H. **V:** 337
Union army **V:** 364
volunteer army **V:** 383
draft deferment **VIII:** 375
draft evasion **IX:** 10, 214, 279–280, 334c; **X:** 325c
antiwar movement— Vietnam **X:** 24
Clinton, William **X:** 65
McGovern, George Stanley **X:** 184
Weather Underground **X:** 318
draft resistance **VII:** 110, 120, 275. *See also* conscientious objectors
draft riots **V: 254–255,** 255, 407c
conscription **V:** 79
elections **V:** 110
employment **V:** 116
homefront **V:** 169
immigration **V:** 176
race and racial conflict **V:** 288
Union army **V:** 364
Women's National Loyal League **V:** 397
women's status and rights **V:** 398
Dragging Canoe **III: 107,** 392c
Cherokee nation **III:** 66
Franklin, state of **III:** 135
Native Americans and the Revolution **III:** 255
Wilderness Road **III:** 378
Dragonwings (Laurence Yep) **IX:** 327
Drake, Daniel **IV:** 230
Drake, Edwin L. **VI:** 145–146, 215

Drake, Sir Francis **I: 110–113,** 111m, *112,* 388c; **II:** 135, 150, 232, 284, 327
Eden, Richard **I:** 118
Elizabeth I **I:** 121
Frobisher, Martin **I:** 133
Hakluyt, Richard, the Elder **I:** 151
Hakluyt, Richard, the Younger **I:** 151
Hawkins, Sir John **I:** 156, 157
Ingram, David **I:** 177
Lane, Ralph **I:** 197
Panama **I:** 277
Roanoke **I:** 314
Spanish Armada **I:** 334
Veracruz **I:** 366
dramaturgy **VII:** 161
Draper, Henry **VI:** 257
Drayandi, Joh. **I:** 336
dreams **I:** 171
Dred: A Tale of the Great Dismal Swamp (Stowe) **IV:** 213; **V:** 339
Dred Scott decision **V: 100–102,** 405c
Buchanan, James **V:** 41
Civil War **V:** 64, 65
Fourteenth Amendment **V:** 138
Missouri Compromise of 1820 **IV:** 238
popular sovereignty **IV:** 286
race and race relations **IV:** 290
Republican Party **IV:** 301; **V:** 301
slavery **IV:** 318; **V:** 329
Supreme Court decision **IV:** 331
Dreier, Margaret **VII:** 205
Dreiser, Theodore **VI:** 136, 178; **VII:** 50, 160, 252
Dresden codex **I:** 45
dress and fashion **IV:** 53, 168; **V: 122–123,** *123,* 170, 251, 253; **VII:** 57–58, **70–71,** 283, 341
dress reform **IV:** 53–54; **V:** 123
Drew, Charles **VIII:** 207
Drew, Daniel **VI:** 117
Drew, John **VI:** 286
Drewry's Bluff **V:** 222
Drexel, Anthony **VI:** 197
Drexel, Morgan & Company **VI:** 197
drills, military
Confederate army **V:** 71–72
54th Massachusetts Regiment **V:** 125

Drinker, Philip **VIII:** 207
drinking age **X:** 112
drive-in movies **IX:** 255
drought **VIII:** 85–87, 405c
Drouillard, George **IV:** 130
Drug Enforcement Agency **X:** 207
drugs/drug abuse **VIII:** 408c; **IX:** 333c; **X:** 5, 81–83, 189, 190, 206–208, 266. *See also* narcotics
Ginsberg, Allen **IX:** 123
Leary, Timothy **IX:** 175–176
LSD **IX:** 183–184
medicine **IX:** 197, 199
miracle drugs **IX:** 205–206
music **IX:** 218
technology **IX:** 295
drug testing **X:** 291
drug trafficking
Bennett, William J. **X:** 35
Bush, George H. W. **X:** 45–46
crime **X:** 81–83
defense policy **X:** 87
Iran-contra affair **X:** 154
Mexico **X:** 193
NAFTA **X:** 223
narcotics **X:** 207
Panama invasion **X:** 231
RICO **X:** 258
drum majors **V:** 243
drums **II:** 239
Drums Along the Mohawk (Edmonds) **VIII:** 193
Drum Taps (Whitman) **V:** 394
"dry" fishing **II:** 118
Drysdale, Hugh **II:** 145
Duala **I:** 52
"dual unionism" **VI:** 170
Duane, James **III:** 88
Duane, William **III:** 29, **107–108; IV:** 42
Dubček, Alexander **IX:** 106; **X:** 156
Dubinsky, David
CIO **VIII:** 69
Hillman, Sidney **VIII:** 145, 146
labor **VIII:** 180
Lewis, John L. **VIII:** 186
Du Bois, W. E. B. **II:** 343; **V:** 166; **VII: 71–72,** 356c, 357c; **VIII:** 227, 411c; **IX:** 220, 261
African Americans **VI:** 6
Boas, Franz **VII:** 33
education, philanthropy and **VI:** 94
Garvey, Marcus **VII:** 106
NAACP **VII:** 198, 199

Niagara Movement **VII:** 214–215
Washington, Booker T. **VI:** 309
Wells-Barnett, Ida Bell **VI:** 312
Dubuque, Julien **IV:** 208
Duchamp, Marcel **VII:** 17, 19
Dudington, Lieutenant **III:** 148
Dudley, Joseph **II:** 94, **95,** 214, 218, 309
Dudley, Thomas **II:** 39, **95–96,** 402
dueling **II:** 96; **IV:** 49, 105, 191; **V:** 385
due process clause **VI:** 64–65, **81–82,** 221, 317
Duer, William **III:** 272
Duet on Ice (Anderson) **X:** 26
Duhare. *See* Cofitachequi
Dukakis, Michael S. **X:** 91, 327c
Albright, Madeleine **X:** 18
Bush, George H. W. **X:** 45
Gore, Albert, Jr. **X:** 133
Horton, Willie (campaign ad) **X:** 143–144
Duke, David **IX:** 200
Duke of Stockbridge (Bellamy) **VI:** 26
Duke Power Company **X:** 135–136
Duke's Laws **II:** 144, 261
Dulany, Daniel **II:** 210; **III: 108,** 332, 373, 391c
Dulles, Allen **IX:** 33, 34
Dulles, John Foster **IX: 82–83,** 83, 209, 274
du Maurier, George **VI:** 312
Dumbarton Oaks Conference **VIII:** 366
Dummer, Jeremiah **II:** 25, **96–97**
Dummer, Jeremiah, Jr. **II:** 96
Dummer, William **II:** 96, 217
"dumping" **VIII:** 5
Dun & Bradstreet **IV:** 333
Dunaway, Faye **IX:** 214
Dunbar, Paul Laurence **VI:** 6, **82–83,** 83
Duncan, Charles **X:** 247
Dunkers **II:** 139
Dunkirk **VIII:** 39
Dunlap, William **III: 108,** 347
Dunmore, John Murray, earl of **III:** 5, **108–109,** 327, 393c. *See also* Lord Dunmore's War
Dunmore's Proclamation **III:** 109
Dunn, Willie **VI:** 274
Dunster, Henry **II:** 84, 155
du Pont, Éleuthère Irénée **IV:** 118, 184, 187; **IX:** 83

Du Pont, Samuel F. **V:** 368
Du Pont Chemical **VIII:** 47, 250
Du Pont Corporation **IX:** 83–84, 216, 293
Du Pont family **VIII:** 14
Dupuy de Lôme, Enrique **VI:** 71
Duquesne Iron Works **VI:** 106
Durán, Diego **I:** 4, 21, 22, **113**
Durand, Asher B. **IV:** 26, 26
Duran Duran **X:** 202
Durant, William C. **VII:** 22, 74; **IX:** 120
Durenburger, Dave **X:** 276
Dürer, Albrecht **I:** **113–114**
Durstine, Roy **VII:** 5
Dust Bowl **VIII:** 85, **85–87**, 86m, 405c, 408c
  agriculture **VIII:** 8
  environmental issues **VIII:** 103
  Ickes, Harold L. **VIII:** 161
  marriage and family life **VIII:** 204
  Mexican Americans **VIII:** 210
  migration **VIII:** 212
  news media **VIII:** 243
  photography **VIII:** 268
  popular culture **VIII:** 274
  Steinbeck, John **VIII:** 339
  transportation **VIII:** 360
Duston, Hannah Emerson **II:** 97
Dutch colonies **II:** 417c
  Delaware **II:** 87
  Delaware Indians **II:** 88, 89
  Glorious Revolution **II:** 141
  Jews **II:** 175
  Leisler's Rebellion **II:** 192–193
  monarchy, British **II:** 232
  New Amsterdam **II:** 249–250
  New Jersey **II:** 252, 253
  New Netherland **II:** 255–257
  Pequot War **II:** 279
  slavery **II:** 339, 342
  Swedish colonies **II:** 365
  women's status and rights **II:** 408
Dutch East India Company **I:** 31, **114–115**, 335
  Dutch Reformed Church **II:** 97
  Hudson, Henry **II:** 158
  New Amsterdam **II:** 249
  New Jersey **II:** 252

New Netherland **II:** 255
New York **II:** 259
Dutch East Indies **VIII:** 398
Dutch-English Wars **II:** 363
Dutch exploration **II:** 68
  Iroquois **I:** 183
  Linschoten, Jan Huygen van **I:** 206–207
  Northeast Passage **I:** 265
  Northwest Passage **I:** 266
Dutch immigrants **II:** 157, 201, 281
Dutch-Indian Wars **II:** **98–99**, 260
Dutchman (play) **IX:** 7
Dutch POWs **VIII:** 282
Dutch Protestants **II:** 144, 252
Dutch Reformed Church **II:** **97–98**; **VIII:** 304
  Frelinghuysen, Theodorus Jacobus **II:** 125
  German Reformed Church **II:** 140
  Great Awakening **II:** 147, 149
  King's College **II:** 184
  Leisler's Rebellion **II:** 192
  New Jersey **II:** 254
  New Netherland **II:** 257
  New York **II:** 260
  Stuyvesant, Peter **II:** 363
Dutch settlers **II:** 65, 259–260, 263, 273, 381
Dutch style houses **II:** 23
Dutch trade
  Akan **I:** 5
  Algonquin **II:** 17
  coffee **I:** 76
  fur trade **II:** 130–131
  Huron **II:** 160
  Iroquois **II:** 168
  Livingston, Robert **II:** 196
  Pequot **II:** 278
Dutch West India Company **I:** 115; **II:** 98
  Dutch-Indian Wars **II:** 98
  Dutch Reformed Church **II:** 97
  Jews **II:** 175
  Kieft, Willem **II:** 182
  Leisler's Rebellion **II:** 192
  Minuit, Peter **II:** 227
  New Amsterdam **II:** 249
  New Netherland **II:** 255–257
  New York **II:** 259, 260
  New York City **II:** 262
  Rensselaerswyck **II:** 319
  Stuyvesant, Peter **II:** 362, 363

Duval, Gabrial **III:** 236
DVD. *See* digital video discs
Dvořák, Antonín **VI:** 128, 202
dwellings. *See* housing
Dwight, Louis **IV:** 278
Dwight, Timothy **III:** 80, **109**; **IV:** 170, 296
Dyer, L. C. **VII:** 360c
Dyer, Mary **II:** **99–100**, 107, 308
dyes **I:** 33, 261
dyestuffs **II:** 43, 65, 166, 284. *See also* indigo
dyewood (brazilwood) trees **I:** 23, 33
Dylan, Bob **IX:** 84, **84–85**, 333c; **X:** 240
  Beat Generation **IX:** 35
  counterculture **IX:** 72
  folk music revival **IX:** 111
  Ginsberg, Allen **IX:** 123
  March on Washington **IX:** 191
  music **IX:** 217–218
  popular culture **IX:** 244
  rock and roll **IX:** 264
dynamic conservatism. *See* modern Republicanism
Dynamic Sociology (Ward) **VI:** 266
dynamite **VI:** 193
dynamos **VI:** 148
dysentery **I:** 108; **II:** 90, 210, 235, 382; **V:** 96, 230, 386

E

Eads, James Buchanan **VI:** 35, 44, **85**
Eads Bridge **VI:** 35, 44, 324c
Eagan, Thomas **VII:** 200
Eagle Forum **X:** 115, 272
Eagleton, Thomas F. **X:** **93**, 184
Eakins, Thomas **V:** 16; **VI:** **85–87**, 86; **VII:** 18
Earhart, Amelia **VIII:** 406c
Earle, Ralph **III:** 22, **111**
Earle, Thomas **IV:** 210
Early, Jubal A. **V:** **103–104**, 407c
  Cedar Mountain, Battle of **V:** 53
  Chancellorsville, Battle of **V:** 54
  Gettysburg, Battle of **V:** 150
  literature **V:** 212
  Longstreet, James **V:** 215–216
  lost cause, the **V:** 217
  Petersburg campaign **V:** 272

Shenandoah Valley:
  Sheridan's campaign **V:** 317, 318
  Washington, D.C. **V:** 390
earth art **X:** 26
Earth Day **X:** 76, 323c
"earthfast" structures **II:** 23
Earth First! Movement **X:** 77
earthquakes **I:** 10, 365; **IV:** 261–262; **X:** 328c
Easley, Ralph **VII:** 201
East, John **X:** 141
East Asians **VIII:** 25
East Bantu **I:** 24, 25
East Coast Indians **II:** 406
Easter Island **I:** 338
Easter massacre at Colfax Courthouse **V:** 375–376
Eastern Abenaki language. *See* Penobscot language
eastern Europe **VIII:** 125, 137; **IX:** 58, 104–106, 232–233, 277. *See also specific countries*
  Clinton, William **X:** 67
  cold war (end of) **X:** 70, 72
  defense policy **X:** 86
  Ford, Gerald R. **X:** 121
  foreign policy **X:** 124
  glasnost **X:** 131
  Iron Curtain **X:** 156, 157
  NATO **X:** 223
  Reagan, Ronald W. **X:** 261
eastern European immigrants **V:** 60, 177, 278; **VI:** 139, 140, 171; **VIII:** 179, 303
  Dillingham Commission **VII:** 69
  Immigration Act of 1917 **VII:** 128
  Mann Act **VII:** 169
  marriage and family life **VII:** 171
  National Origins Act **VII:** 202
  Quota Act **VII:** 245
  science **VII:** 276
  steel industry **VII:** 297
Eastern Long Island Algonquians **I:** 6
Eastern Orthodox **VI:** 243
Eastern State Penitentiary **IV:** 278, 278
Eastern Taino **I:** 342
eastern United States **I:** 253; **II:** 8; **IV:** 117, 230
Eastern Woodlands Indians **II:** 24, 88, 118, 406
East Germany **IX:** 277
  African nations **X:** 12, 13
  cold war (end of) **X:** 70

Ford, Gerald R. **X:** 121
Iron Curtain **X:** 157
NATO **X:** 223
East India Company (British) **I:** **117,** 152, 318, 335; **II:** 155, 158, 259; **III:** 392*c*
Boston Tea Party **III:** 45
British Empire **II:** 41, 44
China trade **III:** 67
clothing **II:** 65
Coercive Acts **III:** 76
Dale, Sir Thomas **II:** 81–82
Duane, William **III:** 107
Hutchinson, Thomas **III:** 171
Maryland **II:** 209
Tea Act **III:** 344
Yale, Elihu **II:** 413
East Indies **I:** 43, 65, 117, 137; **II:** 285; **IV:** 130
East Jersey **II:** 94, 252, 253
Eastman, George **VI:** **87,** 150, **308, 326***c;* **VII:** 134
Eastman, Max **VII:** 114, 173, 253; **X:** 43
East Timor **X:** 307
Eastwood, Clint **X:** 198
Eastwood, Mary **IX:** 223
Eaton, Amos **III:** 321
Eaton, Dorman B. **VI:** 63
Eaton, John, Jr. **V:** **104**
Eaton, Theophilus **II:** 68
Ebenezer, Georgia **II:** 139, 267
Ebenezer Society **IV:** 299
Ebony **X:** 185
Ebony Concerto (Stravinsky) **VIII:** 223
Eccles, Marriner S. **VIII: 89**
Banking Act of 1935 **VIII:** 33, 34
Henderson, Leon **VIII:** 145
Keynesianism **VIII:** 176
recession of 1937–38 **VIII:** 293
TNEC **VIII:** 355
Ecclesiastical Commission of York **II:** 283
EchoStar Communications Corporation **X:** 244
Eckert, John P., Jr. **IX:** 64, 98
E. C. Knight case **VI:** 295
Eclectic Readers (McGuffey) **IV:** 120, 228
ecological imperialism. *See* Columbian Exchange
ecology. *See also* conservation/ conservationism; environmentalism/ environmental policy
Columbian Exchange **I:** 76–78
horses **I:** 169

Madeira **I:** 214
New Spain **I:** 261
Economic Bill of Rights **VIII: 90**
election of 1944 **VIII:** 99
Full Employment Bill **VIII:** 128
liberalism **VIII:** 189
medicine **VIII:** 209
NRPB **VIII:** 233
Roosevelt, Franklin D. **VIII:** 314
Third New Deal **VIII:** 358
economic collapse of 1893 **VII:** 200
Economic Cooperation Act of 1948 **IX:** 194
economic opportunity **VII:** 251
Economic Opportunity Act of 1964 **IX: 87–88,** 334*c*
Community Action Program **IX:** 62–63
Great Society **IX:** 127
Head Start **IX:** 132
Job Corps **IX:** 149–150
labor **IX:** 170
Volunteers in Service to America **IX:** 310
War on Poverty **IX:** 313
Economic Recovery Tax Act of 1981 **X:** 259
Economic Research and Action Project (ERAP) **IX:** 131, 286
Economic Security Bill. *See* Social Security Act
Economic Stabilization Act **VIII:** 371; **IX:** 70
Economic Stabilization Act of 1970 **X:** 313
economy **II: 101–102; III: 111–113,** 112*m,* 397*c;* **IV:** 117, **117–119,** 118*t;* **V: 104–107,** 105*t;* **VI:** xvi; **VII:** xiii, xiv, **73–76; VIII: 90–93,** 91*t,* 176–177, 295–296, 407*c;* **IX: 88–90,** 117–118; **X: 93–96,** 95, 331*c. See also* banking, finance and credit; crash of 1929; trade, domestic and foreign
abolition movement **IV:** 1, 3
Acadia **I:** 2
Acadians **II:** 2
Acosta, José de **I:** 3
Acts of Trade and Navigation **II:** 2–3
advertising **VII:** 4–5; **VIII:** 1
Africa **II:** 4–5

Agricultural Adjustment Act **VIII:** 5
agriculture **II:** 7–13; **III:** 7; **IV:** 9–12; **V:** 6–7; **X:** 15
Algonquin **II:** 17
almshouses **II:** 18
American System **IV:** 17–19
Apalachee **I:** 11
Appalachian Regional Development Act **IX:** 15–16
artisans **II:** 25–26; **III:** 26
Austin, Moses **IV:** 36
automobile industry **VIII:** 30; **X:** 31
Aztecs **I:** 18
baby boom **IX:** 29
baby boomers **X:** 33
banking, investment **VI:** 19–20
banking and credit **II:** 28–29
banking and currency **V:** 22–24
Bank of the United States (First) **III:** 30–31
banks **III:** 32–33
Benin **I:** 28
Berle, Adolf A., Jr. **VIII:** 35
Black Codes **V:** 29
Bonus Bill **IV:** 56
Brain Trust **VIII:** 41
Brazil **I:** 33
British Empire **II:** 41
Brown, Joseph **V:** 39
bubonic plague **I:** 285
Bush, George W. **X:** 48
business **IX:** 44; **X:** 49–51
business and government **VI:** 39–40
business cycles **VI:** 41–42
California gold rush **IV:** 69
California Indians **II:** 49
Caribbean **II:** 53
Caroline affair **IV:** 74–75
carpetbaggers **V:** 50
Carter, James Earl, Jr. **X:** 58
cash-and-carry **VIII:** 53
castas **I:** 62
Castile **I:** 63
Cayuga **I:** 67
Champlain, Samuel de **II:** 56
Charleston **II:** 56, 57
Charles V **I:** 69
Chase, Salmon P. **V:** 56
Church of Jesus Christ of Latter-day Saints **IV:** 81
cities and urban life **II:** 61

Civil War **V:** 63, 67
class **II:** 63
Clinton, George **III:** 75
Clinton, William **X:** 66, 68
Columbian Exchange **I:** 78
Committee for Public Information **VII:** 345
communications **VI:** 61
Conestoga **II:** 67
Confederate navy **V:** 74
Confederate States of America **V:** 77
Confiscation Acts **V:** 78
Congress **VIII:** 66
Connecticut **II:** 69, 70
conscription **V:** 79
conservative coalition **VIII:** 73
conservative movement **X:** 78
consumption **II:** 70–71
convict labor **II:** 72
Cooke, Jay **V:** 81
Copperheads **V:** 82
corporations **III:** 93–94
cotton culture **IV:** 97, 98
Council of Economic Advisors **IX:** 70–71
Coxe, Tench **III:** 96
Coxey's Army **VI:** 67–68
credit cards **IX:** 73
Currency Act **III:** 99; **VII:** 60
currency issue **VI:** 72–73
CWA **VIII:** 62
Davis Bend, Mississippi, freedmen's colony **V:** 91–92
Delaware **II:** 88
demobilization **IX:** 78
Democratic Party **IV:** 108; **V:** 95; **VI:** 77–78; **VIII:** 80
education, primary and secondary **X:** 100
election of 1840 **IV:** 124
elections **IX:** 95
electricity **VII:** 82–83
embargo of 1807 **III:** 117–118
employment **V:** 115–117
encomienda **I:** 122
energy crisis **X:** 103
Era of Good Feelings **IV:** 127
federal income tax **VII:** 92–93
federalism **X:** 113
Federalist Party **III:** 126
Federal Reserve Act **VII:** 93–94

economy (continued)
Federal Trade Commission
Act **VII:** 94
FEPC **VIII:** 109
feudalism **I:** 129–130
First New Deal **VIII:** 122
fishing **II:** 118
Florida **II:** 120
food riots **V:** 129–130
foraging **V:** 130
Ford, Gerald R. **X:** 121
foreign affairs **III:** 131
foreign policy **VI:** 103
Fort Mose **II:** 123
forts **II:** 124
Freedman's Saving Bank
V: 141–142
French colonies **II:** 127,
129
fur trade **II:** 130–131
Georgia **II:** 137–138
globalization **X:** 131–132
Glorious Revolution **II:**
141
Golden Hill, Battle of **III:**
154
government, British
American **II:** 145
Great Depression **VIII:**
138–141
greenbacks **V:** 159
haciendas **I:** 149
Hartford Convention **IV:**
170
homefront **V:** 168
Hoover, Herbert **VIII:**
151
Hoover presidency **VIII:**
153–154
Hutchinson, Anne
Marbury **II:** 161
immigration **IV:** 177; **X:**
148
imperialism **VI:** 142
Inca **I:** 176
indentured servitude **II:**
163–165
industrial development **V:**
180–181
industrialization **IV:** 185
industrial revolution **III:**
177
investments, American,
abroad **VI:** 150
investments, foreign, in the
United States **VI:**
150–151
Jews **VIII:** 172
journalism **II:** 179; **IV:**
197
King Philip's War **II:** 183
Kongo **I:** 195

labor and labor movements
II: 187–190; **III:** 199;
IV: 203–205
labor trends **VI:** 170–171
Laffer curve **X:** 171–172
Le Moyne, Jean-Baptiste,
sieur de Bienville **II:**
193
liberalism **VIII:** 187–189;
X: 174–176
Libertarian Party **X:** 176
literature **VIII:** 191
London Economic
Conference **VIII:**
193–194
lumbering **II:** 201
Mann-Elkins Act **VII:** 170
marriage and family life **V:**
222, 223
Maryland **II:** 210, 211
Massachusetts **II:** 215
McCulloch v. Maryland
IV: 227
media **X:** 187
medicine **X:** 187–188
mercantilism **II:** 221
merchants **II:** 221–222
métis **II:** 223
Mexican immigration **VII:**
182
Mexico **X:** 192, 193
Miantonomo **II:** 224
migration **IV:** 235
military-industrial complex
IX: 203–204
Minuit, Peter **II:** 227
mobilization **VIII:**
213–215
monarchy, British **II:** 232
mortality **II:** 235
MOWM **VIII:** 201
NAFTA **X:** 223
Narragansett **II:** 241
national banking system
VI: 206
national debt **III:** 253
Native Americans **II:** 243;
VI: 206, 208
Navajo **II:** 247
New Deal **VIII:** 239–243
New Frontier **IX:** 230
New Hampshire **II:** 250,
251
New Netherland **II:** 257
New South **VI:** 209–210
New Spain **I:** 261
New York **II:** 260, 262
New York City **V:** 253
NIRA **VIII:** 228
Non-Intercourse Act **III:**
259
NRPB **VIII:** 232

Nullification Controversy
IV: 264
NWLB **VIII:** 233
OPEC **X:** 228–229
OPM **VIII:** 255
OWM **VIII:** 258
Panic of 1792 **III:** 272–273
Panic of 1819 **IV:** 275–276
Panic of 1837 **IV:** 276–277
Panic of 1857 **V:** 264
Pennsylvania **II:** 276
Pequot **II:** 278
Peru **I:** 280
Philadelphia **II:** 281
Philip II **I:** 281
Pinckney, Elizabeth Lucas
II: 284
plantations **V:** 276
plantation system **II:**
286–287
politics in the Roosevelt
era **VIII:** 270
population trends **VIII:**
278
Port Royal, South
Carolina, Experiment **V:**
279–280
postal service **II:** 292
postwar planning **VIII:**
278
poverty **III:** 284–285; **X:**
246
presidency **VIII:** 280
Progressive Party **IX:**
248–249
pueblo **I:** 295
Quakers **II:** 308
railroads **IV:** 292–296; **V:**
289–290; **VI:** 237
Reagan, Ronald W. **X:** 259
Reaganomics **X:** 261
recession of 1937–38 **VIII:**
292–293
Reconstruction **V:** 292, 294
Republican Party **V:** 300,
301
Rhode Island **II:** 321
Roosevelt, Franklin D.
VIII: 312
rum trade **II:** 326
rural life **VII:** 268–269
rust belt **X:** 269
St. Augustine **II:** 327
St. Mary's City **II:** 328
São Tomé **I:** 320
Savannah **II:** 329
scalawags **V:** 307
science and technology **V:**
310
Second New Deal **VIII:**
321
service sector **IX:** 271–272

Seville **I:** 322–323
silver **I:** 325
Singleton, Benjamin **V:**
327
slavery **II:** 341; **III:** 326;
IV: 316–319; **V:**
328–331
slave trade **II:** 343–344
Social Security Act **VIII:**
328
society, British American
II: 349, 350
South Carolina Regulation
III: 330
Spanish colonies **II:** 355,
357, 358
states' rights **V:** 335
steel industry **VII:**
296–298; **VIII:** 338–339
stock market crash (1929)
VIII: 340–341
strikes **V:** 340
sugar **I:** 338–339
Sunbelt **X:** 290
tariffs **III:** 342; **V:** 348;
VII: 305–306
taxation **V:** 349–350; **VIII:**
352
televangelism **X:** 293
temperance movement **IV:**
336
Teotihuacán **I:** 346
Texas **IV:** 337, 339
Third New Deal **VIII:** 358
TNEC **VIII:** 355
tobacco **II:** 373–375
transportation **V:** 354–356
Travis, William Barret **IV:**
345
Tugwell, Rexford G. **VIII:**
361
Tuscarora **II:** 378–379
uniforms **V:** 363
union movement **IX:** 304
Union navy **V:** 370
Van Buren, Martin **IV:**
352
Virginia **II:** 383
Virginia Company of
London **II:** 387
wage and price controls **II:**
389; **X:** 313
wampum **II:** 391
War on Poverty **IX:** 313
Whiskey Rebellion **III:**
375
World War II home front
VIII: 394
Zacatecas **I:** 381
"eco-tage" **X:** 77
ECT (electroconvulsive
therapy) **X:** 190

Ecuador **I:** 10, 175, 277; **II:** 356; **V:** 248; **X:** 228

Eddy, Mary Baker **VI:** 52–53, **87–88**, *88*, 324*c*

Eden, Charles **II:** 34, 369

Eden, Richard **I: 117–118**, 280–281, 343

Edgar Huntly (Brown) **III:** 50

Edgefield Real Estate and Homestead Association **V:** 327

Edgerton, John **VII:** 220

Edict of Nantes **I:** 158, 170; **II:** 130

Edict of Saint-Germain-des-Près (1562) **I:** 169

Edison, Thomas Alva **VI: 88–89**, *89*, 324*c*, 325*c*; **VII:** 107, 190; **IX:** 120; **X:** 210
  banking, investment **VI:** 20
  Bell, Alexander Graham **VI:** 25
  industrial revolution, second **VI:** 146
  inventions and technology **VI:** 147–150
  music **VI:** 204

Edison Electrical Light Company **VII:** 107

Edison Electric Illuminating Company **VI:** 149

Edison General Electric Company **VI:** 305

Edison Lamp Company **VI:** 305

Edison Machine Works **VI:** 305

editorial pages **IV:** 195–196

Edmonds, Emma
  espionage **V:** 118
  literature **V:** 213

Edmonds, Tracy **X:** 203

Edmonds, Walter **VIII:** 193

Edmunds Act of 1882 **VI:** 199

Edmunds-Tucker Act of 1877 **IV:** 110–111

Edmunds-Tucker Act of 1887 **VI:** 199

Edo. *See* Benin

EDS (Electronic Data Systems Corporation) **X:** 234

EDSAC **IX:** 98

Ed Sullivan Show, The **IX:** 36, 244, 295, 334*c*

education **II: 102–105**, *103;* **III: 113–116**, *114;* **IV:** *120*, 120–122, 368; **V: 107–109;** **VI: 89–92**, *90*, 324*c*, 325*c*, 328*c*; **VII: 76–79**, *77*, 361*c*; **VIII: 93–95**, *94;* **IX: 90–92**, 332*c*
  abortion **X:** 3
  AME Church **V:** 5

American Missionary Association **V:** 8

American Philosophical Society **II:** 18

Anglican Church **II:** 20

anti-Catholic riots **IV:** 21

Asian Americans **X:** 28, 30

Aztecs **I:** 19, 20

Benezet, Anthony **II:** 31

Bennett, William J. **X:** 35

BIA **IV:** 180

Bilingual Education Act of 1968 **X:** 35–36

Brown v. Board of Education **IX:** 42–43

Bruce, Blanche K. **V:** 40

Catholics **VIII:** 54

Chase, William Merritt **VI:** 48

Chautauqua Institute **VI:** 49

childhood **II:** 60

children **VIII:** 56

cities and urban life **II:** 61; **IV:** 83

civil rights **VIII:** 61

Civil Rights Act of 1964 **IX:** 57

Clinton, William **X:** 65–66

College of Philadelphia **II:** 66–67

College of William and Mary **II:** 67

Connecticut **II:** 69, 70

Crummell, Alexander **VI:** 71

Cuauhtémoc **I:** 97

Dartmouth College **II:** 83

Dewey, John **VII:** 67–68

dueling **II:** 96

Dutch Reformed Church **II:** 97–98

Eastman, George **VI:** 87

Eaton, John, Jr. **V:** 104

Economic Opportunity Act of 1964 **IX:** 87–88

emancipation **V:** 112

Endecott, John **II:** 107

federal aid to **VI: 92–93**

feminism **X:** 114, 116

Franklin, Benjamin **III:** 135

Freedmen's Bureau **V:** 143

FSA **X:** 110

GI Bill of Rights **VIII:** 131

Great Awakening **II:** 149

Great Migration **VII:** 113

Grimké, Angelina and Sarah **IV:** 164

Hamilton, Alexander **III:** 161

Harper, Frances Ellen Watkins **V:** 164

Harvard College **II:** 155

Hayes, Rutherford B. **VI:** 127

Head Start **IX:** 132

Heathcote, Caleb **II:** 155

Hispanic Americans **X:** 142, 143

home schooling **X: 98**

Howard, O. O. **V:** 173

Hume, Sophia Wigington **II:** 159

Indian Removal Act (1830) **IV:** 183

James, William **VI:** 154–155

Japanese Americans, relocation of **VIII:** 171

Jefferson, Thomas **III:** 183

Jesuits **I:** 189; **II:** 174

Johnson, Samuel **II:** 176, 177

Jomini, Antoine-Henri, baron de **V:** 192

journalism **II:** 178

kindergarten **VI:** 159

King's College **II:** 184–185

Knight, Sarah Kemble **II:** 185–186

labor **II:** 187

labor, child **VI:** 166

Lamy, Jean Baptiste **IV:** 207

Las Casas, Bartolomé de **I:** 199

League of Women Voters **IX:** 175

Leverett, John **II:** 193–194

liberalism **X:** 175

libraries, public, growth of **VI:** 175–176

Lincoln, Abraham **V:** 209

Lincoln, Mary Todd **V:** 211

Livingston, Robert R. **II:** 196

Locke, John **II:** 197

Lockwood, Belva Ann Bennett McNall **VI:** 180

lyceum movement **IV:** 215

Madison, James **III:** 230

Mann, Horace **IV:** 219–220

marriage and family life **II:** 208; **III:** 232; **V:** 223

Massachusetts **II:** 212, 215

Massachusetts School Act **II:** 216–217

McGuffey, William Holmes **IV:** 227–228

media **X:** 184

medicine **V:** 232; **VII:** 179, 180; **X:** 190

migration **VIII:** 212

missions **II:** 229

Model Cities program **IX:** 208

Moody, Dwight Lyman **VI:** 196

Morrill Land-Grant Act **V:** 240–241

Murray, Judith Sargent **III:** 250

Musgrove, Mary Bosomworth **II:** 238

music **IX:** 217

National Endowment for the Humanities **IX:** 221

Native Americans **VII:** 207; **X:** 214–215

New Frontier **IX:** 230

New Jersey **II:** 253

New Woman **VII:** 213–214

Northwest Ordinances **III:** 263

NRA **X:** 212

Pelham, Peter **II:** 272, 273

Pennington, James William Charles **V:** 270

philanthropy and **VI: 93–94**

pragmatism **VI:** 228–229

primary and secondary **X: 98–101**, *99*, 104–105, 200

Princeton College **II:** 298

Protestantism **II:** 302

public **V:** 50

Puerto Ricans **IX:** 251

Puritans **II:** 306

race and racial conflict **X:** 256

Reconstruction **V:** 295

refugees **V:** 298

religion **VI:** 241; **IX:** 257

religious liberty **III:** 300

Republican Party **V:** 301

Revels, Hiram R. **V:** 303

Rhode Island **II:** 321

Roman Catholics **II:** 323

science **II:** 330

scientific management **VII:** 277

Scopes Trial **VII:** 278

Shippen, William, Jr. **II:** 335–336

slavery **IV:** 317

social work **VII:** 290

Society for the Propagation of the Gospel in Foreign Parts **II:** 352–353

South **VIII:** 331

Starbuck, Mary Coffin **II:** 361

Stewart, Maria **IV:** 327

education (continued)
Sumner, William Graham
VI: 281
Taylor, Susie King **V:** 350
technology **IX:** 293
Tennent, Gilbert **II:** 371
Tennent, William, Sr. **II:** 372
Theus, Jeremiah **II:** 373
Thoreau, Henry David **IV:** 342
travel **II:** 377
Tubman, Harriet **V:** 358
Turner, Nat **IV:** 346
Virginia **II:** 385
Ward, Lester Frank **VI:** 307
War on Poverty **IX:** 313
Warren, Mercy Otis **III:** 363
Washington, Booker T. **VI:** 308
Webster, Noah **III:** 370
Wells-Barnett, Ida Bell **VI:** 312
Wheelock, Eleazar **II:** 395–396
Wigglesworth, Edward **II:** 398
Willard, Emma **IV:** 364–366
Williams, Peter, Jr. **IV:** 366
Witherspoon, John **III:** 380
Women's Equity Action League **IX:** 323
women's rights and status **II:** 407; **III:** 383; **IV:** 368; **VI:** 317–318; **VIII:** 384–386; **X:** 320
work, household **VII:** 342
Yale College **II:** 413
youth **VII:** 351
Zumárraga, Juan de **I:** 382
education, higher **IV:** 121; **VI:** 93; **X:** 96–98
affirmative action **X:** 8, 9
African Americans **X:** 10–11
antiwar movement—Vietnam **X:** 24
baby boomers **X:** 33–34
Bakke **X:** 34–35
feminism **X:** 115
Grove City College et al. v. Bell, Secretary of Education, et al. **X:** 136
Jackson State University **X:** 160
medicine **VI:** 191
multiculturalism **X:** 200

Native Americans **X:** 215
Richards, Ellen Henrietta Swallow **VI:** 247
Thomas, M. Carey **VI:** 287–288
women's colleges **VI:** 316
women's rights **VI:** 317
Education Act of 1972 **X:** 320
educational programming **X:** 296
Education Amendments of 1972 **X:** 136, 321
Education Department **X:** 35, 58, 100, 136
Education Flexibility Partnership Act of 1999 **X:** 113
Education for Economic Security Act of 1984 **X:** 104–105
EDVAC **IX:** 64, 98
Edward, HMS **III:** 36, 393c
Edwards, Jonathan **II:** *105,* **105–106,** *148;* **III:** 109
Brainerd, David **II:** 40
Burr, Esther Edwards **II:** 46
Chauncy, Charles **II:** 57
Congregationalists **II:** 68
Edwards, Sarah Pierpont **II:** 106
Enlightenment **II:** 110
Frelinghuysen, Theodorus Jacobus **II:** 125–126
Great Awakening **II:** 147
literature **II:** 195
Philadelphia **II:** 282
Princeton College **II:** 298
Protestantism **II:** 301
"Sinners in the Hands of an Angry God" **II:** 424–425
Edwards, Melvin **X:** 26
Edwards, Sarah Pierpont **II:** **106,** 148
Edwards v. California **VIII:** 409c
Edward VI, king of England **II:** 301
Cabot, Sebastian **I:** 42, 43
Church of England **I:** 74
Mary I **I:** 224
Privy Council **I:** 295
Reformation **I:** 309
EEOC. *See* Equal Employment Opportunity Commission
efficiency **V:** 340; **VI:** 145
efficiency studies **VII:** 74, 76, 357c
Effingham (frigate) **III:** 90
Egan, Patrick **VI:** 50
Egerton, Douglas **III:** 145

Egypt **I:** 14, 185; **V:** 132; **IX:** 146, 147, 277, 288–289, 332c; **X:** 325c
Bush, George H. W. **X:** 46
Camp David accords **X:** 54–55
Carter, James Earl, Jr. **X:** 58
cold war (end of) **X:** 70
foreign policy **X:** 123
Egyptian art **VII:** 19
Ehrlichman, John
Ford, Gerald R. **X:** 120
Mitchell, John N. **X:** 196
United States v. Nixon **X:** 308
Watergate scandal **X:** 316, 317
Eiffel, Gustave **VI:** 276
"Eight, The" **VII:** 18, 357c
Eighteenth Amendment **III:** 346; **VI:** 235; **VII:** 359c; **VIII:** 406c
criminal justice **VII:** 59
elections **VII:** 80
Prohibition **VII:** 241
Volstead Act **VII:** 327
Wilson, Woodrow **VII:** 335
1835, Treaty of **IV:** 378c
Eighth Amendment **X:** 41, 56, 324c
Eighth Army Air Force **VIII:** 12
Eight-Hour movement **VI:** 127, 315
Eight Men Out (movie) **X:** 198
Einhorn, David **VI:** 158, 243
Einstein, Albert **VII:** 275; **VIII:** 408c; **IX:** 139, 236
atomic bomb **VIII:** 29
Letter of 1939 to Franklin D. Roosevelt **VIII:** 422–423
Manhattan Project **VIII:** 200
science **VIII:** 318
Eisenhower, Dwight D. **VII:** 160; **VIII:** 409c; **IX:** 92–93, 93, 315, 331c, 332c
agriculture **IX:** 8
amendments to the Constitution **X:** 19
Americans for Democratic Action **IX:** 14
arms race **IX:** 16
Army-McCarthy hearings **IX:** 19
Atomic Energy Commission **IX:** 24
automobile industry **IX:** 25
Baker v. Carr **IX:** 32
Bay of Pigs **IX:** 33
Brennan, William J. **X:** 40

Brown v. Board of Education **IX:** 43
Bunche, Ralph **IX:** 43–44
Burger, Warren E. **X:** 43–44
CIA **IX:** 50
civil defense **IX:** 53
Civil Rights Act of 1957 **IX:** 54, 55
Civil Rights Act of 1960 **IX:** 55
conservative movement **X:** 79
defense budget **IX:** 77
demobilization **VIII:** 79
Democratic Party **IX:** 79
Dewey, Thomas **IX:** 81
Dulles, John Foster **IX:** 82, 83
economy **VIII:** 92; **IX:** 90
education **IX:** 91
elections **IX:** 94–95
environmental movement **IX:** 101
Faubus, Orval **IX:** 109
Federal Employee Loyalty Program **IX:** 109
government **VIII:** 135
Graham, Billy **IX:** 126
hydrogen bomb **IX:** 140
Indian Claims Commission **IX:** 143
Interstate Highway Act of 1956 **IX:** 144–146
Israel **IX:** 146
Korean War **IX:** 164, 165
liberalism **IX:** 179
Luce, Henry R. **VIII:** 196
McCarthy, Joseph **IX:** 190
military-industrial complex **IX:** 203, 204
mobilization **VIII:** 215
modern Republicanism **IX:** 208–209
NASA **IX:** 219
National Wilderness Preservation Act of 1964 **IX:** 226
Native American movement **IX:** 227–228
NEA, NEH **X:** 209
New Deal **IX:** 229
Nixon, Richard M. **X:** 219
Normandy, invasion of **VIII:** 247, 247
North African campaign **VIII:** 249
Operation Mongoose **IX:** 236
Patton, George **VIII:** 263
Point Four Program **IX:** 243

Reagan, Ronald W. **X:** 258
religion **IX:** 256
Republican Party **IX:** 257, 258
Roosevelt, Eleanor **VIII:** 311
Rosenberg, Julius and Ethel **IX:** 264–265
SANE **IX:** 267
second front **VIII:** 320
segregation **IX:** 271
Sicily **VIII:** 325
Southeast Asia Treaty Organization **IX:** 274
Southern Manifesto **IX:** 276
space policy **X:** 281
Stevenson, Adlai **IX:** 284
Submerged Lands Act **IX:** 287
Taft, Robert A. **VIII:** 349
Termination policy **IX:** 297
Walsh, Lawrence E. **X:** 314
Warren Court **IX:** 315
White Citizens' Councils **IX:** 320
World War II European theater **VIII:** 393
Eisenhower, Milton **VIII:** 171
Eisenhower Doctrine **IX:** 146, 332c
Eisenstadt v. Baird (1972) **X:** 41
Eisenstein, Sergei **VIII:** 309
El Alamein, Second Battle of **VIII:** 393
Elcano, Juan Sebastian de **I:** 56
El Capitan (Sousa) **VI:** 271
El Capitan (Yosemite) **VII:** *19*
elderly **VIII: 95–96; IX:** 196–197, 272, 313; **X:** 245, 246, 290, 327c
 Great Depression **VIII:** 140
 marriage and family life **VIII:** 204
 New Deal **VIII:** 241
 Townsend, Francis E. **VIII:** 358
 unemployment **VIII:** 363
 World War II home front **VIII:** 394
El Dorado **I: 8, 118–119,** 143
election advertising **VIII:** 1
election of 1800 **III: 116–117; IV:** 84, 106
 Adams, John **III:** 3
 Adams, Samuel **III:** 5
 Alien and Sedition Acts **III:** 9
 American Revolution **III:** 13

Ames, Fisher **III:** 13
artisans **III:** 26
Burr, Aaron **III:** 54
cities and urban life **III:** 70
Coxe, Tench **III:** 96
Democratic-Republican Party **III:** 104
Duane, William **III:** 108
Federalist Party **III:** 126
Hamilton, Alexander **III:** 162
Jefferson, Thomas **III:** 185
Judiciary Act of 1801 **III:** 193
national debt **III:** 253
states' rights **III:** 333
Tammany Society **III:** 341
Virginia dynasty **III:** 361
election of 1816 **IV:** 240, 375c
election of 1820 **IV:** 106
election of 1824 **IV:** 376c
 Adams, John Quincy **IV:** 5
 banking and currency **IV:** 42
 Benton, Thomas Hart **IV:** 49
 Calhoun, John C. **IV:** 62
 Clay, Henry **IV:** 87
 Democratic Party **IV:** 106–107
 election of 1828 **IV:** 122–124
 Jackson, Andrew **IV:** 192
 Whig Party **IV:** 363
election of 1828 **IV: 122–124,** 123m, 376c; **V:** 93–94, 117
 Adams, John Quincy **IV:** 5
 American System **IV:** 19
 banking and currency **IV:** 42
 Benton, Thomas Hart **IV:** 49
 Calhoun, John C. **IV:** 62
 Clay, Henry **IV:** 86
 Democratic Party **IV:** 107
 Whig Party **IV:** 363
election of 1832 **IV:** 377c
 American System **IV:** 19
 anti-Masonry **IV:** 24
 Bank of the United States, Second **IV:** 44
 Clay, Henry **IV:** 87
 Fillmore, Millard **IV:** 137
 Jackson, Andrew **IV:** 193
 Whig Party **IV:** 363
election of 1836 **IV:** 377c
 Free-Soil Party **IV:** 150
 Harrison, William Henry **IV:** 170
 Van Buren, Martin **IV:** 351–352

Webster, Daniel **IV:** 360
 Whig Party **IV:** 363
election of 1840 **IV: 124–126,** 125m, 377c; **V:** 333
 banking and currency **IV:** 43
 Democratic Party **IV:** 108
 Free-Soil Party **IV:** 150
 Harrison, William Henry **IV:** 170
 Liberty Party **IV:** 210
 Native Americans **IV:** 256
 Tyler, John **IV:** 348
 Van Buren, Martin **IV:** 352
 Whig Party **IV:** 363
election of 1844 **IV:** 378c
 banking and currency **IV:** 43
 Church of Jesus Christ of Latter-day Saints **IV:** 80
 Clay, Henry **IV:** 87
 Democratic Party **IV:** 108
 Free-Soil Party **IV:** 150
 Houston, Sam **IV:** 175
 Liberty Party **IV:** 210–211
 Manifest Destiny **IV:** 217
 Oregon Treaty of 1846 **IV:** 269
 Polk, James K. **IV:** 283
 Smith, Joseph, Jr. **IV:** 324
 Tyler, John **IV:** 349
 Whig Party **IV:** 364
 Young, Brigham **IV:** 371–372
election of 1848 **IV:** 378c; **V:** 3, 342, 391
 Benton, Thomas Hart **IV:** 49–50
 Cass, Lewis **IV:** 76–77
 Democratic Party **IV:** 108
 Fillmore, Millard **IV:** 137
 Free-Soil Party **IV:** 150
 Liberty Party **IV:** 211
 Scott, Winfield **IV:** 310
 Taylor, Zachary **IV:** 334–335
 Whig Party **IV:** 364
election of 1852
 Buchanan, James **V:** 41
 Civil War **V:** 64
 Fillmore, Millard **IV:** 137–138
 Free-Soil Party **IV:** 151
 Julian, George W. **V:** 194
 Pierce, Franklin **V:** 275
 Scott, Winfield **IV:** 310
 Whig Party **IV:** 364
election of 1854 **IV:** 201–202, 300, 379c
election of 1856 **V:** 405c; **VI:** 78
 Buchanan, James **V:** 41
 Douglas, Stephen A. **V:** 98

employment **V:** 116
Fillmore, Millard **IV:** 138
Frémont, John C. **IV:** 154
Greeley, Horace **V:** 158
Know-Nothing Party **IV:** 202
nativism **V:** 251
Republican Party **IV:** 301
Sumner, Charles **V:** 343
election of 1858 **V:** 98, 264, 377
election of 1860 **V:** 405c; **VI:** 31
 abolition **V:** 4
 Buchanan, James **V:** 42
 Davis, Jefferson **V:** 89
 Democratic Party **IV:** 108; **V:** 94
 Douglas, Stephen A. **V:** 98–99
 Dred Scott decision **V:** 101
 elections **V:** 109
 employment **V:** 116
 Finney, Charles Grandison **IV:** 139
 fire-eaters **V:** 128
 Fort Sumter, South Carolina **V:** 135
 fugitive slave laws **IV:** 155
 Greeley, Horace **V:** 158
 Homestead Act of 1862 **V:** 170
 Know-Nothing Party **IV:** 202
 Lincoln, Abraham **V:** 210
 Manifest Destiny **IV:** 218
 public land policy **IV:** 288
 Republican Party **IV:** 301–302; **V:** 301
 secession **V:** 311, 312
 Seward, William H. **V:** 314
 slavery **IV:** 318; **V:** 330
 states' rights **V:** 336
 Vallandigham, Clement L. **V:** 377
 Welles, Gideon **V:** 391
 Whig Party **IV:** 364
election of 1861 **V:** 110
election of 1862 **V:** 109, 115, 169; **VI:** 31, 108
election of 1863 **V:** 110, 128
election of 1864 **IV:** 139, 154; **V:** 407c
 amnesty, acts of **V:** 8–9
 Atlanta campaign **V:** 19
 Chase, Salmon P. **V:** 56
 Copperheads **V:** 82
 elections **V:** 110
 emancipation **V:** 113
 homefront **V:** 169
 Johnson, Andrew **V:** 187
 Lincoln, Abraham **V:** 211
 Longstreet, James **V:** 215

election of 1864 *(continued)*
   McClellan, George B. **V:** 226
   Nast, Thomas **V:** 247
   Overland campaign **V:** 261
   Petersburg campaign **V:** 272
   Reconstruction **V:** 292
   Republican Party **V:** 302
   Shenandoah Valley: Sheridan's campaign **V:** 317
   Sherman, William T. **V:** 321
   Stanton, Edwin M. **V:** 334
   tactics and strategy **V:** 347
   Union army **V:** 367
   Union League **V:** 367
   Vallandigham, Clement L. **V:** 378
   volunteer army **V:** 384
election of 1866 **IV:** 103; **V:** 30, 178, 293
election of 1868 **V:** 408c; **VI:** 256
   Blair, Francis P., Jr. **V:** 31
   Chase, Salmon P. **V:** 57
   Dana, Charles A. **V:** 88
   Democratic Party **V:** 95
   Fifteenth Amendment **V:** 124
   Grant, Ulysses S. **V:** 156
   Greeley, Horace **V:** 158
   Johnson, Andrew **V:** 189
   Radical Republicans **V:** 289
   Reconstruction **V:** 294
   Reconstruction Acts **V:** 296
   Republican Party **V:** 302
   Sickles, Daniel E. **V:** 327
   Warmoth, Henry C. **V:** 388
election of 1870 **V:** 199
election of 1872 **VI:** 174, 231, 234, 256
   Dana, Charles A. **V:** 88
   Democratic Party **V:** 95
   Early, Jubal A. **V:** 103
   Grant, Ulysses S. **V:** 157
   Greeley, Horace **V:** 158
   Mosby, John Singleton **V:** 242
   Nast, Thomas **V:** 247
   National Labor Union (NLU) **V:** 248
   Republican Party **V:** 302
   Sumner, Charles **V:** 343
   Warmoth, Henry C. **V:** 388
election of 1874 **V:** 95; **VI:** 78
election of 1876 **VI:** 231, 324c
   African Americans **VI:** 5
   Blaine, James Gillespie **VI:** 31

Democratic Party **V:** 95; **VI:** 78
   Greenback-Labor Party **VI:** 120
   Hayes, Rutherford B. **VI:** 125–126
   Julian, George W. **V:** 194
   Reconstruction **V:** 294
   redemption **V:** 297
   Republican Party **V:** 303; **VI:** 246
   Schurz, Carl **VI:** 256
   Scott, Thomas Alexander **VI:** 258
   Tilden, Samuel Jones **VI:** 289
   Wade, Benjamin **V:** 385
   Whiskey Ring **V:** 393
election of 1878 **VI:** 78
election of 1880 **V:** 164; **VI:** 232
   Blaine, James Gillespie **VI:** 31
   Garfield, James Abram **VI:** 108
   Greenback-Labor Party **VI:** 120
   Republican Party **VI:** 246
   Socialist Labor Party **VI:** 268
election of 1884 **VI:** 232
   Blaine, James Gillespie **VI:** 31–32
   Cleveland, Grover **VI:** 58
   Democratic Party **VI:** 78
   Greenback-Labor Party **VI:** 120
   Prohibition Party **VI:** 234
   Republican Party **VI:** 246
   Schurz, Carl **VI:** 257
election of 1888 **VI:** 232
   Blaine, James Gillespie **VI:** 32
   Cleveland, Grover **VI:** 58
   Harrison, Benjamin **VI:** 122
   Socialist Labor Party **VI:** 268
election of 1890 **VI:** 73
election of 1892 **IV:** 51; **VI:** 232
   Blaine, James Gillespie **VI:** 32
   Cleveland, Grover **VI:** 58
   Harrison, Benjamin **VI:** 122
   Omaha platform **VI:** 216
   People's Party **VI:** 222–223
   Populist Party Platform, 1892 **VI:** 346–347
   Prohibition Party **VI:** 234
   Republican Party **VI:** 246

election of 1896 **V:** 379; **VI:** 232; **VII:** 60, 65, 332
   Bryan, William Jennings **VI:** 37, 73
   Cleveland, Grover **VI:** 59
   Democratic Party **VI:** 78
   Free-Silver movement **VI:** 105
   McKinley, William **VI:** 189
   People's Party **VI:** 223
   Republican Party **VI:** 247
   Schurz, Carl **VI:** 257
   Simpson, Jerry **VI:** 262
   Socialist Labor Party **VI:** 268
election of 1900 **VI:** 37, 73, 190, 232–233, 269; **VII:** 80, 266, 355c
election of 1904 **VII:** 80, 356c
election of 1908 **VI:** 37, 73; **VII:** 80, 303, 357c
election of 1912 **VI:** 269; **VII:** 358c; **VIII:** 312
   Cannon, Joseph **VII:** 42
   Democratic Party **VII:** 65–66
   elections **VII:** 80
   Federal Trade Commission Act **VII:** 94
   La Follette, Robert **VII:** 155
   Progressive Party **VII:** 236–237
   progressivism **VII:** 238
   Republican Party **VII:** 263
   Roosevelt, Theodore **VII:** 266
   Taft, William Howard **VII:** 304
   Wilson, Woodrow **VII:** 333
election of 1916 **VII:** 358c; **VIII:** 344
   Budget and Accounting Act **VII:** 36
   elections **VII:** 80
   Hughes, Charles Evans **VII:** 124
   Progressive Party **VII:** 237
   Republican Party **VII:** 263
   Wilson, Woodrow **VII:** 334
election of 1918 **VII:** 66
election of 1920 **VII:** 360c; **VIII:** 312
   Budget and Accounting Act **VII:** 36
   Coolidge, Calvin **VII:** 56–57
   Democratic Party **VII:** 66
   elections **VII:** 80–81
   Harding, Warren G. **VII:** 117–118
   radio **VII:** 254

Republican Party **VII:** 263
   socialism **VII:** 289
election of 1924 **VII:** 360c; **VIII:** 377
   Coolidge, Calvin **VII:** 57
   elections **VII:** 81
   progressivism **VII:** 238
   Republican Party **VII:** 263
election of 1928 **VII:** 66, 81, 287, 361c
   American Federation of Labor **VIII:** 14
   Catholics **VIII:** 53
   Congress **VIII:** 66
   Hoover presidency **VIII:** 153
   Perkins, Frances **VIII:** 265
   politics in the Roosevelt era **VIII:** 270, 271, 272t
   religion **VIII:** 303
   Republican Party **VIII:** 304
   Roosevelt, Franklin D. **VIII:** 312
election of 1930 **VIII:** 66, 305, 312
election of 1932 **VII:** 53, 67, 287–288; **VIII: 96–97**, 406c
   Agricultural Adjustment Act **VIII:** 5
   American Federation of Labor **VIII:** 14
   Baruch, Bernard M. **VIII:** 34
   Berle, Adolf A., Jr. **VIII:** 35
   Bonus Army **VIII:** 39
   Borah, William E. **VIII:** 40
   Communists **VIII:** 65
   Congress **VIII:** 66
   conservatism **VIII:** 71
   conservative coalition **VIII:** 73
   Coughlin, Father Charles E. **VIII:** 75
   Democratic Party **VIII:** 80
   economy **VIII:** 91
   Farley, James A. **VIII:** 111
   Flynn, Edward J. **VIII:** 122
   Garner, John Nance **VIII:** 129
   German Americans **VIII:** 131
   Great Depression **VIII:** 138
   Harriman, Averell **VIII:** 143
   Hillman, Sidney **VIII:** 145
   Hoover, Herbert **VIII:** 151, 152

Hoover presidency **VIII:** 156
Hull, Cordell **VIII:** 159
Ickes, Harold L. **VIII:** 161
Kennedy, Joseph P. **VIII:** 175
La Follette, Robert M., Jr. **VIII:** 182
La Guardia, Fiorello **VIII:** 182
Lewis, John L. **VIII:** 185
Manchuria **VIII:** 199
Moley, Raymond C. **VIII:** 216
New Deal **VIII:** 239–240
Perkins, Frances **VIII:** 265
politics in the Roosevelt era **VIII:** 270, 271, 272*t*
relief **VIII:** 299–300
Relief and Reconstruction Act **VIII:** 302
Republican Party **VIII:** 305
Roosevelt, Eleanor **VIII:** 310
Roosevelt, Franklin D. **VIII:** 312
socialists **VIII:** 327
Thomas, Norman **VIII:** 358
Tugwell, Rexford G. **VIII:** 361
TVA **VIII:** 356
Wagner, Robert F. **VIII:** 372
Wallace, Henry A. **VIII:** 373
Willkie, Wendell L. **VIII:** 378
election of 1934 **VIII:** 67, 81, 305
election of 1936 **VIII: 97,** 407*c*
  American Federation of Labor **VIII:** 14
  American Liberty League **VIII:** 15
  Black Cabinet **VIII:** 38
  Borah, William E. **VIII:** 40
  CIO **VIII:** 70
  Communists **VIII:** 65
  Congress **VIII:** 67
  conservatism **VIII:** 72
  conservative coalition **VIII:** 73
  court-packing plan **VIII:** 76
  Democratic Party **VIII:** 81
  election of 1932 **VIII:** 96
  election of 1940 **VIII:** 98
  Farley, James A. **VIII:** 111
  German Americans **VIII:** 131

Ickes, Harold L. **VIII:** 161
Jews **VIII:** 173
labor **VIII:** 180
La Follette, Robert M., Jr. **VIII:** 182
Landon, Alfred M. **VIII:** 183
Lewis, John L. **VIII:** 186
Long, Huey P. **VIII:** 195
Luce, Henry R. **VIII:** 196
NAACP **VIII:** 227
New Deal **VIII:** 242
Norris, George W. **VIII:** 249
politics in the Roosevelt era **VIII:** 270, 272*t*
Popular Front **VIII:** 276
public opinion polls **VIII:** 284
Republican Party **VIII:** 305
Roosevelt, Franklin D. **VIII:** 313
socialists **VIII:** 327
South **VIII:** 331
Supreme Court **VIII:** 346
Thomas, Norman **VIII:** 358
Townsend, Francis E. **VIII:** 359
Union Party **VIII:** 365
Willkie, Wendell L. **VIII:** 379
election of 1938
  conservatism **VIII:** 72
  conservative coalition **VIII:** 74
  election of 1940 **VIII:** 98
  Flynn, Edward J. **VIII:** 122
  Hopkins, Harry **VIII:** 156
  Republican Party **VIII:** 306
  Roosevelt, Franklin D. **VIII:** 313
election of 1940 **VIII: 97,** 409*c*
  Byrnes, James F. **VIII:** 48
  CIO **VIII:** 70
  Congress **VIII:** 68
  Democratic Party **VIII:** 82
  destroyers-for-bases deal **VIII:** 82, 83
  enemy aliens **VIII:** 103
  Farley, James A. **VIII:** 111
  Flynn, Edward J. **VIII:** 122
  German Americans **VIII:** 131
  Hopkins, Harry **VIII:** 157
  isolationists **VIII:** 166
  Italian Americans **VIII:** 167

Jews **VIII:** 173
Johnson, Hugh S. **VIII:** 174
Kennedy, Joseph P. **VIII:** 176
labor **VIII:** 181
La Guardia, Fiorello **VIII:** 182
Lewis, John L. **VIII:** 186
Luce, Henry R. **VIII:** 196
Polish Americans **VIII:** 269
politics in the Roosevelt era **VIII:** 271, 272*t*
public opinion polls **VIII:** 284
Republican Party **VIII:** 306
Roosevelt, Franklin D. **VIII:** 314
Selective Service **VIII:** 322
socialists **VIII:** 327
Taft, Robert A. **VIII:** 349
Wallace, Henry A. **VIII:** 373
Wheeler, Burton K. **VIII:** 378
Willkie, Wendell L. **VIII:** 378
World War II home front **VIII:** 396
election of 1942 **VIII:** 254, 271–272, 396
election of 1944 **VIII: 97–98,** 410*c*
  Congress **VIII:** 68
  Democratic Party **VIII:** 82
  Economic Bill of Rights **VIII:** 90
  Farley, James A. **VIII:** 111
  Flynn, Edward J. **VIII:** 122
  Full Employment Bill **VIII:** 128
  Hillman, Sidney **VIII:** 146
  labor **VIII:** 181
  OWI **VIII:** 258
  politics in the Roosevelt era **VIII:** 272–273, 272*t*
  public opinion polls **VIII:** 284
  Republican Party **VIII:** 306
  Roosevelt, Franklin D. **VIII:** 314
  socialists **VIII:** 327
  South **VIII:** 332
  Wallace, Henry A. **VIII:** 373
  Willkie, Wendell L. **VIII:** 379

World War II home front **VIII:** 396
Zionism **VIII:** 403
election of 1946 **VIII:** 255
election of 1948 **VIII:** 349, 373–374
election of 1952 **VIII:** 311, 349
election of 1956 **VIII:** 311
election of 1960 **VIII:** 197, 311
elections **V: 109–111; VII:** 69–70, **79–82,** 229, 230; **IX: 94–97,** 96*m*, 330*c*–332*c*; **X: 101–103,** *102*, 327*c*–329*c*. *See also* political campaigns; *specific candidates; specific years*
  abortion **X:** 3
  Agnew, Spiro T. **X:** 14
  amnesty, acts of **V:** 8
  Anderson, John B. **X:** 21
  Bush, George H. W. **X:** 44–46
  Bush, George W. **X:** 47–48
  campaign finance **X:** 53–54
  Carter, James Earl, Jr. **X:** 58, 59
  censorship **X:** 60
  Christian Coalition **X:** 62
  Civil Rights Act of 1964 **IX:** 56
  Clinton, William **X:** 66, 68
  computers **IX:** 64
  conduct of **VI:** 66, **94–95**
  conservative movement **X:** 79, 80
  Democratic Party **V:** 93; **IX:** 79
  Dole, Robert **X:** 90
  Dukakis, Michael **X:** 91
  Eagleton, Thomas F. **X:** 93
  economy **X:** 96
  Ferraro, Geraldine A. **X:** 117
  Fifteenth Amendment **V:** 124
  Ford, Gerald R. **X:** 119
  Gallup Polls **IX:** 118
  gender gap **X:** 128
  Gore, Albert, Jr. **X:** 133, 134
  governors **V:** 152–153
  House of Representatives **X:** 144
  immigration **V:** 176; **X:** 148
  Jackson, Jesse L. **X:** 160
  journalism **IX:** 153
  Judicial Watch **X:** 162
  Kemp, Jack F. **X:** 163
  Kissinger, Henry A. **X:** 165
  Libertarian Party **X:** 176, 177

elections (continued)
McGovern, George Stanley **X:** 184
Mitchell, George **X:** 194, 195
Mondale, Walter F. **X:** 196
neoconservatism **X:** 216
Nixon, Richard M. **X:** 219, 220
NRA **X:** 213
nuclear freeze movement **X:** 224
O'Connor, Sandra Day **X:** 226
political parties **X:** 237, 238
post–Civil War **V:** 110–111
Quayle, J. Danforth **X:** 253
Reagan, Ronald W. **X:** 259, 260
Reform Party **X:** 263, 264
Rehnquist, William H. **X:** 265
Republican Party **IX:** 257–258
Sunbelt **X:** 290
Supreme Court **X:** 291
television **IX:** 297
veterans, Civil War **V:** 379
Wallace, George C. **X:** 314
elective system of college education **VI:** 93
electoral college **IV:** 49, 106
African Americans **III:** 6
election of 1800 **III:** 116
elections **X:** 101–103
Gore, Albert, Jr. **X:** 133, 134
Hamilton, Alexander **III:** 162
Jefferson, Thomas **III:** 185
Libertarian Party **X:** 176
Morris, Gouverneur **III:** 247
political parties **X:** 238
Electoral Commission Act of 1877 **V:** 157; **VI:** 231, 289
Electoral Count Act of 1887 **VI:** 232, 326c
electoral districts **X:** 291
electricity **II:** 194, 277, 331; **VI:** 326c; **VII:** 82, **82–83**; **IX:** 120
architecture **VII:** 16
cities and urban life **VII:** 50
GE **VII:** 107
industrial revolution, second **VI:** 145–147
invention and technology **VII:** 132–133
inventions and technology **VI:** 148

oil industry **VII:** 218
Philadelphia Centennial Exposition **VI:** 224
Tesla, Nikola **VI:** 285
urban transportation **VII:** 317, *318*
work, household **VII:** 342
Electricity Building (Chicago World's Fair) **VI:** *148*
electricity cooperatives **VIII:** 316
electric power **IV:** 308; **VIII:** 284–285, 315–316
electrification **VIII:** 353
electroconvulsive therapy (ECT) **X:** 190
electromagnetism **IV:** 307, 308
Electronic Data Systems Corporation (EDS) **X:** 234
electronic equipment **X:** 273
electronic magazines **X:** 187
Electronic Numerical Integrator and Calculator (ENIAC) **IX:** 63, 64, **97–98**, 269, 295, 329c; **X:** 72
Electronic Privacy Information Center **X:** 245
electronics **IX:** 330c
electronic surveillance **X:** 290
Elementary and Secondary Education Act (ESEA) of 1965 **IX:** 91, **98–99**, 127, 245–246, 334c
elementary school **VIII:** 93
Elements of Military Art and Science (Halleck) **V:** 162
elephant (Republican symbol) **V:** 247
elevated railroads **VI:** 146, 292, 323c
elevators **IV:** 82, 307; **VI:** 149, 326c
Eleventh Amendment **III:** 182, 338, 396c; **IV:** 330
Eli Lilly & Company **X:** 191
Eliot, Charles **VII:** 179
Eliot, Charles William **VI:** 93
Eliot, John **II:** 103, **106–107**, 214, 246, 295–296
Eliot, T. S. **VII:** 360c; **IX:** 183
Elizabeth I, queen of England **I:** **119–122**, *120*, 385c, 387c, 388c; **II:** 39, 231–232, 264, 284, 301
Anglo-Normans **I:** 11
Camden, William **I:** 52
Castile **I:** 64
Church of England **I:** 74
Company of Cathay **I:** 83
De La Warr, Lord **I:** 103
Drake, Sir Francis **I:** 111, 112

East India Company **I:** 117
Frobisher, Martin **I:** 133
Gilbert, Sir Humphrey **I:** 141
Hawkins, Sir John **I:** 156
Henry IV (Henry of Navarre) **I:** 158
Henry VII **I:** 159
Henry VIII **I:** 160
James I **I:** 187
Lane, Ralph **I:** 197
Levant Company **I:** 206
London **I:** 208
Mary I **I:** 224
Privy Council **I:** 295
Puritans **I:** 298
Ralegh, Sir Walter **I:** 303
Reformation **I:** 309
Roanoke **I:** 313
Shakespeare, William **I:** 324
Spanish Armada **I:** 333
Tempest, The **I:** 343
Walsingham, Sir Frances **I:** 371–372
Elizabethan conquest of Ireland **I:** 141
Elizabeth Settlement **I:** 74
El Jaleo (Sargent) **VI:** 256
Elkins Act **VII:** **83–84**, 170, 266, 356c
Ellicott, Joseph **III:** 167
Ellington, Edward Kennedy "Duke" **VII:** 137, 195; **VIII:** 3, **99–100**, *100*, 223
Elliot, Missy **X:** 203
Elliot, Robert Brown **V:** 111
Ellis, Henry **II:** 138
Ellis, Henry Havelock **VII:** **84**
birth control **VII:** 29
Freud, Sigmund **VII:** 102
sexuality **VII:** 283
women's status and rights **VII:** 340
Ellis Island **VI:** 138, 140; **VII:** *125*
Ellison, Ralph **V:** 195; **IX:** 5, 182, 243, 331c
Ellsberg, Daniel **X:** 149, 233, 315
Ellsworth, Elmer Ephraim **V:** 403
Ellsworth, Oliver
Judiciary Act of 1789 **III:** 192
Judiciary Act of 1801 **III:** 193
Marshall, John **III:** 235
Supreme Court **III:** 338
Ellsworth, Solomon, Jr. **IV:** 308
El Mansur **I:** 332
El Mirador **I:** 226, 349

Elmslie, George Grant **VI:** 280
El Paso **IV:** 337
El Portete **I:** 382
El Salvador **I:** 7
cold war (end of) **X:** 71
immigration **X:** 149
Latin America **X:** 173
Reagan, Ronald W. **X:** 260
United Nations **X:** 307
El-Shabaz, El-Hajj Malik. *See* Malcolm X
El Tajín culture **I:** 366
Ely, Richard T. **VI:** 267
Elyot, Hugh **I:** 35
e-mail **X:** 152, 274
emancipation **V:** **111–114**, *112*, 407c
AASS **IV:** 13
abolition/abolition movement **II:** 1, 2; **V:** 1, 3
Benjamin, Judah P. **V:** 28
Black Codes **V:** 29
Brown, Joseph **V:** 39
Chase, Salmon P. **V:** 56
Civil War **V:** 66–67
Colored National Labor Union **V:** 69
conscription **V:** 79
contrabands **V:** 80, 81
Copperheads **V:** 82
Democratic Party **V:** 94
Douglass, Frederick **V:** 100
Eaton, John, Jr. **V:** 104
elections **V:** 109
Emancipation Proclamation **V:** 114–115, 424
Fort Mose **II:** 123
Freedman's Saving Bank **V:** 141–142
Frémont, Jessie Benton **IV:** 152
Frémont, John C. **IV:** 154
Garrison, William Lloyd **V:** 146
Genius of Universal Emancipation **IV:** 161
governors **V:** 153
Greeley, Horace **V:** 158
Hammon, Jupiter **II:** 154
immigration **V:** 176
Johnson, Andrew **V:** 178, 187
Johnson, Anthony **II:** 175
Joint Committee on the Conduct of War **V:** 191
Juneteenth **V:** 194–195
Kelley, William D. **V:** 198
Lincoln, Abraham **V:** 210–211
Louisiana **II:** 200

loyalty oaths **V:** 219
Maryland **II:** 211
McClellan, George B. **V:** 225
Mississippi River **V:** 236
Mount Vernon **II:** 237
New Orleans riot **V:** 252
New York City draft riots **V:** 254, 255
peace movements **V:** 266
race and racial conflict **IV:** 292; **V:** 288
Radical Republicans **V:** 288
Reconstruction **V:** 292
Republican Party **V:** 302
Stanton, Edwin M. **V:** 334
Stevens, Thaddeus **V:** 338
Sumner, Charles **V:** 343
tactics and strategy **V:** 347
Thirteenth Amendment **V:** 352–353
Virginia **II:** 384
Welles, Gideon **V:** 392
Women's National Loyal League **V:** 396, 397
Emancipation Order of 1861 **V:** 406c
Emancipation Proclamation **IV:** 127; **V: 114–115,** 407c, 424
African-American regiments **V:** 4
Antietam, Battle of **V:** 11
Confiscation Acts **V:** 78
Copperheads **V:** 82
emancipation **V:** 111, 113
54th Massachusetts Regiment **V:** 125
foreign policy **V:** 132
governors **V:** 153
homefront **V:** 169
immigration **V:** 176
Juneteenth **V:** 194
Lincoln, Abraham **V:** 210–211
McClellan, George B. **V:** 226
New York City draft riots **V:** 254
prisons **V:** 282
race and racial conflict **V:** 288
Reconstruction **V:** 292
Sherman, William T. **V:** 321
slavery **V:** 330
Thirteenth Amendment **V:** 353
Union army **V:** 367
"Emancipation Proclamation of Preborn Children" (Reagan) **X:** 3–4

Emancipator, The
American Anti-Slavery Society **IV:** 14, 15
Genius of Universal Emancipation **IV:** 160
Liberty Party **IV:** 210
Tappan, Arthur and Lewis **IV:** 333
embargo **V:** 131–132
Embargo Act **III:** 117, 397c, 398c
Embargo Act of 1807 **IV:** 141, 170, 253
embargo of 1807 **III:** *117,* **117–118,** 397c
architecture **III:** 20
Bonaparte, Napoleon **III:** 42
Chesapeake-Leopard affair **III:** 67
economy **III:** 113
Federalist Party **III:** 126
foreign affairs **III:** 131
Gallatin, Albert **III:** 147
Girard, Stephen **III:** 153
industrial revolution **III:** 177
Jefferson, Thomas **III:** 186
Macon, Nathaniel **III:** 226
Macon's Bill No. 2 **III:** 226
Non-Importation Act **III:** 259
Non-Intercourse Act **III:** 259
Orders in Council **III:** 267
population trends **III:** 283
states' rights **III:** 333
Story, Joseph **III:** 334
tariffs **III:** 342
trade **III:** 351
Washington Benevolent Societies **III:** 369
Wilkinson, James **III:** 379
embassies, U.S. **VI:** 104
Emergency Banking Act of 1933 **VIII: 100–101,** *101,* 406c
Banking Act of 1933 **VIII:** 33
Eccles, Marriner S. **VIII:** 89
FDIC **VIII:** 117
RFC **VIII:** 294
Emergency Detention Act **IX:** 144
Emergency Fleet Corporation **VII:** 279
Emergency Highway Energy Conservation Act of 1974 **X:** 112
Emergency Maternity and Infant Care program (EMIC) **VIII:** 56–57

Emergency Price Control Act **VIII:** 254, 371, 409c
Emergency Relief Appropriation Act (ERAA) **VIII: 101–102,** 407c
Congress **VIII:** 67
FAP **VIII:** 114
liberalism **VIII:** 188
RA **VIII:** 307
REA **VIII:** 316
relief **VIII:** 301
Second New Deal **VIII:** 321
Social Security Act **VIII:** 328
WPA **VIII:** 386
Emerson, Edward **V:** 125
Emerson, Irene **V:** 101
Emerson, John **V:** 101
Emerson, Ralph Waldo **IV: 126–127,** *127,* 377c; **V:** 38, 124, 393; **VI:** 172; **VII:** 55
art **IV:** 26
Brook Farm **IV:** 58
Fuller, Margaret **IV:** 155
Hale, Sarah Josepha **IV:** 168
journalism **IV:** 197
literature **IV:** 212
lyceum movement **IV:** 215
religion **IV:** 298, 299
Thoreau, Henry David **IV:** 342
transcendental movement **IV:** 345
EMIC **VIII:** 56–57
Emigrant Aid Society. *See* Massachusetts Emigrant Aid Society
Emigrant's Guide to Oregon and California (Hastings) **IV:** 114
emigrationists. *See* Liberia
Emilio, Luis F. **V:** 125
Emily's List **X:** 116
eminent domain **X:** 250
emissions, automobile **IX:** 26
Emmett, Daniel Decatur **V:** 244
Emperor Jones, The (O'Neill) **VII:** 360c
emphysema **X:** 303
Empire State Building **VIII:** 22, 405c
employment **IV:** 180; **V: 115–117; VIII:** 4, 135t, 281t; **IX:** 334c; **X:** 327c. *See also* unemployment
affirmative action **X:** 8–9
African-American movement **IX:** 4
African Americans **VI:** 6
agriculture **X:** 14

Asian Americans **X:** 28
baby boomers **X:** 33
business **IX:** 44–46
cities and urban life **VI:** 53
civil service reform **VI:** 56–57
Civil War **V:** 66
Colored National Labor Union **V:** 68–69
Council of Economic Advisors **IX:** 70–71
Economic Opportunity Act of 1964 **IX:** 87–88
education **IX:** 92
emancipation **V:** 113
Employment Act of 1946 **IX:** 99–100
Equal Employment Opportunity Commission **IX:** 103
family life **X:** 110
Federal Employee Loyalty Program **IX:** 109–110
feminism **X:** 114, 115
FSA **X:** 110
Griggs et al. v. Duke Power Company **X:** 135–136
immigration **V:** 177; **X:** 147–148
IRCA **X:** 149
Job Corps **IX:** 149–150
labor **IX:** 169–171; **X:** 171
liberalism **X:** 175
Native Americans **V:** 249
New Frontier **IX:** 230
newspapers **VI:** 211, 212
population trends **VI:** 226
President's Commission on the Status of Women **IX:** 246
Prohibition Party **VI:** 234
prostitution **V:** 283–284
Puerto Ricans **IX:** 251
Ray, Charlotte **V:** 291
service sector **IX:** 272
Supreme Court **X:** 291
Union League **V:** 368
Urban League **IX:** 305
War on Poverty **IX:** 313
Women's Equity Action League **IX:** 323
women's rights and status **IX:** 324–325; **X:** 320
Employment Act of 1946 **IX:** 70–71, 88, **99–100,** 329c
Economic Bill of Rights **VIII:** 90
Full Employment Bill **VIII:** 128
Keynesianism **VIII:** 177
Wagner, Robert F. **VIII:** 373

employment contracts **V:** 29
Employment Division v. Smith (1990) **X:** 266
Empower America **X:** 163
"empresarios"
   Alamo, The **IV:** 12
   Austin, Stephen F. **IV:** 36
   Texas **IV:** 338
   Texas Revolution **IV:** 340
Empress of China **III:** 67
encomienda(s) **I: 122; II:** 94
   Aguilar, Francisco de **I:** 4
   Aguilar, Gerónimo (Jerónimo) de **I:** 5
   Charles V **I:** 69
   Columbus, Bartholomew **I:** 79
   conquistadores **I:** 84
   corregidores **I:** 90–91
   Cortés, Hernán **I:** 91, 94
   Cuba **I:** 98
   Ferdinand and Isabella **I:** 128
   haciendas **I:** 150
   Las Casas, Bartolomé de **I:** 198–200
   Mendoza, Antonio de **I:** 231
   New Spain **I:** 258
   Velázquez, Diego de **I:** 364
   Zumárraga, Juan de **I:** 382
encyclicals **VII:** 260
encyclopedias **II:** 177
Endangered Species Act of 1973 **X:** 77, 210, 250, 325c
Endara Galimany, Guillermo **X:** 231
Endeavor (space shuttle) **X:** 282
Endecott, John **II: 107,** 212, 216
end of the world (apocalypse) **I:** 81
endorsements, product **VII:** 295
Endreyas, Gabra **I:** 124
enemy aliens **VIII: 102–103**
   civil liberties **VIII:** 61
   Executive Order 9066 **VIII:** 106–107
   German Americans **VIII:** 130
   Italian Americans **VIII:** 167
   Smith Act **VIII:** 326–327
energy crisis **X: 103–104,** 331c
   business **X:** 49
   Carter, James Earl, Jr. **X:** 58
   economy **X:** 94
   Energy, U.S. Department of **X:** 103
   Ford, Gerald R. **X:** 121
   foreign policy **X:** 122

Energy Department (DOE) **X:** 191
   Carter, James Earl, Jr. **X:** 58
   creation of **X: 103**
   energy crisis **X:** 104
   Human Genome Project **X:** 145–146
energy issues
   automobile industry **X:** 31, 32
   conservation, environmentalism, and environmental policy **X:** 78
   Mexico **X:** 193
Energy Policy Office **X:** 103
Energy Reorganization Act of 1974 **IX:** 24
Energy Research and Development Administration **IX:** 24; **X:** 103
Enforcement Acts **V: 117; VI:** 94
   Ku Klux Klan **V:** 199–200
   Ku Klux Klan Act **V:** 201
   Rainey, Joseph H. **V:** 291
   Reconstruction **V:** 294
   redemption **V:** 296
   United States v. Cruikshank **V:** 375, 376
enforcement clause **V:** 353
enfranchisement **II:** 198. *See also* suffrage
Engel, George **VI:** 127
Engels, Friedrich **V:** 223; **VII:** 146, 229; **IX:** 61
Engel v. Vitale (1962) **IX: 100–101,** 257, 316, 333c
engineering **VI:** 85, 194; **VIII:** 354
Engineering Corps, Union army. *See* Army Corps of Engineers
England **I:** 385c, 387c, 388c; **VI:** 157, 219; **X:** 127, 132. *See also* Great Britain
   Acadia **I:** 2–3
   Acadians **II:** 2
   agriculture **II:** 11
   Andros, Sir Edmund **II:** 19
   Anglican Church **II:** 19
   Anglo-Normans **I:** 10–11
   Battel, Andrew **I:** 27
   black legend **I:** 30–31
   Bristol **I:** 35
   British Empire **II:** 41
   Burgesses, House of **II:** 45
   Castile **I:** 64
   Church of England **I:** 73–74
   convict labor **II:** 71

Cotton, John **II:** 73
crowd action **II:** 77
Drake, Sir Francis **I:** 110–113
Dudley, Joseph **II:** 95
East India Company **I:** 117
economy **II:** 101
Elizabeth I **I:** 119–121
feudalism **I:** 130
fishing **II:** 118
Foxe's *Book of Martyrs* **I:** 132
Gates, Sir Thomas **II:** 135
Henry VII **I:** 159
Henry VIII **I:** 159–160
Hudson, Henry **II:** 158–159
Hudson's Bay Company **II:** 159
Jamaica **I:** 187
James I **I:** 187–188
Jews (Judaism) **I:** 192
Kieft, Willem **II:** 182
land **II:** 191
Las Casas, Bartolomé de **I:** 198
Leisler's Rebellion **II:** 192, 193
London **I:** 208
Maine **II:** 203
Manteo **I:** 220
Mary I **I:** 223–224
monarchy, British **II:** 232
Native Americans **II:** 246
Newport, Christopher **II:** 258
New York City **II:** 263
Parliament **I:** 277
Philip II **I:** 282
Picts **I:** 282
population trends **I:** 290
privateering **II:** 299
Privy Council **I:** 295
Puritans **I:** 298–299
Reformation **I:** 309
Rolfe, John **II:** 322
slavery **I:** 326; **II:** 339
slave trade **II:** 343
Spanish Armada **I:** 333–335
Stuyvesant, Peter **II:** 363
trade and shipping **II:** 375, 376
Wanchese **I:** 372
wolves **II:** 405
English . . . *See also* under British . . .
English Channel **VIII:** 247
English Civil War **II: 107–108,** 418c
   British Empire **II:** 43
   English immigrants **II:** 108

Maryland **II:** 209
Pennsylvania **II:** 275
Roman Catholics **II:** 323
English Cod, An (Chase) **VI:** 49
English colonies/colonization
   Acadia **I:** 3
   Akan **I:** 5
   Anglo-Normans **I:** 11
   Barlowe, Arthur **I:** 26
   Bermuda **I:** 29
   Bermuda Company **I:** 29–30
   Canonicus **II:** 51
   class **II:** 62, 63
   clothing **II:** 64
   crime and punishment **II:** 74
   Dare, Virginia **II:** 82
   Delaware **II:** 86–88
   De La Warr, Lord **I:** 103–104
   disease **II:** 90
   Dominion of New England **II:** 94–95
   Elizabeth I **I:** 121
   Gilbert, Sir Humphrey **I:** 141–142
   Hakluyt, Richard, the Elder **I:** 150–151
   Hakluyt, Richard, the Younger **I:** 151–153
   headright **I:** 157
   indentured servitude **II:** 163
   Iroquois **II:** 169
   Jamestown **II:** 171–173
   King Philip's War **II:** 183–184
   King's College **II:** 184
   King William's War **II:** 185
   Maine **II:** 203
   Maryland **II:** 209–211
   Massachusetts **II:** 212
   Miantonomo **II:** 223–224
   monarchy, British **II:** 232
   Montserrat **I:** 243
   Narragansett **II:** 241
   Native Americans **II:** 243–244
   Nevis **I:** 254
   New Jersey **II:** 253
   New Netherland **II:** 257
   New York **II:** 261–262
   Peckham, Sir George **I:** 279
   Powhatan **I:** 292
   Purchas, Samuel **I:** 297
   Ralegh, Sir Walter **I:** 303–304
   Reformation **I:** 310
   Roanoke **I:** 313–314

St. Mary's City **II:** 328
Sandys, Sir Edwin **I:** 318
Savannah **II:** 329
slavery **II:** 339, 340, 342
smallpox **II:** 345
South Carolina **II:** 353
Spanish colonies **II:** 356
Virginia Company of
    London **II:** 385, 387
Westo **II:** 394
English conquest **II:** 56,
    260–261
English exploration **II:** 115
    Bristol **I:** 35
    Cabot, John **I:** 41–42
    Cabot, Sebastian **I:** 42–43
    Frobisher, Martin **I:**
        133–134
    Ingram, David **I:** 177
    Northeast Passage **I:** 265
    Northwest Passage **I:** 266
"English flies" **II:** 122
English immigrants **II:**
    108–109; IV: 81, 177
    architecture **II:** 23
    Charleston **II:** 56
    gender **II:** 136
    Georgia **II:** 137–138
    government, British
        American **II:** 145
    housing **II:** 157
    indentured servitude **II:**
        164
    Jamestown **II:** 172
    Kieft, Willem **II:** 182
    labor **II:** 187, 188
    limners **II:** 194
    Massachusetts **II:** 212
    Montour, Andrew **II:** 233
    New Jersey **II:** 254
    Philadelphia **II:** 281
    redemptioners **II:** 313
    Virginia **II:** 382, 385
    women's status and rights
        II: 407
English missions **II:** 246
English Reformation **II:** 301
English settlers
    captivity **II:** 51
    Cherokee **II:** 58
    Chesapeake Bay **II:** 58
    Connecticut **II:** 68
    New Netherland **II:** 256,
        257
    New York **II:** 260
    Opechancanough **II:** 268
    Penn, William **II:** 273
    Pequot War **II:** 279–280
    population trends **II:** 291
    Puritans **II:** 304–306
    technology **II:** 369
    Tuscarora War **II:** 379

Virginia **II:** 382
Wingina **II:** 401
women's status and rights
    II: 406, 407
English traders
    Brims **II:** 41
    La Demoiselle **II:** 191
    New Netherland **II:** 255
    Pequot **II:** 278
    Royal African Company **II:**
        325
engraving **I:** 102–103; **II:** 96
"engrossing" **II:** 389
ENIAC. *See* Electronic
    Numerical Integrator and
    Calculator
Enigma machine **VIII:** 64
Enlightenment, American **II:**
    109–110, 179, 194, 276–278,
    282, 330
Enlightenment, the **II:** 316,
    330; **IV:** 121, 277
    Common Sense (Paine)
        III: 78
    Crèvecoeur, J. Hector St.
        John de **III:** 98
    deism **III:** 103
    education **III:** 115
    frontier **III:** 140–141
    George III, king of Great
        Britain **III:** 151
    literature **III:** 214
    poverty **III:** 285
    prisons **III:** 286
    religion **III:** 298
    Unitarianism **III:** 355
    Witherspoon, John **III:**
        380
enlisted men **V:** 368
Enola Gay **VIII:** 29, 146
Enovid **IX:** 242
*Enquiring into the Effects of
    Public Punishments upon
    Criminals and upon Society*
    (Rush) **IV:** 278
Enriquez de Arana, Beatriz **I:**
    80
enrollment, school **VII:** 76, 351;
    VIII: 94
Enrollment Act **V:** 79, 364. *See
    also* Conscription Act of
    1863
Enron Corp. **X:** 96, 331*c*
entail. *See* primogeniture and
    entail
Enterprise, USS **VIII:** 285
*Enterprise for the Americas
    Initiative* **X:** 173
"Entertainer, The" (Joplin) **VII:**
    141, 355*c*
entertainment **IV:** 82, 249–251;
    VI: 95–98, 97, 325*c*; **VII:**

84–87, *86. See* popular
culture; sports and recreation
    advertising **X:** 6
    assassinations **X:** 31
    Barnum, Phineas T. **VI:**
        20–21
    bicycling, 1870–1900 **VI:**
        27–28
    cities and urban life **VIII:**
        59
    Cody, William Frederick
        VI: 59–60
    dime novels **VI:** 80–81
    Houdini, Harry **VII:**
        123–124
    inventions and technology
        VI: 150
    jazz **VII:** 137
    literature **X:** 177
    media **X:** 184–187
    Monroe, Marilyn **IX:**
        209–210
    movie industry **VII:** 190
    movies **VIII:** 217–220; **IX:**
        210–214; **X:** 197–199
    music **VII:** 193–196
    popular culture. *See*
        popular culture
    Presley, Elvis **IX:** 247–248
    radio **VII:** 253–255
    recreation **X:** 262
    sexual revolution **X:** 277
    sports **VII:** 293–295
    sports and recreation **VI:**
        273–275
    television **IX:** 295–297; **X:**
        294–297
    theater **VI:** 285–287
    Tin Pan Alley **VII:** 308–309
    urban transportation **VII:**
        317–318
    USO **VIII:** 366–367
    vaudeville **VII:** 321–322
    Victorianism **VI:** 304
"Enthusiasm Described and
    Caution'd Against" (Chauncy)
    II: 57
entitlements **X:** 175, 176, 259
entrada(s) **I:** 11, 76, 85, 123,
    387*c*
entrepreneurs **VIII:** 46
entropy **VI:** 113
enumerated goods **II:** 3, 102
environment **II: 110–112,** *111;*
    III: 178; **IV:** 69, 163, 187
    Algonquin **II:** 17
    Caribbean **II:** 52
    disease **II:** 90
    food **II:** 121
    forests **II:** 122
    Great Plains Indians **II:**
        149

housing **II:** 157
Inuit **II:** 167
Jamestown **II:** 171
Kalm, Peter **II:** 181
Lining, John **II:** 194
marriage and family life **II:**
    206
Miantonomo **II:** 224
Mittelberger, Gottlieb **II:**
    231
Northwest Coast Indians
    II: 265
religion, Native American
    II: 317
society, British American
    II: 350
Spanish colonies **II:** 355
Virginia **II:** 384
environmentalism/environmenta
    l policy **VI:** 38, 65; **VIII:**
    63–64, 85–87, **103–104; IX:**
    101–102, 334*c;* **X: 76–78,**
    77, 210, 329*c,* 331*c. See also*
    conservation/conservationism
    automobile industry **IX:**
        25, 26; **X:** 31, 32
    Carson, Rachel **IX:** 48, 49
    Clinton, William **X:** 67
    conservative movement **X:**
        79
    energy crisis **X:** 104
    migration **IX:** 203
    Mitchell, George **X:** 195
    NAFTA **X:** 222
    National Outdoor
        Recreation Review
        Board **IX:** 224
    National Wilderness
        Preservation Act of 1964
        IX: 226–227
    NEPA **X:** 210
    OPEC **X:** 229
    property rights **X:** 249–251
    Reagan, Ronald W. **X:**
        260
    science **IX:** 270
    suburbanization **IX:** 288
    Watt, James G. **X:** 317
Environmental Protection
    Agency (EPA) **IX:** 48, 49,
    101; **X:** 323*c*
    conservation,
        environmentalism, and
        environmental policy **X:**
        77
    Nader, Ralph **X:** 205
    NEPA **X:** 210
    property rights **X:** 250
    Ruckelshaus, William D.
        X: 268, 269
Epidemic Intelligence Service
    IX: 198

epidemics. *See* disease and epidemics
Episcopal Church **III:** 189, 397c; **IV:** 297
Episcopalians/Episcopalianism **VI:** 241; **X:** 265
Epistle to the Clergy of the Southern States, An (S. Grimké) **IV:** 164
Epperson v. Arkansas **VII:** 278; **IX:** 257, 334c
Equal Access Act of 1984 **X:** **104–105**
Equal Credit Opportunity Act of 1974 **X:** 325c
Equal Employment Opportunity Act of 1972 **IX:** 99–100; **X:** 8, 256, 324c
Equal Employment Opportunity Commission (EEOC) **IX:** 57, **103**, 223, 325, 334c
  affirmative action **X:** 8
  feminism **X:** 114
  Griggs et al. v. Duke Power Company **X:** 136
  NOW **X:** 210, 211
Equality (Bellamy) **VI:** 26
equal opportunity employment **IX:** 330c
Equal Pay Act of 1963 **IX:** 103, 324, 333c; **X:** 114, 320
equal pay laws **VIII:** 386
Equal Rights **VII:** 253
Equal Rights Amendment (ERA) **VII:** **87–88**, 360c; **VIII:** 383, 386; **IX:** 223, 246, 324; **X:** **105–107**, 106m, 324c, 326c
  abortion **X:** 3
  amendments to the Constitution **X:** 19
  Brennan, William J. **X:** 41
  conservative movement **X:** 79
  feminism **X:** 114–116
  Ferraro, Geraldine A. **X:** 117
  Ford, Gerald R. **X:** 121
  marriage **X:** 183
  Moral Majority **X:** 197
  National Woman's Party **VII:** 205
  NAWSA **VII:** 198
  NOW **X:** 211
  Paul, Alice **VII:** 226
  pro-life and pro-choice movements **X:** 249
  Schlafly, Phyllis **X:** 272
  Steinem, Gloria **X:** 288
  women's rights and status **VII:** 340; **X:** 320–321

Equal Rights Party **VI:** 181, 319
Equatorial Guiana **I:** 127
Equiano, Olaudah **II:** 314, 340, 344, 427–429; **III:** *118*, **118–119**, 395c
Equitable Life Insurance Society **VII:** 142
E.R. (TV program) **X:** 295
ERA. *See* Equal Rights Amendment
ERAA. *See* Emergency Relief Appropriation Act
ERAmerica **X:** 106
Era of Good Feelings **III:** 104, 279; **IV:** 106, **127**, 239
ERAP. *See* Economic Research and Action Project
Erasmus **I:** 50, 322
Eratosthenes **I:** 79
Erdrich, Louise **X:** 177
Ericsson, John **V:** 237
Eric the Red **I:** 145, 263
Erie Canal **III:** 73–74; **IV:** **127–130**, *128*, 375c, 376c; **V:** 355
  agriculture **IV:** 11
  American System **IV:** 18
  Baltimore & Ohio Railroad (B&O) **IV:** 39
  Bonus Bill **IV:** 56
  canal era **IV:** 72–73, 73m
  economy **IV:** 118
  industrialization **IV:** 185
  internal improvements **IV:** 188
  migration **IV:** 235
  railroads **IV:** 293
  science and technology **IV:** 307
Erie Indians **II:** 31, 168, 169
Erie Railroad **V:** 408c
  corruption, political **VI:** 67
  Gould, Jay **VI:** 117, 118
  oil **VI:** 215
  railroads **VI:** 238
Erie School **IV:** 73, 129
Eriksson, Leif **I:** 42, 145, 263, 369, 385c
Erik the Red **I:** 385c
Erlanger, Abraham **VI:** 287
Erlanger Loan **V:** 28
Ervin, Sam, Jr. **X:** 75, 105, 106, 316, 324c
Escalante, Juan de **I:** **123**
Esch-Cummins Act of 1920 **VII:** 360c
Escobedo, Daniel **IX:** 103–104
Escobedo v. Illinois (1964) **IX:** **103–104**, 316, 334c
ESEA. *See* Elementary and Secondary Education Act of 1965

Esenore **II:** 401
Esigie **I:** 28
Eskimo **I:** 145; **II:** 166–167
Esopus Wars **II:** 99, 257
Espejo, Antonio de **I:** 167
espionage **II:** 130; **V:** **117–118**; **VIII:** **104–105**, *105*; **IX:** 330c
  Andrews's Raid **V:** 11
  anticommunism **IX:** 14, 15
  atomic bomb **VIII:** 29
  Boyd, Belle **V:** 34–35
  censorship **VIII:** 55
  Chambers, Whittaker **IX:** 50–51
  CIA **IX:** 50
  Communists **VIII:** 66
  enemy aliens **VIII:** 102
  FBI **VIII:** 115
  FCC **VIII:** 116
  German Americans **VIII:** 131
  Greenhow, Rose O'Neal **V:** 159
  habeas corpus, writ of **V:** 162
  Hiss, Alger **IX:** 133–134
  hydrogen bomb **IX:** 140
  intelligence **VIII:** 164
  Internal Security Act of 1950 **IX:** 143–144
  Manhattan Project **VIII:** 200
  Potsdam Conference **VIII:** 280
  refugees **VIII:** 299
  Rosenberg, Julius and Ethel **IX:** 264–265
  science and technology **V:** 309
  Soviet-American relations **VIII:** 334
  Stimson, Henry L. **VIII:** 340
  Tubman, Harriet **V:** 358
  Van Lew, Elizabeth **V:** 378
Espionage Act **VII:** **88–89**, 359c; **VIII:** 54; **IX:** 263
  Committee for Public Information **VII:** 52, 345
  conscription **VII:** 54
  Debs, Eugene V. **VII:** 65
  Fuel Administration **VII:** 102
  Greenwich Village **VII:** 115
  Haywood, "Big Bill" **VII:** 120
  IWW **VII:** 130
  labor movement **VII:** 153
  New Unionism **VII:** 213

Palmer, A. Mitchell **VII:** 221
  radicalism **VII:** 250
  Schenk v. United States **VII:** 274
  Sedition Act **VII:** 280
  socialism **VII:** 289
Espiritu Santo **I:** 318
ESPN **X:** 284
Es Saheli, Abou-Ishaq Ibrahim **I:** 220, 350
Essais (Michel de Montaigne) **I:** 54
Essay on Crimes and Punishments (Beccaria) **IV:** 277
Essay on the Education of Female Teachers, An (Beecher) **IV:** 120–121
Essex, earl of **I:** 103
Essex, John **II:** 82
Essex, USS **V:** **130**, 152
Essex Decision (1805) **III:** **119**, 397c; **IV:** 151
Estaing, Charles-Henri Theodat, comte d' **III:** **119–120**, 168, 308, 337
Esteban (slave) **IV:** 337
Esteban the Moor **I:** 256, 295–296
Estevan **I:** 383
Estevánico **I:** 38, 88
Estonia **VII:** 323; **IX:** 58, 105; **X:** 281
Esty, Mary **II:** 266
Etchemin. *See* Maliseet
ether **IV:** 230, 307; **V:** 230
Ethical Culture movement **VI:** 158
ethical issues. *See also* values
  Gingrich, Newton L. **X:** 130
  House of Representatives **X:** 144, 145
  Human Genome Project **X:** 146
  Meese, Edwin C. **X:** 191
  religion **X:** 265
  Senate **X:** 276
  Wright, James C., Jr. **X:** 322
Ethics and Public Policy Center **X:** 302
Ethics in Government Act of 1978 **X:** 150
Ethiopia **I:** 75, 104, **123–125**, 189, 293; **VIII:** **105–106**, 124, 239; **X:** 13, 24, 71, 124
ethnicity **VI:** 57, 243, 249
ethnic newspapers **VIII:** 243
ethnic organizations **VII:** **89**
ethnic politics **VIII:** 271

ethnic/racial diversity in British Colonies **III:** 174*m*
ethnic stereotyping **VI:** 97
ethnocentrism **II:** 112, **112–114,** 295
Ettor, Joseph **VII:** 95, 155
Eugene of Savoy, Prince **II:** 267
eugenics
anti-Semitism **VII:** 14
birth control **VII:** 30
race and racial conflict **VII:** 247–248
science **VII:** 276
women's status and rights **VII:** 339
Europe **V:** 16, 131, 132; **VII:** 127
Anglo-Normans **I:** 10–11
animals **II:** 20, 21
architecture **IV:** 27
art **II:** 24, 25; **IV:** 26
art and architecture **I:** 12, 13
Blaeu, Willem **I:** 31
bubonic plague **I:** 285
cabinet of curiosities **I:** 40
cacao **I:** 46
captivity **II:** 51
cities and urban life **VI:** 53
Cody, William Frederick **VI:** 60
coffee **I:** 75
cold war **IX:** 58
Columbian Exchange **I:** 76–78
consumption **II:** 71
corn (maize) **I:** 88
dance **II:** 82
defense policy **X:** 87
Delaware **II:** 87
diseases **I:** 106–107
Dutch East India Company **I:** 114–115
Enlightenment, American **II:** 109
feudalism **I:** 129–130
fishing **II:** 118
and foreign policy **IX:** **104–106**
Franciscans **I:** 132–133
fur trade **II:** 130, 131
GATT **X:** 129
gold **I:** 142
Great Awakening **II:** 147
Holy Roman Empire **I:** 165–166
horses **I:** 168
immigration **IX:** 141; **X:** 147
INF Treaty **X:** 151, 152
inquisition **I:** 178

invention and technology **I:** 179, 180
Islam **I:** 184, 185
jeremiads **II:** 173
Jesuits **I:** 189
Jews **II:** 174–175
Judaism **VI:** 158
literature **II:** 194, 195; **IV:** 211
Marshall Plan **IX:** 194–195
McCormick, Cyrus Hall **IV:** 225
Mercator, Gerhardus **I:** 232
Middle East **IX:** 201
Monroe Doctrine **IV:** 241
monsters **I:** 239–241
nativism **VI:** 209
NATO **IX:** 232–233; **X:** 223–224
New Hampshire **II:** 250
New York **II:** 262
population trends **I:** 290
printing press **I:** 294
science and technology **IV:** 307
Scott, Winfield **IV:** 309
Seven Years' War **II:** 332
slavery **I:** 326, 327; **II:** 338
slave trade **I:** 328; **II:** 343–344
smallpox **I:** 330
Soviet Union **IX:** 277
spinsters **II:** 360
Suleiman I **I:** 339
trade **VI:** 290
trade and shipping **II:** 376
wars of national liberation **IX:** 316
witchcraft **II:** 402
witches **I:** 373–374
European Americans **VI:** 57; **X:** 255–257
European colonialism **IV:** 242; **IX:** 3; **X:** 255–257
European immigrants **V:** 175; **VI:** 57; **VII:** 245, 248, 297; **X:** 255–257. *See also* eastern European immigrants; Southern European immigrants
European Laboratory for Particle Physics (CERN) **X:** 153, 274
European Recovery Program. *See* Marshall Plan
European Space Agency **X:** 283
European theater. *See* World War II European theater
European wars **IV:** 161, 241, 242

Eutaw Springs, Battle of **III:** **120–121,** 156, 232
euthanasia **X:** 264–265, 329*c*
Evacuation Day **III:** 282, 282
Evangelical Alliance **VI:** 279
evangelical Christians **X:** **107–108**
African Americans **X:** 11
amendments to the Constitution **X:** 19
Christian Coalition **X:** 61–62
conservative movement **X:** 79
education, home schooling **X:** 98
ERA **X:** 106
Moral Majority **X:** 197
religion **X:** 265
televangelism **X:** 293–294
Evangelicalism **VIII:** 303–304, 410*c*
Dow, Lorenzo **IV:** 115–116
Finney, Charles Grandison **IV:** 138–139
Liberty Party **IV:** 210
religion **IV:** 296, 297
Second Great Awakening **IV:** 311
Evangelical Lutheran Ministerium of Pennsylvania **II:** 201, 237
evangelical Protestantism **II:** 301, 314; **V:** 2, 299
Evangeline (Longfellow) **IV:** 378*c*
evangelists **VI:** 241; **VII:** 175–176, 301–302
Evans, John **V:** 405*c*
Evans, Linda **X:** 318
Evans, Oliver **IV:** 184, 292, 293
Evans, Walker **VIII:** 24, 268, 275
Evelin, George **II:** 209
"Evening Thought, An" (Hammon) **II:** 154
Eveready Hour (radio show) **VII:** 5
Everest, Wesley **VII:** 130
Everett, Edward **IV:** 15, 196; **VI:** 122
Evers, Medgar **IX:** 6, 253, 333*c*; **X:** 30
Evert, Chris **X:** 262
evolution/evolutionary theory **IV:** 291, 307; **VI:** xvi; **VII:** 355*c*, 361*c*
Darrow, Clarence **VII:** 62
Darwinism and religion **VI:** 75
Marsh, Othniel Charles **VI:** 188

pragmatism **VI:** 228–229
Rauschenbusch, Walter **VII:** 256
religion **VI:** 242; **VII:** 260, 261
science **VI:** 257; **VII:** 275
Scopes Trial **VII:** 277–278
Social Darwinism **VI:** 265
Sumner, William Graham **VI:** 280
Tanner, Benjamin Tucker **VI:** 283
E. W. Clark & Company **V:** 81
Ewe **I:** **125**
Ewedo, Oba **I:** 28
Ewell, Richard Stoddert **V:** **118–119**
Antietam, Battle of **V:** 13
Early, Jubal A. **V:** 103
Gettysburg, Battle of **V:** 147, 150
Longstreet, James **V:** 215
Shenandoah Valley: Jackson's campaign **V:** 316
Wilderness, Battle of the **V:** 395
Ewuare, Oba **I:** 28
Examination of the Constitution of the United States (Coxe) **III:** 96
Excavation (Willem de Kooning) **IX:** 20
excise levies **II:** 41
excise taxes **VIII:** 351
executions **VI:** 128, 196
auto-da-fé **I:** 16
Calvin, John **I:** 50
Caroline, Fort **I:** 57
Church of England **I:** 74
Cortés, Hernán **I:** 95
Cuauhtémoc **I:** 97
Elizabeth I **I:** 120
Henry VIII **I:** 160
Inca **I:** 177
inquisition **I:** 178
Mary I **I:** 224
Raleigh, Sir Walter **I:** 304
witches **I:** 374
executive branch **III:** 12; **VIII:** 281*t*
Executive Order 8802 **VIII:** **106,** 409*c*, 427–428
African Americans **VIII:** 4
civil rights **VIII:** 61, 62
enemy aliens **VIII:** 102
FEPC **VIII:** 109
MOWM **VIII:** 201–202
NAACP **VIII:** 228
race and racial conflict **VIII:** 289

Executive Order 8802
   (*continued*)
      Randolph, A. Philip **VIII:**
         291
      Roosevelt, Franklin D.
         VIII: 314
      World War II home front
         VIII: 394
Executive Order 8985 **VIII:** 55
Executive Order 9066 **VIII:**
   106–107, 409*c*, 428–429
      American Civil Liberties
         Union **VIII:** 13
      Asian Americans **VIII:** 26
      enemy aliens **VIII:** 103
      Executive Reorganization
         Act **VIII:** 107
      Japanese Americans,
         relocation of **VIII:** 171
      Korematsu v. United States
         VIII: 178
Executive Reorganization Act
   VIII: 107–108
      Congress **VIII:** 67
      FCA **VIII:** 112
      government **VIII:** 134
      liberalism **VIII:** 188
      New Deal **VIII:** 241
      NRPB **VIII:** 232
      presidency **VIII:** 281
      Third New Deal **VIII:**
         357
executive veto. *See* veto
   (presidential)
exemption clauses **V:** 79
Exodus **IV:** 297
Exodus of '79 **VI:** 325*c*
exoticism **VI:** 15
expansionism **VI:** 32, 104; **VII:**
   27
      Benton, Thomas Hart **IV:**
         49
      Bent's Fort **IV:** 51
      Democratic Party **IV:** 108
      economy **IV:** 117
      filibustering **V:** 126–127
      Florida **IV:** 140
      foreign policy **IV:** 141–142;
         V: 131, 133
      Hawaiian Islands **IV:**
         171–172
      Horseshoe Bend, Battle of
         IV: 173
      Houston, Sam **IV:** 175
      Kearny, Stephen Watts **IV:**
         200
      Manifest Destiny **IV:** 217,
         218
      Mexican-American War
         IV: 231–234
      Oregon Treaty of 1846 **IV:**
         270

Ostend Manifesto **V:**
   259–260
Perry, Matthew Calbraith
   IV: 279–280
Polk, James K. **IV:** 283
race and race relations **IV:**
   289, 291
Santa Fe Trail **IV:** 306
Seward, William H. **V:**
   315
Ex parte Endo **VIII:** 178, 410*c*
Ex parte Merryman **V:** 161
Ex parte Yarbrough (1884) **VI:**
   163
Expatriation Act **VII:** 41, 127,
   208, 357*c*
*Experiments and Observations
   on the Gastric Juice and
   Physiology of Digestion*
   (Beaumont) **IV:** 230
"expiring republicanism" **IV:**
   241
exploitation **VIII:** 56
exploration **II: 114–115; IV:**
   130–133, 132*m;* **VI:**
   227–228. *See also specific
   headings, e.g.:* English
   exploration
      Bartram, John **II:** 30
      Batts, Thomas **II:** 30–31
      Bering, Vitus Jonassen **II:**
         32
      captivity **II:** 51
      Castillo, Diego del **II:**
         54–55
      Champlain, Samuel de **II:**
         56
      Columbia River **IV:** 93
      Frémont, John C. **IV:**
         153–154
      French colonies **II:** 129
      Fuca, Juan de **II:** 130
      Hudson, Henry **II:**
         158–159
      Indians of the Desert
         Southwest **II:** 165–166
      Inuit **II:** 167
      Jolliet, Louis **II:** 178
      La Salle, René-Robert
         Cavelier, sieur de **II:**
         192
      Le Moyne, Jean-Baptiste,
         sieur de Bienville **II:**
         193
      literature **II:** 195
      Louisiana **II:** 199
      mariners **II:** 204
      Marquette, Jacques **II:**
         205–206
      Minuit, Peter **II:** 226
      Missouri Fur Company **IV:**
         239

monarchy, British **II:**
   231–232
Native Americans **II:** 246
New Hampshire **II:** 250
New Jersey **II:** 252
New York **II:** 259
Nicolet, Jean **II:** 263
Northwest Coast Indians
   II: 266
Pike, Zebulon
   Montgomery **IV:**
   281–282
Smith, Jedediah Strong **IV:**
   321–322
Texas **IV:** 337
White, Andrew **II:** 396
Explosion (Roy Lichtenstein)
   IX: 20
exports/exporting **III:** 8, 87,
   350; **VI:** 103, 150, 290, 291;
   VII: 73–75, 99, 298. *See also*
   trade, domestic and foreign
      agriculture **IV:** 9; **V:** 6; **X:**
         15
      Confederate States of
         America **V:** 76
      cotton culture **IV:** 97
      economy **VI:** 117, 118; **V:**
         104, 107
      homefront **V:** 168
      industrialization **IV:** 184
      Mexico **X:** 192
      slavery **V:** 329
      tariffs **V:** 348
      Union navy **V:** 368–369
Exquemelin, Alexander Olivier
   II: 285
*Extracts for the Virginia
   Charters, with Some Remarks
   upon Them* (Mason) **III:** 237
extremist organizations **IX:**
   334*c. See also* white
   supremacists
      Black Panthers **IX:** 38–39
      Ku Klux Klan **IX:** 166–167
      race and racial conflict **IX:**
         254
      Weathermen **IX:** 318–319
Exxon Valdez oil spill **X:** 327*c*
E-zines **X:** 187
Ezra Church, Battle of **V:** 20

F

FAA. *See* Federal Aviation
   Administration
Fabian Society **VI:** 316; **VII:** 84
"Fabius" **III:** 106
Fable, A (Faulkner) **VIII:** 113
FACE (Freedom of Access to
   Clinic Entrances Act) **X:** 4
Factor, Max **VII:** 58

factories **I:** 23, 65, 114, 117; **III:**
   20; **IV:** 10, 184–187; **V:** 60
Factory Act of 1819 **IV:** 273
factory girls **IV:** 185, 186
factory system, Indian. *See*
   Indian factory system
Fair, Laura **VI:** 115
Fair American, USS **IV:** 199
Fairbanks, Douglas **VII:** 87
Fairbanks, Richard **II:** 292
Fairbanks, Thaddeus **IV:** 308
Fairchild Semiconductor **IX:**
   65
Fair Deal **IX: 107–108,** 330*c*
      Democratic Party **IX:** 79
      New Deal **IX:** 229, 230
      Truman, Harry **IX:** 299,
         300
Fair Employment Practices
   Committee (FEPC) **VIII:**
   109–110; IX: 229, 305–306
      African Americans **VIII:** 4
      civil rights **VIII:** 61
      Executive Order 8802
         VIII: 106
      MOWM **VIII:** 201
      NAACP **VIII:** 228
      race and racial conflict
         VIII: 289
      Randolph, A. Philip **VIII:**
         291
      Roosevelt, Franklin D.
         VIII: 314
      White, Walter **VIII:** 378
      World War II home front
         VIII: 394
Fairfax, Lord **II:** 54
Fairfax Resolves **III:** 237
Fairgrounds Circle **I:** 252
Fair Housing Amendments Act
   of 1988 **X:** 327*c*
Fair Information practices **X:** 74
Fair Labor Standards Act
   (FLSA) **VII:** 3; **VIII:** 110,
   408*c*
      Black, Hugo L. **VIII:** 37
      children **VIII:** 56
      Congress **VIII:** 67
      Hillman, Sidney **VIII:** 146
      New Deal **VIII:** 241
      Perkins, Frances **VIII:** 265
fairness doctrine (television) **X:**
   294
Fair Oaks, Battle of **V:** 173, 274
Fair Play for Cuba Committee
   IX: 238
fairs **III: 123,** 398*c;* **V:** 374
Faleiro, Rui **I:** 215
Falkland Islands **IV:** 242; **X:** 140
Fall, Albert **VII:** 118, 208, 307,
   360*c*
Fallam, Robert **II:** 30–31, 115

Fallen Timbers, Battle of **III:** **123–124,** 396c; **IV:** 168
  Blue Jacket **III:** 41
  Cherokee nation **III:** 66
  Clark, William **III:** 72
  Cornplanter **III:** 92
  Dragging Canoe **III:** 107
  Greenville, Treaty of **III:** 157
  Lewis, Meriwether **III:** 208
  Prophet, the Shawnee **III:** 289
  Red Jacket **III:** 297
  Tecumseh **III:** 345
  Wayne, Anthony **III:** 370
  Wilkinson, James **III:** 379
Falling Water **VIII:** 22, 407c
Fallon, George **IX:** 145
fallout, nuclear **IX:** 23, 24, 180, 192, 267
fallout shelters **IX:** 53
"false face" masks **II:** 24
Falwell, Jerry
  conservative movement **X:** 79
  feminism **X:** 116
  Moral Majority **X:** 197
  televangelism **X:** 293, 294
family, nuclear **VII:** 170–172
Family and Medical Leave Act of 1993 **X:** 328c
family farm communities **II:** 62
Family Law (TV program) **X:** 295
Family Leave and Medical Act of 1993 **X:** 110
family life. *See* marriage and family life
Family Limitation (Sanger) **VII:** 29, 273, 339
family planning
  abortion **X:** 1
  birth control **X:** 36–38
  family life **X:** 109
  feminism **X:** 116
Family Planning Service and Population Research Act of 1970 **X:** 37
family singers **IV:** 250
family size **X:** 28, 30, 109
Family Support Act (FSA) of 1988 **X: 110**
"family values" **X:** 111, 182, 253
Famine Emergency Commission **VIII:** 153
fan, electric **VII:** *133*
Faneuil family **II:** 130
Faneuil Hall **II:** 346
Fang (Fan, Pahouin) **I:** 52, **127**
Fannin, James **IV:** 341
Fanning, Edmund **III:** 261

Fante nation (Africa) **II:** 344
Fantus, Bernard **VIII:** 207
FAP. *See* Federal Art Project
Faraday, Michael **IV:** 307, 308
Farazi, Al- **I:** 140
Fard, Wallace D. **IX:** 214, 257; **X:** 213
Far East **I:** 114, 265–266. *See also* Asia
Farel, Guillaume **I:** 50
Farewell Address of George Washington **III: 124,** 396c
  Hamilton, Alexander **III:** 162
  Neutrality Proclamation **III:** 256
  political parties **III:** 279
  Washington, George **III:** 367
Farewell to Arms, A (Hemingway) **VII:** 166
Farewell to His Troops (Lee) **V:** 427
Farley, James A. **VIII: 110–111**
  Catholics **VIII:** 53
  Democratic Party **VIII:** 81, 82
  election of 1936 **VIII:** 97
  Flynn, Edward J. **VIII:** 122, 123
  Irish Americans **VIII:** 165
  recession of 1937–38 **VIII:** 293
  Roosevelt, Franklin D. **VIII:** 312
Farm Aid concerts **X:** 16
Farm Bloc **VII:** 42, 175
Farm Bureau **VII:** 7
Farm Credit Administration (FCA) **VIII: 111–112**
  Agricultural Adjustment Act **VIII:** 6
  agriculture **VIII:** 8
  Morgenthau, Henry **VIII:** 216
  New Deal **VIII:** 241
  RFC **VIII:** 295
Farmer, James L. **IX:** 66–68; **X: 110–111**
Farmer-Labor Party **VII: 91,** 215, 230; **VIII:** 66, 276
farmers **VIII:** 271
Farmers Alliance **VII:** 332
farmers' alliances **VI: 99–100**
  Lease, Mary Elizabeth **VI:** 173
  national banking system **VI:** 206
  Omaha Platform **VI:** 216
  Patrons of Husbandry **VI:** 221–222
  People's Party **VI:** 222

  Powderly, Terence Vincent **VI:** 227
  Simpson, Jerry **VI:** 262
farmhouses **IV:** 27
farming. *See* agriculture
farm prices **VIII:** 371
Farm Security Administration (FSA) **VIII: 112–113,** 407c
  advertising **VIII:** 1
  agriculture **VIII:** 8
  art and architecture **VIII:** 24
  Congress **VIII:** 67
  New Deal **VIII:** 241
  photography **VIII:** 268
  RA **VIII:** 307
farm tenancy **VI:** 7m
Farnsworth, Philo T. **VII:** 134
Farragut, David Glasgow **V:** *121,* **121–122,** 406c, 407c; **VI:** 79
  elections **V:** 110
  ironclads **V:** 183
  Mississippi River **V:** 234, 235
  Mobile campaign **V:** 236
  monuments **V:** 239
  New Orleans, Battle of **V:** 252
  Porter, David Dixon **V:** 280
  Union navy **V:** 368
  Vicksburg campaign **V:** 380
  Welles, Gideon **V:** 391
Farragut Monument **VI:** 253
Farragut Square **V:** 239
Farrakhan, Louis A. (Louis Eugene Walcott) **IX:** 215; **X:** 111, 329c
  African Americans **X:** 12
  NAACP **X:** 209
  Nation of Islam **X:** 213
  race and racial conflict **X:** 257
Farrell, James T. **VIII:** 165, 191
Farwell, Charles **VI:** 196
fascism **VII:** 101; **VIII:** 19, 124, 276, 334
fashion. *See* dress and fashion
Fasiladas, emperor of Ethiopia **I:** 125
"Fate" (Emerson) **IV:** 126
Fatigue and Efficiency: A Study in Industry (Goldmark) **VII:** 111
"Fat Man" bomb **VIII:** 146, 201
Faubus, Orval **IX:** 43, **108–109,** 209, 271, 276, 332c
Faulkner, William **VII:** 162; **VIII: 113–114,** 192, 405c; **IX:** 181–182, 330c
Fauntroy, Walter **X:** 19
Fauset, Jessie **VII:** 119

Fava, Baron Francesco Saverio **VI:** 185
Favrile Glass **VI:** 288
Fawkes, Guy. *See* Guy Fawkes Day
FBI. *See* Federal Bureau of Investigation
FCA. *See* Farm Credit Administration
FCC. *See* Federal Communications Commission
FCDA. *See* Federal Civil Defense Administration
FDA. *See* Food and Drug Administration
FDIC. *See* Federal Deposit Insurance Corporation
fealty, oath of **I:** 129
fear, freedom from. *See* Four Freedoms
Fear God and Take Your Own Part (Roosevelt) **VII:** 235
Feast of the Dead **I:** 171
feasts and festivals
  Asante **I:** 13
  Aztecs **I:** 20, 21
  Benin **I:** 28
  cacao **I:** 45
  Gutenberg, Johann Gensfleisch zum **I:** 147
  Huitzilopochtli **I:** 170
  Huron **I:** 171
  Inca **I:** 176
  Iroquois **I:** 181
  Tezcatlipoca **I:** 347, 348
Feathered Serpent. *See* Quetzalcoatl
February Revolution **VII:** 270
FEC. *See* Federal Election Commission
FECA. *See* Federal Election Campaign Act of 1971
Federal Aid Highway Act of 1956. *See* Interstate Highway Act of 1956
Federal-Aid Highway Amendments of 1974 **X:** 112
Federal Aid Road Act of 1916 **VII:** 22, 300
Federal Art Project (FAP) **VIII:** 23, *114,* **114–115,** 268
Federal Aviation Act of 1958 **IX:** 28
Federal Aviation Administration (FAA) **IX:** 27, 28, 332c; **X:** 170
federal budget. *See* national budget
Federal Bureau of Investigation (FBI) **VII:** 361c; **VIII: 115**
  Abscam **X:** 4–5
  America First Committee **VIII:** 13

Federal Bureau of Investigation
(*continued*)
  black market **VIII:** 38
  Black Panthers **IX:** 39
  Branch Davidians **X:**
    39–40
  Bunche, Ralph **IX:** 43
  Carmichael, Stokely **IX:** 48
  CIA **IX:** 49
  Clinton, William **X:** 66
  crime **X:** 82
  espionage **VIII:** 104
  FCC **VIII:** 116, 117
  gays and lesbians **IX:** 119
  Hoover, J. Edgar **IX:** 136
  House Un-American
    Activities Committee
    IX: 137
  impeachment **X:** 149–150
  intelligence **VIII:** 164
  Japanese Americans,
    relocation of **VIII:** 172
  militia movement **X:** 194
  narcotics **X:** 207
  Nixon, Richard M. **X:** 219
  OPA **VIII:** 254
  OSS **VIII:** 256
  Reno, Janet **X:** 267
  Robeson, Paul **VIII:** 310;
    IX: 261
  Ruckelshaus, William D.
    X: 268, 269
  Selective Service **VIII:**
    323
  terrorism **X:** 297, 300
Federal Bureau of Labor **VI:**
  162
Federal Cigarette Labeling and
  Advertising Act of 1965 **X:**
  303
Federal Civil Defense
  Administration (FCDA) **IX:**
  52–53
Federal Communications
  Commission (FCC) **VII:** 134;
  VIII: *116*, 116–117, 406c; **X:**
  274, 294
    censorship **VIII:** 55
    New Deal **VIII:** 241
    radio **VIII:** 290
    Welles, Orson **VIII:** 377
Federal Council of Churches
  VI: 267, 279; **VII:** 260
Federal Council on Negro
  Affairs **VIII:** 37
federal debt **VI:** 19; **VII:** 331
federal deficit **VIII:** 351
Federal Deposit Insurance
  Corporation (FDIC) **VIII:**
  117, 406c
    Banking Act of 1933 **VIII:**
      33

Banking Act of 1935 **VIII:**
  34
marriage and family life
  VIII: 204
New Deal **VIII:** 241
Federal Election Campaign Act
  (FECA) of 1971 **X:** 53, 236,
  238, 324c
Federal Election Campaign Act
  of 1974 **X:** 325c
Federal Election Commission
  (FEC)
    campaign finance **X:** 53, 54
    Christian Coalition **X:** 62
    Gingrich, Newton L. **X:**
      130
    PACs **X:** 236
Federal Emergency Relief Act
  VIII: 208, 307
Federal Emergency Relief
  Administration (FERA) **VIII:**
  117–118, 406c
    cities and urban life **VIII:**
      59
    Congress **VIII:** 67
    conservatism **VIII:** 71
    CWA **VIII:** 63
    elderly **VIII:** 95
    First New Deal **VIII:** 122
    FSA **VIII:** 112
    Hopkins, Harry **VIII:** 156
    New Deal **VIII:** 241
    NYA **VIII:** 234
    recreation **VIII:** 296
    relief **VIII:** 301
    RFC **VIII:** 294
    WPA **VIII:** 387
Federal Employee Loyalty
  Program **IX:** 14, **109–110,**
  300, 301, 329c
federal employees **V:** 218
Federal Energy Administration
  X: 103
Federal Farm Board **VIII:** 405c
    Agricultural Adjustment
      Act **VIII:** 7
    agriculture **VIII:** 7
    FCA **VIII:** 111
    Hoover presidency **VIII:**
      153, 154
    Morgenthau, Henry **VIII:**
      216
Federal Farm Loan Act **VII:** 7,
  91–92, 268–269, 334, 359c
Federal Farm Loan Board **VIII:**
  111
Federal Food, Drug, and
  Cosmetic Act of 1962 **IX:** 69
federal funding
    abortion **X:** 3, 4
    African Americans **X:** 10
    birth control **X:** 37

federalism **X:** 112–113
Grove City College et al. v.
  Bell, Secretary of
  Education, et al. **X:** 136
Human Genome Project
  X: 145–146
Internet **X:** 153
marriage **X:** 183
NEA,NEH **X:** 209–210
Reform Party **X:** 263
space policy **X:** 281, 283
Webster v. Reproductive
  Health Services **X:** 319
Federal Highway Act of 1921
  VII: 22
Federal Home Loan Bank Act
  VIII: 150, 154
Federal Housing Administration
  (FHA) **VIII:** **118–119,** 407c;
  IX: 110, 287
    Eccles, Marriner S. **VIII:**
      89
    housing **VIII:** 157
    Italian Americans **VIII:**
      167
    New Deal **VIII:** 241
    RFC **VIII:** 295
    suburbs **VIII:** 342, 343
    USHA **VIII:** 367
federal income tax. *See* income
  tax, federal
Federal Information Act of 1974
  (Privacy Act) **X:** **111–112,**
  325c
federalism **X:** **112–113**
    property rights **X:** 249
    Rehnquist, William H. **X:**
      264
    RICO **X:** 258
Federalism Impact Assessments
  X: 113
Federalist economic policy **IV:**
  363
Federalist furniture style **III:**
  275
Federalist Papers **III:** **124–125,**
  395c
    Federalists **III:** 127
    Hamilton, Alexander **III:**
      161
    Jay, John **III:** 182
    journalism **III:** 191
    literature **III:** 214
    Madison, James **III:**
      228–229
    political parties **III:** 278
    Supreme Court **III:** 338
Federalist Party **III:** **126–127,**
  395c, 397c, 398c; **V:** 41
    Adams, John **III:** 3
    Adams, John Quincy **IV:** 4
    Adams, Samuel **III:** 5

Alien and Sedition Acts
  III: 9
American Revolution **III:**
  13
Ames, Fisher **III:** 13
artisans **III:** 26
Bache, Benjamin Franklin
  III: 29
Bank of the United States
  (First) **III:** 30
banks **III:** 32
Blount, William **III:** 41
Burr, Aaron **III:** 54
Carey, Mathew **III:** 62
Catholics **III:** 63
Chase, Samuel **III:** 65
cities and urban life **III:**
  70
Clinton, DeWitt **III:** 73
Clinton, George **III:** 75
Connecticut Wits **III:** 80
Democratic Party **IV:** 106
Democratic-Republican
  Party **III:** 104
election of 1800 **III:** 116,
  117
embargo of 1807 **III:** 118
Era of Good Feelings **IV:**
  127
Federalists **III:** 127
French Revolution **III:**
  138
Fries's Rebellion **III:** 140
Gerry, Elbridge **III:** 153
Hamilton, Alexander **III:**
  162
Hartford Convention **IV:**
  170, 171
immigration **III:** 173
impeachment **III:** 175
Jackson, Andrew **IV:** 192
Jay, John **III:** 182
Jay's Treaty **III:** 183
journalism **III:** 191, 192
Judiciary Act of 1801 **III:**
  193
King, Rufus **III:** 195
Lee, Henry **III:** 206
liberty tree/pole **III:** 214
literature **III:** 214
Livingston, Robert R. **III:**
  216
Louisiana Purchase **III:**
  218
Lyon, Matthew **III:** 222
Macon, Nathaniel **III:** 226
Madison, Dolley **III:** 227
Marbury v. Madison **III:**
  230
Marshall, John **III:** 235
music **III:** 251
national debt **III:** 253

Otis, Harrison Gray **III:** 268

Panic of 1819 **IV:** 276

Pickering, John **III:** 275–276

political parties **III:** 278, 279

Quasi War **III:** 291–292

Randolph, John **III:** 296

religious liberty **III:** 300

riots **III:** 309

states' rights **III:** 333

Supreme Court **III:** 338

Virginia and Kentucky Resolutions **III:** 360

Virginia dynasty **III:** 361

War of 1812 **IV:** 356

Washington Benevolent Societies **III:** 368–369

Webster, Daniel **IV:** 359

Webster, Noah **III:** 370

West Point **III:** 372

Federalists/Federalism **III:** **127–128,** 128*m;* **V:** 311

anti-Federalists **III:** 15

Bill of Rights **III:** 38, 39

Constitutional Convention **III:** 82

Coxe, Tench **III:** 96

Duane, William **III:** 108

Dwight, Timothy **III:** 109

Federalist Party **III:** 126

Jefferson, Thomas **III:** 185

Madison, James **III:** 228

Paine, Thomas **III:** 272

Pinckney, Charles Cotesworth **III:** 277

political parties **III:** 278

Schuyler, Philip John **III:** 320

Shays's Rebellion **III:** 324–325

Sherman, Roger **III:** 325

Webster, Noah **III:** 370

Federal Land Banks **VII:** 7

Federal Music Project (FMP) **VIII:** **119–120,** 222, 223

federal (neoclassical) architecture **III:** 18

Federal One

FAP **VIII:** 114

FTP **VIII:** 120

FWP **VIII:** 121

relief **VIII:** 301

WPA **VIII:** 387

Federal Power Commission **X:** 103

Federal Radio Act of 1927 **VIII:** 290

Federal Reserve Act **VII:** **93–94,** 358*c;* **VIII:** 34

Democratic Party **VII:** 66

economy **VII:** 75

New Freedom **VII:** 211

Wilson, Woodrow **VII:** 334

Federal Reserve Bank **VII:** 93

Federal Reserve Board **VII:** 93; **X:** 94, 261

Banking Act of 1933 **VIII:** 33

Banking Act of 1935 **VIII:** 33

Eccles, Marriner S. **VIII:** 89

Great Depression **VIII:** 139, 140

recession of 1937–38 **VIII:** 293

stock market crash (1929) **VIII:** 341

Federal Reserve System **VI:** 40, 206; **VIII:** 117

Federal Steel **VI:** 20, 147; **VII:** 297, 319

Federal Suffrage Association **VI:** 317

federal taxes **VIII:** 350

Federal Theatre Project (FTP) **VIII:** **120–121,** 275, 376, 387

Federal Trade Commission (FTC) **IX:** 44; **X:** 7

Federal Trade Commission Act **VII:** **94,** 358*c*

advertising **VII:** 4

Democratic Party **VII:** 66

New Freedom **VII:** 211

progressivism **VII:** 237

Wilson, Woodrow **VII:** 334

Federal Water Pollution Control Act amendments of 1972 **X:** 249–250

Federal Water Quality Administration **IX:** 127

Federal Wilderness Service **X:** 250

Federal Writers' Project (FWP) **VIII:** **121–122,** 193, 222, 399

Federation of American Zionists **VI:** 158

Federation of Islamic Associations **X:** 157

Federation of Organized Trade and Labor Unions of the United States and Canada (FOOTALU) **VI:** 127, 170; **IX:** 11

Federica, Georgia **II:** 267

fee tail. *See* primogeniture and entail

Feingold, Russell **X:** 53

Feke, Robert **II:** 25, **117,** 156, 216, 346

Fell, Margaret **II:** 275, 307

female antislavery societies **IV:** **135–136**

Female Anti-Slavery Society of Philadelphia **IV:** 246, 247, 313

Female Anti-Slavery Society (Salem, Mass.) **IV:** 8, 135

female-headed families **X:** 245, 246, 320

Female Medical College of Pennsylvania **VI:** 318

feme covert status **II:** 406

feme sole status **II:** 406

Feminine Mystique, The (Friedan) **IX:** 71, 114, 115, 183, 223, 324, 333*c;* **X:** 109, 113–114, 320

feminism/feminist movement **VII:** 29, 109, 338, 340; **X:** **113–117.**

amendments to the Constitution **X:** 19

art and architecture **X:** 26

Blackwell, Antoinette Brown **VI:** 30

Brennan, William J. **X:** 41

conservative movement **X:** 79–80

ERA **X:** 105

family life **X:** 109

fashion **V:** 123

feminism **X:** 115, 116

Fifteenth Amendment **V:** 124

Fourteenth Amendment **V:** 139

Friedan, Betty **IX:** 114–116

Gage, Matilda Joslyn **VI:** 107

Ginsburg, Ruth Bader **X:** 130

La Raza Unida **IX:** 171

Latino movement **IX:** 174

League of Women Voters **IX:** 174–175

Mitchell, Maria **VI:** 195

National Organization for Women **IX:** 223; **X:** 211

political parties **X:** 237

pornography **X:** 245

pro-life and pro-choice movements **X:** 249

religion **IX:** 257

Schlafly, Phyllis **X:** 272

Steinem, Gloria **X:** 288

Thomas, M. Carey **VI:** 287

Truth, Sojourner **V:** 357

Women's Equity Action League **IX:** 323–324

Women's National Loyal League **V:** 396

women's rights and status **VI:** 316–318; **IX:** 324, 325; **X:** 320

fencing **II:** 104

Fenians **VI:** 43, 309; **V:** 133

Fenno, John **III:** 29, 191, 395*c*

Fenton, William **VII:** 193

Fenwick, George **II:** 68

Fenwick, John **II:** 252

FEPC. *See* Fair Employment Practices Committee

FERA. *See* Federal Emergency Relief Administration

Ferber, Edna **VII:** 161

Ferdinand, king of Spain **IV:** 303

Ferdinand and Isabella **I:** **127–128,** *128,* 386*c*

cabildo **I:** 38

Cabot, Sebastian **I:** 42

Castile **I:** 63

Cathay (China) **I:** 65

Charles V **I:** 67

Columbus, Bartholomew **I:** 78, 79

Columbus, Christopher **I:** 80–83

corregidores **I:** 90

Cortés, Hernán **I:** 91

Franciscans **I:** 132

Henry VII **I:** 159

Jews (Judaism) **I:** 190

Mary I **I:** 224

Peter Martyr **I:** 280

Ponce de León, Juan **I:** 288

Privileges and Prerogatives Granted to Columbus, 1492 **I:** 389–390

Reconquista **I:** 306

Tordesillas, Treaty of **I:** 358

Ferdinand (brother of Charles V) **I:** 67–69

Ferdinand I, emperor of Germany **I:** 189

Ferguson, Patrick **III:** 196, 197

Ferlinghetti, Lawrence **IX:** 71

Fermi, Enrico **VIII:** 200; **IX:** 139, 237

Fernando (brother of Henry the Navigator) **I:** 157

Fernando Po **I:** **129,** 338

Ferraro, Geraldine A. **X:** 116, **117,** 196, 326*c*

ferries **II:** 377

fertility **II:** **117–118; VII:** 233–235

fertilizer **II:** 118; **IV:** 11

Fessenden, William Pitt **V:** 295

festivals. *See* feasts and festivals
fetal tissue research **X:** 4, 66
Fetherstone, Henry **I:** 297
feudalism **I: 129–130,** 277
Feulner, Edwin J. **X:** 79, 301
Fezzan **I:** 317
fezzes **V:** 403
FHA. *See* Federal Housing Administration
Fhimah, Al Amin Khalifa **X:** 331*c*
Fiat **X:** 32
fiat currency **V:** 23, 24, 105, 106, 159
Fibber McGee and Molly **VIII:** 274
fiber optics **X:** 273–274, 325*c*
Fickey, Edwin **VI:** 145
fiction. *See* literature
fiddles **II:** 239
fiefs **I:** 129–130
Field **X:** 178
Field, Cyrus **V:** 405*c*
Field, James G. **VI:** 223
Field, Marshall **VI:** 78, 79
Field, Stephen J. **VI:** 82, 281
Fielden, Samuel **VI:** 127
Fielding, Henry **II:** 193, 373
Fielding, Lewis **X:** 315, 317
field music **V:** 243
Field of Dreams (movie) **X:** 198
Fields, W. C. **VII:** 321; **VIII:** 217
Fifteenth Amendment **IV:** 15, 289; **V: 123–124,** 408*c*, 428; **VI:** 323*c*; **VII:** 281; **VIII:** 61, 410*c*; **IX:** 311
　Anthony, Susan B. **VI:** 12, 13
　Blackwell, Antoinette Brown **VI:** 30
　Brown, Olympia **VI:** 36
　Catto, Octavius **V:** 53
　Douglass, Frederick **V:** 100
　elections **V:** 109
　elections, conduct of **VI:** 95
　emancipation **V:** 114
　Enforcement Acts **V:** 117
　grandfather clause **VI:** 118, 119
　Harlan, John Marshall **VI:** 122
　Harrison, Benjamin **VI:** 123
　Hayes, Rutherford B. **VI:** 125, 127
　Hoar, George Frisbie **VI:** 130
　NWSA **V:** 248, 249
　Reconstruction **V:** 294
　Republican Party **V:** 302

Stone, Lucy **VI:** 278
Thirteenth Amendment **V:** 353
Truth, Sojourner **V:** 358
United States v. Cruikshank **V:** 375, 376
women's rights and status **V:** 398; **VI:** 317
Fifth Amendment **IV:** 331; **VIII:** 345; **IX:** 132–133, 135, 137, 206, 316; **X:** 271
"fifth column"
　enemy aliens **VIII:** 102
　espionage **VIII:** 104
　German Americans **VIII:** 131
　refugees **VIII:** 299
Fifth Lateran Council **I:** 96
54th Massachusetts Regiment **V: 124–126,** 407*c*
　African-American regiments **V:** 5
　Brown, William Wells **V:** 40
　Carney, William H. **V:** 49
　Douglass, Frederick **V:** 100
　Medal of Honor **V:** 228
　monuments **V:** 239
"Fifty-four forty or fight" **IV:** 217, 270
Fifty-niners **IV:** 145
Fight for the Waterhole (Remington) **VI:** 245–246
"Fighting 99th" Pursuit Squadron **VIII:** 4
Figueroa, José **IV: 136**
Filegate **X:** 162
Filene, Edward **VI:** 78
filibustering **IV:** 137, 142, 219; **V: 126–127,** 260; **X:** 276
filibusters (soldiers) **VI:** 71
Filipino Americans **VIII:** 162; **IX:** 22; **X:** 28, 29, 200, 243
Filipino insurrection **VI: 100,** 125, 190, 272, 328*c*; **VII:** 8
Filipos, Abba **I:** 124
Fillmore, Millard **IV: 136–138,** 137, 379*c*; **V:** 251; **VI:** 198
　Compromise of 1850 **IV:** 95
　Deseret, State of **IV:** 110
　foreign policy **IV:** 143
　Frémont, John C. **IV:** 154
　immigration **IV:** 180
　Know-Nothing Party **IV:** 201, 202
　Perry, Matthew Calbraith **IV:** 279, 280
　Republican Party **IV:** 301
　Taylor, Zachary **IV:** 334–335

Webster, Daniel **IV:** 360
Whig Party **IV:** 364
film. *See* movies/movie industry
film noir **IX:** 212
finance. *See* banking, finance and credit
fines **II:** 75
Finland **II:** 365; **VII:** 323
Finley, Clement A. **V:** 229, 230
Finney, Charles Grandison **IV: 138–139**
　Foster, Abigail Kelley **IV:** 148
　religion **IV:** 296
　Second Great Awakening **IV:** 311
　Weld, Theodore Dwight **IV:** 362
firearms **III:** 376–377; **V:** 180, 387
　Colt, Samuel **IV:** 90–92
　Colt revolver **IV:** 92
　gun control **X:** 136–138
　industrialization **IV:** 184
　Libertarian Party **X:** 176
　militia movement **X:** 193
　NRA **X:** 211–213
　science and technology **IV:** 307
firebombing of Japan **VIII:** 147, 399
fire departments **V:** 61; **VI:** 55
fire-eaters **V: 127–128,** 311, 312, 401
fire escapes **IV:** 82
fire-fighting departments **IV:** 83
Fire in the Flint (White) **VIII:** 378
Fire Next Time, The (James Baldwin) **IX:** 33
fires **II:** 35, 175, 247, 248; **V:** 304, 322; **VI:** 55, 323*c*. *See also* arson; Chicago Fire of 1871
"fireside chats" **VIII:** 409*c*
　Emergency Banking Act of 1933 **VIII:** 101
　New Deal **VIII:** 241
　popular culture **VIII:** 274–275
　radio **VIII:** 289
　Roosevelt, Franklin D. **VIII:** 313
　technology **VIII:** 353
Firestone Company **X:** 32
Firing Line (television show) **X:** 43
First Amendment **V:** 3; **VIII:** 408*c*; **IX:** 80, 100–101, 135, 257, 316; **X:** 324*c*, 326*c*, 327*c*, 330*c*. *See also* free speech; prayer in school
　advertising **X:** 7

　Alien and Sedition Acts **III:** 9
　American Civil Liberties Union **VIII:** 13
　Backus, Isaac **III:** 30
　Bork, Robert **X:** 39
　Brandeis, Louis **VII:** 35
　Breyer, Stephen **X:** 42
　campaign finance **X:** 54
　censorship **VIII:** 54, 55; **X:** 60–61
　civil liberties **VIII:** 60
　Equal Access Act **X:** 104–105
　flag burning **X:** 117, 118
　Holmes, Oliver Wendell **VII:** 123
　Jews **III:** 188
　Madison, James **III:** 228
　PACs **X:** 236
　Pentagon Papers **X:** 233
　pornography **X:** 244, 245
　religion **III:** 298
　religious liberty **III:** 300
　Schenk v. United States **VII:** 274–275
　Sedition Act **VII:** 280
　Supreme Court **VIII:** 347; **X:** 291
　World War II **VIII:** 389
First Continental Congress. *See* Continental Congress, First
First Draft of a Report on the EDVAC (John von Neumann) **IX:** 63, 64
First Great Awakening. *See* Great Awakening
"first Hundred Days" **VIII:** 406*c*
　Agricultural Adjustment Act **VIII:** 5–6
　CCC **VIII:** 63
　presidency **VIII:** 281
　relief **VIII:** 301
　Roosevelt, Franklin D. **VIII:** 313
　TVA **VIII:** 356
First Inter-American Conference **VI:** 220
First Kernstown, Battle of **V:** 316
first ladies **V:** 153–154, 211–212; **VIII:** 310–311
First Louisiana Native Guards. *See* Corps d'Afrique
First Michigan Sharpshooters **V:** 249
First Modern Suite (MacDowell) **VI:** 325*c*
First New Deal. *See* New Deal, First
First New Mexico Volunteer Infantry **IV:** 76

First Puritan Reformation **II:** 305
First South Carolina Volunteers. *See* 33rd U.S. Colored Troops
First Winchester, Battle of **V:** 316
fiscal conservatism **VII:** 262, 263
fiscal policy **VIII:** 89, 216, 292. *See also* Keynesianism
Fischer, Adolph **VI:** 127
Fischl, Eric **X:** 26
Fish, Hamilton **V:** 133, 156
   Canada and the United States **VI:** 43
   Santo Domingo **VI:** 255
   Virginius affair **VI:** 305
   Washington, Treaty of **VI:** 309
Fisher, Bernice **IX:** 66
Fisher, Fred **IX:** 18
fishing **II: 118–119,** *119;* **IV:** 64, 93, 170; **VI:** 26, 43, 65, 309, 310, 323*c*
   Acadians **II:** 2
   Aleut **II:** 16
   Algonquin **II:** 17
   animals **II:** 20
   Azores **I:** 17
   Bristol **I:** 35
   California **I:** 48
   California Indians **II:** 49
   Carib **I:** 56
   Chesapeake Bay **II:** 58
   cod **I:** 74–75
   Cuba **I:** 98
   Delaware **II:** 88–89
   economy **II:** 101
   environment **II:** 110
   Florida **II:** 120
   food **II:** 121, 122
   French colonies **II:** 126
   fur trade **II:** 130
   Huron **I:** 171
   Iroquois **I:** 181
   Maine **II:** 203
   mariners **II:** 204
   Massachusett **I:** 225
   Massachusetts **II:** 212, 215
   Mount Vernon **II:** 237
   Native Americans **II:** 243
   New Hampshire **II:** 250
   New Jersey **II:** 252, 253
   Norse **I:** 264
   Northwest Coast Indians **II:** 265
   Pequot **II:** 278
   Plymouth **II:** 288
   population trends **II:** 290
   Rhode Island **II:** 320, 321
   technology **II:** 369
   trade and shipping **II:** 375, 376

Treaty of Paris **II:** 378
   women's status and rights **II:** 406
fishing industry **X:** 77, 214
"fish-ins" **X:** 214
Fisk, Clinton B. **VI:** 234
Fisk, James (Jim) **V:** 409*c;* **VI:** 67, 117, 118
Fiske, John **VI:** 75, 242, 265, 324*c*
Fiske, Minnie Maddern **VI:** 286
Fiske, Robert B., Jr. **X:** 328*c*
   Clinton, Hillary Rodham **X:** 64
   Clinton, William **X:** 68
   independent counsel **X:** 150
   Starr, Kenneth **X:** 286
Fisk University **V:** 408*c;* **VI:** 5, 94, 202
Fisk University Jubilee Singers **VI:** 6, 202
Fitch, Clyde **VI:** 287
Fitchburg Railroad **IV:** 295
Fithian, Philip **II:** 104
fitness **X:** 286
Fitzgerald, F. Scott **VII:** 161–162, 166–167, *167;* **VIII:** 165; **IX:** 181
Fitzgerald, Zelda **VII:** *167*
Fitzhugh, George **V: 128,** 212, 328
Fitzpatrick, John **VII:** 297, 298
Fitzpatrick, Thomas
   Astor, John Jacob **IV:** 32
   Bidwell, John **IV:** 51
   Bridger, James **IV:** 57
   Fort Laramie **IV:** 143
   mountain men **IV:** 247
   Sublette, William **IV:** 330
Fitzsimmons, Frank **IX:** 293
five-and-ten-cent stores **VI:** 46, 47
Five Civilized Tribes **IV:** 193, 296, 343, 376*c;* **V:** 249, 251; **VI:** 76, 209, 271
"Five Dollar Day" **VII:** 332, 333
Five Forks, Battle of **V: 128–129**
   Appomattox Court House, Virginia **V:** 14
   Chamberlain, Joshua L. **V:** 54
   Lee, Robert E. **V:** 207
   Pickett, George Edward **V:** 274
   Richmond, Virginia **V:** 304
   Sheridan, Philip H. **V:** 319
Five Nations **I:** 387*c,* **II:** 242–243. *See also* Iroquois
   Dekanawideh **II:** 85
   Hiawatha **I:** 160–161

Iroquois **I:** 181–183; **II:** 168, 169
   Mohawk **I:** 238
   Montour, Madame **II:** 233
   Oneida **I:** 271–272
   Onondaga **I:** 272
   Tuscarora **II:** 378–379
   Tuscarora War **II:** 379
Five of Hearts Club **VI:** 1, 160
Five-Power Treaty **VII:** 331
Flack, Audrey **X:** 26
flag burning **X: 117–118,** *118,* 327*c*
   Brennan, William J. **X:** 41
   Scalia, Antonin **X:** 271
   Supreme Court **X:** 291
   White, Byron R. **X:** 319
Flagler, Henry M. **VII:** 296
Flag Protection Act of 1989 **X:** 117–118
"flag riots" **X:** 232
flags **III:** 310–311
flag salute **VIII:** 408*c*
flame-throwers **VIII:** 350
Flamsteed **II:** 40
Flanagan, Hallie **VIII:** 120
Flanagan, John **VI:** 290
Flanders **I:** 232
"Flapper Jane" (Bliven) **VII:** 382–384
Flashman, Edward **II: 119**
Flat Iron Building (New York City) **VI:** *265*
Flaubert, Gustave **VI:** 177
flax **II:** 190, *207,* 253; **IV:** 10
fleas **I:** 285–286
fleet system (trade) **II:** 355, 356
Fleming, Alexander **VIII:** 8, 208; **IX:** 205
Fleming, J. L. **VI:** 311
Fletcher, Alice **VI:** 202
Fletcher, Benjamin **II:** 39, 285
Fletcher, William **V:** 213
Fletcher v. Peck **III:** 237, 338, 388, 398*c;* **IV:** 330
Flexner, Abraham **VI:** 192; **VII:** 179, 290
flight **VI:** 25
Flight (White) **VIII:** 378
"floating fields." *See chinampas*
flood control **VIII:** 103
floods **IV:** 262; **VI:** 107–108, 157
Florence **I:** 204, 235, 327
Florentine Codex **I:** 20, 250, 315, 382
Florida **I: 130–131,** 387*c;* **II: 120–121; III:** 129, 394*c,* 396*c;* **IV:** 375*c;* **V:** 221, 222, 294, 313; **VI:** 4, 156; **IX:** 121–122, 286, 320
   affirmative action **X:** 9
   Apalachee **I:** 11

architecture **II:** 23
Beckwourth, Jim **IV:** 46
British Empire **II:** 43
Bush, George W. **X:** 48
Cabeza de Vaca, Álvar Núñez **I:** 37
Calusa **I:** 49
Caroline, Fort **I:** 57
Choctaw nation **III:** 68
Creek nation **III:** 96
crowd action **II:** 78
Cuba **I:** 98
DeBry, Theodor **I:** 102
Drake, Sir Francis **I:** 111
elections **X:** 102
ERA **X:** 106, 107
foreign affairs **III:** 130, 131
foreign policy **IV:** 142
Fort Mose **II:** 123
Genet, Edmond **III:** 150
Gore, Albert, Jr. **X:** 134
Hispanic Americans **X:** 143
Horseshoe Bend, Battle of **IV:** 173
Indian Removal Act (1830) **IV:** 181
Ingram, David **I:** 177
Jackson, Andrew **IV:** 192
Jay-Gardoqui treaty negotiations **III:** 182
Judicial Watch **X:** 162
Laudonnière, René de **I:** 201
Le Moyne, Jacques **I:** 202
Livingston, Robert R. **III:** 216
Louisiana Purchase **III:** 218
Manifest Destiny **IV:** 218*m*
Massachusetts Emigrant Aid Society **IV:** 224
McGillivray, Alexander **III:** 240
migration **IV:** 235
missions **II:** 230
monarchy, British **II:** 232
Monroe, James **IV:** 240
Nader, Ralph **X:** 206
Narváez, Pánfilo de **I:** 251
Native Americans **II:** 246; **IV:** 256
Native Americans in the War of 1812 **IV:** 259
New Spain **I:** 258
O'Connor, Sandra Day **X:** 226
Oglethorpe, James Edward **II:** 267
Paris, Treaty of **III:** 273
Ponce de León, Juan **I:** 288

Florida *(continued)*
  population trends **X:** 242
  Proclamation of 1763 **III:**
    287
  public land policy **IV:** 287
  Randolph, John **III:** 296
  recreation **X:** 262
  Rehnquist, William H. **X:**
    265
  Reno, Janet **X:** 266
  Roman Catholics **II:** 324
  St. Augustine **II:** 327–328
  San Lorenzo, Treaty of **III:**
    317
  Seminole wars **IV:** 311,
    312
  slave resistance **II:** 337
  Soto, Hernando de **I:** 332
  Souter, David **X:** 279
  Spanish colonies **II:** 355
  Stono Rebellion **II:** 361
  Sunbelt **X:** 290
  Supreme Court **X:** 291
  Taylor, Zachary **IV:** 334
  Texas **IV:** 337–338
  Thomas, Clarence **X:** 302
  Timucua **I:** 351
  tobacco suits **X:** 304
  War of 1812 **IV:** 356
  War of Jenkins' Ear **II:**
    392
  Westo **II:** 394–395
Florida, CSS **V:** 132
Florida, East and West **IV:** xiii,
  139–140, 140*m*
  Adams, John Quincy **IV:** 5
  Adams-Onís Treaty **IV:** 5
  Cuba **IV:** 100
  economy **IV:** 117
  Era of Good Feelings **IV:**
    127
  Gadsden Purchase **IV:** 159
  Seminole wars **IV:** 312
Florida Baptist Institute **VI:** 4
Florida State University **X:** 215
flotilla system (Spain) **I:** 60, 60*m*
flour milling **VI: 101**
Flower, Enoch **II:** 103
Flowers, Gennifer **X:** 162
flowery wars **I:** 17–18, 97, **131,**
  170, 351, 352
Floyd, John **IV:** 259
FLSA. *See* Fair Labor Standards
  Act
Flyer I **VII:** 133
Flynn, Edward J. **VIII:**
  122–123
  Catholics **VIII:** 53
  Democratic Party **VIII:**
    82
  Farley, James A. **VIII:** 110
  Irish Americans **VIII:** 165

Flynn, Elizabeth Gurley **VII:**
  94–95, *95,* 357*c*
  Haywood, "Big Bill" **VII:**
    120
  Lawrence Strike **VII:** 155
  Paterson Strike **VII:** 225
  Sanger, Margaret **VII:** 273
FMP. *See* Federal Music Project
FNLA (Frente Nacional de
  Libertação de Angola) **IX:** 4;
  X: 71
FOIA. *See* Freedom of
  Information Act
Foley, Thomas S. **X: 118–119,**
  328*c*
  Civil Liberties Act of 1988
    X: 63
  Gingrich, Newton L. **X:**
    129
  House of Representatives
    X: 144, 145
  Wright, James C., Jr. **X:** 322
folk music **VI:** 202–203; **VIII:**
  119, 222, 309, 410*c*
folk music revival **IX:** 84–85,
  110–111, 217, 244
Follett, Ken **X:** 234
Follies (Ziegfeld) **VII:** 85, 357*c*
Folsom Man **I:** 254–255
Fon **I:** 101, 125, **131–132**
Fonda, Jane **IX:** 131
Fonda, Peter **IX:** 214
Fonseca, Vincente de **I:** 207
food **II: 121–122; V:** 407*c;* **VI:**
  190–191; **VII:** 177–178,
  243–244; **VIII:** 38, 47, 408*c*
  agriculture **II:** 8
  alcohol **II:** 15
  animals **II:** 21
  Burgesses, House of **II:** 45
  Chesapeake Bay **II:** 58
  Confederate army **V:** 72
  consumption **II:** 70, 71
  crowd actions **II:** 77, 78
  Dale, Sir Thomas **II:** 81
  Delaware **II:** 88
  disease **II:** 90
  economy **II:** 101
  fishing **II:** 118
  foraging **V:** 130
  Gates, Sir Thomas **II:** 135
  gender **II:** 137
  homefront **V:** 168
  impressment **V:** 180
  indentured servitude **II:**
    163
  Indians of the Desert
    Southwest **II:** 165, 166
  Jamestown **II:** 171
  labor **II:** 187, 188, 190
  marriage and family life **II:**
    206

  Maryland **II:** 209, 211
  mills **II:** 225, 226
  Mittelberger, Gottlieb **II:**
    231
  mortality **II:** 235
  Native Americans **II:** 243
  New Jersey **II:** 252
  New York **II:** 262
  North Carolina **II:** 263
  Northwest Coast Indians
    II: 265, 266
  Pocahontas **II:** 288
  population trends **II:** 291
  Powhatan (chief) **II:** 293
  revitalization movements
    II: 320
  Sandys, George **II:** 329
  Savannah **II:** 329
  science and technology **V:**
    310
  Shenandoah Valley:
    Sheridan's campaign **V:**
    318
  slavery **II:** 340
  Smith, John **II:** 346
  society, British American
    II: 349–351
  taverns and inns **II:** 367,
    368
  tenants **II:** 370
  trade and shipping **II:** 375
  Union army **V:** 365
  USCC **V:** 371
  Vicksburg campaign **V:**
    382
  Virginia **II:** 382, 384
  war contracting **V:** 387
  Washington, D.C. **V:** 390
Food, Agriculture,
  Conservation, and Trade Act
  of 1990 **X:** 16
Food and Agriculture Act of
  1965 **IX:** 8, 9, 334*c*
Food and Drug Administration
  (FDA) **VIII:** 1, 123, 208; **IX:**
  332*c;* **X:** 189, 305, 331*c*
Food, Drug, and Cosmetic Act
  VIII: 1, **123,** 208, 408*c*
food exports **VII:** 73
food industry **X:** 6, 14, 15
food products **IV:** 186*m*
food riots **IV:** 277, 352; **V:**
  129–130, 168, 188, 398
Food Stamp Act of 1964 **IX:** 9
Food Stamp program **IX:** 313
food stamps **X:** 135
Fool's Errand, A (Tourgée) **V:**
  354
FOOTALU. *See* Federation of
  Organized Trade and Labor
  Unions of the United States
  and Canada

football **VI: 101–102,** *102,*
  324*c;* **VII:** 258, 293, *293;*
  VIII: 336; **IX:** 255, 280, 281;
  X: 262, 284
Foote, Arthur **VI:** 201
Foote, Henry Stuart **V:** 89
Foote, Shelby **V:** 213
foraging **V: 130–131,** 317, 321,
  322
Foraker, Joseph **VII:** 35
Foraker Act of 1900 **VII:** 355*c*
Foran Act of 1885 **VI:** 66
Forbes, Charles **VII:** 118, 308,
  326, 327
Forbes, John **II:** 332; **III:** 366
Force Bill **IV:** 265
forced labor **I:** 3. *See also*
  slaves/slavery
forceps **IV:** 230
Ford, Betty **X:** 121
Ford, Bill **VII:** 266
Ford, Billy **X:** 231
Ford, Gerald R. **VIII:** 260, **X:**
  119–121, *120,* 324*c,* 325*c*
  African nations **X:** 13
  Albert, Carl B. **X:** 18
  assassinations **X:** 31
  Bush, George H. W. **X:** 45
  Carter, James Earl, Jr. **X:**
    58
  conservative movement **X:**
    79
  defense policy **X:** 86
  détente **X:** 89
  Dole, Robert **X:** 90
  economy **X:** 94
  ERA **X:** 107
  federalism **X:** 112
  foreign policy **X:** 122–123
  Haig, Alexander M., Jr. **X:**
    139
  Helms, Jesse A., Jr. **X:** 141
  impeachment **X:** 150
  Jaworski, Leon **X:** 161
  Kissinger, Henry A. **X:**
    166
  New York City bailout **X:**
    217
  Nixon, Richard M. **X:** 221
  Panama Canal turnover **X:**
    232
  Reagan, Ronald W. **X:** 259
  remarks on taking the oath
    of office **X:** 340–341
  Richardson, Elliot L. **X:**
    268
  Scalia, Antonin **X:** 271
  Strategic Arms Limitation
    Treaties **X:** 289
  Supreme Court **X:** 291
  United Nations **X:** 308
  veto, presidential **X:** 311

wage and price controls **X:** 313

Ford, Henry **VI:** 150, 327c; **VII:** **95–97,** 96, 357c; **IX:** 112
  aircraft industry **VIII:** 11
  America First Committee **VIII:** 12
  anti-Semitism **VII:** 14
  architecture **VII:** 16
  automobile industry **VII:** 21–22
  business **VII:** 38
  economy **VII:** 74
  invention and technology **VII:** 133
  labor **VIII:** 179
  mass production **VII:** 174–175
  nativism **VII:** 209
  rural life **VII:** 268
  technology **VIII:** 353
  TVA **VIII:** 356
  urban transportation **VII:** 318–319
  welfare capitalism **VII:** 333
Ford, James **VIII:** 65
Ford, John **VIII:** 273; **IX:** 211, 213
Ford, Philip **II:** 274
Ford, Richard **X:** 177
Ford, Theodosia **III:** 249
Ford, William Clay **X:** 32
Ford Motor Company **VII:** 21, 174; **VIII:** 30, 70; **IX:** 24, 25, **112,** 259, 294; **X:** 32, 32, 49. See also Model A Ford; Model T Ford
  aviation **VII:** 23–24
  cities and urban life **VII:** 48
  mass production **VII:** 174–175
  welfare capitalism **VII:** 332
Ford Motor Company of Canada **VII:** 135
Fordney-McCumber Tariff **VII:** 75, **97,** 306, 360c; **VIII:** 144
Ford's Theatre **V:** 17, 351
foreclosure (farm) **VIII:** 6–8, 111, 407c
foreclosure (mortgage) **VIII:** 119, 150–151, 157
foreign aid **IX:** 332c, 333c
  abortion **X:** 3
  Africa **IX:** 3–4
  Alliance for Progress **IX:** 10–11
  Boland Amendment **X:** 38
  Grenada, invasion of **X:** 135
  Iran-contra affair **X:** 154
  Marshall Plan **IX:** 194–195

Nicaragua **X:** 218
Panama invasion **X:** 231
Peace Corps **IX:** 241
Point Four Program **IX:** 242–243
South Africa **X:** 280
Soviet Union **X:** 281
United Nations **X:** 307
Foreign Anti-Slavery Society **V:** 146
Foreign Assistance Act of 1967 **X:** 37
Foreign Conspiracy Against the Liberties of the United States (Morse) **IV:** 179
Foreign Corrupt Practices Act of 1977 **X: 121–122,** 325c
foreign investment **IV:** 276; **VI: 150–151; VII: 134–135**
Foreign Miners Tax of 1850 **IV:** 249
foreign policy **I:** 371–372; **III: 130–131; IV: 140–143,** 175; **V: 131–133,** 405c; **VI: 102–104; VII:** 28, **97–101,** 98m; **VIII: 123–126,** 125, 407c, 411c; **IX:** 334c; **X: 122–125,** 123. See also government
  Acheson, Dean **IX:** 1–2
  Africa **IX:** 3–4
  African nations **X:** 12–13
  Agnew, Spiro T. **X:** 14
  Aguinaldo, Emilio **VII:** 8
  Albright, Madeleine K. **X:** 18
  America First Committee **VIII:** 12–13
  Americans for Democratic Action **IX:** 13–14
  Anglo-American relations **VIII:** 16–17
  anticommunism **IX:** 14
  Anti-Imperialist League **VI:** 13
  antiwar movement— Vietnam **X:** 24
  Asia **IX:** 21–22
  Barbary pirates **III:** 35
  Benjamin, Judah P. **V:** 27–28
  Bering Sea dispute **VI:** 26–27
  Big Stick diplomacy **VII:** 27–29
  Black Cabinet **VIII:** 38
  Blaine, James Gillespie **VI:** 31
  Borah, William E. **VIII:** 40
  Boxer Rebellion **VII:** 33–34

Britain, Battle of **VIII:** 43
Buchanan, James **V:** 41
Buchanan, Patrick J. **X:** 42
Bush, George H. W. **X:** 45–46
Canada and the United States **VI:** 43
Carter, James Earl, Jr. **X:** 58–59
cash-and-carry **VIII:** 52–53
Chesapeake-Leopard affair **III:** 66–67
Chilean-American relations **VI:** 49–50
Clark Memorandum **VII:** 50–51
Cleveland, Grover **VI:** 59
Clinton, William **X:** 66–67
cold war **IX:** 57–60; **X:** 70–72
Communists **VIII:** 65
Confederate navy **V:** 73
Confederate States of America **V:** 76
Congress **VIII:** 67, 68
conservatism **VIII:** 72
conservative movement **X:** 79
Constitutional Convention **III:** 82
contras **X:** 80–81
Coolidge, Calvin **VII:** 57
Cuba **VI:** 71–72
de Lôme letter **VI:** 76–77
demobilization **IX:** 78
destroyers-for-bases deal **VIII:** 82
détente **X:** 89–90
dollar diplomacy **VII:** 70
Dulles, John Foster **IX:** 82–83
Eisenhower, Dwight D. **IX:** 92
election of 1940 **VIII:** 98
election of 1944 **VIII:** 99
elections **VII:** 81
Essex decision **III:** 119
Ethiopia **VIII:** 105
Europe **IX:** 104–106
Federal Information Act **X:** 112
filibustering **V:** 126–127
Ford, Gerald R. **X:** 121
Foreign Corrupt Practices Act **X:** 121
German Americans **VIII:** 131
Good Neighbor Policy **VIII:** 132–133
Gore, Albert, Jr. **X:** 133
government **VIII:** 135

Grand Alliance **VIII:** 136–138
Great White Fleet **VII:** 113–114
Haig, Alexander M., Jr. **X:** 139, 140
Haiti **III:** 159
Harriman, Averell **VIII:** 144
Harrison, Benjamin **VI:** 123
Hawaii **VI:** 124
Hay, John Milton **VI:** 125
Hoover, Herbert **VIII:** 152–153
Hoover presidency **VIII:** 154–155
Hopkins, Harry **VIII:** 156
Hull, Cordell **VIII:** 159
imperialism **VI:** 141–143
Iran-contra affair **X:** 154–155
isolationists **VIII:** 165–166
Israel **IX:** 146–147
Italian Americans **VIII:** 167
Jay, John **III:** 181
Jews **VIII:** 173
jingoes **VI:** 157
Johnson, Hugh S. **VIII:** 174
Johnson, Lyndon **IX:** 151
Kennan, George **IX:** 155
Kennedy, Edward M. **X:** 164
Kennedy, John F. **IX:** 158
Kissinger, Henry A. **X:** 165–166
Korean War **IX:** 163–165
Lafayette, marquis de **III:** 201
Landon, Alfred M. **VIII:** 183
Latin America **IX:** 171–172; **X:** 172–174
League of Nations. See League of Nations
Lee, Arthur **III:** 205
Lend-Lease Act **VIII:** 184–185
liberalism **VIII:** 189
Lincoln, Abraham **V:** 211
Little Belt incident **III:** 215–216
Livingston, Robert R. **III:** 216
London Economic Conference **VIII:** 193–194
London Naval Conference **VIII:** 194
Manchuria **VIII:** 199–200

foreign policy (continued)
Mexican invasion **VII:** 183
Mexico **X:** 192–193
Middle East **IX:** 200–201
modern Republicanism **IX:** 209
Monroe Doctrine **IV:** 240–242
Monroe-Pinkney Treaty **III:** 245–246
Morgenthau, Henry **VIII:** 216–217
Munich Conference **VIII:** 220
NATO **IX:** 231–233
Neutrality Acts **VIII:** 238–239
Neutrality Proclamation **III:** 256
New Deal **VIII:** 242
New Frontier **IX:** 230
Nicaragua **X:** 217–218
Nixon, Richard M. **X:** 220
Non-Importation Act **III:** 259
Non-Intercourse Act **III:** 259
Norris, George W. **VIII:** 249
North Vietnam **X:** 224
NSC-68 **IX:** 233–234
Nye Committee **VIII:** 250–251
OPEC **X:** 229
Open Door notes **VI:** 216–217
Open Door Policy. *See* Open Door Policy
Orders in Council **III:** 267–268
Oregon Treaty of 1846 **IV:** 269–271
Ostend Manifesto **V:** 259–260
Panama Canal **VII:** 222–224
Paris, Treaty of **III:** 273
Polish Americans **VIII:** 269
Polk, James K. **IV:** 283
Popular Front **VIII:** 276
postwar planning **VIII:** 278
the presidency **VI:** 230
Progressive Party **IX:** 248
public opinion polls **VIII:** 284
Quasi War **III:** 292–293
Reagan, Ronald W. **X:** 260–261
Republican Party **VIII:** 305

Roosevelt, Franklin D. **VIII:** 312
Roosevelt, Theodore **VII:** 266
Roosevelt Corollary **VII:** 267
Root-Takahira Agreement **VII:** 267–268
Russo-Japanese War **VII:** 271
Samoa **VI:** 254–255
Santo Domingo **VI:** 255
Seward, William H. **V:** 314–315
Siberian Expedition **VII:** 285–286
South Africa **X:** 279–280
Southeast Asia Treaty Organization **IX:** 273–274
Soviet-American relations **VIII:** 333–334
Soviet Union **IX:** 277–279
Spanish-American War **VI:** 272–273
Spanish Civil War **VIII:** 334
Stimson, Henry L. **VIII:** 340
Sumner, Charles **V:** 341, 343
Taft, Robert A. **VIII:** 349
Talleyrand, Prince **III:** 341
Teheran Conference **VIII:** 354–355
terrorism **X:** 301
TNEC **VIII:** 355
trade, foreign **VII:** 309
Truman, Harry **IX:** 299
Truman Doctrine **IX:** 300–301
Tyler, John **IV:** 348
United Nations **VIII:** 365; **X:** 307
Van Buren, Martin **IV:** 352
Venezuela boundary dispute **VI:** 303
Vergennes, comte de **III:** 359–360
Versailles, Treaty of **VII:** 322–324
veterans **VII:** 324, 326
Vietnam War **IX:** 308–310; **X:** 311
Virginius affair **VI:** 305–306
Wallace, Henry A. **VIII:** 373
War of 1812 **IV:** 355–358
Welles, Sumner **VIII:** 377
White Paper **IX:** 320–321

Willkie, Wendell L. **VIII:** 379
World Disarmament Conference **VIII:** 388
World War I **VII:** 343–346
World War II **VIII:** 389
XYZ affair **III:** 385
foreign trade. *See* trade, domestic and foreign
Foreman, George **IX:** 10
Forerunner, The (journal) **VII:** 109
Forest Leaves (Harper) **V:** 164
Forest Management Act of 1897 **VI:** 104, 328c
"forest of kings" **I:** 86
forest preservation **VIII:** 103
Forest Reserve Act of 1891 **VI:** 65, **104,** 327c
forest reserves **VI:** 65, 200
forests **II:** **122–123,** 145, 201, **251,** 265
forests, preservation of **VI:** 65
Forest Service **VII:** 228, 263; **IX:** 16, 226–227
forfeiture (RICO) **X:** 257
"Forgotten Man" **VIII:** 273
"Forgotten War." *See* Korean War
Formosa **VIII:** 399. *See also* Fernando Po; Taiwan
fornication **II:** 228, 409
Forrest, Edwin **V:** 352; **VI:** 286
Forrest, Nathan Bedford **V:** **133–135,** *134,* 407c; **VI:** 163; **VII:** 147
Confederate army **V:** 72
Fort Pillow, Tennessee **V:** 135
Ku Klux Klan **V:** 199
Reconstruction Acts **V:** *295*
Forrestal, James V. **VIII:** **126,** 236
Forsberg, Randall **X:** 224
Fort Amsterdam **II:** 182
Fortas, Abe **IX:** 121, 316; **X:** 41, **125–126,** 323c
Fort Astoria **IV:** 93, 321
Fort Atkinson **IV:** 33–34
Fort Beauséjour **II:** 232
Fort Bridger
Bridger, James **IV:** 57
Donner party **IV:** 114
exploration **IV:** 131
Mormon Trail **IV:** 243
Mormon War **IV:** 244
Fort Brown, Texas **VII:** 35, 356c
Fort Carillon **II:** 332
Fort Caroline, Florida **I:** 130, 201–202, 387c
Fort Christiana **II:** 87, 364, *365*
Fort Clark **IV:** 55

Fort Dearborn **IV:** 259, 356
Fort de Mississippi **II:** 193
Fort Detroit
Cass, Lewis **IV:** 76
Lake Erie, Battle of **IV:** 206
Native Americans **IV:** 256
War of 1812 **IV:** 356
Fort Donelson, Tennessee
Civil War **V:** 66
Confederate army **V:** 73
Forrest, Nathan Bedford **V:** 134
Grant, Ulysses S. **V:** 154, 156
Halleck, Henry W. **V:** 162
Johnston, Albert Sidney **V:** 189
Mississippi River **V:** 234
Orphan Brigade **V:** 258
prisons **V:** 281
Shiloh, Battle of **V:** 323
tactics and strategy **V:** 346
Union navy **V:** 370
Welles, Gideon **V:** 391
Fort Dunmore **III:** 109
Fort Duquesne **II:** 38, 123, 124, 129, 332, 419c; **III:** 146, 149, 366
Fort Edward **II:** 125
Forten, James **II:** 31; **III:** **131–132,** 396c; **IV:** 2, 3, 15, 16
African Americans **III:** 7
antislavery and abolition **III:** 17
Cuffe, Paul **III:** 98, 99
Jones, Absalom **III:** 189
Fort Erie **IV:** 358
Fort Fisher, North Carolina **V:** 280
Fort Frederica **II:** 297
Fort Frontenac **II:** 419c
Fort Gaines, Alabama **V:** 222
Fort Gaspereau **II:** 232
Fort George
Astor, John Jacob **IV:** 31
Astoria **IV:** 33
Scott, Winfield **IV:** 309
War of 1812 **IV:** 356, 358
Fort Gibson, Kansas **V:** 250
Fort Hall **IV:** 71, 131, 267
Fort Harrison **IV:** 334
Fort Henry, Tennessee **IV:** 28, 29, 300, 302
Civil War **V:** 66
Grant, Ulysses S. **V:** 154
Halleck, Henry W. **V:** 162
Johnston, Albert Sidney **V:** 189
Mississippi River **V:** 234
Shiloh, Battle of **V:** 324

tactics and strategy **V:** 346
Welles, Gideon **V:** 391
Fort Hindman, USS **V:** 235
Fort Jackson, Treaty of (1814)
   III: 97; **IV:** 98
Fort James **II:** 192, 261
Fort Johnson, New York **II:**
   177
Fort Laramie **IV: 143–145,**
   144; **VI:** 208
   California Trail **IV:** 71
   Donner party **IV:** 114
   Mormon Trail **IV:** 243
   Native Americans **IV:** 258
   Oregon Trail **IV:** 267
   Sublette, William **IV:** 330
Fort Laramie, Treaty of (1868)
   IV: 144; **V:** 213–214, 408*c;*
   VI: 324*c*
   Black Hills gold rush **VI:**
      29
   Crazy Horse **VI:** 69
   Sioux wars **VI:** 263
   Sitting Bull **VI:** 264
Fort La Tour **I:** 219
Fort Leavenworth **IV:** 33, **145,**
   153, 200
Fort Lee, New Jersey **III:** 155,
   168
Fort Mackinac **IV:** 356, 358
Fort McHenry **IV:** 39, 201
Fort McKenzie **IV:** 17, 55
Fort Meigs **IV:** 169, 259
Fort Mims **IV:** 99, 256, 259
Fort Monroe, Virginia **V:** 267
Fort Mose **II: 123,** 361, 392
Fort Moultrie, South Carolina
   V: 9, 136
Fort Mystic **II:** 243, 278
Fort Nassau **II:** 255
Fort Necessity **II:** 119, **123**
Fort Niagara **II:** 177, 332; **III:**
   146; **IV:** 259, 358
Fort Orange **I:** 183; **II:** 31, 99,
   130–131, 168, 249–250, 255
Fort Oswego **II:** 332
Fort Patrick Henry **III:** 107
Fort Phil Kearny **VI:** 69
Fort Pickering, Tennessee **V:**
   232
Fort Pillow, Tennessee **V:** 134,
   135, 191, 235, 407*c*
Fort Pitt **II:** 76, 124, 233
Fort Randolph **II:** 72
Fort Rosalie **II:** 241, 242
forts **II: 124; V:** 389, 390
   Bacon's Rebellion **II:** 27
   exploration **II:** 115
   French colonies **II:** 126,
      128*m*
   Kieft, Willem **II:** 182
   Native Americans **II:** 246

Oglethorpe, James Edward
   II: 267
   St. Augustine **II:** 327
   Seven Years' War **II:** 332
   slave trade **II:** 343, 344
Fort Scott **IV:** 312
Fort Smith, Arkansas **V:** 250
Fort Stanwix, siege of **III:** 255
Fort Stanwix, Treaty of **II:** 76,
   177; **III: 132,** 392*c*, 394*c*
   Cornplanter **III:** 91–92
   Iroquois Confederacy **III:**
      179
   Ohio Company of Virginia
      III: 265
   Red Jacket **III:** 297
Fort Stephenson **IV:** 169
Fort Stevens **V:** 390
Fort Sumter, South Carolina **V:**
   135–137, *136,* 406*c*
   Anderson, Robert **V:** 9–10
   Beauregard, Pierre **V:** 27
   Civil War **V:** 65
   Confederate States of
      America **V:** 75
   Davis, Jefferson **V:** 89
   Douglas, Stephen A. **V:** 99
   emancipation **V:** 112
   54th Massachusetts
      Regiment **V:** 126
   fire-eaters **V:** 127
   Grant, Ulysses S. **V:** 154
   journalism **V:** 193
   Lee, Robert E. **V:** 205
   Lincoln, Abraham **V:** 210
   secession **V:** 313
   Seward, William H. **V:** 314
   Stanton, Edwin M. **V:** 334
   United States Army Corps
      of Engineers **V:** 371
Fort Sutter **IV:** 51, 115, 332
Fort Ticonderoga **II:** 332; **III:**
   132–133, 393*c*
   Allen, Ethan **III:** 10
   Arnold, Benedict **III:** 21
   Burgoyne, John **III:** 52
   Carleton, Guy **III:** 62
   Continental army **III:** 84
   Deane, Silas **III:** 101
   Dorchester Heights, Battle
      of **III:** 107
   Gage, Thomas **III:** 146
   Gates, Horatio **III:** 149
   Green Mountain Boys **III:**
      156
   Kościuszko, Tadeusz **III:**
      198
   Lyon, Matthew **III:** 222
   Quebec, Battle of **III:** 293
   St. Clair, Arthur **III:** 316
   Saratoga, surrender at **III:**
      318

Schuyler, Philip John **III:**
   320
   Valcour Island, Battle of
      III: 357
   Wayne, Anthony **III:** 369
Fortune, Timothy Thomas
   African Americans **VI:** 6
   civil rights cases **VI:** 56
   newspapers **VI:** 212
   Wells-Barnett, Ida Bell **VI:**
      311
Fortune (magazine) **VIII:** 196,
   284
Fort Vancouver **IV: 145–146**
   Astoria **IV:** 33
   Columbia River **IV:** 93
   McLoughlin, John **IV:**
      229
   Oregon Trail **IV:** 267
   Rocky Mountain Fur
      Company **IV:** 302
   Smith, Jedediah Strong **IV:**
      322
Fort Wagner, South Carolina **V:**
   407*c*
   African-American
      regiments **V:** 5
   54th Massachusetts
      Regiment **V:** 124–126
   marine corps **V:** 222
Fort Washington, capture of **III:**
   133, 155, 167, 376
Fort Wayne, Treaty of **IV:**
   168–169
Fort William Henry **III:** 97
Fort William Henry Massacre
   II: 124–125
Forty-eighters **IV:** 177; **V:** 175
Forty-niners **IV:** *146,* **146–147**
   California gold rush **IV:**
      66–69
   California Trail **IV:** 70
   Fort Laramie **IV:** 143
   gold, discovery and mining
      IV: 162
   lead mines **IV:** 208
   migration **IV:** 236
   Native Americans **IV:** 258
   Oregon Trail **IV:** 267
   South Pass **IV:** 325
49th parallel **IV:** 378*c*
   Adams-Onís Treaty **IV:** 5
   exploration **IV:** 132
   foreign policy **IV:** 142
   Manifest Destiny **IV:** 217
   Webster-Ashburton Treaty
      (1842) **IV:** 360
42nd Massachusetts Infantry
   Regiment **V:** 145
42nd parallel **IV:** 5, 269
Forty-two Articles **II:** 301
Forum magazine **VII:** 19

For Whom the Bell Tolls
   (Hemingway) **VIII:** 192, 335
Fosse, Bob **X:** 241
fossil dating techniques **IX:** 270
fossils **IV:** 308; **VI:** 257
Foster, Abigail Kelley **IV:** 15,
   147–148
Foster, David **X:** 262
Foster, Ezola **X:** 264
Foster, Jodie **X:** 31
Foster, Stephen C. **V: 137–138;**
   VI: 183, 203
Foster, Stephen Symonds **IV:**
   148
Foster, Vincent **X:** 68
Foster, William T. **VIII:** 89
Foster, William Z. **VII:** 297,
   298; **VIII:** 65, 272*t*
Foucault, Jean-Bernard-Léon
   IV: 307
Fountain (Duchamp) **VII:** 19
Fountain of Age, The (Betty
   Friedan) **IX:** 115–116
fountain of youth **I:** 288
Four Freedoms **VIII: 126–127,**
   127, 257, 275
Four Freedoms Speech **VIII:**
   423–427
"Four Horsemen of the
   Apocalypse" **VIII:** 345
442nd Regimental Combat
   Team **VIII:** 26, *26*
Fourier, Charles **IV:** 58, **149**
"Four Indian Kings" **II:** 155
Four-Minute Men **VII:** 52
Four Power Pacific Treaty of
   1921 **VII:** 360*c*
Four-Power Pact **VII:** 331
Fourteen Points **VII:** 359*c;*
   VIII: 28
   Democratic Party **VII:** 66
   League of Nations **VII:**
      156
   progressivism **VII:** 237
   Versailles, Treaty of **VII:**
      323
   Wilson, Woodrow **VII:**
      334
"Fourteen Points" speech
   (Wilson) **VII:** 379–382
Fourteenth Amendment **IV:**
   289; **V: 138–139,** 408*c*,
   427–428; **VI:** 324*c*, 326*c*; **VII:**
   163–164, 281; **VIII:** 37, 61,
   345, 347, 408*c*; **IX:** 42–43,
   104, 121, 259–260; **X:** 324*c*
   amnesty, acts of **V:** 9
   Anthony, Susan B. **VI:** 12,
      13
   Bakke **X:** 34
   banking and currency **V:**
      24

Fourteenth Amendment
(*continued*)
Blackwell, Antoinette
Brown **VI:** 30
Brown, Joseph **V:** 39
civil rights cases **VI:** 55
Douglass, Frederick **V:** 100
due process clause **VI:** 81,
82
emancipation **V:** 114
Enforcement Acts **V:** 117
Fifteenth Amendment **V:**
123, 124
Ginsburg, Ruth Bader **X:**
130
Harlan, John Marshall **VI:**
122
Hayes, Rutherford B. **VI:**
127
Hoar, George Frisbie **VI:**
130
Johnson, Andrew **V:** 178,
188
marriage **X:** 181
Plessy v. Ferguson **VI:** 224
Radical Republicans **V:**
289
Reconstruction **V:** 293, 294
Reconstruction Acts **V:** 296
Rehnquist, William H. **X:**
264, 265
Republican Party **V:** 302
Scalia, Antonin **X:** 271
Stanton, Edwin M. **V:** 334
Stevens, Thaddeus **V:** 338
Stone, Lucy **VI:** 278
Supreme Court **VI:** 281
Thirteenth Amendment **V:**
353
*United States v.
Cruikshank* **V:** 376
veterans, Civil War **V:** 379
women's rights and status
V: 398; **VI:** 317
Fourth of July **III:** 282
*Four Weeks among Some of the
Sioux Tribes* (Welsh) **VI:** 144
Fowlstown **IV:** 312
Fox, Catherine (Kate) **IV:** 299,
325; **VI:** 244
Fox, Charles James **III:** 260
Fox, George **II:** 1, 160, 275,
302, 307, 308
Fox, Gustavus Vasa **V:** 391
Fox, Leah **IV:** 299
Fox, Margaret **IV:** 299, 325; **VI:**
244
Fox, Richard Kyle **VI:** 33
Fox, Vicente **X:** 174, 193
Foxe, John **I:** 132
Foxe's *Book of Martyrs* **I: 132,**
224

Fox Hunt, The (Homer) **VI:** 130
Fox nation **II:** 199; **IV:** 208
Fox News Channel **X:** 241, 296
Fox studios **X:** 197
Frame of Government **II:** 145,
273, 276
France **I:** 387*c*; **III:** 391*c*,
393*c*–398*c*; **VI:** 328*c*; **VII:**
359*c*, 360*c*; **VIII:** 408*c*, 410*c*;
IX: 332*c*
Acadia **I:** 3
Acadians **II:** 2
Adams, John **III:** 2, 3
aircraft industry **VIII:** 10,
11
Algonquin **II:** 17
American Expeditionary
Force **VII:** 9
Asia (foreign policy) **IX:** 21
Atlantic, Battle of the
VIII: 28
Balloon Corps **V:** 21
Benjamin, Judah P. **V:**
27–28
Berlin blockade **IX:** 37
blitzkrieg **VIII:** 39
Bodmer, Karl **IV:** 55
Bonaparte, Napoleon **III:**
41–42
Brazil **I:** 33
British Empire **II:** 41, 43
Bulge, Battle of the **VIII:**
44
Bush, George H. W. **X:** 46
Cabet, Étienne **IV:** 61
Cairo Conference **VIII:** 51
Carey, Mathew **III:** 61
Casablanca Conference
VIII: 52
cash-and-carry **VIII:** 53
Cass, Lewis **IV:** 76
Cayor **I:** 66
Chesapeake-Leopard affair
III: 67
Choctaw nation **III:** 68
Confederate States of
America **V:** 76
Continental navy **III:** 90
Creek nation **III:** 96
Crèvecoeur, J. Hector St.
John de **III:** 97, 98
crowd action **II:** 77
Dawes Plan **VII:** 63
Deane, Silas **III:** 101
deism **III:** 104
economy **III:** 113
election of 1800 **III:** 116
embargo of 1807 **III:** 117
Essex decision **III:** 119
Estaing, comte d' **III:**
119–120
Ethiopia **VIII:** 105

Federalist Party **III:** 126
Ferdinand and Isabella **I:**
128
feudalism **I:** 130
filibustering **V:** 127
Florida **IV:** 139
foreign affairs **III:** 130
foreign policy **IV:** 141; **V:**
131, 132; **VI:** 103; **VII:**
100
Franklin, Benjamin **III:**
135
French alliance **III:** 137
Fries's Rebellion **III:** 140
Fulton, Robert **III:**
141–142
fur trade **IV:** 156
Gallatin, Albert **III:** 147
Genet, Edmond **III:**
149–150
Gerry, Elbridge **III:**
152–153
Ghent, Treaty of (1814) **IV:**
161
Grasse, comte de **III:** 154
Great Plains **III:** 155
Haiti **III:** 159
Hawaii **VI:** 124
Henry IV (Henry of
Navarre) **I:** 158–159
Henry VIII **I:** 160
Holy League **I:** 164
Holy Roman Empire **I:** 165
Huguenots **I:** 169–170
immigration **III:** 173
ironclads **V:** 183
Iroquois Confederacy **III:**
179
isolationists **VIII:** 166
Italian Americans **VIII:**
167
Jay, John **III:** 181
Jefferson, Thomas **III:** 184
Jomini, Antoine-Henri,
baron de **V:** 192
Kalb, baron de **III:** 195
Kellogg-Briand Treaty **VII:**
146
King George's War **II:** 182
Lafayette, marquis de **III:**
200, 201
Lafitte, Jean **IV:** 205
Las Casas, Bartolomé de **I:**
198
lead mines **IV:** 208
Leahy, William D. **VIII:**
184
Lee, Arthur **III:** 205
L'Enfant, Pierre-Charles
III: 207
Lewis and Clark
Expedition **III:** 210

Livingston, Robert R. **III:**
216
London Economic
Conference **VIII:** 193
Louisiana Purchase **III:**
218
Macon's Bill No. 2 **III:** 226
Madison, James **III:** 229
Manifest Destiny **IV:** 218
Marquette, Jacques **II:** 205
Marshall, George C. **VIII:**
206
Marshall, John **III:** 235
Marshall Plan **IX:** 194
Massachusetts **II:** 214
Mexican-American War
IV: 232
Middle East **IX:** 201
Monitor-Merrimack **V:** 237
Monroe, James **IV:** 240
Monroe Doctrine **IV:** 241
Monroe-Pinkney Treaty
III: 245–246
Montour, Madame **II:** 233
Morris, Gouverneur **III:**
247
Munich Conference **VIII:**
220
Native Americans **II:** 246
NATO **IX:** 231–233; **X:**
223
Nazi-Soviet Pact **VIII:** 238
neutrality **VII:** 210
Neutrality Proclamation
III: 256
Nicaragua **X:** 218
Non-Intercourse Act **III:**
259
Normandy, invasion of
VIII: 247, 248
Ohio Company of Virginia
III: 265
Open Door notes **VI:**
216–217
Orders in Council **III:** 267
Ostend Manifesto **V:** 259
Paine, Thomas **III:**
271–272
painting **VI:** 219
Paris, Treaty of **III:** 273
Patton, George **VIII:** 263
Pennsylvania **II:** 276
Pickering, John **III:** 276
Pontiac's Rebellion **III:**
280–281
Popular Front **VIII:** 276
population trends **I:** 290;
III: 283
POWs **VIII:** 281
Príncipe **I:** 293
privateering **II:** 299–300;
III: 287

Quasi War **III:** 291–292
race and racial conflict **V:** 288
Reformation **I:** 309
Republican Party **VIII:** 306
Revolutionary War **III:** 305, 307
Rochambeau, comte de **III:** 310
Roman Catholicism **VI:** 249
Russian Revolution **VII:** 270
science and technology **IV:** 307
Seven Years' War **II:** 332–334
Seward, William H. **V:** 314, 315
Sicily **VIII:** 325
slave trade **II:** 343
Southeast Asia Treaty Organization **IX:** 273–274
space policy **X:** 281
Statue of Liberty **VI:** 275–276
Suez crisis **IX:** 288, 289
Talleyrand, Prince **III:** 341
tariffs **V:** 348
technology **IX:** 294
Teheran Conference **VIII:** 354
Texas **IV:** 337, 338
Texas Revolution **IV:** 339
Treaty of Paris **II:** 378
UN **VIII:** 366
U.S. European foreign policy **IX:** 106
V-E Day **VIII:** 369
Vergennes, comte de **III:** 359–360
Versailles, Treaty of **VII:** 323, 324
Vietnam War **IX:** 308
War of 1812 **IV:** 355
wars of national liberation **IX:** 316
war with Great Britain, 1793–1815. *See* Anglo-French War, 1793–1815
Washington, George **III:** 366
Washington Conference on Naval Disarmament **VII:** 331
West Indies **III:** 372
Wilson, Woodrow **VII:** 334
World Disarmament Conference **VIII:** 388
World War I **VII:** 343

World War II European theater **VIII:** 391
Wright, Richard **VIII:** 400
XYZ affair **III:** 385
Zouaves **V:** 403
Francis, Sam **IV:** 347
Francis, Will **IV:** 347
Franciscans **I: 132–133**
  Apalachee **I:** 11
  Azores **I:** 17
  California **I:** 48, 49
  Calusa **I:** 49
  Florida **I:** 131; **II:** 120
  Hopi **I:** 167
  Jesuits **I:** 189
  missions **II:** 230, 231
  Native Americans **II:** 246
  New Mexico **I:** 256, 257; **II:** 254
  Pueblo Indians **II:** 303
  Pueblo Revolt **II:** 303
  reducción **I:** 306
  religion, Native American **II:** 317
  Roman Catholics **II:** 324
  Sahagún, Bernardino de **I:** 315
  Santa Fe **I:** 319
  Serra, Junípero **II:** 331–332
  Timucua **I:** 351
  Yucatán Peninsula **I:** 379
Francis I, king of France **I:** 50, 57, 204, 339, 367, 387*c*
Francis of Assisi. *See* St. Francis
Francis of Guise **I:** 169
Francis Xavier, St. **I:** 209; **II:** 174
Franco, Francisco **VIII:** 124, 276, 334, 335
Franco-American Convention of 1800 **III:** 397*c*
Franco-American Treaty of 1778 **III:** 385
François de Sales, St. **II:** 244
Franco-Prussian War of 1870–1871 **V:** 25, 319
Frank, Jerome **VIII:** 6
Frank, Leo. *See* Leo Frank case
Frankenthaler, Helen **IX:** 20
Frankfurter, Felix **VII:** 122, 273; **VIII: 127–128; IX:** 1, 31, 100, 315, *315;* **X:** 40, 125, 268
  antimonopoly **VIII:** 17
  Lilienthal, David E. **VIII:** 190
  Supreme Court **VIII:** 346*t*
  Zionism **VIII:** 403
Frank Leslie's Illustrated Newspaper **IV:** 197; **V:** 102, 193, 247
Frank Leslie's Ladies Gazette of Fancy Needle Work **IV:** 197

Franklin, Ann Smith **II: 125,** 299
Franklin, Battle of **V:** 354
Franklin, Benjamin **II:** 14, 419*c;* **III: 133–135,** *134,* 393*c*–395*c;* **IV:** 149, 229; **V:** 1
  Adams, John **III:** 3
  African Americans **II:** 7
  Albany Congress **II:** 14
  American Philosophical Society **II:** 18; **III:** 11
  Bache, Benjamin Franklin **III:** 29
  Bond, Thomas **II:** 33
  Boston **II:** 36
  Carey, Mathew **III:** 61
  Colden, Cadwallader **II:** 66
  College of Philadelphia **II:** 66, 67
  Constitutional Convention **III:** 81
  Continental Congress, Second **III:** 88
  Deane, Silas **III:** 101
  Declaration of Independence **III:** 102
  deism **III:** 103
  disease **II:** 92
  education **II:** 104
  Enlightenment **II:** 109
  Flashman, Edward **II:** 119
  Franklin, Deborah Read **II:** 125
  Franklin, William **III:** 136
  French alliance **III:** 137
  Galloway, Joseph **III:** 148
  German immigrants **II:** 139
  Godfrey, Thomas **II:** 141
  Great Awakening **II:** 149
  Hesselius, John **II:** 156
  Hutchinson, Thomas **III:** 170
  Ingersoll, Jared **III:** 178
  Jay, John **III:** 181
  Jefferson, Thomas **III:** 184
  journalism **II:** 179
  Kalm, Peter **II:** 181
  Knight, Sarah Kemble **II:** 185
  labor and labor movements **III:** 200
  land **II:** 191
  Lee, Arthur **III:** 205
  literature **III:** 215
  Logan, James **II:** 198
  Oliver, Andrew **III:** 267
  Paine, Thomas **III:** 271
  Paris, Treaty of **III:** 273
  Paxton Boys **II:** 272
  Pennsylvania **II:** 276–278

  Philadelphia **II:** 282
  population trends **II:** 291
  postal service **II:** 292–293
  printing and publishing **II:** 299
  Protestant work ethic **II:** 302
  Pulsaki, Casimir **III:** 289
  Quartering Act **III:** 291
  religion, Euro-American **II:** 316
  Rittenhouse, David **II:** 322
  science **II:** 330–331; **III:** 321
  Seven Years' War **II:** 332
  Smith, Robert **II:** 348
  society, British American **II:** 349, 352
  Steuben, Frederick von **III:** 334
  technology **II:** 369
  Townshend Duties **III:** 348
  travel **II:** 377
  voluntary associations **III:** 362
  Webster, Noah **III:** 370
  Weems, "Parson" **III:** 371
  Whately, Thomas **III:** 373
Franklin, Deborah Read **II: 125**
Franklin, James **II:** 299
Franklin, James, Jr. **II:** 258
Franklin, Rosalind **IX:** 269
Franklin, state of **III: 135–136**
Franklin, Stella **VII:** 206, 252
Franklin, William **II:** 372; **III:** 134, **136,** 148
Franklin Institute **IV: 149–150**
Franklin National Bank of New York **IX:** 330*c*
Franks, Bobby **VII:** 62, 158
Franks, David **III:** 187
Frascatoro, Girolamo **I:** 304
Fraser family **IV:** 228
fraud **V:** 408*c*
Frauds Exposed (Comstock) **VI:** 62
Frazier, Charles **V:** 213
Frazier, Joe **IX:** 10
Frazier-Lemke Farm Bankruptcy Act of 1934 **VIII:** 407*c*
Fredendall, Lloyd R. **VIII:** 249
Frederick, Harold **VI:** 177
Frederick III of Saxony (Frederick the Wise) **I:** 211
Fredericksburg, Battle of **V:** 139, **139–141,** 140*m,* 406*c*
  Alexander, Edward P. **V:** 7
  Burnside, Ambrose E. **V:** 45

Fredericksburg, Battle of
   (continued)
      Chamberlain, Joshua L. **V:**
         54
      Early, Jubal A. **V:** 103
      Hancock, Winfield Scott **V:**
         163
      Hill, Ambrose P. **V:** 168
      Hooker, Joseph **V:** 171
      Irish-American regiments
         V: 182
      Jackson, "Stonewall" **V:** 186
      Joint Committee on the
         Conduct of War **V:** 191
      Lee, Robert E. **V:** 206
      Longstreet, James **V:** 215
      Meade, George Gordon **V:**
         226
      Murfreesboro/Stones
         River, Battle of **V:** 242
      photography **V:** 273
      Pickett, George Edward **V:**
         274
      Sickles, Daniel E. **V:** 326
      Walker, Mary Edwards **V:**
         386
      Whitman, Walt **V:** 394
Fredericksburg, Virginia **V:** 267,
   316, 317
Frederick the Great **III:** 334
free African Americans **II:** 260,
   341, 342, 359, 364
Free African Society **III:** 6, 11,
   189, 395*c*
free agency (baseball) **X:** 284
free blacks **IV:** 8–9, 237
Freed, Alan **IX:** 217, 263
Freedman's Saving Bank **V:** 40,
   141–142
freedmen **II:** 383
Freedmen's Aid Society **V:** 104
Freedmen's Bureau **V:**
   142–144, 143*m,* 408*c;* **VI:** 5,
   93, 94, 172
      Black Codes **V:** 30
      contrabands **V:** 81
      Davis Bend, Mississippi,
         freedmen's colony **V:** 92
      Delany, Martin Robinson
         V: 93
      Eaton, John, Jr. **V:** 104
      education **V:** 108
      emancipation **V:** 114
      Fifteenth Amendment **V:**
         124
      Fitzhugh, George **V:** 128
      Freedman's Saving Bank
         V: 141
      Howard, O. O. **V:** 173
      Johnson, Andrew **V:** 188
      Kelley, William D. **V:** 198
      Memphis riot **V:** 232

Reconstruction **V:** 295
      redemption **V:** 296
      Revels, Hiram R. **V:** 303
      Society of Friends **V:** 332
      Special Field Order No. 15
         V: 333
      Stanton, Edwin M. **V:** 334
      Thirteenth Amendment **V:**
         353
Freedmen's Bureau Bill **V:** 178,
   289
Freedmen's Bureaus **IV:** 4
Freedmen's Relief Association
   V: 160
"freedom dues" **II:** 163, 191
Freedom of Access Act of 1984
   X: 105
Freedom of Access to Clinic
   Entrances Act (FACE) **X:** 4
freedom of information **X:** 324*c*
Freedom of Information Act
   (FOIA) **X:** 111–112, 162, 205
freedom of speech **X:** 39, 60–61,
   154
freedom of the press **II:** 153,
   415–416; **X:** 5, 60–61
freedom rides **IX:** *113,*
   113–114, 333*c*
      African-American
         movement **IX:** 5
      Birmingham confrontation
         IX: 38
      Carmichael, Stokely **IX:** 47
      Congress of Racial
         Equality **IX:** 66
      race and racial conflict **IX:**
         253
      Student Nonviolent
         Coordinating
         Committee **IX:** 284
freedom schools **IX:** 207
Freedom's Journal **III:** 131; **IV:**
   15, 194, 366; **VI:** 70
Freedom to Access Clinic
   Entrances Act of 1994
   (FACE) **X:** 249
free labor. *See* labor, free
"free land" **IV:** 288
free love **IV:** 326; **VI:** 317, 319
freeman **II:** 212
Freeman, Orville I. **X:** 196
Freeman's Journal **III:** 139
freemasonry **III: 136–137,** 160,
   361–362; **IV:** 24; **V:** 367
free people of color **II:** 74, 229,
   238
"Freeport Doctrine" **V:** 98–99
Free-Silver movement **V:** 392;
   VI: 104–105; VII: 80
      Altgeld, John Peter **VI:** 10
      Anti-Imperialist League
         VI: 13

bimetallism **VI:** 28
      Bland-Allison Act **VI:** 32
      Bryan, William Jennings
         VI: 37
      Cleveland, Grover **VI:** 59
      Congress **VI:** 63
      Crime of '73 **VI:** 70
      currency issue **VI:** 72, 73
      Democratic Party **VI:**
         77–78
      Greenback-Labor Party
         VI: 120
      Lease, Mary Elizabeth **VI:**
         173
      mugwumps **VI:** 199
      national banking system
         VI: 206
      People's Party **VI:** 223
      political parties, third **VI:**
         226
      presidential campaigns **VI:**
         232
      Sherman, John **VI:** 261
      Simpson, Jerry **VI:** 262
Free Society of Traders **II:** 145,
   189
Free-Soilers
      abolition **V:** 3, 4
      Blair, Francis P., Jr. **V:** 30
      Bleeding Kansas **V:** 31
      Brown, John **V:** 38
      Chase, Salmon P. **V:** 56
      Civil War **V:** 64
      Douglas, Stephen A. **V:**
         98
      Julian, George W. **V:** 194
      Kansas-Nebraska Act of
         1854 **V:** 198
      Republican Party **V:** 300,
         301
      slavery **V:** 328, 330
      Sumner, Charles **V:** 342
      Welles, Gideon **V:** 391
      Whitman, Walt **V:** 393
      Wilmot Proviso **V:** 396
Free-Soil Party **IV: 150–151,**
   151, 379*c*
      abolition movement **IV:** 3
      Benton, Thomas Hart **IV:**
         49–50
      Cass, Lewis **IV:** 77
      Clay, Henry **IV:** 88
      Dana, Richard Henry **IV:**
         103
      Democratic Party **IV:** 108
      Liberty Party **IV:** 210,
         211
      Mann, Horace **IV:** 220
      Republican Party **IV:** 300,
         301
      Taylor, Zachary **IV:** 335
      Whig Party **IV:** 364

free speech **VII:** 359*c;* **VIII:** 85.
   See also First Amendment;
   Four Freedoms
      Brandeis, Louis **VII:** 35
      Espionage Act **VII:** 88
      Greenwich Village **VII:**
         115
      Griffith, D. W. **VII:** 116
      Holmes, Oliver Wendell
         VII: 122
      Schenk v. United States
         VII: 274–275
      Sedition Act **VII:** 280
Free Speech Movement **IX:** 54,
   112–113, 268, 286
Free-State Hotel **IV:** 224
Free Trade and Sailor's Rights
   IV: 151–152
free trappers **IV:** 30, 33
freight boats **IV:** 74
Freiheit **VI:** 167
Frelinghuysen, Frederick **VI:**
   50, 52
Frelinghuysen, Theodorus
   Jacobus **II: 125–126,** 147,
   301
Frémont, Jessie Benton **IV:** 50,
   152–153, 153
Frémont, John C. **IV: 153–154,**
   378*c;* **V:** 405*c,* 406*c*
      Bear Flag Revolt **IV:** 45
      Benton, Thomas Hart **IV:**
         50
      Buchanan, James **V:** 41
      California **IV:** 65
      California Trail **IV:** 71
      Carson, Kit **IV:** 75, 76
      Confiscation Acts **V:** 78
      exploration **IV:** 131–132
      Frémont, Jessie Benton
         IV: 152
      Greeley, Horace **V:** 158
      Halleck, Henry W. **V:**
         162
      Jackson, "Stonewall" **V:**
         185
      Kearny, Stephen Watts **IV:**
         200
      Know-Nothing Party **IV:**
         202
      Larkin, Thomas Oliver **IV:**
         208
      nativism **V:** 251
      Oregon Trail **IV:** 267
      Peninsular campaign **V:**
         267
      Republican Party **IV:** 300;
         V: 301
      Shenandoah Valley:
         Jackson's campaign **V:**
         316, 317
      South Pass **IV:** 325

Stockton, Robert Field **IV:** 328
Union army **V:** 365
French, Daniel Chester **VI:** 259
French, William **V:** 13
French alliance **III: 137–138,** 393*c*, 397*c*
   Catholics **III:** 63
   French Revolution **III:** 138
   Lee, Arthur **III:** 205
   Neutrality Proclamation **III:** 256
   Quasi War **III:** 292
   Revolutionary War **III:** 307
   Rhode Island, Battle of **III:** 308
   Rochambeau, comte de **III:** 310
   Vergennes, comte de **III:** 359–360
   Yorktown, surrender at **III:** 388, 390
French and Indian War **III:** 391*c*; **IV:** 156, 253. *See also* Seven Years' War
   American Revolution **III:** 12
   Brant, Joseph **III:** 48
   Bute, earl of **III:** 55
   campaigns outside of America. *See* Seven Years' War
   Canada **III:** 60
   Carleton, Guy **III:** 62
   Cherokee nation **III:** 66
   Choctaw nation **III:** 68
   Clinton, George **III:** 74
   Coercive Acts **III:** 76
   Cornplanter **III:** 91
   Creek nation **III:** 96
   Crèvecoeur, J. Hector St. John de **III:** 97
   economy **III:** 111
   Estaing, comte d' **III:** 120
   Florida **III:** 129
   foreign affairs **III:** 130
   Fort Ticonderoga **III:** 132–133
   Franklin, Benjamin **III:** 134
   frontier **III:** 141
   Gage, Thomas **III:** 146
   Gates, Horatio **III:** 149
   George III, king of Great Britain **III:** 151
   Grenville, George **III:** 157
   Howe, Richard, Lord **III:** 167
   Howe, Sir William **III:** 168
   Hutchinson, Thomas **III:** 170

Louisiana Purchase **III:** 218
Morgan, Daniel **III:** 246
New Spain (Mexico), northern frontier of **III:** 258
Ohio Company of Virginia **III:** 265
Pitt, William **III:** 277
Pontiac's Rebellion **III:** 280–281
population trends **III:** 283
Proclamation of 1763 **III:** 287
Revere, Paul **III:** 304
St. Clair, Arthur **III:** 315
Schuyler, Philip John **III:** 320
Sugar Act **III:** 337
Townshend Duties **III:** 348
Vergennes, comte de **III:** 359
Washington, George **III:** 366
West Indies **III:** 372
"Yankee Doodle" **III:** 387
Yates, Abraham, Jr. **III:** 387
French Andrew. *See* Montour, Andrew
French burr stones **II:** 225
French Canada **II:** 420*c*
French Clinical School **IV:** 230
French colonies **II: 126–129,** 128*m*, *132*, 200*m*, 419*c*. *See also* New France
   Albany Congress **II:** 14
   art **II:** 25
   Champlain, Samuel de **II:** 126–127
   Colbert, Jean-Baptiste **II:** 129
   crowd action **II:** 78
   exploration **II:** 126, 129
   fishing **II:** 126
   Florida **II:** 120, 121
   forts **II:** 124
   Fort William Henry Massacre **II:** 124–125
   fur trade **II:** 130–132
   Hendrick **II:** 155, 156
   Iroquois **II:** 169
   Jesuits **II:** 174
   King William's War **II:** 185
   La Salle, René-Robert Cavelier, sieur de **II:** 192
   Le Moyne, Jean-Baptiste, sieur de Bienville **II:** 193
   Louisiana **II:** 199–200

Maine **II:** 203
Marquette, Jacques **II:** 205
medicine **II:** 220
mercantilism **II:** 221
miscegenation **II:** 229
missionaries **II:** 127, 129
monarchy, British **II:** 232
Monckton, Robert **II:** 232
Natchez Revolt **II:** 241–242
New Hampshire **II:** 250
New Orleans **II:** 258
New York **II:** 262
Red Shoes **II:** 313
Roman Catholics **II:** 323, 324
Seven Years' War **II:** 129
slavery **II:** 339, 342
theater **II:** 373
trade **II:** 126
trade and shipping **II:** 375
war and warfare **II:** 391
French colonization
   Acadia **I:** 2
   Canary Islands **I:** 53
   Caroline, Fort **I:** 57
   Cartier, Jacques **I:** 59
   Cofitachequi **I:** 76
   Martinique **I:** 223
   Montserrat **I:** 243
   Reformation **I:** 310
French conquest **II:** 61, 251, 267, 353
French exploration **II:** 255, 264
   Cartier, Jacques **I:** 57–59
   Iroquois **I:** 182–183
   Northwest Passage **I:** 266
   Verrazano, Giovanni da **I:** 367
French Huguenots. *See* Huguenots
French immigrants **II: 130; IV:** 163
   Acadians **II:** 2
   architecture **II:** 23
   Louisiana **II:** 199
   métis **II:** 223
   Montour, Andrew **II:** 233
   North Carolina **II:** 265
French missions **II:** 244, 246
French Recollects **II:** 160
French Resistance **VIII:** 257
French Revolution **III: 138–139; IV:** 106, 151
   Adams, John **III:** 3
   Ames, Fisher **III:** 13
   artisans **III:** 26
   Bache, Benjamin Franklin **III:** 29
   Barlow, Joel **III:** 36
   Burke, Edmund **III:** 53
   Canada **III:** 61

Catholics **III:** 63
Chesapeake-Leopard affair **III:** 67
Democratic-Republican Party **III:** 104
Democratic-Republican societies **III:** 105
Dwight, Timothy **III:** 109
embargo of 1807 **III:** 117
Estaing, comte d' **III:** 120
French alliance **III:** 137–138
Genet, Edmond **III:** 149
George III, king of Great Britain **III:** 151
Haiti **III:** 159
Hamilton, Alexander **III:** 162
Husband, Herman **III:** 170
immigration **III:** 173
Jay's Treaty **III:** 182, 183
Jefferson, Thomas **III:** 184
King, Rufus **III:** 195
labor and labor movements **III:** 200
Lafayette, marquis de **III:** 200
liberty tree/pole **III:** 214
Morris, Gouverneur **III:** 247
Neutrality Proclamation **III:** 256
Paine, Thomas **III:** 271–272
popular culture **III:** 282
Priestley, Joseph **III:** 285
Rochambeau, comte de **III:** 310
San Lorenzo, Treaty of **III:** 317
Talleyrand, Prince **III:** 341
Vergennes, comte de **III:** 359
Washington, George **III:** 367
"Yankee Doodle" **III:** 387
French settlers **II:** 418*c*
   clothing **II:** 65
   Creole **II:** 74
   exploration **II:** 114, 115
   Native Americans **II:** 246
   New York **II:** 259
   Nicolet, Jean **II:** 263
   North Carolina **II:** 264
   Protestantism **II:** 300
   Spanish colonies **II:** 356
   Vermont **II:** 381
French traders
   Brims **II:** 41
   Brulé, Étienne **II:** 44
   Cherokee **II:** 58

French traders (continued)
  Chickasaw **II:** 59
  Great Plains Indians **II:**
    150
  Huron **II:** 160
  Iroquois **II:** 168
  La Demoiselle **II:**
    190–191
  Native Americans **II:** 243
  Neolin **II:** 248
  New Hampshire **II:** 251
French Wars of Religion. *See*
  Wars of Religion (France)
French West Indies **II:** 166
Freneau, Philip **III:** 46, **139**,
  214, 215
Frente Nacional de Libertação
  de Angola (FNLA) **IX:** 4
frescos **II:** 25
Freud, Sigmund **VI:** 304; **VII:**
  101–102
  Ellis, Havelock **VII:** 84
  Gilman, Charlotte Perkins
    VII: 109
  Goldman, Emma **VII:** 110
  literature **VII:** 161
  modernism **VII:** 187
  sexuality **VII:** 283
  women's status and rights
    VII: 340
Frick, Henry Clay **VI:**
  105–106; VII: 110, 319
  Carnegie, Andrew **VI:** 44
  Homestead Strike **VI:** 132
  industrial revolution,
    second **VI:** 146
  labor, radical **VI:** 167
Friedan, Betty **IX: 114–116,**
  115, 333*c*, 334*c*
  counterculture **IX:** 71
  family life **X:** 109
  feminism **X:** 113–114
  literature **IX:** 183
  Murray, Pauli **IX:** 216
  National Organization for
    Women **IX:** 223; **X:** 210,
    211
  Steinem, Gloria **X:** 288
  women's rights and status
    IX: 324, 325; **X:** 320
Friedman, Milton **X:** 78
Friedman, William F. **VIII:** 64
Friends (TV program) **X:** 295
Fries's Rebellion **III:** 65,
  139–140, 214, 292, 396*c*
Friml, Rudolph **VII:** 194
Frobisher, Martin **I:** *133,*
  133–135, 134*m*, 388*c*; **II:**
  167
  Company of Cathay **I:** 83
  Drake, Sir Francis **I:** 111
  Greenland **I:** 145

Hakluyt, Richard, the
  Elder **I:** 151
Hakluyt, Richard, the
  Younger **I:** 151
Mandeville, Sir John **I:** 219
Northwest Passage **I:** 266
Frobisher's Strait **I:** 133
frock coat **V:** 122
Froebel, Friedrich **VI:** 159
Frohman, Charles **VI:** 287
Froines, John **X:** 61
From Here to Eternity (Jones)
  VIII: 192, 326; **IX:** 181
*From Puritan
  Days*(MacDowell) **VI:** 183
*From the Virginia Plantation to
  the National Capitol*
  (Langston) **VI:** 172
frontal assaults **V:** 308
frontier **III: 140–141; VI:** 161,
  295, 296, 320, 326*c*. *See also*
  westward expansion
  architecture **III:** 19
  art **IV:** 26
  Atkinson, Henry **IV:** 33–34
  Bacon's Rebellion **II:** 28
  Blount, William **III:** 41
  Boone, Daniel **III:** 42–43
  borderlands **II:** 34–35
  Brackenridge, Hugh
    Henry **III:** 46
  Brown, Charles Brockden
    III: 50
  Carson, Kit **IV:** 75–76
  claim clubs **IV:** 85–86
  Clark, George Rogers **III:**
    71
  Clark, William **III:** 72
  clothing **II:** 64, 65
  Colt, Samuel **IV:** 91
  Colt revolver **IV:** 92
  Cornstalk **II:** 72
  Crèvecoeur, J. Hector St.
    John de **III:** 97
  Crockett, Davy **IV:** 99–100
  Croghan, George **II:** 76
  Deerfield Massacre **II:**
    84–85
  Dragging Canoe **III:** 107
  economy **IV:** 119
  ethnocentrism **II:** 113
  exploration **IV:** 130–133
  Florida **III:** 129
  foreign affairs **III:** 130
  Fort Stanwix, Treaty of **III:**
    132
  French colonies **II:** 129
  German Reformed Church
    II: 140
  Great Awakening **II:** 149
  internal improvements **IV:**
    187–190

Iroquois Confederacy **III:**
  179
Jay's Treaty **III:** 182
King Philip's War **II:** 184
King William's War **II:**
  185
land riots **III:** 201
Lewis, Meriwether **III:**
  208
literature **IV:** 211, 212
Maine **II:** 203
Marshall, John **III:** 235
McRea, Jane **III:** 239
medicine **IV:** 230
migration **IV:** 235–236
Native Americans and the
  Revolution **III:** 255
New Spain (Mexico),
  northern frontier of **III:**
  257
New York **II:** 262
Ostenaco **II:** 269
Paxton Boys **II:** 272
Permanent Indian Frontier
  IV: 279
poverty **III:** 284
Proclamation of 1763 **III:**
  287
Prophet, the Shawnee **III:**
  289
public land policy **IV:** 287
race and racial conflict **III:**
  295
religion **III:** 299; **IV:** 298
rural life **III:** 312
St. Clair, Arthur **III:** 316
Scotch-Irish **III:** 322, 323
Second Great Awakening
  IV: 311
slave resistance **II:** 337
society, British American
  II: 352
South Carolina Regulation
  III: 330
Virginia **II:** 385
Washington, George **III:**
  366
Wayne, Anthony **III:** 369
Whiskey Rebellion **III:**
  375
Wilkinson, James **III:** 379
women's status and rights
  II: 407
Wyoming Valley War **III:**
  384
frontier thesis **II:** 34
Frost, Robert **VIII:** 192
Frothergill, John **III:** 37
fruit trees **II:** 166, 247, 370
Frum, David **X:** 43
fruta madura, la **IV:** 100
Frye, Marquette **IX:** 317

FSA. *See* Family Support Act;
  Farm Security Administration
FSLN. *See* Sandinista Front of
  National Liberation
FTC. *See* Federal Trade
  Commission
FTP. *See* Federal Theatre
  Project
Fuca, Juan de **II: 130**
Fuchs, Klaus **IX:** 140, 264
Fuel Administration **VII:**
  102–103, 344
Fuenmayor, Diego de **I:** 363
Fuerteventura Island **I:** 53
Fugitive Blacksmith
  (Pennington) **V:** 270, 328
Fugitive Slave Act of 1793 **III:**
  396*c;* **IV:** 154; **V:** 56,
  361–362
Fugitive Slave Act of 1850 **IV:**
  379*c,* 411–413; **V:** 405*c;* **VI:**
  171. *See also* Compromise of
  1850
  Brown, William Wells **V:**
    40
  Burns, Anthony **IV:** 59
  Christiana, Pennsylvania,
    riot **V:** 59
  Delany, Martin Robinson
    V: 93
  Democratic Party **V:** 94
  Douglas, Stephen A. **V:** 98
  Fillmore, Millard **IV:** 137
  Free-Soil Party **IV:** 151
  fugitive slave laws **IV:** 155
  Mallory, Stephen R. **V:**
    221
  Mason-Dixon Line **V:** 224
  personal liberty laws **IV:**
    280
  Pierce, Franklin **V:** 275
  race and race relations **IV:**
    290
  Republican Party **V:** 301
  Still, William **IV:** 328
  Stowe, Harriet Beecher **V:**
    338
  Sumner, Charles **V:** 342
  Underground Railroad **V:**
    362
  Webster, Daniel **IV:** 360
  Welles, Gideon **V:** 391
Fugitive Slave Bill **IV:** 334, 335
fugitive slave laws **IV: 154–155**
  abolition movement **IV:** 3
  Compromise of 1850 **IV:**
    93–95
  literature **IV:** 213
  Missouri Compromise of
    1820 **IV:** 237
fugitive slaves. *See* slaves,
  fugitive

fulani bororo **I**: 135
fulani gida **I**: 135
Fulani (Peul, Fula, Fulbe) **I**: 135, 195, 361
Fulbert of Chartres **I**: 129
Fulbright, J. William **X**: 24, 65
Full Employment Bill **VIII**: 128
    Economic Bill of Rights **VIII**: 90
    Keynesianism **VIII**: 177
    liberalism **VIII**: 189
    NRPB **VIII**: 233
    postwar planning **VIII**: 278
    Third New Deal **VIII**: 358
    Wagner, Robert F. **VIII**: 373
Fuller, Margaret **IV**: 155–156
    Brook Farm **IV**: 58
    Emerson, Ralph Waldo **IV**: 126
    journalism **IV**: 194, 197
    literature **IV**: 212
    transcendental movement **IV**: 345
Fuller, Melville W. **VI**: 281
fulling **II**: 225, 369
Fulton, Robert **III**: 141–142, *142*, 216, 321–322, 397*c*; **V**: 355
    agriculture **IV**: 10
    economy **IV**: 118
    industrialization **IV**: 185
    internal improvements **IV**: 188
    science and technology **IV**: 307
Fulton, USS **IV**: 279
Fundamental Constitution for the Government of Carolina (Locke) **II**: 144, 198, 265, 353–354
Fundamentalism **VI**: 75; **VII**: 260, 261–262, 277–278, 355*c*; **VIII**: 71, 72, 302, 303; **IX**: 256; **X**: 3, 197, 294
Fundamental Orders of Government **II**: 68–69
Fundamentals, The **VII**: 261, 355*c*
fund-raising **IV**: 135; **V**: 203, 371, 373–374
Furies, the **X**: 115
furloughs **V**: 79, 96
Furman v. Georgia (1972) **X**: 41, 56, 324*c*
Furnas, Charles **VII**: 23
Furness, Frank **VI**: 15, 279
furniture **I**: 56; **II**: 24, 215; **III**: 275, 324; **IX**: 20
Fur peoples **I**: 102

fur trade **II**: 130–133, *132*; **III**: 142–143, 397*c*; **IV**: 156–158, 157*m*, 375*c*
    Abenaki **I**: 2
    Acts of Trade and Navigation **II**: 3
    Alaska **III**: 8–9
    Alaska, Russia in **II**: 14
    Aleut **II**: 16
    Algonquin **II**: 17
    American Fur Company **IV**: 16–17
    animals **II**: 20–21
    Ashley, William Henry **IV**: 28–30
    Astor, John Jacob **IV**: 30–32
    Astoria **IV**: 32–33
    Beaver Wars **II**: 31
    Bent, Charles **IV**: 47
    Bent, William **IV**: 48
    Bent's Fort **IV**: 50–51
    Bridger, James **IV**: 57
    Brûlé, Étienne **II**: 44
    California Trail **IV**: 70
    Canada **III**: 59–61
    Cayuga **I**: 67
    Champlain, Samuel de **II**: 56
    Chouteau family **IV**: 78–79
    Clark, William **III**: 73
    Columbia River **IV**: 93
    Delaware **II**: 87, 89
    economy **II**: 101
    environment **II**: 110, 111
    ethnocentrism **II**: 113
    exploration **II**: 114, 115; **IV**: 131
    Fort Laramie **IV**: 143, 144
    Fort Vancouver **IV**: 145
    French colonies **II**: 126, 129
    French immigrants **II**: 130
    Great Plains **III**: 155
    habitants **I**: 149
    Hudson's Bay Company **II**: 159
    Huron **II**: 160
    Indian Removal Act (1830) **IV**: 181
    Iroquois **II**: 168–169
    Johnson, Sir William **II**: 177
    Jolliet, Louis **II**: 178
    Kieft, Willem **II**: 182
    King Philip's War **II**: 183
    Livingston, Robert **II**: 196
    Logan, James **II**: 198
    Louisiana **I**: 199
    Maine **II**: 203
    Maliseet **I**: 219
    Massachusetts **II**: 212

    McLoughlin, John **IV**: 228–229
    merchants **II**: 222
    métis **II**: 223
    Miantonomo **II**: 224
    Minuit, Peter **II**: 227
    Missouri Fur Company **IV**: 238–239
    Montagnais-Naskapi **I**: 241
    mountain men **IV**: 247–248
    Native Americans **II**: 243, 246
    Native Americans and the Revolution **III**: 255
    New Hampshire **II**: 250
    New Netherland **II**: 255–257
    New York **II**: 259, 260, 262
    Northwest Coast Indians **II**: 266
    Oneida **I**: 272
    Onondaga **I**: 272
    Oregon Trail **IV**: 267
    Oregon Treaty of 1846 **IV**: 269, 270
    Plymouth **II**: 287
    rendezvous **IV**: 299–300
    Rocky Mountain Fur Company **IV**: 302
    Russian settlements **II**: 326
    Smith, Jedediah Strong **IV**: 320–322
    South Pass **IV**: 324
    Sublette, William **IV**: 329–330
    Sutter, John **IV**: 332
    trade and shipping **II**: 375, 376
    Virginia **II**: 382
Fur Traders Descending the Missouri (Bingham) **IV**: 26
Fusion Party **VIII**: 182
Futurama **VIII**: 22, 244
Futurity Stakes **VI**: 134
FWP. *See* Federal Writers' Project

G

Gable, Clark **VIII**: 218, 408*c*
gable-front and wing **IV**: 27
Gabon **I**: 127, 246–247; **X**: 228
Gabriel's Rebellion **III**: 145–146, 327, 396*c*
Gadsden, Christopher **III**: 329
Gadsden, James **IV**: 159
Gadsden Purchase **IV**: xiii, 159–160, 160*m*, 379*c*; **V**: 275
    economy **IV**: 117
    exploration **IV**: 132

    Guadalupe Hidalgo, Treaty of (1848) **IV**: 166
    Manifest Destiny **IV**: 218*m*
    Santa Anna, Antonio López de **IV**: 304
Gadsden Treaty of 1853 **IV**: 379*c*
Gagarin, Yuri A. **IX**: 219, 278, 294, 333*c*
Gage, Frances Dana **V**: 357
Gage, Matilda Joslyn **V**: 399; **VI**: 107, 224
Gage, Thomas **III**: 146–147
    Burgoyne, John **III**: 51
    Church, Benjamin **III**: 68
    Clinton, Sir Henry **III**: 75
    Continental Congress, First **III**: 87
    Hancock, John **III**: 163
    Howe, Sir William **III**: 168
    Hutchinson, Thomas **III**: 171
    Lexington and Concord, Battles of **III**: 211–213
    Revere, Paul **III**: 304
"gag rule" **X**: 4, 66
Gag Rule (1836) **IV**: 5, 14, 63
Gaines, Edmund P. **IV**: 309, 312
Gaines's Mill, Battle of
    Hood, John Bell **V**: 170
    Irish-American regiments **V**: 181
    Jackson, "Stonewall" **V**: 186
    Meade, George Gordon **V**: 226
    Peninsular campaign **V**: 269
    Pickett, George Edward **V**: 274
Gains v. Canada **IX**: 215
Gaither Report **IX**: 77
Galawedos, king of Ethiopia **I**: 125
Galbraith, John Kenneth **IX**: 13, 69, 90, 117–118, 332*c*
Gale, Leonard **IV**: 245
Galen **II**: 220
Galena, USS **V**: 183
Galibi **I**: 56
Galileo (space probe) **IX**: 220; **X**: 283
Gallatin, Albert **III**: 31, 147–148, 173; **IV**: 253, 269, 375*c*; **VI**: 1
Gallegos, José Manuel **IV**: 207
Gallman, Robert E. **VI**: 145
Galloway, Joseph **III**: 87, 88, 148, 266
Gallup, George Horace **VIII**: 284; **IX**: 118
Gallup Poll **IX**: 118–119

Galton, Francis **VII:** 131
Galveston, Battle of **V: 145**
Galveston, Texas **IV:** 206; **V:** 25, 130, 194
Galveston flood **VI: 107–108**
Galvéz, José de **III:** 57
Gama, Christovão da **I:** 124, 193
Gama, Vasco da **I: 137,** 138*m*, 386*c*
   Cabral, Pedro Álvares **I:** 44
   Dias, Bartholomeu **I:** 105, 106
   invention and technology **I:** 180
   Ramusio, Giovanni Battista **I:** 305
Gamble, James **IV:** 118, 184
gambling **VI:** 21; **VII:** 59, 294; **X:** 263
Gambling Outrages (Comstock) **VI:** 62
games **VII:** 258; **VIII:** 204
game shows (television) **X:** 296
Gandhi, Mahatma Mohandas **IV:** 345; **IX:** 53–54, 284
gangrene **IV:** 230; **V:** 96
gangs **X:** 82, 207, 240
gangsta rap music **X:** 240
Gantt, Edward **III:** 371
Gao **I: 137, 139**
   Askia Muhammad I **I:** 14
   Mansa Musa I **I:** 220
   Songhai **I:** 331, 332
   Taureg **I:** 360
GAO (Government Accounting Office) **X:** 134
GAR. *See* Grand Army of the Republic
Garbo, Greta **VII:** 190; **VIII:** 217, 218
Garden, Alexander **II:** 66, 277, 397
Garden of Eden **I:** 358
Gardiner, Zion **II:** 68
Gardner, Alexander **V:** 35, 36, 273
Gardoqui, Don Diego **III:** 182
Garfield, Harry A. **VII:** 102, 103
Garfield, James Abram **VI: 108–109,** 109, 325*c*
   Arthur, Chester Alan **VI:** 16–17
   Blaine, James Gillespie **VI:** 31
   Civil Rights Act of 1875 **V:** 63
   civil service reform **VI:** 56
   Conkling, Roscoe **VI:** 64
   corruption, political **VI:** 67
   Crédit Mobilier **V:** 84
   Geological Survey, U.S. **VI:** 110

Hancock, Winfield Scott **V:** 164
   the presidency **VI:** 230
   presidential campaigns **VI:** 231, 232
   Republican Party **VI:** 246
   star route frauds **VI:** 275
   Thirteenth Amendment **V:** 353
Garland, Hamlin **VI: 109–110**
   Crane, Stephen **VI:** 68
   Howells, William Dean **VI:** 136
   James, Henry **VI:** 153
   literature **VI:** 177
Garland, Judy **VIII:** 56
garment industry **VIII:** 26
Garner, John Nance **VIII: 129**
   Congress **VIII:** 66
   Democratic Party **VIII:** 80
   election of 1932 **VIII:** 96
   election of 1936 **VIII:** 97
   Farley, James A. **VIII:** 111
   Nye Committee **VIII:** 250
Garner et. al. v. Louisiana **IX:** 273, 333*c*
Garner-Wagner relief bill **VIII:** 299
Garnet, Henry Highland **III:** 159; **V:** 125
Garrett, Bob **VI:** 290
Garrett, Henry Highland **IV:** 261
Garrett, John W. **IV:** 40
Garrett, Mary E. **VI:** 288
Garrett, Richard H. **V:** 33
Garrison, Edward "Snapper" **VI:** 134
Garrison, Lindley **VII:** 202, 236
Garrison, Lucy McKim **VI:** 202
Garrison, William Lloyd **III:** 17, 132; **IV:** 376*c*, 377*c*; **V: 145–147,** *146*
   AASS **IV:** 13–15, 362
   abolition/abolition movement **IV:** 2–3; **V:** 2–4
   ACS **IV:** 16
   African Americans **IV:** 8
   Douglass, Frederick **V:** 100
   female antislavery societies **IV:** 135
   Foster, Abigail Kelley **IV:** 147, 148
   Free-Soil Party **IV:** 150
   Genius of Universal Emancipation **IV:** 160
   Grimké, Angelina and Sarah **IV:** 164
   journalism **IV:** 194
   Liberator editorial, first issue **IV:** 392–393

Liberia **IV:** 209
Liberty Party **IV:** 210
Mott, Lucretia **IV:** 247
Phillips, Wendell **IV:** 280
race and race relations **IV:** 291
Seneca Falls **IV:** 313
Seward, William H. **V:** 314
spiritualism **IV:** 325
Stewart, Maria **IV:** 327
Tappan, Arthur and Lewis **IV:** 334
Thirteenth Amendment **V:** 353
Truth, Sojourner **V:** 357
"Garrisonians" **V:** 100
Garvey, Marcus **VI:** 175; **VII:** 72, *105*, **105–106,** 119, 315–316, 360*c*
Gary, Elbert H. **VI:** 146–147
   steel industry **VII:** 297
   Steel Strike of 1919 **VII:** 298
   U.S. Steel **VII:** 319, 320
   welfare capitalism **VII:** 333
Gary, Joseph **VI:** 10, 127
gas, natural. *See* natural gas
gasoline **VII:** 102; **X:** 104
gasoline rationing
   black market **VIII:** 38
   OPA **VIII:** 254
   rationing **VIII:** 292
   transportation **VIII:** 360
   World War II home front **VIII:** 395
Gaspée affair **III:** 77, **148–149,** 392*c*
Gastonia Strike **VII: 106,** 225
Gaston v. U.S. (1969) **X:** 41
gated communities **IX:** 125
Gates, Bill **X:** 72, 73, *74*
Gates, Horatio **III: 149**
   Arnold, Benedict **III:** 21
   Camden, Battle of **III:** 57–59
   Conway Cabal **III:** 90, 91
   Cornwallis, Lord **III:** 93
   Greene, Nathanael **III:** 155
   Jefferson, Thomas **III:** 184
   Kalb, baron de **III:** 195
   Lafayette, marquis de **III:** 201
   Newburgh conspiracy **III:** 256, 257
   Saratoga, surrender at **III:** 319, 320
   Schuyler, Philip John **III:** 320
   Wilkinson, James **III:** 379
Gates, Sir Thomas **II:** 81, **135–136,** 294

gathering. *See* hunting and gathering
Gatling, Richard **V:** 308
Gatling guns **V:** 308
GATT. *See* General Agreement on Tariffs and Trade
Gauveau, Emile **VII:** 143
gay culture **VII:** 283
Gaye, Marvin **X:** 201
gay rights movement **IX:** 120; **X: 127–128,** 323*c*
   Brennan, William J. **X:** 41
   feminism **X:** 115
   marriage **X:** *182*
   NOW **X:** 211
   political parties **X:** 237
   sexual revolution **X:** 277
   Steinem, Gloria **X:** 288
gays and lesbians **V:** 394; **VII:** 283; **VIII: 129–130,** 377, 389, **395; IX:** 32–33, **119–120,** 162, 325; **X:** 324*c*, 329*c*–331*c*
   art and architecture **X:** 26
   Clinton, William **X:** 66
   defense policy **X:** 87
   feminism **X:** 115, 116
   gay rights movement **X:** 127–128
   Ginsburg, Ruth Bader **X:** 131
   liberalism **X:** 175
   marriage **X:** 183
   multiculturalism **X:** 200, 201
   Powell, Colin L. **X:** 247
   sexual revolution **X:** 277, 278
   Supreme Court **X:** 291
   White, Byron R. **X:** 319
Gazette of the United States **III:** 29, 191, 395*c*
GE. *See* General Electric
Gedi **I: 139**
Geechee culture **II:** 151
Gehrig, Lou **VIII:** 275, 408*c*; **X:** 284
Gehry, Frank **X:** 27
Gell, Monday **IV:** 354
Gemini space program **IX:** 269, 279
gender **II: 136–137**
   affirmative action **X:** 8
   African Americans **II:** 5–6
   Algonquin **II:** 17
   art **II:** 24
   borderlands **II:** 35
   Caribbean **II:** 53
   Cherokee **II:** 57
   childhood **II:** 60
   clothing **II:** 65

crime and punishment **II:** 75

domesticity **II:** 93

education, higher **X:** 97

education, home schooling **X:** 98

ethnocentrism **II:** 113

feminism **X:** 114

gender gap **X:** 128

Hutchinson, Anne Marbury **II:** 161

labor **II:** 188–190

marriage and family life **II:** 206, 208; **X:** 110

Massachusetts School Act **II:** 216

mortality **II:** 234

Musgrove, Mary Bosomworth **II:** 238

North Carolina **II:** 263

NOW **X:** 211

Pennsylvania **II:** 275

Pinckney, Elizabeth Lucas **II:** 284

population trends **II:** 291; **X:** 243

poverty **X:** 246

Powhatan Confederacy **II:** 294

praying towns **II:** 296

printing and publishing **II:** 299

Protestantism **II:** 302

St. Mary's City **II:** 328

slavery **II:** 340–341

society, British American **II:** 349–351

Spanish colonies **II:** 356

tenants **II:** 370

Virginia **II:** 383

Ward, Nancy **II:** 392

women's rights and status **II:** 406–407; **X:** 319–321

gender discrimination **V:** 124, 357

anti-suffragists **VII:** 15

Blackwell, Elizabeth **VI:** 30–31

Bradwell, Myra Colby **VI:** 34

Brown, Olympia **VI:** 35

education **VI:** 91; **VII:** 78

Greenwich Village **VII:** 114

intelligence tests **VII:** 131

labor, woman **VI:** 169

marriage and family life **VIII:** 205; **X:** 183

NOW **X:** 210, 211

race and racial conflict **VII:** 247

Rosie the Riveter **VIII:** 315

Victorianism **VI:** 304

Women's Equity Action League **IX:** 323

women's status and rights **VII:** 340; **IX:** 324–325; **X:** 320, 321

gender gap **X: 128,** 130, 326c

gender-neutral language. *See* inclusive language

gender quotas **X:** 41, 215–216, 325c

gender roles **IX:** 192, 193, 296. *See also* men's roles and status; women's status and rights

General Advertiser, The **III:** 29

General Agreement on Tariffs and Trade (GATT) **X: 129,** 329c

Clinton, William **X:** 67–68

economy **X:** 95–96

foreign policy **X:** 124

World Trade Organization **X:** 321–322

General Agreement on Tariffs and Trade of 1947 **VIII:** 294

General Allotment Act **IX:** 227

General Assembly **VIII:** 402

General Electric (GE) **VI:** 327c; **VII:** 48, **107,** *133,* 232, 253, 355c; **VIII:** 341, 343; **IX:** 24, **120,** 293; **X:** 131, 169

banking, investment **VI:** 20

industrial revolution, second **VI:** 147

inventions and technology **VI:** 149

Morgan, John Pierpont **VI:** 198

Villard, Henry **VI:** 305

General Federation of Women's Clubs **X:** 105

General Foods Corporation **VIII:** 47

General History of the Things of New Spain **I:** *107*

General Jewish Council **VIII:** 19

General Leasing Act of 1920 **VII:** 307

General Managers Association (railroads) **VI:** 236

"General Max" **VIII:** 371

General Motors (GM) **VII:** 22, 74, 241; **VIII:** 407c; **IX: 120–121,** 330c

art and architecture **VIII:** 22

automobile industry **VIII:** 30; **IX:** 24; **X:** 31, 32

business **VIII:** 46; **X:** 49

CIO **VIII:** 69–70

Congress of Industrial Organizations **IX:** 65

cost-of-living adjustment **IX:** 70

DuPont Corporation **IX:** 83

labor **VIII:** 180; **X:** 169

Murray, Philip **VIII:** 221

Nader, Ralph **X:** 205

Perot, H. Ross **X:** 234

Reuther, Walter **IX:** 259

steel industry **VIII:** 338

technology **IX:** 294

General Order No. 3 **V:** 194

General Order No. 9 **V:** 427

General Survey Act of 1824 **IV:** 253

General Theory of Employment, Interest, and Money (Keynes) **VIII:** 176, 407c; **IX:** 70

General Track **VII:** 78

General Trades Union **IV:** 204

generator **IV:** 308

Genet, Edmond **III: 149–150,** 395c

Democratic-Republican societies **III:** 105

foreign affairs **III:** 130

French alliance **III:** 138

French Revolution **III:** 138

Morris, Gouverneur **III:** 247

Neutrality Proclamation **III:** 256

genetic engineering **X:** 15, 16, 191

genetic research **IX:** 269–270

genetics **VII:** 276; **X:** 145–146

Geneva **I:** 50, 51, 309

Geneva Accords **IX:** 308

Geneva Conference of 1962 **IX:** 316

Geneva Conference on Naval Disarmament. *See* Naval Disarmament Conference

Geneva Convention of 1864 **V:** 25, 306

Geneva Convention of 1929 **VIII:** 281, 282

Geneva Convention of 1954 **IX:** 274

Geneva Medical College **IV:** 378c

Genghis Khan **I:** 286

Genius, The (Dreiser) **VII:** 252

Genius of Oblivion, The (Hale) **IV:** 167

Genius of Universal Emancipation **IV: 160–161;** **V:** 145–146

genízaro slaves **II:** 255

Gennett Record Company **VII:** 86

Genoa **I:** 327

genocide **II:** 16

genre painting **V:** 16; **VI:** 219

gens de couleur libre **II:** 74, 229, 238

gente de razón **II:** 356

gente sin razón **II:** 356

gentility **VI:** 176–177

Gentlemen's Agreement **VI:** 141; **VII: 107–108,** 357c

Great White Fleet **VII:** 114

nativism **VII:** 208

race and racial conflict **VII:** 247

Roosevelt, Theodore **VII:** 266

Root-Takahira Agreement **VII:** 267

Geografia (Ptolemy) **I:** 266

geography

Cabot, Sebastian **I:** 42

Cathay (China) **I:** 66

Columbus, Christopher **I:** 79

Hakluyt, Richard, the Younger **I:** 152

mappae mundi **I:** 221

Northwest Passage **I:** 265

Polo, Marco **I:** 287

Geography Made Easy (Morse) **III:** 249

Geography (Ptolemy) **I:** 231, 232

Geological Exploration, U.S. **VI:** 160

Geological Survey, U.S. (USGS) **VI: 110–111,** 325c

conservation **VI:** 65

King, Clarence **VI:** 160

Marsh, Othniel Charles **VI:** 188

mining: metal and coal **VI:** 193

Powell, John Wesley **VI:** 228

science **VI:** 257

geological surveys **VI:** 193

geology **II:** 330; **VI:** 159–160, 199, 228; **VIII:** 318

geophysics **VIII:** 318

George, David **VI:** 3

George, Henry **VI:** 13, **111–112,** 262, 267, 325c; **VII:** 140, 265

George, Milton **VI:** 99

George, Walter F. **VIII:** 295

George I, king of Great Britain **II:** 232

George II, king of Great Britain
II: 58, 232, 375
George III, king of Great
Britain II: 30, 58, 197, 232,
269; III: *150*, **150–151**,
391*c*, 393*c*
   art III: 22
   Brant, Joseph III: 48
   Bute, earl of III: 54
   Catholics III: 63
   Common Sense (Paine)
      III: 77, 78
   corporatism III: 94
   Crèvecoeur, J. Hector St.
      John de III: 97
   Declaration of
      Independence III: 101,
      102
   Declaratory Act III: 103
   Florida III: 129
   French alliance III: 137
   Gage, Thomas III: 146
   Golden Hill, Battle of III:
      153
   Hancock, John III:
      162–164
   Howe, Sir William III: 169
   immigration III: 173
   Johnson, Sir John III: 188
   Lee, Charles III: 205
   Lexington and Concord,
      Battles of III: 211
   liberty tree/pole III: 214
   North, Lord III: 260
   Olive Branch Petition III:
      266
   Paris, Treaty of III: 273
   Pitt, William III: 277
   Proclamation of 1763 III:
      287
   resistance movement III:
      303
   slave trade III: 329
   Stamp Act III: 332
   West, Benjamin III: 371,
      372
   writs of assistance III: 384
George IV, prince regent of
   Great Britain III: 151, 343
Georgetown University VI: 290
*George Washington Parke
   Custis* (barge) V: 21
George White's Scandals VII:
   108
Georgia II: **137–139**, 419*c*; IV:
   376*c*; VI: 4, 163, 296; VII:
   157–158; IX: 132–133, 311
   African Americans II: 6
   agriculture II: 10–12; IV:
      11
   amendments to the
      Constitution X: 19

Carter, James Earl, Jr. X:
   57
cartography V: 51
Cherokee II: 57
Coosa I: 85
economy II: 101
ERA X: 107
Florida II: 121
   La Florida I: 130
foraging V: 130
Fort Mose II: 123
Frémont, John C. IV: 153
gold, discovery and mining
   IV: 162
governors V: 152
homefront V: 169
Hood, John Bell V: 171
Indian Removal Act (1830)
   IV: 181, 183
Johnston, Joseph E. V: 190
migration IV: 235
missions II: 230
Muhlenberg, Henry
   Melchior II: 237
Musgrove, Mary
   Bosomworth II: 238
music II: 239
Native Americans IV: 257
Nullification Controversy
   IV: 263–264
Oglethorpe, James Edward
   II: 267
plantations V: 276
plantation system II: 286
population trends X: 242
Reconstruction V: 294
redemption V: 297
religion, Euro-American
   II: 316
Savannah II: 329
secession V: 313
Seminole wars IV: 312
Sherman, William T. V:
   321
Sherman's March through
   Georgia V: 321–323
slavery II: 342
South Carolina II: 353
Stephens, Alexander H. V:
   336–337
Supreme Court decision
   IV: 330
Timucua I: 351
Tomochichi II: 375
Trail of Tears IV: 344
War of Jenkins' Ear II: 392
Whitefield, George II: 397
Georgia (CIS) X: 281
Georgia Mississippi Company
   III: 388
Georgian architecture II: 23,
   158, 211, 384; III: 18, *19*

"Georgia plan" II: 267
Georgia Sea Islands. *See* Sea
   Islands
Georgia Southwestern Railway
   V: 10
Gephardt, Richard X: 91
Gericke, Wilhelm VI: 23, 183
Germain, Lord III: 62
German American Bund VIII:
   131
German-American regiments V:
   147, 177
German Americans II:
   139–140, 419*c*; IV: 179*t*; VI:
   138, 256, 267; VIII: **130–131**
   canal era IV: 74
   cities and urban life IV: 81;
      V: 60
   civil liberties VIII: 61
   Civil War IV: 180
   Copperheads V: 82
   economy II: 102; IV: 117
   enemy aliens VIII: 102
   English immigrants II: 109
   Espionage Act VII: 88
   German-American
      regiments V: 147
   immigration IV: 177–179;
      V: 175, 176
   indentured servitude II:
      163, 164
   Kaiser, Henry J. VIII: 175
   Know-Nothing Party IV:
      201
   Kuhn, Justus Engelhardt
      II: 186
   labor movements IV: 205
   Lutherans II: 201
   Maine II: 203
   Mittelberger, Gottlieb II:
      231
   Montour, Andrew II: 233
   Muhlenberg, Henry
      Melchior II: 237
   nativism V: 251
   New Jersey II: 253, 254
   New Netherland II: 257
   New York II: 260, 262
   New York City II: 263
   Non-Partisan League VII:
      216
   North Carolina II: 265
   Pacific Railroad Act of
      1862 V: 263
   Philadelphia II: 281
   population trends II: 291;
      V: 277
   Prohibition VII: 240
   race and racial conflict IV:
      292; VIII: 288
   redemptioners II: 313
   religion IV: 298; VIII: 304

Roman Catholics II: 324
South Carolina II: 354
Trading with the Enemy
   Act VII: 311
Virginia II: 385
Wistar, Caspar II: 402
women's status and rights
   II: 407
German imperial territories I:
   67, 68
German Reformed Church II:
   103, 139, **140**
German-Soviet campaign VIII:
   32
German sympathizers VIII: 347
Germantown, Battle of III:
   151, 152*m*; IV: 239
   Cornwallis, Lord III: 93
   Greene, Nathanael III:
      155
   McDougall, Alexander III:
      239
   Pinckney, Charles
      Cotesworth III: 277
   Sullivan, John III: 337
Germany I: 387*c*; II: 365; III:
   166–167, 173, 283; IV: 55,
   307; VI: 328*c*; VII: 358*c*,
   359*c*; VIII: 405*c*, 408*c*–410*c*;
   IX: 105*m*; X: 327*c*. *See also*
   East Germany; Hessians;
   West Germany
   air power VIII: 11, 12
   American Expeditionary
      Force VII: 9
   amphibious warfare VIII:
      15
   Anglo-American relations
      VIII: 16
   Army Air Forces, U.S.
      VIII: 20
   Arnold, "Hap" VIII: 22
   Atlantic, Battle of the
      VIII: 26, 28
   Atlantic Charter VIII: 28
   atomic bomb VIII: 28–29
   automobile industry X:
      31–32
   Axis VIII: 31–32
   Berlin blockade IX: 37
   blitzkrieg VIII: 39
   Bradley, Omar N. VIII: 41
   Britain, Battle of VIII: 43
   Bulge, Battle of the VIII:
      44
   code breaking VIII: 64
   cold war IX: 58
   Committee for Public
      Information VII: 51–52
   conscription VII: 54
   Coolidge, Calvin VII: 57
   Dawes, Charles VII: 63

Dawes Plan **VII:** 63–64
demobilization **VIII:** 79
Democratic Party **VII:** 66
espionage **VIII:** 104
feudalism **I:** 130
Fordney-McCumber Tariff
   VII: 97
foreign policy **VI:** 103;
   VII: 100, 101; **VIII:**
   123–125
gay rights movement **X:**
   127
Grand Alliance **VIII:** 136,
   137
Green Party **X:** 135
Hiroshima and Nagasaki
   VIII: 147
Holocaust **VIII:** 149–150
Holy Roman Empire **I:**
   165, 166
immigration **VII:** 127t;
   VIII: 162
imperialism **VI:** 141
intelligence **VIII:** 164
Iron Curtain **X:** 157
Italian campaign **VIII:** 168
Jews (Judaism) **I:** 190, 192;
   VIII: 173
Judaism **VI:** 158
Kennedy, Joseph P. **VIII:**
   176
kindergarten **VI:** 159
labor **X:** 170
League of Nations **VII:**
   156, 157
Lend-Lease Act **VIII:** 185
Lindbergh, Charles **VII:**
   160
London Naval Conference
   VIII: 194
Lusitania **VII:** 168
Luther, Martin **I:** 211–212
Manchuria **VIII:** 199
Manhattan Project **VIII:**
   200, 201
medicine **VI:** 191
mobilization **VIII:** 215
modernism **VII:** 187
Morgenthau, Henry **VIII:**
   216–217
Munich Conference **VIII:**
   220
Naval Disarmament
   Conference **VII:** 209
Nazi-Soviet Pact **VIII:**
   237–238
neutrality **VII:** 210
Neutrality Acts **VIII:** 239
Normandy, invasion of
   VIII: 247–248
Open Door notes **VI:**
   216–217

OSS **VIII:** 257
Patton, George **VIII:** 263
Polish Americans **VIII:**
   269
politics in the Roosevelt
   era **VIII:** 272
Potsdam Conference **VIII:**
   279–280
POWs **VIII:** 281, 282
Preparedness **VII:** 235
propaganda **VIII:** 282
Reformation **I:** 307, 309
reparations. *See*
   reparations
Republican Party **VII:** 263
Roman Catholicism **VI:**
   249
Russian Revolution **VII:**
   270
Samoa **VI:** 254–255
second front **VIII:** 320
Sedition Act **VII:** 280
Selective Service Act **VII:**
   282
Siberian Expedition **VII:**
   285
Sicily **VIII:** 326
Soviet-American relations
   VIII: 333, 334
Spanish Civil War **VIII:**
   334
sports **VIII:** 337, 338
steel industry **VIII:** 339;
   IX: 282
submarines **VIII:** 342
tariffs **VII:** 306
trade **VI:** 290
trade, foreign **VII:** 310
Trading with the Enemy
   Act **VII:** 311
UN **VIII:** 365
V-E Day **VIII:** 369
Versailles, Treaty of **VII:**
   322–324
Wilson, Woodrow **VII:** 334
witches **I:** 374
World Disarmament
   Conference **VIII:** 388
World War I **VII:** 343–345
World War II **VIII:** 389
   European theater **VIII:**
   391–394
Yalta Conference **VIII:**
   401
Zimmermann telegram
   VII: 353
Zionism **VIII:** 403
Germany, Treaty on the Final
   Settlement with Respect to
   X: 327c
germ theory **IV:** 111; **V:** 310
Gérôme, Jean-Léon **VI:** 45

Geronimo **IV:** 258; **VI:** 14, *112,*
   112–113, 207, 208, 325c,
   326c
Gerry, Elbridge **III:** 81,
   152–153, 277, 385
gerrymandering **IX:** 312
Gershwin, George **VII:** *108,*
   108–109, 361c; **VIII:** 223,
   224
   entertainment **VII:** 85
   jazz **VII:** 137
   music **VII:** 194, 195
   Tin Pan Alley **VII:** 308,
      309
Gerth, Jeff **X:** 328c
Gesell, Gerhard **X:** 315
Gesner, Conrad von **I:** **140**
Gettysburg, Battle of **V:**
   147–150, 149m, 407c
   Alexander, Edward P. **V:** 7
   Armistead, Lewis A. **V:** 15
   brothers' war **V:** 37
   Chamberlain, Joshua L. **V:**
      54
   Civil War **V:** 66
   Copperheads **V:** 82
   desertion **V:** 96
   Early, Jubal A. **V:** 103
   elections **V:** 110
   Ewell, Richard Stoddert **V:**
      119
   foreign policy **V:** 132
   Gettysburg Address **V:**
      151, 424–425
   Hancock, Winfield Scott **V:**
      163
   Hill, Ambrose P. **V:** 168
   Hood, John Bell **V:** 171
   Howard, O. O. **V:** 173
   Irish-American regiments
      V: 182
   ladies aid societies **V:** 204
   Lee, Robert E. **V:** 206
   letters **V:** 208
   Longstreet, James **V:** 215
   Meade, George Gordon **V:**
      227
   Mosby, John Singleton **V:**
      242
   nurses **V:** 256
   Oates, William C. **V:** 257
   Overland campaign **V:** 260
   peace movements **V:** 266
   photography **V:** 273
   Pickett, George Edward **V:**
      274
   refugees **V:** 298
   Sickles, Daniel E. **V:** 327
   Stuart, J. E. B. **V:** 341
   tactics and strategy **V:** 345
   West Point **V:** 373
   Zouaves **V:** 404

Gettysburg Address **V:** 113, 150,
   151, 407c, 424–425
Gettysburg anniversary campout
   V: 379
Gettysburg campaign **V:** 130
Geyer, Enrique Bolanos **X:** 218
Ghana **I: 140–141; II:** 4, 344;
   IX: 3
   Akan **I:** 5
   Asante **I:** 13
   Dagomba **I:** 101
   Ewe **I:** 125
   Fulani **I:** 135
   Gao **I:** 139
   Gold Coast **I:** 143–144
   Gonja **I:** 144
   Guinea-Bissau **I:** 147
   Hausa **I:** 155
   Islam **I:** 184
   Mali **I:** 217
   Mossi **I:** 243
   Sahara **I:** 317
   Sudan **I:** 336–337
Ghazi, Ahmad ibn Ibrahim al- **I:**
   124–125
Ghent, Treaty of (1814) **IV:**
   161–162, 375c, 383–386
   Adams, John Quincy **IV:** 4
   American Fur Company
      IV: 16
   Astor, John Jacob **IV:** 31
   Astoria **IV:** 33
   Canada **III:** 61
   Clay, Henry **IV:** 86
   Constitution, USS **III:** 81
   Dartmoor Prison **IV:** 104
   Decatur, Stephen **IV:** 104
   economy **IV:** 117
   Era of Good Feelings **IV:**
      127
   Florida **III:** 129
   foreign affairs **III:** 131
   foreign policy **IV:** 141
   Free Trade and Sailor's
      Rights **IV:** 152
   French Revolution **III:**
      139
   Gallatin, Albert **III:** 147
   Hartford Convention **IV:**
      171
   impressment **III:** 176
   Kearny, Stephen Watts **IV:**
      200
   Madison, James **III:** 230
   New Orleans, Battle of
      (1815) **IV:** 262
   population trends **III:** 283
   War of 1812 **IV:** 358
   Washington Benevolent
      Societies **III:** 369
   Webster-Ashburton Treaty
      (1842) **IV:** 360

ghettos **I**: 191; **VI**: 140; **VII**: 49–50, 281, 321–322; **VIII**: 5; **IX**: 4, 6, 12, 173, 271, 313
Ghirlandaio **I**: 235
Ghorbanifar, Manucher **X**: 154
Ghormley, Robert L. **VIII**: 246, 330
Ghost Dance movement **II**: 319–320
Ghost Dance religion **VI**: 14, 326c
    Geronimo **VI**: 113
    Native Americans **VI**: 207
    Red Cloud **VI**: 240
    religion **VI**: 245
    Sioux wars **VI**: 263
    Sitting Bull **VI**: 264
Ghost Dance War **VI**: 145, 245
Gibbon, Edward **III**: 302
Gibbons v. Ogden **IV**: 331, 359, 376c
Gibbs, James **II**: 23, 24
Gibbs, Josiah Willard **VI**: 2, **113**, 257, 324c
GI Bill of Rights **VIII**: **131–132**, 410c; *See also* Serviceman's Readjustment Act of 1944
    Congress **VIII**: 68
    demobilization **VIII**: 79
    economy **VIII**: 92
    education **VIII**: 95
    gays and lesbians **VIII**: 130
    housing **VIII**: 159
    Italian Americans **VIII**: 167
    NRPB **VIII**: 233
    NYA **VIII**: 234
    postwar planning **VIII**: 279
    reconversion **VIII**: 295
    WAC **VIII**: 382
    World War II **VIII**: 390
    World War II home front **VIII**: 394
Gibson, Charles Dana **VI**: 137, 185, 326c
Gibson, James **II**: 272
Gibson, James F. **V**: 273
Gibson, Josh **VII**: 295; **VIII**: 336
Gibson Girl **VI**: 137, 185, 326c
Gidden, George R. **IV**: 291
Giddings, Joshua **IV**: 151
Gideon, Clarence Earl **IX**: 121–122; **X**: 196
"Gideon's Band" **V**: 279
Gideon v. Wainwright (1963) **IX**: **121–122**, 333c; **X**: 196
Giffard, Henri **V**: 309
Gifford, Frank **X**: 241
GI Forum **IX**: 173

G.I. Joe (film) **VIII**: 286
Gilbert, Cass **VI**: 313
Gilbert, Sir Humphrey **I**: **141–142**, 388c; **II**: 150, 231–232
    Elizabeth I **I**: 120, 121
    Parmenius, Stephen **I**: 278
    Peckham, Sir George **I**: 279
    Ralegh, Sir Walter **I**: 303
    Walsingham, Sir Frances **I**: 372
Gilbert, Olive **V**: 357
Gilbert and Sullivan **VI**: 203, 271, 286
Gilbert Islands
    amphibious warfare **VIII**: 15
    Halsey, "Bull" **VIII**: 143
    Marines, U.S. **VIII**: 203
    Nimitz, Chester W. **VIII**: 246
    Tarawa **VIII**: 350
    World War II Pacific theater **VIII**: 398
"Gilded Age" **VI**: xv, xvi
Gilded Age: A Tale of Today (Twain & Warner) **VI**: **114–115**, 298
gilded man. *See* El Dorado
Gilder, Richard Watson **VI**: 176, 314
Gillespie, Archibald **IV**: 45
Gillespie, Dizzy **VIII**: 223, 410c
Gillette, King **VI**: 150
Gillette, William **VI**: 287
Gillette v. United States (1971) **X**: 323c
Gilman, Charlotte Perkins **VI**: 177; **VII**: **109**, 229, 338–339
Gilman, Daniel Coit **VI**: 93
Gilman, George F. **VI**: 46–47
Gilmore, Patrick S. **VI**: 128
Gilpatrick, J. **VI**: 134
Gilpin, Thomas **III**: 11
Gimbel, Adam **VI**: 78
Gingrich, Newton L. **X**: **129–130**, 329c
    Clinton, William **X**: 68
    conservative movement **X**: 80
    House of Representatives **X**: 145
    Wright, James C., Jr. **X**: 322
Gingrich Revolution **X**: 68
Ginsberg, Allen **IX**: *122*, **122–123**, 331c
    Beat Generation **IX**: 35–36
    counterculture **IX**: 71, 72
    Kerouac, Jack **IX**: 159, 160
    literature **IX**: 182

music **IX**: 217
    religion **IX**: 256
Ginsburg, Ruth Bader **X**: **130–131**
    abortion **X**: 3
    Supreme Court **X**: 291
    women's rights and status **X**: 321
Giovanni, Nikki **VI**: 83
Giovanni's Room (James Baldwin) **IX**: 32–33
Giovannitti, Arturo **VII**: 95, 155
Girard, Stephen **III**: 31, **153**, 350
Girard Bank **III**: 153
Girard College **IV**: 27
Girl Scouts **VIII**: 298
GIs **VIII**: 2, 79, 286
Gish, Lillian **VIII**: 12
Gist, Christopher **III**: 265
Gist, William Henry **V**: 312
Gitlow v. New York **VII**: 275; **VIII**: 54
Giuliani, Rudolph **X**: 65, 82
glaciers/glaciation **VI**: 199, 200, 257
Gladden, Washington **VI**: **115**, 242, 266
Gladstone, Richard **IX**: 80
Gladwin, Henry **III**: 281
glasnost **X**: 72, **131**, 152, 280
Glass, Carter **VIII**: 33, 34, 111
glass, decorative **VI**: 288
Glass, Hugh **IV**: 57
Glass Ceiling Commission Report **X**: 329c
Glass-Steagall Act. *See* Banking Act of 1933
Glazer, Nathan **X**: 200
Gleanings from the Southland (Cumming) **V**: 85
Glendale, Battle of **V**: 269
Glenn, John **IX**: 236, 278, 294, 333c; **X**: 276
Glidden, Joseph F. **VI**: 20
global economy **VIII**: 42, 92–93, 123, 125, 139, 140, 154
globalization **X**: 131–133, *132*
    Clinton, William **X**: 67
    economy **X**: 94, 96
    World Trade Organization **X**: 321
Globalization Syndrome, The (Mittelman) **X**: 131
Global Military Force Policy of 1998 **X**: 299
global positioning system (GPS) **X**: 275, 281
Global Strategy for Containment of Antimicrobial Resistance **X**: 188

global warming **IX**: 270; **X**: 229
Globe chair **IX**: 20
Globe Theatre **I**: 324
Glorious Revolution **II**: **140–141**, 418c; **III**: 300, 302, 374
    Connecticut **II**: 69
    crowd action **II**: 78
    Dominion of New England **II**: 94
    Leisler's Rebellion **II**: 192
    Maryland **II**: 210
    Massachusetts **II**: 214
    Mather, Cotton **II**: 217
    Mather, Increase **II**: 218
    monarchy, British **II**: 232
    New York **II**: 261
    Protestantism **II**: 300
    religion, Euro-American **II**: 316
    Roman Catholics **II**: 323, 324
    royal colonies **II**: 325
Glover, José **II**: 84
GM. *See* General Motors
GN. *See* Great Northern Railway
GNP. *See* gross national product
Go (John Clellon Holmes) **IX**: 35
Goa **I**: 207; **II**: 174
goats **I**: 53
God and Man at Yale (Buckley) **X**: 43
"God Bless America" **VIII**: 224
Goddard, Robert **VII**: 159
Goddard, William **II**: 292
Goddard Space Flight Center **X**: 281
Godey, Louis **IV**: 167–168, 197
Godey's Lady's Book **IV**: 168, 194, 197; **V**: 122, 338
Godfrey, Thomas **II**: 18, **141**, 277, 282
God in Christ (Bushnell) **IV**: 298
Godkin, Edwin Lawrence **VI**: **115–116**
    Bryce, James **VI**: 38
    magazines **VI**: 185
    mugwumps **VI**: 199
    The Nation **VI**: 205
    newspapers **VI**: 211
    Schurz, Carl **VI**: 257
    Villard, Henry **VI**: 305
gods and goddesses, Native American
    Aataentsic **I**: 1
    Aztecs **I**: 18, 21
    Huitzilopochtli **I**: 170
    Inca **I**: 176

Maya **I:** 227–228
Monte Albán **I:** 242
Natchez **I:** 251
Native American religion
I: 253
Niger River **I:** 263
Quetzalcoatl **I:** 301
Taino **I:** 342
Tezcatlipoca **I:** 347, 348
Tláloc **I:** 352
Toltecs **I:** 355
Yoruba **I:** 377
God That Failed, The (Wright)
VIII: 400
Godwin, Charles **III:** 50
Godwin, E. W. **VI:** 312
Goebbels, Joseph **VIII:** 195,
282
Goethals, George **VII:** 358*c*
gold **I: 142–143,** *143;* **II:** 221,
259; **IV: 162–164;** **V:** 104,
315; **VI:** 194*m,* 324*c,* 327*c*
Akan **I:** 5
Andes Mountains **I:** 10
Asante **I:** 13
Aztecs **I:** 22
Barbados **I:** 26
Beckwourth, Jim **IV:** 47
Bent, William **IV:** 48
Black Hills gold rush **VI:**
29, 263, 264
business cycles **VI:** 42
Cabot, Sebastian **I:** 43
California gold rush **IV:**
66–69, *67,* 68*m*
Cameroon **I:** 52
Cartier, Jacques **I:** 57–59
Casa de Contratación **I:** 59
Castile **I:** 63
Colorado gold rush **IV:**
89–90
Columbian Exchange **I:**
78
Columbus, Christopher **I:**
81, 82
Company of Cathay **I:** 83
Comstock Lode **IV:** 95
Coronado, Francisco **I:** 88
Crime of '73 **VI:** 69–70
Cuba **I:** 98
currency issue **VI:** 72
El Dorado **I:** 118
Forty-niners **IV:** 146–147
Frémont, John C. **IV:** 154
Ghana **I:** 140
Gomes, Diogo **I:** 144
Gould, Jay **VI:** 118
immigration **IV:** 180
Klondike gold rush **VI:**
160–162, *161,* 327*c*
Larkin, Thomas Oliver **IV:**
208

Mali **I:** 217
mining: metal and coal **VI:**
193
Native Americans **IV:** 257,
258
New Mexico **I:** 257
New Spain **I:** 261
Nez Perce War **VI:** 213
"Pike's Peak or Bust" **IV:**
282
Pizarro, Francisco **I:** 283
Ponce de León, Juan **I:**
288
Puerto Rico **I:** 297
silver **I:** 325
Sudan **I:** 337
Sutter, John **IV:** 332
Timbuktu **I:** 350
Velázquez, Diego de **I:**
364
Gold, Harry **IX:** 264
Gold Beach **VIII:** 248
Goldberg, Arthur **IX:** 104, 315;
X: 307
Goldbergs, The (radio show)
VIII: 274, 289
Gold Coast **I:** 5, 104, 142,
143–144, 330; **II:** 4
Golden Age, The **VI:** 25
Golden Age of Piracy **II:** 285
"Golden Bull" (1356) **I:** 165,
190
Golden Castile **I:** 276
"golden circle" of slavery **V:** 127,
259
Golden Gate Park **V:** 258
Golden Hill, Battle of **III:**
153–154, 214, 349, 392*c*
Golden Hind **I:** 110, 111
Golden Horde **I:** 286
*Golden Hour of the Little
Flower* (radio show) **VIII:** 75
Golden Stool legend **I:** 13
Goldiggers of 1933 (film) **VIII:**
274
Goldman, Emma **VI:** 167; **VII:**
109–110, *110,* 360*c*
birth control **VII:** 29
entertainment **VII:** 85
radicalism **VII:** 251
radical press **VII:** 252
women's status and rights
VII: 339
Goldmark, Josephine Clara **VII:**
110–111, 179
gold market **V:** 409*c*
Gold Repeal Resolution of 1933
VIII: 406*c*
gold reserve **VI:** 58–59
gold rush, California. *See*
California gold rush
gold rush, Colorado **V:** 405*c*

gold standard **IV:** 43, 49,
118–119, 377*c;* **V:** 105, 157;
VI: 324*c,* 327*c;* **VII:** 60, 79,
80, 262, 355*c;* **VIII:** 406*c. See
also* specie
bimetallism **VI:** 28, 29
Bretton Woods
Conference **VIII:** 42
Bryan, William Jennings
VI: 37
Crime of '73 **VI:** 69, 70
Democratic Party **VI:** 77
Free-Silver movement **VI:**
105
Garfield, James A. **VI:** 108
Godkin, Edwin Lawrence
VI: 116
Great Depression **VIII:**
139–140
Harrison, Benjamin **VI:**
123
Hayes, Rutherford B. **VI:**
126
London Economic
Conference **VIII:** 193
McKinley, William **VI:** 189
mugwumps **VI:** 199
political parties, third **VI:**
226
Schurz, Carl **VI:** 257
World Disarmament
Conference **VIII:** 388
Gold Standard Act of 1900
bimetallism **VI:** 29
currency issue **VI:** 73
Free-Silver movement **VI:**
105
McKinley, William **VI:** 189
Goldwater, Barry **VIII:** 73; **IX:**
123–124, *296,* 332*c,* 334*c*
advertising **IX:** 3
Buckley, William F., Jr. **X:**
43
conservatism **IX:** 68–69
conservative movement **X:**
79
elections **IX:** 96, 97
liberalism **IX:** 179
modern Republicanism
IX: 209
Reagan, Ronald W. **X:** 258
Republican Party **IX:** 258
Schlafly, Phyllis **X:** 272
Thurmond, J. Strom **X:**
303
golf **VI:** 274–275; **VIII:** 337; **IX:**
281; **X:** 262, 286, 296
golf, miniature **VIII:** 297
Goliad, Texas **IV:** 174, 338, 341
Golikov, Ivan **II:** 326
Gomera Island **I:** 53, 338
Gomes, Diogo **I: 144,** 326, 386*c*

Gomes, Fernão **I:** 142
Gomes, Kiogo **I:** 147
Gomez, Esteban **II:** 259
Gómez, Máximo **VI:** 71
Gómez Farías, Valentín **IV:** 303
Gompers, Samuel **VI: 116–117,**
117, 325*c;* **VIII:** 14; **IX:** 11,
292. *See also* American
Federation of Labor
Adamson Act **VII:** 2
American Federation of
Labor **VI:** 11
Buck's Stove **VII:** 36
Clayton Antitrust Act **VII:**
51
IWW **VII:** 129
labor, radical **VI:** 167
labor movement **VII:** 152,
154
"The labor movement is a
fixed fact" **VI:** 344–346
labor organizations **VI:** 170
National Association of
Manufacturers **VII:** 200
National Civic Federation
VII: 201
National War Labor Board
VII: 204
New Unionism **VII:** 212
Shirtwaist Makers Strike
VII: 285
Socialist Labor Party **VI:**
268
Steel Strike of 1919 **VII:**
298, 299
"Gone to Texas" **IV:** 12
Gone With the Wind (film)
VIII: 217, 408*c*
Gone with the Wind (Mitchell)
V: 213, 217; **VIII:** 193
Gonja **I:** 101, **144**
gonorrhea **V:** 284
Gonzáles, Elián **X:** 162, 330*c*
Gonzáles, Rodolfo "Corky" **IX:**
124–125, 171, 334*c*
Gooch, Daniel **V:** 191
Gooch, William **II:** 145
Good, Sarah **II:** 266
Goodale, Jim **X:** 233
Good Friday Agreement **X:** 69
Goodman, Andrew **IX:** 66, 67,
207, 254, 334*c*
Goodman, Benny **VIII: 132,**
149, 223, 406*c,* 408*c*
Goodman, Paul **X:** 109
Good Neighbor Policy **IV:** 142;
VII: 51; **VIII: 132–133**
Berle, Adolf A., Jr. **VIII:**
35
foreign policy **VIII:** 124
Hull, Cordell **VIII:** 160
Welles, Sumner **VIII:** 377

Good Templar **IV:** 54
"good war" thesis
World War II **VIII:** 389, 390
World War II home front **VIII:** 395
goodwives **II:** 93
Goodyear, Charles **IV:** 118, 184, 307
Goodyear strike of 1936 **VIII:** 69, 180
Goodyear Tire and Rubber **VIII:** 180
Gookin, Charles **II:** 145
Gorbachev, Mikhail **IX:** 17; **X:** 326c
Bush, George H. W. **X:** 46
cold war (end of) **X:** 71, 72
defense policy **X:** 87
foreign policy **X:** 124
glasnost **X:** 131
INF Treaty **X:** 151, 151, 152
Iron Curtain **X:** 156
Reagan, Ronald W. **X:** 260–261
Soviet Union **X:** 280
Gordon, Anna A. **VI:** 315
Gordon, John B. **V:** 39
Gordon, Kermit **X:** 301
Gordon, Mary **X:** 177
Gordon, Patrick **II:** 181
Gordon, Thomas **III:** 79
Gordon-Reed, Annette **III:** 165
Gore, Albert, Jr. **X:** 133, **133–134,** 331c
Bush, George H. W. **X:** 46
Bush, George W. **X:** 48
capital punishment **X:** 56
Clinton, William **X:** 66, 69
Dukakis, Michael **X:** 91
economy **X:** 96
elections **X:** 101–103
Ginsburg, Ruth Bader **X:** 130
Green Party **X:** 135
Horton, Willie (campaign ad) **X:** 143
House of Representatives **X:** 144
Internet **X:** 153
Jackson, Jesse L. **X:** 160
Judicial Watch **X:** 162
Kemp, Jack F. **X:** 163
Nader, Ralph **X:** 206
Persian Gulf War **X:** 235
political parties **X:** 238
Reform Party **X:** 264
Reno, Janet **X:** 267
Supreme Court **X:** 291
Gorée Island **I: 145**
Gorgas, Josiah **V: 151–152,** 356

Gorges, Sir Ferdinando **II:** 203, 250, 360–361
Gorges, William **II:** 150
Gorsuch, Edward **V:** 59
Gorton, Samuel **II: 141–142,** 320–321, 399
Gosden, Freeman **VII:** 254
Gosnold, Bartholomew **I:** 225
gospel music **VIII:** 224
"Gospel of Wealth, The" (Carnegie) **VI:** 326c
Go Tell It on the Mountain (James Baldwin) **IX:** 5, 32, 182, 331c
Gothic Revival **IV:** 27–28
Gotti, John **X:** 82
Gottschalk, Louis Moreau **VI:** 183
Goulart, João **IX:** 172
Gould, Jay **V:** 408c; **VI: 117–118; VII:** 265
corruption, political **VI:** 67
Morgan, John Pierpont **VI:** 197
railroads **VI:** 238
Scott, Thomas Alexander **VI:** 258
Gourges, Dominique de **I:** 202
government **VIII: 133–136,** 135t. *See also* Congress; House of Representatives, U.S.; presidents/presidency; Senate, U.S.; Supreme Court
Abenaki **I:** 2
Acosta, José de **I:** 3
affirmative action **X:** 8
Africa **II:** 4
African Americans **VIII:** 3
Agricultural Adjustment Act **VIII:** 5
agriculture **VIII:** 7
Andros, Sir Edmund **II:** 19
art and architecture **VIII:** 23
Asante **I:** 13
Askia Muhammad I **I:** 14
audiencia **I:** 15–16
Aztecs **I:** 18–19
banking and credit **II:** 29
Benin **I:** 28
black market **VIII:** 38
Boston **II:** 35
Brain Trust **VIII:** 41
Brazil **I:** 33
British American **II: 142–146,** 143m
British Empire **II:** 43
Burgesses, House of **II:** 44–45
business **VI:** 39–41; **IX:** 44, 46
cabildo **I:** 38–39

cacique **I:** 46–47
Calvin, John **I:** 51
Caribbean **II:** 52
Casa de Contratación **I:** 59–61
censorship **VIII:** 54
Cherokee **II:** 57
cities and urban life **IV:** 83–84; **VI:** 55; **IX:** 52
civil service reform **VI:** 56–57
claim clubs **IV:** 85–86
class **II:** 62
Colorado gold rush **IV:** 90
communism **IX:** 61
Communists **VIII:** 65, 66
computers **IX:** 64
Congress **VI:** 63–64; **VIII:** 66
Connecticut **II:** 68–69
corregidores **I:** 90–91
Council of the Indies **I:** 95
Dagomba **I:** 101
defense budget **IX:** 77–78
Delaware **II:** 87–88
De La Warr, Lord **I:** 104
Democratic Party **VIII:** 80
Dominion of New England **II:** 94–95
Dudley, Joseph **II:** 95
economy **IV:** 118; **IX:** 88–89
education, primary and secondary **X:** 98–100
Elementary and Secondary Education Act of 1965 **IX:** 98
and Employment Act of 1946 **IX:** 99
encomienda **I:** 122
Energy, U.S. Department of **X:** 103
environmental issues **VIII:** 103
evangelical Christians **X:** 108
Ewe **I:** 125
Executive Reorganization Act **VIII:** 107–108
Fair Labor Standards Act **VIII:** 110
FCC **VIII:** 116
Federal Employee Loyalty Program **IX:** 109
Federal Information Act **X:** 111–112
federalism **X:** 112–113
gays and lesbians **IX:** 119
globalization **X:** 131–132
Great Depression **VIII:** 140
Huron **I:** 171–172

Igbo **I:** 175
Inca **I:** 176
Indians of the Desert Southwest **II:** 166
Internet **X:** 152–153
Iroquois **I:** 182
Jamestown **II:** 172
John III **I:** 193
Judicial Watch **X:** 162
Keith, William **II:** 181
Kieft, Willem **II:** 182
Kongo **I:** 195
liberalism **VIII:** 187–189; **X:** 174–176
Libertarian Party **X:** 176
literature **VIII:** 193
Locke, John **II:** 197
Mali **I:** 218
Maryland **II:** 209, 210
Massachusett **I:** 225
Maya **I:** 227–228
Mayflower Compact **II:** 219–220
McCarthy, Joseph **IX:** 189–190
Mendoza, Antonio de **I:** 231
mercantilism **II:** 221
military-industrial complex **IX:** 203–204
militia movement **X:** 193
Mississippian culture **I:** 236
modern Republicanism **IX:** 208–209
monarchy, British **II:** 232
Nahua **I:** 249
Native Americans **X:** 214
New Amsterdam **II:** 250
New Deal **IX:** 229–230
New Hampshire **II:** 251–252
New Jersey **II:** 252–253
New Mexico **I:** 257
New Netherland **II:** 257
New Spain **I:** 258–259
New York **II:** 261
Parliament **I:** 277
Pennsylvania **II:** 276
Peru **I:** 280
Philadelphia **II:** 281
Plymouth **II:** 287
postwar planning **VIII:** 278
Powhatan (chief) **II:** 293
Powhatan Confederacy **II:** 294
presidency **VI:** 229–230; **VIII:** 280–281
Privy Council **I:** 295
progressivism in the 1890s **VI:** 233

public health **IX:** 249–250
public opinion polls **VIII:** 283
recreation **VIII:** 296
refugees **VIII:** 298
RFRA **X:** 266
Rhode Island **II:** 321
Roman Catholics **II:** 323
Roosevelt, Franklin D. **VIII:** 312
royal colonies **II:** 325
sachems **II:** 327
science **VIII:** 317
Senegambia **I:** 321
size and cost of **VIII:** 135*t*
Smith, John **II:** 346
society, British American **II:** 349, 350
South Carolina **II:** 353–354
Spanish colonies **II:** 355
States' Rights Party **IX:** 281
Stuyvesant, Peter **II:** 362–363
Submerged Lands Act **IX:** 286–287
Supreme Court **VI:** 281
technology **VIII:** 353
think tanks **X:** 301–302
Third New Deal **VIII:** 357
tobacco suits **X:** 305
unemployment **VIII:** 364
Venice **I:** 364
Virginia Company of London **II:** 387
wage and price controls **VIII:** 371–372
war bonds **VIII:** 374
Ward, Lester Frank **VI:** 307
werowance **I:** 372
women's network **VIII:** 383
women's rights and status **VIII:** 384; **X:** 321
World War II **VIII:** 390
World War II home front **VIII:** 394
WPB **VIII:** 375
Yoruba **I:** 377
Yucatán Peninsula **I:** 378–379
government (state and local) **VIII:** 133–135, 299; **IX: 125**
abortion **X:** 2–3
Agnew, Spiro T. **X:** 14
Baker v. Carr **IX:** 31–32
Birmingham confrontation **IX:** 38
cities and urban life **IX:** 52

Economic Opportunity Act of 1964 **IX:** 87
education, higher **X:** 97
education, primary and secondary **X:** 98–100
ERA **X:** 106–107
Federal Information Act **X:** 112
federalism **X:** 112–113
flag burning **X:** 117, 118
marriage **X:** 181
Medicaid **IX:** 196
political parties **X:** 237, 238
pro-life and pro-choice movements **X:** 248
Rehnquist, William H. **X:** 264
Reynolds v. Simms **IX:** 259–260
Supreme Court **X:** 291
tobacco suits **X:** 304–305
Twenty-sixth Amendment **X:** 306
Government Accounting Office (GAO) **X:** 134
government activism
First New Deal **VIII:** 122
government **VIII:** 134
Morgenthau, Henry **VIII:** 216
Supreme Court **VIII:** 344
World War II home front **VIII:** 395
Government Performance and Results Act of 1993 **X:** 227
government regulation **VII:** xiii.
See also deregulation
advertising **X:** 7–8
Chrysler Corporation Loan Guarantee Act **X:** 62
conservation, environmentalism, and environmental policy **X:** 78
energy crisis **X:** 104
federalism **X:** 113
Gore, Albert, Jr. **X:** 134
Grove City College et al. v. Bell, Secretary of Education, et al. **X:** 136
gun control **X:** 136–138
Libertarian Party **X:** 176
Nader, Ralph **X:** 205
Occupational Safety and Health Act of 1970 **X:** 225
OMB **X:** 227
property rights **X:** 249–250
Reaganomics **X:** 261
television **X:** 294–295
government spending **VIII:** 45, 89, 176, 407*c*

government waste **X:** 57, 58
government workers **VIII:** 106, 109–110, 212
Governo Geral **I:** 33
Governor and Merchants of London Trading into the East Indies. *See* East India Company (British)
Governor Kieft's War **II:** 252, 256, 260
governors **V: 152–153; VIII:** 49, 144, 312
Brown, Joseph **V:** 39
Burnside, Ambrose E. **V:** 44, 45
Butler, Benjamin **V:** 47
Chamberlain, Joshua L. **V:** 54
Chase, Salmon P. **V:** 56
conscription **V:** 79
Coolidge, Calvin **VII:** 56
elections **V:** 109
habeas corpus, writ of **V:** 161
Harding, Warren G. **VII:** 117
Houston, Sam **IV:** 174, 175
Hughes, Charles Evans **VII:** 124
Hull, William **IV:** 175
Jackson, Andrew **IV:** 192
McClellan, George B. **V:** 226
Pinchback, Pinckney B. S. **V:** 275
Pinchot, Gifford **VII:** 228
Polk, James K. **IV:** 283
Reconstruction **V:** 293
Roosevelt, Theodore **VII:** 266
scalawags **V:** 307
Smith, Alfred E. **VII:** 287
states' rights **V:** 336
Stephens, Alexander H. **V:** 337
strikes **V:** 340
territorial **IV:** 154
Union army **V:** 364
volunteer army **V:** 383
Warmoth, Henry C. **V:** 388
Wilson, Woodrow **VII:** 333
women as **X:** 321
Governor's Island Accords **X:** 328*c*
Gowen, Franklin B. **VI:** 195, 196
Goyahkla. *See* Geronimo
GPP (Prolonged Popular War) (Nicaragua) **X:** 217
GPS. *See* global positioning system
Gradation Act of 1854 **IV:** 12

Graduate, The (movie) **IX:** 244
graduate school **VIII:** 95
graduation **IV:** 287
Grady, Henry W. **VI:** 209; **VII:** 332
Graff, Gerald **X:** 177
Graffenried, Christopher, baron de **II: 146–147**
Graham, Billy **VIII:** 303–304, 410*c*; **IX: 125–126**, 255; **X:** 107–108, *293*
Graham, Franklin **X:** *293*
Graham, Frank Porter **X:** 140
Graham, George Rex **IV:** 196
Graham, Isabella **III:** 285
Graham, Sylvester **IV:** 111
Graham's Magazine **IV:** 196
grain combine **IV:** 10
grains **V:** 7, 279
Gramm, Phil **X:** 47, 134–135
grammar schools **IV:** 120
Gramm-Rudman-Hollings Act of 1985 (GRH) **X: 134–135**, 276, 326*c*
Grañ, Ahmad. *See* Ghazi, Ahmad ibn Ibrahim al-
Granada **I:** 80, 81, 128, 174, 185, 306
Gran Canaria Island **I:** 53
Gran Chichimeca **II:** 229
Grand Alliance **VIII: 136–138**
air power **VIII:** 11
Anglo-American relations **VIII:** 17
Army Air Forces, U.S. **VIII:** 21
Atlantic, Battle of the **VIII:** 28
atomic bomb **VIII:** 28, 29
Axis **VIII:** 31, 32
Cairo Conference **VIII:** 51
Casablanca Conference **VIII:** 52
election of 1940 **VIII:** 98
foreign policy **VIII:** 125–126
Hopkins, Harry **VIII:** 157
Italian campaign **VIII:** 168
Lend-Lease Act **VIII:** 184–185
Manhattan Project **VIII:** 200
Marshall, George C. **VIII:** 206
mobilization **VIII:** 214
Nazi-Soviet Pact **VIII:** 238
Normandy, invasion of **VIII:** 247
Popular Front **VIII:** 276
Potsdam Conference **VIII:** 279–280
propaganda **VIII:** 283

Grand Alliance (continued)
   Roosevelt, Franklin D.
      VIII: 314
   second front **VIII:** 320
   Soviet-American relations
      VIII: 333, 334
   Teheran Conference **VIII:**
      354, 355
   V-E Day **VIII:** 369
   World War II **VIII:** 389
   World War II European
      theater **VIII:** 391, 392
   Yalta Conference **VIII:** 401
Grand Army of the Republic
   (GAR) **V:** 408c; **VI:** 58, **118,**
   326c; **VII:** 292, 324
      Civil War **V:** 67
      54th Massachusetts
         Regiment **V:** 126
      monuments **V:** 239
      Taylor, Susie King **V:** 350
      Union army **V:** 367
      veterans, Civil War **V:**
         378–379
Grand Canyon **I:** 90, 156, 167
Grand Coulee Dam **VIII:** 209
grandfather clause **VI:** 95,
   118–119, 327c; **VII:** 358c
Grand National Consolidated
   Trades Union **IV:** 273
Grand Old Party. See
   Republican Party
Grand Ole Opry **VIII:** 222, 224
Grand Portage **II:** 115
Grand Pré **II:** 309
Grand Staircase-Escalante
   National Monument **X:** 250
Grands Voyages **I:** 102
Granganimeo **II:** 264, 401
Grange, Red **VIII:** 336
Granger, Gordon **V:** 194
Granger, Lester **IX:** 305–306
Granger cases **VI:** 82, 281
Granger laws **VI:** 221, 326c
Granger movement **VI:** 40, 99,
   186, 239, 324c. See also
   Patrons of Husbandry
Granite Railway Company **IV:**
   185, 292–293, 295
"grannies" **II:** 225
Grant, Cary **IX:** 212
Grant, Julia Dent **V: 153–154,**
   154
Grant, Madison **VI:** 209; **VII:**
   14, 248
Grant, Ulysses S. **IV:** 103, 234;
   V: 154–158, 155, 406c–408c;
   VI: 323c; **VII:** 303
      Adams, Henry **VI:** 1
      Apache War **VI:** 14
      Appomattox Court House,
         Virginia **V:** 13–15, 14

assassination of Abraham
   Lincoln **V:** 17
Atlanta campaign **V:** 19
Blair, Francis P., Jr. **V:** 30,
   31
Burnside, Ambrose E. **V:**
   45
Butler, Benjamin **V:** 46
Canada and the United
   States **VI:** 43
Chamberlain, Joshua L. **V:**
   54
Chattanooga, Battle of **V:**
   57
Civil Rights Act of 1875 **V:**
   63
civil service reform **VI:** 56
Civil War **V:** 66
Cold Harbor, Battle of **V:**
   68
Confederate States of
   America **V:** 77
Congress **VI:** 63
Conkling, Roscoe **VI:** 64
Corinth, Battle of **V:** 83
corruption, political **VI:** 67
Crédit Mobilier **V:** 84
Dana, Charles A. **V:** 88
Democratic Party **V:** 95
Douglass, Frederick **V:** 100
Early, Jubal A. **V:** 103
Eaton, John, Jr. **V:** 104
education, philanthropy
   and **VI:** 94
elections **V:** 111
Enforcement Acts **V:** 117
espionage **V:** 118
Fifteenth Amendment **V:**
   124
Five Forks, Battle of **V:**
   128–129
foraging **V:** 130
foreign policy **V:** 133; **VI:**
   103, 104
Freedman's Saving Bank
   V: 141
Garfield, James A. **VI:** 108
Godkin, Edwin Lawrence
   VI: 116
Grant, Julia Dent **V:**
   153–154
Greeley, Horace **V:** 158
Greenback-Labor Party
   VI: 120
Halleck, Henry W. **V:** 162
Hancock, Winfield Scott **V:**
   163, 164
Howard, O. O. **V:** 173
impeachment of Andrew
   Johnson **V:** 179
Internal Revenue taxes **VI:**
   147

Johnson, Andrew **V:** 189
Johnston, Albert Sidney **V:**
   189
Joint Committee on the
   Conduct of War **V:** 191
journalism **V:** 194
Ku Klux Klan **V:** 199, 200;
   VI: 163
Ku Klux Klan Act **V:** 201
Lee, Robert E. **V:** 207
Liberal Republican Party
   VI: 173–174
Lincoln, Abraham **V:** 211
literature **V:** 212
Lockwood, Belva Ann
   Bennett McNall **VI:** 180
Lookout Mountain, Battle
   of **V:** 216, 217
Meade, George Gordon **V:**
   227
medicine and hospitals **V:**
   230
Milliken's Bend, Battle of
   V: 232, 233
Mississippi River **V:** 234,
   235
Mobile campaign **V:** 236
Mosby, John Singleton **V:**
   242
Murfreesboro/Stones
   River, Battle of **V:** 242
Nast, Thomas **V:** 247
Native Americans **V:** 249
Nez Perce War **VI:** 213
Overland campaign **V:** 260,
   261
Parker, Ely Samuel **V:** 265
Petersburg campaign **V:**
   270–272
Pickett, George Edward **V:**
   274–275
political parties, third **VI:**
   225
Porter, David Dixon **V:** 280
the presidency **VI:** 230
presidential campaigns **VI:**
   231, 232
prisons **V:** 281
Radical Republicans **V:**
   289
Reconstruction **V:** 294
Reconstruction Acts **V:** 296
redemption **V:** 297
Republican Party **V:** 302;
   VI: 246
Richmond, Virginia **V:** 304
Rosecrans, William S. **V:**
   305
Santo Domingo **VI:** 255
scalawags **V:** 308
Schurz, Carl **VI:** 256
Seward, William H. **V:** 315

Shenandoah Valley:
   Sheridan's campaign **V:**
   317
Sheridan, Philip H. **V:** 318,
   319
Sherman, William T. **V:**
   320, 321
Sherman's March through
   Georgia **V:** 322
Shiloh, Battle of **V:** 323,
   324, 326
Sickles, Daniel E. **V:** 327
Singleton, Benjamin **V:**
   327
Spotsylvania, Battles of **V:**
   333
Stanton, Edwin M. **V:** 334
Stuart, J. E. B. **V:** 341
Sumner, Charles **V:** 343
tactics and strategy **V:** 347
Union army **V:** 367
United States Army Corps
   of Engineers **V:** 371
USCC **V:** 372
Van Lew, Elizabeth **V:** 378
Vicksburg campaign **V:**
   380, 382, 383
Warmoth, Henry C. **V:**
   388
Washington, D.C. **V:** 390
Washington, Treaty of **VI:**
   309
Whiskey Ring **V:** 392, 393
Wilderness, Battle of the
   V: 395
women's rights **VI:** 318
Grant's Tomb **V:** 239
Grapes of Wrath (film) **VIII:**
   217, 274
Grapes of Wrath (Steinbeck)
   VIII: 408c
      Dust Bowl **VIII:** 87
      literature **VIII:** 191, 192
      marriage and family life
         VIII: 204
      migration **VIII:** 212
      Steinbeck, John **VIII:** 339
graphic arts. See illustration,
   photography, and the graphic
   arts
Grasse, François-Joseph-Paul,
   comte de **III: 154,** 310, 390
grasses **I:** 77, 87
Grateful Dead **IX:** 264
Gravano, Salvatore "Sammy the
   Bull" **X:** 82
grave-robbing **IV:** 230
Graves, Thomas **III:** 154
Graves, William S. **VII:** 285
gravestones **II:** 24, 215, 235
gravity railroad **IV:** 292
Gray, Elisha **VI:** 25

Gray, Robert **IV:** 93
Gray, Victoria **IX:** 207
Gray, William **X:** 12
Grayson, Walter **VI:** 100
"gray" v. "blue" **V:** 362
grazing **IV:** 337, 339
"Greaser Act" **IV:** 249
Great American Desert **II:** 149
Great Atlantic and Pacific Tea
    Company (A&P) **VI:** 46–47
Great Awakening **II:** 29,
    147–149, *148,* 419*c;* **III:**
    298, 300, 355; **IV:** 296
    Baptists **II:** 29
    Brainerd, David **II:** 39
    Chauncy, Charles **II:** 57
    Congregationalists **II:** 68
    Dartmouth College **II:** 83
    Davenport, James **II:**
        83–84
    disease **II:** 92
    education **II:** 104–105
    Edwards, Jonathan **II:**
        105–106
    Edwards, Sarah Pierpont
        II: 106
    Frelinghuysen, Theodorus
        Jacobus **II:** 125–126
    German Reformed Church
        II: 140
    Hammon, Jupiter **II:** 153
    journalism **II:** 178
    King's College **II:** 184
    music **II:** 239
    New Jersey **II:** 254
    Osborn, Sarah Haggar
        Wheaten **II:** 268
    Presbyterians **II:** 296
    Princeton College **II:** 298
    Protestantism **II:** 301
    religion, African-American
        II: 314
    Rhode Island **II:** 321–322
    slavery **II:** 342
    society, British American
        II: 351
    Stono Rebellion **II:** 361
    Tennent, Gilbert **II:** 371
    Tennent, William, Jr. **II:**
        372
    Tennent, William, Sr. **II:**
        372
    Virginia **II:** 385
    Wheelock, Eleazar **II:** 395
    Whitefield, George **II:**
        397–398
    Wigglesworth, Edward **II:**
        398
Great Awakening, Second **III:**
    169, 299, 362; **IV: 310,**
    310–311, 311*t;* **V:** 2, 299
    anti-Catholic riots **IV:** 21

anti-Masonry **IV:** 24
Finney, Charles Grandison
    IV: 138
religion **IV:** 296
Republican Party **IV:** 301
Great Basin **IV:** 109
Great Book of Writing **II:** 248
Great Bridge, Battle of **III:** 109
Great Britain **II:** 419*c;* **III:**
    391*c*–398*c;* **IV:** 375*c,* 378*c;*
    VI: 323*c,* 328*c;* **VII:** 359*c,*
    360*c;* **VIII:** 408*c*–411*c;* **IX:**
    332*c;* **X:** 164, 268. *See also*
    British Empire; England;
    United Kingdom
    Acts of Trade and
        Navigation **II:** 2–3
    Adams, John **III:** 2
    Adams, John Quincy **IV:** 4
    Adams, Samuel **III:** 4
    agriculture **V:** 6; **VIII:** 9
    aircraft industry **VIII:** 10,
        11
    Algonquin **II:** 17
    America First Committee
        VIII: 13
    American Expeditionary
        Force **VII:** 9
    American Fur Company
        IV: 16
    American Revolution **III:**
        12
    amphibious warfare **VIII:**
        15
    Andre, John **III:** 13
    Anglo-American relations
        VIII: 16–17
    arms race **IX:** 16
    Arnold, Benedict **III:** 21
    Aroostook War **IV:** 25
    Association, the **III:** 27
    Astoria **IV:** 32, 33
    Atlantic, Battle of the
        VIII: 28
    Atlantic Charter **VIII:** 28
    Audubon, John James **IV:**
        34
    Austin, Moses **IV:** 35
    aviation **IX:** 27, 28
    Baltimore, Battle of **IV:** 39
    banking and credit **II:** 28
    Barbary pirates **III:** 35
    Bear Flag Revolt **IV:** 45
    Beatles **IX:** 36
    Benjamin, Judah P. **V:** 27,
        28
    Bering Sea dispute **VI:**
        26–27
    Berlin blockade **IX:** 37
    Bernard, Francis **III:** 37
    Black Hawk War **IV:** 51,
        52

Blackstone, William **III:**
    39
Blaine, James Gillespie **VI:**
    32
Bonaparte, Napoleon **III:**
    42
Boston Tea Party **III:** 45
Boucher, Jonathan **III:** 46
Boyd, Belle **V:** 35
British Empire **II:** 41–44
Brown, William Wells **V:**
    40
Buchanan, James **V:** 41
Bulge, Battle of the **VIII:**
    44
Burke, Edmund **III:**
    52–53
Bute, earl of **III:** 54
Cairo Conference **VIII:** 51
Camden, William **I:** 51–52
Canada **III:** 61
Carey, Mathew **III:** 61
Carleton, Guy **III:** 62
Caroline affair **IV:** 74–75
Casablanca Conference
    VIII: 52
cash-and-carry **VIII:** 53
Catholics **III:** 63
Cherokee nation **III:** 66
Chesapeake-Leopard affair
    III: 67
Chilean-American
    relations **VI:** 49
Choctaw nation **II:** 61; **III:**
    68
Church of Jesus Christ of
    Latter-day Saints **IV:** 81
Clayton-Bulwer Treaty **IV:**
    88–89
Clinton, Sir Henry **III:**
    75–76
code breaking **VIII:** 64
Columbia River **IV:** 93
Common Sense (Paine)
    III: 78
Confederate States of
    America **V:** 76
Continental army **III:** 85
Continental Congress,
    First **III:** 87
Continental navy **III:** 90
convict labor **II:** 71
Copley, John Singleton **III:**
    91
Cornplanter **III:** 91
Cornwallis, Lord **III:** 92
cotton culture **IV:** 98
Creek nation **III:** 96
Cuba **IV:** 100
Currency Act **III:** 99
Dartmoor Prison **IV:**
    103–104

Dawes Plan **VII:** 63–64
Declaration of
    Independence **III:** 101,
    102
Declaratory Act **III:** 103
deism **III:** 103
Democratic Party **VII:** 66
destroyers-for-bases deal
    VIII: 82, 83
diseases and epidemics **IV:**
    111
Dix, Dorothea **IV:** 113
Dow, Lorenzo **IV:** 116
dueling **II:** 96
Earle, Ralph **III:** 111
economy **III:** 111, 113; **IV:**
    117, 118
emancipation **V:** 114
embargo of 1807 **III:** 117
Equiano, Olaudah **III:**
    118, 119
espionage **VIII:** 104–105
Essex, USS **IV:** 130
Essex decision **III:** 119
Ethiopia **VIII:** 105
ethnocentrism **II:** 112
Eutaw Springs, Battle of
    III: 120–121
exploration **IV:** 132
filibustering **V:** 127
Florida **III:** 129; **IV:** 139
foreign affairs **III:** 130,
    131
foreign policy **IV:** 140–142;
    V: 131, 132; **VI:** 103;
    VII: 100; **VIII:** 124, 125
Fort Stanwix, Treaty of **III:**
    132
Fort Vancouver **IV:** 145
Franklin, Benjamin **III:**
    134, 135
Franklin, William **III:** 136
Free Trade and Sailor's
    Rights **IV:** 151–152
French alliance **III:** 137
French Revolution **III:**
    138–139
Fulton, Robert **III:** 142
fur trade **III:** 142; **IV:** 156
Gage, Thomas **III:**
    146–147
Gallatin, Albert **III:** 147
Galloway, Joseph **III:** 148
Gaspée affair **III:** 148
Genet, Edmond **III:** 149
George III, king of Great
    Britain **III:** 150–151
Ghent, Treaty of (1814) **IV:**
    161–162
Grand Alliance **VIII:** 136,
    137
Grenville, George **III:** 157

Harriman, Averell **VIII:** 143–144

Harrison, Benjamin **VI:** 123

Harrison, William Henry **IV:** 169

Hartford Convention **IV:** 170, 171

Hawaiian Islands **IV:** 171; **VI:** 124

Hay, John Milton **VI:** 125

Hull, William **IV:** 175–176

immigration **VII:** 127t

imperialism **VI:** 141

industrialization **IV:** 184

intelligence **VIII:** 164

investments, foreign **VII:** 134–135

investments, foreign, in the United States **VI:** 150

Irish Americans **VIII:** 165

ironclads **V:** 183

Jackson, Andrew **IV:** 191

Kearny, Stephen Watts **IV:** 200

Kennedy, Joseph P. **VIII:** 175, 176

King, Ernest J. **VIII:** 178

labor and labor movements **III:** 199, 200

Lake Erie, Battle of **IV:** 206, 207

Larkin, Thomas Oliver **IV:** 207

lawyers **III:** 204

Lee, Charles **III:** 205

Lee, Richard Henry **III:** 207

Lend-Lease Act **VIII:** 184–185

Lexington and Concord, Battles of **III:** 211, 212

Liberia **IV:** 209

Limited Test Ban Treaty of 1963 **IX:** 180

literature **IV:** 211

London Economic Conference **VIII:** 193

London Naval Conference **VIII:** 194

Loyalists **III:** 219

Lusitania **VII:** 168

Macon's Bill No. 2 **III:** 226

Madison, James **III:** 229–230

Manchuria **VIII:** 199

Manhattan Project **VIII:** 200

Manifest Destiny **IV:** 217, 218

Marshall Plan **IX:** 194

Mason, George **III:** 237

Mayhew, Jonathan **III:** 238

McKinley, William **VI:** 190

McLoughlin, John **IV:** 229

Mercator, Gerhardus **I:** 232

Mexican-American War **IV:** 232

Middle East **IX:** 201

migration **IV:** 236

Monitor-Merrimack **V:** 237

Monroe, James **IV:** 240

Monroe Doctrine **IV:** 241, 242

Monroe-Pinkney Treaty **III:** 245–246

mountain men **IV:** 247

Munich Conference **VIII:** 220

Native Americans **IV:** 255, 256

Native Americans and the Revolution **III:** 254, 256

Native Americans in the War of 1812 **IV:** 258–260

Naval Disarmament Conference **VII:** 209, 210

Nazi-Soviet Pact **VIII:** 238

neutrality **VII:** 210

Neutrality Proclamation **III:** 256

New Orleans, Battle of (1815) **IV:** 262

New Spain (Mexico), northern frontier of **III:** 258

Non-Importation Act **III:** 259

Non-Intercourse Act **III:** 259

North, Lord **III:** 260

Ohio Company of Virginia **III:** 265

Olive Branch Petition **III:** 266

Open Door notes **VI:** 216–217

Orders in Council **III:** 267

Oregon Treaty of 1846 **IV:** 269–271

Ostenaco **II:** 269

Ostend Manifesto **V:** 259

Otis, James, Jr. **III:** 268

Panama Canal **VII:** 222

Panic of 1837 **IV:** 276

Paris, Treaty of **III:** 273

Patton, George **VIII:** 263

Pennsylvania **II:** 276

Perry, Matthew Calbraith **IV:** 279

Polk, James K. **IV:** 283

Pontiac's Rebellion **III:** 280–281

Popular Front **VIII:** 276

population trends **III:** 283

Potsdam Conference **VIII:** 279

POWs **VIII:** 282

privateering **III:** 287

Proclamation of 1763 **III:** 287

propaganda **VIII:** 283

Quakers **II:** 308; **III:** 291

Quartering Act **III:** 291

Quasi War **III:** 292

race and racial conflict **V:** 288

Red Jacket **III:** 297

republicanism **III:** 302

resistance movement **III:** 303

Revolutionary War **III:** 305, 307

Rhode Island, Battle of **III:** 308

Rocky Mountain Fur Company **IV:** 302

Russian Revolution **VII:** 270

Samoa **VI:** 254, 255

Scotch-Irish **III:** 322

Seabury, Samuel **III:** 323

secession **V:** 311

second front **VIII:** 320

Seminole wars **IV:** 311

Seven Years' War **II:** 332–334

Seward, William H. **V:** 315

Sicily **VIII:** 325, 326

slavery **II:** 339

Smith, Jedediah Strong **IV:** 322

Southeast Asia Treaty Organization **IX:** 273–274

Soviet-American relations **VIII:** 333

Stamp Act **III:** 331–332

Stuart, Gilbert **III:** 335

submarines **VIII:** 342

Suez crisis **IX:** 288–289

Sugar Act **III:** 336

Sumner, Charles **V:** 341, 343

tariffs **V:** 348

Tarleton, Banastre **III:** 343

technology **IX:** 294

Tecumseh **III:** 345

Teheran Conference **VIII:** 354

Texas **IV:** 338

Thames, Battle of the **IV:** 342

Townshend Duties **III:** 348

trade **VI:** 290

trade, foreign **VII:** 310

Treaty of Paris **II:** 378

Truman Doctrine **IX:** 300

UN **VIII:** 365, 366

Union navy **V:** 369

V-E Day **VIII:** 369

Venezuela boundary dispute **VI:** 303

Vergennes, comte de **III:** 359

Versailles, Treaty of **VII:** 323, 324

Victorianism **VI:** 304

Virginia Resolves **III:** 361

Virginius affair **VI:** 305

V-J Day **VIII:** 369

War of 1812 **IV:** 355–358

War of Jenkins' Ear **II:** 392

wars of national liberation **IX:** 316

war with France, 1793–1815. *See* Anglo-French War, 1793–1815

Washington, George **III:** 366

Washington, Treaty of **VI:** 309–310

Washington Conference on Naval Disarmament **VII:** 331

Webster, Daniel **IV:** 360

Webster-Ashburton Treaty (1842) **IV:** 360–361

West, Benjamin **III:** 371

West Indies **III:** 372

Wheatley, Phillis **III:** 373

Whig Party **IV:** 362

Whigs **III:** 374

Wilkes, John **III:** 378

Willkie, Wendell L. **VIII:** 379

Wilson, Woodrow **VII:** 334

World Disarmament Conference **VIII:** 388

World War I **VII:** 343

World War II European theater **VIII:** 391

World War II Pacific theater **VIII:** 398

writs of assistance **III:** 384

Yancey, William Lowndes **V:** 401

Zionism **VIII:** 403

Great Collapse **I:** 275

Great Comet of 1843 **IV:** 308

Great Compromise of 1787 **III:** 82, 228, 395c

Great Depression **V:** 95; **VI:** 79;
VIII: xiii, **138–141,** *139,*
405*c;* **IX:** 88; **X:** 112
advertising **VIII:** 1
African Americans **VIII:**
2–3
Agricultural Adjustment
Act **VIII:** 5–7
Agricultural Marketing Act
VII: 5
agriculture **VII:** 7; **VIII:**
7–8
aircraft industry **VIII:** 9,
10
American Federation of
Labor **VIII:** 14
American Liberty League
VIII: 14
Anglo-American relations
VIII: 16
antimonopoly **VIII:** 17
anti-Semitism **VIII:** 19
art **VII:** 20
art and architecture **VIII:**
22–24
Asian Americans **VIII:** 26
automobile industry **VIII:**
30
Banking Act of 1933 **VIII:**
33
blues **VII:** 32
Bonus Army **VIII:** 39–40
Borah, William E. **VIII:** 40
Brain Trust **VIII:** 41
Bridges, Harry **VIII:** 43
business **VIII:** 45, 47–48
Catholics **VIII:** 53
CCC **VIII:** 63–64
censorship **VIII:** 54
children **VIII:** 56
cities and urban life **VIII:**
57, 58, 60
civil liberties **VIII:** 60
Communists **VIII:** 65
Congress **VIII:** 66, 67
conservatism **VIII:** 71, 73
conservative coalition
VIII: 73
Coolidge, Calvin **VII:** 57
Coughlin, Father Charles
E. **VIII:** 75
Democratic Party **VIII:** 80
DiMaggio, Joe **VIII:** 84
Dust Bowl **VIII:** 87
Eccles, Marriner S. **VIII:**
89
economy **VII:** 76; **VIII:**
91–92
education **VIII:** 93, 94
elderly **VIII:** 95
election of 1932 **VIII:** 96
election of 1936 **VIII:** 97

election of 1940 **VIII:** 98
elections **VII:** 81
Ellington, Duke **VIII:** 100
Emergency Banking Act of
1933 **VIII:** 100
Emergency Relief
Appropriation Act **VIII:**
101–102
ethnic organizations **VII:**
89
FAP **VIII:** 114
FCA **VIII:** 111–112
FDIC **VIII:** 117
FEPC **VIII:** 109
FERA **VIII:** 117–118
FHA **VIII:** 118–119
First New Deal **VIII:** 122
FMP **VIII:** 119–120
Fordney-McCumber Tariff
VII: 97
foreign policy **VII:** 101;
VIII: 123
FSA **VIII:** 112–113
FWP **VIII:** 121
Garner, John Nance **VIII:**
129
German Americans **VIII:**
130
Good Neighbor Policy
VIII: 132
government **VIII:** 133–135
Hawley-Smoot Tariff Act
VIII: 144
HOLC **VIII:** 150–151
Holocaust **VIII:** 150
Hoover, Herbert **VIII:**
151, 152
Hoover presidency **VIII:**
153–156
housing **VIII:** 157–159
immigration **VIII:** 162
Indian Reorganization Act
VIII: 163
Irish Americans **VIII:** 165
Italian Americans **VIII:**
167
Jews **VIII:** 172–173
labor **VIII:** 179
La Follette, Robert M., Jr.
VIII: 182
Lewis, John L. **VIII:** 185
liberalism **VIII:** 187–188
literature **VIII:** 190
London Economic
Conference **VIII:**
193–194
London Naval Conference
VIII: 194
Long, Huey P. **VIII:**
194–195
marriage and family life
VIII: 203–204

McPherson, Aimee
Semple **VII:** 176
medicine **VIII:** 209
Mellon, Andrew **VII:** 180
Mexican Americans **VIII:**
210
Mexican immigration **VII:**
183
Mexican Repatriation
Program **VIII:** 211
Middletown **VII:** 186
migration **VIII:** 212
mobilization **VIII:** 214
movies **VIII:** 217–220
MOWM **VIII:** 201
Murray, Philip **VIII:** 221
music **VIII:** 221, 222
Native Americans **VIII:**
235
Naval Disarmament
Conference **VII:** 209
New Deal **VIII:** 239–243
news media **VIII:** 243,
244
New York World's Fair
(1939–1940) **VIII:** 244
NIRA **VIII:** 228
NRA **VIII:** 231–232
NYA **VIII:** 234
Patton, George **VIII:** 263
photography **VIII:** 268
Polish Americans **VIII:**
269
politics in the Roosevelt
era **VIII:** 270–271
popular culture **VIII:** 273
population trends **VIII:**
276–277
postwar planning **VIII:**
278
presidency **VIII:** 280, 281
Prohibition **VII:** 241
public opinion polls **VIII:**
283
PWA **VIII:** 285–286
RA **VIII:** 307
race and racial conflict
VIII: 287, 288
radicalism **VII:** 251
radical press **VII:** 253
radio **VIII:** 289
rationing **VIII:** 292
REA **VIII:** 315–316
recession of 1937–38 **VIII:**
292–293
Reciprocal Trade
Agreements Act **VIII:**
293–294
reconversion **VIII:** 295
recreation **VIII:** 296–297
refugees **VIII:** 298
relief **VIII:** 299–302

Relief and Reconstruction
Act **VIII:** 302
religion **VIII:** 302–304
Republican Party **VIII:**
305
Revenue Act of 1935 **VIII:**
308
RFC **VIII:** 294–295
Roosevelt, Franklin D.
VIII: 312
shipbuilding **VIII:** 324
Sinclair, Upton **VII:** 287
socialism **VII:** 289
socialists **VIII:** 327
Social Security Act **VIII:**
328–330
social work **VII:** 291
South **VIII:** 331–332
Soviet-American relations
VIII: 333
sports **VIII:** 335
steel industry **VIII:**
338–339
Steinbeck, John **VIII:** 339
STFU **VIII:** 332
stock market crash (1929)
VIII: 340–341
suburbs **VIII:** 342
Sunbelt **VIII:** 343
Supreme Court **VIII:** 345
taxation **VIII:** 351
technology **VIII:** 353
Third New Deal **VIII:**
357–358
Thomas, Norman **VIII:**
358
TNEC **VIII:** 355
Townsend, Francis E.
VIII: 358, 359
trade, foreign **VII:** 310
transportation **VIII:**
359–360
Tugwell, Rexford G. **VIII:**
361
unemployment **VIII:**
363–365
vaudeville **VII:** 322
veterans **VII:** 326
Wagner, Robert F. **VIII:**
372
Welles, Orson **VIII:** 376
women's status and rights
VIII: 384–385
World Disarmament
Conference **VIII:** 388
World War II home front
VIII: 394
Great Duelist, The **IV:** 210
Greater Antilles **II:** 52
Arawak **I:** 12
cacique **I:** 46–47
Columbian Exchange **I:** 77

Greater Antilles (continued)
  Jamaica **I:** 187
  Puerto Rico **I:** 296–297
  Taino **I:** 342
  Velázquez, Diego de **I:** 364
"Greater East Asia Co-
  prosperity Sphere" **VIII:** 31,
  396
"greatest generation" **VIII:** 389
Greatest Show on Earth, The
  VI: 323c
Great Gatsby, The (Fitzgerald)
  VII: 166–167
Great Lakes **II:** 57, 114–115,
  130–131, 375; **III:** 65; **IV:**
  375c, 376c; **V:** 355
  American Fur Company
    IV: 16
  Cass, Lewis **IV:** 76
  fur trade **IV:** 156
  Ghent, Treaty of (1814) **IV:**
    161, 162
  Native Americans in the
    War of 1812 **IV:** 259
  railroads **IV:** 293, 295
  Thames, Battle of the **IV:**
    342
"Great Locomotive Chase" **V:**
  11
Great Migration **II:** 107, 108,
  212; **VI:** 83; **VII:** xiii,
  111–113, 112m, 358c; **VIII:**
  2, 23–24, 61; **IX:** 4
  agriculture **VII:** 7
  blues **VII:** 32
  cities and urban life **VII:**
    48, 49–50
  Harlem Renaissance **VII:**
    119
  literature **VII:** 162
  Locke, Alain **VII:** 164–165
  National Origins Act **VII:**
    202
  popular culture **VII:** 233
  population trends **VII:** 235
  race and racial conflict
    VII: 249
Great Migration (Irish) **IV:** 177,
  180
Great Migration to New
  England **I:** 299
Great Migration (westward) **IV:**
  235
"Great Nation of Futurity"
  (O'Sullivan) **IV:** 217
Great Northern Railway (GN)
  VII: 64, 216
  business and government
    VI: 40
  Hill, James J. **VI:** 129
  Morgan, John Pierpont **VI:**
    197, 198

Pullman Strike **VI:** 236
  railroads **VI:** 237, 239
Great Plains **III:** **154–155,** 258;
  IV: 48, 143, 200; **VIII:** 85–87
Great Plains Indians **II:** 133,
  149–150
Great Pyramid (Pyramid of
  Tepanapa) **I:** 72, 344
Great Railroad Strike (1877) **V:**
  340, 356
Great Salt Lake **X:** 26
  Bridger, James **IV:** 57
  Church of Jesus Christ of
    Latter-day Saints **IV:** 80
  Deseret, State of **IV:** 109
  exploration **IV:** 131, 132
  Frémont, John C. **IV:** 153
  Mormon Trail **IV:** 243,
    243m
  Mormon War **IV:** 244
Great Sedition Trial **VIII:** 326
Great Serpent Mound **I:** 245
Great Sioux Reservation **VI:**
  240, 324c
Great Society **VIII:** 183; **IX:**
  126–127, 334c; **X:** 79, 94,
  175
  economy **IX:** 90
  Elementary and Secondary
    Education Act of 1965
    IX: 98–99
  Johnson, Lyndon **IX:** 151
  Model Cities program **IX:**
    208
  National Endowment for
    the Arts **IX:** 221
  National Endowment for
    the Humanities **IX:** 222
  National Wilderness
    Preservation Act of 1964
    IX: 226
  New Deal **IX:** 230
  Volunteers in Service to
    America **IX:** 310–311
  War on Poverty **IX:**
    313–314
  Wild and Scenic Rivers Act
    of 1968 **IX:** 321–322
great speakers. See huei tlatoani
"Great Stone Bridge" **VI:** 34
Great Strike of 1877 **VI:**
  119–120, 324c
  Hayes, Rutherford B. **VI:**
    126
  Knights of Labor **VI:** 162
  labor: strikes and violence
    VI: 168
  labor organizations **VI:**
    169
  railroads **VI:** 237
  Scott, Thomas Alexander
    VI: 258

Socialist Labor Party **VI:**
  268
Great Swamp Fight **II:** 321
Great Train Robbery, The (film)
  VII: 85, 190, 232
Great War. See World War I
Great White Fleet **VII:**
  113–114, 357c
  foreign policy **VII:** 98
  Gentlemen's Agreement
    VII: 108
  Roosevelt, Theodore **VII:**
    266
  Root-Takahira Agreement
    VII: 268
  Russo-Japanese War **VII:**
    271
  trade, foreign **VII:** 310
"Great White Hope" **VII:** 138
Great White Hope, The (play) **X:**
  241
Grebel, Conrad **I:** 309
Greece **I:** 294; **IV:** 27; **IX:** 194,
  201, 231–233, 248, 300; **X:**
  70, 223
Greek Revival **IV:** 27, 98
Greeks, ancient **II:** 338
Greek War for Independence
  IV: 27
Greeley, Horace **V:** **158,** 407c;
  VI: 323c
  Brook Farm **IV:** 58
  Dana, Charles A. **V:** 88
  Emancipation
    Proclamation **V:** 114
  Fuller, Margaret **IV:** 156
  Grant, Ulysses S. **V:** 157
  Homestead Act of 1862 **V:**
    170
  journalism **IV:** 194
  Liberal Republican Party
    VI: 174
  Lockwood, Belva Ann
    Bennett McNall **VI:** 180
  Massachusetts Emigrant
    Aid Society **IV:** 224
  political parties, third **VI:**
    225
  presidential campaigns **VI:**
    231
  Pulitzer, Joseph **VI:** 235
  race and racial conflict **V:**
    287
  religion **IV:** 299; **VI:** 244
  Republican Party **V:** 302
  Schurz, Carl **VI:** 256
  Sumner, Charles **V:** 343
Green, Duff **IV:** 122
Green, Edith **IX:** 207
Green, Jonas **II:** 178
Green, William **VII:** 11; **VIII:**
  14, 179, 180; **IX:** 66

Greenback-Labor Party **VI:** **120**
  currency issue **VI:** 72
  Great Strike of 1877 **VI:**
    120
  Internal Revenue taxes **VI:**
    147
  Lease, Mary Elizabeth **VI:**
    173
  political parties, third **VI:**
    225–226
  Powderly, Terence Vincent
    VI: 227
  Simpson, Jerry **VI:** 262
  Socialist Labor Party **VI:**
    268
greenbacks **V:** **159;** **VI:** 324c
  banking and currency **V:**
    24
  Chase, Salmon P. **V:** 56
  currency issue **VI:** 72, 73
  economy **V:** 105, 106
  farmers' alliances **VI:** 99
  national banking system
    VI: 206
  Sherman, John **VI:** 261
  Stevens, Thaddeus **V:** 338
Greenbelt **VIII:** 342–343
Greenbelt New Town Program
  VIII: 342–343
  RA **VIII:** 307
  suburbs **VIII:** 342–343
  Tugwell, Rexford G. **VIII:**
    361
Greendale, Wisconsin **VIII:** 343
Greene, Graham **IX:** 212
Greene, Nathanael **III:**
  155–156
  Brandywine, Battle of **III:**
    48
  Church, Benjamin **III:** 68
  Cornwallis, Lord **III:** 93
  Cowpens, Battle of **III:** 95
  Eutaw Springs, Battle of
    III: 120
  Gates, Horatio **III:** 149
  Guilford Courthouse,
    Battle of **III:** 158
  Hamilton, Alexander **III:**
    161
  Lee, Henry **III:** 206
  Long Island, Battle of **III:**
    217
  Revolutionary War **III:**
    305
  Wilkinson, James **III:** 379
Greene, Thomas **II:** 209
"Greenfield Hill" (Dwight) **III:**
  80
Greenglass, David **IX:** 264
Greenglass, Ruth **IX:** 264
Greenhill, James **II:** 220
Greenhills, Ohio **VIII:** 343

greenhouse effect **IX:** 270, 334*c*
Greenhow, Robert **V:** 159
Greenhow, Rose O'Neal **V:** 118, **159–160**
Greenland **I:** 133, **145,** 263, 264, 266, 385*c;* **II:** 166, 167
Green Mountain Boys **III: 156,** 392*c*
   Allen, Ethan **III:** 10
   Clinton, George **III:** 74
   Fort Ticonderoga **III:** 133
   land riots **III:** 202
   Lyon, Matthew **III:** 222
   Young, Thomas **III:** 390
Green Party **X: 135**
   conservation, environmentalism, and environmental policy **X:** 78
   elections **X:** 101, 102
   Nader, Ralph **X:** 206
Greenpeace **X:** 77
Greensboro, North Carolina **IX:** 5, 272–273, 332*c*
"green spaces" **X:** 250
Greenspan, Alan **X:** 95, 96, 331*c*
"Green Spring" faction **II:** 32, 172, 173
Greenville, Treaty of **III: 156–157,** 396*c*
   Blue Jacket **III:** 41
   Fallen Timbers, Battle of **III:** 124
   Lewis, Meriwether **III:** 208
   Tecumseh **III:** 345
   Wayne, Anthony **III:** 370
Greenville *Mountaineer* **V:** 401
Green v. New Kent County (1968) **X:** 41
Greenwich Village **VII: 114–115**
   Haywood, "Big Bill" **VII:** 120
   literature **VII:** 160
   Masses, The **VII:** 173
   modernism **VII:** 188
Greenwood, Isaac **II:** 330
Greer, USS **VIII:** 124
Gregg, David M. **V:** 150
Gregg v. Georgia (1976) **X:** 41, 56
Gregory VII, Pope **I:** 165
Gregory X, Pope **I:** 286
Gregory XIII, Pope **I:** 165
Grenada **II:** 43
   invasion of **X: 135,** 326*c*
   cold war (end of) **X:** 71
   defense policy **X:** 87
   foreign policy **X:** 124
   Latin America **X:** 173

North, Oliver L. **X:** 222
Reagan, Ronald W. **X:** 260
Grenville, George **III: 157–158**
   liberty tree/pole **III:** 214
   Stamp Act **III:** 331, 332
   Sugar Act **III:** 336
   Whately, Thomas **III:** 373
Grenville, Sir Richard **I:** 197, 313–314, 372; **II: 150–151,** 264, **401**
Grenville, William **III:** 182, 183, 396*c*
Grenville Acts **III:** 157
Gresham, Newt **IX:** 8
Gresham, Walter Q. **VI:** 124
Grey, Jane **I:** 224
GRH. *See* Gramm-Rudman-Hollings Act of 1985
Gridley, Richard **III:** 50
Grierson, Benjamin H. **V:** 382
Griffen, Michael **X:** 249
griffes **II:** 229, 237
Griffith, David Wark **VII: 115–116,** 358*c*
   Birth of a Nation **VII:** 30–31
   entertainment **VII:** 85
   Ku Klux Klan **VII:** 147
   movie industry **VII:** 190–191
Griffiths, Martha **X:** 105
Griggs et al. v. Duke Power Company (1971) **X: 135–136**
   affirmative action **X:** 8
   Brennan, William J. **X:** 41
   Burger, Warren E. **X:** 44
   race and racial conflict **X:** 256
Grijalva, Juan de **I:** 6, 96–97, **145–146,** 364
Grimes, James W. **V:** 228
Grimké, Angelina and Sarah **IV:** 14, **164–165,** 368, 395–398; **V:** 331
   AASS **IV:** 362
   abolition movement **IV:** 3
   Bloomer, Amelia **IV:** 54
   female antislavery societies **IV:** 135
   Foster, Abigail Kelley **IV:** 148
   Mott, Lucretia **IV:** 246
   Seneca Falls **IV:** 313
   spiritualism **IV:** 325
Grimké, Charlotte Forten **V: 160**
Grisham, John **X:** 178
Grissom, Virgil **IX:** 219
gristmills **II:** 225, 369; **IV:** 184
Griswold, Roger **III:** 222
Griswold v. Connecticut (1965)
   birth control **X:** 37
   Bork, Robert **X:** 39

Brennan, William J. **X:** 41
Roe v. Wade **X:** 268
sexual revolution **X:** 277
White, Byron R. **X:** 319
grocery store chains **VIII:** 47
Grofé, Ferde **VII:** 108
Groseilliers, sieur des. *See* Chouart, Médard, sieur des Groseilliers
Gross, Samuel **IV:** 230
Gross Clinic, The (Eakins) **VI:** 86–87
gross domestic product **IV:** 117
gross national product (GNP) **VII:** 74; **IX:** 44, 88, 88, 88–89, 272; **X:** 187–188
   economy **VIII:** 91*t,* 92
   Great Depression **VIII:** 140–141
   Keynesianism **VIII:** 177
   mobilization **VIII:** 215
   rationing **VIII:** 292
   recession of 1937–38 **VIII:** 292–293
   taxation **VIII:** 350
   World War II home front **VIII:** 394
Grotius, Hugo **I:** 114, 152
Group of Seventy-Seven **X:** 307
Group of the Cross **I:** 275
Grove City College et al. v. Bell, Secretary of Education, et al. **X: 136**
Groves, Leslie Richard **VIII:** 29, 200, 201; **IX:** 237
Grow, Galusha **V:** 170
Growing Up Absurd (Goodman) **X:** 109
Growing Up in New Guinea (Mead) **VII:** 162, 177
growth centers (urban) **IX:** 16
GRU **VIII:** 164
grunge music **X:** 202, 240
Gua, Pierre du **II:** 2, 126
Guadalajara **I:** 258; **II: 151,** 355
Guadalajara, Diego de **II:** 55
Guadalcanal **VIII: 141,** 409*c,* 410*c*
   Halsey, "Bull" **VIII:** 143
   Marines, U.S. **VIII:** 203
   Solomon Islands **VIII:** 330, 331
   World War II Pacific theater **VIII:** 398
Guadalupe **II:** 94
Guadalupe Hidalgo, Treaty of (1848) **I:** 49; **IV: 165–166,** 378*c,* 404–405
   Bent's Fort **IV:** 51
   California **IV:** 65
   Compromise of 1850 **IV:** 93

Deseret, State of **IV:** 109
   exploration **IV:** 132
   foreign policy **IV:** 142
   Forty-niners **IV:** 147
   immigration **IV:** 177
   Lamy, Jean Baptiste **IV:** 207
   Manifest Destiny **IV:** 218
   Mexican-American War **IV:** 234
   Polk, James K. **IV:** 284
   Santa Anna, Antonio López de **IV:** 304
   Santa Fe Trail **IV:** 306
   Texas **IV:** 339
Guadalupe-Tonantzin **II:** 357
Guadeloupe **II:** 52, 74, 356, 378
Guale **I:** 130, 131; **II:** 120, 246
Guam **VIII:** 202
Guanahani **I:** 81
Guanahatabey **I:** 98; **II:** 52
Guanajuato **II:** 355
Guanches **I:** 214
guarantees **IV:** 225
Guaranty Building (Buffalo, New York) **VI:** 280
guardian spirits **II:** 60
Guard of Honor (Cozzens) **VIII:** 192
Guatemala **II:** 355; **IX:** 50, 60, 172, 331*c;* **X:** 149
   Alvarado, Pedro de **I:** 7, 8
   Díaz de Castillo, Bernal **I:** 106
   Las Casas, Bartolomé de **I:** 199
   Maya **I:** 225–229
   New Spain **I:** 258
   Toltecs **I:** 356
Guatemala City **I:** 258
Guaycura **I:** 48
Guerrero, Gonzalo **I:** 5, 87, **146**
Guerrero, Vincente **IV:** 136
Guerrière, HMS **III:** 81; **IV:** 356
Guerrière, USS **IV:** 328
guerrilla warfare **IV:** 259, 312; **V:** 46, 241, 242, 285–286; **VIII:** 257
Guffey-Snyder Bituminous Coal Act **VIII:** 186, 345
Guggenheim, Simon **VII:** 69
Guggenheim family **VI:** 194
Guggenheim Fund **VII:** 159
Guiana **I:** 12, 118, 119, 303, 304, 388*c;* **II:** 98, 374
guides **IV:** 268
Guide to Holiness (Palmer) **IV:** 296
guilds **I:** 15, 20, 28

Guilford Courthouse, Battle of
III: 158, 158*m*, 394*c*
  Cornwallis, Lord **III:** 93
  Eutaw Springs, Battle of
    III: 120
  Greene, Nathanael **III:**
    156
  Revolutionary War **III:** 305
  Tarleton, Banastre **III:** 343
Guinea **I:** 135, 137, 146; **II:** 348;
  IX: 3
Guinea-Bissau **I: 146–147,** 195,
  327
Guinea islands **I:** 129
Guinn, Joe **IX:** 66
Guinn v. United States **VI:** 119
Guistiniani, Tommaso (Paolo) **I:**
  96
Gulf of Mexico **II:** 115, 178,
  192, 258; **V:** 234, 252
Gulick, Luther **VI:** 275
Gullah **II: 151–152**
gults **I:** 124
Gumo, David **X:** 249
gun control **X: 136–138,** *137,*
  328*c,* 329*c*
  Libertarian Party **X:** 176
  militia movement **X:** 193
  NRA **X:** 212, 213
  Oklahoma City bombing
    X: 228
Gun Control Act of 1968 **X:**
  136, 297
Gun Free School Zones Act of
  1990 **X:** 137
Gunning, Sarah Ogan **IX:** 110,
  111
gunpowder **IV:** 184
Gunpowder Plot **I:** 188
gun rights advocates **X:** 137
guns. *See* firearms
"Gun That Won the West" **IV:**
  92
Gustavus Vasa **II:** 373
Gutenberg, Johann Gensfleisch
  zum **I:** 147, 179, 231, 293
Guthrie, Woody **VIII:** 222, 222,
  224, 410*c;* **IX:** 84, 110, 217
Gutiérrez, José Angel **IX:** 171;
  X: 142
Guy Fawkes Day **III:** 225, 282
Guyot, Arnold Henry **IV:** 290
Guyot, Lawrence **IX:** 207
Guzmán, Nuño de **II:** 151
Gwinn, Mary **VI:** 288

H

habeas corpus, writ of **V:**
  161–162, 407*c*
  Baltimore, Maryland, riots
    V: 22

Confederate States of
  America **V:** 77
Copperheads **V:** 82
Davis, Jefferson **V:** 90
Democratic Party **V:** 94
elections **V:** 109
Enforcement Acts **V:** 117
Ku Klux Klan **V:** 200
Ku Klux Klan Act **V:** 201
Lincoln, Abraham **V:** 210
peace movements **V:** 266
Stanton, Edwin M. **V:**
  334
Habeas Corpus Act of 1863 **V:**
  162, 407*c*
Haber, Al **IX:** 285
Habersham, James **II:** 138
Habib, Philip, C. **X: 139**
habitants **I: 149**
Habitat **IX:** 19
Habitat for Humanity **X:** 59
Habsburg monarchy **I:** 63, 67,
  160; **II:** 355–356
haciendas **I:** 98, 122, **149–150,**
  381; **II:** 52, 355
Hadden, Briton **VIII:** 196
Hadia **II:** 266
hadith **I:** 184
Hadrian **I:** 282
Hadrian IV, Pope **I:** 10
Haeckel, Ernst **X:** 76
Haener, Dorothy **IX:** 223
Hague, Frank **VIII:** 165
Hague, USS **III:** 90
Hague Convention of 1899
  VIII: 281, 282
Hague peace conference (1899)
  VII: 156
Hague peace conference (1907)
  VII: 156
Hague Peace Palace **VI:** 45
Hahn, Jessica **X:** 294
Haida **I: 150**
Haig, Alexander M., Jr. **X:**
  139–140, 141
Hail, Samuel **III:** 160
Hair (musical) **X:** 277
Haiti **I:** 162; **II:** 74, 229; **III:**
  159, 397*c;* **V:** 100; **VI:** 4, 32,
  172; **VII:** 50, 99, 337, 358*c,*
  359*c;* **VIII:** 133; **X:** 328*c*
  abolition movement **IV:** 3
  Bonaparte, Napoleon **III:**
    42
  Clinton, William **X:** 67
  defense policy **X:** 88
  foreign affairs **III:** 130
  Free-Soil Party **IV:** 151
  Hall, Prince **III:** 160
  immigration **X:** 149
  Louisiana Purchase **III:**
    218

Negro Convention
  movement **IV:** 261
Quasi War **III:** 292
U.S. intervention in
  1993–94 **X: 140**
West Indies **III:** 372
Wright, Fanny **IV:** 369
hajj (pilgrimage) **I:** 184, 230
Hakim, Albert **X:** 315
Hakluyt, Richard, the Elder **I:**
  35, 141–142, **150–151,** 266
Hakluyt, Richard, the Younger
  I: 151–153, 388*c*
  Bermuda **I:** 29
  black legend **I:** 30
  Bristol **I:** 35
  DeBry, Theodor **I:** 102
  "Discourse Concerning
    Western Planting, A"
    (1584) **I:** 413–415
  Eden, Richard **I:** 117, 118
  Elizabeth I **I:** 121
  Hakluyt, Richard, the
    Elder **I:** 151
  Harriot, Thomas **I:** 154
  Hawkins, Sir John **I:** 156
  Ingram, David **I:** 177, 178
  invention and technology
    I: 179
  Lane, Ralph **I:** 197
  Mandeville, Sir John **I:** 219
  Mecca **I:** 230
  New World **I:** 262
  Norumbega **I:** 266
  Oviedo y Valdés, Gonzalo
    Fernández de **I:** 273
  Parmenius, Stephen **I:** 278
  printing press **I:** 294
  Purchas, Samuel **I:** 297
  Ramusio, Giovanni Battista
    I: 305
  Spice Islands **I:** 335
  sugar **I:** 338–339
  Walsingham, Sir Frances **I:**
    372
*Hakluytus Posthumus or
  Purchas his Pilgrimes* **I:**
  297–298
Halberstam, David **IX:** 154
Haldeman, H. R.
  Ford, Gerald R. **X:** 120
  Haig, Alexander M., Jr. **X:**
    139
  Mitchell, John N. **X:** 196
  United States v. Nixon **X:**
    308
  Watergate scandal **X:** 316,
    317
Hale, George Ellery **VI:** 258;
  VII: 275–276
Hale, John P. **IV:** 151, 211
Hale, Nathan **III: 159–160**

Hale, Sarah Josepha **IV:** *167,*
  167–168, 197, 213
Hale Telescope **IX:** 278
Haley, Alex **IX:** 7, 334*c;* **X:** 325*c*
half-breed **II:** 223
Half Breeds (Republican Party)
  V: 302; **VI:** 232, 246
"half-free" blacks **II:** 257
"half-freedom" **II:** 257, 260, 262
Half-Way Covenant **II:** 217,
  218, 302, 305, 350, 418*c*
Halifax, North Carolina **VIII:** 62
Hall, A. Oakey **VI:** 298
Hall, Asaph **VI:** 258
Hall, Bob **IX:** 120
Hall, James D. S. **VI:** 4
Hall, Prince **III:** 6, 17, 159,
  160–161
Halleck, Charles **X:** 120
Halleck, Fitz-Greene **IV:** 212
Halleck, Henry Wager **V:**
  162–163
  McClellan, George B. **V:**
    225
  Murfreesboro/Stones
    River, Battle of **V:** 242
  Shenandoah Valley:
    Sheridan's campaign **V:**
    317
  Sheridan, Philip H. **V:** 318
  Sherman, William T. **V:**
    320
  Shiloh, Battle of **V:** 324
  tactics and strategy **V:** 347
Hallidie, Andrew S. **VI:** 292
Hallinan, Vincent **IX:** 249
Hallowell, Norwood **V:** 125
hallucinogens **IX:** 183–184,
  333*c*
Halona, Juan de **I:** 383
Halsey, William F., Jr. **VIII: 143**
  Guadalcanal **VIII:** 141
  King, Ernest J. **VIII:** 177
  Leyte Gulf, Battle for
    VIII: 186–187
  Nimitz, Chester W. **VIII:**
    246
  Solomon Islands **VIII:** 331
  World War II Pacific
    theater **VIII:** 398
Halsted, William S. **VI:** 192
Hamburg American Steamship
  Company **VI:** 257
Hamer, Fannie Lou **IX:**
  129–130, 207
Hamilton, Alexander **II:** 179,
  275–276, 292, 377; **III:** *161,*
  161–162, 394*c,* 395*c,* 397*c;*
  IV: 18, 106, 363; **V:** 311, 348,
  372
  Adams, John **III:** 3
  Ames, Fisher **III:** 13

Annapolis Convention **III:** 14

Bache, Benjamin Franklin **III:** 29

Bank of the United States (First) **III:** 30, 31

banks **III:** 32

Burr, Aaron **III:** 53, 54

Constitutional Convention **III:** 81, 82

Coxe, Tench **III:** 96

Democratic-Republican Party **III:** 104

Democratic-Republican societies **III:** 105

Earle, Ralph **III:** 111

economy **III:** 113

election of 1800 **III:** 116, 117

Federalist Papers **III:** 124, 125

Federalist Party **III:** 126

Federalists **III:** 127

Gallatin, Albert **III:** 147

Genet, Edmond **III:** 150

Husband, Herman **III:** 170

Jefferson, Thomas **III:** 184

journalism **III:** 191

King, Rufus **III:** 195

L'Enfant, Pierre-Charles **III:** 207

Livingston, Robert R. **III:** 216

Madison, James **III:** 228, 229

McDougall, Alexander **III:** 239

national debt **III:** 253

Neutrality Proclamation **III:** 256

Panic of 1792 **III:** 272

Pickering, John **III:** 276

political parties **III:** 279

states' rights **III:** 333

Supreme Court **III:** 338

tariffs **III:** 342

Taylor, John, of Caroline **III:** 344

Washington, District of Columbia **III:** 364

Washington, George **III:** 367

Whiskey Rebellion **III:** 375

Yorktown, surrender at **III:** 390

Hamilton, Andrew **II:** 17, 23, 85, **153**, 415

Hamilton, Henry **III:** 71

Hamilton, James, Jr. **IV:** 264

Hamilton, William **III:** 17

Hamlet (Shakespeare) **V:** 352

Hamlin, Hannibal **IV:** 301; **V:** *302*

Hammerschmidt, John Paul **X:** 65

Hammer v. Dagenhart **VII:** 1, 46, 145, 359*c*

Hammon, Jupiter **II:** 7, **153–154**

Hammond, James Henry **V:** 384

Hammond, John **II:** 163

Hammond, William A. **V:** 230, 256

Hammond (meatpacking company) **VI:** 191

Hampton, Fred **IX:** 39

Hampton, Wade **V:** 276, 297

Hampton Court Conference (1604) **I:** 188

Hampton Institute **VI:** 94

Hampton Roads, Battle of **V:** 406*c*

  ironclads **V:** 184

  marine corps **V:** 222

  Monitor-Merrimack. *See Monitor-Merrimack*

  science and technology **V:** 309

  Union navy **V:** 370

Hanbury, John **III:** 265

Hance, Kent **X:** 47

Hancock, Cornelia **V:** 256

Hancock, John **II:** 215, 334, 348; **III:** **162–164,** *163,* 392*c*

  Adams, Samuel **III:** 5

  Boston Tea Party **III:** 45

  Continental Congress, Second **III:** 88

  Declaration of Independence **III:** 103

  Lexington and Concord, Battles of **III:** 212

  Revere, Paul **III:** 304

  Townshend Duties **III:** 349

Hancock, John M. **VIII:** 295

Hancock, Winfield Scott **V:** **163–164; VI:** 231, 232, 325*c*

  Armistead, Lewis A. **V:** 15

  Gettysburg, Battle of **V:** 148, 150

  Howard, O. O. **V:** 173

  Meade, George Gordon **V:** 227

  Sickles, Daniel E. **V:** 327

  Spotsylvania, Battles of **V:** 333

  Wilderness, Battle of the **V:** 395

Hand, Learned **IX:** 80; **X:** 268

handcarts **IV:** 243

Handel and Haydn Society **VI:** 23

Handgun Control, Inc. **X:** 136–137

handguns **X:** 82, 113, 136–138

handicapped. *See* disabilities, people with

Handsome Lake **II:** 319–320; **III:** 91, **164**

Handy, James A. **VI:** 4

Handy, W. C. **VII:** 194

Hanna, Marcus Alonzo (Hanna, Mark Alonzo) **VI:** **121,** 189

  Anthracite Coal Strike **VII:** 13

  Democratic Party **VII:** 65

  elections **VII:** 80

  Mitchell, John **VII:** 186

  National Civic Federation **VII:** 201

  Republican Party **VII:** 262

Hanno the elephant **I:** 40, **153–154,** 203

Hanoverian monarchs **II:** 232

Hanover Presbytery **II:** 84

Hansberry, Lorraine **IX:** 5, 181, 243, 332*c*

Hansen, Alvin **VIII:** 176

Hanson, Ole **VII:** 279

Hanson, Roger W. **V:** 258

Hardee, William J.

  Bentonville, Battle of **V:** 28

  Cleburne, Patrick Ronayne **V:** 67

  Confederate army **V:** 73

  Sherman's March through Georgia **V:** 323

  tactics and strategy **V:** 345

  uniforms **V:** 363

Hardin, John **III:** 72

Harding, Warren Gamaliel **VII:** xiv, *117,* **117–119,** 360*c*

  AFL **VII:** 11

  Budget and Accounting Act **VII:** 36

  conservatism **VIII:** 71

  Coolidge, Calvin **VII:** 56, 57

  Dawes, Charles **VII:** 63

  Democratic Party **VII:** 66

  elections **VII:** 81

  Fordney-McCumber Tariff **VII:** 97

  foreign policy **VII:** 100

  Hoover, Herbert **VIII:** 151

  Hoover presidency **VIII:** 153

  Hughes, Charles Evans **VII:** 124

  Mellon, Andrew **VII:** 180

  public health **VII:** 243

  Republican Party **VII:** 263

  Sheppard-Towner Act **VII:** 283

  socialism **VII:** 289

  Soldiers' Bonus **VII:** 291

  Taft, William Howard **VII:** 304

  tariffs **VII:** 306

  Teapot Dome **VII:** 307

  United States Shipping Board **VII:** 314

  Veterans Bureau **VII:** 326

  Washington Conference on Naval Disarmament **VII:** 331

  Wheeler, Burton K. **VIII:** 377

Hardinge, Samuel Wylde **V:** 35

"hard money" **IV:** 49; **VI:** 120

Hardtack and Coffee (Billings) **V:** 213

hardware **IV:** 186*m*

Hardy Boys books **IX:** 183

Hare, Robert **III:** 321

Hargis, Billy James **IX:** 256; **X:** 79

Hargous, P. A. **IV:** 159

Hargreave, James **III:** 177

Harkin, Tom **X:** 21

Harkness, S. V. **VII:** 296

Harlan, John Marshall **VI:** 56, **121–122,** 224–225, 281, 327*c;* **IX:** 31, 104, 315

Harlan, Marshall **X:** 264

Harlan brothers **VI:** 27

Harlem (New York) **VIII:** 288, 404; **IX:** 4–7, 32

Harlem Heights, Battle of **IV:** 239

Harlem Railroad **IV:** 352

Harlem Renaissance **VII:** **119–120,** 360*c;* **VIII:** 3, 23

  art **VII:** 19–20

  Great Migration **VII:** 113

  jazz **VII:** 137

  literature **VII:** 162

  Locke, Alain **VII:** 164

  modernism **VII:** 188

  music **VII:** 194

Harlem riot **X:** 255

Harlem Shadows (McKay) **VII:** 360*c*

Harlow, Jean **VIII:** 218

Harmar, Josiah

  Blue Jacket **III:** 41

  Fallen Timbers, Battle of **III:** 123

  Greenville, Treaty of **III:** 157

  Wayne, Anthony **III:** 369

Harmony Society **IV:** 299

Harnack, Adolf von **VI:** 266

Harnett, William Michael **VI:** 138

Harold the Fairheaded, king of Norway **I:** 174

Harper, Frances Ellen Watkins **V: 164**

Harper, William R. **VI:** 49

HarperCollins (Harper and Row) **X:** 178

Harper's Bazaar **V:** 122

Harpers Ferry, West Virginia **V: 164–166,** *165,* 185

Harpers Ferry (battle)
  Antietam, Battle of **V:** 11
  Harpers Ferry, West Virginia **V:** 165
  Jackson, "Stonewall" **V:** 186
  McClellan, George B. **V:** 225
  Shenandoah Valley: Jackson's campaign **V:** 316

Harpers Ferry (John Brown's raid) **IV:** 40, 301, 342; **V:** 405*c*
  abolition **V:** 4
  Booth, John Wilkes **V:** 32
  Brown, John **V:** 37, 38
  Civil War **V:** 64
  Douglass, Frederick **V:** 100
  Harpers Ferry, West Virginia **V:** 165
  Higginson, Thomas Wentworth **V:** 167
  Lee, Robert E. **V:** 205
  slavery **V:** 329
  Stuart, J. E. B. **V:** 341

Harper's Monthly **VI:** 82, 176, 177

Harper's Weekly **VI:** 326*c*
  Dred Scott decision **V:** 101–102
  Garland, Hamlin **VI:** 109
  illustration **VI:** 138
  illustration, photography, and the graphic arts **VI:** 137
  journalism **V:** 193
  Liberal Republican Party **VI:** 174
  Nast, Thomas **V:** 247
  photography **V:** 273
  Reconstruction Acts **V:** 295
  Schurz, Carl **VI:** 257

Harriet Tubman Home for Indigent Aged Negroes **V:** 358

Harriet Tubman, The Moses of Her People (Bradford) **V:** 358

Harrigan, Edward (Ned) **VI:** 203, 287

Harriman, Edward H. **VI:** 19, 129, 197

Harriman, Job **VI:** 269

Harriman, W. Averell **VIII: 143–144**

Harrington, James **III:** 79

Harrington, Mark **VI:** 310

Harrington, Michael **IX:** 62, 67, 90, **130–131,** 313, 333*c*

Harriot, Thomas **I: 154–155,** *179,* 388*c;* **II:** 167, 195, 264, 330, 401
  Algonquians **I:** 6
  DeBry, Theodor **I:** 102
  Hakluyt, Richard, the Younger **I:** 152
  invention and technology **I:** 179
  Lane, Ralph **I:** 197
  Manteo **I:** 220
  Mantoac **I:** 221
  Native American religion **I:** 253
  Picts **I:** 282
  Roanoke **I:** 313, 314
  Secotan **I:** 320, 321
  tobacco **I:** 353
  White, John **I:** 373

Harris, Benjamin **II: 154,** 299

Harris, Charles K. **VI:** 204; **VII:** 309

Harris, Eric **X:** 330*c*

Harris, Isaac **VII:** 312

Harris, Joel Chandler **VI:** 177

Harris, John P. **VII:** 85–86, 191, 356*c*

Harris, Roy **VIII:** 119

Harris, Townsend **V:** 405*c*

Harrison, Benjamin **V:** 241; **VI: 122–123,** *123,* 326*c,* 327*c;* **VII:** 266, 305; **X:** 102
  Bering Sea dispute **VI:** 26
  Blaine, James Gillespie **VI:** 31, 32
  Chilean-American relations **VI:** 50
  Cleveland, Grover **VI:** 58
  conservation **VI:** 65
  corruption, political **VI:** 66
  Forest Reserve Act of 1891 **VI:** 104
  Geological Survey, U.S. **VI:** 110
  Grand Army of the Republic **VI:** 118
  Harlan, John Marshall **VI:** 122
  Mafia incident **VI:** 185–186
  Pan-American Union **VI:** 220
  Powell, John Wesley **VI:** 228

the presidency **VI:** 230
presidential campaigns **VI:** 231, 232
tariff issue **VI:** 284

Harrison, Birge **VI:** 219

Harrison, George **IX:** 36

Harrison, Joseph **IV:** 78

Harrison, Pat **VIII:** 67

Harrison, Peter **II:** 23, **154–155**

Harrison, Wallace **VIII:** 22

Harrison, William Henry **III:** 289, 345, 347, 348, 398*c;* **IV: 168–170,** *169,* 377*c,* 378*c*
  banking and currency **IV:** 43
  Clay, Henry **IV:** 87
  Democratic Party **IV:** 108
  election of 1840 **IV:** 125–126
  Ghent, Treaty of (1814) **IV:** 161
  Lake Erie, Battle of **IV:** 206
  Liberty Party **IV:** 210
  Mexican-American War **IV:** 232
  migration **IV:** 235
  Native Americans **IV:** 255, 256
  Native Americans in the War of 1812 **IV:** 258, 259
  public land policy **IV:** 286
  Thames, Battle of the **IV:** 342
  Tyler, John **IV:** 348
  Van Buren, Martin **IV:** 351, 352
  War of 1812 **IV:** 356
  Webster, Daniel **IV:** 360
  Webster-Ashburton Treaty (1842) **IV:** 361
  Whig Party **IV:** 363

Harrison Anti-Narcotic Act **VII:** 358*c. See also* Narcotics Act

Harrison law. *See* Land Law of 1800

Harris Treaty of 1858 **V:** 405*c*

Harris v. McRae **X:** 3

Hart, Silas **III:** 170

Hart, Tony **VI:** 203

Harte, Bret **V:** 213

Hartford, Connecticut **II:** 68, 154, 157, 363, 417*c*

Hartford, George Huntington **VI:** 46–47

Hartford, Treaty of (1638) **II:** 243–244, 256, 278, 280

Hartford, USS **V:** 121, 239

Hartford Convention **IV:** 127, 161, **170–171,** 356

Democratic-Republican Party **III:** 104

Otis, Harrison Gray **III:** 268

states' rights **III:** 333

Washington Benevolent Societies **III:** 369

Hartford *Evening Press* **V:** 391

Hartford Times **V:** 391

Harvard, John **III:** 169

Harvard Classics **VII:** 5

Harvard College/University **II: 155; III:** 355; **IV:** 121; **VI:** 324*c;* **IX:** 175
  Adams, Henry **VI:** 1
  African Americans **VI:** 6
  Boston **II:** 35
  Brattle, Thomas **II:** 40
  Burgis, William **II:** 46
  Chauncy, Charles **II:** 57
  Connecticut **II:** 70
  Dudley, Thomas **II:** 96
  education **II:** 103, 104
  Endecott, John **II:** 107
  football **VI:** 101
  Levertt, John **II:** 193–194
  lotteries **II:** 199
  Massachusetts **II:** 212
  Massachusetts School Act **II:** 216
  Mather, Cotton **II:** 217
  Mather, Increase **II:** 218
  medicine **VI:** 191
  printing and publishing **II:** 298
  Protestantism **II:** 302
  Pulitzer, Joseph **VI:** 235
  science **II:** 330; **VI:** 258
  Sewall, Samuel **II:** 334
  Smibert, John **II:** 346
  theater **II:** 373
  track and field **VI:** 290
  Washington, Booker T. **VI:** 309
  Wigglesworth, Edward **II:** 398
  Wigglesworth, Michael **II:** 398
  Willard, Samuel **II:** 399

Harvard University Press **II:** 84

Harvey, Sir John **II:** 172, 293, 417*c*

Harvey, William H. **VI:** 29, 73; **VIII:** 272*t*

Hasaw Chan K'awil **I:** 349, 350

Hasenfus, Eugene **X:** 154

Hasidic Jews **VIII:** 303

Hassam, Childe **VI:** 219; **VII:** 18

Hastert, J. Dennis **X:** 145

Hastie, William H. **VIII:** 37, 407*c*

Hastings, Lansford W. **IV:** 114
"Hastings Cutoff" **IV:** 114
Hat Act of 1732 **II:** 3, 203
Hatch, Orrin **X:** 37
Hatch Act **VI:** 8, 92–93; **VIII:** 60, 408c
hate crimes **X:** 82–83
"hate speech" **X:** 271
Hatfield, Mark **X:** 37
Hathaway, Anne **I:** 324
hats **V:** 363, 403–404
Haudenosaunee **II:** 85
Haugen, Gilbert **VII:** 175
Haupt, Herman **V:** *309*
Hauptmann, Bruno **IX:** 136
Hausa **I: 155–156**
    Askia Muhammad I **I:** 14
    Dagomba **I:** 101
    Fang **I:** 127
    Fulani **I:** 135
    Leo Africanus **I:** 203
    Taureg **I:** 361
Hausaland **I:** 155
Havana, Cuba **I:** 98; **II:** 233, 359
Havasupai **I: 156**
Havel, Václav **X:** 156–157
Havemeyer, Henry O. **VI:** 180, 288
Haverly, J. H. **VI:** 95–96
Hawaiian Americans **X:** 243
Hawaiian Islands (Hawaii) **III: 164; IV:** 171, **171–172; V:** 131, 133; **VI: 123–124,** 297, 298, 327c, 328c; **VII:** 107–108, 281
    abortion **X:** 2
    amendments to the Constitution **X:** 19
    Asian Americans **X:** 28–29
    Blaine, James Gillespie **VI:** 32
    Bridges, Harry **VIII:** 43
    California gold rush **IV:** 66
    Cleveland, Grover **VI:** 59
    Executive Order 9066 **VIII:** 106
    exploration **IV:** 133
    Fillmore, Millard **IV:** 137
    foreign policy **IV:** 143; **VI:** 103
    gay rights movement **X:** 128
    Harrison, Benjamin **VI:** 123
    imperialism **VI:** 141
    Kamehameha I **IV:** 199
    Mahan, Alfred Thayer **VI:** 186
    Manifest Destiny **IV:** 219

marriage **X:** 183
Nimitz, Chester W. **VIII:** 246
population trends **X:** 242
religion **IV:** 296
Twain, Mark **VI:** 297, 298
WAVES **VIII:** 380
Hawikuh **I:** 88, 383
Hawker Hurricane **VIII:** 43
Hawkins, Augustus **VII:** 35
Hawkins, Sir John **I: 156–157**
    Drake, Sir Francis **I:** 112
    Drake, Sir Sir Francis **I:** 110
    Elizabeth I **I:** 121
    Hakluyt, Richard, the Elder **I:** 151
    Hakluyt, Richard, the Younger **I:** 151
    Ingram, David **I:** 177, 178
    Lane, Ralph **I:** 197
    slave trade **I:** 329
    Spanish Armada **I:** 334
    tobacco **I:** 353
    Veracruz **I:** 366
Hawks, Howard **IX:** 212
Hawley, Jesse **IV:** 127–128
Hawley-Smoot Tariff Act **VIII: 144,** 405c
    Anglo-American relations **VIII:** 16
    censorship **VIII:** 54, 55
    Congress **VIII:** 66
    foreign policy **VII:** 101; **VIII:** 123
    Good Neighbor Policy **VIII:** 133
    Great Depression **VIII:** 139
    Hoover presidency **VIII:** 153, 154
    London Economic Conference **VIII:** 193
    Reciprocal Trade Agreements Act **VIII:** 293
    Republican Party **VII:** 263
    tariffs **VII:** 306
    trade, foreign **VII:** 310
Hawthorne, Nathaniel **IV:** 379c; **V:** 213; **X:** 179
    Brook Farm **IV:** 58
    Emerson, Ralph Waldo **IV:** 126
    Hale, Sarah Josepha **IV:** 168
    journalism **IV:** 197
    literature **IV:** 212–213
    Manifest Destiny **IV:** 217
    transcendental movement **IV:** 345

Hay, Harry **IX:** 119
Hay, John Milton **VI: 124–125,** 328c; **VII:** 218–219, 223, 224, 356c
    Adams, Henry **VI:** 1
    imperialism **VI:** 142, 143
    King, Clarence **VI:** 160
    literature **VI:** 177
    Mahan, Alfred Thayer **VI:** 186
    McKinley, William **VI:** 189
    Open Door notes **VI:** 216, 217
Hay-Bunau-Varilla Treaty **VII:** 224, 356c; **X:** 232
Hayden, Carl **X:** 105
Hayden, Casey **IX:** 325
Hayden, Ferdinand Vandeveer **VI:** 110
Hayden, Tom **IX: 131–132,** 230–231, 285, 286; **X:** 61
Haydn, Franz Joseph **III:** 252
Hayek, Friedrich A. von **VIII:** 73, **VIII:** 224–225
Hayes, Max **VI:** 269
Hayes, Rutherford Birchard **VI: 125–127,** *126,* 324c; **X:** 102
    Adams, Henry **VI:** 1
    African Americans **VI:** 5
    Arthur, Chester Alan **VI:** 16
    bimetallism **VI:** 29
    Bland-Allison Act **VI:** 32
    Chinese Exclusion Act **VI:** 50
    civil service reform **VI:** 56
    communications **VI:** 62
    Congress **VI:** 63
    Conkling, Roscoe **VI:** 64
    Democratic Party **V:** 95
    education, philanthropy and **VI:** 94
    elections **V:** 111
    Elliot, Robert B. **V:** 111
    Geological Survey, U.S. **VI:** 110
    Grant, Ulysses S. **V:** 157
    Great Strike of 1877 **VI:** 119, 120
    Harlan, John Marshall **VI:** 122
    King, Clarence **VI:** 160
    lobbies and pressure groups **VI:** 180
    Mosby, John Singleton **V:** 242
    Powell, John Wesley **VI:** 228
    the presidency **VI:** 230
    presidential campaigns **VI:** 231, 232
    Reconstruction **V:** 294

redemption **V:** 297
Republican Party **V:** 303; **VI:** 246
Schurz, Carl **VI:** 256
Scott, Thomas Alexander **VI:** 258
Sherman, John **VI:** 261
Solid South **VI:** 270
star route frauds **VI:** 275
Tilden, Samuel Jones **VI:** 289
Van Lew, Elizabeth **V:** 378
Wade, Benjamin **V:** 385
Whiskey Ring **V:** 393
Haymarket riot **VI: 127–128,** *166,* 325c; **VII:** 110
    Altgeld, John Peter **VI:** 10
    Howells, William Dean **VI:** 136
    labor, radical **VI:** 167
    labor organizations **VI:** 170
    Lloyd, Henry Demarest **VI:** 179
    Powderly, Terence Vincent **VI:** 227
Hayne, Robert Y. **IV:** 264, 360, 363, 376c
Haynes, John **II:** 212
Hay-Pauncefote Treaties (1900, 1901) **VI:** 190; **VII:** 222, 355c
Hays, William **III:** 243
Hay's Big Fight **IV:** 92
Hays Commission **VIII:** 274
Hayward, DuBose **VII:** 109
Haywood, William Dudley **VII: 120,** 357c
    Darrow, Clarence **VII:** 62
    Flynn, Elizabeth Gurley **VII:** 95
    IWW **VII:** 130
    labor movement **VII:** 152
    Lawrence Strike **VII:** 155
    New Unionism **VII:** 212, 213
    Paterson Strike **VII:** 225
Hazard of New Fortunes, A (Howells) **VI:** 136
hazardous waste **X:** 78, 113
Hazen, William B. **VI:** 310
HBC. *See* Hudson's Bay Company
HBO. *See* Home Box Office
H. C. Frick and Company **VI:** 105
Heade, Martin Johnson **V:** 16
headright system **I:** 157; **II:** 11, 112, 210, 382
Head Start **IX:** 127, **132,** 313, 334c; **X:** 10, 278
health. *See* medicine and public health
Health, William **III:** 239

Health and Human Services Department **IX:** 222–223

Health Care Security Act **X:** 328c

Health, Education, and Welfare Department (HEW) **IX:** 87, 331c; **X:** 111, 268

health insurance **VIII:** 209, 361, 373

Health Maintenance Organization Act of 1973 **X:** 164

Hearst, George **IV:** 96

Hearst, William Randolph **VI:** 327c; **VII:** 120–122, 121, 124, 141, 142, 267; **VIII:** 305, 377

  de Lôme letter **VI:** 76

  newspapers **VI:** 212

  Pulitzer, Joseph **VI:** 235

  Remington, Frederic **VI:** 245

  yellow journalism **VI:** 321

Hearst newspaper chain **VII:** 141–143

Heart of Atlanta Motel Inc., v. United States **IX:** 132–133, 271, 334c

heart surgery **VIII:** 207–208

Heath, Sir Robert **II:** 265, 353

Heathcote, Caleb **II:** 86

heavy industry **VIII:** 14, 179

Hebert, F. Edward **X:** 144

Hebrew Immigration Aid Society **VI:** 172

Hebrew Union College and Seminary **VII:** 261

Hecker, Friedrich **V:** 147

Hecker, Isaac **IV:** 58; **VI:** 243, 249, 250

Heckewelder equation **II:** 88

Heidelberg Catechism **II:** 140

Heisman Trophy **VIII:** 336

helicopters **IX:** 28, 294

Heller, Joseph **IX:** 181; **X:** 177

"Hell on the Rappahannock" **V:** 244

Hell's Angels **IX:** 244

Helluland **I:** 369

Helm, Leonard **III:** 71

Helms, Jesse A., Jr. **IX:** 200; **X:** 140–141

  abortion **X:** 3

  birth control **X:** 37

  Reagan, Ronald W. **X:** 259

Helsinki Accords (1975) **X:** 86, 89, 121

Helvering, et. al v. Davis **VIII:** 329–330

Hemingway, Ernest **VII:** 161, 162, 166, 361c; **VIII:** 192, 335; **IX:** 181

Hemmings, Madison **III:** 165

Hemmings, Sally **III:** 164–165, 184, 185

hemp **II:** 253; **IV:** 9

Hempel, Amy **X:** 178

Henderson, Fletcher **VII:** 137, 195; **VIII:** 132

Henderson, Leon **VIII:** 144–145

  antimonopoly **VIII:** 18

  Keynesianism **VIII:** 176

  OPA **VIII:** 254–255

  recession of 1937–38 **VIII:** 293

  TNEC **VIII:** 355

  wage and price controls **VIII:** 371

Hendrick **II:** 14, 155–156

Hendrick, Burton J. **IV:** 352

Hendricks, Thomas **VI:** 232

Hendricksen, Cornelis **II:** 274

Hendrix, Jimi **IX:** 111, 218, 244, 264; **X:** 240

Hennessy, David C. **VI:** 185

Henri, Robert **VII:** 18, 20

Henrico College **II:** 103

Henrietta Maria, queen of England **II:** 209

Henry, Aaron **IX:** 207, 284

Henry, Alice **VII:** 206, 252

Henry, Andrew

  Ashley, William Henry **IV:** 28, 29

  Bridger, James **IV:** 57

  exploration **IV:** 131

  Rocky Mountain Fur Company **IV:** 302

Henry, Carl F. H. **IX:** 256

Henry, Joseph **IV:** 308; **VI:** 310

Henry, ninth earl of Northumberland **I:** 155

Henry, O. (Porter, William Sydney) **VI:** 185; **VII:** 356c

Henry, Patrick **II:** 54; **III:** 165–166, 391c, 393c

  anti-Federalists **III:** 14

  Clark, George Rogers **III:** 71

  Constitutional Convention **III:** 81

  Continental Congress, Second **III:** 88

  Lee, Richard Henry **III:** 207

  Madison, James **III:** 227, 229

  Virginia Resolves **III:** 361

Henry, William **III:** 11

Henry II, king of England **I:** 10, 361

Henry II, king of Ireland **I:** 10

Henry III, king of England **I:** 142, 158

Henry IV, king of France (Henry of Navarre) **I:** 158–159; **II:** 126

  Castile **I:** 64

  Ferdinand and Isabella **I:** 127

  Holy Roman Empire **I:** 165

  Huguenots **I:** 170

  Philip II **I:** 282

  Spanish Armada **I:** 334

Henry VII, king of England **I:** 159, 386c; **II:** 231

  Cabot, John **I:** 41, 42

  Cabot, Sebastian **I:** 42

  Church of England **I:** 73

  Columbus, Bartholomew **I:** 78

  Henry VIII **I:** 159

  Patent Granted by King Henry VII to John Cabot and His Sons, March 1496 **I:** 394–395

Henry VIII, king of England **I:** 159–160, 160, 387c; **II:** 19, 231, 301, 316

  Bristol **I:** 35

  Cabot, Sebastian **I:** 42

  Elizabeth I **I:** 119

  Henry VII **I:** 159

  London **I:** 208

  Mary I **I:** 223, 224

  Privy Council **I:** 295

  Reformation **I:** 307, 309

Henry of Guise **I:** 158

Henry Street Settlement **VI:** 259; **VII:** 329

Henry the Navigator, prince of Portugal (Infante Henrique) **I:** 157, 157–158, 385c, 386c

  Canary Islands **I:** 53

  Gomes, Diogo **I:** 144

  slavery **I:** 327

  sugar **I:** 338

Henson, Joshiah **V:** 361

Hepburn, John **II:** 1

Hepburn, Katharine **VIII:** 219; **IX:** 135

Hepburn Act (1906) **VII:** 122, 357c

  Elkins Act **VII:** 84

  Mann-Elkins Act **VII:** 170

  politics **VII:** 230

  Roosevelt, Theodore **VII:** 266

  Steffens, Lincoln **VII:** 299

Hepburn Bill (1902) **VII:** 222

Hepburn v. Griswold **VI:** 72

Herald of Freedom and Gospel Witness (newspaper) **VI:** 20

Herbert, Victor August **VI:** 128–129, 286; **VII:** 85, 194

herbicides **VIII:** 9

herding **I:** 25, 63

Here I Stand (Robeson) **VIII:** 310

Here Is Your War (Pyle) **VIII:** 286

Heritage Foundation **X:** 79, 301–302

Heritage USA **X:** 294

Herkimer, Nicholas **III:** 49

hermaphrodites **I:** 239, 240

Hernandez, Aileen **X:** 211

Hernández, Francisco **I:** 46

Herndon, Angelo **VIII:** 287

Herndon, William H. **V:** 166, 209

Herndon's Lincoln: The True Story of a Great Life (Herndon) **V:** 166

Herodotus **I:** 338

heroic medicine **IV:** 229

Heroic Slave, The (Douglass) **IV:** 212

heroin **VII:** 197; **X:** 206–208

Herold, David E. **V:** 17, 18, 33

Hero Twins **I:** 228

Herrán, Tomas **VII:** 223

Herrman, Augustine **II:** 156

Hersey, John **VIII:** 147

Hershey, Lewis **VIII:** 323, 375

Herter Brothers **VI:** 3

Herzegovina **X:** 85

Heschel, Abraham **VIII:** 303

Hesselius, John **II:** 25, 117, 156

Hessians **III:** 166–167, 393c

  Brandywine, Battle of **III:** 48

  Burgoyne, John **III:** 52

  Greene, Nathanael **III:** 155

  Jersey, HMS **III:** 186

  Jews **III:** 188

  L'Enfant, Pierre-Charles **III:** 207

  Monmouth, Battle of **III:** 245

  Pulaski, Casimir **III:** 290

  Saratoga, surrender at **III:** 320

  Trenton and Princeton, Battles of **III:** 352

  White Plains, Battle of **III:** 376

Heston, Charlton **X:** 212

Hetch Hetchy dam **VII:** 55

Heth, Henry **V:** 148

Heth, Joice **VI:** 21

HEW. *See* Department of Health, Education, and Welfare

Hewitt, Abraham **VII:** 265
Hewitt, Abram S. **VI:** 112
Heylyn, Peter **I:** 297
Heyward, Daniel **II:** 373
Hezbollah **X:** 297
Hezeta, Bruno de **IV:** 93
Hiawatha **I: 160–161,** 182, 272, 387c; **II:** 85, 168
Hickock, "Wild Bill" **V:** 265
Hicks, Elias **IV: 172–173**
Hicks, Thomas **V:** 152, 389
Hicksites **IV:** 172, 246, 314
hidalgo **I:** 323; **II:** 359
hidalguía **I:** 62
Hidatsa nation **I: 161; II:** 77, 150; **III:** 210, 315; **IV:** 55, 113, 377c
Hidden Persuaders, The (Vance Packard) **IX:** 69, 239, 332c
hides and skins **VI:** 291
Hieroglyphic Stairs **I:** 86
Hierro Island **I:** 53
Higgins, Andrew Jackson **VIII:** 324
Higgins Boats **VIII:** 15, 324
Higginson, Thomas Wentworth **IV:** 224; **V: 166–167; VI:** 80, 153
Higgs, William **IX:** 207
higher criticism **VI:** 242
higher education. *See* education, higher
Higher Education Act of 1965 **IX:** 91
"higher law" **V:** 314
Highland Park auto plant **VII:** 22, 96
High Performance Computing Act of 1991 **X:** 153
high schools **V:** 108; **VII:** 76–77, 351, 352
high school students, marijuana use by **X:** 208
Highway Beautification Act **IX:** 151
highways **I:** 175, 176m; **VII:** 22. *See also* interstate highway system
Highway Safety Act **IX:** 26
Hijar, José María **IV:** 136
Hijaz **I:** 230
hijrah **I:** 230
Hill, Ambrose P. **V: 167–168**
   Antietam, Battle of **V:** 13
   Cedar Mountain, Battle of **V:** 53
   Early, Jubal A. **V:** 103
   Gettysburg, Battle of **V:** 147–148
   Longstreet, James **V:** 215
   Peninsular campaign **V:** 269

Wilderness, Battle of the **V:** 395
Hill, Anita Faye **X: 141,** 276, 302, 328c
Hill, D. H. **V:** 13, 28, 281
Hill, Faith **X:** 203
Hill, Harry **VI:** 33
Hill, James J. **V:** 40; **VI:** 19, 40, **129,** 197; **VII:** 216
Hill, Joe **VII:** 95, 252
Hill, Junius **VI:** 23
Hill, Lauryn **X:** 203, 241
Hill, Nathaniel **IV:** 90
Hill, T. Arnold **VIII:** 201
hillbilly music **VIII:** 222
Hill-Burton Act **IX:** 198
Hillman, Sidney **VIII: 145–146**
   American Federation of Labor **VIII:** 14
   CIO **VIII:** 69
   Jews **VIII:** 172
   labor **VIII:** 180, 181
   Lewis, John L. **VIII:** 186
   OPM **VIII:** 255
   socialists **VIII:** 327
Hillquit, Morris **VI:** 268, 269; **VII:** 250
Hilton, Edward **II:** 250
Hilton, William **II:** 250
Himes, Frank T. **VII:** 327
Himmelfarb, Gertrude **X:** 79
Hinckley, John W. **X:** 31, 45, 136
Hinduism **X:** 265
Hine, Lewis **VIII:** 268
hip-hop music **X:** 202, 203, 241
hippies **IX:** 72
Hippocrates **II:** 220
Hirabayashi v. United States **VIII:** 178
Hirohito, emperor of Japan **VIII:** 399, 409c; **IX:** 21
Hiroshima (Hersey) **VIII:** 147
Hiroshima and Nagasaki **VIII:** 29, **146–148,** 147, 148, 201, 411c
   air power **VIII:** 12
   atomic bomb **VIII:** 29
   Axis **VIII:** 32
   Grand Alliance **VIII:** 137
   Manhattan Project **VIII:** 200
   Mariana Islands **VIII:** 202
   Potsdam Conference **VIII:** 280
   Truman's Announcement of the Atomic Bombing of Hiroshima **VIII:** 431–433
   V-J Day **VIII:** 369
   World War II **VIII:** 389
   World War II Pacific theater **VIII:** 399

Hispanic Americans **VII:** 248, 281; **X: 141–143,** 142m. *See also* Mexican Americans
   AIDS **X:** 5
   birthrates **X:** 38
   education, higher **X:** 97
   immigration **X:** 148
   multiculturalism **X:** 200, 201
   Native Americans **X:** 215
   population trends **X:** 243
   poverty **X:** 245, 246
   race and racial conflict **X:** 255, 256
Hispaniola **I: 161–162,** 162m; **II:** 52, 356; **IV:** 141
   adelantado **I:** 3–4
   Alvarado, Pedro de **I:** 6
   audiencia **I:** 15
   Balboa, Vasco Núñez de **I:** 24
   cabildo **I:** 39
   cacique **I:** 46
   Casa de Contratación **I:** 59
   Columbian Exchange **I:** 76
   Columbus, Bartholomew **I:** 78–79
   Columbus, Christopher **I:** 81–83
   conquistadores **I:** 84–85
   Cortés, Hernán **I:** 91
   Cuba **I:** 98
   Dominicans **I:** 110
   Ferdinand and Isabella **I:** 128
   gold **I:** 142
   horses **I:** 167
   Las Casas, Bartolomé de **I:** 198
   Pizarro, Francisco **I:** 283
   Ponce de León, Juan **I:** 288
   smallpox **I:** 331
   sugar **I:** 338
   Taino **I:** 342
   Velázquez, Diego de **I:** 364
Hiss, Alger **IX: 133–134,** 134, 330c; **X:** 219
   anticommunism **IX:** 14
   Chambers, Whittaker **IX:** 50–51
   communism **IX:** 61
   House Un-American Activities Committee **IX:** 137
Histoire d'un voyage faict en la terre du Bresil autrement dite Amerique (Geneva, 1578) (Jean de Léry) **I:** 408–413
Historia Animalium (Conrad von Gesner) **I:** 140

Historia General y Natural de las Indias Occidentales (Oviedo y Valdés) **I:** 272–273
Historia Natural y Moral de las Indias (José de Acosta) **I:** 3
historians **V:** 166, 167; **VI:** 1–2
historical novels **VIII:** 193
historicism **VI:** 15
Historic Plains Indian Culture **II:** 149
historic preservation **VII:** 13
historiography **X:** 200
   Camden, William **I:** 51–52
   Chimalpahin, Domingo Francisco de San Antón Muñón **I:** 71
   Copán **I:** 86
   Díaz de Castillo, Bernal **I:** 106
   Durán, Diego **I:** 113
   Ghana **I:** 140–141
   Ibn Khaldûn **I:** 173–174
   Itzcóatl **I:** 185
   Leo Africanus **I:** 203–204
   Nahua **I:** 249
   Oviedo y Valdés, Gonzalo Fernández de **I:** 272–273
   Sahagún, Bernardino de **I:** 315
History of a Cosmopolite (Dow) **IV:** 116
History of Hungary and the Magyars (Godkin) **VI:** 116
History of New York City (Roosevelt) **VII:** 266
History of the Indies (Bartolomé de Las Casas) **I:** 200
History of the New World (Girolamo Benzoni) **I:** 30
History of the Standard Oil Company (Tarbell) **VII:** 356c
   muckrakers **VII:** 192
   oil industry **VII:** 217
   Standard Oil **VII:** 296
   Tarbell, Ida **VII:** 305
History of the United States during the Administrations of Thomas Jefferson and James Madison (Adams) **VI:** 1
History of Woman Suffrage (Gage, Stanton & Anthony) **VI:** 107; **VII:** 31
history textbooks **V:** 370, 379
Hitchcock, Alfred **IX:** 212
Hitchcock, Ethan Allen **VII:** 203
Hitchcok, George **VI:** 219
Hitler, Adolf **VII:** 121, 157; **VIII:** 31, 407c
   anti-Semitism **VIII:** 19
   Communists **VIII:** 65

Hitler, Adolf (continued)
Coughlin, Father Charles
E. **VIII:** 75
foreign policy **VIII:** 124
Grand Alliance **VIII:** 136
Holocaust **VIII:** 149
isolationists **VIII:** 166
Italian campaign **VIII:** 168
Morgenthau, Henry **VIII:**
216
Munich Conference **VIII:**
220
Nazi-Soviet Pact **VIII:** 238
Normandy, invasion of
VIII: 248
North African campaign
VIII: 249
Owens, Jesse **VIII:** 260
Sicily **VIII:** 325
sports **VIII:** 337
World Disarmament
Conference **VIII:** 388
HIV. See human
immunodeficiency virus
H. L. Hunley, CSS **V:** 74, 310
H. L.V. Matheson. **X:** 17
Hmong immigrants **X:** 28
HMOs **VIII:** 209
H.M.S. Pinafore (Gilbert and
Sullivan) **VI:** 271
Hoar, George Frisbie **VI:** 13,
129–130, 180
hoarding **IV:** 43
Hobbamock (Abamacho) **I:** 225
Hobbes, Thomas **III:** 79, 125
Hobkirk's Hill, Battle of **III:** 120
Hobson, J. A. **VIII:** 41
Hochelaga **I:** 58, 59, **163**
Ho Chi Minh
Asia (and foreign policy)
IX: 21
communism **IX:** 60, 61
Southeast Asia Treaty
Organization **IX:** 274
Soviet Union **IX:** 277
Vietnam War **IX:** 308
wars of national liberation
IX: 317
hockey **VII:** 295; **VIII:** 338; **IX:**
280
Hodgson v. Minnesota (1990) **X:**
17
hoe agriculture **II:** 286–287, 339
Hoey, Jane M. **VIII:** 383
Hoff, Marcian E. **X:** 72, 273
Hoffa, Jimmy **IX:** 12, 292,
292–293, 303, 334c; **X:** 169
Hoffman, Abbie **IX:** 72; **X:** 61
Hoffman, Dustin **IX:** 214
Hoffman, Julius **X:** 61
Hoffman, William **V:** 282
Hoffmann, Albert **IX:** 183

Hogan, James **VI:** 102
Hoge, Jane C. **V:** 204
Hogg, Robert **II:** 247
hogs **I:** 77, 214; **II:** 12, 21, 27,
122, 175, 370
Hohokam **I: 163–164**
Hoke, Robert F. **V:** 28
Holbrook, Josiah **IV:** 215
Holbrooke, Richard **X:** 308
HOLC. See Home Owners
Loan Corporation
Holden, William W. **V:** 199
Holden v. Hardy **VII:** 164
holding companies **VI:** 294, 295
Holiday, Billie **VIII: 148–149,**
223, 406c
holidays **III:** 282; **VII:** 258. See
also feasts and festivals
Holiness movement **VII:** 261
Holladay Overland Stage
Company **IV:** 272
Holland. See Netherlands
Holland Land Company **III:**
167
Holley, Alexander **VI:** 27
Hollings, Ernest **X:** 134–135
Hollis, Thomas **II:** 194
Holly, Buddy **IX:** 263
Hollywood Cemetery **V:** 304
Hollywood film industry **X:** 132,
197–199
Hollywood Production Code **X:**
198
Hollywood Rehabilitation
Committee **IX:** 135
Hollywood Ten **IX:** 61,
134–136, 137, 211–212, 329c
Holmes, John **IV:** 86
Holmes, John Clellon **IX:** 35
Holmes, Oliver Wendell **V:**
70–71; **VII: 122–123,** 355c;
VIII: 313, 346t; **IX:** 133
Brandeis, Louis **VII:** 35
Communist Party **VII:** 52
Lochner v. New York **VII:**
164
Schenk v. United States
VII: 275
Holmes, Oliver Wendell, Sr. **IV:**
113, 215, 308
Holmes, William **II:** 68
Holocaust **VIII:** *149,* **149–150**
anti-Semitism **VIII:** 19
Axis **VIII:** 31
immigration **VIII:** 162
Jews **VIII:** 173
liberalism **VIII:** 189
Morgenthau, Henry **VIII:**
216
refugees **VIII:** 298
World War II **VIII:** 389
Zionism **VIII:** 403

Holt, Joseph **V:** 282
Holy Alliance **IV:** 241
Holy Club **II:** 393, 397
Holy League **I:** 160, **164–165,**
282
Holy Roman Empire **I:** 67, 68,
165–166, 374
homage (feudalism) **I:** 129
home appliances **X:** 273
Home Box Office (HBO) **X:**
241, 296
home economics **VI:** 247
homefront **V: 168–170.** See also
World War II home front
conscription **V:** 79
Davis, Jefferson **V:** 90
economy **V:** 106, 107
employment **V:** 116
habeas corpus, writ of **V:**
162
homespun **V:** 170
impressment **V:** 179–180
ironclad oath **V:** 182–183
journalism **V:** 193
ladies aid societies **V:**
203–204
letters **V:** 208
medicine and hospitals **V:**
230
New York City draft riots
V: 254–255
Pember, Phoebe Yates
Levy **V:** 266–267
race and racial conflict **V:**
287–288
refugees **V:** 299
science and technology **V:**
310
Stanton, Edwin M. **V:**
334
taxation **V:** 349
telegraph **V:** 351
USSC **V:** 373–375
volunteer army **V:** 384
women's status and rights
V: 398
Home Insurance Building **VI:**
149
homeland defense **X:** 23
home offices, OSHA regulations
for **X:** 225
Home Owners Loan
Corporation (HOLC) **VIII:**
150–151
FHA **VIII:** 118–119
housing **VIII:** 157
marriage and family life
VIII: 204
New Deal **VIII:** 241
RFC **VIII:** 295
suburbs **VIII:** 342
USHA **VIII:** 367

Home Owners Refinancing Act
of 1933 **VIII:** 157
Homer, Winslow **V:** 16, 193; **VI:**
130–131, *131,* 185
homespun **V: 170,** 363
Homestead Act of 1862 **IV:** 288;
V: 170–171, *171,* 406c,
421–422
agriculture **V:** 7; **VI:** 8
barbed wire **VI:** 20
homesteading **VI:** 131–132
Lincoln, Abraham **V:** 211
Panic of 1857 **V:** 264
Republican Party **V:** 301
Singleton, Benjamin **V:**
327
Sooners **VI:** 270
homesteading **V:** 142–143; **VI:**
131–132, 270–271
Homestead Law **IV:** 287–288
Homestead Strike **VI: 132,**
327c; **VII:** 110, 297
American Federation of
Labor **VI:** 11
Carnegie, Andrew **VI:** 44
Frick, Henry Clay **VI:** 106
labor, radical **VI:** 167
labor: strikes and violence
VI: 167
labor trends **VI:** 171
"Home, Sweet Home" **V:** 244
homicide **II:** 51, 58, 295, 364,
409; **X:** 10, 56, 82
homophile movement **IX:**
119–120
homosexuality **V:** 394; **VII:** 283;
VIII: 377; **IX:** 32–33, 162.
See also gays and lesbians
Honduras **IV:** 219; **V:** 405c; **X:**
149
Copán **I:** 86
Cortés, Hernán **I:** 94–95
Guerrero, Gonzalo **I:** 146
Maya **I:** 225–229
New Spain **I:** 258
Sandoval, Gonzalo de **I:**
318
Velázquez, Diego de **I:** 364
Honecker, Erich **X:** 157
Hong Kong **V:** 242; **VIII:** 398;
X: 69, 171
honors, military **V:** 227–228
Hood, James **VI:** 4
Hood, John Bell **V: 171–172**
Antietam, Battle of **V:** 13
Atlanta campaign **V:** 19, 20
Confederate army **V:** 73
Forrest, Nathan Bedford
V: 134
Johnston, Joseph E. **V:** 190
Longstreet, James **V:** 215
Oates, William C. **V:** 257

Sherman's March through Georgia **V:** 322
Thomas, George H. **V:** 354
Hood, Raymond **VIII:** 22
Hood, Samuel **III:** 154
Hooftman, Aegidiuss **I:** 232
Hooker, Isabella Beecher **IV:** 325; **VI: 132–133,** 318, 319
Hooker, John **VI:** 132, 133
Hooker, Joseph **V: 172–173,** 407*c*
  Antietam, Battle of **V:** 13
  Balloon Corps **V:** 21
  Burnside, Ambrose E. **V:** 45
  Chancellorsville, Battle of **V:** 54, 55
  Chattanooga, Battle of **V:** 57
  Early, Jubal A. **V:** 103
  Gettysburg, Battle of **V:** 147, 148
  Joint Committee on the Conduct of War **V:** 191
  Lee, Robert E. **V:** 206
  Lookout Mountain, Battle of **V:** 216
  Meade, George Gordon **V:** 226, 227
  prostitution **V:** 284
Hooker, Thomas **II:** 68, 73, 106, **156–157,** 212, 417*c*
Hooks, Benjamin **X:** 208
hoop skirts **V:** 122
Hoosac Tunnel **VI: 133**
Hoover, Herbert Clark **VII:** xiv, 361*c;* **VIII: 151–153,** *152,* 405*c,* 406*c. See also* Hoover presidency
  African Americans **VIII:** 2, 3
  Agricultural Adjustment Act **VIII:** 6–7
  Agricultural Marketing Act **VII:** 5
  agriculture **VIII:** 7
  American Federation of Labor **VIII:** 14
  Anglo-American relations **VIII:** 16
  antimonopoly **VIII:** 17
  Bonus Army **VIII:** 39, 40
  Borah, William E. **VIII:** 40
  Clark Memorandum **VII:** 50
  Communists **VIII:** 65
  Congress **VIII:** 66
  conservatism **VIII:** 71
  Coolidge, Calvin **VII:** 57
  Coughlin, Father Charles E. **VIII:** 75

criminal justice **VII:** 60
  Democratic Party **VIII:** 80–81
  election of 1932 **VIII:** 96
  elections **VII:** 81
  environmental issues **VIII:** 103
  FCA **VIII:** 111
  FCC **VIII:** 116
  foreign policy **VII:** 101; **VIII:** 123
  Garner, John Nance **VIII:** 129
  Good Neighbor Policy **VIII:** 132–133
  government **VIII:** 134
  Great Depression **VIII:** 140
  Hawley-Smoot Tariff Act **VIII:** 144
  HOLC **VIII:** 150
  Hoover presidency **VIII:** 153–156
  immigration **VIII:** 162
  Jones, Jesse H. **VIII:** 174
  labor **VIII:** 179
  Lewis, John L. **VIII:** 185
  London Naval Conference **VIII:** 194
  Manchuria **VIII:** 199
  McNary-Haugen Farm Bill **VII:** 175
  Mellon, Andrew **VII:** 180
  Norris, George W. **VIII:** 248
  OWI **VIII:** 258
  politics in the Roosevelt era **VIII:** 270, 272*t*
  presidency **VIII:** 280
  recreation **VIII:** 296
  refugees **VIII:** 298
  relief **VIII:** 299, 300
  Relief and Reconstruction Act **VIII:** 302
  Republican Party **VII:** 263; **VIII:** 304, 306
  RFC **VIII:** 294
  Roosevelt, Franklin D. **VIII:** 312
  SEC **VIII:** 322
  Smith, Alfred E. **VII:** 287
  Stimson, Henry L. **VIII:** 340
  Supreme Court **VIII:** 344
  tariffs **VII:** 306
  taxation **VIII:** 351
  TVA **VIII:** 356
  World Disarmament Conference **VIII:** 388
Hoover, J. Edgar **VII:** 221, 361*c;* **VIII:** 115; **IX:** *136,* **136–137,** 334*c*

Army-McCarthy hearings **IX:** 18
  Black Panthers **IX:** 39
  Mississippi Freedom Democratic Party **IX:** 207
  Rosenberg, Julius and Ethel **IX:** 264–265
Hoover Dam **VII:** 138; **VIII:** 175
Hoover presidency **VIII: 153–156,** *155*
  Agricultural Adjustment Act **VIII:** 5, 6–7
  agriculture **VIII:** 7
  Anglo-American relations **VIII:** 16
  antimonopoly **VIII:** 17
  Bonus Army **VIII:** 39
  Borah, William E. **VIII:** 40
  Brain Trust **VIII:** 41
  civil rights **VIII:** 61
  Communists **VIII:** 65
  Congress **VIII:** 66
  conservatism **VIII:** 71
  election of 1932 **VIII:** 96
  Emergency Banking Act of 1933 **VIII:** 100
  FCA **VIII:** 112
  FCC **VIII:** 116
  German Americans **VIII:** 130
  Good Neighbor Policy **VIII:** 132
  government **VIII:** 134
  Great Depression **VIII:** 140
  Hawley-Smoot Tariff Act **VIII:** 144
  Hoover, Herbert **VIII:** 151
  immigration **VIII:** 162
  La Follette, Robert M., Jr. **VIII:** 182
  Lewis, John L. **VIII:** 185
  Long, Huey P. **VIII:** 194
  politics in the Roosevelt era **VIII:** 270
  presidency **VIII:** 280–281
  relief **VIII:** 299
  Republican Party **VIII:** 305
  RFC **VIII:** 294
  taxation **VIII:** 351
  Tugwell, Rexford G. **VIII:** 361
  Wagner, Robert F. **VIII:** 372
"Hoovervilles" **VIII:** 155
Hope, Bob **VIII:** 217, 218
Hopewell, Treaty of **II:** 392; **III:** 66

Hopewell culture **I: 166,** 244–245, 252, 385*c*
Hopi nations **I:** 13, 90, **166–167,** 252, 255, 295; **II:** 247, 255, 303; **IV:** 221
Hopkey, Sophia **I:** 394
Hopkins, Esek **III:** 90
Hopkins, Harry L. **VIII: 156–157**
  African Americans **VIII:** 3
  Black Cabinet **VIII:** 37
  CWA **VIII:** 62, 63
  Emergency Relief Appropriation Act **VIII:** 102
  FAP **VIII:** 114
  FERA **VIII:** 118
  Flynn, Edward J. **VIII:** 122
  FSA **VIII:** 112
  FWP **VIII:** 121
  Harriman, Averell **VIII:** 143, 144
  Henderson, Leon **VIII:** 145
  Ickes, Harold L. **VIII:** 161
  Keynesianism **VIII:** 176
  NYA **VIII:** 234
  PWA **VIII:** 285, 286
  recession of 1937–38 **VIII:** 293
  relief **VIII:** 300, 301
  Roosevelt, Eleanor **VIII:** 311
  second front **VIII:** 320
  Social Security Act **VIII:** 328
  TNEC **VIII:** 355
  Wallace, Henry A. **VIII:** 373
  WPA **VIII:** 386, 387
Hopkins, Juliet Opie **V:** 256
Hopkins, Lemuel **III:** 80
Hopkins, Samuel **II:** 269
Hopkins, Stephen **II:** 321
Hopkinson, Francis **II:** 239
Hopkinson, Joseph **IV:** 227
Hopper, Dennis **IX:** 214
Hopper, Edward **VII:** 19, 358*c;* **VIII:** *24,* 25
Hoppin, Augustus **VI:** 115
Hoppus, Edward **II:** 23
Horgan, Stephen **VI:** 212
horizontal integration **VII:** 37, 38. *See also* monopolies
hormone research **IX:** 270
Horne, Lena **IX:** 191
Hornigold, Benjamin **II:** 285, 368
Horowitz, David **X:** 80
horror films **IX:** 213
horsecar lines **VI:** 54, 291–292

horse racing **VI: 133–134;**
VIII: 338
horses **I:** 77, **167–169,** *168,*
273, 329, 377; **III:** 154; **IV:**
337, 344
  animals **II:** 21, 22
  Great Plains Indians **II:**
  150
  Indians of the Desert
  Southwest **II:** 166
  Navajo **II:** 247
  Newport **II:** 258
  taverns and inns **II:** 368
  travel **II:** 377
  war and warfare **II:** 391
Horseshoe Bend, Battle of **III:**
66, 97; **IV: 173**
  Jackson, Andrew **IV:** 191
  Native Americans **IV:** 256
  Native Americans in the
  War of 1812 **IV:** 260
  War of 1812 **IV:** 356
Horsmanden, Daniel **II:** 248
horticulture **II:** 77, 278, 284;
VI: 199, 200. *See also*
agriculture
Horton, Willie **X:** 91, **143–144**
Hospers, John **X:** 176
hospitals **V:** 230, 304, 390; **VII:**
179; **IX:** 198; **X:** 188. *See also*
medicine and public health
Hospital Survey and
Construction Act **IX:** 198
hostages, terrorism and **X:** 297.
See also Iranian hostage crisis
hosts, Internet **X:** 153
Hotchkiss, Jedediah **V:** 51
Hot Five **VII:** 361c
Hot Network **X:** 244
Houdini, Harry **VII:** *123,*
123–124, 355c
Hounsfield, Godfrey **X:** 190
Housatonic, USS **V:** 310
House, Edward **VII:** 156, 263
House, George **IX:** 66
House, Son **VIII:** 223
House Committee on Un-
American Activities (HUAC)
VIII: 408c; **IX: 137–138,**
329c, 334c; **X:** 219
  American Federation of
  Labor **VIII:** 14
  anticommunism **IX:** 14
  Chambers, Whittaker **IX:**
  50
  civil liberties **VIII:** 60
  communism **IX:** 61
  FTP **VIII:** 120
  FWP **VIII:** 121
  Hiss, Alger **IX:** 134
  Hollywood Ten **IX:**
  134–135

House Un-American
  Activities Committee
  VIII: 120
  Ku Klux Klan **IX:** 166
  movies **IX:** 211–212
  Public Utility Holding
  Company Act **VIII:** 285
  Republican Party **VIII:**
  305
  Robeson, Paul **VIII:** 310;
  IX: 261
  Smith Act **VIII:** 326
  Supreme Court **VIII:** 347
  WPA **VIII:** 387
"House Divided" speech
  (Lincoln) **V:** 405c, 411–414
housekeeping **IV:** 367–368
Houseman, John **VIII:** 376
House of Commons
  Cornwallis, Lord **III:** 92
  Franklin, Benjamin **III:**
  134
  impeachment **III:** 175
  Pitt, William **III:** 277
  Tarleton, Banastre **III:**
  343
House of Good Hope **II:** 256
House of Lords **III:** 92, 175,
277
House of Morgan **VI:** 20
House of Representatives, U.S.
III: 397c; **IV:** 378c; **VII:**
356c–358c; **IX:** 331c; **X:**
144–145, 328c. *See also*
specific representatives
  Abscam **X:** 4–5
  Adams, John Quincy **IV:** 5
  Agricultural Adjustment
  Act **VIII:** 5
  Albert, Carl B. **X:** 17, 18
  Ames, Fisher **III:** 13
  Ashley, William Henry **IV:**
  30
  Banking Act of 1935 **VIII:**
  33
  Benton, Thomas Hart **IV:**
  50
  Blaine, James Gillespie **VI:**
  31
  Blair, Francis P., Jr. **V:** 30
  Bland-Allison Act **VI:** 32
  Bryan, William Jennings
  VI: 37
  Bush, George H. W. **X:**
  44–45
  Byrnes, James F. **VIII:** 48
  campaign finance **X:** 54
  Cannon, Joseph **VII:** 42
  Civil Rights Act of 1957
  IX: 54–55
  Civil Rights Act of 1960
  IX: 55, 56

Claiborne, William C. C.
  IV: 84
Clay, Henry **IV:** 86
Clinton, William **X:** 69
Compromise of 1850 **IV:**
  94
Congress **VI:** 63, 64; **VII:**
  53; **VIII:** 67, 68, 68t
Congressional Budget and
  Impoundment Act **X:** 75
Crockett, Davy **IV:** 100
Davis, Jefferson **V:** 88
Dawes Severalty Act **VI:**
  76
Democratic Party **IV:** 106;
  VI: 78; **VII:** 65, 66;
  VIII: 80–82
Douglas, Stephen A. **V:** 98
Douglas, William O. **VIII:**
  85
education, federal aid to
  VI: 92
election of 1800 **III:** 116,
  117
election of 1932 **VIII:** 96
election of 1936 **VIII:** 97
election of 1940 **VIII:** 98
elections **V:** 109, 111; **IX:**
  94–97
Emergency Banking Act of
  1933 **VIII:** 101
ERA **X:** 105–106
Executive Reorganization
  Act **VIII:** 107
Ferraro, Geraldine A. **X:**
  117
Fillmore, Millard **IV:** 137
flag burning **X:** 118
Foley, Thomas S. **X:**
  118–119
Ford, Gerald R. **X:**
  119–120
Fourteenth Amendment
  V: 138
Garfield, James A. **VI:** 108
Garner, John Nance **VIII:**
  129
gay rights movement **X:**
  128
Gingrich, Newton L. **X:**
  129–130
Gore, Albert, Jr. **X:** 133
Harrison, William Henry
  IV: 169
Hearst, William Randolph
  VII: 121
Homestead Act of 1862 **V:**
  170
House Un-American
  Activities Committee
  IX: 137–138
Hull, Cordell **VIII:** 159

impeachment **III:** 175; **X:**
  150
impeachment of Andrew
  Johnson **V:** 178
Jackson, Andrew **IV:** 192
Jefferson, Thomas **III:** 185
Johnson, Andrew **V:** 188
Johnson, Tom **VII:** 140
Joint Committee on the
  Conduct of War **V:** 191
Judiciary Act of 1801 **III:**
  193
Kansas-Nebraska Act of
  1854 **V:** 198
Keating-Owen Act **VII:**
  145
La Guardia, Fiorello **VIII:**
  182
Lincoln, Abraham **V:** 210
Lodge, Henry Cabot **VII:**
  165
Lyon, Matthew **III:** 222
Madison, James **III:** 229
Mann, Horace **IV:** 220
Mann Act **VII:** 169
Marshall, John **III:** 235
NEA,NEH **X:** 209
Neutrality Acts **VIII:** 239
Nixon, Richard M. **X:** 219
Norris, George W. **VIII:**
  248
nuclear freeze movement
  X: 224
O'Neill, Thomas P., Jr. **X:**
  228
Pickering, John **III:** 276
Pierce, Franklin **V:** 275
Pinchback, Pinckney B. S.
  V: 275–276
political parties **X:** 238
political parties, third **VI:**
  225
politics **VII:** 229
politics in the Roosevelt
  era **VIII:** 270–273
population trends **V:** 279
Powell, Adam Clayton **IX:**
  246
presidential campaigns **VI:**
  231
Rainey, Joseph H. **V:** 291
Reagan, Ronald W. **X:** 259
reconversion **VIII:** 295
Reed, Thomas Brackett
  VI: 240, 241
republicanism **III:** 303
Republican Party **V:** 302;
  VII: 262
RFRA **X:** 266
Senate **X:** 275, 276
Seventeenth Amendment
  VII: 69

Sherman, Roger **III:** 325
Sickles, Daniel E. **V:** 326, 327
slavery **IV:** 317
Solid South **VI:** 270
Starr, Kenneth **X:** 287
Stevens, Thaddeus **V:** 338
Story, Joseph **III:** 334
Tyler, John **IV:** 348
Vallandigham, Clement L. **V:** 377
Washington, D.C. **V:** 389
Watergate scandal **X:** 317
Watson, Tom **VII:** 332
Webster, Daniel **IV:** 359
woman suffrage **VII:** 337
Wright, James C., Jr. **X:** 322
House of the Seven Gables (Hawthorne) **IV:** 213, 345
House of Trade. *See* Casa de Contratación
"House of Youth" **I:** 20
House Un-American Activities Committee. *See* House Committee on Un-American Activities
housework. *See* work, household
housing **II:** 23, **157–158; IV:** 82, 98, 260; **VI:** xv, **134–136,** *135;* **VIII: 157–159,** *158,* 407*c;* **IX:** 329*c,* 334*c;* **X:** 175. *See also* tenants
Abenaki **I:** 2
African-American movement **IX:** 4
Aleut **II:** 16
Anglo-Normans **I:** 11
architecture **II:** 22–24
art **II:** 24
art and architecture **I:** 12, 13; **IX:** 19
business **VIII:** 46
California **I:** 48
Carib **I:** 56
chinampas **I:** 72
cities and urban life **VI:** 54; **VIII:** 57–60; **IX:** 52
Economic Opportunity Act of 1964 **IX:** 87
economy **IX:** 90
environment **II:** 110, 111
Fair Deal **IX:** 108
Federal Housing Administration **IX:** 110
FHA **VIII:** 118–119
Gedi **I:** 139
GI Bill of Rights **VIII:** 131–132

government (state and local) **IX:** 125
Haida **I:** 150
Hidatsa **I:** 161
HOLC **VIII:** 150–151
Huron **I:** 170–171
indentured servitude **II:** 163
Indians of the Desert Southwest **II:** 165
iron manufacturing **II:** 167–168
labor **II:** 187, 188
Levitt, William J. **IX:** 176–178
London **I:** 208
low-income. *See* public housing
marriage and family life **II:** 208; **VIII:** 204, 205
Massachuset **I:** 225
Massachusetts **II:** 215
migration **VIII:** 213
Minuit, Peter **II:** 227
Model Cities program **IX:** 208
New Mexico **I:** 255
North Carolina **II:** 264
Northwest Coast Indians **II:** 265
Olmecs **I:** 269
Passamaquoddy **I:** 278
Philadelphia **II:** 281
plantation system **II:** 286
population trends **VI:** 226
Powhatan **I:** 292
prefabricated **IV:** 308
progressivism in the 1890s **VI:** 233
public. *See* public housing
PWA **VIII:** 285
RA **VIII:** 307
race and racial conflict **VII:** 249
Riis, Jacob A. **VI:** 248
Secotan **I:** 320
segregation **VII:** 281
settlement houses **VI:** 259–260
society, British American **II:** 352
sod houses **VI:** 269–270
Southern Christian Leadership Conference **IX:** 276
Stuyvesant, Peter **II:** 363
suburbanization **IX:** 287–288
suburbs **VII:** 300; **VIII:** 342
taverns and inns **II:** 367
Tenochtitlán **I:** 344

Urban League **IX:** 305
urban reform **VII:** 317
USHA **VIII:** 367–368
Venice **I:** 365
Virginia **II:** 382–383
Wagner, Robert F. **VIII:** 372
YMCA **VII:** 350
YWCA **VII:** 349
Zuni **I:** 383
Housing Act of 1937 **VIII:** 157–159, 367, 372, 407*c*
Housing Act of 1968 **IX:** 127
Housing and Urban Development, Department of (HUD) **VIII:** 368; **IX:** 208; **X:** 163, 175
Housing and Urban Development Act of 1965 **IX:** 52, 334*c*
housing industry **VIII:** 138, 342
Houston, Charles **VIII:** 227
Houston, Sam **IV: 173–175,** *174,* 377*c*
Alamo, The **IV:** 13
Austin, Stephen F. **IV:** 37–38
Colt revolver **IV:** 92
election of 1840 **IV:** 124
foreign policy **IV:** 142
Manifest Destiny **IV:** 217
Santa Anna, Antonio López de **IV:** 303–304, *304*
Texas **IV:** 338, 339
Texas, Republic of **IV:** 340, 341
Houston, Texas **X:** 290
Houston, Whitney **X:** 202
Hovey, Frederick **VI:** 274
Howard, Lord Effingham **I:** 112
Howard, Oliver Otis **V: 173–174; VI:** 213
Freedmen's Bureau **V:** 142
Gettysburg, Battle of **V:** 148
Johnson, Andrew **V:** 188
Meade, George Gordon **V:** 227
Sherman's March through Georgia **V:** 322
Howard University **V:** 173, 291; **VI:** 5, 94, 172
Howe, George **I:** 314
Howe, George Augustus, Viscount **II: 158**
Howe, Julia Ward **V: 174,** 244, 398
Howe, Louis McHenry **VIII:** 110, 122, 312
Howe, Richard, Lord **III: 167–168**

Brandywine, Battle of **III:** 48
Howe, Sir William **III:** 169
Lee, Charles **III:** 206
Long Island, Battle of **III:** 217
Sullivan, John **III:** 337
Howe, Sir William **III: 168–169,** 393*c*
Brandywine, Battle of **III:** 47–48
Bunker Hill, Battle of **III:** 50, 51
Burgoyne, John **III:** 52
Cornwallis, Lord **III:** 92
Dorchester Heights, Battle of **III:** 107
Fort Washington, capture of **III:** 133
Franklin, Benjamin **III:** 134
Gage, Thomas **III:** 147
Galloway, Joseph **III:** 148
Germantown, Battle of **III:** 151
Greene, Nathanael **III:** 155
Hale, Nathan **III:** 160
Howe, Richard, Lord **III:** 167, 168
Jersey, HMS **III:** 186
Knox, Henry **III:** 197
Lee, Charles **III:** 206
Long Island, Battle of **III:** 217
Monmouth, Battle of **III:** 244
Revolutionary War **III:** 305
Saratoga, surrender at **III:** 318
Trenton and Princeton, Battles of **III:** 351
Washington, George **III:** 366–367
Wayne, Anthony **III:** 369
White Plains, Battle of **III:** 376
Howe Company **IV:** 184
Howell, Vernon. *See* Koresh, David
Howells, William Dean **VI: 136**
Crane, Stephen **VI:** 68
Dickinson, Emily **VI:** 80
Dunbar, Paul Laurence **VI:** 82
Garland, Hamlin **VI:** 109
Gilded Age, The **VI:** 115
James, Henry **VI:** 153
literature **VI:** 177, 178
Philadelphia Centennial Exposition **VI:** 223–224

Howells, William Dean
(*continued*)
    theater **VI:** 287
    Twain, Mark **VI:** 298
Howes, Edward **I:** 154
Howl (Allen Ginsberg) **IX:** 35,
    71, 122–123, 182, 331*c*
Howlin' Wolf **VIII:** 223
How the Other Half Lives (Riis)
    VI: 135, 137, 248, 326*c*,
    342–343; **VII:** 238
Hoxie, Herbert M. **V:** 84
Hoyt, Beatrix **VI:** 275
Hoyt, William **VI:** 290
HTML (Hyper Text Markup
    Language) **X:** 274
HUAC. *See* House Committee
    on Un-American Activities
    Huang, John **X:** 162
Huascar **I:** 14–15, 177, 283
Huayna Capac **I:** 14
Hubbard, Gardiner **VI:** 25
Hubbell, Webster **X:** 286
Hubble, Edwin **VIII:** 318
Hubble space telescope **X:** 283,
    327*c*
HUD. *See* Housing and Urban
    Development, Department
    of
Hudson, Henry **I:** 114–115, 133,
    265; **II: 158–159,** *159*
    Delaware **II:** 87
    exploration **II:** 115
    fur trade **II:** 130–131
    New Amsterdam **II:** 249
    New Jersey **II:** 252
    New Netherland **II:** 255
    New York **II:** 259
    Pennsylvania **II:** 274
Hudson Bay **I:** 266; **II:** 115,
    130–132, 158, 159, 178, 309
Hudson River **IV:** 128, 295
Hudson River Railroad **IV:**
    352
Hudson River School **IV:** 26; **V:**
    16
Hudson's Bay Company (HBC)
    II: 115, **159,** 375
    Ashley, William Henry **IV:**
        29, 30
    Astor, John Jacob **IV:** 31
    Astoria **IV:** 32, 33
    Bent, Charles **IV:** 47
    Columbia River **IV:** 93
    Fort Vancouver **IV:** 145,
        146
    fur trade **IV:** 156
    McLoughlin, John **IV:**
        228–229
    migration **IV:** 236
    Missouri Fur Company **IV:**
        239

mountain men **IV:** 247,
    248
Oregon Treaty of 1846 **IV:**
    269, 270
rendezvous **IV:** 299
Rocky Mountain Fur
    Company **IV:** 302
Smith, Jedediah Strong **IV:**
    321, 322
Hudson Strait **I:** 83; **II:** 158–159
Hudson Valley riots **III:**
    201–202
huei tlatoani (great speakers) **I:**
    17, 19, 97–99, 185, 237–238
Huelga **X:** 141
Huemac **I:** 356
Huerta, Dolores **IX:** 174, 304
Huerta, Victoriano **VII:** 28,
    184–185
Huexotxingo **I:** 18
Huggins, Charles B. **VIII:** 207
Hugh, Jones **II:** 374
Hughes, Charles Evans **VII:**
    124, 358*c*; **VIII:** 76, 344,
    346, 346*t*; **X:** 130, 198
    Democratic Party **VII:** 66
    elections **VII:** 80
    foreign policy **VII:** 100
    politics **VII:** 230
    Progressive Party **VII:** 237
    Republican Party **VII:** 263
    Washington Conference
        on Naval Disarmament
        VII: 331
    Wilson, Woodrow **VII:** 334
Hughes, Dorothy Pitman **X:**
    288
Hughes, John **III:** 134; **IV:** 23
Hughes, Langston **VII:** 119,
    162; **IX:** 181
Hughes, Lloyd **VI:** 134
Hughes, Sarah Anne **VI:** 296
Hughes, Sarah T. **IX:** *152*
Hughson, John **II:** 247
Hughson, Sarah **II:** 247
Hugo, Victor **V:** 40
Huguenots **I: 169–170,** 387*c*;
    II: 56, 97, 130, 178, 261, 321
    Caroline, Fort **I:** 57
    Castile **I:** 64
    Henry IV (Henry of
        Navarre) **I:** 158
    Laudonnière, René de **I:**
        201–202
    Le Moyne, Jacques **I:** 202
Huitzilopochtli (Huichilobas) **I:**
    170; II: 317
    Aztecs **I:** 17, 18
    Aztlán **I:** 22
    Itzcóatl **I:** 185
    Quetzalcoatl **I:** 301
    Tenochtitlán **I:** 344

Tezcatlipoca **I:** 347
Tláloc **I:** 352
Hulbert, William **VI:** 21
Hull, Cordell **VIII: 159–160**
    Bretton Woods
        Conference **VIII:** 42
    Ethiopia **VIII:** 105
    Good Neighbor Policy
        VIII: 133
    London Economic
        Conference **VIII:** 193
    Manchuria **VIII:** 199
    Neutrality Acts **VIII:** 239
    Reciprocal Trade
        Agreements Act **VIII:**
        294
    Roosevelt, Franklin D.
        VIII: 314
    Spanish Civil War **VIII:**
        335
    Welles, Sumner **VIII:** 377
Hull, Isaac **IV:** 176
Hull, Jane Dee **X:** 321
Hull, William **III:** 398*c*; **IV:**
    175–176
    Cass, Lewis **IV:** 76
    Harrison, William Henry
        IV: 169
    Native Americans in the
        War of 1812 **IV:** 259
    War of 1812 **IV:** 356
Hull-House **VI:** 140, 259, 260,
    326*c*; **VIII:** 383
    Addams, Jane **VII:** 2–3
    criminal justice **VII:** 59
    Kelley, Florence **VII:** 146
    social work **VII:** 289
Humabon, Sultan **I:** 216, 217
Humanae Vitae (Pope Paul VI)
    X: 3, 37
human engineering **VI:** 170
Human Genome Initiative **X:**
    145
human genome map **X:** 190,
    191, 275, 330*c*
Human Genome Project **X:**
    145–146, 187, 191
human immunodeficiency virus
    (HIV) **X:** 5–6, 326*c*
humanism **I:** 287, 322
humanitarian aid **X:** 307
humanitarianism **III: 169–170,**
    291; **VII:** 256
Human Life Amendment
    (1981) **X:** 37
human-potential movement **X:**
    109
human rights **III:** 329; **VIII:**
    411*c*; **X:** 325*c*, 326*c*
    capital punishment **X:** 56
    Carter, James Earl, Jr. **X:**
    58

contras **X:** 80–81
defense policy **X:** 86, 88
détente **X:** 89
foreign policy **X:** 123
Iran-contra affair **X:** 154
Latin America **X:** 173
South Africa **X:** 279
Human Rights **IV:** 14
Human Rights Campaign Fund
    X: 127
Humbard, Rex **X:** 293
Humbolt Current **I:** 279
Hume, Sophia Wigington **II:**
    159–160
Humery, Conrad **I:** 147
humint (human intelligence)
    IX: 49
"humoralism" **II:** 220
Humphrey, Hubert H. **IX: 138,**
    334*c*
    Americans for Democratic
        Action **IX:** 13, 14
    antiwar movement—
        Vietnam **X:** 24
    "Chicago Eight" **X:** 61
    Democratic Party **IX:** 79
    elections **IX:** 95–96
    Kissinger, Henry A. **X:** 165
    McCarthy, Eugene **IX:** 189
    McGovern, George
        Stanley **X:** 184
    Mondale, Walter F. **X:** 196
    National Wilderness
        Preservation Act of 1964
        IX: 226
    neoconservatism **X:** 215
    Nixon, Richard M. **X:** 220
    States' Rights Party **IX:**
        281
    Wallace, George C. **X:** 314
Humphrey, Hubert H., III **X:**
    304
Humphreys, David **III:** 80
Humphreys, Joshua **III:** 80
"hundred-percent corner" **VI:**
    291
Hungary **I:** 374; **II:** 346; **IX:** 58,
    105, 106, 277; **X:** 72, 156, 223
"Hunkers" **IV:** 150
Hunkpapa Sioux nation **VI:** 207,
    263
Hun Sen **X:** 224
Hunt, E. Howard **X:** 43, 316
Hunt, Henry J. **V:** 150
Hunt, Jane **IV:** 314; **V:** 397
Hunt, Jim **X:** 141
Hunt, Richard Morris **VI:** 276
Hunt, Thomas **II:** 360–361
Hunt, Walter **IV:** 308
Hunt, Washington **VI:** 153
Hunt, Wilson Price **IV:** 33
Hunter, David **V:** 125, 358

Hunter, Robert **II:** 198, 233, 234, 415; **V:** 197
Hunter, William **II:** 292
Hunter, William H. **VI:** 4
Hunter (hospital ship) **III:** 139
hunting and gathering **IV:** 64, 156, 182; **VI:** 65
  Abenaki **I:** 2
  Acadia **I:** 2
  Aleut **II:** 16
  Algonquin **II:** 17
  Amazon River **I:** 8
  animals **II:** 21
  Arawak **I:** 12
  California **I:** 48
  California Indians **II:** 49
  Cayuga **I:** 67
  Chesapeake Bay **II:** 58
  Delaware **II:** 89
  Florida **I:** 130
  food **II:** 121
  forests **II:** 122
  Havasupai **I:** 156
  Hohokam **I:** 163
  Huron **I:** 171
  Inuit **II:** 167
  Iroquois **I:** 181; **II:** 168
  Maine **II:** 203
  marriage and family life **II:** 206
  Massachusett **I:** 225
  Mississippian culture **I:** 236–237
  Natchez **I:** 251
  Native Americans **II:** 243
  Navajo **II:** 247
  New Hampshire **II:** 250
  New Jersey **II:** 252
  New Mexico **I:** 254–255
  North Carolina **II:** 263, 264
  Pequot **II:** 278
  South Carolina **II:** 353
  technology **II:** 369
  Tuscarora **II:** 378–379
  wolves **II:** 405
  women's status and rights **II:** 406–407
Huntley, Chet **IX:** 153
Hupa **I:** 48
Huron nation **I:** 1, **170–172,** 183; **II:** 160; **IV:** 156
  agriculture **II:** 8
  Algonquin **II:** 17
  architecture **II:** 22
  Beaver Wars **II:** 31
  Brulé, Étienne **II:** 44
  Dekanawideh **II:** 85
  disease **II:** 90
  exploration **II:** 114
  French colonies **II:** 126
  fur trade **II:** 130–131

Hudson's Bay Company **II:** 159
  Iroquois **II:** 168, 169
  Jesuits **II:** 174
  Montour, Madame **II:** 233
  Native Americans **II:** 243
  New Netherland **II:** 256
  Nicolet, Jean **II:** 263
  religion, Native American **II:** 317–318
hurricanes **VI:** 107–108
Hurston, Zora Neale **VII:** *119;* **VIII:** 3, 192, 193
Hurt, John **IX:** 111
Hus, Jan **I:** 307
Husband, Herman **III:** **170,** 260, **261**
Huske, John **III:** 214
Hussein, king of Jordan **IX:** 147
Hussein, Saddam **IX:** 10, 201
  Bush, George H. W. **X:** 46
  defense policy **X:** 87
  foreign policy **X:** 124
  Jackson, Jesse L. **X:** 160
  Persian Gulf War **X:** 234–236
Hussey, Obed **IV:** 224
Huston, John **IX:** 135
Hut, Hans **I:** 309
Hutcheson, "Big Bill" **VIII:** 14, 186
Hutcheson, Francis **II:** 109
Hutchinson, Anne Marbury **II:** **160–161,** *161,* **417c**
  Coddington, William **II:** 65
  Cotton, John **II:** 73
  Dudley, Thomas **II:** 96
  Dyer, Mary **II:** 99
  Hooker, Thomas **II:** 157
  Massachusetts **II:** 212
  midwives **II:** 225
  Rhode Island **II:** 320
  society, British American **II:** 350
  Wheelwright, John **II:** 396
  Williams, Roger **II:** 399
  Winthrop, John **II:** 402
  women's status and rights **II:** 408
Hutchinson, John **II:** 330
Hutchinson, Thomas **II:** 72, 179; **III:** **170–172,** *171*
  Boston Massacre **III:** 43
  Boston Tea Party **III:** 45
  Franklin, Benjamin **III:** 134
  MacIntosh, Ebenezer **III:** 225
  Oliver, Andrew **III:** 266, 267
  Quincy, Josiah **III:** 293

  riots **III:** 308
  Stamp Act **III:** 332
  voluntary associations **III:** 362
  Warren, Mercy Otis **III:** 363, 364
  Whately, Thomas **III:** 373
  writs of assistance **III:** 384
Hutchinson family **II:** 215
Hutchinson Family Singers **IV:** 250
Hutson, Don **VIII:** 336
Hutton, Bobby **IX:** 39
Hutton, Edward F. **VIII:** 15
Huxley, Aldous **IX:** 183
Huxley, Thomas **VI:** 188
Hyde, Edward, Viscount Cornbury **II:** 98, **162**
Hyde, Henry **X:** 272
Hyde amendment **X:** 2, 3
hydraulic mining **IV:** 69; **VI:** 193
hydroelectric power **VI:** 149, 285, 327c
hydrogen bomb **VIII:** 29; **IX:** **138–140,** *139,* 331c; **X:** 72
  arms race **IX:** 16
  Atomic Energy Commission **IX:** 23
  DuPont Corporation **IX:** 83
  Oppenheimer, J. Robert **IX:** 237
  science **IX:** 270
  technology **IX:** 294
hydropathy **IV:** 230
hymns **V:** 244
hypertext **X:** 153
Hyper Text Markup Language (HTML) **X:** 274

I

Iacocca, Lee **X:** 62
IAM **VII:** 10
"iatrochemistry" **II:** 220
Iberian Peninsula
  Bristol **I:** 35
  Castile **I:** 62–64
  conquistadores **I:** 84
  Islam **I:** 185
  Jews (Judaism) **I:** 190
  Reconquista **I:** 306
Iberville, sieur de. *See* Le Moyne, Pierre, sieur d'Iberville
IBM. *See* International Business Machines
Ibn al-Mukhtar **I:** 350
Ibn Battuta **I:** **173,** 184, 218, 337, 338, 350
Ibn Khaldûn, 'Abd-ar-Rahmân Abû Zayd ibn Muhammad

ibn Muhammad **I:** **173–174,** 217, 337, 340
Ibrahim, Ahmad Ibn **I:** 104
IBRD. *See* International Bank for Reconstruction and Development
IBT. *See* Teamsters Union
ICA. *See* Interstate Commerce Act
Icariens **IV:** 61
ICBMs. *See* intercontinental ballistic missiles
ICC. *See* Indian Claims Commission; Interstate Commerce Commission
ice hockey **VII:** 295
Iceland **I:** 35, **174–175,** 263, 264, 385c; **IX:** 194, 231–233; **X:** 223
Iceman Cometh, The (O'Neill) **VIII:** 192
IC4A (Intercollegiate Association of Amateur Athletes of America) **VI:** 290
Ickes, Harold **X:** 125
Ickes, Harold L. **VIII:** **161–162**
  African Americans **VIII:** 3
  Black Cabinet **VIII:** 37
  civil rights **VIII:** 61
  Emergency Relief Appropriation Act **VIII:** 102
  environmental issues **VIII:** 103
  FHA **VIII:** 119
  Hopkins, Harry **VIII:** 156
  Indian Reorganization Act **VIII:** 163
  NAACP **VIII:** 227
  Native Americans **VIII:** 235
  NIRA **VIII:** 228
  PWA **VIII:** 285
  Roosevelt, Eleanor **VIII:** 311
  Spanish Civil War **VIII:** 335
  Supreme Court **VIII:** *345*
  USHA **VIII:** 367
  Wallace, Henry A. **VIII:** 373
  WPA **VIII:** 386, 387
icons **I:** 13
Idaho **IV:** 93; **VI:** 207, 213, 317; **X:** 107, 194, 242
Idaho Territory **VI:** 51m
Ide, William B. **IV:** 45
Idle Hours (Chase) **VI:** 49
Idris Alooma, Mai **I:** 102, 317
Ife-Ife **I:** 377
Igbo (Ibo) **I:** **175**
Ignatius of Loyola, St. **II:** 174

"I Have a Dream" speech (Martin Luther King, Jr.) **IX:** 161, 191, 275, 351–352
"I Heard the Bells on Christmas Day" **V:** 244
Ihonatiria **II:** 160
Ihuatzio **I:** 343
ILA (Institute for Legislative Action) **X:** 213
ILD. *See* International Labor Defense
ILDF **VII:** 53
Ile-Ife **I:** 377
Ile Oyo **I:** 377
Île Royal. *See* Cape Breton
Île Saint-Jean (Prince Edward Island) **I:** 3; **II:** 2
ILGWU. *See* International Ladies' Garment Workers Union
Illegal Fencing Act of 1885 **VI:** 20
illegal immigrants **IX:** 141–142; **X:** 327*c*
   immigration **X:** 147
   IRCA **X:** 149
   Mexico **X:** 192, *192*, 193
Illinois **II:** 199; **V:** 209–210, 367; **VI:** 221, 318; **IX:** 103–104, 283–284
   Asian Americans **X:** 28
   Beckwourth, Jim **IV:** 46
   Black Hawk War **IV:** 51–53
   canal era **IV:** 74
   capital punishment **X:** 56
   Church of Jesus Christ of Latter-day Saints **IV:** 80
   Deere, John **IV:** 105
   ERA **X:** 106, 107
   Hispanic Americans **X:** 143
   Lovejoy, Elijah **IV:** 214
   migration **IV:** 235
   militia movement **X:** 194
   population trends **X:** 242
   rust belt **X:** 269
Illinois (Hopewell culture) **I:** 166
Illinois & Michigan Canal **IV:** 73*m*
Illinois Central Railroad **V:** 98, 224
Illinois Indians **II:** 31, 169, 174, 206
Illinois Institute of Technology **IX:** 19
illness. *See* disease and epidemics
illustration, photography, and the graphic arts **V:** 247–248; **VI: 137–138**

I Love Lucy **IX:** 244, 331*c*
Ilunga Kalala **I:** 210
ILWU **VIII:** 43
IMF. *See* International Monetary Fund
"immediatists" **IV:** 2–3
Immigrant and the Community, The (Abbott) **VII:** 1
immigrants/immigration **I:** 145, 208; **III: 173–175,** 174*m;* **IV: 177–180,** *178,* 179*t;* **V: 175–177; VI: 138–140,** *139,* 325*c;* **VII:** xiii, *125,* **125–128,** 126*m,* 127*t,* 355*c,* 357*c,* 360*c,* 361*c;* **VIII: 162–163; IX: 141–142,** 331*c;* **X: 147–149,** 148*m,* 326*c,* 328*c. See also* immigration restrictions; *specific groups, e.g.:* English immigrants
   Abbott, Grace **VII:** 1
   Addams, Jane **VII:** 3
   AFL **VII:** 11
   Africa **II:** 4–5
   African Americans **II:** 5
   agriculture **II:** 11–12
   Alien and Sedition Acts **III:** 9
   American Protective Association **VI:** 11
   animals **II:** 20, 21
   anti-Catholic riots **IV:** 21–23, *22*
   anti-Chinese agitation, rise of **IV:** 23
   anti-Semitism **VIII:** 19
   anti-suffragists **VII:** 15
   art and architecture **VI:** 14
   Arthur, Chester Alan **VI:** 17
   Asian-American movement **IX:** 22
   Asian Americans. *See* Asian Americans
   Austin, Stephen F. **IV:** 37
   braceros **IX:** 41
   Cable Act **VII:** 41
   California **IV:** 65
   California gold rush **IV:** 66
   California Trail **IV:** 71
   Canada **III:** 60
   canal era **IV:** 74
   Catholics **III:** 63
   Charleston **II:** 56
   Chinese Exclusion Act of 1882 **VI:** 50–52, 332–334
   CIO **VIII:** 69
   cities and urban life **IV:** 81; **V:** 60; **VI:** 53; **VII:** 48; **VIII:** 59; **IX:** 52
   class consciousness **VI:** 57

Colorado gold rush **IV:** 89, 90
common soldier **V:** 69
Communist Party **VII:** 53
contract labor **VI:** 66
convict labor **II:** 72
Democratic Party **IV:** 108; **VI:** 77; **VII:** 65
Deseret, State of **IV:** 110
Dillingham Commission **VII:** 68–69
dress **VII:** 70
economy **IV:** 117, 119
education **IV:** 121–122; **VI:** 89; **VII:** 76; **VIII:** 93
election of 1940 **VIII:** 98
enemy aliens **VIII:** 102
entertainment, popular **VI:** 97
environment **II:** 112
Erie Canal **IV:** 129
ethnic organizations **VII:** 89
ethnocentrism **II:** 112
food **II:** 121
foreign policy **VI:** 103
Fort Laramie **IV:** 143
Foster, Stephen C. **V:** 137
French colonies **II:** 127
German-American regiments **V:** 147
German Americans. *See* German Americans
gold, discovery and mining **IV:** 163–164
Great Depression **VIII:** 140
Great Migration **VII:** 113
Hispanic Americans **X:** 143
Hoover presidency **VIII:** 153
Immigration Act of 1917 **VII:** 128
Immigration Act of 1965 **IX:** 142
immigration restrictions **VI:** 140–141
imperialism **VI:** 142
indentured servitude **II:** 163–165
intelligence tests **VII:** 131
Internal Security Act of 1950 **IX:** 144
IRCA **X:** 149
Irish-American regiments **V:** 181–182
Irish Americans. *See* Irish Americans
Islam in America **X:** 157
isolationists **VIII:** 166
Italian Americans. *See* Italian Americans

Japanese Americans, relocation of. *See* Japanese Americans, relocation of
journalism **VII:** 141
Judaism **VI:** 158
Know-Nothing Party **IV:** 201, 202
labor and labor movements **III:** 199–200; **IV:** 204; **VII:** 151, 154; **VIII:** 179
labor trends **VI:** 171
land **II:** 192
Lazarus, Emma **VI:** 173
liberalism **VIII:** 187
Mann Act **VII:** 169
mariners **II:** 204
marriage and family life **III:** 233; **VII:** 171
McCarran-Walter Act **IX:** 187–188
Mexican Americans. *See* Mexican Americans
Mexico **X:** 192, 193
Mexico (U.S. relations with) **X:** *192*
migration **VIII:** 212
mortality **II:** 235
movies **VIII:** 217
multiculturalism **X:** 200
music **V:** 245; **VIII:** 223
Nast, Thomas **V:** 247
National Origins Act **VII:** 202
nativism **V:** 251; **VI:** 209; **VII:** 208–209
New Netherland **II:** 256, 257
news media **VIII:** 243
New Woman **VII:** 214
New York City **V:** 253–254
New York City draft riots **V:** 255
Polish Americans. *See* Polish Americans
politics **VII:** 229
popular culture **VII:** 231
population trends **II:** 291; **III:** 283; **V:** 277–279; **VI:** 226; **VII:** 234; **VIII:** 277, 278; **IX:** 245; **X:** 243
Powderly, Terence Vincent **VI:** 227
progressivism **VII:** 238
progressivism in the 1890s **VI:** 233
Prohibition **VII:** 239
Prohibition Party **VI:** 234
Puerto Ricans **IX:** 250
Quota Act. *See* Quota Act

race and race relations **IV:** 289, 292; **VII:** 247
radicalism **VII:** 251
redemptioners **II:** 313
religion **IV:** 296, 298; **VI:** 241, 243; **VII:** 260, 261; **X:** 265
Republican Party **IV:** 301
Roman Catholicism **VI:** 249
Roman Catholics **II:** 323, 324
Russo-Japanese War **VII:** 271
Santa Fe Trail **IV:** 306
science **VII:** 276
Scotch-Irish **III:** 322
Seton, Elizabeth Ann **IV:** 315
skyscrapers **VI:** 264
socialism **VI:** 267, 268
social work **VII:** 291
society, British American **II:** 350
Spanish colonies **II:** 356
Statue of Liberty **VI:** 275–276
steel industry **VII:** 297
Strauss, Levi **IV:** 329
Sunbelt **X:** 290
Swedish colonies **II:** 365
tenants **II:** 370, 371
terrorism **X:** 298
Texas **IV:** 338
Texas Revolution **IV:** 339, 340
Trading with the Enemy Act **VII:** 311
Travis, William Barret **IV:** 346
Triangle Shirtwaist Fire **VII:** 311, 312
Turner, Frederick Jackson **VI:** 295
Union army **V:** 365
vaudeville **VII:** 321–322
Victorianism **VI:** 304
Virginia **II:** 382, 383
welfare capitalism **VII:** 333
Wilderness Road **III:** 378
Wyoming Valley War **III:** 384
YMCA/YWCA **VII:** 349–350
Immigrants' Protective League **VII:** 1
Immigration Act of 1917 **VII:** **128,** 359*c*
   Cable Act **VII:** 41
   Dillingham Commission **VII:** 69
   immigration **VII:** 127

Mexican immigration **VII:** 183
National Origins Act **VII:** 202
nativism **VII:** 208
population trends **VII:** 234
Quota Act **VII:** 245
Immigration Act of 1924 **VII:** 69
Immigration Act of 1965 **IX:** 52, 127, 141, **142,** 245, 334*c*; **X:** 28, 147
Immigration Act of 1990 **X:** 147, 327*c*
Immigration and Nationality Act **X:** 147
Immigration and Naturalization Act of 1990 **X:** 298
Immigration and Naturalization Service (INS) **VII:** 208; **X:** 149, 300
Immigration and Naturalization Service v. Chadha (1983) **X:** 326*c*
Immigration Reform and Control Act (IRCA) of 1986 **X:** 147, **149,** 192, 327*c*
Immigration Restriction League **VI:** 209; **VII:** 127
immigration restrictions **V:** 177; **VI:** 24, 120, **140–141,** 209; **VIII:** 409*c*
   Asian Americans **VIII:** 25
   Catholics **VIII:** 53
   conservatism **VIII:** 71
   Holocaust **VIII:** 150
   Jews **VIII:** 173
   population trends **VIII:** 278
   refugees **VIII:** 298, 299
   religion **VIII:** 303
impeachment **III:** 175; **VI:** 130; **X:** 323*c*, 330*c*
   Albert, Carl B. **X:** 18
   Chase, Samuel **III:** 64, 65
   Clinton, William **X:** 65, 68, 69
   Fortas, Abe **X:** 125, 126
   House of Representatives **X:** 144, 145
   Judiciary Act of 1801 **III:** 193
   Marbury v. Madison **III:** 231
   Nixon, Richard M. **X:** 149–150, 221
   Reno, Janet **X:** 267
   Senate **X:** 276
   Starr, Kenneth **X:** 286, 287
   Supreme Court **III:** 338

United States v. Nixon **X:** 309
   Watergate scandal **X:** 315–317
impeachment of Andrew Johnson **V:** **177–179,** *179,* 408*c*
   Butler, Benjamin **V:** 47
   Chase, Salmon P. **V:** 57
   Civil Rights Act of 1866 **V:** 62
   Dana, Charles A. **V:** 88
   Johnson, Andrew **V:** 189
   Radical Republicans **V:** 289
   Reconstruction **V:** 294
   Reconstruction Acts **V:** 296
   Republican Party **V:** 302
   Seward, William H. **V:** 315
   Stanton, Edwin M. **V:** 334
   Stevens, Thaddeus **V:** 338
   Sumner, Charles **V:** 343
   Wade, Benjamin **V:** 385
Imperato, Ferrante **I:** 40
imperialism **IV:** 171–172, 211, 219; **VI:** **141–143,** 142*m*; **VII:** 27–29, 97–98, 113–114
   Altgeld, John Peter **VI:** 10
   Anti-Imperialist League **VI:** 13
   Bryan, William Jennings **VI:** 37
   foreign policy **VI:** 102, 104
   Hoar, George Frisbie **VI:** 130
   Lease, Mary Elizabeth **VI:** 173
   Liberal Republican Party **VI:** 174
   Mahan, Alfred Thayer **VI:** 185–186
   mugwumps **VI:** 199
   possessions and dependencies **VI:** 142*m*
   Remington, Frederic **VI:** 245
   Schurz, Carl **VI:** 257
   Sherman, John **VI:** 261
   Simpson, Jerry **VI:** 262
   Social Darwinism **VI:** 266
   Social Gospel **VI:** 267
   Spanish-American War **VI:** 272
   Strong, Josiah **VI:** 279
Imperial Japan **VIII:** 389
Imperial Japanese Navy **VIII:** 186, 236, 331
imports/importing **IV:** 270, 276; **V:** 387; **VI:** 66–67, 284–285, 290, 291; **IX:** 25, 282; **X:** 15,

103–104. *See also* tariffs; trade, domestic and foreign
impoundment **X:** 75
impressionists **VI:** 45
impressment **II:** 182, 204, 419*c*; **III:** **175–176;** **IV:** 151–152, 161, 356, 358; **V:** **179–180**
   Attucks, Crispus **III:** 28
   Chesapeake-Leopard affair **III:** 67
   Confederate army **V:** 72
   Confederate States of America **V:** 77
   Davis, Jefferson **V:** 90
   elections **V:** 110
   foreign affairs **III:** 130
   French Revolution **III:** 138
   Jefferson, Thomas **III:** 186
   King, Rufus **III:** 195
   Little Belt incident **III:** 215, 216
   Madison, James **III:** 229
   Monroe-Pinkney Treaty **III:** 245
   slavery **V:** 330
   states' rights **V:** 336
   women's status and rights **V:** 398
imprisonment **V:** 161–162
'Inân, Abû **I:** 174
Inaugural Address (1861) (Davis) **V:** 418–420
Inaugural Address (1933) (Roosevelt) **VIII:** 413
Inaugural Address, First (1861) (Lincoln) **V:** 414–418
Inaugural Address, Second (1865) (Lincoln) **V:** 426–427
Inaugural Address, Second (1997) (Clinton) **X:** 355–357
Inca **I:** **175–177,** *176,* 387*c*
   Acosta, José de **I:** 3
   Alvarado, Pedro de **I:** 7
   Andes Mountains **I:** 10
   art and architecture **I:** 12
   Atahualpa **I:** 14–15
   Cuzco **I:** 99
   El Dorado **I:** 118
   Lima **I:** 206
   Machu Picchu **I:** 213–214
   Peru **I:** 280
   Pizarro, Francisco **I:** 283
   smallpox **I:** 331
Incidents of Travel in Central America, Chiapas, and Yucatan (John L. Stephens) **I:** 86
inclusive language **X:** 115, 116, 211
In Cold Blood (Truman Capote) **IX:** 334*c*

income
    African Americans **X:** 11
    Asian Americans **X:** 28
    baby boomers **X:** 33
    distribution of **VIII:** 138
    farm **VIII:** 7–8
    Native Americans **X:** 215
    poverty **X:** 245–246
    recreation **X:** 261
    sports **X:** 284, 285
    women's rights and status
        X: 320
income gap **X:** 96
income tax, Confederate **V:** 106,
    349
income tax, corporate. *See*
    corporate income tax
income tax, federal **V:** 105, 349;
    VI: 37, 147, 281, 327*c*; **VIII:**
    409*c*; **X:** 193, 259.
        government **VIII:** 136
        Hull, Cordell **VIII:** 159
        Keynesianism **VIII:** 177
        Revenue Act of 1942 **VIII:**
            308
        taxation **VIII:** 351, 352
incorporation **IV:** 84
In Demand (company) **X:** 244
indentured servitude **II:**
    163–165, 418*c*; **III:** 173,
    199, 200, 326; **IV:** 69
        African Americans **II:** 5
        agriculture **II:** 11–12
        animals **II:** 21
        Burgesses, House of **II:** 44
        Chesapeake Bay **II:** 57
        class **II:** 63
        convict labor **II:** 71–72
        economy **II:** 101
        English immigrants **II:** 108
        environment **II:** 112
        ethnocentrism **II:** 113
        gender **II:** 136
        Georgia **II:** 138
        German immigrants **II:**
            139
        iron manufacturing **II:** 168
        Jamestown **II:** 171–172
        Johnson, Anthony **II:** 175,
            176
        labor **II:** 187–189
        land **II:** 191, 192
        marriage and family life **II:**
            207
        Maryland **II:** 210, 211
        miscegenation **II:** 228
        Mittelberger, Gottlieb **II:**
            231
        Moraley, William **II:** 234
        mortality **II:** 235
        mulattoes **II:** 238
        Native Americans **II:** 244

        Negro Plot of 1741 **II:**
            247–248
        North Carolina **II:** 265
        Philadelphia **II:** 282
        plantation system **II:** 286,
            287
        population trends **II:** 291
        postal service **II:** 292
        redemptioners **II:** 313
        St. Mary's City **II:** 328
        slavery **II:** 339
        suffrage **II:** 364
        tobacco **II:** 374, 375
        Virginia **II:** 382–384
        Virginia Company of
            London **II:** 387
        women's status and rights
            II: 407
        Yeardley, Sir George **II:**
            413
Independence, Missouri
    California gold rush **IV:** 66
    California Trail **IV:** 70
    exploration **IV:** 131
    Santa Fe Trail **IV:** 306
Independence Hall **II:** 153; **III:**
    81, **176**
independence movements. *See*
    wars of national liberation
independence of juries **II:** 153
Independent, The **VI:** 24
independent counsel **X: 150–151**
    Clinton, William **X:** 68
    foreign policy **X:** 124
    Iran-contra affair **X:** 154
    Judicial Watch **X:** 162
    Reno, Janet **X:** 267
    Scalia, Antonin **X:** 271
    Starr, Kenneth **X:** 286–287
    Walsh, Lawrence E. **X:**
        314–315
Independent Counsel Act **X:** 150
Independent Journal **III:** 124
Independent Party **X:** 102
Independent Reflector **III:** 217
Independent Treasury Act of
    1846 **IV:** 378*c*
Independent Treasury System
    IV: 43, 119, 124, 284
independent voters **X:** 237–238
Independent Voters' Association
    VII: 216
Index of American Composers
    VIII: 222
Index of Forbidden Books **I:** 96
India **I:** 386*c*; **II:** 41, 43, 44,
    285; **IV:** 111; **VIII:** 17, 398,
    399; **IX:** 22, 274; **X:** 171, 287
        Cathay (China) **I:** 65
        Dutch East India
            Company **I:** 115
        Gama, Vasco da **I:** 137

        Ibn Battuta **I:** 173
        Jesuits **I:** 189
        Linschoten, Jan Huygen
            van **I:** 207
        Prester John **I:** 292
        printing press **I:** 294
        silver **I:** 325
        slave trade **I:** 328
        Sufism **I:** 337
        sugar **I:** 338
Indiana **V:** 153, 209, 331
    abortion **X:** 2
    canal era **IV:** 74
    ERA **X:** 107
    marriage and family life
        IV: 222
    migration **IV:** 235
    Native Americans in the
        War of 1812 **IV:** 258
    personal liberty laws **IV:**
        280
    population trends **X:** 242
    Quayle, J. Danforth **X:** 253
    rust belt **X:** 269
    women's status and rights
        IV: 367
Indian Affairs, Bureau of (BIA)
    IV: 180–181, 187, 376*c*; **V:**
    264, 265; **VIII:** 163, 235; **IX:**
    13, 227, 228, 297, 331*c*; **X:**
    214, 324*c*
        Burke Act **VII:** 37
        Native Americans **VII:**
            206, 207
        segregation **VII:** 280
        Teapot Dome **VII:** 307
Indian Affairs, Office of **VI:**
    143, **143–144**
        Indian Rights Association
            VI: 145
        Native Americans **VI:**
            207–208
        Nez Perce War **VI:** 213
        Schurz, Carl **VI:** 256
"Indiana Hospital" **V:** 386
Indian Americans **X:** 28, 29, 243
Indian Appropriation Act of
    1871 **VI:** 323*c*
Indiana Territory **III:** 398*c*; **IV:**
    168, 169
Indian Bureau. *See* Indian
    Affairs, Office of
Indian Citizenship Act of 1924
    VII: 206, 207, 360*c*
Indian Civil Rights Act of 1968
    IX: 298, 334*c*; **X:** 215
Indian Claims Commission
    (ICC) **IX: 142–143,** 227,
    329*c*
Indian College **II:** 155
Indian corn **I:** 87
Indian Country **IV:** 235

        Indian Education Act of 1972 **X:**
            214–215
        Indian factory system
            American Fur Company
                IV: 16
            Astor, John Jacob **IV:**
                31–32
            BIA **IV:** 180
            fur trade **IV:** 157
        "Indianist" movement (music)
            VI: 202
        "Indian New Deal" **VIII:** 163,
            235–236
        Indian Ocean **II:** 285; **IV:** 130
        Indianola Council **IX:** 320
        Indian removal **IV:** 264
        Indian Removal Act of 1830 **IV:**
            181–183, 182*m,* 376*c,*
            391–392
                BIA **IV:** 181
                internal improvements **IV:**
                    188
                Jackson, Andrew **IV:** 193
                migration **IV:** 235
                Native Americans **IV:** 255,
                    256
                Permanent Indian Frontier
                    IV: 279
                race and race relations **IV:**
                    291
                Seminole wars **IV:** 312
                Supreme Court decision
                    IV: 331
                Trail of Tears **IV:** 343, 344
        Indian Reorganization Act **VIII:**
            13, **163–164,** 235, 236, 406*c*;
            IX: 227
        Indian revolts **II:** 303, 304, 318
        Indian Rights Association **VI:**
            144–145, 207
        Indians. *See* Native Americans
        Indian schools **II:** 67, 83, 103,
            295, 395–396; **VI:** 208
        Indian Self-Determination and
            Education Assistance Act of
            1975 **X:** 214–215
        Indian Sketches (MacDowell)
            VI: 183
        Indians of All Tribes **X:** 323*c*
        Indians of the Desert Southwest
            II: 165–166
        Indian Territory (Oklahoma) **VI:**
            207, 213, 324*c*; **VII:** 357*c*
                BIA **IV:** 181
                Fort Laramie **IV:** 144
                Jackson, Andrew **IV:** 193
                Native Americans **IV:** 256
                Native Americans in the
                    War of 1812 **IV:** 260
                Trail of Tears **IV:** 344
        Indian Tract Manor **II:** 390
        Indian treaties **IV:** 281, 282

Indian wars **VI:** 263
    Reconstruction **V:** 294
    redemption **V:** 297
    rules of war **V:** 306
    tactics and strategy **V:** 346
Indian World (newspaper) **III:** 107
Indies **I:** 84, 95, 335. *See also* East Indies; West Indies
indigenous peoples. *See* Native Americans
indigo **I:** 261; **II: 166,** 419*c*; **IV:** 7, 183; **V:** 1, 276, 329
    Acts of Trade and Navigation **II:** 3
    African Americans **II:** 6
    agriculture **II:** 10
    Charleston **II:** 56
    economy **II:** 101, 102
    labor **II:** 187, 189
    Louisiana **II:** 199, 200
    mercantilism **II:** 221
    merchants **II:** 222
    New Orleans **II:** 258
    Pinckney, Elizabeth Lucas **II:** 284
    plantation system **II:** 286, 287
    slavery **II:** 339
    society, British American **II:** 350
    South Carolina **II:** 354
    Spanish colonies **II:** 355
    tobacco **II:** 374
    trade and shipping **II:** 376
IND (Investigative New Drug) regulations **X:** 189
individualism **V:** 222, 223; **VII:** 185
Indochina **VII:** 338; **VIII:** 398
Indochina Peace Campaign (IPC) **IX:** 131
Indo-China Refugee Act of 1975 **X:** 28
Indonesia **I:** 117; **IX:** 274; **X:** 69, 228–229
"Inducements to the Liking of the Voyage Intended towards Virginia in 40. and 42. Degrees" (Richard Hakluyt, the Elder) **I:** 151
indulgences, sale of **I:** 210–211, 307
industrial accidents **VII:** 297, 342–343
industrial areas **VI:** 54*m*
industrial capacity
    Civil War **V:** 66
    Monitor-Merrimack **V:** 237
    Richmond, Virginia **V:** 303
    war contracting **V:** 387

industrialism **IV:** 98–99
industrialization/Industrial Revolution **III: 177–178,** 395*c*; **IV:** 28, 180, 184, **184–187,** *185,* 186*m;* **V:** 59, 60, 128, **180–181; VI:** xv. *See also* manufacturing and industry
    abolition **V:** 4
    agriculture **IV:** 10; **V:** 7
    architecture **VII:** 16
    child labor **VII:** 44–46
    cities and urban life **IV:** 81–82; **V:** 60, 61; **VII:** 48
    Democratic Party **VI:** 77
    economy **IV:** 118, 119; **V:** 107
    education **IV:** 121–122; **VI:** 90
    foreign policy **VI:** 102; **VII:** 98
    George III, king of Great Britain **III:** 151
    Harpers Ferry, West Virginia **V:** 164
    Haywood, "Big Bill" **VII:** 120
    immigration **IV:** 177; **V:** 175; **VII:** 127
    industrial revolution, second **VI:** 145–147
    IWW **VII:** 129
    journalism **IV:** 197
    labor and labor movements **IV:** 203; **VII:** 151
    labor trends **VI:** 170
    Leo Frank case **VII:** 157
    literature **IV:** 213
    marriage and family life **IV:** 222–223; **V:** 222, 223; **VII:** 171, 172
    mass production. *See* mass production
    Mexican Revolution **VII:** 183
    Morgan, John Pierpont **VI:** 198
    Muller v. Oregon **VII:** 192–193
    New South **VI:** 209–211
    New Unionism **VII:** 212–213
    Nullification Controversy **IV:** 264
    oil industry **VII:** 217
    Owen, Robert **IV:** 272–273
    population trends **III:** 284
    progressivism in the 1890s **VI:** 233
    race and racial conflict **VII:** 248

radicalism **VII:** 250
railroads **VI:** 237
religion **VI:** 241, 242
Republican Party **VI:** 246
science **III:** 321
science and technology **V:** 308, 310
scientific management **VII:** 277
settlement houses **VI:** 259–260
Slater, Samuel **III:** 325–326
socialism **VI:** 267; **VII:** 288
strikes **V:** 340
Strong, Josiah **VI:** 279
Taylor, Frederick W. **VII:** 306–307
Triangle Shirtwaist Fire **VII:** 311–312
welfare capitalism **VII:** 332–333
women's status and rights **IV:** 367
youth **VII:** 350, 351
industrial manpower **VIII:** 375
industrial production **IV:** 117
Industrial Relations Commission (USCIR) **VII:** 2, **128–129,** 152, 154, 212, 358*c*
Industrial Revolution. *See* industrialization/Industrial Revolution
industrial revolution, second **VI: 145–147,** 211, 276
"industrial unionism." *See also* "craft unionism"
    American Federation of Labor **VIII:** 14
    Bridges, Harry **VIII:** 43
    CIO **VIII:** 69
    Hillman, Sidney **VIII:** 146
    labor **VIII:** 179
    Lewis, John L. **VIII:** 186
Industrial Workers of the World (IWW) **VII: 129–131,** *130,* 356*c,* 357*c*
    Committee for Public Information **VII:** 345
    conscription **VII:** 54
    Debs, Eugene V. **VII:** 65
    Espionage Act **VII:** 88
    Flynn, Elizabeth Gurley **VII:** 95
    Greenwich Village **VII:** 115
    labor movement **VII:** 152–154
    Lawrence Strike **VII:** 155–156
    Ludlow Massacre **VII:** 167

Mitchell, John **VII:** 186
National Civic Federation **VII:** 201
New Unionism **VII:** 212, 213
Palmer, A. Mitchell **VII:** 221
Paterson Strike **VII:** 225
preamble to Constitution **VII:** 369
radicalism **VII:** 250, 251
Red Scare **VII:** 259
Russian Revolution **VII:** 270
Sanger, Margaret **VII:** 273
Seattle General Strike **VII:** 279
Sedition Act **VII:** 280
socialism **VII:** 288
Trading with the Enemy Act **VII:** 311
industry. *See* industrialization/Industrial Revolution; manufacturing and industry; mass production
infancy. *See* childhood
Infante Henrique. *See* Henry the Navigator
infant health **VII:** 284
infanticide **I:** 27; **II:** 208
infant mortality **VIII:** 57; **IX:** 249; **X:** 10, 187
infantry **V:** 364
infectious diseases **I:** 106–108, 289. *See also* disease and epidemics
inflation **I:** 61; **IV:** 42, 275; **VI:** 326*c;* **IX:** 70, 90; **X:** 324*c*
    advertising **VIII:** 1
    banking and currency **V:** 23, 24
    bimetallism **VI:** 28
    Confederate States of America **V:** 77
    currency issue **VI:** 72
    economy **V:** 105, 107; **X:** 94, 95
    employment **V:** 116
    energy crisis **X:** 104
    food riots **V:** 129
    Ford, Gerald R. **X:** 121
    Greenback-Labor Party **VI:** 120
    Hayes, Rutherford B. **VI:** 126
    labor **VIII:** 181
    McKinley, William **VI:** 189
    national banking system **VI:** 206
    OPA **VIII:** 254
    Reagan, Ronald W. **X:** 259

inflation *(continued)*
    Reaganomics **X:** 261
    Simpson, Jerry **VI:** 262
    taxation **V:** 349; **VIII:**
        352
    wage and price controls
        VIII: 371; **X:** 313
Influence of Sea Power upon
    History (Mahan) **VII:** 98
influenza **II:** 92, 235, 244; **IV:**
    112, 113
Influenza Epidemic of 1918–19
    VII: 242–243, 359*c*
information exchange **IV:** 82
Information Processing
    Techniques Office (IPTO) **X:**
    152
information technology
    globalization **X:** 131
    media **X:** 184–185
    science and technology **X:**
        273, 275
infrastructure **IV:** 56
In Friendship **IX:** 30
INF Treaty. *See* Intermediate-
    Range and Shorter-Range
    Nuclear Forces Treaty
ingenios **II:** 355
Ingersoll, Jared **III:** **178**
Ingle, Richard **II:** 209, 323
Ingle's Rebellion **II:** 328
Ingram, David **I:** 152, 156,
    177–178, 297
inheritance
    gender **II:** 136, 137
    marriage and family life **II:**
        208
    Maryland **II:** 210
    miscegenation **II:** 228
    primogeniture and entail
        II: 297–298
    society, British American
        II: 350
    Spanish colonies **II:** 357
    tenants **II:** 371
    Van Rensselaer, Maria Van
        Cortlandt **II:** 381
    Warren, Mary Cole **II:**
        392–393
    women's status and rights
        II: 407–408
inheritance tax **VIII:** 308
In Incidents of the Insurrection
    in Western Pennsylvania in
    1794 (Brackenridge) **III:**
    47
injuries, workplace **X:** 225
Inland Steel **IX:** 282
"inner light" **II:** 275, 302, 307,
    410
Inness, George **VI:** 219
Innis, Roy **IX:** 68

Innocents Abroad, The (Twain)
    VI: 298
inns. *See* taverns and inns
Innu. *See* Montagnais-Naskapi
inoculation **II:** 419*c*. *See also*
    smallpox
    Boylston, Zabdiel **II:** 37
    disease **II:** 92
    medicine **II:** 220
    mortality **II:** 235
    printing and publishing **II:**
        299
    smallpox **II:** 345
    Walter, Thomas **II:** 390
Inquiry into the Rights of the
    British Colonies, An (Bland)
    III: 40
inquisition **I:** 178; **II:** 93, 94,
    174, 175
    auto-da-fé **I:** 16
    Calvin, John **I:** 50
    Castile **I:** 63
    Dominicans **I:** 109
    Ferdinand and Isabella **I:**
        128
    Jews (Judaism) **I:** 190, 191
    Yucatán Peninsula **I:** 379
    Zumárraga, Juan de **I:** 382
In re Debs **VI:** 236
In re Lockwood (1893) **VI:** 318
INS. *See* Immigration and
    Naturalization Service
insecticides **VIII:** 9
insider trading **X:** 50
Inspection Act of 1930 **II:** 10
instant messaging **X:** 274
Institute for International
    Economics **X:** 302
Institute for Legislative Action
    (ILA) **X:** 213
Institute for Policy Studies **X:**
    302
Institute for Social and
    Religious Research **VII:** 185
Institutes of the Christian
    Religion (John Calvin) **I:** 50
Instructions of 1786 **III:** 258
insurance **V:** 253; **VI:** 150, 170;
    VII: 325; **VIII:** 209, 265; **IX:**
    334*c;* **X:** 49, 188
    Medicaid **IX:** 196
    Medicare **IX:** 196–197
    public health **IX:** 250
    social **VIII:** 329
Insurance Portability and
    Accountability Act of 1997 **X:**
    164
Insurgent Mexico (Reed) **VII:**
    259
insurrection riots **X:** 255
integrated circuits **IX:** 295,
    332*c;* **X:** 72, 273

integration **IV:** 121, 261; **VI:**
    90–91, 171; **X:** 12, 41, 257.
    See also desegregation;
    horizontal integration;
    vertical integration
    African Americans **VIII:** 4
    censorship **VIII:** 55
    Goodman, Benny **VIII:**
        132
    race and racial conflict
        VIII: 288
integrative cultural diversity **X:**
    257
Intel **X:** 273
intellectual property rights **X:** 74
intelligence **V:** 310, 341; **VIII:**
    164, 409*c*. *See also* espionage
    Berle, Adolf A., Jr. **VIII:**
        35
    code breaking **VIII:** 64–65
    Coral Sea, Battle of the
        VIII: 74
    espionage **VIII:** 104–105
    FBI **VIII:** 115
    FCC **VIII:** 116
    Midway, Battle of **VIII:**
        211
    OSS **VIII:** 256–257
    Pearl Harbor **VIII:**
        263–264
    photography **VIII:** 269
    Sicily **VIII:** 326
    technology **VIII:** 354
    WAVES **VIII:** 379
intelligence tests **VII:** 78, **131**
Inter-Allied Declaration of 1941
    VIII: 365
Inter-American Defense
    College **X:** 173
Inter-American Treaties of 1929
    VIII: 405*c*
Inter-American Treaty of
    Reciprocal Assistance (1974)
    X: 172
Interboro Rapid Transit (IRT)
    VI: 292
Inter Caetera (papal bull) **I:**
    358, 386*c*, 390–392
interchangeable parts **IV:** 91
Intercollegiate Association of
    Amateur Athletes of America
    (IC4A) **VI:** 290
Intercollegiate Football
    Association **VI:** 101
Intercollegiate Society of
    Individualists **X:** 78
intercontinental ballistic missiles
    (ICBMs) **IX:** 16, 270
Interesting Narrative of the Life
    of Olaudah Equiano, or
    Gustavus Vassa, Written by
    Himself **III:** 118, 395*c*

interest rates **VIII:** 34, 341; **X:**
    94–96, 331*c*
Interim Agreement on Strategic
    Offensive Arms **X:** 89, 289
Interior, Department of the **IV:**
    181, **187;** **VII:** 307; **VIII:** 63,
    161; **IX:** 226
    conservation **VI:** 65
    Dawes Severalty Act **VI:**
        76
    Geological Survey, U.S.
        VI: 110, 111
    Indian Affairs, Office of
        VI: 144
    Jackson, Helen Hunt **VI:**
        153
    Schurz, Carl **VI:** 256–257
interior design **VI:** 288
intermarriage **IV:** 366; **V:**
    233–234; **VII:** 248–249. *See*
    also miscegenation
    Cherokee **II:** 58
    ethnocentrism **II:** 113
    fur trade **II:** 130–131
    Jamestown **II:** 171
    Johnson, Sir William **II:**
        177
    Maine **II:** 203
    marriage and family life **II:**
        208
    Pocahontas **II:** 288, 289
    Rolfe, John **II:** 322
    slave codes **II:** 336
    slavery **II:** 342
    South Carolina **II:** 353
    Spanish colonies **II:** 357
    Spanish immigration **II:**
        359
Intermediate-Range and
    Shorter-Range Nuclear
    Forces (INF) Treaty **X:** *151,*
    151–152, 327*c*
    cold war (end of) **X:** 72
    defense policy **X:** 87
    Reagan, Ronald W. **X:** 261
internal improvements **IV:**
    187–190, 189*m*
    American System **IV:** 18
    Bank of the United States,
        Second **IV:** 44
    Bonus Bill **IV:** 56
    Erie Canal **IV:** 130
    National Road **IV:** 253
    Polk, James K. **IV:** 284
    Whig Party **IV:** 362
Internal Revenue Act of 1862 **V:**
    349
Internal Revenue Service (IRS)
    X: 149–150, 162
Internal Revenue taxes **VI:** **147**
Internal Security Act of 1950
    IX: 61, **143–144,** 330*c*

International Association of Machinists (IAM) **VII:** 10

International Bank for Reconstruction and Development (IBRD) **VIII:** 42, 410c. *See also* World Bank

International Brigades **VIII:** 335

International Brotherhood of Electrical Workers **X:** 236

International Brotherhood of Teamsters, Chauffeurs, Warehousemen, and Helpers of America (IBT). *See* Teamsters Union

International Business Machines (IBM) **VIII:** 46; **IX:** 64–65, 97, 216, 334c; **X:** 72, 273, 326c

International Copyright Law of 1891 **VI:** 327c

international economics
    Clinton, William **X:** 67–69
    globalization **X:** 131–132
    United Nations **X:** 307

International Exhibition of Modern Art. *See* Armory Show

International Harvester **VI:** 198; **VII:** 333

International Human Genome Sequencing Consortium **X:** 146

internationalism **VIII:** 123, 366; **IX:** 175

International Jew, The (Ford) **VII:** 14

International Labor Defense Fund (ILDF) **VII:** 53

International Labor Defense (ILD) **VIII:** 227, 319

International Labor Organization **VII:** 360c

International Ladies' Garment Workers Union (ILGWU) **VII: 131–132**
    Asian Americans **VIII:** 26
    ERA **VII:** 87
    Hillman, Sidney **VIII:** 145
    Jews **VIII:** 172
    labor and labor movements **VII:** 152; **VIII:** 180
    Lewis, John L. **VIII:** 186
    National Women's Trade Union League **VII:** 205, 206
    Shirtwaist Makers Strike **VII:** 285

International Longshoremen's and Warehousemen's Union (ILWU) **VIII:** 43

International Migration Society **VI:** 175

international modernism **X:** 27

International Monetary Fund (IMF) **VIII:** 410c; **X:** 132, 192
    Bretton Woods Conference **VIII:** 42
    Eccles, Marriner S. **VIII:** 89
    economy **VIII:** 93
    foreign policy **VIII:** 125
    postwar planning **VIII:** 279

International Organizations Employees Loyalty Board **IX:** 43

International Peace Conference of 1849 **V:** 40

International Planned Parenthood Foundation **VII:** 273

international policeman, U.S. as **X:** 87

International Red Cross **VIII:** 281

international relations. *See* foreign policy

International Space Station **X:** 283

international trade. *See* trade, domestic and foreign

International Treaty Conferences of 1977 **IX:** 12

International Typographical Union **IV:** 203

International Women's Year (IWY) Conference **X:** 116

International Workers Defense League **VII:** 188

International Working People's Association **VI:** 167

Internet **X: 152–154**, 330c. *See also* World Wide Web
    business **X:** 49, 51
    censorship **X:** 60
    Christian Coalition **X:** 61–62
    computers **X:** 74
    economy **X:** 95
    Federal Information Act **X:** 112
    globalization **X:** 131
    Gore, Albert, Jr. **X:** 134
    literature **X:** 178
    media **X:** 187
    music **X:** 203
    popular culture **X:** 239
    pornography **X:** 244, 245
    recreation **X:** 263
    science and technology **X:** 274
    sexual revolution **X:** 277
    television **X:** 296

Internet Explorer program **X:** 330c

Interpretation of Joint Resolution (War Powers Act) **X:** 315

interracial marriage. *See* intermarriage

interstate commerce **IV:** 376c; **VI:** 281, 326c

Interstate Commerce Act (ICA) **VI:** 336–339
    business and government **VI:** 40
    Congress **VI:** 64
    industrial revolution, second **VI:** 146
    Patrons of Husbandry **VI:** 222
    the presidency **VI:** 230
    railroads **VI:** 239
    Sherman Antitrust Act **VI:** 261

Interstate Commerce Commission (ICC) **VI:** 326c, 328c; **VII:** 83, 84, 122, 170, 357c; **IX:** 114
    business and government **VI:** 40
    Hill, James J. **VI:** 129
    railroads **VI:** 239
    Supreme Court **VI:** 281

Interstate Highway Act of 1956 **IX: 144–146,** 332c
    agriculture **IX:** 7
    automobile industry **IX:** 25
    civil defense **IX:** 53
    economy **IX:** 90
    Eisenhower, Dwight D. **IX:** 93
    suburbanization **IX:** 288

interstate highway system **IX:** 145m, 255; **X:** 15

interventionism **VIII:** 313

Intinerario, Voyage ofte Schipvaert naer Oost afte Portugaels Indien (Jan Juygen van Linschoten) **I:** 207

Intolerable Acts **III:** 392c. *See also* Coercive Acts

Intolerance (film) **VII:** 31, 116

Inuit **I:** 133; **II:** 13, 16, 133, **166–167**

Inupiat **II:** 167

Invasion from Mars, The **VIII:** 284

"invention factory" **VI:** 324c

inventions, science, and technology **I: 178–181,** *179;* **II: 330–331, 369–370; III:** 133–134, 141–142, **320–322,** *321;* **IV: 307–309; V: 308–310,** *309;* **VI: 147–150,** *148,* 242, 247, **257–258,** 307; **VII:** xiii, **132–134,** *133,* 261, **275–277; VIII: 317–319, 353–354; IX: 268–271, 293–295; X: 273–275,** *274.* *See also* aviation; computers; electricity
    advertising **VIII:** 1
    agriculture **II:** 9; **IV:** 9; **VI:** 8; **VII:** 6; **VIII:** 8–9; **IX:** 7; **X:** 14–16
    American Philosophical Society **III:** 11, 12
    architecture **IV:** 28; **VII:** 16
    arms race **IX:** 16
    Arnold, "Hap" **VIII:** 22
    art **VII:** 19
    Atomic Energy Commission **IX:** 24
    Balloon Corps **V:** 21–22
    barbed wire **VI:** 20
    Bartram, John **II:** 30
    Bartram, William **III:** 37
    Bell, Alexander Graham **VI:** 25
    Brattle, Thomas **II:** 40
    Bush, Vannevar **VIII:** 44–45
    business **VII:** 38; **VIII:** 46; **X:** 49
    Carter, Landon **II:** 53–54
    Catesby, Mark **II:** 55
    cities and urban life **IV:** 82; **VII:** 48
    Colden, Cadwallader **II:** 66
    Colden, Jane **II:** 66
    Colorado gold rush **IV:** 90
    Comstock Lode **IV:** 96
    Confederate navy **V:** 73
    conservation, environmentalism, and environmental policy **X:** 76–78
    Crèvecoeur, J. Hector St. John de **III:** 98
    Deere, John **IV:** 105–106
    Dow Chemical Corporation **IX:** 82
    Eastman, George **VI:** 87
    economy **IV:** 118; **VII:** 74; **VIII:** 90, 92; **X:** 96
    Edison, Thomas Alva **VI:** 88–89
    education **III:** 114
    Edwards, Jonathan **II:** 105
    Enlightenment **II:** 109, 110
    Erie Canal **IV:** 129
    flour milling **VI:** 101
    FMP **VIII:** 119

inventions, science, and
  technology (*continued*)
    Fordney-McCumber Tariff
      VII: 97
    Franklin Institute **IV:**
      149–150
    Frémont, Jessie Benton
      IV: 152
    General Electric (GE)
      VII: 107; **IX:** 120
    George III, king of Great
      Britain **III:** 151
    Gesner, Conrad von **I:** 140
    globalization **X:** 131–132
    Godfrey, Thomas **II:** 141
    gold, discovery and mining
      IV: 163
    Great Plains Indians **II:**
      150
    Human Genome Project
      X: 145–146
    hydrogen bomb **IX:** 139
    immigration **VI:** 139–140
    industrialization **IV:** 185
    Internet **X:** 152–154
    Inuit **II:** 167
    Jefferson, Thomas **III:**
      184, 185
    Kalm, Peter **II:** 181
    Kinsey, Alfred C. **IX:**
      162–163
    labor, child **VI:** 166
    labor trends **VI:** 170
    Leonardo da Vinci **I:**
      204–205
    Lining, John **II:** 194
    literature **X:** 178
    Logan, James **II:** 198
    magazines **VI:** 185
    mariners **II:** 204
    Massachusetts **II:** 215
    Mather, Cotton **II:** 217
    McCormick, Cyrus Hall
      IV: 224–225
    medicine **III:** 240–241; **IV:**
      229; **IX:** 197–199; **X:**
      187–191
    merchant marine **VI:**
      192–193
    Middletown **VII:** 185
    midwives **II:** 225
    mills **II:** 225, 226
    mining: metal and coal **VI:**
      193, 194
    mobilization **VIII:** 215
    Morse, Samuel F. B. **IV:**
      245–246
    movie industry **VII:** 190
    movies **IX:** 210–211
    music **VIII:** 221; **X:** 202,
      203
    NASA **IX:** 219–220

National Institutes of
  Health **IX:** 222–223
National Road **IV:** 255
Native Americans **II:** 243
newspapers **VI:** 211, 212
New York World's Fair
  (1939–40) **VIII:** 246
OSRD **VIII:** 255–256
Paine, Thomas **III:** 271
Pennsylvania **II:** 274,
  276–277
Philadelphia Centennial
  Exposition **VI:** 223–224
Point Four Program **IX:**
  242–243
Priestley, Joseph **III:** 285
printing press **I:** 293–295
race and race relations **IV:**
  290
radio **VII:** 253–255; **VIII:**
  289–291
religion **VIII:** 303
Rittenhouse, David **II:**
  322; **III:** 309–310
Rush, Benjamin **III:** 312
rust belt **X:** 269
science and technology **IV:**
  307; **VIII:** 317
SDI **X:** 289–290
silver **I:** 325
space exploration **IX:**
  278–279
space policy **X:** 281, 283
Spanish Armada **I:** 334
steel and steel industry **VI:**
  276–278; **VII:** 297
tactics and strategy **V:**
  346
tariffs **VII:** 306
technology **II:** 369; **VIII:**
  353
telegraph **V:** 350–351
Tenochtitlán **I:** 344
Tesla, Nikola **VI:** 285
Webster, Noah **III:** 370
World War II **VIII:** 390
World War II home front
  VIII: 395
Zacatecas **I:** 381
Investigative New Drug (IND)
  regulations **X:** 189
investigative reporting **VI:** 212;
  VII: 141–142
Investiture Controversy **I:** 165
investment, foreign. *See* foreign
  investment
investment banking. *See*
  banking, investment
investments, American, abroad
  VI: 150, 272
Invisible Empire. *See* Ku Klux
  Klan

Invisible Empire (Tourgée) **V:**
  354
Invisible Man, The (Ralph
  Ellison) **IX:** 5, 182, 331*c*
Iola Leroy (Harper) **V:** 164
Ionic columns **IV:** 27
Iouskeha **I:** 1
Iowa **VI:** 221; **X:** 242
  Black Hawk War **IV:** 52,
    53
  claim clubs **IV:** 85
  migration **IV:** 236
  Mormon Trail **IV:** 242
  Native Americans **IV:** 256
  religion **IV:** 299
Iowa Territory **IV:** 153
IPC (Indochina Peace
  Campaign) **IX:** 131
IPTO (Information Processing
  Techniques Office) **X:** 152
Ique **I:** 28
IRA (Irish Republican Army) **X:**
  195
Iran **IX:** 50, 60, 201; **X:** 326*c*
  Farrakhan, Louis A. **X:** 111
  foreign policy **X:** 122
  Iran-contra affair **X:**
    154–155
  Iranian hostage crisis **X:**
    155–156
  North, Oliver L. **X:** 222
  OPEC **X:** 228–229
  Perot, H. Ross **X:** 234
  Reagan, Ronald W. **X:** 260
  terrorism **X:** 297
Iran-contra affair **X: 154–155,**
  327*c*
  Boland Amendment **X:** 38
  Bush, George H. W. **X:** 45
  cold war (end of) **X:** 72
  contras **X:** 81
  economy **X:** 94
  energy crisis **X:** 104
  foreign policy **X:** 124
  independent counsel **X:**
    150
  Mitchell, George **X:** 194,
    195
  North, Oliver L. **X:** 222
  Reagan, Ronald W. **X:** 260
  terrorism **X:** 298
  Tower Commission **X:**
    305–306
  Walsh, Lawrence E. **X:**
    314–315
Iranian hostage crisis **X:** *155,*
  155–156, 326*c*
  Carter, James Earl, Jr. **X:**
    58–59
  economy **X:** 94
  foreign policy **X:** 123
  terrorism **X:** 297

Iraq **IX:** 146; **X:** 328*c*
  Bush, George H. W. **X:** 46
  Clinton, William **X:** 67, 69
  defense policy **X:** 87
  Farrakhan, Louis A. **X:** 111
  foreign policy **X:** 124
  Iranian hostage crisis **X:**
    156
  NATO **X:** 223
  OPEC **X:** 228–229
  Persian Gulf War **X:**
    234–236
  United Nations **X:** 307
IRCA. *See* Immigration Reform
  and Control Act of 1986
Iredell, James **III:** 338
Ireland **I:** 385*c,* 387*c;* **II:** 135,
  150, 151, 338, 387, 405; **IV:**
  115, 241; **V:** 67, 276; **VI:** 309;
  IX: 194; **X:** 69, 195
  Anglo-Normans **I:** 10–11
  art and architecture **I:**
    12–13
  Bristol **I:** 35
  Carey, Mathew **III:** 61
  commonwealthmen **III:**
    80
  Elizabeth I **I:** 120
  Gilbert, Sir Humphrey **I:**
    141
  immigration **III:** 173
  monsters **I:** 239
  population trends **III:** 283
  printing press **I:** 294
  Ralegh, Sir Walter **I:** 303
  Scotch-Irish **III:** 322
Irish, Ned **VIII:** 336
Irish-American regiments (Civil
  War) **V:** 176, 177, **181–182,**
  182
Irish Americans **IV:** 179*t;* **VII:**
  247; **VIII: 164–165.** *See also*
  Scots-Irish immigrants
    anti-Catholic riots **IV:** 21,
      23
    boxing **VI:** 32, 33
    canal era **IV:** 74
    Catholics **VIII:** 53
    cities and urban life **IV:** 81;
      V: 60
    Civil War **IV:** 180
    class consciousness **VI:** 57
    Copperheads **V:** 82
    Democratic Party **VIII:** 80
    diseases and epidemics **IV:**
      111
    economy **IV:** 117
    Erie Canal **IV:** 129
    Farley, James A. **VIII:**
      110–111
    Flynn, Edward J. **VIII:**
      122–123

Forrestal, James V. **VIII:** 126
immigration **IV:** 177–179, *178;* **V:** 175, 176; **VI:** 138
indentured servitude **II:** 164
Irish-American regiments **V:** 181–182
Italian Americans **VIII:** 167
Johnston, Henrietta Deering **II:** 177–178
Kennedy, Joseph P. **VIII:** 175–176
Know-Nothing Party **IV:** 201, 202
labor movements **IV:** 204, 205
Locke, John **II:** 198
Maine **II:** 203
Memphis riot **V:** 232
Molly Maguires **VI:** 195–196
Murray, Philip **VIII:** 221
nativism **V:** 251
Negro Plot of 1741 **II:** 248
New Hampshire **II:** 251
New York City **II:** 263; **V:** 253–254
New York City draft riots **V:** 255
Pacific Railroad Act of 1862 **V:** 263
Philadelphia **II:** 281
population trends **II:** 291; **V:** 277
race and racial conflict **IV:** 292; **VIII:** 288
railroads **V:** 290
Reconstruction Acts **V:** *295*
redemptioners **II:** 313
religion **IV:** 298
Roman Catholicism **VI:** 249
Roman Catholics **II:** 324
transportation **V:** 355
women's status and rights **II:** 407
Zouaves **V:** 403
Irish Brigade **V:** 181–182
Irish Catholics **IV:** 281; **V:** 340
Irish Land Question (George) **VI:** 111
Irish nationalism **V:** 177
Irish potato famine **V:** 175
Irish Republican Army (IRA) **X:** 195
Irish World and American Industrial Liberator **VI:** 111
iron, pig **IV:** 118, 184
Iron Acts **II: 167,** 168, 203

iron and iron manufacturing **I:** 195; **II: 167–168; IV:** 184, 186*m;* **V:** 180, 356; **VI:** 194*m*
artisans **II:** 26
Bessemer process **VI:** 27
Frick, Henry Clay **VI:** 105
industrial revolution, second **VI:** 145
manufacturing and industry **II:** 204
Maryland **II:** 210
Massachusetts **II:** 215
mercantilism **II:** 221
mining: metal and coal **VI:** 193
New Jersey **II:** 253
New South **VI:** 209, 210
steel **VI:** 277
technology **II:** 369
trade **VI:** 291
trusts **VI:** 292
Virginia Company of London **II:** 387
Iron and Steel Institute **VIII:** 317
ironclad oath **V: 182–183,** 218, 219, 292, 385, 406*c*
ironclads **V: 183–184; VI:** 85
Civil War **V:** 66
Confederate navy **V:** 73, 74
Dahlgren, John A. B. **V:** 87
foreign policy **V:** 132
Mallory, Stephen R. **V:** 221
Mississippi River **V:** 234
Mobile campaign **V:** 236
Monitor-Merrimack **V:** 237–239
New Orleans, Battle of **V:** 252
Peninsular campaign **V:** 267
science and technology **V:** 309
Tredegar Iron Works **V:** 356
Union navy **V:** 368, 370
Welles, Gideon **V:** 391
Iron Curtain, collapse of **X: 156–157**
iron foundries **V:** 356
iron lung **VIII:** 207
Iron Molders International Union **V:** 248; **VII:** 36
iron ore **IV:** 361
iron tools **II:** 167, 369, 375
ironware **IV:** 184
Iroquoia (region) **II:** 379
Iroquois **I: 181–183,** 387*c;* **II:** *64,* **168–170,** 169*m,* 419*c;* **IV:** 156, 183, 258. *See also* Five Nations of the Iroquois

Confederation; Six Nations of the Iroquois
agriculture **II:** 8–9
Albany Congress **II:** 14
Algonquin **II:** 17
Andros, Sir Edmund **II:** 19
architecture **II:** 22
art **II:** 24
art and architecture **I:** 12
Beaver Wars **II:** 31
Brulé, Étienne **II:** 44
captivity **II:** 51
Cartier, Jacques **I:** 58
Catawba **II:** 55
Cayuga **I:** 66–67
Cherokee **II:** 57
Chesapeake Bay **II:** 58
Conestoga **II:** 67
Croghan, George **II:** 76
Dekanawideh **II:** 85
De Lancey, James **II:** 85
disease **II:** 90
French colonies **II:** 126–127, 129
gender **II:** 137
Hendrick **II:** 155
Hochelaga **I:** 163
Huron **I:** 171; **II:** 160
Jesuits **II:** 174
Johnson, Sir William **II:** 177
King William's War **II:** 185
Livingston, Robert **II:** 196
Logan, James **II:** 198
marriage and family life **II:** 206
"Mary Jemison's Account of Her Capture by" **II:** 426
Mohawk **I:** 238
monarchy, British **II:** 232
Montagnais-Naskapi **I:** 241
Montour, Andrew **II:** 233
Montour, Madame **II:** 233
Native American religion **I:** 252
Native Americans **II:** 242–243, 246
Neolin **II:** 248
New Hampshire **II:** 251
New Netherland **II:** 255, 256
New York **II:** 259, 260, 262
Nicolet, Jean **II:** 263
North Carolina **II:** 263, 264
Queen Anne's War **II:** 309
religion, Native American **II:** 317
revitalization movements **II:** 320
sachems **II:** 3327

Seneca **I:** 321
Seven Years' War **II:** 332
shamans **II:** 335
smallpox **II:** 345
society, British American **II:** 352
Society for the Propagation of the Gospel in Foreign Parts **II:** 352
Teedyuscung **II:** 370
Tuscarora **II:** 378–379
Tuscarora War **II:** 379
Walking Purchase of 1737 **II:** 389
Weiser, Johann Conrad **II:** 393
women's status and rights **II:** 406
Iroquois Confederacy **III: 178–179,** 392*c*–394*c;* **V:** 265
Brant, Joseph **III:** 48
Cornplanter **III:** 91
Fort Stanwix, Treaty of **III:** 132
Handsome Lake **III:** 164
Lee, Arthur **III:** 205
Native Americans and the Revolution **III:** 254, 255
Pickering, John **III:** 276
Pontiac's Rebellion **III:** 281
Red Jacket **III:** 297
Sullivan, John **III:** 337
Iroquois Homelands, invasion of **III:** 254*m*
Iroquois League **I:** 160–161, 272, 321
Iroquois Wars **IV:** 156
irrigation **II:** 8, 165, 247, 286; **VI:** 228; **VII:** 203–204
IRS. *See* Internal Revenue Service
IRT (Interboro Rapid Transit) **VI:** 292
Irving, Sir Henry **VI:** 286
Irving, Washington **III:** 283; **IV:** 196, 211, 212
Isabella. *See* Ferdinand and Isabella
Isabella, Hispaniola **I:** 39, 82, 161
Ishii, Kikujiro **VII:** 359*c*
Islam **I: 183–185; II:** 4, 314; **VI:** 243; **IX:** 214–215; **X: 157.** *See also* Nation of Islam
Askia Muhammad I **I:** 14
auto-da-fé **I:** 16
Baba, Ahmad **I:** 23
Cabral, Pedro Álvares **I:** 44
Cameroon **I:** 52
Castile **I:** 62
Cathay (China) **I:** 64

Islam (continued)
Cayor **I:** 66
Columbus, Christopher **I:** 81
Dagomba **I:** 101
Darfur **I:** 102
Dengel, Lebna **I:** 104
Djibouti **I:** 109
Ethiopia **I:** 124, 125
Ferdinand and Isabella **I:** 127
Fulani **I:** 135
Gao **I:** 139
Ghana **I:** 141
Guinea-Bisseau **I:** 147
Hausa **I:** 155
Holy League **I:** 164–165
Ibn Battuta **I:** 173
Kotoko **I:** 196
Mali **I:** 217, 218
Mansa Musa I **I:** 220
marabout **I:** 221–223
Mecca **I:** 230
Mossi **I:** 244
Niger River **I:** 263
Philip II **I:** 281
Reconquista **I:** 306
religion **X:** 265
RFRA **X:** 266
Sahara **I:** 317
slavery **I:** 326
slave trade **I:** 328
Songhai **I:** 331
Sudan **I:** 337
Sufism **I:** 337
Suleiman I **I:** 339
Sundiata Keita **I:** 340
Taureg **I:** 360
Timbuktu **I:** 350
Islamic fundamentalism **IX:** 201
Islamic Jihad **X:** 297
Island Carib. *See* Carib
Islands of Devils. *See* Bermuda
Isle La Motte **II:** 381
Isle of the Saints **I:** 34
Isle of Wight **II:** 95
Isles of Shoals **II:** 250
isolationists/isolationism **VIII:** **165–166,** 409c
aircraft industry **VIII:** 10
America First Committee **VIII:** 12–13
Anglo-American relations **VIII:** 16
Atlantic Charter **VIII:** 28
Borah, William E. **VIII:** 40
cash-and-carry **VIII:** 53
Communists **VIII:** 65
Congress **VIII:** 67
conservatism **VIII:** 72
destroyers-for-bases deal **VIII:** 82

election of 1940 **VIII:** 98
Ethiopia **VIII:** 105
foreign policy **VIII:** 123
Hearst, William Randolph **VII:** 121
Hoover, Herbert **VIII:** 152
Johnson, Hiram Warren **VII:** 137–138
labor **VIII:** 181
La Follette, Robert **VII:** 155
La Follette, Robert M., Jr. **VIII:** 182
Lend-Lease Act **VIII:** 184
Luce, Henry R. **VIII:** 196
Manchuria **VIII:** 199
Munich Conference **VIII:** 220
neutrality **VII:** 210
Neutrality Acts **VIII:** 239
Norris, George W. **VIII:** 249
Nye Committee **VIII:** 250
Popular Front **VIII:** 276
Republican Party **VIII:** 305
Roosevelt, Franklin D. **VIII:** 313
socialists **VIII:** 327
Taft, Robert A. **VIII:** 349
Wheeler, Burton K. **VIII:** 377, 378
World Disarmament Conference **VIII:** 388
World War I **VII:** 343
Israel **I:** 22, 113; **VIII:** 173, 366, 403; **IX:** 330c, 332c; **X:** 325c, 330c. *See also* Arab-Israeli conflict
Bunche, Ralph **IX:** 43
Bush, George H. W. **X:** 46
Camp David accords **X:** 54–55
Carter, James Earl, Jr. **X:** 58
Clinton, William **X:** 69
cold war (end of) **X:** 70
energy crisis **X:** 104
foreign policy **X:** 123
and foreign policy **IX:** **146–147**
Haig, Alexander M., Jr. **X:** 140
Iran-contra affair **X:** 154
Jews and Judaism **X:** 161–162
Kissinger, Henry A. **X:** 166
Middle East **IX:** 201
Mitchell, George **X:** 195
OPEC **X:** 229
Suez crisis **IX:** 288, 289
terrorism **X:** 298

Truman, Harry **IX:** 299
United Nations **X:** 307
Israeli-Egyptian Peace Treaty of 1979 **X:** 325c
Isserles, Moses **I:** 192
Isserman, Abraham **IX:** 80
Istanbul **I:** 339
Isthmus of Panama **I:** 276
It (film) **VII:** 87
Italian Americans **VI:** 171; **VII:** 247, 273, 311; **VIII:** 167, **167–168**
Catholics **VIII:** 53
civil liberties **VIII:** 61
DiMaggio, Joe **VIII:** 83–84
enemy aliens **VIII:** 102
World War II home front **VIII:** 395
Italian campaign **VIII:** **168**
amphibious warfare **VIII:** 15
Army, U.S. **VIII:** 19
Axis **VIII:** 31
North African campaign **VIII:** 250
Sicily **VIII:** 325
World War II European theater **VIII:** 393
Italian POWs **VIII:** 282
Italy **II:** 252, 338; **IV:** 156; **V:** 403; **VI:** 184–185, 216, 328c; **VII:** 360c; **VIII:** 393, 409c, 410c; **IX:** 194, 231–233; **X:** 223
Axis **VIII:** 31–32
bubonic plague **I:** 285
cabinet of curiosities **I:** 40
Canary Islands **I:** 53
code breaking **VIII:** 64
diseases **I:** 106
Ethiopia **VIII:** 105
foreign policy **VIII:** 124
Holy League **I:** 164
immigration **VII:** 127t
Italian Americans **VIII:** 167
Jesuits **I:** 189
Jews (Judaism) **I:** 191
Munich Conference **VIII:** 220
Naval Disarmament Conference **VII:** 209
Patton, George **VIII:** 263
population trends **I:** 290
Reformation **I:** 309
Sicily **VIII:** 325–326
slavery **I:** 327
Spanish Civil War **VIII:** 334
submarines **VIII:** 342
Wilson, Woodrow **VII:** 334

World War I **VII:** 343
World War II European theater **VIII:** 391, 392
It Can't Happen Here (Lewis) **VIII:** 120
It Happened One Night (film) **VIII:** 52, 218
Itoyatan **II:** 294
It's a Wonderful Life (film) **VIII:** 52
Iturbide, Agustín de **IV:** 303
Itzá **I:** 70
Itzcóatl **I:** 17, **185,** 342, 351
Iuka, Battle at **V:** 305
Ivan the Terrible **I:** 265
Ives, Charles **VII:** 195
Ives v. South Buffalo Railway Company **VII:** 343
Ivory Cost **II:** 4
IWA (Marxist International Workingmen's Association) **VI:** 267
"I Will Fight No More Forever" speech (Chief Joseph) **VI:** 329–330
Iwo Jima **VIII:** **168–169,** 410c
amphibious warfare **VIII:** 15
Forrestal, James V. **VIII:** 126
Hiroshima and Nagasaki **VIII:** 148
Marines, U.S. **VIII:** 203
Navy, U.S. **VIII:** 236
Nimitz, Chester W. **VIII:** 246
photography **VIII:** 268
World War II Pacific theater **VIII:** 399
IWW. *See* Industrial Workers of the World
IWW Constitution, preamble to **VII:** 369
IWY (International Women's Year) Conference **X:** 116
Ix Chel **I:** 97
Ixtapalpa **I:** 99
Ixtlilxóchitl **I:** 45
Iztapalapa **I:** 317

J

Jack, Homer **IX:** 66
Jack Benny Program (radio show) **VIII:** 274
Jackson, Andrew **IV:** **191–194,** **192,** 375c–377c; **VI:** 205, 229
abolition **V:** 3
Adams, John Quincy **IV:** 5
Adams-Onís Treaty **IV:** 5
American Revolution **III:** 13

American System **IV:** 19
Austin, Stephen F. **IV:** 38
banking and currency **IV:** *41*, 42, 43
Bank of the United States, Second **IV:** 44
Benton, Thomas Hart **IV:** 49
BIA **IV:** 181
Black Hawk War **IV:** 53
Blair, Francis P., Jr. **V:** 30
Bowie, Jim **IV:** 56
Calhoun, John C. **IV:** 62, 63
Cass, Lewis **IV:** 76
Cherokee nation **III:** 66
Claiborne, William C. C. **IV:** 84, 85
Clay, Henry **IV:** 86–87
Creek nation **III:** 97
Crockett, Davy **IV:** 99, 100
Democratic Party **IV:** 107, 108; **V:** 94
Douglas, Stephen A. **V:** 97
economy **IV:** 119
election of 1828 **IV:** 122–124
election of 1840 **IV:** 124
Fillmore, Millard **IV:** 137
Florida **III:** 129; **IV:** 139, 140
foreign policy **IV:** 141, 142
Frémont, Jessie Benton **IV:** 152
frontier **III:** 141
Gadsden Purchase **IV:** 159
Ghent, Treaty of (1814) **IV:** 161
Harrison, William Henry **IV:** 169, 170
Horseshoe Bend, Battle of **IV:** 173
Houston, Sam **IV:** 173, 174
immigration **IV:** 179
Indian Removal Act (1830) **IV:** 183
internal improvements **IV:** 188
Johnson, Andrew **V:** 187
Lafitte, Jean **IV:** 206
liberty tree/pole **III:** 214
Marshall, John **III:** 237
Mexican-American War **IV:** 232
migration **IV:** 235
national debt **III:** 253
Native Americans **IV:** 255–257
Native Americans in the War of 1812 **IV:** 259, 260

New Orleans, Battle of (1815) **IV:** 262
Niles, Hezekiah **III:** 258
Nullification Controversy **IV:** 264–265
Panic of 1837 **IV:** 276
Permanent Indian Frontier **IV:** 279
Pierce, Franklin **V:** 275
political parties **III:** 279
Polk, James K. **IV:** 282
race and race relations **IV:** 291
secession **V:** 311
Seminole wars **IV:** 312
Story, Joseph **III:** 334
Supreme Court decision **IV:** 331
Texas **IV:** 338
Trail of Tears **IV:** 343, 344
Tyler, John **IV:** 348
Van Buren, Martin **IV:** 351
War of 1812 **IV:** 356, 358
Webster, Daniel **IV:** 360
Whig Party **IV:** 362–364
Jackson, Charles Thomas **IV:** 245
Jackson, Claiborne Fox **V:** 152
Jackson, David
  Ashley, William Henry **IV:** 29
  Rocky Mountain Fur Company **IV:** 302
  Smith, Jedediah Strong **IV:** 321
  Sublette, William **IV:** 330
Jackson, Helen Hunt **VI: 153,** 177, *325c,* 330–332
Jackson, Henry **X:** 86, 118
Jackson, Jesse L. **IX:** 274; **X:** *159,* **159–160,** *327c*
  abortion **X:** 3
  African Americans **X:** 12
  NAACP **X:** 208
Jackson, Jimmy Lee **IX:** 284
Jackson, Kate **VI:** 315
Jackson, Michael **X:** 202, 203, 240
Jackson, Mississippi **IX:** 114
Jackson, Rachel **IV:** 123
Jackson, Robert **VIII:** 178, *346t;* **IX:** 315; **X:** 264
Jackson, Shoeless Joe **VII:** 26
Jackson, Thomas J. "Stonewall" **IV:** 40; **V: 185–186,** *186,* **406c, 407c**
  Antietam, Battle of **V:** 11
  Boyd, Belle **V:** 34
  Bull Run, First Battle of **V:** 42
  Bull Run, Second Battle of **V:** 43–44
  cartography **V:** 51

Cedar Mountain, Battle of **V:** 53
Chancellorsville, Battle of **V:** 54, 55
espionage **V:** 118
Ewell, Richard Stoddert **V:** 118, 119
Fredericksburg, Battle of **V:** 139, 141
Harpers Ferry, West Virginia **V:** 165
Hill, Ambrose P. **V:** 168
homefront **V:** 169
Hood, John Bell **V:** 170
Howard, O. O. **V:** 173
Lee, Robert E. **V:** 206
Longstreet, James **V:** 215, 216
McClellan, George B. **V:** 225, 226
monuments **V:** 239
Peninsular campaign **V:** 267, 269
Shenandoah Valley
  Jackson's campaign **V:** 316
  Sheridan's campaign **V:** 317
Stuart, J. E. B. **V:** 341
volunteer army **V:** 383
Jackson 5 **X:** 240
Jackson Hole National Monument **VII:** 13
Jackson State University **IX:** 310; **X: 160**
Jacksonville, Florida **V:** 167
Jacobeans **I:** 74
Jacobellis v. Ohio (1964) **X:** 60
Jacobin clubs **III:** 105
Jacobins **III:** 271
Jacobs, B. F. **VI:** 241
Jacobs, Helen **VIII:** 337
Jacobsen, Cornelis **II:** 274
Jacobsen, David **X:** 154
Jagas **I:** 27
Jagger, Mick **IX:** 218
jail population **X:** 81, 83
jails **II:** 24, 75
Jamaica **I: 83, 187,** 250, 342
  Caribbean **II:** 52, 53
  convict labor **II:** 72
  piracy **II:** 284–286
  Royal African Company **II:** 325
  slavery **II:** 338
  Spanish colonies **II:** 355, 356
  theater **II:** 373
James, duke of York
  government, British American **II:** 144
  New Jersey **II:** 252

New York **II:** 260–261
New York City **II:** 262
Penn, William **II:** 273
Pennsylvania **II:** 274
James, Frank **V:** 46, 285, *408c;* **VI:** 98
James, Harry **VIII:** 326
James, Henry **VI: 153–154;** **VII:** 160; **X:** 179
  Crane, Stephen **VI:** 68
  Howells, William Dean **VI:** 136
  James, William **VI:** 154
  Lazarus, Emma **VI:** 172
  literature **VI:** 178
James, Jesse **V:** 46, 285, *408c*
James, Thomas L. **VI:** 275
James, Wilkie **V:** 125
James, William **VI: 154–155,** *155,* 229, *326c;* **VII:** 229
James I, king of England **I: 187–188,** *388c*
  Acadia **I:** 3
  Bermuda Company **I:** 29
  Calvert, George **II:** 50
  Dale, Sir Thomas **II:** 81
  English Civil War **II:** 108
  Gates, Sir Thomas **II:** 135
  Maryland **II:** 209
  monarchy, British **II:** 232
  Purchas, Samuel **I:** 297
  Ralegh, Sir Walter **I:** 303, 304
  Rolfe, John **II:** 322–323
  Sandys, Sir Edwin **I:** 318
  Shakespeare, William **I:** 324
  tobacco **I:** 353
  Virginia **II:** 382
  Virginia Company of London **II:** 385, 387
  Yeardley, Sir George **II:** 413
James II, king of England **III:** 374; **IV:** 362
  Connecticut **II:** 69
  Delaware **II:** 87
  Dominion of New England **II:** 95
  Glorious Revolution **II:** 140–141
  Harris, Benjamin **II:** 154
  King William's War **II:** 185
  Maryland **II:** 210
  Massachusetts **II:** 214
  Mather, Cotton **II:** 217
  Mather, Increase **II:** 218
  monarchy, British **II:** 232
  New York **II:** 261
  Pennsylvania **II:** 276
  Roman Catholics **II:** 324

James IV, king of Scotland **I:** 159
James VI, king of Scotland. *See*
   James I, king of England
James B. Eads Bridge **VI:** 35,
   44, 324*c*
James River **V:** 303
Jamestown **I:** 388*c*; **II:** 28, 45,
   171–173, 417*c*
   African Americans **II:** 5
   agriculture **II:** 9–10, 12
   Algonquin **II:** 17
   Bacon's Rebellion **II:** 27–28
   Bermuda Company **I:** 29
   Burgesses, House of **II:** 44
   captivity **II:** 51
   Chesapeake Bay **II:** 58
   crowd action **II:** 77
   De La Warr, Lord **I:**
      103–104
   diseases **I:** 108; **II:** 90
   English immigrants **II:** 108
   environment **II:** 111
   Florida **II:** 120
   Gates, Sir Thomas **II:**
      135–136
   German immigrants **II:** 139
   indentured servitude **II:**
      163
   iron manufacturing **II:** 167
   labor **II:** 187–188
   lotteries **II:** 199
   miscegenation **II:** 228
   monarchy, British **II:** 232
   Native Americans **II:** 244
   Newport, Christopher **II:**
      259
   Pilgrims **II:** 283
   Pocahontas **II:** 288
   Powhatan (chief) **II:**
      293–294
   Powhatan Confederacy **II:**
      294–295
   privateering **II:** 299
   Roanoke **I:** 314
   Rolfe, John **II:** 322
   Sandys, Sir Edwin **I:** 318
   slave trade **II:** 343
   Smith, John **II:** 346, 347
   tobacco **II:** 374
   trade and shipping **II:** 375
   travel **II:** 377
   Virginia **II:** 382, 383
   Virginia Company of
      London **II:** 387
"Jane" **IX:** 325
Japan **IV:** 379*c*; **V:** 405*c*; **VI:**
   103, 141, 216–217, 328*c*; **VII:**
   357*c*, 359*c*, 360*c*; **VIII:** 405*c*,
   408*c*–411*c*
   air power **VIII:** 11, 12
   amphibious warfare **VIII:**
      15

Anglo-American relations
   VIII: 16
Army, U.S. **VIII:** 19
Army Air Forces, U.S.
   VIII: 20
Asia (foreign policy) **IX:**
   21
atomic bomb **VIII:** 28–29
automobile industry **X:**
   31–32
Axis **VIII:** 31–32
Bataan Death March **VIII:**
   34–35
Casablanca Conference
   VIII: 52
cash-and-carry **VIII:** 53
Clinton, William **X:** 69
code breaking **VIII:** 64
cold war **IX:** 58
Coral Sea, Battle of the
   VIII: 74
demobilization **VIII:** 79
dollar diplomacy **VII:** 70
economy **X:** 94
energy crisis **X:** 104
espionage **VIII:** 104
Fillmore, Millard **IV:** 137
foreign policy **IV:** 143; **VII:**
   99, 100; **VIII:** 123–126;
   X: 122
Gentlemen's Agreement
   VII: 107–108
globalization **X:** 131
Grand Alliance **VIII:** 136,
   137
Great White Fleet **VII:**
   114
Guadalcanal **VIII:** 141
Halsey, "Bull" **VIII:** 143
Hiroshima and Nagasaki
   VIII: 146–148
Hoover presidency **VIII:**
   155
Hull, Cordell **VIII:** 160
intelligence **VIII:** 164
Iwo Jima **VIII:** 168–169
labor **X:** 170
Latin America **X:** 173
Leyte Gulf, Battle for
   VIII: 186–187
London Naval Conference
   VIII: 194
MacArthur, Douglas **IX:**
   186
Manchuria **VIII:** 199–200
Manifest Destiny **IV:** 219
Mariana Islands **VIII:** 202
Midway, Battle of **VIII:**
   211
Mondale, Walter F. **X:** 197
Munich Conference **VIII:**
   220

Naval Disarmament
   Conference **VII:** 209,
   210
Okinawa **VIII:** 259
OPEC **X:** 229
Open Door Policy **VII:**
   218, 219
Oppenheimer, J. Robert
   IX: 237
OSS **VIII:** 257
Pearl Harbor **VIII:**
   263–265
Perry, Matthew Calbraith
   IV: 279, 280
Philippines **VIII:** 266–267
Philippine Sea, Battle of
   the **VIII:** 267
Potsdam Conference **VIII:**
   279
POWs **VIII:** 281, 282
propaganda **VIII:** 283
Roosevelt, Theodore **VII:**
   266
Root-Takahira Agreement
   VII: 267–268
Russo-Japanese War **VII:**
   271
second front **VIII:** 320
Siberian Expedition **VII:**
   285
Solomon Islands **VIII:**
   330–331
Southeast Asia Treaty
   Organization **IX:** 274
Soviet-American relations
   VIII: 333, 334
space policy **X:** 281, 283
steel industry **VII:** 298;
   VIII: 339; **IX:** 282
Tarawa **VIII:** 350
Teheran Conference **VIII:**
   354
terrorism **X:** 299
Washington Conference
   on Naval Disarmament
   VII: 331
World Disarmament
   Conference **VIII:** 388
World War I **VII:** 343
World War II European
   theater **VIII:** 391
World War II Pacific
   theater **VIII:** 396
Yalta Conference **VIII:**
   401
Japan, surrender of **VIII:** 411*c*
   demobilization **VIII:** 79
   mobilization **VIII:** 215
   Nimitz, Chester W. **VIII:**
      246
   Potsdam Conference **VIII:**
      279, 280

V-J Day **VIII:** 369–370
   WMC **VIII:** 375
   World War II Pacific
      theater **VIII:** 399
Japanese **II:** 174
Japanese Americans **VI:** 141;
   VII: 357*c*; **IX:** 22, 32; **X:** 327*c*
   Asian Americans **VIII:** 25;
      X: 28
   Civil Liberties Act of 1988
      X: 63
   Coolidge, Calvin **VII:** 57
   enemy aliens **VIII:** 102
   Executive Order 9066
      VIII: 106
   Gentlemen's Agreement
      VII: 107–108
   National Origins Act **VII:**
      202
   nativism **VII:** 208, 209
   race and racial conflict
      VII: 249; **VIII:**
      288–289; **X:** 256
   Root-Takahira Agreement
      VII: 267
   Russo-Japanese War **VII:**
      271
Japanese Americans, relocation
   of **VIII:** **171–172,** *172,* 409*c,*
   410*c*
   American Civil Liberties
      Union **VIII:** 13
   Asian Americans **VIII:** 26
   Black, Hugo L. **VIII:** 37
   civil liberties **VIII:** 61
   civil rights **VIII:** 61
   Douglas, William O. **VIII:**
      85
   enemy aliens **VIII:** 103
   espionage **VIII:** 104
   Executive Order 9066
      VIII: 106–107, 428–429
   Frankfurter, Felix **VIII:**
      127
   FSA **VIII:** 113
   *Korematsu v. United
      States. See Korematsu v.
      United States*
   Morgenthau, Henry **VIII:**
      216
   race and racial conflict
      VIII: 288–289
   Roosevelt, Eleanor **VIII:**
      311
   Roosevelt, Franklin D.
      VIII: 314
   Stimson, Henry L. **VIII:**
      340
   Supreme Court **VIII:** 347
   Thomas, Norman **VIII:**
      358
   World War II **VIII:** 389

World War II home front **VIII:** 395

Japanese Evacuation Claims Act **VIII:** 172

Japanese Peace Treaty **IX:** 2, 82, 330*c*

Japan trade **IV:** 379*c*

Jarvis, Frank **VI:** 290

Java **I:** 76, 114

Java, HMS **III:** 81; **IV:** 356

Java Sea, Battle of the **VIII:** 399

Jaworski, Leon **X: 160–161**
    Burger, Warren E. **X:** 44
    Nixon, Richard M. **X:** 221
    United States v. Nixon **X:** 308, 309
    Watergate scandal **X:** 317

Jaws (movie) **X:** 240

Jay, John **III:** *181,* **181–182,** 394*c*–396*c;*
    Continental Congress, First **III:** 87, 88
    election of 1800 **III:** 116
    Federalist Papers **III:** 124, 125
    Federalists **III:** 127
    foreign affairs **III:** 130
    Hamilton, Alexander **III:** 161
    Jay's Treaty **III:** 182
    journalism **III:** 191
    Madison, James **III:** 228
    Marshall, John **III:** 235
    Olive Branch Petition **III:** 266
    Paris, Treaty of **III:** 273
    Stuart, Gilbert **III:** 335
    Supreme Court **III:** 338

Jay Cooke & Company **V:** 81, 107; **VI:** 19, 41, 324*c*

Jay-Gardoqui treaty negotiations **III: 182**

jayhawkers **V:** 31, 32, **186–187,** 285, 328

Jay's Treaty **III: 182–183,** 396*c;* **IV:** 30, 106, 140, 240
    Adams, John **III:** 3
    Ames, Fisher **III:** 13
    Bache, Benjamin Franklin **III:** 29
    Canada **III:** 61
    election of 1800 **III:** 116
    Federalist Party **III:** 126
    foreign affairs **III:** 130
    French alliance **III:** 138
    French Revolution **III:** 138–139
    Fries's Rebellion **III:** 139–140
    fur trade **III:** 142
    Gerry, Elbridge **III:** 153
    Jay, John **III:** 181, 182

Monroe-Pinkney Treaty **III:** 246

Pickering, John **III:** 276

Quasi War **III:** 291

San Lorenzo, Treaty of **III:** 317

Supreme Court **III:** 338

Wilson, James **III:** 380

XYZ affair **III:** 385

jazz **VII: 137,** 361*c;* **VIII:** 406*c,* 408*c,* 410*c;* **IX:** 217, 263; **X:** 201. *See also* ragtime
    African Americans **VIII:** 3
    cities and urban life **VII:** 50
    Ellington, Duke **VIII:** 99–100
    entertainment **VII:** 86
    Gershwin, George **VII:** 108, 109
    Goodman, Benny **VIII:** 132
    Harlem Renaissance **VII:** 120
    Holiday, Billie **VIII:** 148–149
    music **VII:** 194, 195; **VIII:** 221
    popular culture **VII:** 233
    radio **VII:** 254
    Sinatra, Frank **VIII:** 326

Jazz Singer, The (film) **VII:** 87, 191

J. B. Lippincott **X:** 178

JCER **VIII:** 227

J. Edgar Thompson Steel Works **VI:** 146

Jefferson, Blind Lemon **VII:** 32; **VIII:** 223

Jefferson, Joseph, III **VI: 155–156, 286, 287**

Jefferson, Thomas **III:** *183,* **183–186,** 393*c,* 394*c,* 397*c;* **IV:** xiii; **VI:** 176; **X:** 75, 209
    abolition/abolition movement **III:** 15, 16; **V:** 1, 2
    Adams, John **III:** 3
    African Americans **III:** 5
    agriculture **V:** 7
    Alien and Sedition Acts **III:** 9
    American Revolution **III:** 13
    American System **IV:** 18
    Ames, Fisher **III:** 13
    architecture **III:** 20
    artisans **III:** 26
    Astor, John Jacob **IV:** 30
    Austin, Moses **IV:** 35
    Bache, Benjamin Franklin **III:** 29

banking and currency **IV:** 41

Bank of the United States (First) **III:** 31

Banneker, Benjamin **III:** 33, 34

Barbary pirates **III:** 35

Barlow, Joel **III:** 36

Blackstone, William **III:** 40

Bland, Richard **III:** 40

Burr, Aaron **III:** 54

Cass, Lewis **IV:** 76

Chase, Samuel **III:** 65

Chesapeake-Leopard affair **III:** 67

Chouteau family **IV:** 78

cities and urban life **III:** 70

Claiborne, William C. C. **IV:** 84

Clark, William **III:** 72

Clinton, George **III:** 75

College of William and Mary **II:** 67

Constitution, USS **III:** 80

Constitutional Convention **III:** 81

Continental Congress, Second **III:** 88

Cornplanter **III:** 92

corporatism **III:** 94

Coxe, Tench **III:** 96

Declaration of Independence **III:** 102

deism **III:** 103

Democratic Party **IV:** 106; **V:** 93, 94

Democratic-Republican Party **III:** 104

Democratic-Republican societies **III:** 105

Duane, William **III:** 108

economy **III:** 113

education **III:** 114, 115; **IV:** 120

election of 1800 **III:** 116–117

embargo of 1807 **III:** 117, 118

Enlightenment **II:** 109

Federalist Party **III:** 126

Flashman, Edward **II:** 119

foreign affairs **III:** 130, 131

foreign policy **IV:** 141

Freneau, Philip **III:** 139

Fries's Rebellion **III:** 140

Gallatin, Albert **III:** 147

Genet, Edmond **III:** 149, 150

Great Awakening **II:** 149

Haiti **III:** 159

Hamilton, Alexander **III:** 162

Hemmings, Sally **III:** 164–165

Henry, Patrick **III:** 165

Hull, William **IV:** 175

humanitarianism **III:** 170

immigration **III:** 173

internal improvements **IV:** 188

Jackson, Andrew **IV:** 191

Jay's Treaty **III:** 183

journalism **III:** 192

Judiciary Act of 1801 **III:** 193

Lafayette, marquis de **III:** 201

lawyers **III:** 203

Lee, Charles **III:** 205

Lee, Richard Henry **III:** 207

Lewis, Meriwether **III:** 208

Lewis and Clark Expedition **III:** 209, 210

liberty tree/pole **III:** 214

literature **III:** 214, 215

Livingston, Robert R. **III:** 216

Louisiana Purchase **III:** 218

Macon, Nathaniel **III:** 226

Macon's Bill No. 2 **III:** 226

Madison, Dolley **III:** 227

Madison, James **III:** 227, 230

Marshall, John **III:** 235, 236

Mason-Dixon Line **V:** 224

medicine **IV:** 229

Monroe, James **IV:** 240

Monroe Doctrine **IV:** 241

Monroe-Pinkney Treaty **III:** 245, 246

national debt **III:** 253

National Road **IV:** 253

Neutrality Proclamation **III:** 256

Niles, Hezekiah **III:** 258

Non-Importation Act **III:** 259

Non-Intercourse Act **III:** 259

Northwest Ordinances **III:** 261

Nullification Controversy **IV:** 263

Ostenaco **II:** 269

Otis, Harrison Gray **III:** 268

Panic of 1792 **III:** 272

Pennsylvania **II:** 277

Jefferson, Thomas (continued)
   Permanent Indian Frontier
      IV: 279
   Pike, Zebulon
      Montgomery IV: 281
   political parties III: 279
   Priestley, Joseph III: 285
   prisons III: 286
   race and race relations III:
      295; IV: 291
   Randolph, Edmund III:
      296
   Randolph, John III: 296
   religion, Euro-American
      II: 316, 317
   religious liberty III: 300
   Republican Party IV: 300
   Rittenhouse, David II: 322
   St. Clair, Arthur III: 316
   secession V: 311
   slavery V: 328
   slave trade III: 329
   states' rights III: 333
   Story, Joseph III: 334
   Tammany Society III: 341
   tariffs V: 348
   Taylor, John, of Caroline
      III: 344
   Trumbull, John III: 352
   United States Army Corps
      of Engineers V: 370
   Virginia and Kentucky
      Resolutions III: 360
   Virginia dynasty III: 361
   voluntary associations III:
      362
   War of 1812 IV: 355, 356
   Washington Benevolent
      Societies III: 369
   Washington, District of
      Columbia III: 364, 365
   Webster, Noah III: 370
   West Point III: 372, 373;
      V: 372
   Whitney, Eli III: 377
   Wilkinson, James III: 379
   women's rights and status
      III: 383
   Yorktown, surrender at
      III: 388
Jefferson Airplane IX: 111, 218,
   244
Jeffersonian democracy III: 344
Jefferson in Paris (film) III: 164
Jeffersons, The (TV program) X:
   295
Jeffords, James X: 48, 238, 276,
   331c
Jeffries, James (Jim) VII:
   138–139, 139, 294
Jehovah's Witnesses VI: 242;
   VIII: 70–71, 347; X: 265

Jemison, Mary II: 52, 173,
   426–427
Jemmy II: 361
Jen, Gish X: 177
Jenckes, Thomas A. VI: 56
Jenco, Lawrence X: 154
Jenkins, Charles Francis IX: 295
Jenkins, Robert II: 392
Jenkins, W. A., Jr. IX: 38
Jenner, Edward III: 106, 396c
Jennings, Elizabeth VI: 16
Jennings, Solomon II: 390
Jennison, Charles V: 186, 187
Jenny, William Le Baron VI: 14,
   279
Jenrette, John W., Jr. X: 4–5
jeremiads II: 173–174, 305
Jerome, Leonard VI: 134
Jerome Remick Company VII:
   108
Jerry Springer Show (TV
   program) X: 295
Jersey, HMS III: 186–187
Jersey Central Power and Light
   Company IX: 24
Jerusalem I: 81, 262, 292, 358
Jerusalem, Virginia IV: 347, 348
Jervis, John IV: 293
Jesuit College II: 174, 178
Jesuits I: 188–190; II: 174
   Acosta, José de I: 3
   Azores I: 17
   California I: 48
   Calusa I: 49
   Cayuga I: 67
   Chesapeake Bay II: 58
   Counterreformation I: 96
   education II: 102
   Ethiopia I: 125
   Florida I: 131; II: 120
   French colonies II: 126,
      127, 129
   French immigrants II:
      130
   Huron II: 160
   Kongo I: 196
   Loyola, Ignatius I: 209
   Marquette, Jacques II:
      205
   missions II: 229–231
   Montagnais-Naskapi I:
      241
   Native Americans II: 244
   Protestantism II: 300
   reducción I: 306–307
   religion, Native American
      II: 317, 318
   Ricci, Matteo I: 311–312
   Roman Catholics II: 323,
      324
   theater II: 373
   White, Andrew II: 396

Jesup, Thomas S. IV: 312
Jesus Christ I: 348
   Hicks, Elias IV: 172
   religion IV: 298
   Second Great Awakening
      IV: 310
   spiritualism IV: 325
Jet (magazine) X: 185
jet airplanes IX: 26–28, 270,
   294, 331c
jet engines VIII: 353; IX: 120
Jet Propulsion Laboratory X:
   281
Jett, Joan X: 203
Jewett, Sarah Orne VI: 177
Jewish Daily Forward VII: 252
Jewish Enlightenment VI: 158,
   243
Jewish immigrants VII: 358c
   anti-Semitism VII: 13–14
   criminal justice VII: 59
   religion VII: 261
   segregation VII: 281
   Triangle Shirtwaist Fire
      VII: 311
Jews and Judaism I: 190–192,
   386c; II: 174–175, 175; III:
   173, 187–188; IV: 177, 298;
   V: 27–28, 156, 175, 407c; VI:
   57, 139, 157–158, 172–173,
   243, 283; VIII: 172–173,
   410c; IX: 257; X: 161–162
   Alexander VI, Pope I: 6
   anti-Semitism. See anti-
      Semitism
   auto-da-fé I: 16
   Brandeis, Louis VII:
      34–35
   bubonic plague I: 285
   Charleston II: 56
   Columbus, Christopher I:
      81
   conservatism VIII: 72
   Democratic Party VIII: 81
   Dutch Reformed Church
      II: 97
   election of 1936 VIII: 97
   election of 1940 VIII: 98
   ERA X: 106
   Ferdinand and Isabella I:
      127, 128
   German Americans VIII:
      130
   Goodman, Benny VIII:
      132
   Great Awakening II: 147,
      149
   Harrison, Peter II:
      154–155
   Holocaust VIII: 149–150
   immigration VIII: 162
   liberalism VIII: 189

militia movement X: 193
Morgenthau, Henry VIII:
   216
music VII: 193
neoconservatism X: 215
New Deal VIII: 242
New Netherland II: 257
Newport II: 258
New York II: 260
Oglethorpe, James Edward
   II: 267
Philadelphia II: 282
Polish Americans VIII:
   269
politics in the Roosevelt
   era VIII: 271
race and racial conflict
   VII: 247; VIII: 288
refugees VIII: 298, 299
religion VII: 261; VIII:
   303; X: 265
religion, Euro-American
   II: 316
RFRA X: 266
Rhode Island II: 321
Roosevelt, Franklin D.
   VIII: 313
São Tomé I: 320
Spanish Civil War VIII:
   334
Stuyvesant, Peter II: 363
suffrage II: 364
Zionism VIII: 403
Jew's harps IV: 249
JFK (Stone) X: 31
Jiang Jieshi IX: 330c
   Asia (and foreign policy)
      IX: 21
   Cairo Conference VIII: 51
   cold war IX: 58
   Luce, Henry R. VIII: 196
   Soviet Union IX: 277
   White Paper IX: 321
   World War II Pacific
      theater VIII: 398
   Yalta Conference VIII:
      402
jihads
   Askia Muhammad I I: 14
   Ethiopia I: 124
   Fulani I: 135
   Ghana I: 141
   Islam I: 184, 185
   Kaabu kingdom I: 195
   Mossi I: 244
Jim Crow laws VI: 156–157,
   325c; VII: 248, 249, 259, 280,
   281; IX: 4, 42, 215, 220
   African Americans VI: 5,
      6; VIII: 2, 4
   civil rights VIII: 61, 62
   civil rights cases VI: 56

Liberia, immigration to **VI:** 175

Plessy v. Ferguson **VI:** 225

race and racial conflict **VIII:** 287–289

religion **VIII:** 304

South **VIII:** 331

Washington, Booker T. **VI:** 309

World War II home front **VIII:** 395

"Jim Crow" (minstrel acts) **IV:** 376*c*

Jim Kweskin Jug Band **IX:** 111

jingles, advertising **VIII:** 273

jingoes **VI: 157,** 187

Job Corps **IX:** 87, 127, **149–150,** 313, 334*c*

Job Opportunities and Basic Skills (JOBS) **X:** 110

jobs. *See* employment

Jobs, Steven **X:** 72, 273

job segregation **VIII:** 384

Job Training Partnership Act of 1982 **X:** 253

Jocelyn, Simeon **V:** 8

Jockey Club **VI:** 134

Jodrell Bank Observatory **IX:** 278

John XXIII, Pope **IX:** 257

John Birch Society **X:** 43, 79

"John Brown's Body" **V:** 244

John Deere Company **IV:** 105

John I, king of Portugal (João) **I:** 105

John II, king of Portugal (João) **I:** 43, 79, 104, 137, 292, 358

John III, king of Portugal (João) **I:** 33, **192–193**

"Johnny Reb" **V:** 69, 362

John Paul II, Pope **X:** 56, 59

Johns, Jasper **IX:** 20

Johns Hopkins Hospital **VI:** 94

Johns Hopkins University **VI:** 93, 94, 257, 258, 324*c*

Johns Hopkins University Medical School **VI:** 192; **VII:** 179

Johnson, Albert **VII:** 202

Johnson, Andrew **IV:** 138; **V:** *187,* **187–189,** 408*c*

amnesty, acts of **V:** 8, 9

assassination of Abraham Lincoln **V:** 17, 19

Blair, Francis P., Jr. **V:** 30

Civil Rights Act of 1866 **V:** 62

Congress **VI:** 63

Democratic Party **V:** 95

Freedmen's Bureau **V:** 142

Grant, Ulysses S. **V:** 156

impeachment. *See* impeachment of Andrew Johnson

Joint Committee on the Conduct of War **V:** 191

loyalty oaths **V:** 219

Memphis riot **V:** 232

Port Royal, South Carolina, Experiment **V:** 280

the presidency **VI:** 230

Radical Republicans **V:** 288–289

Reconstruction **V:** 292–294

Reconstruction Acts **V:** 295, 296

Republican Party **V:** 302

Schurz, Carl **VI:** 256

Seward, William H. **V:** 315

Sheridan, Philip H. **V:** 319

Sherman, William T. **V:** 321

Sickles, Daniel E. **V:** 327

Special Field Order No. 15 **V:** 332, 333

Stanton, Edwin M. **V:** 334

Stevens, Thaddeus **V:** 338

Sumner, Charles **V:** 343

Thirteenth Amendment **V:** 353

Tilden, Samuel Jones **VI:** 289

Tredegar Iron Works **V:** 356

Wade, Benjamin **V:** 385

Walker, Mary Edwards **V:** 386

Welles, Gideon **V:** 392

Johnson, Anthony **II:** 5, 174, **175–176**

Johnson, Ban **VII:** 294

Johnson, Charles **II:** 285, 369

Johnson, Francis **I:** 298

Johnson, Guy **III:** 48, 188, 255

Johnson, Hiram Warren **VII: 137–138**

Congress **VII:** 54

Progressive Party **VII:** 237

progressivism **VII:** 238

Republican Party **VII:** 263

Taft, William Howard **VII:** 304

Johnson, Hugh S. **VIII:** 34, **173–174,** 228, 231, 232

Johnson, Isaac **II:** 216

Johnson, Jack **VII: 138–139,** *139,* 357*c*

Dempsey, Jack **VII:** 67

entertainment **VII:** 85

Mann Act **VII:** 169–170

sports **VII:** 293–294

Johnson, James **IX:** 108

Johnson, James H. A. **VI:** 4

Johnson, James Weldon **VII:** 199; **VIII:** 227, 378; **IX:** 220

Johnson, Sir John **III: 188–189**

Johnson, Joseph **III:** 255

Johnson, Lady Bird **IX:** 87, **150–151,** *152*

Johnson, Louis **IX:** 233

Johnson, Lyndon B. **IX: 151–153,** *152, 159, 275,* 333*c,* 334*c*

ABM Treaty **X:** 23

Acheson, Dean **IX:** 2

advertising **IX:** 3

affirmative action **X:** 8

Africa **IX:** 4

Alliance for Progress **IX:** 11

amendments to the Constitution **X:** 19

antiwar movement— Vietnam **X:** 24

Appalachian Regional Development Act **IX:** 15

Baruch, Bernard M. **VIII:** 34

Bilingual Education Act of 1968 **X:** 35

birth control **X:** 37

cities and urban life **IX:** 52

Civil Rights Act of 1957 **IX:** 55

Civil Rights Act of 1964 **IX:** 56

Community Action Program **IX:** 62–63

Congress of Racial Equality **IX:** 67

Cox, Archibald, Jr. **X:** 81

defense budget **IX:** 78

Democratic Party **IX:** 79

Economic Opportunity Act of 1964 **IX:** 87

economy **IX:** 90; **X:** 94

education **IX:** 9189

elections **IX:** 95–97

Elementary and Secondary Education Act of 1965 **IX:** 98–99

Ellington, Duke **VIII:** 100

Ford, Gerald R. **X:** 120

Fortas, Abe **X:** 125

Galbraith, John Kenneth **IX:** 117

Goldwater, Barry **IX:** 124

Graham, Billy **IX:** 126

Great Society **IX:** 126–127

Harriman, Averell **VIII:** 144

Harrington, Michael **IX:** 130

Humphrey, Hubert H. **IX:** 138

Israel **IX:** 147

Jaworski, Leon **X:** 161

Job Corps **IX:** 149, 150

Kennedy, John F. **IX:** 157

King, Martin Luther, Jr. **IX:** 161

Kissinger, Henry A. **X:** 165

labor **IX:** 170

Landon, Alfred M. **VIII:** 183

Latin America **IX:** 172; **X:** 172

liberalism **IX:** 179; **X:** 175

March on Washington **IX:** 192

Marshall, Thurgood **IX:** 194

McCarthy, Eugene **IX:** 188, 189

medicine **IX:** 198

Mexico **X:** 192

Mississippi Freedom Democratic Party **IX:** 207

Model Cities program **IX:** 208

NASA **IX:** 219

National Endowment for the Humanities **IX:** 222

National Traffic and Motor Vehicle Safety Act of 1966 **IX:** 225

National Trails Act of 1968 **IX:** 225–226

neoconservatism **X:** 215

New Deal **IX:** 230

O'Neill, Thomas P., Jr. **X:** 228

Oppenheimer, J. Robert **IX:** 237

public health **IX:** 250

race and racial conflict **IX:** 254

SANE **IX:** 267–268

Shriver, Sargent **X:** 278

Southern Christian Leadership Conference **IX:** 275–276

Stevenson, Adlai **IX:** 284

Termination policy **IX:** 298

United Nations **X:** 307

Vietnam War **IX:** 308–310; **X:** 312

Volunteers in Service to America **IX:** 310

Voting Rights Act of 1965 **IX:** 311

War on Poverty **IX:** 313–314

Warren Court **IX:** 315, 316

Johnson, Lyndon B. *(continued)*
  wars of national liberation
    IX: 317
  White Citizens' Councils
    IX: 320
  Wild and Scenic Rivers Act
    of 1968 **IX:** 321–322
Johnson, Mary **II:** 5, 174, 175,
  176
Johnson, Nathaniel **II:** 177
Johnson, Philip **IX:** 19
Johnson, Richard M. **IV:** 169
Johnson, Robert **II:** 34, 224
Johnson, Robert Underwood
  VI: 200
Johnson, Samuel **II: 176–177**
  Anglican Church **II:** 20
  Connecticut **II:** 70
  King's College **II:** 184, 185
  Lennox, Charlotte Ramsay
    II: 193
  Oglethorpe, James Edward
    II: 267
  science **II:** 330
Johnson, Thomas **III:** 338
Johnson, Tom Loftin **VII:**
  139–140, 229, 316
Johnson, Sir William **II:** 76, 83,
  85, 169, **177,** 233
  Brant, Joseph **III:** 48
  Fort Stanwix, Treaty of **III:**
    132
  Johnson, Sir John **III:** 188
  Native Americans and the
    Revolution **III:** 254–255
  Pontiac's Rebellion **III:**
    281
Johnson Doctrine **IX:** 172, 317,
  334*c*
Johnson Electric Company **VII:**
  140
Johnson Hall **II:** 177
Johnson-Reed Act of 1924
  VIII: 25. *See also* National
    Origins Act
Johnson's Island, Ohio **V:** 282
Johnston, Albert Sidney **IV:** 58;
  V: 189
  Beauregard, Pierre **V:** 27
  Confederate army **V:** 73
  Mississippi River **V:** 234
  Shiloh, Battle of **V:** 323,
    324, 326
Johnston, Henrietta Deering **II:**
  25, **177–178**
Johnston, Joseph E. **V:**
  189–190, 406*c*
  Appomattox Court House,
    Virginia **V:** 14
  Atlanta campaign **V:** 19
  Beauregard, Pierre **V:** 27
  Bentonville, Battle of **V:** 28

Chattanooga, Battle of **V:**
  57
  Confederate army **V:** 73
  Five Forks, Battle of **V:**
    129
  Hood, John Bell **V:** 171
  Lee, Robert E. **V:** 205, 207
  Longstreet, James **V:** 214
  Mississippi River **V:** 235
  Peninsular campaign **V:**
    267, 269
  Sherman, William T. **V:**
    321
  Vicksburg campaign **V:** 382
Johnston, Peter **V:** 190
Johnston Act **III:** 8
Johnstone, Anne Hartwell **IX:**
  175
Johnstown flood **VI: 157**
*John Thomas Scopes v. The
  State* **VII:** 386–392
"Join or Die" cartoon (Franklin)
  II: 179
Joint Chiefs of Staff
  Bradley, Omar N. **VIII:** 41
  Leahy, William D. **VIII:**
    184
  OSS **VIII:** 256
  Solomon Islands **VIII:** 331
  World War II Pacific
    theater **VIII:** 398
Joint Committee on Economic
  Recovery (JCER) **VIII:** 227
Joint Committee on
  Reconstruction **V:** 289, 295,
    338
Joint Committee on the
  Conduct of the War **V:**
    190–192
  impeachment of Andrew
    Johnson **V:** 178
  Julian, George W. **V:** 194
  Meade, George Gordon **V:**
    227
  Union army **V:** 365
  Wade, Benjamin **V:** 385
Joint Statement of Principles for
  SALT III **X:** 86
Jolliet, Louis **II:** 115, **178,** *205,*
  206
Jolson, Al **VI:** 96; **VII:** 191
Jomini, Antoine-Henri, baron
  de **V:** 162, **192,** 345
Jones, Absalom **II:** 31; **III: 189,**
  396*c,* 397*c;* **V:** 1
  African Americans **III:** 6
  Allen, Richard **III:** 11
  antislavery and abolition
    III: 17
  slave trade **III:** 329
Jones, Anson **IV:** 338
Jones, Bobby **VIII:** 337

Jones, Catesby **V:** 238
Jones, James **VIII:** 192; **IX:** 181
Jones, Jesse H. **VIII: 174,** 294,
  295, 373
Jones, John Paul **III:** 90,
  189–190, 394*c*
Jones, Joseph **V:** 231
Jones, Leroi **IX:** 7, 334*c. See
  also* Baraka, Amiri
Jones, Mary Harris "Mother"
  VII: 167
Jones, Noble **II:** 138
Jones, Paula Corbin **X:** 329*c,*
  330*c*
  Clinton, William **X:** 68
  impeachment **X:** 150
  Judicial Watch **X:** 162
  Rehnquist, William H. **X:**
    265
  Starr, Kenneth **X:** 287
Jones, Roger **V:** 165
Jones, Seaborn **V:** 396
Jones, Walter **V:** 227
Jones, Walter B. **IX:** 114
Jones, William **IV:** 42, 44; **VI:** 57
Jones Act of 1916 **VII:** 358*c*
Jones Act of 1917 **VII:** 359*c;* **IX:**
  250
Jones Act of 1920 **X:** 142
Jones & Laughlin **IX:** 282
*Jones and Laughlin Steel v.
  NLRB* **VIII:** 69
Jonkman, Bartel **X:** 119
Joplin, Janis **IX:** 72, 218; **X:** 203,
  240
Joplin, Scott **VI:** 204, 328*c;* **VII:**
  140–141, 194, 355*c*
Jordain, Sylvester **I:** 343
Jordan **IX:** 146, 147
Jordan, Barbara **X:** 147, 325*c*
Jordan, Hamilton **X:** 150
Jordan, Michael **X:** *285,*
  285–286
Jorgensen, Jo **X:** 176
Joseph, Chief of Nez Perce **V:**
  173; **VI:** 207, 213, 324*c,*
  329–330
Joslyn Art Museum **IV:** 78
journalism **II: 178–179,** 299;
  III: 190–192, *191;* **IV:**
  194–197, 195*m,* 376*c;* **V:**
  192–194; VII: xiii, **141–143;**
  IX: 153–154, 182, 239
  Adams, Henry **VI:** 1
  advertising **VII:** 4–5
  Bache, Benjamin Franklin
    III: 29
  Beecher-Tilton scandal **VI:**
    24–25
  cities and urban life **IV:** 82
  Crane, Stephen **VI:** 68
  Dana, Charles A. **V:** 88

Duane, William **III:**
  107–108
Freneau, Philip **III:** 139
Fuller, Margaret **IV:** 156
Godkin, Edwin Lawrence
  VI: 115–116
Greeley, Horace **V:** 158
Hale, Sarah Josepha **IV:**
  168
Hearst, William Randolph
  VII: 120–122
Higginson, Thomas
  Wentworth **V:** 167
literature **VI:** 177
Lloyd, Henry Demarest
  VI: 179
Luce, Henry R. **VIII:**
  196–197
Lyon, Matthew **III:** 222
magazines **IV:** 196–197
Marx, Karl **V:** 223–224
Masses, The **VII:** 173
Mauldin, Bill **VIII:** 207
Mencken, H. L. **VII:** 181
muckrakers. *See*
  muckrakers
Nast, Thomas **V:** 247–248
newspapers **IV:** 194–196;
  VI: 211–212
New York City **V:** 253
Niles, Hezekiah **III:**
  258–259
Olmstead, Frederick Law
  V: 257
Paine, Thomas **III:** 271
progressivism **VII:** 238
Pulitzer, Joseph **VI:** 235
Riis, Jacob A. **VI:** 248
science **VII:** 276
science and technology **V:**
  310
Sinclair, Upton **VII:** 286
Spotsylvania, Battles of **V:**
  333
Steffens, Lincoln **VII:** 299
Steinbeck, John **VIII:** 339,
  340
Tarbell, Ida **VII:** 304–305
telegraph **V:** 351
Villard, Henry **VI:** 304
War Revenue Act **VII:**
  330
Webster, Noah **III:** 370
Wells-Barnett, Ida Bell **VI:**
  311–312
Whiskey Ring **V:** 393
White, Walter **VIII:** 378
Whitman, Walt **V:** 393
Wilkes, John **III:** 378
Yancey, William Lowndes
  V: 401
yellow journalism **VI:** 321

Journal of Christian Science **VI:** 88

Journal of Commerce **IV:** 204

Journal of Hospital Life in the Confederate army of Tennessee (Cumming) **V:** 85

Journal of the Franklin Institute **IV:** 149

journals **II:** 46, 179, 185–186, 215, 234

Journey in the Back Country (Olmstead) **V:** 257

Journey in the Seaboard Slave States (Olmstead) **V:** 257

journeymen **II:** 25–26, 63

Journey through Texas (Olmstead) **V:** 257

Joyce, James **VII:** 252; **VIII:** 55

Joyfull Newes out of the Newe Founde Worlde (Nicholas Monardes) **I:** 239

J. P. Morgan & Company **VI:** 197, 327c; **VII:** 64

Juana, queen of Castile **I:** 127

Judah, Theodore D. **V:** 263; **VI:** 180

Judaism. *See* Jews and Judaism

Judaism as a Civilization (Kaplan) **VIII:** 303

Judd, Donald **X:** 26

Judd's Friend **II:** 269

Judeo-Christian tradition **VIII:** 130

Judge, William Quan **VI:** 245

Judges v. Ashcroft, Governor of Missouri (1991) **X:** 113

judicial activism **VII:** 163–164; **VIII:** 37

  Brennan, William J. **X:** 40, 41

  Burger, Warren E. **X:** 44

  Meese, Edwin C. **X:** 191

  Reagan, Ronald W. **X:** 259

judicial appointments **IV:** 330

Judicial Procedures Reform Bill **VIII:** 345, 346. *See also* court-packing

judicial review **IV:** 330

Judicial Watch **X:** **162**

judiciary. *See* courts and judiciary

Judiciary Act of 1789 **III:** **192–193**, 395c; **IV:** 330

  Judiciary Act of 1801 **III:** 193

  Marbury v. Madison **III:** 230–231

  Marshall, John **III:** 236

  Supreme Court **III:** 338

Judiciary Act of 1801 **III:** **193**, 397c

Judiciary Act of 1789 **III:** 192

  Marbury v. Madison **III:** 230

  Marshall, John **III:** 235–236

  Supreme Court **III:** 338

Judith of Bethulia (film) **VII:** 115

Judson, Andrew T. **IV:** 20

Judson, E. C. **IV:** 58

Judson, Edward Z. **VI:** 59

jukeboxes **VIII:** 296

Julian, George Washington **IV:** 151; **V:** 178, 191, **194**

Julius II, Pope **I:** 203, 235

Julius III, Pope **I:** 235

Jumano **II:** 55

Jumbo (elephant) **VI:** 21

Juneteenth **V:** **194–195**

Juneteenth (Ellison) **V:** 195

Jungle, The (Sinclair) **VII:** *286*, 356c

  business **VII:** 39

  Meat Inspection Act **VII:** 178

  Pure Food and Drug Act **VII:** 244

  Sinclair, Upton **VII:** 286

junior high schools **VII:** 78

Juno Beach **VIII:** 248

Junto (Leatherstocking Club) **II:** 18, 33, 141, 277, 278

Jupiter **X:** 283

Jurassic Park (movie) **X:** 198

juries, independence of **II:** 153

"jurisprudence of dignity" **X:** 40

jury duty **VIII:** 386

justice. *See* criminal justice

Justice Department **V:** 242, 294; **VIII:** 18; **IX:** 54–55

  Abscam **X:** 5

  Branch Davidians **X:** 40

  business **X:** 49, 51

  crime **X:** 82

  impeachment **X:** 149–150

  Judicial Watch **X:** 162

  Meese, Edwin C. **X:** 191

  Mitchell, John N. **X:** 195

  narcotics **X:** 206, 207

  Reagan, Ronald W. **X:** 260

  Reno, Janet **X:** 266–267

  Richardson, Elliot L. **X:** 267–268

  RICO **X:** 257, 258

justice system **VIII:** 3

juvenile delinquency

  children **VIII:** 57

  marriage and family life **VIII:** 205

  World War II **VIII:** 389

World War II home front **VIII:** 395

juvenile justice **VII:** 59, 350–351

Juvenile Miscellany **IV:** 167

juvenile offenders **X:** 266, 267

Juzgado de Indios **I:** 15

J. Walter Thompson **VII:** 4

K

Kaabu, kingdom of **I:** 66, **195**, 321–322

Ka'ba **I:** 183, 230

Kachiquels **I:** 227

Kahekili **IV:** 199

Kahn, Albert **VII:** 16, 96

kahunas **IV:** 199

Kaiser, David E. **VII:** 273

Kaiser, Henry J. **VIII:** **175**, 209, 215, 324

Kaiser Permanente **VIII:** 175, 209

Kaiser Shipbuilding **VIII:** 175

Kalakmul **I:** 227, 349

Kalb, Johann, baron de **III:** **195**

Kalenjin **I:** 210

Kaliwa **I:** 48

Kallen, Horace **VII:** 162, 209

Kalm, Peter **II:** **181**

Kalpius, Johannes **II:** 331

Kamehameha I, king of Hawaii **III:** 164; **IV:** 171, **199–200**

Kamehameha III, king of Hawaii **IV:** 172

Kamehameha IV, king of Hawaii **V:** 131

kamikaze **VIII:** 187, 259, 399

Kaminaljuyu **I:** 346

Kampelman, Max **X:** 59–60

Kanagawa, Treaty of **IV:** 280

Kanem-Bornu **I:** 155, 317

Kangaba **I:** 217, 339–340

Kangaroos **VI:** 268

Kansas **I:** 387c; **II:** 160; **V:** 405c, 406c; **IX:** 42–43; **X:** 242. *See also* Bleeding Kansas

  African Americans **VI:** 6

  Brown, John **V:** 37–38

  cattle kingdom **VI:** 46

  claim clubs **IV:** 85

  Democratic Party **IV:** 108

  Fort Leavenworth **IV:** 145

  Frémont, John C. **IV:** 154

  Massachusetts Emigrant Aid Society **IV:** 223–224

  migration **IV:** 235

  Native Americans **V:** 250

  New Mexico **I:** 256

  Simpson, Jerry **VI:** 262

  Singleton, Benjamin **V:** 327

slavery **V:** 328–329

sod houses **VI:** 270

Stone, Lucy **VI:** 278

Stuart, J. E. B. **V:** 341

Truth, Sojourner **V:** 357

Zuni **I:** 383

Kansas Emigrant Aid Society of Ohio **IV:** 223

Kansas-Nebraska Act of 1854 **IV:** 379c; **V:** **197–198**, 405c; **VI:** 261

  abolition **V:** 3

  Benton, Thomas Hart **IV:** 50

  Blair, Francis P., Jr. **V:** 30

  Bleeding Kansas **V:** 31

  Civil War **V:** 64

  Davis, Jefferson **V:** 89

  Democratic Party **IV:** 108; **V:** 94

  Douglas, Stephen A. **V:** 98, 99

  Fort Laramie **IV:** 145

  Greeley, Horace **V:** 158

  jayhawkers **V:** 186

  Lincoln, Abraham **V:** 210

  Massachusetts Emigrant Aid Society **IV:** 223

  Pierce, Franklin **V:** 275

  popular sovereignty **IV:** 285

  Republican Party **IV:** 300; **V:** 300

  Seward, William H. **V:** 314

  slavery **IV:** 318

  Stephens, Alexander H. **V:** 336

  Sumner, Charles **V:** 342

  Wade, Benjamin **V:** 385

  Welles, Gideon **V:** 391

Kansas Regulars **V:** 38

Kansas Territory **IV:** 155, 300, 301, 379c

Kansas v. Hendricks (1997) **X:** 329c

Kant, Immanuel **II:** 109; **IV:** 345

Kanuri **I:** 196

Kaplan, Mordecai **VIII:** 303

Kaplan, Mordechai M. **X:** 161

Karankawa nation **I:** 37

Karlsefni, Thorfinn Thordsson **I:** 369, 385c

Karo, Joseph **I:** 191, 192

Karok **I:** 48

Kasavubu, Joseph **IX:** 317

Kasserine Pass **VIII:** 393

Kati, Mahmud al- **I:** 350

katsina **II:** 317

Kaufman, George S. **VII:** 108

Kaufman, Irving R. **IX:** 264

kayak **II:** 167

Kayak Island **II**: 32
Kayor (Kajor). *See* Cayor
Kazakhstan **X**: 152, 281
KC and the Sunshine Band **X**: 202
KCIA (South Korean Central Intelligence Agency) **X**: 166
KDKA radio (Pittsburgh) **VII**: 254, 360c
Kean, Edmund **V**: 352
Kearns, Jack "Doc" **VII**: 67
Kearny, Stephen Watts **IV**: *200,* **200–201**
    Bent, Charles **IV**: 47
    Bent, William **IV**: 48
    California **IV**: 65
    Carson, Kit **IV**: 75
    Fort Leavenworth **IV**: 145
    Frémont, John C. **IV**: 153
    Mexican-American War **IV**: 234
    Santa Fe Trail **IV**: 306
    Stockton, Robert Field **IV**: 328
Kearsarge, USS **V**: 313
Keating, Charles **X**: 276
"Keating Five" **X**: 276
Keating-Owen Act **VII**: 1, 46, 66, **145**, 358c, 359c
Keayne, Thomas **II**: 389
Kebre Nagast **I**: 123, 124
Kecoughtan **II**: 294
Keeler, James E. **VI**: 258
Keely, Michael **VI**: 20
Keenan, Henry F. **VI**: 177
Keene, Laura **V**: 352
Kefauver, Estes **IX**: 206
Kefauver-Harris Amendments **IX**: 69
Kehew, Mary Morton **VII**: 205
Kehoe, John **VI**: 195, 196
Keira **I**: 102
Keith, B. F. **VI**: 96
Keith, George **II**: 39, 307, 308
Keith, William **II**: 145, **181**
Keithean schism **II**: 308
Kelley, Florence **VII**: **145–146;** **X**: 105
    Addams, Jane **VII**: 3
    Children's Bureau **VII**: 47
    Goldmark, Josephine **VII**: 111
    urban reform **VII**: 317
Kelley, Oliver H. **VI**: 221
Kelley, William D. **V**: **198–199**
Kellogg, Frank **VII**: 43, 146
Kellogg, John Harvey **VI**: 242
Kellogg, William P. **V**: 375
Kellogg-Briand Treaty **VII**: **146–147; VIII**: 220
    Carnegie Endowment **VII**: 43

Coolidge, Calvin **VII**: 57
    foreign policy **VII**: 100–101
    Women's International League for Peace and Freedom **VII**: 338
Kelly, George "Machine Gun" **VIII**: 115
Kelly, King **VI**: 22
Kelly, Richard **X**: 4–5
Kelly, William **VI**: 27
Kelly Air Mail Act **VII**: 23, **147**, 361c
Kel Owey **I**: 317
Kelsey, Frances **IX**: 69
Kemal, Mustafa **VII**: 323
Kemble, Charles and Fanny **V**: 352
Kemp, Jack F. **X**: 35, **163**
Kemp, Robert **IV**: 250
Kempei **VIII**: 164
Kendall, Josias **II**: 209
Kendall, Willmoore **IX**: 68; **X**: 42, 43
Kendrick, Francis **IV**: 21
Kennan, George F. **IX**: 58, 105, **155–156**, 233, 329c, 341–344
Kennedy, Adrienne **IX**: 243
Kennedy, Anthony **X**: 260, 279, 291, 302
Kennedy, Edward M. (Teddy) **X**: **163–164**
    Carter, James Earl, Jr. **X**: 59
    Ginsburg, Ruth Bader **X**: 130
    Quayle, J. Danforth **X**: 253
Kennedy, Jacqueline **IX**: *152,* **156**
Kennedy, John F. **IX**: **156–158,** *157,* 332c–334c
    ABM Treaty **X**: 22
    Acheson, Dean **IX**: 2
    Africa **IX**: 3–4
    Alliance for Progress **IX**: 10
    Appalachian Regional Development Act **IX**: 15
    arms race **IX**: 16
    assassinations **X**: 30, 31
    Baruch, Bernard M. **VIII**: 34
    Bay of Pigs **IX**: 33–35
    Birmingham confrontation **IX**: 38
    CIA **IX**: 50
    civil defense **IX**: 53
    civil disobedience **IX**: 54
    Civil Rights Act of 1964 **IX**: 56
    cold war **IX**: 60

    Community Action Program **IX**: 62
    consumer movement **IX**: 69
    Cox, Archibald, Jr. **X**: 81
    Cuban missile crisis **IX**: 73–75
    defense budget **IX**: 77–78
    Democratic Party **IX**: 79
    economy **IX**: 90
    education **IX**: 91
    elections **IX**: 95; **X**: 101
    Elementary and Secondary Education Act of 1965 **IX**: 98–99
    Engel v. Vitale **IX**: 101
    Federal Housing Administration **IX**: 110
    feminism **X**: 114
    Ford, Gerald R. **X**: 120
    freedom rides **IX**: 114
    Galbraith, John Kenneth **IX**: 117
    Graham, Billy **IX**: 126
    Harriman, Averell **VIII**: 144
    Immigration Act of 1965 **IX**: 142
    Johnson, Lyndon **IX**: 151
    Kennedy, Edward M. **X**: 163
    Kennedy, Joseph P. **VIII**: 176
    Kennedy, Robert **IX**: 158
    King, Martin Luther, Jr. **IX**: 160
    Kissinger, Henry A. **X**: 165
    Latin America **X**: 172
    Limited Test Ban Treaty of 1963 **IX**: 180
    Luce, Henry R. **VIII**: 197
    March on Washington **IX**: 192
    Marshall, Thurgood **IX**: 193
    Meredith, James **IX**: 200
    Mitchell, John N. **X**: 195
    NASA **IX**: 219
    National Endowment for the Arts **IX**: 221
    National Endowment for the Humanities **IX**: 221–222
    National Organization for Women **IX**: 223
    National Wilderness Preservation Act of 1964 **IX**: 226
    New Deal **IX**: 229–230
    New Frontier **IX**: 230
    Nixon, Richard M. **X**: 220
    NOW **X**: 210

    O'Neill, Thomas P., Jr. **X**: 228
    Operation Mongoose **IX**: 236
    Oswald, Lee Harvey **IX**: 237–238
    Peace Corps **IX**: 241
    Powell, Adam Clayton **IX**: 245
    President's Commission on the Status of Women **IX**: 246–247
    race and racial conflict **IX**: 253
    religion **IX**: 256–257
    Roosevelt, Eleanor **VIII**: 311
    SANE **IX**: 267
    science **IX**: 270
    sit-ins **IX**: 273
    Southern Manifesto **IX**: 276
    Soviet Union **IX**: 277
    space exploration **IX**: 278–279
    Stevenson, Adlai **IX**: 284
    technology **IX**: 294
    television **IX**: 297
    Vietnam War **IX**: 308
    Volunteers in Service to America **IX**: 310
    Wallace, George C. **X**: 314
    War on Poverty **IX**: 313
    Warren Court **IX**: 315
    wars of national liberation **IX**: 316, 317
    White, Byron R. **X**: 319
    women's status and rights **IX**: 324
Kennedy, Joseph P. **VIII**: **175–176; IX**: 157
    Catholics **VIII**: 53
    Douglas, William O. **VIII**: 84
    Irish Americans **VIII**: 165
    SEC **VIII**: 322
Kennedy, Robert F. **IX**: **158–159,** *159,* 275, 332c, 334c
    assassinations **X**: 30–31
    elections **IX**: 97
    freedom rides **IX**: 114
    gun control **X**: 136
    Kennedy, Edward M. **X**: 163
    Kennedy, John F. **IX**: 158
    King, Martin Luther, Jr. **IX**: 160
    McCarthy, Eugene **IX**: 189
    Model Cities program **IX**: 208

Operation Mongoose **IX:** 236

race and racial conflict **X:** 255

Teamsters Union **IX:** 292

union movement **IX:** 303

Volunteers in Service to America **IX:** 310

Weathermen **IX:** 319

White, Byron R. **X:** 319

Kennedy Space Center **X:** 281

Kennesaw Mountain, Battle of **V:** 19, 321, 354

Kent, James **IV:** 376c

Kent Island **II:** 50

Kent State University **IX:** 310; **X:** 24, 160, **164,** 323c

Kentucky **II:** 57, 58, 115; **III:** 391c, 392c, 396c; **V:** 405c; **VI:** 4, 122

amendments to the Constitution **X:** 19

Audubon, John James **IV:** 34

Boone, Daniel **III:** 42

brothers' war **V:** 37

Clay, Henry **IV:** 86

Corinth, Battle of **V:** 83

Dragging Canoe **III:** 107

ERA **X:** 107

governors **V:** 152

Liberty Party **IV:** 210

migration **IV:** 235

Mississippi River **V:** 234

Morgan, John Hunt **V:** 240

Orphan Brigade **V:** 258

population trends **X:** 242

religion **IV:** 296, 298

secession **V:** 311

Sherman, William T. **V:** 320

Taylor, Zachary **IV:** 334

Wilderness Road **III:** 378

Wilkinson, James **III:** 379

Kentucky and Virginia Resolutions of 1798 and 1799 **IV:** 263

Kentucky campaign **V:** 67

Kentucky Derby **VI:** 134

Kentucky Resolutions. *See* Virginia and Kentucky Resolutions

Kenya **I:** 139, 210; **X:** 12, 69, 299, 330c

Kenyatta, Jomo **IX:** 261

Keokuk, Chief **IV:** 52, 53

Keoua **IV:** 199

Kepler, Johannes **I:** 155

Keppler, Joseph **VI:** 185

Kern, Jerome **VII:** 85

Kerner, Otto **IX:** 254–255

Kern-McGillicuddy Workmen's Compensation Act **VII:** 359c. *See also* Workmen's Compensation Act

Kerouac, Jack **IX: 159–160,** 332c

Beat Generation **IX:** 35

counterculture **IX:** 71

Ginsberg, Allen **IX:** 122

literature **IX:** 182

religion **IX:** 256

Kerr, Clark **IX:** 112, 113, 268

Kerr-Mills Act of 1960 **IX:** 196

Kesey, Ken **IX:** 35, 182, 184

Kesselring, Albert **VIII:** 168, 325

Key, Francis Scott **III:** 251

Baltimore, Battle of **IV:** 39

Ghent, Treaty of (1814) **IV:** 162

Key nation **I:** 130

Keynes, John Maynard **VII:** 323; **VIII:** 176–177, 407c; **IX:** 70–71, 90

Keynesianism **VIII: 176–177.** *See also* deficit spending

antimonopoly **VIII:** 18

Democratic Party **VIII:** 82

Eccles, Marriner S. **VIII:** 89

economy **VIII:** 92

Full Employment Bill **VIII:** 128

government **VIII:** 136

Great Depression **VIII:** 140

Henderson, Leon **VIII:** 145

Hopkins, Harry **VIII:** 156, 157

liberalism **VIII:** 188, 189

mobilization **VIII:** 215

Morgenthau, Henry **VIII:** 216

New Deal **VIII:** 240, 242

NRPB **VIII:** 232, 233

postwar planning **VIII:** 278

PWA **VIII:** 286

recession of 1937–38 **VIII:** 293

taxation **VIII:** 351, 352

Third New Deal **VIII:** 357–358

TNEC **VIII:** 355, 356

unemployment **VIII:** 364

World War II **VIII:** 390

World War II home front **VIII:** 396

Keys, Donald **IX:** 267

Keystone Bridge Company **VI:** 35, 44

Keystone Kops **VII:** 85, 191

Key to Uncle Tom's Cabin (Stowe) **V:** 339

KGB **VIII:** 104, 164

Khmer Rouge **X:** 224, 325c

Khomeini, Ayatollah Ruhollah **X:** 58, 155, 156

Khrushchev, Nikita **IX:** 333c; **X:** 220

Bay of Pigs **IX:** 33

Cuban missile crisis **IX:** 73–75

Europe (and foreign policy) **IX:** 106

Kennedy, John F. **IX:** 158

Limited Test Ban Treaty of 1963 **IX:** 180

Soviet Union **IX:** 277, 278

wars of national liberation **IX:** 316

Khubilai Khan **I:** 64, 286

Kidd, William **II:** 263, 285, 299

kidnapping **I:** 58, 59, 144; **IV:** 20, 24; **V:** 17, 33, 118. *See also* captivity; slave trade

Kieft, Willem **II:** 99, **182,** 256, 260

Kieft War. *See* Algonquin War

Kiehtan (Chepian) **I:** 225

Kifayat al-Muktal (Ahmad Baba) **I:** 23

Kilby, Jack **X:** 72, 273

Kilenny Statutes **I:** 11

Killdeer Mountain, Battle of **VI:** 264

Killer Angels, The (Shaara) **V:** 213

Kilrain, Jake **VI:** 33

kilts **V:** 363

Kimball, Heber C. **IV:** 322

Kim Dong-Jo **X:** 166

Kim-Il Sung **IX:** 163

Kimmel, Husband E. **VIII:** 177, 237, 264

Kincaid, Thomas C. **VIII:** 177, 186, 246

kindergarten **VI: 159,** 256, 260, 315

Kindergarten Chats (Sullivan) **VI:** 280

Kindred Spirits (Durand) **IV:** 26, *26*

King, Billie Jean **X:** 262

King, Carole **X:** 240

King, Clarence **VI: 159–160**

Adams, Henry **VI:** 1

Geological Survey, U.S. **VI:** 110, 111

Muir, John **VI:** 199

Powell, John Wesley **VI:** 228

science **VI:** 257

King, Coretta Scott **IX:** 95; **X:** 31

King, David **IV:** 97

King, Edward **V:** 350; **VI:** 259

King, Edwin **IX:** 207, 284

King, Ernest J. **VIII: 177–178,** 237, 330, 380

King, John **III:** 240

King, L. Mackenzie **VIII:** 408c

King, Martin Luther, Jr. **IV:** 345; **VIII:** 291; **IX: 160–162,** *161,* 275, 331c–334c; **X:** 326c

African-American movement **IX:** 5

assassinations **X:** 30, 31

Baker, Ella **IX:** 31

Birmingham confrontation **IX:** 37–38

Black Power **IX:** 40

civil disobedience **IX:** 54

elections **IX:** 95

freedom rides **IX:** 114

gun control **X:** 136

Hoover, J. Edgar **IX:** 136

"I Have a Dream" speech **IX:** 351–352

Jackson, Jesse L. **X:** 159

"Letter from Birmingham Jail" **IX:** 344–351

Lewis, John **IX:** 178

March on Washington **IX:** 191

Meredith, James **IX:** 200

Mississippi Freedom Democratic Party **IX:** 207

Parks, Rosa **IX:** 240

race and racial conflict **IX:** 254; **X:** 255

religion **IX:** 256

Robinson, Jackie **IX:** 263

SANE **IX:** 267

segregation **IX:** 271

sit-ins **IX:** 273

Southern Christian Leadership Conference **IX:** 274–276

Steinem, Gloria **X:** 288

Student Nonviolent Coordinating Committee **IX:** 284

Voting Rights Act of 1965 **IX:** 311

Watts uprising **IX:** 318

Weathermen **IX:** 319

King, Mary **IX:** 325

King, Preston **IV:** 151

King, Rodney **X:** 256, 328c

King, Rufus **III:** 81, **195–196;** **IV:** 375c

King, Stephen **X:** 178

"King Andrew I" **IV:** 363

"King Cotton" diplomacy **V:** 76, 131–132
Kingdom of Matthias **V:** 357
Kingdom of New Mexico **II:** 254
Kingdom of Paradise **II:** 297
Kingdom of the Saguenay **I:** 59
King Features Syndicate **VII:** 121
King George's War **II: 182,** 419c; **III:** 136, 170
    agriculture **II:** 10
    British Empire **II:** 41
    Johnson, Sir William **II:** 177
    Massachusetts **II:** 214
    Negro Plot of 1741 **II:** 247
    New Hampshire **II:** 251
    New York **II:** 262
    privateering **II:** 300
King James Bible **IV:** 21, 180
King Philip's War **II:** 183m, **183–184,** 418c
    Connecticut **II:** 68
    Eliot, John **II:** 107
    ethnocentrism **II:** 114
    Massachusetts **II:** 212, 214
    Massachusetts School Act **II:** 216–217
    Mather, Increase **II:** 218
    Metacom **II:** 223
    Narragansett **II:** 241
    Native Americans **II:** 246
    Pequot **II:** 278
    Plymouth **II:** 288
    Rhode Island **II:** 321
    Rowlandson, Mary White **II:** 324
    Sewall, Samuel **II:** 334
    society, British American **II:** 352
King's Chapel, Boston **II:** 154
King's College **II: 184–185**
    Anglican Church **II:** 20
    Dartmouth College **II:** 83
    De Lancey, James **II:** 85
    Dutch Reformed Church **II:** 98
    education **II:** 104–105
    Johnson, Samuel **II:** 177
    Livingston, Philip **II:** 196
Kingsley, Charles **VI:** 266
King's Mountain, Battle of **III:** 93, 196, 196m, **196–197,** 305, 343
Kingston, Maxine Hong **X:** 177
Kingston Trio **IX:** 111, 244
King William's War **II: 185,** 418c
    British Empire **II:** 41
    ethnocentrism **II:** 114
    Massachusetts **II:** 214

monarchy, British **II:** 232
    New Hampshire **II:** 251
    New York **II:** 262
Kinkel, Gottfried **VI:** 256
Kinney, Abbot **VI:** 153
Kino, Eusebio **II:** 115, 284, 300
Kinsey, Alfred C. **IX:** 119, 162, **162–163,** 330c
kinship groups **II:** 265
Kinyoun, Joseph J. **IX:** 222
Kiowa nation **IV:** 47, 79, 306; **VII:** 165–166
Kiowa-Tanoan language **II:** 149
Kircher, Henry **V:** 147
Kirk, George W. **V:** 199
Kirk, Russell **X:** 78
Kirkland, Lane **X:** 169
Kirkland, Reverend **III:** 255
Kirkpatrick, Evron **X:** 216
Kirkpatrick, Jeane
    Bennett, William J. **X:** 35
    conservative movement **X:** 79
    Kemp, Jack F. **X:** 163
    neoconservatism **X:** 216
    United Nations **X:** 308
Kirtland, Ohio **IV:** 79, 323
Kissinger, Henry A. **IX:** 310; **X: 164–166,** 165
    African nations **X:** 13
    cold war **X:** 70
    defense policy **X:** 86
    détente **X:** 89
    Ford, Gerald R. **X:** 120
    foreign policy **X:** 122
    Haig, Alexander M., Jr. **X:** 139
    Latin America **X:** 173
    Nixon, Richard M. **X:** 220
    Perot, H. Ross **X:** 234
    popular culture **X:** 240
    Strategic Arms Limitation Treaties **X:** 289
    Vietnam War **X:** 311, 312
Kissinger Commission Report, The **X:** 173
Kit Carson National Forest **IX:** 298, 334c
"kitchen debate" **X:** 220
Kittaning **II:** 332
Kittrell College **VI:** 4
Kitty Hawk, NC **VII:** 347, 356c
kivas **I:** 383; **II:** 165
Kiwaloo **IV:** 199
KKK. *See* Ku Klux Klan
KLA (Kosovo Liberation Army) **X:** 167
Klamath nation **IX:** 228
Klaw, Mark **VI:** 287
Klayman, Larry **X:** 162
Klebold, Dylan **X:** 330c
Kleindienst, Richard **X:** 264

Klinghoffer, Leon **X:** 298
Klondike gold rush **VI: 160–162,** *161,* 327c
Knapp, Louisa **VI:** 185
Knickerbocker Magazine **IV:** 196
Knickerbocker School **IV:** 212
Knight, Daniel Ridgway **VI:** 138
Knight, Sarah Kemble **II: 185–186,** 215, 377
Knight, Tobias **II:** 369
Knights of Labor **V:** 177; **VI: 162,** 324c, 325c; **VII:** 10, 186, 250
    American Federation of Labor **VI:** 11
    class consciousness **VI:** 57
    contract labor **VI:** 66
    farmers' alliances **VI:** 99
    immigration restrictions **VI:** 141
    Internal Revenue taxes **VI:** 147
    labor, radical **VI:** 167
    labor, woman **VI:** 169
    labor organizations **VI:** 169, 170
    Lease, Mary Elizabeth **VI:** 173
    People's Party **VI:** 222
    Powderly, Terence Vincent **VI:** 227
    railroads **VI:** 237
    Socialist Labor Party **VI:** 268
    Socialist Party **VI:** 269
    Willard, Frances **VI:** 315
Knights of the Golden Circle **V:** 118
Knights of the Southern Circle **V:** 33
Knolle, Henry **VII:** 307
Knollys, Francis **I:** 111
Knot, Richard **II:** 368
Knowles, Charles **II:** 182
Knowlton, Thomas **III:** 160
Know-Nothing Party **IV: 201–202,** *202*
    American Protective Association **VI:** 12
    anti-Catholic riots **IV:** 23
    Democratic Party **IV:** 108
    Fillmore, Millard **IV:** 138
    Harlan, John Marshall **VI:** 121
    Houston, Sam **IV:** 175
    immigration **IV:** 180
    nativism **VI:** 209
    religion **IV:** 298
    Republican Party **IV:** 300–301
    Roman Catholicism **VI:** 249
    Whig Party **IV:** 364

Know-Nothings **V:** 181, 251, 300–301
Knox, Frank **VIII:** 97, 236, 305, 306
Knox, Henry **III:** 69, **197–198,** 276, 393c; **V:** 372
Knox, John **I:** 50, 307
Knox, Philander C. **VII:** 70
Knox, William Franklin **IX:** 283
Knox v. Lee **VI:** 72
Knoxville, siege of **V:** 215
Knoxville, Tennessee **V:** 45, 57, 121
Knudsen, William S. **VIII:** 84, 255
Knyphausen, William von **III:** 48, 245
Kodak **VI:** 87, 326c
Kodak camera **VI:** 137, 150
Kommandatura **IX:** 37
Kongo (Kingdom of) **I: 195–196,** 326, 327, 343
Konkomba **I:** 101
Konoye, Fumimaro **VIII:** 199
Kool and the Gang **X:** 202
Kopechne, Mary Jo **X:** 164
Koran. *See* Qur'an
Korea **V:** 183; **IX:** 21. *See also* Democratic People's Republic of Korea; Republic of Korea
Koreagate **X:** 161, **166**
Korean Americans **X:** 28, 200
Korean War **VIII:** 80, 349, 366; **IX: 163–165,** 164m, *165,* 330c, **331c**
    Acheson, Dean **IX:** 2
    anticommunism **IX:** 14
    Asia (and foreign policy) **IX:** 21
    cold war **IX:** 60
    communism **IX:** 61
    defense budget **IX:** 77
    Eisenhower, Dwight D. **IX:** 92
    MacArthur, Douglas **IX:** 186
    migration **IX:** 202
    military-industrial complex **IX:** 203
    NATO **IX:** 233
    science **IX:** 270
    Soviet Union **IX:** 277
    Truman, Harry **IX:** 299
    veterans **IX:** 307
    White Paper **IX:** 321
Korematsu, Fred **VIII:** 178
Korematsu v. United States **VIII: 178,** 410c
    Asian Americans **VIII:** 26
    Black, Hugo L. **VIII:** 37
    civil liberties **VIII:** 61

Executive Order 9066 **VIII:** 107
Frankfurter, Felix **VIII:** 127
Japanese Americans, relocation of **VIII:** 172
Supreme Court **VIII:** 347
Koresh, David **X:** 39–40, 194
Kornfeld, Artie **X:** 321
Kościuszko, Tadeusz **III: 198,** 393c
Kosovo **X: 166–167,** 330c
    Clinton, William **X:** 69
    Dayton accords **X:** 85
    defense policy **X:** 88
    House of Representatives **X:** 145
    NATO **X:** 224
    United Nations **X:** 307
    War Powers Act **X:** 315
Kosovo Liberation Army (KLA) **X:** 167
Kossi, king of Gao **I:** 331
Kotoko **I:** 52, **196**
Koumbi-Saleh **I:** 141
Koyukon **I:** 252
Kraemer, Fritz **X:** 165–166
Kraenzlein, Alfred **VI:** 290
Kramer, Jack **VIII:** 337
Krimmel, John Lewis **IV:** 26–27
Kristallnacht **VIII:** 149
Kristol, Irving **X:** 215, 216
Kristol, William **X:** 79
Kroc, Ray **IX:** 190–191
Kropotkin, Peter **VII:** 250
Kuapoge pueblo **I:** 319
Kubrick, Stanley **IX:** 213; **X:** 198, 240
Kudlow, Lawrence **X:** 43
Kuhn, Adam **II:** 277
Kuhn, Justus Engelhardt **II:** 25, **186**
Kuhn, Loeb & Company **VI:** 19
Ku Klux Klan (KKK) **V: 199–201,** 200, 408c; **VI:** 181, 182, 323c; **VII:** xiv, **147–149,** 148, 358c; **VIII:** 37, 48, 407c; **IX:** 166, **166–167,** 334c; **X:** 257
    anti-Semitism **VII:** 14
    Birth of a Nation **VII:** 30
    Communist Party **VII:** 53
    Democratic Party **V:** 95
    elections **V:** 111; **VII:** 81
    Enforcement Acts **V:** 117
    Forrest, Nathan Bedford **V:** 133, 135
    Garvey, Marcus **VII:** 106
    Griffith, D. W. **VII:** 115–116
    Ku Klux Klan Act **V:** 201
    lobbying groups **VII:** 162

movie industry **VII:** 191
nativism **VII:** 209
Oates, William C. **V:** 257
race and racial conflict **IX:** 253, 254
Rainey, Joseph H. **V:** 291
Reconstruction **V:** 294
redemption **V:** 297
religion **VII:** 262
Republican Party **V:** 302
scalawags **V:** 308
sharecropping **V:** 316
Southern Manifesto **IX:** 276
Tarbell, Ida **VII:** 305
Tourgée, Albion W. **V:** 354
Union League **V:** 368
United States v. Cruikshank **V:** 375
Universal Negro Improvement Association (UNIA) **VII:** 315
White Citizens' Councils **IX:** 320
Ku Klux Klan Act **V: 201**
    Elliot, Robert B. **V:** 111
    Enforcement Acts **V:** 117
    Ku Klux Klan **V:** 200
    Rainey, Joseph H. **V:** 291
    redemption **V:** 296
Ku Klux Klan cases **VI: 162–163,** 174, 209
Ku Klux Klan Enforcement Act of 1871 **VI:** 163, 323c
Kukulcán **I:** 69, 70, 228, 356
Kumasi **I:** 13
Kurile Islands **VIII:** 402
Kurita, Takeo **VIII:** 143, 186, 187
Kush people **I:** 377
Kuwait
    Bush, George H. W. **X:** 46
    Clinton, William **X:** 67
    defense policy **X:** 87
    NATO **X:** 223
    OPEC **X:** 228–229
    Persian Gulf War **X:** 234–235
    terrorism **X:** 298
    United Nations **X:** 307
Kyoto Protocol **X:** 331c
Kyoto Treaty **X:** 134, 329c
Kyrgyzstan **X:** 281

L

Labbadie, Sylvestre **IV:** 239
labor, free
    Davis Bend, Mississippi, freedmen's colony **V:** 91–92

employment **V:** 116
Fitzhugh, George **V:** 128
Freedmen's Bureau **V:** 142–144
Port Royal, South Carolina, Experiment **V:** 279–280
Republican Party **V:** 301, 302
states' rights **V:** 335
Laboratory School **VII:** 68
labor camps, Soviet **VIII:** 282
labor contracts **V:** 29, 142, 143
Labor Department **VII:** 10, 162; **VIII:** 63, 265, 375; **IX:** 150, 324
Laborers Union **X:** 236
labor/labor movement **II: 187–190,** 190, 418c; **III:** 199, **199–200; IV: 203–205; VI: 169–170,** 325c, 327c; **VII: 151–154,** 152t, 153, 356c–359c, 361c; **VIII: 179–181,** 180, 406c–408c; **IX: 169–171; X: 169–171,** 170. See also employment; industrialization/Industrial Revolution; strikes; unions/union movement; wages
    abolitionism **II:** 1–2
    Adamson Act **VII:** 1–2
    Adkins v. Children's Hospital **VII:** 3
    AFL. See American Federation of Labor
    African Americans **II:** 5–6; **IV:** 7; **VI:** 5, 6; **VIII:** 3
    agriculture **II:** 7, 11–13; **IX:** 8
    Algonquin **II:** 17
    almshouses **II:** 18
    American Federation of Labor **VI:** 11; **VIII:** 14
    American Plan **VII:** 12
    animals **II:** 21–22
    Anthracite Coal Strike **VII:** 12–13
    antimonopoly **VIII:** 17
    artisans **II:** 25–26; **III:** 26
    Asian Americans **VIII:** 26
    automobile industry **VIII:** 30
    braceros **IX:** 41–42
    Bridges, Harry **VIII:** 42–43
    bubonic plague **I:** 286
    Buck's Stove **VII:** 35–36
    business **VIII:** 47
    Byrnes, James F. **VIII:** 48
    Caribbean **II:** 53, 189
    Cherokee **II:** 57

Chesapeake Bay **II:** 58–57, 187–188
child labor **VI:** xv, 165, **165–166**
cities and urban life **VIII:** 58
civil liberties **VIII:** 60
class **II:** 63
class consciousness **VI:** 57
Clayton Antitrust Act. See Clayton Antitrust Act
clothing **II:** 65
Colored National Labor Union **V:** 68–69
Communists **VIII:** 65
Congress **VIII:** 67
Connecticut **II:** 69
conservatism **VIII:** 71
conservative coalition **VIII:** 73
convict labor **II:** 71–72
crowd action **II:** 78
Dale, Sir Thomas **II:** 81
Danbury Hatters **VII:** 61
Darrow, Clarence **VII:** 62
Debs, Eugene V. **VII:** 64–65
Democratic Party **VII:** 66
domesticity **II:** 93
Dutch West India Company **II:** 98
economy **II:** 101; **IV:** 119
election of 1936 **VIII:** 97
election of 1944 **VIII:** 99
employment **V:** 116, 117
encomienda **I:** 122
environment **II:** 112
ERA **VII:** 87; **X:** 105
Fair Labor Standards Act **VIII:** 110
Farmer-Labor Party **VII:** 91
FBI **VIII:** 115
Flynn, Elizabeth Gurley **VII:** 94–95
Ford, Henry **VII:** 96–97
Frick, Henry Clay **VI:** 105
Fuel Administration **VII:** 103
Garner, John Nance **VIII:** 129
Gastonia Strike **VII:** 106
Gates, Sir Thomas **II:** 135
gender **II:** 136, 189, 190
German immigrants **II:** 139
Godkin, Edwin Lawrence **VI:** 116
Goldmark, Josephine **VII:** 111
Gompers, Samuel **VI:** 116–117

labor/labor movement
  (continued)
    Great Migration **VII:**
      111–113
    Great Strike of 1877 **VI:**
      119–120
    Greeley, Horace **V:** 158
    Greenwich Village **VII:**
      114–115
    Harding, Warren G. **VII:**
      118
    Hawaiian Islands **IV:** 172
    Haymarket riot **VI:** 127
    Haywood, "Big Bill" **VII:**
      120
    Hillman, Sidney **VIII:**
      145–146
    Hoover presidency **VIII:**
      154
    housing **II:** 157, 158
    immigration **III:** 173; **IV:**
      179; **V:** 177; **VI:** 140; **X:**
      147, 148
    immigration restrictions
      VI: 141
    indentured servitude **II:**
      163–165
    Industrial Relations
      Commission **VII:**
      128–129
    industrial revolution **III:**
      178
    industrial revolution,
      second **VI:** 145–147
    International Ladies'
      Garment Workers
      Union **VII:** 131–132
    iron manufacturing **II:**
      167–168
    Italian Americans **VIII:**
      167
    IWW **VII:** 129–131
    Jamestown **II:** 171–172
    Jews **VIII:** 172
    Johnson, Hugh S. **VIII:**
      173
    Kaiser, Henry J. **VIII:** 175
    Knights of Labor **VI:** 162
    labor **VIII:** 179
    labor, child **VI:** 166
    labor, woman **VI:** 169
    labor trends **VI:** 171
    La Follette, Robert M., Jr.
      VIII: 182
    Lawrence Strike **VII:**
      155–156
    Lewis, John L. **VIII:**
      185–186
    liberalism **VIII:** 188
    literature **VIII:** 191
    Lloyd, Henry Demarest
      VI: 179

lobbying groups **VII:** 162
Lochner v. New York **VII:**
  163–164
Locke, John **II:** 198
Louisiana **II:** 200
Lower South **II:** 188–189
Ludlow Massacre **VII:**
  167–168
lumbering **II:** 201
manufacturing and
  industry **II:** 203–204
mariners **II:** 204
marriage and family life **II:**
  206
Maryland **II:** 210–211
mass production. *See* mass
  production
Mexican Americans **VIII:**
  210
Mexican immigration **VII:**
  182–183
Middle Colonies and New
  England **II:** 189
Mills, C. Wright **IX:** 204
miscegenation **II:** 228
Mittelberger, Gottlieb **II:**
  231
Molly Maguires **VI:** 195
mortality **II:** 235
muckrakers **VII:** 192
Muller v. Oregon **VII:**
  192–193
Murray, Philip **VIII:** 221
music **II:** 239
NAACP **VIII:** 227
NAFTA **X:** 222
National Association of
  Manufacturers **VII:** 200
National Civic Federation
  VII: 201
National Labor Union
  (NLU) **V:** 248
National War Labor Board
  VII: 204
National Women's Trade
  Union League **VII:**
  205–206
New Mexico **II:** 254
New Netherland **II:** 257
New Unionism **VII:**
  212–213
New York **II:** 260
New York City **II:** 262
NIRA **VIII:** 228
NLRA **VIII:** 229
NLRB **VIII:** 229–231
Norris, George W. **VIII:**
  248
northern United States **IV:**
  203–205
NRA **VIII:** 231
NWLB **VIII:** 233–234

open shop movement. *See*
  open shop movement
OPM **VIII:** 255
Owen, Robert **IV:** 273
OWMR **VIII:** 259
Palmer, A. Mitchell **VII:**
  221
Panic of 1837 **IV:** 277
Passaic Strike **VII:** 224–225
Paterson Strike **VII:** 225
Perkins, Frances **VIII:** 265
Philadelphia **II:** 282
plantation system **II:**
  286–287
Polish Americans **VIII:**
  269
politics in the Roosevelt
  era **VIII:** 271
Popular Front **VIII:** 276
postwar planning **VIII:**
  278
Powderly, Terence Vincent
  VI: 227
Protestant work ethic **II:**
  302
race and racial conflict **II:**
  311; **VIII:** 288
radicalism. *See* radicalism
radical labor **VI:** *166*,
  166–167, 319
radical press **VII:** 252–253
Railroad Administration
  VII: 255
Randolph, A. Philip **VIII:**
  291
recreation **VII:** 258
redemptioners **II:** 313
Red Scare **VII:** 258–259
religion **VIII:** 303
repartimiento **I:** 310–311
Roosevelt, Franklin D.
  VIII: 313
Rosie the Riveter **VIII:**
  315
scientific management
  VII: 277
Seattle General Strike **VII:**
  278–279
Second New Deal **VIII:**
  321
shipbuilding **II:** 335; **VIII:**
  324–325
Shirtwaist Makers Strike
  VII: 284–285
silver **I:** 325
slavery **I:** 325–328; **II:**
  338–342; **IV:** 316–319
slave trade **II:** 343–344
Smith, Alfred E. **VII:** 287
socialism **VI:** 268; **VIII:**
  327
Socialist Party **VI:** 269

social work **VII:** 290
society, British American
  II: 349, 350
South Carolina **II:** 354
southern United States **IV:**
  205
Spanish colonies **II:** 355,
  357–358
Stanton, Elizabeth Cady **V:**
  335
steel industry **VII:** 297;
  VIII: 338
Steel Strike of 1919 **VII:**
  298–299
STFU **VIII:** 332–333
strikes **V:** 339–340
Sumner, William Graham
  VI: 281
Sunbelt **X:** 290
Sunday, Billy **VII:** 302
Taft, William Howard **VII:**
  303
Taylor, Frederick W. **VII:**
  306–307
technology **II:** 369
Tenochtitlán **I:** 345–346
Third New Deal **VIII:** 357
Thomas, Norman **VIII:**
  358
tobacco **II:** 374, 375
trade and shipping **II:** 377
travel **II:** 377
union movement **IX:**
  303–304
United Mine Workers of
  America (UMWA) **VII:**
  313–314
Virginia **II:** 382–{2: }384
Virginia Company of
  London **II:** 387
voluntary associations **III:**
  362
wage and price controls **II:**
  389; **VIII:** 371
Wagner, Robert F. **VIII:**
  372
Wald, Lillian **VII:** 329
welfare capitalism **VII:**
  332–333
Wilson, Woodrow **VII:** 334
woman labor **VI: 169**
women's network **VIII:**
  383
women's status and rights
  II: 406–407; **VII:** 338;
  IX: 324
Workmen's Compensation
  Act **VII:** 342–343
World War II **VIII:** 390
World War II home front
  VIII: 394, 395
Zacatecas **I:** 381

Labor Management Relations Act of 1947. *See* Taft-Hartley Act
labor market **IV:** 201, 291
  Brown, Joseph **V:** 39
  conscription **V:** 79
  Copperheads **V:** 82
  Democratic Party **V:** 94
  New York City draft riots **V:** 254, 255
"Labor Movement Is a Fixed Fact" speech (Gompers) **VI:** 344–346
labor reform **IV:** 273, 281
Labor Reform Party **VI:** 169
labor shortages **V:** 356
labor trends **VI:** 5, 6, 66, **170–171,** 237
labor unions. *See* unions/union movement
labor unrest **VI:** 211
Laboulaye, Edouard de **VI:** 275
Lackawanna Coal and Iron Company **VI:** 168
Laclede, Pierre **IV:** 78
La Demoiselle **II: 190–191**
ladies aid societies **V: 203–204,** 373, 396–397
Ladies' Album **IV:** 167
Ladies Central Relief Committee **V:** 255–256
Ladies' Home Journal **VI:** 2, 138, 185; **VII:** *4,* 142; **VIII:** 343
Ladies' Magazine **IV:** 167
Ladies Professional Golf Association **X:** 262
LaDuke, Winona **X:** 135
Lady Chatterly's Lover (Lawrence) **VIII:** 55
Ladye Annabel; or, The Doom of the Poisoner (Lippard) **IV:** 211
La Farge, John **VIII:** 54
  Adams, Henry **VI:** 1
  Aesthetic movement **VI:** 3
  painting **VI:** 219
  Richardson, Henry Hobson **VI:** 248
Lafayette, Marie-Joseph-Paul-Yves-Roche-Gilbert du Motier, marquis de **III: 200–201,** 394*c*
  Barry, John **III:** 36
  Carey, Mathew **III:** 61
  French Revolution **III:** 138
  Independence Hall **III:** 176
  Kalb, baron de **III:** 195
  Monmouth, Battle of **III:** 244, 245

  Washington, George **III:** 368
  Wayne, Anthony **III:** 369
  Yorktown, surrender at **III:** 388
Lafayette Escadrill **VII:** 23
Laffer, Arthur Betz **X:** 171–172
Laffer curve **X: 171–172**
Lafitte, Jean **IV:** 56, **205–206,** 262
La Florida. *See* Florida
La Follette, Philip **VIII:** 190
La Follette, Robert **VII: 154–155,** 360*c;* **VIII:** 377; **X:** 101
  Congress **VII:** 53–54
  Coolidge, Calvin **VII:** 57
  Democratic Party **VII:** 66
  elections **VII:** 80, 81
  Farmer-Labor Party **VII:** 91
  politics **VII:** 229, 230
  Progressive Party **VII:** 236, 237
  progressivism **VII:** 238
  Republican Party **VII:** 263
  Taft, William Howard **VII:** 303, 304
La Follette, Robert M., Jr. **VIII:** 66, **182,** 299, 305
La Follette, Robert M., Sr. **VIII:** 377
La Follette, Susan **VII:** 340
La Follette's Weekly Magazine **VII:** 155
La Guardia, Fiorello **VIII: 182–183,** 406*c*
  antimonopoly **VIII:** 17
  Berle, Adolf A., Jr. **VIII:** 35
  Italian Americans **VIII:** 167
  MOWM **VIII:** 201
  OCD **VIII:** 253
  taxation **VIII:** 351
  Tugwell, Rexford G. **VIII:** 361
La Guardia Airport **VIII:** 285
Laínez, Diego **I:** 189, 209
Laird, Melvin **X:** 76, 301
laissez-faire economics
  business and government **VI:** 39
  Democratic Party **VI:** 77
  due process clause **VI:** 82
  Godkin, Edwin Lawrence **VI:** 116
  Social Darwinism **VI:** 266
  Sumner, William Graham **VI:** 280
  theory **VII:** 163

laissez-faire liberalism **VIII:** 71, 187
Lake Champlain **II:** 243, 251; **IV:** 356, 375*c*
Lake Champlain, Battle of **IV:** 358
Lake Erie, Battle of **IV:** 169, 206*m,* **206–207,** 356
Lake George **II:** 124, 158, 177
Lake Guatavita **I:** 118
Lake Huron **II:** 129
Lake Michigan **II:** 129, 206, 263
Lake Ontario **IV:** 206
Lake Placid conferences **VI:** 247
Lake Pontchartrain **II:** 258
Lake Simcoe **II:** 160
Lake Winnebago **II:** 206
Lakota **II:** 50; **VI:** 69
Lakota Sioux nation **VI:** 29, 263
L.A. Law (TV program) **X:** 295
Laman, Gary **X:** 275
Lamar, Mirabeau B. **IV:** 175, 338; **V:** 189
Lamarck, Jean-Baptiste **IV:** 34
Lamb, William **VI:** 99
Lambda legal defense **X:** 127
Lamm, Richard **X:** 226
Lamon, Ward Hill **V:** 17
Lamothe, Antoine de, sieur de Cadillac **II:** 193
LaMountain, John **V:** 21
L'Amour, Louis **X:** 178
Lamy, Jean Baptiste **IV: 207**
Lancaster, Burt **IX:** 181
land **II: 191–192; IV:** 12, 25; **IX:** 334*c. See also* public land
  agriculture **II:** 9–12; **X:** 16
  Alaska Native Claim Settlement Act **X:** 17
  Albany Congress **II:** 14
  Algonquin **II:** 17
  Alliance for Progress **IX:** 10–11
  Bacon's Rebellion **II:** 27
  borderlands **II:** 34–35
  Carter, Robert "King" **II:** 54
  Cherokee **II:** 58
  class **II:** 63
  Conestoga **II:** 67
  Cornstalk **II:** 72
  Dutch-Indian Wars **II:** 98–99
  forts **II:** 124
  French colonies **II:** 127
  Georgia **II:** 137, 138
  German immigrants **II:** 139–140
  Gore, Albert, Jr. **X:** 134
  government, British American **II:** 144–146

  Great Plains Indians **II:** 150
  Grenville, Sir Richard **II:** 150
  indentured servitude **II:** 163, 164
  Indian Claims Commission **IX:** 143
  Indians of the Desert Southwest **II:** 165, 166
  Jamestown **II:** 171, 172
  Jemison, Mary **II:** 173
  Johnson, Anthony **II:** 175
  Johnson, Sir William **II:** 177
  Kalm, Peter **II:** 181
  King Philip's War **II:** 184
  labor **II:** 187–189
  Latino movement **IX:** 174
  Livingston, Robert **II:** 196
  manufacturing and industry **II:** 203
  marriage and family life **II:** 207
  Maryland **II:** 210, 211
  Mason, John **II:** 211
  Massachusetts **II:** 212
  merchants **II:** 222
  Metacom **II:** 222
  Minuit, Peter **II:** 227
  Morris, Lewis **II:** 234
  Musgrove, Mary Bosomworth **II:** 238
  Natchez Revolt **II:** 241
  Native American movement **IX:** 227
  Native Americans **II:** 243, 244, 246; **X:** 214
  New Hampshire **II:** 251
  New Jersey **II:** 253
  New Netherland **II:** 255, 256
  New York **II:** 260, 262
  North Carolina **II:** 264
  Opechancanough **II:** 268
  Paxton Boys **II:** 272
  Pennsylvania **II:** 274
  plantation system **II:** 286, 287
  primogeniture and entail **II:** 297–298
  property rights **X:** 249–251
  race and racial conflict **II:** 311
  RFRA **X:** 266
  Rhode Island **II:** 321
  society, British American **II:** 349, 352
  South Carolina **II:** 353
  Spanish colonies **II:** 357
  Submerged Lands Act **IX:** 286–287

land (continued)
  suffrage **II:** 364
  Swedish colonies **II:** 364
  Teedyuscung **II:** 370
  tenants **II:** 370–371
  Termination policy **IX:** 297–298
  Tijerina, Reies López **IX:** 298–299
  tobacco **II:** 375
  Treaty of Paris **II:** 378
  Tuscarora War **II:** 379
  Vermont **II:** 381
  Virginia **II:** 383
  Walking Purchase of 1737 **II:** 389
  war and warfare **II:** 391
  Ward, Nancy **II:** 392
  Winthrop, John **II:** 401
  women's status and rights **II:** 406
Landa, Diego de **I:** 379
Land Act Bill of 1800 **IV:** 168
Land Act of 1796 **IV:** 286, 376c
Land Act of 1820 **IV:** 376c
Land and Water Conservation Fund of 1964 **IX:** 255
land bank **II:** 398
Land Bank versus Silver Bank controversy **II:** 215
land disputes **IV:** 85–86
Land-Grant College Bill. *See* Morrill Land-Grant Act of 1862
land-grant colleges **V:** 7, 108
land grants
  Austin, Stephen F. **IV:** 36–37
  Brent, Margaret Reed **II:** 40
  business and government **VI:** 39
  California **IV:** 64–65
  Creole **II:** 74
  Dale, Sir Thomas **II:** 81
  homesteading **VI:** 131–132
  lobbies and pressure groups **VI:** 180
  Pennsylvania **II:** 275
  railroads **VI:** 238
  Rensselaerswyck **II:** 319
  Scott, Thomas Alexander **VI:** 258
  Texas **IV:** 338
  Texas, Republic of **IV:** 340
  Texas Revolution **IV:** 339
  Virginia **II:** 382
  Virginia Company of London **II:** 387
Landis, James **X:** 125
Landis, James M. **VIII:** 322
Landis, John **VIII:** 253, 254

Landis, Kenesaw Mountain **VII:** 26, 294
Land Law of 1800 **IV:** 286
Land Law of 1820 **IV:** 287
Land League **V:** 177
land leasing **V:** 315
land legislation **IV:** 286–288
"landless Indians" **II:** 223
land mines **V:** 305, 308–309, 346
Landon, Alfred M. **VIII: 183,** 407c
  American Liberty League **VIII:** 15
  Borah, William E. **VIII:** 40
  conservatism **VIII:** 72
  election of 1936 **VIII:** 97
  Farley, James A. **VIII:** 111
  Hoover, Herbert **VIII:** 152
  politics in the Roosevelt era **VIII:** 270, 271
  public opinion polls **VIII:** 284
  Republican Party **VIII:** 305
  Townsend, Francis E. **VIII:** 359
  Willkie, Wendell L. **VIII:** 379
Land Ordinance of 1785 **III:** 394c; **IV:** 286–288; **VI:** 92
land ownership **IV:** 12, 64, 163; **V:** 113, 142, 332–333; **VII:** 206
  Acadia **I:** 2–3
  adelantado **I:** 3–4
  African Americans **VI:** 5
  agriculture **VI:** 8
  Brazil **I:** 33
  entail **I:** 122–123
  feudalism **I:** 129–130
  haciendas **I:** 149
  headright **I:** 157
  invention and technology **I:** 180
  Native Americans **VI:** 206, 207, 209
  Nez Perce War **VI:** 213
  Tlaxcala **I:** 353
  Tordesillas, Treaty of **I:** 358–359, 359m
  Vitoria, Francisco de **I:** 369–370
land policy **IV:** 286–288
land prices **IV:** 18, 19
land riots **III: 201–202**
  North Carolina Regulation **III:** 261
  riots **III:** 309
  Shays's Rebellion **III:** 324–325
  Wyoming Valley War **III:** 384

Landrum, Phil **IX:** 87
Landrum-Griffin Act of 1959 **VIII:** 231; **IX:** 303
land rushes **VI:** 326c
land sales **IV:** 286, 287, 330, 377c
landscape architecture **V:** 257–258
landscape gardening **IV:** 28
landscape painting **IV:** 25–26, 55; **VI:** 219
land speculation **II:** 191, 192; **V:** 170, 180
  agriculture **IV:** 12
  Coxe, Tench **III:** 96
  Holland Land Company **III:** 167
  New Madrid earthquake **IV:** 262
  Ohio Company of Associates **III:** 265
  Ohio Company of Virginia **III:** 265
  Panic of 1819 **IV:** 275
  Panic of 1837 **IV:** 276
  public land policy **IV:** 286
  Yazoo claims **III:** 388
Lane, Franklin **VII:** 203
Lane, James H. **V:** 4, 186
Lane, Ralph **I:** 111–112, **197,** 314, 372; **II:** 151, 401
Lane Seminary **IV:** 362
Lang, Michael **X:** 321
Langdon, F. W. **VI:** 195, 196
Lange, Dorothea **VIII:** 24, 87, 268, 407c
Langley, Samuel P. **VI:** 258
Langley Act **VII:** 243
Langley Research Center **X:** 281
Langston, John Mercer **V:** 125; **VI: 171–172**
languages
  Africa **II:** 4
  Algonquian **I:** 6
  Algonquin **II:** 17
  Arawak **I:** 12
  Bantu **I:** 24, 25
  Benin **I:** 28
  Bilingual Education Act of 1968 **X:** 35–36
  Brulé, Étienne **II:** 44
  California **I:** 48
  California Indians **II:** 49
  Carib **I:** 56
  Chichén Itzá **I:** 70
  computer **IX:** 269
  Creole **II:** 74
  Delaware Indians **II:** 89
  Fernando Po **I:** 129
  Great Plains Indians **II:** 149

Gullah **II:** 151–152
Harriot, Thomas **I:** 154
métis **II:** 223
multiculturalism **X:** 200
Nahuatl **I:** 250
New Netherland **II:** 257
New York **II:** 260
New York City **II:** 262
Nicolet, Jean **II:** 263
Olmecs **I:** 269
political correctness **X:** 236–237
popular culture **X:** 239, 241
Pueblo Indians **II:** 303
slavery **II:** 342
Virginia **II:** 384
Zeisberger, David **II:** 415
Lanham Defense Housing Act **VIII:** 159
Lanier, Sidney **VI:** 178
Lansdale, Edward G. **IX:** 236
Lansing, Robert **VII:** 359c
Lansing-Ishii Agreement of 1917 **VII:** 359c
Lanzarote Island **I:** 53
Laos **IX:** 316–317; **X:** 70, 311, 325c
Laotian Americans **X:** 28
laparoscopic surgery **X:** 190
Lapham, Increase A. **IV:** 309; **VI:** 310
La Plata **IV:** 241
Lapowinsa **II:** 390
Lapu Lapu **I:** 216, 387c
La Raza Unida **IX: 171,** 174; **X:** 142
Lardner, Ring, Jr. **IX:** 134–135, *211*
Largent, Steve **X:** 183
Larkin, Thomas Oliver **IV:** 45, 65, **207–208**
La Roche, Mesgouez de (Troilus de Mesgouez, marquis de La Roche) **II:** 126
Larry King Live **X:** 263
Larson, Jonathan **X:** 242
La Salle, René-Robert Cavelier, sieur de **I:** 115, 129, **192,** 199, 246, 418c
LaSalle, Sieur de **IV:** 337
Las Casas, Bartolomé de **I: 197–201,** 387c; **II:** 93–94
  black legend **I:** 30, 31
  Canary Islands **I:** 53
  Charles V **I:** 69
  Cuba **I:** 98
  Dominicans **I:** 110
  Ferdinand and Isabella **I:** 128
  printing press **I:** 294
  Requerimiento **I:** 311

Sepúlveda, Juan Ginés de **I:** 322
smallpox **I:** 331
Vitoria, Francisco de **I:** 369, 370
Lasch, Christopher **X:** 177
lasers **X:** 273, 275, 289–290
Las Hibueras **I:** 95
Lasker, Albert **VII:** 4, 314
Lassalle, Ferdinand **VI:** 166, 267
Lassalleans
    labor, radical **VI:** 166, 167
    socialism **VI:** 267
    Socialist Labor Party **VI:** 268
    Socialist Party **VI:** 268–269
Last of the Mohicans, The (Cooper) **IV:** 212, 376*c*
Last Rambles Amongst the Indians of the Rocky Mountains and the Andes (Catlin) **IV:** 78
last rites **V:** 256
Las Vegas **X:** 263
latent classicism **X:** 27
Lathrop, Julia **VII:** 1, 47
Latimer, John **I:** 35
Latin America **II:** 342, 356, 359; **IV:** 219; **V:** 131, 259–260; **VII:** 356*c*, 361*c*; **VIII:** 405*c*, 408*c*; **X:** 173. *See also* Central America; South America
    Alliance for Progress **IX:** 10–11
    Blaine, James Gillespie **VI:** 31
    castas **I:** 61–62
    Chilean-American relations **VI:** 49–50
    Clark Memorandum **VII:** 50–51
    dollar diplomacy **VII:** 70
    FCC **VIII:** 116–117
    foreign policy **VI:** 103; **VII:** 99; **VIII:** 124
    and foreign policy **IX:** 171–172
    Good Neighbor Policy **VIII:** 132–133
    haciendas **I:** 149
    Hoover presidency **VIII:** 154
    Hull, Cordell **VIII:** 160
    Leahy, William D. **VIII:** 183
    Mexico **X:** 192–193
    Nicaragua **X:** 217–218
    Pan-American Union **VI:** 220
    Peru **I:** 279–280

Point Four Program **IX:** 242–243
Reciprocal Trade Agreements Act **VIII:** 294
trade, foreign **VII:** 310
United Nations **X:** 307
U.S. relations with **X:** **172–174**
Venezuela boundary dispute **VI:** 303
wars of national liberation **IX:** 317
Welles, Sumner **VIII:** 377
Latin music **X:** 241
Latino movement **IX:** 124–125, **173–174**, 298–299, 327–328
Latrobe, Benjamin Henry **III:** 20, 227
Latvia **VII:** 323; **IX:** 58, 105; **X:** 281
Laud, William **II:** 304
Laudonnière, René de **I:** 57, **201–202**, 202, 348, 351
Laurence, E. O. **VIII:** 318
Laurens, Henry **II:** 222; **III:** **202–203**
Lauste, Eugene **VII:** 190
Lau v. Nichols **X:** 35
"lavender menace" **IX:** 325; **X:** 211
La Venta **I:** 269, 270
law journals **VI:** 34
Lawlor, Charles B. **VI:** 204
lawn tennis **VI:** *274*
Law of Great Peace **II:** 85
Law of the Indies **III:** 19
Lawrence, Amos A. **IV:** 223, 224
Lawrence, Charles **II:** 2
Lawrence, D. H. **VIII:** 55; **IX:** 183
Lawrence, Jacob **VIII:** 23–24
Lawrence, James **IV:** 152
Lawrence, Kansas **IV:** 223–224; **V:** 407*c*
    Bleeding Kansas **V:** 31
    Brown, John **V:** 38
    bushwhackers **V:** 46
    Quantrill, William Clarke **V:** 285
Lawrence, USS **IV:** 206
Lawrence Strike **VII:** **155–156**, 357*c*
    Flynn, Elizabeth Gurley **VII:** 95
    Greenwich Village **VII:** 114–115
    Haywood, "Big Bill" **VII:** 120
    IWW **VII:** 130
    radicalism **VII:** 250
    Sanger, Margaret **VII:** 273

laws. *See also* slave codes; *specific laws*
    African Americans **II:** 7
    British Empire **II:** 43
    Burgesses, House of **II:** 44–45
    Connecticut **II:** 70
    crime and punishment **II:** 76
    De Lancey, James **II:** 85
    education **II:** 103
    government, British American **II:** 144
    mercantilism **II:** 221
    monarchy, British **II:** 232
    Penn, William **II:** 273
    piracy **II:** 285
    slave codes **II:** 336
    slavery **II:** 340, 342
    Spanish colonies **II:** 357
    Stuyvesant, Peter **II:** 363
    suffrage **II:** 364
    taverns and inns **II:** 367–368
    travel **II:** 377
    Virginia **II:** 384
    women's status and rights **II:** 406, 407, 409
Laws, Evander **V:** 257
Laws of Burgos (1512) **I:** 122
Lawson, John **II:** 379
Lawson, John Howard **IX:** 134–135
lawyers **III:** **203–204**; **V:** 27, 28; **VI:** 180–181; **VII:** 61–62, 181
    Blackstone, William **III:** 40
    cities and urban life **III:** 70
    education **III:** 114
    Galloway, Joseph **III:** 148
    Ingersoll, Jared **III:** 178
    Jones, Absalom **III:** 189
    Judiciary Act of 1789 **III:** 192
    Livingston, Robert R. **III:** 216
    Livingston, William **III:** 216–217
    Sons of Liberty **III:** 329
    taverns **III:** 343
    Virginia dynasty **III:** 361
    Wilson, James **III:** 379–380
Lay, Benjamin **II:** 1
Lazarsfeld, Paul **VIII:** 284
Lazarus, Emma **VI:** **172–173**, 276
Lazio, Rick **X:** 65
lead **VI:** 60–61, 145
Leadbelly **VIII:** 221
lead mines **IV:** 35–36, 46, **208–209**

Lead Trust **VI:** 294
Leadville Strike **VI:** 168
League for Social Service **VI:** 279
League of American Wheelmen **VI:** 28
League of Nations **VI:** 37, 261; **VII:** **156–157**, 359*c*, 360*c*; **VIII:** 405*c*
    Borah, William E. **VIII:** 40
    Carnegie Endowment **VII:** 43
    Committee for Public Information **VII:** 346
    Coolidge, Calvin **VII:** 57
    Dawes, Charles **VII:** 63
    Democratic Party **VII:** 66
    Ethiopia **VIII:** 105
    foreign policy **VII:** 100
    Harding, Warren G. **VII:** 117
    Hughes, Charles Evans **VII:** 124
    Hull, Cordell **VIII:** 159
    Johnson, Hiram Warren **VII:** 138
    Lodge, Henry Cabot **VII:** 165
    Manchuria **VIII:** 199
    Naval Disarmament Conference **VII:** 209
    Norris, George W. **VIII:** 248
    postwar planning **VIII:** 279
    Republican Party **VII:** 263
    Taft, William Howard **VII:** 304
    UN **VIII:** 366
    Versailles, Treaty of **VII:** 323, 324
    Wilson, Woodrow **VII:** 334
    Women's International League for Peace and Freedom **VII:** 337
    World Disarmament Conference **VIII:** 388
League of the Ho-dee-nau-sau-nee **II:** 168
League of the Iroquois **I:** 160–161, 182
League of Women Voters (LWV) **VII:** 44, 198, 340; **IX:** **174–175**; **X:** 105
Leahy, William D. **VIII:** **183–184**, 401
leaks, information **X:** 4, 5
Leale, Charles **V:** 18
lean production **X:** 31
Lear, William **X:** 275

Leary, Timothy **IX: 175–176,**
333*c;* **X:** 206, 277
Beat Generation **IX:** 35
counterculture **IX:** 71, 72
Ginsberg, Allen **IX:** 123
LSD **IX:** 183–184
Lease, Mary Elizabeth Clyens
VI: 173
Leatherstocking Club. *See* Junto
Leather-Stocking Tales (Cooper)
IV: 212
Leavenworth, Henry **IV:** 145,
329
Leaves of Grass (Whitman) **IV:**
213, 379*c;* **V:** 393, 394
Leavitt, Joshua **IV:** 210
Lebanon **IX:** 146; **X:** 326*c*
foreign policy **X:** 124
Haig, Alexander M., Jr. **X:**
140
Iran-contra affair **X:** 154
Reagan, Ronald W. **X:**
260
terrorism **X:** 297
Lebrón, Lolita **IX:** 173
LeCler, Chrestien **II:** 422–423
Leclerc, Victor-Emmanuel **III:**
42
Le Compte, Joseph **V:** 231
Lecompton Constitution **V:** 32,
42, 98, 405*c*
Lectures on Revivals of Religion
(Finney) **IV:** 138
Lederer, John **II:** 115
Lederer, Raymond F. **X:** 4–5
Le Duc Tho **X:** 122, 311, 312
Lee, Ang **X:** 240
Lee, Ann **III: 204,** 323, 392*c*
Lee, Arthur **III:** 5, 101, **205,**
266
Lee, Charles **III:** 201,
205–206, 244–245, 343
Lee, Fitzhugh **V:** 129; **VI:** 187
Lee, Harper **IX:** 182
Lee, Henry **III: 206,** 376
Lee, Henry "Light-Horse
Harry" **V:** 205
Lee, Jason **IV:** 145, 229
Lee, John D. **IV:** 81
Lee, Newt **VII:** 157
Lee, Richard Henry **III:** 87,
102, 205, **206–207**
Lee, Robert E. **III:** 206; **IV:**
234; **V: 205,** 205–207,
405*c*–408*c*
Alexander, Edward P. **V:**
7–8
Antietam, Battle of **V:** 11
Appomattox Court House,
Virginia **V:** 13–15, *14*
Beauregard, Pierre **V:** 27
Brown, John **V:** 38

Bull Run, Second Battle of
V: 42–44
Burnside, Ambrose E. **V:**
45
cartography **V:** 51
Cedar Mountain, Battle of
V: 53
Chancellorsville, Battle of
V: 54–56
Civil War **V:** 66
Cold Harbor, Battle of **V:**
68
Confederate army **V:** 72, 73
Confederate States of
America **V:** 77
Davis, Jefferson **V:** 90
desertion **V:** 96
Early, Jubal A. **V:** 103
Ewell, Richard Stoddert **V:**
119
Farewell to His Troops **V:**
427
fire-eaters **V:** 127
Five Forks, Battle of **V:**
129
foraging **V:** 130
Fredericksburg, Battle of
V: 139, 141
Gettysburg, Battle of **V:**
147, 148, 150
governors **V:** 153
Grant, Ulysses S. **V:** 156
Halleck, Henry W. **V:** 162
Hancock, Winfield Scott **V:**
163
Harpers Ferry, West
Virginia **V:** 165
Hill, Ambrose P. **V:** 168
Hood, John Bell **V:** 170
Hooker, Joseph **V:** 171
Jackson, "Stonewall" **V:**
185, 186
Johnston, Joseph E. **V:** 190
literature **V:** 212
Longstreet, James **V:** 215,
216
lost cause, the **V:** 217
McClellan, George B. **V:**
225, 226
Meade, George Gordon **V:**
227
medicine and hospitals **V:**
230
monuments **V:** 239
music **V:** 243
Native Americans **V:** 250
Overland campaign **V:** 260,
261
Peninsular campaign **V:**
269, 270
Petersburg campaign **V:**
270, 272

Pickett, George Edward **V:**
274
Richmond, Virginia **V:** 304
Rosecrans, William S. **V:**
305
Shenandoah Valley:
Jackson's campaign **V:**
316, 317
Shenandoah Valley:
Sheridan's campaign **V:**
317
Sheridan, Philip H. **V:** 318,
319
Spotsylvania, Battles of **V:**
333
Stuart, J. E. B. **V:** 341
tactics and strategy **V:** 346,
347
Union army **V:** 367
United States Army Corps
of Engineers **V:** 370
Washington, D.C. **V:** 389
West Point **V:** 372
Wheeler, Joseph **V:** 392
Wilderness, Battle of the
V: 395
Zouaves **V:** 403
Lee, Spike **X:** 198
Lee, Thomas **III:** 265
Lee's Farewell to His Troops **V:**
427
Leete, Governor **II:** 164
Lee v. Weisman (1992) **X:** 279
Leeward Islands **I:** 342; **II:** 53
Lefebre, E. A. **VI:** 271
legal counsel **IX:** 333*c*, 334*c*
Legal Defense and Education
Fund (NAACP) **IX:** 4, 42,
193
legal dramas **X:** 295
legalization of drugs **X:** 208
Le Gallienne, Eva **VII:** 85
Legal News **VI:** 34
legal profession **VI:** 318
legal realism **X:** 125
legal rights **IV:** 367
Legal Tender Act of 1862 **V:** 24,
105, 159, 406*c;* **VI:** 64, 72,
261
legal tender cases **VI:** 72
"Legend of Sleepy Hollow"
(Irving) **IV:** 212
legend(s). *See also* mythology
black legend **I:** 30–31
Brendan the Navigator,
Saint **I:** 34
Fon **I:** 131–132
Ghana **I:** 140
Henry the Navigator **I:**
157–158
Inca **I:** 175
sugar **I:** 338

Toltecs **I:** 354
Venice **I:** 364
Legion of Honor **IV:** 55
legislative districts **IX:** 334*c*
Baker v. Carr **IX:** 31–32
Reynolds v. Simms **IX:**
259–260
Voting Rights Act of 1965
IX: 312
Warren Court **IX:** 316
Legislative Reorganization Act
of 1970 **X:** 144
legislative representation **IV:** 6
legislators, African-American **V:**
294
Lehár, Franz **VII:** 85, 194
Lehigh Canal **IV:** 73
Lehman, Herbert **IX:** 81
Lehman, John **X:** 221
Leibowitz, Samuel S. **VIII:** 287
Leigh, Vivien **VIII:** 408*c*
Leigh-Mallory, Trafford **VIII:**
248
Leiper, Thomas **IV:** 292
Leiserson Shirtwaist Company
VII: 284
Leisler, Jacob
crowd action **II:** 78
Dominion of New England
II: 95
Dudley, Joseph **II:** 95
Glorious Revolution **II:**
141
government, British
American **II:** 146
King William's War **II:** 185
Leisler's Rebellion **II:**
192–193
New York **II:** 261
Roman Catholics **II:** 324
Youngs, John **II:** 414
Leisler, Peter **II:** 98
Leisler's Rebellion **II:** 77, 78,
185, **192–193,** 261, 418*c*
leisure activities. *See*
entertainment; popular
culture; sports and recreation
Le Jeune, Paul **II:** 127
Leland, John **III:** 34
LeMay, Curtis **IX:** 37; **X:** 20,
314
Lemke, William
Coughlin, Father Charles
E. **VIII:** 75
election of 1936 **VIII:** 97
Long, Huey P. **VIII:** 195
politics in the Roosevelt
era **VIII:** 272*t*
Union Party **VIII:** 365
Lemlich, Clara **VII:** 285
Le Moyne, Jacques **I:** 102, *102,*
201, **202–203,** 351, 373

Le Moyne, Jean-Baptiste, sieur de Bienville **II: 193,** 199
Le Moyne, Pierre, sieur d'Iberville **II:** 246
Lenape. *See* Delaware Indians
Lend-Lease Act **VIII: 184–185,** 409*c*
  agriculture **VIII:** 9
  America First Committee **VIII:** 13
  Arnold, "Hap" **VIII:** 22
  Atlantic, Battle of the **VIII:** 28
  Atlantic Charter **VIII:** 28
  Axis **VIII:** 31
  Cairo Conference **VIII:** 51
  Casablanca Conference **VIII:** 52
  cash-and-carry **VIII:** 53
  Communists **VIII:** 65
  Congress **VIII:** 68
  destroyers-for-bases deal **VIII:** 83
  foreign policy **VIII:** 124
  Four Freedoms **VIII:** 126
  Grand Alliance **VIII:** 136
  Harriman, Averell **VIII:** 143
  Hopkins, Harry **VIII:** 157
  isolationists **VIII:** 166
  La Follette, Robert M., Jr. **VIII:** 182
  mobilization **VIII:** 214
  Morgenthau, Henry **VIII:** 216
  Neutrality Acts **VIII:** 239
  Norris, George W. **VIII:** 249
  Polish Americans **VIII:** 269
  rationing **VIII:** 292
  Roosevelt, Franklin D. **VIII:** 314
  second front **VIII:** 320
  socialists **VIII:** 327
  Soviet-American relations **VIII:** 333
  Taft, Robert A. **VIII:** 349
  Wheeler, Burton K. **VIII:** 378
  Willkie, Wendell L. **VIII:** 379
  World War II European theater **VIII:** 391
L'Enfant, Pierre-Charles **III: 207–208,** 365, 395*c*
Lenin, Vladimir Ilych **VII:** 259, 260, 270, 285; **VIII:** 25; **IX:** 61
Leningrad, siege of **VIII:** 125, 393

Lenni Lenape. *See* Delaware Indians
Lennon, Alton **X:** 140
Lennon, John **IX:** 36, 37; **X:** 31, 240
Lennox, Charlotte Ramsay **II: 193**
Lennox, David **III:** 375
Leno, Jay **X:** 295
Lenope **II:** 86–88, 370
Lenroot, Katherine **VIII:** 383
Leo III, Pope **I:** 165
Leo X (Giovanni de' Medici) **I: 203**
  cabinet of curiosities **I:** 40
  Franciscans **I:** 132
  Hanno the elephant **I:** 153
  invention and technology **I:** 179
  Leo Africanus **I:** 203–204
  Luther, Martin **I:** 211
  Michelangelo **I:** 235
  Reformation **I:** 307
Leo XIII, Pope **VI:** 243, 250; **VII:** 260
Leo Africanus (Giovanni Leoni; al-Hassan ibn Muhammad al-Wazzan al-Zayyati) **I: 203–204**
  Djenne-Djeno **I:** 109
  Gao **I:** 139
  Leo X **I:** 203
  Mali **I:** 218
  Ramusio, Giovanni Battista **I:** 305
  Timbuktu **I:** 350
Leo Frank case **VII: 157–158**
León, Cieza de **I:** 276
Leonard, John **X:** 43
Leonardo da Vinci **I:** 13, **204–205,** 219
Leonardson, Samuel **II:** 97
Leon Fandino, Juan de **II:** 392
Leoni, Giovanni. *See* Leo Africanus
Leonov, Aleksei **IX:** 279
leopard societies **I:** 48
Leopard's Spots (Dixon) **VII:** 30
Leopold, Aldo **IX:** 101, 226–227
Leopold, Nathan **VII:** 62, 361*c*
Leopold and Loeb **VII:** 62, **158,** 361*c*
Leo XIII, Pope **VI:** 243, 250; **VII:** 260
Lepanto, Battle of (1571) **I:** 164–165, 191, 282
Léry, Jean de **I: 205–206**
  cabinet of curiosities **I:** 40
  Histoire d'un voyage faict en la terre du Bresil autrement dite Amerique **I:** 408–413

Linschoten, Jan Huygen van **I:** 207
  Thevet, André **I:** 348
  tobacco **I:** 353
  Tupinambá **I:** 361
lesbian feminism **X:** 115, 116
lesbian rights **X:** 211
lesbians. *See* gays and lesbians
Leslie, Frank **IV:** 197
Leslie Fund **VII:** 198, 337
Les Misérables (musical) **X:** 201
Lesseps, Ferdinand de **VI:** 85
Lesser Antilles
  Arawak **I:** 12
  Barbados **I:** 26
  Carib **I:** 56
  Columbian Exchange **I:** 77
  Martinique **I:** 223
  Montserrat **I:** 243
  Nevis **I:** 254
  Taino **I:** 342
Letcher, John **V:** 130, 153
Letchworth, William Pryor **II:** 173
Le Tort, Anne **II:** 130
Le Tort, Jacques **II:** 130
"Letter from Birmingham Jail" (Martin Luther King, Jr.) **IX:** 38, 54, 161, 333*c*, 344–351
Letterman, David **X:** 295
Letterman, Jonathon **V:** 230
letters **V: 207–208**
  common soldier **V:** 70
  desertion **V:** 95–96
  54th Massachusetts Regiment **V:** 126
  German-American regiments **V:** 147
  Greenhow, Rose O'Neal **V:** 159
  journalism **V:** 193
  Nast, Thomas **V:** 247
  nurses **V:** 256
  Pickett, George Edward **V:** 275
  Union army **V:** 366
  USCC **V:** 372
  USSC **V:** 374
  Wakeman, Sarah Rosetta **V:** 386
  Yancey, William Lowndes **V:** 401
Letters and Notes on the Manners, Customs, and Condition of the North American Indians (Catlin) **IV:** 78
Letters from a Farmer in Pennsylvania to the Inhabitants of the British Colonies (Dickinson) **III:** 105, 349, 392*c*

Letters from an American Farmer (Crèvecoeur) **III:** 97, 98, 214, 394*c*
Letters of a Federal Farmer **III:** 15
Letters on the Equality of the Sexes and the Condition of Women (S. Grimké) **IV:** 164–165
Letters to Catharine Beecher (A. Grimké) **IV:** 165
Let Us Now Praise Famous Men (Agee and Evans) **VIII:** 268
Levant. *See* Turkey
Levant, HMS **III:** 81
Levant Company **I:** 206; **II:** 41
Levasseur, Pierre-Noël **II:** 25
Levertt, John **II: 193–194**
Levison, Stanley **IX:** 30
Levitt, Alfred **IX:** 178, 287
Levitt, William J. **IX:** 19, **176–178,** 203, 287, 329*c*
Levittown **IX:** 177
  art and architecture **IX:** 19
  Levitt, William **IX:** 176–178
  migration **IX:** 203
  suburbanization **IX:** 287
  Urban League **IX:** 305
Levittowns **VIII:** 343; **IX:** 177
  art and architecture **IX:** 19
  Levitt, William **IX:** 176–178
  migration **IX:** 203
  suburbanization **IX:** 287
  Urban League **IX:** 305
Levy, Aaron **II:** 175
Lewinsky, Monica **X:** 330*c*
  Clinton, Hillary Rodham **X:** 65
  Clinton, William **X:** 68, 69
  impeachment **X:** 150
  Judicial Watch **X:** 162
  Starr, Kenneth **X:** 287
  terrorism **X:** 299
Lewis, Andrew **IV:** 239
Lewis, John L. **VII:** 314; **VIII:** 69, *185,* **185–186,** 407*c*, 408*c*; **IX: 178–179**
  American Federation of Labor **VIII:** 14
  Carmichael, Stokely **IX:** 47
  CIO **VIII:** 69, *69*
  Communists **VIII:** 65
  conservatism **VIII:** 73
  freedom rides **IX:** 114
  Hillman, Sidney **VIII:** 145, 146
  labor **VIII:** 179–181, *180*
  March on Washington **IX:** 191
  Murray, Philip **VIII:** 221

Lewis, John L. *(continued)*
  NWLB **VIII:** 234
  race and racial conflict **IX:**
    254
  sit-ins **IX:** 273
  steel industry **VIII:** 338
  Student Nonviolent
    Coordinating
    Committee **IX:** 284, 285
Lewis, Meriwether **II:** 119; **III:**
  72, **208–209.** *See also* Lewis
  and Clark Expedition
  Astor, John Jacob **IV:** 30
  Astoria **IV:** 32
  Chouteau family **IV:** 79
  Columbia River **IV:** 93
  exploration **IV:** 130, 131
Lewis, Oliver **VI:** 134
Lewis, Sinclair **VII:** *161;* **VIII:**
  120, 191, 405*c*
Lewis and Clark Expedition **III:**
  209, **209–211,** 210*m,* 397*c*
  Bodmer, Karl **IV:** 55
  Clark, William **III:** 72
  exploration **II:** 115
  fur trade **III:** 142, 143; **IV:**
    157
  Great Plains **III:** 155
  Jefferson, Thomas **III:**
    185–186
  Kearny, Stephen Watts **IV:**
    200
  Lewis, Meriwether **III:**
    208
  Missouri Fur Company **IV:**
    238
  mountain men **IV:** 247
  Native Americans **IV:** 255
  Oregon Trail **IV:** 267
  Oregon Treaty of 1846 **IV:**
    269
  race and race relations **IV:**
    290
  Sacagawea **III:** 315
Lewis v. United States (1980) **X:**
  136
Lexington (carrier) **VIII:** 74
Lexington, USS **III:** 36, 393*c;* **V:**
  233
Lexington and Concord, Battles
  of **III:** 211*m,* **211–213,** 393*c*
  Adams, Samuel **III:** 4
  Arnold, Benedict **III:** 21
  Bunker Hill, Battle of **III:**
    50
  Clinton, Sir Henry **III:** 75
  Coercive Acts **III:** 77
  committees of
    correspondence **III:** 77
  Continental army **III:** 84
  Earle, Ralph **III:** 111
  foreign affairs **III:** 130

French alliance **III:** 137
Gage, Thomas **III:**
  146–147
Hancock, John **III:** 163
Hessians **III:** 166
minutemen **III:** 243
Paine, Thomas **III:** 271
resistance movement **III:**
  303
Revere, Paul **III:** 304
Revolutionary War **III:**
  305
Washington, George **III:**
  366
Lexington Rifles **V:** 240
Leyden, Ann **II:** 135
Leyenda negra, la. See black
  legend
Leyland, Frederick R. **VI:** 312
Leyte Gulf, Battle for **VIII:**
  186–187
  Halsey, "Bull" **VIII:** 143
  Iwo Jima **VIII:** 168
  Nimitz, Chester W. **VIII:**
    246
  Philippines **VIII:** 267
  World War II Pacific
    theater **VIII:** 399
Libby Prison, Richmond,
  Virginia **V:** 282
libel law **II:** 261, 415–416; **III:**
  191; **X:** 41
liberal arts education **VI:** 94
liberal feminism **X:** 115, 116
liberalism **VII:** 31, 34–35; **VIII:**
  187–189; IX: 13, 68,
  179–180; X: 174–176
  antimonopoly **VIII:** 17
  art and architecture **VIII:**
    25
  Black, Hugo L. **VIII:** 37
  Buckley, William F., Jr. **X:**
    43
  Carter, James Earl, Jr. **X:**
    57
  Catholics **VIII:** 54
  civil rights **VIII:** 62
  Congress **VIII:** 67, 69
  conservatism **VIII:** 71, 72
  conservative coalition
    VIII: 73
  court-packing plan **VIII:**
    76
  Democratic Party **VIII:**
    81, 82
  Economic Bill of Rights
    VIII: 90
  education **VIII:** 93
  election of 1936 **VIII:** 97
  election of 1944 **VIII:** 99
  Frankfurter, Felix **VIII:**
    127

FSA **VIII:** 113
Full Employment Bill
  VIII: 128
Kennedy, Edward M. **X:**
  164
Keynesianism **VIII:** 176,
  177
La Follette, Robert M., Jr.
  VIII: 182
La Guardia, Fiorello **VIII:**
  182
Libertarian Party **X:** 176
neoconservatism **X:** 215
New Deal **VIII:** 240, 242
NRA **VIII:** 231
NRPB **VIII:** 233
OWMR **VIII:** 259
politics in the Roosevelt
  era **VIII:** 271
popular culture **VIII:** 273
pornography **X:** 245
postwar planning **VIII:**
  278
race and racial conflict
  VIII: 289
recession of 1937–38 **VIII:**
  293
Roosevelt, Franklin D.
  VIII: 314
South **VIII:** 331
Supreme Court **VIII:** 345,
  347; **X:** 290
televangelism **X:** 293
Third New Deal **VIII:**
  357, 358
TNEC **VIII:** 355, 356
Wagner, Robert F. **VIII:**
  372
Wallace, Henry A. **VIII:**
  373
World War II home front
  VIII: 396
Liberal Party
  Chase, Salmon P. **V:** 56
  Wilmot Proviso **V:** 396
Liberal Republican Party **VI:**
  173–174, 323*c*
  Adams, Henry **VI:** 1
  Dana, Charles A. **V:** 88
  Grant, Ulysses S. **V:** 156,
    157
  Greeley, Horace **V:** 158
  Julian, George W. **V:** 194
  Lockwood, Belva Ann
    Bennett McNall **VI:**
    180
  mugwumps **VI:** 199
  political parties, third **VI:**
    225
  presidential campaigns **VI:**
    231
  Pulitzer, Joseph **VI:** 235

Republican Party **V:** 302;
  VI: 246
Schurz, Carl **VI:** 256
Sumner, Charles **V:** 343
liberal theology **IV:** 212, 298; **V:**
  300; **VI:** 24, 75; **VII:** 260–262
liberation theology **IX:** 255–256
Liberator, The **III:** 132; **IV:**
  376*c;* **VII:** 253
  AASS **IV:** 14
  abolition movement **IV:** 3
  ACS **IV:** 16
  editorial, first issue **IV:**
    392–393
  Foster, Abigail Kelley **IV:**
    147
  Grimké, Angelina and
    Sarah **IV:** 164
  journalism **IV:** 194
  Stewart, Maria **IV:** 327
Liberator, The (newspaper) **V:** 2,
  3, 100, 146
Liberia **IV:** 2, 3, 15, **209–210,**
  346; **VI:** 4, 70, **174–175,**
  296–297
Liberian Exodus Joint Stock
  Steamship Company **VI:** 175
libertarianism **VIII:** 72
  conservative movement **X:**
    78–80
  militia movement **X:** 193
  pornography **X:** 245
  property rights **X:** 250
Libertarian Party **X: 176–177**
Liberty affair **III:** 163, 349,
  392*c*
Liberty Baptist Theological
  Seminary **X:** 294
Liberty Bonds **VII:** 25, 344
Liberty League. *See* American
  Liberty League
Liberty Men **III:** 202
Liberty Party **IV: 210–211,**
  377*c;* **V:** 3, 146; **VIII:** 272*t;* **X:**
  111
  Free-Soil Party **IV:** 150
  Polk, James K. **IV:** 283
  Republican Party **IV:** 300
  Whig Party **IV:** 364
liberty tree/pole **III:** *213,*
  213–214
  Golden Hill, Battle of **III:**
    153
  McDougall, Alexander **III:**
    239
  Oliver, Andrew **III:** 266
  taverns **III:** 343
libraries **II:** 277, 278, 282, 352;
  VI: 44, **175–176**
Library Company of
  Philadelphia **II:** 18, 33, 109,
  278

Library of Congress **VI:** 176
Libya **I:** 317, 360; **X:** 327c
    African nations **X:** 13
    defense policy **X:** 87
    Farrakhan, Louis A. **X:** 111
    foreign policy **X:** 124
    OPEC **X:** 228–229
    terrorism **X:** 298
Lichtenstein, Roy **IX:** 20, *20*; **X:** 26
Liddy, G. Gordon **X:** 316
Lie, Jonas **VII:** 18
Lieb, Hermann **V:** 233
Lieber, Francis **V:** 305
Lieber Code **V:** 305–306, 384
Lieberman, Joseph I. **X:** *133*, 134, 162
Liege **I:** 102
"life, liberty, and estate" **II:** 197
Life Among the Indians (Catlin) **IV:** 78
Life and Adventures of James P. Beckwourth **IV:** 47
Life and Labor **VII:** 252
Life and Times of Frederick Douglass **V:** 100
life expectancy **II:** 53; **IV:** 7; **V:** 278; **VII:** 234; **VIII:** 95, 278
    medicine **X:** 189
    science and technology **X:** 275
    women's rights and status **X:** 320
Life (magazine) **VIII: 189–190,** 407c
    art and architecture **VIII:** 24
    Luce, Henry R. **VIII:** 196
    photography **VIII:** 268, 269
    recreation **VIII:** 297
    suburbs **VIII:** 343
Life of Washington (Irving) **IV:** 212
Life of Washington, The (Weems) **III:** 371
Ligget, Hunter **VII:** 9
Liggett Group **X:** 303, 304
lightbulb, electric **VI:** 89, 146, 148, 325c; **VII:** 355c
"Light Hose Harry." *See* Lee, Henry
lighting **VI:** 265
Lilienthal, David E. **VIII: 190,** 356; **IX:** 23–24
Lilith Fair **X:** 203
Liliuokalani, queen of Hawaii **IV:** 172; **VI:** 124, 327c
Lilly **IX:** 206
Lily, The (newspaper) **IV:** 53, 54, 378c
Lima **I:** 10, 177, **206,** 280, 283

Limited Test Ban Treaty of 1963 **IX: 180,** 333c
    arms race **IX:** 16
    civil defense **IX:** 53
    hydrogen bomb **IX:** 140
    SANE **IX:** 267
    Soviet Union **IX:** 277
Limits to Growth, The (Club of Rome) **X:** 76
limners **II:** *24*, **194**
limpieza de sangre **II:** 356
Lincoln, Abraham **V: 208–211,** *209,* 405c–408c; **VII:** 31, 305
    abolition **V:** 4
    African-American regiments **V:** 4
    amnesty, acts of **V:** 8
    Anderson, Robert **V:** 9
    Antietam, Battle of **V:** 11, 13
    Appomattox Court House, Virginia **V:** 15
    assassination of **V:** 17–19
    Balloon Corps **V:** 21
    Baltimore, Maryland, riots **V:** 22
    Barton, Clara **V:** 25
    Beauregard, Pierre **V:** 27
    Black Hawk War **IV:** 52
    Blaine, James Gillespie **VI:** 31
    Blair, Francis P., Jr. **V:** 30
    Booth, John Wilkes **V:** 33
    bounty system **V:** 34
    Brady, Mathew **V:** 36
    brothers' war **V:** 37
    Brown, Joseph **V:** 39
    Buchanan, James **V:** 42
    Bull Run, First Battle of **V:** 42
    Bull Run, Second Battle of **V:** 43
    Burnside, Ambrose E. **V:** 45
    Butler, Benjamin **V:** 46
    Chancellorsville, Battle of **V:** 56
    Chase, Salmon P. **V:** 56
    Chattanooga, Battle of **V:** 57
    Civil War **V:** 63, 65, 67
    common soldier **V:** 69
    Confederate States of America **V:** 75
    Confiscation Acts **V:** 78
    Congress **VI:** 63
    conscription **V:** 79
    contrabands **V:** 80, 81
    Copperheads **V:** 82
    Dahlgren, John A. B. **V:** 87
    Dana, Charles A. **V:** 88
    Davis, Jefferson **V:** 89, 90

    Democratic Party **IV:** 108; **V:** 94
    Douglas, Stephen A. **V:** 97–99
    Douglass, Frederick **V:** 100
    Early, Jubal A. **V:** 103
    education, federal aid to **VI:** 92
    elections **V:** 109, 110
    emancipation **V:** 111, 113
    Emancipation Proclamation **V:** 114–115
    Emerson, Ralph Waldo **IV:** 126–127
    employment **V:** 116
    espionage **V:** 118
    54th Massachusetts Regiment **V:** 125, 126
    Fillmore, Millard **IV:** 138
    Finney, Charles Grandison **IV:** 139
    fire-eaters **V:** 128
    foreign policy **V:** 132
    Fort Pillow, Tennessee **V:** 135
    Fort Sumter, South Carolina **V:** 135, 137
    Fredericksburg, Battle of **V:** 139
    Freedman's Saving Bank **V:** 141
    Frémont, Jessie Benton **IV:** 152
    Frémont, John C. **IV:** 154
    fugitive slave laws **IV:** 155
    Garrison, William Lloyd **V:** 146
    Gettysburg, Battle of **V:** 148, 150
    Gettysburg Address **V:** 151, 424–425
    governors **V:** 153
    Grant, Ulysses S. **V:** 156
    Greeley, Horace **V:** 158
    habeas corpus, writ of **V:** 161, 162
    Hale, Sarah Josepha **IV:** 168
    Halleck, Henry W. **V:** 162
    Harpers Ferry, West Virginia **V:** 166
    Hay, John Milton **VI:** 124
    Herndon, William H. **V:** 166
    homefront **V:** 169
    Homestead Act of 1862 **V:** 170
    "House Divided" speech **V:** 411–414
    Howard, O. O. **V:** 173
    Howe, Julia Ward **V:** 174

    Howells, William Dean **VI:** 136
    immigration **IV:** 179
    impeachment of Andrew Johnson **V:** 179
    Inaugural Address, First (1861) **V:** 414–418
    Inaugural Address, Second (1865) (Lincoln) **V:** 426–427
    Irish-American regiments **V:** 181
    Johnson, Andrew **V:** 187
    Joint Committee on the Conduct of War **V:** 191
    journalism **V:** 193
    Juneteenth **V:** 195
    Kansas-Nebraska Act of 1854 **V:** 197–198
    Know-Nothing Party **IV:** 202
    ladies aid societies **V:** 204
    Lee, Robert E. **V:** 205
    Lincoln, Mary Todd **V:** 211–212
    literature **V:** 212
    Longstreet, James **V:** 215
    Lookout Mountain, Battle of **V:** 216
    loyalty oaths **V:** 218–219
    Manifest Destiny **IV:** 218
    Marx, Karl **V:** 223, 224
    McClellan, George B. **V:** 224–226
    Meade, George Gordon **V:** 227
    Medal of Honor **V:** 228
    Mexican-American War **IV:** 232
    Morrill Land-Grant Act **V:** 241
    Murfreesboro/Stones River, Battle of **V:** 242
    music **V:** 244
    Nast, Thomas **V:** 247
    nurses **V:** 256
    Overland campaign **V:** 260, 261
    Pacific Railroad Act of 1862 **V:** 263
    peace movements **V:** 266
    Peninsular campaign **V:** 267, 270
    Petersburg campaign **V:** 272
    Phillips, Wendell **IV:** 281
    the presidency **VI:** 230
    prisons **V:** 281, 282
    Proclamation of Amnesty and Reconstruction **V:** 425–426
    public land policy **IV:** 288

Lincoln, Abraham (*continued*)
  race and race relations **IV:**
    291; **V:** 287
  Radical Republicans **V:**
    288
  Reconstruction **V:** 292
  Reconstruction Acts **V:** 295
  Red River campaign **V:**
    298
  Republican Party **IV:**
    301–302; **V:** 301, 302,
    302
  scalawags **V:** 307
  Schurz, Carl **VI:** 256
  secession **V:** 311–313
  Semmes, Raphael **V:** 313
  Seward, William H. **V:** 314,
    315
  Shenandoah Valley:
    Jackson's campaign **V:**
    316
  Sherman, William T. **V:**
    321
  Sherman's March through
    Georgia **V:** 322, 323
  slavery **IV:** 318; **V:** 329,
    330
  Stanton, Edwin M. **V:** 333,
    334
  states' rights **V:** 336
  Stephens, Alexander H. **V:**
    336
  Stevens, Thaddeus **V:** 338
  Stowe, Harriet Beecher **V:**
    339
  Sumner, Charles **V:** 343
  tactics and strategy **V:** 346,
    347
  Thirteenth Amendment **V:**
    353
  Thomas, George H. **V:** 354
  Truth, Sojourner **V:** 357
  Tyler, John **IV:** 349
  Union army **V:** 364, 365,
    367
  Union League **V:** 367
  Union navy **V:** 368
  USCC **V:** 372
  Vallandigham, Clement L.
    V: 377, 378
  Vicksburg campaign **V:**
    380, 382–383
  volunteer army **V:** 383
  Wade, Benjamin **V:** 385
  Wade-Davis Bill of 1864 **V:**
    385
  war contracting **V:** 387
  Warmoth, Henry C. **V:** 388
  Washington, D.C. **V:**
    388–390
  Welles, Gideon **V:** 391
  Whig Party **IV:** 363, 364

  Whitman, Walt **V:** 394
  Women's National Loyal
    League **V:** 396
Lincoln, Benjamin **III:** 64, 316
Lincoln, Mary Todd **V:** 18, 210,
  211–212, 343; **VI:** 244
Lincoln, Nancy Hanks **V:** 166
Lincoln, Robert Todd **V:** 210,
  212
Lincoln, Willie **V:** 210, 212, 389
Lincoln-Douglas debates **V:** 97,
  98, 210, 405*c*
Lincoln Memorial **V:** 239
Lincoln Memorial **VI:** 259
Lind, Jenny **IV:** 82, 250; **VI:** 21
Lindbergh, Charles Augustus
  VII: 23, **158–160,** *159,* 361*c;*
  VIII: 12, 13, 353; **IX:** 112
Linder, Max **VII:** 191
Linderfelt, Karl **VII:** 168
Lindsay, John **X:** 43, 217
Lindsay, Vachel **VI:** 10
linen manufacturing **I:** 17
lines **V:** 346
Lingg, Louis **VI:** 127
Lining, John **II:** **194**
Linnaeus, Carolus **II:** 66, 181,
  277, 330
linotype **VI:** 137
Linowitz, Sol **X:** 173
Linowitz Commission Report **X:**
  173
Linschoten, Jan Huygen van **I:**
  114, **206–207**
Lippard, George **IV:** 211–212
Lippmann, Walter **VII:** 118;
  VIII: 405*c;* **IX:** 57
liquor **IV:** 335–337
Lisa, Manuel
  Chouteau family **IV:** 79
  fur trade **IV:** 156
  Missouri Fur Company **IV:**
    238–239
  mountain men **IV:** 247
Lisbon, Portugal **I:** **207–208**
  Cabral, Pedro Álvares **I:** 44
  Dias, Bartolomeu **I:** 104,
    105
  Drake, Sir Francis **I:** 112
  Dutch East India
    Company **I:** 114
  slavery **I:** 327
  sugar **I:** 338
Li-schi-tsching **I:** 338
Lister, Joseph **V:** 97, 229, 231;
  VI: 191
Liston, Sonny **IX:** 5, 9, 334*c*
Liszt, Franz **VI:** 183
literacy **III:** 113; **IV:** 120–122,
  368; **V:** 330, 354; **VI:** 211, 296
  African Americans **II:** 7
  childhood **II:** 60

Connecticut **II:** 70
  education **II:** 103, 104
  Puritans **II:** 306
  Society for the Propagation
    of the Gospel in Foreign
    Parts **II:** 352
  women's status and rights
    II: 407
literacy tests **IV:** 202; **VI:** 141;
  VII: 335, 359*c*
Literary Digest **VIII:** 284, 305
literary journals **VII:** 160
literature **II:** 194–195; **III:**
  214–215; IV: 211–214, *213,*
  379*c;* **V:** 212–213; **VI:**
  176–179, 327*c;* **VII:**
  160–162, *161;* **VIII:**
  190–193, 408*c;* **IX:**
  180–183, 334*c;* **X:** 43,
  177–179. *See also* poetry
  Acosta, José de **I:** 3
  African-American
    movement **IX:** 5
  African Americans **II:** 7;
    VI: 6
  Alcott, Louisa May **VI:** 9
  Alger, Horatio **VI:** 9–10
  Beat Generation **IX:** 35
  Brackenridge, Hugh
    Henry **III:** 46, 47
  Brown, Charles Brockden
    III: 49–50
  civil liberties **VIII:** 60
  Comstock, Anthony **VI:**
    62
  Connecticut Wits **III:** 80
  counterculture **IX:** 71
  Crane, Stephen **VI:** 68
  Crèvecoeur, J. Hector St.
    John de **III:** 98
  Dana, Richard Henry **IV:**
    103
  dance **II:** 82
  De Forest, John William
    V: 92
  Dickinson, Emily **VI:**
    79–80
  dime novels **VI:** 80–81
  Dunbar, Paul Laurence
    VI: 82–83
  Eden, Richard **I:** 117–118
  Emerson, Ralph Waldo **IV:**
    126–127
  Faulkner, William **VIII:** 113
  Frémont, Jessie Benton
    IV: 152
  Fuller, Margaret **IV:**
    155–156
  FWP **VIII:** 121
  Garland, Hamlin **VI:**
    109–110
  gays and lesbians **IX:** 119

Gilded Age, The **VI:**
  114–115
Ginsberg, Allen **IX:**
  122–123
Glorious Revolution **II:**
  141
Great Depression **VIII:**
  140
Greenwich Village **VII:**
  115
Hakluyt, Richard, the
  Younger **I:** 151–153
Hale, Sarah Josepha **IV:**
  167–168
Harper, Frances Ellen
  Watkins **V:** 164
Hay, John Milton **VI:**
  124–125
Higginson, Thomas
  Wentworth **V:** 167
Howells, William Dean **VI:**
  136
Irish Americans **VIII:** 165
Jackson, Helen Hunt **VI:**
  153
James, Henry **VI:** 153–154
journalism **II:** 179; **III:**
  190
Lennox, Charlotte Ramsay
  II: 193
Linschoten, Jan Huygen
  van **I:** 207
lost cause, the **V:** 217
Mandeville, Sir John **I:**
  219–220
marriage and family life **II:**
  208; **III:** 232
Massachusetts **II:** 215
Mencken, H. L. **VII:** 181
modernism **VII:** 188
Monardes, Nicholas **I:**
  239
monsters **I:** 239–240
Morton, Thomas **II:** 236
Murray, Judith Sargent
  III: 250
National Endowment for
  the Arts **IX:** 221
National Endowment for
  the Humanities **IX:** 221
Native American
  movement **IX:** 229
Parmenius, Stephen **I:** 278
Pennington, James William
  Charles **V:** 270
Peter Martyr **I:** 280–281
Pigafetta, Antonio **I:** 283
Polo, Marco **I:** 286–288
popular culture **VII:**
  232–233; **IX:** 243
Purchas, Samuel **I:** 297
Quakers **II:** 307

Ramusio, Giovanni Battista **I:** 304–305
religion, African-American **II:** 314
Rowlandson, Mary White **II:** 324–325
Rowson, Susanna **III:** 311
Sandys, George **II:** 329
science **VII:** 276
Shakespeare, William **I:** 323–324
Sinclair, Upton **VII:** 286–287
slavery **V:** 328
Stade, Hans **I:** 336
Steinbeck, John **VIII:** 339–340
Stowe, Harriet Beecher **V:** 338–339
Tempest, The **I:** 343–344
Thevet, André **I:** 348–349
Turell, Jane Colman **II:** 378
Twain, Mark **VI:** 297–298
Tyler, Royall **III:** 352–353
utopianism **VI:** 301
Warren, Mercy Otis **III:** 363–364
Webster, Noah **III:** 370
White, Andrew **II:** 396
Whitman, Walt **V:** 393–394
Wilder, Laura Ingalls **VI:** 314
Wright, Richard **VIII:** 399–400
Yep, Laurence **IX:** 327
Lithuania **I:** 192; **VII:** 323; **IX:** 58, 105; **X:** 124, 281
Little Belt incident **III:** **215–216**
Little Bighorn, Battle of **V:** **213–214,** 251, 319; **VI:** 324c
   Black Hills gold rush **VI:** 29
   Crazy Horse **VI:** 69
   Native Americans **VI:** 207
   Red Cloud **VI:** 240
   Sioux wars **VI:** 263
"Little Boy" bomb **VIII:** 146, 200
Little Caesar (film) **VIII:** 217, 274
"little civil War." *See* Bleeding Kansas
Little Crow **V:** 406c
Little Egypt **VI:** 96
Little House in the Big Woods (Wilder) **VI:** 314
Little Ice Age **I:** 145
Little League Baseball **VIII:** 297
"little New Deals" **VIII:** 134

Little Review (magazine) **VII:** 188, 252
Little Richard **IX:** 263
Little Rock, Arkansas **IX:** 43, 93, 108–109, 276, 332c
Little Round Top. *See* Gettysburg, Battle of
Little Sarah affair **III:** 150
"Little Steel" **VIII:** 70, 181, 221; **IX:** 282
"Little Steel" formula **VIII:** 233, 371
"Little Steel" strikes **VIII:** 338
Little Turtle **III:** 123, 156, 157, 395c; **IV:** 168
Little Walter **VIII:** 223
Little Women (Alcott) **V:** 408c; **VI:** 9
"Litz" wire **VI:** 285
Livermore, Mary A. **V:** 204
livestock **IV:** 10, 11, 65; **V:** 7; **VII:** 177–178. *See also* animals
livestock haciendas **I:** 150
Living Newspapers **VIII:** 120
Livingston, David **VI:** 211
Livingston, Philip **II:** **195–196**
Livingston, Robert **II:** 195, **196**
Livingston, Robert R. **II:** **196–197;** **III:** 129, 142, **216,** 218, 393c
Livingston, William **II:** 184, 185, 196; **III:** **216–217**
Livingstone College **VI:** 5
Livingston family **II:** 381
Living Wage, A (Ryan) **VII:** 260
Lloyd, David **II:** 145, **197,** 276
Lloyd, Edward **I:** 75
Lloyd, Henry **II:** 153
Lloyd, Henry Demarest **VI:** **179,** 294, 325c; **VII:** 265
Lloyd, John **II:** 154
Lloyd, Joseph **II:** 154
Lloyd George, David **VII:** 156, 323, 334
Lloyd's of London **I:** 75
loans **V:** 23; **VII:** 75, 268; **VIII:** 111
lobbies/lobbying **VI:** 118, 144–145, **179–180;** **VII:** **162–163;** **VIII:** 96, 285
   abortion **X:** 3
   agriculture **X:** 16
   American Legion **VII:** 11–12
   Capper-Volstead Act **VII:** 42
   Christian Coalition **X:** 62
   defense policy **X:** 86
   economy **VII:** 75
   elections **VII:** 79
   feminism **X:** 116

medicine **X:** 189, 190
Moral Majority **X:** 197
NAACP **X:** 208
Nader, Ralph **X:** 205
narcotics **X:** 207
NOW **X:** 211
NRA **X:** 212, 213
politics **VII:** 228
race and racial conflict **X:** 256
Reform Party **X:** 263
television **X:** 295
urban transportation **VII:** 319
veterans **VII:** 324
local government. *See* government (state and local)
Lochner, Joseph **VII:** 163
Lochner v. New York **VII:** **163–164,** 193, 356c
Locke, Alain LeRoy **VII:** 33, 119, **164–165**
Locke, John **II:** **197–198; IV:** 62; **VI:** 159
   cities and urban life **II:** 62
   commonwealthmen **III:** 79
   constitutions, state **III:** 82
   Declaration of Independence **III:** 102
   deism **III:** 103
   Edwards, Jonathan **II:** 105
   Enlightenment **II:** 109
   government, British American **II:** 144
   Great Awakening **II:** 147
   King George's War **II:** 182
   North Carolina **II:** 265
   science **II:** 330
   South Carolina **II:** 353
   Yates, Abraham, Jr. **III:** 387
Lockerbie, Scotland **X:** 298, 327c, 331c
Lockhart, Robert **VI:** 274
Lockheed **IX:** 28
locks **IV:** 129, 186m
Lockwood, Belva Ann Bennett McNall **VI:** **180–181,** 318, 325c
Locofocos **IV:** 108, 277
locomotives **VI:** 194
Lodge, Henry Cabot **V:** 117; **VI:** 186; **VII:** **165,** 359c; **IX:** 43, 95, 123
   Committee for Public Information **VII:** 346
   Democratic Party **VII:** 66
   foreign policy **VII:** 100
   League of Nations **VII:** 156
   National Defense Act **VII:** 201

Republican Party **VII:** 263
Versailles, Treaty of **VII:** 324
Wilson, Woodrow **VII:** 335
LodgeNet **X:** 244
lodging **II:** 368, 377. *See also* housing
Loeb, Richard **VII:** 62, 361c
Loeffler, Charles Martin **VI:** 201
Loew, T. S. C. **V:** 309
Loewe, E. W. **VII:** 61
Loewe v. Lawlor **VII:** 357c. *See also* Danbury Hatters
Logan, Adele Hunt **VII:** 200
Logan, James **II:** **198–199**
   Lloyd, David **II:** 197
   Montour, Madame **II:** 233
   Pennsylvania **II:** 277
   Philadelphia **II:** 282
   science **II:** 330
   Walking Purchase of 1737 **II:** 389–390
Logan, John **V:** 365
"Log Cabin and Hard Cider" campaign **IV:** 170
log cabins **II:** 22, 57, 264
"Log College" **II:** 371, 372
logging **VI:** 65, 104; **X:** 77
Lok, Michael **I:** 133, 266; **II:** 130
Lokono. *See* Arawak
Lolita (Vladimir Nabokov) **IX:** 182
Lollobrigida, Gina **IX:** 213
L'Olonnais, François **II:** 285
Lomax, Alan **VIII:** 222, 223
Lomax, John **VIII:** 222
London, England **I:** **208–209**
   Cabot, John **I:** 42
   Cabot, Sebastian **I:** 42, 43
   coffee **I:** 75
   DeBry, Theodor **I:** 102
   East India Company **I:** 117
   Walsingham, Sir Frances **I:** 371
   White, John **I:** 373
London, Jack **VII:** 138, 160, 356c
London Bridge **I:** 208
London *Daily News* **VI:** 116
London Economic Conference (1933) **VIII:** **193–194**
   Anglo-American relations **VIII:** 16
   foreign policy **VIII:** 124
   Hull, Cordell **VIII:** 159
   Moley, Raymond C. **VIII:** 216
   Reciprocal Trade Agreements Act **VIII:** 294

London Economic Conference
(continued)
World Disarmament
Conference **VIII:** 388
London Metropolitan police
model **V:** 61
London Naval Conference
(1930) **VIII: 194**
Anglo-American relations
VIII: 16
foreign policy **VIII:** 123
Hoover presidency **VIII:**
154
Manchuria **VIII:** 199
Stimson, Henry L. **VIII:**
340
World Disarmament
Conference **VIII:** 388
London Society for the
Suppression of Vice **VI:** 62
"Lone Star" state **IV:** *339*
Lone Wolf v. Hitchcock **VII:**
165–166, 207
Long, Breckinridge **VIII:** 150,
298
Long, Edward V. **X:** 93
Long, Huey P. **VII:** 292–293;
VIII: 194–195, 407*c*. *See
also* "Share Our Wealth" Plan
New Deal **VIII:** 241
Revenue Act of 1935 **VIII:**
308
Second New Deal **VIII:**
321
taxation **VIII:** 351
Townsend, Francis E.
VIII: 359
Union Party **VIII:** 365
Long, John **VII:** 266
Long, Maxey **VI:** 290
Long, Stephen H. **IV:** 33
Longfellow, Henry Wadsworth
II: 15, 16, 361; **III:** 304; **IV:**
168, 196, 213, 378*c*; **V:** 244
longhouses **I:** 12, 170–171, 181,
225, 320; **II:** 22, *23*, 157, 160,
206, 259
Long Island, Battle of **III:**
217–218, 393*c*
Barlow, Joel **III:** 35
Clinton, Sir Henry **III:** 75
Cornwallis, Lord **III:** 92
Fort Washington, capture
of **III:** 133
Hale, Nathan **III:** 160
Hamilton, Alexander **III:**
161
Hessians **III:** 167
Howe, Richard, Lord **III:**
167–168
Howe, Sir William **III:** 168
Jersey, HMS **III:** 186

Putnam, Israel **III:** 290
Revolutionary War **III:**
305
Sullivan, John **III:** 337
Trenton and Princeton,
Battles of **III:** 351
Washington, George **III:**
367
Long Island, New York **VIII:**
343
Long Island, Treaty of **III:** 66
Long Island of Holston, Treaty
of **II:** 58
Longley, James B. **X:** 194
"Long Roll, The" **V:** 243
Longstreet, James **V: 214–216,**
406*c*
Alexander, Edward P. **V:** 7,
8
Antietam, Battle of **V:** 11
Armistead, Lewis A. **V:** 15
Bull Run, Second Battle of
V: 43, 44
Chancellorsville, Battle of
V: 54
Chattanooga, Battle of **V:**
57
Chickamauga, Battle of **V:**
58, 59
Fredericksburg, Battle of
V: 139, 141
Gettysburg, Battle of **V:**
147, 148, 150
Hood, John Bell **V:** 171
Lee, Robert E. **V:** 206
Oates, William C. **V:** 257
Pickett, George Edward **V:**
274
scalawags **V:** 307–308
Sickles, Daniel E. **V:** 327
Wilderness, Battle of the
V: 395
"Long Telegram" (George F.
Kennan) **IX:** 105, 155
Longworth, Alice Roosevelt
VIII: 12
Look (magazine) **VIII:** 243, 268
Look Homeward, Angel (Wolfe)
VIII: 191, 405*c*
Looking Backward (Bellamy)
Bellamy, Edward **VI:** 26
business cycles **VI:** 41
literature **VI:** 178
socialism **VI:** 267–268
Socialist Party **VI:** 269
utopianism **VI:** 301
Looking Glass (Nez Perce chief)
VI: 213
Lookout Mountain, Battle of **V:**
216–217
Chattanooga, Battle of **V:**
57

Hooker, Joseph **V:** 173
Longstreet, James **V:** 215
Warmoth, Henry C. **V:** 388
Loomis, Francis B. **VII:** 224
looms **IV:** 184
Lopez, Nancy **X:** 262
López, Narciso **IV:** 101
López de Gómara, Francisco **I:**
106
Lord, Nancy **X:** 176
Lord Dunmore's War **III:** 41,
71, 393*c*
"Lord of Misrule" **II:** 236
lords (feudalism) **I:** 129
Lords of Xibalba **I:** 228
Lords Proprietor over Carolina
II: 265
Loren, Sophia **IX:** 213
Lorentz, Pare **VIII:** 275
Lorenzo the Magnificent **I:** 235
Lorillard Tobacco **X:** 305
Lorimer, William **VII:** 69
Loring, Ellis Gray **IV:** 333
Los Alamos, New Mexico **VIII:**
29, 200, 344, 409*c*
Los Alamos laboratory **IX:** 236,
237
Los Angeles, California **VII:**
176, 191; **VIII:** 410*c*; **IX:** *102,*
317–318, 328; **X:** 328*c*
Catholics **VIII:** 54
children **VIII:** 57
Frémont, John C. **IV:** 153
FTP **VIII:** 120
Kearny, Stephen Watts **IV:**
200
Mexican Americans **VIII:**
210
Mexican Repatriation
Program **VIII:** 211
migration **VIII:** 213
race and racial conflict **VIII:**
288, 289; **X:** 255, 256
Stearns, Abel **IV:** 326
Stockton, Robert Field **IV:**
328
Sunbelt **VIII:** 343; **X:** 290
World War II home front
VIII: 395
zoot-suiters **VIII:** 404
Los Angeles Olympics, 1932
VIII: 338
Los Angeles Times **VII:** 128; **X:**
185
lost cause, the **V: 217–218**
Civil War **V:** 67
literature **V:** 213
Oates, William C. **V:** 257
religion **V:** 300
Richmond, Virginia **V:** 304
UDC **V:** 370
veterans, Civil War **V:** 379

"Lost Colony" **II:** 264–265
Lost Generation **VII:** 120, 161,
166–167
Lott, Eric **VI:** 95, 96
Lott, Trent **X:** 276
Lott Carey Baptist Foreign
Mission Convention **VI:** 4
lotteries **II: 199,** 387; **IV:**
330–331
Louima, Abner **X:** 330*c*
Louis XII, king of France **I:** 204
Louis XIII, king of France **II:**
127
Louis XIV, king of France
French colonies **II:** 129
French immigrants **II:** 130
Glorious Revolution **II:**
141
Jolliet, Louis **II:** 178
King William's War **II:** 185
La Salle, René-Robert
Cavelier, sieur de **II:**
192
Louisiana **II:** 199
Louis XV, king of France **II:**
199
Louis XVI, king of France
French Revolution **III:**
138
Grasse, comte de **III:** 154
Jefferson, Thomas **III:** 184
Lafayette, marquis de **III:**
201
Rochambeau, comte de
III: 310
Vergennes, comte de **III:**
359
Louis, Joe **VIII:** *195,* **195–196,**
275, 337, 408*c*; **IX:** 5
Louisbourg **II:** 124, 182, 194,
214, 232, 332, 419*c*
Louisbourg, capture of **III:** 60,
146, 170
Louisiana **II: 199–200,** 200*m,*
418*c,* 419*c;* **III:** 68, 129, 258;
VI: 324*c;* **VIII:** 194–195; **IX:**
311, 320; **X:** 107, 242, 290
Acadians **II:** 2
African-American
churches, growth of **VI:**
4
African Americans **VI:** 5, 6
amnesty, acts of **V:** 8
art **II:** 25
Beauregard, Pierre **V:** 27
Benjamin, Judah P. **V:** 27
Black Codes **V:** 29
Bowie, Jim **IV:** 56
Butler, Benjamin **V:** 46
cotton culture **IV:** 99
Creole **II:** 74
exploration **II:** 115

Florida **II:** 121; **IV:** 139
French colonies **II:** 126, 129
French immigrants **II:** 130
fur trade **II:** 130–131
grandfather clause **VI:** 119
Harlan, John Marshall **VI:** 122
Hayes, Rutherford B. **VI:** 126
Jim Crow laws **VI:** 156
Jolliet, Louis **II:** 178
Lafitte, Jean **IV:** 205–206
La Salle, René-Robert Cavelier, sieur de **II:** 192
Le Moyne, Jean-Baptiste, sieur de Bienville **II:** 193
migration **IV:** 235
miscegenation **II:** 229
mulattoes **II:** 237, 238
Natchez Revolt **II:** 241–242
Native Americans **II:** 246
New Orleans **II:** 258
New Orleans, Battle of (1815) **IV:** 262
Pinchback, Pinckney B. S. **V:** 275–276
plantations **V:** 276, 277
Plessy v. Ferguson **VI:** 224
public land policy **IV:** 287
race and racial conflict **V:** 287
Reconstruction **V:** 292, 294
redemption **V:** 297
Red River campaign **V:** 297
Red Shoes **II:** 313
refugees **V:** 298
secession **V:** 313
Sheridan, Philip H. **V:** 319
Sherman, William T. **V:** 320
Texas **IV:** 337
trusts **VI:** 294
United States v. Cruikshank **V:** 375–376
Wade-Davis Bill of 1864 **V:** 385
Wakeman, Sarah Rosetta **V:** 386
Zouaves **V:** 403
Louisiana Purchase **III: 218,** 219*m,* 397*c;* **IV:** xiii, 375*c*
Adams-Onís Treaty **IV:** 5
African Americans **III:** 6
Astor, John Jacob **IV:** 30
Astoria **IV:** 32
Austin, Moses **IV:** 35
Bonaparte, Napoleon **III:** 42

Boone, Daniel **III:** 42
Catholics **III:** 63
Clay, Henry **IV:** 86
economy **IV:** 117
exploration **IV:** 130
Florida **III:** 129; **IV:** 139
foreign affairs **III:** 130
foreign policy **IV:** 141
fur trade **III:** 142–143
Jefferson, Thomas **III:** 186
Kearny, Stephen Watts **IV:** 200
Lewis, Meriwether **III:** 208
Lewis and Clark Expedition **III:** 210
Livingston, Robert R. **III:** 216
Manifest Destiny **IV:** 218*m*
Missouri Compromise of 1820 **IV:** 237
Monroe, James **IV:** 240
Native Americans **IV:** 255
New Spain (Mexico), northern frontier of **III:** 258
Oregon Trail **IV:** 267
Pike, Zebulon Montgomery **IV:** 281, 282
public land policy **IV:** 287
Quasi War **III:** 292
Randolph, John **III:** 296
states' rights **III:** 333
Talleyrand, Prince **III:** 341
Texas **IV:** 337
Wilkinson, James **III:** 379
Louisiana Territory **IV:** 78, 84–85
Bonaparte, Napoleon **III:** 42
Clark, William **III:** 72
foreign affairs **III:** 130
Jay-Gardoqui treaty negotiations **III:** 182
Lewis, Meriwether **III:** 208
Quasi War **III:** 292
Louisiana Tigers **V: 218,** 403
Louis-Philippe, king of France **IV:** 61
Louisville, Kentucky **IV:** 23
Louisville Journal **V:** 377
Louverture, Toussaint. *See* Toussaint Louverture
Love, Nancy Harkness **VIII:** 380
Love Canal **X:** 78
Lovejoy, Elijah **IV:** 14, *214,* **214–215,** 280–281, 377*c;* **V:** 3, 146
Lovelace, Francis **II:** 292
Lovell, Sir Bernard **IX:** 278

Lovell, John **I:** 110
Lovett, Robert A. **VIII:** 20, 340
Loving v. Alabama **V:** 234
Loving v. Virginia **X:** 181
Low, Seth **VII:** 201
Low, Will **VI:** 219
Low Countries **II:** 346, 361; **VIII:** 39, 166
Lowe, Thaddeus **V:** 21
Lowell, Francis Cabot **III:** 177, 326; **IV:** 118, 184, 187
Lowell, James Russell **IV:** 196, 213
Lowell, Massachusetts **IV:** 118, 184, 204
Lowell, Robert **IX:** 183
Lowell Mills **IV:** 185, 186
Lower Counties **II:** 87. *See also* Delaware
Lower Creek nation **IV:** 256, 311. *See also* Seminole nation
Lower Pima **II:** 283
Lower South states **IV:** 319, 320; **V:** 311, 361
low-income housing. *See* public housing
Low Level Radioactive Waste Policy Amendments Act of 1985 **X:** 113
Lowndes County Freedom Organization **IX:** 47
Lowry, Robert **VI:** 203
Loyalists **III: 219–221,** 220*m,* 394*c*
American Philosophical Society **III:** 11
Andre, John **III:** 13
Arnold, Benedict **III:** 21
art **III:** 22
artisans **III:** 26
Asbury, Francis **III:** 27
Boucher, Jonathan **III:** 46
Brant, Joseph **III:** 49
Canada **III:** 60
Carleton, Guy **III:** 62
Charleston, siege of **III:** 64
Church, Benjamin **III:** 68–69
cities and urban life **III:** 70
Clinton, George **III:** 75
Clinton, Sir Henry **III:** 75
committees of correspondence **III:** 77
Cornwallis, Lord **III:** 93
Crèvecoeur, J. Hector St. John de **III:** 98
Dulany, Daniel **III:** 108
Dunlap, William **III:** 108
Dunmore, Lord **III:** 109
Eutaw Springs, Battle of **III:** 120
Florida **III:** 129

Franklin, William **III:** 136
freemasonry **III:** 137
Guilford Courthouse, Battle of **III:** 158
Hale, Nathan **III:** 160
immigration **III:** 173
Ingersoll, Jared **III:** 178
Jay's Treaty **III:** 182
Jews **III:** 187
Johnson, Sir John **III:** 188, 189
journalism **III:** 191
King's Mountain, Battle of **III:** 196–197
Livingston, William **III:** 217
Marion, Francis **III:** 231
McRea, Jane **III:** 239
minutemen **III:** 243
Monmouth, Battle of **III:** 244
Native Americans and the Revolution **III:** 255
Oliver, Andrew **III:** 266
Paris, Treaty of **III:** 273
population trends **III:** 283
Quakers **III:** 291
Revolutionary War **III:** 305, 307
Seabury, Samuel **III:** 323
Tarleton, Banastre **III:** 343
Valley Forge, encampment of **III:** 359
Washington, George **III:** 368
Wilson, James **III:** 380
Loyal Nine **III: 221–222,** 391*c*
Adams, Samuel **III:** 4
MacIntosh, Ebenezer **III:** 225
Sons of Liberty **III:** 329
Stamp Act **III:** 332
loyalty investigations **IX:** 43–44, 61, 109–110, 329*c*
loyalty oaths **V:** 8, 182–183, **218–219,** 292, 406*c,* 408*c;* **VIII:** 13, 171, 387
Loyola, Ignatius **I:** 178, 188–189, **209**
LSD **IX:** 175, 176, 182, **183–184; X:** 189, 206
Luba **I: 209–210**
Lucas, Charles **IV:** 49
Lucas, George **X:** 198, 239, 240, 325*c*
Lucas v. South Carolina Coast Council (1992) **X:** 271
Luce, Clare Boothe **VIII:** 197; **IX:** 93, 199, 242
Luce, Henry R. **VIII: 196–197**
Asian Americans **VIII:** 26
Life (magazine) **VIII:** 189

Luce, Henry R. *(continued)*
    Manchuria **VIII:** 199–200
    news media **VIII:** 243
    Republican Party **VIII:**
        306
    Willkie, Wendell L. **VIII:**
        379
Luciano, Charles "Lucky" **IX:**
    81
Ludlow Amendment **VIII:** 166
Ludlow Massacre **VII:** 129,
    167–168, 314, 358*c*
Ludwell, Philip **II:** 32, 172
Ludwell family **II:** 172
Luftwaffe
    air power **VIII:** 11, 12
    Arnold, "Hap" **VIII:** 22
    Britain, Battle of **VIII:** 43,
        44
    Normandy, invasion of
        VIII: 248
Lugue, Hernando de **I:** 283
Luhya **I: 210**
Luisetti, Hank **VIII:** 336
Luker, Kristin **X:** 181
Luks, George **VI:** 321; **VII:** 121
Lull, Ramon **I:** 337
Lumbee nation **V:** 249
lumbering **II:** 201; **IV:** 25; **VI:**
    200
    economy **II:** 101
    Maine **II:** 203
    mills **II:** 225
    New Hampshire **II:** 250
    New Jersey **II:** 253
    trade and shipping **II:** 376
    Virginia Company of
        London **II:** 387
Luminism **V:** 16
Lumumba, Patrice **IX:** 317
Luna, Tristan de **I:** 85, 130
Luna Park (Coney Island, NY)
    VII: *231*
Lundu people **I:** 223
Lundy, Benjamin **IV:** 160–161
Lundy's Lane, Battle of **IV:** 309,
    358
Luque, Hernando de **I:** 276
Luria, Solomon **I:** 192
Lusitania **VII: 168,** 358*c*
    foreign policy **VII:** 100
    National Defense Act **VII:**
        201
    Preparedness **VII:** 235
    World War I **VII:** 343
    Zimmermann telegram
        VII: 353
Luther, Martin **I: 210–212,**
    211, 387*c;* **II:** 140, 201, 300,
    301, 316
    Calvin, John **I:** 50
    Charles V **I:** 68–69

Church of England **I:** 73
Hanno the elephant **I:** 153
Huguenots **I:** 169
invention and technology
    I: 179
Jews (Judaism) **I:** 192
Leo X **I:** 203
printing press **I:** 294
Reformation **I:** 307, 309
Trent, Council of **I:** 360
Lutheranism **I:** 307; **II: 201;**
    VI: 241, 243–244; **VIII:** 166,
    304; **X:** 265
    Dutch Reformed Church
        II: 97
    education **II:** 103
    German immigrants **II:**
        139
    German Reformed Church
        II: 140
    Mittelberger, Gottlieb **II:**
        231
    Muhlenberg, Henry
        Melchior **II:** 237
    New Netherland **II:** 257
    New York **II:** 260
    Protestantism **II:** 301–302
    religion, Euro-American
        II: 316
Luxembourg **VIII:** 39; **IX:** 194,
    231–233; **X:** 223
Luzon Island **VIII:** 16
LWV. *See* League of Women
    Voters
lyceum movement **IV:** 121, **215**
Lyell, Charles **VI:** 242
Lynch, James **VI:** 4, 5
Lynch, John R. **V:** 40
lynchings **V:** 199, 297, 354; **VI:**
    181, **181–182,** 325*c,* 327*c;*
    VII: 360*c;* **IX:** 4, 253. *See
    also* antilynching legislation
    African Americans **VI:** 6;
        VIII: 3
    civil rights **VIII:** 61
    Great Migration **VII:** 113
    Leo Frank case **VII:**
        157–158
    Mafia incident **VI:** 184
    Mormon Church **VI:** 198
    NAACP **VII:** 199
    race and racial conflict
        VII: 249; **VIII:** 287–289
    Red Scare **VII:** 259
    religion **VI:** 244
    Tarbell, Ida **VII:** 305
    Wells-Barnett, Ida Bell **VI:**
        311
    White, Walter **VIII:** 378
Lynch v. Donnelly (1984) **X:**
    326*c*
Lynd, Staughton **IX:** 207

Lyndon B. Johnson Space
    Center **X:** 281
Lynn, Loretta **X:** 203
Lynn, Massachusetts strike
    (1860) **V:** 339–340
Lynn Female Anti-Slavery
    Society **IV:** 147
Lyon, Matthew **III:** 9, **222–223**
Lyon, Nathaniel **V:** 285
Lyon, Phyllis **IX:** 119
Lyrics of Lowly Life (Dunbar)
    VI: 82

M

Maasai **I:** 210
Mabila **I:** 85, **213**
Macao **I:** 66, 312; **II:** 93, 174
MacArthur, Arthur **VI:** 100
MacArthur, Douglas **VIII:** *266,*
    409*c;* **IX:** 21, 58, 163–164,
    185, **185–186,** 330*c*
    amphibious warfare **VIII:**
        15
    Bonus Army **VIII:** 40
    Leyte Gulf, Battle for
        VIII: 186
    Nimitz, Chester W. **VIII:**
        246
    Philippines **VIII:** 266
    Solomon Islands **VIII:**
        330, 331
    Tarawa **VIII:** 350
    World War II Pacific
        theater **VIII:** 398, 399
MacArthur, Douglas, II **X:** 155
Macbeth (Shakespeare) **V:** 352
Macbeth **VIII:** 120, 376
MacBeth Galleries **VII:** 357*c*
Macdonald, Charles **VI:** 274
Macdonough, Thomas **IV:** 358
MacDowell, Edward Alexander
    VI: 183, 201, 202, 325*c*
MacDowell colony **VI:** 23
Macedonia **X:** 167
Macedonian, HMS **IV:** 104, 356
macehualtin **I:** 19, 20
Macfadden, Bernarr **VII:** 143
MacGregor, Gordon **VII:** 135
machine gun **V:** 308, 346
machine politics **V:** 176, 177,
    253; **VI:** 140, **183–184; VII:**
    316
machinery **IV:** 186*m*
Machinists and Aerospace
    Workers Union **X:** 236
Machu Picchu **I:** 12, 175,
    213–214
MacIntosh, Ebenezer **III:** 222,
    225–226
MacKenzie, Alexander **IV:**
    32–33

MacKenzie, William Lyon **IV:**
    74–75
Mackenzie Delta Eskimo **II:** 167
Mackinac **IV:** 259
MacLaury, Bruce **X:** 301
MacMonnies, Frederick **VI:** 259
MacMurrough, Dermot
    (Diarmaid Mac Murchadha)
    I: 10
Macomb, Alexander **III:** 272;
    IV: 310
Macon, Nathaniel **III: 226,** 226
Macon's Bill No. 2 **III: 226,**
    398*c;* **IV:** 355
    Bonaparte, Napoleon **III:**
        42
    foreign affairs **III:** 131
    Macon, Nathaniel **III:** 226
    Non-Intercourse Act **III:**
        259
    Orders in Council **III:** 267
Macready, William Charles **V:**
    352
Macune, Charles W. **VI:** 99
Macy, William **IV:** 123
MAD. *See* Mutually Assured
    Destruction
Madagascar **I:** 44
Madame X (Sargent) **VI:** 256
Maddox, Lester **X:** 20, 57
Madeira **I:** 53, **214,** 338, 385*c;*
    II: 250
Madero, Francisco **VII:** 184,
    357*c*
Madison, Dolley Payne Todd
    III: 226–227, 229, 230
Madison, Dolly **IV:** 77
Madison, James **II:** 317; **III:**
    227–230, 229, 394*c,* 395*c,*
    398*c;* **IV:** 375*c;* **X:** 19
    abolition/abolition
        movement **III:** 16; **V:** 1
    ACS **IV:** 15
    Adams, John Quincy **IV:** 4
    Alien and Sedition Acts
        III: 9
    American System **IV:** 18
    Austin, Moses **IV:** 35
    Bank of the United States,
        Second **IV:** 44
    Bank of the United States
        (First) **III:** 31
    Bill of Rights **III:** 38, 39
    Bonus Bill **IV:** 56
    Brackenridge, Hugh
        Henry **III:** 46
    Clinton, DeWitt **III:** 73
    Clinton, George **III:** 75
    Constitutional Convention
        III: 81, 82
    Continental Congress,
        Second **III:** 88

Democratic Party **IV:** 106;
V: 93
Democratic-Republican
Party **III:** 104
Democratic-Republican
societies **III:** 105
Erie Canal **IV:** 128
Federalist Papers **III:** 124,
125
Federalist Party **III:** 126
Federalists **III:** 127
Florida **III:** 129
foreign affairs **III:** 131
foreign policy **IV:** 141
Gallatin, Albert **III:** 147
Gerry, Elbridge **III:** 153
Ghent, Treaty of (1814) **IV:**
161
Hamilton, Alexander **III:**
161, 162
Hartford Convention **IV:**
171
Hull, William **IV:** 175, 176
Jefferson, Thomas **III:** 184
journalism **III:** 191
Lafitte, Jean **IV:** 206
Liberia **IV:** 209
Macon, Nathaniel **III:** 226
Madison, Dolley **III:** 226,
227
Marbury v. Madison **III:**
230
Marshall, John **III:** 236
Monroe, James **IV:** 240
Monroe Doctrine **IV:** 241
Monroe-Pinkney Treaty
III: 246
national debt **III:** 253
National Road **IV:** 253
Native Americans in the
War of 1812 **IV:** 258
Neutrality Proclamation
III: 256
Niles, Hezekiah **III:** 258
Non-Intercourse Act **III:**
259
Nullification Controversy
IV: 263
Orders in Council **III:** 268
Otis, Harrison Gray **III:**
268
Panic of 1792 **III:** 272
political parties **III:**
278–279
population trends **III:** 283
Randolph, John **III:** 296
states' rights **III:** 333
Story, Joseph **III:** 334
Taylor, John, of Caroline
III: 344
Tippecanoe, Battle of **III:**
348

transportation **V:** 355
Virginia and Kentucky
Resolutions **III:** 360
Virginia dynasty **III:** 361
War Message, 1812 **IV:**
381–383
War of 1812 **IV:** 355
Washington, District of
Columbia **III:** 364
West Point **V:** 372
Madison Avenue **VIII:** 273
Madison Guaranty **X:** 68
Madison Square Garden **VI:** 98;
VII: 105, 225, 315; **VIII:** 19,
336
Madonna (singer) **X:** 202, 203,
240
Madrid, Spain **I:** 45, 281
Madrid, Treaty of (1670) **II:**
356
Maennerchor (Men's Choir) **IV:**
179
Mafia **VI:** 123; **IX:** 136. *See also*
organized crime
Mafia incident **VI: 184–185**
Magalhaes, Pero de **I:** 24
magazines **II:** 38, 193; **IV:**
196–197; **VI:** 2, 137, 176,
185
advertising **VII:** 4; **VIII:** 1;
X: 6, 7
Hearst, William Randolph
VII: 121
journalism **VII:** 142, 143
Life **VIII:** 189–190
literature **X:** 177, 178
Luce, Henry R. **VIII:**
196–197
media **X:** 185–187
neoconservatism **X:** 215,
216
recreation **VIII:** 297
science **VII:** 276
sexuality **VII:** 283
sexual revolution **X:** 277
Magee, Matthew M. **IV:** 33
Magellan, Ferdinand **I:**
215–217, 216*m,* 387*c*
Cabot, Sebastian **I:** 43
caravel **I:** 56
Cathay (China) **I:** 65
Drake, Sir Francis **I:** 111
Pigafetta, Antonio **I:** 283
Maggie: A Girl of the Streets
(Crane) **VI:** 68, 177
Maghreb **I:** 184, 222
magic **I:** 171, 340, 373–374. *See
also* witches/witchcraft
"Magic" code **VIII:** 64, 211
magicians **VII:** 123–124
magnetic resonance imaging
(MRI) **X:** 190

Magnetic Telegraph Company
IV: 246
Magoffin, Beriah **V:** 152
Magruder, Jeb **X:** 316
Magruder, John **V:** 145, 267
Maguzawa **I:** 155
Mahan, Alfred Thayer **VI:** 124,
185–186; VII: 98, 165
Mahan, Asa **IV:** 148
Mahan, Frank **VI:** 275
Mahar, William L. **VI:** 96
Maharishi Mahesh Yogi **IX:** 36
Maher v. Roe (1977) **X:** 3, 247
Mahfuz, emir of Adal **I:** 124
Mahican **II:** 39, 212, 233, 256,
257
Mahican language **I:** 6
Mahone, William **VI:** 172
Mahpiya Luta. *See* Red Cloud
Maidu **I:** 48
mail **IV:** 129, 271–272; **V:** 207,
405*c;* **VI:** 324*c,* 325*c;* **VII:**
147. *See also* Post Office
Department
communications **VI:** 61
corruption, political **VI:** 67
magazines **VI:** 185
newspapers **VI:** 212
Pullman Strike **VI:** 236
mail carriers' strike **X:** 169
Mailer, Norman **VIII:** 192; **IX:**
35, 181, 182, 243, 330*c;* **X:**
177
mail fraud **II:** 292
mail-order houses **VI: 186–187,**
290, **326***c*
Maiman, Theodore H. **X:** 273
Maine **II: 203; III:** 202; **V:**
53–54; **VI:** 31, 240; **X:** 194,
242
Abenaki **I:** 2
Acadia **I:** 2
Aroostook War **IV:** 25
Clay, Henry **IV:** 86
crowd action **II:** 78
French colonies **II:** 126
fur trade **II:** 130–131
King William's War **II:** 185
lumbering **II:** 201
Maliseet **I:** 219
Massachusetts **II:** 214
Missouri Compromise of
1820 **IV:** 237
monarchy, British **II:** 232
Morton, Thomas **II:** 236
Norumbega **I:** 266
Passamaquoddy **I:** 278
shipbuilding **II:** 335
temperance movement **IV:**
336
Verrazano, Giovanni da **I:**
367

War of 1812 **IV:** 358
Webster-Ashburton Treaty
(1842) **IV:** 361
Maine, Remember the **VI:** *187,*
187–188
Maine, USS **VI:** 71, 187, 272,
328*c;* **VII:** 266
Maine Indian Land Claims Act
of 1980 **X:** 195
Maine Indian Settlement Act of
1980 **X:** 214
Maine Woods, The (Thoreau)
IV: 342
mainframe computers **IX:** 64
"maintenance of membership"
rule **VIII:** 233
Main-Travelled Roads (Garland)
VI: 109
Mair, John **I:** 369
maize. *See* corn
Major League Baseball **X:** 262,
284, 328*c*
Majors and Minors (Dunbar)
VI: 82
Makataimeshiekiakiak. *See*
Black Hawk
Makemie, Francis **II:** 296
"Make the World Safe for
Democracy" speech (Wilson)
VII: 376–379
Making of an American, The
(Riis) **VI:** 248
Malabe **I:** 210
Malacca **I:** 335
*Malaeska, The Indian Wife of
the White Hunter* (Stephens)
VI: 80
"Malaise " speech (Carter) **X:**
341–344
malaria **I:** 107, 108; **II:** 90–91,
93, 151, 210, 235, 339; **III:**
106; **IV:** 99, 112; **V:** 96, 97,
230; **VIII:** 208
Malawi **I:** 223
Malaya **VIII:** 398
Malay Archipelago **I:** 114, 115
Malaysia **X:** 69
Malcolm X **IX: 186–187,** *187,*
330*c,* 334*c;* **X:** 30, 111, 213
African-American
movement **IX:** 6, 7
Black Panthers **IX:** 38, 39
Muhammad, Elijah **IX:**
215
Robinson, Jackie **IX:** 263
Malebranche, Nicholas **II:** 105
Malecite, Maleschite. *See*
Maliseet
Mali **I: 217–218; II:** 4
Askia Muhammad I **I:** 14
Djenne-Djeno **I:** 109
Fulani **I:** 135

Mali (continued)
  Gao I: 137, 139
  Ghana I: 140–141
  Gonja I: 144
  Guinea-Bisseau I: 147
  Hausa I: 155
  Henry the Navigator I: 158
  Ibn Battuta I: 173
  Islam I: 184
  Kaabu kingdom I: 195
  Leo Africanus I: 203
  Mansa Musa I I: 220
  Niger River I: 263
  Songhai I: 331, 332
  Sudan I: 336–337
  Sundiata Keita I: 339–340
  Taureg I: 360
  Timbuktu I: 350
Maliki Islam I: 23
Malinche I: 218–219
  Aguilar, Gerónimo
    (Jerónimo) de I: 5
  Aztecs I: 21
  castas I: 61
  Cholula I: 72
  Cortés, Hernán I: 93, 94
  Tabasco I: 341
Maliseet (Etchemin) I: 2, 219,
  278; II: 243
Maliseet language I: 6
Malleus Malificarum I: 374
Mallory, Stephen R. V: 73–75,
  221–222, 237
malls X: 33
malnutrition II: 171; V: 382
Malocello, Lancelotto I: 53
Malone, Annie Turnbo VII: 58
Maltz, Albert IX: 135, 211
Malvern Hill, Battle of V: 406c
  Armistead, Lewis A. V: 15
  Early, Jubal A. V: 103
  Irish-American regiments
    V: 181
  Peninsular campaign V:
    269
Mamluks I: 230
Mammoth Oil Company VII:
  307
Mamprussi I: 243
Manabe, Syukuro IX: 270, 334c
Manabi I: 382
management, scientific. See
  scientific management
Manassas, Battle of. See Bull
  Run/Manassas, First and
  Second Battles of
Man at the Crossroads (Rivera)
  VIII: 25
Manchuria VII: 271; VIII:
  199–200, 405c
  Anglo-American relations
    VIII: 16

foreign policy VIII: 123
Hoover presidency VIII:
  155
POWs VIII: 282
Stimson, Henry L. VIII:
  340
World War II Pacific
  theater VIII: 396
Yalta Conference VIII: 402
Manco Capac I: 99, 175
Manco Inca I: 14, 15, 177
Mandan/Mandan nation I: 161;
  II: 150, 317; III: 210; IV:
  377c
  Bodmer, Karl IV: 55
  Catlin, George IV: 78
  diseases and epidemics IV:
    113
  Fort Laramie IV: 144
  Native Americans IV: 258
mandatory public education
  VII: 361c
Mande I: 141, 217, 339, 340
Mandela, Nelson X: 280
Mandeville, Sir John I: 152,
  219–220, 239, 240, 292
Manding I: 321
Mandinka. See Mande
Mangapeesomon II: 268
Mangi I: 66
Manhattan II: 23, 227
  architecture II: 23
  Dutch-Indian Wars II: 99
  Leisler's Rebellion II: 192
  Minuit, Peter II: 226–227
  New Amsterdam II:
    249–250
  New Netherland II: 255
  New York II: 259, 261
  New York City II: 262
  Protestantism II: 301
Manhattan Indians II: 249
Manhattan Project VIII:
  200–201; IX: 23, 139, 237,
  264–265
  atomic bomb VIII: 29
  business VIII: 47
  Communists VIII: 66
  espionage VIII: 104
  Grand Alliance VIII: 137
  Hiroshima and Nagasaki
    VIII: 146
  intelligence VIII: 164
  Lilienthal, David E. VIII:
    190
  OSRD VIII: 255
  Roosevelt, Franklin D.
    VIII: 314
  Soviet-American relations
    VIII: 333
  Sunbelt VIII: 344
  TVA VIII: 356

Manifest Destiny IV: 217–219,
  218m; VI: 102, 142, 279
  Alamo, The IV: 12
  art IV: 25; V: 16
  Bent, William IV: 48
  Colt revolver IV: 92
  Cuba IV: 101
  Douglas, Stephen A. V: 98
  filibustering V: 126, 127
  foreign policy IV: 142
  Forty-niners IV: 147
  Mexican-American War
    IV: 232
  migration IV: 236
  Native Americans IV: 258
  Oregon Treaty of 1846 IV:
    269
  Pacific Railroad Act of
    1862 V: 264
  race and race relations IV:
    291
  religion V: 299
  Texas IV: 338
Manifesto to the Mexican
  Republic (Figueroa) IV: 136
Manigault, Gabriel II: 373
Manigault family II: 130
manioc I: 31
Manitou. See Mantoac
manitous II: 317, 318
"man-midwives" II: 225
Mann, Horace IV: 83, 120, 121,
  219–220, 220, 377c; V: 108
Mann, Woodrow IX: 109
Mann Act VII: 59, 139,
  169–170, 357c
Mann-Elkins Act VII: 170, 230,
  303, 357c
Man Nobody Knows, The
  (Barton) VII: 5
Man of the Year (Time
  magazine) VIII: 206
mano muerta. See
  primogeniture and entail
Mansa Musa I (Kankan Musa) I:
  220
  Gao I: 139
  Islam I: 184
  Mali I: 217, 218
  Mecca I: 230
  Songhai I: 331
  Timbuktu I: 350
Mansa Sulayman I: 173
Mansa Uli Keita, king of Mali I:
  217
Mansfield, Joseph V: 13, 389
Mansfield, Mike X: 105, 120,
  276
Manship, Paul VII: 19
Manson, Charles X: 31
Manteo I: 220–221, 388c; II:
  264

Barlowe, Arthur I: 26
Harriot, Thomas I: 154
Mantoac I: 221
Roanoke I: 313, 314
Wanchese I: 372
White, John I: 373
Mantoac I: 221, 253
Mantux I: 382
Manual of Military Surgery V:
  231
manual training VII: 77–78
Manuel I, king of Portugal I:
  386c
  Cabral, Pedro Álvares I: 44
  Hanno the elephant I: 153
  John III I: 192–193
  Leo X I: 203
  Magellan, Ferdinand I:
    215
  Vespucci, Amerigo I: 368
manufacturing and industry II:
  203–204; III: 96; IV: 18,
  105, 118; V: 116, 387–388;
  VI: 53, 103, 292; IX: 45m,
  272, 304; X: 269, 290. See
  also specific industries
  Africa II: 4
  automobile industry IX:
    24–26
  business IX: 44
  business cycles VI: 41
  cattle kingdom VI: 46
  cities and urban life IX:
    51–52
  computer IX: 63–65
  Connecticut II: 69
  economy II: 101, 102; VII:
    73
  environment II: 110–111
  Fordney-McCumber Tariff
    VII: 97
  invention and technology
    VII: 132–134
  iron manufacturing II:
    167–168
  Jamestown II: 172
  labor IX: 169
  military-industrial complex
    IX: 203–204
  mills II: 225–226
  Morgan, John Pierpont VI:
    197
  New South VI: 209–210
  Pennsylvania II: 276
  Philadelphia Centennial
    Exposition VI: 223–224
  Rhode Island II: 321
  service sector IX: 271–272
  shipbuilding II: 335
  steel industry VII:
    296–298; IX: 282–283
  technology II: 369

trusts **VI:** 292–295
union movement **IX:**
     303–304
U.S. Steel **VII:** 319–320
manufacturing belt **VI:** 54*m*
manufacturing unemployment
     VIII: 363
manumission **IV:** 1
     abolitionism **II:** 1
     Connecticut **II:** 69
     Creole **II:** 74
     miscegenation **II:** 228, 229
     mulattoes **II:** 238
     slave codes **II:** 336
     slavery **II:** 341, 342
     Spanish colonies **II:** 359
Manuzio, Aldo (Daniel Bomber)
     I: 191
Mao Tse-tung. *See* Mao Zedong
Mao Zedong **VIII:** 196; **IX:** 330*c*
     Asia (and foreign policy)
          IX: 21
     cold war **IX:** 58
     Korean War **IX:** 163, 164
     Soviet Union **IX:** 277
     White Paper **IX:** 321
"Maple Leaf Rag" (Joplin) **VI:**
     328*c*; **VII:** 141, 194
mappae mundi **I:** 29, **221–222,**
     222, 239
Mapplethorpe, Robert **X:** 26,
     209
maps. *See* cartography
maps and mapmaking **VI:** 160,
     227, 228
     art **II:** 25
     Champlain, Samuel de **II:**
          56
     Columbia River **IV:** 93
     exploration **II:** 114, 115;
          IV: 132, 133
     fur trade **IV:** 157
     Jolliet, Louis **II:** 178
     Marquette, Jacques **II:**
          205, 206
     Pennsylvania **II:** 277
     Pike, Zebulon
          Montgomery **IV:**
          281–282
     Wood, William **II:** 410
Maqeda, queen of Sheba **I:** 123
maquiladoras area (Mexico) **X:**
     222
marabout(s) **I:** 66, 184,
     221–223, 337
maranos **I:** 190, 191; **II:** 174
Maravi **I: 223**
Marble, Alice **VIII:** 337
Marbury v. Madison **III:**
     230–231, 397*c;* **IV:** 330
     Federalist Party **III:** 126
     Jefferson, Thomas **III:** 185

Judiciary Act of 1789 **III:**
     192
lawyers **III:** 204
Marshall, John **III:** 236
Supreme Court **III:** 338
Marching Along (Sousa) **VI:** 272
marching music **VI:** 271–272
March of Time (newsreels)
     VIII: 275
March on Washington (1963)
     VIII: 291; **IX: 191–192,** 333*c*
     African-American
          movement **IX:** 5
     Congress of Racial
          Equality **IX:** 67
     King, Martin Luther, Jr.
          IX: 161
     Southern Christian
          Leadership Conference
          IX: 275
     Student Nonviolent
          Coordinating
          Committee **IX:** 285
     Wilkins, Roy **IX:** 322
March on Washington
     Movement (MOWM) **VIII:**
     201–202, 409*c*
     African Americans **VIII:** 4
     civil rights **VIII:** 61
     enemy aliens **VIII:** 102
     Executive Order 8802
          VIII: 106
     FEPC **VIII:** 109
     NAACP **VIII:** 228
     race and racial conflict
          VIII: 289
     Randolph, A. Philip **VIII:**
          291
"March to the Sea." *See*
     Sherman's March through
     Georgia
Marconi, Guglielmo **VII:** 134,
     253
Marcos, Ferdinand E. **X:** 139
Marcus Welby, M.D. (TV
     program) **X:** 295
Marcy, William **IV:** 101; **V:** 260
Mardian, Robert **X:** 308, 317
Mare Liberum (Hugo Grotius)
     I: 114, 152
Margarita Island **I:** 119
*Mariana Griswold Van
     Rensselaer* (Saint-Gaudens)
     VI: 253
Mariana Islands **VIII: 202–203**
     air power **VIII:** 12
     amphibious warfare **VIII:**
          15
     Iwo Jima **VIII:** 168
     Leyte Gulf, Battle for
          VIII: 186
     Navy, U.S. **VIII:** 237

Nimitz, Chester W. **VIII:**
     246
Philippine Sea, Battle of
     the **VIII:** 267
Tarawa **VIII:** 350
World War II Pacific
     theater **VIII:** 398, 399
Mari-Djata. *See* Sundiata Keita
Marie-Galante **II:** 378
marijuana **VII:** 197; **X:** 65, 206,
     208
Marilyn Monroe (Andy Warhol)
     IX: 20
Marin, John **VII:** 20
Marine, James E. **VII:** 31
Marine Band **VI:** 271
mariners **II: 204–205**
     Bonnet, Stede **II:** 34
     class **II:** 63
     crime and punishment **II:**
          74–75
     fishing **II:** 118
     Jews **II:** 174
     King George's War **II:** 182
     Massachusetts **II:** 212
     mercantilism **II:** 221
     mortality **II:** 235
     Newport, Christopher **II:**
          258–259
     Philadelphia **II:** 282
     piracy **II:** 285, 286
     privateering **II:** 299, 300
     Seven Years' War **II:** 333
     slave resistance **II:** 337
     taverns and inns **II:** 368
Mariner space probes **IX:** 220;
     X: 283
Marines, U.S. **IV:** 45, 172; **V:**
     222, 243; **VIII: 203,** 410*c*
     amphibious warfare **VIII:**
          15
     Army, U.S. **VIII:** 19
     demobilization **VIII:** 79
     Guadalcanal **VIII:** 141
     Iwo Jima **VIII:** 169
     King, Ernest J. **VIII:** 177
     Mariana Islands **VIII:** 202
     MOWM **VIII:** 201
     Navy, U.S. **VIII:** 237
     Nimitz, Chester W. **VIII:**
          246
     Okinawa **VIII:** 259
     Philippine Sea, Battle of
          the **VIII:** 267
     Solomon Islands **VIII:** 330
     Tarawa **VIII:** 350
     World War II Pacific
          theater **VIII:** 398
Marion, Francis **III: 231–232,**
     343
Maris, Roger **X:** 284
maritime technologies **I:** 180

Mark (apostle) **I:** 364
Mark V Panther tank **VIII:** 350
marketing **IV:** 105; **VI:** 221–222;
     VIII: 219
market research **VII:** 4, 351;
     VIII: 1, 284
markets **VI:** 8, 61, 292
Markham, William **II:** 285
Markland **I:** 369
Markoe, William **VIII:** 54
maroonage **I:** 261
Marquette, Jacques **II:** 115,
     178, *205,* **205–206,** 324
Marrakech, Morocco **I:** 23
Marrant, John **II:** 148
marriage and family life **II:**
     206–208, *207; ***III: 232–235,**
     234, 311–312, 346, 380–383;
     IV: 220–223, 378*c;* **V:**
     122–123, **222–223; VII:**
     170–173; VIII: 203–205;
     IX: 192–193; X: 109–110,
     181–184, *182,* 331*c.* *See also*
     divorce; intermarriage
     Abenaki **I:** 2
     Acadia **I:** 2
     African Americans **IV:** 7
     agriculture **II:** 8; **IV:** 10
     anticommunism **IX:** 15
     Aztecs **I:** 20
     baby boom **IX:** 29
     baby boomers **X:** 33
     cacao **I:** 45
     California **I:** 48
     captivity **II:** 51–52
     Carib **I:** 56
     castas **I:** 61
     Chichén Itzá **I:** 70
     childhood **II:** 59–60
     Church of England **I:** 73,
          74
     class **II:** 62, 63
     computers **X:** 74–75
     Cortés, Hernán **I:** 94
     Delaware **II:** 89
     domesticity **II:** 93
     education **II:** 103
     ethnocentrism **II:** 113
     family life **X:** 109, 110
     feminism **X:** 114–116
     Ferdinand and Isabella **I:**
          128
     fertility **II:** 117–118
     Friedan, Betty **IX:** 115
     FSA **X:** 110
     fur trade **II:** 130–131
     gay rights movement **X:**
          127, 128
     Great Depression **VIII:**
          140
     Havasupai **I:** 156
     Henry VIII **I:** 160

marriage and family life
(continued)
Holy Roman Empire **I:** 166
homesteading **VI:** 131–132
Huron **II:** 160
Ibn Battuta **I:** 173
Inca **I:** 176
Iroquois **I:** 181–182
Jews (Judaism) **I:** 190
labor **II:** 189; **IX:** 170
land **II:** 191–192
Mali **I:** 218
Maryland **II:** 210
Maya **I:** 228
and *mestizaje* **I:** 233
mestizo **I:** 234
métis **II:** 223
Montagnais-Naskapi **I:** 241
Mormon Church **VI:**
198–199
New Woman **VII:** 213, 214
New York **II:** 259, 261
"the pill" **IX:** 242
plantation system **II:** 287
polygamy **IV:** 284–285
population trends **II:** 291;
VII: 233–234; **VIII:**
277; **IX:** 245
poverty **X:** 246
Powhatan Confederacy **II:**
294, 295
pro-life and pro-choice
movements **X:** 248
Quakers **II:** 308
Quayle, J. Danforth **X:** 253
recreation **X:** 262
Reformation **I:** 310
religion **VI:** 244; **IX:** 257
Roman Catholics **II:** 324
Schlafly, Phyllis **X:** 272
Seneca Falls **IV:** 313
sexuality **VII:** 283
sexual revolution **X:** 278
slavery **II:** 340–341; **IV:**
319
slave trade **I:** 328
society, British American
II: 351
Spanish colonies **II:** 357
spinsters **II:** 360
spiritualism **IV:** 326
Spock, Benjamin **IX:** 279
Steinem, Gloria **X:** 288
suburbanization **IX:**
287–288
television **IX:** 295–297
Texas, Republic of **IV:** 340
Virginia **II:** 383, 385
women's rights and status
II: 406, 408–409; **IV:**
366–368; **VI:** 317; **VIII:**
384–386; **X:** 320

work, household **VII:**
341–342
World War II **VIII:** 389
World War II home front
VIII: 395
Yoruba **I:** 377
Zuni **I:** 383
marriage rate **VIII:** 277, 385,
394
Married Women's Independent
Citizenship Act. *See* Cable
Act
Marriott Hotels **X:** 244
Mars **X:** 283, 329*c*
Marseilles **I:** 75
Marsh, Othniel Charles **VI:** 59,
160, **188,** 257, 258
Marshall, A. D. **X:** 301
Marshall, Burke **IX:** 253
Marshall, Edward **II:** 390
Marshall, George C. **VIII:**
205–207, *206;* **IX:** 190, 194,
203
Army, U.S. **VIII:** 20
atomic bomb **VIII:** 29
Bradley, Omar N. **VIII:** 40
Hopkins, Harry **VIII:** 157
Roosevelt, Franklin D.
VIII: 314
second front **VIII:** 320
Stimson, Henry L. **VIII:**
340
Marshall, James W.
California **IV:** 65
California gold rush **IV:** 66
Forty-niners **IV:** 146
gold, discovery and mining
IV: 162
Sutter, John **IV:** 332
Marshall, John **III:** **235–237,**
236, 397*c;* **X:** 40, 41
Bank of the United States,
Second **IV:** 44
Chase, Samuel **III:** 65
corporations **III:** 94
Dartmouth College case
IV: 104
Federalist Party **III:** 127
Gerry, Elbridge **III:** 152
Jackson, Andrew **IV:** 193
Jay, John **III:** 182
Jefferson, Thomas **III:** 185
Judiciary Act of 1789 **III:**
192
Judiciary Act of 1801 **III:**
193
lawyers **III:** 203, 204
literature **III:** 215
Marbury v. Madison **III:**
230–231
McCulloch v. Maryland
IV: 227

Nullification Controversy
IV: 264
Panic of 1819 **IV:** 275
Pinckney, Charles
Cotesworth **III:** 277
Story, Joseph **III:** 334
Supreme Court **III:** 338
Supreme Court decision
IV: 330
XYZ affair **III:** 385
Yazoo claims **III:** 388
Marshall, Lenore **IX:** 267
Marshall, Martha Stearns **II:** 29
Marshall, Thurgood **VIII:** 227,
228; **IX:** *193,* **193–194,** 334*c;*
X: 291
*Brown v. Board of
Education* **IX:** 42
Kennedy, John F. **IX:** 158
Murray, Pauli **IX:** 215
NAACP **IX:** 220
Warren Court **IX:** 316
Wilkins, Roy **IX:** 322
Marshall Islands
amphibious warfare **VIII:**
15
Halsey, "Bull" **VIII:** 143
Nimitz, Chester W. **VIII:**
246
World War II Pacific
theater **VIII:** 398
Marshall Plan **VIII:** 144,
206–207; **IX:** **194–195,**
195*m,* 330*c,* 339–341
Acheson, Dean **IX:** 1
Alliance for Progress **IX:**
11
business **IX:** 45
cold war **IX:** 58
Europe (and foreign
policy) **IX:** 105
military-industrial complex
IX: 203
NATO **IX:** 232–233
Progressive Party **IX:** 248
Soviet Union **IX:** 277
Truman, Harry **IX:** 299
White Paper **IX:** 321
Mars Pathfinder space mission
X: 283
Martel, Charles **I:** 62, 306
martial discipline **II:** 81
martial law **IV:** 260; **V:** 161, 304,
406*c*
Martian Chronicles, The (Ray
Bradbury) **IX:** 183
Martin, Del **IX:** 119
Martin, Hernán **II:** 54–55
Martin, Luther **III:** 16; **IV:** 227
Martin, Ricky **X:** 241
Martinez, Fray Alonso **I:** 271
Martinez, José Antonio **IV:** 207

Martinique **I:** 76, **223;** **II:** 52,
74, 233, 356, 378
Martin v. Hunter's Lessee **III:**
237, 334; **IV:** 330, 375*c*
Martin v. Wilks (1989) **X:** 63
Martire d'Anghiera, Pietro. *See*
Peter Martyr
martyrs **I:** 132
Marx, Groucho **VIII:** 405*c*
Marx, Karl **IV:** 194; **V:**
223–224; **VII:** 65, 146, 229;
IX: 61
labor, radical **VI:** 166
Social Gospel **VI:** 267
socialism **VI:** 267
Socialist Party **VI:** 268
Victorianism **VI:** 304
Marx Brothers **VIII:** 217, 405*c*
Marxism **VII:** 173; **VIII:** 65; **IX:**
256; **X:** 13
Marxist International
Workingmen's Association
(IWA) **VI:** 267
Marxists **VI:** 166–167, 268
Mary, queen of England **II:** 69,
140, 141, 210, 232, 301
Mary, queen of Scots **I:** 112,
120, 187
Mary I, queen of England **I:**
223–224
Church of England **I:** 74
Henry VII **I:** 159
Henry VIII **I:** 160
Puritans **I:** 298
Reformation **I:** 309
Walsingham, Sir Frances **I:**
371
Maryland **II:** **209–211,** 417*c;*
III: 328, 395*c;* **IV:** 72, 74, 94,
227; **V:** 406*c;* **VI:** 4, 156, 249;
X: 19, 242
agriculture **II:** 10–13
Albany Congress **II:** 14
Baltimore riots **V:** 22
Brent, Margaret Reed **II:**
40
Calvert, George **II:** 50
Calvert, Leonard **II:** 50–51
Chesapeake Bay **II:** 58
class **II:** 63
Conestoga **II:** 67
convict labor **II:** 72
disease **II:** 92
economy **II:** 101
English immigrants **II:**
108
Glorious Revolution **II:**
141
government, British
American **II:** 144
governors **V:** 152
Great Awakening **II:** 148

habeas corpus, writ of **V:** 161

headright in **I:** 157

Herrman, Augustine **II:** 156

Hesselius, John **II:** 156

housing **II:** 157

iron manufacturing **II:** 167

Jesuits **II:** 174

Johnson, Mary **II:** 175

journalism **II:** 178

Kuhn, Justus Engelhardt **II:** 186

Logan, James **II:** 198

Mason-Dixon Line **V:** 224

miscegenation **II:** 228; **V:** 233

mulattoes **II:** 238

Protestantism **II:** 300

Quakers **II:** 308

religion, Euro-American **II:** 316

Roman Catholics **II:** 323

St. Mary's City **II:** 328

Shenandoah Valley: Sheridan's campaign **V:** 317

slave trade **II:** 343

society, British American **II:** 349

Susquehannock War **II:** 364

tenants **II:** 370

Tennent, William, Jr. **II:** 372

tobacco **II:** 374

travel **II:** 377

Virginia **II:** 384

Weiser, Johann Conrad **II:** 393

White, Andrew **II:** 396

women's status and rights **II:** 407

"Maryland, My Maryland" **V:** 244

Maryland's Civil War **II:** 209

Mary of Burgundy **I:** 67

Mashantucket Pequot **II:** 278

Mason, Charles **V:** 224

Mason, George **III:** 16, **237–238,** 329

Mason, James **V:** 132, 197, 241

Mason, John **II:** 68, **211,** 250, 251, 279, 421–422; **V:** 260

Mason, Joseph **IV:** 34

Mason, Lowell **IV:** 250

Mason, Robert Tufton **II:** 312

Mason, William **VI:** 201

Mason-Dixon Line **II:** 274; **V:** 65, 217, **224**

Mason family **II:** 172

Masons **II:** 273; **IV:** 24; **VI:** 265. *See also* Anti-Masonic Party; freemasonry

Massachusett Indians **I:** **224–225; II:** 183, 243, 361

Massachusetts **II:** **212–216,** 213*m*, 418*c;* **V:** 46, 47

Adams, Samuel **III:** 4–5

agriculture **II:** 12

Albany Congress **II:** 14

Aroostook War **IV:** 25

Bernard, Francis **III:** 37

Boston **II:** 35–37

Bradstreet, Anne Dudley **II:** 39

Brook Farm **IV:** 58

Bulfinch, Charles **III:** 50

canal era **IV:** 72

captivity **II:** 51

Coercive Acts **III:** 76

Congregationalists **II:** 68

constitutions, state **III:** 84

Continental Congress, First **III:** 87

Cooke, Elisha, Jr. **II:** 72

crime and punishment **II:** 75

culture and society **II:** 215–216

Day, Stephen **II:** 84

Dominion of New England **II:** 94, 95

Dudley, Joseph **II:** 95

Dukakis, Michael **X:** 91

Dyer, Mary **II:** 99–100

early settlement and growth **II:** 212, 214

economy **IV:** 118, 119

education **IV:** 120, 121

Emerson, Ralph Waldo **IV:** 126, 127

fairs, agricultural **III:** 123

fishing **II:** 118–119

French immigrants **II:** 130

Gerry, Elbridge **III:** 152–153

Glorious Revolution **II:** 141

Gorton, Samuel **II:** 142

government, British American **II:** 144, 145

Great Awakening **II:** 148

Grimké, Angelina and Sarah **IV:** 164

Hall, Prince **III:** 160

Hancock, John **III:** 163

Hartford Convention **IV:** 170

Hooker, Thomas **II:** 156

Horton, Willie (campaign ad) **X:** 143

Howe, George Augustus, Viscount **II:** 158

Hull, William **IV:** 175

Hutchinson, Thomas **III:** 170, 171

industrialization **IV:** 184, 185

industrial revolution **III:** 177

iron manufacturing **II:** 167

Iroquois **II:** 169

King George's War **II:** 182

King Philip's War **II:** 183

King William's War **II:** 185

labor and labor movements **II:** 189; **IV:** 204

land **II:** 191

Leverett, John **II:** 194

Lexington and Concord, Battles of **III:** 211–213

literature **II:** 195

Livingston, Robert **II:** 196

lotteries **II:** 199

lumbering **II:** 201

lyceum movement **IV:** 215

Maine **II:** 203

Mann, Horace **IV:** 219–220

Mason, John **II:** 211

Massasoit **II:** 217

Mather, Cotton **II:** 217

Mather, Increase **II:** 218

Metacom **II:** 222–223

Mexican-American War **IV:** 232

mills **II:** 225

monarchy, British **II:** 232

Morton, Thomas **II:** 236

music **II:** 239

Native Americans **II:** 246

New Hampshire **II:** 251

New Netherland **II:** 256

New York **II:** 260

Oliver, Andrew **III:** 266–267

O'Neill, Thomas P., Jr. **X:** 228

Parris, Samuel **II:** 271

Phillips, Wendell **IV:** 280–281

piracy **II:** 285

Plymouth **II:** 287–288

population trends **X:** 242

primogeniture and entail **II:** 297

Protestantism **II:** 300, 301

provincial period **II:** 214–215

Puritans **II:** 305–306

Quakers **II:** 308

Queen Anne's War **II:** 309

race and race relations **IV:** 291

railroads **IV:** 295

Randolph, Edward **II:** 312

religion, Euro-American **II:** 316

religious liberty **III:** 300

Revere, Paul **III:** 304

Richardson, Elliot L. **X:** 268

Seven Years' War **II:** 333

Sewall, Samuel **II:** 334

Shays's Rebellion **III:** 324

shipbuilding **II:** 335

Story, Joseph **III:** 334

taverns and inns **II:** 367–368

tenants **II:** 371

Thoreau, Henry David **IV:** 342–343

trade and shipping **II:** 375

transcendental movement **IV:** 345

travel **II:** 377

Turell, Jane Colman **II:** 378

Webster, Daniel **IV:** 359–360

Webster-Ashburton Treaty (1842) **IV:** 361

Wheelwright, John **II:** 396

Wigglesworth, Edward **II:** 398

witchcraft **II:** 402

women's status and rights **II:** 409

writs of assistance **III:** 383–384

Massachusetts Anti-Slavery Society **IV:** 377*c;* **V:** 40, 99–100

Massachusetts Bay, Province of **II:** 214

Massachusetts Bay Colony

Boston **II:** 35

Congregationalists **II:** 68

Connecticut **II:** 68

Dudley, Thomas **II:** 95–96

education **II:** 103

Endecott, John **II:** 107

English immigrants **II:** 108

Hutchinson, Anne Marbury **II:** 161

Massachusetts **II:** 212

Native Americans **II:** 243, 246

New Hampshire **II:** 250, 251

Newport **II:** 258

Pequot **II:** 278

Rhode Island **II:** 321

Massachusetts Bay Colony
  (continued)
    society, British American
      II: 349–350
    taverns and inns **II:** 368
    Williams, Roger **II:** 399,
      400
    Winthrop, John **II:**
      401–402
    wolves **II:** 405
    Wood, William **II:** 410
Massachusetts Bay Company **II:**
  216
    Coddington, William **II:**
      65
    education **II:** 102
    fur trade **II:** 130–131
    government, British
      American **II:** 142
    Massachusetts **II:** 212
    praying towns **II:** 295–296
Massachusetts Board of
  Education **IV:** 377c
Massachusetts Court of
  Assistance **II:** 190
Massachusetts Emigrant Aid
  Society **IV: 223–224**
Massachusetts Government Act
  III: 392c
Massachusetts High School Law
  IV: 376c
Massachusetts Institute of
  Technology (MIT) **VI:** 247,
  318; **IX:** 97, 293
Massachusetts language **I:** 6
Massachusetts Metaphysical
  College **VI:** 52
Massachusetts School Act **II:**
  216–217
Massachusetts School Board of
  Education **IV:** 220
Massachusetts Society for the
  Suppression of Intemperance
  (MSSI) **IV:** 335
massacres **I:** 21, 72, 158, 169; **V:**
  135, 285
Massa people **I:** 52
Massasoit **II: 217,** 222, 283,
  287, 360, 361
Massengil Company **VIII:** 123
Masses, The **VII:** 114, **173,** 252,
  259
mass production **III:** 177, 377,
  397c; **IV:** 91, 184; **VII:** xiii,
  173–175, *174;* **IX:** 177–178,
  190, 203
    aircraft industry **VIII:** 11
    American Federation of
      Labor **VIII:** 14
    automobile industry **VII:**
      21–22
    economy **VII:** 74

Ford, Henry **VII:** 96
immigration **VII:** 127
invention and technology
  VII: 132, 133
labor and labor movements
  VII: 151; **VIII:** 179, 180
marriage and family life
  VII: 172
Meat Inspection Act **VII:**
  177–178
New Unionism **VII:** 212
scientific management
  VII: 277
shipbuilding **VIII:** 324
socialism **VII:** 288
master artisans **II:** 26
Master Card **IX:** 73
Masters and Servants Act of
  1850 **IV:** 172
master's degrees **X:** 97, 98
Mast Free Riot **II:** 251
mast trade **II:** 251, 252
Mataafa, king of Samoa **VI:** 255
Matamba **I:** 267
Mateos, Adolfo López **X:** 192
materialism **IX:** 2, 46; **X:** 275
Maternal and Child Health. *See
  also* Title V
maternal death rates **X:** 187
Maternity and Infancy Act. *See*
  Sheppard-Towner Act
Matewan, West Virginia strike
  VII: 314
mathematics **I:** 204–205; **II:**
  141, 277, 322, 330; **VI:** 257
Mather, Cotton **II: 217–218**
    Boston Philosophical
      Society **II:** 37
    Boylston, Zabdiel **II:** 37
    Bradstreet, Anne Dudley
      II: 39
    disease **II:** 92
    Dudley, Joseph **II:** 95
    Duston, Hannah Emerson
      II: 97
    education **II:** 104
    Enlightenment **II:** 110
    journalism **II:** 179
    Massachusetts **II:** 214, 215
    Mather, Increase **II:** 218
    medicine **II:** 220
    Pelham, Peter **II:** 273
    Pennsylvania **II:** 277
    piracy **II:** 286
    printing and publishing **II:**
      299
    Sewall, Samuel **II:** 334
    smallpox **II:** 345
    witchcraft **II:** 402
    wolves **II:** 405
    Yale, Elihu **II:** 413
    Yale College **II:** 413

Mather, Increase **II:** *218,*
  218–219
    Boston **II:** 35
    Boston Philosophical
      Society **II:** 37
    Brattle, Thomas **II:** 40
    Dudley, Joseph **II:** 95
    Leverett, John **II:** 193, 194
    Massachusetts **II:** 214, 215
    Mather, Cotton **II:** 217
    printing and publishing **II:**
      299
    Rowlandson, Mary White
      II: 324
    Sewall, Samuel **II:** 334
    Walter, Thomas **II:** 390
    witchcraft **II:** 402, 403
Mather, John **II:** 218
Mather, Richard **II:** 107
Mather, Stephen **VII:** 203
Mathew, Thomas **II:** 27
Mathews, Henry M. **VI:** 119
Mathews, Shailer **VI:** 102
Mathias, Charles **X:** 24
Matoaka. *See* Pocahontas
matriarchal society **II:** 206
matrilineal inheritance **II:** 120,
  168
matrilineal kinship **II:** 255
matrilineal societies **II:** 160; **IV:**
  221
Matta, Manuel Antonio **VI:** 50
Mattachine Society **IX:** 119; **X:**
  277
Mattaponi nation **II:** 295
Matthews, Robert **V:** 357
Matthijs, Jan **I:** 309
Mauchly, John W. **IX:** 63, 64, 98
Mauldin, Bill **VIII: 207**
Mauritania **I:** 140–141
Maury, Dabney Herndon **V:** 236
Maury, Matthew **V:** 74
Maury, Matthew Fontaine **IV:**
  308
Maximilian, Archduke **V:** 132
Maximilian I **I:** 67
Maximilian von Wied, Prince
  Alexander **IV:** 55, 377c
Maximillian II, Holy Roman
  Emperor **II:** 150
Maximum Freight Rates case
  VI: 40, 239
maximum hour laws **VII:** 3
Maxixcatzin **I:** 353
Max Schmitt in a Single Scull
  (Eakins) **VI:** *86*
Maxtla **I:** 185
Maxwell, James Clerk **VI:** 113
May, Henry **I:** 29
Maya **I: 225–229,** *226m*
    Aguilar, Gerónimo
      (Jerónimo) de **I:** 5

Alvarado, Pedro de **I:** 7
art and architecture **I:** 12,
  13
Aztecs **I:** 21
cacao **I:** 45
Chichén Itzá **I:** 69–71
Cholula **I:** 72
Copán **I:** 86
Córdoba, Francisco
  Hernández de **I:** 86–87
Grijalva, Juan de **I:**
  145–146
Guerrero, Gonzalo **I:** 146
invention and technology
  I: 180
Mexico **I:** 235
Native American religion
  I: 252
New Spain **I:** 258
Olmecs **I:** 270
Palenque **I:** 275
Tabasco **I:** 341
Tikal **I:** 349–350
Tláloc **I:** 352
Yucatán Peninsula **I:** 378
Mayan ruins **IV:** 133
May Day **II:** 236
mayeque **I:** 20
Mayer, Louis B. **IX:** 135
Mayflower (ship) **II:** 15, 16, 38,
  219, 283, 287
Mayflower Compact **II:** *219,*
  219–220, 417c
    Alden, John **II:** 15
    Bradford, William **II:** 38
    Pilgrims **II:** 283
    Plymouth **II:** 287
    Standish, Myles **II:** 361
Mayhew, Jonathan **II:** 20; **III:**
  238–239
Mayhew, Thomas **II:** 246, 295
Mayhew family **II:** 103
Maynard, Robert **II:** 369
MAYO. *See* Mexican America
  Youth Organization
Mayo nation **IV:** 248–249
mayorazgo. See primogeniture
  and entail
mayores **II:** 355
mayors **VI:** 21; **VII:** 139–140
maypole **II:** 236
Mays, Willie **IX:** 5
Maysville Road bill **IV:** 19, 56
Mazey, Emil **IX:** 12
Mazzoli, Romano **X:** 149
Mbundu **I: 229–230**
McAdoo, William **VII:** 81, 255,
  330
McAfee, Mildred **VIII:** 380
McAuliffe, Anthony **VIII:** 44
McAuliffe, Sharon **X:** 283
McCabe, Charles **V:** 174

McCain, John
  Bush, George W. **X:** 48
  campaign finance **X:** 53, 54
  conservative movement **X:** 80
  PACs **X:** 236
  Senate **X:** 276
McCain, John S., Sr. **VIII:** 246
McCann, William **VIII:** 54
McCarran, Patrick J. **IX:** 143, 187
McCarran Act of 1950 **IX:** 14, 330c
McCarran Internal Security Act. *See* Internal Security Act of 1950
McCarran-Walter Act of 1952 **IX:** 141, **187–188,** 331c
McCarthy, Eugene **IX:** 79, 97, 117, **188–189,** 268
McCarthy, Joseph **X:** 215
McCarthy, Joseph R. **VIII:** 182; **IX:** *18,* **189–190,** 330c, 331c
  Americans for Democratic Action **IX:** 14
  anticommunism **IX:** 15
  Army-McCarthy hearings **IX:** 17–19
  communism **IX:** 61
  Eisenhower, Dwight D. **IX:** 93
  Hoover, J. Edgar **IX:** 136
  journalism **IX:** 153
  Kennedy, Robert F. **IX:** 158
  Oppenheimer, J. Robert **IX:** 237
  television **IX:** 297
McCarthyism **IX:** 17, 19, 61, 68, 189, 190
McCartney, Paul **IX:** 36
McCauly, Mary Hays. *See* Molly Pitcher
McClean, John **V:** 101
McClellan, George Brinton **IV:** 138, 234, 310; **V: 224–226,** *225,* 406c; **VI:** 122
  Antietam, Battle of **V:** 11, 13
  Balloon Corps **V:** 21
  Bull Run, First Battle of **V:** 42
  Bull Run, Second Battle of **V:** 42–43
  Burnside, Ambrose E. **V:** 45
  cartography **V:** 51
  Cedar Mountain, Battle of **V:** 53
  Copperheads **V:** 82
  Democratic Party **V:** 94
  elections **V:** 110

espionage **V:** 118
foreign policy **V:** 132
Fredericksburg, Battle of **V:** 139
governors **V:** 152, 153
Hancock, Winfield Scott **V:** 163
homefront **V:** 169
Howard, O. O. **V:** 173
Irish-American regiments **V:** 181
Johnston, Joseph E. **V:** 190
Joint Committee on the Conduct of War **V:** 190, 191
Jomini, Antoine-Henri, baron de **V:** 192
Lee, Robert E. **V:** 206
Meade, George Gordon **V:** 226
medicine and hospitals **V:** 230
peace movements **V:** 266
Peninsular campaign **V:** 267, 269, 270
Rosecrans, William S. **V:** 305
Shenandoah Valley: Jackson's campaign **V:** 316, 317
Shenandoah Valley: Sheridan's campaign **V:** 317
Stanton, Edwin M. **V:** 334
Stuart, J. E. B. **V:** 341
tactics and strategy **V:** 347
Union army **V:** 367
United States Army Corps of Engineers **V:** 370, 371
Vallandigham, Clement L. **V:** 378
Washington, D.C. **V:** 390
West Point **V:** 373
Zouaves **V:** 403
McClellan Committee **IX:** 292–293, 332c
McClellan's Own Story **V:** 226
McClernand, John A. **V:** 388
McClintock, Mary Ann **IV:** 314; **V:** 397
McCloy, John J. **VIII:** 19–20, 340
McClure, Michael **IX:** 71
McClure's Magazine **VII:** 355c
  muckrakers **VII:** 192
  oil industry **VII:** 217
  Rockefeller, John D. **VII:** 265
  Standard Oil **VII:** 296
  Steffens, Lincoln **VII:** 299
  Tarbell, Ida **VII:** 305

McCone, John **IX:** 34
McConnell, Mitch **X:** 54, 236
McCord, James **X:** 316
McCormack, John D. **X:** 144
McCormick, Cyrus Hall **IV: 224–225,** *226,* 376c; **VI:** 196
  agriculture **IV:** 10
  economy **IV:** 118
  industrialization **IV:** 185
  science and technology **IV:** 307
McCormick, Katherine Dexter **IX:** 198–199, 242
McCormick Harvesting Machine Company **VI:** 127
McCormick Theological Seminary **IV:** 225
McCorvey, Norma **X:** 268
McCosh, James **VI:** 93
McCrummell, James C. **IV:** 13
McCulloch, Ben **V:** 265, 285
McCulloch, James **IV:** 44, 227
McCulloch v. Maryland **III:** 237, 338; **IV:** *226,* **227,** 375c
  banking and currency **IV:** 42
  Bank of the United States, Second **IV:** 44
  Supreme Court decision **IV:** 330
  Webster, Daniel **IV:** 359
McCullough, Henry **V:** 233
McCullough, Hugh **V:** 219
McCusker, John J. **II:** 221
McDaniel, David **IV:** 59
McDermott, John **VI:** 274
McDonald, John D. **V:** 393
McDonald, Maurice **IX:** 190, 191
McDonald, Richard **IX:** 190, 191
McDonald's **IX: 190–191,** 330c; **X:** 132
McDonnel Douglas. *See* Douglas Aircraft
McDougal, James **X:** 68
McDougall, Alexander **III:** 74, 154, **239–240**
McDougall, Duncan **IV:** 31, 33
McDowell, Ephraim **III:** 240; **IV:** *231*
McDowell, Irwin
  Balloon Corps **V:** 21
  Bull Run, First Battle of **V:** 42
  McClellan, George B. **V:** 224
  Peninsular campaign **V:** 267
  Shenandoah Valley: Jackson's campaign **V:** 316, 317
  tactics and strategy **V:** 347

McDuffie, George **IV:** 377c
McFarland, Ernest W. **IX:** 123
McFarland, James **III:** 375
McFarlane, Robert **X:** 23, 38
McFate, Yale **IX:** 206
McGillicuddy, Valentine T. **VI:** 240
McGillivray, Alexander **III:** 96, **240**
McGill University **VI:** 101, 289
McGovern, George Stanley **IX:** 117; **X: 184,** 324c
  Clinton, William **X:** 65
  Eagleton, Thomas F. **X:** 93
  Mitchell, George **X:** 194
  Mondale, Walter F. **X:** 196
  Nixon, Richard M. **X:** 220
  Shriver, Sargent **X:** 278
  Steinem, Gloria **X:** 288
McGready, James **IV:** 296
McGuffey, William Holmes **IV:** 120, 167, **227–228**
McGuire, Peter J. **VI:** 167; **VII:** 10
McGwire, Mark **X:** 284
McHenry, Donald **X:** 308
McHenry, James **III:** 116
McHenry, John **V:** 375
McIntire, Carl **IX:** 256
McIntire, Rufus **IV:** 25
McKay, Alexander **IV:** 32–33
McKay, Claude **VII:** 360c
McKay, James C. **X:** 191
McKean, Thomas **III:** 140
McKees Rocks strikes **VII:** 250
McKenney, Thomas L. **IV:** 180–181, 376c
McKenzie, Kenneth **IV:** 16, 17
McKiddy, Cecil **VIII:** 339
McKim, Charles Follen **VI:** 247, 313, 325c
McKim, Mead & White **VI:** 313, 314
McKim, Randolph **V:** 239–240
McKinley, William **IV:** 171, 219; **V:** 379, 392; **VI: 188–190,** *189,* 327c, 328c; **VII:** 355c
  Aguinaldo, Emilio **VII:** 8
  Big Stick diplomacy **VII:** 27
  bimetallism **VI:** 29
  Bryan, William Jennings **VI:** 37
  class consciousness **VI:** 57
  Congress **VI:** 63, 64
  Cuba **VI:** 71
  Currency Act **VII:** 60
  currency issue **VI:** 73
  de Lôme letter **VI:** 76, 77
  Democratic Party **VII:** 65
  elections **VII:** 80

McKinley, William (*continued*)
  foreign policy **VI:** 103, 104; **VII:** 98, 99
  Free-Silver movement **VI:** 105
  Hanna, Marcus Alonzo **VI:** 121
  Hawaii **VI:** 124
  Hay, John Milton **VI:** 125
  imperialism **VI:** 142–143
  Lease, Mary Elizabeth **VI:** 173
  movie industry **VII:** 190
  mugwumps **VI:** 199
  Open Door Policy **VII:** 218, 219
  Panama Canal **VII:** 222
  People's Party **VI:** 223
  Pinchot, Gifford **VII:** 228
  Powderly, Terence Vincent **VI:** 227
  the presidency **VI:** 230
  presidential campaigns **VI:** 231, 232
  Reed, Thomas Brackett **VI:** 240
  Remember the *Maine* **VI:** 187–188
  Republican Party **VI:** 246; **VII:** 262
  Roosevelt, Theodore **VII:** 266
  Schurz, Carl **VI:** 257
  Sherman, John **VI:** 261
  Spanish-American War **VI:** 272
  Taft, William Howard **VII:** 303
  tariff issue **VI:** 284, 285
  Watson, Tom **VII:** 332
McKinley Tariff of 1890 **VI:** 32, 326c; **VII:** 305
  business and government **VI:** 39
  Congress **VI:** 63
  Harrison, Benjamin **VI:** 123
  McKinley, William **VI:** 189
  the presidency **VI:** 230
  Reed, Thomas Brackett **VI:** 240
  tariff issue **VI:** 284
McKissick, Floyd **IX:** 68
McLane, Louis **IV:** 40
McLaughlin, Jim **VI:** 134
McLaughlin, John **X:** 43
McLaughlin, M. Louise **VI:** 3
McLaughlin, Patrick **IV:** 95
McLaughlin, Sarah **X:** 203
McLaurin, Charles **IX:** 207
McLaurin v. Oklahoma State Regents **IX:** 193

McLaws, Lafayette **V:** 13, 165, 215
McLean, Wilmer **V:** 14, 207
McLeod, Alexander **IV:** 74
McLoughlin, John **IV:** 145–146, **228–229**, 268, 322
McLuhan, Marshall **X:** 131
McNair, Lesley **VIII:** 20, 206
McNamara, Frank **IX:** 73, 330c
McNamara, Robert S. **IX:** 112, 308; **X:** 22–24, 233
McNary, Charles **VII:** 175; **VIII:** 98, 305, 306
McNary-Haugen Farm Bill **VII:** 7–8, 138, 163, **175**; **VIII:** 7
McNider, Hanford **VII:** 326
McNutt, Paul V. **VIII:** 374, 375
McParlan, James **VI:** 195
McPherson, Aimee Semple **VII:** **175–176**, *176*, 262
McRea, Jane **III:** **239**
McReynolds, James C. **VIII:** 76, 346t
McTeague (Norris) **VI:** 178
McVeigh, Timothy J. **X:** 329c
  militia movement **X:** 194
  Oklahoma City bombing **X:** 227–228
  terrorism **X:** 299
McVey, Sam **VII:** 138
MCWA (Office of Malaria Control in War Areas) **IX:** 198
MDAs (Model Demonstration Agencies) **IX:** 208
Mead, Margaret **VII:** **176–177**, 361c
  Boas, Franz **VII:** 33
  literature **VII:** 162
  race and racial conflict **VII:** 248
  women's status and rights **VII:** 340
Mead, William R. **VI:** 313, 325c
Meade, George Gordon **V:** **226–227**, 407c
  Fredericksburg, Battle of **V:** 141
  Gettysburg, Battle of **V:** 147, 148, 150
  Hancock, Winfield Scott **V:** 163
  Hooker, Joseph **V:** 171
  Joint Committee on the Conduct of War **V:** 191
  Longstreet, James **V:** 215
  Overland campaign **V:** 260
  Petersburg campaign **V:** 271
  Pickett, George Edward **V:** 274
  Sickles, Daniel E. **V:** 327

Meagher, Thomas Francis **IV:** 180; **V:** 181
Means, Gardiner C. **VIII:** 35
Meany, George **VIII:** 165; **IX:** 11, 12, 66, 259; **X:** 169
measles **II:** 92, 244; **IV:** 158; **V:** 230; **IX:** 199; **X:** 188
meat **VIII:** 38
Meat Inspection Act **VII:** **177–178**, 356c
  muckrakers **VII:** 192
  Pure Food and Drug Act **VII:** 244
  Republican Party **VII:** 263
  Roosevelt, Theodore **VII:** 266
  Sinclair, Upton **VII:** 286
  Steffens, Lincoln **VII:** 299
"Meat Out of the Eater" (Wigglesworth) **II:** 398
meatpacking industry **IV:** 10; **VI:** 46, 190m, **190–191**, 292; **VII:** 244, 286, 356c
meat rationing **VIII:** 254, 395
Mecca **I:** **230**
  Askia Muhammad I **I:** 14
  coffee **I:** 75
  Ibn Battuta **I:** 173
  Ibn Khaldûn **I:** 174
  Islam **I:** 183, 184
  Leo Africanus **I:** 203
  Mali **I:** 217
  Mansa Musa I **I:** 220
MECHA (Movimiento Estudiantil Chicano de Aztlan) **X:** 142
"mechanics" **II:** 74
Mechanics' Union of Trade Associations **IV:** 203, 204
Mechanicsville, Battle of **V:** 186, 226, 269
mechanization **V:** 6, 7; **VI:** 170; **IX:** 7
Medal of Honor **V:** **227–228**
  African-American regiments **V:** 5
  Andrews's Raid **V:** 11
  Carney, William H. **V:** 49
  Chamberlain, Joshua L. **V:** 54
  54th Massachusetts Regiment **V:** 125
  Howard, O. O. **V:** 173
  medicine and hospitals **V:** 231
  Walker, Mary Edwards **V:** 386
medeoulin **I:** 2
media. *See* news media
Median **I:** 184

Medicaid **VIII:** 330; **IX:** 127, 151, **196**, 198, 230, 250, 334c; **X:** 10, 175
medical dramas (TV) **X:** 295
Medical Inquiries and Observations upon the Diseases of the Mind (Rush) **III:** 312
medical schools **VI:** 326c; **VII:** 179, 180; **VIII:** 384, 386
  Blackwell, Elizabeth **VI:** 30, 31
  education, philanthropy and **VI:** 94
  medicine **VI:** 191
  women's rights **VI:** 318
Medicare **VIII:** 330; **IX:** 127, 151, **196–197**, 198, 230, 250, 334c
  abortion **X:** 4
  African Americans **X:** 10
  GRH Act of 1985 **X:** 134, 135
  liberalism **X:** 175
  medicine **X:** 189
  Perot, H. Ross **X:** 234
Medicare Catastrophic Coverage Act of 1988 **X:** 327c
Medici, Catherine de' **I:** 158–159, 169, 348, 361
Medici, Giovanni de'. *See* Leo X
Medici, Lorenzo de' **I:** 367
medicine and public health **II:** **220**; **III:** **240–242**; **IV:** 82, 111–113, 228, **229–231**, *231*, 308, 336, 378c; **V:** **228–232**, *229*, *231*; **VI:** 30–31, **191–192**; **VII:** **178–180**, *179*, **241–243**, 355c; **VIII:** 175, **207–209**, *209*; **IX:** **197–200**, 205–206, 222–223, **249–250**, 295, 331c; **X:** **187–191**, *189*. *See also* Public Health Service
  Abbott, Grace **VII:** 1
  African Americans **X:** 9–10
  agriculture **VIII:** 8–9
  AIDS **X:** 5
  alcohol **II:** 15
  Aleut **II:** 16
  ambergris **I:** 9
  Atomic Energy Commission **IX:** 23, 24
  Barton, Clara **V:** 24–26
  birth control **VII:** 29–30
  Bond, Thomas **II:** 33–34
  Boylston, Zabdiel **II:** 37
  cacao **I:** 46
  Clinton, Hillary Rodham **X:** 64
  Clinton, William **X:** 66
  coffee **I:** 75

Colden, Cadwallader **II:** 66
Cumming, Kate **V:** 85
Delany, Martin Robinson **V:** 93
disease **II:** 90
economy **X:** 94, 95
elderly **VIII:** 95
fertility **II:** 118
Freud, Sigmund **VII:** 101–102
Goldmark, Josephine **VII:** 111
hospitals **V: 228–232**
Kalm, Peter **II:** 181
Kennedy, Edward M. **X:** 164
Kennedy, Robert **IX:** 158
Lining, John **II:** 194
marriage and family life **II:** 207
Medicaid **IX:** 196
Medicare **IX:** 196–197
midwives **II:** 224–225
Monardes, Nicholas **I:** 238–239
mortality **II:** 235
Nader, Ralph **X:** 206
Narcotics Act **VII:** 197–198
Native Americans **II:** 244; **X:** 215
nurses **V:** 255–256
Occupational Safety and Health Act of 1970 **X:** 225
OSRD **VIII:** 256
Pember, Phoebe Yates Levy **V:** 266–267
Point Four Program **IX:** 243
population trends **VII:** 235
Pott, John **II:** 293
public health **IX:** 249–250. *See* public health
Rush, Benjamin **III:** 312
Sanger, Margaret **VII:** 273–274
science **II:** 331; **VII:** 276; **VIII:** 317–318
science and technology **V:** 310; **X:** 275
shamans **II:** 334–335
Sheppard-Towner Act **VII:** 283–284
Shippen, William, Jr. **II:** 335–336
slavery **II:** 342
social work **VII:** 291
space policy **X:** 281
technology **VIII:** 353; **IX:** 295

temperance **III:** 346
tobacco **I:** 353; **II:** 373
tobacco suits **X:** 303–305
USSC **V:** 374
Veterans Bureau **VII:** 326–327
Wald, Lillian **VII:** 329
Walker, Mary Edwards **V:** 386
War on Poverty **IX:** 313
Warren, Joseph **III:** 363
Webster, Noah **III:** 370
witchcraft **II:** 402
Women's Equity Action League **IX:** 323
women's status and rights **II:** 407; **VII:** 340
Medicine Lodge, Treaty of **VII:** 165–166
medicine societies **II:** 335
Medina **I:** 230
Medina, J. H. **IX:** 80
Meditations from the Pen of Mrs. Maria W. Stewart **IV:** 327
Meehan, Marty **X:** 53
Meek, Joe **IV:** 302
Meese, Edwin C., III **X: 191–192**
 Burger, Warren E. **X:** 44
 Haig, Alexander M., Jr. **X:** 139
 Reagan, Ronald W. **X:** 260
Meet Me in St. Louis (film) **VIII:** 218
Meet the Press **IX:** 50, 134, 296
megachurches **X:** 265
Mehrahi, Abdel Baset Ali Mohmed Al **X:** 331c
Meigs, Montgomery C. **V:** 217, 365
Melanchthon, Philipp **I:** 50, 212; **II:** 140
Melchers, Gari **VI:** 219
Mellen, James **IX:** 319
Mellon, Andrew William **VII: 180–181**
 Coolidge, Calvin **VII:** 57
 Fordney-McCumber Tariff **VII:** 97
 Soldiers' Bonus **VII:** 291
 tariffs **VII:** 306
Mellon National Bank **VII:** 180
melodrama **VI:** 286–287
Melville, Herman **IV:** 212, 213; **VI:** 178; **X:** 179
Member of the Third House (Garland) **VI:** 109
Memminger, Christopher **V:** 23, 75, 106
Memoirs (Grant) **V:** 154, 212
Memoirs (Sherman) **V:** 321

Memoirs of Service: Afloat during the War Between the States (Semmes) **V:** 313
Memoirs of the Campaign of the Northwestern Army of the United States: A.D. 1812 **IV:** 176
Memoirs v. Massachusetts (1966) **X:** 244
Memorial Day **V:** 370, 379; **VI:** 118
"Memorial Day Massacre." *See* Republic Steel Memorial Day Massacre
memorial sculptures **VI:** 259
Memphis, Tennessee **X:** 256
 Mississippi River **V:** 235
 prostitution **V:** 283
 Sherman, William T. **V:** 320
 Shiloh, Battle of **V:** 323
Memphis riot **V:** 188, **232**
Memphis Slim **VIII:** 223
Menard, Pierre **IV:** 238–239
Menard, Russell **II:** 221
Mencken, Henry Louis **VII:** 118, 161, **181**, 278; **VIII:** 72, 190
Mendelssohn Glee Club **VI:** 183
Mendex v. Westminster School District **IX:** 173
"Mendians" **IV:** 20
Mendonca, João Furtado de **I:** 27
Mendoza, Antonio de **I: 231**
 Alvarado, Pedro de **I:** 7–8
 Coronado, Francisco **I:** 88
 New Mexico **I:** 256
 New Spain **I:** 259
 Peru **I:** 280
 Zumárraga, Juan de **I:** 382
Mendoza, Luis de **I:** 215
Mendoza, Pedro de **I:** 167–168
Menéndez de Avilés, Pedro **I:** 49, 130, 201, 202; **II:** 120, 327
Menilek **I:** 123
meningitis **IV:** 112
Menlo Park research facility **VII:** 107
Mennonites **II:** 139, 147
Menominee nation **II:** 199; **IX:** 228
Menominee Termination Bill **IX:** 298
men's roles and status
 Abenaki **I:** 2
 Aztecs **I:** 20
 Bahía **I:** 24
 Huron **I:** 171–172
 Ibn Battuta **I:** 173

 Iroquois **I:** 181
 Massachusett **I:** 225
 Montagnais-Naskapi **I:** 241
 Natchez **I:** 251
 repartimiento **I:** 310
 Yoruba **I:** 377
Mental Health Institute **IX:** 197
mental health/mental health reform **III:** 241; **IV:** 113–114, 219, 378c; **IX:** 199, 222; **X:** 189–190
Men without Women (Davis) **VIII:** 25
Mercado Comun del Sur (MERCOSUR) **X:** 174
mercantile colony **II:** 256
mercantilism **II:** 221
 Acts of Trade and Navigation **II:** 2–3
 British Empire **II:** 41
 economy **II:** 101
 French colonies **II:** 129
 Iron Acts **II:** 167
 manufacturing and industry **II:** 204
 Massachusetts **II:** 214
 technology **II:** 369
 wage and price controls **II:** 389
Mercator, Gerhardus **I: 231–233**, 232, 371
Mercator, Rumold **I:** 232
mercenaries **III:** 166–167
Mercer, George **III:** 265
Mercer, Jesse **V:** 299
Mercer, Lucy **VIII:** 310, 312
merchant marine **VI:** 40, **192–193**, 290; **VII:** 314–315
Merchant Marine Act of 1891 **VI:** 40, 193
merchants **II: 221–222**
 Acts of Trade and Navigation **II:** 3
 Alexander, Mary Spratt Provoost **II:** 16–17
 art **II:** 25
 banking and credit **II:** 28
 Boston **II:** 35
 class **II:** 63
 clothing **II:** 65
 Connecticut **II:** 69
 economy **II:** 102
 French colonies **II:** 126
 Georgia **II:** 138
 government, British American **II:** 145
 Guadalajara **II:** 151
 Harris, Benjamin **II:** 154
 Herrman, Augustine **II:** 156
 Hutchinson, Anne Marbury **II:** 161

merchants (*continued*)
  indentured servitude **II:** 165
  Jamestown **II:** 171, 172
  Jews **II:** 175
  Keith, William **II:** 181
  King George's War **II:** 182
  land **II:** 191
  Leisler's Rebellion **II:** 192
  Livingston, Philip **II:** 195–196
  lumbering **II:** 201
  Maryland **II:** 211
  Massachusetts **II:** 214, 215
  New Hampshire **II:** 250
  New Netherland **II:** 255
  Newport **II:** 258
  New York **II:** 259, 262
  New York City **II:** 263
  Philadelphia **II:** 282
  postal service **II:** 292
  privateering **II:** 299
  Rhode Island **II:** 321
  Royal African Company **II:** 325
  Seven Years' War **II:** 333, 334
  shipbuilding **II:** 335
  slave trade **II:** 343
  smuggling **II:** 348–349
  South Carolina **II:** 353
  Spanish colonies **II:** 357
  spinsters **II:** 360
  tobacco **II:** 375
  trade and shipping **II:** 375–377
  Virginia Company of London **II:** 387
merchant ships **II:** 300
mercury **I:** 10; **IV:** 163; **V:** 229
Mercury space program **IX:** 269
Mercury Theater **VIII:** 376, 377
Mercury Theater of the Air **VIII:** 376–377
Meredith, Don **X:** 241
Meredith, James **IX:** 47, **200,** 285, 333*c*, 334*c*
mergers **VI:** 295, 328*c*; **VII:** xiii, 74–75, 216; **X:** 49, 178
Mérida **I:** 379
Merit Network, Inc. **X:** 153
Merrell, Helen **VII:** 185
Merrell, Robert **VII:** 185
Merrill, William E. **V:** 51
Merrimack, CSS **V:** 183, 237, 267
Merritt, Ezekiel **IV:** 45
Merryman, John **V:** 161
Merry Widow (Lehar) **VII:** 194
Mesabi range **IV:** 361
Mesa Verde **I:** 255; **II:** 303
Mescalero Apache **V:** 406*c*

mescaline **X:** 206
mesmerism **IV:** 230
Mesoamerica **I:** 235. *See also specific countries*
Messenger (magazine) **VIII:** 291
mestizaje **I:** 61, **233,** 261, 381–382
mestizos **I:** 61, 62, 233, **233–234,** 261, 320; **II:** 113, 228, 255
Metacom **II:** *222,* **222–223**
  King Philip's War **II:** 183–184
  Massachusetts **II:** 214
  Massasoit **II:** 217
  Plymouth **II:** 287
  Rowlandson, Mary White **II:** 324
  Wetamo **II:** 395
Metacom's War (1675) **II:** 395
Metalious, Grace **IX:** 183
metallurgy **IV:** 90
Metcalfe, Ralph **VIII:** 338
meteorology **VI:** 310
Methodist Church/Methodism **II:** 148, 239, 314, 385, 394; **III:** **242–243;** **V:** 5, 299–300; **VI:** 6; **VII:** 261; **VIII:** 303; **X:** 11, 107, 265
  Allen, Richard **III:** 10–11
  antislavery and abolition **III:** 15
  Asbury, Francis **III:** 26–27
  Dix, Dorothea **IV:** 113
  Dow, Lorenzo **IV:** 115
  education **III:** 115
  Jones, Absalom **III:** 189
  literature **IV:** 211
  Loyalists **III:** 221
  McLoughlin, John **IV:** 229
  religion **III:** 299; **IV:** 296–298
  Second Great Awakening **IV:** 311*t*
Methodist Episcopal churches **VI:** 4, 260
métis **II:** 113, 130–131, **223,** 233
Metro Broadcasting v. Federal Communications Commission (1990) **X:** 9
Metro-Goldwyn-Mayer **VII:** 191
Metropolitan Magazine **VII:** 259
Metropolitan Museum of Art **V:** 16
Metropolitan Opera **VI:** 128; **VIII:** 223; **IX:** 217
Meucci, Antonio **VI:** 149
Mexica. *See* Aztecs

Mexican-American civil rights movement **X:** 141
Mexican Americans **IV:** 163, 248–249; **V:** 7, 279; **VIII:** **210,** 405*c,* 410*c;* **IX:** 334*c;* **X:** 141–143, 177, 200. *See also* Latino movement
  Bent's Fort **IV:** 50
  Catholics **VIII:** 54
  children **VIII:** 57
  cities and urban life **VIII:** 59, 60; **IX:** 52
  civil rights **VIII:** 61, 62
  Figueroa, José **IV:** 136
  FMP **VIII:** 119
  gold, discovery and mining **IV:** 163
  Great Depression **VIII:** 140
  immigration **IV:** 177; **VIII:** 162
  Latino movement **IX:** 173
  Mexican Repatriation Program **VIII:** 211
  migration **VIII:** 213
  race and racial conflict **VIII:** 288, 289
  religion **IV:** 298
  Tijerina, Reies López **IX:** 298–299
  unemployment **VIII:** 363
  United Farm Workers **IX:** 304
  women's status and rights **IX:** 326
  World War II **VIII:** 389
  World War II home front **VIII:** 395
  Young Chicanos for Community Action **IX:** 327–328
  zoot-suiters **VIII:** 403–404
Mexican-American War (1846) **I:** 49; **IV:** **231–234,** 233*m,* 378*c;* **VII:** 353
  abolition **V:** 3
  Adams, John Quincy **IV:** 5
  Anderson, Robert **V:** 9
  Armistead, Lewis A. **V:** 15
  Beauregard, Pierre **V:** 27
  Beckwourth, Jim **IV:** 47
  Bent, Charles **IV:** 47
  Bent, William **IV:** 48
  Bent's Fort **IV:** 51
  Bidwell, John **IV:** 51
  Blair, Francis P., Jr. **V:** 30
  Bragg, Braxton **V:** 36
  Burnside, Ambrose E. **V:** 44
  Calhoun, John C. **IV:** 63
  California **IV:** 65
  California Trail **IV:** 71

  Cass, Lewis **IV:** 77
  Clay, Henry **IV:** 87
  Clayton-Bulwer Treaty **IV:** 88
  Colt, Samuel **IV:** 91
  Colt revolver **IV:** 92
  Compromise of 1850 **IV:** 93
  conscription **V:** 78
  Cooke, Jay **V:** 81
  Davis, Jefferson **V:** 88–89
  Democratic Party **IV:** 108; **V:** 94
  Deseret, State of **IV:** 109
  diseases and epidemics **IV:** 112
  Ewell, Richard Stoddert **V:** 118
  exploration **IV:** 132
  Farragut, David G. **V:** 121
  Fillmore, Millard **IV:** 137
  foreign policy **IV:** 142
  Fort Leavenworth **IV:** 145
  Frémont, John C. **IV:** 153
  Gadsden Purchase **IV:** 159
  Grant, Ulysses S. **V:** 154
  Guadalupe Hidalgo, Treaty of (1848) **IV:** 165–166
  Halleck, Henry W. **V:** 162
  Hancock, Winfield Scott **V:** 163
  Hill, Ambrose P. **V:** 167
  Hooker, Joseph **V:** 171
  immigration **IV:** 177
  Jackson, "Stonewall" **V:** 185
  Johnston, Albert Sidney **V:** 189
  Johnston, Joseph E. **V:** 190
  journalism **IV:** 196; **V:** 192
  Kearny, Stephen Watts **IV:** 200
  Know-Nothing Party **IV:** 201
  Larkin, Thomas Oliver **IV:** 208
  Lee, Robert E. **V:** 205
  Lincoln, Abraham **V:** 210
  Longstreet, James **V:** 214
  Manifest Destiny **IV:** 217, 218
  McClellan, George B. **V:** 224
  Meade, George Gordon **V:** 226
  Monroe Doctrine **IV:** 242
  Morgan, John Hunt **V:** 240
  Mormon Trail **IV:** 243
  Oregon Treaty of 1846 **IV:** 269
  Ostend Manifesto **V:** 260

Perry, Matthew Calbraith **IV:** 279

Pickett, George Edward **V:** 274

Pierce, Franklin **V:** 275

Polk, James K. **IV:** 284

popular sovereignty **IV:** 285

race and race relations **IV:** 291

Rosecrans, William S. **V:** 305

Santa Anna, Antonio López de **IV:** 304

Santa Fe Trail **IV:** 306

Scott, Winfield **IV:** 309, 310

Semmes, Raphael **V:** 313

Stanton, Edwin M. **V:** 333

states' rights **V:** 335

Stearns, Abel **IV:** 326

Stockton, Robert Field **IV:** 328

Sumner, Charles **V:** 342

Sutter, John **IV:** 332

tactics and strategy **V:** 345

Texas **IV:** 339

Thomas, George H. **V:** 353

Vallandigham, Clement L. **V:** 377

Webster, Daniel **IV:** 360

Welles, Gideon **V:** 391

West Point **V:** 372

Whig Party **IV:** 364

Wilmot Proviso **V:** 395

Mexican American Youth Organization (MAYO) **IX:** 171, 174

Mexican Cession **IV:** 218*m*

Mexican Constitution of 1824 **IV:** 174

Mexican immigration **VII:** 127, **182–183,** 235

Mexican invasion **VII: 183,** 358*c;* **VIII:** 173. *See also* Villa, Francisco "Pancho"

American Expeditionary Force **VII:** 9

Big Stick diplomacy **VII:** 28–29

foreign policy **VII:** 99

Mitchell, Billy **VII:** 187

Pershing, John **VII:** 227

Wilson, Woodrow **VII:** 334

Zimmermann telegram **VII:** 353

Mexican Labor Program **IX:** 41–42, 330*c*

Mexican Repatriation Program **VIII:** 60, 162, 210, **211,** 405*c*

Mexican Revolution **IV:** 338, 339; **VII:** 182, 183, **183–185,**

184, 259, 357*c,* 358*c. See also* Villa, Francisco "Pancho"

Mexico **I:** 94*m,* **234–235,** 385*c,* 387*c;* **III:** 57, 258; **IV:** xiii, 378*c;* **V:** 126–127, 132, 315; **VII:** 100, 127*t,* 353, 357*c,* 358*c;* **VIII:** 133, 162, 405*c,* 409*c;* **IX:** 41, 142, 298–299; **X:** 328*c*

Aguilar, Francisco de **I:** 4

Aguilar, Gerónimo (Jerónimo) de **I:** 5

Alamo, The **IV:** 12–13

Alvarado, Pedro de **I:** 8

Apache War **VI:** 14

art and architecture **I:** 13

Austin, Stephen F. **IV:** 36, 37

Aztecs **I:** 17–22

Aztlán **I:** 22

Balboa, Vasco Núñez de **I:** 24

Bear Flag Revolt **IV:** 45

Becknell, William **IV:** 45, 46

Beckwourth, Jim **IV:** 47

Bent, Charles **IV:** 48

Bent's Fort **IV:** 51

Bowie, Jim **IV:** 57

Cabeza de Vaca, Álvar Núñez **I:** 37

cabildo **I:** 39

California **I:** 48–49; **IV:** 64

California missions **IV:** 70

Carson, Kit **IV:** 75

Charles V **I:** 69

Chimalpahin, Domingo Francisco de San Antón Muñón **I:** 71

Cholula **I:** 72

coffee **I:** 76

Córdoba, Francisco Hernández de **I:** 86–87

Coronado, Francisco **I:** 88, 90

Cortés, Hernán **I:** 91–95, 94*m*

Cuba **IV:** 101

Díaz de Castillo, Bernal **I:** 106

economy **IV:** 117; **X:** 95

election of 1840 **IV:** 124

encomienda **I:** 122

Escalante, Juan de **I:** 123

Figueroa, José **IV:** 136

foreign policy **IV:** 142; **VI:** 103; **X:** 124

Forty-niners **IV:** 147

Free-Soil Party **IV:** 150

Frémont, John C. **IV:** 153

fur trade **II:** 133

Gadsden Purchase **IV:** 159–160, 160*m*

Geronimo **VI:** 112, 113

Grijalva, Juan de **I:** 145–146

Hispanic Americans **X:** 141

Houston, Sam **IV:** 174, 175

Huitzilopochtli **I:** 170

immigration **IV:** 177

imperialism **VI:** 142

investments, American, abroad **VI:** 150

IRCA **X:** 149

Itzcóatl **I:** 185

labor **X:** 171

Lamy, Jean Baptiste **IV:** 207

Latin America **X:** 173, 174

Manifest Destiny **IV:** 217–219

Maya **I:** 225–229

Mendoza, Antonio de **I:** 231

Mexican-American War **IV:** 231–234, 233*m*

Monroe Doctrine **IV:** 241

Monte Albán **I:** 241–242

NAFTA **X:** 222–223

Nahua **I:** 249

Nahuatl **I:** 250

Native Americans **II:** 244, 246

New Spain **I:** 258

Olmecs **I:** 269–270

Oregon Treaty of 1846 **IV:** 269

Palenque **I:** 275

Polk, James K. **IV:** 284

printing press **I:** 294

Purchas, Samuel **I:** 297

Ramusio, Giovanni Battista **I:** 305

Sahagún, Bernardino de **I:** 315

Sandoval, Gonzalo de **I:** 317–318

Santa Anna, Antonio López de **IV:** 303–304

Santa Fe Trail **IV:** 305, 306

Serra, Junípero **II:** 331

silver **I:** 325

smallpox **II:** 345

Spanish colonies **II:** 355, 357–359

Stearns, Abel **IV:** 326

Stockton, Robert Field **IV:** 328

Sutter, John **IV:** 332

Tabasco **I:** 341

Tacuba **I:** 342

Tarascan **I:** 343

Taylor, Zachary **IV:** 334

Tenochtitlán **I:** 344–346

Teotihuacán **I:** 346

Texas **IV:** 337–339

Texas Revolution **IV:** 339–341

Tlaxcala **I:** 352–353

Toltecs **I:** 353–358

Travis, William Barret **IV:** 345–346

Tyler, John **IV:** 349

U.S. relations with **X:** *192,* **192–193**

Veracruz **I:** 366

Yucatán Peninsula **I:** 378–379

Zacatecas **I:** 381

Zuni **I:** 383

Mexico City **I:** 258, 259, 382; **II:** 254, 356; **IV:** 234

Mexico City Policy **X:** 3, 4

Meyer, Frank **IX:** 68

Meyer, Grant E. **IX:** 270

Meyer, Russ **IX:** 214

mezzotints **II:** 24, 272–273

MFDP. *See* Mississippi Freedom Democratic Party

Mfume, Kweisi **X:** 209

MI **VIII:** 164

MIA (Montgomery Improvement Association) **IX:** 240

Miami, Florida **X:** 255, 266–267

Miami & Erie Canal **IV:** 73*m*

Miami Indians/Miami nation **II:** 174, 190–191; **III:** 395*c*

Cherokee nation **III:** 66

Dragging Canoe **III:** 107

Greenville, Treaty of **III:** 156–157

Red Jacket **III:** 297

Miantonomo **II: 223–224,** 241, 400

Michael (ship) **I:** 41, 42

Michaelius, Jonas **II:** 97

Michaux Club of Manhattan **VI:** 28

Michelangelo **I:** 13, 204, **235–236**

Michelson, Albert **VII:** 276

Michener, James **X:** 178

Michigan **II:** 206

abortion **X:** 2

amendments to the Constitution **X:** 20

Ford, Gerald R. **X:** 119

militia movement **X:** 194

population trends **X:** 242

rust belt **X:** 269

Michigan Militia Corps **X:** 194

Michigan Territory

Cass, Lewis **IV:** 76

Hull, William **IV:** 175

Michigan Territory (*continued*)
   migration **IV:** 235
   Native Americans in the
      War of 1812 **IV:** 259
   Strang, James Jesse **IV:**
      329
      Thames, Battle of the **IV:**
      342
Michilimackinac **II:** 129, 133,
   178
Michilimackinac Company **IV:**
   16
Mickey Mouse **VIII:** 274
Mickey Mouse Club, The **IX:**
   244
Micmac **I:** 2, 57, 219, 252; **II:**
   243
"Micmac Indian Responds to
   the French, A" (LeCler) **II:**
   422–423
Micmac language **I:** 6
microchips **X:** 72, 73
microcomputers **IX:** 65
Micro Instrumentation
   Telemetry Systems **X:** 72
microprocessing technologies
   computers **X:** 72
   medicine **X:** 190
   science and technology **X:**
      273, 275
microscopes **V:** 231
Microsoft Corporation **X:** 330*c*,
   331*c*
   business **X:** 51
   computers **X:** 72, 73
   economy **X:** 95
   globalization **X:** 131, 132
   television **X:** 296
Microsoft National Broadcasting
   Corporation (MSNBC) **X:**
   241, 296
Microsoft Windows **X:** 273, 330*c*
microwave ovens **IX:** 270, 331*c*;
   X: 273
microwave radiation **X:** 273
Mictlan **I:** 21
Mid-Atlantic states **IV:** 188
Middle Atlantic states **VI:** 53,
   222
Middlebury Female Academy
   IV: 365
middle class **VI:** 2; **VII:** 171,
   230
   advertising **IX:** 2
   baby boom **IX:** 29
   credit cards **IX:** 73
   Federal Housing
      Administration **IX:** 110
   Friedan, Betty **IX:**
      114–116
   marriage and family life
      IX: 192

Mills, C. Wright **IX:** 204
   religion **IX:** 257
Middle Colonies
   African Americans **II:** 6
   banking and credit **II:** 29
   Baptists **II:** 29
   childhood **II:** 60
   disease **II:** 90
   economy **II:** 101
   English immigrants **II:** 108
   Iroquois **II:** 168–170
   labor **II:** 187, 189
   Logan, James **II:** 198
   Lutherans **II:** 201
   marriage and family life **II:**
      206, 208
   mills **II:** 225, 226
   mortality **II:** 235
   New Jersey **II:** 252–254
   population trends **II:** 291
   primogeniture and entail
      II: 297
   religion, Euro-American
      II: 316
   society, British American
      II: 350
   technology **II:** 369
   tenants **II:** 371
   Tennent, William, Sr. **II:**
      372
   trade and shipping **II:** 375
   travel **II:** 377
   Westo **II:** 394–395
Middle East **VIII:** 379, 403; **IX:**
   332*c*. *See also specific
   countries*
   Camp David accords **X:**
      54–55
   Clinton, William **X:** 69
   coffee **I:** 75
   cold war (end of) **X:** 70
   Dulles, John Foster **IX:**
      83
   energy crisis **X:** 103–104
   foreign policy **X:** 122
   and foreign policy **IX:**
      200–201
   Habib, Philip C. **X:** 139
   Ibn Battuta **I:** 173
   invention and technology
      I: 180
   Israel **IX:** 146–147
   Jews (Judaism) **I:** 190
   labor **X:** 170
   NATO **X:** 224
   OPEC **X:** 228–229
   Powell, Colin L. **X:** 247
   Prester John **I:** 292, 293
   Reagan, Ronald W. **X:** 260
   Suez Crisis **IX:** 288–289
   terrorism **X:** 298, 298*m*
   United Nations **X:** 307

middlemen **IV:** 299–300
middle passage **I: 236,** 328; **III:**
   118
   African Americans **II:** 5, 6
   Caribbean **II:** 53
   Johnson, Mary **II:** 175
   mariners **II:** 204
   population trends **II:** 291
   slave resistance **II:** 336
   slave trade **II:** 344
Middlesex Canal **IV:** 72
Middle Temple (London) **I:** 151
Middleton, Arthur **II: 224**
Middleton, Christopher **I:** 266
*Middletown: A Study in
   Modern American Culture*
   (Merrell) **VII:** 171, **185–186**
Middletown in Transition
   (Merrell) **VII:** 186
"midnight judges" **III:** 3, 230,
   236, 397*c*
Midvale Steel **VII:** 297
Midway **V:** 315
Midway, Battle of **VIII:**
   211–212, 409*c*
   code breaking **VIII:** 64
   Coral Sea, Battle of the
      VIII: 74
   Nimitz, Chester W. **VIII:**
      246
   World War II Pacific
      theater **VIII:** 399
midwestern United States **V:** 6,
   176, 278; **IX:** 51
   African-American
      churches, growth of **VI:**
      5
   African Americans **X:** 9
   America First Committee
      VIII: 12, 13
   American Protective
      Association **VI:** 11
   Asian Americans **X:** 29
   cities and urban life **VI:**
      53, 54
   Deere, John **IV:** 105–106
   Dust Bowl **VIII:** 85–87
   education **IV:** 120
   Hispanic Americans **X:**
      143
   immigration **IV:** 178–179
   industrialization **IV:** 187
   isolationists **VIII:** 166
   McCormick, Cyrus Hall
      IV: 225
   Mississippian culture **I:**
      236–237
   mound builders **I:** 244–245
   Patrons of Husbandry **VI:**
      221
   People's Party **VI:** 222
   population trends **X:** 242

property rights **X:** 250
   religion **VIII:** 304
   rust belt **X:** 269
   settlement houses **VI:** 259
   Sunbelt **X:** 290
   World War II **VIII:** 390
midwives **II: 224–225; IV:** 230
   alcohol **II:** 15
   fertility **II:** 118
   marriage and family life **II:**
      208
   medicine **II:** 220
   Shippen, William, Jr. **II:**
      335
   women's status and rights
      II: 409
Mies van der Rohe, Ludwig **IX:**
   19
Mifflin, Thomas **III:** 141
migrant workers **IX:** 173, 174,
   304–305; **X:** 16, 192
migration **IV: 235–236,** 236*m;*
   V: 327; **VI:** 325*c;* **VII:** 48,
   262, 349–350; **VIII:**
   212–213, 408*c;* **IX:**
   201–203, 250, 287–288; **X:**
   9, 290. *See also* Great
   Migration
   African Americans **VI:** 6;
      VIII: 4
   agriculture **VIII:** 7, 8
   Bantu **I:** 24, 25
   Barbados **I:** 26
   cities and urban life **VIII:**
      58–60
   class consciousness **VI:** 57
   consumption **II:** 71
   Cornstalk **II:** 72
   Delaware **II:** 87, 89
   Dust Bowl **VIII:** 87
   ethnocentrism **II:** 112
   FEPC **VIII:** 109
   gays and lesbians **VIII:**
      129, 130
   Great Depression **VIII:**
      140
   housing **VIII:** 158
   labor trends **VI:** 171
   literature **VIII:** 192
   marriage and family life
      VIII: 205
   Mexican Americans **VIII:**
      210
   migration **VIII:** 212
   mobilization **VIII:** 214
   music **VIII:** 223
   North Carolina **II:** 265
   population trends **II:** 290;
      VI: 226; **VIII:** 277
   Puritans **I:** 299
   religion, Euro-American
      II: 317

society, British American **II:** 349, 350
South **VIII:** 332
Spanish colonies **II:** 356
Sunbelt **VIII:** 343–344
transportation **VIII:** 360–361
World War II **VIII:** 390
World War II home front **VIII:** 394
zoot-suiters **VIII:** 404
Migration of the Negro (Lawrence) **VIII:** 24
Mikan, George **VIII:** 336
Milan **I:** 204
Milan Decree **III:** 267
Milborne, Jacob **II:** 141
Miles, Manly **VI:** 8
Miles, Nelson A. **VI:** 213, 263
military. *See* armed forces
military academies **IV:** 145. *See also* United States Military Academy at West Point; United States Naval Academy at Annapolis
military aid
    antiwar movement—Vietnam **X:** 24
    Boland Amendment **X:** 38
    contras **X:** 80–81
military bands **V:** 243–244; **VIII:** 120
military contracts **VIII:** 123
military government **V:** 294
military governors **I:** 3–4
military history **V:** 7–8
military-industrial complex **IX:** **203–204.** *See also* defense budget
    arms race **IX:** 16
    aviation **IX:** 28
    business **IX:** 44, 45
    computers **IX:** 63
    dollar-a-year men **VIII:** 84
    DuPont Corporation **IX:** 83–84
    economy **VIII:** 92; **IX:** 90
    General Electric Company **IX:** 120
    General Motors **IX:** 120–121
    government **VIII:** 135
    Korean War **IX:** 165
    mobilization **VIII:** 215
    Nye Committee **VIII:** 250
military-industrial-university complex **VIII:** 47
Military Memoirs of a Confederate (Alexander) **V:** 7
Military Order of the Loyal Legion of the United States (MOLLUS) **V:** 378

military pensions **IV:** 187
military reform **V:** 191
military supplies
    impressment **V:** 179–180
    ladies aid societies **V:** 203
    science and technology **V:** 310
    Tredegar Iron Works **V:** 356
    Union army **V:** 365
    war contracting **V:** 387
    Washington, D.C. **V:** 390
military training **IV:** 309
Militia Act of 1757 **II:** 324
Militia Act of 1862 **V:** 79, 112–114
militia ground **V:** 38
Militia of Montana **X:** 194
militias/militia movement **IV:** 224, 340; **X:** **193–194**
    citizen-soldier **V:** 62
    Confederate army **V:** 72
    governors **V:** 152
    Morgan, John Hunt **V:** 240
    Oklahoma City bombing **X:** 228
    race and racial conflict **X:** 257
    terrorism **X:** 299
    Washington, D.C. **V:** 389
milk, condensed **IV:** 308
Milken, Michael **X:** 49, 50
Mill, John Stuart **VII:** 131
millennialism **II:** 307; **VI:** 242; **X:** 107
millennium **I:** 81
Miller, Arthur **IX:** 181, *181,* 210, 243, 330c
Miller, Elizabeth Smith **IV:** 54
Miller, Francis Trevelyan **V:** 274
Miller, Glenn **VIII:** 223, 224
Miller, Henry **VIII:** 55
Miller, Joaquin **VI:** 178
Miller, John **VI:** 50
Miller, Lewis **VI:** 49
Miller, Nathan **VIII:** 15
Miller, Phineas **III:** 376
Miller, William **IV:** 299; **VI:** 4, 242
Millerites **IV:** 299
Miller-Tydings Act **VIII:** 18
Miller v. California (1973) **X:** 244
Millet, Francis Davis **VI:** 219
Millet, Jean-François **IV:** 55
Millet, Kate **X:** 320, 323c
Milliken's Bend, Battle of **V:** 5, **232–233**
milling **II:** 203, 210, 215
millionaires **IV:** 187
Million Man March **X:** 111, 213, 329c

mills **II:** **225–226,** *226;* **IV:** 223
    Heathcote, Caleb **II:** 155
    Iron Acts **II:** 167
    Livingston, Philip **II:** 196
    Livingston, Robert R. **II:** 197
    lumbering **II:** 201
    manufacturing and industry **II:** 203
    technology **II:** 369
    tenants **II:** 370
Mills, C. Wright **IX:** 46, **204–205,** 231, 332c
Mills, Marcus **VI:** 100
Mills, Wilbur **IX:** 197
Mills Bill (1888) **VI:** 64
millstones **II:** 225
MILNET **X:** 153
Milosevic, Slobodan **X:** 330c
    Clinton, William **X:** 69
    Dayton accords **X:** 85
    defense policy **X:** 88
    Jackson, Jesse L. **X:** 160
    Kosovo **X:** 166, 167
Milton, Tommy **IX:** 82
Milwaukee **VI:** 53
Milwaukee Braves **X:** 1
Milwaukee Brewers **X:** 1
Mimbres ware **I:** 255
Mind of Primitive Man (Boas) **VII:** 33, 357c
minefields **V:** 221
Mine Owners Protective Association **VI:** 61
mineralogy **II:** 330
mineral resources **IX:** 287
Minersville School District v. Goitis **VIII:** 408c
Ming dynasty **I:** 66, 311–312, 325
miniature golf **VIII:** 297
minicomputers **IX:** 65
Miniconjou Sioux **VI:** 207
Minié, Claude **V:** 308
Minié ball **V:** 308
Minikus, Lee **IX:** 317
minimalism (art) **X:** 26
minimalist school (literature) **X:** 177
Minimal sculpture **IX:** 20
minimum wage **VII:** 3, 87, 360c; **VIII:** 408c; **IX:** 9, 334c; **X:** 68, 176
    Fair Labor Standards Act **VIII:** 110
    Supreme Court **VIII:** 345
    Wallace, Henry A. **VIII:** 373
    women's status and rights **VIII:** 384
mining **IV:** 66, 67, 162, 163, 208; **VI:** **193–194,** 194m;

VII: 356c; **VIII:** 234. *See also* coal/coal industry; gold; lead mines; silver and silver mining
    Anthracite Coal Strike **VII:** 12–13
    California **I:** 49
    Casa de Contratación **I:** 59
    economy **VII:** 75
    industrial revolution, second **VI:** 145
    inventions and technology **VI:** 149
    labor, child **VI:** 165
    labor: strikes and violence **VI:** 168
    labor trends **VI:** 171
    Ludlow Massacre **VII:** 167
    Native Americans **VII:** 206
    New Mexico **I:** 256
    New Spain **I:** 261
    Peru **I:** 280
    slavery **I:** 327
    trusts **VI:** 292
    Zacatecas **I:** 381
Mining Law of 1872 **IV:** 163
miniseries (TV) **X:** 241
ministers **III:** 114, 249
Minister's Wooing (Stowe) **V:** 339
Minkins, Shadrach **IV:** 103, 155
Minnesota **II:** 130–131, 405; **V:** 406c; **VI:** 193, 221
    Akron v. Akron Center for Reproductive Health **X:** 17
    Mondale, Walter F. **X:** 196
    population trends **X:** 242
    tobacco suits **X:** 304
Minnesota, USS **V:** 184, 238
Minnesota Territory **IV:** 236, 379c
Minor, D. Kimball **IV:** 40
Minorca **II:** 43
minorities **X:** 323c, 329c. *See also specific groups*
    advertising **X:** 8
    affirmative action **X:** 8–9
    art and architecture **X:** 26
    Bakke **X:** 34–35
    Clinton, William **X:** 66
    education, higher **X:** 97
    liberalism **X:** 175
    Libertarian Party **X:** 176
    multiculturalism **X:** 200, 201
    television **X:** 297
Minor v. Happersett **VI:** 13, 317, 324c
Minquan Kil **II:** 87
minstrel shows **IV:** 250, 376c; **V:** 138

minstrelsy **VI**: 95–96, 286
Minton, Sherman **IX**: 315
Minuit, Peter **II**: **226–227**, 227, 417*c*
    New Amsterdam **II**: 249, 250
    New Netherland **II**: 255–256
    New York City **II**: 262
    Swedish colonies **II**: 364
minutemen **III**: 77, 146, 211, 212, **243**
Minutemen **X**: 193
Miquelon **II**: 378
Míquic **I**: 72
miracle drugs **IX**: **205–206**, 245, 295
Miranda, Ernesto **IX**: 206
Miranda v. Arizona (1966) **IX**: 104, 194, **206**, 316, 335*c*; **X**: 264, 319
Mirandola, Pico della **I**: 191
Mirror of Liberty, The (magazine) **IV**: 377*c*
MIRVs (multiple independently targeted reentry vehicles) **X**: 85–86
miscegenation **II**: 74, **228–229**, 237–238, 262, 336; **IV**: 289–290; **V**: **233–234**
Mischif (language) **II**: 223
"misery index" **X**: 94, 95
Miss America Pageant **IX**: 325
missile defense system **X**: 71
missile gap **IX**: 60, 95; **X**: 22
Missionary Ridge, Battle of **V**: 36, 258, 318
Mission Indians **VI**: 153
missions and missionaries **II**: **229–231**, 230*m*; **III**: 164; **VI**: 4–5, 124, 196; **IX**: 200–201. *See also* Dominicans; Franciscans; Jesuits; *specific missions, e.g.:* Spanish missions
    Acosta, José de **I**: 3
    Africa **II**: 4
    Alaska, Russia in **II**: 14
    Anglican Church **II**: 20
    Apalachee **I**: 11
    art **II**: 25
    Baptists **II**: 29
    Brainerd, David **II**: 39–40
    British Empire **II**: 43
    California **I**: 48, 49
    California Indians **II**: 49
    California missions **IV**: 69–70
    Calusa **I**: 49
    cities and urban life **II**: 61
    Columbus, Christopher **I**: 82

Counterreformation **I**: 96
diseases **I**: 108
Dominicans **I**: 110; **II**: 93
Durán, Diego **I**: 113
Dyer, Mary **II**: 99–100
Edwards, Jonathan **II**: 106
Eliot, John **II**: 106
Ethiopia **I**: 125
exploration **II**: 115; **IV**: 132
Fang **I**: 127
Figueroa, José **IV**: 136
Florida **I**: 131; **II**: 120
Franciscans **I**: 132–133
French colonies **II**: 126–129, 128*m*
French immigrants **II**: 130
Hawaiian Islands **IV**: 172
Huron **II**: 160
Iroquois **II**: 170
Jesuits **I**: 189; **II**: 174
Kamehameha I **IV**: 199
Kongo **I**: 196
Lamy, Jean Baptiste **IV**: 207
Las Casas, Bartolomé de **I**: 199
literature **IV**: 211
Maine **II**: 203
Marquette, Jacques **II**: 205, 206
Mbundu **I**: 229
McLoughlin, John **IV**: 229
Mexican-American War **IV**: 232
monarchy, British **II**: 232
music **II**: 239
Native American religion **I**: 253–254
Native Americans **II**: 244, 246
New Mexico **I**: 256, 257; **II**: 254
Oñate, Juan de **I**: 271
Oregon Trail **IV**: 267
Pima revolt **II**: 284
praying towns **II**: 295–296
Protestantism **II**: 300
pueblo **I**: 296
reducción **I**: 306–307
religion **IV**: 296
religion, Native American **II**: 317
Ricci, Matteo **I**: 311–312
Santa Fe **I**: 319–320
Serra, Junípero **II**: 331–332
shamans **II**: 335
Society for the Propagation of the Gospel in Foreign Parts **II**: 352–353
Spanish colonies **II**: 356

Texas **IV**: 337
Timucua **I**: 351
Vitoria, Francisco de **I**: 369–370
Wesley, John **II**: 393
Wheelock, Eleazar **II**: 395
White, Andrew **II**: 396
Yucatán Peninsula **I**: 379
Zeisberger, David **II**: 415
mission system **IV**: 311
Mississippi **I**: 251–252; **II**: 60–61; **V**: 408*c*; **VI**: 5, 66, 156
    Black Codes **V**: 29
    brothers' war **V**: 36–37
    Bruce, Blanche K. **V**: 40
    Confederate army **V**: 73
    cotton culture **IV**: 99
    Davis, Jefferson **V**: 88, 89
    ERA **X**: 107
    foraging **V**: 130
    Forrest, Nathan Bedford **V**: 134
    Indian Removal Act (1830) **IV**: 181
    Johnston, Joseph E. **V**: 190
    Meredith, James **IX**: 200
    migration **IV**: 235
    plantations **V**: 276
    population trends **X**: 242
    Reconstruction **V**: 294
    Revels, Hiram R. **V**: 303
    scalawags **V**: 307
    secession **V**: 313
    slave trade, internal **IV**: 320
    tobacco suits **X**: 304
    Trail of Tears **IV**: 344
    Vicksburg campaign **V**: 380–383
    Voting Rights Act of 1965 **IX**: 311, 312
    White Citizens' Councils **IX**: 320
    women's status and rights **IV**: 368
Mississippi (steamer) **VI**: 79
Mississippian **I**: **236–237**
    Cahokia **I**: 47
    Calusa **I**: 49
    Cofitachequi **I**: 76
    Coosa **I**: 85
    Florida **I**: 130
    Mabila **I**: 213
    Natchez **I**: 251
    Native American religion **I**: 252
Mississippi Democratic Party **X**: 196
Mississippi Freedom Democratic Party (MFDP) **IX**: 31, 129, **206–207**, 284, 334*c*; **X**: 196

Mississippi Freedom Summer Project **IX**: 334*c*
    Hamer, Fannie Lou **IX**: 129
    Mississippi Freedom Democratic Party **IX**: 207
    race and racial conflict **IX**: 254
    Savio, Mario **IX**: 268
    Student Nonviolent Coordinating Committee **IX**: 284
    Voting Rights Act of 1965 **IX**: 311
Mississippi River **II**: 205; **III**: 182, 394*c*, 396*c*; **V**: **234–236**, 235, 407*c*; **VI**: 34, 35
    Bruce, Blanche K. **V**: 40
    Chickasaw **II**: 59
    Chouteau family **IV**: 79
    Civil War **V**: 66
    Confederate navy **V**: 74
    contrabands **V**: 80
    Copperheads **V**: 82
    exploration **II**: 115
    Farragut, David G. **V**: 121
    foreign policy **IV**: 140, 141
    Fort Pillow, Tennessee **V**: 135
    Freedmen's Bureau **V**: 142
    French colonies **II**: 129
    Jolliet, Louis **II**: 178
    La Salle, René-Robert Cavelier, sieur de **II**: 192
    lead mines **IV**: 208
    Le Moyne, Jean-Baptiste, sieur de Bienville **II**: 193
    Le Moyne, Pierre, sieur d'Iberville **II**: 246
    Lincoln, Abraham **V**: 209
    Louisiana **II**: 199
    Marquette, Jacques **II**: 205, 206
    Natchez Revolt **II**: 241–242
    Native Americans **II**: 246
    New Madrid earthquake **IV**: 262
    New Orleans **II**: 258
    New Orleans, Battle of **V**: 251–252
    New Orleans, Battle of (1815) **IV**: 262
    Pacific Railroad Act of 1862 **V**: 263
    Permanent Indian Frontier **IV**: 279
    Pike, Zebulon Montgomery **IV**: 281

Porter, David Dixon **V:** 280
railroads **IV:** 293
Red River campaign **V:**
  297, 298
Sherman, William T. **V:**
  320
Shiloh, Battle of **V:** 323
tactics and strategy **V:** 347
Thames, Battle of the **IV:**
  342
transportation **V:** 355
Treaty of Paris **II:** 378
Union navy **V:** 368
Vicksburg campaign **V:**
  380, 382
Welles, Gideon **V:** 391
Mississippi Territory **IV:** 84, 286
Mississippi Valley **V:** 104
Mississippi v. Johnson **V:** 408*c*
Missouri **V:** 405*c*, 406*c;* **VI:** 4
Ashley, William Henry **IV:**
  28, 30
Austin, Moses **IV:** 35
Austin, Stephen F. **IV:** 36
Becknell, William **IV:** 46
Benton, Thomas Hart **IV:**
  49, 50
Blair, Francis P., Jr. **V:** 31
Bridger, James **IV:** 58
bushwhackers **V:** 46
Church of Jesus Christ of
  Latter-day Saints **IV:**
  79–80
Clay, Henry **IV:** 86
ERA **X:** 106, 107
exploration **IV:** 131
federalism **X:** 113
Forty-niners **IV:** 146
governors **V:** 152
jayhawkers **V:** 186, 187
lead mines **IV:** 208
militia movement **X:** 194
Missouri Compromise of
  1820 **IV:** 236–238, 238*m*
Pea Ridge/Elkhorn Tavern,
  Battle of **V:** 265
population trends **X:** 242
public land policy **IV:** 287
Quantrill, William Clarke
  V: 285
Santa Fe Trail **IV:** 305, 306
Smith, Joseph, Jr. **IV:** 323
Union League **V:** 367
*Webster v. Reproductive
  Health Services* **X:** 318
Young, Brigham **IV:** 371
Missouri, Constitution of **IV:**
  388–389
Missouri, Department of the **IV:**
  145
Missouri, USS **VIII:** 246, 370,
  399

Missouri Compromise of 1820
  IV: 236–238, 238*m,*
  375*c*–376*c,* 379*c,* 387–389
  abolition **V:** 2, 3
  Benton, Thomas Hart **IV:**
    50
  Bleeding Kansas **V:** 31
  Civil War **V:** 64
  Clay, Henry **IV:** 86
  Compromise of 1850 **IV:**
    93
  Davis, Jefferson **V:** 89
  Democratic Party **IV:** 108
  Dred Scott decision **V:** 101
  Kansas-Nebraska Act of
    1854 **V:** 197
  Kelley, William D. **V:** 198
  Know-Nothing Party **IV:**
    202
  Mason-Dixon Line **V:** 224
  Monroe, James **IV:** 240
  Panic of 1819 **IV:** 276
  Pierce, Franklin **V:** 275
  popular sovereignty **IV:**
    285
  Republican Party **IV:** 300,
    301; **V:** 301
  slavery **IV:** 317–318
  Supreme Court decision
    IV: 331
  Tyler, John **IV:** 348
  Vesey, Denmark **IV:** 353
Missouri Enabling Act **IV:** 388.
  See also Missouri
  Compromise of 1820
*Missouri ex rel Gaines v.
  Canada* **VIII:** 228, 347, 408*c*
Missouri Fur Company **IV:** 16,
  47, 79, **238–239**
Missouri River **V:** 355
  Astor, John Jacob **IV:** 32
  Bodmer, Karl **IV:** 55
  Catlin, George **IV:** 77
  Chouteau family **IV:** 79
  Missouri Fur Company **IV:**
    239
  Mormon Trail **IV:** 242
Missouri River Basin Project
  VIII: 410*c*
*Miss Ravenel's Conversion from
  Secession to Loyalty* (De
  Forest) **V:** 92, 213
MIT. *See* Massachusetts
  Institute of Technology
mita **I:** 325. *See also* tribute
  system
Mitchell, Arthur W. **VIII:** 2
Mitchell, Charley **VI:** 33
Mitchell, George **IX:** 12, 334*c*
Mitchell, George (John) **X:** 69,
  194–195, 276
Mitchell, Joan **IX:** 20

Mitchell, John **II:** 330; **VI:** 57;
  VII: 186
  Anthracite Coal Strike **VII:**
    12
  Buck's Stove **VII:** 36
  labor movement **VII:** 152
  National Civic Federation
    VII: 201
  New Unionism **VII:** 212
  United Mine Workers of
    America (UMWA) **VII:**
    314
Mitchell, John N. **X: 195–196**
  Ford, Gerald R. **X:** 120
  Nixon, Richard M. **X:** 220
  Richardson, Elliot L. **X:**
    268
  United States v. Nixon **X:**
    308
  Watergate scandal **X:**
    315–317
Mitchell, Louis **II:** 146
Mitchell, Margaret **V:** 213; **VIII:**
  193
Mitchell, Maria **IV:** 308; **VI:**
  194–195, 247, 257
Mitchell, Wesley **IX:** 117
Mitchell, Wesley C. **VI:** 42
Mitchell, William (Billy) **VII:**
  23, **186–187,** 361*c*
Mitford, Jessica **IX:** 69
Mitscher, Marc A. **VIII:** 246
Mittelberger, Gottlieb **II: 231,**
  276, 425–426
Mittelman, James H. **X:** 131
Miwok nation **I:** 48; **IV:** 64
Mixcoatl **I:** 355
mixed crop haciendas **I:** 150
Mixe language **I:** 269
Mixtecs **I:** 7, 99, 242, 352
Mixton War **I:** 256
"the Mobe." *See* National
  Mobilization to End the War
  in Vietnam
Mobile, Alabama **V:** 129
Mobile, Battle of **V:** 121–122
Mobile Bay **V:** 407*c*
  Mallory, Stephen R. **V:** 221
  marine corps **V:** 222
  Mobile campaign **V:** 236
  Union navy **V:** 370
Mobile Bay, Battle of **IV:** 260
Mobile campaign **V:** 110, **236**
Mobile Indians **I:** 333
mobiles **VIII:** 23
mobile telephones **X:** 274–275
mobilization **VIII:** xiii, **213–215**
  advertising **VIII:** 1–2
  African Americans **VIII:** 3
  antimonopoly **VIII:** 18
  automobile industry **VIII:**
    30

Bush, Vannevar **VIII:** 45
business **VIII:** 45, 47, 48
cities and urban life **VIII:**
  59–60
Congress **VIII:** 68
conservatism **VIII:** 73
demobilization **VIII:** 80
dollar-a-year men **VIII:** 84
education **VIII:** 94
elderly **VIII:** 95
Executive Order 8802
  VIII: 106
FEPC **VIII:** 109
Forrestal, James V. **VIII:**
  126
gays and lesbians **VIII:**
  129, 130
government **VIII:** 135
Ickes, Harold L. **VIII:** 161
Irish Americans **VIII:** 165
Kaiser, Henry J. **VIII:** 175
Kennedy, Joseph P. **VIII:**
  176
Keynesianism **VIII:** 177
labor **VIII:** 181
liberalism **VIII:** 188
Mexican Americans **VIII:**
  210
migration **VIII:** 212
Morgenthau, Henry **VIII:**
  216
MOWM **VIII:** 201–202
Murray, Philip **VIII:** 221
Nelson, Donald M. **VIII:**
  238
New Deal **VIII:** 240
NWLB **VIII:** 233
NYA **VIII:** 235
OPA **VIII:** 254
OPM **VIII:** 255
OSRD **VIII:** 255–256
OWI **VIII:** 257
politics in the Roosevelt
  era **VIII:** 272
popular culture **VIII:** 275
postwar planning **VIII:**
  278
presidency **VIII:** 281
rationing **VIII:** 291–292
reconversion **VIII:** 295
Revenue Act of 1942 **VIII:**
  308
RFC **VIII:** 294, 295
shipbuilding **VIII:**
  324–325
steel industry **VIII:** 338
Sunbelt **VIII:** 344
taxation **VIII:** 350, 352
technology **VIII:** 354
Third New Deal **VIII:** 358
TNEC **VIII:** 355
unemployment **VIII:** 364

mobilization (*continued*)
    wage and price controls
        VIII: 371
    Wallace, Henry A. **VIII:**
        373
    White, Walter **VIII:** 378
    WMC **VIII:** 374–375
    World War II home front
        VIII: 394, 395
    WPB **VIII:** 375–376
    zoot-suiters **VIII:** 404
Moby-Dick (Melville) **IV:** 213
Mochizuki v. United States
    (1999) **X:** 63
Moctezuma I Ilhuicamina **I:** 17,
    22, 351
Moctezuma II Xocoyotzin
    (Montezuma) **I:** 92,
    237–238, 387*c*
    Aguilar, Francisco de **I:** 4
    Aztecs **I:** 18, 19, 21
    Cacamatzin **I:** 44, 45
    Cortés, Hernán **I:** 93
    Cuauhtémoc **I:** 97
    Cuitláhuac **I:** 98, 99
    Díaz de Castillo, Bernal **I:**
        106
    Escalante, Juan de **I:** 123
    flowery wars **I:** 131
    Quetzalcoatl **I:** 301
    Sahagún, Bernardino de **I:**
        315
    Tacuba **I:** 342
Moctoli **II:** 246
Model A Ford **VII:** 96
Model Cities program **IX:** 52,
    207–208
Model Demonstration Agencies
    (MDAs) **IX:** 208
"Model of Christian Charity"
    (Winthrop) **II:** 421
Model T Ford **VII:** *21*, 357*c*
    automobile industry **VII:**
        22
    Ford, Henry **VII:** 95, 96
    invention and technology
        VII: 133
    mass production **VII:**
        174–175
    rural life **VII:** 268
    urban transportation **VII:**
        318–319
Modern Chivalry
    (Brackenridge) **III:** 46, 47,
    215
*Modern Corporation and
    Private Property* (Berle and
    Means) **VIII:** 35
Modern Devotion
    (Reformation) **I:** 307
Modern Instance, A (Howells)
    VI: 136

modernism **VI:** 243, 248, 250;
    VII: 187–188; VIII: 22, 303
    Armory Show **VII:** 17
    art **VII:** 18
    Greenwich Village **VII:**
        115
    literature **VII:** 160–161
    Lost Generation **VII:** 166
    music **VII:** 195–196
    religion **VII:** 260
Modernist sculpture **IX:** 20
modernization theories **IX:** 10,
    11
modern liberalism **X:** 174–175
Modern Quarterly **VII:** 253
modern Republicanism **IX:**
    208–209
Modern Times (film) **VIII:** 274
Modern Times, Long Island **IV:**
    359
Modoc nation **IV:** 64
Mod Squad, The (TV program)
    X: 295
Mogollon Culture **I:** 255
Mohammed **I:** 75
Mohave **I:** 48
Mohawk and Hudson Railroad
    IV: 188, 295
Mohawk/Mohawk nation **I:**
    238; III: 48, 178; **IV:** 259
    Algonquin **II:** 17
    Anglican Church **II:** 20
    Beaver Wars **II:** 31
    captivity **II:** 52
    Dekanawideh **II:** 85
    disease **II:** 90
    Dutch-Indian Wars **II:** 99
    Dutch Reformed Church
        II: 98
    Hendrick **II:** 155, 156
    Hiawatha **I:** 160
    Iroquois **I:** 181–183; **II:**
        168–170
    Johnson, Sir William **II:**
        177
    King Philip's War **II:** 184
    Native Americans **II:** 243
    New Netherland **II:** 256
    Oneida **I:** 271
    Seneca **I:** 321
    Society for the Propagation
        of the Gospel in Foreign
        Parts **II:** 352
    Weiser, Johann Conrad **II:**
        393
Mohawk River Valley **III:** 188
Mohegan/Mohegan nation **III:**
    255
    Canonicus **II:** 51
    King Philip's War **II:** 183,
        184
    Mason, John **II:** 211

Miantonomo **II:** 224
    Narragansett **II:** 241
    Pequot **II:** 278
    Pequot War **II:** 279, 280
    wampum **II:** 390
Mohican **II:** 155
moiety **I:** 182
Mojave nation **IV:** 64, 322
molasses **V:** 348
    Acts of Trade and
        Navigation **II:** 3
    Caribbean **II:** 53
    food **II:** 122
    manufacturing and
        industry **II:** 204
    Massachusetts **II:** 215
    mercantilism **II:** 221
    New Hampshire **II:** 250
    Newport **II:** 258
    rum trade **II:** 326
    smuggling **II:** 349
    trade and shipping **II:** 376
Molasses Act **III:** 342
Molasses Act of 1733 **II:** 3, 326,
    349, 419*c*
mold-board plow **II:** 9
Moldova **X:** 281
Molesworth, Robert **III:** 79
Moley, Raymond C. **VIII:**
    215–216
    Berle, Adolf A., Jr. **VIII:**
        35
    Brain Trust **VIII:** 41
    Emergency Banking Act of
        1933 **VIII:** 101
    London Economic
        Conference **VIII:** 193
    Tugwell, Rexford G. **VIII:**
        361
molinillo **I:** 46
MOLLUS (Military Order of
    the Loyal Legion of the
    United States) **V:** 378
Molly Maguires **V:** 177; **VI:**
    195–196
Molly Pitcher **III:** *243*,
    243–244, 245, 393*c*
Molotov, Vyacheslav **VIII:** 320;
    IX: 194
Moltmann, Jurgen **IX:** 256
Momaday, N. Scott **X:** 177
monarchy **III:** 78–79
monarchy, British **II: 231–232**
    Anglican Church **II:** 19
    Glorious Revolution **II:**
        140–141
    Hanovers **II:** 232
    Pelham, Peter **II:** 273
    Quakers **II:** 307
    royal colonies **II:** 325
    Stuarts **II:** 232
    Tudors **II:** 231–232

monarchy, Spanish **II:** 359
Monardes, Nicholas **I:** 40,
    238–239, 353; **II:** 373
monasteries **I:** 12, 73, 123
Monckton, Robert **II: 232–233;**
    III: 149
Moncure, Henry **III:** 230
Mondale, Walter F. **X:**
    196–197, 326*c*
    Albright, Madeleine K. **X:**
        18
    Carter, James Earl, Jr. **X:**
        56–58
    Dole, Robert **X:** 90
    Ferraro, Geraldine A. **X:**
        117
    Reagan, Ronald W. **X:** 260
Monday Night Football **X:** 241,
    296
"Mondo Nuovo" letter of 1504
    (Amerigo Vespucci) **I:**
    395–399
monetary lenders **II:** 222. *See
    also* banking, finance and
    credit
monetary policy **VIII:** 89, 293.
    See also currency; currency
    issue
monetary reform **V:** 302
money. *See* currency
money-back guarantees **IV:** 225
money market **VIII:** 34
money supply **VI:** 41
Mongolia **VIII:** 402
Mongols **I:** 64, 286
Mongrel Tariff (1883) **VI:** 17, 64
Monitor, USS **V:** 183, 184, 237
Monitor-Merrimack **V:** 183–184,
    237*m*, **237–239**, 238, 309,
    370, 406*c*
monitors **V:** 183
Monks Mound **I:** 47
Monmouth, Battle of **III:** 244*m*,
    244–245, 393*c*
    Burr, Aaron **III:** 53
    Clinton, Sir Henry **III:** 75
    Cornwallis, Lord **III:** 93
    Greene, Nathanael **III:** 155
    Lafayette, marquis de **III:**
        201
    Lee, Charles **III:** 205, 206
    Molly Pitcher **III:** 243
Monmouth Court House, Battle
    of **IV:** 239
monoclonal antibodies **X:** 188
monogamy **IV:** 223
monopolies **I:** 261, 322, 323; **IV:**
    17, 32; **VII:** 356*c*, 358*c*. *See
    also* antimonopoly; antitrust
    issues; trusts
    Hepburn Act **VII:** 122
    New Nationalism **VII:** 211

*Northern Securities Co. v.
U.S.* **VII:** 216
Rockefeller, John D. **VII:**
264
Standard Oil **VII:** 295–296
Monopoly (game) **VIII:** 297
monotheism **VIII:** 304
Monro, George **II:** 124
Monroe, Bill **VIII:** 222
Monroe, Harriet **VII:** 188
Monroe, James **II:** 67; **IV:**
239–240, *240,* 375*c,* 376*c;*
VII: 267; **X:** 172
Adams, John Quincy **IV:** 5
American System **IV:** 18
anti-Federalists **III:** 14
architecture **III:** 20
Bulfinch, Charles **III:** 50
Calhoun, John C. **IV:** 62
Democratic Party **IV:** 106
election of 1828 **IV:** 122
Era of Good Feelings **IV:**
127
Essex decision **III:** 119
Florida **III:** 129; **IV:** 139
foreign policy **IV:** 141
Gabriel's Rebellion **III:**
145
industrialization **IV:** 184
King, Rufus **III:** 195
Liberia **IV:** 209
Livingston, Robert R. **III:**
216
Louisiana Purchase **III:**
218
Lyon, Matthew **III:** 223
Macon, Nathaniel **III:** 226
Madison, Dolley **III:** 227
Madison, James **III:** 229,
230
Monroe Doctrine **IV:**
240–242, 389–391
Monroe-Pinkney Treaty
III: 246
National Road **IV:** 253
Panic of 1819 **IV:** 275
Permanent Indian Frontier
IV: 279
political parties **III:** 279
Randolph, John **III:** 296
Virginia dynasty **III:** 361
Monroe, Marilyn **VIII:** 84; **IX:**
209, **209–210,** 213, 244, 330*c*
Monroe Doctrine **III:** 131; **IV:**
5, 142, 240, **240–242,** 376*c,*
389–391; **V:** 314; **VI:** 104,
186, 303; **VII:** 146; **VIII:**
410*c;* **IX:** 172; **X:** 172. *See
also* Roosevelt Corollary
Monroe Doctrine, Roosevelt
Corollary to. *See* Roosevelt
Corollary

Monroe-Pinkney Treaty **III:**
245–246
Monrovia **IV:** 209
Monster and Other Stories, The
(Crane) **VI:** 69
monsters **I:** 219, 221, *239,*
239–241
Monstres et Prodiges, Des
(Ambroise Paré) **I:** 240, 402
Montagnais **I:** 183; **II:** 56, 126,
127, 130–131, 205, 243
Montagnais-Naskapui (Innu) **I:**
241
Montagu, John, fourth earl of
Sandwich **IV:** 171
Montaigne, Michel de **I:** 31, 54
Montana **II:** 76–77; **IV:** 93, 130;
V: 213–214; **VI:** 207–209,
213, 326*c;* **X:** 2, 242
Montana Freemen **X:** 299
Montana Territory **VI:** 51*m*
Montauk Building **VI:** 149
Montauk Indians **II:** 224
Montcalm, Louis-Joseph,
marquis de **II:** 124–125, 129,
158, 333, 405; **III:** 60
Monte Albán **I: 241–242**
Montejo, Francisco de **I:** 146,
227, 378
Montes, Pedro **IV:** 19, 20
Montesarchio, Father de **I:** 343
Montesinos, Fray Antonio de **I:**
110, 369
Montessori, Maria **VII:** 172
Monte Verde **I: 242–243**
Montezuma. *See* Moctezuma II
Xocoyotzin
Montgolfier, Joseph and Jacques
V: 21
Montgomery (frigate) **III:** 90
Montgomery, Alabama **V:** 303
African-American
movement **IX:** 5
freedom rides **IX:** 114
King, Martin Luther, Jr.
IX: 160
Parks, Rosa **IX:** 240
Southern Christian
Leadership Conference
IX: 276
Student Nonviolent
Coordinating
Committee **IX:** 284
Montgomery, Alabama,
Convention (1861) **V:** 75, 94,
401, 406*c*
Montgomery, Benjamin **V:** 91,
92
Montgomery, Bernard Law
VIII: 247, 249, 325
Montgomery, Little Brother
VIII: 223

Montgomery, Richard **III:** 393*c*
Allen, Ethan **III:** 10
Arnold, Benedict **III:** 21
Canada **III:** 60
Carleton, Guy **III:** 62
Quebec, Battle of **III:** 293
Schuyler, Philip John **III:**
320
Montgomery bus boycott **IX:**
30, 240, 331*c*
Montgomery Improvement
Association (MIA) **IX:** 240
Montgomery Ward & Company
VI: 186, 326*c*
*Monthly Magazine and
American Review* **IV:** 196
Montiano, Manuel de **II:** 123
Monticello **III:** 184–186
Montóac. *See* Mantoac
Montour, Andrew **II: 233**
Montour, Henry. *See* Montour,
Andrew
Montour, Madame **II: 233–234**
Montreal **I:** 163; **II:** 127, 175,
232, 333; **III:** 10, 60, 393*c*
Montserrat **I:** 243; **II:** 374
Montt, Pedro **VI:** 50
monuments **V: 239–240; VI:**
259; **VII:** 13, 357*c*
Civil War **V:** 67
Gettysburg, Battle of **V:**
150
Lincoln, Abraham **V:**
208–209
lost cause, the **V:** 217
Pinchback, Pinckney B. S.
V: 276
Richmond, Virginia **V:** 304
veterans, Civil War **V:** 379
volunteer army **V:** 384
Moody, Dwight Lyman **VI:** 75,
196, **196–197,** 241
Moody, Helen Wills **VIII:** 337
Moody, John **II:** 373
Mooney, Tom **VII:** 188
Mooney-Billings case **VII:**
188–189
Moon Is Down (Steinbeck)
VIII: 339
Moon landing **IX:** 269, 279, 294,
333*c*
Moon race **X:** 281, 323*c*
Moor, Joshua **II:** 83
Moor, William **I:** 266
Moore, Alfred **III:** 338
Moore, Alvin **IX:** 206
Moore, Charles **X:** 27
Moore, Gordon **X:** 75
Moore, James **II:** 309
Moore, James, Jr. **II:** 379
Moore, John **II:** 178
Moore, Lorrie **X:** 177

Moore, Mike **X:** 304
Moore, Samuel Preston **V:** 229,
230
Moore School of Electrical
Engineering **IX:** 98
Moore's Law **X:** 75
Moors **I:** 84, 91, 386*c*
Moor's Indian Charity School
II: 83, 395
morale, military **V:** 208, 273,
367
moral economy **II:** 389
Moraley, William **II:** 164, **234**
morality. *See* ethical issues;
values
Moral Majority **X: 197**
abortion **X:** 4
Christian Coalition **X:** 61
evangelical Christians **X:**
108
feminism **X:** 116
televangelism **X:** 294
moral reform **VI:** 233, 234
"moral revival" **X:** 259–260
"moral sense" philosophies **II:**
109
"moral suasion" **V:** 3, 4, 146
Moravians **IV:** 183
education **II:** 103
German immigrants **II:**
139
Lutherans **II:** 201
Montour, Andrew **II:** 233
Montour, Madame **II:**
233
Muhlenberg, Henry
Melchior **II:** 237
music **II:** 239
Zeisberger, David **II:** 415
More, Sir Thomas **I:** 73
Morehouse College **X:** 1
Moreno, Wigberto Jiménez **I:**
354
Morgan, Arthur **VIII:** 190, 356
Morgan, Daniel **III:** 246, 394*c*
Cornwallis, Lord **III:** 93
Cowpens, Battle of **III:** 95
Greene, Nathanael **III:**
156
Guilford Courthouse,
Battle of **III:** 158
Saratoga, surrender at **III:**
320
Morgan, Edwin D. **VI:** 16
Morgan, Frederic **VIII:** 247
Morgan, Harcourt **VIII:** 190,
356
Morgan, Sir Henry **II:** 285
Morgan, James D. **V:** 28
Morgan, John **II:** 277; **III:** 241
Morgan, John Hunt **V:** 45, 46,
72, **240**

Morgan, John Pierpont **VI:**
197–198; VII: 355*c*; **VIII:**
251
  Anthracite Coal Strike **VII:**
    13
  aviation **VII:** 23
  banking, investment **VI:**
    19, 20
  Comstock, Anthony **VI:** 62
  GE **VII:** 107
  Hill, James J. **VI:** 129
  industrial revolution,
    second **VI:** 147
  National Civic Federation
    VII: 201
  Northern Securities Co. v.
    U.S. **VII:** 216
  railroads **VI:** 239
  steel **VI:** 277
  steel industry **VII:** 296–297
  trusts **VI:** 295
  U.S. Steel **VII:** 320
  Villard, Henry **VI:** 305
Morgan, Robin **IX:** 325
Morgan, Thomas Hunt **VII:** 276
Morgan, William **III:** 137; **IV:** 24
Morgenthau, Henry T., Jr. **VIII:**
216–217
  Bretton Woods
    Conference **VIII:** 42
  Eccles, Marriner S. **VIII:**
    89
  FCA **VIII:** 112
  Holocaust **VIII:** 150
  immigration **VIII:** 162
  Jews **VIII:** 173
  Keynesianism **VIII:** 176
  recession of 1937–38 **VIII:**
    293
  refugees **VIII:** 299
  Revenue Act of 1935 **VIII:**
    308
  Social Security Act **VIII:**
    328
  taxation **VIII:** 351
  TNEC **VIII:** 355
  war bonds **VIII:** 374
  Zionism **VIII:** 403
Morgenthau Plan **VIII:**
216–217
Morill Tariff of 1861 **VI:** 39
Moriscos **I:** 164
Morisot, Berthe **VI:** 45
Mormon Battalion **IV:** 109, 243
Mormon Church. *See* Church of
  Jesus Christ of Latter-day
  Saints
Mormon Trail **IV: 242–244,**
  243*m*, 268*m*
Mormon War **IV:** 57–58,
  244–245, 323, 372
morning-after pill. *See* RU-486

Morocco **VIII:** 249, 392
  Baba, Ahmad **I:** 23
  Djenne-Djeno **I:** 109
  Gao **I:** 139
  Ibn Battuta **I:** 173
  marabout **I:** 222
  Sahara **I:** 317
  Songhai **I:** 332
  Timbuktu **I:** 350–351
Moro Insurrection **VII:** 227
Moroni **IV:** 79
morphine **V:** 96–97; **VIII:** 208;
  X: 206
Morrill, Justin **V:** 240–241; **VI:**
  92
Morrill Act of 1890 **VIII:** 94
Morrill Land-Grant Act of 1862
  V: 108, **240–241,** 301, 406*c*
  agriculture **VI:** 8
  education, federal aid to
    VI: 92
  education, higher **VI:** 93
  education, philanthropy
    and **VI:** 94
  women's colleges **VI:** 316
Morrill Tariff Act of 1861 **V:**
  105, 348, 406*c*
Morris (meatpacking company)
  VI: 191
Morris, Gouverneur **III:** 81,
  246–247, 272
Morris, Lewis **II:** 153, 184, **234,**
  253, 415
Morris, Robert **III: 247–248,**
  394*c*
  Bank of North America
    III: 30
  banks **III:** 32
  Barry, John **III:** 36
  Continental Congress,
    Second **III:** 89
  Holland Land Company
    III: 167
  Jews **III:** 188
  Madison, James **III:** 228
  Morris, Gouverneur **III:**
    247
  Newburgh conspiracy **III:**
    256
  Ross, Betsy **III:** 310
Morris, Robert Hunter **II:** 18
Morris, Thomas **IV:** 210
Morris, William **VI:** 3, 172, 248
Morris, William S. **V:** 351
Morris Brown College **VI:** 4
Morris Canal **IV:** 73*m*
Morris-Cosby dispute **II:** 146
Morrison, Frank **VII:** 36
Morrison, Jim **X:** 240
Morrison, Toni **X:** 177, *178*
Morrison, William **IV:** 238–239
Morrison v. Olson (1988) **X:** 271

Morrissey, John **VI:** 134
Morristown, New Jersey,
  encampment of **III:**
  248–249
  Brandywine, Battle of **III:**
    47–48
  Continental army, mutinies
    of **III:** 86
  Greene, Nathanael **III:**
    155
  Howe, Sir William **III:** 168
  Trenton and Princeton,
    Battles of **III:** 352
Morrow, Ann **VII:** 160
Morrow, Dwight **VII:** 23, 147
Morse, Jedidiah **III: 249–250,**
  355
Morse, Samuel F. B. **IV:** *245,*
  245–246, 377*c*; **V:** 35, 251,
  351
  Colt, Samuel **IV:** 91
  economy **IV:** 118
  immigration **IV:** 179
  industrialization **IV:** 185
  science and technology **IV:**
    307
Morse, Wayne **IX:** 99
Morse code **IV:** 245, 307; **V:** 351
mortality **II: 234–236,** *235*
  California Indians **II:** 49
  childhood **II:** 59
  disease **II:** 90, 92
  economy **II:** 101
  fertility **II:** 117
  gender **II:** 136
  indentured servitude **II:**
    164, 165
  Jamestown **II:** 171
  labor **II:** 188
  marriage and family life **II:**
    206–{2: }208, 208
  Maryland **II:** 210
  music **II:** 239
  Plymouth **II:** 287
  population trends **II:** 290,
    291
  Queen Anne's War **II:** 309
  religion, African-American
    II: 314
  Serra, Junípero **II:** 332
  slave trade **II:** 344
  society, British American
    II: 349, 350
  Virginia **II:** 382–{2: }384
  women's status and rights
    II: 407
mortgages **VI:** 135; **VIII:** 407*c*
  Agricultural Adjustment
    Act **VIII:** 6
  FHA **VIII:** 119
  GI Bill of Rights **VIII:**
    131–132

  HOLC **VIII:** 150–151
  housing **VIII:** 157–158
Mortimer, Elias H. **VII:** 327
mortmain. *See* primogeniture
  and entail
Morton, Charles **II:** 330
Morton, "Jelly Roll" (Ferdinand
  LaMenthe) **VII:** 86, 137
Morton, Levi P. **VI:** 276
Morton, Oliver P. **V:** 152, 153;
  VI: 122
Morton, Samuel George **IV:** 290
Morton, Thomas **II:** 107, **236,**
  361
Morton, William Thomas **IV:**
  307; **V:** 230
Morton of Merrymount **II:**
  236
Mosaic browser **X:** 274
Mosaic for X **X:** 153
Mosby, John Singleton **V:** 46,
  72, **241–242**
Moscow **VIII:** 393
Moscow Conference
  Declarations of 1943 **VIII:**
  410*c*
Moses **IV:** 297
Moses, Bob **IX:** 207
mosques **I:** 139, 184, 220, 350
Mosquito Coast **IV:** 88, 89
mosquitoes **I:** 107, 108; **II:** 235,
  414; **III:** 106; **IV:** 111, 112
Mossadegh, Mohammad **IX:** 60,
  201; **X:** 155
Mossi **I:** 14, 101, 109, 144,
  243–244
Most, Johann **VI:** 167; **VII:** 110
Mosto, Alvise Ca'da **I:** 144, 305,
  350
Mother Ann. *See* Lee, Ann
Mother Earth (journal) **VII:**
  110, 252
mothers' pensions **VII: 189,**
  357*c*; **VIII:** 383
  Children's Bureau **VII:** 47
  marriage and family life
    VII: 171–172
  public health **VII:** 243
  social work **VII:** 290–291
Motion Picture Association of
  America **VIII:** 54
Motion Picture Rating System
  (MPRS) **X:** 198, 239
motion pictures. *See*
  movies/movie industry
Motley Crüe **X:** 202
motors, electric **VI:** 146, 148,
  149, 285; **VII:** 83
Motor Vehicle Air Pollution
  Control Act **IX:** 334*c*
Motown Records **IX:** 217; **X:**
  201

Motown Sound **X:** 240
Mott, James **IV:** 314
Mott, Lucretia **IV: 246–247,**
378*c*; **V:** 3, 331, 397
AASS **IV:** 15
African Americans **IV:** 8
Bloomer, Amelia **IV:** 54
female antislavery societies
IV: 135–136
Foster, Abigail Kelley **IV:**
148
Seneca Falls **IV:** 313, 314
women's status and rights
IV: 368
motto, national **IX:** 256
Moulton, Forest R. **VI:** 257
Moulton, Frank **VI:** 24
mound builders **I: 244–246,**
246*m*, 252, 385*c*
Mount, William Sidney **V:** 16
Mountain Meadows massacre
IV: 81, 110
mountain men **IV: 247–248,**
248, 375*c*
Ashley, William Henry **IV:**
28
Beckwourth, Jim **IV:** 46
Bent, Charles **IV:** 47
Bent, William **IV:** 48
Bidwell, John **IV:** 51
Bridger, James **IV:** 57–58
Donner party **IV:** 114
exploration **IV:** 131
Fort Vancouver **IV:** 145
Oregon Trail **IV:** 267
rendezvous **IV:** 299–300
Rocky Mountain Fur
Company **IV:** 302
Sublette, William **IV:**
329–330
Mountbatten, Louis, Lord **VIII:**
398
Mount Holyoke **VI:** 316
Mount Rainier National Park
VI: 65
Mount Vernon **II: 236–237**
Mount Wilson Observatory
VIII: 318
Mount Wollaston **II:** 236
mourning wars **I:** 182; **II:** 31,
51, 244, 345
Moussa (Allakoi) **I:** 217
moveable type **I:** 147, 293–294
movies/movie industry **VI:** 89,
150; **VII:** 190, **190–191,**
356*c*, 358*c*; **VIII: 217–220,**
219, 406*c*, 408*c*, 409*c*; **IX:**
210–214, 229; **X: 197–200,**
325*c*
Beatles **IX:** 36
Birth of a Nation **VII:**
30–31

business **VIII:** 46
Capra, Frank **VIII:** 51–52
censorship **VIII:** 54
children **VIII:** 56
cities and urban life **VIII:**
59
civil liberties **VIII:** 60
Committee for Public
Information **VII:** 52
cosmetics industry **VII:**
58
entertainment **VII:** 85–87
Faulkner, William **VIII:**
113
FMP **VIII:** 119
Griffith, D. W. **VII:**
115–116
Hollywood Ten **IX:**
134–135
invention and technology
VII: 134
Jews **VIII:** 172
media **X:** 185, 187
Monroe, Marilyn **IX:** 209,
210
music **IX:** 216
National Endowment for
the Arts **IX:** 221
news media **VIII:** 243
OWI **VIII:** 258
popular culture **VII:** 232;
VIII: 273–274; **IX:** 244;
X: 239–240, 242
pornography **X:** 244
Presley, Elvis **IX:** 248
Reagan, Ronald W. **X:** 258
recreation **VII:** 257; **VIII:**
296; **IX:** 255; **X:** 263
Robeson, Paul **VIII:**
309–310; **IX:** 261
science **IX:** 270
sexual revolution **X:** 277
Sinatra, Frank **VIII:** 326
technology **VIII:** 353
television **X:** 295–296
vaudeville **VII:** 322
war bonds **VIII:** 374
Welles, Orson **VIII:** 376,
377
World War II home front
VIII: 395
Movimiento Estudiantil
Chicano de Aztlan (MECHA)
X: 142
Mower, Joseph A. **V:** 28
MOWM. *See* March on
Washington Movement
Moynihan, Daniel Patrick **X:**
109, 205, 216, 308
Mozambique **I:** 44, 223; **IX:**
316; **X:** 13, 24, 307
Mozart, Wolfgang **III:** 252

MPLA (Popular Movement for
the Liberation Front of
Angola) **X:** 71
Mpongwe **I: 246–247**
MPRS. *See* Motion Picture
Rating System
*Mr. Buchanan's Administration
on the Eve of the Rebellion*
(Buchanan) **V:** 42
Mr. Coffee **X:** 273
Mr. Deeds Goes to Town (film)
VIII: 52
Mr. Smith Goes to Washington
(film) **VIII:** 52, 218
MRI (magnetic resonance
imaging) **X:** 190
Ms. magazine **IX:** 326; **X:** 185,
288
MSNBC. *See* Microsoft
National Broadcasting
Corporation
MSSI (Massachusetts Society
for the Supression of
Intemperance) **IV:** 335
MTV. *See* Music Television
muckrakers **VI:** 179, 185, 325*c*;
VII: 192, 356*c*
business **VII:** 39
journalism **VII:** 142
Masses, The **VII:** 173
politics **VII:** 229
progressivism **VII:** 238
radical press **VII:** 252
Sinclair, Upton **VII:**
286–287
Standard Oil **VII:** 296
Steffens, Lincoln **VII:** 299
Tarbell, Ida **VII:** 304–305
Mudd, Samuel **V:** 33
Mugoma **I:** 210
mugwumps **VI: 199**
Beecher, Henry Ward **VI:**
24
Blaine, James Gillespie **VI:**
31–32
presidential campaigns **VI:**
232
Republican Party **VI:** 246
Schurz, Carl **VI:** 257
Muhammad (prophet) **I:** 183,
184, 230, 337
Muhammad, Elijah **VIII:** 406*c*;
IX: 9, 186, 187, **214–215,**
257, 330*c*; **X:** 111, 213
Muhammad, Wallace **X:** 111,
213
Muhammad Bounkan Kiria **I:** 14
Muhammad Turé. *See* Askia
Muhammad I
Muhlenberg, Henry Melchior
II: 139, 201, 231, **237,**
301–302

Muir, John **VI:** 65, **199–201,**
200, 326*c*; **VII:** 55, 228, *265*;
IX: 101
mulattoes **I:** 61–62; **II:** 228, 229,
237–238, 342, 357, 359; **III:**
159; **IV:** 237, 289, 290; **V:**
40–41, 83; **VII:** 249
Muldoon, William **VI:** 33
Muller, Curt **VII:** 193
Muller v. Oregon **VII:**
192–193, 357*c*, 369–372
*Adkins v. Children's
Hospital* **VII:** 3
Brandeis, Louis **VII:** 34
Goldmark, Josephine **VII:**
111
Kelley, Florence **VII:** 146
Mullins, Priscilla. *See* Alden,
Priscilla
multiculturalism **II:** 275, 281;
VIII: 275; **X:** 35–36,
200–201
multinational corporations **IX:**
45
multiple independently targeted
reentry vehicles (MIRVs) **X:**
85–86
multiracial residents **II:** 208
mumps **X:** 188
Muncie, Indiana **VII:** 185
Munich Conference (1938)
VIII: 220
Anglo-American relations
VIII: 16
foreign policy **VIII:** 124
isolationists **VIII:** 166
radio **VIII:** 290
Municipal Assistance
Corporation **X:** 217
municipal fiscal crisis of
1931–33 **VIII:** 59
munitions industry **VIII:**
250–251
Munn v. Illinois
business and government
VI: 40
due process clause **VI:** 82
Patrons of Husbandry **VI:**
221
railroads **VI:** 239
Supreme Court **VI:** 281
Munsee **II:** 88, 89, 256, 370
Munsee language **I:** 6
Müntzer, Thomas **I:** 309
Muqaddimah (Ibn Khaldûn) **I:**
174
mural painting **VI:** 219
murder. *See* homicide
"Murder Bay" **V:** 389
Murders in the Rue Morgue
(Poe) **IV:** 378*c*
murder trials **VII:** 158

Murdoch, Rupert **X:** 244, 296
Murfreesboro/Stones River,
  Battle of **V: 242–243**
    Bragg, Braxton **V:** 36
    Cleburne, Patrick Ronayne
      V: 68
    music **V:** 244
    Orphan Brigade **V:** 258
    Rosecrans, William S. **V:**
      305
    Sheridan, Philip H. **V:** 318
    Thomas, George H. **V:** 354
Murphy, Charles (bicyclist) **VI:**
  28
Murphy, Charles F. (Tammany
  boss) **VI:** 225
Murphy, Eddie **X:** 295
Murphy, Frank
    automobile industry **VIII:**
      30
    cities and urban life **VIII:**
      59
    Korematsu v. United States
      VIII: 178
    Supreme Court **VIII:** 346t
Murphy, Isaac **VI:** 134
Murphy, John Francis **VI:** 219
Murphy, John M. **X:** 4–5
Murphy, Thomas **VI:** 16
Murray, Donald **VIII:** 228
Murray, James **IX:** 99
Murray, Judith Sargent Stevens
  III: 250
Murray, Pauli **IX: 215–216,**
  223, 247
Murray, Philip **VIII: 221; IX:**
  11, 66
    CIO **VIII:** 69, 70
    Irish Americans **VIII:** 165
    labor **VIII:** 180, 181
    Lewis, John L. **VIII:** 186
    steel industry **VIII:** 338
Murray, Walter **II:** 373
Murrieta, Joaquín **IV: 248–249**
Murrow, Edward R. **VIII:** 243;
  IX: 153, *153*
Musashi (battleship) **VIII:** 186
Muscogee alliance system **I:** 85
Muscovy Company **I:** 43, 83,
  133, 265; **II:** 158
Museum of Modern Art **VIII:**
  22, 189
museums **V:** 253
Musgrove, Mary Bosomworth
  II: 238, 375
Musharraf, Pervez **X:** 247
music **II: 238–239; III:** 38,
  250–252, 281; **IV:** 39, 179,
  249–251; V: 137–138, 174,
  243–245; VI: 201–204, *202,*
  327c; **VII: 193–196,** *195,*
  357c; **VIII: 221–224,** *222,*

406c, 407c, 410c; **IX:**
  216–218; X: 201–203
    Africa **II:** 4
    African Americans **VI:** 6;
      VIII: 3
    art **II:** 24; **VI: 201–202**
    Beach, Amy **VI:** 22–23
    Beatles **IX:** 36–37
    blues **VII:** 32
    Creole **II:** 74
    Dylan, Bob **IX:** 84–85
    Ellington, Duke **VIII:**
      99–100
    entertainment **VII:** 85, 86
    FMP **VIII:** 119–120
    folk **VI:** 202–203
    folk music revival **IX:**
      110–111
    Gershwin, George **VII:**
      108–109
    Goodman, Benny **VIII:**
      132
    Harlem Renaissance **VII:**
      120
    Herbert, Victor August **VI:**
      128–129
    Holiday, Billie **VIII:**
      148–149
    jazz **VII:** 137
    Joplin, Scott **VII:** 140–141
    MacDowell, Edward
      Alexander **VI:** 183
    Massachusetts **II:** 215
    media **X:** 186
    movies **IX:** 213
    National Endowment for
      the Arts **IX:** 221
    popular **VI:** 203–204
    popular culture **VII:** 233;
      VIII: 273; **IX:** 244; **X:**
      239–241
    Presley, Elvis **IX:** 247, 248
    radio **VII:** 254
    Robeson, Paul **VIII:** 309;
      IX: 261
    rock and roll **IX:** 263–264
    Sinatra, Frank **VIII:** 326
    society, British American
      II: 351
    Sousa, John Philip **VI:**
      271–272
    theater **VI:** 286
    Tin Pan Alley **VII:**
      308–309
    Virginia **II:** 384
    Walter, Thomas **II:** 390
    Woodstock **X:** 321
    World War II home front
      VIII: 395
    zoot-suiters **VIII:** 404
musical instruments **II:** 24, 82,
  239, 273

musical revues **VII:** 357c
musicals **IX:** 213, 216, 243
musical theater **VI:** 203–204; **X:**
  201, 241–242. *See also*
  Broadway
Music Is My Mistress
  (Ellington) **VIII:** 99–100
music publishing **V:** 244
Music Television (MTV) **X:** 326c
    globalization **X:** 132
    music **X:** 202–203
    popular culture **X:** 240
muskets **IV:** 262; **V:** 308, 324
Muskie, Edmund S. **IX:** 138; **X:**
  18, 194, 306
Muskogee. *See* Creek nation
muskrats **II:** 243
Muslims. *See* Islam; Islam in
  America
Muslim Student Association **X:**
  157
Mussolini, Benito **VII:** 121;
  VIII: *31*
    Coughlin, Father Charles
      E. **VIII:** 75
    Ethiopia **VIII:** 105
    Italian Americans **VIII:**
      167
    Italian campaign **VIII:** 168
    Munich Conference **VIII:**
      220
    Sicily **VIII:** 325
    World War II European
      theater **VIII:** 393
mustee **II:** 228
mutinies, in Continental army
  III: 86
mutiny **III:** 86; **IV:** 153
"mutual improvement societies"
  III: 115
Mutually Assured Destruction
  (MAD)
    ABM Treaty **X:** 22, 23
    cold war (end of) **X:** 71
    defense policy **X:** 85
    détente **X:** 89
Muybridge, Eadweard **VI:** 86,
  137–138
M. Witmark & Sons **VI:** 204
My Bondage and My Freedom
  (Douglass) **V:** 100
Myer, Albert J. **VI:** 310
Myers, Abraham C. **V:** 180
Myers, Isaac **V:** 68–69
Myers, Michael O. **X:** 4–5
Myers v. NBC **X:** 5
*My First Days in the White
  House* (Long) **VIII:** 195
*My Imprisonment and the First
  Year of Abolition Rule in
  Washington* (Greenhow) **V:**
  159

"My Old Kentucky Home, Good
  Night" (Foster) **V:** 138
Myrdal, Alva **VIII:** 225
Myrdal, Gunnar **VIII:**
  224–225, 410c; **IX:** 43
    African Americans **VIII:** 5
    civil rights **VIII:** 62
    liberalism **VIII:** 189
    race and racial conflict
      VIII: 287, 289
*My Southern Home; of the
  South and Its People* (Brown)
  V: 40
Mystery, The (newspaper) **V:**
  93
Mystic Fort **II:** 211
mythology
    Aztecs **I:** 17
    Aztlán **I:** 22
    Díaz de Castillo, Bernal **I:**
      106
    El Dorado **I:** 118–119
    Prester John **I:** 292–293
    Sundiata Keita **I:** 339–340
    Yoruba **I:** 377

N

NA (National Association of
  Professional Baseball Players)
  VI: 21
NAACP. *See* National
  Association for the
  Advancement of Colored
  People
NAB. *See* National Association
  of Baseball Clubs; National
  Association of Broadcasters
Nabaga **I:** 144
Nabisco **X:** 49
Nabokov, Vladimir **IX:** 182
NACA **VIII:** 353
NACC (North Atlantic
  Cooperation Council) **X:**
  223
Nacodoches, Battle of **IV:** 57
Nader, Ralph **IX:** 334c; **X:**
  205–206
    Abscam **X:** 5
    automobile industry **IX:**
      25; **X:** 31
    business **IX:** 46
    consumer movement **IX:**
      69
    elections **X:** 101, 102
    General Motors **IX:** 121
    Green Party **X:** 135
    literature **IX:** 182
    National Traffic and Motor
      Vehicle Safety Act of
      1966 **IX:** 225
    political parties **X:** 238

"Nader's Raiders" **X:** 205
NAFTA. *See* North American
    Free Trade Agreement
Nagasaki. *See* Hiroshima and
    Nagasaki
Na Gbewa **I:** 101, 243
Nagumo, Chuichi **VIII:** 264
Nahua **I: 249–250,** 250, 352;
    II: 151
Nahuatl **I: 250**
    Aztlán **I:** 22
    Chimalpahin, Domingo
        Francisco de San Antón
        Muñón **I:** 71
    Cortés, Hernán **I:** 93
    Durán, Diego **I:** 113
    Nahua **I:** 249
    Tabasco **I:** 341
    Tlaxcala **I:** 352, 353
    Toltecs **I:** 354, 355
Naismith, James **VI:** 275; **VII:**
    295
Nakandakarc, Seiju **IX:** *165*
Naked and the Dead, The
    (Mailer) **VIII:** 192; **IX:** 181,
    330*c*
Naked Lunch (William S.
    Burroughs) **IX:** 35, 182
Nakipa **I:** 48
Nalu **I:** 321
Na Luro **I:** 101
NAM. *See* National Association
    of Manufacturers
Namibia **X:** 13
Nancy Drew books **IX:** 183
nanotechnology **X:** 275
Nansemond **II:** 295
Nanticoke **II:** 87, 233, 274,
    295
Nanticoke Federation **II:** 209
Nanticoke language **I:** 6
Nantucket **II:** 361
Nanumba **I:** 243
NAOWS **VII:** 15
napalm **VIII:** 12; **IX:** 82
Napochies **I:** 85
Napoleon Bonaparte. *See*
    Bonaparte, Napoleon
Napoleonic tactics **V:** 308, 345,
    346
Napoleonic Wars **III:** 117, 372;
    IV: 151
Napoleon III **V:** 132, 315
Napster **X:** 74, 330*c*
NARAL. *See* National Abortion
    Rights Action League;
    National Association for the
    Repeal of Abortion Laws
narcotics **V:** 96–97; **VIII:** 149;
    X: 206–208, *207,* 319. *See
    also* drugs/drug abuse; drug
    trafficking

Narcotics Act **VII: 197–198**
Narragansett **I:** 221; **II: 241,**
    400
    Algonquin **II:** 17
    Canonicus **II:** 51
    captivity **II:** 51
    Gorton, Samuel **II:** 142
    King Philip's War **II:** 183
    Massachusetts **II:** 212
    Massasoit **II:** 217
    Miantonomo **II:** 223–224
    Native Americans **II:** 243
    Pequot **II:** 278
    Pequot War **II:** 279, 280
    Rhode Island **II:** 320
    Rowlandson, Mary White
        II: 324
    wampum **II:** 390
    Wetamo **II:** 395
    Williams, Roger **II:** 399,
        400
    Youngs, John **II:** 414
Narragansett language **I:** 6
*Narrative of Arthur Gordon
    Pym* (Poe) **IV:** 213
*Narrative of Col. Ethan Allen's
    Captivity* (Allen) **III:** 10
Narrative of Sojourner Truth **V:**
    357
*Narrative of the Life of David
    Crockett* **IV:** 100
*Narrative of the Life of
    Frederick Douglass, an
    American Slave* **IV:** 9, 212; **V:**
    100, 212, 328
"Narrative of the Proceedings of
    the Black People During the
    Late Awful Calamity in
    Philadelphia" (Jones) **III:**
    189, 396*c*
*Narrative of William W.
    Brown, an American Slave*
    V: 328
narrative relating to Francisco
    Coronado's explorations of
    the Southwest, 1540–1542 **I:**
    400–402
Narváez, Pánfilo de **I: 250–251**
    Apalachee **I:** 11
    Cabeza de Vaca, Álvar
        Núñez **I:** 37
    Cuba **I:** 98
    Florida **I:** 130
    Sandoval, Gonzalo de **I:**
        317
    Timucua **I:** 351
    Velázquez, Diego de **I:**
        364
NASA. *See* National Aeronautic
    and Space Agency; National
    Aeronautics and Space
    Administration

NASCAR (National Association
    for Stock Car Auto Racing) **X:**
    285
NASDAQ **X:** 51
Nash, C. C. **V:** 375
Nash, Diane **IX:** 114
Nash, Gary B. **X:** 200
Nashoba experiment **IV:** 369
Nashville, Battle of **V:** 354
Nashville, Tennessee **V:** 242,
    283, 323, 408*c*; **IX:** 273
Nashville, USS **VII:** 224
Nasi, Doña Gracia **I:** 191
Naskapi. *See* Montagnais-
    Naskapi
NAS (National Academy of
    Sciences) **VI:** 160
Nasser, Gamal Abdel **IX:** 14, 83,
    147, 201, 288, 289
Nast, Thomas **V:** *112,* 193, 194,
    247–248, *295;* **VI:** 52, 323*c*
    class consciousness **VI:**
        57
    Gilded Age, The **VI:** 115
    Liberal Republican Party
        VI: 174
    magazines **VI:** 185
    Tweed Ring **VI:** 298
Natchez **I: 251–252,** 290
    Chickasaw **II:** 59
    Choctaw **II:** 61
    Le Moyne, Jean-Baptiste,
        sieur de Bienville **II:**
        193
    Louisiana **II:** 199, 200
    Natchez Revolt **II:**
        241–242
    Native Americans **II:** 246
Natchez Revolt **II:** 78,
    241–242
Natchez Seminary **VI:** 4
Nathan, George Jean **VII:** 181
Nathan, Tonie **X:** 176
Nation, Carry **VI:** 234
Nation, The **VI:** 205; **VII:** 173;
    VIII: 358
    Bryce, James **VI:** 38
    Godkin, Edwin Lawrence
        VI: 116
    magazines **VI:** 185
    Villard, Henry **VI:** 305
National Abortion Rights Action
    League (NARAL) **X:** 3, 4,
    115, 116
National Academy of Design **IV:**
    77; **VI:** 219; **VII:** 18
National Academy of Sciences
    (NAS) **VI:** 160; **VII:** 276
National Academy of the Arts of
    Design **IV:** 245
National Advertising Review
    Board **X:** 7

National Advisory Committee
    on Aeronautics (NACA)
    VIII: 353; **IX:** 219
National Aeronautics and Space
    Act of 1958 **IX:** 219
National Aeronautics and Space
    Administration (NASA) **IX:**
    219–220, 332*c;* **X:** 152, 281
    arms race **IX:** 16
    aviation **IX:** 28
    computers **IX:** 64
    Eisenhower, Dwight D.
        IX: 93
    science **IX:** 269
    space exploration **IX:**
        278
    technology **IX:** 294
National Air Pollution Control
    Administration **IX:** 127
National Air Quality Control Act
    of 1970. *See* Clean Air Act of
    1970
National American Lyceum **IV:**
    215
National American Woman
    Suffrage Association
    (NAWSA) **V:** 248; **VI:** 326*c;*
    VII: 198, 355*c*
    Anthony, Susan B. **VI:** 13
    Blatch, Harriot **VII:** 31
    Brown, Olympia **VI:** 36
    Catt, Carrie Chapman **VII:**
        44
    National Association of
        Colored Women **VII:**
        200
    National Woman's Party
        VII: 205
    Paul, Alice **VII:** 226
    Shaw, Anna Howard **VI:**
        260, 261
    Stone, Lucy **VI:** 278
    Terrell, Mary Church **VII:**
        308
    Wells-Barnett, Ida Bell **VI:**
        312
    woman suffrage **VII:**
        335–337
    women's rights and status
        VI: 317; **VII:** 339, 340
national anthem **IV:** 39
National Association for Stock
    Car Auto Racing (NASCAR)
    X: 285
National Association for the
    Advancement of Colored
    People (NAACP) **VI:** 7, 136,
    309; **VII: 198–199,** 357*c;*
    VIII: 227–228, 405*c,* 411*c;*
    IX: 220, 333*c;* **X: 208–209**
    African-American
        movement **IX:** 4–5

National Association for the
Advancement of Colored
People (NAACP) *(continued)*
African Americans **VIII:** 2,
4; **X:** 12
Baker, Ella **IX:** 30
*Brown v. Board of
Education* **IX:** 42
civil rights **VIII:** 61, 62
Du Bois, W. E. B. **VII:** 71,
72
Farmer, James L. **X:** 111
Faubus, Orval **IX:**
108–109
feminism **X:** 114
FEPC **VIII:** 109
gun control **X:** 137
Harlem Renaissance **VII:**
119
lobbying groups **VII:** 163
Marshall, Thurgood **IX:**
193
MOWM **VIII:** 201
National Women's Trade
Union League **VII:** 205
Niagara Movement **VII:**
215
Parks, Rosa **IX:** 240
race and racial conflict
VIII: 287, 289
Robinson, Jackie **IX:** 263
Scottsboro Boys **VIII:** 319
sit-ins **IX:** 273
Southern Christian
Leadership Conference
IX: 274
STFU **VIII:** 333
Wald, Lillian **VII:** 329
White, Walter **VIII:** 378
Wilkins, Roy **IX:** 322–323
National Association for the
Advancement of White
People **IX:** 276
National Association for the
Repeal of Abortion Laws
(NARAL) **X:** 248, 249
National Association of Baseball
Clubs (NAB) **VI:** 21
National Association of
Broadcasters (NAB) **X:** 295
National Association of Colored
Women **V:** 164; **VI:** 6; **VII:**
199–200, 308, 340
National Association of
Evangelicals **X:** 108
National Association of
Manufacturers (NAM) **VII:**
200–201
American Plan **VII:** 12
Buck's Stove **VII:** 36
Danbury Hatters **VII:** 61
labor movement **VII:** 151

National Civic Federation
VII: 201
open shop movement **VII:**
219
National Association of
Professional Baseball Players
(NA) **VI:** 21
National Association of Women
Lawyers **X:** 105
National Association Opposed
to Woman Suffrage
(NAOWS) **VII:** 15
National Bank Act (1864) **IV:**
43, 119
National Banking Act of 1863 **V:**
24, 56, 106, 407*c;* **VI:** 72
national banking system **V:** 94,
106; **VI:** 40, 78, 99, **205–206**
National Baptist Convention,
U.S.A. **VI:** 4; **X:** 11
National Baptist Convention of
America **X:** 11
National Barn Dance **VIII:** 222
National Baseball Hall of Fame
VIII: 407*c;* **X:** 1
National Basketball Association
(NBA) **IX:** 281; **X:** 285
National Basketball League **VII:**
295
National Birth Control League
VII: 30
National Black Feminist
Organization **IX:** 326
National Broadcasting
Corporation (NBC) **IX:** 153;
X: 5, 239, 241, 296
entertainment **VII:** 86
journalism **VII:** 143
music **VII:** 195
popular culture **VII:** 232
radio **VII:** 254
national budget **IX:** 44; **X:**
325*c*–327*c,* 330*c.* *See also*
defense budget; federal
funding
antiwar movement—
Vietnam **X:** 24
arms race **X:** 25
Bush, George H. W. **X:** 46
Clinton, William **X:** 68
Congressional Budget and
Impoundment Act **X:**
75
defense policy **X:** 86, 87
economy **X:** 94–96
Ford, Gerald R. **X:** 121
Gingrich, Newton L. **X:**
129–130
Green Party **X:** 135
GRH Act of 1985 **X:**
134–135
OMB **X:** 226–227

Reagan, Ronald W. **X:** 259
Reaganomics **X:** 261
Senate **X:** 276
space policy **X:** 281, 283
National Bureau of Standards
VII: 134
National Cancer Institute **IX:**
222
National Carbon Company **VII:**
5
National Catholic Welfare
Conference **IX:** 99
National Catholic Welfare
Council **VIII:** 54
*National Citizen and the Ballot
Box* (journal) **VI:** 107
National Citizens Rights
Association **V:** 354
National Civic Federation **VII:**
51, 186, **201,** 212
National Coalition of Blacks for
Reparations in America **X:**
256
National Coalition of 100 Black
Women **X:** 141
National Commission on Civil
Disorders **IX:** 254–255
National Commission on
Excellence in Education **X:**
100
National Commission on Law
Observance and
Enforcement **VII:** 60
National Committee for a Sane
Nuclear Policy. *See* SANE
National Committee for
Organizing Iron and Steel
Workers **VII:** 220, 298
National Committee of
Autonomous State Parties **X:**
20
National Committee on
Radiation Protection **IX:** 24
National Conference of Catholic
Bishops **X:** 59–60, 224
National Conference of
Charities and Corrections
VII: 289
National Congress of American
Indians (NCAI) **VIII:** 236;
IX: 227, 228
National Conservation
Commission **VII:** 276
National Consumers League
(NCL) **VII:** 111, 146, 193;
VIII: 83
National Council for the Arts **X:**
209
National Council for the
Humanities **X:** 209
National Council of Catholic
Bishops **X:** 3, 4

National Council of Catholic
Women **X:** 106
National Council of Negro
Women **VIII:** 3, 36
National Council of the Union
Leagues **V:** 368
National Council of Women
VIII: 36
National Council on Disability
X: 21
National Council on the Arts
IX: 221
National Council on the
Humanities **IX:** 221, 222
National Credit Corporation
VIII: 154, 294
National Currency Act (1863)
IV: 43, 119
national debt **III:** **253; IV:** 106,
193; **VI:** 150; **X:** 94, 95
National Defense Act **VII:**
201–202, 236
National Defense
Appropriations Act of 1940
VIII: 68, 214, 408*c*
National Defense Education
Act of 1920 **IX:** 91
National Defense Education
Act of 1957 **IX:** 294
National Defense Education
Act of 1958 **IX:** 91, 332*c*
National Dress Reform
Association (NDRA) **V:** 123
National Education Association
VI: 6; **IX:** 99; **X:** 100, 105
National Emergency Council
VIII: 332
National Endowment for the
Arts and Humanities (NEA;
NEH) **X:** **209–210**
National Endowment for the
Arts (NEA) **IX:** 127, 216,
221, 334*c;* **X:** 209
*National Endowment for the
Arts v. Finley* (1998) **X:** 330*c*
National Endowment for the
Humanities (NEH) **IX:** 127,
221–222, 334*c;* **X:** 35,
209–210
National Enquirer **X:** 185
National Environmental Policy
Act (NEPA) of 1970 **X:** 77,
210, 249, 323*c*
National Era **V:** 339
National Farmers' Alliance and
Industrial Union **VI:** 99, 326*c*
National Farmers Organization
(NFO) **IX:** 8, 331*c*
National Farmers Union **IX:** 8
National Farm Workers
Association (NFWA) **IX:** 174,
304

National Federation of African American Women **VII:** 199

National Federation of Business and Professional Women's Clubs **IX:** 324; **X:** 105

National Federation of Republican Women **X:** 272

National Firearms Act of 1934 **X:** 136, 212

National Flag Conference **X:** 117

National Football League (NFL) **VIII:** 336; **IX:** 280; **X:** 262, 284

National Forest Commission **VII:** 228

National Forest Reserve program **VI:** 65

national forests **IX:** 226–227

National Foundation of the Arts and Humanities Act of 1965 **IX:** 127, 221, 222, 334c; **X:** 209

National Freedmen's Relief Association **V:** 357

National Gazette **III:** 139

National Guard **V:** 340; **VII:** 106, 168, 236; **VIII:** 20

national health insurance **IX:** 107, 138

National Heart Institute **IX:** 197

National Highway Traffic Safety Administration (NHTSA) **IX:** 225

National Hockey League (NHL) **VII:** 295; **VIII:** 338; **IX:** 281

National Housing Act of 1933 **VIII:** 407c

National Housing Act of 1934 **VIII:** 157; **IX:** 110

National Housing Act of 1949 **IX:** 108

National Human Genome Research Institute (NHGRI) **X:** 145–146

national identity **VI:** 201

national income **VIII:** 91t

National Independent (Greenback) Party **VI:** 72

National Indian Youth Council (NIYC) **IX:** 229; **X:** 214

National Industrial Recovery Act (NIRA) **VIII:** **228–229,** 406c, 407c

American Federation of Labor **VIII:** 14

antimonopoly **VIII:** 17

Brain Trust **VIII:** 41

Bridges, Harry **VIII:** 43

Communists **VIII:** 65

Congress **VIII:** 67

conservatism **VIII:** 71

court-packing plan **VIII:** 76

economy **VIII:** 92

First New Deal **VIII:** 122

Ickes, Harold L. **VIII:** 161

Johnson, Hugh S. **VIII:** 173

labor **VIII:** 179

Lewis, John L. **VIII:** 186

liberalism **VIII:** 188

Long, Huey P. **VIII:** 194

New Deal **VIII:** 240

NLRA **VIII:** 229

NLRB **VIII:** 230

NRA **VIII:** 231–232

Perkins, Frances **VIII:** 265

PWA **VIII:** 285

Schechter Poultry Corporation v. United States **VIII:** 317

socialists **VIII:** 327

Supreme Court **VIII:** 345

taxation **VIII:** 351

Tugwell, Rexford G. **VIII:** 361

Wagner, Robert F. **VIII:** 372

National Industrial Union of Textile Workers **VII:** 156

National Institute for Dental Disease **IX:** 197

National Institute for Occupational Safety and Health (NIOSH) **X:** 225

National Institute of Allergy and Infectious Diseases **IX:** 197

National Institute of Mental Health (NIMH) **IX:** 222

National Institute of Neurological Disease and Blindness **IX:** 197

National Institutes of Health (NIH) **VIII:** 208–209; **IX:** 197, **222–223,** 249; **X:** 145–146, 191

National Institutes of Health Revitalization Act of 1994 **X:** 4, 249

National Intelligencer **IV:** 150

nationalism **VI:** 104; **VIII:** 93

Calhoun, John C. **IV:** 62

Era of Good Feelings **IV:** 127

Ghent, Treaty of (1814) **IV:** 162

Taylor, Zachary **IV:** 334–335

nationalism, Irish **V:** 177

Nationalist clubs **VI:** 26

nationalist movements. *See also* wars of national liberation

cold war **IX:** 60

Latin America **IX:** 172

Latino movement **IX:** 173

Middle East **IX:** 201

Suez crisis **IX:** 288–289

Nationalist Party (Spain) **VIII:** 276

Nationalists (Spain) **VIII:** 334

nationalization of industry **VIII:** 133

National Labor Reform Party **V:** 248

National Labor Relations Act (NLRA) **VII:** 124; **VIII:** **229,** 407c; **IX:** 291, 304

American Federation of Labor **VIII:** 14

automobile industry **VIII:** 30

business **VIII:** 47

Byrnes, James F. **VIII:** 48

civil liberties **VIII:** 60

Communists **VIII:** 65

Congress **VIII:** 67

conservatism **VIII:** 72

court-packing plan **VIII:** 76

government **VIII:** 134

labor **VIII:** 180, 181

Lewis, John L. **VIII:** 186

liberalism **VIII:** 188

New Deal **VIII:** 241

NLRB **VIII:** 229–230

NRA **VIII:** 232

Perkins, Frances **VIII:** 265

Roosevelt, Franklin D. **VIII:** 313

Second New Deal **VIII:** 321

socialists **VIII:** 327

steel industry **VIII:** 338

Supreme Court **VIII:** 346

Taft, Robert A. **VIII:** 349

Wagner, Robert F. **VIII:** 372

women's status and rights **VIII:** 384

National Labor Relations Board (NLRB) **VIII:** **229–231,** 230; **X:** 171

Communists **VIII:** 66

NLRA **VIII:** 229

NWLB **VIII:** 233

Wagner, Robert F. **VIII:** 372

National Labor Relations Board v. Jones and Laughlin Steel Corporation **VIII:** 229

National Labor Union (NLU) **V:** 68, 117, **248,** 340; **VI:** 66, 169

National Lawyers Guild **IX:** 80

National Lead and Oil Company of New Jersey **VI:** 294

National League (baseball) **VII:** 25–26, 294; **VIII:** 336; **X:** 284

National League of Professional Base Ball Clubs (NL) **VI:** 21, 22

National Liberation Front (NLF) **IX:** 308–310, 317

National Liberation Front of Angola (FNLA) **X:** 71

National Library of Medicine **IX:** 223

National Manpower Council **IX:** 324

National Military Establishment (NME) **IX:** 224, 225, 329c

National Mobilization to End the War in Vietnam ("the Mobe") **X:** 24, 61

national monuments **VI:** 200; **VII:** 13, 357c; **VIII:** 296

National Motor Vehicle Safety Advisory Council **IX:** 225

national motto **IX:** 256

National Museum of the American Indian Act **X:** 215

National Negro Business League **VI:** 308

National Negro Congress **VIII:** 288

National Opposition Union (UNO) (Nicaragua) **X:** 81, 218

National Organization for the Reform of Marijuana Laws (NORML) **X:** 208

National Organization for Women (NOW) **IX:** 115, 216, **223,** 323, 325, 334c; **X:** **210–211**

abortion **X:** 3, 4

ERA **X:** 105, 106

feminism **X:** 114–116

pro-life and pro-choice movements **X:** 249

Roe v. Wade **X:** 268

Steinem, Gloria **X:** 288

women's rights and status **X:** 320

National Origins Act **VII:** **202,** 361c; **VIII:** 71; **IX:** 141, 142, 187–188

AFL **VII:** 11

anti-Semitism **VII:** 14

Cable Act **VII:** 41

Coolidge, Calvin **VII:** 57

immigration **VII:** 127

Mexican immigration **VII:** 182

nativism **VII:** 208

population trends **VII:** 234

National Origins Act
   (continued)
      race and racial conflict
      VII: 248
National Outdoor Recreation
   Review Commission **IX:**
   223–224, 332*c*
National Packing Company **VI:**
   191
national parks **VI:** 65, 200, 323*c;*
   VII: 13; **VIII:** 103, 296; **IX:**
   255
National Park Service **V:** 239;
   VII: **203,** 266, 276, 359*c;*
   VIII: 296
National Park Service Act **VII:**
   203
National Park system **III:** 176
National Pike. *See* National
   Road
National Police Gazette, The **VI:**
   33
National Prison Reform
   Association **VI:** 127
National Progressive
   Republican League
      Congress **VII:** 54
      elections **VII:** 80
      Johnson, Hiram Warren
         VII: 138
      La Follette, Robert **VII:**
         155
      Progressive Party **VII:** 236
      Republican Party **VII:**
         263
      Taft, William Howard **VII:**
         304
National Prohibition Act. *See*
   Volstead Act
National Prohibition Party **IV:**
   51
National Rainbow Coalition **X:**
   160
National Reclamation Act **VII:**
   203–204, 266, 276
National Recovery
   Administration (NRA) **VII:**
   330; **VIII:** *231,* **231–232**
      advertising **VIII:** 1
      African Americans **VIII:** 3
      antimonopoly **VIII:** 17–18
      automobile industry **VIII:**
         30
      Baruch, Bernard M. **VIII:**
         34
      Brain Trust **VIII:** 41
      children **VIII:** 56
      Fair Labor Standards Act
         VIII: 110
      First New Deal **VIII:** 122
      Harriman, Averell **VIII:**
         143

Henderson, Leon **VIII:**
   145
Hillman, Sidney **VIII:** 145
Johnson, Hugh S. **VIII:**
   173
labor **VIII:** 180
Lewis, John L. **VIII:** 186
New Deal **VIII:** 241
NIRA **VIII:** 228
NLRA **VIII:** 229
PWA **VIII:** 285
*Schechter Poultry
   Corporation v. United
   States* **VIII:** 317
Supreme Court **VIII:** 345
National Reform Party **X:** 263
National Republican Party **IV:**
   193, 360, 363
National Research and
   Education Network (NREN)
   X: 153
National Research Council **VII:**
   277
National Resources Planning
   Board (NRPB) **VIII:**
   232–233; IX: 71
      Congress **VIII:** 68
      Economic Bill of Rights
         VIII: 90
      Executive Reorganization
         Act **VIII:** 107
      GI Bill of Rights **VIII:**
         131
      government **VIII:** 134
      Keynesianism **VIII:** 177
      liberalism **VIII:** 188, 189
      postwar planning **VIII:**
         278, 279
      reconversion **VIII:** 295
      Third New Deal **VIII:** 357
National Review magazine **X:**
   42, 43
National Rifle Association
   (NRA) **X:** **211–213,** *212*
      campaign finance **X:** 54
      gun control **X:** 137
      PACs **X:** 236
National Right to Life
   Committee **X:** 248–249
National Right to Life
   Organization **X:** 116
National Road **III:** 398*c;* **IV:**
   253–255, 254*m;* **V:** 354–355
      agriculture **IV:** 11
      Baltimore & Ohio Railroad
         (B&O) **IV:** 39
      economy **IV:** 117
      internal improvements **IV:**
         188
      migration **IV:** 235
National School Lunch Act of
   1946 **IX:** 9

National Science Foundation
   (NSF) **VIII:** 44, 45; **IX:** 197,
   270, 293, 330*c;* **X:** 153
National Sculpture Society **VI:**
   15
national security **VIII:** 60, 82; **X:**
   233
National Security Act of 1947
   VIII: 126; **IX:** 49, **224–225,**
   248, 299–300, 329*c*
National Security Act of 1949
   IX: 330*c*
National Security Council
   (NSC) **IX:** 329*c,* 330*c. See
   also* NSC-68
      Acheson, Dean **IX:** 2
      African nations **X:** 13
      Boland Amendment **X:** 38
      Cuban missile crisis **IX:** 73
      defense budget **IX:** 77
      Kissinger, Henry A. **X:**
         165
      National Security Act of
         1947 **IX:** 224, 225
      North, Oliver L. **X:**
         221–222
      NSC-68 **IX:** 233–234
      Tower Commission **X:** 306
national security issues **X:** 233
National Security Resources
   Board **IX:** 224
National Service Board for
   Religious Objectors
   (NSBRO) **VIII:** 70
National Service Corps (NSC)
   IX: 310, 311
National Service Trust Act **IX:**
   311
National Space Act of 1958 **X:**
   281
National Spiritualism
   Association **VI:** 244
National Style **IV:** 27
National System of Interstate
   and Defense Highways. *See*
   Interstate Highway Act of
   1956
National Textile Workers' Union
   VII: 106
National Trades Union **IV:** 204
National Traffic and Motor
   Vehicle Safety Act of 1966
   IX: 25, 46, 69, **225,** 334*c;* **X:**
   205
National Trails Act of 1968 **IX:**
   224, **225–226,** 255, 334*c*
National Trails System **IX:**
   225–226, 334*c*
National Trails System Act of
   1983 **X:** 250
National Union for Social
   Justice (NUSJ) **VIII:** 75

National Union for the Total
   Independence of Angola
   (UNITA) **X:** 71
National Unity Party **X:** 21
National Urban League (NUL)
   VI: 7; **X:** 12
National War Labor Board
   (NWLB) **VII:** **204,** 359*c;*
   VIII: **233–234**
      AFL **VII:** 11
      Fuel Administration **VII:**
         102
      labor and labor
         movements **VII:**
         152–154; **VIII:** 181
      mobilization **VIII:** 215
      NLRB **VIII:** 230
      Steel Strike of 1919 **VII:**
         298
      Taft, William Howard **VII:**
         304
      wage and price controls
         VIII: 371, 372
      World War I **VII:** 344
National Wilderness
   Preservation Act of 1964 **IX:**
   101, 224, **226–227,** 321–322,
   334*c;* **X:** 77
National Wildlife Federation
   IX: 101
national wildlife refuges **VI:** 65
National Woman's Party (NWP)
   VII: **204–205,** 359*c*
      Blatch, Harriot **X:** 31
      Catt, Carrie Chapman **VII:**
         44
      ERA **VII:** 87
      Paul, Alice **VII:** 226
      Terrell, Mary Church **VII:**
         308
      woman suffrage **VII:** 336,
         337
      women's status and rights
         VII: 340
National Woman Suffrage
   Association (NWSA) **V:**
   248–249, 409*c;* **VI:** 324*c,*
   326*c;* **VII:** 198
      Anthony, Susan B. **VI:** 12,
         13
      Brown, Olympia **VI:** 36
      Cary, Ann Shadd **V:** 52
      Gage, Matilda Joslyn **VI:**
         107
      Hooker, Isabella Beecher
         VI: 133
      Lockwood, Belva Ann
         Bennett McNall **VI:**
         180
      Ray, Charlotte **V:** 291
      Shaw, Anna Howard **VI:**
         260

Stanton, Elizabeth Cady **V:** 335
Stone, Lucy **VI:** 278
women's rights and status **V:** 398, 399; **VI:** 317
National Women's Law Center **X:** 302
National Women's Party **VI:** 36; **X:** 105
National Women's Political Caucus (NWPC) **IX:** 115; **X:** 115, 116, 211, 288
National Women's Rights Convention (1850) **VI:** 30, 278
National Women's Rights Convention (1852) **VI:** 107
National Women's Rights Convention (1860) **VI:** 30
National Women's Trade Union League (NWTUL) **VII:** **205–206**
  Blatch, Harriot **VII:** 31
  New Woman **VII:** 214
  radical press **VII:** 252
  Shirtwaist Makers Strike **VII:** 285
  Triangle Shirtwaist Fire **VII:** 312
  Wald, Lillian **VII:** 329
  women's status and rights **VII:** 338
National Youth Administration (NYA) **VIII:** **234–235**
  African Americans **VIII:** 3
  Bethune, Mary McLeod **VIII:** 36
  Black Cabinet **VIII:** 37
  children **VIII:** 56
  education **VIII:** 94
  Emergency Relief Appropriation Act **VIII:** 102
  marriage and family life **VIII:** 204
  recreation **VIII:** 296
  relief **VIII:** 301
  Roosevelt, Eleanor **VIII:** 311
  WPA **VIII:** 387
Nation at Risk, A **X:** 100
nation-building policy **IX:** 241; **X:** 18
Nation of Islam **VIII:** 405c, 406c; **IX:** 9, 330c; **X: 213**
  African-American movement **IX:** 5, 7
  African Americans **X:** 12
  Ali, Muhammad **IX:** 9
  Farrakhan, Louis A. **X:** 111
  Jackson, Jesse L. **X:** 160
  Malcolm X **IX:** 186–187

Muhammad, Elijah **IX:** 214–215
NAACP **X:** 208, 209
race and racial conflict **X:** 257
religion **IX:** 257
Native American Association **IV:** 180
Native American Democratic Association **V:** 251
Native American Grave Protection and Repatriation Act **X:** 215
Native American movement **IX:** **227–229**, 334c
Native American religion **I:** **252–254**, 253m; **II:** **317–319**, *318. See also* gods and goddesses, Native American
  Aataentsic **I:** 1
  Aztecs **I:** 17–18, 20, 21
  Cahokia **I:** 47
  calumet **II:** 50
  Cholula **I:** 72
  Cozumel **I:** 96–97
  Crow **II:** 77
  dance **II:** 82
  Dominicans **II:** 93–94
  Eliot, John **II:** 107
  environment **II:** 110
  Great Awakening **II:** 147
  Hopewell culture **I:** 166
  Hopi **I:** 167
  Huitzilopochtli **I:** 170
  Huron **I:** 171; **II:** 160
  Inca **I:** 176
  King Philip's War **II:** 183
  Machu Picchu **I:** 213–214
  Mantoac **I:** 221
  Massachusett **I:** 225
  Maya **I:** 228
  Mississippian culture **I:** 237
  mound builders **I:** 244–246
  Natchez **I:** 251
  Navajo **II:** 247
  Neolin **II:** 248–249
  North Carolina **II:** 264
  Opechancanough **II:** 268
  Powhatan Confederacy **II:** 294
  pueblo **I:** 296
  Pueblo Indians **II:** 303
  Pueblo Revolt **II:** 304
  Quetzalcoatl **I:** 301
  revitalization movements **II:** 319–320
  scalping **II:** 329
  shamans **II:** 334–335
  Teotihuacán **I:** 346
  tobacco **II:** 373
  Toltecs **I:** 355

wampum **II:** 390
Yucatán Peninsula **I:** 379
Zuni **I:** 383
Native American reservations. *See* reservations, Native American
Native Americans **I:** 385c; **II:** *23, 132,* **242–247,** 245m; **III:** 396c–398c; **IV:** **255–258,** 257m, 375c–377c, 379c; **V:** **249–251,** 250m, 405c, 407c, 408c; **VI:** **206–209,** 207m, **208,** 323c–327c; **VII:** **206–208,** *207,* 356c; **VIII:** **235–236,** *236,* 406c, 410c; **X:** **213–215,** 214m, 243, 324c. *See also specific headings*
  Abenaki **I:** 1–2
  abolitionism **II:** 1–2
  agriculture **II:** 7–9, 12
  Alaska **III:** 9
  Alaska Native Claim Settlement Act **X:** 17
  Albany Congress **II:** 14
  Aleut **II:** 16
  Algonquian **I:** 6
  Algonquin **II:** 17
  alliances/assimilation **IV:** 256–257
  American Fur Company **IV:** 17
  American Indian Movement **IX:** 12–13
  Anglican Church **II:** 20
  animals **II:** 20, 21
  Apalachee **I:** 11
  architecture **II:** 22; **III:** 18–19
  art **II:** 24; **IV:** 25; **V:** 16
  Attucks, Crispus **III:** 27–28
  audiencia **I:** 15
  Bacon's Rebellion **II:** 27–28
  Baptists **II:** 29
  Barlowe, Arthur **I:** 26
  Beaver Wars **II:** 31
  Beckwourth, Jim **IV:** 46
  Benezet, Anthony **II:** 31
  Bent, Charles **IV:** 47
  Bent, William **IV:** 48
  Berkeley, Sir William **II:** 33
  BIA **IV:** 180–181
  Bilingual Education Act of 1968 **X:** 36
  Black Hawk War **IV:** 51–53
  Blount, William **III:** 41
  Blue Jacket **III:** 41
  Bodmer, Karl **IV:** 55
  borderlands **II:** 34–35
  Brainerd, David **II:** 39–40

Brant, Joseph **III:** 48–49
Bridger, James **IV:** 58
British Empire **II:** 43
Brown, Charles Brockden **III:** 50
buffalo, extermination of **VI:** 38
Buffalo Soldiers **VI:** 39
Burgoyne, John **III:** 52
Burke Act **VII:** 37
business and government **VI:** 39
Cabeza de Vaca, Álvar Núñez **I:** 37, 38
Cahokia **I:** 47
California **I:** 48; **III:** 57; **IV:** 64–66
California gold rush **IV:** 69
California Indians **II:** 49
California missions **IV:** 70
calumet **II:** 50
Canada **III:** 59–60
cannibalism **I:** 54
captivity **II:** 51–52
Caribbean **II:** 52
Carson, Kit **IV:** 75, 76
Cartier, Jacques **I:** 57–59
Cass, Lewis **IV:** 76
Catawba **II:** 55
Catholics **III:** 63
Catlin, George **IV:** 77–78
Cayuga **I:** 67
Champlain, Samuel de **II:** 56
Cherokee **II:** 57–58
Cherokee nation **III:** 65–66
Chesapeake Bay **II:** 58
Chickasaw **II:** 59
childhood **II:** 60
Choctaw **II:** 60–61
Chouteau family **IV:** 78–79
Civil Liberties Act of 1988 **X:** 63
Clark, George Rogers **III:** 71
Clark, William **III:** 72–73
clothing **II:** 64–65
Coercive Acts **III:** 76
Cofitachequi **I:** 76
College of William and Mary **II:** 67
Colorado gold rush **IV:** 89, 90
Columbian Exchange **I:** 76–78
Columbia River **IV:** 93
Connecticut **II:** 68, 69
consumption **II:** 71
corn (maize) **I:** 87–88
Cornplanter **III:** 91–92
Cornstalk **II:** 72

Native Americans (*continued*)
  corregidores **I:** 91
  cotton culture **IV:** 97, 98
  crafts **II:** 74
  Crazy Horse **VI:** 69
  crime and punishment **II:** 74–75
  Crockett, Davy **IV:** 99
  Crow **II:** 76–77
  crowd action **II:** 77, 78
  cultures **II:** 242–243
  dance **II:** 82
  Dartmouth College **II:** 83
  Dawes Severalty Act **VI:** 76
  Delaware **II:** 86, 88–89
  Democratic Party **IV:** 107–108
  Deseret, State of **IV:** 110
  dime novels **VI:** 81
  disease **II:** 93, 244
  disease and epidemics **I:** 107–108; **II:** 90; **IV:** 113
  Dominicans **I:** 110; **II:** 94
  Dragging Canoe **III:** 107
  Dunmore, Lord **III:** 109
  Dutch-Indian Wars **II:** 98–99
  Dutch Reformed Church **II:** 97–98
  Eaton, John, Jr. **V:** 104
  economy **II:** 243; **IV:** 117
  education **II:** 102–103; **VI:** 90, 91
  Edwards, Sarah Pierpont **II:** 106
  election of 1828 **IV:** 122, 123
  Eliot, John **II:** 106–107
  Enlightenment **II:** 110
  entertainment, popular **VI:** 98
  environment **II:** 110
  ethnocentrism **II:** 112–{2:}114
  European contacts **II:** 243–244
  expansion of the colonies and their role in international politics **II:** 246–247
  exploration **II:** 114; **IV:** 131, 132
  Fallen Timbers, Battle of **III:** 123–124
  fertility **II:** 117–118
  fishing **II:** 118
  Flashman, Edward **II:** 119
  Florida **I:** 130–131; **II:** 120; **III:** 129; **IV:** 139, 140
  FMP **VIII:** 119

food **II:** 121
foreign affairs **III:** 130
foreign policy **IV:** 141
forests **II:** 122
Fort Laramie **IV:** 143–145
forts **II:** 124
Fort Stanwix, Treaty of **III:** 132
Fort Vancouver **IV:** 145
Fort William Henry Massacre **II:** 124
Franklin, state of **III:** 135
Franklin, William **III:** 136
Frémont, John C. **IV:** 153
French colonies **II:** 126–127, 128m, 129
frontier **III:** 140, 141
fur trade **II:** 130–133, *132*; **IV:** 156–158
Gadsden Purchase **IV:** 159
Gates, Sir Thomas **II:** 135
gender **II:** 137
Georgia **II:** 138
Geronimo **VI:** 112–113
Ghent, Treaty of (1814) **IV:** 161, 162
gold, discovery and mining **IV:** 163
Great Plains **III:** 154
Great Plains Indians **II:** 149–150
Greenville, Treaty of **III:** 156–157
Guadalajara **II:** 151
Haida **I:** 150
Handsome Lake **III:** 164
Harriot, Thomas **I:** 154–155
Harrison, William Henry **IV:** 168
Harvard College **II:** 155
Havasupai **I:** 156
Hendrick **II:** 155
Hidatsa **I:** 161
Hoar, George Frisbie **VI:** 130
at Hochelaga **I:** 163
Hohokam **I:** 163–164
Homestead Act of 1862 **V:** 170
Hopewell culture **I:** 166
Hopi **I:** 166–167
horses **I:** 169
Horseshoe Bend, Battle of **IV:** 173
housing **II:** 157
Howard, O. O. **V:** 173
Hudson's Bay Company **II:** 159
Hull, William **IV:** 175–176
Huron **I:** 170–172; **II:** 160
imperialism **VI:** 142

Indian Affairs, Office of **VI:** 143–144
Indian Claims Commission **IX:** 142–143
Indian Removal Act (1830) **IV:** 181–183
Indian Reorganization Act **VIII:** 163
Indian Rights Association **VI:** 144–145
Indians of the Desert Southwest **II:** 165–166
Ingram, David **I:** 177
Inuit **II:** 166–167
iron manufacturing **II:** 167
Iroquois **I:** 181–183; **II:** 168–170
Iroquois Confederacy **III:** 178–179
Jackson, Andrew **IV:** 191, 193
Jackson, Helen Hunt **VI:** 153
Jamestown **II:** 172
Jay's Treaty **III:** 183
Jefferson, Thomas **III:** 185
Johnson, Sir William **II:** 177
Jolliet, Louis **II:** 178
Kieft, Willem **II:** 182
King Philip's War **II:** 183–184
King William's War **II:** 185
Knight, Sarah Kemble **II:** 185–186
labor **II:** 187–189
La Demoiselle **II:** 190–191
Lamy, Jean Baptiste **IV:** 207
land **II:** 191
La Salle, René-Robert Cavelier, sieur de **II:** 192
Las Casas, Bartolomé de **I:** 197–201
lead mines **IV:** 208
Lewis, Meriwether **III:** 208–209
Lewis and Clark Expedition **III:** 209–211
literature **II:** 195; **IV:** 211; **VI:** 177; **X:** 177
Little Bighorn, Battle of **V:** 213–214
Locke, John **II:** 198
Lone Wolf v. Hitchcock **VII:** 165–166
Louisiana **II:** 199
Louisiana Purchase **III:** 218
Mabila **I:** 213
Maliseet **I:** 219

mariners **II:** 204
Marquette, Jacques **II:** 205
marriage and family life **II:** 206, 208; **III:** 232, 235; **IV:** 220–221
Mason, John **II:** 211
Massachusett **I:** 224–225
Massachusetts **II:** 214
Massachusetts School Act **II:** 216–217
Massasoit **II:** 217
McGillivray, Alexander **III:** 240
McRea, Jane **III:** 239
medicine **II:** 220; **III:** 241
merchants **II:** 222
and *mestizaje* **I:** 233
Metacom **II:** 222–223
métis **II:** 223
Mexican-American War **IV:** 232
Miantonomo **II:** 223–224
Middleton, Arthur **II:** 224
midwives **II:** 225
migration **IV:** 235; **VIII:** 213
Minuit, Peter **II:** 226–227
miscegenation **II:** 228
missionaries **II:** 244, 246
missions **II:** 229–231
Mississippian culture **I:** 236–237
Missouri Fur Company **IV:** 239
Mittelberger, Gottlieb **II:** 231
Mohawk **I:** 238
Montagnais-Naskapi **I:** 241
Montour, Madame **II:** 233–234
Moraley, William **II:** 234
mortality **II:** 235–236
Morton, Thomas **II:** 236
mountain men **IV:** 247, 248
movies **IX:** 213
multiculturalism **X:** 200
Musgrove, Mary Bosomworth **II:** 238
music **VI:** 202
Narragansett **II:** 241
Natchez **I:** 251–252
Natchez Revolt **II:** 241–242
Navajo **II:** 247
Neolin **II:** 248–249
New Amsterdam **II:** 249
New Hampshire **II:** 251
New Jersey **II:** 253
New Mexico **II:** 254–255
New Netherland **II:** 256, 257

New Orleans **II:** 258
New Orleans, Battle of
    (1815) **IV:** 262
New Spain **I:** 260
New Spain (Mexico),
    northern frontier of **III:**
    257, 258
New York **II:** 259, 260
Nez Perce War **VI:**
    212–213
Nicolet, Jean **II:** 263
North Carolina **II:**
    263–265
Northwest Coast Indians
    II: 265–266
Northwest Ordinances **III:**
    263
Oglethorpe, James Edward
    II: 267
Ohio Company of Virginia
    III: 265
Oñate, Juan de **I:** 271
Opechancanough **II:** 268
Oregon Trail **IV:** 267, 268
Ostenaco **II:** 269
Paris, Treaty of **III:** 273
Parker, Ely Samuel **V:**
    264–265
Passamaquoddy **I:** 278
Paxton Boys **II:** 272
Pea Ridge/Elkhorn Tavern,
    Battle of **V:** 265
Pennsylvania **II:** 274, 276
Pequot **II:** 278
Pequot War **II:** 279
Permanent Indian Frontier
    IV: 279
Pike, Zebulon
    Montgomery **IV:** 281,
    282
Pilgrims **II:** 283
Pima revolt **II:** 283–284
Plymouth **II:** 287–288
Pocahontas **II:** 288–289
polygamy **IV:** 285
Pontiac's Rebellion **III:**
    280–281
Popé **II:** 290
population **II:** 242, 245m
population trends **I:**
    289–291; **II:** 290; **V:**
    279; **VII:** 234
postal service **II:** 292
Pott, John **II:** 293
Powhatan **I:** 292
Powhatan (chief) **II:** 293
Powhatan Confederacy **II:**
    294–295
praying towns **II:**
    295–296
Proclamation of 1763 **III:**
    287

Prophet, the Shawnee **III:**
    287, 289
Pueblo **II:** 303
pueblo **I:** 295–296
Quakers **III:** 291
race and racial conflict **II:**
    311–312; **III:** 295; **IV:**
    289, 291, 292; **VII:**
    247–249; **VIII:** 289
railroads **V:** 290
recreation **X:** 263
Red Cloud **VI:** 239–240
Red Jacket **III:** 296–297
Red Shoes **II:** 312–313
reducción **I:** 306–307
religion **II:** 317–318; **IV:**
    296; **VI:** 243, 245
Requerimiento **I:** 311
resistance **IV:** 255–256
revitalization movements
    II: 319–320
and the Revolution **III:**
    253–256, 254m
RFRA **X:** 266
Rhode Island **II:** 320
Rocky Mountain Fur
    Company **IV:** 302
Roman Catholics **II:** 323,
    324
rural life **III:** 312
Sacagawea **III:** 315
St. Clair, Arthur **III:** 316
Santa Fe **I:** 319–320
Santa Fe Trail **IV:** 306
scalping **II:** 329–330
Schurz, Carl **VI:** 257
Scotch-Irish **III:** 322
Scott, Winfield **IV:** 310
Secotan **I:** 321
segregation **VII:** 280
Seminole wars **IV:**
    311–312
Seneca **I:** 321
Sepúlveda, Juan Ginés de
    I: 322
Serra, Junípero **II:**
    331–332
Seven Years' War **II:** 332,
    333–334
shamans **II:** 334–335
Sheridan, Philip H. **V:** 319
Sherman, William T. **V:**
    321
silver **I:** 325
Sioux wars **VI:** 263
Sitting Bull **VI:** 263–264
slave resistance **II:** 337
slavery **I:** 326, 327; **II:** 338,
    339
slave trade **II:** 343
smallpox **I:** 330, 331; **II:**
    345

Smith, Jedediah Strong **IV:**
    321, 322
socialism **VI:** 267
society, British American
    II: 349, 351–352
Society for the Propagation
    of the Gospel in Foreign
    Parts **II:** 352
Sooners **VI:** 271
Soto, Hernando de **I:** 333
South Carolina **II:** 353
South Carolina Regulation
    III: 330, 331
South Pass **IV:** 324
Spanish colonies **II:** 357
sports **VII:** 295
Squanto **II:** 360–361
suffrage **II:** 363–364
Supreme Court decision
    IV: 331
Susquehannock War **II:**
    364
Sutter, John **IV:** 332
technology **II:** 369
Tecumseh **III:** 345
Teedyuscung **II:** 370
Termination policy **IX:**
    297–298
Texas **IV:** 337, 338
Texas, Republic of **IV:**
    340
Texas Revolution **IV:** 339
Thames, Battle of the **IV:**
    342
theater **II:** 373
Thoreau, Henry David **IV:**
    342
Timucua **I:** 351
Tippecanoe, Battle of **III:**
    347
tobacco **II:** 373
Tomochichi **II:** 375
trade and shipping **II:**
    375
Trail of Tears **IV:** 343–344
travel **II:** 377
Treaty of Paris **II:** 378
Tuscarora **II:** 378–379
Tuscarora War **II:** 379
Van Rensselaer, Maria Van
    Cortlandt **II:** 381
Virginia **II:** 382, 385
Virginia Company of
    London **II:** 387
Vitoria, Francisco de **I:**
    369–370
war and warfare **II:** 391
Ward, Nancy **II:** 392
War Hawks **IV:** 355
War of 1812 **IV:** 356, 358
Washington, George **III:**
    366

Watie, Stand **V:** 390–391
Wayne, Anthony **III:**
    369–370
Weiser, Johann Conrad **II:**
    393
western United States **IV:**
    257–258
Westo **II:** 394–395
Wheelock, Eleazar **II:**
    395–396
White, Andrew **II:** 396
Wilderness Road **III:** 378
Williams, Roger **II:** 400
wolves **I:** 405
women's rights and status
    II: 406–{2: }410; **III:**
    382; **IV:** 368–369
Woolman, John **II:** 410
World War II **VIII:** 389
yellow fever **II:** 414
Zeisberger, David **II:** 415
Zuni **I:** 383
Native Americans (Caribbean)
    Arawak **I:** 12
    Columbus, Christopher **I:**
        82
    Cortés, Hernán **I:** 91
    encomienda **I:** 122
    Jamaica **I:** 187
    Nevis **I:** 254
    Taino **I:** 342
Native Americans (Central
    America)
    Aztecs **I:** 17–22
    Cabeza de Vaca, Álvar
        Núñez **I:** 38
    Columbus, Christopher **I:**
        82
    encomienda **I:** 122
    Guerrero, Gonzalo **I:** 146
    Maya **I:** 225–229
    Nahua **I:** 249
    Tarascan **I:** 343
    Toltecs **I:** 354–358
Native Americans (South
    America)
    Amazon River **I:** 8
    Arawak **I:** 12
    Brazil **I:** 31
    Carib **I:** 56
    El Dorado **I:** 118
    encomienda **I:** 122
    Inca **I:** 175–177
    Léry, Jean de **I:** 205
    Tupinambá **I:** 361
Native Americans in the War of
    1812 **IV: 258–260**
Native America Party **IV:** 180
Native Son (Wright) **VIII:** 3,
    191, 192, 399, 409c
Native Sons and Daughters of
    the Golden West **VIII:** 26

nativism **III:** 173; **V:** 176, 177, **251**, 254, 255, 300–301; **VI:** 209; **VII:** 11, 14, 124, **208–209**
  American Protective Association **VI:** 11–12
  anti-Catholic riots **IV:** 21, 23
  anti-Semitism **VIII:** 19
  Asian Americans **VIII:** 26
  Catholics **VIII:** 53
  Democratic Party **IV:** 108
  immigration **IV:** 179–180; **VI:** 140; **VIII:** 162
  immigration restrictions **VI:** 140, 141
  Know-Nothing Party **IV:** 201–202
  labor trends **VI:** 171
  race and race relations **IV:** 292
  refugees **VIII:** 298
  religion **VIII:** 303
  Republican Party **IV:** 300–301
NATO. *See* North Atlantic Treaty Organization
"Natural and Civil History of California, A" (Miguel Venegas) **II:** *49*
natural gas **X:** 49, 58, 104
natural history **II:** 110, 277, 330
naturalists/naturalism **IV:** 34–35, 342–343; **VI:** 176, 178
Naturalization Act of 1790 **III:** 173; **IV:** 289
Naturalization Act of 1795 **III:** 396c
Naturalization Act of 1798 **III:** 9, 396c
naturalization law **III:** 173
natural philosophy **II:** 37, 110, 322, 330–331; **IV:** 308
natural resources **VI:** 65
natural selection **VI:** 265
natural theology **II:** 110
Nature (Emerson) **IV:** 126, 212, 345, 377c
Nature's Divine Revelations (Davis) **IV:** 299
nature vs. nurture **VII:** 131
Nauman, Bruce **X:** 26
Nauset **II:** 212, 236
Nautilus (Fulton submarine) **III:** 141
Nautilus, USS **IX:** 23
Nauvoo, Illinois **IV:** **260–261**
  Cabet, Étienne **IV:** 61
  Church of Jesus Christ of Latter-day Saints **IV:** 80
  Deseret, State of **IV:** 109
  Mormon Trail **IV:** 242

  Smith, Joseph, Jr. **IV:** 323–324
  Young, Brigham **IV:** 371, 372
Nauvoo Charter **IV:** 80
Nauvoo Expositor **IV:** 260, 324
Nauvoo temple **IV:** 260
Navagero, Andrea, Girolamo **I:** 304
Navajo code talkers **VIII:** 236, *236*
Navajo nation **I:** 166, 255, 257, 320; **II:** 165, 166, **247**, 303, 317; **IV:** 76, 378c; **V:** 406c; **X:** 215
Naval Disarmament Conference **VII:** 146, **209–210**, 338
naval stores **II:** 201, 221, 222, 224, 251, 376
Naval Stores Act **II:** 265
naval warfare **VIII:** 11. *See* Confederate navy; *Monitor-Merrimack*; Union navy
Navarre **I:** 63, 281
Navidad, Hispaniola **I:** 39, 161
navies **II:** 204, 221, 231
navigation **II:** 141
  Cabot, Sebastian **I:** 42
  Columbus, Bartholomew **I:** 78–79
  Dias, Bartholomeu **I:** 104–106
  Gama, Vasco da **I:** 137
  Henry the Navigator **I:** 158
  invention and technology **I:** 179
Navigation Acts **III:** 322. *See* Acts of Trade and Navigation
Navigationi e Viaggi (Giovanni Battista Ramusio) **I:** 44, 305
Navigatio (Saint Brendan the Navigator) **I:** 34
Navy, U.S. **III:** 190; **IV:** 379c; **VII:** 134, 310; **VIII:** **236–237**, 408c, 410c; **IX:** 77, 329c; **X:** 56–57. *See also* Union navy
  African Americans **VIII:** 3
  air power **VIII:** 11
  amphibious warfare **VIII:** 15
  Annapolis Naval Academy **V:** 373
  Army, U.S. **VIII:** 19
  Arthur, Chester Alan **VI:** 17
  Atlantic, Battle of the **VIII:** 28
  Axis **VIII:** 32
  Casablanca Conference **VIII:** 52
  censorship **VIII:** 55

  Chilean-American relations **VI:** 50
  code breaking **VIII:** 64
  Confederate navy **V:** 74
  Coral Sea, Battle of the **VIII:** 74
  Decatur, Stephen **IV:** 104–105
  demobilization **VIII:** 79
  Dewey, George **VI:** 79
  espionage **VIII:** 104
  Essex, USS **IV:** 130
  foreign policy **IV:** 141; **VI:** 103, 104
  Forrestal, James V. **VIII:** 126
  gays and lesbians **VIII:** 130
  Guadalcanal **VIII:** 141
  King, Ernest J. **VIII:** 177
  Lafitte, Jean **IV:** 205, 206
  Leahy, William D. **VIII:** 183–184
  Leyte Gulf, Battle for **VIII:** 186–187
  Mahan, Alfred Thayer **VI:** 186
  Mariana Islands **VIII:** 202
  Midway, Battle of **VIII:** 211
  mobilization **VIII:** 214
  MOWM **VIII:** 201
  Nimitz, Chester W. **VIII:** 246
  Okinawa **VIII:** 259
  Philippine Sea, Battle of the **VIII:** 267
  Porter, David Dixon **V:** 280
  race and racial conflict **VIII:** 288
  Semmes, Raphael **V:** 313
  shipbuilding **VIII:** 324
  Sicily **VIII:** 325
  Solomon Islands **VIII:** 330
  Stockton, Robert Field **IV:** 328
  submarines **VIII:** 342
  Tarawa **VIII:** 350
  War of 1812 **IV:** 356
  WAVES **VIII:** 379–380
  Welles, Gideon **V:** 391
  World War II **VIII:** 388
  World War II Pacific theater **VIII:** 398
  WPB **VIII:** 375
Navy Department, Confederate **V:** 75, 221–222
Navy Department, United States **V:** 389, 391; **VII:** 266; **VIII:** 312, 376; **IX:** 224
Navy Nurse Corps **VIII:** 380
NAWSA. *See* National American Woman Suffrage Association

Nayler, James **II:** 307
Nazi Ministry of Propaganda and Popular Enlightenment **VIII:** 282
Nazi Party **VIII:** 131, 164
Nazism **VII:** 160. *See also* neo-Nazism
  civil rights **VIII:** 62
  Holocaust **VIII:** 149–150
  Jews **VIII:** 173
  Owens, Jesse **VIII:** 260–261
  refugees **VIII:** 298, 299
  sports **VIII:** 337, 338
Nazism, American **VIII:** 13, 19. *See also* neo-Nazism
Nazi-Soviet Pact **VIII:** **237–238**, 408c
  Axis **VIII:** 31
  Communists **VIII:** 65
  foreign policy **VIII:** 124
  Popular Front **VIII:** 276
  Robeson, Paul **VIII:** 309
  Soviet-American relations **VIII:** 333
  Teheran Conference **VIII:** 354
Nazi sympathizers **VIII:** 72
NBA (National Basketball Association) **IX:** 281; **X:** 285
NBC. *See* National Broadcasting Corporation
NBC Blue **VIII:** 290
NBC Red **VIII:** 290
NCAI **VIII:** 236
NCL. *See* National Consumers League
Ndongo **I:** 229–230, 267, 326
Ndowe **I:** 127
NDRA (National Dress Reform Association) **V:** 123
NEA. *See* National Endowment for the Arts
Neal, Claude **VIII:** 287
Neale, John **II:** 175–176
Neamatha **IV:** 312
NEA (National Endowment for the Arts) **X:** 209
Near East **I:** 114
Near v. Minnesota el rel. Olson **VII:** 275; **VIII:** 55, 405c
Neau, Elias **II:** 7, 352
Nebraska **V:** 31, 197; **VI:** 208; **X:** 107, 242, 330c
Nebraska Territory **IV:** 85, 155, 300
Neebe, Oscar **VI:** 127
Neff, Mary **II:** 97
Negro Air Corps **VIII:** *4*
Negro American Labor Council **VIII:** 291
negro cloth **II:** 65

Negro Convention movement **IV: 261**

Negro Eastern League **VII:** 295

Negroes and the War (OWI) **VIII:** 257–258

Negro fellowship league **VI:** 312

Negro Leagues **VIII:** 336; **IX:** 5, 280; **X:** 1

Negro National League **VII:** 27, 295

Negro Plot of 1741 **II: 7, 247–248,** 262, 263, 337

Negroponte, John D. **X:** 308

Negros. *See* African Americans

Negro Seaman's Act of 1823 **IV:** 354

Negro World **VII:** 315

NEH. *See* National Endowment for the Humanities

Nehru, Jawaharlal **IX:** 54

Nell, William C. **IV:** 379*c*

Nelson, Byron **VIII:** 337

Nelson, Donald M. **VIII: 238**
   dollar-a-year men **VIII:** 84
   mobilization **VIII:** 214
   OPM **VIII:** 255
   OWM **VIII:** 258
   WPB **VIII:** 375–376

Nelson, Gaylord **X:** 76, 93

Nelson, Hugh **IV:** 100

Nelson, Ted **X:** 153

Nelson, Willie **X:** 16

Nemattanew **II:** 268, 295

neoclassical architecture **III:** 18

neoclassical movement **VII:** 17

neoconservatism **IX:** 68–69; **X: 215–216**
   Catholic Bishops' Letter **X:** 59–60
   conservative movement **X:** 79, 80

neoexpressionism **X:** 26

"neo-isolationism" **X:** 24

Neolin **II:** 114, **248–249,** 320; **III:** 281

neo-Nazism **VIII:** 13, 60, 72

Neo-Orthodoxy **VIII:** 304

NEPA. *See* National Environmental Policy Act of 1970

Neptune **X:** 283

Nethercutt, George **X:** 119

Netherlands **III:** 2; **IV:** 4, 156, 280; **VII:** 360*c*; **VIII:** 39, 398; **IX:** 194, 231–233, 316; **X:** 223. *See also* Dutch exploration; Dutch trade
   Blaeu, Willem **I:** 31
   Brazil **I:** 33
   British Empire **II:** 41
   Castile **I:** 64

Dutch East India Company **I:** 114

Gates, Sir Thomas **II:** 135

Gorée Island **I:** 145

Hudson, Henry **II:** 158

invention and technology **I:** 180

Jews **II:** 175

Jews (Judaism) **I:** 192

Las Casas, Bartolomé de **I:** 198

New Netherland **II:** 255, 256

New York **II:** 260

Philip II **I:** 282

Reformation **I:** 309

São Tomé **I:** 320

slave trade **II:** 343

Spanish Armada **I:** 333

Van Rensselaer, Maria Van Cortlandt **II:** 381

Netscape Navigator **X:** 274

Netsilik **II:** 167

networking (telecommunications) **X:** 152, 153, 187, 274

networks, broadcast **VII:** 254

networks, television **X:** 241, 294, 296. *See also specific networks*

Neumann, John von **VIII:** 353; **IX:** 63, 64

Neunendorff, Aldof **VI:** 23

neutrality **VII: 210,** 358*c*
   Committee for Public Information **VII:** 51
   Democratic Party **VII:** 66
   foreign policy **VII:** 99
   Preparedness **VII:** 235
   Wilson, Woodrow **VII:** 334
   World War I **VII:** 343
   Zimmermann telegram **VII:** 353

neutrality, European **V:** 132

Neutrality Acts **VIII: 238–239,** 408*c,* 419–421
   aircraft industry **VIII:** 10
   America First Committee **VIII:** 13
   Anglo-American relations **VIII:** 16
   Borah, William E. **VIII:** 40
   cash-and-carry **VIII:** 52–53
   Congress **VIII:** 67
   destroyers-for-bases deal **VIII:** 83
   Ethiopia **VIII:** 105
   foreign policy **VIII:** 124
   isolationists **VIII:** 166
   La Follette, Robert M., Jr. **VIII:** 182

Munich Conference **VIII:** 220

Nye Committee **VIII:** 250

Popular Front **VIII:** 276

Roosevelt, Franklin D. **VIII:** 313, 314

Spanish Civil War **VIII:** 335

Neutrality Proclamation **III:** 130, **256,** 395*c*–396*c*

Neutrality Treaty of 1977 **X:** 233

Neutral nation **II:** 31, 168, 169

neutral rights **IV:** 356

Nevada **IV:** 95–96; **VI:** 51*m;* **X:** 107, 242

Nevada Test Site (nuclear weapons) **IX:** 23

Nevelson, Louise **IX:** 20

Neville, John **III:** 375

Nevis **I:** 254; **II:** 374

New Age movement **X: 216–217**

New American Poverty, The (Michael Harrington) **IX:** 130

New Amstel **II:** 257

New Amsterdam **II:** *249,* **249–250,** 417*c*
   Delaware **II:** 87
   Dutch-Indian Wars **II:** 99
   Dutch Reformed Church **II:** 97
   fur trade **II:** 130–131
   Herrman, Augustine **II:** 156
   Jews **II:** 175
   Lutherans **II:** 201
   monarchy, British **II:** 232
   New Netherland **II:** 255, 257
   New York **II:** 259
   New York City **II:** 262
   Van Rensselaer, Maria Van Cortlandt **II:** 381

New Andalucía **I:** 118

New Archangel **II:** 326

Newark, New Jersey **IV:** 82

New Bent's Fort **IV:** 48

New Bern **II:** 146–147

New Brunswick, Canada **I:** 219, 278; **IV:** 25

Newburgh conspiracy **III: 256–257**

Newcastle, duke of **III:** 54

New Christian Right **X:** 79

"New Colossus, The" (Lazarus) **VI:** 173, 276

Newcombe, Don **IX:** 260

New Deal **III:** 365; **VIII:** xiii, **239–243,** 406*c*–408*c;* **IX:** 330*c;* **X:** 174. *See also* New Deal, First; New Deal, Second; New Deal, Third

African Americans **VIII:** 3

Agricultural Adjustment Act **VIII:** 5–6

agriculture **VIII:** 7, 8; **IX:** 8

American Federation of Labor **VIII:** 14

American Liberty League **VIII:** 14–15

Americans for Democratic Action **IX:** 13

antimonopoly **VIII:** 17–18

anti-Semitism **VIII:** 19

art **VII:** 20

art and architecture **VIII:** 22, 23

Asian Americans **VIII:** 26

automobile industry **VIII:** 30

Banking Act of 1933 **VIII:** 33

Banking Act of 1935 **VIII:** 33–34

Baruch, Bernard M. **VII:** 25; **VIII:** 34

Bethune, Mary McLeod **VIII:** 36

Black, Hugo L. **VIII:** 37

Black Cabinet **VIII:** 37

Borah, William E. **VIII:** 40

Brain Trust **VIII:** 41

Brandeis, Louis **VII:** 35

Bridges, Harry **VIII:** 43

business **VIII:** 47, 48

Byrnes, James F. **VIII:** 48

Catholics **VIII:** 53, 54

CCC **VIII:** 63–64

children **VIII:** 56

cities and urban life **VIII:** 58–60

civil rights **VIII:** 61

Communists **VIII:** 65

Congress **VIII:** 66–68

conservatism **VIII:** 72, 73

conservative coalition **VIII:** 73, 74

Coughlin, Father Charles E. **VIII:** 75

court-packing plan **VIII:** 76–77

criminal justice **VII:** 60

CWA **VIII:** 62–63

Democratic Party **VIII:** 81, 82; **IX:** 79

Dempsey, Jack **VII:** 67

dollar-a-year men **VIII:** 84

Douglas, William O. **VIII:** 84

Dust Bowl **VIII:** 87

Eccles, Marriner S. **VIII:** 89

New Deal (continued)
 economy **VIII**: 91–92; **IX**: 88
 education **VIII**: 93
 elderly **VIII**: 95
 election of 1932 **VIII**: 96
 election of 1936 **VIII**: 97
 election of 1944 **VIII**: 99
 Emergency Banking Act of 1933 **VIII**: 100–101
 Emergency Relief Appropriation Act **VIII**: 101–102
 environmental issues **VIII**: 103
 ethnic organizations **VII**: 89
 Executive Reorganization Act **VIII**: 107
 Fair Deal **IX**: 107
 FAP **VIII**: 114
 FBI **VIII**: 115
 FCA **VIII**: 111–112
 FCC **VIII**: 116
 FDIC **VIII**: 117
 FHA **VIII**: 118–119
 FMP **VIII**: 119–120
 folk music revival **IX**: 110
 Food, Drug, and Cosmetic Act **VIII**: 123
 Four Freedoms **VIII**: 127
 Frankfurter, Felix **VIII**: 127
 FSA **VIII**: 112–113
 FTP **VIII**: 120–121
 FWP **VIII**: 121
 Garner, John Nance **VIII**: 129
 German Americans **VIII**: 131
 government **VIII**: 134, 135
 Great Depression **VIII**: 138, 140, 141
 Harriman, Averell **VIII**: 143
 Hearst, William Randolph **VII**: 121
 Henderson, Leon **VIII**: 144, 145
 Hillman, Sidney **VIII**: 145
 HOLC **VIII**: 150–151
 Hoover, Herbert **VIII**: 152
 Hoover presidency **VIII**: 153
 Hopkins, Harry **VIII**: 156–157
 House Un-American Activities Committee **IX**: 137
 housing **VIII**: 157
 Hughes, Charles Evans **VII**: 124

 Ickes, Harold L. **VIII**: 161
 Indian Reorganization Act **VIII**: 163
 influence of **IX**: **229–230**
 Irish Americans **VIII**: 165
 Italian Americans **VIII**: 167
 Jews **VIII**: 173
 Johnson, Hugh S. **VIII**: 173
 Jones, Jesse H. **VIII**: 174
 Kennedy, Joseph P. **VIII**: 176
 Keynesianism **VIII**: 176–177
 labor **VIII**: 179
 La Follette, Robert M., Jr. **VIII**: 182
 La Guardia, Fiorello **VIII**: 182
 Landon, Alfred M. **VIII**: 183
 Lewis, John L. **VIII**: 186
 liberalism **VIII**: 187, 188; **IX**: 179
 Lilienthal, David E. **VIII**: 190
 literature **VIII**: 192
 London Economic Conference **VIII**: 193
 Long, Huey P. **VIII**: 194
 marriage and family life **VIII**: 204
 Mexican Repatriation Program **VIII**: 211
 modern Republicanism **IX**: 208
 Moley, Raymond C. **VIII**: 216
 Morgenthau, Henry **VIII**: 216
 Murray, Philip **VIII**: 221
 NAACP **VIII**: 227
 Native Americans **VIII**: 235
 Nelson, Donald M. **VIII**: 238
 Neutrality Acts **VIII**: 239
 news media **VIII**: 243
 NIRA **VIII**: 228
 NLRB **VIII**: 229–231
 Norris, George W. **VIII**: 248
 NRA **VIII**: 231–232
 NRPB **VIII**: 232
 NYA **VIII**: 234
 OWI **VIII**: 258
 Perkins, Frances **VIII**: 265
 photography **VIII**: 268
 Polish Americans **VIII**: 269
 politics in the Roosevelt era **VIII**: 270, 271

 popular culture **VIII**: 273, 275
 Popular Front **VIII**: 276
 presidency **VIII**: 280, 281
 progressivism **VII**: 238
 propaganda **VIII**: 283
 Public Utility Holding Company Act **VIII**: 284
 PWA **VIII**: 285–286
 RA **VIII**: 307
 REA **VIII**: 315–316
 recession of 1937–38 **VIII**: 292, 293
 Reciprocal Trade Agreements Act **VIII**: 293–294
 relief **VIII**: 299
 Relief and Reconstruction Act **VIII**: 302
 religion **VIII**: 303, 304
 Republican Party **VIII**: 305, 306; **IX**: 258
 Revenue Act of 1935 **VIII**: 307–308
 RFC **VIII**: 294
 Roosevelt, Eleanor **VIII**: 311
 Roosevelt, Franklin D. **VIII**: 312
 Schechter Poultry Corporation v. United States **VIII**: 317
 SEC **VIII**: 321–322
 Second New Deal **VIII**: 321
 Smith, Alfred E. **VII**: 288
 socialists **VIII**: 327
 Social Security Act **VIII**: 328–330
 South **VIII**: 331–332
 stock market crash (1929) **VIII**: 341
 Supreme Court **VIII**: 344–347
 Taft, Robert A. **VIII**: 349
 taxation **VIII**: 350–352
 technology **VIII**: 354
 Third New Deal **VIII**: 357–358
 Thomas, Norman **VIII**: 358
 TNEC **VIII**: 355
 Townsend, Francis E. **VIII**: 358
 transportation **VIII**: 360
 Tugwell, Rexford G. **VIII**: 361
 TVA **VIII**: 356–357
 unemployment **VIII**: 363, 364
 Union Party **VIII**: 365
 USHA **VIII**: 367–368

 Wagner, Robert F. **VIII**: 372, 373
 Wallace, Henry A. **VIII**: 373
 War Industries Board **VII**: 330
 Wheeler, Burton K. **VIII**: 377–378
 Willkie, Wendell L. **VIII**: 378, 379
 women's network **VIII**: 383
 women's status and rights **VIII**: 384
 WPA **VIII**: 386–388
New Deal, First **VIII**: **122**
 Agricultural Adjustment Act **VIII**: 5
 antimonopoly **VIII**: 17
 Brain Trust **VIII**: 41
 Congress **VIII**: 67
 conservatism **VIII**: 71
 Coughlin, Father Charles E. **VIII**: 75
 economy **VIII**: 92
 FERA **VIII**: 118
 liberalism **VIII**: 188
 Moley, Raymond C. **VIII**: 216
 New Deal **VIII**: 241
 NRA **VIII**: 231–232
 PWA **VIII**: 285–286
 relief **VIII**: 301
 Roosevelt, Franklin D. **VIII**: 313
 Schechter Poultry Corporation v. United States **VIII**: 317
 Social Security Act **VIII**: 328
 Wallace, Henry A. **VIII**: 373
New Deal, Second **VIII**: **321**
 antimonopoly **VIII**: 18
 Banking Act of 1935 **VIII**: 33–34
 Byrnes, James F. **VIII**: 48
 Congress **VIII**: 67
 conservatism **VIII**: 72
 liberalism **VIII**: 188
 Long, Huey P. **VIII**: 195
 New Deal **VIII**: 241
 NLRB **VIII**: 230
 NYA **VIII**: 234
 Public Utility Holding Company Act **VIII**: 284–285
 relief **VIII**: 301
 Republican Party **VIII**: 305
 Revenue Act of 1935 **VIII**: 307–308

Roosevelt, Franklin D.
VIII: 313
*Schechter Poultry
Corporation v. United
States* **VIII:** 317
Social Security Act **VIII:**
328–330
Union Party **VIII:** 365
New Deal, Third **VIII:**
357–358
Executive Reorganization
Act **VIII:** 107
Full Employment Bill
VIII: 128
Keynesianism **VIII:** 176
liberalism **VIII:** 188
New Deal **VIII:** 242
recession of 1937–38 **VIII:**
293
TNEC **VIII:** 355
New Democracy **VII:** 34
New Democrats **X:** 133, 234,
237
New Echota, Georgia **IV:** 344,
377c
New Echota, Treaty of **IV:** 344,
377c; **V:** 390
New Economic Policy **X:** 94,
313
Newell, Robert **IV:** 302
New England **II:** 213m; **VIII:**
390; **X:** 242. *See also*
Dominion of New England
AASS **IV:** 362
African-American
churches, growth of **VI:**
4
African Americans **II:** 6
agriculture **II:** 12–13; **V:** 6;
VI: 8
Anglican Church **II:** 19,
20
animals **II:** 21
architecture **II:** 23; **III:**
18–20
Baptists **II:** 29; **III:** 34
Bulfinch, Charles **III:** 50
captivity **II:** 51
childhood **II:** 60
class **II:** 62
clothing **II:** 64
Congregationalists **II:** 68
Connecticut **II:** 68–70
Deerfield Massacre **II:**
84–85
Democratic-Republican
Party **III:** 104
disease **II:** 90–92
domesticity **II:** 93
Dominion of New England
II: 94–95
Dudley, Joseph **II:** 95

Dummer, Jeremiah **II:**
96–97
economy **IV:** 118
education **II:** 103; **III:**
113, 115; **IV:** 120; **V:**
108
English Civil War **II:** 108
English immigrants **II:**
108
environment **II:** 110–111
ethnocentrism **II:** 114
exploration **II:** 115
Federalist Party **III:** 126
fertility **II:** 117
fishing **II:** 118–119
foreign policy **IV:** 141
French immigrants **II:** 130
fur trade **II:** 130–131
gender **II:** 137
Ghent, Treaty of (1814) **IV:**
161
Glorious Revolution **II:**
141
government, British
American **II:** 142
Great Awakening **II:** 147,
148
Hartford Convention **IV:**
170, 171
housing **II:** 157
immigration restrictions
VI: 141
indentured servitude **II:**
165
industrialization **IV:** 184,
187
internal improvements **IV:**
188
iron manufacturing **II:** 167
Iroquois **II:** 168
King George's War **II:** 182
King Philip's War **II:** 183
Knight, Sarah Kemble **II:**
185–186
labor **II:** 189
land riots **III:** 201–202
Liberty Party **IV:** 210
limners **II:** 194
literature **IV:** 213
lumbering **II:** 201
lyceum movement **IV:** 215
manufacturing and
industry **II:** 204
marriage and family life **II:**
206–208
Massachuset Indians **I:**
224–225
Massachusetts **II:** 214
Metacom **II:** 223
mortality **II:** 234, 235
Native Americans **II:** 243,
246

New Amsterdam **II:** 250
New Hampshire **II:**
250–252
New Jersey **II:** 253
New South **VI:** 210
New York **II:** 260, 262
Panic of 1819 **IV:** 275
Patrons of Husbandry **VI:**
222
Pequot War **II:** 279
population trends **II:**
290–291, 298
praying towns **II:** 295–296
primogeniture and entail
II: 297
Protestantism **II:** 302
Puritans **I:** 299; **II:** 306
Quakers **II:** 308
Queen Anne's War
II: 309
railroads **IV:** 295
religion **II:** 316; **III:** 298;
IV: 297–298
religion, Native American
II: 317
religious liberty **III:**
300–301
Rhode Island **II:** 320–322
rum trade **II:** 326
scalping **II:** 329
secession **V:** 311
Slater, Samuel **III:**
325–326
Smith, John **II:** 347
society, British American
II: 349–350
spinsters **II:** 360
Squanto **II:** 360
Stuyvesant, Peter **II:** 363
suffrage **II:** 364
tariffs **V:** 348
tenants **II:** 371
trade and shipping
II: 376
travel **II:** 377
Virginia Company of
London **II:** 387
War Hawks **IV:** 355
War of 1812 **IV:** 356
Warren, Josiah **IV:** 358
Webster, Daniel **IV:** 359
Welles, Gideon **V:** 391
witchcraft **II:** 402
women's rights and status
II: 406, 407, 409; **III:**
381
Youngs, John **II:** 414
New England Anti-Slavery
Society **IV:** 3, 8, 148
New England Company **II:** 216
New England Confederation **II:**
51, 68, 94, 212, 287

New England Emigrant Aid
Company **IV:** 223, 224; **V:** 31
New England Farm **IV:** 27
New England Farmhouse **IV:**
27
New England Female Medical
College **VI:** 318
New England Mississippi Land
Company **III:** 388
New England Non-Resistant
Society **IV:** 147
*New England Psalm Singer: or
American Chorister* (Billings)
III: 38
"New England Renaissance" **IV:**
212
New England school (music)
VI: 201
New England Woman Suffrage
Association **VI:** 36, 133
"new fire ceremony" **I:** 21
Newfoundland **I:** 385c, 388c; **II:**
50, 163, 209, 232, 309; **III:**
394c. *See also* Vinland
Cabot, John **I:** 41
Cartier, Jacques **I:** 57
Cathay (China) **I:** 65
Gilbert, Sir Humphrey **I:**
142
Parmenius, Stephen **I:** 278
Peckham, Sir George **I:**
279
Vinland **I:** 369
New Fourteenth Street Theater
VI: 203
New France **I:** 149, 219, 387c.
See also Canada; Quebec
British Empire **II:** 43
Brulé, Étienne **II:** 44
Champlain, Samuel de **II:**
56
French colonies **II:** 128m
Hendrick **II:** 155
Huron **II:** 160
Jesuits **II:** 174
Jolliet, Louis **II:** 178
Monckton, Robert **II:** 232
theater **II:** 373
New Freedom **VII: 210–211**
agriculture **VII:** 7
elections **VII:** 80
Federal Farm Loan Act
VII: 92
Federal Trade
Commission Act
VII: 94
New Nationalism **VII:**
212
progressivism **VII:** 238
rural life **VII:** 268
Wilson, Woodrow **VII:**
333–334

New Frontier **IX:** 16, **230**, 230, **230**, 230, 241
New Frontier Media **X:** 244
New Galicia **I:** 258
New Grenada **I:** 118; **II:** 356; **IV:** 378c. *See also* Colombia
New Guinea **I:** 114; **VIII:** 15, 330, 398
New Hampshire **II: 250–252;** **III:** 188; **IV:** 104; **V:** 275; **X:** 206, 242
   Abenaki **I:** 2
   Albany Congress **II:** 14
   disease **II:** 92
   Dominion of New England **II:** 94
   Dudley, Joseph **II:** 95
   education **II:** 103
   food **II:** 122
   Great Awakening **II:** 149
   lumbering **II:** 201
   mills **II:** 225
   monarchy, British **II:** 232
   Randolph, Edward **II:** 312
   Vermont **II:** 381
   Wheelwright, John **II:** 396
New Harmony, Indiana
   Owen, Robert **IV:** 273
   religion **IV:** 299
   Warren, Josiah **IV:** 358
   Wright, Fanny **IV:** 369
New Harmony *Gazette* **IV:** 369
New Haven, Connecticut **II:** 68–70; **IV:** 184
   Massachusetts **II:** 212
   Massachusetts School Act **II:** 216
   Rhode Island **II:** 321
   society, British American **II:** 350
   Winthrop, John **II:** 402
   Yale College **II:** 413
New Helvetia, California **IV:** 332
New Hope Church, Battle of **V:** 19
New Hospital and London School of Medicine for Women **VI:** 31
New Icaria **IV:** 61
"new immigration" **V:** 278; **VI:** 138–139
New Industrial State, The (John Kenneth Galbraith) **IX:** 117
New Ironsides, USS **V:** 183
New Jersey **II: 252–254,** 418c; **V:** 226; **VI:** 53, 294; **VII:** 257; **X:** 20, 143, 242
   agriculture **II:** 11
   architecture **II:** 23
   Bernard, Francis **III:** 37–38

Brainerd, David **II:** 40
Carteret, Philip **II:** 54
Delaware **II:** 89
economy **II:** 101
English immigrants **II:** 108
Franklin, William **III:** 136
Frelinghuysen, Theodorus Jacobus **II:** 125
Glorious Revolution **II:** 141
government, British American **II:** 144
Great Awakening **II:** 147
housing **II:** 157
Hyde, Edward, Viscount Cornbury **II:** 162
iron manufacturing **II:** 167
Kalm, Peter **II:** 181
Livingston, William **III:** 216–217
Logan, James **II:** 198
Morris, Lewis **II:** 234
Penn, William **II:** 273
population trends **II:** 291
Powhatan Confederacy **II:** 295
Quakers **II:** 308
slavery **II:** 338
Smith, Robert **II:** 348
suffrage **III:** 336
taverns and inns **II:** 367
Tennent, Gilbert **II:** 371
Tennent, William, Jr. **II:** 372
travel **II:** 377
women's rights and status **II:** 407; **III:** 381
New Jersey Plan **III:** 82, 395c
"new journalism" **VI:** 212
"Newlanders" **II:** 231
Newlands, Francis G. **VII:** 203
Newlands Act. *See* National Reclamation Act
New Laws (1542) **I:** 122, 199–200, 370
New Left **IX: 230–231,** 333c; **X:** 215, 216
   Hayden, Tom **IX:** 131
   Mills, C. Wright **IX:** 205
   SANE **IX:** 267
   Students for a Democratic Society **IX:** 286
   women's status and rights **IX:** 325
New Light Log College **II:** 254
New Lights
   Chauncy, Charles **II:** 57
   Congregationalists **II:** 68
   Connecticut **II:** 70
   Davies, Samuel **II:** 84
   Great Awakening **II:** 148
   Presbyterians **II:** 296

Princeton College **II:** 298
   Tennent, Gilbert **II:** 371
   Tennent, William, Jr. **II:** 372
New London, Connecticut **II:** 12, 84, 186
New London Society for Trade and Commerce **II:** 69
New Look policy **IX:** 82–83, 140
New Lost City Ramblers **IX:** 111
New Madrid earthquake **IV:** 47, **261–262,** 306
Newman, Charles **X:** 177
New Men of Power (C. Wright Mills) **IX:** 204
New Mexico **I: 254–257,** 255, 388c; **II: 254–255; IV:** xiii; **V:** 7, 406c; **VI:** 14, 112; **X:** 143, 215, 242
   agriculture **II:** 9
   Alvarado, Pedro de **I:** 8
   art **II:** 25
   Becknell, William **IV:** 45
   Bent, Charles **IV:** 47–48
   Bent's Fort **IV:** 51
   Clay, Henry **IV:** 87, 88
   Compromise of 1850 **IV:** 93–95, 94m
   Coronado, Francisco **I:** 88
   De Vargas, Diego **II:** 89
   exploration **II:** 115; **IV:** 130
   Fort Leavenworth **IV:** 145
   Great Plains Indians **II:** 150
   Guadalupe Hidalgo, Treaty of (1848) **IV:** 165–166
   Hopi **I:** 167
   Indians of the Desert Southwest **II:** 165–166
   Lamy, Jean Baptiste **IV:** 207
   Manifest Destiny **IV:** 218
   Mexican-American War **IV:** 232, 234
   missions **II:** 229, 231
   Native Americans **II:** 244, 246
   New Spain **I:** 258
   Oñate, Juan de **I:** 271
   pueblo **I:** 295–296
   Pueblo Indians **II:** 303
   Pueblo Revolt **II:** 303–304
   Roman Catholics **II:** 324
   Santa Fe **I:** 319–320
   Santa Fe Trail **IV:** 305
   Taylor, Zachary **IV:** 335
   Texas **IV:** 339
   Zuni **I:** 383
New Mexico Territory **VI:** 51m
New Model Army **II:** 108

new modernism **X:** 27
New Nationalism **VII: 211–212**
   elections **VII:** 80
   Federal Trade Commission Act **VII:** 94
   New Freedom **VII:** 210
   Progressive Party **VII:** 236
   progressivism **VII:** 238
   Roosevelt, Theodore **VII:** 266
   Taft, William Howard **VII:** 304
New Negro, An Interpretation (Locke) **VII:** 119, 164
New Netherland **II: 255–257,** 256m
   British Empire **II:** 41
   Delaware **II:** 87
   Dutch-Indian Wars **II:** 98–99
   Dutch West India Company **II:** 98
   government, British American **II:** 144
   Herrman, Augustine **II:** 156
   Hudson, Henry **II:** 159
   Kieft, Willem **II:** 182
   Leisler's Rebellion **II:** 192
   Minuit, Peter **II:** 226–227
   New Amsterdam **II:** 250
   New Jersey **II:** 252, 253
   New York **II:** 259–260
   Pennsylvania **II:** 274
   Stuyvesant, Peter **II:** 362–363
   Youngs, John **II:** 414
New Netherland Company **II:** 255
New Orange **II:** 261, 262
New Orleans **II: 258,** 419c; **III:** 396c; **V:** 407c; **VI:** 185, 203; **VII:** 137; **X:** 137
   architecture **II:** 23
   Beauregard, Pierre **V:** 27
   Benjamin, Judah P. **V:** 27–28
   Butler, Benjamin **V:** 46
   Choctaw nation **III:** 68
   cities and urban life **II:** 61; **IV:** 82
   Claiborne, William C. C. **IV:** 85
   Corps d'Afrique **V:** 83
   Creole **II:** 74
   diseases and epidemics **IV:** 112
   Farragut, David G. **V:** 121
   foreign policy **IV:** 141
   French colonies **II:** 129
   gender **II:** 137

Hood, John Bell **V:** 171
Le Moyne, Jean-Baptiste, sieur de Bienville **II:** 193
Lewis and Clark Expedition **III:** 210
Lincoln, Abraham **V:** 209
Longstreet, James **V:** 215
Louisiana **II:** 199, 200
Louisiana Purchase **III:** 218
marine corps **V:** 222
Marquette, Jacques **II:** 205
Mississippi River **V:** 234
Pinchback, Pinckney B. S. **V:** 275–276
railroads **IV:** 293, 295
San Lorenzo, Treaty of **III:** 317
scalawags **V:** 308
slavery **II:** 338
Treaty of Paris **II:** 378
Warmoth, Henry C. **V:** 388
New Orleans, Battle of (1815) **IV: 262–263,** 263m, 375c
Bowie, Jim **IV:** 56
Era of Good Feelings **IV:** 127
foreign policy **IV:** 141
Ghent, Treaty of (1814) **IV:** 161
Jackson, Andrew **IV:** 191–192
Lafitte, Jean **IV:** 205–206
Native Americans **IV:** 256
Panic of 1819 **IV:** 276
War of 1812 **IV:** 358
New Orleans, Battle of (Civil War) **V: 251–252,** 406c
Mississippi River **V:** 234
Porter, David Dixon **V:** 280
Union navy **V:** 370
Welles, Gideon **V:** 391
New Orleans, Jackson, and Great Northern Railroad **V:** 27
New Orleans, Louisiana, riot **V:** 188, **252–253**
Newport, Christopher **II: 258–259**
Newport, Rhode Island **II: 258; III:** 308, 310; **V:** 373
architecture **II:** 23
cities and urban life **II:** 61
Coddington, William **II:** 66
Dyer, Mary **II:** 99
Franklin, Ann Smith **II:** 125
Harrison, Peter **II:** 154
Jews **II:** 175
journalism **II:** 178

Osborn, Sarah Haggar Wheaten **II:** 268
piracy **II:** 285
privateering **II:** 300
Rhode Island **II:** 320, 321
Smibert, John **II:** 346
society, British American **II:** 350
Newport Jazz Festival **VIII:** 100
New Republic, The **VIII:** 373
new Republicanism. *See* modern Republicanism
New Republicans **X:** 119
New Right **IX:** 209; **X:** 79–80, 141, 197, 259
newsboys **VI:** 165; **VII:** 45
news magazine television shows **X:** 296
news media **VIII: 243–244; X: 184–187,** *186. See also* journalism; magazines; newspapers; radio
advertising **VIII:** 1; **X:** 6–8
Appalachian Regional Development Act **IX:** 15
art and architecture **VIII:** 24
Birmingham confrontation **IX:** 38
Buckley, William F., Jr. **X:** 43
censorship **X:** 60–61
Christian Coalition **X:** 62
civil liberties **VIII:** 60
Congress **VIII:** 68
evangelical Christians **X:** 108
FBI **VIII:** 115
globalization **X:** 132
gun control **X:** 136–137
House of Representatives **X:** 144
Life (magazine) **VIII:** 189–190
literature **X:** 177
Luce, Henry R. **VIII:** 196–197
Pentagon Papers **X:** 233
presidency **VIII:** 281
Quayle, J. Danforth **X:** 253
radio **VIII:** 290
sexual revolution **X:** 277, 278
television **IX:** 295–297; **X:** 294–297
World War II **VIII:** 389
New South **V:** 50, 181, 315–316; **VI:** 77, **209–211,** 210m, 284
New Spain **I: 258–262,** 260m; **II:** 303, 331, 358, 359; **IV:** 70.

See also Spanish colonies/ colonization
Aguilar, Francisco de **I:** 4
castas **I:** 61–62
Cortés, Hernán **I:** 91, 94, 95
Council of the Indies **I:** 95
Mendoza, Antonio de **I:** 231
Mexico **I:** 234–235
New Mexico **I:** 254–257
northern frontier **III:** 257m, **257–258**
silver **I:** 325
slavery **I:** 327
slave trade **I:** 330
Veracruz **I:** 366
Zacatecas **I:** 381
Zumárraga, Juan de **I:** 382
newspapers **II:** 38, 178, 292, 299, 415; **IV:** 224, 376c; **VI: 211–212,** 327c; **VII:** 120–122, 330; **VIII:** 1, 243, 284; **IX:** 153. *See also* journalism
advertising **VI:** 2; **X:** 6
African Americans **VI:** 6
boxing **VI:** 33
censorship **X:** 60
cities and urban life **IV:** 82
Colorado gold rush **IV:** 90
communications **VI:** 62
Crummell, Alexander **VI:** 70
election of 1828 **IV:** 122
Genius of Universal Emancipation **IV:** 160–161
illustration, photography, and the graphic arts **VI:** 137
Indian Removal Act (1830) **IV:** 183
journalism **IV:** 194–196
media **X:** 185
Memphis riot **V:** 232
miscegenation **V:** 233
The Nation **VI:** 205
Native Americans **IV:** 257
neoconservatism **X:** 215
New York City **V:** 253
Pentagon Papers **X:** 233
Pulitzer, Joseph **VI:** 235
Remember the *Maine* **VI:** 187
Tappan, Arthur and Lewis **IV:** 333
telegraph **V:** 351
Washington, Booker T. **VI:** 309
Woodhull, Victoria **VI:** 318

news programs (television) **X:** 296
newsreels **VII:** 121; **VIII:** 54–55, 275
New Sweden. *See* Swedish colonies
New Sweden Company **II:** 87, 88, 364
Newsweek (magazine) **VIII:** 243; **X:** 237
New Toledo **I:** 283
Newton, Huey P. **IX:** 7, 38, 39, 334c
Newton, Sir Isaac
Brattle, Thomas **II:** 40
Edwards, Jonathan **II:** 105
Enlightenment **II:** 109
Great Awakening **II:** 147
journalism **II:** 179
Rittenhouse, David **II:** 322
science **II:** 330
Newton, John **II:** 239
Newtonianism **II:** 330–331
New Unionism **VI:** 170; **VII: 212–213,** 357c; **VIII:** 145
Adamson Act **VII:** 1–2
AFL **VII:** 10
Flynn, Elizabeth Gurley **VII:** 94–95
Haywood, "Big Bill" **VII:** 120
IWW **VII:** 129–131
labor movement **VII:** 152–154
Lawrence Strike **VII:** 155
National Civic Federation **VII:** 201
New View of Society (Owen) **IV:** 273
"New Vision" **IX:** 122
New Woman **VII:** *213,* **213–214,** 342
New World **I: 262–263**
Alexander VI, Pope **I:** 6
cabinet of curiosities **I:** 40
cannibalism **I:** 53–54
Castile **I:** 63
Columbian Exchange **I:** 76–78
conquistadores **I:** 84–85
Council of the Indies **I:** 95
Franciscans **I:** 132
printing press **I:** 294
Vespucci, Amerigo **I:** 368
New York (state) **II: 259–262,** 418c; **III:** 393c; **IV:** 375c; **IX:** 81, 100–101, 297
abortion **X:** 2
African Americans **II:** 7
agriculture **II:** 8, 11–13; **IV:** 11
Albany Congress **II:** 14

New York (continued)
Andros, Sir Edmund **II**: 19
anti-Masonry **IV**: 24
architecture **II**: 23
Asian Americans **X**: 28, 29
Beaver Wars **II**: 31
Bilingual Education Act of 1968 **X**: 36
Bonus Bill **IV**: 56
Brainerd, David **II**: 39
British settlement **II**: 261–262
canal era **IV**: 72–73
Cayuga **I**: 67
Cleveland, Grover **VI**: 58
Clinton, DeWitt **III**: 73–74
Clinton, George **III**: 74–75
Clinton, Hillary Rodham **X**: 65
Colden, Cadwallader **II**: 66
Conkling, Roscoe **VI**: 64
Connecticut **II**: 69
conservation **VI**: 65
Cornplanter **III**: 91
corruption, political **VI**: 67
Crèvecoeur, J. Hector St. John de **III**: 97–98
crowd action **II**: 78
Davenport, James **II**: 83, 84
Declaration of Independence **III**: 102
De Lancey family **II**: 86
Dominion of New England **II**: 94, 95
Dow, Lorenzo **IV**: 115, 116
Dudley, Joseph **II**: 95
Dutch settlement **II**: 259–260
economy **II**: 101
election of 1800 **III**: 116
English conquest **II**: 260–261
Erie Canal **IV**: 127–130
exploration **II**: 259
Federalist Papers **III**: 125
Finney, Charles Grandison **IV**: 138
first inhabitants **II**: 259
Fort Stanwix, Treaty of **III**: 132
French colonies **II**: 126–127
French immigrants **II**: 130
Garfield, James A. **VI**: 108
German immigrants **II**: 139
Glorious Revolution **II**: 141

government, British American **II**: 144, 146
Great Awakening **II**: 147, 148
Hamilton, Andrew **II**: 153
Handsome Lake **III**: 164
Heathcote, Caleb **II**: 155
Hendrick **II**: 155
Hispanic Americans **X**: 143
Holland Land Company **III**: 167
housing **II**: 157
Howe, George Augustus, Viscount **II**: 158
Hudson, Henry **II**: 158, 159
Huron **II**: 160
Hyde, Edward, Viscount Cornbury **II**: 162
indentured servitude **II**: 164
Iroquois **I**: 181–183; **II**: 168
Iroquois Confederacy **III**: 178–179
Jay, John **III**: 182
Jemison, Mary **II**: 173
Johnson, Sir William **II**: 177
Kalm, Peter **II**: 181
King George's War **II**: 182
King Philip's War **II**: 184
King's College **II**: 184–185
King William's War **II**: 185
labor **II**: 189
land riots **III**: 201–202
Leisler's Rebellion **II**: 192–193
Lennox, Charlotte Ramsay **II**: 193
limners **II**: 194
Livingston, Philip **II**: 195–196
Livingston, Robert R. **II**: 196–197
Logan, James **II**: 198
Lutherans **II**: 201
mills **II**: 225
Mohawk **I**: 238
monarchy, British **II**: 232
Montour, Andrew **II**: 233
Montour, Madame **II**: 233
Morris, Lewis **II**: 234
Native Americans **II**: 243
Native Americans and the Revolution **III**: 255
New Amsterdam **II**: 250
New Hampshire **II**: 251
New Jersey **II**: 253
New Netherland **II**: 256
New York City **II**: 262–263
NRA **X**: 212

Onondaga **I**: 272
population trends **II**: 291; **III**: 284; **X**: 242
primogeniture and entail **II**: 297
prisons **III**: 286
Protestantism **II**: 301
Quakers **II**: 308
Quartering Act **III**: 291
Queen Anne's War **II**: 309
Red Jacket **III**: 297
religion **IV**: 296
Roman Catholics **II**: 324
Seneca **I**: 321
slave resistance **II**: 337
Smith, Joseph, Jr. **IV**: 322
society, British American **II**: 350
spiritualism **IV**: 325
Stuyvesant, Peter **II**: 362
suffrage **II**: 364
Supreme Court decision **IV**: 331
Tennent, William, Sr. **II**: 372
Tilden, Samuel Jones **VI**: 289
trusts **VI**: 294
Tuscarora **II**: 378–379
Tuscarora War **II**: 379
Van Buren, Martin **IV**: 351
Van Rensselaer, Maria Van Cortlandt **II**: 381
Vermont **II**: 381
Verrazano, Giovanni da **I**: 367
war **II**: 262
Willard, Emma **IV**: 365–366
witchcraft **II**: 402
women's status and rights **II**: 408
Woodstock **X**: 321
Yates, Abraham, Jr. **III**: 387–388
Youngs, John **II**: 414
Zenger, John Peter **II**: 415
New York, New Haven & Hartford Railroad **IV**: 293, 295
New York Age **VI**: 212
New York Anti-Slavery Society **V**: 40
New York Associated Press **VI**: 62
New York Athletic Club **VI**: 33
New York Central railroad (NYC)
    banking, investment **VI**: 19
    economy **IV**: 118
    Gould, Jay **VI**: 117
    industrialization **IV**: 185

internal improvements **IV**: 188
Morgan, John Pierpont **VI**: 197
oil **VI**: 215
Vanderbilt, Cornelius **IV**: 353
New York Central Railway v. White **VII**: 343
New York City **II**: 262–263; **III**: 392c, 394c, 395c; **IV**: 377c; **V**: 60, **253–254**; **VI**: 323c; **VII**: 48, 339; **VIII**: 406c, 410c; **IX**: 30, 202–203, 250
    African-American churches, growth of **VI**: 4
    Alexander, Mary Spratt Provoost **II**: 16–17
    almshouses **II**: 18
    Anglican Church **II**: 20
    anti-Catholic riots **IV**: 23
    Armory Show **VII**: 17
    art and architecture **VIII**: 22, 25
    Ashcan school **VII**: 20
    bailout **X**: **217**, 325c
    boxing **VI**: 33
    Bradford, William **II**: 39
    Brady, Mathew **V**: 35–36
    Burgis, William **II**: 45
    canal era **IV**: 73
    cities and urban life **II**: 61, 62; **IV**: 81–84, 83; **VI**: 53
    class **II**: 62–63
    Clinton, DeWitt **III**: 73
    Colden, Jane **II**: 66
    corruption, political **VI**: 66
    crafts **II**: 73–74
    Crèvecoeur, J. Hector St. John de **III**: 98
    crime **X**: 82
    criminal justice **VII**: 58
    crowd action **II**: 78
    De Lancey family **II**: 86
    Democratic Party **VI**: 77
    disease and epidemics **II**: 91, 92; **IV**: 111, 112
    draft riots **V**: 254–255
    economy **X**: 96
    education **IV**: 121
    entertainment, popular **VI**: 95, 96
    Erie Canal **IV**: 129
    feminism **X**: 114
    Ferraro, Geraldine A. **X**: 117
    Fort Washington, capture of **III**: 133
    French immigrants **II**: 130

FTP **VIII:** 120, 121

gay rights movement **X:** 127

George, Henry **VI:** 111–112

Godkin, Edwin Lawrence **VI:** 116

Golden Hill, Battle of **III:** 153

Gompers, Samuel **VI:** 116–117

Hamilton, Alexander **III:** 161

Hancock, Winfield Scott **V:** 164

Harlem Renaissance **VII:** 119–120

Heathcote, Caleb **II:** 155

housing **VI:** 135; **VIII:** *158*

immigration **IV:** 177, 178; **V:** 176; **VI:** 138, 140

industrialization **IV:** 185

Jersey, HMS **III:** 186–187

Jews **II:** 175; **III:** 187, 188

Johnson, Samuel **II:** 177

journalism **II:** 178

King's College **II:** 184–185

Knox, Henry **III:** 197

labor and labor movements **II:** 187; **IV:** 203, 204

La Guardia, Fiorello **VIII:** 182

Lee, Charles **III:** 205, 206

Leisler's Rebellion **II:** 192

L'Enfant, Pierre-Charles **III:** 207

liberty tree/pole **III:** 214

Lincoln, Abraham **V:** 210

Livingston, Philip **II:** 196

Long Island, Battle of **III:** 217

machine politics **VI:** 184

McClellan, George B. **V:** 226

McDougall, Alexander **III:** 239

monuments **V:** 239

Morris, Lewis **II:** 234

mortality **II:** 235

movies **X:** 197

mulattoes **II:** 238

music **VI:** 201

Nast, Thomas **V:** 247

nativism **V:** 251

Negro Plot of 1741 **II:** 247–248

New Jersey **II:** 253

newspapers **VI:** 211

New York **II:** 259

nurses **V:** 256

Olmstead, Frederick Law **V:** 257

penitentiary movement **IV:** 278

piracy **II:** 285

Plunkitt, George Washington **VI:** 225

population trends **II:** 292; **III:** 283–284; **V:** 278; **VI:** 226

postal service **II:** 292

printing and publishing **II:** 299

privateering **II:** 300

prostitution **V:** 283

race and racial conflict **VIII:** 288

railroads **IV:** 293, 295

Ray, Charlotte **V:** 291

Riis, Jacob A. **VI:** 248

Roosevelt, Theodore **VII:** 265–266

Seton, Elizabeth Ann **IV:** 315–316

settlement houses **VI:** 259

Sickles, Daniel E. **V:** 326

skyscrapers **VI:** 264, 265

slave resistance **II:** 337

Smith, Alfred E. **VII:** 287

society, British American **II:** 350

Society for the Propagation of the Gospel in Foreign Parts **II:** 352

Stewart, Maria **IV:** 327

strikes **V:** 340

suffrage **III:** 336

temperance movement **IV:** 337

theater **II:** 373; **V:** 352

Thomas, Norman **VIII:** 358

trade and shipping **II:** 377

transportation **V:** 355, 356

transportation, urban **VI:** 292

travel **II:** 377–378

Tweed Ring **VI:** 298–299

UN **VIII:** 366

urban reform **VII:** 317

Van Rensselaer, Maria Van Cortlandt **II:** 381

vaudeville **VII:** 321–322

V-J Day **VIII:** 370

Weather Underground **X:** 318

yellow fever **II:** 414

Zouaves **V:** 403

New York City Crystal Palace Exhibition (1853) **IV:** 84

New York City draft riots **V:** **254–255,** 255, *407c*

conscription **V:** 79

employment **V:** 116

homefront **V:** 169

immigration **V:** 176

race and racial conflict **V:** 288

Union army **V:** 364

Women's National Loyal League **V:** 397

women's status and rights **V:** 398

New York City Fire Department **V:** 403

New York County Courthouse **VI:** 67

New York Daily News **VII:** 143

New York Daily Tribune **V:** 223

New Yorker, The (magazine) **VII:** 161; **VIII:** 147

New York Evening Post **V:** 391

Godkin, Edwin Lawrence **VI:** 116

newspapers **VI:** 211

Schurz, Carl **VI:** 257

Villard, Henry **VI:** 305

New York *Free Enquirer* **IV:** 369

New York *Freiheit* **VI:** 167

New York Herald **IV:** 82, 194; **V:** 192, 193; **VI:** 211, 304

New York Herald-Tribune **VIII:** 339, *405c*

New York Hospital **II:** 196

New York Illustrated News **V:** 247

New York Infirmary for Women and Children **VI:** 31

New York Journal **IV:** 194, 197; **VI:** *327c*

de Lôme letter **VI:** 76–77

labor, child **VI:** 165

Pulitzer, Joseph **VI:** 235

Spanish-American War **VI:** 272

yellow journalism **VI:** 321

New York *Journal American* **VII:** 142

New York Journal of Commerce **IV:** 333

New York Kansas League **IV:** 223

New York Ledger **VI:** 80

New York magazine **X:** 288

New York Manumission Society **III:** *394c;* **IV:** 15

New York Married Women's Property Act **IV:** *378c*

New York Morning Journal **VI:** 321; **VII:** 121

New York Packet **III:** 124

New York Philharmonic Symphony Orchestra **IV:** 179; **VI:** 201; **VIII:** *410c*

New York Police Department **VII:** 266

New York Post **VIII:** 378

New York Press **VI:** 321

New York Protestant Association **V:** 251

New York Public Library **VI:** 176

New York Redstockings **IX:** 325

New York Republican Party **VI:** 16

New York Seventh Regiment **V:** 389

New York Society for the Suppression of Vice **VI:** 62, 198

New York Society Library **II:** 196

New York State Constitution **II:** 196

New York State Reservation at Niagara Falls **VI:** 65

New York Stock Exchange **V:** 253; **VIII:** 91, 341

New York Suffrage Society **V:** 398

New York Sun **IV:** 82, 194, 196; **V:** 88; **VI:** 211, 212

New York Supreme Court **II:** 85–86

New York Times **VI:** 116, 119, 212; **VII:** 141

German-American regiments **V:** 147

journalism **V:** 193

media **X:** 185

Pentagon Papers **X:** 233

photography **V:** 273

political correctness **X:** 237

science and technology **X:** 275

Tourgée, Albion W. **V:** 354

Watergate scandal **X:** 315

New York Times v. Sullivan (1964) **X:** 41

New York Times v. United States (1971) **X:** 41, 60, 233, *324c*

New York Transcript **IV:** 195

New York Tribune **IV:** 156, 194–196; **V:** *407c*

Blackwell, Antoinette Brown **VI:** 30

Dana, Charles A. **V:** 88

Greeley, Horace **V:** 158

illustration, photography, and the graphic arts **VI:** 137

journalism **V:** 193

newspapers **VI:** 211

race and racial conflict **V:** 287

Villard, Henry **VI:** 304

New York v. United States
(1992) **X:** 113
New York Weekly **VI:** 80
New York *World* **V:** 233; **VI:**
327*c*; **VII:** 121, 141, 142
boxing **VI:** 33
labor, child **VI:** 165
Lease, Mary Elizabeth **VI:**
173
newspapers **VI:** 211
yellow journalism **VI:** 321
New York World's Fair
(1939–40) **VIII: 244–246,**
245, 408*c*; **IX:** 295
advertising **VIII:** 1
art and architecture **VIII:**
22
suburbs **VIII:** 343
technology **VIII:** 353
New York World's Fair (1964)
IX: 67
New York Yankees **VII:** 295;
VIII: 83–84
New Zealand **IX:** 273–274; **X:**
135
Nezahualcóyotl **I:** 45, 185, 250
Nezahualpilli **I:** 45
Nez Perce nation **III:** 211
Nez Perce War **V:** 173, 251; **VI:**
207, **212–213,** 324*c*
NFL. *See* National Football
League
NFO. *See* National Farmers
Organization
NFWA. *See* National Farm
Workers Association
Ngbanya **I:** 144
NGOs. *See* nongovernmental
organizations
NHGRI (National Human
Genome Research Institute)
X: 145–146
NHL. *See* National Hockey
League
NHTSA (National Highway
Traffic Safety Administration)
IX: 225
Niagara, USS **IV:** 206
Niagara Bible Conference **VI:**
75
Niagara Falls **II:** 115
Niagara Frontier **IV:** 356
Niagara Movement **VII:** 72,
199, **214–215,** 356*c*
Niagara Movement Declaration
of Principles **VII:** 367–369
Niagara River **IV:** 356, 358
Niani, Mali **I:** 218
Niantic **II:** 241, 320
Nicaragua **IV:** 88, 89, 142, 219,
379*c*; **V:** 7, 127, 131, 133,
405*c*; **VI:** 32; **VII:** 357*c*;

VIII: 133, 340; **X:** 326*c,*
327*c*
Big Stick diplomacy **VII:**
28
Boland Amendment **X:** 38
cold war (end of) **X:** 71, 72
contras **X:** 80–81
dollar diplomacy **VII:** 70
foreign policy **VII:** 99; **X:**
124
Iran-contra affair **X:** 154
Latin America **X:** 173
North, Oliver L. **X:** 222
Panama Canal **VII:** 222
Reagan, Ronald W. **X:** 260,
261
U.S. relations with **X:**
217–218
Women's International
League for Peace and
Freedom **VII:** 337
Nicholas II, czar of Russia **VII:**
156, 259, 267
Nicholette, Charles **II:** 209
Nicholls, Richard **II:** 144, 257,
261
Nichols, Mike **IX:** 214
Nichols, Terry L. **X:** 194,
227–228, 299
Nicholson, Francis **II:** 55, 95,
210, 328, 354
Nicholson, William **II:** 224
Nickas **II:** 76
Nickelodeon **X:** 296
nickelodeons **VII:** 86, 191, 257,
356*c*
Nicklaus, Jack **X:** 262, 286
Nickles, Don **X:** 183
Nicodemus, Kansas **V:** 327
Nicolay, John **VI:** 124, 125
Nicolet, Jean **II:** 115, **263**
Nicollet, Joseph **IV:** 153
Nicuesa, Diego de **I:** 276
Niebuhr, H. Richard **VIII:** 304
Niebuhr, Reinhold **VIII:** 304;
IX: 13, 14
Nielson, Patty **X:** *137*
Niger **I:** 135, 155, 360
Nigeria **I:** 4; **X:** 122, 228–229
Calabar **I:** 47–48
Fulani **I:** 135
Hausa **I:** 155
Igbo **I:** 175
Kotoko **I:** 196
Oyo **I:** 273
Yoruba **I:** 377
Niger River **I:** 14, 137, 139,
217–218, **263**
Niger River Valley **I:** 108–109
Nigger, The (film) **VII:** 249
"nigger heaven" **VI:** 3
night baseball **VIII:** 335

Nighthawks (Hopper) **VIII:** *24,*
25
Nightingale, Florence **V:** 230
Nightingale, Taylor **VI:** 311
"Night of Terror" **VII:** 205
NIH. *See* National Institutes of
Health
Nike X. *See* Sentinel Defense
System
Nike Zeus project **X:** 22
Niles, Hezekiah **III: 258–259**
Niles' Weekly Register **III:** 258;
IV: 197
NIMH (National Institute of
Mental Health) **IX:** 222
Nimitz, Chester W. **VIII:**
246–247, 409*c*
Coral Sea, Battle of the
VIII: 74
King, Ernest J. **VIII:** 177
Marines, U.S. **VIII:** 203
Midway, Battle of **VIII:**
211
World War II Pacific
theater **VIII:** 398
Niña **I:** 55
99th Pursuit Squadron **VIII:** 21
Nine-Power Pact **VII:** 331, 360*c*
Nine-Power Treaty **VIII:** 199
Nineteenth Amendment **VI:** 30,
36; **VII:** 360*c*
anti-suffragists **VII:** 15
Blatch, Harriot **VII:** 31–32
Cable Act **VII:** 41
Catt, Carrie Chapman **VII:**
44
Committee for Public
Information **VII:** 346
Coolidge, Calvin **VII:** 56
elections **VII:** 79
marriage and family life
VII: 171
NAWSA **VII:** 198
Paul, Alice **VII:** 226
politics **VII:** 229
Wilson, Woodrow **VII:**
335
woman suffrage **VII:** 337
women's status and rights
VII: 340
Ninety-five Theses **II:** 201
Ninigret **II:** 241
Ninigret II **II:** 241
NIOSH (National Institute for
Occupational Safety and
Health) **X:** 225
Nipmuc **II:** 183, 212, 320
NIRA. *See* National Industrial
Recovery Act
Nirenberg, Marshall W. **IX:** 270
Nirvana (music group) **X:** 202,
240

Nissan automobiles **IX:** 25; **X:**
31
nitrous oxide **IV:** 230
Nitze, Paul H. **IX:** 233
Nixon, Richard M. **VIII:** 100;
IX: 331*c,* 332*c,* 334*c;* **X:**
218–221, *219,* 323*c*–325*c*
ABM Treaty **X:** 22–23
affirmative action **X:** 8
African nations **X:** 13
Agnew, Spiro T. **X:** 14
Albert, Carl B. **X:** 18
antiwar movement—
Vietnam **X:** 24
arms race **IX:** 16
birth control **X:** 37
Bork, Robert **X:** 39
Brennan, William J. **X:** 41
Buchanan, Patrick J. **X:** 42
Burger, Warren E. **X:** 44
Bush, George H. W. **X:** 45
Chambers, Whittaker **IX:**
50
"Chicago Eight" **X:** 61
cold war (end of) **X:** 70
Congressional Budget and
Impoundment Act **X:**
75
conscription **X:** 76
conservation,
environmentalism, and
environmental policy **X:**
77
conservatism **IX:** 69
conservative movement **X:**
79
Cox, Archibald, Jr. **X:** 81
defense policy **X:** 85
détente **X:** 89
Dewey, Thomas **IX:** 81
Dole, Robert **X:** 90
economy **X:** 94
Eisenhower, Dwight D.
IX: 92
elections **IX:** 94–95, 97; **X:**
101
Energy, U.S. Department
of **X:** 103
energy crisis **X:** 103, 104
Farmer, James L. **X:** 111
Federal Information Act
X: 112
federalism **X:** 112
Ford, Gerald R. **X:** 119,
120
foreign policy **X:** 122
Goldwater, Barry **IX:** 123
Graham, Billy **IX:** 126
Hiss, Alger **IX:** 134
Hoover, J. Edgar **IX:** 136
House of Representatives
X: 144

House Un-American Activities Committee **IX:** 137

impeachment **X:** 149–150

Jackson State University **X:** 160

Jaworski, Leon **X:** 161

journalism **IX:** 154

Kennedy, Edward M. **X:** 163–164

Kennedy, John F. **IX:** 157

Kent State University **X:** 164

Kissinger, Henry A. **X:** 165

Koreagate **X:** 166

labor **X:** 169

Latin America **IX:** 172; **X:** 172

Leary, Timothy **IX:** 175–176

liberalism **IX:** 180; **X:** 175

McGovern, George Stanley **X:** 184

Mitchell, John N. **X:** 195–196

narcotics **X:** 206

neoconservatism **X:** 216

NEPA **X:** 210

New Left **IX:** 231

Occupational Safety and Health Act of 1970 **X:** 225

OMB **X:** 226–227

Panama Canal turnover **X:** 232

Pentagon Papers **X:** 233

political parties **X:** 237

Powell, Lewis **X:** 247

property rights **X:** 249

race and racial conflict **X:** 256

Reagan, Ronald W. **X:** 259

Rehnquist, William H. **X:** 264

Republican Party **IX:** 257, 258

resignation speech **X:** 338–340

Richardson, Elliot L. **X:** 267, 268

Robinson, Jackie **IX:** 263

Ruckelshaus, William D. **X:** 269

"Silent Majority" speech **X:** 333–334

South Africa **X:** 279

space policy **X:** 283

Strategic Arms Limitation Treaties **X:** 289

Supreme Court **X:** 290

Teamsters Union **IX:** 293

television **IX:** 297

Thurmond, J. Strom **X:** 303

United Nations **X:** 307

United States v. Nixon **X:** 308–309

veto, presidential **X:** 311

Vietnam War **IX:** 310; **X:** 311, 312

Volunteers in Service to America **IX:** 311

wage and price controls **X:** 313

Wallace, George C. **X:** 314

War Powers Act **X:** 315

Watergate scandal **X:** 315–317

Nixon Doctrine **X:** 85, 122, 173

NIYC (National Indian Youth Council) **IX:** 229

Niza, Fray Marcos de **I:** 88, 256, 295–296, 383

Nkongolo **I:** 209–210

Nkrumah, Kwame **IX:** *43*

NL. *See* National League of Professional Base Ball Clubs

NLF. *See* National Liberation Front

NLRA. *See* National Labor Relations Act; National Labor Relations Act of 1935

NLRB. *See* National Labor Relations Board

NLU. *See* National Labor Union

Nmantambu **I:** 243

NME. *See* National Military Establishment

Noad, king of Ethiopia **I:** 124

Nobel Peace Prize **VII:** 356*c;* **VIII:** 160, 206, 207

Addams, Jane **VII:** 3

Dawes, Charles **VII:** 63

foreign policy **VII:** 99

Great White Fleet **VII:** 114

Russo-Japanese War **VII:** 271

Women's International League for Peace and Freedom **VII:** 337

Nobel Prize **VII:** 276; **IX:** 43, 330*c*

Nobel Prize (economic science) **VIII:** 224–225

Nobel Prize (literature) **VIII:** 113, 192, 339, 405*c*, 407*c*, 408*c*

nobility **I:** 3–4, 19, 20, 84, 169, 323; **II:** 297, 359. *See also* social classes

Nobody Knows My Name (James Baldwin) **IX:** 33

Noche Triste (Sad Night) **I:** 7, 22, 45, 97

no-fault divorce **X:** 181, 183, 259, 323*c*

Noli, Antonio de **I:** 147

Nombre de Dios **I:** 277

nonaggression treaty. *See* Nazi-Soviet Pact

nonfiction **VIII:** 121

nongovernmental organizations (NGOs) **X:** 76–77

Non-Importation Act **III:** 226, **259,** 267, 397*c*

Non-Intercourse Act **III: 259,** 259, 398*c*

Bonaparte, Napoleon **III:** 42

embargo of 1807 **III:** 118

foreign affairs **III:** 131

Orders in Council **III:** 267

noninterventionism **IV:** 242; **VIII:** 124, 199, 305

Non-Partisan League **VII:** 91, **215–216,** 230, 288

CIO **VIII:** 70

Hillman, Sidney **VIII:** 146

labor **VIII:** 180

Lewis, John L. **VIII:** 186

Non-Separatist Puritans **II:** 283

nonviolence doctrine

African-American movement **IX:** 6

civil disobedience **IX:** 53–546

Congress of Racial Equality **IX:** 66–68

King, Martin Luther, Jr. **IX:** 160–162

Lewis, John **IX:** 178

sit-ins **IX:** 273

Southern Christian Leadership Conference **IX:** 274–276

Student Nonviolent Coordinating Committee **IX:** 284–285

Students for a Democratic Society **IX:** 286

Watts uprising **IX:** 318

Wilkins, Roy **IX:** 322–323

Nookta **II:** 266

Norcross, Gerald **V:** 168

Norfolk, Virginia **IV:** 112

Noriega, Manuel Antonio **X:** 327*c*

Bush, George H. W. **X:** 45–46

defense policy **X:** 87

foreign policy **X:** 124

Panama invasion **X:** 231

normal schools **IV:** 220

Normandy, invasion of **VIII:** *16, 247,* **247–248,** 410*c*

air power **VIII:** 11–12

amphibious warfare **VIII:** 15, 16, *16*

Anglo-American relations **VIII:** 17

Army, U.S. **VIII:** 19

Bradley, Omar N. **VIII:** 41

Bulge, Battle of the **VIII:** 44

Italian campaign **VIII:** 168

King, Ernest J. **VIII:** 177

Navy, U.S. **VIII:** 236

Patton, George **VIII:** 263

photography **VIII:** 269

second front **VIII:** 320

shipbuilding **VIII:** 324

tanks **VIII:** 350

Teheran Conference **VIII:** 355

World War II European theater **VIII:** 393

Normans **I:** 10–11, 385*c*

Norman v. Reed (1992) **X:** 279

NORML (National Organization for the Reform of Marijuana Laws) **X:** 208

Norplant **X:** 36

Norris, Frank **VI:** 81, 178; **VII:** 38–39, 160

Norris, George W. **VII:** 42, 54; **VIII: 248–249**

antimonopoly **VIII:** 17

Congress **VIII:** 66

Republican Party **VIII:** 305

TVA **VIII:** 356

Norris, William **IV:** 307

Norris-La Guardia Act **VIII:** 406*c*

antimonopoly **VIII:** 17

Hoover presidency **VIII:** 154

labor **VIII:** 179

La Guardia, Fiorello **VIII:** 182

Norris (Norreys), Sir John **I:** 112

Norse **I: 263–265,** 264*m,* 385*c*

Cabot, John **I:** 42

cod **I:** 74

Greenland **I:** 145

Iceland **I:** 174–175

Vinland **I:** 369

North, Frederick, Lord **III:** 76, **259–260,** 335, 349

North, Oliver L. **X: 221–222**

Boland Amendment **X:** 38

foreign policy **X:** 124

Iran-contra affair **X:** 154–155

North, Oliver L *(continued)*
   Mitchell, George **X:** 194, 195
   Walsh, Lawrence E. **X:** 314, 315
North Africa **IX:** 201
North African campaign **VIII:** **249–250**, *250*, 409*c*, 410*c*
   amphibious warfare **VIII:** 15
   Army, U.S. **VIII:** 19
   Axis **VIII:** 31–32
   Bradley, Omar N. **VIII:** 41
   Casablanca Conference **VIII:** 52
   Italian campaign **VIII:** 168
   Patton, George **VIII:** 263
   second front **VIII:** 320
   submarines **VIII:** 342
   tanks **VIII:** 349–350
   World War II European theater **VIII:** 392
North America. *See also specific areas, e.g.:* Canada, Texas
   Acadia **I:** 2–3
   Blaeu, Willem **I:** 31
   Cabot, John **I:** 41
   Cabot, Sebastian **I:** 42
   Cartier, Jacques **I:** 57–59
   Columbian Exchange **I:** 77
   corn (maize) **I:** 87–88
   Dutch East India Company **I:** 115
   Latin America **X:** 173
   NAFTA **X:** 222–223
   Waldseemüller, Martin **I:** 371
North American Free Trade Agreement (NAFTA) **X:** **222–223**, 328*c*
   Bush, George H. W. **X:** 46
   Clinton, William **X:** 67
   economy **X:** 95
   foreign policy **X:** 124
   globalization **X:** 132
   labor **X:** 171
   Latin America **X:** 173, 174
   Mexico **X:** 192
North American Review **IV:** 196; **VI:** 1, 176
North Anna, Battle of **V:** 168
North Atlantic Cooperation Council (NACC) **X:** 223
North Atlantic Treaty Organization (NATO) **VIII:** 207; **IX:** **231–233**, 232*m*, 330*c*; **X:** **223–224**, 327*c*, 330*c*
   Acheson, Dean **IX:** 1
   Africa **IX:** 3
   arms race **IX:** 16
   Berlin blockade **IX:** 37

Clinton, William **X:** 67, 69
cold war **IX:** 58, 60
Dayton accords **X:** 85
defense policy **X:** 86, 88
Eisenhower, Dwight D. **IX:** 92
Europe (and foreign policy) **IX:** 105–106
foreign policy **X:** 124–125
Haig, Alexander M., Jr. **X:** 139
INF Treaty **X:** 151
Iron Curtain **X:** 156, 157
Kosovo **X:** 166, 167
militia movement **X:** 193
Reagan, Ronald W. **X:** 260
Truman, Harry **IX:** 299
North Briton, The **III:** 378
North Carolina **I:** 388*c*; **II:** **263–265**; **III:** 392*c*; **IV:** 162, 191; **IX:** 311, 320; **X:** 106, 107, 242
   African-American churches, growth of **VI:** 4
   African Americans **VI:** 6
   agriculture **II:** 11
   Alamance, Battle of **III:** 8
   Catawba **II:** 55
   Cherokee **II:** 57, 58
   Cofitachequi **I:** 76
   colonization **II:** 265
   Franklin, state of **III:** 135–136
   governors **V:** 152
   Guilford Courthouse, Battle of **III:** 158
   Husband, Herman **III:** 170
   Iroquois **II:** 168
   Jews **III:** 188
   Jim Crow laws **VI:** 156
   King's Mountain, Battle of **III:** 196–197
   Ku Klux Klan **V:** 199; **VI:** 163
   "Lost Colony" **II:** 264–265
   lumbering **II:** 201
   Mantoac **I:** 221
   miscegenation **II:** 228
   mulattoes **II:** 238
   music **II:** 239
   New South **VI:** 210
   original inhabitants **II:** 263–264
   Ostenaco **II:** 269
   Porter, David Dixon **V:** 280
   Quakers **II:** 308
   Reconstruction **V:** 294
   redemption **V:** 297
   religion, Euro-American **II:** 316

society, British American **II:** 352
South Carolina **II:** 353, 354
taverns and inns **II:** 367
Teach, Edward **II:** 369
Tourgée, Albion W. **V:** 354
Tuscarora **II:** 378
Tuscarora War **II:** 379
Virginia Company of London **II:** 387
Wingina **II:** 401
North Carolina Algonquians **I:** 6
North Carolina campaigns **V:** 45
North Carolina Regulation **III:** 170, **260–261**, 392*c*
North Dakota **I:** 161; **IV:** 258; **VI:** 208, 326*c*; **VII:** 215–216; **X:** 242, 243
northeastern United States **II:** 62, 157, 168–170; **IV:** 11, 117; **V:** 193, 278; **IX:** 51
   American Protective Association **VI:** 11
   Asian Americans **X:** 29
   cities and urban life **VI:** 53
   Hispanic Americans **X:** 143
   labor **X:** 171
   national banking system **VI:** 206
   Norumbega **I:** 266–267
   People's Party **VI:** 223
   population trends **X:** 242
   poverty **X:** 246
   rust belt **X:** 269
   settlement houses **VI:** 259
Northeast Passage **I:** 43, 83, 114, **265;** **II:** 158
Northern Alliance (Afghanistan) **X:** 125
Northern Andes **I:** 10
Northern Cheyenne nation **VI:** 69
Northern colonies **II:** 340, 407–408
Northern Ireland **X:** 195
Northern Pacific Railroad (NPRR) **V:** 81; **VII:** 216
   Hill, James J. **VI:** 129
   Morgan, John Pierpont **VI:** 197, 198
   railroads **VI:** 237, 239
   Villard, Henry **VI:** 305
Northern Securities case **VI:** 19, 239; **VII:** 39, 211, **216,** 266, 356*c*
Northern Securities Company
   banking, investment **VI:** 19
   Hill, James J. **VI:** 129
   Morgan, John Pierpont **VI:** 198
   railroads **VI:** 239

Northern Spectator **V:** 158
Northern Star, The **IV:** 212
northern United States **II:** 6, 7, 9, 13, 20; **VI:** 209; **VIII:** 279, 367; **X:** 9
   abolition **V:** 3
   African-American movement **IX:** 4
   African Americans **IV:** 8; **VI:** 5, 6
   agriculture **IV:** 9, 10; **V:** 6
   cities and urban life **V:** 59
   Civil War **V:** 67
   common soldier **V:** 70
   contract labor **VI:** 66
   Copperheads **V:** 81–82
   Democratic Party **IV:** 108; **V:** 95
   economy **IV:** 117, 119; **V:** 104–107
   elections **V:** 109
   employment **V:** 115–116
   fugitive slave laws **IV:** 154, 155
   Grimké, Angelina and Sarah **IV:** 164
   habeas corpus, writ of **V:** 161–162
   industrial development **V:** 180–181
   industrialization **IV:** 187
   labor movements **IV:** 203–205
   migration **IX:** 201
   Nullification Controversy **IV:** 264
   Panic of 1837 **IV:** 277
   polygamy **IV:** 285
   popular sovereignty **IV:** 285
   population trends **V:** 279; **VI:** 226
   race and race relations **IV:** 291
   railroads **IV:** 295, 296
   religion **VI:** 242
   Republican Party **IV:** 300
   slavery **IV:** 316
   states' rights **V:** 335
   tariffs **V:** 348
   taxation **V:** 349–350
   telegraph **V:** 351
   Underground Railroad **V:** 362
   Union League **V:** 367
   Urban League **IX:** 305–306
   Weld, Theodore Dwight **IV:** 362
North Korea. *See* Democratic People's Republic of Korea
North Pole **VII:** 357*c*, 361*c*

Northrup, Lucius B. **V:** 180
North Salem, New York **IV:** 184
North Star (newspaper) **IV:** 14;
V: 3, 100
North Vietnam **IX:** 21, 308–310,
334*c*; **X:** 325*c*
cold war (end of) **X:** 70
foreign policy **X:** 122
U.S. relations with **X: 224**
Vietnam War **X:** 311–312
Weather Underground **X:**
317, 318
Northwest Coast Indians **II:**
265–266
North West Company
American Fur Company
IV: 16
Astor, John Jacob **IV:** 30,
31
Astoria **IV:** 32, 33
fur trade **IV:** 156
McLoughlin, John **IV:** 228
mountain men **IV:** 247
rendezvous **IV:** 299
Northwest Company **IV:** 93
Northwestern Alliance **VI:** 99,
100, 222
northwestern United States **II:**
130–131; **IV:** 140; **VI:** 207,
213; **X:** 214, 290
northwestern United States,
Native American religion in
I: 253
Northwestern University **VI:**
191
Northwestern Virginia Railroad
IV: 40
Northwest Indian
Confederation **III:** 396*c*
Northwest Indian War **III:**
123–124
Northwest Ordinance of 1787 **V:**
1
abolition/abolition
movement **IV:** 1
Missouri Compromise of
1820 **IV:** 237
Mormon War **IV:** 244
slavery **IV:** 316
Northwest Ordinances **III:**
261–263, 262*m,* 395*c*
abolition/abolition
movement **III:** 16
African Americans **III:** 6
Articles of Confederation
III: 25
Continental Congress,
Second **III:** 89
education **III:** 114
Jefferson, Thomas **III:** 184
Northwest Passage **I: 265–266,**
388*c;* **II:** 115, 130, 150, 158;

III: 185, 209–211; **IV:** 93,
171
Bristol **I:** 35
Cabot, Sebastian **I:** 42, 43
Cartier, Jacques **I:** 57–59
Cathay (China) **I:** 65
Company of Cathay **I:** 83
Frobisher, Martin **I:**
133–134
Northwest Territories **III:**
262*m,* 315, 316, 394*c*–396*c*
abolition movement **IV:** 1
Cass, Lewis **IV:** 76
economy **IV:** 117
foreign policy **IV:** 141
Harrison, William Henry
IV: 168
Native Americans **IV:** 255,
256
public land policy **IV:** 286
*Northwood: A Tale of New
England* (Hale) **IV:** 167
Norton, Charles Eliot **VI:** 15
Norton, Ken **IX:** 10
Norumbega **I: 266–267,** 367
Norway **I:** 145, 174, 175, 264;
VIII: 28, 39; **IX:** 194,
231–233; **X:** 223
Norwegian settlers **II:** 257
Norwood (Beecher) **VI:** 24
no-strike pledge **VIII:** 146
Notes of a Native Son (James
Baldwin) **IX:** 33
"Notes of Eight Years Travel
Amongst the North American
Indians" (Catlin) **IV:** 78
Notes on Canada West (Cary) **V:**
52
Notes on Coinage (Jefferson)
III: 184
Notes on the State of Virginia
(Jefferson) **III:** 33–34, 184,
214; **V:** 2
Notorious B.I.G. **X:** 240
Nott, Josiah Clark **IV:** 290–291
Nova Belgica et Anglia Nova"
(map) **I:** 31
Novak, Kim **IX:** 212
Novak, Michael **X:** 301
Nova Scotia **II:** 43, 130, 148,
185, 232; **III:** 219, 221, 394*c.*
See also Louisbourg
Nova Zembla **I:** 265
novels **IV:** 167, 211–213, 379*c;*
V: 213, 217
No Vitals **II:** 77
NOW. *See* National
Organization for Women
NOW v. Scheidler (1994) **X:** 211
Noyes, John Humphrey **IV:** 299
NPRR. *See* Northern Pacific
Railroad

NPT. *See* Nuclear
Nonproliferation Treaty
NRA. *See* National Recovery
Administration; National
Rifle Association
NREN (National Research and
Education Network) **X:** 153
NRPB. *See* National Resources
Planning Board
NSBRO (National Service
Board for Religious
Objectors) **VIII:** 70
NSC. *See* National Security
Council; National Service
Corps
NSC-68 **IX:** 2, 77, 203,
233–234, 330*c*
NSF. *See* National Science
Foundation
NSFNET **X:** 153
N'Sync **X:** 202, 241
nuclear arms race **VIII:** 29
nuclear energy **VII:** 25; **IX:**
23–24, 293, 294
atomic bomb **VIII:** 29
Baruch, Bernard M. **VIII:**
34
environmental issues **VIII:**
104
Lilienthal, David E. **VIII:**
190
nuclear family. *See* family,
nuclear
nuclear freeze movement **X:** 23,
59, **224**
Nuclear Nonproliferation Treaty
(NPT) **IX:** 140, 334*c;* **X:** 25
nuclear physics **VIII:** 318
Nuclear Regulatory
Commission **IX:** 24
nuclear test ban **IX:** 180, 267
Nuclear Test Ban Treaty **VIII:**
144
nuclear weapons **IX:** 333*c;* **X:**
327*c. See also* atomic bomb;
hydrogen bomb
ABM Treaty **X:** 22–23
arms race **IX:** 16–17; **X:** 25
Atomic Energy
Commission **IX:** 23–24
aviation **IX:** 28
civil defense **IX:** 52–53
cold war **IX:** 60
Cuban missile crisis **IX:**
73–75
defense policy **X:** 85, 86
DuPont Corporation **IX:**
83–84
foreign policy **X:** 122, 124
Gore, Albert, Jr. **X:** 134
hydrogen bomb **IX:**
138–140

INF Treaty **X:** 151–152
Kissinger, Henry A. **X:** 165
Limited Test Ban Treaty of
1963 **IX:** 180
military-industrial complex
IX: 203
NATO **X:** 223
nuclear freeze movement
X: 224
Rosenberg, Julius and
Ethel **IX:** 264–265
SANE **IX:** 267–268
science **IX:** 268–269
Strategic Arms Limitation
Treaties **X:** 288–289
technology **IX:** 294
U.S. facilities for **IX:** 17*m*
*Nuclear Weapons and Foreign
Policy* (Kissinger) **X:** 165
Nude Descending a Staircase
(Duchamp) **VII:** 17
nudity **X:** 239, 277
Nueces River **IV:** 232, 334
Nugent, Maude **VI:** 204
NUL (National Urban League)
VI: 7
nullification **IV:** 360, 363, 376*c,*
377*c;* **V:** 94, 311, 348
Nullification Controversy **IV:**
124, 193, **263–265**
Nullification Crisis of 1832–33
V: 311
Nunavut **II:** 167
Nunez, Jacob **II:** 267
Nunn, Sam **X:** 140
"Nunna daul Tsuny" **IV:** 344
Nupe **I:** 273
Nuremberg Laws **VIII:** 149
Nuremberg Trials **VII:** 147
Nurenberg Chronicle
(Hartmann Schedel) **I:** 240
Nurse, Rebecca **II: 266**
*Nurse and Spy in the Union
army* (Edmonds) **V:** 118, 213
nurses/nursing **IV:** 114, 316; **V:**
255–256; VII: 111, 329
Barton, Clara **V:** 24–26
Bickerdyke, "Mother" **V:**
28–29
Civil War **V:** 66
Cumming, Kate **V:** 85
disease and epidemics **V:**
97
homefront **V:** 169
ladies aid societies **V:** 203
medicine and hospitals **V:**
230, 231
Pember, Phoebe Yates
Levy **V:** 266–267
Taylor, Susie King **V:** 350
Tubman, Harriet **V:** 358
USCC **V:** 371

nurses/nursing (continued)
Walker, Mary Edwards **V:** 386
Whitman, Walt **V:** 393
women's status and rights **V:** 398
Nurse's Settlement **VII:** 329
nursing homes **X:** 189
nursing schools **VII:** 111
Nusbaum, Aaron **VI:** 186
NUSJ **VIII:** 75
Nutimus **II:** 390
nutrition. See food
nuts **II:** 121, 122
Nutten Island **II:** 249
N. W. Ayer and Son **VII:** 4
NWLB. See National War Labor Board
NWP. See National Woman's Party; National Women's Party
NWPC. See National Women's Political Caucus
NWSA. See National Woman Suffrage Association
NWTUL. See National Women's Trade Union League
NYA. See National Youth Administration
Nyagse **I:** 101
NYC. See New York Central railroad
Nye, Gerald P.
antimonopoly **VIII:** 17
Neutrality Acts **VIII:** 239
Nye Committee **VIII:** 250
Spanish Civil War **VIII:** 335
Nye, Russel B. **VI:** 96
Nye Committee **VIII:** 67, 166, 239, **250–251**
nylon **VIII:** 47
NYNEX **X:** 50m
NYPD Blue (TV program) **X:** 277, 278, 295
Nzinga, queen of Angola (Nzinga Mbande, or Ana de Sousa, or Dona Anna de Sousa) **I:** 229, **267**
Nzinga a Nkuwu, king of Kongo **I:** 196
Nzinga Mbembe, king of Kongo **I:** 196

O

OAA. See Old-Age Assistance Program
Oacpicagigua, Luis **II:** 284
OAI. See Old-Age Insurance Program
Oak and Ivory (Dunbar) **VI:** 82

Oakley, Annie
Cody, William Frederick **VI:** 59
entertainment, popular **VI:** 98
Native Americans **VI:** 209
Sitting Bull **VI:** 264
Oak Ridge, Tennessee **VIII:** 344, 356
"Oaks, The" **II:** 224
OAS. See Organization of American States
OASI **VIII:** 330
Oates, Joyce Carol **X:** 177
Oates, William C. **V:** **257**
oath of fealty (feudalism) **I:** 129
oats **II:** 370
Oaxaca (Antequera) **I:** 258; **II:** 357
oba **I:** 28
Oberlin College **VI:** 316
Burns, Anthony **IV:** 59
Finney, Charles Grandison **IV:** 139
Foster, Abigail Kelley **IV:** 148
Tappan, Arthur and Lewis **IV:** 333
Weld, Theodore Dwight **IV:** 362
Oberlin Rescuers **V:** 2
"Objections to the Federal Constitution" (Mason) **III:** 237, 238
obscenity **VII:** 29, 84
Bork, Robert **X:** 39
Brennan, William J. **X:** 40
censorship **X:** 60
pornography **X:** 244–245
Supreme Court **X:** 291
Observants (Franciscans) **I:** 132
observatories **II:** 322
obsidian trade **I:** 346, 356
Ocala demands **VI:** 222
OCCA. See Organized Crime Control Act of 1970
Occom, Samson **II:** 395, 396; **III:** 255
occult **II:** 331
Occupational Safety and Health Act of 1970 **X:** 77, 210, **225**, 323c
Occupational Safety and Health Administration (OSHA) **X:** 205, 225
Occupational Safety and Health Review Commission (OSHRC) **X:** 225
occupational status
African Americans **X:** 11
Asian Americans **X:** 28, 30

women's rights and status **X:** 320
occupations **IX:** 169–170, 170
OCD. See Office of Civil Defense; Office of Civilian Defense
oceanography **IV:** 308
Ochs, Adolph **VI:** 212; **VII:** 141
Ockenga, Harold **IX:** 256; **X:** 107–108
O'Connor, Sandra Day **X:** **225–226**, 226, 326c
Reagan, Ronald W. **X:** 260
Rehnquist, William H. **X:** 264
Souter, David **X:** 279
Supreme Court **X:** 291
Thomas, Clarence **X:** 302
Webster v. Reproductive Health Services **X:** 318
women's rights and status **X:** 321
O'Connor, William **V:** 394
OCR (Office for Civil Rights) **X:** 14
Ocracoke Inlet, North Carolina **II:** 369
octli **I:** 45
October Revolution **VII:** 100, 259, 270
October War of 1973 **X:** 54
Octopus, The (Norris) **VII:** 38–39
octoroon **II:** 229, 237
Octoroon, The (Boucicault) **V:** 352
Odanak **II:** 244
Odd Fellows **VI:** 265
Odell, Moses **V:** 191
Odets, Clifford **VIII:** 191
Oduduwa **I:** 273, 377
Odwira **I:** 13
OEO. See Office of Economic Opportunity
OEPC. See Organization of Petroleum Exporting Countries
Of Cabbages and Kings (Henry) **VII:** 356c
Offenbach, Jacques **VI:** 271
offense (military) **V:** 345
Office for Civil Rights (OCR) **X:** 14
Office of Bilingual and Minority Language Affairs **X:** 36
Office of Censorship **VIII:** 55
Office of Civil and Defense Mobilization **IX:** 53
Office of Civil Defense (OCD) **IX:** 53, 333c
Office of Civilian Defense (OCD) **VIII:** 182–183, 253, **253–254; IX:** 52

Office of Defense Mobilization **IX:** 53
Office of Defense Transportation **VIII:** 360
Office of Economic Opportunity (OEO) **IX:** 62, 87
Office of Economic Stabilization **VIII:** 49, 254, 371
Office of Emergency Planning **IX:** 53
Office of Federal Contract Compliance **X:** 8
Office of Indian Affairs **IV:** 181
Office of Indian Trade **IV:** 180
Office of Information and Regulatory Affairs **X:** 227
Office of Intergovernmental Affairs **X:** 14
Office of Malaria Control in War Areas (MCWA) **IX:** 198
Office of Management and Budget (OMB) **X:** 134–135, **226–227**
Office of National Drug Control Policy **X:** 35
Office of Naval Intelligence **VIII:** 164
Office of Price Administration (OPA) **VIII:** **254–255**, 409c
black market **VIII:** 38
Congress **VIII:** 68
Henderson, Leon **VIII:** 145
labor **VIII:** 181
mobilization **VIII:** 215
NWLB **VIII:** 233
OPM **VIII:** 255
rationing **VIII:** 292
wage and price controls **VIII:** 371
women's status and rights **VIII:** 386
World War II home front **VIII:** 396
WPB **VIII:** 375
Office of Price Administration and Civilian Supply (OPACS) **VIII:** 371
Office of Production Management (OPM) **VIII:** **255**
Harriman, Averell **VIII:** 143
Hillman, Sidney **VIII:** 146
labor **VIII:** 181
mobilization **VIII:** 214
Nelson, Donald M. **VIII:** 238
Office of Radio Research (ORR) **VIII:** 284

Office of Redress
   Administration (ORA) **X**: 63
Office of Scientific Research
   and Development (OSRD)
   VIII: 255–256
   atomic bomb **VIII**: 29
   Bush, Vannevar **VIII**: 45
   Manhattan Project **VIII**:
      200
   mobilization **VIII**: 215
   World War II home front
      VIII: 395
Office of Strategic Services
   (OSS) **VIII**: 105, 164,
   256–257, *257*, 283, 409*c*; **IX**:
   49
Office of War Information
   (OWI) **VIII: 257–258**, 409*c*
   advertising **VIII**: 1
   art and architecture **VIII**:
      24
   censorship **VIII**: 55
   Four Freedoms **VIII**: 127
   movies **VIII**: 218
   news media **VIII**: 243
   OSS **VIII**: 256
   photography **VIII**: 268
   popular culture **VIII**: 275
   propaganda **VIII**: 283
   public opinion polls **VIII**:
      284
Office of War Mobilization
   (OWM) **VIII: 258**
   Byrnes, James F. **VIII**: 49
   Congress **VIII**: 68
   mobilization **VIII**: 214
   reconversion **VIII**: 295
   sports **VIII**: 338
   WMC **VIII**: 375
   WPB **VIII**: 375, 376
Office of War Mobilization and
   Reconversion (OWMR) **VIII**:
   215, **258–259**, 296, 375
officers, political appointment of
   V: 365, 366, 383
Of Human Bondage (film) **VIII**:
   219
Of Thee I Sing (Gershwin) **VII**:
   108; **VIII**: 224
Ogdensburg Declaration of
   1940 **VIII**: 408*c*
Ogden v. Gibbons **III**: 142
Oglala Lakota **VI**: 69
Oglala Sioux nation
   Black Hills gold rush **VI**:
      29
   Crazy Horse **VI**: 69
   Native Americans **VI**: 207
   Red Cloud **VI**: 239–240
Oglethorpe, James Edward **II**:
   137, 238, 239, **267–268**, 297,
   375, 392, 394

O'Hara, John **VIII**: 165
Oh! Calcutta (musical) **X**: 277
Ohio **II**: 190–191, 248
   affirmative action **X**: 9
   *Akron v. Akron Center for
      Reproductive Health* **X**:
      16–17
   amendments to the
      Constitution **X**: 19–20
   Cass, Lewis **IV**: 76
   Chase, Salmon P. **V**: 56
   Church of Jesus Christ of
      Latter-day Saints **IV**: 79
   Harrison, William Henry
      IV: 169, 170
   Hayes, Rutherford B. **VI**:
      125
   internal improvements **IV**:
      188
   Liberty Party **IV**: 210
   McKinley, William **VI**: 189
   migration **IV**: 235
   National Road **IV**: 253
   oil **VI**: 215
   population trends **X**: 242
   rust belt **X**: 269
   trusts **VI**: 294
   Vallandigham, Clement L.
      V: 377–378
   volunteer army **V**: 383
   Wade, Benjamin **V**: 385
Ohio, Hopewell culture in **I**:
   166
Ohio & Erie Canal **IV**: 73*m*
Ohio Company of Associates
   III: 237, **265**
Ohio Company of Virginia **III**:
   265
Ohio Indians **II**: 76, 87, 114;
   III: 132
Ohio Life Insurance Company
   of Cincinnati **V**: 104
Ohio River **IV**: 40, 237, 293; **V**:
   355
Ohio River Valley **IV**: 117, 181,
   183, 235, 253
*Ohio v. Akron Center for
   Reproductive Health* (1990)
   X: 17
Ohio Valley **VI**: 4
Ohke Pueblo **I**: 319
Ohrlin, Glenn **IX**: 111
"Oh! Susannah" (Foster) **V**: 137
Oidores **I**: 15
oil conservation **VIII**: 103
oil embargo **VIII**: 105
oil/oil industry **II**: 225; **VI**:
   145–146, **215–216**, *216*,
   293–294, 323*c*; **VII**: *217*,
   217–218, 355*c*; **VIII**: 133;
   IX: 201, 286–287
   air power **VIII**: 12

Alaska Native Claim
   Settlement Act **X**: 17
business **VIII**: 46–47; **X**:
   49
Carter, James Earl, Jr. **X**:
   58
economy **VII**: 75; **X**: 94
Energy, U.S. Department
   of **X**: 103
energy crisis **X**: 103–104
foreign policy **VIII**: 124
Fuel Administration **VII**:
   102
Gore, Albert, Jr. **X**: 134
labor **X**: 170
Mexico **X**: 192
OPEC **X**: 228–229
Persian Gulf War **X**: 234
Rockefeller, John D. **VII**:
   264–265
Standard Oil **VII**: 295–296
Sunbelt **X**: 290
Teapot Dome **VII**:
   307–308
wage and price controls **X**:
   313
Zionism **VIII**: 403
oil spills **X**: 77
Ojeda, Alonso de **I**: 276, 368,
   386*c*
Ojibwa nation **II**: 17; **V**: 249
Ojo Caliente Reservation (New
   Mexico) **VI**: 14, 112
"OK" **IV**: 125
Okeechobee, Battle of **IV**: 334
O'Keefe, Georgia **VI**: 48; **VII**:
   20
oki **I**: 171
Okinawa **VIII**: **259**, 410*c*
   amphibious warfare **VIII**:
      15
   Hiroshima and Nagasaki
      VIII: 148
   Iwo Jima **VIII**: 169
   Marines, U.S. **VIII**: 203
   Navy, U.S. **VIII**: 236
   Nimitz, Chester W. **VIII**:
      246
   tanks **VIII**: 350
   World War II Pacific
      theater **VIII**: 399
Oklahoma **II**: 87; **V**: 390; **VI**:
   326*c*; **VII**: 357*c*; **VIII**: 87,
   212
   cotton culture **IV**: 98
   ERA **X**: 107
   grandfather clause **VI**:
      119
   Indian Removal Act (1830)
      IV: 183
   Jim Crow laws **VI**: 156
   migration **IV**: 235

Native Americans **IV**: 256;
   VI: 209; **X**: 215
population trends **X**: 242
Seminole wars **IV**: 312
Sooners **VI**: 270–271
Sunbelt **X**: 290
Trail of Tears **IV**: 344
Oklahoma! (Rodgers and
   Hammerstein) **VIII**: 224
Oklahoma City bombing **X**: 194,
   227, **227–228**, 299, 329*c*
Oklahoma City National
   Memorial **X**: 228
okra **II**: 122
O'Laughlin, Michael **V**: 17
Olcott, Henry Steel **VI**: 245
Old-Age and Survivors
   Insurance (OASI) **VIII**: 330
Old-Age Assistance Program
   (OAA). *See* Title I
Old-Age Benefits. *See* Title II
Old-Age Insurance Program
   (OAI) **VIII**: 95, 329–330
old age pension movement
   VIII: 330
Old-Age Revolving Pensions,
   Ltd. **VIII**: 359
"Old Briton." *See* La Demoiselle
Old Charter of 1629 **II**: 218
Old Deluder Satan Act **II**: 212,
   216
Oldenburg, Claes **IX**: 20
Old English. *See* Anglo-
   Normans
Older Americans Act of 1965 **X**:
   14
"Old Folks Concerts" **IV**: 250
Old Guard Republicans
   Cannon, Joseph **VII**: 42
   Congress **VII**: 53
   Coolidge, Calvin **VII**: 57
   Progressive Party **VII**: 236,
      237
   Republican Party **VII**: 263
   Taft, William Howard **VII**:
      303, 304
"old immigration" **V**: 278; **VI**:
   138
"Old Ironsides." *See
   Constitution*, USS
"Old Kinderhook" **IV**: 125
Old Lights
   Congregationalists **II**: 68
   Connecticut **II**: 70
   Great Awakening **II**: 148
   New Jersey **II**: 254
   Presbyterians **II**: 296
   Tennent, Gilbert **II**: 371
   Wigglesworth, Edward **II**:
      398
Old North Church (Boston) **II**:
   24, 217, 218; **III**: 212

Old Northwest
    Free-Soil Party **IV:** 151
    Harrison, William Henry
        IV: 169
    Hull, William **IV:** 175
    migration **IV:** 235
    public land policy **IV:** 286
"Old Rough and Ready" **IV:** 334
Olds, Ransom E. **VII:** 21
Old School doctrine **IV:** 225
Olds Motor Vehicle Company
    IX: 120
Old South Church **III:**
    265–266, 390
Old Spanish Trail **IV:** 131
*Old Swimmin' Hole and 'Leven
    More Poems* (Riley) **VI:** 178
Old-Time Gospel Hour, The **X:**
    294
"Old Tippecanoe" **IV:** 125
Old Town Folks (Stowe) **V:** 339
Olid, Cristóbal **I:** 364
Olive Branch Petition **III: 266**
Oliver, Andrew **III: 266–267**
    liberty tree/pole **III:** 213
    Loyal Nine **III:** 222
    MacIntosh, Ebenezer **III:**
        225
    Stamp Act **III:** 332
Oliver, James **VI:** 8
Oliver, Joe "King" **VII:** 137, 194
Oliver, Robert **III:** 350
Olivi, Giovanni Battista **I:** 40
Ollokot **VI:** 213
Olmecs **I: 269–270,** 270, 385c
    art and architecture **I:** 13
    Aztecs **I:** 21
    cacao **I:** 45
    Quetzalcoatl **I:** 301
    Tabasco **I:** 341
    Tláloc **I:** 352
    Veracruz **I:** 366
Olmstead, Frederick Law **III:**
    365; **IV:** 28, 98; **V:** 61,
    257–258, 373; **VI:** 65
Olmstead v. United States **VII:**
    361c
Olmsted, Vaux & Co. **VI:** 319
Olney, Richard **VI:** 236, 303;
    VII: 64
Olorun **I:** 377
Olson, Culbert L. **VII:** 188
Olustee, Battle of **V:** 126
Olympia, USS **VI:** 79
Olympic Games **VI:** 290; **X:**
    326c. *See also* Summer
    Olympic games
        Carter, James Earl, Jr. **X:**
            58
        cold war (end of) **X:** 71
        foreign policy **X:** 123
        recreation **X:** 262

television **X:** 296
    terrorism **X:** 299
Olympic Games (Berlin, 1936)
    VIII: 260–261, 275, 338,
    407c
Olympic Games (Los Angeles,
    1932) **VIII:** 338
Omaha **IV:** 242
Omaha Beach **VIII:** 248
Omaha platform **VI:** 100, **216,**
    222, 327c
O'Mahoney, Joseph C. **VIII:**
    355
O'Malley, Walter **IX:** 280, 332c
Omar, Mullah **X:** 331c
OMB. *See* Office of
    Management and Budget
omnibus **IV:** 82; **V:** 59
Omnibus Act of 1950 **IX:** 197
Omnibus Budget Reconciliation
    Act **X:** 16
Omnibus Crime Control and
    Safe Streets Act of 1994 **X:**
    82–83
Omnibus Trade and
    Competitiveness Act of 1988
    X: 121–122
Omni Hotels **X:** 244
Onassis, Aristotle **IX:** 156
Oñate, Juan de **I:** 257, **271,** 319,
    383, 388c; **II:** 246, 254
"one-drop rule" **VII:** 248–249
One Feather, Vivian **IX:** 229
114 Songs (Ives) **VII:** 195
Oneida, New York **IV:** 299
Oneida nation **I:** 160, 181–183,
    271–272; III: 178, 179,
    255
        Conestoga **II:** 67
        Dekanawideh **II:** 85
        Iroquois **II:** 168, 170
        Native Americans **II:** 243
        New Netherland **II:** 256
        society, British American
            II: 352
        Tuscarora **II:** 379
        Tuscarora War **II:** 379
Oneida Perfectionist
    Community **VI:** 301
O'Neill, Eugene **VII:** 85, 161,
    360c; **VIII:** 165, 192, 407c;
    IX: 181, 261
O'Neill, Thomas P., Jr. ("Tip")
    X: 144, 166, **228,** 325c
ONE (journal) **IX:** 119
One World (Willkie) **VIII:** 379
Onigbogi **I:** 273
Onís, Luís de **IV:** 5
*Only Method of Attracting
    Everyone to the True
    Religion, The* (Bartolomé de
    Las Casas) **I:** 199

Onondaga nation **I:** 160,
    181–183, **272,** 321; **II:** 85,
    168, 243, 256, 415; **III:** 178
OnStar system **X:** 275
Ontario **I:** 405
"on the charity" **II:** 137
"On the Constitution"
    (Franklin) **III:** 135, 395c
On the Origin of Species
    (Darwin) **IV:** 291; **VI:** 75,
    242, 265
"On the Question of Slavery"
    speech **IV:** 377c
On the Road (Jack Kerouac) **IX:**
    35, 71, 159, 182, 332c
On the Waterfront (movie) **IX:**
    303
"On to Richmond" **V:** 367
OPA. *See* Office of Price
    Administration
OPACS (Office of Price
    Administration and Civilian
    Supply) **VIII:** 371
op art **IX:** 20; **X:** 26
Opata **II:** 229
OPEC. *See* Organization of
    Petroleum Exporting
    Countries
Opechancanough **II: 268,** 417c,
    418c
        ethnocentrism **II:** 114
        Native Americans **II:** 244
        Powhatan (chief) **II:** 294
        Powhatan Confederacy **II:**
            294, 295
        Virginia **II:** 382
Open Door notes **VI: 216–217,**
    328c; **VIII:** 199
        Hay, John Milton **VI:** 125
        imperialism **VI:** 143
        Mahan, Alfred Thayer **VI:**
            186
        McKinley, William **VI:**
            190
Open Door Policy **VII:**
    218–219, 355c, 357c, 360c
        Boxer Rebellion **VII:** 33,
            34
        foreign policy **VII:** 98
        Great White Fleet **VII:**
            114
        Hughes, Charles Evans
            VII: 124
        nativism **VII:** 208
        Root-Takahira Agreement
            VII: 267
        Russo-Japanese War **VII:**
            271
        trade, foreign **VII:** 310
        Washington Conference
            on Naval Disarmament
            VII: 331

open hearth furnace **VI:** 27,
    276–277
open-pit mining **VI:** 193
open shop movement **VII:**
    219–220
        American Plan **VII:** 12
        Anthracite Coal Strike **VII:**
            13
        Farmer-Labor Party **VII:**
            91
        labor movement **VII:** 152
        Ludlow Massacre **VII:** 168
        National Association of
            Manufacturers **VII:** 200
        National War Labor Board
            VII: 204
        Seattle General Strike **VII:**
            279
        U.S. Steel **VII:** 320
opera **VII:** 141; **VIII:** 223; **IX:**
    216–217; **X:** 201
Operation Barbarossa **VIII:** 393
Operation Bingo **IX:** 236
Operation Bolero **VIII:** 320
Operation Bootstrap **IX:** 173,
    250, 329c
Operation Breadbasket **X:** 159
Operation Desert Shield **X:** 235
Operation Desert Storm. *See*
    Persian Gulf War
Operation Dirty Trick **IX:** 236
Operation Dixie **IX: 235–236,**
    329c
Operation Good Times **IX:** 236
Operation Husky **VIII:** 325
Operation Just Cause **X:**
    231–232
Operation Midnight Climax **IX:**
    183
Operation Mongoose **IX:** 35, 73,
    75, **236**
Operation Musketeer Revise
    IX: 289
Operation Neptune **VIII:** 248
Operation Overlord **IX:** 92
        amphibious warfare **VIII:**
            16
        Normandy, invasion of
            VIII: 247
        second front **VIII:** 320
        Teheran Conference **VIII:**
            354, 355
Operation Rescue **X:** 249
Operation Roundup **VIII:** 320
Operation Sledgehammer **VIII:**
    320
Operation Torch **VIII:** 249,
    392–393; **IX:** 92
Operation Zapata **IX:** 34
operettas
        Herbert, Victor August **VI:**
            128–129

music **VI:** 203
Sousa, John Philip **VI:** 271
theater **VI:** 286
Opitchapam **II:** 294
opium **IV:** 230; **VII:** 197; **X:** 206
OPM. *See* Office of Production Management
Oppenheimer, J. Robert **VIII:** 29, 146, 200, 409*c*; **IX:** 139, 140, **236–237**
opportunity liberalism **X:** 175
optical processors **X:** 75
optics **II:** 277, 330
oral contraceptives **IX:** 198–199, 242, 270, 295, 332*c*; **X:** 36
Oral Roberts Evangelical Association **X:** 294
oral tradition **II:** 195
Oran **I:** 174; **VIII:** 393
Oranyan **I:** 273
ORA (Office of Redress Administration) **X:** 63
Oration on the Abolition of the Slave Trade (Williams) **IV:** 366
orchards **V:** 7
Order No. 11 **V:** 407*c*
Order No. 28 **V:** 407*c*
Orders in Council **III:** 131, **267–268; IV:** 151
Ordinance of 1784 **III:** 184
Ordinance of 1785. *See* Land Ordinance of 1785
Ordinance of Nullification **IV:** 354
Ordinances of Discovery and Settlement (1573) **I:** 200
ordnance, Confederate **V:** 151–152
Oregon **X:** 19, 214, 242
Chinese workers in **VI:** 51*m*
Native Americans **VI:** 207
Nez Perce War **VI:** 213
Patrons of Husbandry **VI:** 221
Oregon & California Railroad **VI:** 305
Oregon Boundary Treaty **IV:** 403–404
Oregon Country **IV:** xiii, 29*m*, 229, 236
Oregon Joint Occupation Treaty (1827) **IV:** 229
Oregon Steam and Navigation Company **VI:** 305
Oregon Territory **IV:** 375*c*
Adams-Onís Treaty **IV:** 5
American Fur Company **IV:** 16
Astoria **IV:** 32–33
Bidwell, John **IV:** 51

Calhoun, John C. **IV:** 63
Clayton-Bulwer Treaty **IV:** 88
Columbia River **IV:** 92, 93
Compromise of 1850 **IV:** 94*m*
diseases and epidemics **IV:** 113
exploration **IV:** 132
foreign policy **IV:** 142
Fort Vancouver **IV:** 145
Manifest Destiny **IV:** 217, 218*m*
Massachusetts Emigrant Aid Society **IV:** 224
Monroe Doctrine **IV:** 242
Oregon Trail **IV:** 267
Polk, James K. **IV:** 283
Rocky Mountain Fur Company **IV:** 302
South Pass **IV:** 325
Oregon Trail **IV: 267–269,** 268*m*, 378*c*
California Trail **IV:** 70
Columbia River **IV:** 93
exploration **IV:** 131, 132
Fort Laramie **IV:** 143
Fort Leavenworth **IV:** 145
Forty-niners **IV:** 146
Frémont, John C. **IV:** 153
McLoughlin, John **IV:** 229
migration **IV:** 236
Mormon Trail **IV:** 243
mountain men **IV:** 248
Native Americans **IV:** 258
Smith, Jedediah Strong **IV:** 321
Sublette, William **IV:** 330
Oregon Treaty of 1846 **IV: 269–271,** 270*m*, 378*c*, 403–404; **VI:** 309
Adams-Onís Treaty **IV:** 5
Clayton-Bulwer Treaty **IV:** 88
economy **IV:** 117
exploration **IV:** 132
foreign policy **IV:** 142
Fort Laramie **IV:** 144
Fort Vancouver **IV:** 146
Manifest Destiny **IV:** 217
Polk, James K. **IV:** 283
Oregon v. Mitchell (1970) **X:** 19
Orellana, Francisco de **I:** 8, 9, 33
organ harvesting **X:** 146
Organic Act of 1897 **VI:** 65
organic compounds, synthetic **IV:** 307
Organization of American States (OAS) **VI:** 220; **IX:** 172, 330*c*
Latin America **X:** 172, 173
Mexico **X:** 192
Nicaragua **X:** 218

Organization of Petroleum Exporting Countries (OPEC) **X: 228–229,** 324*c*
automobile industry **X:** 31
economy **X:** 94
energy crisis **X:** 103–104
labor **X:** 170
wage and price controls **X:** 313
organized crime **VII:** 60, 241; **VIII:** 38, 167, 217–218; **IX:** 81, 136, 293, 303; **X:** 4, 82, 257–258
Organized Crime Control Act (OCCA) of 1970 **X:** 82, 257, 297, 323*c*
Organized Crime Strike Force (FBI) **X:** 4–5
organized labor. *See* labor/labor movement; unions/union movement
organs **II:** 239
organ transplants **IX:** 198; **X:** 190
Original Bantu **I:** 24, 25
Original Dixieland Jazz Band **VII:** 194
original sin **VIII:** 304
O'Riley, Peter **IV:** 95
Orinoco River **I:** 82, 368, 386*c*
Oriskany, Battle of **III:** 49, 188
Orkney Islands **I:** 263
Orlando, Vittorio **VII:** 323, 334
Orleans, Territory of **IV:** 84–85
Ormiston, Kenneth **VII:** 176
Ormond (Brown) **III:** 49
Ornithological Biography, The (Audubon) **IV:** 34
Ornitz, Samuel **IX:** 135, *211*
Orompoto **I:** 273
orphanages **II:** 397
Orphan Brigade **V: 258**
orphans **V:** 358
Orpheum Circuit **VI:** 96
ORR **VIII:** 284
orreries **II:** 322
Ortega, Daniel **X:** 218
Orteig, Raymond **VII:** 159
Ortelius, Abraham **I:** 51, 232
Orthodox Judaism **VI:** 158, 243; **VIII:** 303; **X:** 161, 265
Orthodox Quakers **IV:** 172
orthodox theology **VI:** 75
Orungu **I:** 247
Osage nation **IV:** 78–79, 282; **VI:** 209, 271
Osbon, B. S. **V:** 193
Osborn, Alex **VII:** 5
Osborn, Fairfield **IX:** 101
Osborn, Sarah Haggar Wheaten **II: 268–269**
Osborne, Sir Edward **I:** 206

Osceola **IV:** 256, 312, 377*c*
Osei Tutu **I:** 13
OSHA. *See* Occupational Safety and Health Administration
OSHRC (Occupational Safety and Health Review Commission) **X:** 225
Osmond, Henry **IX:** 183
OSRD. *See* Office of Scientific Research and Development
OSS. *See* Office of Strategic Services
Ostenaco **II: 269**
Ostend Manifesto **IV:** 101; **V:** 41, 131, 259, **259–260**
Osterhaus, Peter **V:** 147
Ostfriedland (battleship) **VII:** 187
O'Sullivan, John **IV:** 142, 217, 219
O'Sullivan, Mary Kenney **VII:** 205
O'Sullivan, Timothy H. **V:** 36, 273
Oswald, Lee Harvey **IX:** 158, **237–238,** *238*, 334*c*
Oswego, New York **II:** 262
Otermín, Antonio de **II:** 303
Othello **VIII:** 309–310, 410*c*
Other America, The (Michael Harrington) **IX:** 62, 90, 130, 313, 333*c*
"otherness, cult of" **X:** 176, 201
Other People's Money (Brandeis) **VII:** 34
Otis, Elisha **IV:** 82, 307; **VI:** 149, 326*c*
Otis, Harrison Gray **III:** 173, **268**
Otis, James, Jr. **II:** 215; **III: 268–269,** 391*c*
antislavery and abolition **III:** 16
Hutchinson, Thomas **III:** 171
Revere, Paul **III:** 304
Warren, Mercy Otis **III:** 363
writs of assistance **III:** 384
Otis, James, Sr. **II:** 72; **III:** 171
Otis family **II:** 215
Ottawa **II:** 31, 174, 191, 205, 246; **III:** 281; **V:** 249
Ottoman Empire **I:** 339; **II:** 150, 346
Ottoman Turks
Holy League **I:** 164, 165
Islam **I:** 185
Jews (Judaism) **I:** 191
Ouagadougou (Wegadugu) **I:** 243
Oubry **I:** 243

Ouedraogo (Wedraogo) **I:** 243
ouija boards **IV:** 325
Ould, Robert **V:** 281
Our Country: Its Possible Future and Its Present Crisis (Strong) **VI:** 142, 267, 279, 325c
Our Flirtations (Sousa) **VI:** 271
Our Land and Land Policy (George) **VI:** 111
Our Plundered Planet (Fairfield Osborn) **IX:** 101
Ousamequin **II:** 217
Outacite **II:** 269
Outcault, Richard **VI:** 321; **VII:** 121
"outdoor" relief system **II:** 18
Outdoor Resources Review commission **IX:** 322
Outer Banks **II:** 263–265
Outerbridge, Mary **VI:** 273
Outlines of the Cosmic Philosophy (Fiske) **VI:** 75, 242
out-of-wedlock births **X:** 181, 182
ouvidor **I:** 33
Ovando, Nicolas de **I:** 82, 91, 288
ovariotomy **IV:** 231
Overhill Cherokee Treaty **III:** 66
Overland campaign **V: 260–261**
    Cold Harbor, Battle of **V:** 68
    Ewell, Richard Stoddert **V:** 119
    Grant, Ulysses S. **V:** 156
    homefront **V:** 169
    Lee, Robert E. **V:** 207
    Lincoln, Abraham **V:** 211
    Petersburg campaign **V:** 270
    Spotsylvania, Battles of **V:** 333
    Stuart, J. E. B. **V:** 341
    Union army **V:** 367
    Wilderness, Battle of the **V:** 395
overland mail **IV: 271–272,** 272
Overland Mail Company **IV:** 271–272
Overland Trail **IV:** 131
overpopulation
    abortion **X:** 1
    birth control **X:** 37
    gay rights movement **X:** 127
    pro-life and pro-choice movements **X:** 248
overproduction, agricultural **IX:** 8–9

overseer **IV:** 98
Overseers of the Poor (Philadelphia) **II:** 282
Over-Soul **IV:** 345
overtime **VIII:** 110
Overton Act **VII:** 255
Oviedo y Valdés, Gonzalo Fernández de **I:** 29, 207, **272–273,** 305
Ovington, Mary White **VI:** 309
Owen, Chandler **VIII:** 291
Owen, Robert **IV: 272–273**
    industrialization **IV:** 185
    religion **IV:** 299
    Warren, Josiah **IV:** 358
    Wright, Fanny **IV:** 369
Owen, Ruth Bryan **VIII:** 383, 384
Owens, Jesse **VIII:** *260,* **260–261,** 275, 338, 407c; **IX:** 5
OWI. *See* Office of War Information
OWM. *See* Office of War Mobilization
OWMR. *See* Office of War Mobilization and Reconversion
Ox-Bow Trail **IV:** 132
Oxenham, John **I:** 277
Oxford **I:** 75, 152, 278
Oxford Methodists **II:** 393
Oya **I:** 263
Oyo **I:** 101, 125, **273,** 377
Oyster Creed power plant **IX:** 24
Ozawa, Jisaburo **VIII:** 267
Ozick, Cynthia **X:** 178
Ozma, Agnes **VII:** 261
Ozolua **I:** 28

P

Pabst, Daniel **VI:** 15
PAC. *See* political action committee
Pacaritambo **I:** 175
Pace v. Alabama **V:** 234
Pachacuti **I:** 99, 175, 176, 213–214
Pacific coast **II:** 382
Pacific Crest Trail **IX:** 226
Pacific Fur Company
    American Fur Company **IV:** 16
    Astor, John Jacob **IV:** 31
    Astoria **IV:** 32
    Columbia River **IV:** 93
Pacific Islander Americans
    Asian Americans **X:** 28, 30
    education, higher **X:** 97
    population trends **X:** 243

Pacific Northwest **II:** 118; **IV:** 378c
    exploration **IV:** 132
    Fort Vancouver **IV:** 145
    McLoughlin, John **IV:** 228–229
    Oregon Treaty of 1846 **IV:** 269–271
    Rocky Mountain Fur Company **IV:** 302
Pacific Ocean **I:** 24, 25m, 215–216, 276, 386c; **V:** 133; **VI:** 141
    foreign policy **IV:** 143
    Hawaiian Islands **IV:** 171–172
    Manifest Destiny **IV:** 219
    Perry, Matthew Calbraith **IV:** 280
Pacific Railroad **IV:** 118
Pacific Railroad Act of 1862 **V:** 84, 107, **263–264,** 301, 406c, 422–424
Pacific Railroad of Missouri (PRRM) **V:** 263, 264
Pacific Railway Act of 1862 **VI:** 179–180
Pacific Telesis Group **X:** 50m
Pacific theater. *See* World War II Pacific theater
pacifists/pacifism **II:** 275, 302, 307; **III:** 291; **V:** 266, 331–332; **VIII:** 54
    Addams, Jane **VII:** 3
    foreign policy **VII:** 101
    Wald, Lillian **VII:** 329
    Women's International League for Peace and Freedom **VII:** 337–338
Packard, Vance **IX:** 46, 69, 182, **239–240,** 332c
Packenham, Edward **IV:** 358
packet boats **IV:** 74
Packwood, Bob **X:** 276
"Pact of Steel" **VIII:** 31
Padilla, Juan de **I:** 167
Padres, José María **IV:** 136
Page, James **II:** 173
Page, Thomas Nelson **V:** 217
Page, William **V:** 35
pagers **IX:** 270
Pahlavi, Mohammad Reza
    Carter, James Earl, Jr. **X:** 58
    Iranian hostage crisis **X:** 155, 156
    terrorism **X:** 297
Pahouin. *See* Fang
Paige, Satchel **VII:** 295; **VIII:** 336
Paik, Nam June **X:** 26
Paine, H. E. **VI:** 310

Paine, John Knowles **VI:** 201
Paine, Lewis **V:** 17, 18, 315
Paine, Thomas **II:** 62, 119, 232; **III: 271–272,** 272, 393c
    antislavery and abolition **III:** 16
    artisans **III:** 26
    Barlow, Joel **III:** 36
    Burke, Edmund **III:** 53
    Common Sense (Paine) **III:** 77–79
    corporatism **III:** 94
    deism **III:** 104
    Franklin, Benjamin **III:** 134, 135
    journalism **III:** *191*
    literature **III:** 214, 215
    Morse, Jedidiah **III:** 249
    republicanism **III:** 302
    resistance movement **III:** 303
painkillers **V:** 96–97
painting **II:** 24, 25; **IV:** 26, 34–35, 54–55, 77–78; **V:** 16; **VI: 219–220; IX:** 19–20. *See also* portraiture
    art and architecture **VI:** 15
    Cassatt, Mary **VI:** 45
    Chase, William Merritt **VI:** 48–49
    Eakins, Thomas **VI:** 85–87
    Homer, Winslow **VI:** 130–131
    Jefferson, Joseph, III **VI:** 156
    Remington, Frederic **VI:** 245–246
    Whistler, James Abbott McNeill **VI:** 312
Paipai **I:** 48
Paiute nation **IV:** 115; **VI:** 198
Pakenman, Edward **IV:** 262
Pakistan **VIII:** 366; **IX:** 273–274; **X:** 164, 247
Palace of the Sun **I:** 99
Palace Theatre, New York **VI:** 96
Palacios Rubios, Juan López de **I:** 311, 369
Paladanus, Bernard **I:** 40
Palatine **II:** 97, 139, 146, 147, 261
Palaus **VIII:** 246
Palazzo della Signoria **I:** 204
Palazzo Vendramin-Calergi **I:** 365
Palenque **I:** 12, 69, 252, **275,** 349
palenques **II:** 359
Paleo-Indians **I:** 385c; **II:** 149
paleontology **VI:** 188, 257

Palestine **I:** 294; **VI:** 173; **VIII:** 403; **IX:** 146, 201, 330*c*; **X:** 54, 69, 195, 330*c*
Palestine Implementation Commission **IX:** 43
Palestine Liberation Organization (PLO)
    Camp David accords **X:** 54
    Habib, Philip C. **X:** 139
    neoconservatism **X:** 215
    terrorism **X:** 298
Palfrey, John **IV:** 196
Palfrey, Sarah **VIII:** 337
Palladio, Andrea **II:** 23; **III:** 185
Palma Island **I:** 53, 338
Palmer, Alexander Mitchell **VII:** **221,** 360*c*
    Communist Party **VII:** 52
    Coolidge, Calvin **VII:** 56
    Democratic Party **VII:** 66
    elections **VII:** 81
    Fuel Administration **VII:** 103
    labor movement **VII:** 153
    New Unionism **VII:** 213
    radicalism **VII:** 251
    Red Scare. *See* Red Scare
    Russian Revolution **VII:** 270
    socialism **VII:** 289
    Trading with the Enemy Act **VII:** 311
    women's status and rights **VII:** 340
Palmer, Arnold **X:** 262, 286
Palmer, John E. **VI:** 204
Palmer, John M. **V:** 285
Palmer, Mitchell **IX:** 136
Palmer, Nathaniel Brown **IV:** 133, 375*c*
Palmer, Phoebe **IV:** 296
Palmer Raids **VII:** 273, 360*c*.
    See also Red Scare
Palomar Observatory **IX:** 278
Pamunkey **II:** 268, 294, 295; **V:** 249
pan-Africanism **IV:** 354; **VI:** 71; **VII:** 72; **IX:** 48
Panama **I:** 275–277; **II:** 356; **IV:** 88, 146, 378*c*; **V:** 133, 315; **VI:** 125; **VII:** 27–28, 99, 356*c*, 358*c*; **IX:** 172
    Balboa, Vasco Núñez de **I:** 24
    Bush, George H. W. **X:** 45–46
    Canal Zone turnover **X:** **232–233**
    Columbus, Bartholomew **I:** 79
    Columbus, Christopher **I:** 82

defense policy **X:** 87
Drake, Sir Francis **I:** 110, 112
foreign policy **X:** 124
invasion of **X:** **231–232,** 232*m*, 327*c*
Latin America **X:** 172
Pizarro, Francisco **I:** 283
Powell, Colin L. **X:** 247
smallpox **I:** 331
Panama, Isthmus of **I:** 386*c*
Panama Canal **V:** 133; **VI:** 85; **VII:** 222, **222–224,** 223*m*, 356*c*, 358*c*; **VIII:** 408*c*
    Big Stick diplomacy **VII:** 27–28
    Carter, James Earl, Jr. **X:** 58
    Ford, Gerald R. **X:** 121
    foreign policy **VII:** 99; **X:** 123
    Latin America **X:** 173
    National Association of Manufacturers **VII:** 200
    Panama Canal **VII:** 222–224
    Roosevelt, Theodore **VII:** 266
    turnover of **X:** **232–233,** 330*c*
Panama Canal Treaty of 1977 **X:** 233, 325*c*
Panama Congress of 1826 **VI:** 220
Panama Defense Forces (PDF) **X:** 231
pan-amalgamation process **IV:** 96
Pan-American Conference of 1889–1890 **VI:** 32, 123; **X:** 172
Pan-American Conference of 1933 **VIII:** 133, 160
Pan American Petroleum and Transportation Company **VII:** 307
Pan-American Union **VI:** 44, **220**
Pan American World Airways **VII:** 160
Panay, USS **VIII:** 199
Pancoast, Henry S. **VI:** 144
pandemics. *See* disease and epidemics
Panic of 1792 **III:** **272–273,** 395*c*
Panic of 1819 **III:** 33, 113, 351; **IV:** **275–276; VI:** 41
    agriculture **IV:** 12
    Alamo, The **IV:** 12
    American System **IV:** 18

Ashley, William Henry **IV:** 28
Audubon, John James **IV:** 34
Austin, Moses **IV:** 36
banking and currency **IV:** 42
Bank of the United States, Second **IV:** 44
Benton, Thomas Hart **IV:** 49
economy **IV:** 119
Era of Good Feelings **IV:** 127
industrialization **IV:** 185
migration **IV:** 235
public land policy **IV:** 286
Travis, William Barret **IV:** 345
Turner, Nat **IV:** 346
Panic of 1837 **IV:** **276–277; V:** 37, 401; **VI:** 41
    banking and currency **IV:** 42
    Bank of the United States, Second **IV:** 44
    Church of Jesus Christ of Latter-day Saints **IV:** 79
    economy **IV:** 119
    election of 1840 **IV:** 124
    Florida **IV:** 140
    Harrison, William Henry **IV:** 170
    industrialization **IV:** 185
    internal improvements **IV:** 188
    labor movements **IV:** 204
    marriage and family life **IV:** 222
    McCormick, Cyrus Hall **IV:** 224
    Tappan, Arthur and Lewis **IV:** 333
    Van Buren, Martin **IV:** 352
    Whig Party **IV:** 363
Panic of 1857 **IV:** 119, 301; **V:** **264**
    Cooke, Jay **V:** 81
    economy **V:** 104, 107
    employment **V:** 116
    Sherman, William T. **V:** 320
Panic of 1873 **VI:** 324*c*
    banking, investment **VI:** 19
    business cycles **VI:** 41–42
    Cooke, Jay **V:** 81
    economy **V:** 107
    entertainment, popular **VI:** 96
    Freedman's Saving Bank **V:** 141
    Grant, Ulysses S. **V:** 157

Greenback-Labor Party **VI:** 120
national banking system **VI:** 206
National Labor Union (NLU) **V:** 248
Patrons of Husbandry **VI:** 221
redemption **V:** 297
Scott, Thomas Alexander **VI:** 258
steel **VI:** 277
Tredegar Iron Works **V:** 356
trusts **VI:** 292
Villard, Henry **VI:** 305
Panic of 1884 **VI:** 41, 206
Panic of 1893 **VI:** 327*c*; **VII:** 65
    business cycles **VI:** 41
    Coxey's Army **VI:** 67
    currency issue **VI:** 73
    Democratic Party **VI:** 78
    Klondike gold rush **VI:** 161
    McKinley, William **VI:** 189
    national banking system **VI:** 206
    the presidency **VI:** 230
    railroads **VI:** 238
    Republican Party **VI:** 246
    steel **VI:** 277
    Villard, Henry **VI:** 305
    World's Columbian Exposition **VI:** 320
Panic of 1907 **VI:** 198; **VII:** 93
Pankhurst, Emmeline **VII:** 336
Pánuco **I:** 146
Papago **II:** 165
Papegoja, Armgard **II:** 365
paper currency. *See* bluebacks; greenbacks
paper/paper manufacturing **I:** 293; **II:** 225; **IV:** 186*m*
Papua New Guinea **I:** 338
PA (Press Association of the Southern States) **V:** 193
parables **II:** 152
Paracelsus **II:** 220
Paraguay **I:** 38, 306; **II:** 229; **X:** 174
Paramount **IX:** 210
Paramount Records **VII:** 32
paranormal **X:** 217
Pardo, Juan **I:** 76, 85, 130
pardons, presidential. *See* presidential pardons
Paré, Ambroise **I:** 40, 240, 402
Paredes, Mariano **IV:** 234
parental consent (abortion) **X:** 3, 17
Parham, Charles **VII:** 261
Paris **I:** 75

Paris, Declaration of (1856) **V:** 131
Paris, liberation of **VIII:** 410c
Paris, Pact of **VII:** 361c
Paris, Treaty of (1763) **II:** 121, 126, **378,** 420c; **IV:** 337
 Acadians **II:** 2
 British Empire **II:** 41
 French colonies **II:** 129
 Louisiana **II:** 199
 Pennsylvania **II:** 276
 Seven Years' War **II:** 334
 Vermont **II:** 381
Paris, Treaty of (1783) **III: 273,** 274m, 391c, 394c; **IV:** 25, 139, 337, 360
 Adams, John **III:** 2
 Canada **III:** 60, 61
 Choctaw nation **III:** 68
 Continental Congress, Second **III:** 89
 Florida **III:** 129
 foreign affairs **III:** 130
 frontier **III:** 141
 Grasse, comte de **III:** 154
 Iroquois Confederacy **III:** 179
 Jay, John **III:** 181
 Jay's Treaty **III:** 182
 journalism **III:** 191
 labor and labor movements **III:** 200
 Laurens, Henry **III:** 203
 Louisiana Purchase **III:** 218
 Loyalists **III:** 221
 Native Americans and the Revolution **III:** 256
 Pontiac's Rebellion **III:** 281
 San Lorenzo, Treaty of **III:** 317
 Vergennes, comte de **III:** 359
 Washington, George **III:** 367
Paris, Treaty of (1856) **V:** 74
Paris, Treaty of (1898) **VI:** 37, 71, 328c
Parish, David **III:** 153
Paris Peace Accord (1973) **X:** 324c
 détente **X:** 89
 Nixon, Richard M. **X:** 220
 Vietnam War **X:** 311, 312
Paris Peace Conference (1849) **V:** 40
Paris Peace Conference (1918) **VII:** 359c
 Democratic Party **VII:** 66
 League of Nations **VII:** 156

Lodge, Henry Cabot **VII:** 165
 Versailles, Treaty of **VII:** 322
 Wilson, Woodrow **VII:** 334
Paris Peace Talks (Vietnam) **VIII:** 144
parity **IX:** 8
Park, Robert **VII:** 248
Park Chung Hee **X:** 166
Parke Davis **IX:** 206
Parker, Alton B. **VII:** 80, 201, 356c
Parker, Charlie **VIII:** 223, 410c
Parker, Ely Samuel **V:** 15, 249, 250, **264–265**
Parker, Horatio **VI:** 201; **VII:** 194
Parker, John **II:** 224; **III:** 212
Parker, John H. **V:** 18
Parker, John J. **VIII:** 405c; **IX:** 220
 African Americans **VIII:** 2
 civil rights **VIII:** 61
 NAACP **VIII:** 227
 Supreme Court **VIII:** 344
 White, Walter **VIII:** 378
Parker, Robert **II:** 176
Parker, Theodore **IV:** 298
Parker, William **V:** 59
Parker's Ferry, Battle of **III:** 232
Parkinson, Kenneth W. **X:** 308, 317
Parkman, Francis **IV:** 196
parks, public **V:** 61, 257–258
Parks, Rosa **IX:** 5, 113, **240–241,** 271, 331c
Parks, William **II:** 178
Park Tong Sun **X:** 166
Parliament **I: 277; III:** 391c, 392c
 British Empire **II:** 43
 Currency Act **III:** 99
 Drake, Sir Francis **I:** 111
 Elizabeth I **I:** 119
 English Civil War **II:** 108
 government, British American **II:** 144, 146
 Hawkins, Sir John **I:** 156
 Henry VII **I:** 159
 Henry VIII **I:** 160
 Mary I **I:** 224
 Otis, James, Jr. **III:** 268
 Privy Council **I:** 295
 Quartering Act **III:** 291
 Vice Admiralty Courts **III:** 360
 Wilkes, John **III:** 378–379
Parliamentary Gaols Committee **II:** 137
Parmenius, Stephen **I:** 142, **278,** 388c

parochial schools **IV:** 315, 316; **V:** 176; **VI:** 91–92; **IX:** 98
parole camps **V:** 281
Parris, Samuel **II: 271,** 402
Parsons, Albert **VI:** 127
Parsons, Charles **VI:** 138
Parsons, Theophilus **IV:** 4
Parsons, William **II:** 18
Parsons' Cause **II: 271–272;** **III:** 40, 166
partial birth abortion **X:** 4, 42, 279, 330c
partible inheritance **II:** 297
participatory democracy **IX:** 286
"particular plantations" **II:** 387
parties. *See* political parties
partisan politics **III:** 175
Partisan Rangers **V:** 241
Partnership for a New Generation of Vehicles (PNGV) **X:** 32
partnership for peace (NATO) **IX:** 233
Partnership for Peace (PFP) **X:** 223
Parton, Dolly **X:** 203
part-time employment **IX:** 272
party unity **IV:** 127
Pasgoula **II:** 246
Paspahegh, queen of the Powhatan **I:** 135
Paspahegh nation **II:** 294
Paspiheigh **II:** 171, 172
Passaic Strike **VII: 224–225,** 361c
Passamaquoddy **I:** 219, **278; II:** 243
Passamaquoddy language **I:** 6
Passing of the Armies (Chamberlain) **V:** 54
Passing of the Great Race (Grant) **VII:** 14, 248
Passionate Pilgrim, The (James) **VI:** 154
Passion Flowers (Howe) **V:** 174
Pasteur, Louis **V:** 97
Pastor, Tony **VI:** 96, 203
Patagonia **I:** 283
Patawamake **II:** 288
PATCO (Professional Air Traffic Controllers Association) strike **X:** 170
Patent Arms Manufacturing Company **IV:** 91
patent disputes **VI:** 25, 149, 150
Patent Granted by King Henry VII to John Cabot and His Sons, March 1496 **I:** 394–395
patent medicine **IV:** 230; **VII:** 197
Patent of 1621 **II:** 220
Patent Office **IV:** 11

patents **II:** 369; **IV:** 187, 224, 225, 245, 308, 377c; **VI:** 147, 220
paternalism **III:** 94
paternal society **II:** 136
Paterson, William **III:** 192, 338
Paterson Strike **VII:** 115, 120, 130, **225**
"Pathfinder, The." *See* Frémont, John C.
Pathfinder mission **X:** 329c
Patients' Bill of Rights Act of 2001 **X:** 164
Patman, Wright **X:** 144
Patman Bonus Bill **VIII:** 39
Patowmack Company **IV:** 72
patriarchal society **II:** 206
patrilineal kinship **II:** 255
patriotism **VI:** 157
"patriot movement" **X:** 227–228
patronage **IV:** 150; **VI:** 108, 174; **VII:** 324. *See also* civil service reform
 Bruce, Blanche K. **V:** 40–41
 impeachment of Andrew Johnson **V:** 178
 Longstreet, James **V:** 216
 Republican Party **V:** 302
 scalawags **V:** 307
patronato real **I:** 262
Patrons of Husbandry **VI:** 99, 221, **221–222,** 239
patroonships **II:** 227, 256, 257, 260, 319, 381
Patterson, John **IX:** 114
Patterson, Robert B. **IX:** 320
Patterson, Robert P. **VIII:** 19, 340
Patterson v. McLean Credit Union (1989) **X:** 63
Pattie, James Ohio **IV:** 131
Pattie, Sylvester **IV:** 131
Pattison, Robert **VI:** 132
Patton, Charlie **VII:** 32; **VIII:** 223
Patton, George S., Jr. **VII:** 9; **VIII: 263,** 409c
 African Americans **VIII:** 4
 Bulge, Battle of the **VIII:** 44
 Mauldin, Bill **VIII:** 207
 North African campaign **VIII:** 249
 Sicily **VIII:** 325
 tanks **VIII:** 349
Patuxet **II:** 287, 360–361
Pátzcuaro **I:** 343
Paul, Alice **VI:** 36; **VII: 225–226,** 359c, 360c; **X:** 19, 105
 ERA **VII:** 87

National Woman's Party **VII:** 204, 205

NAWSA **VII:** 198

woman suffrage **VII:** 336, 337

women's status and rights **VII:** 340

Paul, William **IV:** 354

Paulding, James Kirke **IV:** 212

Paul III, Pope **I:** 188, 209, 212, 235–236, 359–360

Pauling, Linus **IX:** 267

Paulists **VI:** 249

Paul IV, Pope **I:** 191

Paul Quinn College **VI:** 4

"Paul Revere's Ride" (Longfellow) **III:** 304

Paul VI, Pope **X:** 3, 37

Pawnee nation **II:** 255; **IV:** 282

pawnships **II:** 71

Pawnshop, The (film) **VII:** 359c

Paxton Boys **II:** 67, **272**, 274, 415

Payne, Daniel A. **VI:** 4

Payne, David L. **VI:** 270

Payne-Aldrich Tariff Act **VI:** 39; **VII: 226–227**, 357c

Congress **VII:** 53

Progressive Party **VII:** 236

Republican Party **VII:** 263

Taft, William Howard **VII:** 303–304

tariffs **VII:** 305

payroll tax **VIII:** 329

PBS. *See* Public Broadcasting Service

PCSW. *See* President's Commission on the Status of Women (1961)

PDF (Panama Defense Forces) **X:** 231

Peabody, Elizabeth **IV:** 155

Peabody, Francis Greenwood **VI:** 266

Peabody, George **VI:** 94, 150

Peabody Education Fund **VI:** 94

Peabody Museum **VI:** 188

peace activism **VI:** 181

Peace Corps **IX:** 158, 230, **241–242**, 311, 333c; **X:** 278

Peace Democrats. *See also* Copperheads

McClellan, George B. **V:** 226

peace movements **V:** 266

Vallandigham, Clement L. **V:** 377

Women's National Loyal League **V:** 396

peace efforts (Catholic Bishops' Letter) **X:** 59–60

peacekeeping activities (UN) **X:** 307

peace movements **V: 265–266; VII:** 43, 101, 146–147, 358c

Peace of Augsburg (1555) **I:** 212, 307

Peace Parties **V:** 169

Peace! Peace! (Spring) **V:** 266

peace pipes **II:** 50

peaches **II:** 8

Peachtree Creek, Battle of **V:** 354

Peach Tree War **II:** 99

Peach War **II:** 252

Peacock Room **VI:** 312

Peale, Charles Willson **III:** 22–24, 176, **273, 275**, 366

peanuts **II:** 121; **VI:** 45

Pearce, Charles Sprague **VI:** 15

Pea Ridge/Elkhorn Tavern, Battle of **V:** 73, 250, **265**, 391

Pearl Harbor **VIII: 263–265, *264***, 409c

aircraft industry **VIII:** 11

air power **VIII:** 11

America First Committee **VIII:** 13

Anglo-American relations **VIII:** 17

Asian Americans **VIII:** 26

Axis **VIII:** 31

Bataan Death March **VIII:** 35

Communists **VIII:** 65

Coral Sea, Battle of the **VIII:** 74

"Day of Infamy" speech **VIII:** 428

enemy aliens **VIII:** 102

espionage **VIII:** 104

Executive Order 9066 **VIII:** 107

foreign policy **VIII:** 124, 125

Halsey, "Bull" **VIII:** 143

Hiroshima and Nagasaki **VIII:** 147

intelligence **VIII:** 164

isolationists **VIII:** 166

Japanese Americans, relocation of **VIII:** 171

King, Ernest J. **VIII:** 177

labor **VIII:** 181

La Follette, Robert M., Jr. **VIII:** 182

Manchuria **VIII:** 200

Manhattan Project **VIII:** 200

Mariana Islands **VIII:** 202

Marines, U.S. **VIII:** 203

Marshall, George C. **VIII:** 206

mobilization **VIII:** 214

Navy, U.S. **VIII:** 237

Neutrality Acts **VIII:** 239

news media **VIII:** 243

Nimitz, Chester W. **VIII:** 246

OCD **VIII:** 253

OSS **VIII:** 256

radio **VIII:** 290

Republican Party **VIII:** 306

Roosevelt, Franklin D. **VIII:** 314

shipbuilding **VIII:** 324

Thomas, Norman **VIII:** 358

World War II **VIII:** 388

World War II home front **VIII:** 395

World War II Pacific theater **VIII:** 396, 398

Pearl Harbor naval base **V:** 133

Pearl Jam **X:** 240

pearls **I:** 29

Pearson, Isaac **II:** 234

Peary, Robert E. **VII:** 357c

Peasants' Rebellion (1525) **I:** 307

Peck, Gregory **IX:** 182

Peck, Jim **IX:** 114

Peckham, Sir George **I: 279; II:** 163

Peckham, Rufus **VII:** 164

Pecora, Ferdinand **VIII:** 322

Pecos **I:** 88, 90

Pedee **II:** 55

Pedrarias. *See* Dávilar, Pedrarias

Pedro the Cruel **I:** 174

Peek, George N. **VIII:** 6, 12, 34

Peel, Robert **IV:** 270

Pegg, Thomas **V:** 250

Peirce, Charles **VI:** 229

Peirson, Elijah **V:** 357

Peleliu **VIII:** 15

Pelham, Henry **II:** 273

Pelham, Peter **II:** 25, 194, 215, **272–273; III:** 91

pellagra **II:** 382

Pell grants **X:** 136

Pember, Phoebe Yates Levy **V: 266–267**

Pemberton, Isaac **II:** 307

Pemberton, John C.

Confederate army **V:** 73

Johnston, Joseph E. **V:** 190

Milliken's Bend, Battle of **V:** 232

Mississippi River **V:** 235

Vicksburg campaign **V:** 380, 382

Pemisapan. *See* Wingina

Pender, William Dorsey **V:** 148

Pendergast, Tom **VIII:** 165

Pendleton, Edmund **III:** 88

Pendleton Act of 1883 **VI:** 63, 325c

Pendleton Civil Service Reform Act of 1883

Arthur, Chester Alan **VI:** 17

civil service reform **VI:** 56

Garfield, James A. **VI:** 109

Hanna, Marcus Alonzo **VI:** 121

Hayes, Rutherford B. **VI:** 126

Hoar, George Frisbie **VI:** 130

pendulums **IV:** 307

Penecute **II:** 30

Penguin Group **X:** 178

penicillin **VIII:** 8–9, 47, 208; **IX:** 205, 295; **X:** 188

Peninsular campaign **V: 267–270**, *268m*, 406c

Balloon Corps **V:** 21

cartography **V:** 51

Cedar Mountain, Battle of **V:** 53

governors **V:** 153

Hooker, Joseph **V:** 171

Howard, O. O. **V:** 173

Irish-American regiments **V:** 181, *182*

McClellan, George B. **V:** 225

Meade, George Gordon **V:** 226

medicine and hospitals **V:** 230

Mosby, John Singleton **V:** 242

Sickles, Daniel E. **V:** 326

tactics and strategy **V:** 347

Union army **V:** 367

Washington, D.C. **V:** 390

peninsulares **I:** 259; **II:** 356, 359

penitentiary movement **IV: 277–279**, *278*

Penn, Arthur **IX:** 214

Penn, John **II:** 389, 390; **III:** 11, 316, 379

Penn, Richard **III:** 266

Penn, Thomas **II:** 389, 390

Penn, William **II: 273–274, *275*, 418c; III:** 300

Conestoga **II:** 67

Delaware **II:** 87–88

education **II:** 103

Enlightenment **II:** 109

French immigrants **II:** 130

gender **II:** 136

government, British American **II:** 144–145

Penn, William (*continued*)
Hamilton, Andrew **II:** 153
Hume, Sophia Wigington **II:** 160
land **II:** 191
Lloyd, David **II:** 197
Logan, James **II:** 198
monarchy, British **II:** 232
New Jersey **II:** 252, 253
Pennsylvania **II:** 274–277
Philadelphia **II:** 281, 282
Quakers **II:** 307, 308
religion, Euro-American **II:** 317
Roman Catholics **II:** 324
Swedish colonies **II:** 365
Pennacook **II:** 212
Penn Central Transportation v. New York City (1978) **X:** 250
Penn family **V:** 224, 227
Pennington, James William Charles **V: 270,** 328
Penn-Meade trial of 1670 **II:** 273
Pennsylvania **II: 274–278,** 418*c;* **III:** 394*c,* 396*c;* **V:** 407*c;* **X:** 331*c*
abolitionism **II:** 1–2
agriculture **II:** 11, 13
Albany Congress **II:** 14
architecture **II:** 23
Audubon, John James **IV:** 34
Bank of North America **III:** 30
Benezet, Anthony **II:** 32
Bradford, William **II:** 39
Brainerd, David **II:** 39–40
Buchanan, James **V:** 41
Campbell, Thomas **IV:** 72
canal era **IV:** 74
captivity **II:** 52
Catlin, George **IV:** 77
College of Philadelphia **II:** 67
Conestoga **II:** 67
constitutions, state **III:** 84
Cornstalk **II:** 72
Croghan, George **II:** 76
Delaware **II:** 87
economy **II:** 101, 276
education **II:** 103
election of 1800 **III:** 116
English immigrants **II:** 108
Enlightenment **II:** 109
Enlightenment, American **II:** 276–278
exploration **II:** 274
foraging **V:** 130
foreign policy **X:** 125
Forten, James **III:** 131
forts **II:** 124

Franklin, Benjamin **III:** 133–135
French colonies **II:** 129
French immigrants **II:** 130
Fries's Rebellion **III:** 139–140
Gallatin, Albert **III:** 147
gender **II:** 136
German immigrants **II:** 139–140
German Reformed Church **II:** 140
Gettysburg, Battle of **V:** 147–150
government, British American **II:** 144, 145
Great Awakening **II:** 147
Haiti **III:** 159
Husband, Herman **III:** 170
indentured servitude **II:** 165
Independence Hall **III:** 176
industrialization **IV:** 184
iron manufacturing **II:** 167, 168
Iroquois **II:** 168
Jesuits **II:** 174
Jews **III:** 188
Johnstown flood **VI:** 157
Jones, Absalom **III:** 189
Kalm, Peter **II:** 181
Keith, William **II:** 181
labor **II:** 189
land **II:** 191
Lloyd, David **II:** 197
Logan, James **II:** 198
Longstreet, James **V:** 215
Lutherans **II:** 201
machine politics **VI:** 184
Mason-Dixon Line **V:** 224
mills **II:** 225
mining: metal and coal **VI:** 193
miscegenation **II:** 228
Mittelberger, Gottlieb **II:** 231
Molly Maguires **VI:** 195–196
monarchy, British **II:** 232
Montour, Andrew **II:** 233
Montour, Madame **II:** 233, 234
Morris, Robert **III:** 247–248
Muhlenberg, Henry Melchior **II:** 237
music **II:** 239
National Road **IV:** 255
Native Americans **II:** 246
Neolin **II:** 248

New Jersey **II:** 253
oil **VI:** 215
penitentiary movement **IV:** 278
Penn, William **II:** 273–275
Philadelphia **II:** 281–282
politics **II:** 276
population trends **II:** 291; **X:** 242, 243
Powhatan Confederacy **II:** 295
prisons **III:** 286
Protestantism **II:** 300–302
Quakers **II:** 275, 276, 308; **III:** 291
redemptioners **II:** 313
religion **II:** 275–276; **IV:** 298
religion, Euro-American **II:** 316, 317
religious liberty **III:** 300
Rittenhouse, David **II:** 322
Roman Catholics **II:** 323–324
rum trade **II:** 326
rust belt **X:** 269
St. Clair, Arthur **III:** 315–316
Seven Years' War **II:** 276, 332
Smith, Robert **II:** 348
society, British American **II:** 350
Society of Friends **V:** 331
Stevens, Thaddeus **V:** 337, 338
Stuart, J. E. B. **V:** 341
suffrage **II:** 364
taverns and inns **II:** 368
Teedyuscung **II:** 370
tenants **II:** 371
Tennent, William, Jr. **II:** 372
Tennent, William, Sr. **II:** 372
travel **II:** 377
Union army **V:** 367
Walking Purchase of 1737 **II:** 389–390
Weiser, Johann Conrad **II:** 393
Whiskey Rebellion **III:** 375–376
women's status and rights **II:** 407
Wyoming Valley War **III:** 384
Zouaves **V:** 404
Pennsylvania Abolition Society **III:** 393*c;* **IV:** 15, 16
Pennsylvania Academy of the Fine Arts **IV:** 77; **VI:** 48, 220

Pennsylvania anthracite strikes (1873) **V:** 340
Pennsylvania Canal **IV:** 73*m*
Pennsylvania Constitution of 1776 **II:** 322
Pennsylvania Gazette **III:** 133
Pennsylvania Herald **III:** 61
Pennsylvania Hospital **II:** 33–34, 109, 220, 282, 336
Pennsylvania Magazine, The **III:** *191,* 271
Pennsylvania Main Line Canal **IV:** 73
Pennsylvania Railroad (PRR) **VII:** 297
banking, investment **VI:** 19
Carnegie, Andrew **VI:** 44
corruption, political **VI:** 67
economy **IV:** 118
Great Strike of 1877 **VI:** 119
industrialization **IV:** 185
Lloyd, Henry Demarest **VI:** 179
Morgan, John Pierpont **VI:** 197
National Road **IV:** 255
newspapers **VI:** 212
oil **VI:** 215
railroads **IV:** 295
Scott, Thomas Alexander **VI:** 258
Pennsylvania State House **II:** 23
Pennsylvania Turnpike **VI:** 197
penny papers/penny press **IV:** 82, 194–196, 213; **V:** 192; **VI:** 2
Penobscot **II:** 243
Penobscot (Eastern Abenaki) language **I:** 6, 219
Penobscot nation **II:** 243
Penrose, Boies **VI:** 184
Pensacola, Florida **II:** 120; **IV:** 112, 139
Pension Arrears Act of 1879 **VI:** 118
pensions **V:** 256, 358, 379; **VI:** 118, 123; **VII:** 324; **VIII:** 95
Pentagon **VIII:** 19, 20; **IX:** 64, 236; **X:** 331*c*
Bush, George W. **X:** 48
defense policy **X:** 88
foreign policy **X:** 125
Powell, Colin L. **X:** 247
Senate **X:** 276
terrorism **X:** 297, 300
Pentagon Papers **IX:** 154; **X:** 41, 60, **233,** 315
Pentecostalism **VII:** 176, 261, 262; **VIII:** 302, 304; **IX:** 256; **X:** 265

Peonage Abolition Act of 1867 **V:** 408*c*

People, The (newspaper) **VI:** 268

People magazine **X:** 186

People of the Longhouse **II:** 168

People's Convention of Friends of Free Territory **IV:** 150

People's Party (Populist Party) **V:** 47; **VI:** **222–223,** 327*c;* **VII:** 332; **IX:** 279–280

Bellamy, Edward **VI:** 26

bimetallism **VI:** 29

Bryan, William Jennings **VI:** 37

currency issue **VI:** 73

Democratic Party **VI:** 78

farmers' alliances **VI:** 100

Free-Silver movement **VI:** 105

Garland, Hamlin **VI:** 109

Greenback-Labor Party **VI:** 120

Internal Revenue taxes **VI:** 147

Lease, Mary Elizabeth **VI:** 173

Lloyd, Henry Demarest **VI:** 179

national banking system **VI:** 206

Omaha Platform **VI:** 216

political parties, third **VI:** 226

Populist Party Platform, 1892 **VI:** 346–34

Powderly, Terence Vincent **VI:** 227

Simpson, Jerry **VI:** 262

Willard, Frances **VI:** 315

People's Republic of China. *See* China

People's Republic of the Congo **X:** 13

People United to Serve Humanity. *See* PUSH

People v. Hall **IV:** 292

Peoria **II:** 206

Pepperell, William **II:** 214

Pequot **II:** **278**

Canonicus **II:** 51

Connecticut **II:** 68

Endecott, John **II:** 107

forts **II:** 124

land **II:** 191

Mason, John **II:** 211

Miantonomo **II:** 224

Narragansett **II:** 241

Native Americans **II:** 243–244

wampum **II:** 390

Pequot War **II:** *279,* **279–280,** 417*c*

Canonicus **II:** 51

Connecticut **II:** 68

Endecott, John **II:** 107

Hutchinson, Anne Marbury **II:** 161

King Philip's War **II:** 183

Mason, John **II:** 211

Massachusetts **II:** 212

Miantonomo **II:** 224

Narragansett **II:** 241

Native Americans **II:** 243

Pequot **II:** 278

Perabo, Ernst **VI:** 23

Peralta, Don Pedro de **I:** 319

Percy, George **I:** 318; **II:** 135, 171

Percy, Hugh **III:** 213

Pereira Coutinho, Francisco **I:** 23

Peress, Irving **IX:** 18

Perestrello, Rafael **I:** 65

perestroika **X:** 72, 280

Pérez, Juan **I:** 150, 266

perfectionism **IV:** 299

performance art **X:** 26

perfumes **I:** 9

Pericu **I:** 48

periodicals. *See* magazines; newspapers

Perisphere. *See* Trylon and Perisphere

Perkins, Edward **X:** 308

Perkins, Frances **VII:** 287; **VIII:** **265–266,** 406*c*

Democratic Party **VIII:** 81

Dewson, "Molly" **VIII:** 83

Fair Labor Standards Act **VIII:** 110

labor **VIII:** 180

New Deal **VIII:** 241

NLRA **VIII:** 229

Social Security Act **VIII:** 328

Wagner, Robert F. **VIII:** 372

women's network **VIII:** 383

women's status and rights **VIII:** 384

Perkins, John **IV:** 308

Perkins, William **II:** 73

Perle, Richard **X:** 79, 216

Permanent Indian Frontier **IV:** 236, **279**

Permanent Joint Board of Defense **VIII:** 408*c*

Pernambuco **II:** 98

Perot, H. Ross **X:** **233–234,** 328*c,* 329*c*

Bush, George H. W. **X:** 46

Clinton, William **X:** 66, 68

elections **X:** 101, 102

political parties **X:** 238–239

Reform Party **X:** 263

Perry, Benjamin F. **V:** 401

Perry, Matthew Calbraith **IV:** 137, 143, 219, **279–280,** 379*c*

Perry, Oliver Hazard

Harrison, William Henry **IV:** 169

Lake Erie, Battle of **IV:** 206–207

Perry, Matthew Calbraith **IV:** 279

War of 1812 **IV:** 356

Perry, William **X:** 88, 174

Perry Mason (TV program) **X:** 295

Perryville, Battle of **V:** 66

Pershing, John J. **VII:** **227,** 358*c,* 359*c;* **VIII:** 173, 206

American Expeditionary Force **VII:** 8–9

conscription **VII:** 54

Dawes, Charles **VII:** 63

foreign policy **VII:** 98

Mexican invasion **VII:** 183

Mitchell, Billy **VII:** 187

Selective Service Act **VII:** 282

Wilson, Woodrow **VII:** 334

Zimmermann telegram **VII:** 353

Persia (Iran) **I:** 337, 338

Persian Gulf War **VIII:** 207; **IX:** 10, 201; **X:** **234–236,** 235*m,* 327*c,* 328*c*

Bush, George H. W. **X:** 44, 46

defense policy **X:** 87

foreign policy **X:** 124

Gore, Albert, Jr. **X:** 133

Powell, Colin L. **X:** 246

United Nations **X:** 307

personal liberty laws **IV:** 95, 154, 155, **280**

Personal Memoirs (Grant) **V:** 154, 157

Personal Responsibility and Work Opportunity Reconciliation Act of 1996 **X:** 113

Peru **I:** **279–280,** 385*c,* 387*c;* **II:** 93, 354, 358; **IV:** 241; **VI:** 49, 50; **X:** 46, 220

Acosta, José de **I:** 3

Andes Mountains **I:** 10

Balboa, Vasco Núñez de **I:** 24

Cabeza de Vaca, Álvar Núñez **I:** 38

Charles V **I:** 69

conquistadores **I:** 85

Council of the Indies **I:** 95

El Dorado **I:** 118, 119

encomienda **I:** 122

horses **I:** 168

Inca **I:** 175

Lima **I:** 206

Mendoza, Antonio de **I:** 231

Panama **I:** 277

Pizarro, Francisco **I:** 283

printing press **I:** 294

Ramusio, Giovanni Battista **I:** 305

slavery **I:** 327

Soto, Hernando de **I:** 332

Valdivia, Pedro de **I:** 363

Peruschi, Mario de **I:** 153

pesquisa **I:** 128

Pestalozzi, Johann **VI:** 159

Petananuet **II:** 395

"pet banks" **IV:** 119

Peter, Paul, and Mary **IX:** 111, 191

Peter Martyr (Pietro Martire d'Anghiera) **I:** 118, **280–281,** 305, 338, 343, 387*c*

Petersburg, siege of **V:** 407*c*

Hill, Ambrose P. **V:** 168

homefront **V:** 169

Lee, Robert E. **V:** 207

Oates, William C. **V:** 257

Petersburg campaign **V:** 271–272

Washington, D.C. **V:** 390

Petersburg, Virginia

Appomattox Court House, Virginia **V:** 14

Burnside, Ambrose E. **V:** 45

Five Forks, Battle of **V:** 129

Sheridan, Philip H. **V:** 319

Petersburg campaign **V:** **270–273,** *271,* 272*m*

Chamberlain, Joshua L. **V:** 54

Hancock, Winfield Scott **V:** 163

Meade, George Gordon **V:** 227

Native Americans **V:** 249

Overland campaign **V:** 261

Peterson, Douglas B. **X:** 224

Peterson, Esther **IX:** 223, 246, 324

Peterson, Scott C. **X:** 244

Peterson's Ladies' National Magazine **IV:** 197

Peterson v. City of Greenville **IX:** 273

Peter the Great, emperor of
   Russia **II:** 32
Petits Voyages **I:** 102
Petrarch **I:** 365
petroglyphs **I:** 296; **II:** 24
petroleum/petroleum industry.
   See gasoline; gasoline
   rationing; oil
Pettigrew, James Johnston
      Fort Sumter, South
         Carolina **V:** 136
      Gettysburg, Battle of **V:**
         150
      Pickett, George Edward **V:**
         274
      volunteer army **V:** 384
Petun **II:** 31, 168, 169
Peul. *See* Fulani
pewter **II: 280–281**
peyote **X:** 266
Peyton Place (Grace Metalious)
   IX: 183
Pfizer Corporation **VIII:** 208;
   IX: 206
PFP. *See* Partnership for Peace
PGA. *See* Professional Golfers
   Association
Phagan, Mary **VII:** 157
phalanstery/phalanxes **IV:** 58,
   149
Phantom of the Opera, The
   (musical) **X:** 201
pharmaceutical industry **V:** 231;
   VIII: 47; **IX:** 205–206. *See
   also* medicine and public
   health
Ph.D. degrees **VI:** 93
Phelps, Elizabeth Stuart **VI:** 177
Philadelphia, capture of **III:**
   168–169
Philadelphia, Pennsylvania **I:**
   108; **II: 281–283; III:** 392*c*,
   396*c*
      ACS **IV:** 15
      agriculture **II:** 13
      Allen, Richard **III:** 10–11
      almshouses **II:** 18
      AME Church **V:** 5
      American Philosophical
         Society **II:** 18
      Anglican Church **II:** 20
      anti-Catholic riots **IV:** 21
      architecture **II:** 23–24
      Arnold, Benedict **III:** 21
      Baltimore & Ohio Railroad
         (B&O) **IV:** 40
      Bond, Thomas **II:** 33
      Carey, Mathew **III:** 61–62
      Catto, Octavius **V:** 52
      cities and urban life **II:** 61,
         62; **III:** *69*; **IV:** 81; **V:**
         61; **VI:** 53

class **II:** 62–63
Colden, Cadwallader **II:**
   66
College of Philadelphia **II:**
   66–67
Cornwallis, Lord **III:** 92
corruption, political **VI:** 66
crafts **II:** 73–74
Declaration of
   Independence **III:** *102*
Democratic-Republican
   societies **III:** 105
disease and epidemics **II:**
   91, 92; **III:** 106; **IV:**
   112
Duane, William **III:** 108
Eakins, Thomas **VI:** 85–87
economy **II:** 102
Feke, Robert **II:** 117
Forten, James **III:** 131
Franklin, Benjamin **III:**
   133–134
Franklin, Deborah Read
   II: 125
Franklin Institute **IV:** 149
Galloway, Joseph **III:** 148
German immigrants **II:**
   139
German Reformed Church
   II: 140
Girard, Stephen **III:** 153
Godfrey, Thomas **II:** 141
Hale, Sarah Josepha **IV:**
   168
Hamilton, Alexander **III:**
   161
Hamilton, Andrew **II:**
   153
Hesselius, John **II:** 156
Hume, Sophia Wigington
   II: 160
immigration **IV:** 180
Independence Hall **III:**
   176
industrialization **IV:** 185
industrial revolution **III:**
   178
Ingersoll, Jared **III:** 178
Jews **II:** 175
Jones, Absalom **III:** 189
journalism **II:** 178
Kalm, Peter **II:** 181
Keith, William **II:** 181
Know-Nothing Party **IV:**
   201
labor and labor movements
   II: 187, 189; **IV:** 203,
   204
ladies aid societies **V:** 204
Lloyd, David **II:** 197
Logan, James **II:** 198
lotteries **II:** 199

mills **II:** 225
miscegenation **II:** 228
Moraley, William **II:** 234
mortality **II:** 235
Muhlenberg, Henry
   Melchior **II:** 237
mulattoes **II:** 238
music **VI:** 201
New Jersey **II:** 253
Panic of 1819 **IV:** 275
penitentiary movement **IV:**
   277
Penn, William **II:** 274
Pennsylvania **II:** 274–{2:
   }276, 276, 277–278
piracy **II:** 285
population trends **III:**
   283–284
postal service **II:** 292
Presbyterians **II:** 296
printing and publishing **II:**
   299
Quakers **II:** 308
railroads **IV:** 292, 293, 295
redemptioners **II:** 313
religion **IV:** 297
Rittenhouse, David **III:**
   310
Roman Catholics **II:** 324
settlement houses **VI:** 259
shipbuilding **II:** 335
slave resistance **II:** 337
Smith, Robert **II:** 347–348
society, British American
   II: 350
Still, William **IV:** 327–328
taverns and inns **II:** 367,
   368
Tennent, Gilbert **II:** 371
Tennent, William, Jr. **II:**
   372
Tennent, William, Sr. **II:**
   372
theater **II:** 373; **III:** *347*
trade and shipping **II:** 377
travel **II:** 377
Tubman, Harriet **V:** 358
Weiser, Johann Conrad **II:**
   393
Wistar, Caspar **II:** 402
witchcraft **II:** 403
yellow fever **II:** 414
Philadelphia, USS **III:** 35, 397*c*;
   IV: 104
Philadelphia & Reading
   Railroad **IV:** 295
Philadelphia Anti-Slavery
   Society **IV:** 135, 164; **V:** 331
Philadelphia Artisans **II:** 18
Philadelphia Association **II:** 29
*Philadelphia Baptist Association
   v. Hart's Executors* **III:** 170

Philadelphia Centennial
   Exposition (1876) **VI:**
   223–224, 324*c*
      Anthony, Susan B. **VI:** 13
      Bell, Alexander Graham
         VI: 25
      communications **VI:** 62
      department stores **VI:** 78
      Gage, Matilda Joslyn **VI:**
         107
      painting **VI:** 220
Philadelphia Female Anti-
   Slavery Society **IV:** 8
Philadelphia Museum of Art **V:**
   16
Philadelphia Negro, The (Du
   Bois) **VII:** 71
Philadelphia Orchestra **VI:** 201
Philadelphia Plan **X:** 8, 323*c*
Philadelphia Public Ledger **IV:**
   196
Philadelphia Society for the
   Abolition of Slavery **V:** 1
Philadelphia Story (film) **VIII:**
   219
Philadelphia Yearly Meeting
   (Quakers) **II:** 1–2, 31–32,
   104, 308, 410
Philanthropist, The **IV:** 160
philanthropy **VI:** 44, 87, 93–94;
   VII: 180–181, 265; **VIII:** 174,
   318
Philip, King. *See* Metacom
Philip II, king of Spain **I:**
   281–282
      cabildo **I:** 39
      Caroline, Fort **I:** 57
      Casa de Contratación **I:**
         60, 61
      Castile **I:** 63, 64
      Charles V **I:** 68, 69
      Drake, Sir Francis **I:** 111,
         112
      Elizabeth I **I:** 121
      Henry IV (Henry of
         Navarre) **I:** 158
      Holy League **I:** 164
      Las Casas, Bartolomé de **I:**
         200
      Lisbon **I:** 208
      Mary I **I:** 224
      Spanish Armada **I:** 333,
         334
Philip IV, king of Spain **I:** 323
Philip Morris **X:** 305
Philippine Rebellion of 1899 **VI:**
   13
Philippines **I:** 114, 216–217,
   258, 283, 387*c*; **II:** 93; **IV:**
   219; **VI:** 328*c*; **VII:** 355*c*,
   358*c*; **VIII:** 266, **266–267,**
   406*c*, 409*c*, 410*c*; **IX:**

273–274; **X:** 69, 122, 125, 139
  Aguinaldo, Emilio **VII:** 8
  amphibious warfare **VIII:** 15, 16
  Anti-Imperialist League **VI:** 13
  Army, U.S. **VIII:** 19
  Asian Americans **VIII:** 26
  Bataan Death March **VIII:** 34–35
  Bryan, William Jennings **VI:** 37
  Dewey, George **VI:** 79
  Filipino insurrection **VI:** 100
  foreign policy **VI:** 104; **VII:** 98
  Halsey, "Bull" **VIII:** 143
  Hay, John Milton **VI:** 125
  Hoar, George Frisbie **VI:** 130
  immigration **VIII:** 162
  imperialism **VI:** 142, 143
  intelligence **VIII:** 164
  Leyte Gulf, Battle for **VIII:** 186–187
  Lodge, Henry Cabot **VII:** 165
  Mahan, Alfred Thayer **VI:** 186
  McKinley, William **VI:** 190
  mugwumps **VI:** 199
  Navy, U.S. **VIII:** 237
  Nimitz, Chester W. **VIII:** 246
  Open Door Policy **VII:** 218
  Pearl Harbor **VIII:** 263
  Pershing, John **VII:** 227
  POWs **VIII:** 282
  Roosevelt, Theodore **VII:** 266
  Schurz, Carl **VI:** 257
  segregation **VII:** 281
  southern demagogues **VII:** 292
  Spanish-American War **VI:** 272
  Stimson, Henry L. **VIII:** 340
  Taft, William Howard **VII:** 303
  Tarawa **VIII:** 350
  WMC **VIII:** 375
  World War II Pacific theater **VIII:** 398, 399
Philippine Sea, Battle of the **VIII: 267**
  air power **VIII:** 11
  Leyte Gulf, Battle for **VIII:** 186

Mariana Islands **VIII:** 202
Nimitz, Chester W. **VIII:** 246
World War II Pacific theater **VIII:** 399
Philippine Wars **V:** 306; **VII:** 98
Philipse, Frederick **II:** 285, 348
"Philip the Signer" **II:** 196
Phillips, David Graham **VII:** 69, 192
Phillips, Howard **X:** 20
Phillips, Sam **IX:** 247
Phillips, Wendell **IV:** 14, 59, **280–281; V:** 100, 124
philosophy **II:** 197–198, 277, 297; **IV:** 149; **VI:** 154, 155, 228–229; **VII:** 67–68; **X:** 216–217
Philosophy of Individuality, The (Blackwell) **VI:** 30
Phips, Sir William
  Brattle, Thomas **II:** 40
  King William's War **II:** 185
  Massachusetts **II:** 214
  Mather, Cotton **II:** 217
  Mather, Increase **II:** 218
  piracy **II:** 285
  witchcraft **II:** 402, 403
Phoenix **X:** 290
"phonic" educational method **IV:** 228
phonograph/phonograph records **VI:** *89, 324c;* **VII:** 194, 195, 254. *See also* recorded music
  Bell, Alexander Graham **VI:** 25
  Edison, Thomas Alva **VI:** 89
  inventions and technology **VI:** 150
  Sousa, John Philip **VI:** 271–272
Photographic History of the Civil War (Miller) **V:** 274
Photographic Sketchbook of the War (Gardner) **V:** 273
Photographic Views of Sherman's Campaign (Barnard) **V:** 273
photography **V:** 16, 35–36, **273–274,** 308; **VI:** *326c;* **VII:** 134; **VIII:** *268,* **268–269,** *407c;* **X:** 26
  art and architecture **VIII:** 24
  Eakins, Thomas **VI:** 86
  Eastman, George **VI:** 87
  illustration, photography, and the graphic arts **VI:** 137

inventions and technology **VI:** 150
Life (magazine) **VIII:** 189
lynching **VI:** 182
news media **VIII:** 243
popular culture **VIII:** 275
RA **VIII:** 307
Riis, Jacob A. **VI:** 248
World War II **VIII:** 389
photorealists **X:** 26
phrenology **IV:** 230
PHS. *See* Public Health Service
Phyfe, Duncan **III:** 26, **275**
physical anthropology **IV:** 290
physical chemistry **VI:** *324c*
Physical Geography of the Sea (Maury) **IV:** 308
physician-assisted suicide **X:** 265
physicians **IV:** 230; **X:** 187–188
physico-theology **II:** 110, 330
physics **II:** 330; **VI:** 113, 257; **VIII:** 318
Piazza d'Italia, New Orleans (Moore) **X:** 27
Pickawillany **II:** 191
Pickens, Francis **V:** 136, 137
Pickering, John **III:** 116, 175
Pickering, Thomas **X:** 308
Pickering, Timothy **III:** 118, 235, **275–276**
Pickett, George Edward **V:** **274–275**
  Armistead, Lewis A. **V:** 15
  Five Forks, Battle of **V:** 129
  Gettysburg, Battle of **V:** 150
  Richmond, Virginia **V:** 304
"Pickett's Charge"
  Alexander, Edward P. **V:** 7
  Gettysburg, Battle of **V:** 150
  Hancock, Winfield Scott **V:** 163
  Lee, Robert E. **V:** 206
  Longstreet, James **V:** 215
  Pickett, George Edward **V:** 274
  tactics and strategy **V:** 345
Pickford, Mary **VII:** 232
Picknell, William Lamb **VI:** 219
Pico, Pío **IV:** 45
pictographs **II:** 24
Picts **I:** 155, **282**
picture brides **VII:** 108
pidgin language **II:** 151
piece work **VII:** 155
Piedfroid **II:** 190
Piedmont region
  Catawba **II:** 55
  Native Americans **II:** 246
  North Carolina **II:** 263

South Carolina **II:** 353
Tuscarora **II:** 378
Tuscarora War **II:** 379
Virginia **II:** 385
Pieh, Sengbe **IV:** 19
Pierce, Edward **V:** 279
Pierce, Franklin **IV:** *379c;* **V:** **275**
  Bleeding Kansas **V:** 32
  Buchanan, James **V:** 41
  Clayton-Bulwer Treaty **IV:** 89
  Cuba **IV:** 101
  Davis, Jefferson **V:** 89
  Democratic Party **IV:** 108
  Dix, Dorothea **IV:** 114
  foreign policy **IV:** 142; **V:** 131
  Gadsden Purchase **IV:** 159
  Julian, George W. **V:** 194
  Kansas-Nebraska Act of 1854 **V:** 198
  Manifest Destiny **IV:** 218
  Ostend Manifesto **V:** 260
  Republican Party **IV:** 300
  Scott, Winfield **IV:** 310
Pierce, John **II:** 220
Pierce, Joseph **III:** 197
Pierce, William **II:** 323
Pierce Patent **II:** 287
Pierce v. Society of the Sisters **VII:** *361c*
Pierson, Abraham **II:** 413
pietism **II:** 125, 147, 237, 282
Pigafetta, Antonio **I:** 215, 216, **283**
pig iron **IV:** 118, 184; **VI:** 27
Pigot, John **III:** 308
pigs. *See* hogs
Pike, Zebulon Montgomery **III:** 155; **IV:** 130, **281–282**
Pike's Peak
  Atkinson, Henry **IV:** 33
  Colorado gold rush **IV:** 89
  exploration **IV:** 130
  Pike, Zebulon Montgomery **IV:** 282
Pike's Peak gold rush **V:** *405c*
"Pike's Peak or Bust" **IV: 282**
Pilcher, Joshua **IV:** 239
Pilgrim, USS **IV:** 103
Pilgrimage (Samuel Purchas) **I:** 297–298
Pilgrims **II:** *219,* **283**
  agriculture **II:** 12
  Alden, John **II:** 15
  Alden, Priscilla **II:** 16
  captivity **II:** 51
  Congregationalists **II:** 68
  fur trade **II:** 130–131
  literature **II:** 195
  Massachusetts **II:** 212

Pilgrims (continued)
    Massasoit **II:** 217
    Mayflower Compact **II:**
      219–220
    music **II:** 238–239
    piracy **II:** 285
    Plymouth **II:** 287–288
    population trends **II:** 290
    Squanto **II:** 360, 361
    Standish, Myles **II:** 361
"pill, the" **IX:** 198–199, **242,**
  270, 295; **X:** 36
pilli **I:** 19
pillorying **II:** 208
Pima **II:** 165, 229
Pima Atlas **II:** 283
Pima Bajas **II:** 283
Pima revolt **II:** 78, **283–284**
Pinchback, Pinckney B. S. **V:**
  275–276; VI: 5
Pinchot, Gifford **VI:** 65; **VII:**
  227–28
    conservationism **VII:** 55
    Progressive Party **VII:** 236
    Republican Party **VII:** 263
    Taft, William Howard **VII:**
      304
Pinckney, Charles Cotesworth
  III: 116, 152, *276,* **276–277,**
  385, 397*c,* 398*c*
Pinckney, Elizabeth Lucas **II:**
  56, 136, 166, **284**
Pinckney, Thomas **III:** 317
Pinckney's Treaty of 1795 **IV:**
  20, 140
pineapples **II:** 121
Pine Ridge Agency **VI:** 240, 245
Pine Ridge Reservation **VI:** 207;
  X: 214
Pingree, Hazen **VII:** 316
Pinkerton, Allan **V:** 118
Pinkerton Detective Agency **VI:**
  327*c*
    Coeur d'Alene miners'
      strike **VI:** 61
    Homestead Strike **VI:** 132
    labor: strikes and violence
      VI: 167
    Molly Maguires **VI:** 195
Pinkney, William **III:** 246; **IV:**
  227
Pinochet, Augusto **X:** 325*c*
Pinta **I:** 55
Pinzón, Vicente Yáñez **I:** 8, 32*m*
"Pioneer Band" **IV:** 243
Pioneer Hi-Bred International
  IX: 84
pioneers **IV:** 242, 249
Pioneers, The (Cooper) **IV:** 212
Pioneer space program **X:** 283
pipelines, oil **VI:** 215
pipes **II:** 374

pipiltin **I:** 19
pirates/piracy **I:** 34–35, 110,
  193, 277, 281–282, 320; **II:**
  284–286; IV: 205–206
    Bonnet, Stede **II:** 34
    Chesapeake Bay **II:** 57
    Florida **II:** 120
    mariners **II:** 204
    North Carolina **II:** 265
    South Carolina **II:** 354
    Spanish colonies **II:** 356
    Teach, Edward **II:**
      368–369
PIRGs. *See* public interest
  research groups
Piscataway **I:** 292; **II:** 50, 209,
  328, 364
Pistole Free Dispute **II:** 54
pistols **IV:** 307
Pitcairn, John **III:** 212
pitch **II:** 201, 265
Pitcher, Molly. *See* Molly
  Pitcher
pit houses **I:** 255
Pitt, William **II:** 119, 332, 405;
  III: 277–278
    Bute, earl of **III:** 54
    Mayhew, Jonathan **III:**
      238
    Townshend Duties **III:**
      348
    Wilkes, John **III:** 378
Pitts, John and Hiram **IV:** 308
Pittsburgh, Pennsylvania **IV:** 81;
  VIII: 58; **X:** 269
Pittsburgh Gazette **III:** 46
Pittsburgh Manifesto **VI:** 167
Pittsburgh Pirates **VII:** 301
Pittsburgh platform (Judaism)
  VI: 158
Pittsburgh Steelers **X:** 319
Pittsburgh Symphony Orchestra
  VI: 128
Pittsburg Landing, Tennessee **V:**
  324, 325*m*
Pius V, Pope **I:** 120, 164
Pius IX, Pope **IV:** 22, 114; **VI:**
  249
Pius X, Pope **VII:** 260
Pius XII, Pope **VIII:** 53
Pizarro, Francisco **I: 283–285,**
  284*m,* 285, 387*c;* **II:** 359
    Andes Mountains **I:** 10
    Atahualpa **I:** 14, 15
    Balboa, Vasco Núñez de **I:**
      24
    conquistadores **I:** 84
    Cuzco **I:** 99
    El Dorado **I:** 118
    gold **I:** 143
    Inca **I:** 177
    Lima **I:** 206

    Panama **I:** 277
    Peru **I:** 280
    Soto, Hernando de **I:** 332
    Valdivia, Pedro de **I:** 363
Pizarro, Gonzalo **I:** 119
Pizza Connection **X:** 82
PL. *See* Players League;
  Progressive Labor Party
placer mining **IV:** 67, 90, 162,
  163; **VI:** 193
plague (bubonic) **I: 285–286**
    Cathay (China) **I:** 64
    Cholula **I:** 72
    Columbian Exchange **I:** 77
    diseases **I:** 106, 107
    Iceland **I:** 175
    Léry, Jean de **I:** 205
    population trends **I:** 290
    Shakespeare, William **I:**
      324
    Tlaxcala **I:** 353
Plains Indians **II:** 24, 50, 77,
  391; **III:** 154, 155, 397*c;* **IV:**
  145, 158, 258, 377*c;* **V:**
  213–214; **VI:** 38, 208
Plains of Abraham **III:** 60, 97,
  130
Plains-Woodland period **II:** 149
Plains-Woodland to Plains
  Culture **II:** 149
Planck, Max **VII:** 275
*Plan for Improving Female
  Education* (Willard) **IV:** 365
planned obsolescence **IX:** 239
Planned Parenthood Federation
  of America **VII:** 30, 243,
  359*c;* **IX:** 199, 242; **X:** 36,
  248, 249
*Planned Parenthood of Central
  Missouri v. Danforth* **X:** 3,
  16–17
*Planned Parenthood of
  Southeastern Pennsylvania v.
  Casey* (1992)
    *Akron v. Akron Center for
      Reproductive Health* **X:**
      17
    Rehnquist, William H. **X:**
      264
    Souter, David **X:** 279
    *Webster v. Reproductive
      Health Services* **X:** 319
    White, Byron R. **X:** 319
planning, postwar. See postwar
  planning
Plan of Union **II:** 419*c*
Plantation Act of 1740 **III:** 173
plantations/plantation system **II:**
  286–287; V: 276–277, 277
    abolition **V:** 1
    Acts of Trade and
      Navigation **II:** 3

    agriculture **II:** 12, 13; **IV:**
      10; **V:** 6
    Black Codes **V:** 29
    Bruce, Blanche K. **V:** 40
    Byrd family **II:** 47
    Caribbean **II:** 53
    cities and urban life **II:** 61
    class **II:** 63, 64
    contrabands **V:** 81
    Davis Bend, Mississippi,
      freedmen's colony **V:** 91
    economy **II:** 101
    education **II:** 104; **V:** 108
    food **II:** 122
    Freedmen's Bureau **V:** 142
    gender **II:** 136, 137
    Georgia **II:** 138
    government, British
      American **II:** 144, 145
    Gullah **II:** 151
    Harpers Ferry, West
      Virginia **V:** 165
    housing **II:** 157
    indentured servitude **II:**
      164, 165
    Indian Removal Act (1830)
      IV: 183
    iron manufacturing **II:**
      167–168
    Jamestown **II:** 172
    Johnson, Anthony **II:** 175
    Johnson, Mary **II:** 175
    labor **II:** 187, 189
    labor movements **IV:** 205
    marriage and family life **II:**
      207–208
    Maryland **II:** 211
    Middleton, Arthur **II:** 224
    midwives **II:** 225
    Mount Vernon **II:** 236–237
    Native Americans **IV:**
      256–257
    New Orleans **II:** 258
    Nullification Controversy
      IV: 264
    Panic of 1819 **IV:** 275
    Panic of 1837 **IV:** 277
    Port Royal, South
      Carolina, Experiment **V:**
      279–280
    primogeniture and entail
      II: 297
    race and racial conflict **V:**
      287
    Red River campaign **V:**
      297
    refugees **V:** 298
    Rhode Island **II:** 321
    rum trade **II:** 326
    sharecropping **V:** 315–316
    Sherman, William T. **V:**
      321

Sherman's March through Georgia **V:** 322–323
slavery **II:** 338, 342; **IV:** 318; **V:** 329
slave trade **II:** 343
society, British American **II:** 349
South Carolina **II:** 354
Spanish colonies **II:** 355, 358–359
Special Field Order No. 15 **V:** 332
travel **II:** 377
Tubman, Harriet **V:** 358
Underground Railroad **V:** 361
Virginia **II:** 382–385
women's status and rights **II:** 407
Yancey, William Lowndes **V:** 401
Plantin, Chrisophe **I:** 232
plants. *See also* agriculture
Columbian Exchange **I:** 76–78
Harriot, Thomas **I:** 154, 155
Plantson, Anthony **IV:** 308
platform mounds **I:** 237, 244–245
Platform of the American Anti-Imperialist League (1899) **VI:** 357–358
Platt, Charles Adams **VI:** 15
Platt, Thomas C. **VII:** 266
Platt Amendment **VI:** 72, 143; **VII:** 27, 99, 267, 355c; **VIII:** 133
Platte River **IV:** 164
Plattsburgh, Battle of **IV:** 358
Playboy **X:** 185
Playboy Club (New York) **X:** 288
Playboy Enterprises **X:** 244
Players Association (baseball) **X:** 284
Players League (PL) **VI:** 22
PLC (Public Lands Commission) **VI:** 110
"Plea for Captain Brown, A" (Thoreau) **IV:** 342
Pledge of Allegiance **IX:** 256
Plessy, Homer J. **V:** 354; **VI:** 224
Plessy v. Ferguson **V:** 139, 241, 354; **VI:** **224–225**, 327c, 349–354; **VII:** 281; **VIII:** 5, 61; **IX:** 42, 193, 220, 271, 276
African Americans **VI:** 6
civil rights cases **VI:** 56
due process clause **VI:** 81–82
education **VI:** 90

Harlan, John Marshall **VI:** 122
Jim Crow laws **VI:** 156
Supreme Court **VI:** 281
Pliny the Elder **I:** 239
PLO. *See* Palestine Liberation Organization
Ploscowe, Morris **VII:** 60
plows **II:** 9; **IV:** 10, 105, 185, 224; **V:** 308; **VI:** 8
"plumbers" **X:** 315–316
Plumed Serpent. *See* Quetzalcoatl
Plunkitt, George Washington **VI:** 67, 184, **225**
Plunkitt of Tammany Hall (Riordon) **VI:** 225
plutonium **VIII:** 29, 200
Plymouth **I:** 298; **II:** **287–288**
agriculture **II:** 12
alcohol **II:** 15
Alden, John **II:** 15
Alden, Priscilla **II:** 16
Algonquin **II:** 17
Bradford, William **II:** 38–39
captivity **II:** 51
Congregationalists **II:** 68
Dominion of New England **II:** 94
fishing **II:** 118–119
King Philip's War **II:** 183
Massachusetts **II:** 212, 214
Massachusetts School Act **II:** 216
Massasoit **II:** 217
Mayflower Compact **II:** 220
Metacom **II:** 222–223
Morton, Thomas **II:** 236
New Netherland **II:** 256
Pilgrims **II:** 283
Puritans **II:** 304
Rhode Island **II:** 321
Squanto **II:** 360–361
Standish, Myles **II:** 361
Virginia Company of London **II:** 387
Winthrop, John **II:** 402
wolves **II:** 405
Plymouth Church (Brooklyn, New York) **VI:** 24, 25
Plymouth Company **II:** 347
Plymouth Council for New England **II:** 386m
pneumonia **II:** 92, 235; **IV:** 112; **V:** 96, 230
pneumonic plague **I:** 285
PNGV (Partnership for a New Generation of Vehicles) **X:** 32
Po, Fernão do **I:** 52, 129
Poage, W. R. **X:** 144

Pocahontas **I:** 221; **II:** **288–289**, 289, 417c; **VII:** 248
captivity **II:** 51
Dale, Sir Thomas **II:** 81
Gates, Sir Thomas **II:** 135
miscegenation **II:** 228
Native Americans **II:** 244
Powhatan (chief) **II:** 294
Powhatan Confederacy **II:** 295
Rolfe, John **II:** 322, 323
Smith, John **II:** 347
pochteca **I:** 19–20
pocket veto **V:** 385–386; **X:** 311
Pocumtuck **II:** 212
Podhoretz, Norman **X:** 79, 215, 216
Poe, Edgar Allan **IV:** 197, 211, 213, 217, 378c; **V:** 372
Poems and Translations Written between the Ages of Fourteen and Sixteen (Lazarus) **VI:** 172–173
Poems for Our Children (Hale) **IV:** 167
poetry **II:** 39, 298, 357, 398; **III:** 139, 311, 373–374; **IV:** 167, 379c; **VII:** 161, 188; **VIII:** 192; **X:** 178
African Americans **VI:** 6
Dickinson, Emily **VI:** 79–80
Grimké, Charlotte Forten **V:** 160
Harper, Frances Ellen Watkins **V:** 164
Hay, John Milton **VI:** 124
Howe, Julia Ward **V:** 174
Jackson, Helen Hunt **VI:** 153
Lazarus, Emma **VI:** 172–173
literature **VI:** 178
Whitman, Walt **V:** 393–394
Poetry: A Magazine of Verse **VII:** 188
Poindexter, John **X:** 38, 154, 314–315
Point Four Program **IX:** 45–46, **242–243**
Point Lévis **II:** 233
Point Pleasant, Battle of **II:** 72
Poison (music group) **X:** 202
Pokanocket **II:** 217
Poland **I:** 192, 374; **II:** 365; **III:** 198, 205, 289; **VII:** 323; **VIII:** 408c; **IX:** 58, 105, 106, 277
air power **VIII:** 11
blitzkrieg **VIII:** 39
cold war (end of) **X:** 71, 72
foreign policy **VIII:** 124
Grand Alliance **VIII:** 137

Haig, Alexander M., Jr. **X:** 140
Holocaust **VIII:** 149, 150
Iron Curtain **X:** 156
isolationists **VIII:** 166
NATO **X:** 223
Nazi-Soviet Pact **VIII:** 237, 238
Potsdam Conference **VIII:** 280
POWs **VIII:** 281
Reagan, Ronald W. **X:** 260
Soviet-American relations **VIII:** 333
Teheran Conference **VIII:** 354
Yalta Conference **VIII:** 401, 402
Polemical Works (Dow) **IV:** 116
police **IV:** 180; **V:** 61; **IX:** 103–104, 206, 316, 334c
Police (music group) **X:** 240
Police Firearms Instructor certification program **X:** 212
polio **VIII:** 312; **IX:** 199, 250–251; **X:** 188
polio vaccine **IX:** 199, 331c
Polish Americans **VIII:** 53, 98, **269–270**
Polish Relief Commission **VIII:** 153
political action committee (PAC) **VIII:** 70, 146, 181; **X:** 53, 130, 143, **236**
political advertising **IX:** 3
political appointment of officers **V:** 365, 366
political campaigns **VI:** **230–233**, 231t, 232, 323c–327c. *See also* campaign finance; elections
advertising **X:** 8
African Americans **VI:** 5
Altgeld, John Peter **VI:** 10
American Independent Party **X:** 20
Anti-Imperialist League **VI:** 13
Arthur, Chester Alan **VI:** 16–17
Burger, Warren E. **X:** 43
campaign finance **X:** 53–54
Carter, James Earl, Jr. **X:** 57–58
class consciousness **VI:** 57
Cleveland, Grover **VI:** 58, 59
Conkling, Roscoe **VI:** 64
corruption, political **VI:** 66, 67
currency issue **VI:** 72, 73
Dukakis, Michael **X:** 91

political campaigns (continued)
Farmer, James L. **X:** 111
Ferraro, Geraldine A. **X:** 117
Ford, Gerald R. **X:** 121
Free-Silver movement **VI:** 105
Green Party **X:** 135
Hanna, Marcus Alonzo **VI:** 121
Harlan, John Marshall **VI:** 121–122
Harrison, Benjamin **VI:** 122
Hayes, Rutherford B. **VI:** 125–126
Horton, Willie (campaign ad) **X:** 143–144
McKinley, William **VI:** 189
mugwumps **VI:** 199
Nader, Ralph **X:** 206
Nixon, Richard M. **X:** 219–220
People's Party **VI:** 222–223
Perot, H. Ross **X:** 233–234
presidential campaigns **VI:** **230–233**
Prohibition Party **VI:** 234
Republican Party **VI:** 246–247
Schlafly, Phyllis **X:** 272
Shriver, Sargent **X:** 278
Tilden, Samuel Jones **VI:** 289
Wallace, George C. **X:** 313
political correctness **X:** **236–237**
censorship **X:** 60–61
conservative movement **X:** 80
multiculturalism **X:** 200
political exiles **III:** 126–127, 173
political machines **VI:** 95; **VII:** 316
political parties **III:** **278–280,** 397c; **VII:** 65–67, 236–237, 262–263; **X:** **237–239.** See also specific parties
abolition **V:** 3
American Independent Party **X:** 20
civil service reform **VI:** 56, 57
Civil War **V:** 64
Confederate States of America **V:** 75, 77
Congress **VI:** 63
conservation, environmentalism, and environmental policy **X:** 78

Democratic Party **IV:** 106–109
election of 1800 **III:** 116
elections **V:** 109; **X:** 101
elections, conduct of **VI:** 94
Farewell Address of George Washington **III:** 124
Free-Soil Party **IV:** 150–151
French Revolution **III:** 138
Green Party **X:** 135
Hispanic Americans **X:** 142
homefront **V:** 169
journalism **III:** 191
Know-Nothing Party **IV:** 201–202
labor movements **IV:** 204
Libertarian Party **X:** 176–177
Liberty Party **IV:** 210–211
music **III:** 251
nativism **V:** 251
Perot, H. Ross **X:** 233–234
political parties **X:** 237–239
Reform Party **X:** 263–264
Republican Party **IV:** 300–302
Sunbelt **X:** 290
tariffs **III:** 342
Washington, George **III:** 367
Whig Party **IV:** 362–364
political parties, third **VI:** **225–226**
Greenback-Labor Party **VI:** 120
Liberal Republican Party **VI:** 173–174
People's Party **VI:** 222–223
Populist Party platform, 1892 **VI:** 346–347
Prohibition Party **VI:** 233–235
Socialist Labor Party **VI:** 268
Socialist Party **VI:** 268–269
political reform **VI:** 115–116
political refugees **VIII:** 298–299
political science **VI:** 38
political theory
Bland, Richard **III:** 40
Blount, William **III:** 40–41
Clinton, DeWitt **III:** 73–74
commonwealthmen **III:** 79–80
corporatism **III:** 94–95
Coxe, Tench **III:** 96
Dwight, Timothy **III:** 109

Mason, George **III:** 237–238
Morris, Gouverneur **III:** 246–247
Murray, Judith Sargent Stevens **III:** 250
Paine, Thomas **III:** 271–272
Story, Joseph **III:** 334–335
Taylor, John, of Caroline **III:** 344
Wilson, James **III:** 379–380
Yates, Abraham, Jr. **III:** 387–388
politics **VI:** xv, 326c; **VII:** **228–230; VIII: 270–273,** 272. See also Congress; elections; government; political parties
affirmative action **X:** 9
agriculture **II:** 7
Akan **I:** 5
Alexander, Mary Spratt Provoost **II:** 17
Alien and Sedition Acts **III:** 9
almshouses **II:** 18
American Revolution **III:** 12–13
Americans for Democratic Action **IX:** 13
Andros, Sir Edmund **II:** 19
Annapolis Convention **III:** 14
anti-Federalists **III:** 14–15
art and architecture **I:** 12–13
Arthur, Chester Alan **VI:** 16
Articles of Confederation **III:** 24–25
Asian-American movement **IX:** 22
Association, the **III:** 27
audiencia **I:** 15
baby boomers **X:** 33
banking and credit **II:** 29
Benin **I:** 28
Berkeley, Lady Frances **II:** 32
Beverley, Robert **II:** 33
Bill of Rights **III:** 38–39
Black Panthers **IX:** 38
Blaine, James Gillespie **VI:** 31–32
Boston **II:** 37
Burgesses, House of **II:** 45
Byrd, William II **II:** 47
Catholics **VIII:** 53–54
Charles V **I:** 69

Cherokee **II:** 58
Cincinnati, Order of **III:** 69
cities and urban life **II:** 61; **III:** 70; **VIII:** 59
civil service reform **VI:** 56
class consciousness **VI:** 57
Common Sense (Paine) **III:** 77–79
communism **IX:** 60–62
Congress **VI:** 63; **VII:** 53–54
conservatism **IX:** 68–69
conservative movement **X:** 78–80
Constitutional Convention **III:** 81–82
constitutions, state **III:** 82–84
Continental Congress, First **III:** 86–88
Continental Congress, Second **III:** 88–89
Cooke, Elisha, Jr. **II:** 72
Copán **I:** 86
corruption, political **VI:** 66–67
Council of the Indies **I:** 95
Dagomba **I:** 101
Declaration of Independence **III:** 101–103
De Lancey, James **II:** 85–86
De Lancey family **II:** 86
Democratic-Republican societies **III:** 104–105
encomienda **I:** 122
energy crisis **X:** 104
Enlightenment **II:** 110
evangelical Christians **X:** 108
Ewe **I:** 125
Farewell Address of George Washington **III:** 124
Farley, James A. **VIII:** 110–111
farmers' alliances **VI:** 99–100
federalism **X:** 112–113
Federalist Papers **III:** 124–125
Federalist Party **III:** 126–127
Federalists **III:** 127
feminism **X:** 116
Ferdinand and Isabella **I:** 128
feudalism **I:** 129–130
Flynn, Edward J. **VIII:** 122–123

forts **II:** 124
French colonies **II:** 127
fur trade **II:** 130–131
gay rights movement **X:** 127–128
gender gap **X:** 128
German immigrants **II:** 140
globalization **X:** 131–132
Great Depression **VIII:** 140
haciendas **I:** 149–150
Hanna, Marcus Alonzo **VI:** 121
Heathcote, Caleb **II:** 155
Hendrick **II:** 155
Herrman, Augustine **II:** 156
Hispanic Americans **X:** 142, 143
Hutchinson, Anne Marbury **II:** 161
impeachment **III:** 175
Iroquois **I:** 182; **II:** 168
Italian Americans **VIII:** 167
Jackson, Jesse L. **X:** 159, 160
Jews **VIII:** 173
journalism **II:** 179; **III:** 190–192
La Raza Unida **IX:** 171
League of Women Voters **IX:** 174–175
liberalism **VIII:** 187–189; **IX:** 179–180; **X:** 174–176
Livingston, Philip **II:** 196
Livingston, Robert **II:** 196
Lloyd, David **II:** 197
lobbying groups **VII:** 162–163
Locke, John **II:** 197–198
Logan, James **II:** 198
machine politics **VI:** 183–184
Massachusetts **II:** 214–215
Mather, Cotton **II:** 217
Mather, Increase **II:** 218
media **X:** 187
Mendoza, Antonio de **I:** 231
merchants **II:** 222
métis **II:** 223
Middleton, Arthur **II:** 224
militia movement **X:** 193–194
Mills, C. Wright **IX:** 205
Mississippi Freedom Democratic Party **IX:** 206–207
Moctezuma II **I:** 237

modern Republicanism **IX:** 208–209
Moral Majority **X:** 197
Morris, Lewis **II:** 234
multiculturalism **X:** 200–201
music **X:** 201–202
Nader, Ralph **X:** 205–206
Native Americans **II:** 243, 246
nativism **VI:** 209
NEA,NEH **X:** 209
neoconservatism **X:** 215–216
New Deal **VIII:** 239–243
New Hampshire **II:** 251
New Left **IX:** 230–231
Newport, Christopher **II:** 259
New Spain **I:** 258–259, 262
newspapers **VI:** 211, 212
New York **II:** 261
OPEC **X:** 229
Patrons of Husbandry **VI:** 221
Paxton Boys **II:** 272
Pennsylvania **II:** 276
Plunkitt, George Washington **VI:** 225
Polish Americans **VIII:** 269–270
political correctness **X:** 236–237
political parties **III:** 278–279
popular culture **III:** 282–283
Pott, John **II:** 293
presidency **VIII:** 281
presidential campaigns **VI:** 230–233
Privy Council **I:** 295
Progressive Party **VII:** 236–237; **IX:** 248–249
progressivism in the 1890s **VI:** 233
Prohibition Party **VI:** 234
Quakers **II:** 308
republicanism **III:** 301–303
Rhode Island **II:** 321
Rittenhouse, David **II:** 322
Roosevelt, Franklin D. **VIII:** 312
Sahara **I:** 317
Schlafly, Phyllis **X:** 271–272
Seventeenth Amendment **VII:** 69–70
Shakespeare, William **I:** 324

slave trade **II:** 344; **III:** 329
society, British American **II:** 349, 350
South Carolina **II:** 353
states' rights **III:** 333
States' Rights Party **IX:** 281–282
Steinem, Gloria **X:** 288
suffrage **II:** 364; **III:** 335–336
Supreme Court **III:** 337–339
Tammany Society **III:** 341
tariffs **VII:** 305–306
televangelism **X:** 293, 294
television **IX:** 297
tenants **II:** 370–371
Venice **I:** 364
Virginia **II:** 384–385
Washington, District of Columbia **III:** 364–365
Washington Benevolent Societies **III:** 368–369
Whigs **III:** 374–375
women's rights and status **III:** 382–383; **X:** 321
Yoruba **I:** 377
Youngs, John **II:** 414
Zenger, John Peter **II:** 415
Polk, James K. **IV:** 282–284, 283, 378c
  Bear Flag Revolt **IV:** 45
  Buchanan, James **V:** 41
  Carson, Kit **IV:** 75
  Clay, Henry **IV:** 87
  Clayton-Bulwer Treaty **IV:** 88
  Colt revolver **IV:** 92
  Democratic Party **IV:** 108; **V:** 94
  foreign policy **IV:** 142
  Fort Vancouver **IV:** 145
  Forty-niners **IV:** 146
  Free-Soil Party **IV:** 150
  Frémont, John C. **IV:** 153
  Guadalupe Hidalgo, Treaty of (1848) **IV:** 165
  Houston, Sam **IV:** 175
  Larkin, Thomas Oliver **IV:** 208
  Liberty Party **IV:** 211
  Manifest Destiny **IV:** 217, 218
  Mexican-American War **IV:** 232, 234
  Monroe Doctrine **IV:** 242
  Oregon Treaty of 1846 **IV:** 269, 270
  Ostend Manifesto **V:** 260
  Pierce, Franklin **V:** 275
  Stanton, Edwin M. **V:** 333

Taylor, Zachary **IV:** 334
Tyler, John **IV:** 349
Whig Party **IV:** 364
Wilmot Proviso **V:** 395, 396
Polk, Leonidas L. **V:** 58, 73; **VI:** 222
Pollack, Ben **VIII:** 132
Pollock, Jackson **VIII:** 23, 25, 114; **IX:** 19, 20
Pollock v. Farmers' Loan and Trust Company **VI:** 147, 281; **VII:** 92
poll taxes **V:** 291; **VI:** 95; **VII:** 248; **VIII:** 36; **IX:** 312, 334c
pollution **V:** 355. *See* conservation/conservationism; environmentalism/ environmental policy
Polly decision **III:** 119
Polo, Don José **VI:** 305
Polo, Maffeo **I:** 286
Polo, Marco **I:** 286–288, 287m
  Cathay (China) **I:** 64, 66
  Columbus, Christopher **I:** 79
  Ramusio, Giovanni Battista **I:** 305
  sugar **I:** 338
Polo, Nicolò **I:** 286
Pol Pot **X:** 325c
polygamy **IV:** 284–285; **VI:** 198–199, 244
  Church of Jesus Christ of Latter-day Saints **IV:** 79–81
  Deseret, State of **IV:** 109–111
  marriage and family life **IV:** 223
  Mormon War **IV:** 244
  religion **IV:** 298, 299
  Smith, Joseph, Jr. **IV:** 324
  Young, Brigham **IV:** 371, 372
polygenesis **IV:** 290
Polynesians **III:** 164
Pomeroy, Samuel C. **IV:** 224; **VI:** 114, 115
Pomo **I:** 48
Ponca nation **VI:** 153
Ponce de León, Juan **I:** 288, 386c
  adelantado **I:** 3–4
  Caiusa **I:** 49
  conquistadores **I:** 84
  Florida **I:** 130
  Puerto Rico **I:** 297
Poniatowski, Stanislaus, king of Poland **III:** 205
Pontiac **III:** 281, 391c
  ethnocentrism **II:** 114
  Iroquois **II:** 169

Pontiac (*continued*)
Native Americans **II:** 247
Neolin **II:** 248
revitalization movements **II:** 320
Treaty of Paris **II:** 378
Pontiac's Rebellion **III:** 280*m*, **280–281**, 391*c*
Croghan, George **II:** 76
Gage, Thomas **III:** 146
Johnson, Sir John **III:** 188
Johnson, Sir William **II:** 177
Neolin **II:** 248
Pennsylvania **II:** 276
Proclamation of 1763 **III:** 287
Putnam, Israel **III:** 290
Seven Years' War **II:** 334
Pony Express **IV:** 145, 268*m*, 271, 272; **V:** 405*c*
Poole, Dave **V:** 46
Poole, Elijah. *See* Muhammad, Elijah
Poole, Frederick C. **VII:** 286
Poole, William F. **VI:** 176
pools, railroad **VI:** 293
poorhouses. *See* almshouses
Poor Pay More, The (David Caplovitz) **IX:** 69
Poor People's Campaign **IX:** 276
Poor People's March on Washington **V:** 195; **IX:** 124, 161, 298
Poor Richard's Almanack **II:** 302, 419*c*; **III:** 133
pop art **IX:** 20; **X:** 26
popcorn **II:** 8
Popé **II: 289–290**
Indians of the desert Southwest **II:** 166
Native Americans **II:** 244
Pueblo Indians **II:** 303
Pueblo Revolt **II:** 304
Pope, John **V:** 406*c*
Bull Run, Second Battle of **V:** 42–44
Cedar Mountain, Battle of **V:** 53
Jackson, "Stonewall" **V:** 186
Lee, Robert E. **V:** 206
McClellan, George B. **V:** 225
Pope (Catholic). *See specific popes*
Pope Day **III:** 225
Popenoe, David **X:** 182
Popham Colony **II:** 299
pop music **X:** 201, 240
Popol Vuh **I:** 45, 228
pop sculpture **IX:** 20

Populaire, Le **IV:** 61
popular culture **III:** 251–252, **281–283**, *282;* **V:** 351–352; **VII: 230–233**, *231;* **VIII: 273–275**, *274;* **IX: 243–244;** **X: 239–242**, *240. See also* entertainment; music
advertising **VIII:** 1
Beatles **IX:** 36
business **VIII:** 46
children **VIII:** 56
cities and urban life **VII:** 50
counterculture **IX:** 71–72
evangelical Christians **X:** 108
folk music revival **IX:** 110–111
Great Depression **VIII:** 140
jazz **VII:** 137
Jews **VIII:** 172
Life (magazine) **VIII:** 189–190
literature. *See* literature
Luce, Henry R. **VIII:** 196–197
McDonald's **IX:** 190–191
media **X:** 184–187
movies **VIII:** 217–220; **IX:** 210–214; **X:** 197–199
news media **VIII:** 243–244
New York World's Fair (1939–40) **VIII:** 244–246
photography **VIII:** 268–269
radio **VIII:** 289–291
recreation **VII:** 256–258; **VIII:** 296–298; **IX:** 255; **X:** 261–263
rock and roll **IX:** 263–264
Sinatra, Frank **VIII:** 326
sports **VII:** 293–295; **VIII:** 335–338; **X:** 284–286
television **IX:** 295–297; **X:** 294–297
World War II home front **VIII:** 395
"popular" fiction **X:** 177
Popular Front **VIII:** 65, 238, **275–276**
Popular Movement for the Liberation Front of Angola (MPLA) **X:** 71
popular music **IV:** 250–251; **VI:** 203–204; **VII:** 233
Popular Party **II:** 197
Popular Science magazine **VIII:** 56
popular sovereignty **IV: 285–286**, 379*c*

Cass, Lewis **IV:** 77
Democratic Party **IV:** 108
Guadalupe Hidalgo, Treaty of (1848) **IV:** 166
Massachusetts Emigrant Aid Society **IV:** 223
Republican Party **IV:** 300
population crisis **VII:** 273
population trends **I: 288–291;** **II:** 43, **290–292**, 291*t*, 420*c;* **III: 283–284; IV:** 177–178; **V:** 175–177, **277–279**, *278;* **VI: 226–227; VII: 233–235,** 234*m;* **VIII: 276–278; IX:** 7, 8, 29–30, 202*m*, **244–245; X: 242–244**, 243*m. See also* Great Migration; immigrants/immigration; overpopulation
Acadians **II:** 2
African Americans **II:** 6; **IV:** 8*m;* **VI:** 5; **X:** 9, 10*m*
agriculture **II:** 11
Amazon River **I:** 8
Andes Mountains **I:** 10
anti-Chinese agitation, rise of **IV:** 23
Asian Americans **X:** 28–30, 29*m*
baby boomers **X:** 33
birthrates **X:** 38
Boston **II:** 35, 37
bubonic plague **I:** 285
California **IV:** 65
California gold rush **IV:** 69
California Indians **II:** 49
Caribbean **II:** 52
Charleston **II:** 57
Chickasaw **II:** 59
children **VIII:** 55–57
Choctaw **II:** 60
cities and urban life **II:** 62; **IV:** 81; **VI:** 53; **VIII:** 57–58
Columbian Exchange **I:** 77–78
Comstock Lode **IV:** 96
Conestoga **II:** 67
Connecticut **II:** 69
Coosa **I:** 85
cotton culture **IV:** 97, 98
Delaware **II:** 88
disease and epidemics **I:** 106, 108; **II:** 90
economy **IV:** 117, 119
education **IV:** 120, 121
English immigrants **II:** 108
fertility **II:** 117–118
Florida **I:** 131
food **II:** 121
German immigrants **II:** 139

Great Depression **VIII:** 140
Hispanic Americans **X:** 142, 142*m*
Hispaniola **I:** 162
Hohokam **I:** 164
horses **I:** 167–168
housing **VI:** 134
Huron **I:** 170
industrialization **IV:** 185, 187
Iroquois **I:** 183
Islam in America **X:** 157
Jews and Judaism **X:** 162
Judaism **VI:** 158
Kalm, Peter **II:** 181
Kieft, Willem **II:** 182
King Philip's War **II:** 183, 184
Las Casas, Bartolomé de **I:** 201
Lima **I:** 206
Lisbon **I:** 207
London **I:** 208
Louisiana **II:** 199
mariners **II:** 204
marriage and family life **II:** 207, 208
Maryland **II:** 210
Massachusetts **II:** 212, 214, 216
migration **IV:** 235, 236, 236*m. See* migration
missions **II:** 229, 230
Monte Albán **I:** 242
mortality **II:** 234–236
Natchez **I:** 251
Native Americans **II:** 242, 245*m;* **X:** 215
Negro Plot of 1741 **II:** 247
New Hampshire **II:** 251, 252
New Jersey **II:** 252, 253
New Mexico **II:** 255
New Netherland **II:** 257
New Orleans **II:** 258
Newport **II:** 258
New Spain **I:** 260
New York **II:** 260
New York City **II:** 263
Norse **I:** 264
North Carolina **II:** 264
Penn, William **II:** 274
Pennsylvania **II:** 275
Pequot War **II:** 280
Philadelphia **II:** 281
Powhatan Confederacy **II:** 295
progressivism in the 1890s **VI:** 233
Pueblo Indians **II:** 303
Pueblo Revolt **II:** 304

Rhode Island **II:** 321
Roman Catholics **II:** 323–324
Serra, Junípero **II:** 332
Seville **I:** 323
skyscrapers **VI:** 264
slavery **II:** 338, 340
smallpox **II:** 345
South Carolina **II:** 354
Spanish colonies **II:** 356, 357
Spanish immigration **II:** 359
spinsters **II:** 360
Suleiman I **I:** 339
Sunbelt **X:** 290
Swedish colonies **II:** 364
Taino **I:** 342
Tenochtitlán **I:** 344, 346
Teotihuacán **I:** 346
Texas **IV:** 338, 339
Texas, Republic of **IV:** 340
Tikal **I:** 349
Tlaxcala **I:** 353
tobacco **II:** 375
Virginia **II:** 382, 384
World War II **VIII:** 390
Populist Party. *See* People's Party
Populists/Populism
anti-Semitism **VII:** 14
Democratic Party **VII:** 65
Farmer-Labor Party **VII:** 91
Non-Partisan League **VII:** 215
segregation **VII:** 281
southern demagogues **VII:** 292–293
Watson, Tom **VII:** 331–332
Porcher, Francis P. **V:** 231
Porgy and Bess (Gershwin) **VII:** 108–109, 195; **VIII:** 223, 309
pork **IV:** 9
pornography **VI:** 62; **X:** **244–245**
Bork, Robert **X:** 39
Brennan, William J. **X:** 40
censorship **X:** 60
Christian Coalition **X:** 61
computers **X:** 74
Internet **X:** 153–154
RICO **X:** 258
sexual revolution **X:** 277, 278
Porras, Francisco **I:** 167
Porres, St. Martín de **I:** **291**
porringers **II:** 280
portable communications **X:** 274
Port Chicago incident **VIII:** 288
Porter, Cole **VIII:** 224

Porter, David **IV:** 130, 152
Porter, David Dixon **V:** **280–281**
Annapolis Naval Academy **V:** 373
Milliken's Bend, Battle of **V:** 233
Union navy **V:** 368
Vicksburg campaign **V:** 382
Welles, Gideon **V:** 391
Porter, Edwin Stratton **VII:** 85, 190
Porter, Fitz-John **V:** 21, 269
Porter, Henry **IV:** 347
Porter, Horace **V:** 261
Porter, John **V:** 13
Porter, Noah **VI:** 93
Porter, Paul **X:** 125
Porter, William David **V:** 37
Porter, William Sydney (O. Henry) **VI:** 185
Porterfield, E. E. **VII:** 189
Port Folio **IV:** 196
Port Hudson, Louisiana
African-American regiments **V:** 5
De Forest, John William **V:** 92
Farragut, David G. **V:** 121
Mississippi River **V:** 235–236
Vicksburg campaign **V:** 382
Port Huron Statement, The (Tom Hayden) **IX:** 131, 230–231, 285, 286, 333*c*
Port Moresby **VIII:** 398
Portolá, Gaspar de **II:** 49, 331; **IV:** 69
Porto Santo **I:** 169
Portrait of a Lady (James) **VI:** 177
Portrait of the Assassin (Ford and Stiles) **X:** 120
portrait photography **V:** 35, 273
portraiture **IV:** 245
art **II:** 24, 25; **III:** 22; **IV:** 77; **V:** 16; **VII:** 17–18
Bodmer, Karl **IV:** 55
Dummer, Jeremiah **II:** 96
Feke, Robert **II:** 117
Hesselius, John **II:** 156
Johnston, Henrietta Deering **II:** 177–178
Kuhn, Justus Engelhardt **II:** 186
limners **II:** 194
painting **VI:** 219
Sargent, John Singer **VI:** 255–256
Theus, Jeremiah **II:** 373
Port Republic, Battle of **V:** 317

Port Royal, South Carolina **I:** 3; **II:** 95, 114, 126, 185, 309; **V:** 391
Port Royal, South Carolina, Experiment **V:** 113, **279–280**
Portsmouth, Treaty of **VII:** 99, 267, 271
Portugal **I:** 385*c*, 386*c*; **II:** 204, 338, 343; **VII:** 360*c*; **IX:** 194, 231–233, 316; **X:** 71, 223
Alexander VI, Pope **I:** 6
Amazon River **I:** 8
Azores **I:** 16
Battel, Andrew **I:** 27
Benin **I:** 28
Cabral, Pedro Álvares **I:** 43–44
Cameroon **I:** 52–53
Dengel, Lebna **I:** 104
Dutch East India Company **I:** 114
East India Company **I:** 117
Ethiopia **I:** 124, 125
Ferdinand and Isabella **I:** 128
Fernando Po **I:** 129
Gama, Vasco da **I:** 137
Henry the Navigator **I:** *157*
invention and technology **I:** 179–180
Jesuits **I:** 189
Jews (Judaism) **I:** 191
John III **I:** 192–193
Lisbon **I:** 207–208
Philip II **I:** 282
slavery **I:** 327
slave trade **I:** 328
Spice Islands **I:** 335
Tordesillas, Treaty of **I:** 358
Portuguese colonization **I:** 189
Akan **I:** 5
Azores **I:** 16
Bahía **I:** 23–24
Brazil **I:** 31–34
Dominicans **II:** 94
Gorée Island **I:** 145
Jesuits **II:** 174
Jews **II:** 175
John III **I:** 193
Madeira **I:** 214
Maravi **I:** 223
Mbundu **I:** 229
Nzinga **I:** 267
Reformation **I:** 310
São Tomé **I:** 320
slavery **I:** 326–327; **II:** 338, 339, 342
Portuguese exploration **II:** 259
Barbados **I:** 26
Bermuda **I:** 29
Brazil **I:** 33
Canary Islands **I:** 53

caravel **I:** 56
Cathay (China) **I:** 64–66
Dias, Bartholomeu **I:** 104–106
Fernando Po **I:** 129
gold **I:** 142
Gold Coast **I:** 143–144
Gomes, Diogo **I:** 144
Guinea-Bisseau **I:** 146–147
Henry the Navigator **I:** 158
Kongo **I:** 195–196
Magellan, Ferdinand **I:** 215–217
Northeast Passage **I:** 265
Príncipe **I:** **293**, 293
Ricci, Matteo **I:** 311–312
Sahara **I:** 317
Portuguese settlers **II:** 286
Portuguese traders **II:** 166
Portumma Castle **I:** 13
Posados de Puerto Rico v. Tourism Co. (1986) **X:** 7
Posner, Richard **X:** 330*c*
possessions, U.S. **VI:** 142*m*
Post, Amy and Isaac **IV:** 325
postal rates **VII:** 330
postal service **II:** **292–293**
Post-Dispatch **VI:** 235
posters **VIII:** 1
postmasters general **II:** 292
postmillennialism **X:** 107
postmodernism **X:** 27, 178
Postmortem: New Evidence in the Case of Sacco and Vanzetti (Young and Kaiser) **VII:** 273
Post Office Department **II:** 292–293; **V:** 30; **VII:** 23, 24, 147, 252. *See also* mail; mail service
communications **VI:** 61
Comstock, Anthony **VI:** 62
Harrison, Benjamin **VI:** 122–123
mail-order houses **VI:** 186
star route frauds **VI:** 275
post roads **II:** 215
postwar era **VIII:** 343, 354, 355
postwar planning **VIII:** **278–279**, 410*c*
foreign policy **VIII:** 125
Full Employment Bill **VIII:** 128
GI Bill of Rights **VIII:** 131–132
Keynesianism **VIII:** 177
mobilization **VIII:** 215
NRPB **VIII:** 232
Potsdam Conference **VIII:** 279–280
reconversion **VIII:** 295–296

postwar planning (continued)
unemployment **VIII:** 365
World War II home front
VIII: 396
Yalta Conference **VIII:**
401
potash **II:** 387
potatoes **I:** 77, 78, 112, 176, 197;
II: 121, 251
potato famine **IV:** 177, 298; **V:**
175
Potawatomi nation **II:** 199,
246
potlatch **II:** 266
"pot likker" **II:** 122
Potomac **II:** 295
Potomac River **V:** 11, 13, 148,
389, 390
Potosí **I:** 10, 280, **291–292,** 325,
327; **II:** 355
Potsdam Conference (1945)
VIII: 279, **279–280,** 410c;
IX: 277, 299
Anglo-American relations
VIII: 17
Arnold, "Hap" **VIII:** 22
atomic bomb **VIII:** 29
foreign policy **VIII:**
125–126
Forrestal, James V. **VIII:**
126
Grand Alliance **VIII:** 137
Hiroshima and Nagasaki
VIII: 146, 148
Leahy, William D. **VIII:**
184
Marshall, George C. **VIII:**
206
Soviet-American relations
VIII: 334
V-J Day **VIII:** 369
Potsdam Declaration **VIII:** 29,
137
Pott, John **II: 293**
Pottawatomie Rifles **V:** 38
Potter, John **V:** 218
pottery **I:** 13; **II:** 24, 247
Poughkeepsie Bridge **VI:** 35
Pound, Ezra **VII:** 188
Pound, Roscoe **VII:** 122
POUR (President's Organization
for Unemployment Relief)
VIII: 299
poverty **III: 284–285; IV:** 98,
183, 273; **V:** 254; **VI:** 5, 6,
326c; **VII:** 290; **IX:** 333c; **X:**
245–246, 246, 326c. See also
war on poverty
African Americans **X:** 10
agriculture **VIII:** 9
almshouses **II:** 18
Anglican Church **II:** 20

Appalachian Regional
Development Act **IX:**
15, 16
Asian Americans **X:** 28,
30
cities and urban life **II:** 62;
III: 71; **IX:** 52
Community Action
Program **IX:** 62–63
crime and punishment **II:**
75
economy **II:** 102; **IX:** 90
elderly **VIII:** 95
FSA **VIII:** 112
Georgia **II:** 137–138
Gonzáles, Rodolfo "Corky"
IX: 124–125
Great Society **IX:**
126–127
Harrington, Michael **IX:**
130
humanitarianism **III:** 169
Jackson, Jesse L. **X:** 160
labor **II:** 187
marriage **X:** 182, 183
Massachusetts **II:** 214
Medicaid **IX:** 196
métis **II:** 223
Model Cities program **IX:**
207–208
Native Americans **VIII:**
235; **X:** 215
New Frontier **IX:** 230
Oglethorpe, James Edward
II: 267
Osborn, Sarah Haggar
Wheaten **II:** 268
Philadelphia **II:** 282
St. Augustine **II:** 327
Scotch-Irish **III:** 322
society, British American
II: 350
Southern Christian
Leadership Conference
IX: 276
temperance **III:** 346
tenants **II:** 370
Virginia Company of
London **II:** 387
Volunteers in Service to
America **IX:** 310
War on Poverty **IX:**
313–314
"poverty gap" **X:** 246
Poverty Point **I:** 244
Powderly, Terence Vincent **VI:**
162, **227,** 268
Powell, Adam Clayton **IX:** 200,
245–246
Powell, Colin L. **X: 246–247,**
247, 327c, 331c
defense policy **X:** 87

Haiti, U.S. intervention in
X: 140
United Nations **X:** 308
Powell, John Wesley **VI:** 110,
111, 160, **227–228,** 257
Powell, Lewis **X: 247–248.** See
Paine, Lewis
Bakke **X:** 34
Bork, Robert **X:** 39
Rehnquist, William H. **X:**
264
Supreme Court **X:** 290,
291
Powell v. Alabama **VIII:** 13,
406c
power elite **IX:** 204, 205
Power Elite, The (C. Wright
Mills) **IX:** 204, 332c
power loom **IV:** 184
power plants, nuclear. See
nuclear energy
Powhatan (chieftain) **II:**
293–294
captivity **II:** 51
Dale, Sir Thomas **II:** 81
Gates, Sir Thomas **II:** 135
Jamestown **II:** 172
literature **II:** 195
Native Americans **II:** 244
Opechancanough **II:** 268
Pocahontas **II:** 288, 289
Powhatan Confederacy **II:**
294, 295
Rolfe, John **II:** 322
Smith, John **II:** 347
Virginia **II:** 382
Powhatan, USS **V:** 137
Powhatan Confederacy **II:**
242–243, **294–295**
Chesapeake Bay **II:** 58
Dale, Sir Thomas **II:** 81
Jamestown **II:** 171
miscegenation **II:** 228
Native Americans **II:** 244
Smith, John **II:** 347
Virginia **II:** 382
Powhatan Indians **I: 292,** 314,
372; **II:** 417c
Algonquin **II:** 17
Bacon's Rebellion **II:** 27
Dale, Sir Thomas **II:** 81
environment **II:** 112
ethnocentrism **II:** 114
Opechancanough **II:** 268
Pocahontas **II:** 288, 289
Powhatan Confederacy **II:**
294
Sandys, George **II:** 329
Smith, John **II:** 346–347
Virginia Company of
London **II:** 387
Wingina **II:** 401

Powhatan language **I:** 6
Powhatan-Renape Indians **II:**
288, 295
POWs. See prisoners of war
powwows **I:** 225
Poyas, Peter **IV:** 354
pragmatism **VI:** 155, **228–229;**
VII: 67–68
Prague Spring **IX:** 106
Prairie Farmer magazine **IV:**
105
Prairie School **VII:** 346
Praise the Lord (PTL) Club **X:**
294
Prang, Louis **VI:** 138
Pratt, Charles **VI:** 27–28
Pratt, Matthew **III:** 371
Pratte, Chouteau and Company
IV: 17
Pratz, Antoine Simon le Page du
I: 251
prayer in school **IX:** 100–101,
256, 257, 316, 333c
conservative movement **X:**
80
Equal Access Act **X:**
104–105
Reagan, Ronald W. **X:** 259
Souter, David **X:** 279
televangelism **X:** 293
"Prayer of Twenty Millions"
(Greeley) **V:** 407c
praying towns **II: 295–296**
Brainerd, David **II:** 40
Eliot, John **II:** 107
ethnocentrism **II:** 114
Massachusetts **II:** 214
Native Americans **II:** 246
religion, Native American
II: 317
Preakness Stakes **VI:** 134
Preble, Edward **IV:** 130
predestination **I:** 50, 51; **II:** 316
preemption **IV:** 190, 287
Preemption Act of 1830 **IV:** 12
Preemption Act of 1841 **IV:** 12,
85–86, 287
prehistoric humans **I:** 242,
254–255, 316
prejudice **IV:** 8, 9, 317; **V:** 99,
291, 350. See also
discrimination
Preliminary Emancipation
Proclamation **V:** 169
premarital sex **VII:** 283
Prence, Thomas **II:** 287
Prentiss, B. M. **V:** 326
preparationism **II:** 157
Preparedness **VII: 235–236**
Adamson Act **VII:** 2
Lodge, Henry Cabot **VII:**
165

Mooney-Billings case **VII:** 188

National Defense Act **VII:** 201

Selective Service Act **VII:** 282

Presbyterians/Presbyterianism **II: 296–297; III:** 322; **V:** 185; **VI:** 242; **VII:** 261; **VIII:** 303; **X:** 265

Campbell, Thomas **IV:** 71–72

Finney, Charles Grandison **IV:** 138

French immigrants **II:** 130

Great Awakening **II:** 148–149

Liberty Party **IV:** 210

Lovejoy, Elijah **IV:** 214, 215

McCormick, Cyrus Hall **IV:** 225

McGuffey, William Holmes **IV:** 228

New Hampshire **II:** 251

New Jersey **II:** 253, 254

Protestantism **II:** 301

religion **IV:** 297

revitalization movements **II:** 320

Second Great Awakening **IV:** 311*t*

Smith, Joseph, Jr. **IV:** 322

Tennent, Gilbert **II:** 371–372

Tennent, William, Jr. **II:** 372

Tennent, William, Sr. **II:** 372

Virginia **II:** 385

Whig Party **IV:** 362

Prescott, Richard **III:** 337

Prescott, Samuel **III:** 304

Prescott, William **III:** 50

prescription drugs **X:** 189, 190

preservation **VI:** 65, 199–200; **IX:** 255, 321–322, 334*c. See also* environmentalism/ environmental policy

preserving food **II:** 122

President, USS **III:** 215, 216; **IV:** 104, 328

Presidential Address to a Joint Session of Congress and the American People (George W. Bush) **X:** 359–362

presidential ballots **X:** 42

presidential campaigns. *See* political campaigns

Presidential Medal of Freedom **VIII:** 100, 178, 260

presidential pardons **X:** 325*c*

amnesty, acts of **V:** 9

fire-eaters **V:** 128

Ford, Gerald R. **X:** 120

impeachment of Andrew Johnson **V:** 178

Johnson, Andrew **V:** 188

Nixon, Richard M. **X:** 221

Semmes, Raphael **V:** 313

Tredegar Iron Works **V:** 356

Walsh, Lawrence E. **X:** 315

Weather Underground **X:** 318

presidential Reconstruction **V:** 292–294

Presidential Succession Act of 1886 **VI:** 130

President's Commission on the Status of Women (1961) (PCSW) **IX:** 175, 216, 223, **246–247,** 324

President's Committee on Civil Rights **IX:** 329*c*

President's Committee on Rural Poverty **IX:** 9

President's Gold Medal **VIII:** 100

President's Organization for Unemployment Relief (POUR) **VIII:** 299

presidents/presidency **VI: 229–230,** 323*c;* **VIII: 280–281,** 281*t*

Budget and Accounting Act **VII:** 36–37

Congress **VII:** 53; **VIII:** 66

Congressional Budget and Impoundment Act **X:** 75

Executive Reorganization Act **VIII:** 107–108

government **VIII:** 134, 136

Hartford Convention **IV:** 171

impeachment **X:** 149–150

New Deal **VIII:** 241

NRPB **VIII:** 232

OMB **X:** 226, 227

OWMR **VIII:** 259

political parties **X:** 237, 238

Rehnquist, William H. **X:** 264

veto, presidential **X:** 311

War Powers Act **X:** 315

World War II **VIII:** 390

presidios **II:** 255

Presley, Elvis **IX:** *247,* **247–248,** 332*c*

movies **IX:** 213–214

music **IX:** 217

popular culture **IX:** 244

rock and roll **IX:** 263

Press Association of the Southern States (PA) **V:** 193

press gangs **II:** 182; **III:** 175, 176

pressure groups. *See* lobbies/lobbying

Prester John **I: 292–293**

Behaim, Martin **I:** 27

Dias, Bartholomeu **I:** 104

Ethiopia **I:** 123, 125

Henry the Navigator **I:** 158

mappae mundi **I:** 221

Preston, Frances **X:** 203

Preston, John S. **V:** 96

Preston, Thomas **III:** 43

preventive crime-fighting **X:** 266–267

Priber, Christian Gottlieb **II: 297**

Pribilof Islands **VI:** 26, 27

Price, Byron **VIII:** 55, 258

Price, John **V:** 2; **VI:** 171

Price, Sterling **V:** 83, 265, 285

Price-Anderson Act of 1957 **IX:** 24

price controls. *See* wage and price controls

price fixing **IX:** 44, 206

price supports **VII:** 175; **VIII:** 7–9, 406*c;* **IX:** 8

price wars **VI:** 293

Priestley, Joseph **III: 285**

Prigg v. Pennsylvania **IV:** 280

primary education. *See* education, primary and secondary

Primitive Methodists **IV:** 116

primogeniture and entail **I:** 28, **122–123,** 166; **II: 297–298,** 407

Primrose and West minstrel company **VI:** 95

Prince (singer) **X:** 240

Prince (slave) **II:** 247

Prince, Lucy Terry **II:** 7, 195, **298**

Prince, Sally **II:** 46

Prince, Thomas **II:** 215

Prince Edward Island **I:** 3; **II:** 2

Princeton, Battle of **III:** 161; **IV:** 175. *See also* Trenton and Princeton, Battles of

Princeton, New Jersey **III:** 176

Princeton, USS **VIII:** 186

Princeton College/University **II:** 149, 184, 254, **298,** 335, 371, 372; **III:** 380; **IV:** 308; **VI:** 93, 101, *102,* 289, 290, 324*c*

Principall Navigations, Voyages, Traffiques and discoveries of the English Nation, The (Richard Hakluyt, the Younger) **I:** 152, 177

Príncipe **I:** 129, **293**

Principles of Management, The (Taylor) **VII:** 38, 357*c*

Principles of Psychology, The (James) **VI:** 154, 155, 326*c*

Pring, Martin **I:** 225; **II:** 250

Prinstein, Meyer **VI:** 290

printing and publishing **II: 298–299;** **V:** 244, 253; **VI:** 185, 204, 211–212. *See also* journalism; literature

Bradford, Cornelia Smith **II:** 38

Bradford, William **II:** 39

cities and urban life **II:** 61

Day, Stephen **II:** 84

Enlightenment **II:** 109

Franklin, Ann Smith **II:** 125

German immigrants **II:** 139

Harris, Benjamin **II:** 154

Massachusetts **II:** 212

Pelham, Peter **II:** 272–273

Zenger, John Peter **II:** 415

printing press **I: 293–295,** *294;* **IV:** 196, 213, 214; **V:** 192, 308

art and architecture **I:** 13

black legend **I:** 30

DeBry, Theodor **I:** 102

Gutenberg, Johann Gensfleisch zum **I:** 147

Huguenots **I:** 169

invention and technology **I:** 179, 180

Jews (Judaism) **I:** 191, 192

Mercator, Gerhardus **I:** 231

monsters **I:** 240

Reformation **I:** 307

Vespucci, Amerigo **I:** 368

Zumárraga, Juan de **I:** 382

Printz, Johan **II:** 274, 365

Printz v. United States (1997) **X:** 113, 329*c*

prison camps, Union **V:** 11

Prisoners from the Front (Homer) **VI:** 130

prisoners of war (POWs) **IV:** 103–104; **V:** 281–282; **VIII:** 34–35, 250, **281–282;** **IX:** 164; **X:** 234, 312, *312*

Andersonville Prison **V:** 10–11

assassination of Abraham Lincoln **V:** 17

Booth, John Wilkes **V:** 33

espionage **V:** 118

Greenhow, Rose O'Neal **V:** 159

ironclad oath **V:** 182–183

Morgan, John Hunt **V:** 240

prisoners of war *(continued)*
  prisons **V:** 281–283
  Walker, Mary Edwards **V:** 386
prison reform **IV:** 219; **VI:** 315
prisons **III: 285–286; IV:** 103–104; **V:** 10–11, **281–283,** 304; **VI:** 66; **X:** 81, 83
"Prison Ship, The" (Freneau) **III:** 139
prison ships **III:** 139, 186–187
Pritchard, Gullah Jack **IV:** 354
Privacy Act. *See* Federal Information Act of 1974
privateering **II: 299–300,** 300; **III: 286–287; IV:** 39, 152, 358; **V:** 315
  Barry, John **III:** 36
  Continental navy **III:** 90
  Dutch West India Company **II:** 98
  economy **III:** 111
  Florida **II:** 121
  impressment **III:** 175
  King George's War **II:** 182
  mariners **II:** 204
  McDougall, Alexander **III:** 239
  Newport, Christopher **II:** 258
  New York City **II:** 263
  North Carolina **II:** 264
  Paine, Thomas **III:** 271
  piracy **II:** 286
  Revolutionary War **III:** 307
  Teach, Edward **II:** 368
  Virginia Company of London **II:** 387
private property **VI:** 301
privatization **X:** 188
Privileges and Prerogatives Granted to Columbus, 1492 **I:** 389–390
Privy Council **I:** 103, 277, **295; II:** 43, 142
probability sampling **IX:** 118
probation **VII:** 59
"Problem, The" (Emerson) **IV:** 126
Problem of Civilization Solved (Lease) **VI:** 173
processing tax **VIII:** 6
Proclamation Line **II:** 342
Proclamation of 1763 **II:** 276, 334, 342, 385, 392, 420c; **III: 287,** 288m, 391c
  Canada **III:** 60
  Coercive Acts **III:** 76
  Fort Stanwix, Treaty of **III:** 132
  frontier **III:** 141

Iroquois Confederacy **III:** 179
  Ohio Company of Virginia **III:** 265
  Scotch-Irish **III:** 322
Proclamation of Amnesty and Reconstruction **V:** 407c, 425–426
Proclamations of Amnesty **V:** 407c
  amnesty, acts of **V:** 8, 9
  impeachment of Andrew Johnson **V:** 178
  Port Royal, South Carolina, Experiment **V:** 280
  Reconstruction **V:** 292
Procter, William **IV:** 118, 184
Procter & Gamble **VIII:** 46
Proctor, Henry **IV:** 169, 207, 256, 342
Procuranda Indorum Salute, De (José de Acosta) **I:** 3
Producers, The (musical) **X:** 242
product endorsements **VII:** 295
product integraph **IX:** 97
Production Code Administration **VIII:** 54
productivity **VI:** 145, 170
"pro-family" movement **X:** 271, 272
Professional Air Traffic Controllers Association (PATCO) strike **X:** 170
Professional Golfers Association (PGA) **VIII:** 337; **X:** 286
professionalization **VI:** 192
professional sports teams **IX:** 280
Profiles in Courage (John F. Kennedy) **IX:** 157
Program for Economic Recovery **X:** 261
programming, computer **IX:** 63–65, 98, 269
programming, radio **VII:** 254
Progress and Poverty (George) **VI:** 111, 325c; **VII:** 140
Progressive Baptist Convention **X:** 11
progressive education **VIII:** 93
Progressive Era **VI:** 40, 115
  AFL **VII:** 10–11
  antimonopoly **VIII:** 17
  anti-Semitism **VII:** 14
  Brandeis, Louis **VII:** 34–35
  Buck's Stove **VII:** 35–36
  criminal justice **VII:** 58–60
  Dewey, John **VII:** 68
  Dillingham Commission **VII:** 68–69

Elkins Act **VII:** 83–84
  environmental issues **VIII:** 103
  Federal Trade Commission Act **VII:** 94
  Flynn, Elizabeth Gurley **VII:** 94–95
  Gilman, Charlotte Perkins **VII:** 109
  intelligence tests **VII:** 131
  Johnson, Hiram Warren **VII:** 137–138
  journalism **VII:** 141
  Keating-Owen Act **VII:** 145
  Kelley, Florence **VII:** 145–146
  liberalism **VIII:** 187
  marriage and family life **VII:** 172
  Mooney-Billings case **VII:** 188
  mothers' pensions **VII:** 189
  Narcotics Act **VII:** 197–198
  National Women's Trade Union League **VII:** 205–206
  New Woman **VII:** 214
  Perkins, Frances **VIII:** 265
  Rauschenbusch, Walter **VII:** 255–256
  Supreme Court **VIII:** 344
progressive income tax **VII:** 93
Progressive Labor Party (PL) **IX:** 318–319; **X:** 317
Progressive Party **VII: 236–237,** 358c, 360c; **IX:** 14, 79, 94, **248–249,** 330c. *See also* National Progressive Republican League
  Children's Bureau **VII:** 47
  Coolidge, Calvin **VII:** 57
  Democratic Party **VII:** 66
  elections **VII:** 80, 81
  Federal Trade Commission Act **VII:** 94
  Johnson, Hiram Warren **VII:** 138
  La Follette, Robert **VII:** 154, 155
  La Follette, Robert M., Jr. **VIII:** 182
  La Guardia, Fiorello **VIII:** 182
  New Freedom **VII:** 211
  New Nationalism **VII:** 211
  Payne-Aldrich Tariff Act **VII:** 227
  politics **VII:** 230
  progressivism **VII:** 238

Republican Party **VII:** 263
  Roosevelt, Theodore **VII:** 266
  Taft, William Howard **VII:** 304
  tariffs **VII:** 305
  Wallace, Henry A. **VIII:** 373, 374
  Wheeler, Burton K. **VIII:** 377
Progressive reform **VI:** 173
Progressive Republicans **VIII:** 166, 248
progressive taxation **VI:** 147
progressivism in the 1890s **VI:** 115, 179, 205, **233,** 261–262
progressivism/Progressive reform **VI:** 266; **VII:** xiii, **237–238**
  Addams, Jane **VII:** 2–3
  Adkins v. Children's Hospital **VII:** 3
  AFL **VII:** 10
  Borah, William E. **VIII:** 40
  Budget and Accounting Act **VII:** 36
  business **VII:** 39
  Cannon, Joseph **VII:** 42
  child labor **VII:** 45–46
  Clayton Antitrust Act. *See* Clayton Antitrust Act
  Congress **VII:** 53
  conservationism **VII:** 55–56
  conservatism **VIII:** 71
  Coolidge, Calvin **VII:** 56
  Debs, Eugene V. **VII:** 64
  education **VII:** 76
  elections **VII:** 81
  Farmer-Labor Party **VII:** 91
  Harding, Warren G. **VII:** 118
  Hepburn Act **VII:** 122
  Hoover, Herbert **VIII:** 151–152
  Hoover presidency **VIII:** 153
  Industrial Relations Commission **VII:** 128
  journalism **VII:** 141–142
  Kelley, Florence **VII:** 145–146
  La Follette, Robert. *See* La Follette, Robert
  La Follette, Robert M., Jr. **VIII:** 182
  Lochner v. New York **VII:** 163
  Mann Act **VII:** 169
  Mann-Elkins Act **VII:** 170
  Masses, The **VII:** 173

mothers' pensions **VII:** 189
muckrakers **VII:** 192
Muller v. Oregon **VII:**
192–193
National Association of
Colored Women **VII:**
199–200
NAWSA **VII:** 198
New Freedom **VII:**
210–211
New Nationalism **VII:** 211
New Unionism **VII:** 212
New Woman **VII:** 214
Payne-Aldrich Tariff Act
VII: 226
Pinchot, Gifford **VII:** 228
politics **VII:** 229
Progressive Party **VII:**
236–237
Prohibition **VII:** 238–241
Pure Food and Drug Act
VII: 243–244
radicalism **VII:** 251
recreation **VII:** 258
Republican Party **VII:** 263;
VIII: 305
Roosevelt, Theodore **VII:**
265–266
science **VII:** 275
Seventeenth Amendment
VII: 69–70
Sheppard-Towner Act **VII:**
283–284
Sinclair, Upton **VII:** 286
Smith, Alfred E. **VII:** 287
socialism **VII:** 288
social work **VII:** 289–291
Steffens, Lincoln **VII:** 299
Taft, William Howard **VII:**
304
tariffs **VII:** 305
Triangle Shirtwaist Fire
VII: 311–312
Underwood-Simmons
Tariff **VII:** 313
urban reform **VII:**
316–317
Wald, Lillian **VII:** 329
Wilson, Woodrow **VII:**
333–334
women's status and rights
VII: 340
Workmen's Compensation
Act **VII:** 342–343
youth **VII:** 350
Prohibition **IV:** 336; **V:** 176; **VI:**
233; **VII: 238–241,** *239,*
240m, 359c; **VIII:** 296, 351,
406c. See also Eighteenth
Amendment
agriculture **VII:** 7
criminal justice **VII:** 59–60

elections **VII:** 80, 81
Lost Generation **VII:** 166
Mencken, H. L. **VII:** 181
progressivism **VII:** 238
radicalism **VII:** 250
Smith, Alfred E. **VII:** 287
Volstead Act **VII:** 327–328
Prohibition Party **VI:** 226,
233–235, *234,* 315; **VII:** 80,
358c
"Project C." *See* Birmingham
(Alabama) confrontation
Project Mercury **IX:** 219, 236
Proletarios (Nicaragua) **X:** 217
Pro-Life Action League **X:** 249
pro-life and pro-choice
movements **X:** 2, **248–249**
abortion **X:** 1–4
birth control **X:** 37
conservative movement **X:**
79
Roe v. Wade **X:** 268
Webster v. Reproductive
Health Services **X:** 319
Prolonged Popular War (GPP)
(Nicaragua) **X:** 217
Promise of American Life, The
(Croly) **VII:** 211
propaganda **V:** 282; **VII:** 51–52,
344, 345, *359c;* **VIII:**
282–283; IX: 52–53, 320
advertising **VIII:** 1–2
Capra, Frank **VIII:** 52
censorship **VIII:** 55
FTP **VIII:** 120
movies **VIII:** 218
news media **VIII:** 243
OSS **VIII:** 257
OWI **VIII:** 257
popular culture **VIII:** 273
war bonds **VIII:** 374
property crimes **X:** 81
property ownership
California Indians **II:** 49
crime and punishment **II:**
76
government, British
American **II:** 145
Locke, John **II:** 198
New Hampshire **II:** 251
Philadelphia **II:** 282
primogeniture and entail
II: 297–298
slavery **II:** 338, 341
society, British American
II: 351
South Carolina **II:** 353
Spanish colonies **II:** 357
suffrage **II:** 364
Virginia **II:** 384
women's status and rights
II: 408, 409

property rights **I:** 128, 326; **IV:**
378*c;* **VI:** 12, 135, 281, 317,
325*c;* **X: 249–251**
African Americans **IV:** 9
agriculture **IV:** 12
Amistad incident **IV:** 20,
21
computers **X:** 74
conservation,
environmentalism, and
environmental policy **X:**
78
marriage and family life
IV: 222
Scalia, Antonin **X:** 271
Supreme Court decision
IV: 331
women's status and rights
IV: 368
property tax **V:** 106; **VIII:** 59
Prophecy Conferences **VI:** 75
Prophet, the Shawnee **III: 287,**
289, 345, 347–348, 397*c,*
398*c;* **IV:** 256, 258. *See also*
Tenskwatawa
Prophetstown **IV:** 169, 255–256,
258
proportional representation **X:**
41
Proposition 209 (California) **X:**
9
proprietary grants **II:** 11, 191,
203, 209
proprietary rights **II:** 197,
209–210
proprietary rule **II:** 144–146,
210, 224, 234, 253, 265
"Proprietor of Livingston
Manor" **II:** 196
Prosser, Gabriel **III:** 7; **V:** 328
Prosser, Thomas **III:** 145
Prosser Slave Rebellion **IV:** 316
prostitution **IV:** 129; **V:**
283–284, 304, 352; **VI:** 169,
233
criminal justice **VII:** 59
Mann Act **VII:** 169
public health **VII:** 242
YWCA **VII:** 349
protectionism **III:** 177; **IV:**
376*c;* **V:** 348; **VI:** 180, 189,
284; **VIII:** 123, 144. *See also*
tariff issue; tariffs
Protestant, The (newspaper) **V:**
251
Protestant Association **II:** 141,
210
Protestantism **I:** 387*c;* **II:**
300–302; III: 63, 188; **VII:**
260, 261–262, 268, 349–350.
See also Counterreformation;
Fundamentalism;

Reformation; *specific*
denominations
abortion **X:** 3, 4
African Americans **X:** 11
anti-Catholic riots **IV:**
21–23
Austin, Stephen F. **IV:** 37
auto-da-fé **I:** 16
black legend **I:** 30
Blackwell, Antoinette
Brown **VI:** 29–30
Calvin, John **I:** 49–51
Calvinism **II:** 300
Chautauqua Institute **VI:**
49
Church of England **I:**
73–74
Civil War **V:** 64
clothing **II:** 65
conflict with Catholicism
II: 300
Congregationalists **II:**
67–68
conservatism **VIII:** 71
Counterreformation **I:**
95–96
Democratic Party **IV:** 108;
VIII: 80
denominationalism **II:**
300–301
Dow, Lorenzo **IV:** 115–116
Dutch Reformed Church
II: 97–98
Dutch West India
Company **II:** 98
education **II:** 102–103
Elizabeth I **I:** 120–121
English Reformation **II:**
301
Enlightenment **II:**
109–110
evangelical **II:** 301
evangelical Christians **X:**
107
Finney, Charles Grandison
IV: 138–139
Foxe's Book of Martyrs **I:**
132
French immigrants **II:** 130
Gates, Sir Thomas **II:** 135
German immigrants **II:**
139
Glorious Revolution **II:**
140
Graffenried, Christopher,
baron de **II:** 146
Great Awakening **II:**
147–149
Hakluyt, Richard, the
Elder **I:** 151
Hakluyt, Richard, the
Younger **I:** 152

Protestantism (continued)
  Hendrick II: 155
  Henry IV (Henry of
    Navarre) I: 158–159
  Huguenots I: 169–170
  immigration IV: 180; V:
    176
  imperialism VI: 142
  Jesuits I: 189
  Know-Nothing Party IV:
    201
  Loyola, Ignatius I: 209
  Lutheranism II: 301–302
  Mary I I: 224
  Maryland II: 209
  Massachusetts II: 212
  monarchy, British II: 231
  Moody, Dwight Lyman VI:
    196–197
  Native Americans II: 244,
    246
  nativism V: 251
  Philadelphia II: 282
  Philip II I: 282
  politics in the Roosevelt
    era VIII: 271
  praying towns II: 295–296
  Presbyterians II: 296
  Protestant work ethic II:
    302
  Puritans I: 298–299; II:
    302, 304–306
  Quakers II: 302
  religion V: 299–300; VI:
    241–243; VIII: 302,
    303; X: 265
  religion, Euro-American
    II: 316
  Republican Party IV: 301
  Roman Catholicism II:
    323; VI: 249
  St. Mary's City II: 328
  Second Great Awakening
    IV: 310–311
  slavery II: 342
  Social Darwinism VI: 266
  Social Gospel VI: 266–267
  society, British American
    II: 351
  Spanish Civil War VIII:
    334
  strikes V: 340
  Strong, Josiah VI: 279
  suffrage II: 364
  Sumner, William Graham
    VI: 280
  televangelism X: 293
  Trent, Council of I:
    359–360
  Victorianism VI: 304
  Virginia II: 385
  Whig Party IV: 362

Protestant Reformation II: 19,
  314, 316
Protestant Separatism II: 38
Protestant work ethic II: 302
protest music VIII: 222
protests. See demonstrations,
  protests, and rallies
"protest votes" X: 238–239
Providence (sloop) III: 190
Providence, Rhode Island II:
  417c
  Baptists II: 29
  Canonicus II: 51
  Coddington, William II: 66
  Newport II: 258
  Rhode Island II: 320, 321
  travel II: 378
  Williams, Roger II: 399
Providence Island, Bahamas II:
  368, 374
Provincetown Harbor II: 219
Provincetown Players VII: 115
Provincial Freeman (newspaper)
  V: 52
Provisional Confederate
  Congress. See Confederate
  Congress
Provisional Junta of National
  Reconstruction (Nicaragua)
  X: 218
proxy wars X: 124
PRR. See Pennsylvania Railroad
PRRM. See Pacific Railroad of
  Missouri
Prussia II: 332, 365, 378; IV: 4,
  241
Pryor, Arthur VI: 271
Pryor, Ralph IX: 166
psalms II: 239
psilocybin X: 206
psychedelic drugs IX: 183–184
psychedelic rock IX: 218, 264
psychiatry III: 312; IX: 199; X:
  189
psychic powers X: 216
psychoanalysis VII: 101–102,
  252
psychological warfare VIII: 282
psychology VI: 154–155, 326c;
  VII: 101–102, 158, 290; VIII:
  284; X: 109
Psychology of Sex (Ellis) VII:
  102
psychotropic drugs X: 189, 190,
  206
PT 109 IX: 157
PT boats VIII: 324
PTL (Praise the Lord) Club X:
  294
Ptolemy I: 231, 232, 266
public accommodations, ADA
  requirements for X: 21

public assistance II: 18, 282. See
  also almshouses
Public Broadcasting Service
  (PBS) X: 184, 296
public buildings II: 23
Public Citizen IX: 69; X: 205
public domain IV: 286–288
public education V: 195, 337;
  VI: 89–92. See also education
  cities and urban life IV: 83
  education IV: 120
  Hawaiian Islands IV: 172
  literature IV: 213
  Mann, Horace IV:
    219–220
  McGuffey, William
    Holmes IV: 228
Public Enemy (film) VIII: 217,
  218
public health. See medicine and
  public health
Public Health Service VII: 179,
  356c; VIII: 329, 406c, 418;
  IX: 222–223. See also Title VI
  Children's Bureau VII: 47
  public health VII: 242, 243
  Sheppard-Towner Act VII:
    284
  veterans VII: 325
public housing VIII: 407c
  cities and urban life VIII:
    59
  housing VIII: 158–159
  PWA VIII: 285
  USHA VIII: 367, 368
  Wagner, Robert F. VIII:
    372
public interest research groups
  (PIRGs) X: 77, 205
public land VI: 5, 8, 131–132,
  228, 327c
Public Land Act of 1800 IV: 275
public land policy IV: 286–288,
  287t
  Cabet, Étienne IV: 61
  economy IV: 117
  election of 1828 IV: 122
  internal improvements IV:
    190
  lead mines IV: 208–209
  migration IV: 235
  New Madrid earthquake
    IV: 262
  Panic of 1819 IV: 275, 276
  Panic of 1837 IV: 276
public land sales IV: 377c, 378c
Public Lands Commission
  (PLC) VI: 110
public morals VI: 62
public opinion polls VIII:
  283–284, 407c; IX: 118
  advertising VIII: 1

anti-Semitism VIII: 19
election of 1940 VIII: 98
election of 1944 VIII: 99
Farley, James A. VIII: 111
Full Employment Bill
  VIII: 128
Jews VIII: 173
liberalism VIII: 189
Munich Conference VIII:
  220
popular culture VIII: 275
postwar planning VIII:
  278
refugees VIII: 298
Republican Party VIII:
  305
Spanish Civil War VIII:
  334
World War II home front
  VIII: 396
public schools IV: 21, 37, 377c
  education, home schooling
    X: 98
  education, primary and
    secondary X: 98–101
public services IV: 82–84
public speaking
  African Americans IV: 9
  Douglass, Frederick V:
    99–100
  Foster, Abigail Kelley IV:
    148
  Harper, Frances Ellen
    Watkins V: 164
  Higginson, Thomas
    Wentworth V: 167
  Howard, O. O. V: 173
  lyceum movement IV: 215
  Phillips, Wendell IV: 281
  Seneca Falls IV: 313
  women's status and rights
    IV: 368
  Wright, Fanny IV: 369
public transportation. See urban
  transportation
Public Utility Holding Company
  Act (PUHCA) VIII:
  284–285
  antimonopoly VIII: 18
  Black, Hugo L. VIII: 37
  Second New Deal VIII:
    321
  Willkie, Wendell L. VIII:
    379
public works VI: 68; VIII:
  405c–407c
Public Works Administration
  (PWA) VIII: 285–286
  Black Cabinet VIII: 37
  CWA VIII: 63
  environmental issues VIII:
    103

FHA **VIII:** 119
Ickes, Harold L. **VIII:** 161
Native Americans **VIII:** 235
NIRA **VIII:** 228
NRA **VIII:** 232
USHA **VIII:** 367
Public Works of Art Project (PWAP) **VIII:** 23
publishing **X:** 178, 185. *See also* printing and publishing
Puebla **I:** 258
Pueblo **I: 295–296,** *296;* **II: 303; IV:** 76
    art and architecture **I:** 12
    De Vargas, Diego **II:** 89
    Great Plains Indians **II:** 150
    Hopi **I:** 166
    Indians of the Desert Southwest **II:** 165
    missions **II:** 229
    Native Americans **II:** 244
    Navajo **II:** 247
    New Mexico **I:** 254, 255; **II:** 254, 255
    Oñate, Juan de **I:** 271
    Pueblo Revolt **II:** 304
    religion, Native American **II:** 317, 318
Pueblo Lands Act **VII:** 208
Pueblo Revolt **I:** 167, 257, 296; **II: 303–304,** 418*c*
    agriculture **II:** 9
    crowd action **II:** 78
    Great Plains Indians **II:** 150
    missions **II:** 230
    Native Americans **II:** 244
    Navajo **II:** 247
    New Mexico **II:** 254
    Popé **II:** 289–290
    Pueblo Indians **II:** 303
puerperal fever **IV:** 113, 308; **VI:** 191
Puerto Rican Americans **X:** 141–143, 200
Puerto Rican Legal Defense and Education Fund **IX:** 250–251
Puerto Ricans **IX:** 52, 173, **250–251,** 331*c. See also* Latino movement
Puerto Rico **I:** 82, 288, **296–297,** 342, 386*c;* **II:** 52; **V:** 104; **VI:** 104, 130, 189–190, 328*c;* **VII:** 355*c,* 359*c,* 360*c;* **VIII:** 184, 361; **IX:** 173, 250, 329*c;* **X:** 141, 142
PUHCA. *See* Public Utility Holding Company Act

Pulitzer, Albert **VI:** 321
Pulitzer, Joseph **VI: 235,** 327*c;* **VII:** 121, 141
    boxing **VI:** 33
    newspapers **VI:** 211, 212
    Statue of Liberty **VI:** 276
    yellow journalism **VI:** 321
Pulitzer Prize **VI:** 110, 235; **VII:** 85, 108, 195; **VIII:** 113, 207, 286
Pullman, George M. **VI:** 235; **VII:** 64
Pullman Car Company **VI:** 59, 149; **VIII:** 291
Pullman Strike (1894) **VI: 235–236,** 327*c;* **VII:** 62, 64–65, 201
    Altgeld, John Peter **VI:** 10
    Cleveland, Grover **VI:** 59
    Great Strike of 1877 **VI:** 119, 120
    Howells, William Dean **VI:** 136
    labor: strikes and violence **VI:** 168
    Lloyd, Henry Demarest **VI:** 179
    railroads **VI:** 237
    Socialist Party **VI:** 268
    World's Columbian Exposition **VI:** 320
Pullo **I:** 321
Pulsaki, Casimir **III: 289–290**
pumpkin papers **IX:** 51, 134
pumpkins **II:** 8, 121
punch **II:** 215
punishment. *See* crime and punishment
punk rock **X:** 240
Purchas, Samuel **I: 297–298**
    art and architecture **I:** 13
    Battel, Andrew **I:** 27
    black legend **I:** 30
    Ingram, David **I:** 177
    Ramusio, Giovanni Battista **I:** 305
    Spice Islands **I:** 335
Pure Food and Drug Act **VII: 243–244,** 356*c*
    business **VII:** 39
    Meat Inspection Act **VII:** 178
    muckrakers **VII:** 192
    Narcotics Act **VII:** 197
    Republican Party **VII:** 263
    Roosevelt, Theodore **VII:** 266
    Sinclair, Upton **VII:** 286
    Steffens, Lincoln **VII:** 299
purge of anti-New Dealers. *See* election of 1938
purging **IV:** 229

"Puritan-Pequot War, John Mason's Account of" **II:** 421–422
Puritan Reformation, Second **II:** 305
Puritans/Puritanism **I: 298–299,** *299;* **II: 65, 304–306,** *305,* 417*c,* 418*c;* **IV:** 213
    alcohol **II:** 15
    Anglican Church **II:** 19, 20
    Baptists **II:** 29
    Bermuda Company **I:** 29
    Boston **II:** 35
    Bradstreet, Anne Dudley **II:** 39
    Brent, Margaret Reed **II:** 40
    Burr, Esther Edwards **II:** 46
    Calvin, John **I:** 51
    childhood **II:** 60
    Church of England **I:** 74
    clothing **II:** 65
    Congregationalists **II:** 68
    domesticity **II:** 93
    Dominion of New England **II:** 94
    Dudley, Thomas **II:** 96
    dueling **II:** 96
    Dutch Reformed Church **II:** 97
    education **II:** 103
    Elizabeth I **I:** 121
    Endecott, John **II:** 107
    English Civil War **II:** 107
    English immigrants **II:** 108
    environment **II:** 111
    government, British American **II:** 144, 145
    Harvard College **II:** 155
    Hutchinson, Anne Marbury **II:** 161
    Iroquois **II:** 170
    jeremiads **II:** 173–174
    labor **II:** 190
    literature **II:** 195
    Locke, John **II:** 198
    marriage and family life **II:** 208
    Maryland **II:** 209
    Massachusetts **II:** 212, 214, 216
    Massachusetts Bay Company **II:** 216
    Mather, Increase **II:** 218
    midwives **II:** 225
    monarchy, British **II:** 232
    Morton, Thomas **II:** 236
    music **II:** 239
    Native Americans **II:** 243

New Hampshire **II:** 250–252
New Jersey **II:** 252, 253
New York **II:** 260
Parris, Samuel **II:** 271
Pelham, Peter **II:** 273
Pennsylvania **II:** 275
Pequot War **II:** 280
Pilgrims **II:** 283
praying towns **II:** 295
Presbyterians **II:** 296
Protestantism **II:** 300–302
Protestant work ethic **II:** 302
religion, Euro-American **II:** 316
Sewall, Samuel **II:** 334
society, British American **II:** 349–350
theater **II:** 373
Wheelwright, John **II:** 396
Wigglesworth, Michael **II:** 398
Willard, Samuel **II:** 399
Williams, Roger **II:** 399
Winthrop, John **II:** 401–402
witchcraft **II:** 402
women's status and rights **II:** 408, 409
Wood, William **II:** 410
Purple Heart **V:** 228
Purple machine **VIII:** 64
Purviance, Edna **VII:** *190*
Purvis, Robert **IV:** 13; **V:** 125, 361
Pushmahata **IV:** 262
PUSH (People United to Serve Humanity) **X:** 159, 160
Putnam, Ann **II:** 266
Putnam, Israel **III:** 50, 53, 217, **290**
Putnam, Rufus **III:** 265
Putún Maya **I:** 341
PWA. *See* Public Works Administration
PWAP (Public Works of Art Project) **VIII:** 23
"Pygmie rebellion" **II:** 209
pygmies **I:** 52
Pyle, Ernie **VIII:** 40, 207, 243, **286**
Pyle, Howard **VI:** 137
Pynchon, Thomas **X:** 177
Pyramid of Tepanapa. *See* Great Pyramid
pyramids
    art and architecture **I:** 12
    Cholula **I:** 72
    Cozumel **I:** 96
    Huitzilopochtli **I:** 170

pyramids (*continued*)
　invention and technology
　　I: 180
　Olmecs **I:** 269
　Palenque **I:** 275
　Tikal **I:** 349
　Toltecs **I:** 356

Q

Qatar **X:** 228–229
Qclass **II:** 104
Quack **II:** 337
quackery **IV:** 229–231
Quadequina **II:** 217
quadrant **II:** 141
quadroons **II:** 229, 237
Quaker City: or, The Monks of Monk-Hall (Lippard) **IV:** 212
Quakers **II: 307–309,** 418*c;* **III:** 291, **291, 291–292,** 393*c;* **IV:** 148, 172–173; **V: 331–332;** **VI:** 31, 244. *See also* Hicksites
　AASS **IV:** 13
　abolition/abolition movement **II:** 1–2; **III:** 15–16; **IV:** 1; **V:** 1
　African Americans **III:** 5; **IV:** 8
　architecture **II:** 23
　artisans **III:** 26
　Bartram, John **II:** 30
　Bartram, William **III:** 37
　Benezet, Anthony **II:** 31–32
　Boone, Daniel **III:** 42
　Bradford, William **II:** 39
　Carteret, Philip **II:** 54
　Christiana, Pennsylvania, riot **V:** 59
　cities and urban life **II:** 62
　clothing **II:** 65
　Connecticut **II:** 70
　Cuffe, Paul **III:** 98
　Delaware **II:** 88
　dueling **II:** 96
　Dutch Reformed Church **II:** 97
　Dyer, Mary **II:** 99–100
　education **II:** 103
　Endecott, John **II:** 107
　English immigrants **II:** 108
　Enlightenment **II:** 110
　Franklin, Benjamin **III:** 134
　gender **II:** 136, 137
　Genius of Universal Emancipation **IV:** 160
　Gorton, Samuel **II:** 142
　government, British American **II:** 144, 145
　Great Awakening **II:** 147, 148

Greene, Nathanael **III:** 155
Grimké, Angelina and Sarah **IV:** 164
Hammon, Jupiter **II:** 153
Handsome Lake **III:** 164
Hume, Sophia Wigington **II:** 159–160
Husband, Herman **III:** 170
immigration **III:** 173
indentured servitude **II:** 165
Indian Removal Act (1830) **IV:** 183
Jones, Absalom **III:** 189
Kalm, Peter **II:** 181
Lee, Ann **III:** 204
Liberty Party **IV:** 210
Lloyd, David **II:** 197
Logan, James **II:** 198
Loyalists **III:** 219
Madison, Dolley **III:** 226
marriage and family life **II:** 208; **III:** 233
Maryland **II:** 210
Morris, Lewis **II:** 234
Mott, Lucretia **IV:** 246, 247
New Hampshire **II:** 251
New Jersey **II:** 252–{2: }254
New Netherland **II:** 257
Newport **II:** 258
New York **II:** 260
Niles, Hezekiah **III:** 258
North Carolina Regulation **III:** 260
Paine, Thomas **III:** 271
Paxton Boys **II:** 272
peace movements **V:** 266
Penn, William **II:** 273
Pennington, James William Charles **V:** 270
Pennsylvania **II:** 274, 275
Philadelphia **II:** 281
Plymouth **II:** 287
Protestantism **II:** 302
religion **II:** 316; **III:** 297; **IV:** 296
Rhode Island **II:** 321
Roman Catholics **II:** 324
Ross, Betsy **III:** 310
Scotch-Irish **III:** 322
Seneca Falls **IV:** 313–315
Shakers **III:** 323
slavery **III:** 327
society, British American **II:** 350, 351
spiritualism **IV:** 325
Starbuck, Mary Coffin **II:** 361

Stuyvesant, Peter **II:** 363
Truth, Sojourner **V:** 358
Tubman, Harriet **V:** 358
Underground Railroad **V:** 361
West, Benjamin **III:** 371
Willard, Samuel **II:** 399
Wistar, Caspar **II:** 402
women's status and rights **II:** 408–409
Woolman, John **II:** 410
Quanistagua (Caristauga) **II:** 67
Quanopin **II:** 395
Quantrill, William Clarke **V:** 46, **285–286,** 407*c*
Quantrill's Raiders **V:** 285
Quantum computers **X:** 75
quantum mechanics **VIII:** 318
quantum theory **VII:** 275
Quarry, Robert **II:** 197
Quartering Act **III:** 153, 154, 214, **292,** 348, 391*c,* 392*c*
Quarterly Anti-Slavery Magazine **IV:** 14
quartz mining **IV:** 69, 90, 163
quasars **IX:** 278
Quasi War **III: 292–293,** 396*c,* 397*c*
　Adams, John **III:** 3
　Alien and Sedition Acts **III:** 9
　Bache, Benjamin Franklin **III:** 29
　Barry, John **III:** 36
　Chauncey, Isaac **III:** 65
　Constitution, USS **III:** 80
　Continental navy **III:** 90
　Democratic-Republican Party **III:** 104
　Duane, William **III:** 108
　election of 1800 **III:** 116
　Federalist Party **III:** 126
　foreign affairs **III:** 130
　French alliance **III:** 138
　French Revolution **III:** 139
　Fries's Rebellion **III:** 140
　Jay's Treaty **III:** 183
　privateering **III:** 287
　rural life **III:** 312
　Talleyrand, Prince **III:** 341
　XYZ affair **III:** 385
Quay, Matthew **VI:** 66, 184
Quayle, J. Danforth **X:** 45, *45,* 91, **253–254**
Quebec **I:** 183; **II:** 417*c,* 419*c*
　Acadians **II:** 2
　Champlain, Samuel de **II:** 56
　exploration **II:** 114
　Flashman, Edward **II:** 119
　French colonies **II:** 126–127, 129

French immigrants **II:** 130
fur trade **II:** 130–131
Huron **II:** 160
Inuit **II:** 167
Jesuits **II:** 174
Jolliet, Louis **II:** 178
King William's War **II:** 185
Marquette, Jacques **II:** 205
Monckton, Robert **II:** 233
Native Americans **II:** 246
New Netherland **II:** 256
Queen Anne's War **II:** 309
Seven Years' War **II:** 332, 333
Wolfe, James **II:** 405
wolves **II:** 405
Quebec, Battle of **III: 293**
　Arnold, Benedict **III:** 21
　Carleton, Guy **III:** 62
　Crèvecoeur, J. Hector St. John de **III:** 97
　Morgan, Daniel **III:** 246
　Revolutionary War **III:** 307
　Schuyler, Philip John **III:** 320
Quebec Act **II:** 174; **III:** 392*c*
　Canada **III:** 60
　Carleton, Guy **III:** 62
　Coercive Acts **III:** 76
　frontier **III:** 141
　Proclamation of 1763 **III:** 287
Quebec Conference **VIII:** 393
Queen Anne's War **II: 309,** 419*c*
　British Empire **II:** 41
　Deerfield Massacre **II:** 84–85
　ethnocentrism **II:** 114
　iron manufacturing **II:** 167
　Massachusetts **II:** 214
　Mather, Increase **II:** 218
　monarchy, British **II:** 232
　New York **II:** 262
　privateering **II:** 299–300
　Teach, Edward **II:** 368
Queen Charlotte Islands **I:** 150
Queensbury, marquis of **VI:** 33
Queen's College **II:** 98, 104–105. *See also* Rutgers
Queenston Heights **IV:** 309
Queenston Heights, Battle of **III:** 61
Queer as Folk (TV program) **X:** 295
Quelch, John **II:** 285
Quemado pueblo (Aqua Fria) **I:** 319
Querini, Vincenzo (Pietro) **I:** 96
Quesada, Gaspar de **I:** 215

Quest for Common Learning, The (Carnegie Foundation) **X:** 99–100
Quetzalcoatl **I: 301**
  Aztecs **I:** 21
  Chichén Itzá **I:** 69
  Cholula **I:** 72
  Cortés, Hernán **I:** 93
  Durán, Diego **I:** 113
  Maya **I:** 228
  Moctezuma II **I:** 237
  Monte Albán **I:** 242
  Toltecs **I:** 355
Quiahuiztlan **I:** 352
Quiché Maya **I:** 7, 227, 258
"Quids" **III:** 226
quietism **II:** 307
quilombos **II:** 359
Quilting Frolic (Krimmel) **IV:** 26
Quimby, Phineas Parkhurst **VI:** 52, 88
Quincy, Josiah **III: 293–294**, 392*c*
  Adams, John **III:** 2
  Boston Massacre **III:** 43
  Boston Tea Party **III:** 45
  embargo of 1807 **III:** 118
quinine **VIII:** 208
Quinn, Paul **VI:** 4
Quinnapin **II:** 324
Quinnipiac **II:** 68
quinto **I:** 261
quipus **I:** 176
Quiriguá **I:** 86
Quiripi language **I:** 6
Quitman, John A. **IV:** 101
Quito **I:** 14–15
quitrents **II:** 79, 191, 209, 210, 253, 387
Quivira **I:** 90, 256, 271
quiz shows (television) **X:** 296
Quorum of the Twelve Apostles **IV:** 109, 261
Quota Act **VII: 245,** 360*c*
  AFL **VII:** 11
  anti-Semitism **VII:** 14
  Coolidge, Calvin **VII:** 57
  immigration **VII:** 127
  Mexican immigration **VII:** 182
  National Origins Act **VII:** 202
  nativism **VII:** 208
  population trends **VII:** 234
  race and racial conflict **VII:** 248
quotas **VIII:** 162, 298
  agriculture **IX:** 8
  immigration **IX:** 141
  Immigration Act of 1965 **IX:** 142

McCarran-Walter Act **IX:** 187–188
Qur'an (Koran) **I:** 183–184, 222, 337
Quraysh **I:** 183, 230

R

RA. *See* Resettlement Administration
Rabbinic Judaism **I:** 192
rabbits **I:** 214
Raca, Soliman Mutapha **I:** 75
Race, The (TV program) **X:** 295
race and racial conflict **II: 311–312,** 418*c*; **III:** 174*m*, **295; IV: 289–292,** 291; **V: 287–288,** 407*c*; **VI:** 327*c*; **VII:** xiv, 14, 27, 33, **247–250,** 292, 359*c*; **VIII: 287–289,** 405*c*, 409*c*, 410*c*; **IX:** 6, 7, **253–255,** 254; **X: 255–257,** 257. *See also* abolition/abolition movement; slave rebellions/resistance; slaves/slavery
  abolition movement **IV:** 1–3
  affirmative action **X:** 8
  African-American movement **IX:** 6*m*
  African Americans **II:** 5–7; **IV:** 8; **VI:** 5–7; **VIII:** 5; **X:** 9–12
  American Civil Liberties Union **VIII:** 13
  anti-Semitism **VII:** 13–15
  Bacon's Rebellion **II:** 27–28
  Baker v. Carr **IX:** 31
  Baldwin, James **IX:** 32
  baseball **VII:** 27
  Birmingham confrontation **IX:** 37–38
  Birth of a Nation **VII:** 30–31
  Black Power **IX:** 40–41
  Boas, Franz **VII:** 32–33
  Brownsville Riot **VII:** 35
  Brown v. Board of Education **IX:** 42
  Caribbean **II:** 53
  Catto, Octavius **V:** 52, 53
  cities and urban life **VIII:** 60; **IX:** 52
  civil rights **VIII:** 62
  Civil Rights Act of 1964 **IX:** 56–57
  Civil Rights Act of 1991 **X:** 63
  class consciousness **VI:** 57
  Colorado gold rush **IV:** 90

  Colored National Labor Union **V:** 68–69
  Creole **II:** 74
  Crummell, Alexander **VI:** 70
  Delany, Martin Robinson **V:** 92–93
  Democratic Party **VI:** 77
  Du Bois, W. E. B. **VII:** 71–72
  Dunbar, Paul Laurence **VI:** 82–83
  education **IV:** *120*
  enemy aliens **VIII:** 102
  entail **I:** 122–123
  ethnocentrism **II:** 113, 114
  Executive Order 8802 **VIII:** 106
  Farrakhan, Louis A. **X:** 111
  federalism **X:** 112
  FEPC **VIII:** 109
  Fifteenth Amendment **V:** 124
  Gentlemen's Agreement **VII:** 107–108
  government **VIII:** 134–135
  Grant, Ulysses S. **V:** 156
  Great Migration **VII:** 111–113
  Griffith, D. W. **VII:** 115–116
  Harlem Renaissance **VII:** 119–120
  intelligence tests **VII:** 131
  Jackson, Jesse L. **X:** 160
  Jackson State University **X:** 160
  Johnson, Andrew **V:** 188
  Johnson, Anthony **II:** 176
  Johnson, Hiram Warren **VII:** 138
  Johnson, Jack **VII:** 138, 139
  Kennedy, John F. **IX:** 158
  Ku Klux Klan **V:** 199–201; **VII:** 147–149
  labor: strikes and violence **VI:** 168
  labor trends **VI:** 171
  Leo Frank case **VII:** 157
  liberalism **VIII:** 189
  Locke, Alain **VII:** 164
  lost cause, the **V:** 218
  lynchings. *See* lynchings
  marriage **X:** 181
  Mauldin, Bill **VIII:** 207
  Memphis riot **V:** 232
  Mencken, H. L. **VII:** 181
  mestizaje **I:** 233
  mestizo **I:** 233–234
  migration **VIII:** 213
  militia movement **X:** 193–194

  miscegenation **II:** 228; **V:** 233–234
  music **X:** 201
  Myrdal, Gunnar **VIII:** 224–225
  NAACP. *See* National Association for the Advancement of Colored People
  National Association of Colored Women **VII:** 199–200
  Nation of Islam **X:** 213
  nativism **VII:** 208–209
  New Orleans riot **V:** 252
  New York City draft riots **V:** 254–255
  Niagara Movement **VII:** 214–215
  Paxton Boys **II:** 272
  Pennsylvania **II:** 275
  Plessy v. Ferguson **VI:** 224–225
  political correctness **X:** 237
  popular culture **VIII:** 275
  population trends **VIII:** 277–278; **X:** 243
  postwar planning **VIII:** 279
  praying towns **II:** 296
  race and racial conflict **X:** 255–257
  scalawags **V:** 307, 308
  Scalia, Antonin **X:** 271
  Scottsboro Boys **VIII:** 319–320
  segregation. *See* segregation
  sharecropping **V:** 316
  Singleton, Benjamin **V:** 327
  slave resistance **II:** 336–338
  slavery **I:** 327–328; **II:** 338–342; **V:** 328–331
  slave trade **II:** 343
  Social Darwinism **VI:** 266
  society, British American **II:** 349
  South **VIII:** 332
  South Africa **X:** 279–280
  southern demagogues **VII:** 292–293
  strikes **V:** 340
  suburbs **VIII:** 343
  Taylor, Susie King **V:** 350
  Terrell, Mary Church **VII:** 308
  Trail of Tears **IV:** 343
  Truth, Sojourner **V:** 357
  Turner, Henry McNeal **VI:** 297

race and racial conflict
(*continued*)
Wallace, George C. **X:** 313,
314
Washington, Booker T. **VI:**
308–309
Watts uprising **IX:**
317–318
White, Walter **VIII:** 378
White Citizens' Councils
IX: 319–320
women's status and rights
IX: 326
World's Columbian
Exposition **VI:** 320
World War II **VIII:** 389
World War II home front
VIII: 395
Wright, Richard **VIII:** 400
zambos **I:** 381–382
zoot-suiters **VIII:** 403–404
Race Riot (Andy Warhol) **IX:**
20
racial quotas **X:** 325*c*
Bakke **X:** 34–35
Brennan, William J. **X:** 41
neoconservatism **X:**
215–216
race and racial conflict **X:**
256
racial theories **IV:** 290–292
Racketeer Influenced and
Corrupt Organizations Act
(RICO) of 1970 **X: 257–258,**
323*c*
abortion **X:** 4
crime **X:** 82
NOW **X:** 211
pro-life and pro-choice
movements **X:** 249
tobacco suits **X:** 305
racketeering **X:** 50
Rackham, Calico Jack **II:** 286
radar **VIII:** 390
Radar Range **X:** 273
Radcliffe College **VI:** 316
radicalism **IV:** 273; **VII:**
250–251; IX: 14; **X:** 215
American Federation of
Labor **VIII:** 14
American Legion **VII:**
11–12
Bridges, Harry **VIII:** 43
civil liberties **VIII:** 60
Debs, Eugene. *See* Debs,
Eugene Victor
Farmer-Labor Party **VII:**
91
Goldman, Emma **VII:**
109–110
Greenwich Village **VII:**
114–115

Haywood, "Big Bill" **VII:**
120
IWW **VII:** 129–131
liberalism **VIII:** 187
Mooney-Billings case **VII:**
188–189
nativism **VII:** 208, 209
New Unionism **VII:** 212
Non-Partisan League **VII:**
215
Paul, Alice **VII:** 226
Red Scare **VII:** 258–259
Russian Revolution **VII:**
270–271
Sacco and Vanzetti **VII:**
273
Seattle General Strike **VII:**
279
socialism. *See* socialists/
socialism
southern demagogues **VII:**
293
radical press **VI:** 116, 167; **VII:**
251–253
Flynn, Elizabeth Gurley
VII: 94
Goldman, Emma **VII:** 110
Greenwich Village **VII:**
114
literature **VII:** 160
Masses, The **VII:** 173
muckrakers **VII:** 192
Reed, John **VII:** 259–260
Sinclair, Upton **VII:**
286–287
Steffens, Lincoln **VII:** 299
Trading with the Enemy
Act **VII:** 311
Radical Reconstruction **V:** 408*c*
Freedmen's Bureau **V:** 144
Garrison, William Lloyd **V:**
147
Ku Klux Klan Act **V:** 201
Mallory, Stephen R. **V:**
222
race and racial conflict **V:**
288
Stevens, Thaddeus **V:** 338
veterans, Civil War **V:** 379
radical reform **III:** 87, 170
radical Reformation **I:** 309
Radical Republicans **V:**
288–289, 408*c;* **VI:** 256, 270,
317
amnesty, acts of **V:** 8
assassination of Abraham
Lincoln **V:** 19
Black Codes **V:** 29
Blair, Francis P., Jr. **V:** 30
Butler, Benjamin **V:** 46–47
Civil Rights Act of 1866 **V:**
62

Civil Rights Act of 1875 **V:**
63
Civil War **V:** 66
Copperheads **V:** 82
Democratic Party **V:** 95
Greeley, Horace **V:** 158
homefront **V:** 169
impeachment of Andrew
Johnson **V:** 177–179
Johnson, Andrew **V:** 188
Joint Committee on the
Conduct of War **V:** 191
journalism **V:** 194
Julian, George W. **V:** 194
Lincoln, Abraham **V:** 211
loyalty oaths **V:** 219
Memphis riot **V:** 232
New Orleans riot **V:** 252
Reconstruction **V:** 292, 293
Reconstruction Acts **V:**
295, 296
Republican Party **V:** 302
Seward, William H. **V:** 315
Sheridan, Philip H. **V:** 319
Sickles, Daniel E. **V:** 327
slavery **V:** 330
Stanton, Edwin M. **V:** 334
Stevens, Thaddeus **V:**
337–338
Sumner, Charles **V:** 343
Thirteenth Amendment **V:**
353
Wade, Benjamin **V:** 385
Wade-Davis Bill of 1864 **V:**
385–386
West Point **V:** 372
"radical Whigs" **II:** 146
radio **VII: 253–255,** 360*c,*
361*c;* **VIII: 289–291,** 290,
405*c,* 408*c;* **IX:** 263, 280, 297,
320; **X:** 6, 7, 186–187
advertising **VII:** 4–5; **VIII:**
1
business **VIII:** 46
Catholics **VIII:** 53
censorship **VIII:** 54, 55
Congress **VIII:** 69
Coughlin, Father Charles
E. **VIII:** 75
electricity **VII:** 83
Ellington, Duke **VIII:** 100
entertainment **VII:** 86
FCC **VIII:** 116
FMP **VIII:** 119
Goodman, Benny **VIII:**
132
government **VIII:** 134
Great Migration **VII:** 113
invention and technology
VII: 134
Jews **VIII:** 172
journalism **VII:** 143

Long, Huey P. **VIII:** 195
marriage and family life
VIII: 204
McPherson, Aimee
Semple **VII:** 176
music **VII:** 195; **VIII:** 221,
223
New Deal **VIII:** 241
news media **VIII:** 243
OSS **VIII:** 256
OWI **VIII:** 257
popular culture **VII:** 232;
VIII: 273–275
propaganda **VIII:** 283
public opinion polls **VIII:**
283
race and racial conflict
VIII: 287
recreation **VIII:** 296, 297
religion **VII:** 262; **VIII:**
303
Roosevelt, Franklin D.
VIII: 313
technology **VIII:** 353
Tin Pan Alley **VII:** 309
vaudeville **VII:** 322
Welles, Orson **VIII:**
376–377
World War II home front
VIII: 395
radioactive dating techniques
IX: 270
Radio Act of 1927 **VII:** 134,
143; **VIII:** 116
radio astronomy **VIII:** 318; **IX:**
278
Radio City Music Hall **VIII:** 22
Radio Corporation of America
(RCA) **VII:** 86, 253, 254;
VIII: 244, 341; **IX:** 65
Radio Free Europe **VIII:** 36
radioisotope tracers **X:** 190
radiological contamination **IX:**
23, 24, 255
radio stations, minority-owned
X: 9
Radisson, Pierre Esprit **II:** 115,
159
RAF. *See* Royal Air Force
*Ragged Dick: Or Street Life in
New York* (Alger) **VI:** 10
ragtime **VI:** 204; **VII:** 140–141,
194, 309
Railroad Administration **VII:**
11, **255**
railroad regulation **VI:** 324*c,*
328*c*
business and government
VI: 40
Democratic Party **VI:** 77
Sherman, John **VI:** 261
Supreme Court **VI:** 281

railroads **III:** 177; **IV:** **292–296,** *293,* 294*m,* 376*c;* **V:** **289–290,** *290,* 408*c,* 409*c;* **VI:** xv, **237–239,** 238*m, 239,* 324*c;* **VII:** 356*c,* 358*c–360c;* **VIII:** 359–360; **IX:** 7, 146, 294; **X:** 275. *See also* transcontinental railroad
  Adamson Act **VII:** 1, 2
  agriculture **IV:** 11; **VI:** 7–9
  Andrews's Raid **V:** 11
  Baltimore & Ohio Railroad (B&O) **IV:** 39–40
  Bruce, Blanche K. **V:** 40
  buffalo, extermination of **VI:** 38
  bushwhackers **V:** 46
  business **VII:** 38–39
  business and government **VI:** 39–40
  business cycles **VI:** 41
  canal era **IV:** 74
  carpetbaggers **V:** 50
  cattle kingdom **VI:** 46
  Chinese Exclusion Act **VI:** 50
  Church of Jesus Christ of Latter-day Saints **IV:** 81
  cities and urban life **IV:** 82; **V:** 59
  Civil War **V:** 66
  Colorado gold rush **IV:** 90
  communications **VI:** 61
  Copperheads **V:** 82
  corruption, political **VI:** 66–67
  Darrow, Clarence **VII:** 62
  economy **IV:** 118; **V:** 104, 107
  Elkins Act **VII:** 83–84
  entertainment, popular **VI:** 97
  exploration **IV:** 132, 133
  farmers' alliances **VI:** 99
  filibustering **V:** 127
  flour milling **VI:** 101
  Forrest, Nathan Bedford **V:** 134
  Fort Laramie **IV:** 145
  Gadsden Purchase **IV:** 159–160
  Gould, Jay **VI:** 117–118
  Grant, Ulysses S. **V:** 156
  Great Migration **VII:** 113
  Greeley, Horace **V:** 158
  Hayes, Rutherford B. **VI:** 126
  Hepburn Act **VII:** 122
  Hill, James J. **VI:** 129
  homefront (Civil War) **V:** 168
  homesteading **VI:** 132

Hoosac Tunnel **VI:** 133
immigration **V:** 176
industrial development **V:** 181
industrialization **IV:** 185
industrial revolution, second **VI:** 145
internal improvements **IV:** 188, 189*m,* 190
inventions and technology **VI:** 149–150
journalism **IV:** 196
Knights of Labor **VI:** 162
lobbies and pressure groups **VI:** 179
mail-order houses **VI:** 186
Mann-Elkins Act **VII:** 170
meatpacking **VI:** 190–191
Mexican-American War **IV:** 234
Mexican immigration **VII:** 182
Mexican Revolution **VII:** 184
Mississippi River **V:** 234, 236
Morgan, John Hunt **V:** 240
Morgan, John Pierpont **VI:** 197–198
Mormon Trail **IV:** 243
Morse, Samuel F. B. **IV:** 246
National Road **IV:** 255
Native Americans **V:** 251; **VII:** 206
New South **VI:** 209, 210
newspapers **VI:** 212
New York City **V:** 253
Northern Securities Co. v. U.S. **VII:** 216
oil **VI:** 215
Pacific Railroad Act of 1862 **V:** 263–264
Panic of 1857 **V:** 264
Patrons of Husbandry **VI:** 221, 222
Petersburg campaign **V:** 271
Plessy v. Ferguson **VI:** 224
Pullman Strike **VI:** 235–236
Railroad Administration **VII:** 255
Rockefeller, John D. **VII:** 264
Roosevelt, Theodore **VII:** 266
Santa Fe Trail **IV:** 305
scalawags **V:** 307
science and technology **IV:** 307–308; **V:** *309,* 310
Scott, Thomas Alexander **VI:** 258

Sheridan, Philip H. **V:** 318
Sherman's March through Georgia **V:** 322
Shiloh, Battle of **V:** 323
Sooners **VI:** 270
Stevens, Thaddeus **V:** 337, 338
suburbs **VII:** 300, 301
tactics and strategy **V:** 346
trade **VI:** 290
transportation **V:** 355
trusts **VI:** 292, 293
Vanderbilt, Cornelius **IV:** 352–353
Villard, Henry **VI:** 305
Washington, D.C. **V:** 389
Wells-Barnett, Ida Bell **VI:** 311
Wilson, Woodrow **VII:** 334
railroads, elevated **VI:** 146
railroad securities **VI:** 19
Railroad Shopmen's Strike of 1922 **VII:** 2, 11, 118
"rainbow coalition" **X:** 160
Rainey, Gertrude "Ma" **VII:** 194, 195
Rainey, Joseph H. **V:** **290–291**
rain forests **I:** 8
Rains, Claude **VIII:** *219*
Rains, Joseph **V:** 308
Rainy Day (Longfellow & Beach) **VI:** 23
Raisin in the Sun, A (Lorraine Hansbury) **IX:** 5, 181, 332*c*
Rajai, Ali **X:** 156
Raleigh, Sir Walter **I:** **303–304,** *304,* 388*c;* **II:** 151, 232, 264, 265, 284
  Barlowe, Arthur **I:** 26
  Drake, Sir Francis **I:** 111
  El Dorado **I:** 119
  Elizabeth I **I:** 121
  Gilbert, Sir Humphrey **I:** 141
  Hakluyt, Richard, the Elder **I:** 151
  Hakluyt, Richard, the Younger **I:** 151
  Harriot, Thomas **I:** 154, 155
  Lane, Ralph **I:** 197
  Manteo **I:** 220
  Requerimiento **I:** 311
  Roanoke **I:** 313, 314
  Spanish Armada **I:** 335
  Thevet, André **I:** 348
  Wanchese **I:** 372
  White, John **I:** 373
Raleigh Institute **VI:** 4
rallies. *See* demonstrations, protests, and rallies
Ramirez, Mannie **X:** 284

Ramona (Jackson) **VI:** 153
Ramsay, Sir Bertram **VIII:** 247–248
Ramsey, David **II:** 179
Ramusio, Giovanni Battista (Giambattista) **I:** **304–305,** 305
  Cabral, Pedro Álvares **I:** 44
  corn (maize) **I:** 88
  Hakluyt, Richard, the Younger **I:** 152
  Leo Africanus **I:** 204
  Oviedo y Valdés, Gonzalo Fernández de **I:** 273
  Peter Martyr **I:** 280
  printing press **I:** 294
  Timbuktu **I:** 350
  Venice **I:** 365
ranchers/ranching **IV:** 51; **V:** 170; **VI:** 20
rancho system
  California **IV:** 64–65
  California missions **IV:** 70
  Dana, Richard Henry **IV:** 103
  Larkin, Thomas Oliver **IV:** 207
Rand, Ayn **X:** 78
Randall, Samuel J. **VI:** 232
Rand Corporation **X:** 301
Randolph, A. Philip **VII:** 106; **VIII:** **291,** 409*c*
  African Americans **VIII:** 4
  civil rights **VIII:** 61
  Executive Order 8802 **VIII:** 106
  FEPC **VIII:** 109
  MOWM **VIII:** 201–202
  NAACP **VIII:** 228
  race and racial conflict **VIII:** 288, 289
  White, Walter **VIII:** 378
Randolph, Edmund **II:** 67, 348; **III:** **295–296,** 395*c*
  Constitutional Convention **III:** 82
  Madison, James **III:** 228
  Mason, George **III:** 238
  Neutrality Proclamation **III:** 256
  Pickering, John **III:** 276
  Wilkinson, James **III:** 379
Randolph, Edward **II:** 94, 95, **312**
Randolph, George Wythe **V:** 66, 75
Randolph, John **III:** **296;** **IV:** 355; **VI:** 1
  embargo of 1807 **III:** 118
  Non-Importation Act **III:** 259

Randolph, John (continued)
    Non-Intercourse Act III:
        259
    Taylor, John, of Caroline
        III: 344
Randolph, Peyton III: 88
Random Access Memory
    (RAM) IX: 64
Random House X: 178
Rangel, Charles B. IX: 246
Ranger, USS III: 90, 190
Rankin, Jeanette VII: 358c;
    VIII: 166
Rankin, John IX: 135, 137
Ransdell Act of 1930 IX: 222
rape II: 409; X: 81
rape crisis centers X: 115
rap music X: 201–203, 240
Rapp, George IV: 299
Rappahannock II: 295
Rarick, John C. X: 20
Raritan II: 182
Raskob, John J. VIII: 15
rate wars IV: 40
Rathbone, Henry Reed V: 18,
    33
Rather, Dan X: 296
rationalism II: 147, 193–194;
    IV: 72
ration coupons, counterfeit
    VIII: 38
rationing (energy crisis) X: 104
rationing (World War II) VIII:
    291–292
    black market VIII: 38
    Henderson, Leon VIII:
        145
    marriage and family life
        VIII: 205
    mobilization VIII: 215
    OPA VIII: 254–255
    OWMR VIII: 259
    politics in the Roosevelt
        era VIII: 272
    reconversion VIII: 295
    recreation VIII: 297
    transportation VIII: 360
    women's status and rights
        VIII: 386
    World War II VIII: 389
    World War II home front
        VIII: 394, 395
rats I: 77, 285
Rauh, Joseph IX: 13, 207
Raulston, John T. VII: 278
Rauschenbusch, Walter VI: 266,
    267; VII: 255–256, 260
Rauwolf, Leonhard I: 75
R.A.V. v. City of St. Paul (1992)
    X: 271
"Raven, The" (Poe) IV: 213
Ravitch, Diane X: 201

Rawdon, Lord Francis III: 120
Rawlins, John A. V: 239
raw materials V: 356
Ray, Charlotte V: 291
Ray, James Earl X: 30, 31
Ray, Robert W. X: 287
Rayburn, Sam VIII: 284
Raylton, Tace Sowle II: 39
Raymond, Henry J. V: 257, 408c
Raynal, Abbé III: 98
Raynolds, William IV: 58
RCA. See Radio Corporation of
    America
RCA Victor VII: 86
REA. See Rural Electrification
    Administration
reactors. See nuclear energy
Read, Deborah III: 134, 136
Read, Mary II: 286
reading VIII: 297
Reading, Pennsylvania II: 332
Reagan, John H. V: 75, 221
Reagan, Ronald W. IX: 13; X:
    258–261, 259, 326c, 327c
    ABM Treaty X: 22, 23
    abortion X: 3–4
    African nations X: 13
    Anderson, John B. X: 21
    arms race IX: 17; X: 25
    assassinations X: 30, 31
    Bennett, William J. X: 35
    Boland Amendment X: 38
    Bork, Robert X: 39
    Buchanan, Patrick J. X: 42
    Buckley, William F., Jr. X:
        42, 43
    Bush, George H. W. X: 45
    business X: 49
    campaign finance X: 53
    Carter, James Earl, Jr. X:
        59
    Catholic Bishops' Letter X:
        59
    Civil Liberties Act of 1988
        X: 63
    cold war (end of) X: 71, 71
    conservatism IX: 69
    conservative movement X:
        78–80
    contras X: 80
    defense policy X: 86–87
    détente X: 90
    Dole, Robert X: 90
    economy X: 94–95
    education, primary and
        secondary X: 100
    elections X: 101
    ERA X: 107
    federalism X: 112–113
    feminism X: 116
    Ferraro, Geraldine A. X:
        117

Ford, Gerald R. X: 121
    foreign policy X: 123–124
    Free Speech Movement
        IX: 113
    Gore, Albert, Jr. X: 133
    Grenada, invasion of X:
        135
    GRH Act of 1985 X: 135
    gun control X: 136
    Habib, Philip C. X: 139
    Haig, Alexander M., Jr. X:
        139
    Helms, Jesse A., Jr. X: 141
    Hollywood Ten IX: 135
    House of Representatives
        X: 144
    immigration X: 148
    independent counsel X:
        150
    INF Treaty X: 151, 151,
        152
    Iran-contra affair X:
        154–155
    Iranian hostage crisis X:
        156
    Kemp, Jack F. X: 163
    Kennedy, Edward M. X:
        164
    labor X: 170
    Laffer curve X: 172
    Latin America X: 173
    Meese, Edwin C. X: 191
    Mexico X: 192
    military-industrial complex
        IX: 204
    Mitchell, George X: 195
    Mondale, Walter F. X: 196
    Moral Majority X: 197
    NAACP X: 208
    NEA,NEH X: 209
    neoconservatism X: 216
    NEPA X: 210
    Nicaragua X: 218
    Nixon, Richard M. X: 221
    North, Oliver L. X: 222
    nuclear freeze movement
        X: 224
    O'Connor, Sandra Day X:
        226
    OMB X: 227
    O'Neill, Thomas P., Jr. X:
        228
    Panama invasion X: 231
    Persian Gulf War X: 235
    political parties X: 237,
        238
    pro-life and pro-choice
        movements X: 249
    property rights X: 250
    Reaganomics X: 261
    Rehnquist, William H. X:
        264

    remarks at the
        Brandenburg Gate X:
        344–347
    Republican Party IX: 258
    Scalia, Antonin X: 271
    SDI X: 289
    Senate X: 276
    South Africa X: 279, 280
    Soviet Union X: 280
    Starr, Kenneth X: 286
    Strategic Arms Limitation
        Treaties X: 289
    Supreme Court X: 291
    terrorism X: 298
    think tanks X: 302
    Thurmond, J. Strom X:
        303
    Tower Commission X:
        305–306
    United Nations X: 308
    veto, presidential X: 311
    Walsh, Lawrence E. X:
        315
    Watt, James G. X: 317
Reagan Doctrine X: 260
Reaganomics X: 95, 261
real-estate speculation IV: 276
realism VI: 176, 177, 287; VIII:
    25
reality television shows X: 241,
    295
reaper IV: 10, 118, 226, 376c
    agriculture IV: 10
    economy IV: 118
    industrialization IV: 185
    McCormick, Cyrus Hall
        IV: 224–225
    science and technology IV:
        307
Reason the Only Oracle of God
    (Allen) III: 104
rebates VI: 40; VII: 83, 264,
    356c
rebellions II: 89, 290. See also
    slave rebellions/resistance
Rebel Private: Front and Rear
    (Fletcher) V: 213
Rebel without a Cause IX: 244
De Rebus Oceanicis et Nove
    Orbe decades tres (Peter
    Martyr) I: 280
Recco, Niccoloso da I: 53
recession, post–Revolutionary
    War
    banks III: 33
    economy III: 113
    Shays's Rebellion III: 324
    trade III: 349–350
recession of 1833–34 IV: 193,
    363
recession of 1921–22 VII: xiv,
    106, 224

recession of 1937–38 **VIII:**
 292–293, 408*c*
 antimonopoly **VIII:** 18
 automobile industry **VIII:**
  30
 CIO **VIII:** 70
 Congress **VIII:** 67
 conservatism **VIII:** 72
 conservative coalition
  VIII: 74
 Democratic Party **VIII:** 82
 Eccles, Marriner S. **VIII:**
  89
 economy **VIII:** 92
 Full Employment Bill
  VIII: 128
 Great Depression **VIII:**
  138
 Henderson, Leon **VIII:**
  145
 HOLC **VIII:** 151
 Hopkins, Harry **VIII:** 156
 Johnson, Hugh S. **VIII:**
  174
 Keynesianism **VIII:** 176
 labor **VIII:** 181
 liberalism **VIII:** 188
 mobilization **VIII:** 214
 Morgenthau, Henry **VIII:**
  216
 New Deal **VIII:** 240
 NYA **VIII:** 234
 politics in the Roosevelt
  era **VIII:** 271
 Republican Party **VIII:** 306
 Roosevelt, Franklin D.
  VIII: 313
 steel industry **VIII:** 338
 taxation **VIII:** 352
 Third New Deal **VIII:** 357
 TNEC **VIII:** 355
 unemployment **VIII:** 364
 WPA **VIII:** 387
recession of 1970s–1980s **X:**
 94–96, 229, 324*c*, 331*c*
reciprocal trade agreements **VI:**
 189
Reciprocal Trade Agreements
 Act **VIII: 293–294,** 406*c*
 Good Neighbor Policy
  VIII: 133
 Hull, Cordell **VIII:**
  159–160
 London Economic
  Conference **VIII:** 193
Recohockrians. *See* Westo
Recollections of the Civil War
 (Dana) **V:** 88
Recollet missionaries **II:** 130
reconcentrado policy **VI:** 71
Reconquista **I: 306,** 386*c*
 adelantado **I:** 3–4

Castile **I:** 62–64
Columbus, Christopher **I:**
 81
Ferdinand and Isabella **I:**
 128
 inquisition **I:** 178
 Jews (Judaism) **I:** 190
 New Spain **I:** 261
Reconstruction **IV:** 4, 261, 292;
 V: 291–295, 293*m,*
 407*c*–408*c;* **VI:** 324*c;* **VIII:**
 61, 80. *See also* Radical
 Reconstruction; Radical
 Republicanism; Radical
 Republicans
 abolition **V:** 4
 African Americans **VI:** 5
 AME Church **V:** 5
 amnesty, acts of **V:** 8, 9
 assassination of Abraham
  Lincoln **V:** 19
 banking and currency **V:**
  24
 Birth of a Nation **VII:** 30
 Black Codes **V:** 29–30
 Blaine, James Gillespie **VI:**
  31
 Blair, Francis P., Jr. **V:**
  30–31
 Brown, Joseph **V:** 39
 Butler, Benjamin **V:** 46–47
 carpetbaggers **V:** 49–50
 Chamberlain, Joshua L. **V:**
  54
 Chase, Salmon P. **V:** 57
 Civil Rights Act of 1875 **V:**
  62–63
 Congress **VI:** 63
 Congressional
  Reconstruction **V:** 294
 Corps d'Afrique **V:** 84
 Davis Bend, Mississippi,
  freedmen's colony **V:** 92
 Democratic Party **V:** 95;
  VI: 77
 economy **V:** 107
 education **V:** 108
 education, philanthropy
  and **VI:** 93–94
 elections **V:** 110, 111
 Elliot, Robert B. **V:** 111
 emancipation **V:** 114
 Enforcement Acts **V:** 117
 Fifteenth Amendment **V:**
  124
 foreign policy **V:** 132
 Freedmen's Bureau **V:**
  142–144
 Garrison, William Lloyd **V:**
  147
 Godkin, Edwin Lawrence
  VI: 116

Grant, Ulysses S. **V:** 156,
 157
Great Migration **VII:** 112
Greeley, Horace **V:** 158
Griffith, D. W. **VII:** 116
Grimké, Charlotte Forten
 V: 160
Hancock, Winfield Scott **V:**
 163
Hayes, Rutherford B. **VI:**
 125, 126
Howard, O. O. **V:** 173
impeachment of Andrew
 Johnson **V:** 177–179
industrial development **V:**
 181
Johnson, Andrew **V:** 188
Joint Committee on the
 Conduct of War **V:** 191
journalism **V:** 194
Julian, George W. **V:** 194
Kelley, William D. **V:** 198
Ku Klux Klan **V:** 199; **VI:**
 162; **VII:** 147
Ku Klux Klan Act **V:** 201
Langston, John Mercer **VI:**
 172
Liberia, immigration to **VI:**
 174
Lincoln, Abraham **V:** 211
Longstreet, James **V:** 215
loyalty oaths **V:** 218–219
Memphis riot **V:** 232
miscegenation **V:** 233–234
movie industry **VII:** 191
Nast, Thomas **V:** 247
Native Americans **V:** 251
New Orleans riot **V:** 252
Oates, William C. **V:** 257
Pinchback, Pinckney B. S.
 V: 275–276
plantations **V:** 277
Port Royal, South
 Carolina, Experiment **V:**
 279, 280
the presidency **VI:** 229,
 230
presidential
 Reconstruction **V:**
 292–294
Proclamation of Amnesty
 and Reconstruction **V:**
 425–426
race and racial conflict
 VII: 249
Radical Republicans **V:**
 288–289
Reconstruction Acts **V:**
 295–296
redemption **V:** 294–297
Republican Party **V:** 302,
 303; **VI:** 246

scalawags **V:** 307–308
Seward, William H. **V:** 315
Sheridan, Philip H. **V:** 319
Sickles, Daniel E. **V:** 327
slavery **V:** 330–331
Society of Friends **V:** 332
Solid South **VI:** 270
Stanton, Edwin M. **V:** 334
Stevens, Thaddeus **V:** 338
Sumner, Charles **V:** 343
Thirteenth Amendment **V:**
 353
Tilden, Samuel Jones **VI:**
 289
UDC **V:** 370
Union League **V:** 367, 368
*United States v.
 Cruikshank* **V:** 375–376
Wade, Benjamin **V:** 385
Wade-Davis Bill of 1864 **V:**
 385–386
Warmoth, Henry C. **V:** 388
wartime Reconstruction **V:**
 292
Welles, Gideon **V:** 391–392
women's status and rights
 V: 399
Reconstruction, second **IX:** 220
Reconstruction Act of 1867 **VI:**
 296
Reconstruction Acts **V:** 295,
 295–296, 408*c*
 amnesty, acts of **V:** 9
 Freedmen's Bureau **V:** 144
 impeachment of Andrew
  Johnson **V:** 178
 Radical Republicans **V:**
  289
 Reconstruction **V:** 294
 Sheridan, Philip H. **V:** 319
Reconstruction Amendments **V:**
 302, 343. *See also* Fifteenth
 Amendment; Fourteenth
 Amendment; Thirteenth
 Amendment
Reconstruction Finance
 Corporation (RFC) **VIII:**
 294–295, 405*c*
 Congress **VIII:** 66
 Emergency Banking Act of
  1933 **VIII:** 101
 FCA **VIII:** 111
 Hoover, Herbert **VIII:** 152
 Hoover presidency **VIII:**
  154
 Jones, Jesse H. **VIII:** 174
 mobilization **VIII:** 215
 relief **VIII:** 299
 Relief and Reconstruction
  Act **VIII:** 302
 Wagner, Robert F. **VIII:**
  372

Reconstructionism (Jews and Judaism) **X:** 161
reconversion **VIII: 295–296**
    aircraft industry **VIII:** 11
    automobile industry **VIII:** 30
      Baruch, Bernard M. **VIII:** 34
      Congress **VIII:** 68
      demobilization **VIII:** 79
      labor **VIII:** 181
      mobilization **VIII:** 215
      Nelson, Donald M. **VIII:** 238
      OSRD **VIII:** 256
      OWMR **VIII:** 258–259
      postwar planning **VIII:** 278–279
      steel industry **VIII:** 339
      V-J Day **VIII:** 370
      World War II home front **VIII:** 396
      WPB **VIII:** 376
recorded music **VIII:** 119, 132, 222, 223. *See also* phonograph/phonograph records
recording industry **X:** 202, 203
Recording Industry Association of America (RIAA) **X:** 330*c*
recreation. *See* sports and recreation
recruitment **V:** 153
Rector, Henry **V:** 152
Red Army
      POWs **VIII:** 281
      second front **VIII:** 320
      World War II European theater **VIII:** 391, 393
      Yalta Conference **VIII:** 401
Red Army GRU **VIII:** 104
Red Badge of Courage (Crane) **VI:** 68, 177
Redbank, Battle of **III:** 167
Red Cloud **V:** 408*c*; **VI: 239–240**
      Crazy Horse **VI:** 69
      Native Americans **VI:** 206, 208
      Sioux wars **VI:** 263
      Sitting Bull **VI:** 264
Red Cross **V:** 24, 25; **VI:** 157; **VII:** 282; **VIII:** *300,* 386. *See also* International Red Cross
"redeemed" states **VI:** 5
"redeemers" **V:** 291
redemption **V: 296–297**
      carpetbaggers **V:** 50
      Fifteenth Amendment **V:** 124

Reconstruction **V:** 291, 292, 294–295
    Republican Party **V:** 302
    scalawags **V:** 308
    Society of Friends **V:** 332
    Union League **V:** 368
    United States v. Cruikshank **V:** 375
redemptioners **II:** 164, **313,** 324; **III:** 199, 200
Redes **I:** 144
redistribution of income **VIII:** 308, 407*c. See also* "Share Our Wealth" Plan
Red Jacket **III:** 92, **296–297,** 297; **IV:** 375*c*
"red-lining" **VIII:** 119
Red Power **IX:** 12, 228, 229
Red River Basin **IV:** 218*m*
Red River campaign **V:** 280, **297–298,** 386
Reds (film) **VII:** 260
Red Scare **VII:** xiv, **258–259,** 360*c;* **VIII:** 43, 310, 327; **IX:** 14, 61, 137–138, 140
    AFL **VII:** 11
    Committee for Public Information **VII:** 52, 345
    Communist Party **VII:** 52
    Debs, Eugene V. **VII:** 65
    Democratic Party **VII:** 66
    Gilman, Charlotte Perkins **VII:** 109
    Goldman, Emma **VII:** 110
    labor movement **VII:** 153
    National Civic Federation **VII:** 201
    New Unionism **VII:** 213
    open shop movement **VII:** 220
    Palmer, A. Mitchell **VII:** 221
    Passaic Strike **VII:** 224
    politics **VII:** 230
    population trends **VII:** 234
    radicalism **VII:** 250, 251
    radical press **VII:** 252
    Russian Revolution **VII:** 270
    Sacco and Vanzetti **VII:** 273
    Seattle General Strike **VII:** 279
    socialism **VII:** 289
    Women's International League for Peace and Freedom **VII:** 337
    women's status and rights **VII:** 340
Red Scare, second **IX:** 66
Red Scout **II:** 77

Red Sea **II:** 285
Red Shoes **II:** 61, **312–313**
Red Sticks
    Horseshoe Bend, Battle of **IV:** 173
    Native Americans **IV:** 256
    Native Americans in the War of 1812 **IV:** 259
    Seminole wars **IV:** 312
Red Stick War of 1812–14 **IV:** 173. *See also* Creek War
Red Summer **VII:** 359*c*
reducción **I:** 3, **306–307**
Redwood Library **II:** 154
Reed, James **IV:** 114, 115
Reed, John **VII:** 52, **259–260**
Reed, Ralph **X:** 61
Reed, Stanley F. **VIII:** 346*t;* **IX:** 315, *315*
Reed, Thomas Brackett **VI:** 64, **240–241,** 262, 284
Reed rules (House of Representatives) **VI:** 240
"reefers" **VI:** 190–191
reenactments, Civil War **V:** 404
Reese, Jack **IV:** 347
Reese, Pee Wee **IX:** 262
Reeve, Tapping **III:** 203; **IV:** 62, 77, 219
reexport trade **III:** 113, 119, 350
referendums **VII:** 229
Reflections on the Revolution in France (Burke) **III:** 53, 271
reforestation **VIII:** 63
reform **VIII:** 40, 134, 235. *See also specific headings, e.g.:* social reform
    American Missionary Association **V:** 8
    Bloomer, Amelia **IV:** 53
    Catto, Octavius **V:** 52–53
    Democratic Party **IV:** 108
    Dix, Dorothea **IV:** 113–114
    education **IV:** 120–122
    fashion **V:** 123
    Greeley, Horace **V:** 158
    Harper, Frances Ellen Watkins **V:** 164
    Hicks, Elias **IV:** 172–173
    journalism **IV:** 194
    labor movements **IV:** 203, 204
    literature **IV:** 212
    Owen, Robert **IV:** 272–273
    penitentiary movement **IV:** 277–278
    prostitution **V:** 283
    religion **V:** 299
    Second Great Awakening **IV:** 311
    slavery **IV:** 317

Still, William **IV:** 328
Whiskey Ring **V:** 392
women's status and rights **IV:** 366, 368; **V:** 397
Reformation **I: 307–310,** 308*m,* 387*c*
    art and architecture **I:** 12
    Calvin, John **I:** 50, 51
    Counterreformation **I:** 95–96
    Dominicans **I:** 109–110
    Dürer, Albrecht **I:** 113–114
    Foxe's *Book of Martyrs* **I:** 132
    inquisition **I:** 178
    Jesuits **I:** 189
    Jews (Judaism) **I:** 191, 192
    Leo X **I:** 203
    Léry, Jean de **I:** 205
    Luther, Martin **I:** 210–212
    Puritans **I:** 298
    Trent, Council of **I:** 359, 360
Reformation, English **II:** 301
Reformed churches **I:** 307, 309
Reformers (Republican Party) **VI:** 246
Reform Judaism **IV:** 298; **VI:** 158, 243; **VII:** 261; **VIII:** 303; **X:** 161, 265
reform legislation **VIII:** 372
Reform Party **X: 263–264**
    Buchanan, Patrick J. **X:** 42
    elections **X:** 102
    Perot, H. Ross **X:** 234
refrigeration **IV:** 308; **VI:** 190–191
Refugee Act of 1980 **X:** 28
refugees **V: 298–299; VIII: 298–299; X:** 67, 147, 163
    Acadians **II:** 2
    anti-Semitism **VIII:** 19
    Civil War **V:** 67
    contrabands **V:** 80, 81
    elections **V:** 110
    food riots **V:** 129
    Freedmen's Bureau **V:** 142
    French immigrants **II:** 130
    German Americans **VIII:** 130
    German immigrants **II:** 139
    Graffenried, Christopher, baron de **II:** 146
    Holocaust **VIII:** 150
    Huron **II:** 160
    immigration **VIII:** 162
    Jews **II:** 175; **VIII:** 173
    Natchez Revolt **II:** 242
    Native Americans **V:** 250
    Navajo **II:** 247

Petersburg campaign **V:** 272

Polish Americans **VIII:** 270

race and racial conflict **V:** 287

Reconstruction **V:** 291

Richmond, Virginia **V:** 304

Roosevelt, Franklin D. **VIII:** 314

Special Field Order No. 15 **V:** 332

Zionism **VIII:** 403

Regan, Donald **X:** 154

Regents of the University of California v. Allan Bakke. See Bakke (1978)

reggae music **X:** 241

regidores **I:** 39

regionalism **VIII:** 25

Regular Baptists **II:** 29

regulation **VII:** 34, 83–84, 122; **VIII:** 71, 123

Regulations for the Army of the Confederate States **V:** 363

Regulations for the Order and Discipline of the Troops of the United States **III:** 334

Regulations for the Uniform and Dress of the Army of the United States **V:** 363

Regulations of 1772 **III:** 258

regulator movements **III:** 322. *See also* North Carolina Regulation; South Carolina Regulation

Regulators **II:** 265

regulatory legislation **VI:** 324c, 326c

   Interstate Commerce Act of 1887 **VI:** 336–339

   People's Party **VI:** 223

   railroads **VI:** 239

   Supreme Court **VI:** 281

Rehabilitation Act of 1973 **IX:** 103; **X:** 20–21

Rehnquist, William H. **X:** **264–265**, 327c

   Brennan, William J. **X:** 40, 41

   Burger, Warren E. **X:** 44

   Ginsburg, Ruth Bader **X:** 130

   Reagan, Ronald W. **X:** 260

   Roe v. Wade **X:** 268

   Scalia, Antonin **X:** 271

   Supreme Court **X:** 290, 291

   Thomas, Clarence **X:** 302

   Webster v. Reproductive Health Services **X:** 318

Reich, Robert **X:** 62

Reid, John **VI:** 274

Reid, Thomas **IV:** 71

Reid, Whitelaw **V:** 82; **VI:** 211

Reign of Terror **III:** 310

relação **I:** 33

Relaciones (Chimalpahin) **I:** 71

relativity theory **VII:** 275

relief **III:** 285, 355; **VII:** 260; **VIII:** **299–302**, *300*, 387

   African Americans **VIII:** 3

   art and architecture **VIII:** 23

   Bonus Army **VIII:** 39

   Bridges, Harry **VIII:** 43

   CCC **VIII:** 63

   children **VIII:** 56

   cities and urban life **VIII:** 58

   Communists **VIII:** 65

   Congress **VIII:** 66

   conservatism **VIII:** 73

   conservative coalition **VIII:** 73

   CWA **VIII:** 62–63

   Democratic Party **VIII:** 81

   economy **VIII:** 91–92

   Emergency Relief Appropriation Act **VIII:** 101–102

   FAP **VIII:** 114

   FERA **VIII:** 117–118

   First New Deal **VIII:** 122

   FMP **VIII:** 119–120

   FTP **VIII:** 120–121

   FWP **VIII:** 121

   government **VIII:** 134

   Great Depression **VIII:** 140

   Hoover, Herbert **VIII:** 152

   Hoover presidency **VIII:** 154

   Hopkins, Harry **VIII:** 156–157

   immigration **VIII:** 162

   Keynesianism **VIII:** 176

   liberalism **VIII:** 188

   marriage and family life **VIII:** 204

   medicine **VIII:** 208

   Mexican Americans **VIII:** 210

   Mexican Repatriation Program **VIII:** 211

   Native Americans **VIII:** 235

   New Deal **VIII:** 240

   NRPB **VIII:** 232

   NYA **VIII:** 234

   Perkins, Frances **VIII:** 265

   PWA **VIII:** 285

   recession of 1937–38 **VIII:** 293

   recreation **VIII:** 296

Relief and Reconstruction Act **VIII:** 302

   religion **VIII:** 304

   Republican Party **VIII:** 305

   RFC **VIII:** 294

   Roosevelt, Franklin D. **VIII:** 312, 313

   Second New Deal **VIII:** 321

   Thomas, Norman **VIII:** 358

   unemployment **VIII:** 363

   Wagner, Robert F. **VIII:** 372

   Wallace, Henry A. **VIII:** 373

   women's status and rights **VIII:** 384

   WPA **VIII:** 386–388

Relief and Reconstruction Act **VIII:** 302, 405c

   Congress **VIII:** 66

   FERA **VIII:** 118

   Hoover presidency **VIII:** 154

   relief **VIII:** 299

   RFC **VIII:** 294

   Wagner, Robert F. **VIII:** 372

relief work **V:** 28–29

religion **II:** **314–317**, 315m; **III:** **297–299**, *298, 301*, 397c; **IV:** **296–299**, *297*; **V:** **299–300**; **VI:** **241–245**, *244*; **VII:** **260–262**; **VIII:** **302–304**; **IX:** **255–257**; **X:** **265**. *See also specific headings*

   abolition **V:** 3

   Africa **II:** 4

   African-American **II:** **313–314**

   African-American churches, growth of **VI:** 3–5

   African Americans **II:** 7; **IV:** 7, 7–8; **VI:** 6; **X:** 11–12

   agriculture **IV:** 10

   Allen, Richard **III:** 10–11

   AME Church **V:** 5–6

   American Missionary Association **V:** 8

   Anglican Church **II:** 19–20

   animals **II:** 20

   anti-Catholic riots **IV:** 21–23

   anti-Semitism **VII:** 13–15; **VIII:** 18–19

   art **II:** 25

   Asbury, Francis **III:** 26–27

   Baptists **II:** 29; **III:** 34–35

Beecher, Henry Ward **VI:** 23–24

birth control **X:** 37

Blackwell, Antoinette Brown **VI:** 29–30

Boston **II:** 35

Boylston, Zabdiel **II:** 37

Branch Davidians **X:** 39–40

Brattle, Thomas **II:** 40

Brazil **I:** 31

Brown, John **V:** 37

Brown, Olympia **VI:** 35–36

cacao **I:** 45

California missions **IV:** 70

Campbell, Thomas **IV:** 71–72

Carib **I:** 56

Cary, Ann Shadd **V:** 52

Castile **I:** 62

Charles V **I:** 68–69

Chauncy, Charles **II:** 57

Chichén Itzá **I:** 70

Civil War **V:** 64

clothing **II:** 65

Columbus, Christopher **I:** 81

Common Sense (Paine) **III:** 78

Connecticut **II:** 70

conservative movement **X:** 79, 80

corn (maize) **I:** 88

Cotton, John **II:** 73

Counterreformation **I:** 95–96

crime and punishment **II:** 75

Cuzco **I:** 99

dance **II:** 82

Darwinism and religion **VI:** 75

deism **III:** 103–104

Dow, Lorenzo **IV:** 115–116

Eddy, Mary Baker **VI:** 87–88

education **II:** 103; **III:** 113–115; **IV:** 121; **V:** 108

elections **IX:** 95

Elementary and Secondary Education Act of 1965 **IX:** 98

Eliot, John **II:** 107

Engel v. Vitale **IX:** 100–101

Enlightenment **II:** 109, 110

Equal Access Act **X:** 104–105

Euro-American **II:** **314–317**

religion (*continued*)

Finney, Charles Grandison **IV:** 138–139

French immigrants **II:** 130

German Reformed Church **II:** 140

Gladden, Washington **VI:** 115

Gorton, Samuel **II:** 141–142

Graham, Billy **IX:** 125–126

Great Awakening **II:** 147–149

Hammon, Jupiter **II:** 153–154

Handsome Lake **III:** 164

Harlem Renaissance **VII:** 120

Hawaii **III:** 164

Hicks, Elias **IV:** 172–173

Hooker, Thomas **II:** 156–157

Human Genome Project **X:** 146

humanitarianism **III:** 169–170

Hume, Sophia Wigington **II:** 159–160

Husband, Herman **III:** 170

Hutchinson, Anne Marbury **II:** 160–161

Igbo **I:** 175

Indian Removal Act (1830) **IV:** 183

industrial revolution **III:** 178

inquisition **I:** 178

Islam **I:** 183–185; **X:** 157

James, William **VI:** 155

Jefferson, Thomas **III:** 184

jeremiads **II:** 173–174

Jesuits **II:** 174

King's College **II:** 184–185

Kongo **I:** 196

Lamy, Jean Baptiste **IV:** 207

land **II:** 191

Lee, Ann **III:** 204

Leverett, John **II:** 193–194

liberalism **X:** 174

Lutherans **II:** 201

marriage and family life **II:** 208

Maryland **II:** 209, 210

Massachusetts **II:** 212

Massachusetts Bay Company **II:** 216

Mather, Cotton **II:** 217–218

Mather, Increase **II:** 218

Mayhew, Jonathan **III:** 238

McPherson, Aimee Semple **VII:** 175–176

Mexican Americans **VIII:** 210

missions **II:** 229–231

Mormon War **IV:** 244

Morse, Jedidiah **III:** 249–250

music **III:** 250; **IV:** 250

National Endowment for the Humanities **IX:** 221

Nation of Islam **X:** 213

Native Americans **I:** 252–254; **VI:** 207

nativism **V:** 251

New Age movement **X:** 216–217

New Jersey **II:** 253–254

New Netherland **II:** 257

New Spain **I:** 261–262

New World **I:** 263

New York **II:** 260

nurses **V:** 256

Osborn, Sarah Haggar Wheaten **II:** 268–269

Owen, Robert **IV:** 273

Panic of 1857 **V:** 264

peace movements **V:** 266

penitentiary movement **IV:** 278

Pennington, James William Charles **V:** 270

Pennsylvania **II:** 275–276

Philadelphia **II:** 282

Pilgrims **II:** 283

popular culture **III:** 282

Priestley, Joseph **III:** 285

Puritans **II:** 304–306

race and race relations **IV:** 290, 291

Ralegh, Sir Walter **I:** 303

Rauschenbusch, Walter **VII:** 255–256

religious liberty **III:** 300–301

RFRA **X:** 266

science **II:** 330

science and technology **X:** 275

Scientology **X:** 266

Scopes Trial **VII:** 277–278

Seabury, Samuel **III:** 323

Second Great Awakening **IV:** 310–311

slavery **II:** 342; **IV:** 319; **V:** 328

slave trade **II:** 344

Smith, Joseph, Jr. **IV:** 322–324

Social Darwinism **VI:** 265–266

society, British American **II:** 351

Spanish colonies **II:** 357

spiritualism **IV:** 325–326

Starbuck, Mary Coffin **II:** 361

Strang, James Jesse **IV:** 328–329

Stuyvesant, Peter **II:** 363

suburbanization **IX:** 287

Sunday, Billy **VII:** 301–302

televangelism **X:** 293–294

temperance **III:** 346

temperance movement **IV:** 336

Tennent, Gilbert **II:** 371–372

Tennent, William, Jr. **II:** 372

Tennent, William, Sr. **II:** 372

Texas, Republic of **IV:** 340

Thoreau, Henry David **IV:** 342

Truth, Sojourner **V:** 356–357

Turner, Nat **IV:** 346–347

USCC **V:** 371–372

Victorianism **VI:** 304

Virginia **II:** 384, 385

voluntary associations **III:** 361, 362

Walter, Thomas **II:** 390

Wheelwright, John **II:** 396

White, Andrew **II:** 396

Whitefield, George **II:** 397–398

Williams, Peter, Jr. **IV:** 366

witchcraft **II:** 402–404

witches **I:** 373–374

wolves **II:** 405

women's status and rights **II:** 406, 408–409

World War II home front **VIII:** 395

YMCA/YWCA **VII:** 349–350

Young, Brigham **IV:** 371–373

Religious Freedom Restoration Act of 1993 (RFRA) **X: 266**

Religious Land Use and Institutionalized Persons Act of 2000 **X:** 266

religious liberty **II:** 201; **III: 300–301**, 394*c*; **VIII:** 408*c*, 410*c. See also* Four Freedoms

Backus, Isaac **III:** 29–30

Baptists **II:** 29; **III:** 35

Bill of Rights **III:** 38

Calvert, George **II:** 50

Catholics **III:** 63

Common Sense (Paine) **III:** 79

commonwealthmen **III:** 80

Enlightenment **II:** 109

French immigrants **II:** 130

German immigrants **II:** 139

Gorton, Samuel **II:** 141–142

government, British American **II:** 142, 144, 145

Great Awakening **II:** 147

Jews **III:** 187, 188

Madison, James **III:** 227, 228

Methodism **III:** 242

New Hampshire **II:** 251

Newport **II:** 258

New York **II:** 260

Northwest Ordinances **III:** 263

Penn, William **II:** 273

Philadelphia **II:** 282

Quakers **II:** 307

religion **III:** 298

religion, Euro-American **II:** 317

Rhode Island **II:** 321

Roman Catholics **II:** 323, 324

Taylor, John, of Caroline **III:** 344

Williams, Roger **II:** 399–400

religious music **X:** 201

religious orders, disputes among **I:** 15–16

religious persecution **V:** 175

religious pluralism **VIII:** 302

religious revivalism **X:** 1

Religious Right **X:** 293

Religious Rights Watch **X:** 62

relocation camps **VIII:** 13. *See also* Japanese Americans, relocation of

relocation policies **IX:** 229, 298

Relocation Program. *See* Termination policy

remarks at the Brandenburg Gate (Reagan) **X:** 344–347

Remarks on Prisons and Prison Discipline in the United States (Dix) **IV:** 114

remarks on taking the oath of office (Ford) **X:** 340–341

Remarks on the History of England (Bolingbroke) **III:** 278

remarks to the Fourth World Conference on Women (Albright) **X:** 353–355

Rembrandt **I:** 192
Remington, Frederic **V:** 16; **VI:** 137, **245–246**, 259, 326*c*
Remond, Charles Lenox **IV:** 377*c*
Remsen, Ira **VI:** 257
Renaissance **I:** 3, 13, 204–205, 235–236, 364–366
Renaut, Philippe **IV:** 208
rendezvous **IV: 299–300**
  Ashley, William Henry **IV:** 28–30
  Beckwourth, Jim **IV:** 46
  Bent, Charles **IV:** 47
  exploration **IV:** 131
  Fort Laramie **IV:** 143
  McLoughlin, John **IV:** 229
  Missouri Fur Company **IV:** 239
  mountain men **IV:** 247–248
  Rocky Mountain Fur Company **IV:** 302
  Smith, Jedediah Strong **IV:** 321, 322
  South Pass **IV:** 324
  Sublette, William **IV:** 330
renegados **I:** 230
Reno, Janet **X: 266–267**, 267, 328*c*
  Branch Davidians **X:** 39, 40
  Clinton, Hillary Rodham **X:** 64
  Clinton, William **X:** 68
  feminism **X:** 116
  Judicial Watch **X:** 162
  tobacco suits **X:** 305
Reno, Marcus **V:** 214
Reno, Nevada **X:** 263
Renoir, Auguste **VI:** 45
Reno v. ACLU (1997) **X:** 329*c*
  censorship **X:** 60
  Internet **X:** 154
  pornography **X:** 245
Rensselaer, Kiliaen van **II:** 260, 319
Rensselaer Polytechnic Institute **IX:** 293
Rensselaerswyck **II:** 256, 260, **319**, 319*m*, 381
rents **II:** 78, 81
reparations **X:** 327*c*
  Civil Liberties Act of 1988 **X:** 63
  Coolidge, Calvin **VII:** 57
  Dawes, Charles **VII:** 63
  Dawes Plan **VII:** 63–64
  Executive Order 9066 **VIII:** 107
  foreign policy **VII:** 100, 101

Great Depression **VIII:** 139
  Hoover presidency **VIII:** 154
  Potsdam Conference **VIII:** 279–280
  race and racial conflict **X:** 256
  trade, foreign **VII:** 310
  Yalta Conference **VIII:** 401
repartimiento **I: 310–311**
  corregidores **I:** 91
  haciendas **I:** 150
  New Spain **I:** 261
  Peru **I:** 280
  Potosí **I:** 291
  slavery **I:** 327
repartimiento de mercancias **II:** 357–358
repatriation of slaves. *See* slaves, colonization/repatriation of
Repeal Amendment. *See* Twenty-first Amendment
repeating rifles **V:** 308
reporters **IV:** 196; **VII:** 141, 304–305. *See also* journalism; muckrakers
Report of the Exploring Expedition to Oregon and California (Frémont) **IV:** 153
Report on Manufactures (Hamilton) **V:** 348
Repository of Religion and Literature **V:** 5
representation, legislative **IV:** 6
Representation of Facts, A (Laurens) **III:** 203
repression **VII:** 311
reproductive rights **X:** 324*c*, 330*c*
  abortion **X:** 1–4
  birth control **X:** 36–38
  NOW **X:** 211
  political parties **X:** 237
  pro-life and pro-choice movements **X:** 248–249
  Roe v. Wade **X:** 268
Republican elephant **V:** 247
republicanism **III: 301–303; IV:** 241–242
  American Revolution **III:** 12
  anti-Federalists **III:** 15
  art **III:** 23
  Cincinnati, Order of **III:** 69
  cities and urban life **III:** 70
  commonwealthmen **III:** 79
  Connecticut Wits **III:** 80
  Constitutional Convention **III:** 82

corporatism **III:** 95
  Federalist Papers **III:** 125
  Federalists **III:** 127
  foreign affairs **III:** 130
  freemasonry **III:** 137
  French Revolution **III:** 138
  frontier **III:** 140–141
  Gerry, Elbridge **III:** 152
  immigration **III:** 173
  Kościuszko, Tadeusz **III:** 198
  labor and labor movements **III:** 200
  Livingston, William **III:** 217
  Murray, Judith Sargent **III:** 250
  Paine, Thomas **III:** 271
  Peale, Charles Willson **III:** 275
  theater **III:** 347
  Witherspoon, John **III:** 380
  women's rights and status **III:** 382
Republican National Convention of 1880 **VI:** 261
Republican National Convention of 1888 **VI:** 261
Republican National Convention of 1960 **IX:** 123
Republican National Convention of 1964 **IX:** 123
Republican Party **IV: 300–302**, 379*c*; **V: 300–303**, *302*, 405*c*, 408*c*; **VI: 246–247**, 323*c*; **VII: 262–264**, 357*c*; **VIII: 304–307; IX: 257–258; X:** 116
  abolition/abolition movement **IV:** 3; **V:** 3, 4
  abortion **X:** 3, 4
  African Americans **VIII:** 2–3
  amendments to the Constitution **X:** 19
  America First Committee **VIII:** 12
  American Liberty League **VIII:** 15
  American System **IV:** 18
  Anthony, Susan B. **VI:** 12
  Anthracite Coal Strike **VII:** 13
  Army-McCarthy hearings **IX:** 17
  Arthur, Chester Alan **VI:** 16
  Atlanta campaign **V:** 19
  Barton, Clara **V:** 24
  Benton, Thomas Hart **IV:** 49, 50

Blaine, James Gillespie **VI:** 31–32
  Blair, Francis P., Jr. **V:** 30
  Borah, William E. **VIII:** 40
  Brown, Joseph **V:** 39
  Bruce, Blanche K. **V:** 40
  Buchanan, James **V:** 41, 42
  Buchanan, Patrick J. **X:** 42
  Bush, George W. **X:** 47, 48
  business and government **VI:** 39
  Butler, Benjamin **V:** 46
  Cannon, Joseph **VII:** 42
  carpetbaggers **V:** 49–50
  Chase, Salmon P. **V:** 56
  Christian Coalition **X:** 62
  Civil Rights Act of 1875 **V:** 63
  Civil Rights Act of 1957 **IX:** 54
  Civil War **V:** 64–65
  class consciousness **VI:** 57
  Clinton, William **X:** 68
  common soldier **V:** 70
  Congress **VI:** 63; **VII:** 53; **VIII:** 66, 67, 68*t*
  Conkling, Roscoe **VI:** 64
  conservatism **VIII:** 71; **IX:** 68, 69
  conservative coalition **VIII:** 73, 74
  conservative movement **X:** 79
  Coolidge, Calvin **VII:** 56, 57
  Copperheads **V:** 82
  corruption, political **VI:** 66, 67
  Crédit Mobilier **V:** 84
  Currency Act **VII:** 60
  Davis, Jefferson **V:** 89
  Davis Bend, Mississippi, freedmen's colony **V:** 92
  Dawes, Charles **VII:** 63
  Democratic Party **IV:** 108; **V:** 94; **VI:** 78; **VII:** 65, 66; **VIII:** 80, 82
  Dole, Robert **X:** 90–91
  Douglas, Stephen A. **V:** 98
  Douglass, Frederick **V:** 100
  Dred Scott decision **V:** 101
  Economic Opportunity Act of 1964 **IX:** 87
  education, federal aid to **VI:** 92
  Elkins Act **VII:** 83, 84
  Elliot, Robert B. **V:** 111
  employment **V:** 116, 117
  ERA **X:** 105, 107
  evangelical Christians **X:** 108
  exploration **IV:** 132

Republican Party (continued)
    federal income tax **VII:** 92
    Fifteenth Amendment **V:** 124
    54th Massachusetts Regiment **V:** 126
    filibustering **V:** 127
    Fillmore, Millard **IV:** 138
    fire-eaters **V:** 128
    Ford, Gerald R. **X:** 119–121
    Fordney-McCumber Tariff **VII:** 97
    foreign policy **VII:** 100
    Foster, Abigail Kelley **IV:** 148
    Fourteenth Amendment **V:** 138
    Free-Soil Party **IV:** 151
    Frémont, Jessie Benton **IV:** 152
    Frémont, John C. **IV:** 153, 154
    fugitive slave laws **IV:** 155
    Garfield, James A. **VI:** 108
    gender gap **X:** 128
    German Americans **VIII:** 130
    Gingrich, Newton L. **X:** 129
    governors **V:** 153
    Grand Army of the Republic **VI:** 118
    Grant, Ulysses S. **V:** 156–157
    Great Depression **VIII:** 140
    Greeley, Horace **V:** 158
    Hanna, Marcus Alonzo **VI:** 121
    Harding, Warren G. **VII:** 118
    Harlan, John Marshall **VI:** 122
    Harrison, Benjamin **VI:** 122
    Hawley-Smoot Tariff Act **VIII:** 144
    Hay, John Milton **VI:** 125
    Hayes, Rutherford B. **VI:** 125, 126–127
    Helms, Jesse A., Jr. **X:** 140–141
    Herndon, William H. **V:** 166
    Hillman, Sidney **VIII:** 146
    Hispanic Americans **X:** 143
    Hoar, George Frisbie **VI:** 129, 130
    homefront **V:** 169
    Homestead Act of 1862 **V:** 170
    Hoover, Herbert **VIII:** 151
    Hoover presidency **VIII:** 153
    House of Representatives **X:** 144, 145
    Howard, O. O. **V:** 173
    immigration **X:** 148
    impeachment of Andrew Johnson **V:** 177, 179
    Internal Security Act of 1950 **IX:** 143
    isolationists **VIII:** 166
    Johnson, Andrew **V:** 187, 188
    Johnson, Hiram Warren **VII:** 138
    journalism **V:** 193
    Julian, George W. **V:** 194
    Kansas-Nebraska Act of 1854 **V:** 197
    Kelley, William D. **V:** 198
    Kemp, Jack F. **X:** 163
    Ku Klux Klan **V:** 199
    labor **VIII:** 179
    La Follette, Robert **VII:** 154–155
    La Follette, Robert M., Jr. **VIII:** 182
    La Guardia, Fiorello **VIII:** 182
    Landon, Alfred M. **VIII:** 183
    Langston, John Mercer **VI:** 171, 172
    Lewis, John L. **VIII:** 185
    liberalism **IX:** 179–180; **X:** 175–176
    Liberty Party **IV:** 210
    Lincoln, Abraham **V:** 208, 210
    lobbying groups **VII:** 163
    Longstreet, James **V:** 215
    Luce, Henry R. **VIII:** 196
    machine politics **VI:** 184
    marriage and family life **X:** 110, 182
    Marx, Karl **V:** 223
    miscegenation **V:** 233
    modern Republicanism **IX:** 208–209
    Moley, Raymond C. **VIII:** 216
    Mormon War **IV:** 244
    Morrill Land-Grant Act **V:** 241
    mugwumps **VI:** 199
    Murray, Philip **VIII:** 221
    NAACP **VIII:** 227
    Nader, Ralph **X:** 205
    Nast, Thomas **V:** 247–248
    national banking system **VI:** 205
    nativism **V:** 251
    neoconservatism **X:** 216
    New Freedom **VII:** 211
    newspapers **VI:** 211
    New York City draft riots **V:** 254, 255
    Nicaragua **X:** 218
    Nixon, Richard M. **X:** 219
    Norris, George W. **VIII:** 248
    NRA **X:** 213
    OPA **VIII:** 254
    Ostend Manifesto **V:** 260
    OWI **VIII:** 258
    Panic of 1819 **IV:** 276
    Panic of 1857 **V:** 264
    Payne-Aldrich Tariff Act **VII:** 226
    People's Party **VI:** 223
    Perot, H. Ross **X:** 234
    Pinchback, Pinckney B. S. **V:** 276
    Pinchot, Gifford **VII:** 228
    political parties **X:** 237–239
    political parties, third **VI:** 226
    politics **VII:** 228–229
    politics in the Roosevelt era **VIII:** 270–272, 272t
    Popular Front **VIII:** 276
    presidential campaigns **VI:** 230–232
    Progressive Party **VII:** 236
    Prohibition Party **VI:** 234
    pro-life and pro-choice movements **X:** 249
    public land policy **IV:** 288
    public opinion polls **VIII:** 284
    Radical Republicans **V:** 288–289
    Rainey, Joseph H. **V:** 290–291
    Reagan, Ronald W. **X:** 258
    Reconstruction **V:** 291, 293, 294
    redemption **V:** 296, 297
    Reed, Thomas Brackett **VI:** 240
    Roosevelt, Theodore **VII:** 265
    scalawags **V:** 307
    Schlafly, Phyllis **X:** 272
    Schurz, Carl **VI:** 256
    secession **V:** 311
    Senate **X:** 275, 276
    Seventeenth Amendment **VII:** 69
    Seward, William H. **V:** 314
    Sherman, John **VI:** 261
    Singleton, Benjamin **V:** 327
    slavery **V:** 330
    Solid South **VI:** 270
    Southeast Asia Treaty Organization **IX:** 274
    Stanton, Edwin M. **V:** 334
    Stanton, Elizabeth Cady **V:** 334–335
    states' rights **V:** 335
    Stearns, Abel **IV:** 326
    Stevens, Thaddeus **V:** 337
    Stimson, Henry L. **VIII:** 340
    Stone, Lucy **VI:** 278
    Sunday, Billy **VII:** 302
    Supreme Court **VIII:** 344
    tactics and strategy **V:** 346
    Taft, Robert A. **VIII:** 349
    Taft, William Howard **VII:** 303
    tariff issue **VI:** 284
    tariffs **V:** 348; **VII:** 305, 306
    Teapot Dome **VII:** 308
    Thirteenth Amendment **V:** 353
    Tourgée, Albion W. **V:** 354
    Townsend, Francis E. **VIII:** 359
    TVA **VIII:** 356
    UN **VIII:** 366
    Union League **V:** 367–368
    United States v. Cruikshank **V:** 375, 376
    veterans **VII:** 324
    Veterans Bureau **VII:** 327
    Vietnam War **X:** 312
    volunteer army **V:** 384
    Wade, Benjamin **V:** 385
    Wallace, Henry A. **VIII:** 373
    war contracting **V:** 387
    Warmoth, Henry C. **V:** 388
    War Revenue Act **VII:** 331
    Welles, Gideon **V:** 391
    Whig Party **IV:** 364
    Whiskey Ring **V:** 393
    Willkie, Wendell L. **VIII:** 378, 379
    Wilmot Proviso **V:** 396
    Wilson, Woodrow **VII:** 333
    women's status and rights **V:** 398
    World War II home front **VIII:** 396
Republicans. *See* Democratic-Republican Party
Republicans (Spain) **VIII:** 334, 335
Republic of China. *See* Taiwan

Republic of Korea (South Korea) **IX:** 21, 60; **X:** 139, 166, 328c.
See also Korean War
Clinton, William **X:** 67, 69
cold war (end of) **X:** 70
foreign policy **X:** 122
republic of letters **II:** 109, 330
Republic of San Joaquin del Río Chama **IX:** 298
Republic of the Congo **I:** 343
Republic Steel **IX:** 282
Republic Steel Memorial Day Massacre **VIII:** 54, 221
Requerimiento (The Requirement), 1513 **I: 311,** 388c, 399–400
Coronado, Francisco **I:** 88
Cortés, Hernán **I:** 92–93
Inca **I:** 177
New Spain **I:** 262
Resaca, Battle of **V:** 19
Rescued from an Eagle Nest (film) **VII:** 115
research **VII:** 107, 133–134, 159–160, 355c; **VIII:** 46–47
computers **X:** 72
medicine **X:** 188
National Endowment for the Humanities **IX:** 221
National Institutes of Health **IX:** 222–223
"the pill" **IX:** 242
public health **IX:** 250
science **IX:** 268–271
technology **IX:** 293
think tanks **X:** 301–302
research laboratories **VII:** 355c; **VIII:** 46
reservations, Native American **IV:** 264, 279; **VII:** 307; **IX:** 227–229, 297–298; **X:** 214, 214m, 263
Apache War **VI:** 14
Crazy Horse **VI:** 69
Dawes Severalty Act of 1887 **VI:** 334–336
Indian Affairs, Office of **VI:** 144
Native Americans **VI:** 206
Red Cloud **VI:** 240
Sioux wars **VI:** 263
Reserve Officers Training Corps (ROTC) **V:** 241; **IX:** 91
Resettlement Administration (RA) **VIII: 307,** 407c
agriculture **VIII:** 8
Dust Bowl **VIII:** 87
Emergency Relief Appropriation Act **VIII:** 102
FSA **VIII:** 112
suburbs **VIII:** 342

Tugwell, Rexford G. **VIII:** 361
residencia **I:** 91, 128, 259
resident aliens **VIII:** 408c
resignation speech (Nixon) **X:** 338–340
resistance movement **III: 303–304**
Adams, Samuel **III:** 4
African Americans **III:** 6
American Revolution **III:** 12
artisans **III:** 26
Attucks, Crispus **III:** 28
Chase, Samuel **III:** 64
cities and urban life **III:** 69–70
commonwealthmen **III:** 79
Deane, Silas **III:** 101
Dickinson, John **III:** 105
Dunmore, Lord **III:** 109
economy **III:** 111
foreign affairs **III:** 130
Gage, Thomas **III:** 146
Golden Hill, Battle of **III:** 153–154
Grenville, George **III:** 157
Hancock, John **III:** 163
Jews **III:** 187
journalism **III:** 192
Laurens, Henry **III:** 203
Lexington and Concord, Battles of **III:** 211
liberty tree/pole **III:** 213–214
literature **III:** 214
Loyal Nine **III:** 221–222
MacIntosh, Ebenezer **III:** 225–226
McDougall, Alexander **III:** 239
music **III:** 251
Old South Church **III:** 265
Otis, James, Jr. **III:** 268
popular culture **III:** 282
Quakers **III:** 291
Quartering Act **III:** 291
Quincy, Josiah **III:** 293–294
riots **III:** 309
Stamp Act **III:** 331–332
suffrage **III:** 336
tariffs **III:** 342
taverns **III:** 343
Townshend Duties **III:** 349
Virginia Resolves **III:** 361
Warren, Joseph **III:** 363
Washington, George **III:** 366

women's rights and status **III:** 382
Young, Thomas **III:** 390
Resistance to Civil Government (Thoreau) **IV:** 342
Resolution, HMS **IV:** 171
Resor, Helen Lansdowne **VII:** 4
Resource Conservation and Recovery Act of 1976 **X:** 78
restaurants **X:** 6
"restoration" **V:** 188
restoration colonies **II:** 144
Restorationists **II:** 252; **IV:** 72
Restoration Movement **IV:** 298
Resumption Act of 1875 **VI:** 261
Resurrection Boulevard (TV program) **X:** 295
retail business **VII:** 75; **VIII:** 47
advertising **X:** 6
baby boomers **X:** 34
business **X:** 51
economy **X:** 94
Reuther, Walter P. **VIII:** 180, 327; **IX:** 11, 13, 14, **258–259,** 331c; **X:** 169
revelations **IV:** 322, 323
Revels, Hiram R. **V:** 303; **VI:** 5, 323c
Revenue Act of 1921 **VII:** 180
Revenue Act of 1932 **VIII:** 351
Revenue Act of 1934 **VIII:** 351
Revenue Act of 1935 **VIII: 307–308**
antimonopoly **VIII:** 18
Congress **VIII:** 67
conservatism **VIII:** 72
New Deal **VIII:** 241
Roosevelt, Franklin D. **VIII:** 313
Second New Deal **VIII:** 321
taxation **VIII:** 351
Union Party **VIII:** 365
Revenue Act of 1936 **VIII:** 352
Revenue Act of 1937 **VIII:** 352
Revenue Act of 1938 **VIII:** 352
Revenue Act of 1942 **VIII:** 177, **308–309,** 352, 395, 409c
Revenues Act of 1663 **II:** 3
Revere, Paul **II:** 215, 216; **III:** 304, 304, 393c
Boston Massacre (engraving) **III:** 44
Church, Benjamin **III:** 68
Hancock, John **III:** 163
Lexington and Concord, Battles of **III:** 212
Suffolk Resolves **III:** 335
Warren, Joseph **III:** 363
reverse discrimination **X:** 9, 256
revitalization movements **II: 319–320**

revivalism **VI:** 197, 241; **VII:** 261
Dow, Lorenzo **IV:** 115–116
Edwards, Jonathan **II:** 105–106
Edwards, Sarah Pierpont **II:** 106
Know-Nothing Party **IV:** 201
Philadelphia **II:** 282
Presbyterians **II:** 296
Puritans **II:** 306
religion **IV:** 296
revitalization movements **II:** 319–320
Second Great Awakening **IV:** 310–311
society, British American **II:** 351
Wesley, John **II:** 394
Revolution, The (newspaper) **V:** 248; **VI:** 12, 107
Revolutionary War **III: 305–307,** 306m, 393c, 394c.
See also American Revolution
Adams, John **III:** 2
Adams, Samuel **III:** 4
African Americans **III:** 5
agriculture **III:** 7, 8
Alamance, Battle of **III:** 8
American Revolution **III:** 12
antislavery and abolition **III:** 15, 17
architecture **III:** 18
Arnold, Benedict **III:** 21
art **III:** 22–23
Articles of Confederation **III:** 24
Asbury, Francis **III:** 27
Backus, Isaac **III:** 30
Baptists **III:** 34
Barbary pirates **III:** 35
Barlow, Joel **III:** 35–36
Barry, John **III:** 36
Blount, William **III:** 40
Blue Jacket **III:** 41
Boone, Daniel **III:** 42
Brackenridge, Hugh Henry **III:** 46
Brandywine, Battle of **III:** 47–48
Brant, Joseph **III:** 48–49
Bunker Hill, Battle of **III:** 50–51
Burgoyne, John **III:** 51–52
Burr, Aaron **III:** 53
camp followers **III:** 59
Canada **III:** 60
Carleton, Guy **III:** 62
Catholics **III:** 63
Chase, Samuel **III:** 64
Cherokee nation **III:** 66

Revolutionary War (continued)
  Choctaw nation **III:** 68
  Cincinnati, Order of **III:** 69
  cities and urban life **III:** 70
  Clark, George Rogers **III:** 71
  Clinton, Sir Henry **III:** 75–76
  committees of correspondence **III:** 77
  Connecticut Wits **III:** 80
  conscription **V:** 78
  Continental army, mutinies of **III:** 86
  Continental Congress, Second **III:** 88
  Cornplanter **III:** 91
  Cornwallis, Lord **III:** 92
  Coxe, Tench **III:** 96
  Creek nation **III:** 96
  Crèvecoeur, J. Hector St. John de **III:** 98
  Cuffe, Paul **III:** 98
  Deane, Silas **III:** 101
  Declaration of Independence **III:** 102
  Dickinson, John **III:** 106
  disease and epidemics **III:** 106
  Dorchester Heights, Battle of **III:** 107
  Dragging Canoe **III:** 107
  Dunmore, Lord **III:** 109
  economy **III:** 111, 113
  Estaing, comte d' **III:** 119–120
  Eutaw Springs, Battle of **III:** 120–121
  Florida **III:** 129
  Forten, James **III:** 131
  Fort Ticonderoga **III:** 133
  Fort Washington, capture of **III:** 133
  Franklin, William **III:** 136
  freemasonry **III:** 137
  French alliance **III:** 137–138
  French Revolution **III:** 138
  Freneau, Philip **III:** 139
  Gage, Thomas **III:** 146–147
  Galloway, Joseph **III:** 148
  Gates, Horatio **III:** 149
  George III, king of Great Britain **III:** 150
  Gerry, Elbridge **III:** 152
  Girard, Stephen **III:** 153
  Grasse, comte de **III:** 154
  Greene, Nathanael **III:** 155–156
  Green Mountain Boys **III:** 156

Guilford Courthouse, Battle of **III:** 158
  Hale, Nathan **III:** 159–160
  Hamilton, Alexander **III:** 161
  Hancock, John **III:** 163
  Handsome Lake **III:** 164
  Hessians **III:** 166–167
  Howe, Richard, Lord **III:** 167–168
  Howe, Sir William **III:** 168–169
  Hull, William **IV:** 175
  humanitarianism **III:** 169
  Husband, Herman **III:** 170
  Hutchinson, Thomas **III:** 170
  immigration **III:** 173
  Independence Hall **III:** 176
  industrial revolution **III:** 177
  Iroquois Confederacy **III:** 179
  Jay's Treaty **III:** 182
  Jersey, HMS **III:** 186–187
  Jews **III:** 187
  Johnson, Sir John **III:** 188–189
  Jones, Absalom **III:** 189
  Jones, John Paul **III:** 190
  journalism **III:** 191, 192
  Kalb, baron de **III:** 195
  King's Mountain, Battle of **III:** 196
  Knox, Henry **III:** 197
  Kościuszko, Tadeusz **III:** 198
  labor and labor movements **III:** 199–200
  Lafayette, marquis de **III:** 200–201
  land riots **III:** 202
  Lee, Ann **III:** 204
  Lee, Arthur **III:** 205
  Lee, Henry **III:** 206
  L'Enfant, Pierre-Charles **III:** 207
  Lexington and Concord, Battles of **III:** 211–213
  liberty tree/pole **III:** 214
  literature **III:** 214
  Livingston, Robert R. **III:** 216
  Long Island, Battle of **III:** 217–218
  Loyalists **III:** 219, 221
  Lyon, Matthew **III:** 222
  Marion, Francis **III:** 231–232
  Marshall, John **III:** 235

Mason, George **III:** 237
  McDougall, Alexander **III:** 239
  McGillivray, Alexander **III:** 240
  Medal of Honor **V:** 228
  Methodism **III:** 242
  minutemen **III:** 243
  Molly Pitcher **III:** 243–244
  Monmouth, Battle of **III:** 244–245
  Monroe, James **IV:** 239
  Morgan, Daniel **III:** 246
  Morris, Robert **III:** 247
  Morristown, New Jersey, encampment of **III:** 248–249
  music **III:** 251
  national debt **III:** 253
  Native Americans and the Revolution **III:** 253–256
  Newburgh conspiracy **III:** 256
  North, Lord **III:** 259, 260
  North Carolina Regulation **III:** 261
  Old South Church **III:** 266
  Otis, James, Jr. **III:** 268
  Paris, Treaty of **III:** 273
  Peale, Charles Willson **III:** 273, 275
  Pickering, John **III:** 276
  Pinckney, Charles Cotesworth **III:** 276, 277
  popular culture **III:** 282
  population trends **III:** 283
  privateering **III:** 286–287
  Pulsaki, Casimir **III:** 289–290
  Putnam, Israel **III:** 290
  Quakers **III:** 291
  Quincy, Josiah **III:** 293
  Randolph, Edmund **III:** 295–296
  Red Jacket **III:** 296–297
  Rhode Island, Battle of **III:** 308
  riots **III:** 309
  Rittenhouse, David **III:** 310
  Rochambeau, comte de **III:** 310
  Ross, Betsy **III:** 310
  Rowson, Susanna **III:** 311
  rules of war **V:** 305
  rural life **III:** 312
  Rush, Benjamin **III:** 312
  St. Clair, Arthur **III:** 315–316
  Sampson, Deborah **III:** 316–317

San Lorenzo, Treaty of **III:** 317
  Saratoga, surrender at **III:** 317–320
  science **III:** 320, 321
  Seabury, Samuel **III:** 323
  Seminole wars **IV:** 311
  Shays's Rebellion **III:** 324
  slavery **III:** 326, 327
  slave trade **III:** 329
  states' rights **III:** 333
  Stuart, Gilbert **III:** 335
  suffrage **III:** 336
  Sullivan, John **III:** 337
  tactics and strategy **V:** 346
  tariffs **III:** 342
  Tarleton, Banastre **III:** 342–343
  taverns **III:** 343
  Taylor, John, of Caroline **III:** 344
  Tecumseh **III:** 345
  temperance **III:** 346
  theater **III:** 347
  trade **III:** 349
  Trenton and Princeton, Battles of **III:** 351–352
  Trumbull, John **III:** 352
  Unitarianism **III:** 355
  United States Army Corps of Engineers **V:** 370
  Valley Forge, encampment of **III:** 357–359
  Vergennes, comte de **III:** 359
  voluntary associations **III:** 362
  Washington, George **III:** 365–368
  Wayne, Anthony **III:** 369
  Webster-Ashburton Treaty (1842) **IV:** 360
  West Indies **III:** 372
  West Point **III:** 372; **V:** 372
  Whigs **III:** 375
  White Plains, Battle of **III:** 376
  Wilderness Road **III:** 378
  Wilkes, John **III:** 379
  Wilkinson, James **III:** 379
  women's rights and status **III:** 382–383
  "Yankee Doodle" **III:** 387
  Yates, Abraham, Jr. **III:** 387
  Yorktown, surrender at **III:** 388–390
  Young, Thomas **III:** 390
Revolutionary Youth Movement (RYM) **X:** 317
revues, musical **VII:** 85, 357c
Reynolds, John **II:** 138; **IV:** 53

Reynolds, John F. **V:** 148, 173, 226, 227
Reynolds, Malvina **IX:** 287
Reynolds v. Simms (1966) **IX:** 32, **259–260,** 316, 334*c*
Rezanov, Nikolai **II:** 326; **III:** 8
RFC. *See* Reconstruction Finance Corporation
RFRA (Religious Freedom Restoration Act of 1993) **X:** **266**
Rhapsody in Blue (Gershwin) **VII:** 108, 195, 361*c*
Rhee, Syngman **IX:** 163, 164
Rheet, Robert Barnwell **IV:** 264; **V:** 127, 311
Rhett, William **II:** 34
Rhinelander, Kip **VII:** 143
Rhode Island **II: 320–322,** 321, *400;* **III:** 395*c;* **IV:** 184, 378*c;* **V:** 44, 45; **X:** 2, 242
  agriculture **II:** 13
  Albany Congress **II:** 14
  Baptists **II:** 29
  Butterworth, Mary Peck **II:** 46
  Coddington, William **II:** 65, 66
  Dominion of New England **II:** 94
  education **II:** 103
  Estaing, comte d' **III:** 120
  Franklin, Ann Smith **II:** 125
  Gaspée affair **III:** 148
  Gorton, Samuel **II:** 142
  Great Awakening **II:** 149
  Greene, Nathanael **III:** 155
  Harrison, Peter **II:** 154
  Hutchinson, Anne Marbury **II:** 161
  Jews **III:** 188
  Massachusetts **II:** 212
  Massasoit **II:** 217
  Miantonomo **II:** 223–224
  mills **II:** 225
  monarchy, British **II:** 232
  Narragansett **II:** 241
  Newport **II:** 258
  Osborn, Sarah Haggar Wheaten **II:** 268
  piracy **II:** 285
  primogeniture and entail **II:** 297
  Protestantism **II:** 301, 302
  Quakers **II:** 307–308
  religion, Euro-American **II:** 316, 317
  slavery **II:** 338
  Smith, Robert **II:** 348
  trade and shipping **II:** 376
Williams, Roger **II:** 399
wolves **II:** 405
Rhode Island, Battle of **III: 308**
  Greene, Nathanael **III:** 155
  Howe, Richard, Lord **III:** 168
  Lafayette, marquis de **III:** 201
  Sullivan, John **III:** 337
Rhodes, James **X:** 164
Rhodesia **X:** 70
rhythm and blues **VIII:** 224; **IX:** 217, 263; **X:** 201
RIAA (Recording Industry Association of America) **X:** 330*c*
Ribault, Jean **I:** 57, 201
Ribicoff, Abraham **IX:** 225
Ricci, Matteo **I:** 66, 189, **311–312,** *312;* **II:** 174
rice **I:** 150; **III:** 326, 328; **V:** 1, 276, 329
  Acts of Trade and Navigation **II:** 3
  African Americans **II:** 6; **IV:** 7
  agriculture **II:** 10, 12; **IV:** 9, 11
  British Empire **II:** 43
  Charleston **II:** 56
  cotton culture **IV:** 97
  economy **II:** 101–102
  food **II:** 122
  Georgia **II:** 138
  Gullah **II:** 151
  indigo **II:** 166
  Johnston, Henrietta Deering **II:** 178
  labor **II:** 187, 188–189
  Le Moyne, Jean-Baptiste, sieur de Bienville **II:** 193
  Louisiana **II:** 200
  marriage and family life **II:** 208
  mercantilism **II:** 221
  merchants **II:** 222
  Middleton, Arthur **II:** 224
  plantation system **II:** 286, 287
  slavery **II:** 339; **IV:** 318
  society, British American **II:** 350
  South Carolina **II:** 354
  trade and shipping **II:** 376
Rice, Dan **IV:** 376*c*
Rice, Edwin **VII:** 107
Rich, Sir Robert **II:** 322, 347, 387
Richard, Mark **X:** 178
Richard III, king of England **I:** 159
Richards, Ann **X:** 47
Richards, Ellen Henrietta Swallow **VI:** 195, **247,** 318
Richards, Theodore **VII:** 276
Richardson, Bill **X:** 308
Richardson, Elliot L. **X:** **267–268,** 324*c*
  Bork, Robert **X:** 39
  Cox, Archibald, Jr. **X:** 81
  Nixon, Richard M. **X:** 221
  Ruckelshaus, William D. **X:** 269
  Watergate scandal **X:** 316
Richardson, Henry Hobson **VI:** **247–248,** 313
Richardson, Israel **V:** 13
Richardson Romanesque style **VI:** 247, 248
Rich family **II:** 387
Richmond, Mary **VII:** 290
Richmond, Virginia **III:** 184, 185, 394*c*, 396*c;* **V: 303–305,** *304*
  Appomattox Court House, Virginia **V:** 14
  assassination of Abraham Lincoln **V:** 17
  Beauregard, Pierre **V:** 27
  Benjamin, Judah P. **V:** 28
  Bull Run, First Battle of **V:** 42
  Butler, Benjamin **V:** 46
  cartography **V:** 51
  Cedar Mountain, Battle of **V:** 53
  Cold Harbor, Battle of **V:** 68
  Confederate States of America **V:** 75, 77
  Davis, Jefferson **V:** 90
  economy **V:** 107
  employment **V:** 116
  Ewell, Richard Stoddert **V:** 118
  Five Forks, Battle of **V:** 129
  food riots **V:** 129–130
  Fredericksburg, Battle of **V:** 139
  homefront **V:** 169
  Jackson, "Stonewall" **V:** 185, 186
  Johnston, Joseph E. **V:** 190
  Lee, Robert E. **V:** 207
  Longstreet, James **V:** 214
  Louisiana Tigers **V:** 218
  Mallory, Stephen R. **V:** 221
  McClellan, George B. **V:** 225
  medicine and hospitals **V:** 230
  Monitor-Merrimack **V:** 237
  monuments **V:** 239
  nurses **V:** 256
  Overland campaign **V:** 261
  Peninsular campaign **V:** 267, 269, 270
  Petersburg campaign **V:** 270, 272
  photography **V:** 273
  prostitution **V:** 283
  refugees **V:** 298
  Shenandoah Valley: Jackson's campaign **V:** 316
  Shenandoah Valley: Sheridan's campaign **V:** 317
  Spotsylvania, Battles of **V:** 333
  tactics and strategy **V:** 347
  Tredegar Iron Works **V:** 356
  Van Lew, Elizabeth **V:** 378
  veterans, Civil War **V:** 379
  Washington, D.C. **V:** 389
Richmond bread riots of 1863 **V:** 116
Richmond *Enquirer* **V:** 128
Richmond Grays **V:** 32
Rickenbacker, Eddie **VIII:** 12
Rickey, Branch **IX:** 5, **260,** 262–263, 280
Rickover, Hyman G. **VI:** 188; **IX:** 24
RICO. *See* Racketeer Influenced and Corrupt Organizations Act
Ride, Sally **X:** 326*c*
Ridge, John **IV:** 344
Ridgway, Matthew **IX:** 164
Riegle, Donald **X:** 276
Riesman, David **IX:** 46
Rieve, Emil **IX:** 11
Rifle and Light Infantry Tactics (Hardee) **V:** 345
rifles **IV:** 262; **V:** 45, 308, 345
Rigdon, Sidney **IV:** 323
Riggs, Bobby **VIII:** 337
right of discovery doctrine **II:** 191
Rights of Man, The (Paine) **III:** 53, 271
Rights of the British Colonies (Otis) **III:** 16, 391*c*
rights revolution **X:** 175, 176
right to counsel **X:** 319. *See also* Sixth Amendment
Right to Life Amendment **X:** 249
right to privacy
  abortion **X:** 1, 2
  birth control **X:** 37
  Bork, Robert **X:** 39

right to privacy (continued)
  Brennan, William J. **X:** 41
  computers **X:** 74
  Federal Information Act
    X: 111–112
  Roe v. Wade **X:** 268
  White, Byron R. **X:** 319
"Right to Work, The" (Baker)
  VII: 192
Riis, Jacob A. **VI: 248–249,**
  326c; **VII:** 238; **VIII:** 268
  housing **VI:** 135
  How the Other Half Lives
    VI: 342–343
  photography **VI:** 137
  progressivism in the 1890s
    VI: 233
  Social Gospel **VI:** 267
Riley, James Whitcomb **VI:** 178
Riley, William Bell **VII:** 261
Ring Dance **II:** 82
Ringling Bros. Circus **VI:** 97
Rio Belen **I:** 82
Rio Conference of American
  Republics **VIII:** 116–117,
  133, 377
Rio de Janeiro **I:** 33
Rio Grande
  Guadalupe Hidalgo, Treaty
    of (1848) **IV:** 165, 166
  Mexican-American War
    IV: 232, 234
  Taylor, Zachary **IV:** 334
  Texas **IV:** 337
Rio Pact **IX:** 172, 329c; **X:** 172
Riordon, William L. **VI:** 225
riots **II:** 253, 356; **III: 308–309,**
  392c; **IV:** 201; **V:** 407c; **VI:**
  325c; **VII:** xiv, 359c; **VIII:**
  410c; **IX:** 6m, 52, 152,
  317–318, 333c, 334c; **X:** 325c,
  328c, 330c
  Africa **IX:** 4
  African-American
    movement **IX:** 6, 6m
  African Americans **VIII:** 5
  Alamance, Battle of **III:** 8
  Attucks, Crispus **III:** 28
  Boston Massacre **III:** 43–44
  Brownsville Riot **VII:** 35
  Catto, Octavius **V:** 53
  "Chicago Eight" **X:** 61
  children **VIII:** 57
  Chinese Exclusion Act **VI:**
    50
  Christiana, Pennsylvania,
    riot **V:** 59
  cities and urban life **III:**
    70; **VIII:** 58; **IX:** 52
  employment **V:** 116
  gay rights movement **X:**
    127

Gentlemen's Agreement
  VII: 107
Great Migration **VII:** 113
Hayden, Tom **IX:** 131
Haymarket riot **VI:**
  127–128
impressment **III:** 175
Jackson State University **X:**
  160
Johnson, Lyndon **IX:** 152
Kent State University **X:**
  164
land riots **III:** 201–202
Latino movement **IX:** 173
MacIntosh, Ebenezer **III:**
  225
Mayhew, Jonathan **III:**
  238
Memphis riot **V:** 232
Mexican Americans **VIII:**
  210
New Orleans riot **V:** 252
North Carolina Regulation
  III: 261
Panama Canal turnover **X:**
  232
popular culture **III:** 282
race and racial conflict **V:**
  288; **VII:** 249; **VIII:**
  288; **IX:** 254; **X:**
  255–256
Remember the *Maine* **VI:**
  187
resistance movement **III:**
  303
Roman Catholicism **VI:**
  249
Root-Takahira Agreement
  VII: 267
Shays's Rebellion **III:**
  324–325
Sons of Liberty **III:** 330
South **VIII:** 332
South Carolina Regulation
  III: 330–331
Stamp Act **III:** 332
Watts uprising **IX:**
  317–318
Weather Underground **X:**
  318
Wells-Barnett, Ida Bell **VI:**
  312
World's Columbian
  Exposition **VI:** 320
World War II **VIII:** 389
World War II home front
  VIII: 395
zoot-suiters **VIII:** 403–404
Ripken, Cal, Jr. **X:** 284
Ripley, George **IV:** 58, 155, 212
"Rip Van Winkle" (Irving) **IV:**
  212

Rip Van Winkle (play,
  Boucicault) **VI:** 156, 287
Risalah **I:** 184
*Rise and Fall of the Confederate
  Government, The* (Davis) **V:**
  90, 212
Rise of Silas Lapham, The
  (Howells) **VI:** 136
Rising Glory of America, The
  (Brackenridge and Freneau)
  III: 46, 139
Ritalin **X:** 190
Ritchie, Thomas **IV:** 107
Ritchie v. People **VII:** 193
rites of passage **II:** 60
Ritschl, Albrecht **VI:** 266
Rittenhouse, David **II:** 277,
  322; III: 11, **309–310,** 321,
  321
Rittenhouse, William **II:** 39
rituals. *See* ceremonies and
  rituals
Rivera, Diego **VIII:** 25
Rivera, Geraldo **X:** 295
Rivera, Primo de **VI:** 100
River and Harbor Act (1882)
  VI: 17
river defense **V:** 74
River Indians **II:** 88
river mining **IV:** 69
River Rouge auto plant **VII:** 22,
  48, 133; **VIII:** *230*
rivers **II:** 377; **IX:** 321–322
R. J. Reynolds **X:** 49, 305
RKO Pictures **VIII:** 377
RNA **IX:** 269
roads **II:** 35, 111, 377; **IV:** 18,
  19, 56, 187–190, 189m; **VII:**
  319
Road to Serfdom (von Hayek)
  VIII: 73
Roanoke **I: 313–314,** 388c
  Barlowe, Arthur **I:** 26
  DeBry, Theodor **I:** 102
  Hakluyt, Richard, the
    Younger **I:** 152
  Harriot, Thomas **I:** 154,
    155
  Lane, Ralph **I:** 197
  Manteo **I:** 220
  Ralegh, Sir Walter **I:** 303
  Spanish Armada **I:** 335
  White, John **I:** 372
Roanoke (Roanoac) Indians **I:**
  292, *313*, 314, 372
  Algonquin **II:** 17
  Dare, Virginia **II:** 82
  Grenville, Sir Richard **II:**
    150, 151
  monarchy, British **II:** 232
  North Carolina **II:**
    264–265

population trends **II:** 290
Virginia Company of
  London **II:** 387
Wingina **II:** 294; **II:** 401
Roanoke Island **II:** 58, 299, 401;
  V: 27, 346
Robb, Charles **X:** 222
"robber barons" **VI:** 117–118
robbery **X:** 81
Robbins, Harold **X:** 178
Robert-Houdin, Jean-Eugène
  VII: 124
Roberto, Holden **IX:** 4
Roberts, John **X:** 321
Roberts, Lawrence G. **X:** 152
Roberts, Oral **X:** 293, 294
Roberts, Owen J. **VIII:** 76, 178,
  344, 346, 346t
Robertson, Edward V. **IX:** 224
Robertson, Marion Gordon
  "Pat"
  Bush, George H. W. **X:** 45
  Christian Coalition **X:** 61,
    62
  conservative movement **X:**
    79
  evangelical Christians **X:**
    107
  televangelism **X:** 293, 294
Roberval, Jean-François de la
  Rocque, sieur de **I:** 59
Robeson, Paul **VII:** 360c; **VIII:**
  309, **309–310,** 410c; **IX:** 211,
  261–262
Robespierre, Maximilian **III:**
  138, 272, 310
Robins, Mary Dreier **VII:** 205
Robinson, Charles **IV:** 223, 224
Robinson, Jackie **VIII:** 336; **IX:**
  262, **262–263,** 329c
  African-American
    movement **IX:** 5
  March on Washington **IX:**
    191
  Rickey, Branch **IX:** 260
  sports **IX:** 280
  television **IX:** 297
Robinson, James R. **IX:** 66
Robinson, John **II:** 68, 283
Robinson, Mack **VIII:** 338
Robinson, Theodore **VI:** 219
Robinson-Patman Act of 1936
  VIII: 18
Robinson v. California (1962) **X:**
  319
Robison, James **X:** 293
robotic lasers **X:** 275
robotic surgery **X:** 190
Rochambeau, Jean-Baptiste-
  Donatien de Vimeur, comte
  de **III:** 154, **310,** 343, 390
Roche, Josephine **VIII:** 383

Rochefort, Joseph P., Jr. **VIII:** 64
Rochester, New York **X:** 157
Rochester, New York, Women's Rights Convention of 1848 **V:** 397
Rochester North Star **V:** 93
rock and roll **VIII:** 224; **IX:** **263–264,** 331c, 332c; **X:** 201–203, 240, 321
Beatles **IX:** 36–37
music **IX:** 217
popular culture **IX:** 244
Presley, Elvis **IX:** 247–248
"Rock Around the Clock" **IX:** 263
Rockefeller, John D. **VI:** 323c, 325c; **VII:** *264,* **264–265,** 356c, 359c
business **VII:** 38
education, philanthropy and **VI:** 94
industrial revolution, second **VI:** 145, 146
muckrakers **VII:** 192
oil **VI:** 215
oil industry **VII:** 217
Republican Party **VII:** 263
Standard Oil **VII:** 295–296
steel industry **VII:** 296
Tarbell, Ida **VII:** 305
trusts **VI:** 293
Washington, Booker T. **VI:** 308
Rockefeller, John D., III **X:** 36
Rockefeller, John D., Jr.
American Plan **VII:** 12
Industrial Relations Commission **VII:** 129
Ludlow Massacre **VII:** 167, 168
open shop movement **VII:** 220
Sunday, Billy **VII:** 302
Rockefeller, Nelson **IX:** 124, 209, 258, *296*
Ford, Gerald R. **X:** 120
Kissinger, Henry A. **X:** 165
Latin America **X:** 172
New York City bailout **X:** 217
Rockefeller, William **VII:** 296
Rockefeller Center **VIII:** 22, 25
Rockefeller family **VIII:** 25
Rockefeller Foundation **VII:** 265, 276
Rockefeller Report on the Americas **X:** 172–173
"rocker," gold **IV:** 163
rocketry **IX:** 278, 294
Rockingham, Lord **III:** 52, 157, 332

Rockne, Knute **VIII:** 336
Rockwell, Norman **VIII:** 25, 127
Rockwood, Ebenezer **VI:** 129
Rocky Mountain Fur Company **IV:** **302**
Ashley, William Henry **IV:** 29
Astor, John Jacob **IV:** 32
Beckwourth, Jim **IV:** 46
Bridger, James **IV:** 57
Sublette, William **IV:** 330
Rocky Mountain News **IV:** 90
Rocky Mountains **IV:** 376c
American Fur Company **IV:** 17
Ashley, William Henry **IV:** 28–29, 29m
Atkinson, Henry **IV:** 33
Carson, Kit **IV:** 75
Chouteau family **IV:** 79
exploration **IV:** 131
Missouri Fur Company **IV:** 239
rendezvous **IV:** 299–300
Smith, Jedediah Strong **IV:** 321
South Pass **IV:** 324
Roden, Ben **X:** 39
Roden, George **X:** 39
Roden, Lois **X:** 39
rodents **II:** 21
Rodgers, Jimmy **VIII:** 222
Rodgers, Richard **VIII:** 224
Rodham Clinton, Hillary. *See* Clinton, Hillary Rodham
Rodman, Isaac **V:** 13
Rodman, Peter **X:** 43
Rodney, George **III:** 154
Rodríguez, Agustín **I:** 256
Rodriguez, Alex **X:** 284
Roebling, John Augustus **IV:** 308; **VI:** 35
Roebling, Washington **VI:** 35
Roebuck, Alvah Curtis **VI:** 186
Roethke, Theodore **IX:** 183
Roe v. Wade (1973) **X:** **268,** 324c, 335–338
abortion **X:** 1–4
birth control **X:** 37
Bork, Robert **X:** 39
Brennan, William J. **X:** 41
Burger, Warren E. **X:** 44
conservative movement **X:** 79
feminism **X:** 115
Ginsburg, Ruth Bader **X:** 130–131
Powell, Lewis **X:** 247
pro-life and pro-choice movements **X:** 248, 249
Reagan, Ronald W. **X:** 259

Rehnquist, William H. **X:** 264
Souter, David **X:** 279
Supreme Court **X:** 291
Webster v. Reproductive Health Services **X:** 318
White, Byron R. **X:** 319
women's rights and status **X:** 320
Rogers, Edith **VIII:** 381
Rogers, Ginger **VII:** 108
Rogers, John **III:** 215, 216
Rogers, Robert **II:** 158, 251; **IV:** 93
Rogers, Roy **VIII:** 218, 222
Rogers, Will **VIII:** 80, 218, 274
Roldan, Francisco **I:** 79, 82
Rolfe, John **II:** **322–323,** 417c; **VII:** 248
agriculture **II:** 8, 10
captivity **II:** 51
Dale, Sir Thomas **II:** 81
environment **II:** 112
Gates, Sir Thomas **II:** 135
Jamestown **II:** 171, 172
labor **II:** 188
miscegenation **II:** 228
Native Americans **II:** 244
Pocahontas **II:** 288–289
Powhatan Confederacy **II:** 295
tobacco **II:** 374
Virginia **II:** 382
Rolfe, Rebecca. *See* Pocahontas
Rolfe, Thomas **II:** 289, 323
roll calls **V:** 96
Rolling Stones, the **IX:** 218, 244, 264; **X:** 202, 240
"Roll of Honor," Confederate **V:** 228
Roma **VIII:** 149
Roman Catholic Church/Roman Catholicism **I:** 387c; **II:** **323–324; III:** 63; **V:** 176, 251, 340; **VI:** 141, **249–250,** 325c; **VII:** 65, 260–261, 287; **VIII:** **53–54; IX:** 256–257. *See also* Counterreformation; Reformation; *specific orders, e.g.:* Franciscans
abortion **X:** 3
Alexander VI, Pope **I:** 6
American Protective Association **VI:** 11–12
anti-Catholic riots **IV:** 21–23, 22
architecture **III:** 19
Austin, Moses **IV:** 36
Austin, Stephen F. **IV:** 37
auto-da-fé **I:** 16
birth control **X:** 37
black legend **I:** 30

Bowie, Jim **IV:** 57
Brent, Margaret Reed **II:** 40
California missions **IV:** 70
Canada **III:** 60
capital punishment **X:** 56
Carey, Mathew **III:** 61
Carleton, Guy **III:** 62
Carson, Kit **IV:** 75
Castile **I:** 63, 64
Chesapeake Bay **II:** 58
Church of England **I:** 73–74
Coercive Acts **III:** 76
conservatism **VIII:** 72
conservative movement **X:** 79
Coughlin, Father Charles E. **VIII:** 74–76
Counterreformation **I:** 95–96
Democratic Party **IV:** 106; **VIII:** 80, 81
Dominicans **I:** 109–110
Dominion of New England **II:** 95
Dow, Lorenzo **IV:** 115
Dutch Reformed Church **II:** 97
education **VI:** 91–92
election of 1936 **VIII:** 97
Elizabeth I **I:** 120, 121
encomienda **I:** 122
ERA **X:** 106
Ethiopia **I:** 125
Ferdinand and Isabella **I:** 128
Florida **II:** 120
Fort Mose **II:** 123
Foxe's *Book of Martyrs* **I:** 132
Frémont, John C. **IV:** 154
French alliance **III:** 137
French colonies **II:** 126, 127
French immigrants **II:** 130
Glorious Revolution **II:** 140–141
Great Awakening **II:** 147, 149
Hanno the elephant **I:** 153
Henry IV (Henry of Navarre) **I:** 158–159
Henry VIII **I:** 160
Holy League **I:** 164–165
immigration **III:** 173; **IV:** 179, 180
Indians of the Desert Southwest **II:** 166
inquisition **I:** 178
Irish Americans **VIII:** 164, 165

Roman Catholic Church/Roman
  Catholicism (*continued*)
    Iroquois **II:** 170
    isolationists **VIII:** 166
    Italian Americans **VIII:**
      167
    James I **I:** 188
    Jesuits **I:** 188–189; **II:** 174
    Jews **II:** 174
    Know-Nothing Party **IV:**
      201
    Lamy, Jean Baptiste **IV:**
      207
    Leo X **I:** 203
    Locke, John **II:** 198
    Luther, Martin **I:** 210–211
    Lutherans **II:** 201
    MacIntosh, Ebenezer **III:**
      225
    Marquette, Jacques **II:** 205
    Mary I **I:** 224
    Maryland **II:** 209, 210
    Mexican Americans **VIII:**
      210
    missions **II:** 229–231
    monarchy, British **II:** 231,
      232
    Native Americans **II:** 244,
      246
    nativism **VI:** 209
    Negro Plot of 1741 **II:** 248
    New Deal **VIII:** 242
    New Mexico **II:** 254
    New Spain **I:** 261–262
    Panama invasion **X:** 231
    Pennsylvania **II:** 275, 276
    Philadelphia **II:** 282
    politics in the Roosevelt
      era **VIII:** 271
    Porres, St. Martín de **I:**
      291
    Protestantism **II:** 300, 301
    Puritans **I:** 298
    race and race relations **IV:**
      292
    religion **II:** 314, 316; **III:**
      299; **IV:** 296–298; **VI:**
      241, 243; **VIII:** 302,
      303; **X:** 265
    Republican Party **IV:** 300,
      301
    Requerimiento **I:** 311
    Roe v. Wade **X:** 268
    Roosevelt, Franklin D.
      VIII: 313
    St. Mary's City **II:** 328
    Santa Anna, Antonio
      López de **IV:** 303
    Scotch-Irish **III:** 322
    Seton, Elizabeth Ann **IV:**
      315–316
    slavery **II:** 342

  Spanish Civil War **VIII:**
    334, 335
  Spanish colonies **II:**
    356–357
  suffrage **II:** 364
  Texas, Republic of **IV:** 340
  Thevet, André **I:** 348
  Trent, Council of **I:**
    359–360
  Union Party **VIII:** 365
  Vitoria, Francisco de **I:** 369
  Whig Party **IV:** 362
  Zumárraga, Juan de **I:** 382
Roman Catholic Legion of
  Decency **VIII:** 54
Roman Empire **II:** 338; **III:** 302
Romania **I:** 294; **IX:** 58, 105; **X:**
  72, 157
romanticism **IV:** 229
Rome **I:** 235–236, 327
Rome, ancient **III:** 302
Rome, liberation of **VIII:** 393,
  410c
Rome-Berlin-Tokyo Axis **VIII:**
  31, 396. *See also* Axis
*Romer, Governor of Colorado,
  et al. v. Evans et al.* (1997) **X:**
  131, 329c
Rommel, Erwin **VIII:** 248, 249,
  349–350
Rooney, John **IX:** 100–101
Rooney, Mickey **VIII:** 56, 218
Roosevelt, Eleanor **VIII:**
  310–312, **311,** 411c; **IX:** 13,
  14, 267, 324; **X:** 114, 210
    African Americans **VIII:** 3
    Baruch, Bernard M. **VIII:**
      34
    Bethune, Mary McLeod
      VIII: 36
    Black Cabinet **VIII:** 37
    Bonus Army **VIII:** 40
    civil rights **VIII:** 61
    Democratic Party **VIII:**
      81
    Dewson, "Molly" **VIII:** 83
    FBI **VIII:** 115
    MOWM **VIII:** 201
    NAACP **VIII:** 227
    NYA **VIII:** 234
    OCD **VIII:** 254
    Perkins, Frances **VIII:**
      265
    Roosevelt, Franklin D.
      VIII: 312
    Wallace, Henry A. **VIII:**
      373
    WAVES **VIII:** 379–380
    women's network **VIII:**
      383
    women's status and rights
      VIII: 384

Roosevelt, Franklin Delano **III:**
  365; **VIII:** xiii, **312–315,** *314,*
  406c–410c; **X:** 311
    Acheson, Dean **IX:** 1
    African-American
      movement **IX:** 4
    African Americans **VIII:** 3,
      4
    Agricultural Adjustment
      Act **VIII:** 5–6
    agriculture **VIII:** 8
    aircraft industry **VIII:**
      10–11
    America First Committee
      VIII: 12
    American Federation of
      Labor **VIII:** 14; **IX:** 11
    American Liberty League
      VIII: 14, 15
    Americans for Democratic
      Action **IX:** 13
    Anglo-American relations
      VIII: 16–17
    antimonopoly **VIII:** 17, 18
    Antiquities Act **VII:** 13
    anti-Semitism **VIII:** 19
    Army, U.S. **VIII:** 19
    Arnold, "Hap" **VIII:** 22
    art **VII:** 20
    Asian Americans **VIII:** 26
    Atlantic Charter **VIII:** 28
    atomic bomb **VIII:** 29
    aviation **VII:** 24
    Banking Act of 1933 **VIII:**
      33
    Banking Act of 1935 **VIII:**
      33
    Baruch, Bernard M. **VII:**
      25; **VIII:** 34
    Berle, Adolf A., Jr. **VIII:**
      35
    Bethune, Mary McLeod
      VIII: 36
    Black, Hugo L. **VIII:** 36,
      37
    Black Cabinet **VIII:** 37
    Bonus Army **VIII:** 40
    Brain Trust **VIII:** 41, 42
    Brandeis, Louis **VII:** 35
    Bush, Vannevar **VIII:** 44,
      45
    Byrnes, James F. **VIII:** 48
    Cairo Conference **VIII:** 51
    Casablanca Conference
      VIII: 52
    cash-and-carry **VIII:** 53
    Catholics **VIII:** 53, 54
    CCC **VIII:** 63
    censorship **VIII:** 55
    CIO **VIII:** 70
    cities and urban life **VIII:**
      59

civil defense **IX:** 52
civil rights **VIII:** 61
Clark Memorandum **VII:**
  51
communism **IX:** 61
Communists **VIII:** 65
Congress **VIII:** 67
conscientious objectors
  VIII: 70
conservatism **VIII:** 71, 72
conservative coalition
  VIII: 73, 74
Coolidge, Calvin **VII:** 57
Coughlin, Father Charles
  E. **VIII:** 75
court-packing plan **VIII:**
  76–77
CWA **VIII:** 62, 63
"Day of Infamy" speech
  VIII: 428
Democratic Party **VII:** 67;
  VIII: 80–82
Dempsey, Jack **VII:** 67
destroyers-for-bases deal
  VIII: 82
Dewson, "Molly" **VIII:** 83
dollar-a-year men **VIII:** 84
Douglas, William O. **VIII:**
  84
Dust Bowl **VIII:** 87
Eccles, Marriner S. **VIII:**
  89
Economic Bill of Rights
  VIII: 90
economy **VIII:** 91
education **VIII:** 94
elderly **VIII:** 95
election of 1932 **VIII:** 96
election of 1936 **VIII:** 97
election of 1940 **VIII:** 98
election of 1944 **VIII:**
  98–99
Emergency Banking Act of
  1933 **VIII:** 100, 101
Emergency Relief
  Appropriation Act **VIII:**
  101
environmental issues **VIII:**
  103
Ethiopia **VIII:** 105
Executive Order 8802
  VIII: 106, 427–428
Executive Order 9066
  VIII: 106, 107, 428–429
Executive Reorganization
  Act **VIII:** 107–108
Fair Labor Standards Act
  VIII: 110
FAP **VIII:** 114
Farley, James A. **VIII:** 110,
  111
FBI **VIII:** 115

FCA **VIII:** 111
FCC **VIII:** 116
FDIC **VIII:** 117
FEPC **VIII:** 109
FERA **VIII:** 117, 118
First Inaugural Address, 1933 **VIII:** 413–415
First New Deal **VIII:** 122
Flynn, Edward J. **VIII:** 122
foreign policy **VII:** 101; **VIII:** 123–125
Forrestal, James V. **VIII:** 126
Four Freedoms **VIII:** 126–127
Four Freedoms speech **VIII:** 423–427
Frankfurter, Felix **VIII:** 127
FSA **VIII:** 112
Full Employment Bill **VIII:** 128
Garner, John Nance **VIII:** 129
German Americans **VIII:** 131
GI Bill of Rights **VIII:** 131
Good Neighbor Policy **VIII:** 132, 133
government **VIII:** 133–136
Grand Alliance **VIII:** 136, 137
Great Depression **VIII:** 138, 140
Harriman, Averell **VIII:** 143, 144
Hearst, William Randolph **VII:** 121
Henderson, Leon **VIII:** 144, 145
Hillman, Sidney **VIII:** 145, 146
Hiroshima and Nagasaki **VIII:** 147
HOLC **VIII:** 150
Holocaust **VIII:** 150
Hoover, Herbert **VIII:** 152
Hoover presidency **VIII:** 153, 156
Hopkins, Harry **VIII:** 156
housing **VIII:** 157
Hughes, Charles Evans **VII:** 124
Hull, Cordell **VIII:** 159
Ickes, Harold L. **VIII:** 161
immigration **VIII:** 162
Indian Reorganization Act **VIII:** 163
Irish Americans **VIII:** 165
isolationists **VIII:** 166
Italian Americans **VIII:** 167

Japanese Americans, relocation of **VIII:** 171
Jews **VIII:** 173
Johnson, Hugh S. **VIII:** 173, 174
Jones, Jesse H. **VIII:** 174
Kennedy, Joseph P. **VIII:** 175, 176
Keynesianism **VIII:** 176, 177
King, Ernest J. **VIII:** 178
labor **VIII:** 179–181, *180*
La Follette, Robert M., Jr. **VIII:** 182
La Guardia, Fiorello **VIII:** 182
Landon, Alfred M. **VIII:** 183
Leahy, William D. **VIII:** 183, 184
Lend-Lease Act **VIII:** 184
Lewis, John L. **VIII:** 185–186
liberalism **VIII:** 188, 189
Lilienthal, David E. **VIII:** 190
Lindbergh, Charles **VII:** 160
London Economic Conference **VIII:** 193
Long, Huey P. **VIII:** 194, 195
MacArthur, Douglas **IX:** 185
Manchuria **VIII:** 199
Manhattan Project **VIII:** 200
Marshall, George C. **VIII:** 206
medicine **VIII:** 208, 209
Mellon, Andrew **VII:** 180
mobilization **VIII:** 214
Moley, Raymond C. **VIII:** 215
Morgenthau, Henry **VIII:** 216
movies **VIII:** 219
MOWM **VIII:** 201
Munich Conference **VIII:** 220
Murray, Philip **VIII:** 221
NAACP **VIII:** 227
Navy, U.S. **VIII:** 236
Nelson, Donald M. **VIII:** 238
Neutrality Acts **VIII:** 239
New Deal **VIII:** 239–243; **IX:** 229–230
news media **VIII:** 243
NIRA **VIII:** 228
NLRA **VIII:** 229
NLRB **VIII:** 230

Norris, George W. **VIII:** 248–249
North African campaign **VIII:** 249
NRA **VIII:** 231
NRPB **VIII:** 232
NWLB **VIII:** 233
NYA **VIII:** 234
Nye Committee **VIII:** 250
OCD **VIII:** 253
OPA **VIII:** 254
OPM **VIII:** 255
Oppenheimer, J. Robert **IX:** 236
OSRD **VIII:** 255
OSS **VIII:** 256
OWI **VIII:** 257, 258
OWM **VIII:** 258
OWMR **VIII:** 259
Perkins, Frances **VIII:** 265
Philippines **VIII:** 266
Polish Americans **VIII:** 269, 270
politics in the Roosevelt era **VIII:** 270–273, 272*t*
popular culture **VIII:** 273, 274
Popular Front **VIII:** 276
postwar planning **VIII:** 278, 279
Potsdam Conference **VIII:** 279, 280
presidency **VIII:** 280, 281
propaganda **VIII:** 283
public opinion polls **VIII:** 284
Public Utility Holding Company Act **VIII:** 284, 285
PWA **VIII:** 285
RA **VIII:** 307
race and racial conflict **VIII:** 289
radio **VIII:** 289
Randolph, A. Philip **VIII:** 291
rationing **VIII:** 292
recession of 1937–38 **VIII:** 292, 293
Reciprocal Trade Agreements Act **VIII:** 293–294
reconversion **VIII:** 295
recreation **VIII:** 296
refugees **VIII:** 298
relief **VIII:** 299–301
religion **VIII:** 303, 304
Republican Party **VIII:** 305
Revenue Act of 1935 **VIII:** 307–308
Revenue Act of 1942 **VIII:** 308, 309

RFC **VIII:** 294, 295
Roosevelt, Eleanor **VIII:** 310–311
Schechter Poultry Corporation v. United States **VIII:** 317
SEC **VIII:** 322
second front **VIII:** 320
Second New Deal **VIII:** 321
Selective Service **VIII:** 322, *323*
Seventeenth Amendment **VII:** 69
Smith, Alfred E. **VII:** 287–288
Smith Act **VIII:** 326
socialists **VIII:** 327
Social Security Act **VIII:** 328, 329
South **VIII:** 331, 332
Soviet-American relations **VIII:** 333, 334
Spanish Civil War **VIII:** 335
sports **VIII:** 335
Standard Oil **VII:** 296
States' Rights Party **IX:** 281
STFU **VIII:** 333
Stimson, Henry L. **VIII:** 340
suburbs **VIII:** 342
Sunbelt **VIII:** 343
Supreme Court **VIII:** 344, *345*, 346
Taft, Robert A. **VIII:** 349
taxation **VIII:** 350, 351
technology **VIII:** 353
Teheran Conference **VIII:** 354
television **IX:** 295
Third New Deal **VIII:** 357–358
Thomas, Norman **VIII:** 358
TNEC **VIII:** 355
Townsend, Francis E. **VIII:** 358, 359
transportation **VIII:** 360
Truman, Harry **IX:** 299
Tugwell, Rexford G. **VIII:** 361
TVA **VIII:** 356
UN **VIII:** 365, 366
Union Party **VIII:** 365
USHA **VIII:** 367
USO **VIII:** 366
wage and price controls **VIII:** 371
Wagner, Robert F. **VIII:** 372

Roosevelt, Franklin Delano (*continued*)

Wallace, Henry A. **VIII:** 373

war bonds **VIII:** 374

WAVES **VIII:** 379–380

Welles, Sumner **VIII:** 377

Wheeler, Burton K. **VIII:** 377–378

White, Walter **VIII:** 378

Willkie, Wendell L. **VIII:** 378

WMC **VIII:** 374, 375

women's network **VIII:** 383

women's status and rights **VIII:** 384, 385

World Disarmament Conference **VIII:** 388

World War II **VIII:** 388

World War II European theater **VIII:** 391

World War II home front **VIII:** 396

WPA **VIII:** 386–388

Yalta Conference **VIII:** 401, 402, *402*

Zionism **VIII:** 403

Roosevelt, Theodore **V:** 247, 248, 315, 354; **VI:** 328*c*; **VII:** xiii, *28*, 265, **265–266,** 355*c*–358*c*; **IX:** 185

Anthracite Coal Strike **VII:** 12, 13

Antiquities Act **VII:** 13

Big Stick diplomacy **VII:** 27–28

Brownsville Riot **VII:** 35

business **VII:** 39

business and government **VI:** 40

Cannon, Joseph **VII:** 42

Children's Bureau **VII:** 47

Congress **VI:** 64; **VII:** 53

conservationism **VII:** 55

Coolidge, Calvin **VII:** 56

Democratic Party **VII:** 66

Dewey, George **VI:** 79

dollar diplomacy **VII:** 70

elections **VII:** 80

Elkins Act **VII:** 83–84

Federal Trade Commission Act **VII:** 94

foreign policy **VII:** 98, 99

Gentlemen's Agreement **VII:** 107–108

Geronimo **VI:** 113

Good Neighbor Policy **VIII:** 132

Great White Fleet **VII:** 113–114

Hanna, Marcus Alonzo **VI:** 121

Harrison, Benjamin **VI:** 123

Hay, John Milton **VI:** 125

Hepburn Act **VII:** 122

Holmes, Oliver Wendell **VII:** 123

Hughes, Charles Evans **VII:** 124

Johnson, Hiram Warren **VII:** 138

La Follette, Robert **VII:** 155

Lease, Mary Elizabeth **VI:** 173

Lodge, Henry Cabot **VII:** 165

Mahan, Alfred Thayer **VI:** 186

Mann-Elkins Act **VII:** 170

McKinley, William **VI:** 190

Meat Inspection Act **VII:** 178

Mitchell, John **VII:** 186

Morgan, John Pierpont **VI:** 198

muckrakers **VII:** 192

Muir, John **VI:** 200

National Defense Act **VII:** 201, 202

National Park Service **VII:** 203

National Reclamation Act **VII:** 203

Native Americans **VI:** 208

New Freedom **VII:** 210, 211

New Nationalism **VII:** 211–212

Norris, George W. **VIII:** 248

Northern Securities Co. v. U.S. **VII:** 216

oil industry **VII:** 217

Open Door Policy **VII:** 219

Panama Canal **VII:** 222, 224

Payne-Aldrich Tariff Act **VII:** 226

Pinchot, Gifford **VII:** 227

politics **VII:** 230

Powderly, Terence Vincent **VI:** 227

Preparedness **VII:** 235

Progressive Party **VII:** 236, 237

progressivism **VII:** 238

Pure Food and Drug Act **VII:** 244

Republican Party **VII:** 263

Riis, Jacob A. **VI:** 248

Roosevelt Corollary **VII:** 267

Root-Takahira Agreement **VII:** 267

Rough Riders **VI:** 250–251, *251*

Russo-Japanese War **VII:** 271

science **VII:** 276

Sherman Antitrust Act **VI:** 262

Sinclair, Upton **VII:** 286

Spanish-American War **VI:** 272

Steffens, Lincoln **VII:** 299

"Strenuous Life" speech **VII:** 363–367

Taft, William Howard **VII:** 303, 304

trade, foreign **VII:** 310

United Mine Workers of America (UMWA) **VII:** 314

veterans **VII:** 324

Washington, Booker T. **VI:** 309

Wilson, Woodrow **VII:** 333

Roosevelt Coalition

Democratic Party **VIII:** 82

election of 1936 **VIII:** 97

election of 1940 **VIII:** 98

election of 1944 **VIII:** 99

labor **VIII:** 179

politics in the Roosevelt era **VIII:** 273

women's status and rights **VIII:** 384

Roosevelt Corollary **IV:** 142; **VII:** 50, 99, 266, **267,** 356*c*; **VIII:** 132–133

Root, Elihu **VII:** 99, 135; **VIII:** 340

Root, George F. **V:** 244

Roots (miniseries) **X:** 241, 325*c*

Root-Takahira Agreement **VII:** 99, 266, **267–268,** 271, 357*c*

root vegetables **II:** 121

rope manufacturing **IV:** 186*m*

Roper, Elmo **VIII:** 284

ropewalks **II:** 26

Rose, Ernestine **V:** 396, 398

Rose (Anshutz) **VII:** 18

Rosebud, Battle of the **VI:** 324*c*

Black Hills gold rush **VI:** 29

Crazy Horse **VI:** 69

Sioux wars **VI:** 263

Sitting Bull **VI:** 264

Rosecrans, William S. **IV:** 40; **V:** **305**

Chattanooga, Battle of **V:** 57

Chickamauga, Battle of **V:** 58, 59

Corinth, Battle of **V:** 83

Lookout Mountain, Battle of **V:** 216

Murfreesboro/Stones River, Battle of **V:** 242, 243

Thomas, George H. **V:** 354

Rosenberg, Julius and Ethel **IX:** 14, 61, 136, 140, **264–265,** 330*c*

Rosenberg, W. L. **VI:** 269

Rosenman, Joel **X:** 321

Rosenthal, Joe **VIII:** 169, 268

Rosenwald, Julius **VI:** 186

Rosie the Riveter **VIII: 315**

aircraft industry **VIII:** 11

women's status and rights **VIII:** 385

World War II **VIII:** 390

World War II home front **VIII:** 394

Ross, Alexander **IV:** 93

Ross, Betsy **III: 310–311**

Ross, George **III:** 310

Ross, John **IV:** 344; **V:** 390, 391

Ross, Nellie Tayloe **VIII:** 384

Ross, Robert **IV:** 39

Rosselli, Johnny **IX:** 236

Rossetti, William Michael **V:** 394

Rostenkowski, Dan **X:** 145

ROTC. *See* Reserve Officers Training Corps

Roth, Philip **X:** 177

Rothafel, "Roxy" **VIII:** 22

Rothko, Mark **VIII:** 25; **IX:** 19–20

Roth v. United States (1957) **X:** 40–41, 60, 244

Rough Riders **V:** 392; **VI:** **250–251,** *251,* 272, 328*c*; **VII:** 266

Rousseau, Jean-Jacques **III:** 135; **VI:** 159

Rousseau, Théodore **IV:** 34, 55

Rovaag, Karl F. **X:** 196

Rowell, George P. **VI:** 2

Rowland, Henry **VI:** 113

Rowland, John **II:** 372

Rowlandson, Mary White **II:** 51, 195, **324–325**

Rowson, Susanna Haswell **III:** 281, **311**

Royal African Company **II:** 188, 198, **325,** 339

Royal Air Force (RAF) **VIII:** 11, 43–44

royal colonies **II:** 144, **325–326**
  Dominion of New England **II:** 94
  Georgia **II:** 137
  Maryland **II:** 210
  New York **II:** 261
  North Carolina **II:** 265
  Rhode Island **II:** 321
  Roman Catholics **II:** 323
  Savannah **II:** 329
  Virginia **II:** 382
  Virginia Company of London **II:** 387
royal fifth **I:** 69, 323, 327; **II:** 359
"Royal Greens" **III:** 188
royal land distribution **II:** 11
Royal Navy **II:** 251, 259, 369
Royal Society of London
  Bartram, John **II:** 30
  Boston Philosophical Society **II:** 37
  Boylston, Zabdiel **II:** 37
  Brattle, Thomas **II:** 40
  Byrd, William II **II:** 47
  Catesby, Mark **II:** 55
  Pennsylvania **II:** 277
  science **II:** 330
Rozelle, Pete **X:** 284
Rozier, Ferdinand **IV:** 34
RU-486 (morning-after pill) **X:** 4, 36, 331*c*
rubber/rubber industry **IV:** 118, 184, 307; **VII:** 75; **VIII:** 69, 292, 409*c*
Rubenstein, Arthur **VIII:** 223
Rubin, Jerry **IX:** 72; **X:** 61
Rubinstein, Helena **VII:** 58
Ruby, Jack **IX:** 238, *238*
Ruby Ridge, Idaho **X:** 194
Ruckelshaus, William D. **X:** **268–269,** 324*c*
  Bork, Robert **X:** 39
  Cox, Archibald, Jr. **X:** 81
  Nixon, Richard M. **X:** 221
  Richardson, Elliot L. **X:** 268
  Watergate scandal **X:** 316
Rudd, Mark **IX:** 319; **X:** 317
Rudman, Warren **X:** 134–135, 279
Rudyard, Thomas **II:** 54
Ruef, Abraham **VII:** 138
Ruffin, Edmund **V:** 127, 170, 311
Ruffin, Josephine St. Pierre **VI:** 6; **VII:** 199
Ruggieri, Michele **I:** 312
Ruggles, David **IV:** 377*c*
Ruggles, Timothy **III:** 332
Rugova, Ibrahim **X:** 167
Ruiz, José **IV:** 19, 20
Rule of 1756 **III:** 119

rules of war **V:** 130, 179–180, **305–306,** 384
Ruml, Beordsley **VIII:** 309
rum trade **II:** **326**
  alcohol **II:** 15
  Caribbean **II:** 53
  food **II:** 122
  manufacturing and industry **II:** 204
  Massachusetts **II:** 215
  merchants **II:** 222
  New Hampshire **II:** 250
  Newport **II:** 258
  smuggling **II:** 349
  taverns and inns **II:** 368
runaway slaves. *See* slaves, fugitive
Rundstedtr, Gerd von **VIII:** 248
Run Island **I:** 335
Runyon v. McCrary et al. (1976) **X:** 325*c*
Rural Electrification Administration (REA) **VIII:** **315–316**
  agriculture **VIII:** 8
  Emergency Relief Appropriation Act **VIII:** 102
  Public Utility Holding Company Act **VIII:** 285
  RFC **VIII:** 294
rural life **II:** 25, 356, 407; **III:** 284, 285, **311–312;** **IV:** 7, 19, 316–319; **VII:** **268–270,** *269;* **IX:** 7, 15; **X:** 101
  cities and urban life **VI:** 53
  communications **VI:** 61
  housing **VI:** 135
  kindergarten **VI:** 159
  mail-order houses **VI:** 186
  national banking system **VI:** 206
  population trends **VI:** 226
  railroads **VI:** 237
Rush, Benjamin **III:** **312–313,** 392*c,* 396*c;* **IV:** 277–278
  Allen, Richard **III:** 11
  antislavery and abolition **III:** 16
  medicine **III:** 241
  prisons **III:** 286
  slave trade **III:** 329
  temperance **III:** 346
Rush, Howard **VIII:** 208
Rush, Richard **IV:** 269
Rush-Bagot Agreement of 1817 **IV:** 375*c*
Rusher, William **X:** 20, 43
Ruskin, John **VI:** 259, 266, 312
Russel, Cabot **V:** 125
Russell, Andrew J. **V:** 273
Russell, Bill **X:** 285

Russell, Charles Taze **VI:** 242
Russell, Henry **IV:** 250
Russell, Lillian **VI:** 96
Russell, Richard B. **X:** 140
Russell, William Green **IV:** 89
Russell, William H. **IV:** 114
Russia **III:** 8–9, 289; **V:** 133, 315, 408*c;* **VI:** 103, 216–217, 328*c;* **IX:** 61. *See also* Soviet Union
  ABM Treaty **X:** 23
  Adams, John Quincy **IV:** 4
  Alaska, Russia in **II:** 13–14
  Aleut **II:** 16
  Bering, Vitus Jonassen **II:** 32
  Cabot, Sebastian **I:** 43
  California **IV:** 64
  Clinton, William **X:** 66–67, 69
  defense policy **X:** 87
  diseases and epidemics **IV:** 111
  exploration **II:** 115; **IV:** 132
  Figueroa, José **IV:** 136
  foreign policy **IV:** 142; **VII:** 100; **X:** 124
  fur trade **I:** 133; **IV:** 156
  Goldman, Emma **VII:** 109–110
  Great White Fleet **VII:** 114
  INF Treaty **X:** 152
  Jews (Judaism) **I:** 192
  Manifest Destiny **IV:** 217
  Monroe Doctrine **IV:** 241, 242
  NATO **X:** 223
  Northeast Passage **I:** 265
  Open Door Policy **VII:** 219
  printing press **I:** 294
  Red Scare **VII:** 258
  Reed, John **VII:** 259
  Root-Takahira Agreement **VII:** 267
  Russo-Japanese War **VII:** 271
  Seven Years' War **II:** 332
  Siberian Expedition **VII:** 285–286
  Soviet Union **X:** 281
  space policy **X:** 283
  Treaty of Paris **II:** 378
  Versailles, Treaty of **VII:** 324
  World Trade Organization **X:** 321, 322
  World War I **VII:** 343
Russian-American Company **II:** 14, 326; **IV:** 241

Russian Company **II:** 41
Russian explorers **II:** 167
Russian fur traders **II:** 266
Russian Revolution **VII:** **270–271,** 359*c,* 360*c;* **VIII:** 187. *See also* Bolshevik Revolution; Bolsheviks
  Committee for Public Information **VII:** 52
  Communist Party **VII:** 52
  foreign policy **VII:** 100
  Masses, The **VII:** 173
  Palmer, A. Mitchell **VII:** 221
  radicalism **VII:** 251
  Red Scare **VII:** 258
  Reed, John **VII:** 259
  Seattle General Strike **VII:** 278, 279
  Siberian Expedition **VII:** 285
  socialism **VII:** 289
Russian settlements **II:** **326**
Russian settlers **IV:** 241
Russian-Ukraine Trilateral Statement and Annex (1994) **X:** 124
Russo-Japanese War **VII:** **271,** 356*c*
  foreign policy **VII:** 99
  Great White Fleet **VII:** 114
  Open Door Policy **VII:** 219
  Roosevelt, Theodore **VII:** 266
  Root-Takahira Agreement **VII:** 267
Russo-Japanese War of 1904–1905 **VIII:** 64, 164, 402
Russwurm, John B. **IV:** 15, 194, 376*c*
rust belt **IX:** 51; **X:** **269,** 290
Rustichello of Pisa **I:** 286, 287
Rustin, Bayard **IX:** 30, 67
Rust v. Sullivan **X:** 318–319
Rutgers College/University **II:** 149; **VI:** 101. *See also* Queen's College
Ruth, Babe **VII:** 26, *26,* 294–295, 361*c;* **VIII:** 275, 335; **X:** 1
Rutherford, Joseph Franklin **VI:** 242
Rutledge, Ann **V:** 166
Rutledge, John **III:** 338
Rutledge, Wiley B. **VIII:** 346*t*
Rwanda **X:** 67, 88, 307
Ryan, George H. **X:** 56
Ryan, John **VII:** 260
Ryan, Father John A. **VIII:** 54, 165

Ryan, Paddy **VI:** 33
Ryder, Albert Pinkham **VI:** 219
Ryder, Charles W. **VIII:** 249
rye **II:** 276
RYM (Revolutionary Youth
 Movement) **X:** 317
Ryswick, Treaty (Peace) of
 (1697) **II:** 185, 356

S

Sá, Mem de **I:** 33
Sabin, Albert B. **IX:** 199
Sabin, Pauline **VII:** 241
Sabine Crossroads **V:** 297
Sabine Pass **V:** 228
Sabine River **IV:** 5, 337, 338
saboteurs **VIII:** 115
Sabradin **I:** 124
Sacagawea **III:** 72, 208–211,
 315, 397c
sacatras 2: 229, 237
Sacco and Vanzetti **VII:** 53,
 273, 361c
sachems **I:** 225; **II: 327**
 Aleut **II:** 16
 Canonicus **II:** 51
 ethnocentrism **II:** 113
 Iroquois **II:** 168
 Miantonomo **II:** 223–224
 Narragansett **II:** 241
 Pequot War **II:** 280
 wampum **II:** 390
 Wetamo **II:** 395
 women's status and rights
  II: 406
Sacher, Harry **IX:** 80
sack coat **V:** 122
Sac nation **II:** 199; **IV:** 33–34,
 51–53, 208, 256
Sacramento, California **IV:** 66,
 332
Sacramento Valley **IV:** 131
sacrifices **II:** 317
 Aztecs **I:** 17–18
 Battel, Andrew **I:** 27
 Cahokia **I:** 47
 Chichén Itzá **I:** 69, 70
 Cozumel **I:** 97
 flowery wars **I:** 131
 Ghana **I:** 140
 Hopewell culture **I:** 166
 Huitzilopochtli **I:** 170
 Maya **I:** 228
 Quetzalcoatl **I:** 301
 Tezcatlipoca **I:** 347, 348
Sacsahuaman **I:** 99
Sadat, Anwar el- **X:** 54–55, 55,
 58
al-Sa'di, 'Abd al-Rahman, ibn'
 Abd Allah ibn **I:** 350
Sad Night. *See* Noche Triste

Safdie, Moshe **IX:** 19
Safe Drinking Water Act of
 1974 **X:** 77–78, 205, 210, 250
Safeguard program **X:** 23
Safer, Morley **IX:** 154
safety issues
 automobile industry **IX:**
  25–26, 225; **X:** 31, 32
 Nader, Ralph **X:** 205
 Occupational Safety and
  Health Act of 1970 **X:**
  225
safety pin **IV:** 308
Safford, Laurence F. **VIII:** 64
SAG (Screen Actors Guild) **X:**
 258
Sagard, Gabriel **II:** 44
Saguenay, Kingdom of the **I:** 59
Sahagún, Bernardino de **I:** 250,
 315, 382
Sahara **I:** 52, **315–317,** 316m,
 328, 386c
sailors. *See* mariners
St. Andrew's Benevolent society
 II: 196
St. Augustine **I:** 130–131, 189,
 201, 298, 387c; **II: 327–328**
 architecture **II:** 23
 cities and urban life **II:** 61
 Florida **II:** 120, 121
 Fort Mose **II:** 123
 Gates, Sir Thomas **II:** 135
 Middleton, Arthur **II:** 224
 Oglethorpe, James Edward
  II: 267
 Queen Anne's War **II:** 309
 Stono Rebellion **II:** 361
St. Bartholomew's Day
 Massacre (1572) **I:** 158, 169,
 371
St. Brendan (island) **I:** 27
St. Catherine's Island **II:** 238
St. Christopher **II:** 227
St. Clair, Arthur **III: 315–316,**
 395c; **IV:** 168
 Blue Jacket **III:** 41
 Fallen Timbers, Battle of
  III: 123
 Greenville, Treaty of **III:**
  157
 Lyon, Matthew **III:** 222
 Wayne, Anthony **III:** 369
St. Clair, James **X:** 309, 317
St. Clement's Island **II:** 50
St. Croix River **IV:** 25
Saint-Domingue **II:** 53, 74, 338,
 355, 356
St. Dominic **I:** 188, 209
Sainte-Marie-du-Salte **II:** 205
Saintes, Battle of the **III:** 154,
 372
Saint-Esprit **II:** 205

St. Eustatius **II:** 98
St. Francis **I:** 132, 188, 209
Saint-Gaudens, Augustus **V:**
 124, 239; **VI: 253,** 254, 259,
 314
St.-Germain-en-Laye **II:** 127
Saint-Ignace **II:** 206
St. John, John P. **VI:** 234
St. John River **IV:** 25
St. Joseph, Missouri **IV:** 66, 70
St. Kitts **II:** 374
St. Lawrence River **I:** 57, 58
St. Leger, Abastenia **VII:** 18
St. Leger, Barry
 Brant, Joseph **III:** 49
 Burgoyne, John **III:** 51, 52
 Johnson, Sir John **III:** 188
 Saratoga, surrender at **III:**
  318
St. Louis, Missouri **VI:** 85
 American Fur Company
  IV: 16
 Ashley, William Henry **IV:**
  29, 30
 Astor, John Jacob **IV:** 31,
  32
 Astoria **IV:** 33
 Atkinson, Henry **IV:** 33
 Austin, Moses **IV:** 36
 Benton, Thomas Hart **IV:**
  49
 Bodmer, Karl **IV:** 55
 Chouteau family **IV:** 78
 cities and urban life **IV:** 82,
  84
 fur trade **IV:** 157
 industrialization **IV:** 187
 mountain men **IV:** 247
 Pike, Zebulon
  Montgomery **IV:** 281
 Sublette, William **IV:** 330
St. Louis, Missouri Fur
 Company **IV:** 238
St. Louis Browns **VI:** 22
St. Louis Cardinals **IX:** 260
St. Louis Gazette **IV:** 247, 320
St. Louis Observer **IV:** 214
St. Louis World's Fair (1904)
 VI: 113, 208
Saint-Lusson, Simon Daumont
 II: 178
St. Martin-in-the-Fields church
 (London) **II:** 24
St. Mary's City **II: 328**
 Brent, Margaret Reed **II:**
  40
 Calvert, Leonard **II:** 50
 Chesapeake Bay **II:** 58
 Maryland **II:** 209, 210
 Roman Catholics **II:** 323
St. Mary's River **V:** 167
Saint Paul, Minnesota **X:** 115

St. Paul, Minneapolis &
 Manitoba Railway **VI:** 129
St. Paul & Pacific Railroad **VI:**
 129
St. Paul's Cathedral (London) **I:**
 208
St. Peter's Basilica **I:** 236
St. Phillips Episcopal Church,
 New York City **IV:** 366
St. Pierre (island) **II:** 378
saints **I:** 40, 188, 209, 291; **II:**
 94; **IV:** 315–316. *See also*
 specific saints
Saint-Sauveur **I:** 3
Saint Sebastian **I:** 27
St. Thomas's African Episcopal
 Church **III:** 189
St. Vincent **II:** 43
St. Vrain, Ceran **IV:** 47, 48, 50
Saipan **VIII:** 202
Salado **I:** 164
Salary Grab Act of 1873 **VI:** 130
Salazar y Mendoza, José
 Francisco Xavier **II:** 25
Salem, Massachusetts **II:** 212,
 214, 418c
 Endecott, John **II:** 107
 French immigrants **II:** 130
 Massachusetts Bay
  Company **II:** 216
 music **II:** 238
 Nurse, Rebecca **II:** 266
 Quakers **II:** 308
 travel **II:** 378
Salem witchcraft trials **II:** *404*
 Brattle, Thomas **II:** 40
 crime and punishment **II:**
  74
 Parris, Samuel **II:** 271
 Sewall, Samuel **II:** 334
 society, British American
  II: 350
 Willard, Samuel **II:** 399
 witchcraft **II:** 402–403
 women's status and rights
  II: 409
sales tax **VIII:** 352
Salina **I:** 48
Salinas, Carlos **X:** 192
Salinger, J. D. **IX:** 182, 243
Salisbury, Lord **VI:** 303
Salk, Jonas E. **IX:** 199, 295,
 331c
Salle, David **X:** 26
Sally Hemmings (Chase-
 Riboud) **III:** 164
Salmagundi **X:** 177
Salmerón, Alfonso **I:** 189, 209
Salmon, Lucy Maynard **VII:** 161
Salomon, Haym **III:** 187–188
saloons **IV:** 129, 249; **VI:** 96
salsa music **X:** 203

salt **I**: 52, 53, 337; **II**: 376
SALT (Strategic Arms
    Limitation Talks) **IX**: 16
SALT I; SALT II. *See* Strategic
    Arms Limitation Treaties
Saltbox architecture **II**: 215
salt fish **II**: 258
Salt Lake City, Utah
    Deseret, State of **IV**: 109
    Mormon War **IV**: 244
    South Pass **IV**: 325
    Young, Brigham **IV**: 372
Salt Lake region **IV**: 236
Saltonstall, Sir Richard **II**: 216
salt poisoning **I**: 108
Salvador, Brazil **I**: 24
Salvation Army **VI**: 266
Salzburgers **II**: 139, 267
Salzman, Jack **VI**: 81
samba music **X**: 203
same-sex marriages **X**: 183, 331*c*
Samoa **VI**: 32, 123, **254–255**
Samoset **II**: 283, 360
Sampson, Deborah **III**: *316*,
    316–317
San Antonio (ship) **I**: 215
San Antonio, Texas **II**: 61; **IV**:
    337, 339, 341, 346; **X**: 290
Sanburg, Carl **VIII**: 192
San Carlos Reservation
    (Arizona) **VI**: 14, 112, 207
Sánchez, Alfonso **IX**: 298
Sánchez, David **IX**: 327, 328
Sand County Almanac, A (Aldo
    Leopold) **IX**: 101
Sand Creek Massacre **IV**: 47,
    48; **V**: 407*c*
Sandford, John **IV**: 331
San Diego, California **II**: 231,
    331; **IV**: 69, 75; **X**: 290
San Diego Chargers **X**: 163
Sandinista Front of National
    Liberation (FSLN) **X**: 326*c*
    contras **X**: 80
    foreign policy **X**: 124
    Iran-contra affair **X**: 154
    Latin America **X**: 173
    Nicaragua **X**: 217–218
Sandino, Augusto César **X**:
    217–218
Sandler, Bernice **X**: 115
Sandoval, Gonzalo de **I**:
    317–318
Sandwich Islands. *See* Hawaiian
    Islands
Sandys, Sir Edwin **I**: **318–319**;
    II: 44, 347, 387
Sandys, George **II**: 142,
    328–329
SANE (National Committee for
    a Sane Nuclear Policy) **IX**:
    267–268, 279

San Felipe, Texas **IV**: 346
Sanford, Edward T. **VIII**: 346*t*
Sanford, John F. A. **V**: 101
San Francisco, California
    anti-Chinese agitation, rise
        of **IV**: 23
    Asian Americans **VIII**: 26
    California **IV**: 65, 66
    California gold rush **IV**: 69
    cities and urban life **II**: 61
    Comstock Lode **IV**: 96
    diseases and epidemics **IV**:
        111
    filibustering **V**: 127
    Forty-niners **IV**: 146
    Frémont, Jessie Benton
        IV: 152
    George, Henry **VI**: 111
    gold, discovery and mining
        IV: 163
    Larkin, Thomas Oliver **IV**:
        207
    LSD **IX**: 184
    missions **II**: 231
    Monroe Doctrine **IV**: 241
    Strauss, Levi **IV**: 329
    transportation, urban **VI**:
        292
San Francisco Examiner **VII**:
    121
San Francisco school system
    Gentlemen's Agreement
        VII: 107, 108
    Root-Takahira Agreement
        VII: 267
    Russo-Japanese War **VII**:
        271
    segregation **VII**: 281
San Gabriel **I**: 257, 319
Sanger, Margaret **VII**:
    273–274, 358*c*, 359*c*; **IX**:
    198–199, 242; **X**: 36
    birth control **VII**: 29, 30
    "Children's Era" speech
        VII: 384–386
    Ellis, Havelock **VII**: 84
    Flynn, Elizabeth Gurley
        VII: 95
    public health **VII**: 243
    women's status and rights
        VII: 339
Sanger, William **V**: 283
Sanibel Island **I**: 288
San Ildefonso, Treaty of **III**: 42
"sanitary fairs" **V**: 374
sanitation **IV**: 111; **VI**: 191, 192,
    323*c*
San Jacinto, Battle of **IV**: 338,
    341
San Jacinto, USS **V**: 132, 369
San Juan, New Mexico **I**: 319
San Juan, Puerto Rico **I**: 297

San Juan Bautista **I**: 82. *See also*
    Puerto Rico
San Juan de los Caballeros **I**:
    257, 271
San Juan Ulúa **I**: 93, 156, 334
San Juan Hill **V**: 392; **VII**: 266
San Juan Hill, Battle of **VI**: *251*,
    272, 328*c*
San Juan Islands **VI**: 43, 309,
    310
San Juan pueblo **II**: 254,
    289–290, 304
Sankey, Ira **VI**: 197, 203
San Lorenzo **I**: 269
San Lorenzo, Treaty of **III**: 130,
    182, **317**, 396*c*; **IV**: 139
Sanlúcar de Barrameda **I**: 387*c*
San Marco, Church of **I**: 364,
    365
San Mateo **I**: 57
San Pascual, Battle of **IV**: 75
San Salvador **I**: 79, 81
Santa Anna **V**: 395
Santa Anna, Antonio López de
    IV: **303–304**, *304*
    Alamo, The **IV**: 12–13
    Austin, Stephen F. **IV**: 37
    Bowie, Jim **IV**: 57
    Crockett, Davy **IV**: 100
    Figueroa, José **IV**: 136
    Gadsden Purchase **IV**: 159
    Guadalupe Hidalgo, Treaty
        of (1848) **IV**: 165
    Houston, Sam **IV**: 174
    Manifest Destiny **IV**: 217
    Mexican-American War
        IV: 234
    Scott, Winfield **IV**: 310
    Taylor, Zachary **IV**: 334
    Texas **IV**: 338
    Texas, Republic of **IV**: 340,
        341
    Travis, William Barret **IV**:
        346
*Santa Clara v. Southern Pacific
    Railroad Company* **VI**: 82,
    326*c*
Santa Claus **V**: 247; **VI**: 211
Santa Cruz **II**: 255. *See also*
    Cozumel
Santa Fe **I**: 254, 257, **319–320**;
    II: 89, 254, 255, 303; **IV**: 337,
    338
    Becknell, William **IV**: 45
    Bent, Charles **IV**: 47
    Bent's Fort **IV**: 50, 51
    exploration **IV**: 131
    Lamy, Jean Baptiste **IV**:
        207
    Smith, Jedediah Strong **IV**:
        322
Santa Fe Railroad **VI**: 237

Santa Fe Trail **IV**: 305*m*,
    305–307
    Becknell, William **IV**: 46
    Bent's Fort **IV**: 50
    Carson, Kit **IV**: 75
    exploration **IV**: 131
    Fort Leavenworth **IV**: 145
    Sutter, John **IV**: 332
Santa Maria **I**: 55, 81
Santayana, George **VI**: 178
Santee and Cooper Canal **IV**:
    72
Santee Sioux nation **IV**: 379*c*; **V**:
    406*c*
Santiago (ship) **I**: 215
Santiago (town) **I**: 363
Santo Domingo **I**: 162; **II**: 355;
    IX: 317
    audiencia **I**: 15
    cabildo **I**: 39
    Columbus, Bartholomew
        I: 78, 79
    Columbus, Christopher **I**:
        82
    Douglass, Frederick **V**: 100
    foreign policy **V**: 133
    Grant, Ulysses S. **V**: 156
    Hispaniola **I**: 161, 162
    Oviedo y Valdés, Gonzalo
        Fernández de **I**: 272,
        273
    Sumner, Charles **V**: 343
Santo Domingo, proposed
    annexation of **VI**: 104, **255**,
    256
Santo Domingo Annexation
    Treaty of 1870 **VI**: 103
Santo Domingo pueblo **I**: 271
Sanudo, Marin **I**: 365
São Francisco River **I**: 31
São Jorge da Mina **I**: 142, 144
Sao kingdom **I**: 52
São Tomé **I**: 129, 293, **320**, 338
Sapiro, Aaron **VII**: 14
Saponi **II**: 55
Saratoga, First Battle of **III**:
    137, 318*m*
Saratoga, Second Battle of **III**:
    319*m*
Saratoga, surrender at **III**:
    317–320, 318*m*, 319*m*, 393*c*
    Arnold, Benedict **III**: 21
    Brant, Joseph **III**: 49
    Burgoyne, John **III**: 51–52
    Carleton, Guy **III**: 62
    Clinton, George **III**: 75
    Clinton, Sir Henry **III**: 75
    Conway Cabal **III**: 90–91
    Deane, Silas **III**: 101
    Gates, Horatio **III**: 149
    Green Mountain Boys **III**:
        156

Saratoga, surrender at
(*continued*)
Howe, Richard, Lord **III:**
168
Howe, Sir William **III:**
169
Kościuszko, Tadeusz **III:**
198
Lee, Arthur **III:** 205
Lyon, Matthew **III:** 222
McRea, Jane **III:** 239
Morgan, Daniel **III:** 246
Native Americans and the
Revolution **III:** 255
North, Lord **III:** 260
Revolutionary War **III:**
305, 307
Schuyler, Philip John **III:**
320
Valcour Island, Battle of
III: 357
Vergennes, comte de **III:**
359
Washington, George **III:**
367
"Yankee Doodle" **III:** 387
Saratoga, USS **V:** 121
Sargent, Aaron A. **VI:** 180
Sargent, John Singer **V:** 16; **VI:**
219, **255–256; VII:** 18
Sargent, Winthrop **IV:** 84
Sarter, Caesar **III:** 5
Sartoris (Faulkner) **VIII:** 405c
Sassacus **II:** 211, 280
Sassamon, John **II:** 183,
222–223
satellite communications
globalization **X:** 131
science and technology **X:**
274
SDI **X:** 289–290
space policy **X:** 281
satellite dishes **X:** *274*
satellites **IX:** 16, 28, 98, 278
satellite television
popular culture **X:** 239
pornography **X:** 244
science and technology **X:**
273
television **X:** 296
satire **VI:** 95, 114–115
SATs (Scholastic Aptitude Tests)
X: 99
Sattelihu, Andreas. *See*
Montour, Andrew
Saturday Evening Post **IV:** 196
Saturday Night Massacre **X:**
324c
Cox, Archibald, Jr. **X:** 81
independent counsel **X:**
150
Jaworski, Leon **X:** 161

Richardson, Elliot L. **X:**
268
Ruckelshaus, William D.
X: 269
Watergate scandal **X:** 317
Saturiba **I:** 201
Saturn **VI:** 258; **X:** 283
satyagraha **IX:** 53–54
Saudi Arabia **VIII:** 403
Iran-contra affair **X:** 154
OPEC **X:** 228–229
Persian Gulf War **X:**
234–235
terrorism **X:** 299
Sauk nation **II:** 199. *See* Sac
nation
Saul, Ralph **IX:** *165*
Sault **II:** 263
Sault Ste. Marie **II:** 178
Saunders, Barry **VI:** 163
Saur, Christopher **II:** 139
Savage's Station, Battle of **V:** 181
Savannah, Georgia **II:** **329; IV:**
112
animals **II:** 21
Georgia **II:** 137, 138
Jews **II:** 175
marine corps **V:** 222
Oglethorpe, James Edward
II: 267
Sherman, William T. **V:** 321
Sherman's March through
Georgia **V:** 321–323
Special Field Order No. 15
V: 332
Taylor, Susie King **V:** 350
Tomochichi **II:** 375
Wesley, John **II:** 393
Whitefield, George **II:** 397
Savannah, USS **IV:** 307
Savannah Indians **II:** 395
Saving Private Ryan (movie) **X:**
198
savings, personal **VIII:** 92
savings and loan crisis
Bush, George H. W. **X:** 46
business **X:** 50
Clinton, William **X:** 68
Sunbelt **X:** 290
Savio, Mario **IX:** 54, 112, 113,
268
Savoy Declaration **II:** 68
sawmills **II:** 225, 369
saws **IV:** 184
Saxton, Rufus **V:** 332
Saybrook Platform of 1708 **II:**
70
Sayler's Creek, Battle of **V:** 222
Sayles, John **X:** 198
scalawags **V:** **307–308**
carpetbaggers **V:** 49, 50
Longstreet, James **V:** 215

Reconstruction **V:** 291,
294
Republican Party **V:** 302
scale, platform **IV:** 308
Scali, John **X:** 308
Scalia, Antonin **X:** **271**
Ginsburg, Ruth Bader **X:**
130
independent counsel **X:**
150
Reagan, Ronald W. **X:** 260
Rehnquist, William H. **X:**
264
Supreme Court **X:** 291
Thomas, Clarence **X:** 302
scalping **II:** 97, 124, 272,
329–330
scalplock **II:** 329
Scandinavia **I:** 263–264, 307,
385c; **VIII:** 39, 166
Scandinavian Americans **IV:**
301; **VI:** 138; **VIII:** 304
Scandinavian settlers **II:** 260
Scarface (film) **VIII:** 217
Scarlet Letter, The (Hawthorne)
IV: 213, 345, 379c
Scarsdale, Manor of **II:** 155
*Schechter Poultry Corporation
v. United States* **VIII:** **317,**
407c
antimonopoly **VIII:** 18
Fair Labor Standards Act
VIII: 110
First New Deal **VIII:** 122
NIRA **VIII:** 228
NRA **VIII:** 232
Supreme Court **VIII:** 345
Schedel, Hartmann **I:** 240
Schenk v. United States **VII:** 52,
123, **274–275**
schepens **II:** 257
Schiff, Jacob **VI:** 19, 129, 197;
VII: 329
Schine, David **IX:** 18
Schlafly, Fred **X:** 79
Schlafly, Phyllis **X:** **271–272**
ABM Treaty **X:** 22
amendments to the
Constitution **X:** 19
Christian Coalition **X:** 62
conservative movement **X:**
79
ERA **X:** 106, 107
feminism **X:** 115–116
Helms, Jesse A., Jr. **X:** 141
Panama Canal turnover **X:**
233
Reagan, Ronald W. **X:** 259
women's rights and status
X: 320
Schlamm, Willi **X:** 43
Schlatter, Michael **II:** 139, 140

Schlesinger, Arthur M., Jr. **IX:**
13; **X:** 201
Schlesinger, Benjamin **VII:** 132
Schlesinger, James R. **X:** 86,
103, 104
Schmalkaldic League **I:** 212
Schmeling, Max **VIII:** 195–196,
337, 408c
Schneiderman, Rose **VII:** 206,
312
Schoenberg, Arnold **VIII:** 223
Schofield, John M. **V:** 322
Scholastic Aptitude Tests (SATs)
X: 99
Scholasticism **II:** 277
Schomburgk, Robert **VI:** 303
School and Society, The
(Dewey) **VII:** 68
school attendance **IV:** 120
schoolbooks **IV:** 120; **V:** 370, 379
school busing programs
Brennan, William J. **X:** 41
Burger, Warren E. **X:** 44
Kennedy, Edward M. **X:**
164
race and racial conflict **X:**
256
school desegregation **IX:** 332c
Brennan, William J. **X:** 41
*Brown v. Board of
Education* **IX:** 42–43
Civil Rights Act of 1957
IX: 55
Faubus, Orval **IX:** 108–109
Latino movement **IX:** 173
modern Republicanism
IX: 209
Murray, Pauli **IX:** 215
NAACP **IX:** 220
race and racial conflict **IX:**
253; **X:** 256
Supreme Court **X:** 290
Thurmond, J. Strom **X:**
303
Wallace, George C. **X:** 313,
314
Warren Court **IX:** 316
White Citizens' Councils
IX: 319–320
schools **VII:** 76, 78, 207, 351;
VIII: 235. *See also* education
schools, consolidation of **IX:** 125
schools, parochial **IV:** 315, 316
school shootings **X:** 137, 213
schout **II:** 257
Schubert, Franz **VI:** 203
Schuller, Robert **X:** 293
Schultz, George **X:** 141
Schurz, Carl **IV:** 180; **V:** *50*, 157,
302; **VI:** **256–257**
Forest Reserve Act of 1891
VI: 104

Hayes, Rutherford B. **VI:** 126

King, Clarence **VI:** 160

Liberal Republican Party **VI:** 174

mugwumps **VI:** 199

Nez Perce War **VI:** 213

Villard, Henry **VI:** 304, 305

Schurz, Margaretha **VI:** 159

Schuurman, Jacobus **II:** 125

Schuyler, Elizabeth **III:** 161

Schuyler, George **IX:** 30

Schuyler, Louisa Lee **V:** 255

Schuyler, Philip **II:** 332

Schuyler, Philip John **III:** 149, 188, 318–319, **320**

Schuyler family **II:** 381

Schwab, Charles **VII:** 297, 320

Schwab, Eugene **VI:** 127

Schwartz, Fred C. **IX:** 256

Schwartzchild & Sulzberger **VI:** 191

Schwarz, Charles **X:** 330*c*

Schwarz, Fred **X:** 79

Schwarzenegger, Arnold **X:** 198

Schwarzkopf, Norman **X:** 235, 247

Schwenkfelders **II:** 139

Schwerner, Michael **IX:** 66, 67, 207, 254, 334*c*

Schwieger, Walter **VII:** 168

Sciapods **I:** 221

science. *See* inventions, science, and technology

Science (journal) **VI:** 25

Science: The Endless Frontier (Bush) **VIII:** 44, 45, 255

Science and Health (Eddy) **VI:** 52, 88, 324*c*

science fiction books **IX:** 327

science fiction movies **IX:** 213

Science in World War II **VIII:** 255

scientific management **VI:** 145, 170; **VII: 277**, 357*c*

automobile industry **VII:** 22

business **VII:** 38

economy **VII:** 74

Ford, Henry **VII:** 96

invention and technology **VII:** 133

IWW **VII:** 129

labor movement **VII:** 151

mass production **VII:** 173

New Unionism **VII:** 212

progressivism **VII:** 237

science **VII:** 276

steel industry **VII:** 297

Taylor, Frederick W. **VII:** 306–307

Scientific Revolution **II:** 330

Scientology **X:** 266

sciopodes **I:** 239

SCLC. *See* Southern Christian Leadership conference

Sclopsis, Federico **VI:** 310

Scofield, Cyrus Ingerson **VI:** 75, 243

Scofield Reference Bible **VI:** 75

Scopes, John **VI:** 37; **VII:** 62, 278, 361*c*

Scopes Trial **VI:** 37; **VII: 277–278**, 361*c*; **VIII:** 71

Darrow, Clarence **VII:** 62

John Thomas Scopes v. The State **VII:** 386–392

Mencken, H. L. **VII:** 181

religion **VII:** 261

science **VII:** 275

scorched-earth policy. *See* "total war"

Scorpion (prison ship) **III:** 139

Scorsese, Martin **X:** 198, 239, 240

Scotland **I:** 10, 187, 282, 309, 385*c*; **II:** 28, 41, 43, 108, 232, 405; **III:** 379; **VI:** 150; **X:** 329*c*

Scots-Irish immigrants **II:** 11, 263, 419*c*; **III:** 141, 173, 188, **322–323**

economy **II:** 102

English immigrants **II:** 109

indentured servitude **II:** 164

Maine **II:** 203

Montour, Andrew **II:** 233

New Hampshire **II:** 251

New Jersey **II:** 253

New York **II:** 261, 262

New York City **II:** 263

North Carolina **II:** 265

Paxton Boys **II:** 272

Pennsylvania **II:** 274

Philadelphia **II:** 281

population trends **II:** 291

Presbyterians **II:** 296

South Carolina **II:** 354

Virginia **II:** 385

women's status and rights **II:** 407

Scott, Adrian **IX:** 135

Scott, Dred **IV:** 301. *See also Dred Scott* decision

Scott, Hugh **X:** 276

Scott, Isaac E. **VI:** 15

Scott, Ridley **X:** 240

Scott, Thomas Alexander **VI: 258**

Carnegie, Andrew **VI:** 44

Great Strike of 1877 **VI:** 119

Hayes, Rutherford B. **VI:** 126

oil **VI:** 215

Scott, Winfield **IV:** *309,* **309–310**, 377*c*–379*c*

Aroostook War **IV:** 25

Balloon Corps **V:** 21

Black Hawk War **IV:** 53

Civil War **V:** 66

Fillmore, Millard **IV:** 137

Fort Sumter, South Carolina **V:** 137

Guadalupe Hidalgo, Treaty of (1848) **IV:** 165

habeas corpus, writ of **V:** 161

Jackson, "Stonewall" **V:** 185

Lee, Robert E. **V:** 205

McClellan, George B. **V:** 224

Medal of Honor **V:** 228

Mexican-American War **IV:** 234

monuments **V:** 239

Polk, James K. **IV:** 284

Porter, David Dixon **V:** 280

Santa Anna, Antonio López de **IV:** 304

Seminole wars **IV:** 312

tactics and strategy **V:** 345, 347

Union army **V:** 367

Webster-Ashburton Treaty (1842) **IV:** 360

Whig Party **IV:** 364

Scottish Highlanders **II:** 267

Scottsboro Boys **VIII:** *319,* **319–320**, 405*c*, 406*c*

African Americans **VIII:** 3

American Civil Liberties Union **VIII:** 13

Bethune, Mary McLeod **VIII:** 36

civil rights **VIII:** 61

Communists **VIII:** 65

NAACP **VIII:** 227

race and racial conflict **VIII:** 287

Scouts of the Prairies (Buntline) **VI:** 59

Scowcroft, Brent **X:** 306

Scranton, William **X:** 308

Screen Actors Guild (SAG) **X:** 258

screen printing **VI:** 212

Scripps, Edward W. **VI:** 212; **VII:** 142, 276

Scripps-Howard newspaper chain **VII:** 142; **VIII:** 286

Scruggs, William L. **VI:** 303

SCS. *See* Soil Conservation Service

Scudder, Vida **VI:** 259

Scudder's American Museum **VI:** 21

Scull, Nicolas **II:** 277

sculpture **II:** 25; **VI:** 15, 253, **258–259**; **VIII:** 22–23; **IX:** 20; **X:** 26

scurvy **I:** 2, 59; **II:** 90, 182; **V:** 230

SD. *See* Sicherheitsdienst

SDI. *See* Strategic Defense Initiative

SDP. *See* Social Democratic Party

SDS. *See* Students for a Democratic Society

Sea Around Us, The (Rachel Carson) **IX:** 49

Seabiscuit **VIII:** 338

Seabury, Samuel **III: 323**

sea charts. *See* cartography

"sea dogs" **II:** 284, 299

Seagram Building (New York) **IX:** 19

Sea Islands **II:** 151; **IV:** 354

Freedmen's Bureau **V:** 142

Port Royal, South Carolina, Experiment **V:** 280

Sherman's March through Georgia **V:** 323

Special Field Order No. 15 **V:** 332–333

Seale, Bobby **IX:** 7, 38, 39, 334*c*; **X:** 61

seal hunting **VI:** 26, 27

sealskins **II:** 133, 159

seamen laws **IV:** 151

séances **IV:** 325

sea otters **II:** 14, 16, 326

Searles, John E., Jr. **VI:** 180

Sears, Richard **VI:** 274

Sears, Richard Warren **VI:** 186

Sears, Roebuck and Company **VI:** 186; **VIII:** 341

Sears Tower **X:** 27

seashore **VII:** 257

"seasoning time" **II:** 235

SEATO. *See* Southeast Asia Treaty Organization

sea travel **IV:** 324

Seattle **X:** 330*c*

Seattle General Strike **VII:** 270, **278–279**, 359*c*

Seattle Metal Trades Council **VII:** 279

Sea Venture **I:** 29

Seaver, James Everett **II:** 173

SEC. *See* Securities and Exchange Commission

Seceder Church **IV:** 71, 72

secession **V: 310–313**, 312*m*, 406*c*
  abolition **V:** 4
  Alexander, Edward P. **V:** 7
  Baltimore, Maryland, riots **V:** 22
  Beauregard, Pierre **V:** 27
  Benjamin, Judah P. **V:** 27
  Booth, John Wilkes **V:** 33
  Brown, Joseph **V:** 39
  Buchanan, James **V:** 42
  Chesnut, Mary B. **V:** 58
  Civil War **V:** 65
  Confederate army **V:** 71
  Confederate States of America **V:** 75
  Copperheads **V:** 82
  Davis, Jefferson **V:** 89
  Democratic Party **IV:** 108; **V:** 94
  Early, Jubal A. **V:** 103
  employment **V:** 116
  fire-eaters **V:** 127, 128
  Forrest, Nathan Bedford **V:** 134
  Fort Sumter, South Carolina **V:** 135
  Greeley, Horace **V:** 158
  habeas corpus, writ of **V:** 161
  Hartford Convention **IV:** 170–171
  Houston, Sam **IV:** 175
  ironclad oath **V:** 182
  Jackson, "Stonewall" **V:** 185
  Johnson, Andrew **V:** 187, 188
  Lee, Robert E. **V:** 205
  Lincoln, Abraham **V:** 210
  Longstreet, James **V:** 214
  Mallory, Stephen R. **V:** 221
  Morrill Land-Grant Act **V:** 241
  Oates, William C. **V:** 257
  Pacific Railroad Act of 1862 **V:** 263
  public land policy **IV:** 288
  Reconstruction **V:** 291
  redemption **V:** 296
  Republican Party **IV:** 301–302; **V:** 301
  Richmond, Virginia **V:** 303
  Seward, William H. **V:** 314
  slavery **IV:** 318; **V:** 330
  states' rights **V:** 335–336
  Stephens, Alexander H. **V:** 336
  Sumner, Charles **V:** 343
  tariffs **V:** 348
  UDC **V:** 370
  Washington, D.C. **V:** 389

Yancey, William Lowndes **V:** 401
Secession Ordinances **V:** 128
Second Amendment **V:** 62; **X:** 137, 193
secondary education. *See* education, primary and secondary
secondary schools **IV:** 121; **VIII:** 94
Second Coming of Christ **IV:** 298, 299; **VI:** 242–243, 283
Second Continental Congress. *See* Continental Congress, Second
second front **VIII: 320–321,** 409*c*, 410*c*
  Anglo-American relations **VIII:** 17
  Casablanca Conference **VIII:** 52
  foreign policy **VIII:** 125
  Grand Alliance **VIII:** 137
  Hopkins, Harry **VIII:** 157
  Italian campaign **VIII:** 168
  Lend-Lease Act **VIII:** 185
  Marshall, George C. **VIII:** 206
  Normandy, invasion of **VIII:** 247
  Sicily **VIII:** 325
  Soviet-American relations **VIII:** 334
  Teheran Conference **VIII:** 354
  World War II European theater **VIII:** 391
Second Great Awakening. *See* Great Awakening, Second
Second Inaugural Address (Clinton) **X:** 355–357
second industrial revolution. *See* industrial revolution, second
Second New Deal. *See* New Deal, Second
Second Stage, The (Betty Friedan) **IX:** 115
Secord, Richard **X:** 315
Secotan (Secoton) **I: 320–321; II:** 401
secretaries of agriculture. *See* Agriculture Department
secretaries of state. *See* State Department
secretaries of war. *See* War Department
secret ballot **VI:** 95
Secret Diary of Harold L. Ickes **VIII:** 162
Secret Service **V:** 118; **X:** 149–150

secret service (England) **I:** 371, 372
"Secret Six" **V:** 38
secret societies **I:** 48; **VI:** 195–196, 221
sectionalism **VI:** 295–296
secularization **IV:** 70
Secularization Law of 1833 **IV:** 136
Securities Act of 1933 **VIII:** 322, 406*c*
Securities and Exchange Act of 1934 **VIII:** 321, 322, 406*c*
Securities and Exchange Commission (SEC) **VIII: 321–322,** 406*c;* **X:** 49
  Catholics **VIII:** 53
  Douglas, William O. **VIII:** 84
  Henderson, Leon **VIII:** 145
  Kennedy, Joseph P. **VIII:** 175–176
  New Deal **VIII:** 241
  Public Utility Holding Company Act **VIII:** 285
  stock market crash (1929) **VIII:** 341
securities fraud **V:** 408*c*
securities market reforms **VIII:** 35
security, corporate **X:** 74
Security Council **VIII:** 366, 401
Seddon, James A. **V:** 75
Sedgwick, Catharine Maria **IV:** 213
Sedgwick, John **V:** 13, 54
Sedima, S.P.R.L. v. Imrex Co. (1985) **X:** 258
Sedition Act **VII: 280,** 359*c;* **VIII:** 54
  Committee for Public Information **VII:** 52, 345
  conscription **VII:** 54
  Debs, Eugene V. **VII:** 65
  Fuel Administration **VII:** 102
  Palmer, A. Mitchell **VII:** 221
  radicalism **VII:** 250
  Schenk v. United States **VII:** 274
  socialism **VII:** 289
Seeger, Pete **IX:** 110–111, *111,* 217, 244
Segal, George **X:** 26
Segovia **I:** 190
segregation **II:** 114; **III:** 242; **VI:** 327*c;* **VII: 280–282; VIII:** 409*c;* **IX: 271,** 331*c,* 333*c. See also* desegregation; school desegregation

African-American movement **IX:** 4–5
African-American regiments **V:** 4
African Americans **VI:** 6; **VIII:** 3
AME Church **V:** 5
Army, U.S. **VIII:** 20
Arthur, Chester Alan **VI:** 16
Baker v. Carr **IX:** 31–32
baseball **VII:** 27
Birmingham confrontation **IX:** 37–38
Black Codes **V:** 30
Brown v. Board of Education **IX:** 42–43
Carter, James Earl, Jr. **X:** 57
CCC **VIII:** 63
cities and urban life **VII:** 50
civil rights **VIII:** 62
Civil Rights Act of 1964 **IX:** 57
civil rights cases **VI:** 56
Democratic Party **IX:** 79
Du Bois, W. E. B. **VII:** 72
education **VI:** 90
Federal Housing Administration **IX:** 110
Fourteenth Amendment **V:** 139
freedom rides **IX:** 113–114
Gentlemen's Agreement **VII:** 107
Great Migration **VII:** 111, 112
Jim Crow laws **VI:** 156–157
Johnson, Jack **VII:** 138
liberalism **X:** 175, 176
Malcolm X **IX:** 187
Mississippi Freedom Democratic Party **IX:** 206–207
Morrill Land-Grant Act **V:** 241
MOWM **VIII:** 201
Murray, Pauli **IX:** 215
Myrdal, Gunnar **VIII:** 225
NAACP **VII:** 199; **IX:** 220; **X:** 208
Operation Dixie **IX:** 235–236
Progressive Party **IX:** 249
race and racial conflict **VII:** 248, 249; **VIII:** 287, 288; **IX:** 253–255; **X:** 256
Randolph, A. Philip **VIII:** 291

religion **IX:** 256
Rickey, Branch **IX:** 260
Robinson, Jackie **IX:**
    262–263
sit-ins **IX:** 272–273
South Africa **X:** 279–280
Southern Manifesto **IX:**
    276
sports **VII:** 295; **IX:** 280
States' Rights Party **IX:**
    281
suburbs **VIII:** 343
Tanner, Benjamin Tucker
    VI: 283
Terrell, Mary Church **VII:**
    308
theater **V:** 352
Thurmond, J. Strom **X:**
    303
Tourgée, Albion W. **V:** 354
Universal Negro
    Improvement
    Association (UNIA)
    VII: 316
WAC **VIII:** 381
Wallace, George C. **X:** 313,
    314
Wilkins, Roy **IX:** 322
Wilson, Woodrow **VII:** 334
woman suffrage **VII:** 335
Seigenthaler, John **IX:** 114
seigneurs **I:** 149
Seinfeld (TV program) **X:** 295
Selassie, Haile **VIII:** 105
Selden, George **VI:** 150; **VII:** 96
selective serotonin reuptake
    inhibitors (SSRIs) **X:** 190
Selective Service **VIII:**
    322–324, 323, 409c; **X:** 76
    Army, U.S. **VIII:** 20
    civil liberties **VIII:** 60–61
    conscientious objectors
        VIII: 70–71
    foreign policy **VIII:** 124
    mobilization **VIII:** 214
    Roosevelt, Franklin D.
        VIII: 314
    socialists **VIII:** 327
    Wheeler, Burton K. **VIII:**
        378
    Willkie, Wendell L. **VIII:**
        379
    WMC **VIII:** 374, 375
    World War II home front
        VIII: 394
Selective Service Act **VII: 282,**
    359c; **VIII:** 409c
    American Expeditionary
        Force **VII:** 9
    Communists **VIII:** 65
    Congress **VIII:** 68
    conscription **VII:** 54

demobilization **VIII:** 79
La Follette, Robert M., Jr.
    VIII: 182
Norris, George W. **VIII:**
    249
Preparedness **VII:** 236
Selective Service **VIII:**
    322–324
Stimson, Henry L. **VIII:**
    340
Taft, Robert A. **VIII:** 349
World War I **VII:** 344
Selective Training and Service
    Act of 1940. *See* Selective
    Service Act
self-fulfillment, pursuit of
    family life **X:** 109, 110
    feminism **X:** 114
    New Age movement **X:**
        217
    recreation **X:** 261
self-governing charters **II:** 232
self-government **II:** 257
self-incrimination. *See* Fifth
    Amendment
self-mutilation **I:** 13
"Self-Reliance" (Emerson) **IV:**
    345
Selkirk, earl of **III:** 190
Selma, Alabama **IX:** 275, 284,
    311, 334c
semiconductor chips **IX:** 65
Seminole nation **II:** 352; **IV:**
    377c; **V:** 167; **VI:** 209. *See*
    also Five Civilized Tribes
    foreign policy **IV:** 142
    Horseshoe Bend, Battle of
        IV: 173
    Indian Removal Act (1830)
        IV: 181, 182m
    Jackson, Andrew **IV:** 192
    Native Americans **IV:** 256
    Native Americans in the
        War of 1812 **IV:** 260
    New Orleans, Battle of
        (1815) **IV:** 262
    race and race relations **IV:**
        291
    Taylor, Zachary **IV:** 334
    Trail of Tears **IV:** 343
Seminole Treaty **IV:** 377c
Seminole War
    Bragg, Braxton **V:** 36
    Johnston, Joseph E. **V:** 190
    Mallory, Stephen R. **V:** 221
    Meade, George Gordon **V:**
        226
    Sherman, William T. **V:**
        319
Seminole War, First (1817) **IV:**
    375c
    foreign policy **IV:** 142

Horseshoe Bend, Battle of
    IV: 173
Native Americans **IV:** 256
Seminole wars **IV:**
    311–312
Seminole War, First and Second
    IV: 311–312
Seminole War, Second
    (1835–42) **IV:** 377c
    Beckwourth, Jim **IV:** 46
    Colt, Samuel **IV:** 91
    election of 1840 **IV:** 124
    Florida **IV:** 140
    Native Americans **IV:** 256
    Scott, Winfield **IV:** 310
    Seminole wars **IV:** 312
    Taylor, Zachary **IV:** 334
Seminole War, Third (1855–58)
    IV: 256, 312
Semmelweis, Ignaz P. **IV:** 113,
    308
Semmes, Raphael **V:** 74, **313**
senado da câmara **I:** 33
Senate, U.S. **IX:** 331c; **X:**
    275–277, 326c, 331c. *See*
    also specific Senators
    abolition **V:** 4
    Abscam **X:** 4–5
    Adams, John Quincy **IV:** 4
    Adams-Onís Treaty **IV:** 5
    Agricultural Adjustment
        Act **VIII:** 5
    Army-McCarthy hearings
        IX: 19
    Banking Act of 1935 **VIII:**
        34
    Benjamin, Judah P. **V:** 27
    Benton, Thomas Hart **IV:**
        49
    Blaine, James Gillespie **VI:**
        31
    Blair, Francis P., Jr. **V:** 31
    Borah, William E. **VIII:** 40
    Bork, Robert **X:** 39
    Brown, Joseph **V:** 39
    Bruce, Blanche K. **V:** 40
    Bush, George W. **X:** 48
    Byrd, Robert **X:** 51
    Byrnes, James F. **VIII:** 48
    Calhoun, John C. **IV:** 63
    campaign finance **X:** 54
    Carter, James Earl, Jr. **X:**
        59
    Cass, Lewis **IV:** 76, 77
    Chase, Salmon P. **V:** 56
    Chesnut, Mary B. **V:** 58
    Civil Rights Act of 1957
        IX: 55
    Civil Rights Act of 1960
        IX: 55, 56
    Civil Rights Act of 1964
        IX: 56

Claiborne, William C. C.
    IV: 85
Clay, Henry **IV:** 87, 88
Clayton-Bulwer Treaty **IV:**
    89
Clinton, DeWitt **III:** 73
Compromise of 1850 **IV:**
    94
Congress **VI:** 63, 64; **VII:**
    53; **VIII:** 67, 68, 68t
Congressional Budget and
    Impoundment Act **X:** 75
Dana, Richard Henry **IV:**
    103
Democratic Party **V:** 94;
    VII: 65; **VIII:** 80–82
Dole, Robert **X:** 90
Douglas, Stephen A. **V:** 98
Eagleton, Thomas F. **X:** 93
education, federal aid to
    VI: 92
election of 1932 **VIII:** 96
election of 1936 **VIII:** 97
election of 1940 **VIII:** 98
elections **IX:** 94–97
Emergency Banking Act of
    1933 **VIII:** 101
ERA **X:** 105, 106
Fillmore, Millard **IV:** 137
flag burning **X:** 118
foreign policy **VII:** 100
Frémont, John C. **IV:** 154
Gadsden Purchase **IV:** 159
Gingrich, Newton L. **X:**
    129
Gore, Albert, Jr. **X:** 133
Harding, Warren G. **VII:**
    117
Harrison, William Henry
    IV: 169
Helms, Jesse A., Jr. **X:**
    140–141
Hill, Anita Faye **X:** 141
House of Representatives
    X: 145
Houston, Sam **IV:** 174, 175
impeachment **III:** 175; **X:**
    150
impeachment of Andrew
    Johnson **V:** 177, 178,
    179
Jackson, Andrew **IV:** 191
Johnson, Andrew **V:** 188,
    189
Johnson, Hiram Warren
    VII: 138
Joint Committee on the
    Conduct of War **V:** 191
Kansas-Nebraska Act of
    1854 **V:** 197, 198
Keating-Owen Act **VII:**
    145

Senate, U.S. (continued)
Kellogg-Briand Treaty **VII:** 146
Kennedy, Edward M. **X:** 163–164
La Follette, Robert **VII:** 155
Lincoln, Abraham **V:** 210
Lodge, Henry Cabot **VII:** 165
Mallory, Stephen R. **V:** 221
McGovern, George Stanley **X:** 184
Medal of Honor **V:** 228
Mitchell, George **X:** 194–195
Mondale, Walter F. **X:** 196
NEA,NEH **X:** 209
Neutrality Acts **VIII:** 239
Nixon, Richard M. **X:** 219
NLRA **VIII:** 229
Norris, George W. **VIII:** 248
nuclear freeze movement **X:** 224
Oregon Treaty of 1846 **IV:** 270
OWM **VIII:** 258
Pacific Railroad Act of 1862 **V:** 263
Pickering, John **III:** 276
Pierce, Franklin **V:** 275
Pinchback, Pinckney B. S. **V:** 275–276
political parties **X:** 238
political parties, third **VI:** 225
politics **VII:** 229
politics in the Roosevelt era **VIII:** 270–273
population trends **V:** 279
the presidency **VI:** 230
presidential campaigns **VI:** 231
Public Utility Holding Company Act **VIII:** 285
Quayle, J. Danforth **X:** 253
Reagan, Ronald W. **X:** 259, 260
Reconstruction **V:** 294
reconversion **VIII:** 295
republicanism **III:** 302–303
Republican Party **V:** 302; **VII:** 262
Revels, Hiram R. **V:** 303
RFRA **X:** 266
Schurz, Carl **VI:** 256
Sherman, Roger **III:** 325
Starr, Kenneth **X:** 287
Stockton, Robert Field **IV:** 328

Sumner, Charles **V:** 341–343
Supreme Court **X:** 291
Teamsters Union **IX:** 292–293
Thomas, Clarence **X:** 302
Thurmond, J. Strom **X:** 303
Tyler, John **IV:** 348
Van Buren, Martin **IV:** 351
Wade, Benjamin **V:** 385
Wagner, Robert F. **VIII:** 372–373
Watergate scandal **X:** 316
Wheeler, Burton K. **VIII:** 378
Wilmot Proviso **V:** 396
woman suffrage **VII:** 337
Senate Foreign Relations Committee **VII:** 165
Senate majority leader **VIII:** 66, 349
Seneca Falls Women's Rights Convention of 1848 **IV:** 313–315, 378c; **VI:** 12, 107; **X:** 113
Bloomer, Amelia **IV:** 53
Declaration of Sentiments **IV:** 405–407
Douglass, Frederick **V:** 100
female antislavery societies **IV:** 136
Fuller, Margaret **IV:** 156
Mott, Lucretia **IV:** 247
NWSA **V:** 248
Stanton, Elizabeth Cady **V:** 334
women's status and rights **IV:** 368; **V:** 397
Seneca Haudenosaunee. See Iroquois
Seneca nation **I:** 160, 181–183, 321; **IV:** 259, 375c; **V:** 249, 264
Beaver Wars **II:** 31
Brulé, Étienne **II:** 44
captivity **II:** 52
Conestoga **II:** 67
Cornplanter **III:** 91
Dekanawideh **II:** 85
Handsome Lake **III:** 164
Iroquois **II:** 168, 169
Iroquois Confederacy **III:** 178
Jemison, Mary **II:** 173
Native Americans **II:** 243
New Netherland **II:** 256
Pickering, John **III:** 276
Pontiac's Rebellion **III:** 281
Senegal **I:** 66, 135, 195; **II:** 43, 74, 200, 229, 343

Senegambia **I:** 66, 185, 321–322, 327, 329, 330; **II:** 4
seniority **VII:** 54
Sennett, Mack **VII:** 85, 191
sensationalism **VI:** 211, 235, 327c. See also yellow journalism
Sentinel Defense System (Nike X) **X:** 22–23, 132
Separate Baptists **II:** 29
"separate but equal" doctrine **VI:** 224–225, 349–354. See also Brown v. Board of Education; Plessy v. Ferguson
separation of church and state. See church and state, separation of
separatist movement **IX:** 6, 7
Separatists **I:** 298; **II:** 212, 219, 236, 283, 304
Sephardic Jews **I:** 191, 192; **II:** 174, 175
September 11, 2001, terrorist attacks **X:** 328c
Bush, George W. **X:** 48
defense policy **X:** 88
economy **X:** 96
foreign policy **X:** 125
Powell, Colin L. **X:** 247
Senate **X:** 276
terrorism **X:** 297, 300
septicemia **IV:** 230
Sepúlveda, Juan Ginés de **I:** 200, 322
Sequeira, Diogo Lopes de **I:** 335
sequels, movie **X:** 198
sequence-controlled calculator **IX:** 97
sequestration **X:** 134, 135
Sequoia National Park **VI:** 65
Sequoyah **IV:** 257, 376c
Serapis, HMS **III:** 90, 190, 394c
Serbia **VII:** 343; **X:** 329c, 330c
Albright, Madeleine K. **X:** 18
Clinton, William **X:** 69
Dayton accords **X:** 85
defense policy **X:** 88
Serer **I:** 321
serfs **I:** 20
Sgt. Pepper's Lonely Hearts Club Band (Beatles) **X:** 36
"serious" literature **X:** 177
sermons **II:** 173–174
Serra, Junípero **II:** 331, 331–332; **IV:** 64, 69
Serra, Richard **X:** 26
Serrano, Andres **X:** 209
servants **VII:** 172
Servetus, Michael **I:** 50
service industries **X:** 94, 171

Serviceman's Readjustment Act of 1944 (G.I. Bill) **IX:** 78, 90, 91, 307
service sector **IX:** 44, 45, 52, 90, 271–272
Services of Colored Americans in the Wars of 1776 and 1812 (Nell) **IV:** 379c
sesame **II:** 122
Seton, Elizabeth Ann **IV:** 315, 315–316
Seton, William **IV:** 315
settlement house movement **VI:** 259–260, 326c; **VIII:** 310
Addams, Jane **VII:** 2–3
Aesthetic movement **VI:** 3
criminal justice **VII:** 59
education **VI:** 92
immigration **VI:** 140
New Woman **VII:** 214
progressivism in the 1890s **VI:** 233
religion **VII:** 260
Riis, Jacob A. **VI:** 248
social work **VII:** 289
Wald, Lillian **VII:** 329
Seven Cities of Cíbola
New Mexico **I:** 256
pueblo **I:** 295
Ramusio, Giovanni Battista **I:** 305
Zuni **I:** 383
Seven Cities of Gold **I:** 88
Seven Days' Battle
Balloon Corps **V:** 22
homefront **V:** 169
Jackson, "Stonewall" **V:** 186
Lee, Robert E. **V:** 206
Longstreet, James **V:** 215
McClellan, George B. **V:** 225
Peninsular campaign **V:** 270
700 Club, The **X:** 294
Seven Pines, Battle of
Armistead, Lewis A. **V:** 15
Johnston, Joseph E. **V:** 190
Lee, Robert E. **V:** 205–206
Longstreet, James **V:** 215
Peninsular campaign **V:** 269
Seven Sisters (oil companies) **VII:** 218, 296
Seventeenth Amendment **VII:** 335, 358c. See also direct election of senators
Seventh-Day Adventist Church **IV:** 299; **VI:** 242
73rd U.S. Colored Infantry **V:** 84
Seven Years' War **II:** 332–334, 333m, 419c, 420c; **IV:** 139,

156. *See also* French and
Indian War
    Acadians **II:** 2
    Braddock, Edward **II:** 38
    British Empire **II:** 41
    Bute, earl of **III:** 55
    captivity **II:** 52
    Cherokee **II:** 58
    Clinton, Sir Henry **III:** 75
    Cornstalk **II:** 72
    Cornwallis, Lord **III:** 92,
        93
    Croghan, George **II:** 76
    De Lancey, James **II:** 85
    exploration **II:** 115
    Flashman, Edward **II:** 119
    Florida **II:** 121
    Fort Necessity **II:** 123
    forts **II:** 124
    Fort William Henry
        Massacre **II:** 124, 125
    French colonies **II:** 126,
        129
    fur trade **II:** 132
    Georgia **II:** 138
    government, British
        American **II:** 146
    Howe, George Augustus,
        Viscount **II:** 158
    Iroquois **II:** 169
    Johnson, Sir William **II:**
        177
    journalism **II:** 178, 179
    King's College **II:** 184–185
    Lee, Charles **III:** 205
    Livingston, Philip **II:** 195
    Massachusetts **II:** 214
    McDougall, Alexander **III:**
        239
    Mittelberger, Gottlieb **II:**
        231
    Monckton, Robert **II:**
        232–233
    Montour, Andrew **II:** 233
    Native Americans **II:** 247
    Neolin **II:** 248
    New Hampshire **II:** 251
    New York **II:** 262
    North Carolina **II:** 264
    Ostenaco **II:** 269
    Pennsylvania **II:** 274, 276
    privateering **II:** 300
    Quakers **II:** 308
    Roman Catholics **II:** 323,
        324
    society, British American
        II: 352
    South Carolina **II:** 353
    Spanish colonies **II:** 359
    Steuben, Frederick von
        III: 334
    Teedyuscung **II:** 370

Treaty of Paris **II:** 378
Tuscarora **II:** 379
Virginia **II:** 385
Walking Purchase of 1737
    II: 390
Wolfe, James **II:** 404–405
Severn, Battle of **II:** 209
Sevier, John **II:** 392; **III:**
    135–136
Seville **I: 322–323**
    Casa de Contratación **I:**
        59, 60
    Council of the Indies **I:** 95
    gold **I:** 142
    slavery **I:** 327
    Vespucci, Amerigo **I:** 367
Sewall, Arthur M. **VI:** 223
Sewall, Samuel **II:** 1, *1*, 96, 215,
    334, 346
Seward, William H. **IV:** 94–95,
    363; **V: 313–315,** *314*, 406*c*,
    408*c*; **VI:** 31
    abolition **V:** 4
    assassination of Abraham
        Lincoln **V:** 17
    Blair, Francis P., Jr. **V:** 30
    Dred Scott decision **V:** 101
    employment **V:** 116
    foreign policy **V:** 131–133
    Fort Sumter, South
        Carolina **V:** 137
    Greeley, Horace **V:** 158
    Republican Party **V:** 301
    slavery **V:** 329
    Stanton, Edwin M. **V:** 334
    Sumner, Charles **V:** 343
    Welles, Gideon **V:** 391
"Seward's Folly" **V:** 133, 315
sewer districts **IX:** 125
sewer systems **VI:** 54–55
sewing machine **V:** 181, 308,
    310
sex, premarital **VII:** 283
Sex and the City **X:** 241
Sexes Throughout Nature, The
    (Blackwell) **VI:** 30
Sexias, Gershom **II:** 175
Sex Pistols **X:** 240
sex roles/sexual equality. *See*
    gender
Sexton, Anne **IX:** 183
sexual abuse **IV:** 319, 367
*Sexual Behavior in the Human
    Female* (Alfred C. Kinsey) **IX:**
    163
*Sexual Behavior in the Human
    Male* (Alfred C. Kinsey) **IX:**
    163, 330*c*
sexual conduct **IV:** 171
sexual harassment **X:** 329*c*
    Clinton, William **X:** 68
    Hill, Anita Faye **X:** 141

Judicial Watch **X:** 162
NAACP **X:** 209
Rehnquist, William H. **X:**
    265
Starr, Kenneth **X:** 287
Thomas, Clarence **X:** 302
sexual identity scale **IX:** 162
Sexual Inversion (Ellis) **VII:** 84
sexuality **IV:** 369; **V:** 283–284;
    VI: 304; **VII:** 102, **282–283;**
    VIII: 273, 274
    AIDS **X:** 5–6
    birth control. *See* birth
        control
    Ellis, Havelock **VII:** 84
    feminism **X:** 116
    gay rights movement **X:**
        127
    gays and lesbians **IX:**
        119–120
    Goldman, Emma **VII:** 110
    Kinsey, Alfred C. **IX:**
        162–163
    marriage **X:** 182
    "the pill" **IX:** 242
    Presley, Elvis **IX:** 247–248
    Sanger, Margaret **VII:**
        273–274
    women's status and rights
        VII: 339
sexually transmitted diseases **V:**
    283, 284; **VII:** 242
sexual mores **IV:** 326
    birth control. *See* birth
        control
    Committee for Public
        Information **VII:** 346
    Ellis, Havelock **VII:** 84
    entertainment **VII:** 87
    Freud, Sigmund **VII:** 101,
        102
    radicalism **VII:** 251
    radical press **VII:** 252
    recreation **VII:** 256–257
    sexuality **VII:** 283
    women's status and rights
        VII: 339, 340
Sexual Politics (Millet) **X:** 320,
    323*c*
sexual revolution **X: 277–278**
    birth control **X:** 36
    censorship **X:** 60
    family life **X:** 109
    gay rights movement **X:**
        127
    marriage **X:** 181
Seymour, Horatio **V:** 31, 79,
    189, 408*c*; **VI:** 289
Seymour, Jane **I:** 74, 160
Seymour, John **II:** 210
Seymour, William **VII:** 261
Sforza, Lodovico **I:** 204

*Sgt. Pepper's Lonely Hearts
    Club Band* (Beatles) **IX:** 36
Shaara, Michael **V:** 213
Shadow, The **VIII:** 376
Shadows of Our Social System
    (Blackwell) **VI:** 30
Sha'fi, Al- **I:** 184
Shaftesbury, earl of. *See* Cooper,
    Anthony Ashley, Lord
Shaheen, Jeanne **X:** 321
Shakers **III:** 204, **323–324,**
    392*c*; **IV:** 299, 308
Shakespeare, William **I:** 118,
    323–325, 343–344; **II:** 135,
    373; **V:** 352
Shakespeare's plays **VI:** 286
Shakur, Tupac **X:** 240
shallops **II:** 130–131, 377
shamans **I:** 2, 31; **II:** *318,*
    334–335
    Huron **II:** 160
    medicine **II:** 220
    midwives **II:** 225
    Native Americans **II:** 246
    religion, Native American
        II: 317
    women's status and rights
        II: 408
Shame of the Cities, The
    (Steffens) **VII:** 140, 192, 299
Shamokin **II:** 233
Shango (Chango) **I:** 263, 273
Shannon, HMS **IV:** 152, 358
Shannon, James A. **IX:** 222
sharecropping **V: 315–316; VII:**
    111–112; **VIII:** 407*c*; **IX:** 7–8
    African Americans **VIII:** 2
    Agricultural Adjustment
        Act **VIII:** 6
    agriculture **V:** 6
    banking and currency **V:**
        24
    Black Codes **V:** 30
    carpetbaggers **V:** 50
    Communists **VIII:** 65
    employment **V:** 116
    Freedmen's Bureau **V:** 143
    Ku Klux Klan **V:** 199
    plantations **V:** 276, 277
    population trends **V:** 279
    race and racial conflict
        VIII: 288
    Reconstruction **V:** 294
    Singleton, Benjamin **V:** 327
    slavery **V:** 331
    South **VIII:** 332
    STFU **VIII:** 332–333
"Share Our Wealth" Plan **VIII:**
    407*c*
    Long, Huey P. **VIII:** 195
    Revenue Act of 1935 **VIII:**
        308

"Share Our Wealth" Plan
    (continued)
        Second New Deal **VIII:**
            321
        taxation **VIII:** 351
        Union Party **VIII:** 365
Sharpe, George H. **V:** 118
Sharpeville massacre (South
    Africa) **IX:** 4; **X:** 279
Sharpsburg. *See* Antietam/
    Sharpsburg, Battle of
Sharpton, Al **X:** 12
Shasta nation **I:** 48 **IV:** 64
Shaw, Anna Howard **VI:** *260*,
    260–261; **VII:** 44, 198, 335
Shaw, George Bernard **VI:** 62
Shaw, Josephine **V:** 203
Shaw, Lemuel **IV:** 204
Shaw, Robert Gould **VI:** 253
    African-American
        regiments **V:** 5
    Carney, William H. **V:** 49
    54th Massachusetts
        Regiment **V:** 124–126
    Washington, D.C. **V:** 389
Shaw Memorial **VI:** 253, *254*
Shawnee nation **III:** 393*c*
    Blue Jacket **III:** 41
    captivity **II:** 52
    Cornstalk **II:** 72
    Croghan, George **II:** 76
    Dragging Canoe **III:** 107
    Dunmore, Lord **III:** 109
    foreign policy **IV:** 141
    Harrison, William Henry
        IV: 168–169
    Jemison, Mary **II:** 173
    Montour, Andrew **II:** 233
    Native Americans **IV:** 255
    Native Americans and the
        Revolution **III:** 255
    Native Americans in the
        War of 1812 **IV:** 258
    New Orleans, Battle of
        (1815) **IV:** 262
    Paxton Boys **II:** 272
    Pennsylvania **II:** 274
    revitalization movements
        II: 320
    Tecumseh **III:** 345
Shawnee Prophet, the. *See*
    Prophet, the Shawnee. *See
    also* Tenskwatawa
Shaw v. Hunt (1996) **X:** 329*c*
Shaw v. Reno (1993) **X:** 328*c*
Shays, Christopher **X:** 53, 54,
    236
Shays's Rebellion **III: 324–325,**
    394*c;* **IV:** 175
    Connecticut Wits **III:** 80
    Constitutional Convention
        III: 82

economy **III:** 113
literature **III:** 215
riots **III:** 309
Sullivan, John **III:** 337
Tyler, Royall **III:** 353
Shearer, William K. **X:** 20
Sheeler, Charles **VI:** 48
Sheen, Fulton J. **VIII:** 53; **IX:**
    257
sheep **II:** 12, 166, 247, 370, 405
sheet music **IV:** 250; **V:** 137;
    VII: 308–309
Sheftall, Mordecai **III:** 187
Shelby, Isaac **III:** 107
Shelby, Joe **V:** 285
Sheldon, Ronald **VI:** 290
Shelikhov, Grigorii **II:** 326; **III:**
    8
Shelley v. Kraemer **IX:** 42
shellfish **II:** 121
shell trade **I:** 11
Shelton, Robert M., Jr. **IX:** *166,*
    166–167
Shenandoah (dirigible) **VII:** 187
Shenandoah, CSS **V:** 74
Shenandoah Valley: Jackson's
    campaign **V: 316–317**
    Boyd, Belle **V:** 34
    cartography **V:** 51
    Ewell, Richard Stoddert **V:**
        118
    Jackson, "Stonewall" **V:**
        185
    Peninsular campaign **V:**
        267, 269
Shenandoah Valley: Sheridan's
    campaign **V: 317–318,** 347
Shepard, Alan B. **IX:** 219, 278,
    278, 294, 333*c*
Shepard, Jeremiah **II:** 408
Shepard, Sam **X:** 242
Sheppard, Morris **VII:** 241
Sheppard-Towner Act **VII:**
    283–284; VIII: 208
    Abbott, Grace **VII:** 1
    Children's Bureau **VII:** 47
    ERA **VII:** 88
    Kelley, Florence **VII:** 146
    public health **VII:** 243
    women's status and rights
        VII: 340
Sherard, William **II:** 55
Sherbert v. Verner (1963) **X:** 266
Sheridan, Philip H. **IV:** 180; **V:**
    318–319; VI: 98, 213
    Appomattox Court House,
        Virginia **V:** 14
    Early, Jubal A. **V:** 103
    elections **V:** 110
    Five Forks, Battle of **V:** 129
    Grant, Ulysses S. **V:** 156
    monuments **V:** 239

Mosby, John Singleton **V:**
    242
Petersburg campaign **V:**
    272
Shenandoah Valley:
    Sheridan's campaign **V:**
    317–318
    tactics and strategy **V:** 347
    Wilderness, Battle of the
        V: 395
Sherman, Cindy **X:** 26
Sherman, John **V:** 288, 320; **VI:**
    73, 108, 232, **261**
Sherman, Roger **III:** 87, 228,
    325, 393*c,* 395*c*
Sherman, William T. **V:**
    319–321, *320,* 407*c;* **VI:** 39,
    213
    Anderson, Robert **V:** 10
    Andersonville Prison **V:** 10
    Atlanta campaign **V:** 19, 20
    Bentonville, Battle of **V:** 28
    Blair, Francis P., Jr. **V:** 30
    Chattanooga, Battle of **V:**
        57
    Civil War **V:** 66
    Copperheads **V:** 82
    elections **V:** 110
    emancipation **V:** 113
    foraging **V:** 130
    Forrest, Nathan Bedford
        V: 133
    Freedmen's Bureau **V:** 142
    Georgia. *See* Sherman's
        March through Georgia
    German-American
        regiments **V:** 147
    Grant, Ulysses S. **V:** 156
    homefront **V:** 169
    Hood, John Bell **V:** 171
    Howard, O. O. **V:** 173
    Johnston, Joseph E. **V:** 190
    journalism **V:** 193–194
    Lookout Mountain, Battle
        of **V:** 216
    March to the Sea. *See*
        Sherman's March
        through Georgia
    Native Americans **V:** 249
    Overland campaign **V:** 260
    Petersburg campaign **V:** 272
    photography **V:** 273
    Port Royal, South
        Carolina, Experiment **V:**
        280
    Red River campaign **V:**
        298
    Shiloh, Battle of **V:** 324,
        326
    Special Field Order No. 15
        V: 332
    tactics and strategy **V:** 347

Thomas, George H. **V:** 354
Union army **V:** 367
Vicksburg campaign **V:** 380
Wheeler, Joseph **V:** 392
Sherman Antitrust Act of 1890
    VI: 261–262, 326*c,* 327*c,*
    343–344; **VII:** 356*c,* 358*c*
    Buck's Stove **VII:** 36
    business **VII:** 39
    business and government
        VI: 40
    Capper-Volstead Act **VII:**
        42
    Clayton Antitrust Act **VII:**
        51
    Danbury Hatters **VII:** 61
    Debs, Eugene V. **VII:** 65
    Harlan, John Marshall **VI:**
        122
    Harrison, Benjamin **VI:**
        123
    Hill, James J. **VI:** 129
    Hoar, George Frisbie **VI:**
        130
    labor movement **VII:** 152
    *Northern Securities Co. v.
        U.S.* **VII:** 216
    oil industry **VII:** 217
    the presidency **VI:** 230
    progressivism **VII:** 237
    Pullman Strike **VI:** 236
    railroads **VI:** 239
    Reed, Thomas Brackett
        VI: 240
    Sherman, John **VI:** 261
    Standard Oil **VII:** 296
    Supreme Court **VI:** 281
    Tarbell, Ida **VII:** 305
    trusts **VI:** 294, 295
Sherman Monument **VI:** 253
Sherman Silver Purchase Act of
    1890 **VI:** 326*c,* 327*c*
    bimetallism **VI:** 29
    Bland-Allison Act **VI:** 32
    Bryan, William Jennings
        VI: 37
    business cycles **VI:** 42
    Cleveland, Grover **VI:**
        58–59
    Crime of '73 **VI:** 70
    currency issue **VI:** 73
    Free-Silver movement **VI:**
        105
    Harrison, Benjamin **VI:**
        123
    the presidency **VI:** 230
    Sherman, John **VI:** 261
Sherman's March through
    Georgia **V: 321–323,** 322*m,*
    407*c*
    Blair, Francis P., Jr. **V:** 30
    cartography **V:** 51

foraging **V:** 130
Hood, John Bell **V:** 171
Native Americans **V:** 249
Orphan Brigade **V:** 258
plantations **V:** 276
rules of war **V:** 306
Sherman, William T. **V:** 321
Special Field Order No. 15 **V:** 332
tactics and strategy **V:** 347
Wheeler, Joseph **V:** 392
Sherman tank **VIII:** 349–350
Sherrill, Charles **VI:** 290
Shetland Islands **I:** 263
Shields, James **V:** 185, 316
Shi'i Muslims **I:** 184
Shikellamy **II:** 393
Shiloh, Battle of **V: 323–326,** 325m, 406c
Beauregard, Pierre **V:** 27
Bickerdyke, "Mother" **V:** 29
Bragg, Braxton **V:** 36
Civil War **V:** 66
Cleburne, Patrick Ronayne **V:** 67
common soldier **V:** 70
Confederate army **V:** 73
Cumming, Kate **V:** 85
Forrest, Nathan Bedford **V:** 134
German-American regiments **V:** 147
Grant, Ulysses S. **V:** 156
homefront **V:** 169
Johnston, Albert Sidney **V:** 189
Mississippi River **V:** 234
Morgan, John Hunt **V:** 240
Orphan Brigade **V:** 258
Sherman, William T. **V:** 320
Thomas, George H. **V:** 354
Shiloh (Foote) **V:** 213
Shiloh National Military Park **V:** 239
Shinnecock Hills Golf Club **VI:** 274, 275
shipbuilding **II: 335; V:** 236; **VI:** 193; **VIII: 324–325**
Acts of Trade and Navigation **II:** 3
artisans **II:** 26
Atlantic, Battle of the **VIII:** 28
Boston **II:** 35
Chesapeake Bay **II:** 58
CIO **VIII:** 70
Connecticut **II:** 69
economy **II:** 101
environment **II:** 110–111

forests **II:** 122
Kaiser, Henry J. **VIII:** 175
labor **VIII:** 181
Maine **II:** 203
manufacturing and industry **II:** 203, 204
Maryland **II:** 210
Massachusetts **II:** 214, 215
medicine **VIII:** 209
migration **VIII:** 213
mobilization **VIII:** 215
monarchy, British **II:** 231
Navy, U.S. **VIII:** 237
New Hampshire **II:** 250
Newport **II:** 258
Plymouth **II:** 288
St. Mary's City **II:** 328
slave trade **II:** 343
society, British American **II:** 350
South **VIII:** 332
steel industry **VIII:** 339
Sunbelt **VIII:** 344
trade and shipping **II:** 376, 377
Shippen, Margaret **III:** 21
Shippen, William, Jr. **II: 335–336; III:** 241
Shipping Act of 1916 **VII:** 314
shipping industry **VI:** 192–193; **VII:** 314–315
ships **II:** 300, 336, 343, 356. *See also* warships
brigantine **I:** 34–35
caravel **I:** 55, 55–56
invention and technology **I:** 179–180
Norse **I:** 263
Spanish Armada **I:** 334
Shirley, William **II:** 17, 85, 182, 214; **III:** 170
Shirtwaist Makers Strike **VII: 284–285,** 357c
International Ladies' Garment Workers Union **VII:** 132
National Women's Trade Union League **VII:** 205
Triangle Shirtwaist Fire **VII:** 311–312
Wald, Lillian **VII:** 329
Shock, Albert **VI:** 28
Shockley, William **IX:** 64, 330c; **X:** 72
"shoddy" **V:** 362–363, 387
shoe manufacturing **V:** 180
shoes **V:** 363; **VIII:** 292
Shokaku **VIII:** 74
shopping malls **X:** 33
Short, Walter **VIII:** 264
Short Account of the Destruction of the Indies

(Bartolomé de Las Casas) **I:** 387c
shortages **VIII:** 394
short sword **I:** 356–357
Shoshone nation **III:** 210–211, 315
Shotts, John **VI:** 274
Shotwell, James T. **VII:** 43, 101, 146
Shouse, Jouett **VIII:** 15
Show Boat (Ferber) **VII:** 161
Show Boat (Kern-Hammerstein) **VII:** 85; **VIII:** 309
Shreve, Lamb and Harmon **VIII:** 22
Shriver, Robert Sargent, Jr. **X:** 93, 184, **278**
Shriver, Sargent **IX:** 132, 241
Shtueree **II:** 55
Shuffle Along (Sissle and Blake) **VII:** 85
Shulhan Arukh **I:** 191–192
Shulush Homa. *See* Red Shoes
Shute, Samuel **II:** 217
Shuteree **II:** 379
Shuttlesworth, Fred **IX:** 38, 191
Shy, John **III:** 305
Sibbes, Richard **II:** 73
Siberian Expedition **VII:** 270, **285–286**
Sibley, H. H. **V:** 73, 406c
Sicherheitsdienst (SD) **VIII:** 164, 263
Sicily **I:** 67; **VIII: 325–326,** 410c
amphibious warfare **VIII:** 15
Army, U.S. **VIII:** 19
Bradley, Omar N. **VIII:** 41
Casablanca Conference **VIII:** 52
Italian campaign **VIII:** 168
North African campaign **VIII:** 250
second front **VIII:** 320
World War II European theater **VIII:** 393
"Sick Chicken" decision. *See Schechter Poultry Corporation v. United States*
sickle-cell disease **II:** 91
Sickles, Daniel E. **V: 326–327; VI:** 231
Gettysburg, Battle of **V:** 148, 150
Meade, George Gordon **V:** 227
monuments **V:** 239
prostitution **V:** 284
Sidney, Algernon **II:** 273
Sidney, Sir Henry **I:** 141

Sidonia, Median **I:** 334
Siemens-Martin open-hearth process **VI:** 27, 276–277
Sierra Club **VI:** 65, 200; **VII:** 55; **VIII:** 103; **IX:** 101, 226
Sierra Leone **I:** 142, 156, 330; **II:** 4; **III:** 98, 99; **IV:** 21, 333; **VI:** 4; **X:** 307
Sierra Nevada
California Trail **IV:** 70
exploration **IV:** 131
Forty-niners **IV:** 146
gold, discovery and mining **IV:** 163
Murrieta, Joaquín **IV:** 248–249
Smith, Jedediah Strong **IV:** 322
Sigel, Franz **V:** 147, 265
Signal Corps **VII:** 382
Sigourney, Lydia **IV:** 167
Sigsbee, Charles D. **VI:** 187
Sikh **X:** 266
Sikonese. *See* Ciconicin
Silent Majority **IX:** 231, 258
"Silent Majority" speech (Nixon) **X:** 323c, 333–334
Silent Sentinels **VII:** 226, 336
Silent Spring (Carson) **IX:** 48, 49, 69, 101, 182, 270, 333c; **X:** 76, 210
silicon chip **X:** 324c
silk **I:** 29; **II:** 43, 225, 226; **VI:** 291
Silko, Leslie Marmon **X:** 177
Silla **I:** 321
Sillery Kahnawake **II:** 244
Sillery mission **II:** 127
Silliman, Benjamin **IV:** 308
silos **VI:** 8
Silver, Gray **VII:** 42
silver and silver mining **I: 325; II:** 221, 355, 358; **IV:** 43, 95–96, 118–119, 305; **V:** 105; **VI:** 194m; **VII:** 262; **VIII:** 5, 75
Andes Mountains **I:** 10
Cabot, Sebastian **I:** 43
Casa de Contratación **I:** 61
Castile **I:** 63
Charles V **I:** 69
Coeur d'Alene miners' strike **VI:** 60–61
Columbian Exchange **I:** 78
Coronado, Francisco **I:** 88
Crime of '73 **VI:** 69–70
currency issue **VI:** 72
Djibouti **I:** 109
Free-Silver movement **VI:** 104–105
gold **I:** 143
Mexico **I:** 235

silver and silver mining
   (continued)
      mining: metal and coal **VI**: 193
      New Spain **I**: 261
      Panama **I**: 277
      Peru **I**: 280
      Pizarro, Francisco **I**: 283
      Potosí **I**: 291
      Seville **I**: 323
      slavery **I**: 327
      Zacatecas **I**: 381
silver coin **IV**: 118–119
silver (currency) **IV**: 43. *See also* specie
      bimetallism **VI**: 28, 29
      Bland-Allison Act **VI**: 32
      business cycles **VI**: 42
      Crime of '73 **VI**: 69–70
      currency issue **VI**: 72, 73
      Democratic Party **VI**: 77–78
"Silver Kings" **IV**: 96
Silver Shirt League **VIII**: 19
silversmiths **II**: 215
Simmons, Robert J. **V**: 125
Simmons, William J. **VI**: 311
Simms, M. O. **IX**: 259–260
Simms, Willie **VI**: 134
Simon, Neil **X**: 242
Simon, William **X**: 103, 120, 301
Simon & Garfunkel **X**: 240
Simon and Schuster **X**: 178
Simons, Arthur D. **X**: 234
Simons, Elwin L. **IX**: 270
Simpson, Alan **X**: 149
Simpson, George **IV**: 228–229
Simpson, Howard N. **IV**: 112
Simpson, Jerry **VI**: **262–263**
Simpson, O. J. **X**: 60, 257, 329*c*
Simpson Mazzoli Act. *See* Immigration Reform and Control Act
Sinan **I**: 339
Sinatra, Frank **VIII**: 223, 224, **326**; **IX**: 13, 181, 216, 244; **X**: 240
Sinclair, Harry **VII**: 307
Sinclair, Upton **VII**: *286*, **286–287**, 356*c*
      business **VII**: 39
      literature **VII**: 160
      Meat Inspection Act **VII**: 178
      muckrakers **VII**: 192
      Pure Food and Drug Act **VII**: 244
      Steffens, Lincoln **VII**: 299
Singapore **VIII**: 398
Singer Manufacturing Company **VI**: 150

singing **IV**: 249
Singing Master's Assistant, or Key to Practical Music (Billings) **III**: 38
"singing plow" **IV**: 10
"single-member" district election system **X**: 238
"single tax" **VI**: 111, 325*c*
single-tax **VII**: 140
Singleton, Benjamin **V**: **327–328**; **VI**: 325*c*
Singleton, John **X**: 198
"Sinners in the Hands of an Angry God" (Edwards) **II**: 424–425
Sino-Japanese War **VIII**: 124, 164
Siouan **II**: 50, 149, 242–243
Sioux nation **II**: 150; **III**: 154, 210; **IV**: 53, 143, 144, 281; **V**: 213, 214, 408*c*; **VI**: *208*, 324*c*, 326*c*; **X**: 215
      Black Hills gold rush **VI**: 29
      buffalo, extermination of **VI**: 38
      Crazy Horse **VI**: 69
      Native Americans **VI**: 206–207
      Red Cloud **VI**: 239
      Sioux wars **VI**: 263
Sioux wars **IV**: 145; **VI**: **263**
      Black Hills gold rush **VI**: 29
      buffalo, extermination of **VI**: 38
      Crazy Horse **VI**: 69
      Native Americans **VI**: 206–208
      Red Cloud **VI**: 240
      Sitting Bull **VI**: 264
Sirhan, Bishara Sirhan **IX**: 159; **X**: 31
Sirica, John J. **X**: 220, 309, 316, 317
Sissle, Noble **VII**: 85
Sister Carrie (Dreiser) **VI**: 178; **VII**: 160
Sisters Freehold **II**: 40
Sistine Chapel **I**: 235, 236
site sculpture **X**: 26
sit-ins **IX**: **272–273**, 332*c*, 333*c*
      African-American movement **IX**: 5
      civil disobedience **IX**: 54
      Congress of Racial Equality **IX**: 67
      Free Speech Movement **IX**: 112
      King, Martin Luther, Jr. **IX**: 160

race and racial conflict **IX**: 253
Savio, Mario **IX**: 268
Student Nonviolent Coordinating Committee **IX**: 284
Sitobu **I**: 101, 243
Sitting Bull **V**: 214; **VI**: **263–264**, *264*, 324*c*
      Black Hills gold rush **VI**: 29
      Buffalo Soldiers **VI**: 39
      Cody, William Frederick **VI**: 60
      entertainment, popular **VI**: 98
      Native Americans **VI**: 207–209
      religion **VI**: 245
      Sioux wars **VI**: 263
situation comedies **IX**: 244, 296
Six-Day War of 1967 **IX**: 147; **X**: 54, 161–162
Six Nations of the Iroquois **I**: 181; **III**: 92, 255. *See also* Iroquois Confederacy
      Dekanawideh **II**: 85
      Johnson, Sir William **II**: 177
      New York **II**: 262
      North Carolina **II**: 264
      Tuscarora **II**: 379
      Tuscarora War **II**: 379
six-shooter **IV**: 307
1646, Treaty of **II**: 244
Sixteenth Amendment **VI**: 147; **VII**: 93, 263, 313, 358*c*; **VIII**: 351
Sixth Amendment **IX**: 103–104, 121–122, 206, 316
Sixth Massachusetts Infantry **V**: 22, 389
Sixth U.S. Colored Infantry **V**: 53
Six Towns (southern) Choctaw **II**: 60–61
63rd U.S. Colored Troops **V**: 104
Siyon, Amda **I**: 124
Sketch Book (Irving) **IV**: 212
Sketches of American Character (Hale) **IV**: 167
Skidmore, Thomas **IV**: 204
skiing **X**: 262
Skiko **II**: 401
skilled labor **IV**: 179, 203; **V**: 116; **VII**: 10, 12
skirmishing **V**: 346
Skylab space station **IX**: 220; **X**: 283
Skyline Drive (Virginia) **VIII**: 285

skyscrapers **VI**: **264–265**, *265*; **VII**: 16, 48, 50; **VIII**: 22, 405*c*; **X**: 27
      art and architecture **VI**: 14
      Bessemer process **VI**: 27
      chain stores **VI**: 47
      inventions and technology **VI**: 149
Slany, John **II**: 360–361
slash-and-burn **I**: 8, 12, 31
Slater, John **VI**: 94
Slater, Samuel **III**: **325–326**, 395*c*; **IV**: 118, 184
      economy **III**: 113
      immigration **III**: 173
      industrial revolution **III**: 177
      science **III**: 321
Slater Fund **VI**: 94
Slater Mill **III**: 20, 395*c*
Slaughterhouse cases **V**: 139; **VI**: 82, 281
"Slaughter Mountain" **V**: 53
slave catchers **V**: 224, 361–362
slave codes **II**: **336**, 418*c*, 419*c*
      African Americans **II**: 5
      Caribbean **II**: 53
      Great Awakening **II**: 148
      Le Moyne, Jean-Baptiste, sieur de Bienville **II**: 193
      New York City **II**: 263
      plantation system **II**: 286
      slave resistance **II**: 337
      slavery **II**: 338, 340, 342
      society, British American **II**: 349, 350
      South Carolina **II**: 354
      Stono Rebellion **II**: 361
slave rebellions/resistance **I**: 261, 330; **II**: **336–338**, 419*c*; **III**: 397*c*; **IV**: 7, 376*c*; **V**: 328
      African Americans **II**: 7; **III**: 7; **IV**: 7
      agriculture **II**: 12
      childhood **II**: 60
      crowd action **II**: 78
      Gabriel's Rebellion **III**: 145
      labor movements **IV**: 205
      New York **II**: 262
      New York City **II**: 263
      plantation system **II**: 286
      race and racial conflict **II**: 311
      religion **IV**: 297
      slavery **II**: 342; **III**: 327; **IV**: 316, 319
      slave trade **II**: 344
      society, British American **II**: 350, 351
      South Carolina **II**: 354

Stono Rebellion **II**: 361–362

Turner, Nat **IV**: *347*, 347–348

Vesey, Denmark **IV**: 353–354

West Indies **III**: 372

"Slavery in Massachusetts" (Thoreau) **IV**: 342

slaves, colonization/repatriation of **IV**: 375*c*; **VI**: 174–175

abolition/abolition movement **III**: 17; **IV**: 1–2; **V**: 1, 4

Cuffe, Paul **III**: 98, 99

Delany, Martin Robinson **V**: 93

Emancipation Proclamation **V**: 115

Forten, James **III**: 132

Garrison, William Lloyd **V**: 146

Jefferson, Thomas **III**: 184

Jones, Absalom **III**: 189

Liberia **IV**: 209–210

Liberty Party **IV**: 210

Negro Convention movement **IV**: 261

Pennington, James William Charles **V**: 270

race and race relations **IV**: 291; **V**: 288

religion **IV**: 296

slavery **V**: 328

slaves, fugitive **IV**: 139, 280, 311–312, 375*c*, 379*c*; **VI**: 125

African Americans **II**: 7

childhood **II**: 60

clothing **II**: 65

crowd action **II**: 78

Florida **II**: 120, 121

Fort Mose **II**: 123

slave resistance **II**: 337

Stono Rebellion **II**: 361

slaves as nurses **V**: 256

Slave's Friend **IV**: 14

Slaves in Algiers (Rowson) **III**: 311

slaves in Confederate military **V**: 76, 90

slave smuggling **IV**: 56

slaves/slavery **I**: **325–328**, 386*c*; **II**: **338–342**, *339*, **374**; **III**: **326–328**, *327*, 395*c*, 396*c*; **IV**: xiii, **316–319**, *317*, 318*m*, 375*c*–379*c*; **V**: **328–331**, 329*m*, *330*, 405*c*; **VII**: 280; **IX**: 271. *See also* forced labor

AASS **IV**: 13–15

abolition/abolition movement **II**: 1–2; **III**: 15; **IV**: 1–4; **V**: 1–4

ACS **IV**: 15–16

Africa **II**: 4

African-American churches, growth of **VI**: 3, 4

African-American regiments **V**: 4

African Americans **II**: 5–7; **III**: 5; **IV**: 6–9

agriculture **II**: 12, 13; **III**: 7; **IV**: 10, 11; **V**: 6

Alamo, The **IV**: 12

alcohol **II**: 15

Allen, Richard **III**: 10

AME Church **V**: 5

American Missionary Association **V**: 8

American System **IV**: 19

Amistad incident **IV**: 19–21

Anglican Church **II**: 20

animals **II**: 21

assassination of Abraham Lincoln **V**: 17

Austin, Stephen F. **IV**: 37

Aztecs **I**: 20

Bahía **I**: 24

Baltimore, Battle of **IV**: 39

Baltimore, Maryland, riots **V**: 22

Barbados **I**: 26

Beckwourth, Jim **IV**: 46

Beecher, Henry Ward **VI**: 24

Benezet, Anthony **II**: 31–32

Benton, Thomas Hart **IV**: 49–50

Bermuda Company **I**: 29–30

Blair, Francis P., Jr. **V**: 30

Bleeding Kansas **V**: 31–32

Booth, John Wilkes **V**: 32, 33

Brown, John **V**: 37–38

Brown, Joseph **V**: 39

Brown, William Wells **V**: 39–40

Bruce, Blanche K. **V**: 40–41

bubonic plague **I**: 286

Buchanan, James **V**: 41, 42

Burns, Anthony **IV**: 59

Butler, Benjamin **V**: 46

Cabeza de Vaca, Álvar Núñez **I**: 37

Calhoun, John C. **IV**: 63

California **IV**: 64, 65

Canary Islands **I**: 53

captivity **II**: 51

Carib **I**: 56

Caribbean **II**: 52

Cary, Ann Shadd **V**: 52

Cass, Lewis **IV**: 77

castas **I**: 61–62

Charleston **II**: 57

Chase, Salmon P. **V**: 56

Chesapeake Bay **II**: 57

Chesnut, Mary B. **V**: 58

childhood **II**: 60

Choctaw **II**: 61

Christiana, Pennsylvania, riot **V**: 59

cities and urban life **II**: 61–62

Civil Rights Act of 1866 **V**: 62

civil rights cases **VI**: 55–56

Civil War **V**: 63–67

Clark, William **III**: 73

class **II**: 63–64

Clay, Henry **IV**: 86–88

Clayton-Bulwer Treaty **IV**: 88

clothing **II**: 64, 65

common soldier **V**: 69

Compromise of 1850 **IV**: 93–95, 94*m*

Confederate States of America **V**: 75

Confiscation Acts **V**: 78

Connecticut **II**: 69

contrabands **V**: 80–81

Corps d'Afrique **V**: 83

cotton culture **IV**: 97–99

crafts **II**: 74

crime and punishment **II**: 74–76

Cuba **IV**: 101

Cuffe, Paul **III**: 99

Dana, Richard Henry **IV**: 103

dance **II**: 82

Davis, Jefferson **V**: 89, 90

Davis Bend, Mississippi, freedmen's colony **V**: 91–92

Declaration of Independence **III**: 102

Delaware **II**: 88

Democratic Party **IV**: 106–108; **V**: 93, 94; **VI**: 77

disease and epidemics **II**: 91; **IV**: 112

Douglas, Stephen A. **V**: 98–99

Douglass, Frederick **V**: 99–100

Dred Scott decision **V**: 100–102

Dunmore, Lord **III**: 108, 109

Dutch Reformed Church **II**: 97

economy **II**: 102; **IV**: 119; **V**: 105, 106

education **IV**: 121; **V**: 108

election of 1840 **IV**: 124

elections **V**: 109

emancipation **V**: 111–114

Emancipation Proclamation **V**: 114–115, 424

Emerson, Ralph Waldo **IV**: 126–127

employment **V**: 115, 116

encomienda **I**: 122

entertainment, popular **VI**: 96

environment **II**: 112

Equiano, Olaudah **III**: 118

Era of Good Feelings **IV**: 127

ethnocentrism **II**: 114

female antislavery societies **IV**: 135

Ferdinand and Isabella **I**: 128

fertility **II**: 117–118

filibustering **V**: 126, 127

Fillmore, Millard **IV**: 136, 137

fire-eaters **V**: 127–128

Fitzhugh, George **V**: 128

Florida **III**: 129

food **II**: 122

foreign policy **IV**: 142; **V**: 131, 132

Fort Mose **II**: 123

Franklin, Benjamin **III**: 135

Free-Soil Party **IV**: 150

fugitive slave laws **IV**: 154–155

Gabriel's Rebellion **III**: 145

Gadsden Purchase **IV**: 159

Garrison, William Lloyd **V**: 146

gender **II**: 137

Genius of Universal Emancipation **IV**: 160–161

Georgia **II**: 137–138

Gold Coast **I**: 144

Great Awakening **II**: 148

Greeley, Horace **V**: 158

Grimké, Angelina and Sarah **IV**: 164–165

Guadalupe Hidalgo, Treaty of (1848) **IV**: 165–166

Gullah **II**: 151–152

haciendas **I**: 149–150

Haiti **III**: 159

slaves/slavery *(continued)*
Hall, Prince **III:** 160
Hammon, Jupiter **II:** 153
Harpers Ferry, West
    Virginia **V:** 165
Hemmings, Sally **III:**
    164–165
Hispaniola **I:** 162
homefront **V:** 169
housing **II:** 157
Houston, Sam **IV:** 175
humanitarianism **III:** 170
indentured servitude **II:**
    164–165
Indian Removal Act (1830)
    IV: 183
Indians of the Desert
    Southwest **II:** 166
industrial development **V:**
    181
iron manufacturing **II:**
    168
Jackson, Andrew **IV:** 191
Jamestown **II:** 172
Jay, John **III:** 182
Jefferson, Thomas **III:**
    183, 184, 186
Johnson, Andrew **V:** 187
Johnson, Mary **II:** 175
Jones, Absalom **III:** 189
Kansas-Nebraska Act of
    1854 **V:** 197–198
Kelley, William D. **V:** 198
King Philip's War **II:** 184
Know-Nothing Party **IV:**
    201, 202
labor and labor movements
    II: 187–189; **III:** 199;
    IV: 203, 205
Langston, John Mercer **VI:**
    171, 172
Las Casas, Bartolomé de **I:**
    200
Laurens, Henry **III:**
    202–203
lead mines **IV:** 208
Lee, Richard Henry **III:**
    207
Le Moyne, Jean-Baptiste,
    sieur de Bienville **II:**
    193
Leo Africanus **I:** 203
Liberia **IV:** 209
Liberia, immigration to **VI:**
    174
Liberty Party **IV:** 211
Lincoln, Abraham **V:**
    208–210
literature **II:** 195; **IV:** 213;
    V: 212, 213
Locke, John **II:** 198
lost cause, the **V:** 217

Louisiana **II:** 199, 200
Lovejoy, Elijah **IV:** 214
lumbering **II:** 201
Madeira **I:** 214
Madison, James **III:** 228,
    230
Mali **I:** 218
Mallory, Stephen R. **V:** 221
Manifest Destiny **IV:** 218
Mann, Horace **IV:** 220
manufacturing and
    industry **II:** 204
marriage and family life **II:**
    206, 208; **III:** 233–235;
    IV: 221
Martinique **I:** 223
Maryland **II:** 210–211
Mason-Dixon Line **V:** 224
Massachusetts **II:** 214
Massachusetts Emigrant
    Aid Society **IV:** 223–224
McClellan, George B. **V:**
    225
Mecca **I:** 230
Metacom **II:** 223
Methodism **III:** 242
Mexican-American War
    IV: 232
middle passage **I:** 236
Middleton, Arthur **II:** 224
midwives **II:** 225
migration **IV:** 236
miscegenation **II:** 228; **V:**
    233
Mississippi River **V:** 236
Missouri Compromise of
    1820 **IV:** 236–238, 238*m*
Monroe, James **IV:** 240
Mormon War **IV:** 244
mortality **II:** 235
Mott, Lucretia **IV:** 247
Mount Vernon **II:** 237
mulattoes **II:** 238
music **II:** 239
Nast, Thomas **V:** 247
Natchez **I:** 251
Natchez Revolt **II:**
    241–242
Native Americans **II:** 243,
    246; **IV:** 256, 257; **V:**
    249, 251
Navajo **II:** 247
Negro Plot of 1741 **II:**
    247–248
New Jersey **II:** 253
New Netherland **II:** 257
New Orleans **II:** 258
New York **II:** 260, 262
New York City **II:** 262
North Carolina **II:** 265
Northwest Ordinances **III:**
    263

Oglethorpe, James Edward
    II: 267
"Olaudah Equiano's
    Account of his Capture
    and Enslavement" **II:**
    427–429
Olmstead, Frederick Law
    V: 257
Oñate, Juan de **I:** 271
Ostend Manifesto **V:** 259,
    260
Panama **I:** 277
Panic of 1819 **IV:** 276
Penn, William **II:** 273–274
Pennsylvania **II:** 275
Pequot **II:** 278
Pequot War **II:** 280
personal liberty laws **IV:**
    280
Petersburg campaign **V:**
    271
Philadelphia **II:** 282
Phillips, Wendell **IV:** 281
Pierce, Franklin **V:** 275
plantations **V:** 276
plantation system **II:** 286,
    287
Polk, James K. **IV:** 283
polygamy **IV:** 285
popular sovereignty **IV:**
    285–286
population trends **II:**
    291–292; **III:** 284; **V:**
    279
Port Royal, South
    Carolina, Experiment **V:**
    279–280
Powhatan Confederacy **II:**
    295
prisons **V:** 282
Protestantism **II:** 302
public land policy **IV:** 287
Pueblo Indians **II:** 303
Quakers **II:** 308–309
Queen Anne's War **II:** 309
race and race relations **III:**
    295; **IV:** 289–291; **V:**
    287–288
Reconstruction **V:** 291, 292
Reconstruction Acts **V:** 295
refugees **V:** 298, 299
religion **III:** 299; **IV:** 296;
    V: 299–300
religion, African-American
    II: 313–314
Republican Party **IV:** 300,
    301; **V:** 300, 301
Rhode Island **II:** 321
rural life **III:** 312
St. Augustine **II:** 327–328
St. Mary's City **II:** 328
scalawags **V:** 307, 308

secession **V:** 311
Seville **I:** 323
Sewall, Samuel **II:** 334
Seward, William H. **V:** 314
sharecropping **V:** 315
Sherman, William T. **V:**
    321
Sherman's March through
    Georgia **V:** 322–323
Singleton, Benjamin **V:** 327
slave codes **II:** 336
slave resistance **II:**
    336–338
slave trade **III:** 328–329
slave trade, internal **IV:**
    319–320
Smith, Venture **II:** 348
society, British American
    II: 350, 351
Society for the Propagation
    of the Gospel in Foreign
    Parts **II:** 352
South Carolina **II:**
    353–354
South Carolina Regulation
    III: 330, 331
Spanish colonies **II:**
    358–359
Special Field Order No. 15
    V: 332–333
states' rights **V:** 335–336
Stephens, Alexander H. **V:**
    336, 337
Stewart, Maria **IV:** 327
Stono Rebellion **II:** 361
Sudan **I:** 337
sugar **I:** 338
Supreme Court decision
    IV: 331
Tappan, Arthur and Lewis
    IV: 333–334
tariffs **V:** 348
Taureg **I:** 360–361
taverns and inns **II:** 368
Taylor, John, of Caroline
    III: 344
Taylor, Susie King **V:** 350
Taylor, Zachary **IV:** 334,
    335
Texas **IV:** 338–339
Texas, Republic of **IV:** 341
theater **V:** 352
Thirteenth Amendment **V:**
    352–353
Thoreau, Henry David **IV:**
    342
Timbuktu **I:** 350
tobacco **II:** 375
Truth, Sojourner **V:**
    356–358
Tubman, Harriet **V:**
    358–359

Turner, Nat **IV:** 346–348
Tuscarora War **II:** 379
UDC **V:** 370
Underground Railroad **V:** 361–362
Vallandigham, Clement L. **V:** 377
Vesey, Denmark **IV:** 353–354
Virginia **II:** 382–384
Vitoria, Francisco de **I:** 369
Wade-Davis Bill of 1864 **V:** 385
War of Jenkins' Ear **II:** 392
Washington, George **III:** 367
Webster, Daniel **IV:** 360
West Indies **III:** 372
Whig Party **IV:** 364
Whitney, Eli **III:** 376, *377*
Wilmot Proviso **V:** 395–396
Women's National Loyal League **V:** 396
women's rights and status **II:** 406, 407; **III:** 382, 383; **IV:** 366–367; **VI:** 317
Woolman, John **II:** 410–411
Wright, Fanny **IV:** 369
Yancey, William Lowndes **V:** 401
Yeardley, Sir George **II:** 413
Young, Brigham **IV:** 372
zambos **I:** 382
slave trade **I: 328–330,** 329*m,* 386*c;* **II:** 341*m, 343,* **343–345,** 344*t,* 417*c*–419*c;* **III: 328–329,** 329, 396*c;* **VII:** 31
　abolition/abolition movement **III:** 16; **IV:** 1
　Africa **II:** 4–5
　African Americans **III:** 5
　Amistad incident **IV:** 19–21
　Benin **I:** 28
　Boston **II:** 35
　Brazil **I:** 33
　British Empire **II:** 41
　Cabeza de Vaca, Álvar Núñez **I:** 38
　Calabar **I:** 47–48
　Cameroon **I:** 52–53
　Canary Islands **I:** 53
　Caribbean **II:** 53
　Cayor **I:** 66
　Charleston **II:** 57
　Columbian Exchange **I:** 78
　Columbus, Christopher **I:** 82

cotton culture **IV:** 99
Creek nation **III:** 96
Cuba **I:** 98; **IV:** 100
Dahomey **I:** 101–102
disease **II:** 92
Djibouti **I:** 109
Dutch West India Company **II:** 98
economy **II:** 101
Enlightenment **II:** 110
Equiano, Olaudah **III:** 118, 119
Fang **I:** 127
Flashman, Edward **II:** 119
Fon **I:** 132
Ghana **I:** 140
Gomes, Diogo **I:** 144
Gorée Island **I:** 145
Guinea-Bissau **I:** 147
Haiti **III:** 159
Hawkins, Sir John **I:** 156
Igbo **I:** 175
Islam **I:** 185
Johnson, Mary **II:** 175
Jones, Absalom **III:** 189
Kaabu kingdom **I:** 195
Kongo **I:** 196
labor **II:** 188, 189
Laurens, Henry **III:** 202
Locke, John **II:** 198
Luba **I:** 210
manufacturing and industry **II:** 204
mariners **II:** 204
marriage and family life **III:** 233
Massachusetts **II:** 215
Mbundu **I:** 229–230
merchants **II:** 222
mortality **II:** 235
Mpongwe **I:** 246, 247
Natchez Revolt **II:** 241
New Jersey **II:** 253
New Netherland **II:** 257
Newport **II:** 258
New York **II:** 260
Nzinga **I:** 267
Oyo **I:** 273
population trends **I:** 290; **III:** 284
Príncipe **I:** 293
Quakers **II:** 309
race and racial conflict **II:** 311
Royal African Company **II:** 325
São Tomé **I:** 320
Savannah **II:** 329
Senegambia **I:** 322
slavery **II:** 338–340; **III:** 326
and slavery **I:** 326–327

slave trade, internal **IV:** 319
smallpox **I:** 330
Spanish Armada **I:** 334
sugar **I:** 339
Supreme Court decision **IV:** 331
Tappan, Arthur and Lewis **IV:** 333
Taureg **I:** 360
Téké **I:** 343
trade and shipping **II:** 375, 376
Tuscarora **II:** 378
Virginia **II:** 384
Yoruba **I:** 377
slave trade, internal **IV: 319–320**
　Clay, Henry **IV:** 88
　Compromise of 1850 **IV:** 93, 94
　Liberty Party **IV:** 211
　Taylor, Zachary **IV:** 335
Slave Trade Abolition Act of 1807 **III:** 397*c*
Slick, Grace **X:** 203
Slidell, John **V:** 131, 132, 241
Sloan, Alfred P. **VII:** 22; **VIII:** 15; **IX:** 121
Sloan, Dolly **VII:** 115
Sloan, John **VII:** 18, 115
Sloane, Sir Hans **II:** 30, 55
Sloane, William Milligan **VI:** 290
Sloat, John **IV:** 328
Slocum, Henry W. **V:** 28, 150, 322
Sloo, A. G. **IV:** 159
SLP. *See* Socialist Labor Party
slum clearance **VIII:** 59
slums **VI:** 135, 233, 248
Small, Albion W. **VI:** 267
"small beer" **II:** 15, 122
smallpox **I: 330–331; II:** *91,* **345; III:** 396*c;* **IV:** 377*c;* **V:** 230; **IX:** 199
　Atahualpa **I:** 14
　Aztecs **I:** 22
　Bodmer, Karl **IV:** 55
　Boylston, Zabdiel **II:** 37
　Catawba **II:** 55
　Choctaw **II:** 61
　cities and urban life **III:** 70; **IV:** 82
　Cozumel **I:** 97
　Cuauhtémoc **I:** 97
　Cuitláhuac **I:** 98
　disease and epidemics **I:** 107, 108; **II:** 90–92; **III:** 106; **IV:** 113
　Enlightenment **II:** 110
　Fort William Henry Massacre **II:** 124

fur trade **IV:** 158
Harrison, William Henry **IV:** 168
Iceland **I:** 175
Iroquois **I:** 183
King George's War **II:** 182
La Demoiselle **II:** 191
Massachusetts **II:** 215
Mather, Cotton **II:** 217
Mather, Increase **II:** 218
medicine **III:** 241
mortality **II:** 235
Native Americans **II:** 244; **IV:** 258
North Carolina **II:** 264
Pizarro, Francisco **I:** 283
population trends **II:** 290
religion, Native American **II:** 318
Seven Years' War **II:** 333–334
South Carolina **II:** 353
Tenochtitlán **I:** 346
Warren, Joseph **III:** 363
small towns **VI:** 135
Smart Set, The **VII:** 181
Smeal, Eleanor **X:** 106
smelting industry **IV:** 90
Smibert, John **II:** 25, 154, 216, 273, **345–346**
Smiley, Jane **X:** 177
Smith, Adam **II:** 119, 221
Smith, Alfred E. **VII:** 66, 81, **287–288,** 312, 361*c;* **X:** 228
　American Liberty League **VIII:** 15
　Catholics **VIII:** 53
　conservatism **VIII:** 71
　Democratic Party **VIII:** 80
　Dewson, "Molly" **VIII:** 83
　Irish Americans **VIII:** 165
　Italian Americans **VIII:** 167
　Norris, George W. **VIII:** 248
　Perkins, Frances **VIII:** 265
　Polish Americans **VIII:** 269
　politics in the Roosevelt era **VIII:** 270, 271, 272*t*
　religion **VIII:** 303
　Republican Party **VIII:** 305
　Roosevelt, Franklin D. **VIII:** 312
　Wagner, Robert F. **VIII:** 372
Smith, Bessie **VII:** 86, 194, 195; **VIII:** 149
Smith, David **IX:** 20
Smith, Edmund Kirby **V:** 232
Smith, "Extra Billy" **V:** 153

Smith, Francis **III:** 212, 213
Smith, Gerald L. K.
      conservatism **VIII:** 72
      Coughlin, Father Charles
           E. **VIII:** 75
      Long, Huey P. **VIII:** 195
      Union Party **VIII:** 365
Smith, Gerard **X:** 289
Smith, Gerrit **IV:** 150, 210
Smith, Gustavus W. **V:** 323
Smith, Harry **VI:** 6
Smith, Hoke **VI:** 111
Smith, Holland M. **VIII:** 202,
      203, 350
Smith, Hyrum
      Church of Jesus Christ of
           Latter-day Saints **IV:** 80
      Deseret, State of **IV:** 109
      Nauvoo, Illinois **IV:** 261
      Smith, Joseph, Jr. **IV:** 324
Smith, Jedediah Strong **IV:**
      320–322, 321m
      Ashley, William Henry **IV:**
           28, 29, 29m
      Beckwourth, Jim **IV:** 46
      Bridger, James **IV:** 57
      California Trail **IV:** 70
      exploration **IV:** 131
      Fort Vancouver **IV:** 145
      McLoughlin, John **IV:** 229
      mountain men **IV:** 247
      Rocky Mountain Fur
           Company **IV:** 302
      South Pass **IV:** 324, 325
      Sublette, William **IV:** 329
Smith, John **I:** 154, 225, 388c;
      II: 346–347, 347
      agriculture **II:** 8
      captivity **II:** 51
      Chesapeake Bay **II:** 58
      exploration **II:** 115
      Grenville, Sir Richard **II:**
           150
      Jamestown **II:** 171
      journalism **II:** 179
      literature **II:** 195
      New Hampshire **II:** 250
      Opechancanough **II:** 268
      Pennsylvania **II:** 274
      Pocahontas **II:** 288, 289
      Powhatan (chief) **II:** 293,
           294
      Powhatan Confederacy **II:**
           295
      Squanto **II:** 360–361
Smith, John G. **X:** 20
Smith, Joseph **V:** 238; **VI:** 198,
      244
Smith, Joseph, Jr. **IV: 322–324,**
      323, 376c
      Church of Jesus Christ of
           Latter-day Saints **IV:**
           79–80

Deseret, State of **IV:** 109
Mormon Trail **IV:** 243m
Mormon War **IV:** 244
Nauvoo, Illinois **IV:**
      260–261
polygamy **IV:** 285
religion **IV:** 298
Strang, James Jesse **IV:**
      329
Young, Brigham **IV:** 371,
      372
Smith, Julian **VIII:** 350
Smith, Kate **VIII:** 224
Smith, Kirby **V:** 73, 83, 297, 298
Smith, Lydia H. **V:** 337
Smith, Mamie **VII:** 194
Smith, Matthew **II:** 272
Smith, Nathan Davis **IV:** 231,
      308
Smith, Robert **II:** 298, **347–348**
Smith, Roger **X:** 234
Smith, Ruby Doris **IX:** 114
Smith, Theobald **VI:** 191
Smith, Sir Thomas **II:** 163, 224,
      387
Smith, Tommie **IX:** 40, 41
Smith, Venture **II: 348**
Smith, W. Eugene **VIII:** 268
Smith, William **II:** 66–67, 153,
      281; **III:** 371
Smith, William French **X:** 260
Smith, Willis **X:** 140
Smith Act (Smith Alien
      Registration Act) **VII:** 95;
      VIII: 55, 60, 102, **326–327,**
      408c; **IX:** 80, 331c
Smith and Wesson **X:** 137–138
Smith College **VI:** 316
Smith-Connally Act **VIII:** 410c
      conservatism **VIII:** 73
      labor **VIII:** 181
      Lewis, John L. **VIII:** 186
      NWLB **VIII:** 234
Smith Gerrit **IV:** 224
Smithson, Robert **X:** 26
Smithsonian Institution **IV:** 78,
      308; **V:** 389; **VI:** 110, 111
Smith v. Allwright **VIII:** 61,
      228, 347, 410c
smog **IX:** 101, 102, 334c
smoking **X:** 303–305. See also
      antismoking
smoothbore muskets **V:** 308
smuggling **I:** 61; **II: 348–349;**
      III: 130; **X:** 149
      Acts of Trade and
           Navigation **II:** 3
      Boston **II:** 35
      British Empire **II:** 44
      Rhode Island **II:** 321
      Seven Years' War **II:** 334
      War of Jenkins' Ear **II:** 392

Smythe, Sir Thomas **I:** 117, 318;
      II: 347
Snap the Whip (Homer) **VI:** 130
SNCC. See Student Nonviolent
      Coordinating Committee
Snead, Sam **VIII:** 337
Snell, Bertrand **VIII:** 305
Snoop Dogg **X:** 240
Snow, John **IV:** 111
Snow White and the Seven
      Dwarfs (film) **VIII:** 219, 408c
snuff **II:** 374
Snyder, Gary **IX:** 35, 71, 256
soap **IV:** 184
Sobran, Joseph **X:** 43
soccer **X:** 285
social activism **IV:** 342; **VIII:**
      406c
social change **VIII:** 268
social classes **IV:** 187; **X:** 11
      Aztecs **I:** 18–20
      Benin **I:** 28
      cacao **I:** 45
      cacique **I:** 46
      Cahokia **I:** 47
      Carib **I:** 56
      castas **I:** 61–62
      Castile **I:** 63
      entail **I:** 122–123
      Gonja **I:** 144
      habitants **I:** 149
      Haida **I:** 150
      Hopewell culture **I:** 166
      Inca **I:** 176
      Mossi **I:** 244
      New Spain **I:** 259–260
      Secotan **I:** 320
      Seville **I:** 323
      Taino **I:** 342
      Taureg **I:** 360–361
      zambos **I:** 381–382
social contract theory **II:** 197
social criticism **VII:** 160
Social Darwinism **VI: 265–266;**
      VII: 32, 109, 256; **VIII:** 72
      Adams, Henry **VI:** 1–2
      immigration restrictions
           VI: 141
      imperialism **VI:** 142
      nativism **VI:** 209
      Sumner, William Graham
           VI: 280–281
Social Democracy of America
      VI: 268, 269
Social Democratic Party (SDP)
      VI: 269; **VII:** 65, 250, 251,
      288
Social Destiny of Man: Or,
      Theory of the Four
      Movements (Fourier) **IV:** 149
Social Diagnosis (Richmond)
      VII: 290

social experiments **IV:** 61, 126
"social fascists" **VIII:** 276
Social Gospel **VI: 266–267;**
      VII: 185, 255–256, 260; **VIII:**
      35
      Beecher, Henry Ward **VI:**
           24
      Gladden, Washington **VI:**
           115
      religion **VI:** 241–242
      Strong, Josiah **VI:**
           278–279
social insurance **VIII:** 329
socialist feminism **X:** 115
Socialist International **V:** 340
Socialist Labor Party (SLP) **VI:**
      268; VII: 65, 250, 288
      labor, radical **VI:** 167
      political parties, third **VI:**
           226
      Powderly, Terence Vincent
           VI: 227
      socialism **VI:** 267
      Socialist Party **VI:** 268
Socialist Party **VI:** 26, 167,
      268–269; VII: 355c, 358c
      Communist Party **VII:** 53
      Debs, Eugene V. **VII:** 65
      election of 1932 **VIII:** 96
      Espionage Act **VII:** 88
      Farmer-Labor Party **VII:**
           91
      Haywood, "Big Bill" **VII:**
           120
      IWW **VII:** 130
      labor movement **VII:** 152,
           154
      National Civic Federation
           VII: 201
      Non-Partisan League **VII:**
           215
      politics in the Roosevelt
           era **VIII:** 270, 272t
      Popular Front **VIII:** 276
      radicalism **VII:** 250, 251
      Randolph, A. Philip **VIII:**
           291
      Russian Revolution **VII:**
           270
      Sedition Act **VII:** 280
      Shirtwaist Makers Strike
           VII: 285
      Sinclair, Upton **VII:** 287
      socialism **VII:** 288, 289
      socialists **VIII:** 327
      STFU **VIII:** 333
      Thomas, Norman **VIII:**
           358
      Trading with the Enemy
           Act **VII:** 311
socialists/socialism **VI:**
      267–268; VII: 288–289;

VIII: 113, 173, **327–328; X:** 174, 258
Agricultural Adjustment Act **VIII:** 6
Bellamy, Edward **VI:** 26
Communist Party **VII:** 52
Communists **VIII:** 65
Debs, Eugene V. **VII:** 64–65
Du Bois, W. E. B. **VII:** 72
elections **VII:** 80
Ellis, Havelock **VII:** 84
Flynn, Elizabeth Gurley **VII:** 94
Gilman, Charlotte Perkins **VII:** 109
Gladden, Washington **VI:** 115
Gompers, Samuel **VI:** 116
labor, radical **VI:** 166, 167
Masses, The **VII:** 173
Non-Partisan League **VII:** 215
politics **VII:** 229
Popular Front **VIII:** 276
Russian Revolution **VII:** 270–271
Sinclair, Upton **VII:** 286
Socialist Party **VI:** 268
Thomas, Norman **VIII:** 358
utopianism **VI:** 301
Willard, Frances **VI:** 316
Woodhull, Victoria **VI:** 319
Socialist Workers Party **VIII:** 326
Social Justice magazine **VIII:** 76
social life **IV:** 10; **VI:** 207, 221.
See also cities and urban life; class
Algonquin **II:** 17
American Philosophical Society **II:** 18
California Indians **II:** 49
Caribbean **II:** 53
Charleston **II:** 56–57
Connecticut **II:** 70
consumption **II:** 71
Crow **II:** 77
dance **II:** 82
Delaware **II:** 88–89
Massachusetts **II:** 215
Morton, Thomas **II:** 236
music **II:** 238–239
plantation system **II:** 287
Powhatan Confederacy **II:** 294
Quakers **II:** 308
slave codes **II:** 336
slavery **II:** 338, 340–341
Spanish colonies **II:** 356–357, 359

taverns and inns **II:** 367–368
theater **II:** 373
tobacco **II:** 374
Virginia **II:** 384
social occasions **IV:** 247–248
social organizations **IV:** 8
social realists **VIII:** 25
social reconstructionism **VIII:** 93
social reform **III:** 169–170; **IV:** 219–220, 335–337; **VI:** 325*c*.
See also reform
art **VII:** 18–19
cities and urban life **VII:** 50
Comstock, Anthony **VI:** 62
George, Henry **VI:** 111–112
Knights of Labor **VI:** 162
labor, child **VI:** 166
labor, woman **VI:** 169
Langston, John Mercer **VI:** 171–172
Lease, Mary Elizabeth **VI:** 173
Liberal Republican Party **VI:** 174
Lloyd, Henry Demarest **VI:** 179
Lodge, Henry Cabot **VII:** 165
muckrakers **VII:** 192
newspapers **VI:** 211
New Woman **VII:** 213
pragmatism **VI:** 228–229
progressivism in the 1890s **VI:** 233
Rauschenbusch, Walter **VII:** 255–256
Schurz, Carl **VI:** 256–257
settlement houses **VI:** 259–260
Social Gospel **VI:** 266–267
trusts **VI:** 294
Villard, Henry **VI:** 304–305
Wald, Lillian **VII:** 329
Ward, Lester Frank **VI:** 307
Willard, Frances **VI:** 315–316
Social Revolutionary Party **VI:** 167
Social Salvation (Gladden) **VI:** 115
Social Security **VIII:** 73, 96, 293; **IX:** 229, 230, 313; **X:** 246
Social Security Act **VII:** 124; **VIII: 328–330,** 329, 407*c*, 415–419; **IX:** 196, 197

advertising **VIII:** 1
African Americans **X:** 10
birth control **X:** 37
business **VIII:** 46
children **VIII:** 56
Congress **VIII:** 67
conservatism **VIII:** 72
court-packing plan **VIII:** 76
elderly **VIII:** 95
election of 1936 **VIII:** 97
Emergency Relief Appropriation Act **VIII:** 101
government **VIII:** 134
liberalism **VIII:** 188; **X:** 175
marriage and family life **VIII:** 204
medicine **VIII:** 208; **X:** 189
New Deal **VIII:** 241
Perkins, Frances **VIII:** 265
relief **VIII:** 301
Roosevelt, Franklin D. **VIII:** 313
Second New Deal **VIII:** 321
Supreme Court **VIII:** 346
taxation **VIII:** 351
Townsend, Francis E. **VIII:** 358, 359
Tugwell, Rexford G. **VIII:** 361
Union Party **VIII:** 365
Willkie, Wendell L. **VIII:** 379
women's network **VIII:** 383
women's status and rights **VIII:** 384
WPA **VIII:** 387
Social Security Act of 1950 **IX:** 108
Social Security Amendments of 1965 **IX:** 334*c*
Social Security Board **VIII:** 83, 330
social services **V:** 371–372; **X:** 112–113
social status. *See* class
social structure. *See* community life
social welfare **VI:** 326*c*; **VII:** 283–284; **VIII:** 328–330
social work **VII: 289–291**
Abbott, Grace **VII:** 1
Children's Bureau **VII:** 47
ethnic organizations **VII:** 89
progressivism **VII:** 238
Wald, Lillian **VII:** 329

Société Français des Peintres-Graveurs **VI:** 45
society, British American **II: 349–352**
artisans **II:** 25–26
class **II:** 63
crowd action **II:** 77–78
environment **II:** 112
Society for a More Beautiful National Capital **IX:** 151
Society for Propagating the Gospel among Indians **II:** 398
Society for the Improvement and Colonization of East European Jews **VI:** 173
Society for the Promotion of Temperance **IV:** 296
Society for the Propagation of the Gospel in Foreign Parts (SPG) **II: 352–353**
African Americans **II:** 6–7
Anglican Church **II:** 20
education **II:** 104
Heathcote, Caleb **II:** 155
Johnston, Henrietta Deering **II:** 177
King's College **II:** 184–185
religion, Euro-American **II:** 316
Society for the Suppression of Vice **V:** 394; **VII:** 143, 283
Society in Scotland for Propagating Christian Knowledge **II:** 40
Society of American Artists **VI:** 48, 220; **VII:** 18
Society of American Musicians and Composers **VI:** 183
Society of American Women Composers **VI:** 23
Society of Faces **I:** 181
Society of Friends. *See* Quakers
Society of Jesus **II:** 174, 244.
See also Jesuits
Society of Missionary Priests of St. Paul the Apostle **VI:** 249
"sociocracy" **VI:** 307
sociology **VI:** 307; **VII:** 248; **IX:** 204–205
Sociology of the South: or the Failure of Free Society (Fitzhugh) **V:** 128, 212, 328
sod houses **VI:** 269, **269–270**
soft drinks **VIII:** 47
soft-money contributions **VI:** 120; **X:** 236
software **IX:** 65; **X:** 73, 152, 153
Sogolon **I:** 339
soil-bank program **IX:** 8, 331*c*
soil conservation **IV:** 11, 99

soil conservation (continued)
    Agricultural Adjustment
        Act **VIII**: 6
    agriculture **VIII**: 8
    environmental issues **VIII**:
        104
    Ickes, Harold L. **VIII**: 161
Soil Conservation and Domestic
    Allotment Act **VIII**: 6, 8,
    407c
Soil Conservation Service (SCS)
    VIII: 87, 103
soil erosion **VIII**: 405c
Soil Erosion Service **VIII**: 87,
    103
soil exhaustion **II**: 383; **IV**: 235
Sojourner lander **X**: 283
Sokoloff, Nikolai **VIII**: 119
solar calendars **I**: 21
Soldiers' Adjusted Compensation
    Act. *See* Soldiers' Bonus
Soldiers Aid Society **IV**: 54
Soldiers' Bonus **VII**: 230,
    291–292, 325–327, 361c
soldiers' homes **V**: 379
Soldier's Pay (Faulkner) **VII**:
    162; **VIII**: 113
Solidarity (IWW journal) **VII**:
    252
Solidarity movement (Poland)
    X: 71, 156, 260
"solidism" **II**: 220
Solid South **VI**: 77, **270**
Solinus **I**: 239
Solomon, king of Jerusalem **I**:
    123
Solomon Islands **I**: 338; **VIII**:
    330–331, 409c
    Coral Sea, Battle of the
        VIII: 74
    Guadalcanal **VIII**: 141
    Halsey, "Bull" **VIII**: 143
    Marines, U.S. **VIII**: 203
    World War II Pacific
        theater **VIII**: 398
Solzhenitsyn, Alexander **X**: 141
Somalia **X**: 328c
    African nations **X**: 12, 13
    Clinton, William **X**: 66
    cold war (end of) **X**: 71
    defense policy **X**: 88
    foreign policy **X**: 124
    United Nations **X**: 307
Somers, Sir George **I**: 29–30
Somers Island Company. *See*
    Bermuda Company
Somers Isles. *See* Bermuda
Sommervell, Brehon B. **VIII**:
    20, 206
Somoza, Anastasio **X**: 80, 173,
    217, 218, 326c
Somoza, Luis **X**: 217

Somoza, Tachito **X**: 217, 218
Somozas **IX**: 10
sonar **IX**: 270
Sondheim, Stephen **X**: 241–242
Songhai **I**: **331–332**; **II**: 4
    Askia Muhammad I **I**: 14
    Baba, Ahmad **I**: 23
    Djenne-Djeno **I**: 109
    Fulani **I**: 135
    Gao **I**: 137, 139
    Hausa **I**: 155
    Islam **I**: 184
    Leo Africanus **I**: 203
    Mali **I**: 218
    Mossi **I**: 243–244
    Sahara **I**: 317
    slavery **I**: 326
    Sudan **I**: 336–337
    Timbuktu **I**: 350
Song of the Sierras (Miller) **VI**:
    178
Songs of a Semite (Lazarus) **VI**:
    172
Soninke **I**: 140
Sonni Ali. *See* Sunni Ali Ber
Sonni Bakari Da'o **I**: 14
*Son of the Forest: The
    Experience of William Apess,
    a Native of the Forest* **IV**: 211
Son of the Middle Border
    (Garland) **VI**: 110
Sons of Dan **IV**: 79
Sons of Liberty **III**: **329–330**;
    V: 377
    Adams, Samuel **III**: 4
    artisans **III**: 26
    Boston Tea Party **III**: 45
    committees of
        correspondence **III**: 77
    Democratic-Republican
        societies **III**: 105
    Golden Hill, Battle of **III**:
        153
    liberty tree/pole **III**:
        213–214
    Loyal Nine **III**: 221
    Putnam, Israel **III**: 290
    resistance movement **III**:
        303
    Revere, Paul **III**: 304
    Stamp Act **III**: 332
    taverns **III**: 343
Sons of the Confederate
    Veterans **V**: 217, 379
Sony **X**: 273
Sony v. Universal (1984) **X**: 273,
    326c
Sooners **VI**: **270–271**
Sopranos, The (TV program) **X**:
    241, 295
Sorge, Richard **VIII**: 104
sorghum **II**: 122

Sorko **I**: 137
"sorts" **II**: 281–282. *See also*
    class
Sosso **I**: 141, 217, 340
Soto, Hernando de **I**: 332,
    332–333, 387c; **II**: 21, 59, 61
    Apalachee **I**: 11
    Cofitachequi **I**: 76
    Coosa **I**: 85
    Florida **I**: 130
    Mabila **I**: 213
    Natchez **I**: 251
    Panama **I**: 276
    Ponce de León, Juan **I**:
        288
    Timucua **I**: 351
Soule, Pierre **V**: 260
soul liberty **II**: 29
soul music **X**: 201, 241
Souls of Black Folk (Du Bois)
    VII: 71, 356c
Soul Train **X**: 202
Sound and the Fury (Faulkner)
    VIII: 113, 405c
soundtracks, movie **X**: 201
soup kitchens **VIII**: 299
"Sources of Soviet Conduct"
    (George F. Kennan) **IX**: 155,
    341–344
Sousa, John Philip **VI**: 204,
    271–272, 327c
Sousa, Martím Afonso De **I**: 193
Sousa, Tomé de **I**: 33
Sousa Band **VI**: 327c
sousaphone **VI**: 271
Souter, David **X**: 41, **278–279**,
    291
South Africa **VI**: 4; **IX**: 4; **X**:
    327c
    African nations **X**: 13
    cold war (end of) **X**: 71
    foreign policy **X**: 122
    United Nations **X**: 307
    U.S. relations with **X**:
        279–280
South African National Party **X**:
    279
South America **II**: 2, 285, 332,
    337, 338–342; **IV**: 142,
    241–242; **V**: 276; **VIII**: 410c.
    See also specific countries
    Amazon River **I**: 8
    Andes Mountains **I**: 9–10
    Columbian Exchange **I**: 77
    Columbus, Christopher **I**:
        82
    corn (maize) **I**: 87–88
    Waldseemüller, Martin **I**:
        371
South American descent,
    Americans of **X**: 143
Southampton, earl of **II**: 347

Southampton County, Virginia
    IV: 346–348
South Carolina **II**: **353–354**,
    418c; **III**: 394c; **IV**: 376c; **V**:
    406c; **VI**: 324c, 327c; **IX**: 114,
    272–273, 311, 320; **X**: 107,
    242
    African-American
        churches, growth of **VI**:
        4
    African Americans **II**: 6, 7;
        VI: 5
    agriculture **II**: 10–12; **IV**:
        11
    American System **IV**: 19
    Anderson, Robert **V**: 9
    Apalachee **I**: 11
    banking and credit **II**: 29
    Black Codes **V**: 29
    Calhoun, John C. **IV**:
        62–63
    Camden, Battle of **III**:
        57–59
    canal era **IV**: 72
    Catawba **II**: 55
    Charleston **II**: 56–57
    Cherokee **II**: 57
    class **II**: 63–64
    Clay, Henry **IV**: 87
    Cofitachequi **I**: 76
    Cornwallis, Lord **III**: 93
    Cowpens, Battle of **III**: 95
    crowd action **II**: 78
    Democratic Party **V**: 94
    economy **II**: 101
    Elliot, Robert B. **V**: 111
    Enforcement Acts **V**: 117
    Eutaw Springs, Battle of
        III: 120–121
    fire-eaters **V**: 127–128
    La Florida **I**: 130
    foraging **V**: 130
    Fort Mose **II**: 123
    Fort Sumter, South
        Carolina **V**: 135–137
    French immigrants **II**: 130
    Georgia **II**: 137, 138
    government, British
        American **II**: 145
    Great Awakening **II**: 148
    Greene, Nathanael **III**:
        156
    Grimké, Angelina and
        Sarah **IV**: 164
    Gullah **II**: 151–152
    Haiti **III**: 159
    Hayes, Rutherford B. **VI**:
        126
    Higginson, Thomas
        Wentworth **V**: 167
    Hume, Sophia Wigington
        II: 159–160

indigo **II:** 166
Jackson, Andrew **IV:** 191, 193
Jim Crow laws **VI:** 156
Johnston, Henrietta Deering **II:** 177
Ku Klux Klan **V:** 200
labor **II:** 188–189
land **II:** 191
Lining, John **II:** 194
manufacturing and industry **II:** 204
Marion, Francis **III:** 231–232
marriage and family life **IV:** 222
mercantilism **II:** 221
merchants **II:** 222
Mexican-American War **IV:** 232
Middleton, Arthur **II:** 224
miscegenation **II:** 228–229
mulattoes **II:** 238
Musgrove, Mary Bosomworth **II:** 238
Native Americans **II:** 353–354
Nullification Controversy **IV:** 264–265
Oglethorpe, James Edward **II:** 267
Ostenaco **II:** 269
Pinckney, Charles Cotesworth **III:** 276–277
Pinckney, Elizabeth Lucas **II:** 284
plantations **V:** 276
plantation system **II:** 286
population trends **II:** 291–292
Queen Anne's War **II:** 309
Rainey, Joseph H. **V:** 290–291
Reconstruction **V:** 294
redemption **V:** 296, 297
Republican Party **IV:** 302
secession **V:** 311–313
Sherman, William T. **V:** 321
shipbuilding **II:** 335
slave codes **II:** 336
slave resistance **II:** 337
slavery **II:** 342; **III:** 328; **IV:** 318; **V:** 330
slave trade **III:** 329
society, British American **II:** 351, 352
Stono Rebellion **II:** 361–362
suffrage **II:** 364
tariffs **V:** 348

Teach, Edward **II:** 369
Theus, Jeremiah **II:** 373
Tuscarora **II:** 378
Tuscarora War **II:** 379
Tyler, John **IV:** 348
Vesey, Denmark **IV:** 353–354
War of Jenkins' Ear **II:** 392
Webster, Daniel **IV:** 360
women's status and rights **IV:** 367
South Carolina Exposition **IV:** 376c
South Carolina Leader **V:** 111
South Carolina Railroad **IV:** 295
South Carolina Regulation **III:** **330–331,** 392c
South Carolina Secession Convention of 1860 **V:** 312
South Carolina Society **II:** 373
South Dakota **II:** 115; **IV:** 131; **V:** 408c; **VI:** 29, 208, 209, 240, 324c, 326c; **X:** 107, 215, 242
Southeast Asia Treaty Organization (SEATO) **IX:** 83, 92, **273–274,** 317, 331c
Southeastern Ceremonial Complex **I:** 237
southeastern United States **II:** 55, 90, 394–395; **IV:** 181–183, 182m, 343–344; **X:** 171
Mississippian culture **I:** 236–237
mound builders **I:** 244–245
Southeby, William **II:** 1
Southern Andes **I:** 10
Southern Baptist Convention **IV:** 296–297, 311t; **V:** 299; **VIII:** 302, 304
Southern Bivouac magazine **V:** 258
Southern Christian Leadership Conference (SCLC) **IX:** **274–276,** 332c, 333c; **X:** 159
African-American movement **IX:** 5
Baker, Ella **IX:** 30–31
Birmingham confrontation **IX:** 37–38
civil disobedience **IX:** 54
King, Martin Luther, Jr. **IX:** 160, 161
Parks, Rosa **IX:** 240
race and racial conflict **IX:** 253
sit-ins **IX:** 273
Voting Rights Act of 1965 **IX:** 311
southern colonial houses **IV:** 27
southern colonies
Baptists **II:** 29

class **II:** 63
dueling **II:** 96
economy **II:** 101–102
English immigrants **II:** 108
plantation system **II:** 286–287
primogeniture and entail **II:** 297
slavery **II:** 338, 340, 342
society, British American **II:** 350–351
Southern Cotton Manufacturers **VII:** 46
"Southern Cross" **V:** 26
"Southern Crusade" **X:** 208
southern demagogues **VII:** **292–293**
southern European immigrants **V:** 60, 177, 278; **VI:** 139, 140, 171; **VIII:** 303
Dillingham Commission **VII:** 69
Immigration Act of 1917 **VII:** 128
Mann Act **VII:** 169
marriage and family life **VII:** 171
National Origins Act **VII:** 202
Quota Act **VII:** 245
science **VII:** 276
steel industry **VII:** 297
Southern Farmers' Alliance **VI:** 99, 100, 222, 227
Southern Historical Society **V:** 217
Southern Historical Society Papers **V:** 216
Southern Homestead Act of 1866 **V:** 142
Southern Literary Messenger **IV:** 197
Southern Manifesto **IX:** 108, 220, 253, **276–277,** 331c; **X:** 303
Southern Methodists **V:** 299–300
Southern Pacific Railroad **IV:** 306; **VI:** 67, 197, 237
Southern Quarterly Review **IV:** 197
Southern Regional Council **VIII:** 279, 289
Southern Review **IV:** 197
southern rights **IV:** 63
Southern States Industrial Council **IX:** 235
Southern Tenant Farmers Union (STFU) **VIII:** **332–333**
Agricultural Adjustment Act **VIII:** 6

Bethune, Mary McLeod **VIII:** 36
race and racial conflict **VIII:** 288
socialists **VIII:** 327
South **VIII:** 332
Thomas, Norman **VIII:** 358
Southern Textile Manufacturers **VII:** 145
southern United States **V:** 408c; **VI:** 5, 209–211, 270; **VII:** 248, 249, 292–293; **VIII:** **331–332,** 405c. *See also* Confederate States of America; Lower South states; New South; Upper South states
abolition **V:** 1–2
African-American movement **IX:** 4
African Americans **IV:** 6, 8; **VI:** 5, 6; **VIII:** 2, 3; **X:** 9
Agricultural Adjustment Act **VIII:** 6
agriculture **II:** 11, 12; **IV:** 9, 10; **V:** 6; **VI:** 8
America First Committee **VIII:** 13
amnesty, acts of **V:** 8
Anglican Church **II:** 20
Asian Americans **X:** 29
banking and credit **II:** 28
Black Codes **V:** 29
Booth, John Wilkes **V:** 32–33
carpetbaggers **V:** 49–50
cities and urban life **V:** 59; **IX:** 51
civil rights **VIII:** 61–62
Civil War **V:** 67
Colored National Labor Union **V:** 69
common soldier **V:** 70
Confederate States of America **V:** 75–77
Congress **VIII:** 66, 67
Congress of Industrial Organizations **IX:** 66
conservative coalition **VIII:** 73
contract labor **VI:** 66
CWA **VIII:** 63
Davis, Jefferson **V:** 88–90
Democratic Party **IV:** 109; **VIII:** 80–82
Dow, Lorenzo **IV:** 115, 116
economy **IV:** 117–119; **V:** 104–105; **VIII:** 92
education **IV:** 120; **V:** 108
education, federal aid to **VI:** 92

southern United States
(*continued*)
education, philanthropy
and **VI:** 93–94
election of 1936 **VIII:** 97
election of 1940 **VIII:** 98
election of 1944 **VIII:** 99
elections **V:** 109
elections, conduct of **VI:**
95
employment **V:** 115, 116
Fair Labor Standards Act
VIII: 110
Faulkner, William **VIII:**
113
FEPC **VIII:** 109, 110
FERA **VIII:** 118
Forrest, Nathan Bedford
V: 133–135
Freedmen's Bureau **V:**
142–144
fugitive slave laws **IV:**
154–155
government **VIII:** 134–135
grandfather clause **VI:**
118–119
Great Awakening **II:** 147,
148
Grimké, Angelina and
Sarah **IV:** 164
Hartford Convention **IV:**
170
Hayes, Rutherford B. **VI:**
126, 127
Hillman, Sidney **VIII:** 146
Hispanic Americans **X:**
143
homefront **V:** 168
Horseshoe Bend, Battle of
IV: 173
impeachment of Andrew
Johnson **V:** 178
industrial development **V:**
181
industrialization **IV:** 184
isolationists **VIII:** 166
journalism **V:** 193
Ku Klux Klan **V:** 199–201
labor and labor movements
II: 188–189; **IV:** 205; **X:**
171
Langston, John Mercer **VI:**
172
Lease, Mary Elizabeth **VI:**
173
literature **VIII:** 191, 192
lost cause, the **V:** 217–218
loyalty oaths **V:** 218–219
lynchings. *See* lynchings
marriage and family life **II:**
207–208; **VIII:** 205
Mason-Dixon Line **V:** 224

McCormick, Cyrus Hall
IV: 225
migration **IV:** 235; **IX:**
201–202
miscegenation **V:** 233–234
monuments **V:** 239
Morrill Land-Grant Act **V:**
241
mortality **II:** 234–235
mulattoes **II:** 238
Myrdal, Gunnar **VIII:** 225
NAACP **VIII:** 227–228
Native Americans **II:** 244
Native Americans in the
War of 1812 **IV:** 258
New South **VI:** 209–211
Nullification Controversy
IV: 263–265
Operation Dixie **IX:**
235–236
Panic of 1819 **IV:** 275
Panic of 1837 **IV:** 277
People's Party **VI:** 222, 223
Plessy v. Ferguson **VI:** 225
politics in the Roosevelt
era **VIII:** 270
polygamy **IV:** 285
popular sovereignty **IV:**
285
population trends **V:**
278–279; **VIII:** 277; **X:**
242
postwar planning **VIII:**
279
poverty **X:** 245, 246
race and racial conflict
VIII: 287–288
Radical Republicans **V:**
288–289
railroads **IV:** 296
Reconstruction **V:** 291–295
religion **V:** 299; **VI:** 241,
242; **VIII:** 302, 304
Republican Party **IV:** 301;
VI: 246; **VIII:** 306
rock and roll **IX:** 263
Roosevelt, Franklin D.
VIII: 313
rust belt **X:** 269
scalawags **V:** 307–308
Scottsboro Boys **VIII:**
319–320
secession **V:** 310–313
segregation **IX:** 271
shipbuilding **VIII:** 325
slavery **IV:** 316–319
slave trade, internal **IV:**
319–320
socialists **VIII:** 327
Solid South **VI:** 270
Southern Manifesto **IX:**
276

states' rights **V:** 335, 336
STFU **VIII:** 332–333
Sunbelt **VIII:** 343
Supreme Court **VIII:** 347
tariffs **V:** 348
technology **VIII:** 353
Thirteenth Amendment **V:**
353
travel **II:** 377
Union League **V:** 368
*United States v.
Cruikshank* **V:** 375–376
USHA **VIII:** 367
Voting Rights Act of 1965
IX: 311
War Hawks **IV:** 355
White Citizens' Councils
IX: 319–320
Wilmot Proviso **V:** 396
World War II **VIII:** 390
World War II home front
VIII: 394
Wright, Richard **VIII:** 399
zoot-suiters **VIII:** 404
Southern Woman's Story, A
(Pember) **V:** 267
South Fork Dam **VI:** 157
South Improvement Company
VI: 146, 215
South Korea. *See* Republic of
Korea
South Korean Central
Intelligence Agency (KCIA)
X: 166
South Mountain, Battle of **V:**
226
South Orkney Islands **IV:** 133
South Pacific **VI:** 254–255
South Pacific (Rodgers and
Hammerstein) **VIII:** 224
South Pass **IV: 324–325**
California Trail **IV:** 70, 71
Carson, Kit **IV:** 75
exploration **IV:** 131
Forty-niners **IV:** 146
Oregon Trail **IV:** 267
Smith, Jedediah Strong **IV:**
321, 322
Sublette, William **IV:** 330
South Side Railroad **V:** 129
South Vietnam **IX:** 21, 308–310,
317, 331c, 333c; **X:** 324c,
325c
cold war (end of) **X:** 70
foreign policy **X:** 122
Vietnam War **X:** 311–312
Southwestern Bell Corp. **X:** 50m
southwestern United States **IV:**
378c; **VI:** 4, 324c; **X:** 9, 171
agriculture **II:** 8, 9
Bent, Charles **IV:** 47–48
Bent, William **IV:** 48

Bent's Fort **IV:** 50–51
civil rights **VIII:** 62
Coronado, Francisco **I:** 88
economy **IV:** 117
environmental issues **VIII:**
104
exploration **IV:** 131, 132
Gadsden Purchase **IV:**
159–160
gender **II:** 136
Great Plains Indians **II:**
150
housing **II:** 157
Kearny, Stephen Watts **IV:**
200
Lamy, Jean Baptiste **IV:**
207
Manifest Destiny **IV:**
217–218
Mexican Americans **VIII:**
210
Mexican Repatriation
Program **VIII:** 211
migration **IV:** 236
Native Americans **II:** 246
Navajo **II:** 247
New Mexico **I:** 254–257;
II: 254–255
Protestantism **II:** 300
pueblo **I:** 295–296
Santa Fe Trail **IV:** 305–306
Smith, Jedediah Strong **IV:**
322
Toltecs **I:** 357
Southwest Fur Company **IV:** 16
Southworth, Alice **II:** 39
Southworth, Mrs. E.D.E.N. **IV:**
213
Sovereign, James P. **VI:** 167
Soviet-American relations **VIII:**
333–334, 406c
Anglo-American relations
VIII: 17
atomic bomb **VIII:** 29
Bretton Woods
Conference **VIII:** 42
Casablanca Conference
VIII: 52
demobilization **VIII:** 80
foreign policy **VIII:** 124
Grand Alliance **VIII:** 137
Harriman, Averell **VIII:**
144
Hiroshima and Nagasaki
VIII: 148
Hopkins, Harry **VIII:** 157
isolationists **VIII:** 166
Lend-Lease Act **VIII:**
184–185
liberalism **VIII:** 189
Manhattan Project **VIII:**
200

Nazi-Soviet Pact **VIII:** 238
Potsdam Conference **VIII:** 280
second front **VIII:** 320
Teheran Conference **VIII:** 355
UN **VIII:** 366
V-J Day **VIII:** 370
World War II **VIII:** 389
Yalta Conference **VIII:** 401
Soviet Union **VIII:** 406c, 408c–411c; **IX:** 329c–333c; **X:** 326c–328c. *See also* cold war; Russia; Russian Revolution
ABM Treaty **X:** 22–23
Acheson, Dean **IX:** 1, 2
Africa **IX:** 3, 4
African nations **X:** 12–13
Americans for Democratic Action **IX:** 13
Anglo-American relations **VIII:** 17
anticommunism **IX:** 14
antiwar movement—Vietnam **X:** 24
arms race **IX:** 16–17; **X:** 25
Asia (foreign policy) **IX:** 21
Atlantic Charter **VIII:** 28
atomic bomb **VIII:** 29
aviation **IX:** 28
Axis **VIII:** 31
Bay of Pigs **IX:** 33–35
Berlin blockade **IX:** 37
blitzkrieg **VIII:** 39
breakup of **X: 280–281**
Bretton Woods Conference **VIII:** 42
Bush, George H. W. **X:** 46
Cairo Conference **VIII:** 51
Camp David accords **X:** 54
Carter, James Earl, Jr. **X:** 58
Casablanca Conference **VIII:** 52
Catholic Bishops' Letter **X:** 60
CIA **IX:** 50
cold war (end of) **X:** 70–72
communism **IX:** 61
Communists **VIII:** 65
conservative movement **X:** 79
Cuban missile crisis **IX:** 73–75
defense policy **X:** 85–87
détente **X:** 89–90
Dulles, John Foster **IX:** 82–83
espionage **VIII:** 104
Ford, Gerald R. **X:** 121
foreign policy **VIII:** 124–126; **X:** 122–124

and foreign policy **IX: 277–278**
Forrestal, James V. **VIII:** 126
Gastonia Strike **VII:** 106
glasnost **X:** 131
Goldman, Emma **VII:** 110
Grand Alliance **VIII:** 136, 137
Haig, Alexander M., Jr. **X:** 140
Harriman, Averell **VIII:** 144
Haywood, "Big Bill" **VII:** 120
Hiroshima and Nagasaki **VIII:** 146
Holocaust **VIII:** 149
Hull, Cordell **VIII:** 160
INF Treaty **X:** 151–152
intelligence **VIII:** 164
Internet **X:** 152
Iron Curtain **X:** 156, 157
Jews and Judaism **X:** 161
Kennan, George **IX:** 155
Kennedy, Edward M. **X:** 164
Kissinger, Henry A. **X:** 166
Korean War **IX:** 163–165
League of Nations **VII:** 157
Lend-Lease Act **VIII:** 184–185
Limited Test Ban Treaty of 1963 **IX:** 180
Manchuria **VIII:** 200
Manhattan Project **VIII:** 200
Marshall Plan **IX:** 194
McGovern, George Stanley **X:** 184
Middle East **IX:** 201
military-industrial complex **IX:** 203
movies **IX:** 212–213
NATO **IX:** 232, 233; **X:** 223
Nazi-Soviet Pact **VIII:** 237–238
Nicaragua **X:** 218
Nixon, Richard M. **X:** 220
North Vietnam **X:** 224
NSC-68 **IX:** 233–234
nuclear freeze movement **X:** 224
Oswald, Lee Harvey **IX:** 237
Patton, George **VIII:** 263
Polish Americans **VIII:** 270
Potsdam Conference **VIII:** 279, 280

POWs **VIII:** 281
Progressive Party **IX:** 248, 249
propaganda **VIII:** 283
Reagan, Ronald W. **X:** 258–261
Reuther, Walter **IX:** 259
Robeson, Paul **VIII:** 309, 310; **IX:** 261
Rosenberg, Julius and Ethel **IX:** 264–265
science **IX:** 270
second front **VIII:** 320
socialists **VIII:** 327
space exploration **IX:** 278, 279
space policy **X:** 281
Spanish Civil War **VIII:** 334
Steffens, Lincoln **VII:** 299
Strategic Arms Limitation Treaties **X:** 288–289
submarines **VIII:** 342
Suez crisis **IX:** 289
technology **IX:** 294
Teheran Conference **VIII:** 354
Truman, Harry **IX:** 299
United Nations **VIII:** 365, 366; **X:** 307
U.S. European foreign policy **IX:** 104–106
U.S. Latin American foreign policy **IX:** 172
and U.S. defense budget **IX:** 77
V-J Day **VIII:** 369
Wallace, Henry A. **VIII:** 373, 374
wars of national liberation **IX:** 316
White Paper **IX:** 321
Willkie, Wendell L. **VIII:** 379
World War II **VIII:** 389
World War II European theater **VIII:** 391
Yalta Conference **VIII:** 401
Sowle, Andrew **II:** 39
SPAB (Supply Priorities and Allocation Board) **VIII:** 255
Space Advisory Committee **X:** 14
space exploration **IX: 278–279,** 333c
aviation **IX:** 28
NASA **IX:** 219–220
New Frontier **IX:** 230
science **IX:** 268–269
technology **IX:** 294
space policy **X:** 14, **281–283,** 282

space program **X:** 152, 326c, 327c
space shuttle **IX:** 220; **X:** 283
space telescope **X:** 283, 327c
Spain **I:** 386c, 388c; **III:** 394c, 396c, 397c; **IV:** 375c; **VI:** 323c, 327–328c; **VII:** 8, 97; **VIII:** 276
Adams-Onís Treaty **IV:** 5–6
adelantado **I:** 3–4
Alamo, The **IV:** 12
Alexander VI, **I:** 6
Amistad incident **IV:** 19–21
Anti-Imperialist League **VI:** 13
architecture **III:** 19
Austin, Moses **IV:** 36
Austin, Stephen F. **IV:** 36
auto-da-fé **I:** 16
Becknell, William **IV:** 45
Blaeu, Willem **I:** 31
Bowie, Jim **IV:** 56
Brazil **I:** 31, 33
bubonic plague **I:** 285
Buchanan, James V. **V:** 41
cabildo **I:** 38–39
Cabot, Sebastian **I:** 43
cacao **I:** 46
California **III:** 57
California missions **IV:** 69–70
Caroline, Fort **I:** 57
Casa de Contratación **I:** 59–61
Castile **I:** 62–64
Charles V **I:** 67–69
Choctaw nation **III:** 68
Chouteau family **IV:** 78
Clark, William **III:** 72
Columbus, Christopher **I:** 80
corregidores **I:** 90
Creek nation **III:** 96
Cuba **IV:** 100–101
de Lôme letter **VI:** 76–77
Dewey, George **VI:** 79
Drake, Sir Francis **I:** 110
Dutch East India Company **I:** 114
Essex decision **III:** 119
exploration **IV:** 132
Ferdinand and Isabella **I:** 127–128
Filipino insurrection **VI:** 100
Florida **III:** 129; **IV:** 139
foreign affairs **III:** 130, 131
foreign policy **IV:** 140, 142; **V:** 131, 133; **VI:** 104
fur trade **IV:** 156

Spain (continued)
Gates, Sir Thomas II: 135
gender II: 136
Georgia II: 138
globalization X: 131
gold I: 142
Great Plains III: 155
Great Plains Indians II: 150
Haiti III: 159
Holy League I: 164
horses I: 168
Ibn Battuta I: 173
Indians of the Desert Southwest II: 165
inquisition I: 178
Islam I: 184
Jay, John III: 181
Jay-Gardoqui treaty negotiations III: 182
Jesuits I: 189
Jews (Judaism) I: 190, 191
Lafitte, Jean IV: 205
land II: 191
Las Casas, Bartolomé de I: 198, 200
Lee, Arthur III: 205
Lewis and Clark Expedition III: 209
Louisiana Purchase III: 218
Manifest Destiny IV: 218
mariners II: 204
Mary I, queen of England I: 224
McGillivray, Alexander III: 240
McKinley, William VI: 189
Middleton, Arthur II: 224
monarchy, British II: 231
Monroe, James IV: 240
Monroe Doctrine IV: 241–242
Monroe-Pinkney Treaty III: 245–246
Native Americans IV: 256
Native Americans in the War of 1812 IV: 259, 260
NATO X: 223
Negro Plot of 1741 II: 247
New Hampshire II: 250
Newport, Christopher II: 258
New Spain I: 258–262
New Spain (Mexico), northern frontier of III: 257–258
Nicaragua X: 218
Oregon Treaty of 1846 IV: 269

Ostend Manifesto V: 259–260
Paris, Treaty of III: 273
Philip II I: 281–282
population trends I: 290
Potosí I: 291
privateering II: 299–300; III: 287
Quasi War III: 292
Reformation I: 309
Remember the Maine VI: 187–188
San Lorenzo, Treaty of III: 317
Santa Anna, Antonio López de IV: 303
Seminole wars IV: 311
Seven Years' War II: 332
Seville I: 322–323
Seward, William H. V: 314
silver I: 325
slavery II: 338
slave trade II: 343
Spanish-American War VI: 272–273
Spanish Armada I: 333–335
terrorism X: 297
Texas IV: 337
Texas Revolution IV: 339
Tordesillas, Treaty of I: 358
Treaty of Paris II: 378
Virginius affair VI: 305–306
War of Jenkins' Ear II: 392
West Indies III: 372
Wilkinson, James III: 379
Spalding, Albert VI: 21
Spalding, Lyman IV: 113
Spanish America. See also New Spain
audiencia I: 15–16
black legend I: 30–31
Cabeza de Vaca, Álvar Núñez I: 37
cabildo I: 38, 39
California I: 48–49
Charles V I: 69
corregidores I: 90–91
encomienda I: 122
La Florida I: 130–131
haciendas I: 149–150
Peru I: 280
repartimiento I: 310
Requerimiento I: 311
Spanish-American War IV: 143, 219; VI: 272–273, 273m, 328c; VIII: 177, 183, 266
Balloon Corps V: 22
Barton, Clara V: 25
Big Stick diplomacy VII: 27

Bryan, William Jennings VI: 37
Crane, Stephen VI: 68
Cuba VI: 71
Dewey, George VI: 79
foreign policy V: 131, 133; VII: 97, 98
Hay, John Milton VI: 125
Hearst, William Randolph VII: 121
imperialism VI: 142–143
investments, American, abroad VI: 150
Lodge, Henry Cabot VII: 165
McKinley, William VI: 189–190
Mitchell, Billy VII: 187
Ostend Manifesto V: 260
Panama Canal VII: 222
Pershing, John VII: 227
the presidency VI: 230
Remember the Maine VI: 187–188
Remington, Frederic VI: 245
Roosevelt, Theodore VII: 266
Roosevelt Corollary VII: 267
Rough Riders VI: 250
rules of war V: 306
southern demagogues VII: 292
veterans VII: 324
Wheeler, Joseph V: 392
Spanish Armada I: 333–335, 388c; II: 151, 231, 265, 284
Castile I: 64
Drake, Sir Francis I: 111, 112
Elizabeth I I: 121
Frobisher, Martin I: 133
Philip II I: 282
Roanoke I: 314
White, John I: 373
Spanish Civil War VIII: 334–335
foreign policy VIII: 124
Neutrality Acts VIII: 239
Popular Front VIII: 276
Robeson, Paul VIII: 309
Spanish colonies/colonization II: 354–359, 358m
art II: 25
Bermuda I: 28–29
borderlands II: 34
cacique I: 46–47
Canary Islands I: 53
Caribbean II: 52
castas I: 61
Castile I: 63

class II: 62
crowd action II: 78
Dominicans II: 94
Florida II: 120–121
Fort Mose II: 123
French colonies II: 128m
fur trade II: 130–131
Guadalajara II: 151
Hispaniola I: 161
Indians of the Desert Southwest II: 166
Jesuits II: 174
Jews II: 174–175
medicine II: 220
and mestizaje I: 233
mestizo I: 233–234
miscegenation II: 228
missions II: 229–231
Nahua I: 249
Navajo II: 247
New Mexico I: 256–257; II: 254–255
Oviedo y Valdés, Gonzalo Fernández de I: 272–273
Pima revolt II: 284
piracy II: 284–285
Popé II: 289–290
printing and publishing II: 299
Pueblo Revolt II: 303–304
Puerto Rico I: 297
Reformation I: 310
repartimiento I: 310
Roman Catholics II: 323, 324
Sepúlveda, Juan Ginés de I: 322
slavery I: 327; II: 338, 339, 342
slave trade II: 343
theater II: 373
Spanish conquest II: 244, 254–255, 267, 309
Spanish exploration IV: 64, 93, 337
Amazon River I: 8, 9
Andes Mountains I: 10
Apalachee I: 11
Barbados I: 26
Cabeza de Vaca, Álvar Núñez I: 37
Cabot, Sebastian I: 42–43
Cathay (China) I: 64
Chickasaw II: 59
cities and urban life II: 61
Columbus, Christopher I: 79–83
conquistadores I: 84–85. See also conquistador(es)
Cozumel I: 96

Cuba **I:** 97–98
Cuitláhuac **I:** 99
El Dorado **I:** 118–119
exploration **II:** 114
Indians of the Desert
    Southwest **II:** 165–166
Jamaica **I:** 187
North Carolina **II:** 264
Northeast Passage **I:** 265
Northwest Passage **I:** 266
Panama **I:** 275–276
Ponce de León, Juan **I:**
    288
Protestantism **II:** 300
Pueblo Indians **II:** 303
South Carolina **II:** 353
Vespucci, Amerigo **I:** 367,
    368
Spanish Flu Epidemic **VII:**
    242–243, 359*c*
Spanish immigration **II:** 23,
    359–360
Spanish missions **II:** 43, 49, 120,
    244, 246, 247; **IV:** 64
Spanish settlers **II:** 9, 327, 382
Spanish traders **II:** 41, 166, 266
Sparkman, John **IX:** 95
SPARS (Coast Guard) **VIII:** 386
Spartan missiles **X:** 22
Spaulding, Elbridge G. **V:** 159
Spaulding, Eliza **IV:** 325
Speaker of the House **IV:**
    282–283; **VII:** 42, 356*c;* **VIII:**
    66, 96, 129
speakers. *See tlatoani*
Spears, Britney **X:** 202, 241
Special Field Order No. 15 **V:**
    332–333
    Freedmen's Bureau **V:** 142
    Port Royal, South
        Carolina, Experiment **V:**
        280
    Sherman, William T. **V:**
        321
    Sherman's March through
        Georgia **V:** 323
Special Field Order No. 67 **V:**
    322
special interest groups. *See*
    lobbies/lobbying
Special Operations Executive
    (Great Britain) **VIII:**
    104–105
"special relationship" **VIII:** 16
Special Service Organization
    (Japan) **VIII:** 104
specie **IV:** 44, 118–119, 276,
    277, 377*c;* **V:** 23, 24, 159
Specie Circular of 1836 **IV:**
    42–43, 119, 276, 377*c*
Specie Resumption Act of 1875
    V: 157; **VI:** 72, 120, 324*c*

spectography **VII:** 276
speculation. *See also* land
    speculation
    agriculture **IV:** 12
    banking and currency **IV:**
        42, 43
    claim clubs **IV:** 85–86
    Era of Good Feelings **IV:**
        127
    Erie Canal **IV:** 129
    Gadsden Purchase **IV:** 159
    Panic of 1819 **IV:** 275
    Panic of 1837 **IV:** 276
speech, freedom of. *See* First
    Amendment; Four
    Freedoms; free speech
spelling **III:** 370
Spellman, Francis Joseph **VIII:**
    53
Spencer, Herbert
    Darwinism and religion
        VI: 75
    James, William **VI:** 154
    literature **VI:** 178
    pragmatism **VI:** 228
    religion **VI:** 242
    Social Darwinism **VI:** 266
    Sumner, William Graham
        VI: 280
Spencer, Lilly Martin **V:** 16
Spencer, Percy **X:** 273
Spence v. Washington **X:** 117
sperm whales **I:** 9
SPG. *See* Society for the
    Propagation of the Gospel in
    Foreign Parts
sphere of influence, Soviet
    foreign policy **VIII:** 125
    Nazi-Soviet Pact **VIII:** 238
    Soviet-American relations
        VIII: 334
    Yalta Conference **VIII:**
        401, 402
"Sphinx, The" (Emerson) **IV:**
    126
Spice Girls **X:** 202
Spice Islands **I:** 44, **335,** 365
spices **II:** 122
spice trade **I:** 43–44, 114, 335
Spielberg, Steven **X:** 198, *199,*
    239, 240
spies. *See* espionage
Spies, August **VI:** 127
Spillane, Mickey **IX:** 183
Spinks, Leon **IX:** 10
spinning jenny **III:** 177
Spinoza, Baruch **I:** 192
spinsters **II: 360**
Spiral Jetty (Smithson) **X:** 26
"spiriting" **II:** 204
Spirit of St. Louis **VII:** 23, 158,
    159, *159*

Spirit of the Times, The **IV:** 211
spirits (alcohol) **II:** 15
"spirits" (indentured servitude)
    II: 164
Spiritual Exercises (Ignatius
    Loyola) **I:** 188, 209
spiritualists/spiritualism **IV:** 273,
    299, **325–326; VI:** 243, 244,
    318, 319; **VII:** 124
spirituality **X:** 216–217
spirituals **VIII:** 309
Spitzbergen **I:** 114
Spock, Benjamin **IX:** 267,
    279–280, 329*c;* **X:** 33
Spoil of Office, A (Garland) **VI:**
    109
"Spoils Conference" **VII:** 24
spoils system **IV:** 108, 123, 192;
    V: 156, 302; **VI:** 56, 58, 126.
    See also patronage
Spokane Indians **I:** 253
Spooner Act **VII:** 356*c*
Sporting Life **VI:** 22
Sporting News **VI:** 22
Sport of the Gods, The (Dunbar)
    VI: 83
sports and recreation **V:** 192; **VI:**
    273–275, *274;* **VII:**
    256–258, *257,* **293,** *293,*
    293–295; **VIII: 296–298,**
    297, **335–338,** *337;* **IX: 255,**
    280–281, 332*c;* **X:** 186,
    261–263, *262,* **284–286,** *286*
    African-American
        movement **IX:** 5
    baseball **VI:** 21–22; **VII:**
        25–27; **VIII:** 335–336
    basketball **VIII:** 336
    bicycling **VI:** 27–28
    boxing **VI:** 32–34; **VIII:**
        336–337
    cities and urban life **VII:**
        50; **VIII:** 59
    Dempsey, Jack **VII:** 67
    DiMaggio, Joe **VIII:**
        83–84
    football **VI:** 101–102; **VIII:**
        336
    golf **VIII:** 337
    hockey **VIII:** 338
    horse racing **VI:** 133–134;
        VIII: 338
    Japanese Americans,
        relocation of **VIII:** 171
    Johnson, Jack **VII:** 138–139
    Louis, Joe **VIII:** 195–196
    marriage and family life
        VIII: 204
    media **X:** 186
    National Outdoor
        Recreation Review
        Board **IX:** 223–224

National Trails Act of 1968
    IX: 225–226
news media **VIII:** 243
Owens, Jesse **VIII:**
    260–261
popular culture **VII:** 232;
    VIII: 273–275; **X:** 241
recreation **VII:** 256,
    257–258; **VIII:** 296; **IX:**
    255; **X:** 261–262
television **IX:** 297; **X:** 296
tennis **VIII:** 337
tobacco suits **X:** 305
track and field **VI:**
    289–290; **VIII:** 337–338
USO **VIII:** 366–367
war bonds **VIII:** 374
women's rights and status
    X: 321
work, household **VII:** 342
World War II home front
    VIII: 395
YMCA **VIII:** 350
Sports Illustrated (magazine)
    VIII: 196; **X:** 186
Spotswood, Alexander **II:** 115,
    292, 369
Spotsylvania, Battles of **V: 333,**
    407*c*
    Burnside, Ambrose E. **V:**
        45
    Chamberlain, Joshua L. **V:**
        54
    Early, Jubal A. **V:** 103
    Grant, Ulysses S. **V:** 156
    Hancock, Winfield Scott **V:**
        163
    Hill, Ambrose P. **V:** 168
    homefront **V:** 169
    Irish-American regiments
        V: 182
    Lee, Robert E. **V:** 207
    Louisiana Tigers **V:** 218
    Meade, George Gordon **V:**
        227
    Overland campaign **V:** 261
    Stuart, J. E. B. **V:** 341
spotted fever **IV:** 112
Sprague, Frank J. **VI:** 149
Spring, Lindley **V:** 266
Springfield Bicycle Club **VI:** *28*
Springsteen, Bruce **X:** 202, *202,*
    240
Spring Wells Treaty **IV:** 169
Sprint missiles **X:** 22
Spruance, Raymond A.
    King, Ernest J. **VIII:** 177
    Nimitz, Chester W. **VIII:**
        246
    Philippine Sea, Battle of
        the **VIII:** 267
    Tarawa **VIII:** 350

Sputnik satellites **IX:** 28, 91, 219, 278, 332*c*
spying. *See* espionage
spy planes **IX:** 28
Squanto **I:** 286; **II:** 38, 51, 130–131, 283, 287, **360–361**
Square Deal **VII:** 84, 170
"square-set" timbering process **IV:** 96
squash **II:** 8, 77, 121, 165
squatters **II:** 11, 192, 381, 385; **IV:** 85–86, 100, 344
Squibb **VIII:** 208
Squier, Ephriam George **IV:** 308
SSI **VIII:** 330
SSRIs (selective serotonin reuptake inhibitors) **X:** 190
Stack, Carol **X:** 109
Stadacona **I:** 58, 59
Stade, Hans (Staden) **I:** 54–55, **335–336,** 361
Stagecoach (film) **VIII:** 273
stagecoaches **II:** 377; **IV:** 255, 271
Stager, Anson **V:** 351
stagflation
   Carter, James Earl, Jr. **X:** 58
   economy **X:** 94
   Ford, Gerald R. **X:** 121
   O'Neill, Thomas P., Jr. **X:** 228
stained glass **VI:** 288
"stainless banner" **V:** 26
Stalin, Joseph **VII:** 270; **VIII:** 410*c*
   Anglo-American relations **VIII:** 17
   Asia (and foreign policy) **IX:** 21
   atomic bomb **VIII:** 29
   Cairo Conference **VIII:** 51
   Casablanca Conference **VIII:** 52
   cold war **IX:** 58
   communism **IX:** 61
   Communists **VIII:** 65
   Europe (and foreign policy) **IX:** 105, 106
   Grand Alliance **VIII:** 137
   Harriman, Averell **VIII:** 144
   Hopkins, Harry **VIII:** 157
   Italian campaign **VIII:** 168
   Korean War **IX:** 163
   Nazi-Soviet Pact **VIII:** 238
   Potsdam Conference **VIII:** 279
   POWs **VIII:** 282
   propaganda **VIII:** 283
   Robeson, Paul **VIII:** 310
   Roosevelt, Franklin D. **VIII:** 314

second front **VIII:** 320
Soviet-American relations **VIII:** 334
Soviet Union **IX:** 277
Teheran Conference **VIII:** 354
Truman Doctrine **IX:** 300
United Nations (UN) **VIII:** 365, 366
V-E Day **VIII:** 369
Wallace, Henry A. **VIII:** 374
White Paper **IX:** 321
World War II European theater **VIII:** 391, 392
Yalta Conference **VIII:** 401, 402, *402*
Stalingrad, Battle of **VIII:** 125, 320
Stallone, Sylvester **X:** 198
Stalwarts (Republican Party) **V:** 302
   Arthur, Chester Alan **VI:** 16
   Conkling, Roscoe **VI:** 64
   Garfield, James A. **VI:** 108
   presidential campaigns **VI:** 232
   Republican Party **VI:** 246
Stamp Act **II:** 196, 334; **III:** *331*, **331–332,** 391*c*
   Adams, John **III:** 2
   Adams, Samuel **III:** 4
   American Revolution **III:** 12
   artisans **III:** 26
   Association, the **III:** 27
   Attucks, Crispus **III:** 28
   Bernard, Francis **III:** 37, 38
   Bland, Richard **III:** 40
   Burke, Edmund **III:** 52
   Bute, earl of **III:** 55
   Chase, Samuel **III:** 64
   cities and urban life **III:** 69
   Continental Congress, First **III:** 87
   Currency Act **III:** 99
   Declaratory Act **III:** 103
   Dickinson, John **III:** 105
   Dulany, Daniel **III:** 108
   economy **III:** 111
   Franklin, Benjamin **III:** 134
   Franklin, William **III:** 136
   Galloway, Joseph **III:** 148
   Golden Hill, Battle of **III:** 153
   Grenville, George **III:** 157
   Hancock, John **III:** 163
   Henry, Patrick **III:** 166

Hutchinson, Thomas **III:** 171
Ingersoll, Jared **III:** 178
Jews **III:** 187
journalism **III:** 191
Laurens, Henry **III:** 203
Lee, Richard Henry **III:** 207
liberty tree/pole **III:** 213–214
Livingston, William **III:** 217
Loyal Nine **III:** 221, 222
MacIntosh, Ebenezer **III:** 225
Mason, George **III:** 237
Mayhew, Jonathan **III:** 238
McDougall, Alexander **III:** 239
Oliver, Andrew **III:** 266–267
Otis, James, Jr. **III:** 268
Pitt, William **III:** 277
resistance movement **III:** 303
Revere, Paul **III:** 304
riots **III:** 308, 309
Sons of Liberty **III:** 329, 330
Stamp Act Congress **III:** 332–333
theater **III:** 347
Townshend Duties **III:** 348
Virginia Resolves **III:** 361
Whately, Thomas **III:** 373
Young, Thomas **III:** 390
Stamp Act Congress **II:** 196; **III:** **332–333,** 391*c*
   Dickinson, John **III:** 105
   Grenville, George **III:** 157
   Hancock, John **III:** 163
   resistance movement **III:** 303
   Stamp Act **III:** 332
Stamp Act Crisis **II:** 179
stamp mills **IV:** 96
stamps, postage **II:** 292, 293
stamp tax **II:** 181, 292
standard of living. *See also* poverty
   agriculture **IX:** 7, 9
   Appalachian Regional Development Act **IX:** 15
   cost-of-living adjustment **IX:** 70
   United Farm Workers **IX:** 304
Standard Oil **VI:** 146, 179, 325*c;* **VII:** **295–296,** 356*c,* 357*c*
   business **VII:** 38

muckrakers **VII:** 192
New Nationalism **VII:** 211
Northern Securities Co. v. U.S. **VII:** 216
oil industry **VII:** 217–218
Prohibition **VII:** 241
Republican Party **VII:** 263
Rockefeller, John D. **VII:** 264
Roosevelt, Theodore **VII:** 266
Steffens, Lincoln **VII:** 299
Tarbell, Ida **VII:** 305
Standard Oil Company of New Jersey et al v. United States **VII:** 357*c*
Standard Oil of New Jersey **VI:** 215, 294
Standard Oil of Ohio **VI:** 215, 293–294, 323*c*
Standard Oil Trust Agreement **VI:** 293–294
Standing Bear **VI:** 153
Standish, Myles **II:** 15, 16, 236, **361**
Stanford, Leland **VI:** 94
Stanford-Binet intelligence test **VII:** 131
Stanford University **VI:** 94; **X:** 215
Stanislaw II, king of Poland **III:** 289
Stanley, Henry **VI:** 211
Stanley Cup **VII:** 295
Stanleyville airlift (Congo) **IX:** 4
Stanton, Edwin M. **V:** **333–334,** 408*c*
   Andrews's Raid **V:** 11
   Appomattox Court House, Virginia **V:** 15
   assassination of Abraham Lincoln **V:** 18
   Boyd, Belle **V:** 34
   Dana, Charles A. **V:** 88
   54th Massachusetts Regiment **V:** 125
   governors **V:** 153
   impeachment of Andrew Johnson **V:** 177–179
   Johnson, Andrew **V:** 188–189
   Medal of Honor **V:** 228
   prisons **V:** 282
   Reconstruction Acts **V:** 296
   Shenandoah Valley: Sheridan's campaign **V:** 317
   Sherman, William T. **V:** 321
   Special Field Order No. 15 **V:** 332
   telegraph **V:** 351

Union army **V:** 365
war contracting **V:** 387
Washington, D.C. **V:** 390
Welles, Gideon **V:** 391
Stanton, Elizabeth Cady **IV:**
378c; **V: 334–335**, 335, 409c;
VII: 31, 198, 335
  AASS **IV:** 15
  abolition **V:** 3
  Anthony, Susan B. **VI:** 12,
  13
  Blackwell, Antoinette
  Brown **VI:** 30
  Bloomer, Amelia **IV:** 53, 54
  Brown, Olympia **VI:** 36
  female antislavery societies
  IV: 136
  Fourteenth Amendment
  V: 139
  Gage, Matilda Joslyn **VI:**
  107
  Hooker, Isabella Beecher
  VI: 133
  Mott, Lucretia **IV:** 247
  NWSA **V:** 248
  Seneca Falls **IV:** 314, 315
  Stone, Lucy **VI:** 278
  temperance movement **IV:**
  336
  women's colleges **VI:** 316
  women's rights and status
  IV: 368; **V:** 397–399; **VI:**
  317
  Woodhull, Victoria **VI:** 318
Stanton, Harriet **IV:** 315
Stanton, Henry B. **IV:** 314, 362
Staper, Richard **I:** 206
staple crop haciendas **I:** 150
Staples Act of 1663 **II:** 3
Starbuck, Mary Coffin **II: 361**
Stark, Harold R. **VIII:** 237
Star of the West **V:** 136
Starr, Ellen Gates **VI:** 140, 233,
259
Starr, Kenneth **X: 286–287**,
328c, 330c
  Clinton, Hillary Rodham
  X: 64
  Clinton, William **X:** 68, 69
  independent counsel **X:**
  150
  Reno, Janet **X:** 267
Starr, Ringo (Richard Starkey)
IX: 36
star route frauds **VI:** 17, 67, **275**
Starr Report **X:** 287
"Stars and Bars" **V:** 26
"Stars and Stripes" **V:** 26
Stars and Stripes (newspaper)
VIII: 207
"Star Spangled Banner" **III:**
251; **IV:** 39, 162, 201

START. *See* Strategic Arms
  Reduction Treaty
"Star Wars." *See* Strategic
  Defense Initiative
Star Wars (movie) **X:** 198, 240,
325c
Stassen, Harold **X:** 43
state banks **IV:** 41, 42, 275; **VI:**
205–206
state constitutions **VI:** 5
State Department **IV:** 351, 360;
V: 41, 131, 159; **VI:** 5, 31, 32,
37, 103; **VII:** 124, 135; **IX:**
189–190, 233–234, 320–321
  Albright, Madeleine K. **X:**
  18
  Berle, Adolf A., Jr. **VIII:** 35
  Byrnes, James F. **VIII:** 48,
  49
  Communists **VIII:** 66
  FCC **VIII:** 116, 117
  Haig, Alexander M., Jr. **X:**
  139
  Hull, Cordell **VIII:** 159
  Kissinger, Henry A. **X:** 166
  Marshall, George C. **VIII:**
  206
  Moley, Raymond C. **VIII:**
  216
  Powell, Colin L. **X:** 246,
  247
  Spanish Civil War **VIII:**
  335
  Stimson, Henry L. **VIII:**
  340
  Zionism **VIII:** 403
State Department, Confederate
V: 27–28, 75
state government. *See*
  government (state and local)
statehood **X:** 19
state legislatures **VII:** 69
Statement on Fundamentals of
  American Foreign Policy
  VIII: 411c
states' rights **III: 333; IV:** 376c,
377c; **V: 335–336; VI:** 92;
VII: 169; **VIII:** 82
  abolition **V:** 3
  Baker v. Carr **IX:** 31
  Bank of the United States
  (First) **III:** 31
  Bork, Robert **X:** 39
  Brown, Joseph **V:** 39
  Calhoun, John C. **IV:** 63
  Civil Rights Act of 1964
  IX: 56, 57
  common soldier **V:** 69
  Compromise of 1850 **IV:**
  94, 95
  Confederate States of
  America **V:** 75

conscription **V:** 79
Davis, Jefferson **V:** 88, 90
Democratic Party **V:** 94
election of 1828 **IV:** 122
election of 1840 **IV:** 124
elections **V:** 109, 110
federalism **X:** 112–113
Federalist Party **III:** 126
fire-eaters **V:** 127, 128
Gideon v. Wainwright **IX:**
121–122
governors **V:** 152
Hancock, Winfield Scott **V:**
163
Hartford Convention **IV:**
170–171
impeachment of Andrew
  Johnson **V:** 178
Jackson, Andrew **IV:** 191,
193
Johnson, Andrew **V:** 188
liberalism **X:** 175
lost cause, the **V:** 217
Macon, Nathaniel **III:** 226
Madison, James **III:** 229
Marshall, John **III:** 237
McCulloch v. Maryland
IV: 227
modern Republicanism
IX: 209
Native American
  movement **IX:** 228
Nullification Controversy
IV: 263–265
Otis, Harrison Gray **III:**
268
Pickering, John **III:** 275
Pierce, Franklin **V:** 275
polygamy **IV:** 285
Randolph, John **III:** 296
Reconstruction Acts **V:** 296
secession **V:** 311
slavery **IV:** 317, 318
States' Rights Party **IX:**
281
Stephens, Alexander H. **V:**
337
Story, Joseph **III:** 334
Submerged Lands Act **IX:**
286–287
Taylor, John, of Caroline
III: 344
Thurmond, J. Strom **X:**
303
Vallandigham, Clement L.
V: 377
Virginia and Kentucky
  Resolutions **III:** 360
*Webster v. Reproductive
  Health Services* **X:**
318–319
Welles, Gideon **V:** 392

Whig Party **IV:** 363
Yancey, William Lowndes
V: 401
States' Rights Party (Dixiecrats)
VIII: 82, 189; **IX:** 14, 79, 94,
179, 258, **281–282**, 330c; **X:**
303
state universities **VI:** 92
Statue of Liberty **VI:** 173, 211,
275–276, 276, 321, 326c
Status Seekers, The (Vance
Packard) **IX:** 239
Statute for Religious Freedom
II: 317; **III:** 184
Statute of Artificers (1562) **II:**
389
Steagall, Henry **VIII:** 33
Steamboat Act of 1838 **V:** 355
Steamboat Act of 1852 **V:** 355
steamboats **III:** 142, 177, 322
  agriculture **IV:** 10–11
  economy **IV:** 117–118
  Forty-niners **IV:** 147
  immigration **IV:** 177, 178
  industrialization **IV:** 185
  Mexican-American War
  IV: 234
  migration **IV:** 235
  National Road **IV:** 253
  railroads **IV:** 293
  science and technology **IV:**
  307
  Vanderbilt, Cornelius **IV:**
  352
steam engines **III:** 177; **V:** 368
steam locomotives **IV:** 40, 292,
307
steam plows **VI:** 8
steam power **III:** 11; **IV:** 81–82,
117–118, 292; **VI:** 149
steamship lines **VI:** 140
steamships **V:** 175, 355
Stearns, Abel **IV: 326–327**
Stearns, George L. **V:** 125
Stedman, Edmund Clarence **VI:**
176
Steel, Danielle **X:** 178
Steele, Frederick **V:** 236
steel plow **IV:** 10
steel/steel industry **IV:** 105; **V:**
356; **VI:** xv, **276–278**, 277m,
327c; **VII: 296–298**,
298–299; **VIII: 338–339**,
407c; **IX:** 66, **282–283**, 331c;
X: 94, 269. *See also specific
headings, e.g.:* Bethlehem
Steel
  automobile industry **VIII:**
  30
  banking, investment **VI:** 20
  Bessemer process **VI:** 27
  bridges **VI:** 34–35

steel/steel industry (continued)
    Carnegie, Andrew **VI:** 44
    CIO **VIII:** 69
    economy **VIII:** 92
    Frick, Henry Clay **VI:** 105
    industrial revolution,
        second **VI:** 145–147
    inventions and technology
        VI: 149
    labor **VIII:** 180, 181
    Lewis, John L. **VIII:** 186
    mobilization **VIII:** 214
    Morgan, John Pierpont **VI:**
        198
    Murray, Philip **VIII:** 221
    New South **VI:** 209, 210
    skyscrapers **VI:** 264, 265
    trade **VI:** 291
    trusts **VI:** 292, 295
    WPB **VIII:** 375
Steel Strike of 1919 **VII:**
    298–299, 360*c*
    AFL **VII:** 11
    Committee for Public
        Information **VII:** 52
    labor movement **VII:** 153
    New Unionism **VII:** 213
    open shop movement **VII:**
        220
    steel industry **VII:**
        297–298
    U.S. Steel **VII:** 320
Steelworkers Organizing
    Committee (SWOC)
    CIO **VIII:** 69, 70
    labor **VIII:** 180
    Murray, Philip **VIII:** 221
    steel industry **VIII:** 338
Steffens, Lincoln **VII:** 140, 192,
    198, **299,** 355*c*
Steichen, Edward **VIII:** 268
Steiglitz, Alfred **VII:** 161
Stein, Gertrude **VII:** 160–161,
    166; **IX:** 181
Stein, Herbert **X:** 301
Steinbeck, John **VIII: 339–340,**
    408*c*; **IX:** 181
    Dust Bowl **VIII:** 87
    literature **VIII:** 191–192
    marriage and family life
        VIII: 204
    migration **VIII:** 212
Steinem, Gloria **IX:** 115, 326; **X:**
    211, **287–288**
Steiner, George **X:** 178
Steinfels, Peter **X:** 215
stem cell research **X:** 146, 331*c*
Stenberg v. Carhart (2000) **X:**
    42, 264, 279, 330*c*
Stenberg v. Planned Parenthood
    (2000) **X:** 130
Stengstacke, John **IX:** 13

Stennis, John **X:** 81
Stephens, Alexander Hamilton
    V: 336–337; VII: 332
    Civil War **V:** 63
    Confederate States of
        America **V:** 75, 77
    Davis, Jefferson **V:** 90
    elections **V:** 110
    homespun **V:** 170
    Johnson, Andrew **V:** 188
    Kansas-Nebraska Act of
        1854 **V:** 198
Stephens, Ann Sophia **VI:** 80
Stephens, George E. **V:** 125
Stephens, John Lloyd **I:** 86, 225;
    IV: 133
Stephens, John W. **V:** 199
Stephens, Samuel **II:** 32
Stephens, Thomas **II:** 138
Stephens, Uriah **VI:** 162
Stephens, William **II:** 267
Stephens, William D. **VII:** 188
Stephenson, David **VII:** 148
Steptoe, E. W. **IX:** 207
sterilization **VII:** 30
Stern, David **IV:** 329
Stettheimer, Florine **VII:** 19
Stettinius, Edward **IX:** 283
Steuben, Baron Frederick von
    III: 86, 201, **334,** 359, 393*c*
Steunenberg, Frank **VII:** 62,
    120
Stevens, Alzina P. **VI:** 10
Stevens, David **VI:** 4
Stevens, Edwin A. **IV:** 295
Stevens, John **IV:** 293
Stevens, John L. **IV:** 171; **VI:**
    124
Stevens, John Paul **X:** 131, 291
Stevens, Nettie **VII:** 276
Stevens, Robert **X:** 331*c*
Stevens, Robert L. **IV:** 295, 307
Stevens, Thaddeus **IV:** 363; **V:**
    337–338, 408*c*
    impeachment of Andrew
        Johnson **V:** 177
    Radical Republicans **V:**
        288, 289
    Reconstruction **V:** 292
    Republican Party **V:** 302
    Sumner, Charles **V:** 343
Stevens, Thomas **VI:** 28
Stevenson, Adlai, III **X:** 24
Stevenson, Adlai E. **VIII:** 311;
    IX: *283*, **283–284,** 331*c*,
    332*c*; **X:** 219–220, 287
    Democratic Party **IX:** 79
    elections **IX:** 94, 95
    Free Speech Movement
        IX: 112
    Powell, Adam Clayton **IX:**
        245

Stevenson, Carter L. **V:** 57, 216
Steward, Theophilus G. **VI:** 4,
    283
Steward v. Davis **VIII:** 329
Stewart, Alexander **III:** 120, 121
Stewart, Alexander H. **VI:** 78
Stewart, Alexander P. **V:** 28
Stewart, Jimmy **VIII:** 218, *219;*
    IX: 212
Stewart, Julius L. **VI:** 219
Stewart, Maria **IV: 327**
Stewart, Potter **IX:** 31, 100, 104,
    315
Stewart, William **VI:** 115
STFU. *See* Southern Tenant
    Farmers Union
Stieglitz, Alfred **VII:** 18, 20,
    356*c;* **VIII:** 24, 268
Stiles, Ezra **II:** 142, 331
Stiles, John R. **X:** 120
Still, William **IV: 327–328; V:**
    361
Stilwell, Joseph W. **VIII:** 398
Stimson, Henry L. **VII:** 201,
    353; **VIII: 340**
    Army, U.S. **VIII:** 19
    Executive Order 9066
        VIII: 107
    Hoover presidency **VIII:**
        155
    Manchuria **VIII:** 199
    Marshall, George C. **VIII:**
        206
    Reciprocal Trade
        Agreements Act **VIII:**
        294
    Republican Party **VIII:**
        306
    Selective Service **VIII:** 323
Stimson Doctrine **VIII:** 123,
    199, 405*c*
sting operations **X:** 4–5
stock car racing **X:** 285
Stockdale, James **X:** 263
stockholders **II:** 191
stock market crash of 1929. *See*
    crash of 1929
stock market reports **V:** 192,
    253, 351
stocks/stock market **IV:** 96; **VII:**
    xiv; **VIII:** 406*c;* **X:** 327*c*
    banking, investment **VI:** 20
    business **X:** 50, 51
    economy **X:** 95, 96
    Gould, Jay **VI:** 117–118
    industrial revolution,
        second **VI:** 146
    trusts **VI:** 295
stock tickers **VI:** 89
Stockton, California **IV:** 66
Stockton, Robert Field **IV:** 65,
    153, 200, **328**

Stoddard, Richard Henry **VI:**
    176
Stoddard, Solomon **II:** 105, 217,
    218, 305
Stoddert, Benjamin **III:** 291
Stokes, Carl **X:** 256
Stokowski, Leopold **VI:** 79
Stone, Barton W. **IV:** 72, 298
Stone, Charles P. **V:** 191, 389
Stone, Harlan Fiske **VIII:** 76,
    345, 346, 346*t*, 409*c*
Stone, John **II:** 279
Stone, Kate **V:** 287, 298
Stone, Lucy **IV:** 148, 378*c;* **V:**
    248, 396, 398; **VI: 278; VII:**
    198, 335
    Anthony, Susan B. **VI:** 12
    Blackwell, Antoinette
        Brown **VI:** 30
    Brown, Olympia **VI:** 36
    Mitchell, Maria **VI:** 195
    women's rights **VI:** 317
Stone, Oliver **X:** 31
Stone, William **II:** 209
stone carving **I:** 86
Stoneites **IV:** 299
Stoneman, George **V:** 54
Stone Mountain, Georgia **V:** 239
Stonewall, CSS **V:** 183
Stonewall riots (New York City)
    X: 127, 277, 323*c*
Stono Rebellion **II: 361–362**
    African Americans **II:** 7
    agriculture **II:** 12
    Charleston **II:** 57
    crowd action **II:** 78
    Fort Mose **II:** 123
    journalism **II:** 178
    slave resistance **II:** 337
    slavery **II:** 342
    South Carolina **II:** 354
    War of Jenkins' Ear **II:** 392
STOP ERA
    amendments to the
        Constitution **X:** 19
    conservative movement **X:**
        79
    ERA **X:** 106
    feminism **X:** 115–116
    Schlafly, Phyllis **X:** 272
    women's rights and status
        X: 321
Story, Joseph **III:** 236,
    334–335, 388; **IV:** 331,
    398–402
storytelling **II:** 60, 351
Stoughton, Edwin H. **V:** 242
Stover, Charles B. **VI:** 259
Stowe, Harriet Beecher **IV:**
    379*c;* **V: 338–339,** *339;* **VI:**
    24, 286
    AASS **IV:** 14

abolition **V:** 4
Civil War **V:** 64
Fitzhugh, George **V:** 128
literature **IV:** 213; **V:** 212
race and race relations **IV:** 291
religion **IV:** 296
theater **V:** 352
Truth, Sojourner **V:** 357
Strachan, Gordon **X:** 308
Strachey, William **I:** 343; **II:** 135, 288
straight pins **IV:** 184
Strait of Gibraltar **I:** 306
Straits of Magellan **I:** 110, 215, 217; **IV:** 146
Strang, James Jesse **IV:** **328–329**
"Strange Fruit" **VIII:** 149
"Strangites" **IV:** 329
Strasberg, Lee **IX:** 210
Strasbourg **I:** 50
Strasser, Adolph **VI:** 116–117; **VII:** 10
Strategic Arms Limitation Talks (SALT) **IX:** 16
Strategic Arms Limitation Treaties (SALT I; SALT II) **X:** **288–289**
Strategic Arms Limitation Treaty (SALT I) **X:** 324c
ABM Treaty **X:** 22–23
arms race **X:** 25
cold war (end of) **X:** 70
defense policy **X:** 85
détente **X:** 89
foreign policy **X:** 122
Kissinger, Henry A. **X:** 165–165
Nixon, Richard M. **X:** 220
Strategic Arms Limitation Treaty (SALT II) **X:** 325c
Carter, James Earl, Jr. **X:** 58
cold war (end of) **X:** 71
defense policy **X:** 86
détente **X:** 89
foreign policy **X:** 123
Helms, Jesse A., Jr. **X:** 141
Strategic Arms Reduction Treaty (START)
arms race **X:** 25
cold war (end of) **X:** 72
foreign policy **X:** 124
INF Treaty **X:** 151, 152
Reagan, Ronald W. **X:** 261
Strategic Arms Limitation Treaties **X:** 289
Strategic Defense Initiative (SDI) ("Star Wars") **X:** **289–290**
ABM Treaty **X:** 23

cold war (end of) **X:** 71
defense policy **X:** 87
Powell, Colin L. **X:** 247
Reagan, Ronald W. **X:** 260, 261
strategic sufficiency policy **X:** 85
strategy. *See* tactics and strategy
strategy, Confederate **V:** 346
strategy, Union **V:** 346–348
Stratemeyer, Edward **IX:** 183
Straus, Nathan **VI:** 78, 79
Strauss, Leo **X:** 78, 215
Strauss, Levi **IV:** **329**
Stravinsky, Igor **VIII:** 223
Strayhorn, Billy **VIII:** 100
streamlined trains **VIII:** 360
Streetcar Named Desire, A (Tennessee Williams) **IX:** 329c
streetcars **VI:** 54, 149, 292
AFL **VII:** 10
cities and urban life **VII:** 49, 50
Johnson, Tom **VII:** 140
urban reform **VII:** 316–317
Street v. New York (1969) **X:** 117
"Strenuous Life" speech (Roosevelt) **VII:** 363–367
streptomycin **IX:** 205
Stricker, John **IV:** 39
Strickland, William **IV:** 27
strikebreaking **VII:** 36, 51, 249
strikes **III:** 200; **IV:** 152, 203, 204, 258; **V:** 116, 158, **339–340**, 356; **VI:** **167–169**, 168m, 324c, 327c; **VII:** 357c, 358c, 360c, 361c; **VIII:** 406c, 407c, 410c; **X:** 326c, 328c. *See also* boycotts
AFL **VII:** 11
agriculture **X:** 16
American Federation of Labor **VI:** 11; **VIII:** 14; **IX:** 11
American Plan **VII:** 12
Anthracite Coal Strike **VII:** **12–13,** 356c
automobile industry **VIII:** 30
Boston Police Strike of 1919 **VII:** 56
Bridges, Harry **VIII:** 43
Buck's Stove **VII:** 35–36
CIO **VIII:** 69–70
civil liberties **VIII:** 60
Cleveland, Grover **VI:** 59
Cloak Makers' Strike **VII:** 132
Coeur d'Alene miners' strike **VI:** 60–61

Committee for Public Information **VII:** 52
Congress of Industrial Organizations **IX:** 65–66
conservatism **VIII:** 73
conservative coalition **VIII:** 74
Cripple Creek strike **VII:** 120, 129
Darrow, Clarence **VII:** 62
Debs, Eugene V. **VII:** 64–65
Democratic Party **VIII:** 82
Flynn, Elizabeth Gurley **VII:** 95
Frick, Henry Clay **VI:** 105–106
Gastonia Strike **VII:** **106,** 225
Gompers, Samuel **VI:** 117
Great Strike of 1877 **VI:** 119–120
Greenwich Village **VII:** 114–115
Hayes, Rutherford B. **VI:** 126
Haymarket riot **VI:** 127
Haywood, "Big Bill" **VII:** 120
Hispanic Americans **X:** 141
Homestead Strike **VI:** 132; **VII:** 110, 297
International Ladies' Garment Workers Union **VII:** 132
IWW **VII:** 129, 130
King, Martin Luther, Jr. **IX:** 161–162
Knights of Labor **VI:** 162
labor, child **VI:** 165–166
labor and labor movements. *See* labor/ labor movement
labor organizations **VI:** 170
labor trends **VI:** 171
Lawrence Strike **VII:** **155–156,** 357c
Lewis, John L. **VIII:** 186
Ludlow Massacre **VII:** 167–168
Matewan, West Virginia strike **VII:** 314
McKees Rocks strikes **VII:** 250
Mitchell, John **VII:** 186
muckrakers **VII:** 192
Murray, Philip **VIII:** 221
National Civic Federation **VII:** 201
National Women's Trade Union League **VII:** 205

New Unionism **VII:** 212, 213
NLRB **VIII:** 231
NWLB **VIII:** 233, 234
open shop movement **VII:** 220
Passaic Strike **VII:** **224–225,** 361c
Paterson Strike **VII:** 115, 120, 130, **225**
Pullman Strike **VI:** 235–236
Pullman Strike of 1894 **VII:** 62, 64–65, 201
radicalism **VII:** 250
railroads **VI:** 237
Railroad Shopmen's Strike of 1922 **VII:** 2, 11, 118
Red Scare **VII:** 259
Roosevelt, Theodore **VII:** 266
Russian Revolution **VII:** 270
Sanger, Margaret **VII:** 273
Scott, Thomas Alexander **VI:** 258
Seattle General Strike **VII:** 270, **278–279,** 359c
Shirtwaist Makers Strike **VII:** **284–285,** 357c
sports **X:** 284
steel industry **VII:** 297–298; **VIII:** 338; **IX:** 282
Steel Strike of 1919 **VII:** **298–299,** 360c
Steinem, Gloria **X:** 288
Taft-Hartley Act **IX:** 291
Teamsters Union **IX:** 292
Triangle Shirtwaist Fire **VII:** 311–312
union movement **IX:** 303
United Farm Workers **IX:** 304–305
United Mine Workers of America (UMWA) **VII:** 314
U.S. Steel **VII:** 319, 320
Wald, Lillian **VII:** 329
Strike! (Vorse) **VII:** 106
strip cropping **IX:** 7
strip malls **IX:** 288
Strong, Caleb **III:** 192
Strong, George Templeton **V:** 366, 373
Strong, Josiah **VI:** **278–279,** 279, 325c
Darwinism and religion **VI:** 75
imperialism **VI:** 142
religion **VI:** 242
Social Darwinism **VI:** 266
Social Gospel **VI:** 267

Strong, William L. **VII:** 266
Strongbow, Richard (Strigul de Clare) **I:** 10
Strong, Theodore **III:** 321
Struggle of the Two Natures of Man (Barnard) **VI:** 259
Stryker, Roy **VIII:** 268
Stuart, Charles **IV:** 362
Stuart, George H. **V:** 371
Stuart, Gilbert **III:** 22, **335**, 396*c*
Stuart, J. E. B. **V: 340–341**, 406*c*
    Antietam, Battle of **V:** 13
    Chancellorsville, Battle of **V:** 55
    Confederate army **V:** 72
    Gettysburg, Battle of **V:** 148, 150
    Mosby, John Singleton **V:** 241, 242
    Richmond, Virginia **V:** 304
    Sheridan, Philip H. **V:** 318
Stuart, John **III:** 96, 254, 255, 281; **V:** 274
Stuart, John Todd **V:** 209
Stuart, R. Douglas, Jr. **VIII:** 12
Stuart, Robert
    American Fur Company **IV:** 17
    Ashley, William Henry **IV:** 29
    exploration **IV:** 131
    South Pass **IV:** 324
Stuart & Company **IV:** 184
Stuart monarchs **II:** 232
student activism **IX:** 334*c*
    education **IX:** 92
    Free Speech Movement **IX:** 112–113
    Hayden, Tom **IX:** 131
    La Raza Unida **IX:** 171
    New Left **IX:** 230–231
    race and racial conflict **IX:** 253
    sit-ins **IX:** 272–273
    Student Nonviolent Coordinating Committee **IX:** 284–285
    Students for a Democratic Society **IX:** 285–286
Student Nonviolent Coordinating Committee (SNCC) **IX: 284–285**, 285, 332*c*–334*c*
    African-American movement **IX:** 5, 6
    Baker, Ella **IX:** 31
    Black Panthers **IX:** 39
    Black Power **IX:** 40–41

    Carmichael, Stokely **IX:** 47–48
    Congress of Racial Equality **IX:** 66, 67
    freedom rides **IX:** 113–114
    Hamer, Fannie Lou **IX:** 129
    Lewis, John **IX:** 178–179
    Mississippi Freedom Democratic Party **IX:** 207
    NAACP **IX:** 220
    race and racial conflict **IX:** 253–254
    sit-ins **IX:** 273
    Voting Rights Act of 1965 **IX:** 311
    women's status and rights **IX:** 325
Students for a Democratic Society (SDS) **IX:** *285*, **285–286**, 333*c*; **X:** 317
    Hayden, Tom **IX:** 131
    Mills, C. Wright **IX:** 205
    New Left **IX:** 230–231
    Weathermen **IX:** 318–319
    women's status and rights **IX:** 325
Student War Loans Program **VIII:** 94
Studs Lonigan trilogy (Farrell) **VIII:** 165, 191
Stukly, Sir Lewis **II:** 323
Sturges v. Crowninshield **III:** 237
Sturgis, Samuel **V:** 13
Stuyvesant, Peter **II: 362–363**, 363
    Dutch-Indian Wars **II:** 99
    Herrman, Augustine **II:** 156
    Jews **II:** 175
    Kieft, Willem **II:** 182
    New Amsterdam **II:** 250
    New Netherland **II:** 257
    New York **II:** 260, 261
    Pennsylvania **II:** 274
Sublette, Andrew **IV:** 46–47
Sublette, Milton **IV:** 247, 302, 330
Sublette, William **IV: 329–330**
    American Fur Company **IV:** 17
    Bridger, James **IV:** 57
    Fort Laramie **IV:** 143
    mountain men **IV:** 247
    Rocky Mountain Fur Company **IV:** 302
    Smith, Jedediah Strong **IV:** 321

Sublette brothers **IV:** 32
submarines **III:** 141–142; **V:** 74, 310; **VIII: 342; IX:** 24, 293, 331*c. See also* U-boats
    Atlantic, Battle of the **VIII:** 26, 28
    foreign policy **VII:** 100
    King, Ernest J. **VIII:** 177
    Lusitania **VII:** 168
    Nimitz, Chester W. **VIII:** 246
    Pearl Harbor **VIII:** 264
    Philippine Sea, Battle of the **VIII:** 267
    World War I **VII:** 343
    World War II Pacific theater **VIII:** 399
    Zimmermann telegram **VII:** 353
Submerged Lands Act of 1953 **IX: 286–287**, 331*c*
subscription libraries **II:** 278, 282
subsidies **VI:** 193; **VIII:** 9; **IX:** 8, 334*c. See also* price supports
subsistence crops **V:** 279
substitutes. *See* commutation
subtreasury policy **IV:** 277
subtreasury system
    farmers' alliances **VI:** 99
    national banking system **VI:** 206
    Omaha Platform **VI:** 216
    political parties, third **VI:** 226
suburbs/suburbanization **V:** 59, 60; **VI:** 14, 79, 135; **VII: 299–301**, 318, 341; **VIII: 342–343; IX: 287–288; X:** 33
    automobile industry **IX:** 25
    cities and urban life **VIII:** 58–60
    economy **IX:** 90
    environmental issues **VIII:** 104
    FHA **VIII:** 119
    GI Bill of Rights **VIII:** 132
    housing **VIII:** 158
    Levitt, William J. **IX:** 176–178
    marriage and family life **IX:** 192
    migration **VIII:** 212; **IX:** 202–203
    National Outdoor Recreation Review Board **IX:** 223–224
    population trends **VIII:** 277
    RA **VIII:** 307
    World War II **VIII:** 390

World War II home front **VIII:** 394
Subversive Activities Control Act **IX:** 144
subway trains **V:** 356; **VI:** 292
Sudan **I:** 102, 173, 184, 203–204, 326, **336–337; X:** 330*c*
    African nations **X:** 12
    Clinton, William **X:** 69
    terrorism **X:** 299
Sudentenland **VIII:** 220
Suez Canal **IX:** 146, 332*c*
Suez crisis **IX:** 277, 288*m*, **288–289**, 332*c*
Suffolk Resolves **III:** 86, 87, 146, **335**, 363, 392*c*
suffrage **II: 363–364; III:** 64, **335–336**, 341, *381*, 383. *See also* African-American suffrage; voting rights; woman suffrage
    Boston **II:** 35
    Brent, Margaret Reed **II:** 40
    Burgesses, House of **II:** 45
    class consciousness **VI:** 57
    government, British American **II:** 142, 146
    Hooker, Thomas **II:** 157
    Jews **II:** 175
    labor, radical **VI:** 166
    Maryland **II:** 209–211
    Massachusetts **II:** 212, 214
    New Hampshire **II:** 251
    New Netherland **II:** 257
    Plymouth **II:** 287
    Roman Catholics **II:** 323
    tenants **II:** 370–371
    Virginia **II:** 384
Sufism **I:** 135, 184, 337, **337–338**
sugar **I: 338–339; IV:** 9, 97, 100; **VI:** 124, 291, 292, 327*c;* **VIII:** 38
    Acts of Trade and Navigation **II:** 3
    agriculture **II:** 11
    Bahía **I:** 23–24
    Brazil **I:** 33
    British Empire **II:** 43
    Canary Islands **I:** 53
    Caribbean **II:** 53
    consumption **II:** 71
    Dutch West India Company **II:** 98
    haciendas **I:** 149–150
    indentured servitude **II:** 164
    Jamaica **I:** 187
    labor **II:** 189
    Le Moyne, Jean-Baptiste, sieur de Bienville **II:** 193
    Madeira **I:** 214

Martinique **I:** 223
mercantilism **II:** 221
Montserrat **I:** 243
Nevis **I:** 254
New Hampshire **II:** 250
New Spain **I:** 261
Príncipe **I:** 293
Puerto Rico **I:** 297
rum trade **II:** 326
São Tomé **I:** 320
slavery **I:** 327; **II:** 338
smuggling **II:** 349
Spanish colonies **II:** 355
tobacco **II:** 374
Treaty of Paris **II:** 378
Sugar Act **III: 336–337,** 391*c*
   Bernard, Francis **III:** 37
   Currency Act **III:** 99
   Dickinson, John **III:** 105
   Grenville, George **III:** 157
   Hancock, John **III:** 163
   Otis, James, Jr. **III:** 268
   resistance movement **III:** 303
   Stamp Act Congress **III:** 333
   tariffs **III:** 342
   Vice Admiralty Courts **III:** 360
   West Indies **III:** 372
   Whately, Thomas **III:** 373
Sugaree **II:** 55, 379
sugar plantations **III:** 6; **V:** 259, 276
Sugar Trust **VI:** 180, 294
suicide bombers **X:** 297
Sulayman, Shaykh
   Dagomba **I:** 101
   Darfur **I:** 102
Suleiman I (Süleyman) **I: 339**
   Islam **I:** 185
   Jews (Judaism) **I:** 191
Suleiman II **I:** 191
sulfa drugs **VIII:** 208
sulky plows **VI:** 8
Sullivan, Ed **IX:** *36;* **X:** 202
Sullivan, John **II:** 173; **III: 337,** 394*c*
   Brandywine, Battle of **III:** 48
   Brant, Joseph **III:** 49
   Cornplanter **III:** 91
   Estaing, comte d' **III:** 120
   Howe, Richard, Lord **III:** 168
   Iroquois Confederacy **III:** 179
   Native Americans and the Revolution **III:** 255
   Red Jacket **III:** 297
   Rhode Island, Battle of **III:** 308

Sullivan, John L. **VI:** 33, *33,* 34, 325*c;* **VII:** 138
Sullivan, Leonor **X:** 106
Sullivan, Louis H. **VI:** 85, **279–280,** 320; **VII:** 16, 346
Sully, Thomas **V:** 16
Sulsey, Joseph **V:** 125
Sumanguru **I:** 141, 217, 339, 340
Sumatra **I:** 335
"Summary View of the Rights of British America" **III:** 183
Summer, Donna **X:** 202, 240
Summer Olympic games (1960) **IX:** 9
Summer Olympic games (1968) **IX:** *40,* 40–41
Summer Olympic games (1988) **IX:** 165
Summer Olympic games (1996) **IX:** 10
Summer on the Lakes (Fuller) **IV:** 156
Summit of the Americas **X:** 174
Sumner, Charles **IV:** 150; **V: 341–343,** *342,* 405*c*
   abolition **V:** 4
   amnesty, acts of **V:** 8
   Bleeding Kansas **V:** 31
   Canada and the United States **VI:** 43
   Civil Rights Act of 1875 **V:** 63
   Elliot, Robert B. **V:** 111
   Emancipation Proclamation **V:** 114
   foreign policy **V:** 133
   impeachment of Andrew Johnson **V:** 177
   the presidency **VI:** 230
   Radical Republicans **V:** 288, 289
   Reconstruction **V:** 292
   Republican Party **V:** 301, 302
   Santo Domingo **VI:** 255
   slavery **V:** 329
   Stevens, Thaddeus **V:** 338
   Turner, Henry McNeal **VI:** 296
   Wade, Benjamin **V:** 385
   Washington, Treaty of **VI:** 309
   Women's National Loyal League **V:** 397
Sumner, Edwin V. **V:** 13
Sumner, William Graham **VI: 280–281**
   James, William **VI:** 154
   pragmatism **VI:** 228
   Social Darwinism **VI:** 266

Ward, Lester Frank **VI:** 307
Sumpter Banner **IV:** 98
sumptuary laws **II:** 65, 215
Sumter, CSS **V:** 313
sun **VI:** 258
Sun Also Rises, The (Hemingway) **VII:** 162, 166, 361*c*
Sunbelt **VIII: 343–344; IX:** 51, 202, 203; **X: 290**
   aircraft industry **VIII:** 11
   economy **VIII:** 92
   migration **VIII:** 212
   mobilization **VIII:** 214
   population trends **VIII:** 277
   shipbuilding **VIII:** 325
   South **VIII:** 332
   World War II **VIII:** 390
   World War II home front **VIII:** 394
Sunday, William Ashley, Jr. **VII:** 262, *301,* **301–302**
Sunday, Women Drying Their Hair (Sloan) **VII:** 18
Sunday schools **IV:** 114, 296, 311; **VI:** 196, 241
Sundiata Keita (Sundjata or Mari-Djata) **I:** 141, 217, 220, **339–340**
sunflowers **II:** 8
Sunkist **VII:** *4*
Sunni Ali Ber **I:** 14, 109, 218, 243, 331–332
Sunni Islam **I:** 184; **X:** 213
"sunshine" rules **X:** 144
Sununu, John **X:** 279
Super Bowl **X:** 284, 296
Superfund **X:** 78
superheroes **VIII:** 275
Superman **VIII:** 275
Supermarine Spitfire **VIII:** 43
supermarkets **VIII:** 47
supernatural **X:** 217
Supplemental Security Income (SSI) **VIII:** 330
supplies. *See* military supplies
Supply Priorities and Allocation Board (SPAB) **VIII:** 255
supply-side economics **X:** 95, 172, 261
Suppression of the African Slave Trade in the United States, 1638–1870 (Du Bois) **VII:** 71
Supremacy Clause (U.S. Constitution) **X:** 112, 113
Supreme Court **III: 337–339,** 396*c,* 397*c;* **IV: 330–331,** 375*c–377c;* **V:** 405*c;* **VI: 281–282,** 325*c–328c;* **VII:** 358*c,* 359*c;* **VIII: 344–347,**

345, 346*t,* 405*c,* 407*c–410c;* **IX:** 334*c;* **X: 290–291,** 323*c,* 326*c,* 329*c. See also specific cases*
   abortion **X:** 1–3
   Abscam **X:** 5
   Adkins v. Children's Hospital **VII:** 3
   advertising **X:** 7
   affirmative action **X:** 8–9
   African-American movement **IX:** 4–6
   African Americans **VI:** 6; **VIII:** 2
   Agricultural Adjustment Act **VIII:** 6
   agriculture **VIII:** 8; **IX:** 8
   Ali, Muhammad **IX:** 10
   American Civil Liberties Union **VIII:** 13
   Amistad incident **IV:** 20
   antimonopoly **VIII:** 17–18
   Asian Americans **VIII:** 26
   banking, investment **VI:** 19
   banking and currency **IV:** 42
   Bank of the United States, Second **IV:** 44
   Bill of Rights **III:** 39
   Black, Hugo L. **VIII:** 36–37
   Bork, Robert **X:** 39
   Bradwell, Myra Colby **VI:** 34
   Brandeis, Louis **VII:** 34
   Brennan, William J., Jr. **X:** 40–42
   Breyer, Stephen **X:** 42
   Burger, Warren E. **X:** 43–44
   Bush, George W. **X:** 48
   business and government **VI:** 40
   Byrnes, James F. **VIII:** 48, 49
   capital punishment **X:** 56
   censorship **VIII:** 54; **X:** 60
   Chase, Salmon P. **V:** 56–57
   Chase, Samuel **III:** 64, 65
   child labor **VII:** 46
   civil liberties **VIII:** 61
   civil rights **VIII:** 61
   Civil Rights Act of 1875 **V:** 63
   civil rights cases **VI:** 55–56
   Civil War **V:** 65
   Clinton, William **X:** 68, 69
   Compromise of 1850 **IV:** 93
   Conkling, Roscoe **VI:** 64–65
   conservatism **VIII:** 72

Supreme Court (continued)
corporations III: 94
court-packing plan VIII:
76–77
currency issue VI: 72
Dartmouth College case
IV: 104
Democratic Party IV: 108
Douglas, William O. VIII:
84–85
Dred Scott decision V:
100–102
due process clause VI:
81–82
education III: 115; VI: 90
elections X: 102
Equal Employment
Opportunity
Commission IX: 103
ERA X: 107
Executive Order 9066
VIII: 107
Fair Labor Standards Act
VIII: 110
Federal Employee Loyalty
Program IX: 110
federal income tax VII: 92
federalism X: 113
First New Deal VIII: 122
Food, Drug, and Cosmetic
Act VIII: 123
Fortas, Abe X: 125–126
Frankfurter, Felix VIII:
127
freedom rides IX: 113–114
fugitive slave laws IV: 154,
155
gay rights movement X:
127
gays and lesbians IX: 119
Ginsburg, Ruth Bader X:
130–131
Gore, Albert, Jr. X: 134
government VIII: 133,
134, 136
grandfather clause VI: 119
GRH Act of 1985 X: 134
habeas corpus, writ of V:
161
Hamilton, Alexander III:
162
Harlan, John Marshall VI:
121–122
Henderson, Leon VIII:
145
Hill, Anita Faye X: 141
Hill, James J. VI: 129
Holmes, Oliver Wendell
VII: 122–123
House Un-American
Activities Committee
convictions IX: 137

Hughes, Charles Evans
VII: 124
humanitarianism III: 170
impeachment III: 175
Internal Revenue taxes VI:
147
Internet X: 153–154
Irish Americans VIII: 165
Jackson, Andrew IV: 193
Jaworski, Leon X: 161
Jay, John III: 181, 182
Jim Crow laws VI: 156
Judiciary Act of 1789 III:
192
Judiciary Act of 1801 III:
193
Keating-Owen Act VII:
145
Korematsu v. United States
VIII: 178
Ku Klux Klan VI: 163
labor and labor movements
VII: 152, 154; VIII: 180
lawyers III: 204
Lochner v. New York VII:
163–164
Lockwood, Belva Ann
Bennett McNall VI: 180
Marbury v. Madison III:
230–231
Marshall, John III:
235–237
Marshall, Thurgood IX:
193–194
McCulloch v. Maryland
IV: 227
miscegenation V: 234
Missouri Compromise of
1820 IV: 238
Mitchell, John N. X: 195
Mondale, Walter F. X: 196
Mormon Church VI:
198–199
Muller v. Oregon VII: 193
NAACP VIII: 227; IX:
220
Native Americans IV: 257;
X: 214
NIRA VIII: 228
NLRA VIII: 229
NLRB VIII: 230
Northern Securities Co. v.
U.S. VII: 216
NRA VIII: 231, 232
Nullification Controversy
IV: 264
O'Connor, Sandra Day X:
225–226
Panic of 1819 IV: 275
Parks, Rosa IX: 240
Patrons of Husbandry VI:
221, 222

Pentagon Papers X: 233
personal liberty laws IV:
280
Pinckney, Charles
Cotesworth III: 277
Plessy v. Ferguson VI:
224–225, 349–354
politics VII: 229
popular culture X: 239
popular sovereignty IV:
286
pornography X: 244
Powell, Adam Clayton IX:
246
Powell, Lewis X: 247
presidency VIII: 281
property rights X: 250
Pullman Strike VI: 236
race and race relations IV:
290, 292; VIII: 287; X:
256
railroads VI: 239
Reagan, Ronald W. X: 260
Rehnquist, William H. X:
264–265
Republican Party IV: 301;
VII: 263
RFRA X: 266
Robeson, Paul IX: 262
Roe v. Wade X: 335–338
Roosevelt, Franklin D.
VIII: 313
Scalia, Antonin X: 271
Schechter Poultry
Corporation v. United
States VIII: 317
science and technology X:
273
Scottsboro Boys VIII: 319
Sherman Antitrust Act VI:
262
Smith Act VIII: 326
Social Security Act VIII:
329–330
Souter, David X: 278, 279
Stanton, Edwin M. V: 334
Starr, Kenneth X: 286–287
steel industry IX: 282
Story, Joseph III: 334
Submerged Lands Act IX:
287
Taft, William Howard VII:
303, 304
Tappan, Arthur and Lewis
IV: 333
taxation VIII: 351–352
Thomas, Clarence X: 302
Tourgée, Albion W. V: 354
Trail of Tears IV: 344
TVA VIII: 356
Twenty-sixth Amendment
X: 306

United States v.
Cruikshank V: 375–376
United States v. Nixon X:
309
Vallandigham, Clement L.
V: 378
Voting Rights Act of 1965
IX: 312
Wagner, Robert F. VIII:
372
Walsh, Lawrence E. X:
315
Warren Court IX: 315–316
Washington, District of
Columbia III: 365
Watergate scandal X: 317
Webster, Daniel IV: 359
Webster v. Reproductive
Health Services X:
318–319
White, Byron R. X: 319
White, Walter VIII: 378
Wilson, James III: 380
women's rights and status
VI: 317, 318; X: 321
Yazoo claims III: 388
surgery IV: 230, 307; V: 97, 231,
386; X: 190, 275. See also
medicine and public health
Suriname I: 192; II: 98
surpluses, agricultural. See crop
surplus
Surratt, John V: 17
Surratt, Mary V: 18
Surround Sound X: 273
surveying II: 292, 410; III: 310;
IV: 153, 286; VI: 160, 228.
See also Geological Survey,
U.S.
Survey magazine VII: 18
surveys. See public opinion polls
Survival of the American Indian
Association X: 214
survival of the fittest. See Social
Darwinism
Survivor (TV program) X: 295
Susann, Jacqueline X: 178
suspension bridge IV: 308
Susquehanna Coal Company
VI: 194
Susquehannah II: 27, 31, 168,
169, 370
Susquehannah treaty of 1652 II:
210
Susquehannock II: 58, 67, 274,
364, 383
Susquehannock War II: 364
Susu I: 321
Sutherland, George VIII: 76,
345, 346t
Sutherland, Thomas X: 297
Sutro, Adolph IV: 96

Sutter, John **IV: 332**
 California **IV:** 65
 California gold rush **IV:** 66
 California Trail **IV:** 71
 Forty-niners **IV:** 146
 gold, discovery and mining **IV:** 162, 163
swaddling **II:** 60
Swaggart, Jimmy **X:** 197, 293, 294
Swahili culture **I:** 139
"Swamp Fox, The." *See* Marion, Francis
Swan, Abraham **II:** 23
Swan, Judge **IX:** 80
Swank, James M. **VI:** 180
Swann, Thomas **IV:** 40
Swann v. Charlotte-Mecklenburg County School Board (1971) **X:** 44, 256, 323c
Swansea, Massachusetts King Philip's War **II:** 183
sweatshops **VII:** 146
Sweatt v. Painter **IX:** 42, 193
Sweden **II:** 88; **IX:** 194
Swedenborgians **VI:** 244
Swedish colonies **II:** 256m, **364–365,** *365,* 417c
 Delaware **II:** 87, 88
 Dutch-Indian Wars **II:** 99
 New Jersey **II:** 252, 253
 New Netherland **II:** 256, 257
 Pennsylvania **II:** 274
 Protestantism **II:** 301
 Swedish colonies **II:** 364–365
Swedish exploration **II:** 181, 274
Swedish immigrants **II:** 156, 201
Swedish merchants **I:** 5
Swedish settlers **II:** 65, 182, 273, 363
Swedish traders **II:** 133
Swedish West India Company **II:** 227
Sweeney, John **X:** 171, 329c
Sweeny, Peter B. **VI:** 298
sweet potatoes **I:** 77; **VI:** 45
Sweetwater (Laurence Yep) **IX:** 327
Swift, Gustavus F. **VI:** 191; **VII:** 38
Swimming Hole, The (Eakins) **VI:** 87
swing **VIII:** 404
Swing Era **VIII:** 223
Swing Landscape (Davis) **VIII:** 25
Swiss immigrants **II:** 146–147, 164, 265, 281, 354

Swiss settlers **II:** 97, 260
Switzerland **I:** 309; **V:** 25; **IX:** 194; **X:** 321
SWOC. *See* Steelworkers Organizing Committee
Sword Beach **VIII:** 248
Sybil, HMS **III:** 36
Sybil, The: A Review of the Tastes, Errors, and Fashions of Society **V:** 123
Sykes, George **V:** 148
Syllabus of a Course of Lectures in Chemistry (Rush) **III:** 312, 392c
Sylvis, William **V:** 68, 248
Symbionese Liberation Army **X:** 297
symphonies **VI:** 23
symphony orchestras **IX:** 216; **X:** 201
syndicalism **VII:** 289
syndicates **VI:** 19; **VII:** 241
Synopsis of Birds of North America (Audubon) **IV:** 34
synthetic materials **VIII:** 47, 318, 390
syphilis **I:** 77, 107; **II:** 90; **V:** 283, 284; **VIII:** 123, 208, 406c
Syracuse Convention. *See* National Women's Rights Convention (1852)
Syracuse University **VI:** 191
Syria **IX:** 146, 147; **X:** 70, 160
Systematic Treatise on the Principal Diseases of the Interior Valley of North America (Drake) **IV:** 230
System of Surgery (Gross) **IV:** 230
Syula **I:** 218
Szilard, Leo **VIII:** 200; **IX:** 236

T

Tabascan Indians **I:** 92–93
Tabasco **I:** 5, 21, 145, 218, **341**
tabloid TV **X:** 295
Tacoma Building, Chicago **VI:** 265
tactics and strategy **V: 345–348**
 Balloon Corps **V:** 21–22
 cartography **V:** 51–52
 Confederate strategy **V:** 346
 Dahlgren, John A. B. **V:** 87
 foraging **V:** 130
 Jomini, Antoine-Henri, baron de **V:** 192
 Lincoln, Abraham **V:** 211
 Longstreet, James **V:** 215

science and technology **V:** 308
 tactics **V:** 345–346
 Union strategy **V:** 346–348
Tacuba (Tlacopan) **I:** 17, 22, 185, **342**
Tadodaho **I:** 182
Tadoussac **I:** 278; **II:** 126, 127, 130–131
Taft, Robert **X:** 105
Taft, Robert A. **VIII:** 72, 98, 306, **349; IX:** 99, 100, 258
Taft, William Howard **VII: 303–304,** *304,* 357c, 358c; **VIII:** 340, 344, 346t, 349
 Big Stick diplomacy **VII:** 28
 Budget and Accounting Act **VII:** 36
 business **VII:** 39
 Cannon, Joseph **VII:** 42
 Children's Bureau **VII:** 47
 Congress **VII:** 53
 criminal justice **VII:** 60
 Democratic Party **VII:** 66
 dollar diplomacy **VII:** 70
 elections **VII:** 80
 Federal Trade Commission Act **VII:** 94
 foreign policy **VII:** 99
 Hughes, Charles Evans **VII:** 124
 Industrial Relations Commission **VII:** 128
 labor movement **VII:** 154
 La Follette, Robert **VII:** 155
 Mann-Elkins Act **VII:** 170
 National War Labor Board **VII:** 204
 New Freedom **VII:** 211
 Payne-Aldrich Tariff Act **VII:** 226
 Pinchot, Gifford **VII:** 228
 Progressive Party **VII:** 236–237
 progressivism **VII:** 238
 Republican Party **VII:** 263
 Roosevelt, Theodore **VII:** 266
 tariffs **VII:** 305
 Wilson, Woodrow **VII:** 333
Taft-Hartley Act of 1947 **IX: 291,** 329c
 American Federation of Labor **IX:** 11
 Congress of Industrial Organizations **IX:** 65–66
 Fair Deal **IX:** 107
 labor **VIII:** 181
 Lewis, John L. **VIII:** 186
 NLRB **VIII:** 231

Progressive Party **IX:** 249
Taft, Robert A. **VIII:** 349
Teamsters Union **IX:** 292
 union movement **IX:** 303
Tahlequah, Kansas **V:** 250
Tahontaenrat **I:** 170–172
Taignoagny **I:** 58, 59
tailoring industry **VII:** 151
tailors **IV:** 204
Taino language **I:** 56
Taino nation **I: 342–343; II:** 52
 Arawak **I:** 12
 cacique **I:** 46–47
 Carib **I:** 56
 Cuba **I:** 98
 Hispaniola **I:** 161, 162
 Jamaica **I:** 187
 Nevis **I:** 254
 Puerto Rico **I:** 296, 297
 smallpox **I:** 331
Taiwan **IX:** 21, 321, 330c; **X:** 58, 154
Taiwanese Americans **X:** 200
Tajikistan **X:** 281
Takahira, Kogoro **VII:** 267
"Take the A Train" (Strayhorn) **VIII:** 100
Takrur **I:** 14
Takrurumanguru **I:** 141
Talbot v. Seeman **III:** 236
"talented tenth" **VII:** 71
Taliaferro, Lawrence **V:** 101
Taliban **X:** 125, 300, 331c
Taliwa, Battle of **II:** 391
talk shows **X:** 295
Talleyrand-Périgord, Charles-Maurice, prince de Bénévent (Prince Talleyrand) **III:** 29, 153, **341,** 385
Tallmadge, James **IV:** 237
Talmadge, Eugene **VII:** 293
Talmud **I:** 191
Tamaese, king of Samoa **VI:** 254
Tammany Hall **V:** 176, 247, 326; **VII:** 69, 81, 287; **VIII:** 182
 Cleveland, Grover **VI:** 58
 Democratic Party **VI:** 77
 Gilded Age, The **VI:** 114
 Godkin, Edwin Lawrence **VI:** 116
 immigration **VI:** 140
 machine politics **VI:** 184
 Plunkitt, George Washington **VI:** 225
 Tilden, Samuel Jones **VI:** 289
 Tweed Ring **VI:** 298
Tammany Society **III: 341–342,** 395c
Tamoanchan **I:** 269
Tan, Amy **X:** 177
Tandy Corporation **X:** 72, 273

Taney, Roger **IV**: 377*c*; **V**: 101
  Amistad incident **IV**: 20
  banking and currency **IV**: 42
  Republican Party **IV**: 301
  Supreme Court decision **IV**: 331
TANF **VIII**: 330
Tanger **I**: 157
tanks **VIII**: **349–350**
  Army, U.S. **VIII**: 20
  automobile industry **VIII**: 30
  blitzkrieg **VIII**: 39
  mobilization **VIII**: 215
Tanner, Benjamin Tucker **VI**: 175, **283–284**, 296
Tanner, Henry O. **VI**: 6, 219
Tanner, James **VI**: 123
tanneries **II**: 26
Tanzania **X**: 69, 299, 330*c*
Taoism **IV**: 298
Taos, New Mexico **I**: 90; **IV**: 50, 75, 76, 131
Taos Indian rebellion **IV**: 51
Taos Indians **IV**: 48, 51
Taos Pueblo **I**: *296;* **II**: 136
Tappan, Arthur and Lewis **IV**: 3, 13, 15, **333–334**, 362
Tappan, Lewis **IV**: 20, 21; **V**: 3, 8
Tappanhannock **II**: 329
"Taps after Tattoo" **V**: 243
tar **II**: 201, 265
Tarantino, Quentin **X**: 240
Tarascan **I**: 234, 258, **343**
Tarawa **VIII**: 15, 203, **350**, 398
Tarbell, Ida Minerva **VII**: **304–305**, 356*c*
  muckrakers **VII**: 192
  oil industry **VII**: 217
  Rockefeller, John D. **VII**: 265
  Standard Oil **VII**: 296
  Steffens, Lincoln **VII**: 299
tariff nullification **V**: 311
Tariff of Abominations **IV**: 19, 62, 123, 376*c*; **V**: 94, 348
Tariff of 1824 **IV**: 276, 376*c*
Tariff of 1828 **IV**: 376*c*; **V**: 348
Tariff of 1832 **IV**: 377*c*
Tariff of 1833 **IV**: 377*c*; **V**: 348
Tariff of 1857 **V**: 264
Tariff of 1861 **V**: 349
tariff reform **VII**: 313, 333–334
tariffs **III**: 342, *342;* **IV**: 378*c*; **V**: **348–349**; **VI**: **284–285**, 326*c*, 328*c*; **VII**: xiv, **305–306**, 357*c*, 360*c*; **VIII**: 405*c*, 406*c*; **X**: 129, 327*c*
  Agricultural Adjustment Act **VIII**: 5

American System **IV**: 18–19
Arthur, Chester Alan **VI**: 17
banking and currency **IV**: 42
Blaine, James Gillespie **VI**: 31, 32
Bretton Woods Conference **VIII**: 42
Bryan, William Jennings **VI**: 37
business and government **VI**: 39, 40
Calhoun, John C. **IV**: 62, 63
Carey, Mathew **III**: 61, 62
class consciousness **VI**: 57
Clay, Henry **IV**: 86, 87
Cleveland, Grover **VI**: 58
Congress **VI**: 64; **VII**: 53; **VIII**: 66
Democratic Party **IV**: 108; **V**: 94; **VI**: 77, 78; **VII**: 65
economy **III**: 113; **IV**: 118; **V**: 105; **VII**: 73, 75
election of 1828 **IV**: 123
elections **VII**: 80
federal income tax **VII**: 92
Fordney-McCumber Tariff **VII**: 97
foreign policy **V**: 133; **VII**: 101; **VIII**: 123
Gallatin, Albert **III**: 147
Godkin, Edwin Lawrence **VI**: 116
Grant, Ulysses S. **V**: 156
Great Depression **VIII**: 139
Greeley, Horace **V**: 158
Harding, Warren G. **VII**: 117
Hawley-Smoot Tariff Act **VIII**: 144
Hoover presidency **VIII**: 153
Hull, Cordell **VIII**: 159–160
industrialization **IV**: 184
industrial revolution **III**: 177
industrial revolution, second **VI**: 145
investments, American, abroad **VI**: 150
investments, foreign **VII**: 135
Jackson, Andrew **IV**: 193
Lawrence Strike **VII**: 156
Liberal Republican Party **VI**: 174

lobbies and pressure groups **VI**: 180
lobbying groups **VII**: 163
Lodge, Henry Cabot **VII**: 165
London Economic Conference **VIII**: 193
Macon, Nathaniel **III**: 226
New Freedom **VII**: 211
newspapers **VI**: 211
Nullification Controversy **IV**: 264–265
Oregon Treaty of 1846 **IV**: 270
Panic of 1819 **IV**: 276
Panic of 1857 **V**: 264
Payne-Aldrich Tariff Act **VII**: 226–227
Polk, James K. **IV**: 284
Progressive Party **VII**: 236
Reciprocal Trade Agreements Act **VIII**: 293–294
Republican Party **V**: 301, 302; **VI**: 246–247; **VII**: 262, 263
secession **V**: 311
Sherman, John **VI**: 261
Social Darwinism **VI**: 266
steel **VI**: 277
Stephens, Alexander H. **V**: 336
Stevens, Thaddeus **V**: 338
Sumner, William Graham **VI**: 281
Taft, William Howard **VII**: 303–304
taxation **V**: 349
trade **III**: 351
trade, foreign **VII**: 309, 310
Tyler, John **IV**: 348
Underwood-Simmons Tariff **VII**: 313
veterans **VII**: 324
Wallace, Henry A. **VIII**: 373
Webster, Daniel **IV**: 360
Wheeler, Joseph **V**: 392
Whig Party **IV**: 363
Tariq, al- **I**: 306
Tarleton, Banastre **III**: **342–343**, 394*c*
  Charleston, siege of **III**: 64
  Cornwallis, Lord **III**: 93
  Cowpens, Battle of **III**: 95
  Greene, Nathanael **III**: 156
  Jefferson, Thomas **III**: 184
  Morgan, Daniel **III**: 246
  Revolutionary War **III**: 305

Tarrentine **II**: 130
Tarryington, duchess and duke of **II**: 119
Tascaluza **I**: 213
Tashfin, Yusuf ibn **I**: 184
Tashtasick **II**: 51
Tashunca-uitco. *See* Crazy Horse
Task Force on National Health Care Reform **X**: 64
task system **II**: 12, 321
Tatamy, Moses (Tunda) **II**: 40
Taureg **I**: 350
taverns and inns **II**: **367–368**; **III**: **343–344**
  cities and urban life **III**: 70
  consumption **II**: 71
  journalism **III**: 190
  Massachusetts **II**: 215
  music **III**: 251
  New York City **II**: 262
  pewter **II**: 280
  popular culture **III**: 281
  postal service **II**: 292
  travel **II**: 377
Tawiscaron **I**: 1
taxation **III**: 24–25; **IV**: 375*c*; **V**: **349–350**; **VI**: 37, 147, 281, 284–285, 325*c*, 327*c*; **VIII**: **350–353**, 409*c*; **X**: 327*c*. *See also* income tax, federal
  Acts of Trade and Navigation **II**: 3
  agriculture **II**: 11
  almshouses **II**: 18
  animals **II**: 21
  antimonopoly **VIII**: 18
  banking and currency **V**: 23
  Bonus Bill **IV**: 56
  British Empire **II**: 41
  Bush, George W. **X**: 48
  Castile **I**: 63–64
  Charles V **I**: 69
  cities and urban life **IV**: 84; **VIII**: 57
  Civil War **V**: 66
  Confederate States of America **V**: 77
  Congressional Budget and Impoundment Act **X**: 75
  conservatism **VIII**: 72
  Cuba **IV**: 101
  Dagomba **I**: 101
  economy **V**: 105, 106; **X**: 95, 96
  education **IV**: 120; **V**: 108
  education, primary and secondary **X**: 99
  elections **V**: 110
  federal income tax **VII**: 92–93

federalism **X:** 113
Ford, Gerald R. **X:** 121
government **VIII:** 136
government, British
    American **II:** 144, 145
Great Awakening **II:** 147
homefront **V:** 169
Hoover presidency **VIII:**
    154
Interstate Highway Act of
    1956 **IX:** 145
invention and technology
    I: 180
Johnson, Anthony **II:** 175
Johnson, Mary **II:** 175
Kemp, Jack F. **X:** 163
Keynesianism **VIII:** 176
Kieft, Willem **II:** 182
Laffer curve **X:** 171–172
Libertarian Party **X:** 176
Maryland **II:** 210
Massachusetts School Act
    II: 216
McCulloch v. Maryland
    IV: 227
Mellon, Andrew **VII:** 180
Middleton, Arthur **II:** 224
militia movement **X:** 193,
    194
mobilization **VIII:** 215
Morgenthau, Henry **VIII:**
    216
New Deal **VIII:** 240
New Netherland **II:** 256
NIRA **VIII:** 228
Parsons' Cause **II:**
    271–272
postal service **II:** 292
Reagan, Ronald W. **X:** 259,
    260
Reaganomics **X:** 261
recession of 1937–38 **VIII:**
    293
Revenue Act of 1935 **VIII:**
    307–308
Revenue Act of 1942 **VIII:**
    308
Roman Catholics **II:** 323,
    324
Santa Fe Trail **IV:** 306
Senate **X:** 276
Seven Years' War **II:** 334
smuggling **II:** 348
Spanish colonies **II:** 357
states' rights **V:** 336
Stephens, Alexander H. **V:**
    337
Supreme Court **X:** 290
tariffs **V:** 348
Termination policy **IX:** 297
Thoreau, Henry David **IV:**
    342

Virginia **II:** 385
Wallace, Henry A. **VIII:**
    373
War Revenue Act **VII:**
    330–331
Whiskey Ring **V:** 392–393
World War I **VII:** 344
World War II home front
    VIII: 395
taxation, proportionate **IV:** 171
Taxation: The People's Business
    (Mellon) **VII:** 180
taxation without representation
    III: 108, 111, 157
tax cuts **VII:** 331
taxes (state and local) **VIII:** 350
"tax-in-kind" **V:** 349
tax reform **VII:** 140, 180; **VIII:**
    216
Tax Reform Act of 1986 **X:** 327*c*
Tayasal **I:** 227
Taylor, Bayard **VI:** 224
Taylor, Charles H. J. **VI:** 175
Taylor, Frederick Winslow **VI:**
    145, 170; **VII: 306–307,**
    357*c. See also* scientific
    management
        business **VII:** 38
        economy **VII:** 74
        Ford, Henry **VII:** 96
        mass production **VII:**
            173–174
        scientific management
            VII: 277
        steel industry **VII:** 297
Taylor, Glen **IX:** 248
Taylor, John, of Caroline **III:**
    228, 279, **344**
Taylor, Major **VI:** 28
Taylor, Nathaniel W. **IV:** 298
Taylor, Paul S. **VIII:** 268
Taylor, Richard **V:** 51, 233, 297,
    298
Taylor, Susie King **V:** 256, **350**
Taylor, William
    literature **X:** 178
Taylor, Zachary **IV: 334–335,**
    335, 335, 378*c,* 379*c;* **V:** 88
        Cass, Lewis **IV:** 77
        Clayton-Bulwer Treaty **IV:**
            88
        Colt, Samuel **IV:** 91
        Compromise of 1850 **IV:**
            95
        Deseret, State of **IV:** 110
        Fillmore, Millard **IV:** 137
        Free-Soil Party **IV:** 150
        Guadalupe Hidalgo, Treaty
            of (1848) **IV:** 165
        immigration **IV:** 180
        Mexican-American War
            IV: 232–234

Santa Anna, Antonio
    López de **IV:** 304
Scott, Winfield **IV:** 310
Seminole wars **IV:** 312
Whig Party **IV:** 364
"Taylorism" **IV:** 298
tea **II:** 43, 44, 71
Tea Act **III: 344–345,** 392*c*
    American Revolution **III:**
        12
    Boston Tea Party **III:** 45
    Burke, Edmund **III:** 52
    cities and urban life **III:** 69
    Coercive Acts **III:** 76
    committees of
        correspondence **III:** 77
    Franklin, Benjamin **III:**
        134
    North, Lord **III:** 260
    Old South Church **III:**
        266
    resistance movement **III:**
        303
    riots **III:** 309
Teach, Edward **II:** 34, 285,
    368–369
teacher education **IV:** 220
teaching hospitals **VI:** 94
"teach-ins" **X:** 24
Team Drivers International
    Union **IX:** 292
Teamsters Union **IX:** 292,
    292–293, 332*c,* 334*c;* **X:** 236
    American Federation of
        Labor **IX:** 12
    Reuther, Walter **IX:** 259
    union movement **IX:** 303
    United Farm Workers **IX:**
        305
Teapot Dome **VII:** 57, 118,
    307–308, 327, 360*c;* **VIII:**
    344
El Teatro Campesino **IX:** 174
Tebbell, John **X:** 185
technology. *See* inventions,
    science, and technology
technology industries **X:** 51
technology transfer **X:** 260
Tecumseh **III: 345,** 397*c,* 398*c;*
    IV: 375*c*
    Black Hawk War **IV:** 51
    Blue Jacket **III:** 41
    Cherokee nation **III:** 66
    Creek nation **III:** 97
    Dragging Canoe **III:** 107
    foreign policy **IV:** 141
    Ghent, Treaty of (1814) **IV:**
        161, 162
    Harrison, William Henry
        IV: 169
    Hull, William **IV:** 175
    migration **IV:** 235

Native Americans **IV:** 255,
    256
Native Americans in the
    War of 1812 **IV:** 258,
    259
Prophet, the Shawnee **III:**
    287, 289
Thames, Battle of the **IV:**
    342
Tippecanoe, Battle of **III:**
    347, 348
War of 1812 **IV:** 356
Tedder, Arthur **VIII:** 325
Teedyuscung **II: 370**
teenagers **VIII:** 56, 205
teetotalism **IV:** 336
Teheran Conference (1943)
    VIII: 354–355, 410*c*
    Anglo-American relations
        VIII: 17
    Cairo Conference **VIII:** 51
    foreign policy **VIII:** 125
    Grand Alliance **VIII:** 137
    Harriman, Averell **VIII:**
        144
    Hopkins, Harry **VIII:** 157
    Leahy, William D. **VIII:**
        184
    Normandy, invasion of
        VIII: 247
    Roosevelt, Franklin D.
        VIII: 314
    second front **VIII:** 320
    Soviet-American relations
        VIII: 334
    UN **VIII:** 365
    World War II European
        theater **VIII:** 393
    Yalta Conference **VIII:**
        401
Tejano music **X:** 203
Tekakwitha, Kateri **II:** 318
Téké **I: 343**
Tekesta **I:** 130
Tekrur **I:** 321
telecommunications **VII:** 357*c*
    ADA **X:** 21
    computers **X:** 74–75
    medicine **X:** 190
    pornography **X:** 244, 245
    space policy **X:** 281
Telecommunications Act of
    1996 **X:** 245, 274, 329*c*
telegraph **IV:** 377*c;* **V: 350–351,**
    405*c*
    Andrews's Raid **V:** 11
    Appomattox Court House,
        Virginia **V:** 15
    Atlanta campaign **V:** 19
    Balloon Corps **V:** 21
    Baltimore, Maryland, riots
        V: 22

telegraph (*continued*)
　Civil War **V:** 66
　communications **VI:** 61–62
　economy **IV:** 118
　Edison, Thomas Alva **VI:** 89
　Fort Laramie **IV:** 145
　industrialization **IV:** 185
　journalism **IV:** 196; **V:** 192
　Knights of Labor **VI:** 162
　Mexican-American War **IV:** 234
　Morse, Samuel F. B. **IV:** 245–246
　Mosby, John Singleton **V:** 242
　newspapers **VI:** 212
　New York City **V:** 253
　New York City draft riots **V:** 254
　Panic of 1857 **V:** 264
　science and technology **IV:** 307; **V:** 308, 310
　tactics and strategy **V:** 346
　Washington, D.C. **V:** 389
　Weather Bureau, U.S. **VI:** 310
Telegraph **IV:** 122
Telegraph Plateau **IV:** 308
Telenet **X:** 152
telephone **V:** 351; **VI:** 324*c;* **VII:** 253; **VIII:** 353; **IX:** 270; **X:** 274–275
　Bell, Alexander Graham **VI:** 25
　business cycles **VI:** 41
　communications **VI:** 62
　Edison, Thomas Alva **VI:** 89
　industrial revolution, second **VI:** 147
　inventions and technology **VI:** 149
　newspapers **VI:** 212
　Philadelphia Centennial Exposition **VI:** 224
telescope **IX:** 278; **X:** 283, 327*c*
televangelism **X:** 197, 265, **293**, **293–294**
television **VII:** 134; **VIII:** 1, 353, 405*c;* **IX:** **295–297**, 332*c–334c;* **X:** **294–297**. *See also* cable television
　advertising **IX:** 2, 2, 3
　Army-McCarthy hearings **IX:** 19
　Beatles **IX:** 36
　Buchanan, Patrick J. **X:** 42
　censorship **X:** 60
　Christian Coalition **X:** 61
　cities and urban life **IX:** 52
　elections **IX:** 95

General Electric Company **IX:** 120
　Horton, Willie (campaign ad) **X:** 143–144
　House of Representatives **X:** 144
　journalism **IX:** 153–154
　McCarthy, Joseph **IX:** 190
　media **X:** 184–{10: }187, 187
　movies **X:** 197, 199
　music **X:** 202–203
　Nixon, Richard M. **X:** 220
　Persian Gulf War **X:** 235
　political parties **X:** 239
　popular culture **IX:** 243–244; **X:** 239, 241
　race and racial conflict **X:** 257
　recreation **IX:** 255; **X:** 261–{10: }263
　religion **IX:** 255, 257
　science **IX:** 270
　science and technology **X:** 273
　Senate **X:** 276
　sexual revolution **X:** 277
　sports **IX:** 280; **X:** 284
　Student Nonviolent Coordinating Committee **IX:** 284
　suburbanization **IX:** 287
　technology **IX:** 295
　televangelism **X:** 293–294
　Vietnam War **IX:** 309
　Weathermen **IX:** 319
　White Citizens' Councils **IX:** 320
television rating system **X:** 241
television stations, minority-owned **X:** 9
Teller, Edward **VIII:** 200; **IX:** 139; **X:** 289
Teller Amendment **VI:** 71, 72, 273
temperance movement **III:** **346–347**, 398*c;* **IV:** xiii, **335–337**, 378*c;* **VI:** 324*c. See also* Woman's Christian Temperance Union; Women's war
　Blackwell, Antoinette Brown **VI:** 30
　Bloomer, Amelia **IV:** 53, 54
　Delany, Martin Robinson **V:** 93
　Democratic Party **IV:** 108
　Handsome Lake **III:** 164
　Harper, Frances Ellen Watkins **V:** 164
　humanitarianism **III:** 169

Langston, John Mercer **VI:** 171
Lovejoy, Elijah **IV:** 214
Mann, Horace **IV:** 219
Mott, Lucretia **IV:** 246
New Woman **VII:** 214
NWSA **V:** 248
Prohibition **VII:** 238–241
Prohibition Party **VI:** 233–235
religion **IV:** 296
Shaw, Anna Howard **VI:** 260
spiritualism **IV:** 326
Sunday, Billy **VII:** 302
Truth, Sojourner **V:** 357
Volstead Act **VII:** 327
voluntary associations **III:** 362
Weems, "Parson" **III:** 371
Willard, Frances **VI:** 315–316
women's status and rights **IV:** 368; **V:** 399
Tempest, The **I:** **343–344**
Temple, Shirley **VIII:** 56, 217, 406*c*
temples **I:** 13, 18, 252, 275, 344, 349
Temporary Aid to Needy Families (TANF) **VIII:** 330
Temporary National Economic Committee (TNEC) **VIII:** **355–356**
　antimonopoly **VIII:** 18
　Henderson, Leon **VIII:** 145
　New Deal **VIII:** 242
　recession of 1937–38 **VIII:** 293
Temptations **IX:** 217
Ten American Painters **VI:** 220
tenancy **VI:** 5, 7*m*
tenant farmers **V:** 316; **VIII:** 65; **IX:** 7–8
tenants **II:** **370–371**
　crowd action **II:** 78
　Maryland **II:** 209
　New Jersey **II:** 253
　New York **II:** 261
　Penn, William **II:** 273
　society, British American **II:** 350
　Van Rensselaer, Maria Van Cortlandt **II:** 381
　Virginia **II:** 384
　Virginia Company of London **II:** 387
Tenda **I:** 321
Ten Days That Shook the World (Reed) **VII:** 259
Tendile **I:** 93

tenements **V:** 60, 97; **VIII:** *58*
Tenerife Island **I:** 53
Tennant, William **III:** 322
Tennent, Gilbert **II:** 125–126, 268, 301, *371*, **371–372**; **III:** 298
Tennent, Gilbert, Jr. **II:** 84
Tennent, John **II:** 301
Tennent, William, Jr. **II:** 301, **372**
Tennent, William, Sr. **II:** 147, 298, 301, 371, **372**
Tennessee **II:** 57–59, 353; **III:** 40–41, 107, 135–136; **V:** 406*c–408c;* **VI:** 156, 210; **IX:** 31, 273, 320; **X:** 107, 242
　Benton, Thomas Hart **IV:** 49
　Chattanooga, Battle of **V:** 57
　Claiborne, William C. C. **IV:** 84
　Coosa in **I:** 85
　Corinth, Battle of **V:** 83
　Crockett, Davy **IV:** 99–100
　Forrest, Nathan Bedford **V:** 134
　Fort Pillow, Tennessee **V:** 135
　Hood, John Bell **V:** 171
　Houston, Sam **IV:** 174
　impeachment of Andrew Johnson **V:** 177
　Jackson, Andrew **IV:** 191
　Johnson, Andrew **V:** 187, 189
　Ku Klux Klan **V:** 199
　Lookout Mountain, Battle of **V:** 216–217
　migration **IV:** 235
　Mississippi River **V:** 234, 235
　Morgan, John Hunt **V:** 240
　Murfreesboro/Stones River, Battle of **V:** 242–243
　Native Americans in the War of 1812 **IV:** 259
　Orphan Brigade **V:** 258
　Polk, James K. **IV:** 282, 283
　Reconstruction **V:** 292
　secession **V:** 311
　Sheridan, Philip H. **V:** 318
　Sherman, William T. **V:** 320
　Shiloh, Battle of **V:** 323–326
　Singleton, Benjamin **V:** 327
　tactics and strategy **V:** 347
　Thomas, George H. **V:** 354

Tennessee Coal, Iron, & Railroad Company **VI:** 198
Tennessee Militia **IV:** 49
Tennessee River **V:** 234, 323, 326
Tennessee Valley Authority (TVA) **VIII: 356–357,** 357, 406c
   agriculture **VIII:** 8
   Black, Hugo L. **VIII:** 37
   conservatism **VIII:** 71
   environmental issues **VIII:** 103
   Lilienthal, David E. **VIII:** 190
   New Deal **VIII:** 241
   Norris, George W. **VIII:** 248
   REA **VIII:** 316
   Willkie, Wendell L. **VIII:** 378–379
tennis **VI:** 273–274, 274; **VIII:** 337; **IX:** 280, 281; **X:** 262
Tenoch **I:** 344
Tenochtitlán **I: 344–346,** 345m, 387c
   Alvarado, Pedro de **I:** 6–7
   Aztecs **I:** 17, 18, 21
   Aztlán **I:** 22
   Cacamatzin **I:** 45
   chinampas **I:** 72
   Codex Aubin **I:** 400
   Columbian Exchange **I:** 77
   Cortés, Hernán **I:** 93, 94
   Cuauhtémoc **I:** 97
   Cuitláhuac **I:** 98, 99
   Escalante, Juan de **I:** 123
   Huitzilopochtli **I:** 170
   invention and technology **I:** 180
   Itzcóatl **I:** 185
   Mexico **I:** 234
   Moctezuma II **I:** 237
   New Spain **I:** 258
   Olmecs **I:** 270
   Quetzalcoatl **I:** 301
   Sandoval, Gonzalo de **I:** 317–318
   Tacuba **I:** 342
   Tezcatlipoca **I:** 348
   Tláloc **I:** 352
   Tlaxcala **I:** 352, 353
"Ten Per Cent Plan" **V:** 8, 292
Tenskwatawa **II:** 319–320. See also Prophet, the Shawnee
   Catlin, George **IV:** 77
   Harrison, William Henry **IV:** 169
   Native Americans **IV:** 256
   Native Americans in the War of 1812 **IV:** 258, 259

Tenth Amendment **X:** 112, 137
Tenure of Office Act of 1867 **V:** 408c
   impeachment of Andrew Johnson **V:** 178
   Johnson, Andrew **V:** 188–189
   Radical Republicans **V:** 289
   Reconstruction Acts **V:** 296
   Stanton, Edwin M. **V:** 334
Tenure of Office of Act, repeal of **VI:** 130
Ten Years' War **VI:** 71
Teoniahigarawe **II:** 155
Teotihuacán **I: 346–347,** 347m
   Aztecs **I:** 21
   Copán **I:** 86
   Maya **I:** 226
   Monte Albán **I:** 242
   Quetzalcoatl **I:** 301
   Tikal **I:** 349
   Tláloc **I:** 352
   Toltecs **I:** 355
Tepanecs **I:** 17, 185, 342
Tepeticpac **I:** 352
Tequesta **I:** 49; **II:** 120
Tercerista insurrectionists (Nicaragua) **X:** 217
Teresa of Ávila, Saint **I:** 96
Tereshkova, Valentina **IX:** 279
Termination of the State of War with Germany **IX:** 330c
Termination policy **IX:** 12, 143, 227–229, **297–298,** 331c
Ternate **I:** 335
Terra da Veracruz **I:** 44
Terrell, Mary Church **VI:** 6; **VII:** 199–200, **308**
Terrill, Edwin **V:** 285
Terrill, James **V:** 37
Terrill, William **V:** 37
terrorism **V:** 111, 117; **VI:** 181–182, 195–196, 311, 325c; **X: 297–301,** 298m, 299, 300, 323c, 326c–331c
   Anglo-Normans **I:** 11
   Bush, George W. **X:** 47, 48
   Clinton, William **X:** 66, 67, 69
   defense policy **X:** 87–89
   economy **X:** 96
   Elizabeth I **I:** 120
   foreign policy **X:** 124, 125
   Iran-contra affair **X:** 154
   Iranian hostage crisis **X:** 155–156
   militia movement **X:** 194
   North, Oliver L. **X:** 221–222
   Oklahoma City bombing **X:** 227–228

Persian Gulf War **X:** 236
Powell, Colin L. **X:** 247
RICO **X:** 258
Senate **X:** 276
Weather Underground **X:** 317–318
Terry, Alfred H. **V:** 214, 280
Terry, Luther **IX:** 249, 333c
Tesla, Nikola **VI:** 146, 147, 149, **285,** 326c, 327c
Tesla coil **VI:** 149
Tesla Electric Company **VI:** 285
test pilots **VIII:** 380–381
teteuhctin **I:** 19
Tet Offensive **IX:** 152, 310, 334c
Teton Sioux nation **V:** 213
tetracyclines **IX:** 205
Tetzel, Johann **I:** 211; **II:** 93
Tew, Thomas **II:** 285
Tewa Pueblo **I:** 295
Tewksbury, John Walter **VI:** 290
Texas **II:** 419c; **III:** 258; **IV:** xiii, **337–339,** 339, 377c, 378c; **VI:** 46, 215; **IX:** 171, 174, 286, 320
   Act of Annexation **IV:** 402–403
   Adams-Onís Treaty **IV:** 5
   agriculture **II:** 9
   art **II:** 25
   Asian Americans **X:** 28
   Austin, Moses **IV:** 36
   Austin, Stephen F. **IV:** 36–38
   Bear Flag Revolt **IV:** 45
   Becknell, William **IV:** 46
   Bent's Fort **IV:** 51
   Bilingual Education Act of 1968 **X:** 36
   Bowie, Jim **IV:** 56–57
   Branch Davidians **X:** 39–40
   Bush, George W. **X:** 47
   Cabet, Étienne **IV:** 61
   Cabeza de Vaca, Álvar Núñez **I:** 37
   Calhoun, John C. **IV:** 63
   Carson, Kit **IV:** 76
   Castillo, Diego Del **II:** 54–55
   Clay, Henry **IV:** 87, 88
   Colt revolver **IV:** 92
   Compromise of 1850 **IV:** 93, 94, 94m
   Coronado, Francisco **I:** 88
   cotton culture **IV:** 99
   Democratic Party **IV:** 108; **V:** 94
   economy **IV:** 117
   election of 1840 **IV:** 124
   foreign policy **IV:** 142
   Free-Soil Party **IV:** 150

Gadsden Purchase **IV:** 160m
Galveston, Battle of **V:** 145
Guadalupe Hidalgo, Treaty of (1848) **IV:** 165–166
Hispanic Americans **X:** 143
Houston, Sam **IV:** 173–175
IRCA **X:** 149
Johnston, Albert Sidney **V:** 189
Juneteenth **V:** 194–195
Ku Klux Klan **V:** 199
Larkin, Thomas Oliver **IV:** 208
La Salle, René-Robert Cavelier, sieur de **II:** 192
Manifest Destiny **IV:** 217–218, 218m
medicine **X:** 190
Mexican-American War **IV:** 232–234
migration **IV:** 236
militia movement **X:** 194
missions **II:** 229, 231
Oregon Treaty of 1846 **IV:** 269, 270
overland mail **IV:** 272
plantations **V:** 276
Polk, James K. **IV:** 283, 284
population trends **X:** 242
Reconstruction **V:** 294
Red River campaign **V:** 297
refugees **V:** 298
Roe v. Wade **X:** 268
Roman Catholics **II:** 324
Santa Fe Trail **IV:** 305, 306
secession **V:** 313
Stockton, Robert Field **IV:** 328
Sumner, Charles **V:** 342
Sunbelt **X:** 290
Supreme Court **X:** 291
Taylor, Zachary **IV:** 334, 335
Texas **IV:** 338
Texas Revolution **IV:** 339–341
Travis, William Barret **IV:** 345–346
Tyler, John **IV:** 348–349
Van Buren, Martin **IV:** 352
Webster, Daniel **IV:** 360
Whig Party **IV:** 364
Wilmot Proviso **V:** 395
Wright, James C., Jr. **X:** 322
Texas & Pacific Railroad (T&P) **VI:** 180, 258
Texas Constitutional Militia **X:** 194

Texas Instruments **IX:** 65; **X:** 273
Texas Rangers **IV:** 91, 92, 377*c*
Texas Rangers (baseball team) **X:** 47
Texas Revolution **IV:** 339, **339–342,** 377*c*
  Alamo, The **IV:** 12–13
  Austin, Stephen F. **IV:** 37–38
  Bent's Fort **IV:** 50–51
  Bowie, Jim **IV:** 57
  Colt, Samuel **IV:** 91
  Crockett, Davy **IV:** 100
  election of 1840 **IV:** 124
  foreign policy **IV:** 142
  Houston, Sam **IV:** 173–175
  Manifest Destiny **IV:** 217–218
  Mexican-American War **IV:** 232
  Santa Anna, Antonio López de **IV:** 303–304
  Santa Fe Trail **IV:** 306
  Texas **IV:** 338
  Texas Declaration of Independence **IV:** 393–394
  Travis, William Barret **IV:** 346
Texas v. Johnson (1989) **X:** 327*c*
  Brennan, William J. **X:** 41
  flag burning **X:** 117
  Scalia, Antonin **X:** 271
  White, Byron R. **X:** 319
Texcoco **I:** 17, 44–45, 185, 342, 352
Textbook of the Origin and History of Colored People (Pennington) **V:** 270
textiles/textile industry **II:** 166, 190, 225, 226, 375; **III:** 395*c*; **V:** 123, 170; **VI:** 165, 209, 210; **VIII:** 48; **X:** 94. *See also* cotton
  agriculture **V:** 6
  architecture **III:** 20
  Castile **I:** 63
  child labor **VII:** 44
  Confederate States of America **V:** 76
  cotton culture **IV:** 97–98
  economy **III:** 113; **IV:** 118, 119
  fashion **V:** 123
  foreign policy **V:** 131
  Gastonia Strike **VII:** 106
  immigration **IV:** 179
  industrial development **V:** 180, 181
  industrialization **IV:** 184–187, 186*m*

industrial revolution **III:** 177, 178
IWW **VII:** 130
Keating-Owen Act **VII:** 145
Kongo **I:** 195
labor movements **IV:** 204
Lawrence Strike **VII:** 155–156
Panic of 1857 **V:** 264
Passaic Strike **VII:** 224
Paterson Strike **VII:** 225
pueblo **I:** 295
scalawags **V:** 307
Slater, Samuel **III:** 325–326
Whitney, Eli **III:** 376
Zacatecas **I:** 381
Textile Workers Organizing Committee **VIII:** 146
Tezcatlipoca **I:** 301, **347, 348,** 352, 355
Tezozomoc **I:** 17
Thadodaho (Atotarho) **I:** 161
Thai Americans **X:** 200
Thailand **IX:** 273–274; **X:** 69
thalidomide **IX:** 69; **X:** 189
Thames, Battle of the **III:** 289, 345; **IV:** **342**
  Cass, Lewis **IV:** 76
  Ghent, Treaty of (1814) **IV:** 161
  Lake Erie, Battle of **IV:** 207
  Native Americans **IV:** 256
  Native Americans in the War of 1812 **IV:** 259
  War of 1812 **IV:** 356
Thanksgiving **II:** 217, 283, 287; **IV:** 168
Thatcher, Margaret **X:** 260, 261
Thaw, Harry **VI:** 314
Thayer, Abbott Handerson **VI:** 15; **VII:** 17
Thayer, Eli **IV:** 223
Thayer, Martin **VI:** 102
Thayer, Sylvanus **V:** 372
theater **I:** 324, 343–344; **II:** 62, **373; III:** **347,** 347, 395*c;* **V:** 32–33, 138, 253, **351–352;** **VI:** **285–287,** 287; **VIII:** 376, 407*c,* 410*c;* **IX:** 221, 243, 261, 332*c;* **X:** 201, 239, 241–242. *See also* Broadway
  cities and urban life **III:** 70
  Cody, William Frederick **VI:** 59
  Dunlap, William **III:** 108
  entertainment **VII:** 85

Gershwin, George **VII:** 108
Greenwich Village **VII:** 115
Jefferson, Joseph, III **VI:** 155–156
  music **VI:** 203–204; **VII:** 194
  popular culture **III:** 281; **VII:** 231
  Sousa, John Philip **VI:** 271
  Tyler, Royall **III:** 352–353
  vaudeville **VII:** 321–322
  Victorianism **VI:** 304
  Warren, Mercy Otis **III:** 363–364
Theatre Owners Booking Association (TOBA) **VI:** 96
Theatrum Orbis Terrarum sive Novus Atlas (Willem and Joan Blaeu) **I:** 31
theft **II:** 76; **V:** 130
Their Eyes Were Watching God (Hurston) **VIII:** 3, 192
theocracy **IV:** 244, 372
Theodore Thomas Orchestra **VI:** 201
Theology for the Social Gospel (Rauschenbusch) **VI:** 267
Theory and Practice of Landscape Gardening, The (Downing) **IV:** 28
THEORYNET **X:** 153
Theosophical Society **VI:** 244–245
Theosophists **VI:** 243
thermodynamics **VI:** 113
thermometer, clinical **V:** 231
These Are Our Lives **VIII:** 121
The Thinker: Portrait of Louis N. Kenton (Eakins) **VII:** 18
Theus, Jeremiah **II:** 25, **373**
Thevet, André **I:** **348–349**
  cabinet of curiosities **I:** 40
  Cosmographie Universelle **I:** 403–408
  Léry, Jean de **I:** 205
  printing press **I:** 294
  tobacco **I:** 353
  Tupinambá **I:** 361
The Way They Go to California **IV:** *146*
Theyanoquin **II:** 155
Thieu, Nguyen Van **IX:** 309
think tanks **X:** 79, **301–302**
Thin Red Line, The (James Jones) **IX:** 181
Third International **VII:** 360*c*
Third New Deal. *See* New Deal, Third
third parties. *See* political parties, third

third-party candidates **X:** 101–102. *See also specific parties*
third-party movement **VII:** 80, 91
Third Provincial Council of Lima **I:** 3
Third World **IX:** 50, 316
Third World Marxists **IX:** 319
Thirteenth Amendment **IV:** 4; **V:** **352–353,** 408*c;* **VIII:** 61; **IX:** 132–133
  abolition **V:** 4
  Civil Rights Act of 1866 **V:** 62
  civil rights cases **VI:** 55, 56
  Civil War **V:** 66
  Confiscation Acts **V:** 78
  Douglass, Frederick **V:** 100
  emancipation **V:** 111, 113, 114
  Emancipation Proclamation **V:** 115
  employment **V:** 117
  Enforcement Acts **V:** 117
  Fourteenth Amendment **V:** 138
  Garrison, William Lloyd **V:** 146
  Harlan, John Marshall **VI:** 122
  Johnson, Andrew **V:** 188
  Lincoln, Abraham **V:** 211
  Plessy v. Ferguson **VI:** 224
  race and racial conflict **V:** 288
  Reconstruction **V:** 293
  Republican Party **V:** 302
  slavery **V:** 330
  women's rights **VI:** 317
33rd U.S. Colored Troops **V:** 167, 256, 350
Thirty-nine Articles **I:** 74, 120; **II:** 301
Thirty Years View (Benton) **IV:** 50
This Is the Army (Berlin) **VIII:** 224
"This Land Is Your Land" (Guthrie) **VIII:** 224
Thom, Mel **IX:** 229
Thomas, Augustus **VI:** 287
Thomas, Cal **X:** 62
Thomas, Clarence **X:** **302,** 328*c*
  African Americans **X:** 12
  Ginsburg, Ruth Bader **X:** 130
  Hill, Anita Faye **X:** 141
  NAACP **X:** 208
  Senate **X:** 276
  Supreme Court **X:** 291
Thomas, Elmer **VIII:** 5

Thomas, Ernest **IX:** 66, 67
Thomas, George H. **V: 353–354**
   Chattanooga, Battle of **V:** 57
   Chickamauga, Battle of **V:** 58
   Hood, John Bell **V:** 171
   Lookout Mountain, Battle of **V:** 216
   Sherman's March through Georgia **V:** 322
Thomas, Henry **IX:** 114
Thomas, J. B. **IV:** 237
Thomas, J. Parnell **IX:** 135, 137
Thomas, John **IV:** 299
Thomas, Lorenzo **V:** 178
Thomas, M. Carey **VI:** 247, **287–288,** 316
Thomas, Norman **VIII: 358**
   Agricultural Adjustment Act **VIII:** 6
   election of 1932 **VIII:** 96
   election of 1936 **VIII:** 97
   politics in the Roosevelt era **VIII:** 270, 272*t*
   socialists **VIII:** 327
   STFU **VIII:** 333
Thomas, Philip E. **IV:** 40
Thomas, Theodore **VI:** 183, 201
Thomas, Vivien **VIII:** 207
Thomas B. Harms publishers **VI:** 204
Thomas Bray's Associates **II:** 104
Thomas Edison Laboratories **VII:** 190
Thomas Jefferson and Sally Hemmings: An American Controversy (Gordon-Reed) **III:** 165
Thomas Proviso **IV:** 237–238
Thompson, Benjamin, Count Rumford **III:** 321
Thompson, David **I:** 161; **II:** 250; **IV:** 93
Thompson, Sir Eric **I:** 225
Thompson, Frank, Jr. **X:** 4–5
Thompson, J. W. (construction contractor) **VII:** 327
Thompson, J. Walter (advertising executive) **VI:** 2; **VII:** 4
Thompson, Jacob **V:** 118
Thompson, James **IX:** 104
Thompson, Meldrum **X:** 279
Thompson, Tommy **X:** *308*
Thomson, Charles **III:** 11
Thomson, Elihu **VI:** 148
Thomson-Houston Electric Company **VI:** 148, 149
Thomson-Urrutia Treaty **VII:** 358*c*

Thoreau, Henry David **IV: 342–343,** *343,* 378*c,* 379*c;* **VII:** 55; **IX:** 53
   art **IV:** 26
   "Civil Disobedience" **IV:** 407–410
   literature **IV:** 212
   lyceum movement **IV:** 215
   religion **IV:** 299
   transcendental movement **IV:** 345
   Warren, Josiah **IV:** 358
Thorn, Jonathan **IV:** 33
thornbacks **II:** 360
Thorne, Robert **I:** 35
Thorne, Robert, the Younger **I:** 35
Thorne, Thomas **I:** 35
Thorne, William **I:** 35
Thornton, James **VI:** 204
Thorpe, Jim **VII:** *293,* 295
"Thoughts on African colonization" (Garrison) **IV:** 16
Thoughts on Art (Emerson) **IV:** 26
Thoughts on Government (Adams) **III:** 2
"Thousand Points of Light" speech (George H. W. Bush) **X:** 347–351
thrashings **II:** 208
332nd Fighter Group **VIII:** 4
three-fifths compromise **IV:** 237
Three Little Pigs (film) **VIII:** 219
Three Mile Island **X:** 325*c*
Three Soldiers (Dos Passos) **VII:** 162
Three Years in Mississippi (James Meredith) **IX:** 200
thresher **IV:** 10, 308
threshers **VI:** 8
Throckmorton, Elizabeth (Bess) **I:** 303, 304
Thumb, Tom **VI:** 21
Thurmond, J. Strom **IX:** 330*c;* **X: 303**
   Americans for Democratic Action **IX:** 13, 14
   Democratic Party **IX:** 79
   elections **IX:** 94
   liberalism **IX:** 179
   Republican Party **IX:** 258
   States' Rights Party **IX:** 281, 282
   White Citizens' Councils **IX:** 320
Tidewater region
   agriculture **II:** 10–11
   disease **II:** 90
   Opechancanough **II:** 268

plantation system **II:** 286, 287
population trends **II:** 298
primogeniture and entail **II:** 297
slavery **II:** 338, 339, 342
Virginia **II:** 384, 385
Tidore **I:** 335
Tierra del Fuego **II:** 242
Tierre Firme **I:** 24, 276
Tiffany, Louis Comfort **VI:** 3, 220, **288–289**
Tiffany and Company **VI:** 3, 15, 78, 288
Tiffany Foundation **VI:** 288
Tiffany Studios **VI:** 288
Tiger Rifles **V:** 218
Tiguex **I:** 90
Tijerina, Reies López ("El Tigre") **IX:** 124, 174, **298–299**
Tikal **I: 349–350**
   art and architecture **I:** 12
   Chichén Itzá **I:** 69
   Copán **I:** 86
   Maya **I:** 227
   Native American religion **I:** 252
   Teotihuacán **I:** 346
Tikas, Louis **VII:** 168
Tilden, Samuel J. **VI: 289,** 324*c*
   Democratic Party **V:** 95; **VI:** 78
   Hayes, Rutherford B. **VI:** 125, 126
   Julian, George W. **V:** 194
   libraries, public, growth of **VI:** 176
   presidential campaigns **VI:** 231
   Reconstruction **V:** 294
   Republican Party **V:** 303
   Scott, Thomas Alexander **VI:** 258
   Tweed Ring **VI:** 298
Till, Emmett **IX:** 253
Tillman, Ben **VII:** 292
Tillotson, John **II:** 109
Tilted Arc (Serra) **X:** 26
Tilton, Elizabeth **VI:** 24, 25, 133
Tilton, Theodore **VI:** 24, 25, 319
timber **II:** 260
Timber and Stone Act of 1878 **VI:** 39
Timber Culture Act of 1873 **VI:** 323*c*
Timbuktu **I: 350–351**
   Askia Muhammad I **I:** 14
   Baba, Ahmad **I:** 23
   Djenne-Djeno **I:** 109
   Leo Africanus **I:** 203
   Mansa Musa I **I:** 220

Songhai **I:** 332
Taureg **I:** 360
Time (magazine) **VIII:** 196, 206, 243
Time, Inc. **VIII:** 196; **X:** 49
"time store" **IV:** 359
Time-Warner **X:** 51, 178, 244
Timucua **I:** 130, 131, 201, 202, **351;** **II:** 120
Timuca Indians (Le Moyne engraving) **I:** *202*
tin **I:** 10
tindamba **I:** 101
Tinicum Island **II:** 274
"Tin Lizzie." *See* Model T
Tin Pan Alley **VI:** 204; **VII:** 108, 137, 194, 195, **308–309**
Tipai **I:** 48
Tipaldo case **VIII:** 345
Tippecanoe, Battle of **III:** 141, 289, 345, **347–348,** 348*m,* 398*c;* **IV:** 169, 258, 356
"Tippecanoe and Tyler too!"
   election of 1840 **IV:** 126
   Harrison, William Henry **IV:** 170
   Tyler, John **IV:** 348
   Van Buren, Martin **IV:** 352
Tippit, J. D. **IX:** 238
tires/tire industry **VIII:** 254, 292; **X:** 49
Tisquantum. *See* Squanto
tissue grafts **X:** 5
Titanic **VII:** 357*c*
Titanic (movie) **X:** 240
Title I (Old-Age Assistance) **VIII:** 95, 96, 329, 415–416
Title II (Old-Age Benefits) **VIII:** 329, 416
Title III (Unemployment Compensation) **VIII:** 329, 361, 416
Title IV (Aid to Dependent Children) **VIII:** 329, 416–417
Title V (Maternal and Child Health) **VIII:** 56, 329, 417–418
Title VI (Public Health Service) **VIII:** 329, 418. *See also* Public Health Service
Title IX (Prohibition of Sex Discrimination) **X:** 334–335
Title X (Aid to the Blind) **VIII:** 329, 418–419
Tito, Josip **IX:** 106, 277, 300; **X:** 166, 167
Tituba **II:** 271, 402
Tizatlan **I:** 352
Tlacacla (Tlacaélel) **I:** 17, 131, 185, **351–352**
tlacatechtli **I:** 97
tlacohtin **I:** 20

Tlacopan. *See* Tacuba
Tláloc **I:** 170, 301, 344, **352**
tlamacazcalli **I:** 20
Tlapa **I:** 4
Tlatelolco **I:** 17, 315, 344
tlatoani (speakers) **I:** 17, 19, 352
Tlaxcala **I: 352–353**
    Aztecs **I:** 18
    Cholula **I:** 72
    Cuauhtémoc **I:** 97
    flowery wars **I:** 131
    Nahua **I:** 249
    Sandoval, Gonzalo de **I:** 317
Tlemcen **I:** 174
tlepochcalli **I:** 20
Tlingit **I:** 150; **II:** 266, 326
TNCs. *See* transnational corporations
TNEC. *See* Temporary National Economic Committee
Toaché **II:** 44
tobacco **I: 353–354**, *354*, 387*c;* **II: 373–375**, *374*, 417*c,* 418*c;* **III:** 7, 166, 326; **VI:** 8, 209, 210. *See also* antismoking
    abolition **V:** 1
    Acts of Trade and Navigation **II:** 3
    advertising **X:** 324*c*
    African Americans **II:** 6; **IV:** 7
    agriculture **II:** 8, 10, 12, 13; **IV:** 9, 10; **V:** 6
    Bermuda Company **I:** 29, 30
    Brent, Margaret Reed **II:** 40
    British Empire **II:** 43
    calumet **II:** 50
    Carter, Robert "King" **II:** 54
    Chesapeake Bay **II:** 57, 58
    class **II:** 63
    College of William and Mary **II:** 67
    convict labor **II:** 72
    cotton culture **IV:** 97
    Crow **II:** 77
    crowd action **II:** 78
    Delaware **II:** 88
    De La Warr, Lord **I:** 104
    Drake, Sir Francis **I:** 112
    economy **II:** 101, 102
    environment **II:** 112
    Gates, Sir Thomas **II:** 135
    Glorious Revolution **II:** 141
    government, British American **II:** 145
    headright **I:** 157

indentured servitude **II:** 164
Indian Removal Act (1830) **IV:** 183
Jamestown **II:** 171, 172
Johnson, Anthony **II:** 175
Kieft, Willem **II:** 182
labor **II:** 187, 188
Lane, Ralph **I:** 197
Le Moyne, Jean-Baptiste, sieur de Bienville **II:** 193
Louisiana **II:** 200
marriage and family life **II:** 208
Maryland **II:** 210, 211
Massachusetts **II:** 215
mercantilism **II:** 221
merchants **II:** 222
miscegenation **II:** 228
monarchy, British **II:** 232
Monardes, Nicholas **I:** 239
Mount Vernon **II:** 237
Native American religion **I:** 252
Native Americans **II:** 244
New York **II:** 260
North Carolina **II:** 265
Northwest Coast Indians **II:** 265
Opechancanough **II:** 268
Parsons' Cause **II:** 271–272
plantations **V:** 276
plantation system **II:** 286, 287
religion, Native American **II:** 317
Rhode Island **II:** 321
Rolfe, John **II:** 322
St. Mary's City **II:** 328
Sandys, Sir Edwin **I:** 318
slavery **II:** 339; **IV:** 318; **V:** 329
Spanish colonies **II:** 355
tenants **II:** 370
trade and shipping **II:** 376
travel **II:** 377
Virginia **II:** 382–385
Virginia Company of London **I:** 387
Tobacco Inspection Act **II:** 78
Tobacco nation **II:** 8
Tobacco Road (Caldwell) **VIII:** 191
tobacco suits **X: 303–305**, *304*, 329*c*
Tobago **II:** 43
TOBA (Theatre Owners Booking Association) **VI:** 96
Tobias, Sheila **X:** 115
Tobin, Dan **IX:** 292

toboggan **II:** 167
Tocqueville, Alexis de **IV:** 229, 308, 377*c;* **V:** 40
Todd, Francis **V:** 145–146
Todd, George **V:** 46, 285
Todd, John **III:** 226
Togo **I:** 13, 101, 125, 243, 377
Togo, Heihachiro **VII:** 271
To Have and Have Not (Hemingway) **VIII:** 192
Tohono O'odham (Papago) **I:** 164; **II:** 165, 166
Tohopeka. *See* Horseshoe Bend, Battle of
Tojo, Hideki **VIII:** 199, 202
To Kill a Mockingbird (Harper Lee) **IX:** 182
Tokugawa shogun **IV:** 143, 219
"Tokyo Rose" **VIII:** 283
Tokyo Round (GATT) **X:** 129
Tolan, Eddie **VIII:** 338
Toledo, Don Francisco de **I:** 3
Toleration Act of 1649 **II:** 209
Toli Tenegela **I:** 322
Toll, Robert C. **VI:** 96
Toltecs **I: 354–358**, 355*m*
    Chichén Itzá **I:** 69, 70
    Cholula **I:** 72
    Itzcóatl **I:** 185
    Maya **I:** 227
    Mexico **I:** 234
    Nahua **I:** 249
    Nahuatl **I:** 250
    Quetzalcoatl **I:** 301
    Tabasco **I:** 341
T-O maps **I:** 262, **358**
tomatoes **I:** 78; **II:** 121
Tombouctou. *See* Timbuktu
Tomistas Islands **I:** 326–327
Tomlinson, Ray **X:** 152
Tomochichi **II:** 137, 138, 238, **375**
Tomocommo **II:** 289
Tompkins, Sally Louisa **V:** 231
Tom Swift books **VII:** 276
Tom Thumb (locomotive)
    Baltimore & Ohio Railroad (B&O) **IV:** 40
    economy **IV:** 118
    industrialization **IV:** 185
    railroads **IV:** 293
    science and technology **IV:** 307
Tom Watson's Magazine **VII:** 332
Tonatiuh **I:** 6
Tonawanda Seneca nation **V:** 264, 265
Tonti, Henri **II:** 129, 246
Tony Orlando and Dawn **X:** 240
tools **II:** 26, 222, 259
Tools, Robert **X:** 190, 275

Toombs, Robert **V:** 90; **VII:** 332
Topiltzin **I:** 355
topographical studies **IV:** 153
Topographic Engineering Corps **V:** 370–371
topographic views **II:** 25
Tordesillas, Treaty of **I: 358–359**, 359*m*, 386*c*
    Alexander VI, Pope **I:** 6
    Azores **I:** 16
    Brazil **I:** 31, 33
    Cabot, Sebastian **I:** 43
    Cabral, Pedro Álvares **I:** 44
    Leo X **I:** 203
    Spice Islands **I:** 335
    Vitoria, Francisco de **I:** 369
To Reclaim a Legacy (Bennett) **X:** 209
Tories **III:** 307, 374. *See also* Loyalists
torpedoes **V:** 221, 310
Torquemada **I:** 190
Torrijos Herrera, Omar **X:** 231, 232
Tortilla Flat (Steinbeck) **VIII:** 339
torture
    Huron **I:** 171
    inquisition **I:** 178
    Mercator, Gerhardus **I:** 232
    witches **I:** 374
Toscanelli, Paolo dal Pozzo **I:** 65, 287
Toscanini, Arturo **VII:** 194; **VIII:** 223
totalitarianism **VIII:** 73
"total war" **I:** 226
    rules of war **V:** 305, 306
    Shenandoah Valley: Sheridan's campaign **V:** 317
    Sherman, William T. **V:** 321
    Sherman's March through Georgia **V:** 321–323
    tactics and strategy **V:** 347
    Union army **V:** 367
totem poles **I:** 150; **II:** 24
Totonacs **I:** 93, 123
Toure, Kwame. *See* Carmichael, Stokely
Tourgée, Albion W. **V: 354; VI:** 177, 224
tourism **IV:** 129; **VII:** 203; **X:** 96, 262, 290
Touro Synagogue (Newport, RI) **III:** 187, 188
Toussaint Louverture **III:** 159; **IV:** 141
Tovar, Pedro de **I:** 90, 167
Toward a Democratic Left (Michael Harrington) **IX:** 130

Tower, John Goodwin **X:** 305–306

Tower Commission **X:** 154, 222, **305–306**

Tower of London **I:** 119, 303, 304

Town Act of 1662 **II:** 172

Town and the City, The (Jack Kerouac) **IX:** 160

Towne, Laura **V:** 280

town fathers **II:** 62

Townley, Arthur C. **VII:** 215

town planning **VI:** 53–54

Townsend, Francis E. **VIII: 358–359**

    Coughlin, Father Charles E. **VIII:** 75

    elderly **VIII:** 95

    Long, Huey P. **VIII:** 195

    New Deal **VIII:** 241

    Social Security Act **VIII:** 328

    Union Party **VIII:** 365

Townsend Movement **VIII:** 95

Townsend Plan **VIII:** 330, 359

Townshend, Charles **III:** 348, 349

Townshend Duties **III: 348–349,** 392*c*

    American Revolution **III:** 12

    Association, the **III:** 27

    Bernard, Francis **III:** 37

    Coercive Acts **III:** 76

    committees of correspondence **III:** 77

    Dickinson, John **III:** 105

    economy **III:** 111

    Franklin, Benjamin **III:** 134

    Gaspée affair **III:** 148

    Golden Hill, Battle of **III:** 154

    Laurens, Henry **III:** 203

    Lee, Richard Henry **III:** 207

    Livingston, William **III:** 217

    North, Lord **III:** 260

    Otis, James, Jr. **III:** 268

    Quartering Act **III:** 291

    resistance movement **III:** 303

    tariffs **III:** 342

    Tea Act **III:** 344

townships **IV:** 286

Toynbee Hall **VI:** 259

Toyota **IX:** 25; **X:** 31

toys **II:** 208

track and field **VI: 289–290; VIII:** 337–338

tracking, school **VII:** 78

Tracy, Edward **X:** 297

trade, domestic and foreign **II: 375–377,** 376*m;* **III: 349–351,** 350*;* **IV:** 376*c;* **V:** 405*c;* **VI: 290–291,** 326*c,* 328*c;* **VII: 309–311; VIII:** 91. *See also* fur trade; tariffs

    Acadians **II:** 2

    Acts of Trade and Navigation **II:** 2–3

    Adams, John **III:** 2

    Africa **II:** 4

    agriculture **II:** 8, 10–13; **VI:** 8–9; **VII:** 6, 7

    Akan **I:** 5

    Alaska, Russia in **II:** 14

    Albany Congress **II:** 14

    Algonquin **II:** 17

    Ames, Fisher **III:** 13

    animals **II:** 20–21

    Apalachee **I:** 11

    Arthur, Chester Alan **VI:** 17

    Asante **I:** 13

    Azores **I:** 17

    Bahía **I:** 23–24

    Barry, John **III:** 36

    Battel, Andrew **I:** 27

    Beaver Wars **II:** 31

    Becknell, William **IV:** 45–46

    Benin **I:** 28

    Bent, Charles **IV:** 47

    Bent, William **IV:** 48

    Bent's Fort **IV:** 50–51

    Bermuda Company **I:** 29–30

    Bernard, Francis **III:** 37

    BIA **IV:** 180

    Blaine, James Gillespie **VI:** 31, 32

    Bonaparte, Napoleon **III:** 42

    Boston **II:** 35

    Boxer Rebellion **VII:** 33

    Brazil **I:** 33

    brigantine **I:** 34–35

    Brims **II:** 41

    Bristol **I:** 35

    British Empire **II:** 41, 43–44

    Brûlé, Étienne **II:** 44

    Burke, Edmund **III:** 52

    Cabot, Sebastian **I:** 43

    Cahokia **I:** 47

    California **III:** 57; **IV:** 65

    California Indians **II:** 49

    Calusa **I:** 49

    Canada and the United States **VI:** 43

    canal era **IV:** 72–74

    caravel **I:** 55

    Caribbean **II:** 52, 53

    Cartier, Jacques **I:** 57, 58

    Casa de Contratación **I:** 59–61

    Castile **I:** 63

    Catawba **II:** 55

    Cathay (China) **I:** 66

    Charleston **II:** 56, 57

    Charles V **I:** 69

    Cherokee **II:** 58

    Chesapeake Bay **II:** 58

    Chesapeake-Leopard affair **III:** 67

    Chichén Itzá **I:** 70

    Chickasaw **II:** 59

    China trade **III:** 67–68

    Choctaw nation **III:** 68

    Cholula **I:** 72

    Chouteau family **IV:** 78–79

    cities and urban life **II:** 61; **III:** 69–70; **VI:** 53

    Clark, William **III:** 72

    Clayton-Bulwer Treaty **IV:** 88

    Columbus, Christopher **I:** 82

    Conestoga **II:** 67

    Confederate States of America **V:** 77

    Connecticut **II:** 68, 69

    Copán **I:** 86

    corporations **III:** 94

    cotton culture **IV:** 97, 98

    Croghan, George **II:** 76

    Cuba **IV:** 100–101

    Dagomba **I:** 101

    Dana, Richard Henry **IV:** 103

    Dawes Plan **VII:** 63–64

    Declaration of Independence **III:** 101

    Delaware **II:** 87, 88

    disease **II:** 92

    Djenne-Djeno **I:** 108–109

    Dutch East India Company **I:** 114–115

    Dutch West India Company **II:** 98

    East India Company **I:** 117

    economy **II:** 101, 102; **III:** 111, 113; **IV:** 117, 118; **VII:** 73–75; **X:** 95, 96

    embargo of 1807 **III:** 117–118

    environment **II:** 111–112

    Erie Canal **IV:** 129

    Essex decision **III:** 119

    fishing **II:** 118, 119

    Florida **II:** 120, 121; **III:** 129

    food **II:** 122

    foreign affairs **III:** 130–131

    foreign policy **V:** 131–133; **VI:** 103; **VII:** 97–99, 101; **X:** 124

    forts **II:** 124

    Franklin, Benjamin **III:** 134

    French alliance **III:** 137

    French colonies **II:** 126, 127, 129

    French Revolution **III:** 138

    fur trade **II:** 133; **IV:** 156–158

    Gage, Thomas **III:** 146

    Gama, Vasco da **I:** 137

    Gao **I:** 137, 139

    Gaspée affair **III:** 148

    GATT **X:** 129

    Georgia **II:** 138

    Ghana **I:** 140, 141

    Ghent, Treaty of (1814) **IV:** 161–162

    globalization **X:** 131–132

    Gold Coast **I:** 144

    Gonja **I:** 144

    Graffenried, Christopher, baron de **II:** 147

    Great Plains **III:** 155

    Great Plains Indians **II:** 150

    Greenland **I:** 145

    Guinea-Bisseau **I:** 147

    Hakluyt, Richard, the Elder **I:** 151

    Hancock, John **III:** 163

    Hartford Convention **IV:** 170, 171

    Hausa **I:** 155

    Hawaii **III:** 164

    Heathcote, Caleb **II:** 155

    Henry the Navigator **I:** 158

    Hopewell culture **I:** 166

    Hudson's Bay Company **II:** 159

    imperialism **VI:** 143

    indigo **II:** 166

    industrial revolution **III:** 177

    investments, American, abroad **VI:** 150

    investments, foreign, in the United States **VI:** 150–151

    Iroquois **I:** 181, 183

    Jamestown **II:** 171, 172

    Jay, John **III:** 182

    Jay-Gardoqui treaty negotiations **III:** 182

    Jews **III:** 187

    John III **I:** 193

trade, domestic and foreign
(*continued*)
Johnson, Sir William **II:** 177
King George's War **II:** 182
Kongo **I:** 196
labor **II:** 190
Larkin, Thomas Oliver **IV:** 207
Latin America **X:** 173–174
Levant Company **I:** 206
Lisbon **I:** 207–208
London **I:** 208
Macon, Nathaniel **III:** 226
Macon's Bill No. 2 **III:** 226
Manifest Destiny **IV:** 219
Maravi **I:** 223
mariners **II:** 204
Massachusetts **II:** 212, 214, 215
Massachusetts Bay Company **II:** 216
mercantilism **II:** 221
merchant marine **VI:** 192–193
merchants **II:** 221–222
Mexico **X:** 192
Minuit, Peter **II:** 226–227
Mississippian culture **I:** 237
Mohawk **I:** 238
monarchy, British **II:** 232
Monroe Doctrine **IV:** 241
Monroe-Pinkney Treaty **III:** 245
Morton, Thomas **II:** 236
Mossi **I:** 244
Mpongwe **I:** 247
NAFTA **X:** 222–223
Native Americans **II:** 243, 246
Native Americans and the Revolution **III:** 255
Navajo **II:** 247
New Hampshire **II:** 250
New Jersey **II:** 252, 253
New Netherland **II:** 255, 257
New Spain **I:** 261
New York **II:** 259, 260, 262
New York City **II:** 263; **V:** 253
Nicaragua **X:** 218
Nixon, Richard M. **X:** 220
Non-Importation Act **III:** 259
Non-Intercourse Act **III:** 259
North Carolina **II:** 263–264
North Vietnam **X:** 224

Northwest Coast Indians **II:** 266
Olmecs **I:** 269
OPEC **X:** 228–229
Open Door notes **VI:** 216–217
Orders in Council **III:** 267
Oyo **I:** 273
Panama **I:** 277
Pan-American Union **VI:** 220
Panic of 1857 **V:** 264
Peckham, Sir George **I:** 279
Penn, William **II:** 274
Pequot **II:** 278
Perry, Matthew Calbraith **IV:** 280
Peru **I:** 280
Philadelphia **II:** 281
piracy **II:** 284–286
Plymouth **II:** 288
primogeniture and entail **II:** 297
privateering **II:** 299–300; **III:** 287
Privy Council **I:** 295
pueblo **I:** 295
Randolph, Edward **II:** 312
Red Shoes **II:** 313
rendezvous **IV:** 299–300
Rensselaerswyck **II:** 319
Revolutionary War **III:** 307
Rhode Island **II:** 321
rum trade **II:** 326
San Lorenzo, Treaty of **III:** 317
Santa Fe Trail **IV:** 305–306
secession **V:** 311
Senegambia **I:** 321, 322
Seven Years' War **II:** 334
Seville **I:** 322–323
shipbuilding **II:** 335
slavery **V:** 329
slave trade **I:** 328–330
smuggling **II:** 348–349
society, British American **II:** 349, 350
South Africa **X:** 280
South Carolina **II:** 353, 354
Spanish colonies **II:** 355, 356
Stamp Act **III:** 332
Stearns, Abel **IV:** 326–327
steel industry **VII:** 298
Swedish colonies **II:** 365
Tabasco **I:** 341
tariff issue **VI:** 284–285
tariffs **III:** 342; **V:** 348
television **X:** 295

Tenochtitlán **I:** 345
Timbuktu **I:** 350
Toltecs **I:** 355, 357
Tomochichi **II:** 375
trusts **VI:** 292–295
Tuscarora **II:** 378
Tuscarora War **II:** 379
Underwood-Simmons Tariff **VII:** 313
Union navy **V:** 368–369
Venice **I:** 364, 365
Virginia **II:** 382
wage and price controls **II:** 389
wampum **II:** 390
war and warfare **II:** 391
War of 1812 **IV:** 355
West Indies **III:** 372
Wingina **II:** 401
World War I **VII:** 343
WTO **X:** 321–322
trade, reciprocal **VIII:** 193
trade balance **VI:** 150, 151
Dawes Plan **VII:** 63–64
economy **VII:** 75
tariffs **VII:** 306
trade, foreign **VII:** 309
trade deficit **III:** 99, 111
Trade Expansion Act of 1962 **VIII:** 294
Trade Reform Act of 1974 **X:** 325*c*
trade routes
Askia Muhammad I **I:** 14
Azores **I:** 16
Calabar **I:** 48
Cuzco **I:** 99
Darfur **I:** 102
Ethiopia **I:** 123, 124
Gao **I:** 137, 139
Islam **I:** 184
Mali **I:** 217–218
Mecca **I:** 230
Niger River **I:** 263
Sahara **I:** 316, 317
Songhai **I:** 332
Sudan **I:** 337
trades **II:** 35–36, 73–74
Tradescant, John **I:** 40
Trade Union Education League **VII:** 132
trade unions. *See* labor/labor movement; unions/union movement
trading posts **II:** 115, 279. *See* factories (trading posts)
trading rights **IV:** 156
Trading with the Enemy Act **VII:** 311
conscription **VII:** 54
Greenwich Village **VII:** 115

journalism **VII:** 142
radical press **VII:** 252
World War I **VII:** 344
traditional conservatism **X:** 78, 79
traditional music **VIII:** 222
"traditional values"
family life **X:** 110
Farrakhan, Louis A. **X:** 111
marriage **X:** 182
Traditional Values Coalition **X:** 266
Tragabigzanda, Charatza **II:** 346
T-rail **IV:** 307
Trail of Broken Treaties **X:** 324*c*
Trail of Tears **IV:** **343–345**
BIA **IV:** 181
cotton culture **IV:** 98
Indian Removal Act (1830) **IV:** 182*m*, 183
Jackson, Andrew **IV:** 193
Native Americans **IV:** 257
Nullification Controversy **IV:** 264
Train, George Francis **VI:** 12, 278
training **V:** 365
Traits of American Life (Hale) **IV:** 167
Transactions of the American Philosophical Society **III:** 11
transatlantic telegraph **V:** 405*c*
transatlantic trade **II:** 376
transatlantic voice transmission **VII:** 253
Transcendental Club **IV:** 345
transcendental movement **IV:** **345**, 377*c*, 379*c;* **V:** 16; **VI:** 249; **VII:** 55
art **IV:** 26
Brook Farm **IV:** 58
Emerson, Ralph Waldo **IV:** 126
Fuller, Margaret **IV:** 155
journalism **IV:** 196–197
literature **IV:** 212
religion **IV:** 299
Seneca Falls **IV:** 314
Thoreau, Henry David **IV:** 342
transcontinental railroad **IV:** 272, 325, 372; **V:** 406*c*, 409*c;* **VI:** 237
Cooke, Jay **V:** 81
Crédit Mobilier **V:** 84–85
Davis, Jefferson **V:** 89
Douglas, Stephen A. **V:** 98
elections **V:** 109
immigration **V:** 177
Pacific Railroad Act of 1862 **V:** 263–264, 422–424

railroads **V:** 290
Republican Party **V:** 301
transportation **V:** 355
United States Army Corps
of Engineers **V:** 371
Transcontinental Railroad
Surveys **IV:** 132, 133
Transcontinental Treaty. *See*
Adams-Onís Treaty
transformers, electric **VI:** 149
transistors **IX:** 64, 293, 295,
330*c*; **X:** 72
Transitional period, the **II:** 149
translators. *See* interpreters
transnational corporations
(TNCs) **X:** 131–132, 173
transportation **V:** 354–356; **VII:**
300–301, 309–310, 341; **VIII:**
359–361, *360*. *See also*
automobiles/automobile
industry; aviation; railroads
ADA **X:** 21
agriculture **IV:** 10–11; **V:** 6;
VIII: 9; **IX:** 7; **X:** 15
aircraft industry **VIII:**
9–11
American System **IV:** 18
automobile industry **VIII:**
30; **IX:** 24–26
aviation **IX:** 26–28
Boston **II:** 35
Brazil **I:** 31
business cycles **VI:** 41
canal era **IV:** 72–74
Chesapeake Bay **II:** 58
cities and urban life **IV:** 82;
V: 59; **VI:** 53
Confederate army **V:** 72
Confederate States of
America **V:** 77
Congress of Racial
Equality **IX:** 66
convict labor **II:** 71
economy **IV:** 117–118; **V:**
105; **IX:** 90
environment **II:** 111
Erie Canal **IV:** 127–130
food riots **V:** 129, 130
freedom rides **IX:** 113–114
globalization **X:** 131
Halleck, Henry W. **V:** 162
Hoosac Tunnel **VI:** 133
immigration **V:** 175–176
Inca **I:** 175, 176*m*
industrial development **V:**
181
industrialization **IV:** 185
internal improvements **IV:**
187–190
Interstate Highway Act of
1956 **IX:** 144–146
ladies aid societies **V:** 204

London **I:** 208
merchant marine **VI:**
192–193
Mexican-American War
IV: 234
migration **IV:** 235
Mississippi River **V:** 234
National Traffic and Motor
Vehicle Safety Act of
1966 **IX:** 225
New Orleans, Battle of **V:**
252
New South **VI:** 210
Niger River **I:** 263
Pacific Railroad Act of
1862 **V:** 263–264
Puerto Rico **I:** 296
railroads **IV:** 292–296; **V:**
289–290; **VI:** 237–239
science and technology **X:**
275
shipbuilding **II:** 335
technology **VIII:** 353; **IX:**
294
Tenochtitlán **I:** 344
theater **V:** 352
trade and shipping **II:** 377
travel **II:** 377
Union army **V:** 365
Vicksburg campaign **V:**
380
World War II home front
VIII: 394
transportation, urban **V:** 356;
VI: 54, 118, *291*, **291–292**;
VII: **317–319**. *See also*
streetcars; trolleys
Transportation Department
(DOT) **IX:** 225; **X:** 112
Trans World Airlines **IX:** 27
Transylvania **II:** 346
Transylvania Company **III:**
392*c*, 393*c*
Boone, Daniel **III:** 42
Cherokee nation **III:** 66
Dragging Canoe **III:** 107
Wilderness Road **III:** 378
Traore, Tiramakhan **I:** 195
trapping **IV:** 46. *See also* fur
trade
trapping brigade **IV:** 29, 30
travel **II:** **377–378**; **VI:** 185,
237; **VIII:** 297
art **IV:** 25
California Trail **IV:** 70–71
Erie Canal **IV:** 129
exploration **II:** 115
French colonies **II:** 127
Graffenried, Christopher,
baron de **II:** 146
Great Plains Indians **II:**
149, 150

indentured servitude **II:**
163–165
industrialization **IV:** 185
Kalm, Peter **II:** 181
Knight, Sarah Kemble **II:**
185–186
mariners **II:** 204
Massachusetts **II:** 215
Ostenaco **II:** 269
postal service **II:** 292
redemptioners **II:** 313
taverns and inns **II:**
367–368
Traveler from Altruria
(Howells) **VI:** 178
Travelgate **X:** 162
travel industry **IX:** 255; **X:** 96
Travels (Bartram) **III:** 37, 395*c*
*Travels in New England and
New York* (Dwight) **III:**
109
*Travels in the Interior of
America* (Maximilian) **IV:** 55
Travers, William **VI:** 134
Travers Stakes **VI:** 134
Travis, Hark **IV:** 347
Travis, Joseph **IV:** 347–348
Travis, William Barret **IV:** 13,
57, 341, **345–346**
Travis plantation **II:** 173
travois **II:** 149
Traynor, William J. **VI:** 11–12
treason **V:** 334; **X:** 56
Treason of the Senate (Phillips)
VII: 69, 192
treasury, independent. *See*
Independent Treasury
System
Treasury Department **III:** 147,
162; **IV:** 42–44, 286, 377*c*,
378*c*; **VI:** 42, 261; **VII:** 180;
VIII: 406*c*
Chase, Salmon P. **V:** 56
Communists **VIII:** 66
greenbacks **V:** 159
Morgenthau, Henry **VIII:**
216
recession of 1937–38 **VIII:**
293
Revenue Act of 1942 **VIII:**
308–309
taxation **VIII:** 351
war bonds **VIII:** 374
Whiskey Ring **V:** 393
women's status and rights
V: 398
Treasury Department,
Confederate
Confederate States of
America **V:** 75
economy **V:** 106
Fitzhugh, George **V:** 128

women's status and rights
V: 398
treaties **II:** 169, 244; **IV:** 51,
255, 257. *See also under
specific name, e.g.: Big Tree,
Treaty of*
Treblinka **VIII:** 150
Tredegar Iron Works **V:** 181,
303, **356**, 387
Tree, Ellen **V:** 352
Treemonisha (Joplin) **VII:** 141
"Tree of Peace" **II:** 31, 169
Trenchard, John **III:** 79
Trent, Council of **I:** 96, 109,
189, **359–360**; **II:** 174
Trent Affair
foreign policy **V:** 132
Seward, William H. **V:** 315
Sumner, Charles **V:** 343
Union navy **V:** 369
Trenton, Battle of **IV:** 175, 239
Trenton and Princeton, Battles
of **III:** **351–352**, 393*c*
Cornwallis, Lord **III:** 92
Greene, Nathanael **III:**
155
Hessians **III:** 167
Howe, Richard, Lord **III:**
168
Knox, Henry **III:** 197
Revolutionary War **III:**
305
St. Clair, Arthur **III:** 316
Sullivan, John **III:** 337
Washington, George **III:**
367
Wilkinson, James **III:** 379
treponematosis **I:** 107
Tresca, Carlo **VII:** 95
Tres Zapotes **I:** 270
Triangle Shirtwaist Company
VII: 284
Triangle Shirtwaist Fire **VII:**
311–312, 357*c*; **VIII:** 372
Goldmark, Josephine **VII:**
111
International Ladies'
Garment Workers
Union **VII:** 132
Shirtwaist Makers Strike
VII: 285
Workmen's Compensation
Act **VII:** 342, 343
triangle trade **II:** 52, 215, 258,
321, 326, 343–344
tribelets **II:** 49
tribute system **II:** 254, 255, 357
Acosta, José de **I:** 3
Aztecs **I:** 18, 19, 21
Benin **I:** 28
Columbus, Bartholomew
I: 78–79

tribute system (continued)
   encomienda **I:** 122
   Ethiopia **I:** 124
   Inca **I:** 176
   Maravi **I:** 223
   Mossi **I:** 244
   Nahua **I:** 249
   Powhatan **I:** 292
Trident Conference **VIII:** 320
Trident missile **X:** 22
Triennial Convention **V:** 299
Trilateral Commission **X:** 173
Trilling, Lionel **X:** 43, 215
Trimble, Isaac **V:** 150
Trinidad **I:** 12, 119; **II:** 52
Trinidad (ship) **I:** 215, 216
Trinitarian denomination **II:** 68
Trinity Church, Boston **VI:** 219, 248, 313
Trinity Church, New York City **IV:** 28
Tripartate Pact **VIII:** 124, 409c
Tripartite Union **VI:** 4
Triple Alliance **I:** 342, 352
Triple Crown races **VI:** 134
Tripoli **IV:** 130
Tripoli War **III:** 35, 65, 80–81, 397c
Tripp, Linda **X:** 68, 287
Tri-Quarterly **X:** 177
Trist, Nicholas P. **IV:** 165, 234
Troilus de Mesgouez, marquis de La Roche **II:** 126
Trois Rivières, Battle of **III:** 62
trolleys **IV:** 82; **VI:** 291, 292; **VII:** 318
Tropic of Cancer (Miller) **VIII:** 55
Trotsky, Leon **VII:** 270
Trott, Perient **I:** 30
Troy, New York, strike (1869) **V:** 340
Troy Female Academy **IV:** 365–366
Truchement **II:** 44
trucks/trucking **VII:** 301; **IX:** 7
True Civilization, an Immediate Necessity (Warren) **V:** 266
True History of the Conquest of Mexico (Bernal Díaz del Castillo) **I:** 106
True History of the Conquest of New Spain (Bernal Díaz del Castillo) **I:** 344
True Reporte of the Late discoveries and Possession . . . . of Newfound Landes, A (Sir Humphrey Gilbert) **I:** 279
True Story magazine **VII:** 143
Truman, Harry S. **VII:** 25; **VIII:** 410c, 411c; **IX:** 94, 299,

299–300, 329c–331c; **X:** 75, 76, 311
   Acheson, Dean **IX:** 1, 2
   African Americans **VIII:** 4
   Americans for Democratic Action **IX:** 13, 14
   Announcement of the Atomic Bombing of Hiroshima **VIII:** 431–433
   Asia (foreign policy) **IX:** 21
   atomic bomb **VIII:** 29
   Atomic Energy Commission **IX:** 23
   Baruch, Bernard M. **VIII:** 34
   Berlin blockade **IX:** 37
   braceros **IX:** 41
   Bradley, Omar N. **VIII:** 41
   Bush, Vannevar **VIII:** 45
   Byrnes, James F. **VIII:** 49
   CIA **IX:** 49
   civil defense **IX:** 52
   cold war **IX:** 57–58
   communism **IX:** 61
   Congress **VIII:** 69
   Congress of Industrial Organizations **IX:** 66
   conservatism **IX:** 68
   Council of Economic Advisors **IX:** 71
   defense budget **IX:** 77
   demobilization **VIII:** 79
   Democratic Party **IX:** 79
   Dennis v. United States **IX:** 80
   Dewey, Thomas **IX:** 81
   Eisenhower, Dwight D. **IX:** 92
   election of 1944 **VIII:** 99
   elections **IX:** 94
   Fair Deal **IX:** 107–108
   Flynn, Edward J. **VIII:** 122
   Forrestal, James V. **VIII:** 126
   FSA **VIII:** 113
   Full Employment Bill **VIII:** 128
   Grand Alliance **VIII:** 137
   Hillman, Sidney **VIII:** 146
   Hiroshima and Nagasaki **VIII:** 146–148
   Hiss, Alger **IX:** 134
   Hoover, Herbert **VIII:** 153
   Hopkins, Harry **VIII:** 157
   hydrogen bomb **IX:** 139
   Ickes, Harold L. **VIII:** 161
   Internal Security Act of 1950 **IX:** 143–144
   Israel **IX:** 146
   Jones, Jesse H. **VIII:** 174

   King, Ernest J. **VIII:** 178
   Korean War **IX:** 164
   Landon, Alfred M. **VIII:** 183
   Leahy, William D. **VIII:** 184
   Lend-Lease Act **VIII:** 185
   Lilienthal, David E. **VIII:** 190
   MacArthur, Douglas **IX:** 186
   Manhattan Project **VIII:** 201
   Marshall, George C. **VIII:** 206
   Marshall Plan **IX:** 194
   McCarran-Walter Act **IX:** 188
   Medicare **IX:** 196
   medicine **VIII:** 209; **IX:** 197
   Morgenthau, Henry **VIII:** 217
   NATO **IX:** 232–233
   New Deal **IX:** 229, 230
   NSC-68 **IX:** 233–234
   Oppenheimer, J. Robert **IX:** 237
   OWI **VIII:** 258
   Perkins, Frances **VIII:** 265
   Point Four Program **IX:** 242–243
   Potsdam Conference **VIII:** 279, 280
   Progressive Party **IX:** 248, 249
   public health **IX:** 250
   Randolph, A. Philip **VIII:** 291
   Roosevelt, Eleanor **VIII:** 311
   Roosevelt, Franklin D. **VIII:** 314
   Rosenberg, Julius and Ethel **IX:** 264–265
   science **IX:** 270
   Southeast Asia Treaty Organization **IX:** 274
   Soviet-American relations **VIII:** 334
   States' Rights Party **IX:** 281
   steel industry **IX:** 282
   Stevenson, Adlai **IX:** 284
   Stimson, Henry L. **VIII:** 340
   Submerged Lands Act **IX:** 287
   Taft, Robert A. **VIII:** 349
   Taft-Hartley Act **IX:** 291
   Truman Doctrine **IX:** 300–301
   union movement **IX:** 303

   Urban League **IX:** 305
   USHA **VIII:** 368
   V-E Day **VIII:** 369
   V-J Day **VIII:** 369
   Wallace, Henry A. **VIII:** 373
   WAVES **VIII:** 380
   White Paper **IX:** 321
   Zionism **VIII:** 403
Truman Doctrine **IX: 300–301,** 329c, 337–339
   cold war **IX:** 58
   Korean War **IX:** 163
   Middle East **IX:** 201
   Progressive Party **IX:** 248
   Truman, Harry **IX:** 299
Trumbo, Dalton **IX:** 135, 211, 212
Trumbull, J. Hammond **VI:** 115
Trumbull, John (artist) **III:** 22, 23, **352,** 394c, 396c
Trumbull, John (writer) **III:** 80, 215
Trumbull, Lyman **V:** 62
truss bridges **VI:** 35
Trustees of Dartmouth College v. Woodward. See Dartmouth College v. Woodward
trusts **VI: 292–295,** 325c–328c; **VII:** 129, 264, 295–296, 357c. *See also* antimonopoly; antitrust issues; monopolies; Standard Oil
   business and government **VI:** 39, 40
   due process clause **VI:** 82
   Eastman, George **VI:** 87
   Elkins Act **VII:** 83–84
   industrial revolution, second **VI:** 146
   Lloyd, Henry Demarest **VI:** 179
   Morgan, John Pierpont **VI:** 198
   newspapers **VI:** 211
   oil **VI:** 215
   Republican Party **VII:** 263
   Roosevelt, Theodore **VII:** 266
   Sherman Antitrust Act **VI:** 261–262, 343–344
   Taft, William Howard **VII:** 303
Truth, Sojourner **IV:** 9, 291, 378c, 379c; **V: 356–358,** 357, 398; **VII:** 335
Truthful History and Description of a Landscape of Wild, Naked, Cruel Man-Eating People in the New World of America (Hans Stade) **I:** 336

truth in advertising **VIII:** 1
Truxton, Thomas **III:** 36
Trylon and Perisphere **VIII:** 22, 244, *245*
Tryon, William **III:** 170, 261
Tsalagi. *See* Cherokee Nation
Tsenacommacah **II:** 293, 294
Tsenacomoco **I:** 292
Tshombe, Moise **IX:** 4
Tuareg **I:** 317, **360–361**
tuberculosis **I:** 107; **II:** 235; **III:** 106; **V:** 97; **VII:** 242
    Clay, Henry **IV:** 88
    diseases and epidemics **IV:** 112
    Dix, Dorothea **IV:** 113
    Thoreau, Henry David **IV:** 342
Tubman, Harriet **IV:** 9, 378*c;* **V:** 3, *358,* **358–359,** 361
Tucker, Jim Guy **X:** 286
Tucker, Thomas **V:** 1
Tudor dynasty **I:** 159–160, 223–224
Tudor monarchs **II:** 231–232
Tughluq, Muhammad ibn **I:** 173
Tugwell, Rexford G. **VIII: 361**
    Agricultural Adjustment Act **VIII:** 5
    Berle, Adolf A., Jr. **VIII:** 35
    Brain Trust **VIII:** 41
    FSA **VIII:** 112
    NRA **VIII:** 231
    RA **VIII:** 307
Tuke, Samuel **IV:** 113
Tukolor **I:** 135, 321
Tula **I:** 354–358
Tullahoma campaign **V:** 68, 305
Tunisia **VIII:** 392, 393
Tunjur **I:** 102
Tunney, Gene **VII:** 67, 258, 294; **VIII:** 336
Tupelo, Battle of **V:** 134
Tupí-Guaraní **I:** 31
Tupinambá **I: 361**
    Bahía **I:** 24
    Brazil **I:** 33
    cannibalism **I:** 54
    Léry, Jean de **I:** 205
    Pigafetta, Antonio **I:** 283
    Stade, Hans **I:** 335, 336
    tobacco **I:** 353
Tupper, Benjamin **III:** 265
turbans **V:** 403
Turé, Ismail **I:** 14
Turell, Ebenezer **II:** 378
Turell, Jane Colman **II: 378**
Turk, the **I:** 90
Turkey **V:** 308; **VII:** 323; **VIII:** 51; **X:** 223. *See also* Ottoman Empire
    coffee **I:** 75

cold war **IX:** 60
Cuban missile crisis **IX:** 73, 75
Ethiopia **I:** 124–125
Jews (Judaism) **I:** 191
Levant Company **I:** 206
Marshall Plan **IX:** 194
Middle East **IX:** 201
NATO **IX:** 231–233
printing press **I:** 294
Progressive Party **IX:** 248
Sufism **I:** 337
Truman Doctrine **IX:** 300
turkeys **II:** 121
Turkish wheat **I:** 87
Turkmenistan **X:** 281
Turnbow, Hartman **IX:** 207
Turner, Frederick Jackson **II:** 34–35; **VI: 295–296,** 320
Turner, Henry McNeal **VI: 296–297**
    African-American churches, growth of **VI:** 4
    Crummell, Alexander **VI:** 70
    Liberia, immigration to **VI:** 175
    Tanner, Benjamin Tucker **VI:** 283, 284
Turner, Nat **III:** 145; **IV:** 63, 205, 297, 319, **346–348,** *347,* 376*c;* **V:** 2, 64, 328
Turner, Richard "Kelly" **VIII:** 202, 246, 330
Turner, Samuel **IV:** 346
Turner, Tina **X:** 203
Turner, William **VII:** 168
Turner Broadcasting Systems **X:** 1
turning maneuvers **V:** 345–346
turnouts **IV:** 203
turnpikes **IV:** 117, 187–188
turpentine **II:** 201, 265
Turquoise Road **I:** 255, 357
turtles **I:** 30
Tuscarora nation **I:** 181; **II: 378–379; III:** 179; **IX:** 297
    Catawba **II:** 55
    Cherokee **II:** 58
    Conestoga **II:** 67
    Dekanawideh (Deganawidah) **II:** 85
    Iroquois **II:** 168
    North Carolina **II:** 263–265
    Tuscarora War **II:** 379
Tuscarora War **II:** 264, 352, 378, **379**
Tuskegee Airmen **VIII:** 4, 21
Tuskegee experiments **VIII:** 208, 406*c;* **X:** 329*c*

Tuskegee Institute **VI:** 6, 45, 308, 325*c,* 327*c*
Tusugu **I:** 243
Tutelo **II:** 233
tutors **V:** 108
Tututepec **I:** 7
Tuxedo Unionism **IX:** 170, 303
Tuzultán **I:** 199
TVA. *See* Tennessee Valley Authority
Twachtman, John **VI:** 219
Twain, Mark **IV:** 98; **V:** 213, 408*c;* **VI:** xv, 114–115, 177, 178, 297, **297–298,** 325*c;* **X:** 179, 209
Tweed, William M. **V:** 176, 194, 253; **VI:** 299, 323*c*
    corruption, political **VI:** 67
    Gilded Age, The **VI:** 114
    Plunkitt, George Washington **VI:** 225
    Tilden, Samuel Jones **VI:** 289
    Tweed Ring **VI:** 298–299
Tweed Ring **VI: 298–299,** 299
    corruption, political **VI:** 67
    Gould, Jay **VI:** 117, 118
    presidential campaigns **VI:** 231
    Tilden, Samuel Jones **VI:** 289
12th Army Group **VIII:** 41
Twelfth Amendment **III:** 117, 185, 397*c*
Twentieth Amendment **VIII:** 406*c*
Twenty-fifth Amendment **X:** 120
Twenty-first Amendment **VI:** 235; **VII:** 328; **VIII:** 406*c*
Twenty-Four **I:** 323
Twenty-fourth Amendment **IX:** 312, 334*c*
Twenty-Negro Law (Twenty-Slave Law) **V:** 79, 276
22nd Regiment of U.S. Colored Troops **V:** 5
Twenty-seventh Amendment **X:** 19–20
Twenty-sixth Amendment **X:** 19, **306,** 324*c*
Twenty-third Amendment **X:** 19
Twenty Years at Hull-House (Addams) **VII:** 214, 260
Twide, Richard **I:** 177
Twightwees **II:** 76
Twi language **I:** 13
Twisted Hair **III:** 211
2,4,-D **VIII:** 9
291 Gallery **VII:** 356*c*
Twopenny Act of 1755 **II:** 271–272; **III:** 40, 166

Two Years Before the Mast (Dana) **IV:** 65, 70, 103
Tydings-McDuffie Act **VIII:** 26, 162, 406*c*
Tyler, John **IV: 348–349,** *349,* 378*c*
    banking and currency **IV:** 43
    Calhoun, John C. **IV:** 63
    Clay, Henry **IV:** 87
    election of 1840 **IV:** 126
    Harrison, William Henry **IV:** 170
    Liberty Party **IV:** 210
    Mexican-American War **IV:** 232
    Stockton, Robert Field **IV:** 328
    Webster, Daniel **IV:** 360
    Webster-Ashburton Treaty (1842) **IV:** 361
    Whig Party **IV:** 363, 364
Tyler, Royall **III:** 347, **352–353,** 395*c*
typesetting **VI:** 137
Types of Mankind (Nott & Gidden) **IV:** 291
typewriters **VI:** 224
typhoid **I:** 108; **II:** 90, 171, 235, 382; **IV:** 57, 112; **V:** 96, 97, 389
Tyron, William **III:** 8
Tzintzuntzan **I:** 343

U

U-20 **VII:** 168
UAW. *See* United Auto Workers
U-boats **VII:** 210, 343, 353, 358*c;* **VIII:** 410*c*
    Atlantic, Battle of the **VIII:** 28
    destroyers-for-bases deal **VIII:** 82
    foreign policy **VIII:** 124
    Navy, U.S. **VIII:** 236
    OCD **VIII:** 253
    shipbuilding **VIII:** 324
    submarines **VIII:** 342
    WAVES **VIII:** 380
UCV. *See* United Confederate Veterans
Udall, Stewart **IX:** 322
UDC. *See* United Daughters of the Confederacy
Udo **I:** 28
UFW. *See* United Farm Workers
Ujeda, Alonso de **I:** 32*m*
Ukraine **VIII:** 393; **X:** 124, 152, 281

Ulster Scots. *See* Scots-Irish immigrants
Ultra code **VIII:** 64, 326
Ulysses (Joyce) **VII:** 252; **VIII:** 55
UMA (United Mexican Students) **X:** 142
UMW. *See* United Mine Workers
UMWA. *See* United Mine Workers of America
UN. *See* United Nations
Unangan **II:** 16
Uncas **II:** 211, 224, 280
"Uncle Sam" **IV:** 162
Uncle Tom's Cabin (Stowe, novel) **IV:** 14, 213, 296, 362, 379c; **V:** 339
  abolition **V:** 4
  Civil War **V:** 64
  literature **V:** 212
Uncle Tom's Cabin (Stowe, play) **V:** 352; **VI:** 286
Uncovered Wagon, The (film) **VII:** 191
Underground Railroad **IV:** 376c, 378c; **V: 361–362; VI:** 24, 171
  abolition **V:** 3
  African Americans **IV:** 9
  AME Church **V:** 5
  American Missionary Association **V:** 8
  Brown, John **V:** 37
  Brown, William Wells **V:** 39, 40
  Carney, William H. **V:** 49
  Christiana, Pennsylvania, riot **V:** 59
  fugitive slave laws **IV:** 154
  Mason-Dixon Line **V:** 224
  Mott, Lucretia **IV:** 247
  Pennington, James William Charles **V:** 270
  Ray, Charlotte **V:** 291
  religion **IV:** 296
  slavery **V:** 328
  Society of Friends **V:** 331
  Still, William **IV:** 327–328
  Tappan, Arthur and Lewis **IV:** 334
  Tubman, Harriet **V:** 358
Underground Railroad, The (Still) **IV:** 328
Underhill, John **II:** 99
Under the Horse Chestnut (Cassatt) **VI:** 45
Under the Sea Wind (Rachel Carson) **IX:** 48
Underwood-Simmons Tariff **VII: 313,** 358c
  New Freedom **VII:** 211

tariffs **VII:** 305–306
Wilson, Woodrow **VII:** 334
Underwood Tariff Act **VIII:** 159
underworld
  Aztecs **I:** 21
  Maya **I:** 228
  Yucatán Peninsula **I:** 378
"undeserving" poor **VIII:** 118
undistributed profits tax **VIII:** 352
Unemployed Councils **VIII:** 65
unemployment **IV:** 277; **V:** 264; **VI:** 67–68, 324c, 327c; **VIII: 363–365,** 364t, 405c, 406c; **X:** 326c, 331c
  African Americans **VIII:** 3
  Bonus Army **VIII:** 39
  business **VIII:** 45
  children **VIII:** 56
  cities and urban life **VIII:** 58
  civil liberties **VIII:** 60
  Communists **VIII:** 65
  Congress **VIII:** 66
  conservatism **VIII:** 71
  CWA **VIII:** 63
  economy **VIII:** 91, 91t, 92; **X:** 94–96
  elderly **VIII:** 95
  Emergency Relief Appropriation Act **VIII:** 101
  FEPC **VIII:** 109
  FERA **VIII:** 117–118
  Ford, Gerald R. **X:** 121
  government **VIII:** 134
  Great Depression **VIII:** 138, 140
  Hoover presidency **VIII:** 154
  immigration **VIII:** 162
  Keynesianism **VIII:** 177
  labor **VIII:** 179
  marriage and family life **VIII:** 204
  Mexican Americans **VIII:** 210
  Mexican Repatriation Program **VIII:** 211
  New Deal **VIII:** 240
  NRPB **VIII:** 232
  NYA **VIII:** 234
  politics in the Roosevelt era **VIII:** 270
  population trends **VIII:** 277
  poverty **X:** 246
  Reagan, Ronald W. **X:** 259
  Reaganomics **X:** 261

recession of 1937–38 **VIII:** 293
recreation **VIII:** 296
Relief and Reconstruction Act **VIII:** 302
steel industry **VIII:** 338
wage and price controls **X:** 313
Wagner, Robert F. **VIII:** 372
women's status and rights **VIII:** 384
World War II home front **VIII:** 394
unemployment compensation. *See* Title III
unemployment insurance **VII:** 11
UNESCO (United Nations Educational, Scientific, and Cultural Organization) **X:** 307
Unexpected Legacy of Divorce, The (Wallerstein) **X:** 110
Unfunded Mandates Reform Act of 1995 **X:** 113
UNIA. *See* Universal Negro Improvement Association
unicameral legislature **II:** 419c
uniforms **V:** 362, **362–364,** 363
  Annapolis Naval Academy **V:** 373
  common soldier **V:** 70
  Confederate army **V:** 72
  economy **V:** 106
  54th Massachusetts Regiment **V:** 125
  industrial development **V:** 181
  ladies aid societies **V:** 203
  rules of war **V:** 305
  Shiloh, Battle of **V:** 324
  Union army **V:** 364, 365
  volunteer army **V:** 383
  war contracting **V:** 387
  Zouaves **V:** 403–404
union, colonial **II:** 14
Union army **V: 364–367,** 366, 407c
  abolition **V:** 4
  African-American regiments **V:** 4–5
  Anderson, Robert **V:** 9–10
  Andrews's Raid **V:** 11
  Antietam, Battle of **V:** 11, 13
  Atlanta campaign **V:** 19
  Balloon Corps **V:** 21
  Baltimore, Maryland, riots **V:** 22
  Baltimore & Ohio Railroad (B&O) **IV:** 40
  battle flags **V:** 26

Beauregard, Pierre **V:** 27
Bentonville, Battle of **V:** 28
Bickerdyke, "Mother" **V:** 28–29
Blair, Francis P., Jr. **V:** 30
bounty system **V:** 34
brothers' war **V:** 37
Bull Run, First Battle of **V:** 42
Burnside, Ambrose E. **V:** 44–45
Butler, Benjamin **V:** 46
Carney, William H. **V:** 49
cartography **V:** 51
Catto, Octavius **V:** 52
Chamberlain, Joshua L. **V:** 53–54
Chase, Salmon P. **V:** 56
Chattanooga, Battle of **V:** 57
Chickamauga, Battle of **V:** 58
Cold Harbor, Battle of **V:** 68
common soldier **V:** 69
Confiscation Acts **V:** 78
conscription **V:** 80
contrabands **V:** 80–81
Corps d'Afrique **V:** 84
Davis Bend, Mississippi, freedmen's colony **V:** 91–92
Deere, John **IV:** 105
Delany, Martin Robinson **V:** 93
desertion **V:** 96
Eaton, John, Jr. **V:** 104
economy **V:** 106, 107
emancipation **V:** 111, 112
Emancipation Proclamation **V:** 114
espionage **V:** 117–118
foraging **V:** 130
Frémont, Jessie Benton **IV:** 152
German-American regiments **V:** 147
Gettysburg, Battle of **V:** 147–150
Gettysburg Address **V:** 151
Grant, Ulysses S. **V:** 154, 156
Halleck, Henry W. **V:** 162–163
Hancock, Winfield Scott **V:** 163–164
Harpers Ferry, West Virginia **V:** 165–166
Higginson, Thomas Wentworth **V:** 166, 167
Hooker, Joseph **V:** 171–172

Howard, O. O. **V:** 173
industrial development **V:** 181
Irish-American regiments **V:** 181–182
Jackson, "Stonewall" **V:** 185
jayhawkers **V:** 187
Johnson, Andrew **V:** 187
Joint Committee on the Conduct of War **V:** 191
letters **V:** 207
Longstreet, James **V:** 215
McClellan, George B. **V:** 224–226
Meade, George Gordon **V:** 226–227
Milliken's Bend, Battle of **V:** 232
Mississippi River **V:** 234, 235
Mosby, John Singleton **V:** 241
Murfreesboro/Stones River, Battle of **V:** 242–243
Nast, Thomas **V:** 247
Native Americans **V:** 249, 250
New York City draft riots **V:** 255
Overland campaign **V:** 260–261
Parker, Ely Samuel **V:** 265
plantations **V:** 276
race and racial conflict **V:** 287, 288
railroads **V:** 289
Reconstruction **V:** 292
Revels, Hiram R. **V:** 303
Rosecrans, William S. **V:** 305
rules of war **V:** 305, 306
Santa Fe Trail **IV:** 306
science and technology **V:** 310
Shenandoah Valley: Sheridan's campaign **V:** 317
Sheridan, Philip H. **V:** 318–319
Sherman, William T. **V:** 319–321
Sherman's March through Georgia **V:** 322
Sickles, Daniel E. **V:** 326–327
slavery **V:** 330
Special Field Order No. 15 **V:** 332
Stanton, Edwin M. **V:** 334
tactics and strategy **V:** 345–347

telegraph **V:** 351
Thirteenth Amendment **V:** 352
Thomas, George H. **V:** 353–354
uniforms **V:** 362–363
Union navy **V:** 370
USCC **V:** 371–372
USSC **V:** 373–375
veterans, Civil War **V:** 378–379
Vicksburg campaign **V:** 380, 382
volunteer army **V:** 383
Wakeman, Sarah Rosetta **V:** 386
war contracting **V:** 387
Warmoth, Henry C. **V:** 388
Washington, D.C. **V:** 390
Welles, Gideon **V:** 391
West Point **V:** 373
Wilderness, Battle of the **V:** 395
Women's National Loyal League **V:** 396–397
Zouaves **V:** 403
Union army Medical Bureau **V:** 229
Union Canal **IV:** 73
Union College **VI:** 290
Unionists **V:** 182
Union Labor Party **VI:** 112, 173, 262
Union Labor Press **VI:** 173
Union League **V:** 294, 296, **367–368,** 396
Union League Club **VI:** 276
Union marine corps **V:** 222
Union Mills **VI:** 44
Union navy **V: 368–370,** 369, 406*c,* 407*c*
   African-American regiments **V:** 5
   Confederate navy **V:** 74
   Dahlgren, John A. B. **V:** 87
   Farragut, David G. **V:** 121–122
   Galveston, Battle of **V:** 145
   ironclads **V:** 183, 184
   Mississippi River **V:** 234
   Monitor-Merrimack **V:** 237
   Porter, David Dixon **V:** 280
   Port Royal, South Carolina, Experiment **V:** 279
   science and technology **V:** 309
   tactics and strategy **V:** 347
   Vicksburg campaign **V:** 380, 382
   Welles, Gideon **V:** 391–392

Union of American Hebrew Congregations **VI:** 158, 243
Union of Textile Workers **VII:** 225
Union Pacific Railroad **IV:** 58, 269; **V:** 409*c*
   Blaine, James Gillespie **VI:** 31
   business and government **VI:** 40
   corruption, political **VI:** 67
   Crédit Mobilier **V:** 84–85
   Gould, Jay **VI:** 118
   immigration **V:** 177
   lobbies and pressure groups **VI:** 179
   Morgan, John Pierpont **VI:** 197
   mugwumps **VI:** 199
   Pacific Railroad Act of 1862 **V:** 263
   presidential campaigns **VI:** 232
   railroads **V:** 290; **VI:** 237, 238
   Scott, Thomas Alexander **VI:** 258
   transportation **V:** 355
Union Party **VIII: 365**
   conservatism **VIII:** 72
   Coughlin, Father Charles E. **VIII:** 75
   election of 1936 **VIII:** 97
   Long, Huey P. **VIII:** 195
   politics in the Roosevelt era **VIII:** 272*t*
   Townsend, Francis E. **VIII:** 359
Union Quartermaster Department **V:** 365
unions/union movement **IV:** 119, 187; **VII:** 162, 281, 358*c*; **IX: 303–304,** 329*c. See also* labor/labor movement; strikes; *specific unions*
   agriculture **IX:** 8; **X:** 16
   American Federation of Labor **IX:** 11–12
   automobile industry **IX:** 24–25
   braceros **IX:** 41
   business **IX:** 46
   campaign finance **X:** 53
   Clinton, William **X:** 67
   Colored National Labor Union **V:** 68–69
   Congress of Industrial Organizations **IX:** 65–66
   cost-of-living adjustments **IX:** 70
   crime **X:** 82

   economy **IX:** 90; **X:** 94
   education, primary and secondary **X:** 100
   employment **V:** 116
   immigration **V:** 177; **X:** 148
   labor **IX:** 170–171; **X:** 169–{10: }171
   NAFTA **X:** 222
   National Labor Union (NLU) **V:** 248
   Operation Dixie **IX:** 235–236
   PACs **X:** 236
   political parties **X:** 238
   Reuther, Walter **IX:** 258–259
   service sector **IX:** 272
   sports **X:** 284
   steel industry **IX:** 282
   strikes **V:** 340
   Sunbelt **X:** 290
   Taft-Hartley Act **IX:** 291
   Teamsters Union **IX:** 292–293
   United Farm Workers **IX:** 304–305
Union Temperance Society of Moreau and Northumberland **III:** 398*c*
Union Trust Company **VII:** 180
UNITA (National Union for the Total Independence of Angola) **X:** 71
Unitarianism **II:** 68, 194; **III:** 249, 285, **355; IV:** 212, 297–298
United Airlines **VII:** 147; **IX:** 27, 64
United Arab Emirates **X:** 228–229
United Auto Workers (UAW) **VIII:** 407*c;* **IX:** 330*c;* **X:** 31, 169, 236
   African Americans **VIII:** 3
   American Federation of Labor **IX:** 11
   automobile industry **VIII:** 30; **IX:** 24–25
   CIO **VIII:** 69–70
   Congress of Industrial Organizations **IX:** 65
   cost-of-living adjustment **IX:** 70
   labor **VIII:** 180
   Murray, Philip **VIII:** 221
   Reuther, Walter **IX:** 258–259
   women's status and rights **IX:** 324
United Colonies of New England **II:** 418*c*

United Confederate Veterans
(UCV)
  Civil War **V:** 67
  lost cause, the **V:** 217
  monuments **V:** 239
  veterans, Civil War **V:** 379
United Conference of Mayors
  VIII: 406c
United Daughters of the
  Confederacy (UDC) **V: 370**
  Cumming, Kate **V:** 85
  lost cause, the **V:** 217
  monuments **V:** 239
  veterans, Civil War **V:** 379
United Farm Workers (UFW)
  IX: 174, 304, **304–305,** 334c
United Front (Berkeley) **IX:** 112
United Fruit Company **VII:** 310
United Glass Company **II:** 402
United Hatters Union **VII:** 61
United Kingdom **IX:** 194,
  231–233, 294; **X:** 330c. See
  also specific countries
  globalization **X:** 131
  Mitchell, George **X:** 195
  NATO **X:** 223
  Reaganomics **X:** 261
United Mastodon Minstrels **VI:**
  95–96
United Mexican Students
  (UMA) **X:** 142
United Mine Workers of
  America (UMWA) **VII:**
  313–314, 356c
  American Federation of
    Labor **VI:** 11
  Anthracite Coal Strike **VII:**
    12
  class consciousness **VI:** 57
  Fuel Administration **VII:**
    103
  labor, child **VI:** 166
  labor and labor movements
    VII: 152; **VIII:** 180, 181
  labor trends **VI:** 171
  Lewis, John L. **VIII:** 185,
    186
  Ludlow Massacre **VII:** 167
  Mitchell, John **VII:** 186
  Murray, Philip **VIII:** 221
  National Civic Federation
    VII: 201
  New Unionism **VII:** 212
  NWLB **VIII:** 234
  Red Scare **VII:** 259
United Nations (UN) **VII:** 138,
  156, 157; **VIII: 365–366,**
  411c; **X:** 329c
  Africa **IX:** 3, 4
  African nations **X:** 13
  Albright, Madeleine K. **X:**
    18

American Indian
  Movement **IX:** 12
Asia (foreign policy) **IX:** 21
Atlantic Charter **VIII:** 28
Baruch, Bernard M. **VIII:**
  34
Bretton Woods
  Conference **VIII:** 42
Bunche, Ralph **IX:** 43, 44
Bush, George H. W. **X:** 45
Camp David accords **X:**
  54
Carter, James Earl, Jr. **X:**
  59
Catholic Bishops' Letter **X:**
  59
Congress **VIII:** 68
defense policy **X:** 87
demobilization **VIII:** 79
Dulles, John Foster **IX:** 82
foreign policy **VIII:** 125
globalization **X:** 132
Grand Alliance **VIII:** 137
Haiti, U.S. intervention in
  X: 140
Hull, Cordell **VIII:** 160
isolationists **VIII:** 166
Israel **IX:** 146
Korean War **IX:** 163–165
La Guardia, Fiorello **VIII:**
  183
League of Women Voters
  IX: 175
liberalism **VIII:** 189
Mariana Islands **VIII:**
  202
militia movement **X:** 193
Morgenthau, Henry **VIII:**
  216
Nimitz, Chester W. **VIII:**
  246
Persian Gulf War **X:** 235,
  236
postwar planning **VIII:**
  279
religion **IX:** 256
Republican Party **IX:** 258
Roosevelt, Eleanor **VIII:**
  311
Roosevelt, Franklin D.
  VIII: 314
South Africa **X:** 279
Soviet-American relations
  VIII: 334
Stevenson, Adlai **IX:** 283,
  284
Taft, Robert A. **VIII:** 349
U.S. participation since
  1968 **X: 307–308**
Welles, Sumner **VIII:** 377
White, Walter **VIII:** 378
White Paper **IX:** 321

World War II **VIII:** 389
Yalta Conference **VIII:**
  401–402
United Nations Atomic Energy
  Commission **VII:** 25
United Nations Charter **VIII:**
  366
United Nations Committee on
  Human Rights **VIII:** 411c
United Nations Economic
  Commission for Europe
  VIII: 224
United Nations Educational,
  Scientific, and Cultural
  Organization (UNESCO) **X:**
  307
United Nations Human Rights
  Commission **X:** 117, 172
United Nations Monetary and
  Financial Conference. See
  Bretton Woods Conference
United Nations of the tribes.
  See National Congress of
  American Indians
United Nations Relief and
  Rehabilitation Administration
  (UNRRA) **VIII:** 42
United Negro Improvement
  Association (UNIA) **IX:** 214
United Party (South Africa) **X:**
  279
United Press **VII:** 143
United Press International
  (UPI) **IV:** 196; **IX:** 153
United Provinces **II:** 260
United Service Organizations
  (USO) **VIII:** 224, 297–298,
  366–367, 367, 386, 409c; **IX:**
  210
United Society of Believers in
  Christ's Second Awakening
  IV: 299
United States, USS **III:** 36; **IV:**
  104, 356
United States–Chinese Treaty of
  1858 **V:** 405c
United States Army Regulation,
  1857 **V:** 71
United States Bank of
  Pennsylvania **IV:** 44
United States Centennial
  Exposition **V:** 399
United States Christian
  Commission (USCC) **V:**
  371–372
  ladies aid societies **V:** 204
  letters **V:** 207
  religion **V:** 300
  Women's National Loyal
    League **V:** 396
United States Colored Troops
  (USCT) **V:** 4, 125, 367

United States Constitution. *See*
  Constitution, U.S.
United States Football League
  (USFL) **X:** 284
United States Housing
  Authority (USHA) **VIII:**
  367–368, 407c
  cities and urban life **VIII:**
    59
  Congress **VIII:** 67
  FHA **VIII:** 119
  housing **VIII:** 158
  New Deal **VIII:** 241
  PWA **VIII:** 285
  Wagner, Robert F. **VIII:**
    372
United States Magazine **III:** 46
*United States Magazine and
  Democratic Review* **IV:** 217
United States Military Academy
  at West Point **III:** 317,
  372–373, 394c; **V: 372–373**
  Alexander, Edward P. **V:** 7
  Anderson, Robert **V:** 9
  Annapolis Naval Academy
    V: 373
  Armistead, Lewis A. **V:** 15
  Beauregard, Pierre **V:** 26,
    27
  Bragg, Braxton **V:** 36
  Burnside, Ambrose E. **V:**
    44
  citizen-soldier **V:** 62
  Davis, Jefferson **V:** 88
  Early, Jubal A. **V:** 103
  espionage **V:** 117
  Ewell, Richard Stoddert **V:**
    118
  Gorgas, Josiah **V:** 151
  Grant, Ulysses S. **V:** 154
  Halleck, Henry W. **V:** 162
  Hancock, Winfield Scott **V:**
    163
  Hill, Ambrose P. **V:** 167
  Hood, John Bell **V:** 170
  Hooker, Joseph **V:** 171
  Howard, O. O. **V:** 173
  Jackson, "Stonewall" **V:**
    185
  Johnston, Albert Sidney **V:**
    189
  Johnston, Joseph E. **V:** 190
  Joint Committee on the
    Conduct of War **V:** 191
  Jomini, Antoine-Henri,
    baron de **V:** 192
  Lee, Robert E. **V:** 205
  Longstreet, James **V:** 214
  McClellan, George B. **V:**
    224
  Meade, George Gordon **V:**
    226

Pickett, George Edward **V:** 274

Rosecrans, William S. **V:** 305

Sheridan, Philip H. **V:** 318

Sherman, William T. **V:** 319

Stuart, J. E. B. **V:** 341

tactics and strategy **V:** 345

Thomas, George H. **V:** 353

uniforms **V:** 362

Union army **V:** 365

United States Army Corps of Engineers **V:** 370

Wheeler, Joseph **V:** 392

United States Military Telegraph Service **V:** 351

United States Mint **II:** 322

United States National Museum **IV:** 78

United States Naval Academy at Annapolis **V:** 280–281, **373**

"United States of America," origin of name **III:** 25

United States Postal Service **V:** 207. *See also* Post Office Department

United States Public Health Service. *See* Public Health Service

United States Sanitary Commission (USSC) **V:** **373–375,** *374*

Bickerdyke, "Mother" **V:** 29

disease and epidemics **V:** 97

homefront **V:** 169

ladies aid societies **V:** 204

medicine and hospitals **V:** 230

nurses **V:** 256

Olmstead, Frederick Law **V:** 258

Women's National Loyal League **V:** 396

women's status and rights **V:** 398

United States Shipping Board **VII:** 4, **314–315**

United States Steel Corporation **VII: 319–320,** 355*c*; **IX:** 282, 305

banking, investment **VI:** 20

barbed wire **VI:** 20

bridges **VI:** 35

business **VII:** 37–38

CIO **VIII:** 70

industrial revolution, second **VI:** 147

Morgan, John Pierpont **VI:** 198

Murray, Philip **VIII:** 221

Northern Securities Co. v. U.S. **VII:** 216

open shop movement **VII:** 220

steel **VI:** 277–278

steel industry **VII:** 297, 298; **VIII:** 338

Steel Strike of 1919 **VII:** 298

stock market crash (1929) **VIII:** 341

trusts **VI:** 295

welfare capitalism **VII:** 333

United States v. Butler **VIII:** 345, 407*c*

United States v. C. C. Nash and Others **V:** 375–376

United States v. Cruikshank **V:** 117, 139, 201, **375–376; VI:** 163

United States v. Curtiss-Wright Export Corporation **VIII:** 407*c*

United States v. Darby Lumber Co. **VIII:** 110

United States v. E. C. Knight Company **VI:** 327*c;* **VII:** 216

business and government **VI:** 40

Harlan, John Marshall **VI:** 122

Sherman Antitrust Act **VI:** 262

Supreme Court **VI:** 281

United States v. Eichman (1990) **X:** 41, 118, 271, 319

United States v. Harris **VI:** 163

United States v. Libellants and Claimants of the Schooner Amistad **IV:** 398–402

United States v. Lopez (1995) **X:** 137, 302

United States v. Nixon (1974) **X:** **308–309**

Burger, Warren E. **X:** 44

Jaworski, Leon **X:** 161

Nixon, Richard M. **X:** 221

Supreme Court **X:** 291

Watergate scandal **X:** 317

United States v. Reese **V:** 117, 376; **VI:** 163

United States v. Turkette (1981) **X:** 258

United States v. Virginia et al. (1996) **X:** 329*c*

United States v. Washington Post (1971) **X:** 324*c*

United Steelworkers of America (USWA) **VIII:** 221; **IX:** 66, 282; **X:** 171

United Steelworkers v. Weber (1979) **X:** 8–9

United Textile Workers (UTW) **VII:** 155, 224–225

United War Work **VII:** 5

United We Stand Committee **X:** 234

UNIVAC **IX:** *63,* 64, 331*c*

Universal Declaration of Human Rights **VIII:** 311

Universal Expositions **VI:** 220

Universal Franchise Association **VI:** 180

Universalis Cosmographia (Martin Waldseemüller) **I:** 371

Universalism **II:** 57

Universalist Church **IV:** 325–326; **VI:** 35, 36

Universal Negro Improvement Association (UNIA) **VII:** 72, 105–106, 119, **315–316,** 360*c*

Universal Studios **X:** 197

"Universal Suffrage" speech **IV:** 376*c*

universities **VI:** 92–94. *See also* education, higher; *specific universities*

University Hospital **VI:** 191

University of Alabama **X:** 314

University of California **X:** 9

University of California, Berkeley **IX:** 112–113, 268, 270, 286, 334*c*

University of California, San Diego **X:** 211

University of Chicago **VI:** 94; **VII:** 68

University of Lingen **II:** 125

University of Michigan **VI:** 191

University of Mississippi **IX:** 200, 320, 333*c*

University of North Carolina **IX:** 215

University of Pennsylvania **II:** 33, 104, 282, 322, 335; **VI:** 101, 191; **IX:** 63, 97, 98, 329*c;* **X:** 72

University of Texas Law School **X:** 9

University of Virginia **III:** 115, 186

University Settlement **VI:** 259

UNO. *See* National Opposition Union (Nicaragua)

UNRRA **VIII:** 42

Unruly Calf, The (Homer) **VI:** *131*

Unsafe at Any Speed (Nader) **IX:** 25, 69, 121, 182–183, 225, 334*c;* **X:** 31, 205

unskilled labor **IV:** 179; **V:** 116; **VII:** 151; **VIII:** 69, 167. *See also* "industrial unionism"

Updike, John **X:** 177

Up from Slavery (Washington) **V:** 213; **VI:** 308

UPI (United Press International) **IX:** 153

Upjohn, Richard Mitchell **IV:** 27–28

Upjohn's Rural Architecture **IV:** 28

Upper Creek nation **IV:** 256

Upper Pima **II:** 283

Upper South states **IV:** 301, 319–320; **V:** 311, 313, 361

Upshaw, William D. **VIII:** 272*t*

Upsi, Erik **I:** 369

Upward Bound **IX:** 313

upward mobility **V:** 301; **VI:** 57

uranium **VIII:** 29, 200

Uranus **X:** 283

Urban Institute **X:** 302

urbanization. *See* cities and urban life

urban landscape style **VII:** 18

Urban League **VII:** 119; **IX:** **305–306**

urban realists **VII:** 18

urban reform **VII: 316–317**

elections **VII:** 79

Johnson, Tom **VII:** 139–140

politics **VII:** 228

progressivism **VII:** 238

urban riots **IX:** 6*m,* 52, 152, 317–318

urban transportation **IV:** 82; **V:** 356; **VII: 317–319,** *318. See also* streetcars

cities and urban life **VII:** 49

electricity **VII:** 82–83

Johnson, Tom **VII:** 140

suburbs **VII:** 300–301

urban reform **VII:** 316–317

work, household **VII:** 341

Ursuline order **II:** 130, 373; **IV:** 21

Uruguay **I:** 38, 43

Uruguay Conference. *See* Pan-American Conference of 1933

Uruguay Round (GATT) **X:** 129, 174, 321–322

USA (Dos Passos) **VII:** 166

USA Patriot Act of 2001 **X:** 300

USA Today **X:** 185

U.S.A. trilogy (Dos Passos) **VIII:** 191

U.S.-Canada Free-Trade Agreement Implementation Act of 1988 **X:** 327c
U.S.-Canadian Convention of 1903 **VII:** 356c
USCC. *See* United States Christian Commission
USCIR. *See* Industrial Relations Commission
USCT. *See* United States Colored Troops
U.S. Department of . . . . *See specific heading, e.g.:* Agriculture Department
USENET **X:** 153
USFL (United States Football League) **X:** 284
USGA (U.S. Golf Association) **VI:** 274
U.S. Geological Survey. *See* Geological Survey, U.S.
U.S.-German Peace Treaty of 1921 **VII:** 360c
U.S. Golf Association (USGA) **VI:** 274
USGS. *See* Geological Survey, U.S.
USHA. *See* United States Housing Authority
U.S.-Kiowa Treaty **VII:** 356c
U.S. Lawn Tennis Association (USLTA) **VI:** 274
Us magazine **X:** 186
USO. *See* United Service Organizations
USO (United Service Organization) **IX:** 210
U.S. Pharmacopoeia **IV:** 113
USSC. *See* United States Sanitary Commission
Usselinx, Willem **II:** 98
USSR. *See* Soviet Union; Union of Soviet Socialist Republics
U.S. Term Limits, Inc., v. Thornton (1995) **X:** 113, 302, 329c
USW (United Steel Workers) **X:** 171
USWA. *See* United Steel Workers of America
U.S. Women's Open Championship **X:** 262
Utah **I:** 255; **VI:** 317
    abortion **X:** 2
    ERA **X:** 107
    marriage **X:** 183
    population trends **X:** 242
    property rights **X:** 250
Utah Beach **VIII:** 248
Utah Territory **VI:** 51m, 198, 199, 244

Church of Jesus Christ of Latter-day Saints **IV:** 80–81
Clay, Henry **IV:** 87, 88
Compromise of 1850 **IV:** 94m, 95
Deseret, State of **IV:** 109–111
exploration **IV:** 132
marriage and family life **IV:** 222
migration **IV:** 236
Mormon Trail **IV:** 243m
Mormon War **IV:** 244–245
Native Americans **IV:** 258
Nauvoo, Illinois **IV:** 261
polygamy **IV:** 285
religion **IV:** 298
South Pass **IV:** 325
Taylor, Zachary **IV:** 335
women's status and rights **IV:** 367
Young, Brigham **IV:** 372
Utah War **IV:** 81, 110; **VI:** 198
Ute/Ute nation **I:** 166; **II:** 247; **IV:** 76, 110; **VI:** 145
utilities, electric **VI:** 146, 148
utility companies **VII:** 83, 317, 341–342; **VIII:** 284–285, 356
Uto-Aztecan language **II:** 149
Utopia, Ohio **IV:** 359
utopian communities/utopianism **II:** 297; **IV:** 273, 299; **V:** 357; **VI:** 26, **301**; **VII:** 286
    Brook Farm **IV:** 58
    Fourier, Charles **IV:** 149
    Fuller, Margaret **IV:** 155
    Owen, Robert **IV:** 273
    transcendental movement **IV:** 345
    Warren, Josiah **IV:** 358–359
    Wright, Fanny **IV:** 369
Utrecht, Treaty (Peace) of (1713) **I:** 3; **II:** 2, 309, 419c
Uttamatamakin (Tomocommo) **II:** 289
Uttamatomakking **II:** 322
UTW. *See* United Textile Workers
U2 (music group) **X:** 202
UUNET **X:** 153
UWSA (United We Stand America) **X:** 263
Uxmal **I:** 378
Uzbekistan **X:** 281

V

VA (Veterans Administration) **VIII:** 131; **IX:** 287

vacations **VII:** 258; **VIII:** 297; **X:** 262
Vaccination Assistance Act **IX:** 198
vaccines **III:** 106; **IX:** 197–199, 250–251, 295; **X:** 5, 188–189
vacuum domicilium **II:** 191
vacuum tube **VII:** 355c
Vagrancy Act of 1547 **I:** 326
Vail, Alfred **IV:** 245, 307
Valcour Island, Battle of **III:** 21, 62, **357**, 357m
Valdez, Luis **IX:** 174
Valdivia (town) **I:** 363
Valdivia, Pedro de **I:** **363**
Valencia **I:** 327
Valentino, Rudolph **VII:** 87, 190
Valesh, Eva McDonald **VII:** 285
Vallandigham, Clement L. **V:** **377–378**
    Burnside, Ambrose E. **V:** 45
    Copperheads **V:** 82
    elections **V:** 110
    homefront **V:** 169
    peace movements **V:** 266
Valle, Pietro delle **I:** 75
Vallejo, Mariano **IV:** 45
Valley Forge **IV:** 239
Valley Forge, encampment of **III:** **357–359**, 358, 393c
    Continental army **III:** 86
    Greene, Nathanael **III:** 155
    Howe, Sir William **III:** 168
    Kalb, baron de **III:** 195
    Knox, Henry **III:** 197
    Lafayette, marquis de **III:** 201
    Marshall, John **III:** 235
    Pulsaki, Casimir **III:** 289
    Steuben, Frederick von **III:** 334
    Sullivan, John **III:** 337
    Washington, Martha **III:** 368
Valparaiso, Treaty of (1883) **VI:** 50
values. *See also* ethical issues; sexual mores
    abortion **X:** 1
    birth control **X:** 36, 37
    Carter, James Earl, Jr. **X:** 57
    censorship **X:** 60
    common soldier **V:** 69
    Comstock, Anthony **VI:** 62
    conservative movement **X:** 78–80
    cosmetics industry **VII:** 58
    criminal justice **VII:** 59
    Democratic Party **IV:** 108

dress **VII:** 70–71
    education **IV:** 120–121; **V:** 107, 108; **VI:** 91
    entertainment, popular **VI:** 96, 98
    Farrakhan, Louis A. **X:** 111
    foreign policy **X:** 122
    gays and lesbians **VIII:** 130
    Greenwich Village **VII:** 114–115
    Hale, Sarah Josepha **IV:** 168
    immigration restrictions **VI:** 141
    labor, child **VI:** 166
    liberalism **X:** 176
    Liberty Party **IV:** 210
    literature **VI:** 176
    marriage and family life **IV:** 221, 222; **V:** 222, 223; **VIII:** 204, 205; **X:** 110, 181
    Middletown **VII:** 185–186
    Moral Majority **X:** 197
    movie industry **VII:** 190
    movies **X:** 197–199
    NAACP **X:** 208
    narcotics **X:** 206
    penitentiary movement **IV:** 277–278
    polygamy **IV:** 284–285
    popular culture **VII:** 230; **VIII:** 273
    pornography **X:** 244, 245
    prostitution **V:** 283–284
    recreation **VII:** 256–257
    religion **V:** 299, 300
    rural life **VII:** 269
    sexuality **VII:** 282–283
    sexual revolution **X:** 277–278
    slavery **V:** 328
    spiritualism **IV:** 326
    Sumner, Charles **V:** 342
    televangelism **X:** 293
    Victorianism **VI:** 303–304
    volunteer army **V:** 384
    WAVES **VIII:** 380
    women's status and rights **IV:** 368
    Wright, Fanny **IV:** 369
    YMCA/YWCA **VII:** 349–350
Values Party (New Zealand) **X:** 135
Van Allen, William **VIII:** 22
Van Buren, Martin **III:** 74, 279, 341; **IV:** 351, **351–352**, 377c; **VI:** 289
    abolition **V:** 3
    American System **IV:** 19
    Amistad incident **IV:** 20

anti-Masonry **IV:** 24
banking and currency **IV:** 43
Benton, Thomas Hart **IV:** 49–50
Calhoun, John C. **IV:** 62
Caroline affair **IV:** 74–75
Cass, Lewis **IV:** 77
Democratic Party **IV:** 107, *107*, 108; **V:** 94
election of 1828 **IV:** 122–124
election of 1840 **IV:** 124–126
Free-Soil Party **IV:** 150
Harrison, William Henry **IV:** 170
Jackson, Andrew **IV:** 192
Mexican-American War **IV:** 232
Oregon Treaty of 1846 **IV:** 269
Panic of 1837 **IV:** 277
Polk, James K. **IV:** 283
Stanton, Edwin M. **V:** 333
Taylor, Zachary **IV:** 335
Welles, Gideon **V:** 391
Whig Party **IV:** 363
Vance, Cyrus **X:** 55, 58
Vance, Zebulon B.
Confederate States of America **V:** 77
conscription **V:** 79
elections **V:** 110
governors **V:** 152, 153
peace movements **V:** 266
states' rights **V:** 336
vancomycin-resistant enterococci (VRE) **X:** 188
Vancouver, George **I:** 266; **IV:** 93
Vandalia, Illinois **IV:** 117
Vandenberg, Arthur H. **X:** 119
Vandenberg Resolution **X:** 223
Vanderbilt, Arthur **X:** 40
Vanderbilt, Cornelius **IV:** 88, 118, **352–353**, *353*, 378*c*; **V:** 127, 408*c*; **VI:** 117, 267, 318
Vanderbilt, W. H. **VI:** 19
Van der Donck **II:** 156
Vandergrift, Alexander A. **VIII:** 330
Vanderlyn, Pieter **II:** 25
Van Devanter, Willis **VIII:** 76, 345, 346, 346*t*
Van Dorn, Earl **V:** 73, 83, 265
Van Dyck, Sir Anthony **II:** 25
Vane, Charles **II:** 369
Vane, Henry **II:** 35, 212, 402
Van Halen **X:** 203
vanilla **I:** 261
vanishing-frontier thesis **VI:** 295, 296

Van Lew, Elizabeth **V:** 118, **378**
Vann, Robert **VIII:** 37
Van Patter, Philip **VI:** 268
Van Rensselaer, Maria Van Cortlandt **II:** **381**
Van Ronk, Dave **IX:** 111
Vanzetti, Bartolomeo **VII:** 361*c*. *See* Sacco and Vanzetti
Varennes, Pierre Gaultier de, sieur de la Vérendrye **I:** 161; **II:** 115
Vargas Zapata Luján Ponce de León, Diego de. *See* De Vargas, Diego
variety shows **IX:** 244
variola. *See* smallpox
variolation **II:** 92
Varuna, USS **V:** 252
Vasari, Giorgio **I:** 204
Vasquez, Louis **IV:** 57
Vassa, Gustavus. *See* Equiano, Olaudah
vassals **I:** 129
Vassar, Matthew **VI:** 195
Vassar College **VI:** 195, 316
Vatican **I:** 153, 203
Vatican Councils **VI:** 249, 250
Vatican II **VI:** 250; **IX:** 257
vaudeville **VI:** 96–97, 203, *287;* **VII:** **321–322,** *322;* **VIII:** 289
entertainment **VII:** 85
Johnson, Jack **VII:** 139
popular culture **VII:** 231
Tin Pan Alley **VII:** 309
Vaughan family **II:** 252
Vaux, Calvert **V:** 257, 258; **VI:** 65
VCRs. *See* videocassette recorders
Veblen, Thorstein **IX:** 117
Vector Analysis (Gibbs) **VI:** 257
V-E Day **VIII:** 185, 338, **369,** 394
Vedder, Elihi **VI:** 219
vegetable greens **II:** 122
vegetables **II:** 253, 370, 376
Velasco, Treaty of **IV:** 304, 341
Velázquez, Diego de **I:** **363–364**
Alvarado, Pedro de **I:** 7
Aztecs **I:** 21
cabildo **I:** 39
Córdoba, Francisco Hernández de **I:** 86, 87
Cortés, Hernán **I:** 91, 93, 94
Cuba **I:** 98
Escalante, Juan de **I:** 123
Grijalva, Juan de **I:** 145

Narváez, Pánfilo de **I:** 250–251
Veracruz **I:** 366
velodromes **VI:** 28
venereal disease **IV:** 171; **VII:** 242
Venezuela **I:** 10, 24, 199, 277, 386*c;* **II:** 355, 356; **IV:** 101; **VI:** 103; **IX:** 172; **X:** 220, 228–229
Venezuela boundary dispute **VI:** 59, 123, **303**
Venice **I:** **364–366**
art and architecture **I:** 12
Cabot, Sebastian **I:** 42
Cabral, Pedro Álvares **I:** 44
coffee **I:** 75
Holy League **I:** 164, 165
Islam **I:** 185
Jews (Judaism) **I:** 191
printing press **I:** 294
Ramusio, Giovanni Battista **I:** 304
slavery **I:** 327
Venice Company **I:** 206
VEP. *See* Voter Education Project
Veracruz, Mexico **I:** **366**
cabildo **I:** 39
Cacamatzin **I:** 45
Cortés, Hernán **I:** 93
Cuauhtémoc **I:** 97
Escalante, Juan de **I:** 123
Grijalva, Juan de **I:** 146
Guadalupe Hidalgo, Treaty of (1848) **IV:** 165
Mexican-American War **IV:** 234
New Spain **I:** 258
Panama **I:** 277
Sandoval, Gonzalo de **I:** 317
Scott, Winfield **IV:** 310
Veragua **I:** 79
Verapaz **I:** 199
Vérendrye, sieur de la. *See* Varennes, Pierre Gaultier de, sieur de la Vérendrye
Vergennes, Charles Gravier, comte de **III:** 135, 137, **359–360**
Verhulst, Willem **II:** 255
Vermont **II:** 114, **381; III:** 392*c*, 395*c;* **IV:** 105, 299, 365; **V:** 240, 241; **X:** 183, 242, 331*c*
Abenaki **I:** 2
deism **III:** 104
Green Mountain Boys **III:** 156
land riots **III:** 201–202
Lyon, Matthew **III:** 222
suffrage **III:** 336

Vermont Central Railroad **IV:** 295
Vermont Journal **III:** 222
Verney, Russ **X:** 263
Verrazano, Giovanni da **I:** 2, 225, 266, **367**, 367*m*, 368*m*, 387*c;* **II:** 252, 259
Verrazano, Girolamo da **I:** 266
Verrochio **I:** 204
Versailles, Treaty of (1783) **I:** 243
Versailles, Treaty of (1919) **VII:** **322–324,** 359*c*, 360*c;* **VIII:** 269, 388
Baruch, Bernard M. **VII:** 25
Committee for Public Information **VII:** 346
Dawes, Charles **VII:** 63
Dawes Plan **VII:** 63, 64
Democratic Party **VII:** 66
foreign policy **VII:** 100, 101
Hughes, Charles Evans **VII:** 124
Johnson, Hiram Warren **VII:** 138
League of Nations **VII:** 156, 157
Lodge, Henry Cabot **VII:** 165
Naval Disarmament Conference **VII:** 209
Republican Party **VII:** 263
trade, foreign **VII:** 310
Wilson, Woodrow **VII:** 335
vertical ecology **I:** 280
vertical integration **VI:** 146; **VII:** 37, 133, 319
Very Brief Account of the Destruction of the Indies, The (Bartolomé de Las Casas) **I:** 199
Vesey, Denmark **III:** 145, 327; **IV:** 205, 297, **353–354,** 376*c*
Vesey, Joseph **IV:** 353
Vespucci, Amerigo **I:** **367, 368,** 386*c*
Brazil **I:** 32*m*, 33
"Mondo Nuovo" letter of 1504 **I:** 395–399
New World **I:** 262
Ramusio, Giovanni Battista **I:** 305
Waldseemüller, Martin **I:** 371
Vessy, Denmark **V:** 328
Vetch, Samuel **II:** 309
veterans **VII:** **324–326,** *325;* **IX:** **307–308; X:** 175
American Legion **VII:** 11–12

veterans (continued)
  Committee for Public
    Information **VII:** 346
  public health **VII:** 243
  Veterans Bureau **VII:**
    326–327
veterans, African-American **V:**
  252, 368
veterans, Civil War **V: 378–380,**
  408c; **VI:** 118, 180, 326c
  Andersonville Prison **V:** 11
  bounty system **V:** 34
  Civil War **V:** 67
  common soldier **V:** 70
  conscription **V:** 79
  54th Massachusetts
    Regiment **V:** 126
  Johnston, Joseph E. **V:**
    190
  ladies aid societies **V:** 204
  Longstreet, James **V:** 215,
    216
  lost cause, the **V:** 217
  monuments **V:** 239
  Mosby, John Singleton **V:**
    242
  nurses **V:** 256
  Oates, William C. **V:** 257
  Orphan Brigade **V:** 258
  Pacific Railroad Act of
    1862 **V:** 263
  railroads **V:** 290
  Rosecrans, William S. **V:**
    305
  Sherman, William T. **V:**
    321
  Society of Friends **V:** 332
  Taylor, Susie King **V:** 350
  transportation **V:** 355
  Union army **V:** 367
veterans, War of 1812 **IV:** 287
veterans, World War I **VIII:** 39,
  263, 406c
veterans, World War II **VIII:**
  386, 410c
Veterans Administration (VA)
  VIII: 131; **IX:** 287
Veterans Bureau **VII: 326–327**
  Harding, Warren G. **VII:**
    118
  politics **VII:** 230
  public health **VII:** 243
  Soldiers' Bonus **VII:** 292
  Teapot Dome **VII:** 307
  veterans **VII:** 325
Veterans of Foreign Wars
  (VFW) **VII:** 324, 326
veto (presidential) **VI:** 230; **X:**
  311, 327c
  banking and currency **IV:**
    42
  Democratic Party **IV:** 108

Ford, Gerald R. **X:**
  120–121
Gingrich, Newton L. **X:**
  129
National Road **IV:** 253
Polk, James K. **IV:** 282,
  284
pro-life and pro-choice
  movements **X:** 249
public land policy **IV:**
  287–288
Radical Republicans **V:** 289
Reconstruction **V:** 292–294
Reconstruction Acts **V:** 296
Thirteenth Amendment **V:**
  353
Wade-Davis Bill of 1864 **V:**
  385–386
War Powers Act **X:** 315
Whig Party **IV:** 363
VFW. See Veterans of Foreign
  Wars
Viacom **VI:** 178
vice **VI:** 96
vice admiralty courts **II:** 285;
  III: 360
vice presidency **III:** 3, 185; **VII:**
  63
vice presidency, Confederate **V:**
  337
viceroyalties **II:** 355
viceroy system **I:** 15, 95, 258,
  259
Vicksburg, siege of **V:** 382, 407c
Vicksburg campaign **V:**
  380–383, 381m, 407c
  Blair, Francis P., Jr. **V:** 30
  Civil War **V:** 66
  Copperheads **V:** 82
  elections **V:** 110
  foraging **V:** 130
  Grant, Ulysses S. **V:** 156
  homefront **V:** 169
  Johnston, Joseph E. **V:** 190
  medicine and hospitals **V:**
    230
  Milliken's Bend, Battle of
    V: 232–233
  Mississippi River **V:** 235
  nurses **V:** 256
  Orphan Brigade **V:** 258
  Parker, Ely Samuel **V:** 265
  Porter, David Dixon **V:** 280
  Sherman, William T. **V:**
    320–321
  Union navy **V:** 370
  United States Army Corps
    of Engineers **V:** 371
  Warmoth, Henry C. **V:** 388
  West Point **V:** 373
Victor Herbert Orchestra **VI:**
  128

Victoria **I:** 43, 56, 215–217, 387c
Victorian culture **IV:** 222
Victorianism **VI: 303–304**
  dime novels **VI:** 81
  Eakins, Thomas **VI:** 86
  entertainment, popular **VI:**
    98
  literature **VI:** 176, 178
  theater **VI:** 286
Victorio (Apache war chief) **VI:**
  14
Victor Talking Machine
  Company **VII:** 86
Victory (magazine) **VIII:** 258
video cameras **X:** 273
videocassette recorders (VCRs)
  X: 239, 241, 273
videocassette recordings
  movies **X:** 199
  music **X:** 202–203
  pornography **X:** 244
  recreation **X:** 263
  sexual revolution **X:** 277
video games **X:** 263
Vienna **I:** 75
Vienna, Congress of **III:** 341
Viet Cong. See National
  Liberation Front
Vietnam **VIII:** 340; **IX:** 92, 274;
  X: 329c. See also North
  Vietnam; South Vietnam
  Ford, Gerald R. **X:** 121
  foreign policy **X:** 124
  Reagan, Ronald W. **X:** 261
  Vietnam War **X:** 312
Vietnamese Americans **X:** 28,
  200
Vietnamization policy **IX:** 310;
  X: 122, 311, 324c
Vietnam War **IX:** 308m,
  308–310, 309, 334c; **X:** 312,
  323c, 324c
  Acheson, Dean **IX:** 2
  Albert, Carl B. **X:** 18
  Ali, Muhammad **IX:** 9, 10
  Americans for Democratic
    Action **IX:** 14
  anticommunism **IX:** 14
  antiwar movement **X:** 24
  Asian Americans **X:** 28
  Clinton, William **X:** 65
  cold war **IX:** 60
  communism **IX:** 61–62
  conscription **X:** 76
  defense budget **IX:** 78
  Democratic Party **IX:** 79
  détente **X:** 89
  Dow Chemical
    Corporation **IX:** 82
  Eagleton, Thomas F. **X:** 93
  end of U.S. involvement **X:**
    311–312

foreign policy **X:** 122
Gonzáles, Rodolfo "Corky"
  IX: 124–125
Habib, Philip C. **X:** 139
Hayden, Tom **IX:** 131
Humphrey, Hubert H. **IX:**
  138
and immigration **IX:** 141
Johnson, Lyndon **IX:**
  151–152
journalism **IX:** 154
Kennedy, Edward M. **X:**
  163–164
Kennedy, John F. **IX:** 158
King, Martin Luther, Jr.
  IX: 161
Kissinger, Henry A. **X:** 166
Latin America **X:** 172
McGovern, George
  Stanley **X:** 184
movies **X:** 198
music **X:** 202
Nixon, Richard M. **X:** 220
North Vietnam **X:** 224
O'Neill, Thomas P., Jr. **X:**
  228
Pentagon Papers **X:** 233
political parties **X:** 237
Republican Party **IX:** 258
rock and roll **IX:** 264
SANE **IX:** 267, 268
Southeast Asia Treaty
  Organization **IX:** 274
Soviet Union **IX:** 277
television **IX:** 297
Twenty-sixth Amendment
  X: 306
veterans **IX:** 307
War Powers Act **X:** 315
wars of national liberation
  IX: 317
Weather Underground **X:**
  317, 318
Young Chicanos for
  Community Action **IX:**
  328
Vietnam War Memorial **IX:**
  307–308
View of the Causes and
  Consequences of the
  American Revolution
  (Boucher) **III:** 46
Views of Society and Manners in
  America (Wright) **IV:** 369
vigilante groups **III:** 330–331;
  V: 199–201
Viguerie, Richard **X:** 20
Vikings **I:** 241, 263, 264m, 385c;
  II: 338
Viking space program **IX:** 220;
  X: 283
Vilcabamba **I:** 15, 177

Villa, Francisco "Pancho" **VII:** 357c, 358c
  Big Stick diplomacy **VII:** 28–29
  foreign policy **VII:** 99
  Mexican invasion **VII:** 183
  Mexican Revolution **VII:** 184, 185
  Reed, John **VII:** 259
  Wilson, Woodrow **VII:** 334
  Zimmermann telegram **VII:** 353
Villa de la Navidad **I:** 81
Village of Equity, Ohio **IV:** 359
Village People, the **X:** 202, 240
Villard, Henry **VI:** 147, **304–305**
Villard, Oswald Garrison **VI:** 309
Villa Rica de la Vera Cruz. *See* Veracruz
Villiers, George **I:** 188
Vincent, John H. **VI:** 49, 241
Vincent, Strong **V:** 148
Vinland **I:** 35, 263, **369,** 385c
Vinson, Fred **IX:** 42, 315; **X:** 319
Vinson Naval Act **VIII:** 408c
Vio (Cajetan), Tommaso de **I:** 109
violence **IV:** 69, 79
Violence Against Women Act **X:** 330c
Violent Crime Control and Law Enforcement Act of 1994 **X:** 137
violins **II:** 239
virginals **II:** 239
Virginia **II:** **45, 382–385,** 383m, 417c; **III:** 394c, 396c; **IV:** 376c, 379c; **V:** 406c, 407c; **IX:** 311; **X:** 107, 242
  African Americans **II:** 5; **III:** 6; **VI:** 6
  agriculture **II:** 8, 10, 11; **IV:** 10
  Albany Congress **II:** 14
  Andros, Sir Edmund **II:** 19
  Anglican Church **II:** 19
  antislavery and abolition **III:** 15–16
  architecture **II:** 23
  Bacon's Rebellion **II:** 27–28
  Berkeley, Lady Frances **II:** 32
  Berkeley, Sir William **II:** 32–33
  Beverley, Robert **II:** 33
  Bland, Richard **III:** 40
  Braddock, Edward **II:** 38
  Brent, Margaret Reed **II:** 40

Bull Run/Manassas, First and Second Battles of **V:** 42–44
Burgesses, House of **II:** 44–45
bushwhackers **V:** 46
Byrd, William II **II:** 47
Byrd family **II:** 47
Calvert, Leonard **II:** 50
captivity **II:** 51
Carter, Landon **II:** 53–54
Carter, Robert "King" **II:** 54
Catawba **II:** 55
Cedar Mountain, Battle of **V:** 53
Chancellorsville, Battle of **V:** 54
Cherokee **II:** 57, 58
class **II:** 63
clothing **II:** 65
College of William and Mary **II:** 67
Compromise of 1850 **IV:** 94
Conestoga **II:** 67
Confederate army **V:** 72
Confederate States of America **V:** 75
convict labor **II:** 72
Cornstalk **II:** 72
crime and punishment **II:** 75
crowd action **II:** 78
Culpeper, Thomas, Lord **II:** 79
Dale, Sir Thomas **II:** 81
Davies, Samuel **II:** 84
disease **II:** 90
Drake, Sir Francis **I:** 111–112
Early, Jubal A. **V:** 103
economy **II:** 101
education **II:** 103; **III:** 115
English Civil War **II:** 108
English immigrants **II:** 108
Enlightenment **II:** 109
environment **II:** 110–112
ethnocentrism **II:** 114
exploration **II:** 115
Five Forks, Battle of **V:** 128–129
food **II:** 122
Fort Necessity **II:** 123
Fredericksburg, Battle of **V:** 139–141
French colonies **II:** 129
Gabriel's Rebellion **III:** 145
Gates, Sir Thomas **II:** 135–136

Glorious Revolution **II:** 141
government, British American **II:** 142, 144, 145
governors **V:** 153
Great Awakening **II:** 147, 148
Harpers Ferry, West Virginia **V:** 164–166
headright **I:** 157
Henry, Patrick **III:** 165–166
Hill, Ambrose P. **V:** 167–168
housing **II:** 157
humanitarianism **III:** 170
impeachment of Andrew Johnson **V:** 178
iron manufacturing **II:** 167
Iroquois **II:** 168, 169
Jackson, "Stonewall" **V:** 185
Jamestown **II:** 171–173
Jefferson, Thomas **III:** 183, 184
Jews **III:** 188
Jim Crow laws **VI:** 156
Johnson, Anthony **II:** 175
Johnson, Mary **II:** 175
Johnston, Joseph E. **V:** 190
labor **II:** 187–188
land **II:** 191, 192
Lane, Ralph **I:** 197
Lee, Robert E. **V:** 205
Longstreet, James **V:** 214
lost cause, the **V:** 217
lotteries **II:** 199
Madison, James **III:** 227
Maryland **II:** 209
Mason, George **III:** 237
Mayflower Compact **II:** 219
mills **II:** 225
miscegenation **II:** 228; **V:** 233
monarchy, British **II:** 232
Monroe, James **IV:** 239, 240
Morgan, Daniel **III:** 246
mortality **II:** 235
Mosby, John Singleton **V:** 241–242
mulattoes **II:** 238
Native Americans **II:** 243, 244, 246
New Amsterdam **II:** 250
New Hampshire **II:** 250
Newport, Christopher **II:** 259
New South **VI:** 210
North Carolina **II:** 265

Opechancanough **II:** 268
Ostenaco **II:** 269
Overland campaign **V:** 260, 261
Parsons' Cause **II:** 271–272
Peninsular campaign **V:** 267–270
Petersburg campaign **V:** 270–273
piracy **II:** 285
plantations **V:** 276
plantation system **II:** 287
population trends **II:** 291; **III:** 284
Pott, John **II:** 293
Powhatan (chief) **II:** 293
Powhatan Confederacy **II:** 295
Protestantism **II:** 301
Quakers **II:** 308
race and race relations **IV:** 289
Ralegh, Sir Walter **I:** 303
Reconstruction **V:** 292, 294
redemption **V:** 297
refugees **V:** 299
religion, Euro-American **II:** 316, 317
religious liberty **III:** 300
Rolfe, John **II:** 322
Sandys, George **II:** 328–329
secession **V:** 311
Seven Years' War **II:** 332
Shenandoah Valley: Jackson's campaign **V:** 316–317
Shenandoah Valley: Sheridan's campaign **V:** 317–318
slave codes **II:** 336
slavery **III:** 326
slave trade **II:** 343
slave trade, internal **IV:** 320
Smith, John **II:** 346
Smith, Robert **II:** 348
society, British American **II:** 349
spinsters **II:** 360
Spotsylvania, Battles of **V:** 333
suffrage **II:** 364
Susquehannock War **II:** 364
tactics and strategy **V:** 347
Teach, Edward **II:** 368, 369
tenants **II:** 371
Tennent, William, Jr. **II:** 372

Virginia *(continued)*
  theater **II:** 373
  tobacco **II:** 374
  trade and shipping **II:** 376
  travel **II:** 377
  Turner, Nat **IV:** 346–348
  Tuscarora War **II:** 379
  Tyler, John **IV:** 348
  Washington, D.C. **V:** 389, 390
  Weiser, Johann Conrad **II:** 393
  Wilderness, Battle of the **V:** 395
  witchcraft **II:** 402, 403
  wolves **II:** 405
  women's rights and status **II:** 407; **VI:** 318
  Wyatt, Sir Francis **II:** 411
  Yeardley, Sir George **II:** 413–414
Virginia, CSS
  brothers' war **V:** 37
  ironclads **V:** 183, 184
  Monitor-Merrimack **V:** 237
  Peninsular campaign **V:** 267
  science and technology **V:** 309
  Tredegar Iron Works **V:** 356
Virginia Algonquians **I:** 6, 77–78
Virginia and Kentucky
  Resolutions **III: 360; V:** 311
    Alien and Sedition Acts **III:** 9
    Jefferson, Thomas **III:** 185
    Madison, James **III:** 229
    states' rights **III:** 333
    Taylor, John, of Caroline **III:** 344
Virginia Bill of Rights **III:** 393*c*
Virginia City, Nevada **IV:** 96
Virginia Company **I:** 29, 30, 152, 318
  Berkeley, Sir William **II:** 32
  Burgesses, House of **II:** 44
  Dale, Sir Thomas **II:** 81
  environment **II:** 112
  Gates, Sir Thomas **II:** 135
  Pocahontas **II:** 289
  Smith, John **II:** 347
  Yeardley, Sir George **II:** 413
Virginia Company of London **II: 385–387,** 386*m,* 417*c*
  agriculture **II:** 9
  environment **II:** 111
  government, British American **II:** 142

indentured servitude **II:** 163
  Jamestown **II:** 171, 172
  labor **II:** 188
  lotteries **II:** 199
  Maryland **II:** 209
  monarchy, British **II:** 232
  Newport, Christopher **II:** 259
  Rolfe, John **II:** 322
  Smith, John **II:** 346
  Virginia **II:** 382
Virginia Company of Plymouth **II:** 386*m,* 387, 417*c*
Virginia Convention, second **III:** 166, 393*c*
Virginia Declaration of Rights **III:** 38
Virginia dynasty **III: 361**
Virginia House of Burgesses **III:** 391*c*
  committees of correspondence **III:** 77
  Dunmore, Lord **III:** 109
  Lee, Richard Henry **III:** 206–207
  Mason, George **III:** 237
  Stamp Act **III:** 332
  Virginia Resolves **III:** 361
  Washington, George **III:** 366
Virginia Military Institute (VMI) **V:** 185; **X:** 131, 329*c*
Virginia Plan **III:** 395*c*
  Constitutional Convention **III:** 82
  Madison, James **III:** 228
  Randolph, Edmund **III:** 296
Virginia Racial Integrity Act **VII:** 248–249
Virginia Resolves **III: 361,** 391*c*
Virginia Slave Code **II:** 384
Virginia State Board of Pharmacy v. Virginia Citizens consumer Council (1976) **X:** 7
Virginia v. United States (1996) **X:** 131
Virgin Islands **II:** 53
Virginius affair **V:** 156; **VI:** 71, 272, **305–306,** 323*c*
Virgin of Guadalupe **I:** 262
virgin soil epidemics **I:** 108, 175, 183, 330–331; **II:** 90, 345
Visa **IX:** 330*c*
Vision of Columbus, The (Barlow) **III:** 36
visita **I:** 259
Visiting Nurse Service **VI:** 259
VISTA. *See* Volunteers in Service to America

Vitoria, Francisco de **I:** 109, **369–370**
Viviparous Quadrupeds of North America, The (Audubon) **IV:** 35
Vizcaíno, Sebastián **I:** 132
V-J Day **VIII: 369–370**
  demobilization **VIII:** 79
  Hiroshima and Nagasaki **VIII:** 146
  Lend-Lease Act **VIII:** 185
  Marines, U.S. **VIII:** 203
  World War II home front **VIII:** 396
Vlag, Piet **VII:** 173
VMI. *See* Virginia Military Institute
vocal music **IV:** 179, 250
vocational education **VII:** 77–78, 352; **VIII:** 94, 235
Voice of America **VIII:** 283
volcanoes **I:** 10
Volcker, Paul **X:** 94, 95, 259
Volkswagen **IX:** 25, 332*c;* **X:** 31
Vollmer, August **VII:** 58
Volpe, Justin **X:** 330*c*
Volstead, Andrew J. **VII:** 327
Volstead Act **VII:** 59, 241, **327–328,** 359*c*
volta do mar **I:** 180
Voltaire **III:** 103, 109
voluntarism **II:** 201
voluntary associations **III: 361–362**
  Franklin, Benjamin **III:** 133
  humanitarianism **III:** 169
  popular culture **III:** 281
  religion **III:** 299
Voluntary Parenthood League **VII:** 29
volunteer army **V: 383–384**
  bounty system **V:** 34
  Confederate army **V:** 71
  conscription **V:** 80
  Halleck, Henry W. **V:** 162
  Union army **V:** 364
Volunteers in Service to America (VISTA) **IX:** 87, 241, **310–311,** 334*c;* **X:** 278
Volunteer's Journal **III:** 61
Volvo **X:** 32
Von der Ahe, Chris **VI:** 22
von Hayek, Friedrich **X:** 78
von Mises, Ludwig **X:** 140
voodoo **IV:** 297
Voorhis, Jerry **X:** 219
Voree colony **IV:** 329
Vorse, Mary Heaton **VII:** 106
Vorwarts **VI:** 268
Voskhod space program **IX:** 279

vote recorders **VI:** 89
Voter Education Project (VEP) **IX:** 178, 306
voter turnout **V:** 109
voting **VI:** 66, 127, 231, 232; **X:** 326*c. See also* elections; suffrage
  gender gap **X:** 128
  NAACP **X:** 208
  political parties **X:** 238
voting age **X:** 19, 101, 324*c*
voting rights **IV:** 376*c;* **VIII:** 228, 347, 384; **IX:** 332*c,* 334*c. See also* African-American suffrage; suffrage; woman suffrage
  AASS **IV:** 15
  African Americans **IV:** 8
  Civil Rights Act of 1957 **IX:** 55
  Civil Rights Act of 1960 **IX:** 55–56
  Civil Rights Act of 1964 **IX:** 56
  Democratic Party **IV:** 106
  feminism **X:** 113, 114
  Hamer, Fannie Lou **IX:** 129
  King, Martin Luther, Jr. **IX:** 161
  Lewis, John **IX:** 178
  Meredith, James **IX:** 200
  race and racial conflict **IV:** 289; **IX:** 254
  Student Nonviolent Coordinating Committee **IX:** 284
  Twenty-sixth Amendment **X:** 306
  Voting Rights Act of 1965 **IX:** 311–312
Voting Rights Act of 1965 **IX: 311–312,** 334*c;* **X:** 255, 306
  African-American movement **IX:** 5
  Great Society **IX:** 127
  Johnson, Lyndon **IX:** 151
  King, Martin Luther, Jr. **IX:** 161
  race and racial conflict **IX:** 254
  segregation **IX:** 271
  Southern Christian Leadership Conference **IX:** 276
  Southern Manifesto **IX:** 276
  Student Nonviolent Coordinating Committee **IX:** 284
Voting Rights Act of 1970 **X:** 19, 306

votive paintings **II:** 25
Voyage et Aventures de Lord William Carisdell en Icarie **IV:** 61
Voyager space program **IX:** 220; **X:** 283
voyageurs **I:** 149; **II:** 130–131
VRE (vancomycin-resistant enterococci) **X:** 188
vulcanizing rubber **IV:** 118

W

WAAC **VIII:** 381
Wabanaki **I:** 2; **II:** 203
Wabash & Erie Canal **IV:** 73*m*
Wabash v. Illinois **VI:** 40, 222, 281, 326*c*
WAC. *See* Women's Army Corps
Waco, Texas **X:** 194, 267, 328*c*
Wade, Benjamin Franklin **V:** 385
  amnesty, acts of **V:** 8
  Fort Pillow, Tennessee **V:** 135
  impeachment of Andrew Johnson **V:** 178, 179
  Joint Committee on the Conduct of War **V:** 191
  Kansas-Nebraska Act of 1854 **V:** 198
  Morrill Land-Grant Act **V:** 241
  Radical Republicans **V:** 288
  Republican Party **V:** 302
  Wade-Davis Bill of 1864 **V:** 385, 386
Wade-Davis Bill of 1864 **V:** 292, **385–386,** 407*c*–408*c*
Wadsworth, James W. **X:** 105
Wagadu **I:** 140
wage and price controls **II:** 221, 368, **389; VIII: 371–372,** 409*c;* **X:** 94, 103, **313,** 324*c*
  black market **VIII:** 38
  mobilization **VIII:** 215
  Murray, Philip **VIII:** 221
  NRA **VIII:** 231
  NWLB **VIII:** 233
  OPA **VIII:** 254–255
  reconversion **VIII:** 295
wage discrimination **V:** 125; **VI:** 169, 171
wage labor
  Democratic Party **IV:** 108
  industrialization **IV:** 185
  slavery **IV:** 316, 319
  women's status and rights **IV:** 367
wages **IV:** 203, 222; **V:** 116, 340, 383; **VI:** 117, 140, 170; **VIII:**

3, 110, 407*c*, 408*c;* **X:** 246, 291
  Adamson Act **VII:** 2
  Adkins v. Children's Hospital **VII:** 3
  cost-of-living adjustment **IX:** 70
  economy **VII:** 76
  Fair Deal **IX:** 108
  Fuel Administration **VII:** 103
  labor **IX:** 170
  Progressive Party **IX:** 249
  Soldiers' Bonus **VII:** 291
  union movement **IX:** 303
  women's status and rights **IX:** 324
Wagner, Richard **VI:** 203
Wagner, Robert **VII:** 287; **VIII: 372–373; IX:** 99
  Congress **VIII:** 66, 67
  Democratic Party **VIII:** 81
  labor **VIII:** 180
  medicine **VIII:** 209
  NIRA **VIII:** 228
  NLRA **VIII:** 229
  NRA **VIII:** 231
  PWA **VIII:** 285
  relief **VIII:** 299
  USHA **VIII:** 367, 368
Wagner Act. *See* National Labor Relations Act
Wagner-Murray-Dingall bill **VIII:** 372–373
Wagner Public Housing Act. *See* Housing Act of 1937
Wagner-Steagall Act **VIII:** 407*c*
wagon making **II:** 101
Wahunsonacock. *See* Powhatan (chief)
Wainwright, Jonathan M. **VIII:** 267
Waite, Morrison R. **V:** 376; **VI:** 281
Waiting for Lefty (Odets) **VIII:** 191
Wakeman, George **V:** 233
Wakeman, Sarah Rosetta **V:** 386
Waksman, Selman **VIII:** 208; **IX:** 205
Walcott, Charles Doolittle **VI:** 111
Walcott, Louis Eugene. *See* Farrakhan, Louis A.
Wald, Lillian **VI:** 259; **VII:** 47, 198, **329**
Walden (Thoreau) **IV:** 379*c*
  literature **IV:** 212
  religion **IV:** 299
  Thoreau, Henry David **IV:** 342, *343*

  transcendental movement **IV:** 345
Waldenbooks **X:** 178
Waldron, Francis X. *See* Dennis, Eugene
Waldron family **II:** 252
Waldseemüller, Martin **I:** 368, **371**
Wales **I:** 10, 11, 385*c*
"Walk against Fear" **IX:** 285
Walker, David **IV:** 2, 3, 16, 376*c;* **V:** 2, 3
Walker, Edwin **VI:** 236
Walker, John G. **V:** 13, 165
Walker, Johnny (drum major) **V:** 243
Walker, Joseph **IV:** 131
Walker, Leroy Pope **V:** 137
Walker, Madam C. J. **VII:** 58, 355*c*
Walker, Mary Edwards **V:** 228, 231, **386–387,** 387
Walker, Samuel **IV:** 91, 92
Walker, William **IV:** 89, 219; **V:** 126–127, 405*c*
"Walker Colt" **IV:** 91
Walker Commission **X:** 61
Walker Tariff Act of 1846 **IV:** 378*c*
Walker War **IV:** 110
Walking Purchase of 1737 **II:** 191, 274, 370, **389–390,** 393
Wallace, George C. **VII:** 293; **IX:** 333*c;* **X: 313–314**
  American Independent Party **X:** 20
  Carter, James Earl, Jr. **X:** 57
  Democratic Party **IX:** 79
  elections **IX:** 97; **X:** 101
  Great Society **IX:** 127
  liberalism **IX:** 179
  McGovern, George Stanley **X:** 184
  Nixon, Richard M. **X:** 220
  political parties **X:** 238
  Southern Manifesto **IX:** 276
  Student Nonviolent Coordinating Committee **IX:** 284
  third-party candidates **X:** 102
  White Citizens' Councils **IX:** 320
Wallace, Henry A. **VI:** 45; **VIII: 373–374,** 407*c;* **IX:** 330*c*
  Agricultural Adjustment Act **VIII:** 5, 6
  agriculture **VIII:** 8
  Americans for Democratic Action **IX:** 13, 14

  Democratic Party **IX:** 79
  election of 1940 **VIII:** 98
  election of 1944 **VIII:** 99
  elections **IX:** 94
  FSA **VIII:** 112
  Hopkins, Harry **VIII:** 157
  Jones, Jesse H. **VIII:** 174
  Keynesianism **VIII:** 176
  Progressive Party **IX:** 248, 249
  Reciprocal Trade Agreements Act **VIII:** 294
  RFC **VIII:** 295
  Roosevelt, Franklin D. **VIII:** 314
  Social Security Act **VIII:** 328
  States' Rights Party **IX:** 281
  Zionism **VIII:** 403
Wallace, Henry C. **VI:** 45; **VII:** 175
Wallace, Lurleen **X:** 314
Wallace, Mike **IX:** 187
Wallach, E. Robert **X:** 191
Wallerstein, Judith **X:** 110
Walling, William English **VII:** 205
Walloons **II:** 249, 255, 257, 259
Wall Street **II:** 363; **IV:** 276; **V:** 84, 253, 264; **VI:** 117–118. *See also* stocks/stock market
Wall Street Journal **X:** 185
Wal-Mart **X:** 49, 95
Walpole, Horace **II:** 193
Walpole, Robert **II:** 137, 145, 210, 415; **III:** 79, 277, 375
walrus **I:** 264
Walsh, Frank **VII:** 128, 204
Walsh, Lawrence E. **X:** 150, 154, 222, **314–315**
Walsh, Thomas **VIII:** 165; **X:** 105
Walsh-Healy Government Contract Act of 1936 **VIII:** 407*c*
Walsingham, Sir Francis **I:** 152, **371–372**
Walt Disney Studios **VIII:** 408*c*
Walter, Francis **IX:** 187
Walter, Thomas **II:** 239, **390**
Walter, Thomas Ustick **IV:** 27
Walters, Vernon **X:** 308
Wampanoag
  Algonquin **II:** 17
  captivity **II:** 51
  King Philip's War **II:** 183
  Massachusetts **II:** 212, 214
  Massasoit **II:** 217
  Metacom **II:** 222–223
  Native Americans **II:** 246

Wampanoag (continued)
    Plymouth **II:** 287
    Rhode Island **II:** 320
    Squanto **II:** 360
    Wetamo **II:** 395
wampum **I:** 182, 183; **II:**
    390–391
    art **II:** 24
    Dekanawideh
        (Deganawidah) **II:** 85
    King Philip's War **II:** 183
    Miantonomo **II:** 224
    Narragansett **II:** 241
    Native Americans **II:** 243
    Pequot **II:** 278
    Pequot War **II:** 279
Wamsutta
    Massasoit **II:** 217
    Metacom **II:** 222
    Plymouth **II:** 287
    Wetamo **II:** 395
Wanamaker, John **VI:** 62, 78, 79
Wanchese **I:** 26, 154, 220, 313,
    372, 388c; **II:** 264
Wanga kingdom **I:** 210
Wangara **I:** 218
Wanghia, Treaty of **IV:** 378c
want, freedom from. See Four
    Freedoms
Wappo **I:** 48
War Admiral **VIII:** 338
war against terrorism **X:** 88–89,
    125, 247, 300
war and warfare **II:** 391; **VI:**
    323c, 324c. See also cold war;
    foreign policy; specific wars
    Acadians **II:** 2
    Algonquin **II:** 17
    Anti-Imperialist League
        VI: 13
    British Empire **II:** 41, 43
    Catholic Bishops' Letter **X:**
        59–60
    Chickasaw **II:** 59
    Choctaw **II:** 61
    Cuba **VI:** 71
    Dale, Sir Thomas **II:** 81
    Filipino insurrection **VI:**
        100
    Howe, George Augustus,
        Viscount **II:** 158
    Iroquois **II:** 169
    Mason, John **II:** 211
    monarchy, British **II:** 232
    Native Americans **II:** 243,
        244; **VI:** 206–208
    New York **II:** 262
    Powhatan Confederacy **II:**
        295
    Pueblo Revolt **II:** 303–304
    Red Cloud **VI:** 239–240
    Red Shoes **II:** 313

Remember the Maine **VI:**
    187–188
Rhode Island **II:** 321
scalping **II:** 329–330
smallpox **II:** 345
Stuyvesant, Peter **II:** 363
terrorism **X:** 299
Treaty of Paris **II:** 378
War Powers Act **X:** 315
Westo **II:** 395
War between Britain and
    France. See Anglo-French
    War, 1793–1815
war bonds **VIII:** **374**
    advertising **VIII:** 1–2
    mobilization **VIII:** 215
    recreation **VIII:** 298
    sports **VIII:** 337
    women's status and rights
        VIII: 386
    World War II home front
        VIII: 395
war contracting **V:** **387–388**
war crimes **V:** 282
Ward, Aaron Montgomery **VI:**
    186
Ward, Artemas **III:** 50
Ward, Charles B. **VI:** 204
Ward, Hamilton **VII:** 265
Ward, Holcombe **VI:** 274
Ward, John M. **VI:** 22
Ward, John Q. A. **VI:** 259
Ward, Lester Frank **VI:** 266,
    307; VII: 109, 338
Ward, Nancy **II:** **391–392**
Ward, Samuel **II:** 321; **VI:** 180
Ward, Samuel Ringgold **V:** 52
war debt **V:** 138, 293; **VIII:** 139,
    154
        Fordney-McCumber Tariff
            VII: 97
        Revolutionary War **III:** 89
        tariffs **VII:** 306
        trade, foreign **VII:** 310
        War Revenue Act **VII:** 330
War Democrats **V:** 110, 211
War Department **IV:** 180–181,
    309; **V:** 362–363; **VI:** 258;
    VII: 303, 347; **VIII:** 340; **IX:**
    224
        Army, U.S. **VIII:** 20
        CCC **VIII:** 63
        code breaking **VIII:** 64
        Dana, Charles A. **V:** 88
        Freedmen's Bureau **V:** 142
        industrial development **V:**
            181
        ladies aid societies **V:** 204
        Lee, Robert E. **V:** 205
        Little Bighorn, Battle of **V:**
            214
        Mississippi River **V:** 234

public opinion polls **VIII:**
    284
Stanton, Edwin M. **V:** 334
Stimson, Henry L. **VIII:**
    340
Washington, D.C. **V:** 389
WMC **VIII:** 375
WPB **VIII:** 376
War Department, Confederate
    V: 27, 75, 180
Wardley Society **III:** 323
Wardman, Ervin **VI:** 321
Ward's Cove Packing Company
    v. Antonio (1989) **X:** 9, 63,
    264
Ware, Charles Pickard **VI:** 202
Ware, Henry **III:** 249, 355
Warehouse Act (Illinois) **VI:** 221
war ethic **I:** 62
War for Independence. See
    American Revolution
War for the Black Hills. See
    Black Hills, War for the
War for the Bozeman Trail. See
    Bozeman Trail, War for the
War Hawks **IV:** **355**
    American System **IV:** 18
    Calhoun, John C. **IV:** 62
    Clay, Henry **IV:** 86
    War of 1812 **IV:** 356
Warhol, Andy **IX:** 20; **X:** 26
war housing **VIII:** 159
War Industries Board (WIB)
    VII: **329–330; IX:** 203
    American Expeditionary
        Force **VII:** 9
    Baruch, Bernard M. **VII:**
        25; **VIII:** 34
    Committee for Public
        Information **VII:** 345
    dollar-a-year men **VIII:** 84
    Fuel Administration **VII:**
        102
    Johnson, Hugh S. **VIII:**
        173
    NIRA **VIII:** 228
    NRA **VIII:** 231
    World War I **VII:** 344
war industry **V:** 77. See defense
    production
War is Kind (Crane) **VI:** 68, 178
War Labor Board. See National
    War Labor Board
War Manpower Commission
    (WMC) **VIII:** **374–375**
    FEPC **VIII:** 109
    mobilization **VIII:** 214
    NWLB **VIII:** 233
    NYA **VIII:** 234
    Selective Service **VIII:** 323
War Message, 1812 (Madison)
    IV: 381–383

Warmoth, Henry Clay **V:** **388**
Warm Springs Apache **VI:** 14
Warm Springs Reservation **VI:**
    14
Warner, Charles Dudley **VI:** xv,
    114, 115, 177, 298
Warner, John **X:** 222
Warner, Susan **IV:** 213
Warner (company) **X:** 49
Warner Brothers **VII:** 191
Warner-Lambert **X:** 7
War of 1812 **III:** 398c; **IV:**
    355–358, 357m, 375c; **VII:**
    92
        Adams-Onís Treaty **IV:** 5
        agriculture **IV:** 11
        American Fur Company
            IV: 16
        American System **IV:** 18
        architecture **III:** 20
        Ashley, William Henry **IV:**
            28
        Astor, John Jacob **IV:** 31
        Astoria **IV:** 32, 33
        Baltimore, Battle of **IV:** 39
        banking and currency **IV:**
            41–42
        Bank of the United States,
            Second **IV:** 44
        Barbary pirates **III:** 35
        Benton, Thomas Hart **IV:**
            49
        Black Hawk War **IV:** 51
        Bonaparte, Napoleon **III:**
            42
        Bonus Bill **IV:** 56
        Calhoun, John C. **IV:** 62
        Caroline affair **IV:** 74
        Cass, Lewis **IV:** 76
        Chauncey, Isaac **III:** 65
        Cherokee nation **III:** 66
        Chesapeake-Leopard affair
            III: 67
        Choctaw nation **III:** 68
        Chouteau family **IV:** 79
        Claiborne, William C. C.
            IV: 85
        Clark, William **III:** 72
        Clay, Henry **IV:** 86
        Columbia River **IV:** 93
        conscription **V:** 78
        Constitution, USS **III:** 81
        Continental navy **III:** 90
        Cornplanter **III:** 92
        Creek nation **III:** 96
        Dartmoor Prison **IV:**
            103–104
        Decatur, Stephen **IV:** 104
        Democratic Party **IV:** 106
        Democratic-Republican
            Party **III:** 104
        economy **III:** 113; **IV:** 117

Era of Good Feelings **IV:** 127

Essex, USS **IV:** 130

Essex decision **III:** 119

Farragut, David G. **V:** 121

Federalist Party **III:** 126

Florida **III:** 129

foreign affairs **III:** 131

foreign policy **IV:** 141

Free Trade and Sailor's Rights **IV:** 151–152

French Revolution **III:** 139

frontier **III:** 141

Fulton, Robert **III:** 142

fur trade **III:** 142

Gallatin, Albert **III:** 147

Ghent, Treaty of (1814) **IV:** 161–162

Girard, Stephen **III:** 153

Harrison, William Henry **IV:** 169, 170

Hartford Convention **IV:** 170

Houston, Sam **IV:** 174

Hull, William **IV:** 175–176

impressment **III:** 175, 176

Indian Removal Act (1830) **IV:** 183

industrialization **IV:** 184

industrial revolution **III:** 177

Iroquois Confederacy **III:** 178, 179

Jackson, Andrew **IV:** 191–192

Jefferson, Thomas **III:** 186

journalism **III:** 192

Kearny, Stephen Watts **IV:** 200

King, Rufus **III:** 195

Lafitte, Jean **IV:** 205–206

Lake Erie, Battle of **IV:** 206–207

lead mines **IV:** 208

Little Belt incident **III:** 215, 216

Lyon, Matthew **III:** 222–223

Macon, Nathaniel **III:** 226

Macon's Bill No. 2 **III:** 226

Madison, James **III:** 230

McCulloch v. Maryland **IV:** 227

migration **IV:** 235

Missouri Fur Company **IV:** 239

Monroe, James **IV:** 240

Monroe-Pinkney Treaty **III:** 245

Mott, Lucretia **IV:** 246

mountain men **IV:** 247

national debt **III:** 253

National Road **IV:** 253

Native Americans **IV:** 255, 256, 258–260

New Orleans, Battle of (1815) **IV:** 262

Non-Importation Act **III:** 259

Orders in Council **III:** 267

Otis, Harrison Gray **III:** 268

Panic of 1819 **IV:** 275

Panic of 1837 **IV:** 276

Paris, Treaty of **III:** 273

Pickering, John **III:** 276

Pike, Zebulon Montgomery **IV:** 282

political parties **III:** 279

population trends **III:** 283

prisons **V:** 281

privateering **III:** 287

Prophet, the Shawnee **III:** 289

public land policy **IV:** 286

race and race relations **IV:** 291

Red Jacket **III:** 297

riots **III:** 309

rural life **III:** 312

Scott, Winfield **IV:** 309

secession **V:** 311

South Pass **IV:** 324

states' rights **III:** 333

Taylor, Zachary **IV:** 334

Tecumseh **III:** 345

Thames, Battle of the **IV:** 342

trade **III:** 351

Vanderbilt, Cornelius **IV:** 352

War Hawks **IV:** 355

Webster, Daniel **IV:** 359

War of Jenkins' Ear **II:** 41, **392**

War of the Austrian Succession **II:** 182

War of the League of Augsburg **II:** 185

War of the Three Henries **I:** 158

War of the Worlds (Wells) **VIII:** 408c

FCC **VIII:** 116

public opinion polls **VIII:** 284

radio **VIII:** 290

Welles, Orson **VIII:** 376–377

war on crime **X:** 206

war on drugs **X:** 35, 82, 207

War on Poverty **IX: 313–314,** 334c; **X:** 35–36, 175

Appalachian Regional Development Act **IX:** 15–16

cities and urban life **IX:** 52

Community Action Program **IX:** 62–63

Economic Opportunity Act of 1964 **IX:** 87–88

Elementary and Secondary Education Act of 1965 **IX:** 99

Head Start **IX:** 132

Job Corps **IX:** 149–150

New Deal **IX:** 230

Volunteers in Service to America **IX:** 310

War Powers Act of 1973 **X:** 18, **315,** 324c

War Production Board (WPB) **VIII: 375–376; IX:** 205

automobile industry **VIII:** 30

Baruch, Bernard M. **VIII:** 34

Congress **VIII:** 68

dollar-a-year men **VIII:** 84

Hillman, Sidney **VIII:** 146

mobilization **VIII:** 214

Nelson, Donald M. **VIII:** 238

OPA **VIII:** 254

OPM **VIII:** 255

OWM **VIII:** 258

rationing **VIII:** 292

reconversion **VIII:** 295

zoot-suiters **VIII:** 404

Warraghiyagey **II:** 177

War Refugee Board (WRB) **VIII:** 410c

Holocaust **VIII:** 150

immigration **VIII:** 162

Jews **VIII:** 173

Morgenthau, Henry **VIII:** 216

refugees **VIII:** 299

War Relocation Authority (WRA) **VIII:** 171, 172

Warren, Earl **IX: 314–315,** 315, 331c

Baker v. Carr **IX:** 31

Brennan, William J. **X:** 40, 41

Brown v. Board of Education **IX:** 42

Burger, Warren E. **X:** 44

Eisenhower, Dwight D. **IX:** 93

elections **IX:** 94

Engel v. Vitale **IX:** 100

gays and lesbians **IX:** 119

Meese, Edwin C. **X:** 191

Miranda v. Arizona **IX:** 206

NAACP **IX:** 220

Oswald, Lee Harvey **IX:** 238

Reynolds v. Simms **IX:** 260

Supreme Court **X:** 290

Warren Court **IX:** 315–316

Warren, Fred **VII:** 286

Warren, Gouverneur K. **V:** 129, 148

Warren, John **IV:** 307

Warren, Joseph **III: 363**

Gage, Thomas **III:** 146

Old South Church **III:** 265

Revere, Paul **III:** 304

Suffolk Resolves **III:** 335

Warren, Joshua **V:** 266

Warren, Josiah **IV: 358–359**

Warren, Mary Cole **II: 392–393**

Warren, Mercy Otis **III:** 215, **363–364**

Warren, Sir Peter **II:** 86, 182

Warren, Robert Penn **IX:** 182

Warren, William **VI:** 156

Warren Bridge Company **IV:** 331

Warren Commission **IX:** 334c; **X:** 120

Warren Court **IX:** 31, 132–133, 271, **315–316**

Warrenton, Virginia **V:** 386

War Revenue Act **VII:** 142, **330–331,** 344

Warrior, Clyde **IX:** 229

warrior tradition

Aztecs **I:** 20

conquistadores **I:** 84

Dahomey **I:** 102

feudalism **I:** 129–130

flowery wars **I:** 131

Huron **I:** 171

War Risk Insurance **VII:** 325

Warsaw ghetto **VIII:** 150

Warsaw Pact **IX:** 58, 105, 106, 232m, 277, 331c; **X:** 156, 223, 327c

Warsaw Treaty **X:** 152

warships **V:** 183–184, 368, 391

warships, steam **III:** 142

wars of national liberation **IX: 316–317**

Wars of Religion (France) **I:** 64, 169, 170, 282

Wars of the Roses **I:** 159

Wartime Civil Control Administration (WCCA) **VIII:** 171

Wartime Prohibition Act **VII:** 240

wartime Reconstruction **V:** 292

Warwick, earl of. *See* Rich, Sir Robert

war widows **V:** 67

Washburn, Cadwallader Colden **VI:** 101

Washburn & Moen Manufacturing Company **VI:** 20

Washington (state)
abortion **X:** 2
Foley, Thomas S. **X:** 119
Native Americans **X:** 214, 215
population trends **X:** 242

Washington, Booker T. **V:** 213, 358; **VI: 307–309,** *308,* 325*c,* 327*c;* **VII:** 71, 72, 199, 215; **IX:** 220
African Americans **VI:** 6
"Atlanta Compromise" speech **VI:** 348–349
Carver, George Washington **VI:** 45
Native Americans **VI:** 207
Wells-Barnett, Ida Bell **VI:** 312

Washington, Bushrod **III:** 338

Washington, District of Columbia **III:** *364,* **364–365,** 395*c,* 397*c;* **IV:** 375*c;* **V:** **388–390,** 407*c;* **VI:** 4, 318; **VIII:** 39–40, 212, 406*c. See* District of Columbia (D.C.); March on Washington Movement
act abolishing slave trade **IV:** 413
amendments to the Constitution **X:** 19
Antietam, Battle of **V:** 13
Appomattox Court House, Virginia **V:** 15
architecture **III:** 18, 20
assassination of Abraham Lincoln **V:** 17
Baltimore, Maryland, riots **V:** 22
Baltimore & Ohio Railroad (B&O) **IV:** 40
Barton, Clara **V:** 24
Beauregard, Pierre **V:** 27
Brady, Mathew **V:** 36
Bulfinch, Charles **III:** 50
Bull Run, First Battle of **V:** 42
Cary, Ann Shadd **V:** 52
Chesnut, Mary B. **V:** 58
Clay, Henry **IV:** 88
Compromise of 1850 **IV:** 93, 94
contrabands **V:** 80
Cornplanter **III:** 92
Dana, Charles A. **V:** 88
Douglass, Frederick **V:** 100
Duane, William **III:** 108

Early, Jubal A. **V:** 103
economy **IV:** 117
emancipation **V:** 112
employment **V:** 116
espionage **V:** 118
feminism **X:** 115
Fifteenth Amendment **V:** 124
foreign policy **IV:** 141
Freedman's Saving Bank **V:** 141
Frémont, Jessie Benton **IV:** 152
Ghent, Treaty of (1814) **IV:** 161
Grant, Ulysses S. **V:** 156
habeas corpus, writ of **V:** 161
Halleck, Henry W. **V:** 162
Herndon, William H. **V:** 166
Hooker, Joseph **V:** 171
Jackson, Jesse L. **X:** 160
Jefferson, Thomas **III:** 185
Key, Francis Scott **IV:** 201
L'Enfant, Pierre-Charles **III:** 207
Liberty Party **IV:** 211
Lincoln, Abraham **V:** 208–209
Lincoln, Mary Todd **V:** 212
McClellan, George B. **V:** 224, 225
monuments **V:** 239
Mosby, John Singleton **V:** 241
population trends **X:** 242, 243
prostitution **V:** 283, 284
Ray, Charlotte **V:** 291
Republican Party **V:** 301
Revels, Hiram R. **V:** 303
Shenandoah Valley: Jackson's campaign **V:** 316
Shenandoah Valley: Sheridan's campaign **V:** 317
Sherman, William T. **V:** 319
Sickles, Daniel E. **V:** 326
Stanton, Edwin M. **V:** 334
Supreme Court **III:** 338
theater **V:** 351
Truth, Sojourner **V:** 357
Union army **V:** 367
Wakeman, Sarah Rosetta **V:** 386
War of 1812 **IV:** 356, 358
Whiskey Ring **V:** 393
Whitman, Walt **V:** 394

Washington, George **I:** 214; **III: 365–368,** *366,* 393*c*–396*c;* **X:** 209
Adams, John **III:** 2, 3
Adams, John Quincy **IV:** 4
Andre, John **III:** 14
animals **II:** 22
anti-Masonry **IV:** 24
antislavery and abolition **III:** 16
Arnold, Benedict **III:** 21
Articles of Confederation **III:** 25
Bache, Benjamin Franklin **III:** 29
banks **III:** 32
Barry, John **III:** 36
Blount, William **III:** 41
Braddock, Edward **II:** 38
Brandywine, Battle of **III:** 47
Burgoyne, John **III:** 52
Burr, Aaron **III:** 53
Chase, Samuel **III:** 64, 65
Cherokee nation **III:** 66
Cincinnati, Order of **III:** 69
Clinton, Sir Henry **III:** 75
Constitutional Convention **III:** 81
Continental army **III:** 85
Continental army, mutinies of **III:** 86
Continental Congress, First **III:** 87
Continental Congress, Second **III:** 88
Continental navy **III:** 90
Conway Cabal **III:** 90–91
Cornplanter **III:** 92
Cornwallis, Lord **III:** 92
Cowpens, Battle of **III:** 95
deism **III:** 103–104
Democratic Party **IV:** 106
Democratic-Republican societies **III:** 104, 105
Dorchester Heights, Battle of **III:** 107
Fallen Timbers, Battle of **III:** 123
Farewell Address **III:** 124
Federalist Party **III:** 126
Flashman, Edward **II:** 119
Fort Necessity **II:** 123
Fort Washington, capture of **III:** 133
French colonies **II:** 129
French Revolution **III:** 138
Fulton, Robert **III:** 141
Gallatin, Albert **III:** 147
Gates, Horatio **III:** 149

Genet, Edmond **III:** 149
Germantown, Battle of **III:** 151
Grasse, comte de **III:** 154
Greene, Nathanael **III:** 155, 156
Greenville, Treaty of **III:** 157
Hamilton, Alexander **III:** 161, 162
Hancock, John **III:** 163
Harpers Ferry, West Virginia **V:** 164
Henry, Patrick **III:** 166
Howe, Richard, Lord **III:** 168
Howe, Sir William **III:** 168
Independence Hall **III:** 176
Iroquois Confederacy **III:** 179
Jay, John **III:** 182
Jay's Treaty **III:** 183
Jefferson, Thomas **III:** 184
Jersey, HMS **III:** 187
Jews **III:** 188
Judiciary Act of 1789 **III:** 192
Kalb, baron de **III:** 195
Knox, Henry **III:** 197
Lafayette, marquis de **III:** 201
land **II:** 191
Laurens, Henry **III:** 202
Lee, Charles **III:** 205
Lee, Henry **III:** 206
Lee, Richard Henry **III:** 207
L'Enfant, Pierre-Charles **III:** 207
Long Island, Battle of **III:** 217
Madison, James **III:** 229
Marshall, John **III:** 235
Mason, George **III:** 237
McDougall, Alexander **III:** 239
Medal of Honor **V:** 228
Monmouth, Battle of **III:** 244, 245
Monroe, James **IV:** 239, 240
Morgan, Daniel **III:** 246
Morris, Gouverneur **III:** 247
Morristown, New Jersey, encampment of **III:** 248–249
Mount Vernon **II:** 236–237
music **III:** 251
Native Americans and the Revolution **III:** 255

Neutrality Proclamation **III:** 256

Newburgh conspiracy **III:** 256, 257

Peale, Charles Willson **III:** 275

Pickering, John **III:** 276

Pinckney, Charles Cotesworth **III:** 276, 277

political parties **III:** 279

popular culture **III:** 282

Pulsaki, Casimir **III:** 289

Putnam, Israel **III:** 290

Randolph, Edmund **III:** 296

republicanism **III:** 302

Revolutionary War **III:** 305, 307

Rittenhouse, David **III:** 310

Rochambeau, comte de **III:** 310

Ross, Betsy **III:** 310, 311

Rush, Benjamin **III:** 312

St. Clair, Arthur **III:** 316

Schuyler, Philip John **III:** 320

Seven Years' War **II:** 332

slavery **III:** *327*

slave trade **III:** 329

Steuben, Frederick von **III:** 334

Stuart, Gilbert **III:** 335

Sullivan, John **III:** 337

Supreme Court **III:** 338

tactics and strategy **V:** 346

tariffs **V:** 348

theater **III:** 347

Trenton and Princeton, Battles of **III:** 351–352

Valley Forge, encampment of **III:** 357–359

Virginia dynasty **III:** 361

Washington, District of Columbia **III:** 364

Washington, Martha **III:** 368

Washington Benevolent Societies **III:** 369

Wayne, Anthony **III:** 369

Weems, "Parson" **III:** 371

West Point **III:** 372; **V:** 372

Whiskey Rebellion **III:** 376

White Plains, Battle of **III:** 376

Wilson, James **III:** 380

Yorktown, surrender at **III:** 390

Washington, John **II:** 364

Washington, Margaret Murray **VII:** 199

Washington, Martha Dandridge Custis **III:** 335, 359, 366, **368**

Washington, Treaty of (1871) **V:** 156; **VI:** 43, **309–310**, 323*c*

Washington, USS **III:** 90; **IV:** 19

Washington Benevolent Societies **III: 368–369**

Washington Conference on Naval Disarmament **VII: 331**

    foreign policy **VII:** 100

    Harding, Warren G. **VII:** 118

    Lodge, Henry Cabot **VII:** 165

    Naval Disarmament Conference **VII:** 209

Washington Globe **V:** 30

Washington National Park **VI:** 65

Washington Post **X:** 185

Washington Post March (Sousa) **VI:** 271

Washington State v. Glucksberg (1997) **X:** 265

Washington Territory **IV:** 92, 93, 379*c*; **VI:** 51*m*

WASP. *See* Women Airforce Service Pilots

Wasserstein, Wendy **X:** 242

waste, government **X:** 57, 58

Waste Land, The (Eliot) **VII:** 360*c*

Waste Makers, The (Vance Packard) **IX:** 239

watch industry **IX:** 44

water **II:** 14–15; **IV:** 162–163; **VII:** 203–204

    Chichén Itzá **I:** 69

    diseases **I:** 107, 108

    Gedi **I:** 139

    pueblo **I:** 295

    Yucatán Peninsula **I:** 378

Water-Cure Journal **V:** 123

water districts **IX:** 125

watered stock **VI:** 117

Wateree **II:** 55

Watergate scandal **IX:** 154; **X: 315–317**, *316*, 324*c*, 325*c*.

    See also Saturday Night Massacre

    Agnew, Spiro T. **X:** 14

    Albert, Carl B. **X:** 18

    Bork, Robert **X:** 39

    Burger, Warren E. **X:** 44

    conservative movement **X:** 79

    Cox, Archibald, Jr. **X:** 81

    economy **X:** 94

    Ford, Gerald R. **X:** 120

    Haig, Alexander M., Jr. **X:** 139

    House of Representatives **X:** 144

    impeachment **X:** 149–150

    independent counsel **X:** 150

    Jaworski, Leon **X:** 160–161

    media **X:** 185

    Mitchell, John N. **X:** 196

    Nixon, Richard M. **X:** 220–221

    OMB **X:** 227

    Richardson, Elliot L. **X:** 268

    Ruckelshaus, William D. **X:** 269

    Supreme Court **X:** 291

    United States v. Nixon **X:** 308–309

Waterman, Louis **VI:** 150

watermelon **II:** 8, 122

water mills **II:** *226*

Water Pollution Control Act of 1972 **X:** 77, 210

water power **IV:** 184

water-powered mills **II:** 225

Water Quality Act of 1965 **IX:** 46, 334*c*

Waters, Muddy **VIII:** 223

"watershed war" thesis **VIII:** 389–390

water systems **VI:** 54–55

water transportation **II:** 377

waterways **IV:** 117–118, 127–130

waterworks **IV:** 82–83

Watie, Stand **V:** 265, **390–391**

Watkins, Sam **V:** 213

Watkins, William **IV:** 16

Watonga Treaty **III:** 66

Watres Act **VII:** 24

Watson, Claude A. **VIII:** 272*t*

Watson, Elkanah **III:** 123, 398*c*

Watson, Gregory D. **X:** 20

Watson, James D. **IX:** 269, 295

Watson, John **VII:** 4

Watson, Thomas E. **VI:** 37, 222, 223; **VII:** 292, **331–332**

Watson and the Shark (Copley) **III:** 23

Watson-Parker Act of 1926 **VII:** 361*c*

Watt, James **III:** 177

Watt, James G. **X:** 260, **317**

wattle and daub **II:** 157, 171

Watts, John **II:** 86

Watts uprising (1965) **IX:** 208, 254, **317–318**, *318*, 334*c*; **X:** 255

WAVES. *See* Women Accepted for Volunteer Emergency Service

Wa-Wan Press **VI:** 202

Waxaklahum-Ubah-K'awil **I:** 86

Waxhaw **II:** 55

Wayland Seminary **VI:** 4

Waymouth, George **I:** 133

Wayne, Anthony **III: 369–370**, 396*c*; **IV:** 168, 281

    Blue Jacket **III:** 41

    Brandywine, Battle of **III:** 48

    Clark, William **III:** 72

    Fallen Timbers, Battle of **III:** 123, 124

    Greenville, Treaty of **III:** 157

    Lewis, Meriwether **III:** 208

    Pulsaki, Casimir **III:** 289

    Washington, George **III:** 367

    Wilkinson, James **III:** 379

Wayne, John **IX:** 213

Waynesboro, Battle of **V:** 318

Ways and Means Committee **III:** 296; **IV:** 282; **V:** 338

WCAR. *See* Women's Central Association for Relief

WCCA **VIII:** 171

WCTU. *See* Woman's Christian Temperance Union

We (Lindbergh) **VII:** 159

WEAF radio (New York City) **VII:** 254

WEAL (Women's Equity Action League) **X:** 114

wealth **VI:** 44

    cities and urban life **II:** 62

    crime and punishment **II:** 76

    distribution of **IV:** 119, 185, 187, 367; **V:** 107, 181

    Philadelphia **II:** 282

    Protestant work ethic **II:** 302

    science **II:** 330

    slave trade **II:** 343

    smuggling **II:** 348

    society, British American **II:** 350, 351

    Spanish colonies **II:** 356

    Spanish immigration **II:** 359

Wealth against Commonwealth (Lloyd) **VI:** 179; **VII:** 265

"Wealth" Essay (Carnegie) **VI:** 339–342

"Wealth Tax" **VIII:** 307–308, 351

Weapemeoc **II:** 401
weapon quality **VIII:** 215
weapons **IV:** 186m. *See also specific headings*
   Carib **I:** 56
   Chichén Itzá **I:** 70
   Confederate army **V:** 72
   conquistadores **I:** 85
   crime **X:** 82
   Dahlgren, John A. B. **V:** 87
   defense policy **X:** 85–88
   forts **II:** 124
   French colonies **II:** 127
   fur trade **II:** 133
   Gorgas, Josiah **V:** 151–152
   Great Plains Indians **II:** 150
   gun control **X:** 136–138
   Harpers Ferry, West Virginia **V:** 164
   Huron **II:** 160
   Inuit **II:** 167
   invention and technology **I:** 180
   merchants **II:** 222
   militia movement **X:** 193, 194
   Morton, Thomas **II:** 236
   Native Americans **II:** 243
   Neolin **II:** 248
   NRA **X:** 213
   Opechancanough **II:** 268
   Persian Gulf War **X:** 235
   Reagan, Ronald W. **X:** 260
   science and technology **V:** 308
   Shiloh, Battle of **V:** 324
   Supreme Court **X:** 291
   technology **II:** 369
   Toltecs **I:** 356–357
   trade and shipping **II:** 375
   Tuscarora War **II:** 379
   Union army **V:** 365
   Union navy **V:** 368
   Valdivia, Pedro de **I:** 363
   Virginia **II:** 384
   war and warfare **II:** 391
weapons of mass destruction **X:** 236
"Wearing of the Grey" **V:** 244
Weason, Jack **II:** 30
weather **II:** 194, 331
Weather Bureau **IV:** 308; **VI:** 311, 323c
Weather Underground **IX:** 231, 286, **318–319,** 319; **X:** 297, 317, **317–318,** 317–318, 323c
Weaver, James B. **VI:** 327c
   currency issue **VI:** 72
   Greenback-Labor Party **VI:** 120
   People's Party **VI:** 222–223

presidential campaigns **VI:** 231
Weaver, John **VII:** 35
Weaver, Randy **X:** 194, 228
Weaver, Richard **X:** 78
Weaver, Robert C. **VIII:** 37, 227
Weavers, the **IX:** 110–111, 217
weaving **II:** 247
Webb, Edwin **VII:** 88, 280
Webber, Andrew Lloyd **X:** 203, 242
Webbers Falls **V:** 391
Webb-Kenyon Act **VII:** 358c
Weber, Max **IX:** 256
Weber, Vin **X:** 35
Weber and Fields **VI:** 96
Webster, Daniel **IV:** 359, **359–360,** 376c, 378c; **V:** 263, 342
   Cass, Lewis **IV:** 76
   Compromise of 1850 **IV:** 94
   Dartmouth College case **IV:** 104
   election of 1840 **IV:** 124
   Free-Soil Party **IV:** 150
   McCulloch v. Maryland **IV:** 227
   Nullification Controversy **IV:** 264
   Oregon Treaty of 1846 **IV:** 269
   Taylor, Zachary **IV:** 335
   Tyler, John **IV:** 348
   Webster-Ashburton Treaty (1842) **IV:** 361
   Whig Party **IV:** 362–364
Webster, Joseph P. **VI:** 203
Webster, Noah **III:** 80, 114, **370,** 394c; **IV:** 120
Webster, Peletiah **III:** 247
Webster-Ashburton Treaty (1842) **IV:** 25, 269, 360, **360–362,** 361m, 378c
Webster v. Reproductive Health Services (1989) **X:** **318–319,** 327c
   O'Connor, Sandra Day **X:** 226
   Rehnquist, William H. **X:** 264
   White, Byron R. **X:** 319
WebTV **X:** 263
Wedderburn, Alexander **III:** 134
Weddington, Sarah **X:** 114–115
"We Do Our Part" **VIII:** 231, 232
Wedraogo (Ouedraogo) **I:** 243
Weed, Thurlow **IV:** 224, 363; **V:** 158

weeds **I:** 77
Weeks, Edwin Lord **VI:** 219
Weeks, John D. **VII:** 337
Weeks v. Southern Bell (1969) **X:** 115, 211
Weems, "Parson" Mason Locke **III:** 215, 365, **370–371**
Weetamoo **II:** 324
Wefers, Bernie **VI:** 290
Wegadugu (Ouagadougou) **I:** 243
Weigel, George **X:** 60
Weiland (Brown) **III:** 49
Weill, Kurt **VIII:** 223
Weimar Republic **VII:** 323, 324
Weinberg, Jack **IX:** 112
Weinberger, Caspar **X:** 86, 247, 315
Weiner, Lee **X:** 61
Weir, Benjamin **X:** 154
Weir, J. Alden **VI:** 219; **VII:** 18
Weisberg, Bernard **IX:** 104
Weisbord, Albert **VII:** 224–225
Weiser, Johann Conrad **II:** 233, **393;** **III:** 136
Weiss, Carl A. **VIII:** 195
Welch, Joseph **IX:** 18–19
Welch, Robert **X:** 79
Welch, Thomas **II:** 115
Weld, Angelina Grimké **V:** 396
Weld, Theodore Dwight **IV:** 362
   AASS **IV:** 14
   abolition movement **IV:** 3
   Foster, Abigail Kelley **IV:** 148
   Grimké, Angelina and Sarah **IV:** 165
   Tappan, Arthur and Lewis **IV:** 333
Weld, William **X:** 191
Welde, Thomas **II:** 107
Wele **I:** 210
welfare **IV:** 180; **X:** 329c
   Clinton, William **X:** 66
   FSA **X:** 110
   GRH Act of 1985 **X:** 135
   liberalism **X:** 174
welfare capitalism **VII:** 12, 201, 290, **332–333**
welfare state **VIII:** xiii, 408c
   conservatism **VIII:** 72
   conservative coalition **VIII:** 73
   Democratic Party **VIII:** 82
   Executive Reorganization Act **VIII:** 107
   government **VIII:** 134
   Republican Party **VIII:** 306
   Wagner, Robert F. **VIII:** 373

Welles, Gideon **V:** 368, **391–392**
Welles, Orson **VIII:** 376, **376–377,** 408c, 409c; **IX:** 212
   FCC **VIII:** 116
   FTP **VIII:** 120
   public opinion polls **VIII:** 284
   radio **VIII:** 290
Welles, Sumner **VIII:** 133, 159, **377**
Wellesley College **VI:** 316
"well-made plays" **VI:** 287
Wells, Fargo and Company **IV:** 271–272
Wells, H. G. **VIII:** 376, 408c
Wells, Herman **IX:** 163
Wells-Barnett, Ida Bell **V:** 399; **VI:** 6, 182, *311,* **311–312,** 327c; **VII:** 198, 199
Welsh, Herbert **VI:** 144–145
Wenbera, Bati Del **I:** 125
Wendat **II:** 160. *See* Huron/Huron nation
Wene, Ntine **I:** 195
Wentworth, Benning **II:** 252
Wentworth, John **II:** 83
Werdel, Thomas H. **IX:** 282
werowances **I:** **372;** **II:** 113, 288, 293, 294, 346, 347
Werowocomoco (capital) **II:** 293, 294
Werowocomoco Indians **II:** 295
Wesberry v. Sanders **IX:** 32
"We Shall Overcome" **IX:** 38, 111, 191, 217, 273
Wesley, Charles **II:** 393, 397
Wesley, John **II:** **393–394,** *394;* **III:** 242
   Great Awakening **II:** 147, 148
   music **II:** 239
   Philadelphia **II:** 282
   Whitefield, George **II:** 397
Wessaguscus **II:** 236
West, Benjamin **II:** 119; **III:** **371–372**
   art **III:** 22, 23
   Earle, Ralph **III:** 111
   Peale, Charles Willson **III:** 273
   Stuart, Gilbert **III:** 335
   Trumbull, John **III:** 352
West, Cornel **X:** 12
West, Mae **VII:** 321; **VIII:** 55
West, Sir Thomas **II:** 81
West Bantu **I:** 24, 25
West Berlin **IX:** 37
Westbrook, T. R. **VII:** 265
West Coast, U.S. **VIII:** 409c
   Executive Order 9066 **VIII:** 106–107

migration **VIII:** 213
population trends **VIII:** 277
Sunbelt **VIII:** 343
West Countrymen **II:** 135
Westendorf, Thomas Paine **VI:** 203
West End Street Railway (Boston) **VI:** 291
western Choctaw **II:** 60–61
Western Emigration Society **IV:** 51
western Europe **IX:** 104–106
  cold war **IX:** 58
  energy crisis **X:** 104
  foreign policy **X:** 122
  immigration **X:** 147
  Latin America **X:** 173
  Marshall Plan **IX:** 194–195
  Middle East **IX:** 201
  NATO **IX:** 232–233
  OPEC **X:** 229
  Powell, Colin L. **X:** 247
Western Federation of Miners (WFM) **VI:** 61; **VII:** 120, 129, 167
western fiction **V:** 213
western Hemisphere. *See* New World
Western Inland Lock Navigation Company **IV:** 72, 127
Western Museum **IV:** 34
Western Railroad of Massachusetts **IV:** 295
westerns (movies) **VII:** 191; **IX:** 212–213
Western School **VIII:** 24
Western Taino **I:** 342
Western Territory **III:** 184
Western Union Telegraph Company **IV:** 246
  communications **VI:** 61
  Gould, Jay **VI:** 118
  industrial revolution, second **VI:** 147
  inventions and technology **VI:** 149
  Tesla, Nikola **VI:** 285
western United States **VI:** 324c; **VIII:** 62, 92, 390
  African-American churches, growth of **VI:** 5
  African Americans **VI:** 6
  agriculture **IV:** 10
  American Protective Association **VI:** 11
  art **V:** 16
  Asian Americans **X:** 29
  Bear Flag Revolt **IV:** 45
  cities and urban life **V:** 59, 60; **VI:** 54; **IX:** 51

communications **VI:** 61
Deseret, State of **IV:** 109–111
  economy **IV:** 117
  Geological Survey, U.S. **VI:** 110
  Hispanic Americans **X:** 143
  immigration **V:** 176
  Kearny, Stephen Watts **IV:** 200
  lyceum movement **IV:** 215
  migration **IX:** 202
  Mississippi River **V:** 234
  Native Americans **IV:** 257–258; **VI:** 209
  Panic of 1819 **IV:** 275
  People's Party **VI:** 222, 223
  Pike, Zebulon Montgomery **IV:** 281–282
  population trends **V:** 278, 279; **X:** 242
  Powell, John Wesley **VI:** 228
  property rights **X:** 250
  public land policy **IV:** 287
  railroads **VI:** 237
  Remington, Frederic **VI:** 245–246
  science and technology **IV:** 307
  Strauss, Levi **IV:** 329
  Urban League **IX:** 305–306
  War Hawks **IV:** 355
  Young, Brigham **IV:** 371–373
West Germany **IX:** 37, 58, 194, 231–233, 330c
  cold war (end of) **X:** 70
  economy **X:** 94
  foreign policy **X:** 124
  Iron Curtain **X:** 157
  NATO **X:** 223
  Nicaragua **X:** 218
West Indian colonies **II:** 187
West Indian immigrants **II:** 145
West Indians **II:** 340
West Indies **III: 372**, 396c; **V:** 132, 348
  African Americans **III:** 5
  Arawak **I:** 12
  art and architecture **I:** 13
  Barbados **I:** 26
  Barry, John **III:** 36
  black legend **I:** 30
  British Empire **II:** 44
  cannibalism **I:** 54
  Caribbean **II:** 52
  Cathay (China) **I:** 65

Charles V **I:** 69
Chauncey, Isaac **III:** 65
Clinton, Sir Henry **III:** 75
Connecticut **II:** 69
conquistadores **I:** 84
Creole **II:** 74
Cuba **I:** 97–98
disease and epidemics **III:** 106
Drake, Sir Francis **I:** 110, 111
encomienda **I:** 122
Estaing, comte d' **III:** 120
foreign affairs **III:** 130
Freneau, Philip **III:** 139
Gates, Horatio **III:** 149
George III, king of Great Britain **III:** 151
Girard, Stephen **III:** 153
Grasse, comte de **III:** 154
Hamilton, Alexander **III:** 161
impressment **III:** 176
indentured servitude **II:** 164
Jay, John **III:** 182
Jones, John Paul **III:** 190
labor **II:** 188
Loyalists **III:** 219
lumbering **II:** 201
manufacturing and industry **II:** 204
Massachusetts **II:** 214, 215
mills **II:** 225
Native Americans **II:** 243, 246
New Hampshire **II:** 250
Newport **II:** 258
New York **II:** 262
New York City **II:** 263
Penn, William **II:** 274
population trends **III:** 283
privateering **III:** 287
Quasi War **III:** 291
Revolutionary War **III:** 307
Royal African Company **II:** 325
rum trade **II:** 326
slave resistance **II:** 337
slavery **II:** 338, 339
slave trade **III:** 328
smuggling **II:** 349
Society for the Propagation of the Gospel in Foreign Parts **II:** 352–353
Sugar Act **III:** 336, 337
Teach, Edward **II:** 368
temperance **III:** 346
trade **III:** 350
trade and shipping **II:** 375, 376

Treaty of Paris **II:** 378
Van Rensselaer, Maria Van Cortlandt **II:** 381
Westinghouse, George **V:** 409c; **VI:** 146, 149, 285, 326c
Westinghouse Corporation **VI:** 147; **VII:** 232, 253–254; **IX:** 24
West Jersey **II:** 94, 252, 253, 418c
West Jersey Society **II:** 253
Westminster Abbey **II:** 158
Westminster Confession **II:** 296
West New Jersey Concessions and Agreements of 1676 **II:** 273
Westo **II:** 375, **394–395**
Weston, Edward **VIII:** 268
Weston, Thomas **II:** 283
Westo War of 1680 **II:** 395
West Point. *See* United States Military Academy at West Point
West Point, Virginia **II:** 268
West Side Story **IX:** 244
West Virginia **II:** 72; **V:** 152, 164–166, 305, 407c; **VI:** 215; **X:** 242, 243, 304
West Virginia State Board of Education v. Barnette **VIII:** 410c
westward expansion **III:** 398c; **V:** 213; **VII:** 55. *See also* frontier
  agriculture **V:** 6, 7
  art **IV:** 25, 26
  Baltimore & Ohio Railroad (B&O) **IV:** 39
  barbed wire **VI:** 20
  Becknell, William **IV:** 45–46
  Bent, Charles **IV:** 47–48
  Bent, William **IV:** 48
  Bent's Fort **IV:** 50–51
  Bidwell, John **IV:** 51
  Blue Jacket **III:** 41
  Bridger, James **IV:** 57–58
  buffalo, extermination of **VI:** 38
  Buffalo Soldiers **VI:** 39
  business and government **VI:** 39
  California gold rush **IV:** 66
  Democratic Party **IV:** 108
  Donner party **IV:** 114–115
  Douglas, Stephen A. **V:** 98
  economy **IV:** 117
  foreign policy **IV:** 141; **V:** 131
  Fort Laramie **IV:** 143–145
  Forty-niners **IV:** 146–147
  fur trade **IV:** 156–158

westward expansion (continued)
Greeley, Horace **V:** 158
homefront **V:** 168
Homestead Act of 1862 **V:** 170–171
Indian Affairs, Office of **VI:** 144
Indian Removal Act (1830) **IV:** 181
Jay-Gardoqui treaty negotiations **III:** 182
Jay's Treaty **III:** 182–183
Jefferson, Thomas **III:** 185–186
letters **V:** 207
literature **V:** 213
Louisiana Purchase **III:** 218
lyceum movement **IV:** 215
Manifest Destiny **IV:** 217, 218m
migration **IV:** 235–236
Mormon Trail **IV:** 242–243
National Road **IV:** 253–255
Native Americans **IV:** 255; **V:** 251
Native Americans in the War of 1812 **IV:** 258
Nauvoo, Illinois **IV:** 261
Oregon Trail **IV:** 267–269
overland mail **IV:** 271–272
overland routes **IV:** 268m
Pacific Railroad Act of 1862 **V:** 263–264
Permanent Indian Frontier **IV:** 279
plantations **V:** 276
poverty **III:** 284
public land policy **IV:** 286–288
railroads **IV:** 292–296; **V:** 290
religion **III:** 299
Santa Fe Trail **IV:** 305–306
Scotch-Irish **III:** 323
secession **V:** 311
Sioux wars **VI:** 263
sod houses **VI:** 269–270
Sooners **VI:** 270–271
South Pass **IV:** 324–325
Strauss, Levi **IV:** 329
Tecumseh **III:** 345
transportation **V:** 354–356
United States Army Corps of Engineers **V:** 371
Wilderness Road **III:** 378
Wyoming Valley War **III:** 384
Wetamo **II: 395**
wetbacks **IX:** 41

"wet" fishing **II:** 118
Wetherald, Richard **IX:** 270, 334c
Wethersfield, Connecticut **II:** 68
"wet plate" photographic process **V:** 35
"We Wear the Mask" (Dunbar) **VI:** 83
Weyler y Nicholau, Valeriano **VI:** 71
Weyrich, Paul **X:** 79, 197, 301
WFL (World Football League) **X:** 284
WFM. See Western Federation of Miners
Whaam! (Roy Lichtenstein) **IX:** 20
whale oil **I:** 29
whales **I:** 9
whaling **II:** 20, 118, 204, 265; **III:** 99, 164; **IV:** 172, 199, 280
Wharton, Edith **VI:** xv; **VII:** 160; **VIII:** 191
Whately, Thomas **III: 373**
"What We Want" program **IX:** 39
wheat **I:** 77, 150, 214; **IV:** 10, 11, 275; **V:** 7; **VI:** 8–9
agriculture **II:** 11, 13
Indians of the Desert Southwest **II:** 166
Maryland **II:** 210, 211
merchants **II:** 222
Mount Vernon **II:** 237
New Jersey **II:** 252
Pennsylvania **II:** 276
tenants **II:** 370
Wheat, Chatam Roberdau **V:** 403
wheat farming **VIII:** 85–87
Wheatley, Phillis **II:** 7, 154, 314; **III:** 5, 214, **373–374**, 374, 392c
Wheatstone, Charles **IV:** 307
Wheeler, Burton K. **VIII:** 284, 306, **377–378**
Farmer-Labor Party **VII:** 91
politics **VII:** 230
progressivism **VII:** 238
Teapot Dome **VII:** 308
Wheeler, Candace **VI:** 288
Wheeler, George Montague **VI:** 110
Wheeler, Joseph **V:** 258, 323, **392,** 392
Wheeler, Wayne **VII:** 327
Wheeler-Howard Indian Reorganization Act. See Indian Reorganization Act

Wheeler-Rayburn Act. See Public Utility Holding Company Act
Wheelock, Eleazar **II:** 83, 103, **395–396**
Wheelwright, John **II:** 161, 250, **396**
"When Lilacs Last in the Dooryard Bloom'd" (Whitman) **V:** 394
"When Malindy Sings" (Dunbar) **VI:** 82
Whewell, William **IV:** 308
Whig-American Party **IV:** 138
Whig Party **III: 374–375; IV: 362–364,** 377c, 378c; **V:** 405c
AASS **IV:** 362
abolition **V:** 3
African Americans **III:** 5
Alamance, Battle of **III:** 8
American System **IV:** 19
anti-Masonry **IV:** 24
art **III:** 23
Ashley, William Henry **IV:** 30
banking and currency **IV:** 43
Benjamin, Judah P. **V:** 27
Cass, Lewis **IV:** 77
Catholics **III:** 63
Civil War **V:** 64
Clay, Henry **IV:** 87
commonwealthmen **III:** 79
Crockett, Davy **IV:** 100
Democratic Party **IV:** 108; **V:** 94
Douglas, Stephen A. **V:** 98
education **IV:** 120
election of 1840 **IV:** 124–126
elections **V:** 109
Fillmore, Millard **IV:** 137
freemasonry **III:** 137
Free-Soil Party **IV:** 150
Freneau, Philip **III:** 139
fugitive slave laws **IV:** 155
Golden Hill, Battle of **III:** 154
Greeley, Horace **V:** 158
Green Mountain Boys **III:** 156
Harlan, John Marshall **VI:** 121
Harrison, William Henry **IV:** 168, 170
Henry, Patrick **III:** 165
Herndon, William H. **V:** 166
internal improvements **IV:** 188

Jackson, Andrew **IV:** 193
Jay, John **III:** 181
Jews **III:** 187
Julian, George W. **V:** 194
Kansas-Nebraska Act of 1854 **V:** 197, 198
King's Mountain, Battle of **III:** 196
Know-Nothing Party **IV:** 201, 202
labor movements **IV:** 204
Liberty Party **IV:** 210
Lincoln, Abraham **V:** 209, 210
Livingston, Robert R. **III:** 216
Livingston, William **III:** 217
Mann, Horace **IV:** 219, 220
Mexican-American War **IV:** 232
minutemen **III:** 243
national banking system **VI:** 205
nativism **V:** 251; **VI:** 209
Nauvoo, Illinois **IV:** 260
Niles, Hezekiah **III:** 258
North, Lord **III:** 260
Oregon Treaty of 1846 **IV:** 269–270
Otis, James, Jr. **III:** 268
Panic of 1837 **IV:** 276, 277
political parties **III:** 278
Polk, James K. **IV:** 283
popular sovereignty **IV:** 285
the presidency **VI:** 229
Republican Party **IV:** 300, 301; **V:** 300, 301
Revolutionary War **III:** 307
scalawags **V:** 307
Scott, Winfield **IV:** 310
Seward, William H. **V:** 314
states' rights **V:** 335
Stearns, Abel **IV:** 326
Stephens, Alexander H. **V:** 336
Stevens, Thaddeus **V:** 337
suffrage **III:** 336
Sumner, Charles **V:** 342
Taylor, Zachary **IV:** 334
theater **III:** 347
Tyler, John **IV:** 348
Van Buren, Martin **IV:** 351, 352
Wade, Benjamin **V:** 385
Webster, Daniel **IV:** 360
Whip Inflation Now (WIN) **X:** 94
Whirling Dervishes. See Sufism

Whiskey Rebellion **III:** **375–376,** 396*c*
  Brackenridge, Hugh Henry **III:** 47
  Democratic-Republican societies **III:** 105
  Gallatin, Albert **III:** 147
  Husband, Herman **III:** 170
  Lee, Henry **III:** 206
  Lewis, Meriwether **III:** 208
  liberty tree/pole **III:** 214
  Morgan, Daniel **III:** 246
  riots **III:** 309
  Washington, George **III:** 367
Whiskey Ring **V:** 157, **392–393;** **VI:** 67, 147
Whistler, James McNeill **V:** 16, 372; **VI: 312,** 323*c*
  art and architecture **VI:** 15
  Chase, William Merritt **VI:** 49
  illustration **VI:** 138
  painting **VI:** 220
Whistler's Mother (portrait) **VI:** 3, *313*
Whitaker, Alexander **II:** 288
Whitcomb, Edgar **X:** 253
White, Alfred T. **VI:** 233
White, Andrew **II: 396**
White, Byron **IX:** 100, 104, 315; **X:** 268, 291, **319**
White, Edward **IX:** 219, 279
White, Ellen Gould Harmon **VI:** 242
White, Garland H. **VI:** 4
White, George L. **VI:** 202
White, Harry Dexter **VIII:** 42
White, Horace **VI:** 257
White, Hugh Lawson **IV:** 363
White, John **I:** *179, 313,* **372–373,** 388*c;* **II:** 58, 82, 265
  DeBry, Theodor **I:** 102
  Harriot, Thomas **I:** 154, 155
  Lane, Ralph **I:** 197
  Native American religion **I:** 253
  Roanoke **I:** 313, 314
  Secotan **I:** 320, 321
White, Kevin **X:** 93
White, Stanford **VI:** 247, 253, 259, 313, **313–314,** 325*c*
White, Walter **VIII: 378; IX:** 261, 322
  civil rights **VIII:** 61
  FEPC **VIII:** 109
  MOWM **VIII:** 201
  NAACP **VIII:** 227

Roosevelt, Eleanor **VIII:** 311
White Army **VII:** 285
White Bird **VI:** 213
"White Christmas" **VIII:** 224
White Citizens' Council **IX:** 240, 276, **319–320; X:** 57
"white city" **VI:** 320
White Collar (C. Wright Mills) **IX:** 204
white-collar work **VIII:** 385
Whitefield, George **II: 397–398,** 419*c;* **III:** 298
  Dartmouth College **II:** 83
  Davenport, James **II:** 83
  education **II:** 104–105
  Edwards, Jonathan **II:** 105–106
  Frelinghuysen, Theodorus Jacobus **II:** 125–126
  Great Awakening **II:** 147, 148
  Hammon, Jupiter **II:** 153
  Philadelphia **II:** 282
  Princeton College **II:** 298
  Protestantism **II:** 301
  Tennent, Gilbert **II:** 371
  Wesley, John **II:** 393
  Wigglesworth, Edward **II:** 398
White House **III:** *364;* **IV:** 161, 162, 375*c;* **V:** 212, 389
White House Office on Environmental Policy **X:** 210
White Indians **II:** 78
White Leagues **V:** 319
Whiteman, Paul **VII:** 86, 195
White Mountain Apaches **I:** 253
White Oak Swamp, Battle of **V:** 186
White Paper (on China) **IX:** 21, **320–321**
White Plains, Battle of **III: 376**
  Fort Washington, capture of **III:** 133
  Greene, Nathanael **III:** 155
  Hamilton, Alexander **III:** 161
  Hessians **III:** 167
  Howe, Sir William **III:** 168
  McDougall, Alexander **III:** 239
  Revolutionary War **III:** 305
  Rochambeau, comte de **III:** 310
"White Rabbit" (Jefferson Airplane) **IX:** 218
white race **IV:** 289, 291, 292; **VII:** 247, 280

White Slave Traffic Act. *See* Mann Act
White Sticks **IV:** 256, 259
white supremacists **V:** 156, 199–201, 316, 408*c;* **VI:** 77; **VII:** 358*c;* **X:** 257
  Ku Klux Klan **VII:** 147
  race and racial conflict **VII:** 248
  segregation **VII:** 281
  southern demagogues **VII:** 292
Whitewater Canal **IV:** 73
Whitewater investigation **X:** 328*c*
  Clinton, Hillary Rodham **X:** 64
  Clinton, William **X:** 68
  impeachment **X:** 150
  independent counsel **X:** 150–151
  Starr, Kenneth **X:** 286–287
"White Woman of the Genesee, the" **II:** 173
Whitgift, John **I:** 298
Whitman, Christine Todd **X:** 321
Whitman, Malcolm **VI:** 274
Whitman, Marcus **IV:** 145, 229
Whitman, Narcissa **IV:** 145, 325
Whitman, Walt **IV:** 26, 213, 217, 379*c;* **V:** 256, **393–395,** *394;* **VI:** 178; **IX:** 183
  agriculture **III:** 7
  industrial revolution **III:** 177
  science **III:** 322
  slavery **III:** 327
Whitney, Eli, Jr. **IV:** 91
Whitney, Josiah D. **VI:** 199
Whitney, Richard **VIII:** 322
Whitney, Silas **IV:** 292
Whitney Museum **VIII:** 22
Whitney v. California **VII:** 35
Whittaker, Charles E. **IX:** 31, 315
Whittier, John Greenleaf **IV:** 13, 362
WHO. *See* World Health Organization
Who, The **IX:** 111, 244
wholesale business **VII:** 75
whooping cough **X:** 188
Who's Afraid of Virginia Woolf? (movie) **X:** 239
Who Wants to Be a Millionaire? (TV program) **X:** 296
Why Change Your Wife? (film) **VII:** 87

Whydah **I:** 102
Whytt, Robert **II:** 194
Why We Fight (films) **VIII:** 51, 52, 218
"Why Women Should Vote" (Addams) **VII:** 372–376
WIB. *See* War Industries Board
Wichita Indians **I:** 90
Wickersham, George W. **VII:** 60
Wickersham Commission **VII:** 60
Wickes, Lambert **III:** 90
wickiups **I:** 48
Wicocomoco nation **II:** 295
Wide, Wide World, The (Warner) **IV:** 213
"Wide Awake Clubs" **V:** 301
Widmar v. Vincent **X:** 104
widows **II:** 136, 137
widows, war **V:** 67
Wiggins, Ella Mae **VII:** 106
Wiggins, James Russell **X:** 307
Wiggins Amendment **X:** 105–106
Wigglesworth, Edward **II: 398**
Wigglesworth, Michael **II:** 195, 215, **398–399**
wigs **II:** 215
wigwams **I:** 225, 278; **II:** 22, 23, 157
Wilberforce, William **III:** 98
Wilberforce University **V:** 5; **VI:** 4
Wilcox, Orlando **V:** 13
Wild and Scenic Rivers Act of 1968 **IX:** 224, 255, **321–322,** 334*c;* **X:** 77
wildcat banks **IV:** 119, 275
Wild Coast **II:** 98
Wilde, Oscar **VI:** 15
Wilder, Laura Ingalls **VI: 314**
wilderness **IV:** 25
Wilderness, Battle of the **V: 395**
  Burnside, Ambrose E. **V:** 45
  Early, Jubal A. **V:** 103
  Grant, Ulysses S. **V:** 156
  Hancock, Winfield Scott **V:** 163
  Hill, Ambrose P. **V:** 168
  homefront **V:** 169
  Lee, Robert E. **V:** 207
  Longstreet, James **V:** 215
  Meade, George Gordon **V:** 227
  Native Americans **V:** 249
  Overland campaign **V:** 261
Wilderness Act of 1964. *See* National Wilderness Preservation Act of 1964
Wilderness Road **II:** 115; **III: 378**

Wilderness Society **IX:** 226

Wild Free-Roaming Horse and Burro Act of 1971 **X:** 77

wildlife management and preservation **VI:** 65; **X:** 77

Wild West Shows **VI:** 97–98. *See also* Buffalo Bill's Wild West Show

Wiles, Irving R. **VI:** 219

Wiley, Bell **V:** 95

Wiley, George **IX:** 68

Wiley, Harvey **VII:** 244

Wilfong, George **IV:** 172

Wilhelm I, emperor of Germany **VI:** 310

Wilkes, Charles **IV:** 133; **V:** 132, 369

Wilkes, John **III:** 277, **378–379**

Wilkins, Roy **IX:** 275, **322–323**

Wilkinson, James **III:** 54, **379**; **IV:** 85, 281, 282, 309

Wilkins scientific group **IX:** 269

Will, George **X:** 43

Willamette Valley **IV:** 131, 236

Willard, Emma (Hart) **IV:** **364–366**, *365*

Willard, Frances **V:** 407*c*; **VI:** 234, *315*, **315–316**, 317, 324*c*

Willard, Jess **VII:** 67, 139, 294

Willard, John **IV:** 365

Willard, Samuel **II:** 37, **399**

Willaston, John **II:** 156

Willes, Richard **I:** 117

Willey, Norman **VI:** 61

William III, king of England
British Empire **II:** 41
Connecticut **II:** 69
Dominion of New England **II:** 95
Glorious Revolution **II:** 140, 141
King William's War **II:** 185
Leisler's Rebellion **II:** 192
Maryland **II:** 210
Massachusetts **II:** 214
Mather, Increase **II:** 218
monarchy, British **II:** 232
New York **II:** 261
St. Mary's City **II:** 328

William and Mary College **III:** 115

William Clobbery and Company **II:** 209

William L. Sublette Company **IV:** 29

William of Orange. *See* William III, king of England

Williams, Aubrey **VIII:** 37, 234

Williams, Bert **VI:** 97

Williams, Eunice **II:** 52

Williams, Hank **VIII:** 224

Williams, Harrison A., Jr. **X:** 4–5, 276

Williams, Hosea **IX:** 254

Williams, James Douglas **VI:** 122

Williams, John **II:** 85

Williams, Nelson **IV:** 347

Williams, Peter **III:** 17; **VI:** 4, 70

Williams, Peter, Jr. **IV:** **366**

Williams, Robin **X:** 295

Williams, Roger **I:** 221; **II:** **399–400**, *400*, 417*c*
Baptists **II:** 29
Canonicus **II:** 51
Dudley, Thomas **II:** 96
education **II:** 103
ethnocentrism **II:** 113
Massachusetts **II:** 212
Miantonomo **II:** 224
Newport **II:** 258
Pequot War **II:** 279
Rhode Island **II:** 320, 321
society, British American **II:** 350
Winthrop, John **II:** 402
wolves **II:** 405

Williams, Tennessee **IX:** 181, 243, 329*c*

Williams Act of 1968 **X:** 49

Williamsburg, Battle of
Early, Jubal A. **V:** 103
Hancock, Winfield Scott **V:** 163
Longstreet, James **V:** 215
Peninsular campaign **V:** 267
Pickett, George Edward **V:** 274

Williamsburg, Virginia **III:** 183, 184
Jamestown **II:** 173
journalism **II:** 178
Ostenaco **II:** 269
Smith, Robert **II:** 348
theater **II:** 373
Virginia **II:** 384, 385

Williams College **II:** 199, 298; **VI:** 290

William's Fort **IV:** 48

Williamson, John **II:** 394

Williams-Steiger Act. *See* Occupational Safety and Health Act of 1970

William the Silent **I:** 333

William Wilson & Son Company **V:** 228

Willich, August **V:** 147

Willing, Thomas **III:** 30

Willis Woodward **VI:** 204

Willkie, Wendell L. **VIII:** **378–379**, 409*c*; **IX:** 81

CIO **VIII:** 70
election of 1940 **VIII:** 98
election of 1944 **VIII:** 99
Ickes, Harold L. **VIII:** 161
isolationists **VIII:** 166
Johnson, Hugh S. **VIII:** 174
labor **VIII:** 181
Lewis, John L. **VIII:** 186
Luce, Henry R. **VIII:** 196
Murray, Philip **VIII:** 221
politics in the Roosevelt era **VIII:** 271, 272*t*
Republican Party **VIII:** 306
Roosevelt, Franklin D. **VIII:** 314
Selective Service **VIII:** 322
Taft, Robert A. **VIII:** 349
TVA **VIII:** 356

Willoughby, Sir Hugh **I:** 265

Willow Run, Michigan aircraft plant **VIII:** 11

Wills, Bob **VIII:** 222

Wills, Garry **X:** 43

Wilmington, North Carolina **V:** 36

Wilmot, David **IV:** 108, 150, 151; **V:** 3, 395, 396

Wilmot Proviso **IV:** 150, 165–166, 285, 378*c*; **V:** 3, 64, **395–396**

WILPF. *See* Women's International League for Peace and Freedom

Wilson, Alexander **III:** 321; **IV:** 34

Wilson, August **X:** 241

Wilson, Benjamin **II:** 125

Wilson, Charles E. **IX:** 204

Wilson, Edmund Beecher **VII:** 276

Wilson, George **IV:** 354

Wilson, Henry **IV:** 150, 151; **V:** 141, 228

Wilson, Jack **VI:** 245

Wilson, James **III:** 89, 135, 338, **379–380**; **VI:** 45

Wilson, John **II:** 35, 73

Wilson, M. L. **VIII:** 5

Wilson, Pete **X:** 148

Wilson, Sloan **IX:** 46

Wilson, Teddy **VIII:** 149

Wilson, Woodrow **VII:** xiii, **333–335**, *334*, 358*c*, 359*c*; **IX:** 61; **X:** 101
Adamson Act **VII:** 2
AFL **VII:** 10
agriculture **VII:** 7
Atlantic Charter **VIII:** 28
Baruch, Bernard M. **VII:** 25; **VIII:** 34

Big Stick diplomacy **VII:** 28–29

Brandeis, Louis **VII:** 34

Bryan, William Jennings **VI:** 37

Budget and Accounting Act **VII:** 36

Cannon, Joseph **VII:** 42

chain stores **VI:** 47

Clayton Antitrust Act **VII:** 51

Committee for Public Information **VII:** 51, 346

Congress **VII:** 53

conscription **VII:** 54

Coolidge, Calvin **VII:** 56

Dawes, Charles **VII:** 63

Debs, Eugene V. **VII:** 65

Democratic Party **VII:** 66

elections **VII:** 80

Espionage Act **VII:** 88

FCA **VIII:** 111

Federal Farm Loan Act **VII:** 92

Federal Reserve Act **VII:** 93–94

Federal Trade Commission Act **VII:** 94

foreign policy **VII:** 99, 100

"Fourteen Points" speech **VII:** 379–382

Fuel Administration **VII:** 102

Hoover, Herbert **VIII:** 151

Hughes, Charles Evans **VII:** 124

Hull, Cordell **VIII:** 159

Immigration Act of 1917 **VII:** 128

Industrial Relations Commission **VII:** 128

League of Nations **VII:** 156, 157

lobbying groups **VII:** 162

Lockwood, Belva Ann Bennett McNall **VI:** 181

Lodge, Henry Cabot **VII:** 165

Lost Generation **VII:** 166

Ludlow Massacre **VII:** 168

"Make the World Safe For Democracy" speech **VII:** 376–379

Mexican invasion **VII:** 183

Mexican Revolution **VII:** 185

Mooney-Billings case **VII:** 188

National Defense Act **VII:** 201, 202

National Park Service **VII:** 203

National War Labor Board **VII:** 204

National Woman's Party **VII:** 205

nativism **VII:** 208

neutrality **VII:** 210

New Freedom **VII:** 210–211

New Nationalism **VII:** 211–212

New Unionism **VII:** 212

Nye Committee **VIII:** 251

open shop movement **VII:** 220

Palmer, A. Mitchell **VII:** 221

Paul, Alice **VII:** 226

politics **VII:** 230

Preparedness **VII:** 235–236

Progressive Party **VII:** 237

progressivism **VII:** 237, 238

Prohibition **VII:** 240

Railroad Administration **VII:** 255

Red Scare **VII:** 258–259

Republican Party **VII:** 262, 263

Roosevelt, Franklin D. **VIII:** 312

rural life **VII:** 268

Sedition Act **VII:** 280

Selective Service Act **VII:** 282

Seventeenth Amendment **VII:** 69

Siberian Expedition **VII:** 285

socialism **VII:** 289

Steel Strike of 1919 **VII:** 298, 299

Taft, William Howard **VII:** 304

tariffs **VII:** 305

taxation **VIII:** 351

trade, foreign **VII:** 310

Trading with the Enemy Act **VII:** 311

UN **VIII:** 366

Underwood-Simmons Tariff **VII:** 313

Versailles, Treaty of **VII:** 323

Volstead Act **VII:** 327

War Industries Board **VII:** 329, 330

Washington, Booker T. **VI:** 309

woman suffrage **VII:** 336, 337

Workmen's Compensation Act **VII:** 343

World War I **VII:** 343–344

Zimmermann telegram **VII:** 353

Wilson Dam **VIII:** 356

Wilson-Gorman Tariff of 1894 **VI:** 327c; **VII:** 92

business and government **VI:** 39

Congress **VI:** 64

Internal Revenue taxes **VI:** 147

tariff issue **VI:** 284

Wilson's Creek, Battle of **V:** 285, 391

WIN (Whip Inflation Now) **X:** 94

Winchell, Walter **VIII:** 243

Winchester, James **IV:** 169

Winder, John **V:** 282

wind instruments **II:** 239

Windward Islands **II:** 52

wine **II:** 15, 376; **IV:** 336

Winfrey, Oprah **X:** 295

Wingate, George **X:** 212

Wingina **I:** 372; **II:** 264, 294, **401**

Wings (music group) **X:** 240

Winnebago **II:** 199, 263

Winnebago nation **IV:** 33–34, 52

Winsor, Justin **VI:** 176

Winter Quarters, Nebraska **IV:** 242, 243

Winthrop, John **II: 401–402,** *402*

Boston **II:** 35

Bradford, William **II:** 39

Bradstreet, Anne Dudley **II:** 39

Dudley, Thomas **II:** 96

Endecott, John **II:** 107

government, British American **II:** 142

Hutchinson, Anne Marbury **II:** 161

jeremiads **II:** 174

journalism **II:** 179

literature **II:** 195

Massachusetts **II:** 212

Massachusetts Bay Company **II:** 216

Mather, Cotton **II:** 217

"Model of Christian Charity" **II:** 421

postal service **II:** 292

Wheelwright, John **II:** 396

Williams, Roger **II:** 399

Winthrop, John, IV **II:** 330

Winthrop, John, Jr. **II:** 68, 69

Winthrop, Robert C. **V:** 342

Wintu **I:** 48

wireless communications **X:** 75

WIRES **VIII:** 382

wire service **IV:** 196

wiretapping **VII:** 361c

Wirt, William **IV:** 24, 227

Wirtz, Lenny **X:** 262

Wirz, Henry **V:** 10, 11, 239, 282

Wisconsin **II:** 168; **IV:** 51, 52, 235, 236, 329, 376c, 377c; **VI:** 221; **VII:** 154–155; **X:** 127, 242

Wisconsin v. Yoder (1972) **X:** 266

Wisconsin Woman Suffrage Association (WWSA) **VI:** 36

Wise, Henry A. **V:** 226, 271

Wise, Isaac Mayer **IV:** 298; **VI:** 158, 243

Wise, John **V:** 21

Wise, Stephen S. **VI:** 158; **VII:** 261; **VIII:** 173

Wistar, Caspar **II: 402–403**

witches/witchcraft **I:** 96, 171, 225, *373,* **373–374; II: 403–404,** *404,* 418c; **III:** 282

crime and punishment **II:** 74, 75

King William's War **II:** 185

marriage and family life **II:** 207

Massachusetts **II:** 214

Mather, Cotton **II:** 217

midwives **II:** 225

Nurse, Rebecca **II:** 266

Parris, Samuel **II:** 271

Plymouth **II:** 287

Popé **II:** 290

science **II:** 331

Sewall, Samuel **II:** 334

spinsters **II:** 360

Willard, Samuel **II:** 399

women's status and rights **II:** 409

Witherspoon, John **III:** 227, **380**

withholding system **VIII:** 177, 308–309, 409c

Without Sanctuary **VI:** 182

Witness (photographic exhibit) **VI:** 182

Witt, Christopher **II:** 331

Witt, Shirley Mill **IX:** 229

Wittenmyer, Annie **V:** 371, 399

Wiyot **I:** 48

Wizard of Oz (film) **VIII:** 220

WLS radio **VIII:** 222

WMC. *See* War Manpower Commission

WNBA (Women's National Basketball Association) **X:** 285

Wobblies. *See* Industrial Workers of the World

Wococon Island **II:** 264

Wöhler, Friedrich **IV:** 307

Wokokan **I:** 197

Wolcott, Oliver **III:** 96

Wolfe, George C. **X:** 241

Wolfe, James **II:** 119, 129, 233, 333, **404–405,** 419c; **III:** 60, 62

Wolfe, Thomas **VIII:** 191, 405c

Wolfe, Tom **IX:** 182, 184; **X:** 177

"wolf packs" **VIII:** 28

Wolfskill, William **IV:** 131

Wolfson, Warren **IX:** 103, 104

Wolgemut, Michael **I:** 113

Wollaston, Captain **II:** 236

Wolof **I:** 66, 321, 322

Wolsey, Thomas **I:** 73, 160

wolves **II:** 22, 122, 159, **405–406**

Woman, Church, and State (Gage) **VI:** 107

Woman in the Nineteenth Century (Fuller) **IV:** 155–156, 345

Woman Rebel (magazine) **VII:** 29, 273, 339

Woman's Bible **VI:** 317

Woman's Christian Temperance Union (WCTU) **IV:** 337; **V:** 164, 399; **VI:** 324c; **VII:** 214, 239, 240, 327

Prohibition Party **VI:** 234, 235

Shaw, Anna Howard **VI:** 260

Willard, Frances **VI:** 315, 316

women's rights **VI:** 317

Woman's Journal **VI:** 278

Woman's National Liberal Union **VI:** 107

Woman's Peace Party **VII:** 44, 337

Woman's Record: or, Sketches of All Distinguished Women from "the Beginning" till A.D. 1850 (Hale) **IV:** 168

woman suffrage **IV:** 378c; **V:** 124; **VI:** 323c, 324c; **VII:** xiii, **335–337,** 336m, *339,* 359c, 360c; **VIII:** 384

Adkins v. Children's Hospital **VII:** 3

Anthony, Susan B. **VI:** 12–13

Susan B. Anthony's speech on **VI:** 329

woman suffrage (continued)
  anti-suffragists **VII:** 15
  Blackwell, Antoinette
    Brown **VI:** 30
  Blatch, Harriot **VII:** 31–32
  Bloomer, Amelia **IV:** 54
  Bradwell, Myra Colby **VI:**
    34
  Brown, Olympia **VI:** 35–36
  Cable Act **VII:** 41
  Catt, Carrie Chapman **VII:**
    43–44
  Committee for Public
    Information **VII:** 346
  Deseret, State of **IV:**
    110–111
  elections **VII:** 79
  elections, conduct of **VI:**
    95
  Flynn, Elizabeth Gurley
    VII: 94
  Fourteenth Amendment
    V: 139
  Grimké, Angelina and
    Sarah **IV:** 164
  Hale, Sarah Josepha **IV:**
    168
  Hoar, George Frisbie **VI:**
    130
  Hooker, Isabella Beecher
    VI: 132–133
  Howe, Julia Ward **V:** 174
  Lease, Mary Elizabeth **VI:**
    173
  Liberty Party **IV:** 210
  Lockwood, Belva Ann
    Bennett McNall **VI:** 181
  magazines **VI:** 185
  marriage and family life
    VII: 171
  Mitchell, Maria **VI:** 195
  National Association of
    Colored Women **VII:**
    200
  National Woman's Party
    VII: 204–205
  National Women's Trade
    Union League **VII:** 206
  NAWSA. See National
    American Woman
    Suffrage Association
  New Woman **VII:** 214
  Non-Partisan League **VII:**
    215
  NWSA **V:** 248–249
  Paul, Alice **VII:** 225–226
  Philadelphia Centennial
    Exposition **VI:** 224
  politics **VII:** 228, 230
  progressivism **VII:** 237
  race and race relations **IV:**
    289

  radicalism **VII:** 250
  radical press **VII:** 253
  Ray, Charlotte **V:** 291
  Shaw, Anna Howard **VI:**
    260–261
  Stanton, Elizabeth Cady **V:**
    334
  Stone, Lucy **VI:** 278
  Tarbell, Ida **VII:** 305
  Terrell, Mary Church **VII:**
    308
  Walker, Mary Edwards **V:**
    386
  Wells-Barnett, Ida Bell **VI:**
    312
  Willard, Frances **VI:** 315
  Wilson, Woodrow
    VII: 335
  women's rights and status
    V: 397–399; **VI:** 317;
    VII: 338–340
  Woodhull, Victoria **VI:**
    318
  YWCA **VII:** 349
Woman Suffrage Amendment.
  See Nineteenth Amendment
Woman Voter **VII:** 253
women **VI:** 323c. See also
  women's status and rights
  Aesthetic movement **VI:** 3
  agriculture **II:** 8, 9
  aircraft industry **VIII:** 11
  Aleut **II:** 16
  American Federation of
    Labor **VI:** 11
  Army, U.S. **VIII:** 20
  Army Air Forces, U.S.
    VIII: 21
  art **II:** 24
  art and architecture **VI:** 14
  automobile industry **VIII:**
    30
  aviation **VIII:** 406c
  clothing **II:** 64, 65
  crime and punishment **II:**
    75
  crowd action **II:** 77
  Delaware **II:** 88
  economy **II:** 101, 102
  fertility **II:** 117–118
  Gates, Sir Thomas **II:** 135
  in government **VIII:** 242,
    406c
  Hoar, George Frisbie **VI:**
    130
  Italian Americans **VIII:**
    167
  Knights of Labor **VI:** 162
  labor **VIII:** 181
  magazines **VI:** 185
  marriage and family life
    VIII: 205

  migration **VIII:** 213
  in military **VII:** 54
  Moraley, William **II:** 234
  newspapers **VI:** 212
  Philadelphia Centennial
    Exposition **VI:** 224
  piracy **II:** 286
  population trends **II:** 290
  progressivism in the 1890s
    VI: 233
  Prohibition Party **VI:** 234
  Protestantism **II:** 302
  Quakers **II:** 307, 308
  religion, Native American
    II: 318
  Rosie the Riveter **VIII:**
    315
  sachems **II:** 327
  shipbuilding **VIII:** 325
  slave trade **II:** 343, 344
  society, British American
    II: 349
  South Carolina **II:** 353
  Spanish colonies **II:** 356,
    359
  Spanish immigration **II:**
    359
  Tanner, Benjamin Tucker
    VI: 283
  unemployment **VIII:**
    363–364
  WAC **VIII:** 381–382
  WASP **VIII:** 380–381
  WAVES **VIII:** 379–380
  witchcraft **II:** 402
  women's status and rights
    VIII: 384, 385
  World War II home front
    VIII: 394–395
  Zeisberger, David **II:** 415
Women Accepted for Volunteer
  Emergency Service (WAVES)
  VIII: 379–380, 386
Women Airforce Service Pilots
  (WASP) **VIII:** 21, **380–381**,
  386
Women and Economics
  (Gilman) **VII:** 109, 339
Women in Publishing **X:** 115
Women in Radio and Electrical
  Service (WIRES) **VIII:** 382
Women's Armed Forces
  Integration Act **VIII:** 382
Women's Armed Services Act
  VIII: 380
Women's Army Auxiliary Corps
  (WAAC) **VIII:** 381
Women's Army Corps (WAC)
  VIII: 20, **381–382**, 382, 386
Women's Central Association for
  Relief (WCAR) **V:** 97,
  203–204, 255–256, 373

  women's colleges **V:** 108; **VI:** 91,
    316, 317
  Women's Council of 1808 **II:**
    392
  "Women's Declaration of 1876"
    VI: 13
  Women's Economic Equity Act
    of 1984 **X:** 117
  Women's Equity Action League
    (WEAL) **IX: 323–324; X:**
    114, 115
  Women's Era Club **VI:** 311
  Women's Exchange **VI:** 15
  women's history **VII:** 32
  Women's International League
    for Peace and Freedom
    (WILPF) **VII:** 198, 308,
    337–338, 340
  "Women's Lesser Duties"
    speech (Willard) **V:** 407c
  women's liberation movement
    IX: 325
    feminism **X:** 114, 115
    pro-life and pro-choice
      movements **X:** 249
    Steinem, Gloria **X:** 288
  Women's Loyal National League
    VI: 12
  Women's Medical College of
    Pennsylvania **IV:** 231
  Women's Medical College of the
    New York Infirmary **VI:** 31,
    318
  women's movement **X:** 320
  Women's National Basketball
    Association (WNBA) **X:** 285
  Women's National Loyal League
    V: 396–397
  Women's National Soccer Team
    X: 285
  women's network **VIII: 383**
    Democratic Party **VIII:** 81
    Dewson, "Molly" **VIII:** 83
    Perkins, Frances **VIII:** 265
    Roosevelt, Eleanor **VIII:**
      310
  Women's Organization for
    National Prohibition Reform
    (WONPR) **VII:** 241
  Women's Relief Corps **V:** 350
  Women's Rights Convention of
    1848. See Seneca Falls
    Women's Rights Convention
    of 1848
  Women's Rights Project
    (ACLU) **X:** 130
  women's shelters **X:** 115
  women's status and rights **II:**
    406–410, 408; **III: 380–383**,
    381; **IV:** xiii, 247, **366–369**,
    368, 378c, 379c; **V: 397–399**;
    VI: 316–318, 324c; **VII:**

338–341, *339;* **VIII:**
383–386, *385;* **IX: 324–326;**
X: 319–321, 329c. *See also*
feminism/feminist
movement; gender
discrimination
AASS **IV:** 15, 362
Abbott, Grace **VII:** 1
Abenaki **I:** 2
abolition/abolition
    movement **IV:** 3; **V:** 3
abortion **X:** 1–4
Adams, Abigail **III:** 1
Adkins v. Children's
    Hospital **VII:** 3
Africa **II:** 4
African Americans **IV:** 7, 8
agriculture **IV:** 10
alcohol **II:** 15
Algonquin **II:** 17
Alvarado, Pedro de **I:** 8
amendments to the
    Constitution **X:** 19
anti-suffragists **VII:** 15
Aztecs **I:** 20
baby boomers **X:** 33
Bahía **I:** 24
Baptists **II:** 29
Barton, Clara **V:** 24–26
birth control **X:** 36. *See*
    birth control
birthrates **X:** 38
Black Power **IX:** 41
Blackwell, Antoinette
    Brown **VI:** 29–30
Blatch, Harriot **VII:** 31–32
Bloomer, Amelia **IV:** 53–54
Bradwell, Myra Colby **VI:**
    34
Brent, Margaret Reed **II:**
    40
Brown, Olympia **VI:** 35–36
Burgis, William **II:** 46
Cable Act **VII:** 41
California gold rush **IV:**
    68–69
Carib **I:** 56
Caribbean **II:** 53
Cary, Ann Shadd **V:** 52
CCC **VIII:** 63
Cherokee **II:** 57
cities and urban life **II:** 61
Civil War **V:** 66
class **II:** 62
Clinton, William **X:** 66
Colden, Jane **II:** 66
community **II:** 409–410
conservative movement **X:**
    80
consumption **II:** 71
cosmetics industry **VII:**
    57–58

Cumming, Kate **V:** 85
Dahomey **I:** 102
Declaration of Sentiments
    IV: 405–407
dime novels **VI:** 81
domesticity **II:** 93
Douglass, Frederick **V:** 100
dress **VII:** 70–71
education **III:** 114–115;
    IV: 120–121; **VI:** 91;
    VII: 78
education, higher **X:** 97
Enlightenment **II:** 110
ERA **VII:** 87–88; **X:**
    105–107
Ewe **I:** 125
fashion **V:** 122–123
female antislavery societies
    IV: 135–136
feminism **X:** 113–116
Flynn, Elizabeth Gurley
    VII: 95
Foster, Abigail Kelley **IV:**
    147–148
Fourteenth Amendment
    V: 139
Franciscans **I:** 132
Franklin, Ann Smith **II:**
    125
Frémont, Jessie Benton
    IV: 152
Friedan, Betty **IX:**
    114–116
Fuller, Margaret **IV:**
    155–156
Gage, Matilda Joslyn **VI:**
    107
gender **II:** 136, 137
gender gap **X:** 128
German immigrants **II:**
    139
Gilman, Charlotte Perkins
    VII: 109
Glorious Revolution **II:**
    141
Goldmark, Josephine **VII:**
    111
Great Awakening **II:** 148
Great Plains **III:** 154–155
Grimké, Angelina and
    Sarah **IV:** 164–165
Grimké, Charlotte Forten
    V: 160
Haida **I:** 150
Hale, Sarah Josepha **IV:**
    167–168
Hooker, Isabella Beecher
    VI: 132
horses **I:** 169
humanitarianism **III:** 170
Hume, Sophia Wigington
    II: 160

Huron **I:** 171–172; **II:** 160
Hutchinson, Anne
    Marbury **II:** 161
Ibn Battuta **I:** 173
Indian Removal Act (1830)
    IV: 182–183
industrialization **IV:** 185
inheritance **II:** 407–408
International Ladies'
    Garment Workers
    Union **VII:** 132
Iroquois **I:** 181; **II:** 168
Islam in America **X:** 157
Jamestown **II:** 172
Jemison, Mary **II:** 173
Jews (Judaism) **I:** 191
Johnson, Anthony **II:** 175
Johnson, Mary **II:** 175
Johnston, Henrietta
    Deering **II:** 177–178
journalism **II:** 178
Knight, Sarah Kemble **II:**
    185
labor **II:** 189–190; **IX:**
    169–170
labor, woman **VI:** 169
ladies aid societies **V:**
    203–204
land **II:** 191–192
Langston, John Mercer **VI:**
    171
Latino movement **IX:** 174
League of Women Voters
    IX: 174–175
liberalism **VIII:** 189; **X:**
    175
Libertarian Party **X:** 176
literature **IV:** 213; **V:** 213
Livingston, Robert R. **II:**
    196
Locke, John **II:** 198
Lockwood, Belva Ann
    Bennett McNall **VI:**
    180–181
Mali **I:** 218
Mann, Horace **IV:** 220
manufacturing and
    industry **II:** 203–204
marriage and family life **II:**
    206; **III:** 232, 235; **IV:**
    221–222; **VII:** 170–172;
    VIII: 204; **IX:** 192; **X:**
    109, 181
Maryland **II:** 210
Massachuset **I:** 225
Massachusetts School Act
    II: 216
medicine **IV:** 230–231;
    VII: 180
merchants **II:** 222
and *mestizaje* **I:** 233
midwives **II:** 224–225

Mitchell, Maria **VI:** 195
Montagnais-Naskapi **I:** 241
mortality **II:** 235
mothers' pensions **VII:**
    189
Mott, Lucretia **IV:**
    246–247
Muller v. Oregon **VII:**
    192–193
multiculturalism **X:** 200,
    201
Murray, Judith Sargent
    III: 250
Musgrove, Mary
    Bosomworth **II:** 238
music **X:** 203
Natchez **I:** 251
National Association of
    Colored Women **VII:**
    199–200
National Organization for
    Women **IX:** 223
National Woman's Party
    VII: 204–205
National Women's Trade
    Union League **VII:**
    205–206
New Deal **VIII:** 242
New Netherland **II:** 257
New Orleans, Battle of **V:**
    252
newspapers **VI:** 211
New Woman **VII:** 213–214
New York **II:** 261, 262
New York City **II:** 263
North Carolina **II:** 263,
    264
NOW **X:** 210–211
NWSA **V:** 248–249
Osborn, Sarah Haggar
    Wheaten **II:** 268–269
Pennsylvania **II:** 275
Perkins, Frances **VIII:**
    265
Phillips, Wendell **IV:** 281
Pinckney, Elizabeth Lucas
    II: 284
Pocahontas **II:** 288–289
politics **VII:** 229–230
polygamy **IV:** 284–285
population trends **VIII:**
    278
Powhatan Confederacy **II:**
    294–295
President's Commission on
    the Status of Women
    IX: 246–247
Prohibition **VII:** 241
prostitution **V:** 283–284
Ray, Charlotte **V:** 291
recreation **X:** 262
relief **VIII:** 301

women's status and rights
(*continued*)
    religion **II:** 408–409; **V:**
        299; **IX:** 257
    Revolutionary War **III:**
        307
    Roe v. Wade **X:** 268
    Roosevelt, Eleanor **VIII:**
        310–311
    Rosie the Riveter **VIII:**
        315
    rural life **III:** 312
    Sampson, Deborah **III:**
        316–317
    Sanger, Margaret **VII:**
        273–274
    Schlafly, Phyllis **X:** 272
    Seneca Falls **IV:** 313–315
    service sector **IX:** 272
    Shaw, Anna Howard **VI:**
        260–261
    slavery **IV:** 319
    society, British American
        II: 349–351
    Spanish colonies **II:** 357
    spinsters **II:** 360
    spiritualism **IV:** 326
    sports **X:** 285
    Stanton, Elizabeth Cady **V:**
        334–335
    Starbuck, Mary Coffin **II:**
        361
    Steinem, Gloria **X:** 287,
        288
    Stewart, Maria **IV:** 327
    Stone, Lucy **VI:** 278
    Students for a Democratic
        Society **IX:** 286
    suburbanization **IX:**
        287–288
    Sufism **I:** 337
    temperance movement **IV:**
        336
    tenants **II:** 370
    Terrell, Mary Church **VII:**
        308
    travel **II:** 377
    Truth, Sojourner **V:**
        356–358
    Turell, Jane Colman **II:**
        378
    USSC **V:** 373, 375
    Van Lew, Elizabeth **V:**
        378
    Van Rensselaer, Maria Van
        Cortlandt **II:** 381
    Victorianism **VI:** 304
    Virginia **II:** 383
    WAC **VIII:** 381–382
    Wakeman, Sarah Rosetta
        V: 386
    Wald, Lillian **VII:** 329

Walker, Mary Edwards **V:**
    386
Ward, Nancy **II:** 392
Warren, Mercy Otis **III:**
    363–364
WASP **VIII:** 380–381
WAVES **VIII:** 379–380
Weathermen **IX:** 319
Wells-Barnett, Ida Bell **VI:**
    311–312
Willard, Emma **IV:**
    364–366
witches **I:** 374
woman suffrage **VII:**
    335–337
women's colleges **VI:** 316
Women's Equity Action
    League **IX:** 323–324
Women's International
    League for Peace and
    Freedom **VII:** 337–338
Women's National Loyal
    League **V:** 396–397
women's network **VIII:**
    383
Woodhull, Victoria **VI:**
    318–319
work **II:** 406–407
work, household **VII:**
    341–342
World War II **VIII:** 389,
    390
Wright, Fanny **IV:** 369
Yoruba **I:** 377
YWCA **II:** 349
Women's Strike for Equality **IX:**
    115; **X:** 211, 288
Women's Studies programs **X:**
    115, 200, 211
Women's war **VI:** 233–234, 324*c*
women voters **VIII:** 271. *See
    also* woman suffrage
Wonder, Stevie **IX:** 217; **X:** 240
WONPR **VII:** 24
wood **II:** 24, 215, 250. *See also*
    lumbering
Wood, Abraham **II:** 30, 115
Wood, Ed **IX:** 213
Wood, Grant **VIII:** 25
Wood, Leonard **VI:** 250; **VII:**
    235
Wood, Natalie **IX:** *212*
Wood, Robert E. **VIII:** 12
Wood, William **II:** **410**
Woodbridge, John **II:** 39
Woodbury Facial Soap **VII:** 4
Woodhull, Victoria **IV:** 326; **V:**
    399; **VI:** **318–319**, 323*c*
    Beecher, Henry Ward **VI:**
        24
    Beecher-Tilton scandal **VI:**
        24, 25

Hooker, Isabella Beecher
    VI: 133
Lockwood, Belva Ann
    Bennett McNall **VI:** 180
socialism **VI:** 267
Stone, Lucy **VI:** 278
women's rights **VI:** 317
Woodhull, Claflin and Company
    VI: 318
Woodhull and Claflin's Weekly
    VI: 24, 267, 318, 319, 323*c*
Woodin, William H. **VIII:** 216
Woodland Indians **II:** 328
"Woodnotes" (Emerson) **IV:**
    126
Woods, Thomas **II:** 30
Woods, Tiger **X:** 262, 285, 286,
    296
Woodstock music festival **IX:**
    111, *217*, 218, 244; **X:** 277,
    321, 323*c*
Woodstock Ventures, Inc. **X:**
    321
Woodville, Richard Caton **V:** 16
Woodward, C. Vann **X:** 201
Woodward, Henry **II:** 394
Woodward, Robert (Bob) **X:** 44,
    185, 196
woodworking **II:** 204
wool **IV:** 10
Woolen Act of 1699 **II:** 3, 203
woolen goods **II:** 221
woolen manufacturing **IV:** 118,
    184
Woolley, Mary **VII:** 338
Woolman, John **II:** 2, 31, 110,
    253, 309, **410–411**
Woolson, Albert **V:** 379
wool trade **I:** 63
Woolworth, Frank W. **VI:** 46, 47
Woolworth Building **VI:** 47
Woolworth department stores
    IX: 272–273, 332*c*
Worcester, Samuel **IV:** 344
Worcester Convention. *See*
    National Women's Rights
    Convention (1850)
Worcester v. Georgia **IV:** 257,
    331
"word" educational method **IV:**
    228
Worden, John L. **V:** 183, 184,
    238
Wordsworth, William **IV:** 345
work. *See* employment;
    labor/labor movement
Work, Henry C. **V:** 244; **VI:** 203
work, household **VII:** 172, *341*,
    341–342
workers' compensation **VII:** 11,
    359*c*
"working class" **VII:** 185

working conditions **IV:** 185–186
working hours **II:** 26
Workingman's Friend **VI:** 116
Workingmen's Benevolent
    Association **VI:** 195, 196
Workingmen's Parties **VI:** 120
Workingmen's Party of
    Philadelphia **IV:** 204
Workingmen's Party of the
    United States (WPUS) **V:**
    340; **VI:** 268
working women **VII:** 205–206
Workingwomen's Protective
    Group **V:** 116
Workmen's Compensation Act
    VII: 334, **342–343**
work slowdowns **IV:** 203
Works Progress Administration
    (WPA) **VIII:** **386–388**, *387*,
    407*c*; **IX:** 30
    advertising **VIII:** 1
    art and architecture **VIII:**
        25
    Black Cabinet **VIII:** 37
    CCC **VIII:** 64
    children **VIII:** 56
    cities and urban life **VIII:**
        59
    Congress **VIII:** 68
    conservatism **VIII:** 72
    CWA **VIII:** 63
    Emergency Relief
        Appropriation Act **VIII:**
        102
    FAP **VIII:** 114
    FBI **VIII:** 115
    FMP **VIII:** 119
    FTP **VIII:** 120
    FWP **VIII:** 121
    Henderson, Leon **VIII:**
        145
    Hopkins, Harry **VIII:** 156
    Johnson, Hugh S. **VIII:**
        173
    literature **VIII:** 193
    music **VIII:** 222
    Native Americans **VIII:**
        235
    New Deal **VIII:** 241
    NYA **VIII:** 234
    popular culture **VIII:** 273
    PWA **VIII:** 285
    REA **VIII:** 316
    recession of 1937–38 **VIII:**
        293
    recreation **VIII:** 296
    relief **VIII:** 301
    Roosevelt, Eleanor **VIII:**
        311
    Second New Deal **VIII:**
        321
    transportation **VIII:** 360

World Anti-Slavery Conference
of 1843 **V:** 270
World Anti-Slavery Convention
IV: 136, 246, 313–314
World Bank
Bretton Woods
Conference **VIII:** 42
Eccles, Marriner S. **VIII:**
89
economy **VIII:** 93
foreign policy **VIII:** 125
postwar planning **VIII:**
279
World Columbian Exposition
(1893) **VII:** 15, 140–141
World Community of Islam in
the West **X:** 111
World Council of Churches **IX:**
256
World Court **VII:** 43, 138, 156;
VIII: 75
World Cup (soccer) **X:** 285
World Disarmament
Conference (1932–34) **VIII:**
388, 405c
foreign policy **VIII:** 123
Hoover presidency **VIII:**
154
London Naval Conference
VIII: 194
World Football League (WFL)
X: 284
World Health Organization
(WHO) **IX:** 199; **X:** 5, 188
"World of Tomorrow" **VIII:**
408c
World Parliament of Religions
VII: 260
World's Columbian Exposition
(Chicago, 1893) **V:** 258; **VI:**
148, 319, **319–320**
art and architecture **VI:** 15
Beach, Amy **VI:** 23
Carver, George
Washington **VI:** 45
Cassatt, Mary **VI:** 45
Cody, William Frederick
VI: 60
entertainment, popular **VI:**
96
industrial revolution,
second **VI:** 146
painting **VI:** 220
Richards, Ellen Henrietta
Swallow **VI:** 247
Saint-Gaudens, Augustus
VI: 253
sculpture **VI:** 259
Sousa, John Philip **VI:** 271
Strong, Josiah **VI:** 279
Sullivan, Louis H. **VI:** 280
Tesla, Nikola **VI:** 285

Tiffany, Louis Comfort **VI:**
288
Victorianism **VI:** 304
Wells-Barnett, Ida Bell **VI:**
311
World Series (baseball) **X:** 284,
296, 328c
World's Temperance
Convention of 1853 **VI:** 30
World Trade Center **X:** 328c,
331c
Bush, George W. **X:** 48
Clinton, William **X:** 66
defense policy **X:** 88
economy **X:** 96
foreign policy **X:** 125
Powell, Colin L. **X:** 247
Senate **X:** 276
terrorism **X:** 297, 298, *299,*
300
World Trade Organization
(WTO) **X: 321–322,** 329c,
330c
economy **X:** 96
foreign policy **X:** 124
GATT **X:** 129
globalization **X:** 132
World War I **V:** 306; **VII:**
xiii–xiv, **343–346,** *344,* 345m,
358c–360c
Adamson Act **VII:** 2
Addams, Jane **VII:** 3
advertising **VII:** 4–5
AFL **VII:** 11
African Americans **VIII:** 2
Agricultural Marketing Act
VII: 5
agriculture **VII:** 7
American Civil Liberties
Union **VIII:** 13
American Expeditionary
Force **VII:** 8–9
American Legion **VII:**
11–12
architecture **VII:** 16
Arnold, "Hap" **VIII:** 21
Atlantic Charter **VIII:** 28
aviation **VII:** 23
Baruch, Bernard M. **VII:**
25; **VIII:** 34
baseball **VII:** 26
blitzkrieg **VIII:** 39
blues **VII:** 32
Borah, William E. **VIII:** 40
Bryan, William Jennings
VI: 37
Bryce, James **VI:** 38
Cable Act **VII:** 41
Catt, Carrie Chapman **VII:**
44
censorship **VIII:** 54, 55
civil liberties **VIII:** 60

code breaking **VIII:** 64
Committee for Public
Information **VII:** 51–52
conscription **VII:** 54–55
conservatism **VIII:** 71
Dawes, Charles **VII:** 63
Dawes Plan **VII:** 63–64
Debs, Eugene V. **VII:** 65
Democratic Party **VII:** 66
economy **VII:** 73–74
education **VII:** 78
elections **VII:** 80
Espionage Act. *See*
Espionage Act
ethnic organizations **VII:**
89
federal income tax **VII:** 93
Fordney-McCumber Tariff
VII: 97
foreign policy **VII:** 99–101;
VIII: 123
Forrestal, James V. **VIII:**
126
Fuel Administration **VII:**
102
German Americans **VIII:**
131
Goldman, Emma **VII:** 110
Great Depression **VIII:**
139
Great Migration **VII:** 113
Greenwich Village **VII:**
115
Halsey, "Bull" **VIII:** 143
Harding, Warren G. **VII:**
117, 118
Harlem Renaissance **VII:**
120
Haywood, "Big Bill" **VII:**
120
Hillman, Sidney **VIII:** 145
Hoover, Herbert **VIII:** 151
Hoover presidency **VIII:**
153
immigration **VII:** 124
Immigration Act of 1917
VII: 128
intelligence tests **VII:** 131
invention and technology
VII: 133
investments, foreign **VII:**
135
investments, foreign, in the
United States **VI:** 151
isolationists **VIII:** 166
IWW **VII:** 130
Johnson, Hiram Warren
VII: 138
Johnson, Hugh S. **VIII:**
173
journalism **VII:** 142–143
King, Ernest J. **VIII:** 177

labor movement **VII:**
152–153
La Follette, Robert **VII:**
155
La Guardia, Fiorello **VIII:**
182
Landon, Alfred M. **VIII:**
183
League of Nations **VII:**
156
Leahy, William D. **VIII:**
183
liberalism **VIII:** 187
literature **VII:** 161
lobbying groups **VII:** 163
Lodge, Henry Cabot **VII:**
165
Lost Generation **VII:** 166
Lusitania **VII:** 168
Marshall, George C. **VIII:**
206
Mitchell, Billy **VII:** 187
modernism **VII:** 188
movie industry **VII:** 191
Murray, Philip **VIII:** 221
National Association of
Manufacturers **VII:** 200
National Civic Federation
VII: 201
National War Labor Board
VII: 204
National Woman's Party
VII: 204–205
nativism **VII:** 208
NAWSA **VII:** 198
neutrality **VII:** 210
Neutrality Acts **VIII:** 239
New Nationalism **VII:** 212
New Unionism **VII:**
212–213
Nimitz, Chester W. **VIII:**
246
Non-Partisan League **VII:**
216
Norris, George W. **VIII:**
248
Nye Committee **VIII:** 250,
251
open shop movement **VII:**
219
Palmer, A. Mitchell **VII:**
221
Pershing, John **VII:** 227
Polish Americans **VIII:**
269
politics **VII:** 230
popular culture **VII:** 232
population trends **VII:** 234
postwar planning **VIII:**
279
Preparedness **VII:**
235–236

World War I (continued)
  progressivism **VII:** 238
  Prohibition **VII:** 239–240
  public health **VII:** 242, 243
  Quota Act **VII:** 245
  race and racial conflict
    VII: 249
  radicalism **VII:** 250, 251
  radical press **VII:** 252
  radio **VII:** 253
  Railroad Administration
    VII: 255
  Randolph, A. Philip **VIII:**
    291
  reconversion **VIII:** 295
  recreation **VII:** 258
  Red Scare **VII:** 258
  Reed, John **VII:** 259
  relief **VIII:** 300
  Republican Party **VII:** 263
  rural life **VII:** 268–269
  Russian Revolution **VII:**
    270
  Schenk v. United States
    VII: 274–275
  science **VII:** 276
  Seattle General Strike **VII:**
    279
  Sedition Act **VII:** 280
  Selective Service **VIII:** 322
  Selective Service Act **VII:**
    282
  Shaw, Anna Howard **VI:**
    261
  Sheppard-Towner Act **VII:**
    284
  shipbuilding **VIII:** 324
  Sinclair, Upton **VII:** 286
  socialism **VII:** 289
  socialists **VIII:** 327
  Soldiers' Bonus **VII:**
    291–292
  Solomon Islands **VIII:** 330
  Sousa, John Philip **VI:** 271
  steel industry **VII:** 297
  Stimson, Henry L. **VIII:**
    340
  submarines **VIII:** 342
  Taft, Robert A. **VIII:** 349
  Taft, William Howard **VII:**
    304
  tariffs **VII:** 306
  taxation **VIII:** 351
  Terrell, Mary Church **VII:**
    308
  trade, foreign **VII:** 310
  Trading with the Enemy
    Act **VII:** 311
  TVA **VIII:** 356
  United States Shipping
    Board **VII:** 314
  USO **VIII:** 366

U.S. Steel **VII:** 320
Versailles, Treaty of **VII:**
    322–324
veterans **VII:** 324–326
Veterans Bureau **VII:**
    326–327
War Industries Board **VII:**
    329–330
War Revenue Act **VII:**
    330–331
Washington Conference
    on Naval Disarmament
    VII: 331
WAVES **VIII:** 379
Wilson, Woodrow **VII:**
    334
woman suffrage **VII:** 337
Women's International
    League for Peace and
    Freedom **VII:** 337–338
women's status and rights
    VII: 340
Workmen's Compensation
    Act **VII:** 343
World War II European
    theater **VIII:** 391
Wright Brothers **VII:** 348
Zimmermann telegram
    VII: 353
World War II **VI:** 79; **VIII:** xiii,
    388–391, 409c; **IX:** 330c. *See
    also* World War II European
    theater; World War II home
    front; World War II Pacific
    theater
  advertising **VIII:** 1–2
  African Americans **VIII:**
    3–5
  agriculture **VIII:** 7–9
  aircraft industry **VIII:**
    9–11
  air power **VIII:** 11–12
  America First Committee
    VIII: 12–13
  American Civil Liberties
    Union **VIII:** 13
  American Federation of
    Labor **VIII:** 14
  amphibious warfare **VIII:**
    15–16
  antimonopoly **VIII:** 17, 18
  anti-Semitism **VIII:** 19
  Army, U.S. **VIII:** 19–20
  Army Air Forces, U.S.
    VIII: 20–21
  Arnold, "Hap" **VIII:** 21–22
  art and architecture **VIII:**
    22, 24
  Asian-American movement
    IX: 22
  Asian Americans **VIII:** 25,
    26

Atlantic Charter **VIII:** 28
atomic bomb **VIII:** 28–29
automobile industry **VIII:**
    30
Axis **VIII:** 31–32
baby boom **IX:** 29
Baruch, Bernard M. **VII:**
    25; **VIII:** 34
Berle, Adolf A., Jr. **VIII:**
    35
Black Cabinet **VIII:** 38
Borah, William E. **VIII:** 40
Bretton Woods
    Conference **VIII:** 42
Bush, Vannevar **VIII:** 44,
    45
business **VIII:** 45–48; **IX:**
    44
Byrnes, James F. **VIII:** 49
Capra, Frank **VIII:** 51, 52
cash-and-carry **VIII:** 53
Catholics **VIII:** 53–54
CCC **VIII:** 64
censorship **VIII:** 54, 55
children **VIII:** 56
CIA **IX:** 49
CIO **VIII:** 70
cities and urban life **VIII:**
    57–60
civil liberties **VIII:** 60
civil rights **VIII:** 61–62
code breaking **VIII:** 64–65
Communists **VIII:** 65, 66
Congress **VIII:** 66, 67–68
conscientious objectors
    VIII: 70–71
conservatism **VIII:** 71,
    72–73
conservative coalition
    VIII: 74
Coughlin, Father Charles
    E. **VIII:** 75–76
demobilization **VIII:**
    79–80
Democratic Party **VIII:** 82
DiMaggio, Joe **VIII:** 84
dollar-a-year men **VIII:** 84
Dust Bowl **VIII:** 87
Eccles, Marriner S. **VIII:**
    89
Economic Bill of Rights
    VIII: 90
economy **VIII:** 92; **IX:** 88
education **VIII:** 93–94
Eisenhower, Dwight D.
    IX: 92
elderly **VIII:** 95–96
ENIAC **IX:** 98
espionage **VIII:** 104–105
Ethiopia **VIII:** 105
Executive Order 8802
    VIII: 106

Executive Order 9066
    VIII: 106–107
FAP **VIII:** 114
FBI **VIII:** 115
FCC **VIII:** 116
FEPC **VIII:** 109
FMP **VIII:** 120
Ford Motor Company **IX:**
    112
foreign policy **VII:** 101;
    VIII: 123–126
Forrestal, James V. **VIII:**
    126
Four Freedoms **VIII:** 126
FSA **VIII:** 113
Full Employment Bill
    VIII: 128
FWP **VIII:** 121
gays and lesbians **VIII:**
    129, 130; **IX:** 119
German Americans **VIII:**
    130, 131
GI Bill of Rights **VIII:**
    131–132
Good Neighbor Policy
    VIII: 133
government **VIII:** 133,
    135–136
Grand Alliance **VIII:**
    136–138
Great Depression **VIII:**
    140–141
Harriman, Averell **VIII:**
    143–144
Hillman, Sidney **VIII:** 146
HOLC **VIII:** 151
Holocaust **VIII:** 149–150
Hoover, Herbert **VIII:** 153
Hopkins, Harry **VIII:** 156,
    157
housing **VIII:** 157–159
Hull, Cordell **VIII:** 159,
    160
Ickes, Harold L. **VIII:** 161
intelligence **VIII:** 164
Irish Americans **VIII:** 165
isolationists **VIII:** 165–166
Italian Americans **VIII:**
    167
Jews **VIII:** 173
Jones, Jesse H. **VIII:** 174
Kaiser, Henry J. **VIII:** 175
Kennedy, Joseph P. **VIII:**
    176
Keynesianism **VIII:** 176,
    177
King, Ernest J. **VIII:**
    177–178
Kissinger, Henry A. **X:** 165
labor **VIII:** 179, 181
Landon, Alfred M. **VIII:**
    183

Leahy, William D. **VIII:** 183–184

Lend-Lease Act **VIII:** 184–185

Lewis, John L. **VIII:** 186

liberalism **VIII:** 188

Life (magazine) **VIII:** 189–190

Lilienthal, David E. **VIII:** 190

Lindbergh, Charles **VII:** 160

literature **VIII:** 191, 192

London Naval Conference **VIII:** 194

Louis, Joe **VIII:** 196

Luce, Henry R. **VIII:** 196

MacArthur, Douglas **IX:** 185–186

Manhattan Project **VIII:** 200–201

marriage and family life **VIII:** 204–205

Marshall, George C. **VIII:** 205–207

Mauldin, Bill **VIII:** 207

medicine **VIII:** 208, 209

Mexican Americans **VIII:** 210

Mexican Repatriation Program **VIII:** 211

migration **VIII:** 212–213

military-industrial complex **IX:** 203

Mitchell, Billy **VII:** 187

mobilization **VIII:** 213–215

Morgenthau, Henry **VIII:** 216

MOWM **VIII:** 201–202

Munich Conference **VIII:** 220

Murray, Philip **VIII:** 221

music **VIII:** 221, 223, 224

Myrdal, Gunnar **VIII:** 225

NAACP **VIII:** 228

Native Americans **VIII:** 235, 236

Naval Disarmament Conference **VII:** 209

Navy, U.S. **VIII:** 236–237

Nazi-Soviet Pact **VIII:** 238

Nelson, Donald M. **VIII:** 238

Neutrality Acts **VIII:** 239

New Deal **VIII:** 240, 242

news media **VIII:** 243, 244

New York World's Fair (1939–40) **VIII:** 244, 246

NLRB **VIII:** 230

Norris, George W. **VIII:** 249

NRA **X:** 212

NRPB **VIII:** 232

NWLB **VIII:** 233–234

OPM **VIII:** 255

OSRD **VIII:** 255–256

OSS **VIII:** 256–257

OWI **VIII:** 257–258

Pearl Harbor **VIII:** 263–265

photography **VIII:** 268–269

Polish Americans **VIII:** 269–270

politics in the Roosevelt era **VIII:** 270–273

popular culture **VIII:** 275

population trends **VIII:** 277–278

postwar planning **VIII:** 278–279

POWs **VIII:** 281–282

presidency **VIII:** 280, 281

propaganda **VIII:** 282–283

public opinion polls **VIII:** 284

Pyle, Ernie **VIII:** 286

race and racial conflict **VIII:** 287–289

radio **VIII:** 289, 290

Randolph, A. Philip **VIII:** 291

recreation **VIII:** 296–298

refugees **VIII:** 298–299

relief **VIII:** 302

religion **VIII:** 302–304

Republican Party **VIII:** 305, 306

Revenue Act of 1942 **VIII:** 308

RFC **VIII:** 294

Roosevelt, Eleanor **VIII:** 311

Roosevelt, Franklin D. **VIII:** 313, 314

Rosie the Riveter **VIII:** 315

science **VIII:** 317–319

Second New Deal **VIII:** 321

Selective Service **VIII:** 322–324

shipbuilding **VIII:** 324–325

Sinatra, Frank **VIII:** 326

socialists **VIII:** 327

Social Security Act **VIII:** 330

South **VIII:** 332

Soviet-American relations **VIII:** 333

sports **VIII:** 335–338

steel industry **VIII:** 338–339

Steinbeck, John **VIII:** 339

Stevenson, Adlai **IX:** 283

Stimson, Henry L. **VIII:** 340

submarines **VIII:** 342

suburbs **VIII:** 342

Sunbelt **VIII:** 343

Supreme Court **VIII:** 347

Taft, Robert A. **VIII:** 349

tanks **VIII:** 349–350

taxation **VIII:** 352

technology **VIII:** 353–354

Teheran Conference **VIII:** 354

television **IX:** 295

Third New Deal **VIII:** 357, 358

Thomas, Norman **VIII:** 358

TNEC **VIII:** 355

transportation **VIII:** 360–361

Truman, Harry **IX:** 299

TVA **VIII:** 356

UN **VIII:** 365, 366

unemployment **VIII:** 363

USO **VIII:** 366–367

V-E Day **VIII:** 369

Versailles, Treaty of **VII:** 323

veterans **IX:** 307

V-J Day **VIII:** 369–370

WAC **VIII:** 381–382

Wagner, Robert F. **VIII:** 372–373

Wallace, Henry A. **VIII:** 373

war bonds **VIII:** 374

WASP **VIII:** 380–381

WAVES **VIII:** 379–380

Wheeler, Burton K. **VIII:** 378

White, Walter **VIII:** 378

Willkie, Wendell L. **VIII:** 379

women's status and rights **VIII:** 385

Wright, Richard **VIII:** 400

Yalta Conference **VIII:** 401

Zionism **VIII:** 403

zoot-suiters **VIII:** 404

World War II European theater **VIII:** **391–394,** 392*m,* 408*c,* 410*c*

air power **VIII:** 11

amphibious warfare **VIII:** 15

Anglo-American relations **VIII:** 16–17

Army Air Forces, U.S. **VIII:** 21

Axis **VIII:** 31–32

blitzkrieg **VIII:** 39

Bradley, Omar N. **VIII:** 40–41

Britain, Battle of **VIII:** 43

Bulge, Battle of the **VIII:** 44

Casablanca Conference **VIII:** 52

election of 1940 **VIII:** 98

Italian campaign **VIII:** 168

Marshall, George C. **VIII:** 206

Mauldin, Bill **VIII:** 207

medicine **VIII:** 208

mobilization **VIII:** 214

Navy, U.S. **VIII:** 236

Nazi-Soviet Pact **VIII:** 237–238

Normandy, invasion of **VIII:** 247–248

North African campaign **VIII:** 249

Patton, George **VIII:** 263

politics in the Roosevelt era **VIII:** 272

Pyle, Ernie **VIII:** 286

Roosevelt, Franklin D. **VIII:** 314

second front **VIII:** 320

Sicily **VIII:** 325–326

submarines **VIII:** 342

Teheran Conference **VIII:** 354

V-E Day **VIII:** 369

World War II **VIII:** 389

World War II home front **VIII:** **394–396**

advertising **VIII:** 1–2

Asian Americans **VIII:** 26

black market **VIII:** 38

children **VIII:** 57

civil liberties **VIII:** 60–61

enemy aliens **VIII:** 102–103

Henderson, Leon **VIII:** 145

Japanese Americans, relocation of **VIII:** 171–172

Korematsu v. United States **VIII:** 178

mobilization **VIII:** 214

NRPB **VIII:** 233

OCD **VIII:** 253–254

OPA **VIII:** 254–255

OWM **VIII:** 258

OWMR **VIII:** 258–259

World War II home front
(continued)
    politics in the Roosevelt
      era **VIII:** 272
    public opinion polls **VIII:**
      284
    rationing **VIII:** 291–292
    recreation **VIII:** 297
    Rosie the Riveter **VIII:**
      315
    Smith Act **VIII:** 326–327
    wage and price controls
      VIII: 371–372
    WMC **VIII:** 374–375
    World War II **VIII:** 390
    WPB **VIII:** 375–376
World War II Pacific theater
  VIII: 396–399, 397*m,*
  409*c*–411*c*
    air power **VIII:** 11, 12
    amphibious warfare **VIII:**
      15
    Army, U.S. **VIII:** 19
    Army Air Forces, U.S.
      VIII: 21
    atomic bomb **VIII:** 28–29
    Axis **VIII:** 32
    Bataan Death March **VIII:**
      34–35
    Cairo Conference **VIII:** 51
    Casablanca Conference
      VIII: 52
    code breaking **VIII:** 64
    Coral Sea, Battle of the
      VIII: 74
    Guadalcanal **VIII:** 141
    Halsey, "Bull" **VIII:** 143
    Hiroshima and Nagasaki
      VIII: 146–148
    Iwo Jima **VIII:** 168–169
    King, Ernest J. **VIII:** 177
    Lend-Lease Act **VIII:** 185
    Leyte Gulf, Battle for
      VIII: 186–187
    Manchuria **VIII:** 199–200
    Mariana Islands **VIII:** 202
    Marines, U.S. **VIII:** 203
    medicine **VIII:** 208
    Midway, Battle of **VIII:**
      211
    mobilization **VIII:** 214
    Navy, U.S. **VIII:** 236–237
    Nimitz, Chester W. **VIII:**
      246
    Okinawa **VIII:** 259
    Pearl Harbor **VIII:**
      263–265
    Philippines **VIII:** 266–267
    Philippine Sea, Battle of
      the **VIII:** 267
    politics in the Roosevelt
      era **VIII:** 272

Potsdam Conference **VIII:**
  280
POWs **VIII:** 282
Pyle, Ernie **VIII:** 286
Roosevelt, Franklin D.
  VIII: 314
shipbuilding **VIII:** 324
Solomon Islands **VIII:**
  330–331
Soviet-American relations
  VIII: 333
submarines **VIII:** 342
Tarawa **VIII:** 350
Teheran Conference **VIII:**
  354
V-E Day **VIII:** 369
V-J Day **VIII:** 369–370
World War II **VIII:** 388
World War II European
  theater **VIII:** 391
Yalta Conference **VIII:**
  401
World Wide Web (WWW)
  business **X:** 51
  Gore, Albert, Jr. **X:** 134
  Internet **X:** 153
  pornography **X:** 244, 245
  science and technology **X:**
    274
World Women's Party **VII:** 226
Worth, William J. **IV:** 312
"worthy poor" **II:** 137, 267
Wouk, Herman **VIII:** 192; **X:**
  178
Wounded Knee, South Dakota
  IX: 13, 228; **X:** 214, 324*c*
Wounded Knee massacre **VI:**
  207, 245, 263, 326–327*c*
Wovoka **VI:** 245, 326*c*
Wowinchopunk **II:** 171
Wozniak, Stephen **X:** 72, 273
WPA. *See* Works Progress
  Administration
WPB. *See* War Production
  Board
WRA. *See* War Relocation
  Authority
WRB. *See* War Refugee Board
Wren, Sir Christopher **II:** 24,
  67, 385
Wrenn, Robert **VI:** 274
Wright, Benjamin **IV:** 73, 129
Wright, Cleo **VIII:** 288
Wright, Fanny **IV: 369**
Wright, Fielding **IX:** 281
Wright, Frank Lloyd **VI:** 280;
  VII: 16, **346; VIII:** 22, *23,*
  343, 407*c*
Wright, Harry **VI:** 21
Wright, Henry **IV:** 148
Wright, James C., Jr. **X:** 129,
  144, 145, **322**

Wright, Martha C. **IV:** 314; **V:**
  397
Wright, Orville and Wilbur. *See*
  Wright brothers
Wright, Richard **VIII:** 3, 121,
  191, 193, **399–400,** 400*c;* **IX:**
  5, 32, 33, 182
Wright, Susan Weber **X:** 329*c*
Wright brothers **VI:** 150; **VII:**
  23, 133, *347,* **347–348,** 356*c;*
  VIII: 21
Write, June **II:** 135
writing **I:** 225, 226, 228–229;
  VIII: 407*c*
writing systems **IV:** 257, 376*c*
writ of habeas corpus **IV:** 280
writs of assistance **II:** 215; **III:**
  171, 268, **383–384**
writs of mandamus **III:** 192
WSM radio **VIII:** 222
WTO. *See* World Trade
  Organization
wunderkammer **I:** 40
W. W. Norton **X:** 178
WWSA (Wisconsin Woman
  Suffrage Association) **VI:** 36
WWW. *See* World Wide Web
Wyandanch **II:** 224
Wyandot **II:** 76, 160
Wyant, Alexander Helwig **VI:**
  219
Wyatt, Sir Francis **II:** 329, **411**
Wycliffe, John **I:** 307
Wye River Memorandum **X:** 69
Wyeth, Nathaniel Jarvis **IV:** 131
Wygant v. Jackson (1986) **X:** 9
Wynette, Tammy **X:** 203
Wyoming **II:** 76–77; **IV:** 57, 130;
  V: 398–399; **VI:** 208, 317; **X:**
  242
Wyoming Territory **VI:** 51*m,* 65,
  215
Wyoming Valley War **III:** 309,
  384
Wytfliet, Cornelius **I:** 266
Wythe, George **III:** 183; **IV:** 86

X

xenophobia. *See* nativism
xenotransplantation **X:** 5
X-Files, The **X:** 31
Xibalba **I:** 228
Xicallanco **I:** 341
Xicotencatl the Elder **I: 375**
Xicotencatl the Younger **I:** 99,
  375
Ximenez de Quesada, Gonzalo
  I: 119
Xiutecuhtli **I:** 21, 347
Xochimilco **I:** 72
Xochiyaotl. *See* flowery wars

X-ray technology **VII:** 355*c;*
  VIII: 207, 317
XYZ affair **III: 385,** 396*c;* **IV:**
  141
    Alien and Sedition Acts
      III: 9
    Bache, Benjamin Franklin
      III: 29
    Federalist Party **III:** 126
    foreign affairs **III:** 130
    Gallatin, Albert **III:** 147
    Gerry, Elbridge **III:** 153
    immigration **III:** 173
    Marshall, John **III:** 235
    Pickering, John **III:** 276
    Pinckney, Charles
      Cotesworth **III:** 276,
      277
    Quasi War **III:** 291
    Talleyrand, Prince **III:**
      341

Y

Yakima **I:** 48
Yale, Elihu **II: 413**
Yale College/University **II: 413;**
  III: 80, 109; **IV:** 121, 296; **VI:**
  324*c;* **X:** 43
    Brainerd, David **II:** 39
    Connecticut **II:** 70
    Davenport, James **II:** 83
    education **II:** 104
    Edwards, Jonathan **II:** 105
    football **VI:** 101, 102, *102*
    Gibbs, Willard **VI:** 113
    Johnson, Samuel **II:** 176
    Livingston, Philip **II:** 195,
      196
    lotteries **II:** 199
    Marsh, Othniel Charles
      VI: 188
    medicine **VI:** 191
    science **VI:** 257, 258
    Tennent, Gilbert **II:** 371
    track and field **VI:** 289,
      290
    Wheelock, Eleazar **II:** 395
    Wigglesworth, Edward **II:**
      398
    Yale, Elihu **II:** 413
Yale Divinity School **IV:** 298
Yalta Agreement **VIII:** 429–431
Yalta Conference (1945) **VIII:**
  401–402, *402,* 410*c*
    Byrnes, James F. **VIII:** 49
    foreign policy **VIII:** 125
    Grand Alliance **VIII:** 137
    Harriman, Averell **VIII:**
      144
    Hiroshima and Nagasaki
      VIII: 148

Hopkins, Harry **VIII**: 157
Leahy, William D. **VIII**: 184
Polish Americans **VIII**: 270
Potsdam Conference **VIII**: 279, 280
Roosevelt, Franklin D. **VIII**: 314
Soviet-American relations **VIII**: 334
Teheran Conference **VIII**: 355
UN **VIII**: 366
Yalta Agreement **VIII**: 429–431
Yamacraw **II**: 138, 375
Yamamoto, Isoroku **VIII**: 263
Yamasee **I**: 130, 131
  Brims **II**: 41
  Charleston **II**: 56
  Middleton, Arthur **II**: 224
  North Carolina **II**: 265
  Queen Anne's War **II**: 309
  Society for the Propagation of the Gospel in Foreign Parts **II**: 352
  South Carolina **II**: 353, 354
Yamasee War **II**: 137, 178, 352, 419*c*
Yamashita, Tomoyuki **VIII**: 267
yams **II**: 122
Yana **I**: 48
ya-na **I**: 101
Yancey, Jimmy **VIII**: 223
Yancey, William Lowndes **V**: 127, 128, 311, **401–402**
Yanenga **I**: 243
"Yankee Doodle" **III**: 251, **387**
Yaocomico **II**: 209
Yáotl **I**: 347
Yap Treaty of 1922 **VII**: 360*c*
Yaqui nation **IV**: 248–249
Yarbrough, Joseph **VI**: 163
Yatenga **I**: 243
Yates, Abraham, Jr. **III**: **387–388**
Yax Ch'aktel Xok **I**: 349
Yaxchilan **I**: 252
Yax-K'uk'-Mo' **I**: 86
Yax Pasah **I**: 86
Yazoo claims **III**: 237, 296, **388**
Yeardley, Sir George **II**: 44, 268, **413–414**
Year of American Travel, A (Frémont) **IV**: 152
Yeats, James **II**: 390
yellow bile (choler) **II**: 220
"yellow dog" contracts **VI**: 167; **VII**: 200; **VIII**: 17, 179, 406*c*
"Yellow Feather" **II**: 217

yellow fever **I**: 107, 108; **II**: **414**; **III**: 396*c*; **IV**: 111–112, 315; **VI**: 55, 324*c*
  Allen, Richard **III**: 11
  Brown, Charles Brockden **III**: 49
  Colden, Cadwallader **II**: 66
  disease and epidemics **II**: 91, 92; **III**: 106; **V**: 97
  Duane, William **III**: 108
  Galveston, Battle of **V**: 145
  Hood, John Bell **V**: 171
  Jones, Absalom **III**: 189
  Lining, John **II**: 194
  Madison, Dolley **III**: 226
  medicine **III**: 241
  mortality **II**: 235
  Nast, Thomas **V**: 248
  Rush, Benjamin **III**: 312
  smallpox **II**: 345
Yellow Hand **VI**: 59
yellow journalism **VI**: 212, 235, 272, **321**, 327*c*; **VII**: 121, 141
"Yellow Kid" **VI**: 321
"Yellow Peril" **VII**: 107, 114, 267, 271
Yellowstone National Park **VI**: 65, 104; **VII**: 55, 203
Yellowstone National Park Act of 1872 **VI**: 323*c*
Yellowstone River **IV**: 33, 239
Yellow Tavern, Battle of **V**: 341
Yeltsin, Boris
  ABM Treaty **X**: 23
  Clinton, William **X**: 66–67
  foreign policy **X**: 124
  Soviet Union **X**: 280
Yemen **I**: 75; **X**: 299–300, 331*c*
Yep, Laurence **IX**: **327**
Yippies **IX**: 72
Yi Sun Shin **V**: 183
YMCA. *See* Young Men's Christian Association
Yokuts **I**: 48
Yom Kippur War (1973)
  cold war (end of) **X**: 70
  energy crisis **X**: 104
  Jews and Judaism **X**: 161–162
  OPEC **X**: 229
York (slave) **III**: 72, 73
York, duke of **II**: 250
Yorktown, siege of **V**: 267, 371
Yorktown, surrender at **III**: **388–390**, 389*m*, 394*c*
  Clinton, Sir Henry **III**: 76
  Continental army **III**: 86
  Continental Congress, Second **III**: 89
  Cornwallis, Lord **III**: 92, 93

Cowpens, Battle of **III**: 95
  French alliance **III**: 137
  Grasse, comte de **III**: 154
  Greene, Nathanael **III**: 155
  Guilford Courthouse, Battle of **III**: 158
  Hamilton, Alexander **III**: 161
  Lafayette, marquis de **III**: 201
  Lee, Henry **III**: 206
  North, Lord **III**: 260
  Paris, Treaty of **III**: 273
  Revolutionary War **III**: 305, 307
  Rochambeau, comte de **III**: 310
  Steuben, Frederick von **III**: 334
  Tarleton, Banastre **III**: 343
  Vergennes, comte de **III**: 359
  Washington, George **III**: 367
  West Indies **III**: 372
Yorktown, USS **VIII**: 74, 211, 285
Yoruba **I**: 28, 273, **377–378**
Yorubaland **I**: 377
Yosemite National Park **VI**: 65, 200, 326*c*; **VII**: 19, 55, 203
Yo Soy Joaquín (Rodolfo Gonzáles) **IX**: 124, 125, 334*c*
Yost, Charles **X**: 308
You Can't Go Home Again (Wolfe) **VIII**: 191
Young, Andrew **X**: 12, 279, 308
Young, Brigham **IV**: *371*, **371–373**; **VI**: 198, 244
  Church of Jesus Christ of Latter-day Saints **IV**: 80–81
  Deseret, State of **IV**: 109, 110
  exploration **IV**: 132
  Mormon Trail **IV**: 242–243, 243*m*
  Mormon War **IV**: 244, 245
  Nauvoo, Illinois **IV**: 261
  religion **IV**: 298
  Smith, Joseph, Jr. **IV**: 323
  Strang, James Jesse **IV**: 329
Young, Ewing **IV**: 75, 131
Young, John **IV**: 171, 199
Young, Thomas **III**: **390**
Young, Whitney M. **IX**: 306
Young, William **II**: 277; **VII**: 273
"Young America" movement **IV**: 217

Young Chicanos for Community Action **IX**: **327–328**, 334*c*
Younger, Cole **V**: 46, 285; **VI**: 98
Younger, Robert **V**: 46
Young Lords **IX**: 173, 251, 334*c*; **X**: 142
Young Men's Christian Association (YMCA) **VII**: 50, 257, 302, **349–350**
  Comstock, Anthony **VI**: 62
  education **VI**: 92
  Moody, Dwight Lyman **VI**: 196
  Social Gospel **VI**: 266
Young Negroes' Cooperative League **IX**: 30
Youngs, John **II**: **414**
Young Turks **X**: 119–120
Young Women's Christian Association (YWCA) **VII**: 50, 257, **349–350**
Youth International Party (Yippies) **IX**: 72
youth market
  popular culture **X**: 239
  television **X**: 295
  tobacco suits **X**: 304, 305
youth rebellion. *See also* counterculture
  family life **X**: 109
  sexual revolution **X**: 277
Ysopete **I**: 90
Y2K **X**: 233
Yucatán Peninsula **I**: 378*m*, **378–379**, 387*c*
  Aguilar, Francisco de **I**: 4
  Aguilar, Gerónimo (Jerónimo) de **I**: 5
  Alvarado, Pedro de **I**: 6
  Chichén Itzá **I**: 69–71
  Córdoba, Francisco Hernández de **I**: 86
  Cuba **I**: 98
  Grijalva, Juan de **I**: 145
  Guerrero, Gonzalo **I**: 146
  Maya **I**: 225–229
  Mexico **I**: 234–235
  New Spain **I**: 258
  smallpox **I**: 331
  Velázquez, Diego de **I**: 364
Yugoslavia **VI**: 285; **VII**: 323; **IX**: 58, 105, 277; **X**: 329*c*
  Albright, Madeleine K. **X**: 18
  Dayton accords **X**: 85
  defense policy **X**: 88
  Kosovo **X**: 166–167
  NATO **X**: 223
Yuki **I**: 48
Yuma nation **III**: 57; **IV**: 64
Yup'ik Eskimo **II**: 167
Yurok **I**: 48

YWCA. *See* Young Women's Christian Association

Z

Zacatecas **I:** 258, **381; II:** 355
Zacharias, Ellis M. **VIII:** 126
Zahniser, Howard **IX:** 101
Zaire **X:** 12
Zaldívar, Don Juan de **I:** 271
Zambia **I:** 209–210, 223
zambo(s) **I:** 62, 233, 234, 261, **381–382**
Zapata, Emiliano **VII:** 184, 185, 357c
Zapotecs **I:** 242, 352
Zar'a Ya'qob **I:** 124
Zargun, Mahmud ibn **I:** 23, 351
Za Yassibou **I:** 220
Zayyati, al-Hassan ibn Muhammad al-Wazzan al-. *See* Leo Africanus

Zea mays **I:** 87
Zeila, Djibouti **I:** 109, 124
Zeisberger, David **II: 415**
Zemeckis, Robert **X:** 198
Zen Buddhism **IX:** 256
Zenger, John Peter **II: 415–416,** 419c; **III:** 191
    Alexander, Mary Spratt Provoost **II:** 17
    De Lancey, James **II:** 85
    Hamilton, Andrew **II:** 153
    journalism **II:** 178
    Morris, Lewis **II:** 234
    New York **II:** 261
"zero-sum game" **II:** 221
Zerrahn, Carl **VI:** 23
Ziegfeld, Florenz **VII:** 85, 357c
Zigler, Edward **IX:** 132
Zimmermann, Arthur **VII:** 353
Zimmermann telegram **VII:** 100, 210, 343, **353,** 359c

zinc **VI:** 145
Zinzendorf, Count Nicholas Ludwig von **II:** 201, 237
Zionism **VI:** 158; **VIII:** 172, **403**
Zion's Cooperative Mercantile Institution **IV:** 372
Zola, Emile **VI:** 177
zoning **VII:** 317
zoology **I:** 140; **II:** 330
zoonosis **X:** 5
zoot-suiters **VIII: 403–404,** 410c
    children **VIII:** 57
    Mexican Americans **VIII:** 210
    migration **VIII:** 213
    race and racial conflict **VIII:** 288
    World War II home front **VIII:** 395

Zoot-Suit Riots **VIII:** 288, 289, 410c
Zoquean language **I:** 269
Zouaves **V:** 244, 362, **403–404,** 404
Zuara, Eanes de **I:** 158
Zuikaku **VIII:** 74
Zumárraga, Juan de **I: 382–383**
Zuni **I:** 13, 88, 167, 255, 295, **383; II:** 247
Zuni pueblos **II:** 303
Zurara, Gomes Eannes de **I:** 327, 328
Zwaanendeal **II:** 87
Zwicker, Ralph **IX:** 18
Zwingli, Huldrych **I:** 298, 307
Zwingli, Ulrich **II:** 140
Zworykin, Vladimir K. **VII:** 134; **IX:** 295